DO THE RIGHT THING

Readings in Applied Ethics and Social Philosophy

SECOND EDITION

Edited by **Francis J. Beckwith**
Trinity International University

WADSWORTH

THOMSON LEARNING

Australia • Canada • Mexico • Singapore • Spain
United Kingdom • United States

ABOUT THE EDITOR: **Francis J. Beckwith** is Associate Professor of Philosophy, Culture, and Law, Trinity Graduate School, Trinity International University, where he holds adjunct appointments in Trinity Law School and Trinity Evangelical Divinity School. A graduate of Washington University School of Law in St. Louis (Master of Juridical Studies) and Fordham University (PhD, MA in philosophy), he is the author or editor of several books as well as the author of scholarly articles that have been published in journals such as *Journal of Law, Medicine, and Ethics, Social Theory and Practice, Journal of Social Philosophy, Journal of Church and State, International Philosophical Quarterly, Public Affairs Quarterly,* and *Logos.*

Philosophy Editor: Peter Adams
Assistant Editor: Kara Kindstrom
Editorial Assistant: Chalida Anusasananan
Marketing Manager: Dave Garrison
Print Buyer: Robert King
Permissions Editor: Stephanie Keough-Hedges

Production Service: Shepherd, Inc.
Copy Editor: Jane C. Morgan
Cover Designer: Yvo Reziebos
Cover Printer: Von Hoffmann Graphics
Compositor: Shepherd, Inc.
Printer: Von Hoffmann Graphics

ISBN 0-534-54335-9

Library of Congress Cataloging-in-Publication Data

Do the right thing : readings in applied ethics and social philosophy / [edited by] Francis J. Beckwith.-- 2nd ed.
    p. cm.
  Includes bibliographical references.
  ISBN 0-534-54335-9
  1. Applied ethics. 2. Ethical problems.
3. United States--Moral conditions. I. Beckwith Francis.

BJ1031 .D6 2001
170--dc21   00-053445

For more information, contact
Wadsworth/Thomson Learning
10 Davis Drive
Belmont, CA 94002-3098
USA

For more information about our products, contact us:
Thomson Learning Academic Resource Center
1-800-423-0563
http://www.wadsworth.com

International Headquarters
Thomson Learning
International Division
290 Harbor Drive, 2nd Floor
Stamford, CT 06902-7477
USA

UK/Europe/Middle East/South Africa
Thomson Learning
Berkshire House
168-173 High Holborn
London WC1V 7AA
United Kingdom

Asia
Thomson Learning
60 Albert Complex, #15-01
Singapore 189969

Canada
Nelson Thomson Learning
1120 Birchmount Road
Scarborough, Ontario M1K 5G4
Canada

To my brothers, James and Patrick,
and my sister, Elizabeth Ann,
the first three pages in our parents'
book of virtues.

Contents

III. Issues of Social Justice and Personal Liberty   385

* Indicates new essays and sections for second edition.

Preface

The idea for the first edition of this book came to me when I was teaching at the University of Nevada, Las Vegas (1989–1996). During my time at UNLV, I taught a course in applied ethics, "Contemporary Moral Issues." Among the many reasons I wanted to put this book together was to provide to professors and students a text that was balanced in its selections in both quantity and quality that was also accessible and philosophically rigorous. In addition, given the influence of philosophical reasoning on contemporary jurisprudence, and given the importance of the moral dimension of the legal issues that deeply affect our public life (e.g., censorship, affirmative action, abortion), I wanted the text to include court decisions. This is why both editions include a number of U.S. Supreme Court opinions as well as essays on the legal dimensions of the moral issue being discussed. As a result, this book has three features that make it an ideal textbook for courses in applied ethics and social philosophy as well as a supplementary textbook in jurisprudence, philosophy of law, political and social philosophy, and social problems.

Balanced and Respectful Treatments. No one ideological or partisan point of view dominates the text or the issues discussed in it. Introductions, chapter summaries, and study questions were written with the express purpose of exposing students to different points of view in a fair and impartial manner.

Cutting Edge Contemporary Issues and Essays. Although this book contains issues found in most other applied ethics textbooks (e.g., abortion, euthanasia, affirmative action), it also includes important essays concerning those issues that are truly on the cutting edge of what's being published in applied ethics, social philosophy, and jurisprudence (e.g., religion and the public square, cloning, same-sex marriage).

Accessible and Interdisciplinary. An effort was made to include essays that are philosophically rigorous yet accessible to the ordinary student. Philosophers make up barely a majority of the book's contributors. Legal scholars, political scientists, economists, physicians, and Supreme Court justices are well represented.

This text is divided into three major parts: (I) Ethical Theory, Ethical Practice, and the Public Square; (II) Issues of Life and Death, and (III) Issues of Social Justice and Personal Liberty.

Part I (Ethical Theory, Ethical Practice, and the Public Square) covers theoretical and practical issues some philosophers believe are necessary in order to be able to discuss the moral and social issues of Parts II and III. Part I consists of four sections. Section A covers the issue of moral relativism. Ethical theory is the topic of Section B, containing essays on Kantianism, Utilitarianism, Natural Law, and Virtue Theory. Section C takes on the question of God and morality. State neutrality, religion, and morality are the focus of Section D. It is perhaps the hottest topic in contemporary social and legal philosophy. It is included in Part I because it deals with important theoretical questions surrounding the practical application in law of particular ethical positions (e.g., abortion, gay rights).

Part II (Issues of Life and Death) covers issues that touch on the question of what is a human life and when if ever is it morally justified to take such a life. Section A deals with the issue of Abortion. Euthanasia and Physician-Assisted Suicide will be discussed in Section B. Section C (Creating and Experimenting with Life at the Margins) contains essays on fetal tissue transplantation and human cloning. The death penalty will be the focus of Section D.

Part III (Issues of Social Justice and Personal Liberty) deals with issues that have wide-range ramifications for the future of our society and how we are to define and apply concepts such as liberty, justice, and equality. The issues covered in Part III are among the most politically volatile of our time: Affirmative Action (Section A), Economic and Social Justice (Section B), Censorship and Freedom of Expression (Section C), and Homosexuality (Section D).

In addition to the general introduction to the text, I have written a substantial introduction for each of the sections (including brief introductions for the three major parts), author bios (when appropriate), summaries and discussion questions for each chapter, a list for further reading for each of the sections, and suggested words for InfoTrac, so that students may search for other essays that contain perspectives not found in this text.

This text is structured so that each entry presents a different perspective on the issue (though not always an *opposite* perspective). It is not a pro/con anthology, since many of these issues do not lend themselves to such a false dichotomy. Rather, it is framed as a philosophical dialogue, a polite interaction between the proponents of differing views. I have strived to edit a text that presents a balanced approach to each of these issues.

NEW TO THIS EDITION

In response to suggestions from several readers, I have made changes for this second edition that I believe make it a better text. I dropped some issues and essays in order to replace them with the following. First, Part I includes a new essay on moral relativism (in Section A) as well as a much more informed discussion on ethical theory including new essays (in Section B) by Immanuel Kant, John Stuart Mill, and Susan Dimock (on Thomas Aquinas's Natural Law Theory). A defense of virtue theory by William Kilpatrick, which originally appeared in a different section in the first edition, is included with the new essays in the ethical theory section. I have included a section (C) on God and morality as well as a section (D) on state neutrality, religion, and morality. Second, Part II includes a new U.S. Supreme Court decision (*Washington v. Glucksberg* [1997]) and an article by Paul Chamberlain (both in Section B) as well as a significant revision of Section C (Creating and Experimenting with Life at the Margins), which now deals with the issues of fetal tissue transplantation as well as cloning. A new section (D), on the topic of the death penalty, has been added. Third, Part III has undergone many changes. A new Supreme Court decision (*Adarand v. Pena* [1997]) has been added to Section A (Affirmative Action). An essay by Susan Moller Okin has been added to Section B (Economic and Social Justice). Okin's essay appeared in the first edition, but in a different section. Section C (Censorship and Freedom of Expression) includes the controversial Minneapolis anti-pornography ordinances of the mid-1980s, an expansion of Catharine MacKinnon's piece that appeared in the first edition, and a new essay by Robert Bork, a conservative legal scholar, defending the permissibility of censorship. Section D (Homosexuality) includes a new Supreme Court decision (*Romer v. Evans* [1996]), new essays by Michael Pakaluk, Robert P. George, and Angela Bolte, a renamed subsection (Homosexuality and the Morality of Discrimination), and a new subsection on same-sex marriage. And finally, all the introductions and bibliographies and some of the discussion questions and author biographies have been updated—some significantly revised.

INFOTRAC

Because most of the issues in this book are ones for which many articles and book reviews continue to be published, and because it is inevitable that I did not include an instructor's favorite essay or topic, this text has been designed so that the instructor may be able to use it with **InfoTrac,** an on-line full text library that contains over 600 publications and 800,000 articles. After the introduction to each issue in this book is a list of **key words.** They are suggested words that the student or instructor may want to put in the InfoTrac search engine if he or she is looking for more information or different arguments concerning the issue. **InfoTrac** is very easy to access via the Internet. Simply point your web browser to:

www.Infotrac-college.com/wadsworth/

When you arrive, enter your ID number and fill out the registration form. After you are registered, you may want to conduct a search. InfoTrac allows you to do so by employing Easy Search or by subject, key word, publication date, or journal name. Instructors may want to supplement the readings from this text with news stories, op-ed pieces, magazine essays, or professional journal articles that can be accessed via InfoTrac.

ACKNOWLEDGMENTS

The first edition of this book would not have been possible without the enthusiasm, encouragement, and patience of the publishers, Nancy and Art Bartlett. Thanks to the careful and thoughtful editorial work of Peter Adams and Kara Kindstrom (both at Wadsworth) Publishers, this second edition would not have come to be. It is deeply gratifying to work with people who truly care about providing university and college professors with outstanding texts. I would like to also thank the following readers who provided insightful comments, which resulted in a number of key changes in the text in the first edition before it went to press: Louis P. Pojman (University of Mississippi), Dianne N. Irving (DeSales School of Theology), Henry R. West (Macalester College), Caroline J. Simon (Hope College), Joseph DeMarco (Cleveland State University) and Marina Oshana (California State University, Sacramento). For the second edition, the following reviewers provided many helpful suggestions, some of which have been incorporated in the text: Raymond Dennehy, University of San Francisco; Melinda Roberts, College of New Jersey; Lucia Palmer, University of Delaware; Larry Simon, Bowdoin College; David Fletcher, Wheaton College; William O. Stephens, Creighton University. Finally, special thanks to my wife, Frankie, for her continued love and support.

Introduction

Recently my wife and I were visiting the home of some friends of ours. They are a charming couple with two children and a pet. They are decent people who truly care about their family, friends, and community. When we walked into their living room I noticed something on their coffee table, something that I believe is truly symbolic of the age in which we live. On the coffee table rested two books, the latter on top of the former: *The Book of Virtues* and *The Bridges of Madison County*. The first is a collection of writings, edited by former U.S. Secretary of Education William J. Bennett, extolling the importance of living virtuously. The latter is a novel about a woman in a small town who commits adultery with a romantic and alluring stranger while her husband is out of town. I believe that these books symbolize two apparently contrary impulses that dominate popular culture in North America: we decry the rise of incivility and the absence of personal and public virtue in our fellow citizens and elected officials, while on the other hand we do not want to appear "judgmental" because we suspect that personal morality is relative, a matter of taste.

Yet, it seems that people everywhere and in every place agree that we should all strive to do the right thing, that is, to do what is morally appropriate or obligatory in a given situation or circumstance. Where people disagree, however, is over the question of *what exactly is* the right thing to do. In some cases there is little if no disagreement. For example, it is uncontroversial to claim that Mother Teresa is morally superior to Adolf Hitler, that torturing three-year-olds for fun is evil, that giving 10 percent of one's financial surplus to an invalid is praiseworthy, that raping a woman is morally wicked, and that providing food and shelter for one's spouse and children is a good thing. But why do we make these moral judgments rather than their opposites? And why is that on some issues—such as abortion, euthanasia, affirmative action, and homosexuality—there is impassioned disagreement? The purpose of this text is to guide the student through some of the great moral ideas and great moral debates of the present day so that he or she can arrive at a reasoned answer to these and other questions.

In October 1992 I participated in a panel discussion sponsored by the Clark County Bar Association of Southern Nevada, *Sex, Laws, and Videotapes: Morality in the Media*.

The purpose of the panel was to discuss the issue of the moral responsibility of the media, focusing for the most part on sex, violence, and obscenity. The participants represented a potpourri of interests and professions: two radio shock jocks, two attorneys, owner of a phone sex line, general manager of a local television station, a home school mom, a Christian radio disk jockey, a television reporter, and me, a philosopher. The moderator was the incoming president of the bar association, a David Letterman wannabe who was very entertaining and quite fair. Throughout the discussion I agreed with most of the participants that government censorship was not the answer to our problems. However, I did say that that does not preclude the media from morally evaluating the content of their programming and being concerned about how such programming may influence young people and society as a whole. At that point, a young woman in the audience raised her hand and asked me the question, "Who are you to judge?" This was a rhetorical question, not really meant to be answered (She was really making the *claim:* "Beckwith you have no right to make moral judgments about society"). But I answered it anyway: "I am a rational human person who is aware of certain fundamental principles of logic and moral reasoning. I think I'm qualified." This response absolutely shocked her. I went on to say, "Your claim that I have no right to make judgments is itself a judgment about me. Your claim, therefore, is self-refuting." Although our exchange brought the audience to laughter, the young woman's question was a very serious one raised by many people in our contemporary culture. It is a question which apparently assumes that when it comes to the discussion of moral issues there are no right or wrong answers and no inappropriate or appropriate judgments, no reasonable or rational way by which make moral distinctions. There are only subjective opinions, no different from opinions about one's favorite ice cream flavor, football team, or movie star.

But the young woman in the audience did not fully comprehend the scope of her denial. For to deny that one can make moral distinctions one must deny the legitimacy of the uncontroversial moral judgments listed above. That is, one must admit that Mother Teresa is no more or less moral than Adolf Hitler, torturing three-year-olds for fun is neither good nor evil, giving 10 percent of one's financial surplus to an invalid is neither praiseworthy nor blameworthy, raping a woman is not right or wrong, and providing food and shelter for one's spouse and children is neither a good thing nor a bad thing.

When people deny that we can reason about moral matters, they give up much more than they had ever imagined. It is no secret that people disagree, sometimes vehemently, over a variety of moral and social issues, just as do the contributors to this text. But many of us, including all the contributors to this volume (no matter how differently they approach the subject), agree on at least one thing: we can reason about moral matters.

APPROACHES TO THE STUDY OF MORALITY AND ETHICS

Four different approaches to the study of morality and ethics have dominated the literature. The following diagram outlines these four approaches.[1]

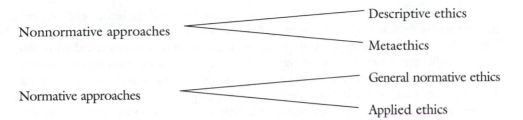

Nonnormative approaches — Descriptive ethics / Metaethics

Normative approaches — General normative ethics / Applied ethics

The first two approaches are called *nonnormative approaches* since they examine morality without concern for making judgments as to what is morally right or wrong; that is, they take no moral positions. The second two approaches are called *normative approaches* since they concern making judgments as to what is morally right or wrong; that is, they take moral positions. When a person makes a *normative* moral judgment, she is saying that a particular act, rule, principle, law, behavior, or person is right or wrong, appropriate or inappropriate, in some sense in violation or in accordance with particular ethical principles, rules, intuitions or examples of morality. For instance, if David were to say, "Frank is wrong in not helping the homeless," David would be making a normative moral judgment. In contrast, a nonnormative analysis of morality and ethics would be quite different; it would not involve a moral judgment of rightness or wrongness, but may entail an evaluation of moral terms (e.g., "What does David mean when he says that Frank is wrong in not helping the homeless?") or a non-judgmental description of moral activity (e.g., "David says that Frank is wrong in not helping the homeless."). Let us look at each of these types of approaches in greater detail.

1. Nonnormative Approaches. There are two nonnormative approaches: descriptive ethics and metaethics. *Descriptive ethics* concerns what sociologists, anthropologists, and historians often do in their study and research: describe and sometimes try to explain the moral and ethical practices and beliefs of certain societies and cultures. In their descriptions and explanations, sociologists, anthropologists, and historians do not make judgments about the morality of the practices and beliefs. For example, the observation that a particular culture may sanction infanticide (the killing of infants) because it does not believe that children are human persons is not a moral judgment; it is simply a description and an explanation of the practice.

Metaethics (which literally means "above ethics") focuses on the analysis of the meanings of the central terms used in ethical reasoning and decision-making, such as "good," "bad," "duty," "right," etc. Like descriptive ethics, it does not involve the making of normative moral judgments. Metaethical inquiries attempt to answer questions of meaning, such as the following. What do people mean when they say some action or behavior is morally wrong? Do they mean "society disapproves" or do they mean "it violates somebody's fundamental rights?" When people make a moral claim, such as "helping the homeless is good," do they mean that the act itself has the moral property of "goodness" that is just as real as a physical property such as the homeless person's property of "height"?

Although nonnormative issues in ethics are important and are in fact raised in some places in this text (especially in Part I), the chief focus of this book is on normative ethics.

2. Normative Approaches. There are two normative approaches to ethics: general normative ethics and applied ethics. *General normative ethics* is concerned with ethical theory and the study of moral systems. It is not so much concerned with discovering whether a particular act is right or wrong (e.g., "What position on affirmative action is the most ethical?"), but rather, discovering the moral theory or moral system which best establishes and/or confirms our moral intuitions about certain actions, such as the wrongness of murder and thievery. The two most prominent categories of ethical theories are *deontological* and *utilitarian*. Tom Beauchamp broadly characterizes utilitarian theories:

> Some philosophers have argued that there is one and only one fundamental principle determining right action. It is, roughly, the following: An action is morally right if, and only if, it produces at least as great a balance of value over disvalue as any available alternative action. This principle is known as the "principle of utility," and philosophers who subscribe to it are referred to as "utilitarians."[2]

Although there are many different versions of utilitarianism,[3] all versions judge the moral rightness or wrongness of an act or moral rule by its nonmoral results; for example, does it result in more pleasure than pain or more benefit than harm.

Nonutilitarians, though not dismissing the importance of results, stress the intrinsic moral rightness or wrongness of a particular act, motive, virtue, habit, or moral rule. Beauchamp writes:

> Nonutilitarians claim that one or more fundamental principles of ethics differ from the principle of utility. These are usually principles of strict obligation, such as "Never treat another person merely as a means to your own goals." This principle means that it is immoral, for example, to deceive, coerce, or fail to consult with others merely in order to promote your goals. Many philosophers who accept a nonutilitarian account of principles of moral obligation are referred to as "deontologists."[4]

There are many different versions of deontological ethics,[5] though all seem to agree that what makes an act, motive, habit, or moral rule intrinsically right or wrong is not its results but whether it is consistent with fundamental moral duties, prima facia obligations, a universal moral principle (e.g., the golden rule, or Kant's categorical imperative), and/or natural moral law.

Thus, both the utilitarian and the deontologist may agree that in general killing human persons is wrong, but for entirely different reasons. The utilitarian may decry homicide because it denies a human person, in most instances, a future of possible happiness and/or pleasure. The deontologist, on the other hand, may condemn homicide because human persons have an intrinsic right to life that cannot be violated except when a higher moral duty is demanded (e.g., a just war, self-defense).

Ethical theory will be covered in Part I of this text; Parts II and III focus on *applied ethics,* the area of study that deals with specific moral and social issues such as abortion, euthanasia, affirmative action, and homosexuality. It will become evident as we study each one of these issues that the disputants in defending their cases appeal to particular moral principles, rules, virtues, and so on. Thus, ethical theory plays an integral part in the study of applied ethics.

WRONG WAYS STUDENTS LOOK AT MORAL ISSUES

Oftentimes when students first begin to study ethics and contemporary moral issues they become overwhelmed by the disagreements and the level of the sophistication of the disputants. This causes many students to throw up their hands and say, "There are no answers to be found. Morality is just subjective." I believe that this frustration occurs because of at least three reasons: (1) students overrate the amount of disagreement, (2) students ignore values disputants have in common, including the far greater number of issues on which people agree and the many past moral problems that have been "solved," and (3) students erroneously appeal to personal autonomy as an "easy way out."

   1. Students overrate the amount of disagreement. Although it is evident that people disagree about certain moral issues, the number of legitimate options per issue is very limited. That is to say, it does not follow from disagreement that "anything goes." For example, on the issue of preferential treatment in hiring (which comes under the broader issue of "affirmative action"), some people who support this position argue that a less qualified, though adequately qualified, candidate ought to be hired for a job over more qualified candidates if the less qualified candidate is part of a minority group whose members have suffered discrimination in the past (e.g., blacks, women, Hispanics, Native Americans). On the other hand, some opponents of this view argue that preferential treatment is unfair since it penalizes someone (e.g., a white male) who most likely never engaged in discrimination against anyone let alone the minority person receiving the preferential treatment.

   Notice that neither says that fairness, justice, equality, and merit have no bearing on this issue. Neither side is saying that it is morally justified for an employer to choose an employee solely on the basis of his or her race. Rather, each side appeals to the values of fairness, justice, equality, and merit but applies them differently. For example, each side believes that merit is important in evaluating potential employees (i.e., they should be minimally qualified), but the supporters of preferential treatment believe that considerations of past injustice and unfairness against the group to which the potential employee belongs demands that she be hired in the interest of equality. On the other hand, the opponents of preferential treatment believe that group membership is irrelevant to the question of whether an applicant is the best qualified candidate in a *particular case* (merit), since it is the individual and not the group who is being hired. And in the interest of fairness and justice, it would be morally wrong to deny someone (e.g., a white male) a job when he is the most qualified for it, for to engage in a practice that denies someone what he deserves and to give that desert to someone who does not deserve it is to deny the wronged applicant equal treatment.

   What is interesting here is that the values of fairness, justice, equality, and merit limit the number of different positions one can take on the issue of preferential treatment. There are roughly two major positions on this issue and a couple of minor viewpoints. But certainly it does not follow from this that "anything goes." Common values and facts are the parameters within which disputants debate this issue.

   This is true of other issues as well. Concerning abortion, the death penalty, and euthanasia there are roughly 3 or 4 major positions on each issue. Consequently, the student should not infer from impassioned disagreement that any position is as good as any other. In other words, anarchic moral relativism does not follow from disagreement on certain moral issues.

2. Students ignore the values disputants have in common, including the far greater number of issues on which people agree and the many past moral problems that have been "solved." By focusing only on different viewpoints on moral issues, the student is sometimes given the mistaken impression that all moral conflicts are in some sense insoluble. In discussing moral conflicts in the United States we tend to focus our attention on contemporary issues such as abortion, euthanasia, and affirmative action, over which there is obviously wide and impassioned disagreement. However, we ignore the fact that disputants in these moral debates hold a number of values in common (as we saw on the issue of "preferential treatment"). Take for example the two main positions taken in the debate over abortion: pro-life and pro-choice.

First, each side believes that all human persons possess certain inalienable rights regardless of whether their governments protect these rights. That is why both sides appeal to what each believes is a fundamental right. The pro-life advocate appeals to "life" whereas the pro-choice advocate appeals to "liberty" (or "choice").

Second, each side believes that its position best exemplifies its opponent's fundamental value. The abortion-rights advocate does not deny that "life" is a value, but argues that his position's appeal to human liberty is a necessary ingredient by which an individual can pursue the fullest and most complete life possible. Furthermore, more sophisticated pro-choice advocates argue that the unborn are not human persons. And for this reason, the unborn do not have a right to life if their life hinders the liberty of a being who is a person (i.e., the pregnant woman). Others argue that even if the unborn entity is a human person, it has no right to use the body of another against that person's will, since such a usage of another's body demands of that person great risk and sacrifice, one that goes beyond any ordinary moral obligation. Hence, since a pregnant woman is not morally obligated to put herself at great risk and to make a significant sacrifice for another, she is morally justified in removing her unborn offspring even if such a removal results in its death.

On the other hand, the pro-life advocate does not eschew "liberty." She believes that all human liberty is limited by another human person's right to life. For example, one has a right to freely pursue any goal one believes is consistent with one's happiness, such as attending a Los Angeles Lakers basketball game. However, one has no right to freely pursue this goal at the expense of another's life or liberty, such as running over pedestrians with one's car so that one can get to the game on time. And of course, the pro-life advocate argues that the unborn are persons with a full right to life. And since the act of abortion typically results in the death of the unborn, abortion, unless the mother's life is in danger (since it is a prima facie greater good that one person should live rather than two die), is not morally justified.

It is apparent then that the main dispute in the abortion debate does not involve differing values, but disagreement about both the application of these values and the truth of certain facts. The pro-choice advocate does not deny that human persons have a right to life. He just believes that this right to life is not extended to the unborn since they are not human persons and/or their existence demands that another (the pregnant woman) is asked to make significant nonobligatory sacrifices. The pro-life advocate does not deny that human persons have the liberty to make choices that they believe are in their best interests. She believes that this liberty does not entail the right to choose abortion since such a choice conflicts with the life, liberty, and interests of another human person (the fetus), which is defenseless, weak, and vulnerable, and has a natural claim upon its parents' care, both pre- and post-natally.

Since there is a common ground between two moral positions that are often depicted as absolutely polarized, we can coherently reason and argue about the issue of abortion. And since there is a common ground of values, the question as to which position is correct rests on which one is best established by the facts and is consistent with our common values.

We also sometimes ignore the fact that there are a great number of issues on which almost all North Americans agree (e.g., it is wrong to torture babies for fun, to molest six-year-old children, to commit rape) and that a number of past moral conflicts have been solved (e.g., slavery, women's suffrage, forced segregation). Thus, by focusing our attention on disagreements, our perception is skewed. James Rachels points out how such a mistaken focus can also be applied to other disciplines:

> If we think of questions like *this* [e.g., abortion, euthanasia, affirmative action], it is easy to believe that "proof" in ethics is impossible. The same can be said of the sciences. There are many complicated matters that physicists cannot agree on; and if we focused our attention entirely on *them* we might conclude that there is no "proof" in physics. But of course, many simpler matters in physics *can* be proven, and about those all competent physicists agree. Similarly, in ethics there are many matters far simpler than abortion about which all reasonable people must agree.[6]

3. Students erroneously appeal to personal autonomy as an "easy way out." Instead of actually wrestling with arguments for and against a particular moral position, students give into the temptation to reduce the dispute to a question of "personal preference" or "subjective opinion." Take for example the issue of whether certain interest groups have a right to boycott products that are advertised on television programs these groups find to be morally inappropriate, especially for children. The usual argument in response to these groups is the following, "If you don't like a particular program, you don't have to watch it. You can always change the channel." But is this response really compelling? After all, these groups are not *merely* saying that they personally find these programs offensive; rather, they are saying something a bit more subtle and profound: these programs convey messages and create a moral climate that will affect others, especially children, in a way that is adverse to the public good. Hence, what bothers these groups is that *you* and *your children* will not change the channel. Furthermore, it bothers these people that there is probably somewhere in America an unsupervised ten-year-old watching the Jerry Springer Show or the Howard Stern Radio Show. Most of these people fear that their ten-year-olds may have to socially interact with, and possibly date in the near future, the unsupervised ten-year-old. Frankly, there are many thoughtful and reflective people who do not believe that such a parental concern is totally unjustified, especially in light of what we know about how certain forms of entertainment and media affect people. Therefore, the question cannot be relegated to a question of one's personal preference or autonomy. The appropriate question is what sort of social action is permissible and would best serve the public good.

Some have suggested that as long as these groups do not advocate state censorship, but merely apply social and economic pressures to private corporations and businesses (which civil rights and feminist groups have done for quite some time), a balance of freedoms is achieved. All are free to pursue their interests within the confines of constitutional protection, although all must be willing to suffer the social and economic consequences for their actions. This, according to some, best serves the public good. Notice that this response does not resort to "personal autonomy" or "personal preference," but takes seriously the values of freedom of expression, the public good, and individual rights, and attempts to uphold these values in a way that is believed to be consistent and fair.

Consider one more example. In the debate over abortion rights, many people who support these rights are fond of telling those who oppose abortion: "Don't like abortion, then don't have one." This request reduces the abortion debate to one of subjective preference, which is clearly a mistake, since those who oppose abortion do so because they believe that the fetus during most if not all of a woman's pregnancy is a human person with a right to life. This is why when the pro-lifer hears the pro-choicer tell her that if she doesn't like abortion she doesn't have to have one, it sounds to her as if the pro-choicer is saying, "Don't like murder, then don't kill any innocent persons." Understandably, the pro-lifer is not persuaded by such rhetoric.

Certainly the pro-lifer's arguments may be flawed, but the pro-choice advocate does not attack those flawed arguments when he reduces the debate to one of subjective preference. In any disagreement over such a serious issue as abortion, it is incumbent for those on all sides to present *reasons* for their views rather than merely appealing to personal autonomy, especially when the issue in dispute is whether it is permissible for people to exercise personal autonomy, that is, "Should women have the right to abort their fetuses?"

NOTES

1. This diagram is taken from Tom L. Beauchamp, *Philosophical Ethics: An Introduction to Moral Philosophy,* 2nd ed. (New York: McGraw-Hill, 1991), 33. Professor Beauchamp's work in this area is state of the art.
2. Ibid., 35.
3. See Louis Pojman, *Ethics: Discovering Right and Wrong* (Belmont, CA: Wadsworth, 1990), chapter 6.
4. Beauchamp, *Philosophical Ethics,* 35.
5. See Pojman, *Ethics,* chapter 5.
6. James Rachels, "Some Basic Points about Arguments," in *The Right Thing to Do: Basic Readings in Moral Philosophy,* ed. James Rachels (New York: Random House, 1989), 40.

Part I

Ethical Theory, Ethical Practice, and the Public Square

General Introduction to Part I

If your neighbor calls you at 3 A.M. telling you that he is stranded twenty miles away with a flat tire and needs a lift home, do you have a moral obligation to pick him up? If you are a non-Jew in Nazi Germany and you are hiding Jews in your home who are going to be sent to a concentration camp, is it right to tell the Nazi soldiers, when they come to your door inquiring, that you are not hiding Jews in your home? Is this falsehood morally justified? Are we our brothers' keepers? What is the scope of our moral obligation to others? Do we have a right, and possibly an obligation, to prevent practices in other cultures that we perceive as violating fundamental human rights? Do I have a right to shape the law in light of moral beliefs that are connected to my religious tradition? Can morality exist without God? These and other questions are answered within the framework of an ethical theory together with our intuitions about ethical practice on both a social and personal level.

Consequently, before we can deal with *applied ethics* we must first confront the issue of *ethical theory* and how we can put these *theories* into practice, that is, apply them to the particular issues covered in this text. In this part we will cover a number of important topics relating to ethical theory and ethical practice. One topic that is essential to confront is the issue of ethical relativism. It is fashionable in contemporary North America to be an ethical relativist. We hear it in the rhetorical question, "Who are you to judge?" Most people who espouse this view assume (usually without argument) that ethical relativism is more tolerant, open-minded, and consistent with our observations about the world than its chief rival, ethical objectivism, which is perceived by some to breed intolerance, narrow-mindedness, and moral imperialism. Section A, which contains two essays, deals with the issue of ethical relativism vs. ethical objectivism.

Section B concerns the issue of ethical theory. Throughout the history of philosophy a number of philosophers have put forth ethical theories in order to better explain how we come to the moral conclusions we do about such things as killing, lying, sexuality, obligation, and rights. Philosophers have also been concerned about how these theories influence how we make ethical decisions. This section contains four essays that are representative of four different schools of thought in ethical theory: Kantianism, utilitarianism, natural law theory, and virtue ethics.

The question of God and morality is the focus of Section C. This section contains one essay, a transcript from a debate that took place in 1988 on the campus of the University of Mississippi. The participants take opposing views on the question of whether God is necessary for the existence of objective moral laws.

Section D concerns an area of our public life in which morality, law, and religion intersect. The authors of the two essays in this section take differing views on the relationship between one's religiously grounded moral beliefs and whether one has a right to shape the law in a way that reflects those beliefs.

For Further Reading

Hadley Arkes, *First Things: An Inquiry into the First Principles of Morals and Justice* (Princeton: Princeton University Press, 1986).

Tom L. Beauchamp, *Philosophical Ethics: An Introduction to Moral Philosophy,* 2nd ed. (New York: McGraw-Hill, 1991).

Francis J. Beckwith and Gregory P. Koukl, *Relativism: Feet Firmly Planted in Mid-Air* (Grand Rapids, MI: Baker, 1998).

Robert P. George, ed., *Natural Law, Liberalism, and Morality* (New York: Oxford University Press, 1996).

Alasdair MacIntyre, *A Short History of Ethics* (New York: Macmillan, 1966).

———, *After Virtue* (Notre Dame, IN: University of Notre Dame Press, 1981).

———, *Whose Justice? Which Rationality?* (Notre Dame, IN: University of Notre Dame Press, 1988).

J.P. Moreland, *Scaling tie Secular City* (Grand Rapids, MI: Baker, 1987), 103–32, 240–48.

Kai Nielsen, *Ethics Without God,* rev. ed. (Buffalo, NY: Prometheus, 1989).

Louis P. Pojman, ed., *Ethical Theory: Classical and Contemporary Readings,* 3rd ed. (Belmont, CA: Wadsworth, 1998).

———, *Ethics: Discovering Right and Wrong,* 3rd ed. (1998).

Christina Hoff Sommers and Fred Sommers, eds. *Vice and Virtue in Everyday Life: Introductory Readings in Ethics,* 3rd ed. (New York: Harcourt Brace Jovanovich, 1993).

Bernard Williams, *Morality: An Introduction to Ethics* (New York: Harper & Row, 1972).

SECTION A

Relativism versus Objectivism

Introduction to Section A

Moral relativism is the view that there are no objective moral norms or values that transcend either culture or the individual. Moral claims are merely opinions, personal preferences, cultural rules, and/or emotive exclamations. This seems to be borne out by the findings of anthropology, sociology, and history as well as by our personal experience. For example, many people who live in India do not eat cattle, whereas many North Americans eat beef; some people think that homosexuality is morally correct while others do not; some cultures practice polygamy while many practice monogamy; there is enormous disagreement about the morality of abortion, euthanasia, and social justice; many people are morally offended by hardcore pornography while others consume it on a regular basis with no apparent moral offense.

Moral objectivism is the view that there are objective moral norms and values that transcend both culture and the individual. The Declaration of Independence seems to presuppose this view when it says that "we hold these truths to be self-evident, that all men are created equal, that they are endowed by their Creator with certain unalienable rights, that among these are life, liberty and the pursuit of happiness."[1] That is to say, any culture or nation that violates any of these unalienable rights is morally wrong. Just like moral relativism, moral objectivism seems to be consistent with our observations and intuitions. For example, it seems obvious that Mother Teresa was objectively a better person than Adolf Hitler; providing food and shelter for one's spouse and children is a good thing; torturing babies for fun is always and everywhere morally wrong; some cultural practices are inherently wicked (e.g., Nazi Holocaust, racial apartheid, rape); helping those less fortunate than ourselves is virtuous; and there can exist real moral reformers, such as Martin Luther King, Jr., and the prophets of the Jewish Tanuch (the Christian Old Testament), who serve as prophetic voices to reprimand their cultures for having drifted from a true moral practice based on fundamental moral law.

The moral objectivist is usually stereotyped as narrow-minded, intolerant, and dogmatic, since she believes that there is only one set of objectively true moral values (or laws), whereas the moral relativist is usually portrayed as open-minded, tolerant, and non-dogmatic, since he believes that there are a diverse number of alternative moral systems each of which is valid for the person, culture, or nation that embraces it. But these stereotypes are far from accurate and irrelevant to the question of each view's plausibility, because it is the views' defenders that are being described rather than the views' merits. For example, the author of the bestseller, *The Closing of the American Mind*, Allan Bloom, observes that "there is one thing a professor can be absolutely certain of: almost every student entering the university believes, or says he believes, that truth is relative. The students, of course, cannot defend their opinion. It is something with which they have been indoctrinated."[2] Bloom called this the "closing of the American mind" because by dogmatically asserting that there is no moral truth, the student has closed his or her mind to the possibility of knowing moral truth if in fact it does exist.

Of course, the sophisticated moral relativist does not believe he is closed-minded; in fact, he has looked at the findings of anthropologists, sociologists, and historians and has concluded that cultures, nations, and individuals have strikingly different views of morality. For this reason, he denies that there is such a thing as objective moral truth.

This section contains two pieces: The first essay (Chapter 1) is by the late anthropologist, Ruth Benedict. She argues from anthropological data that moral relativism is the correct view and that moral objectivism conflicts with the evidence. Francis J. Beckwith, in this section's second essay (Chapter 2), challenges relativism by showing what he believes are its shortcomings.

Keywords: moral relativism, subjectivism, postmodern ethics, moral disagreement, cultural relativism, moral objectivism, moral absolutism.

NOTES

1. "The Declaration of Independence (1776)," in *The Constitution of the United States and Related Documents,* ed. Martin Shapiro (Northbrook, IL: AHM Publishing, 1973), 78.
2. Allan Bloom, *The Closing of the American Mind* (New York: Simon & Schuster, 1987), 25.

For Further Reading

Hadley Arkes, "The Fallacies of Cultural Relativism; or, Abbott and Costello Meet the Anthropologist," chapter 7 of *First Things: An Inquiry into the First Principles of Morals and Justice* by Hadley Arkes (Princeton: Princeton University Press, 1986).

Francis J. Beckwith and Gregory P. Koukl, *Relativism: Feet Firmly Planted in Mid-Air* (Grand Rapids, MI: Baker, 1998).

Francis J. Beckwith, "The Epistemology of Political Correctness," *Public Affairs Quarterly* 8.4 (1994).

Ruth Benedict, *Patterns of Culture* (New York: Houghton Mifflin 1934).

"The Declaration of Independence (1776)," in *The Constitution of the United States and Related Documents,* ed. Martin Shapiro (Northbrook, IL: AHM Publishing, 1973).

Stanley Fish, "There's No Such Thing as Free Speech and It's a Good Thing, Too," in *Are You Politically Correct?: Debating America's Cultural Standards,* eds. Francis J. Beckwith and Michael Bauman (Amherst, NY: Prometheus, 1993).

Gilbert Harman, "Moral Relativism Defended," *Philosophical Review* 84 (1975).

Michael Krausz and Jack W. Meiland, eds., *Relativism: Cognitive and Moral* (Notre Dame, IN: University of Notre Dame Press, 1982).

John Ladd, ed. *Ethical Relativism* (Belmont, CA: Wadsworth, 1973).

John T. Tilley, "Cultural Relativism," *Human Rights Quarterly: A Comparative International Journal of the Social Sciences, Humanities and Law* 22.2 (May 2000).

———, "The Problem of Normative Cultural Relativism," *Ratio Juris* 11 (1998)

David B. Wong, *Moral Relativity* (Berkeley: University of California Press, 1984).

1   A Defense of Moral Relativism

RUTH BENEDICT

Ruth Benedict (1887–1948) taught at Columbia University and was one of the foremost American anthropologists. She was the author of numerous scholarly articles. Among her published books is *Patterns of Culture* (1934).

Professor Benedict argues that morality is merely conventional, that is, morality is a useful term to indicate socially approved customs, nothing more and nothing less. For Professor Benedict, there are no transcultural objective moral principles to which all people everywhere and in every place are obligated to subscribe; morality is culturally relative. Like styles of clothing and rules of etiquette, moral rules and moral values differ from culture to culture. For example, in the southern United States there was a time when slavery was considered moral whereas today it is looked upon as an evil institution; some cultures approve homosexual behavior whereas other cultures do not; in India it is considered immoral to eat cattle whereas in North America and Europe people devour steaks and hamburgers without a second thought. What is considered "normalcy" in one society may be considered "abnormalcy" in another. Since there are no universal objective moral norms, and since morality is the result of a culture's evolution, Professor Benedict maintains that "modern civilization, from this point of view, becomes not a necessary pinnacle of human achievement but one entry in a long series of possible adjustments." Thus, no culture can be said to be morally better than any other.

Reprinted by permission from Journal of General Psychology 10 (1934): 59–82.

MODERN SOCIAL ANTHROPOLOGY HAS become more and more a study of the varieties and common elements of cultural environment and the consequences of these in human behavior. For such a study of diverse social orders primitive peoples fortunately provide a laboratory not yet entirely vitiated by the spread of a standardized worldwide civilization. Dyaks and Hopis, Fijians and Yakuts are significant for psychological and sociological study because only among these simpler peoples has there been sufficient isolation to give opportunity for the development of localized social forms. In the higher cultures the standardization of custom and belief over a couple of continents has given a false sense of the inevitability of the particular forms that have gained currency, and we need to turn to a wider survey in order to check the conclusions we hastily base upon this near-universality of familiar customs. Most of the simpler cultures did not gain the wide currency of the one which, out of our experience, we identify with human nature, but this was for various historical reasons, and certainly not for any that gives us as its carriers a monopoly of social good or of social sanity. Modern civilization, from this point of view, becomes not a necessary pinnacle of human achievement but one entry in a long series of possible adjustments.

These adjustments, whether they are in mannerisms like the ways of showing anger, or joy, or grief in any society, or in major human drives like those of sex, prove to be far more variable than experience in any one culture would suggest. In certain fields, such as that of religion or of formal marriage arrangements, these wide limits of variability are well known and can be fairly described. In others it is not yet possible to give a generalized account, but that does not absolve us of the task of indicating the significance of the work that has been done and of the problems that have arisen.

One of these problems relates to the customary modem normal-abnormal categories and our conclusions regarding them. In how far are such categories culturally determined, or in how far can we with assurance regard them as absolute? In how far can we regard inability to function socially as diagnostic of abnormality, or in how far is it necessary to regard this as a function of the culture?

As a matter of fact, one of the most striking facts that emerge from a study of widely varying cultures is the ease with which our abnormals function in other cultures. It does not matter what kind of "abnormality" we choose for illustration, those which indicate extreme instability, or those which are more in the nature of character traits like sadism or delusions of grandeur or of persecution, there are well-described cultures in which these abnormals function at ease and with honor, and apparently without danger or difficulty to the society. . . .

The most notorious of these is trance and catalepsy. Even a very mild mystic is aberrant in our culture. But most peoples have regarded even extreme psychic manifestations not only as normal and desirable, but even as characteristic of highly valued and gifted individuals. This was true even in our own cultural background in that period when Catholicism made the ecstatic experience the mark of sainthood. It is hard for us, born and brought up in a culture that makes no use of the experience, to realize how important a role it may play and how many individuals are capable of it, once it has been given an honorable place in any society. . . .

Cataleptic and trance phenomena are, of course, only one illustration of the fact that those whom we regard as abnormals may function adequately in other cultures. Many of our culturally discarded traits are selected for elaboration in different societies. Homosexuality is an excellent example, for in this case our attention is not constantly diverted, as in the consideration of trance, to the interruption of routine activity which it implies. Homosexuality poses the problem very simply. A tendency toward this trait in our culture exposes an individual to all the conflicts to which all aberrants are always exposed, and we tend to identify the consequences of this conflict with homosexuality. But these consequences are obviously local and cultural. Homosexuals in many societies are not incompetent, but they may be such if the culture asks adjustments of them that would strain any man's vitality. Wherever homosexuality has been given an honorable place in any society, those to whom it is congenial have filled adequately the honorable roles society assigns to them. Plato's *Republic* is, of course, the most convincing statement of such a reading of homosexuality. It is presented as one of the major means to the good life, and it was generally so regarded in Greece at that time.

The cultural attitude toward homosexuals has not always been on such a high ethical plane, but it has been very varied. Among many American Indian tribes there exists the institution of the berdache, as the French called them. These men-women were men who at puberty or thereafter took the dress and the occupations of women. Sometimes they married other men and lived with them. Sometimes they were men with no inversion, persons of weak sexual endowment who chose this role to avoid the jeers of the women. The berdaches were never regarded as of first-rate supernatural power, as similar men-women were in Siberia, but rather as leaders in women's occupations, good healers in certain diseases, or, among certain tribes, as the genial organizers of social affairs. In any case, they were socially placed. They were not left exposed to the conflicts that visit the deviant who is excluded from participation in the recognized patterns of his society.

The most spectacular illustrations of the extent to which normality may be culturally defined are those cultures where an abnormality of our culture is the cornerstone of their social structure. It is not possible to do justice to these possibilities in a short discussion. A recent study of an island of northwest Melanesia by Fortune describes a society built upon traits which we regard as beyond the border of paranoia. In this tribe the exogamic groups look upon each other as prime manipulators of black magic, so that one marries always into an enemy group which remains for life one's deadly and unappeasable foes. They look upon a good garden crop as a confession of theft, for everyone is engaged in making magic to induce into his garden the productiveness of his neighbors'; therefore no secrecy in the island is so rigidly insisted upon as the secrecy of a man's harvesting of his yams. Their polite phrase at the acceptance of a gift is, "And if you now poison me, how shall I repay you this present?" Their preoccupation with poisoning is constant; no woman ever leaves her cooking pot for a moment untended. Even the great affinal economic exchanges that are characteristic of this Melanesian culture area are quite altered in Dobu since they are incompatible with this fear and distrust that pervades the culture. They go farther and people the whole world outside their own quarters with such malignant spirits that all-night feasts and ceremonials simply do not occur here. They have even rigorous religiously enforced customs that forbid the sharing of seed even in one family group. Anyone else's food is deadly poison to you, so that communality of stores is out of the question. For some months before harvest the whole society is on the verge of starvation, but if one falls to the temptation and eats up one's seed yams, one is an outcast and a beachcomber for life. There is no coming back. It involves, as a matter of course, divorce and the breaking of all social ties.

Now in this society where no one may work with another and no one may share with another, Fortune describes the individual who was regarded by all his fellows as crazy. He was not one of those who periodically ran amok and, beside himself and frothing at the mouth, fell with a knife upon anyone he could reach. Such behavior they did not regard as putting anyone outside the pale. They did not even put the individuals who were known to be liable to these attacks under any kind of control. They merely fled when they saw the attack coming on and kept out of the way. "He would be all right tomorrow." But there was one man of sunny, kindly disposition who liked work and liked to be helpful. The compulsion was too strong for him to repress it in favor of the opposite tendencies of his culture. Men and women never spoke of him without laughing; he was silly and simple and definitely crazy. Nevertheless, to the ethnologist used to a culture that has, in Christianity, made his type the model of all virtue, he seemed a pleasant fellow. . . .

. . . Among the Kwakiutl it did not matter whether a relative had died in bed of disease, or by the hand of an enemy, in either case death was an affront to be wiped out by the death of another person. The fact that one had been caused to mourn was proof that one had been put upon. A chief's sister and her daughter had gone up to Victoria, and either because they drank bad whiskey or because their boat capsized they never came back. The chief called together his warriors, "Now I ask you, tribes, who shall wail? Shall I do it or shall another?" The spokesman answered, of course, "Not you, Chief. Let some other of the tribes." Immediately they set up the war pole to announce their intention of wiping out the injury, and gathered a war party. They set out, and found seven men and two children asleep and killed them. "Then they felt good when they arrived at Sebaa in the evening."

The point which is of interest to us is that in our society those who on that occasion would feel good when they arrived at Sebaa that evening would be the definitely abnormal. There would be some, even in our society, but it is not a recognized and approved mood under the circumstances. On the Northwest Coast those are favored and fortunate to whom that mood under those circumstances is congenial and those to whom it is repugnant are unlucky. This latter minority can register in

their own culture only by doing violence to their congenial responses and acquiring others that are difficult for them. The person, for instance, who, like a Plains Indian whose wife has been taken from him, is too proud to fight, can deal with the Northwest Coast civilization only by ignoring its strongest bents. If he cannot achieve it, he is the deviant in that culture, their instance of abnormality.

This headhunting that takes place on the Northwest Coast after a death is no matter of blood revenge or of organized vengeance. There is no effort to tie up the subsequent killing with any responsibility on the part of the victim for the death of the person who is being mourned. A chief whose son has died goes visiting wherever his fancy dictates, and he says to his host, "My prince has died today, and you go with him." Then he kills him. In this, according to their interpretation, he acts nobly because he has not been downed. He has thrust back in return. The whole procedure is meaningless without the fundamental paranoid reading of bereavement. Death, like all the other untoward accidents of existence, confounds man's pride and can only be handled in the category of insults.

Behavior honored upon the Northwest Coast is one which is recognized as abnormal in our civilization, and yet it is sufficiently close to the attitudes of our own culture to be intelligible to us and to have a definite vocabulary with which we may discuss it. The megalomaniac paranoid trend is a definite danger in our society. It is encouraged by some of our major preoccupations, and it confronts us with a choice of two possible attitudes. One is to brand it as abnormal and reprehensible, and is the attitude we have chosen in our civilization. The other is to make it an essential attribute of ideal man, and this is the solution in the culture of the Northwest Coast.

These illustrations, which it has been possible to indicate only in the briefest manner, force upon us the fact that normality is culturally defined. An adult shaped to the drives and standards of either of these cultures, if he were transported into our civilization, would fall into our categories of abnormality. He would be faced with the psychic dilemmas of the socially unavailable. In his own culture, however, he is the pillar of society, the end result of socially inculcated mores, and the problem of personal instability in his case simply does not arise.

No one civilization can possibly utilize in its mores the whole potential range of human behavior. Just as there are great numbers of possible phonetic articulations, and the possibility of language depends on a selection and standardization of a few of these in order that speech communication may be possible at all, so the possibility of organized behavior of every sort, from the fashions of local dress and houses to the dicta of a people's ethics and religion, depends upon a similar selection among the possible behavior traits. In the field of recognized economic obligations or sex tabus this selection is as nonrational and subconscious a process as it is in the field of phonetics. It is a process which goes on in the group for long periods of time and is historically conditioned by innumerable accidents of isolation or of contact of peoples. In any comprehensive study of psychology, the selection that different cultures have made in the course of history within the great circumference of potential behavior is of great significance.

Every society, beginning with some slight inclination in one direction or another, carries its preference farther and farther, integrating itself more and more completely upon its chosen basis, and discarding those types of behavior that are uncongenial. Most of those organizations of personality that seem to us most incontrovertibly abnormal have been used by different civilizations in the very foundations of their institutional life. Conversely the most valued traits of our normal individuals have been looked on in differently organized cultures as aberrant. Normality, in short, within a very wide range, is culturally defined. It is primarily a term for the socially elaborated segment of human behavior in any culture; and abnormality, a term for the segment that that particular civilization does not use. The very eyes with which we see the problem are conditioned by the long traditional habits of our own society.

It is a point that has been made more often in relation to ethics than in relation to psychiatry. We do not any longer make the mistake of deriving the morality of our locality and decade directly from the inevitable constitution of human nature. We do not elevate it to the dignity of a first principle. We recognize that morality differs in every society, and is a convenient term for socially approved habits. Mankind has always preferred to say, "It is morally good," rather than "It is habitual," and the fact of this preference is matter enough for a critical science of ethics. But historically the two phrases are synonymous.

The concept of the normal is properly a variant of the concept of the good. It is that which society has approved. A normal action is one which falls well within the limits of expected behavior for a particular society. Its variability among different peoples is essentially a function of the variability of the behavior patterns that different societies have created for themselves, and can never be wholly divorced from a consideration of culturally institutionalized types of behavior.

Each culture is a more or less elaborate working-out of the potentialities of the segment it has chosen. In so far as a civilization is well integrated and consistent within itself, it will tend to carry farther and farther, according to its nature, its initial impulse toward a particular type of action, and from the point of view of any other culture those elaborations will include more and more extreme and aberrant traits.

Each of these traits, in proportion as it reinforces the chosen behavior patterns of that culture, is for that culture normal. Those individuals to whom it is congenial either congenitally, or as the result of childhood sets, are accorded prestige in that culture, and are not visited with the social contempt or disapproval which their traits would call down upon them in a society that was differently organized. On the other hand, those individuals whose characteristics are not congenial to the selected type of human behavior in that community are the deviants, no matter how valued their personality traits may be in a contrasted civilization.

The Dobuan who is not easily susceptible to fear of treachery, who enjoys work and likes to be helpful, is their neurotic and regarded as silly.

On the Northwest Coast the person who finds it difficult to read life in terms of an insult contest will be the person upon whom fall all the difficulties of the culturally unprovided for. The person who does not find it easy to humiliate a neighbor, nor to see humiliation in his own experience, who is genial and loving, may, of course, find some unstandardized way of achieving satisfactions in his society, but not in the major patterned responses that his culture requires of him. If he is born to play an important role in a family with many hereditary privileges, he can succeed only by doing violence to his whole personality. If he does not succeed, he has betrayed his culture; that is, he is abnormal.

I have spoken of individuals as having sets toward certain types of behavior, and of these sets as running sometimes counter to the types of behavior which are institutionalized in the culture to which they belong. From all that we know of contrasting cultures it seems clear that differences of temperament occur in every society. The matter has never been made the subject of investigation, but from the available material it would appear that these temperament types are very likely of universal recurrence. That is, there is an ascertainable range of human behavior that is found wherever a sufficiently large series of individuals is observed. But the proportion in which behavior types stand to one another in different societies is not universal. The vast majority of individuals in any group are shaped to the fashion of that culture. In other words, most individuals are plastic to the molding force of the society into which they are born. In a society that values trance, as in India, they will have supernormal experience. In a society that institutionalizes homosexuality, they will be homosexual. In a society that sets the gathering of possessions as the chief human objective, they will amass property. The deviants, whatever the type of behavior the culture has institutionalized, will remain few in number, and there seems no more difficulty in molding the vast malleable majority to the "normality" of what we consider an aberrant trait, such as delusions of reference, than to the normality of such accepted behavior patterns as acquisitiveness. The small proportion of the number of the deviants in any culture is not a function of the sure instinct with which that society has built itself upon the fundamental sanities, but of the universal fact that, happily, the majority of mankind quite readily take any shape that is presented to them. . . .

Discussion Questions

1. Present and explain Professor Benedict's defense of ethical relativism. How does she account for the existence of morality in any particular society or culture?
2. Since, according to Professor Benedict, no culture can be said to be morally better than any other, is she able to condemn apartheid in South Africa, slavery throughout history, and the Holocaust, all of which were or are morally acceptable to the society that practiced or practice them?
3. Professor Benedict maintains that cultural diversity proves ethical relativism. Do you agree with this position? Explain and defend your answer.

You can locate InfoTrac-College Education articles about this chapter by accessing the InfoTrac-College Edition website (http://www.infotrac-college.com/wadsworth/). Using the InfoTrac-College Edition subject guide, enter the search terms relevant to this chapter, and then read abstracts for relevant articles.

2   A Critique of Moral Relativism

FRANCIS J. BECKWITH

Francis J. Beckwith is Associate Professor of Philosophy, Culture, and Law, Trinity Graduate School, Trinity International University, where he holds adjunct appointments in Trinity Law School and Trinity Evangelical Divinity School. Among his books are *Relativism: Feet Firmly Planted in Mid-Air* (1998), *Abortion and the Sanctity of Human Life* (2000), and *The Abortion Controversy 25 Years After Roe v. Wade: A Reader,* 2nd ed. (1998).

In this essay Professor Beckwith critiques moral relativism. He begins with an analysis of the nature of moral claims in which he shows how moral relativism has affected the way in which we talk about controversial moral issues. He then goes on to critique the two arguments most often used to defend moral relativism: (1) the argument from cultural and individual differences; and (2) the argument from tolerance. Concerning the former, Beckwith believes there are four problems with it: (a) relativism does not follow from disagreement; (b) disagreement counts against relativism; (c) disagreement is overrated; and (d) absurd consequences follow from moral relativism. In dealing with the argument from tolerance, Professor Beckwith provides four criticisms, all of which maintain that tolerance (rightly understood) is actually *incompatible* with relativism: (a) tolerance supports objective morality, not relativism; (b) relativism is itself a closed-minded and intolerant position; (c) relativism is judgmental, exclusivist, and partisan; and (d) the "tolerance" of moral relativism either condones barbarism or is self-refuting. Beckwith concludes his essay by stating that "moral relativism is a philosophical failure."

MORAL RELATIVISM IS THE view that when it comes to questions of morality, there is no absolute or objective right and wrong; moral rules are merely personal preferences or the result of one's cultural, sexual, or ethnic orientation. Many people see relativism as necessary for promoting tolerance, nonjudgmentalism, and inclusiveness, for they think if one believes one's moral position is correct and others' incorrect, one is close-minded and intolerant. I will argue in this essay that not only do the argu-ments for relativism fail, but that relativism itself cannot live up to its own reputation, for it is promoted by its proponents as the only correct view on morality. This is why relativists typically do not tolerate nonrelativist views, judge those views as mistaken, and maintain that relativism is exclusively right.

I will first briefly discuss how moral relativism has affected our ability to engage in moral discourse. I will then present and critique two arguments for moral relativism.

This essay, published here by permission of its author, is adapted from the essay, "Why I Am Not a Relativist," which appears in the book Why I Am a Christian, eds. Norman L. Geisler and Paul Hoffman (Grand Rapids, MI: Baker, 2001).

MORAL RELATIVISM AND MORAL DISCOURSE

Moral relativism has stunted our ability to grasp the nature of moral claims. People in our culture often confuse *preference-claims* with *moral-claims* or reduce the latter to the former. To understand what I mean by this, consider two statements:[1]

1. I like vanilla ice cream
2. Killing people without justification is wrong.

The first statement is a preference-claim, since it is a description of a person's subjective taste. It is not a *normative* claim. It is not a claim about what one ought or ought not to do. It is not saying, "Since I like vanilla ice cream, the government ought to coerce you to eat it as well" or "Everyone in the world ought to like vanilla ice cream too." A claim of subjective preference tells us nothing about what one ought to think or do. For example, if someone were to say, "I like to torture children for fun," this would tell us nothing about whether it is wrong or right to torture children for fun.

The second claim, however, is quite different. It has little if anything to do with what one likes or dislikes. In fact, one may prefer to kill another person without justification and still know that it is morally wrong to do so. This statement is a moral-claim. It is not a descriptive claim, for it does not tell us what, why, or how things are, or how a majority of people in fact behave and think. Nor is it a preference-claim, for it does not tell us what anyone's subjective preference may be or how one prefers to behave and think. Rather, it is a claim about what persons ought to do, which may be contrary to how persons in fact behave and how they prefer to behave.

Unfortunately, the espousal of moral relativism has made it difficult for many people in our culture to distinguish between preference-claims and moral-claims. Rather than pondering and struggling with arguments for and against a particular moral perspective, people sometimes reduce the disagreement to a question of "personal preference" or "subjective opinion." Take for example the debate over abortion rights.[2] Many who defend a woman's right to abortion (pro-choicers) sometimes tell those who oppose abortion rights (pro-lifers): "Don't like abortion, then don't have one." This request reduces the abortion debate to a preference-claim. That is, the objective moral rightness or wrongness of abortion (i.e., whether or not it involves the unjustified killing of an innocent human person) is declared, without argument, not relevant. But this is clearly a mistake, for those who oppose abortion do so because they believe that the fetus during most if not all of a woman's pregnancy is a human person with a right to life and it is generally wrong, both objectively and universally, to violate a person's right to life. For this reason, when the pro-lifer hears the pro-choicer tell her that if she doesn't like abortion she doesn't have to have one, it sounds to her as if the pro-choicer is saying, "Don't like murder, then don't kill any innocent persons." Understandably, the pro-lifer, committed to objective moral norms, finds such rhetoric perplexing as well as unpersuasive. Of course, many sophisticated pro-choice advocates are opponents of moral relativism as well.[3] But it just seems that in the popular debate pro-choicers tend to reduce the question of abortion to a question of preference and thus seem to have been more affected by moral relativism than have their opponents. (But they are not completely affected, for they do appeal to "fundamental rights" which are typically grounded in some objective morality). It is true that the pro-lifer's arguments may be flawed, but the pro-choice advocate does not critique those flawed arguments when he mistakenly turns a serious moral disagreement into a debate over preferences.

ARGUMENTS FOR MORAL RELATIVISM

There are two arguments that are often used to defend moral relativism. The first is the argument from cultural and individual differences and the second is the argument from tolerance.

1. Argument from cultural and individual differences. In this argument, the relativist concludes that there are no objective moral norms because cultures and individuals disagree on moral issues. In order to defend this premise the relativist typically cites a number of examples, such as cross-cultural and intra-cultural differences over the morality of sexual practices, abortion, war, and capital punishment. In the words of Hadley Arkes, an opponent of moral relativism: "In one society, a widow is burned on the funeral pyre of her husband; in another, she is burned on the beach in Miami. In one society, people complain to the chef about the roast beef; in another, they send back the roast beef and eat the chef."[4] There are at least four problems with this argument.

a. Relativism does not follow from disagreement. The fact that people disagree about something does not mean that there is no truth. For example, if you and I were to disagree on the question of whether or not the earth is round, our disagreement would certainly not be proof that the earth has *no* shape. The fact that a skin-head (a type of young Neo-Nazi) and I may disagree on the question of whether we should treat people equally and with fairness, is certainly not sufficient reason to conclude that equality and fairness are not objective moral values. Even if individuals and cultures hold no values in common, it does not follow from this that nobody is right or wrong about the correct values. That is, there could be a mistaken individual or culture, such as Adolf Hitler and Nazi Germany.

If the mere fact of disagreement were sufficient to conclude that objective norms do not exist, then we would have to believe that there is no objectively correct position on such issues as slavery, genocide, and child molestation, for the slave owner, genocidal maniac, and pedophile have an opinion that differs from the one held by those of us who condemn their actions. In the end, moral disagreement proves nothing.

b. Disagreement counts against relativism. Suppose, however, that the relativist, despite the logical failure of this case, sticks to his guns and maintains that disagreement over objective norms proves the correctness of relativism. But this will not work. For the relativist has set down a principle—disagreement means there is no truth—that unravels his own case. After all, some of us believe that relativism is a mistaken view. We, in other words, *disagree* with the relativist over the nature of morality. We believe that objective moral norms exist whereas the relativist does not. But, according to the relativist's own principle—disagreement means there is no truth—he ought to abandon his opinion that relativism is the correct position. And to make matters worse for the relativist, his principle is a proposition for which there is not universal agreement, and thus on its own grounds must be rejected. As Arkes points out, "My disagreement establishes that the proposition [i.e., disagreement means there is no truth] does not enjoy a universal assent, and by the very terms of the proposition, that should be quite sufficient to determine *its own invalidity*."[5]

c. Disagreement is overrated. Although it is true that people and cultures disagree on moral issues, it does not follow from this that they do not share the same values or that there are not moral norms that are binding on all nations in all times and in all places. Take for example the Salem witch trials. There was a time in colonial days in Massachusetts when certain individuals were put to death as punishment for practicing witchcraft. We do not execute witches today, but not because our moral norms have changed. Rather, the reason why we don't execute witches is because we do not believe, as the seventeenth century residents of Massachusetts did, that the practice of witchcraft has a fatal affect upon the community. But suppose that we had good evidence that the practice of witchcraft did affect people in the same way that second-hand cigarette smoke effects the nonsmoker. We would alter the practice of our values to take into consideration this factual change. We may set up nonwitch sections in restaurants and ban the casting of spells on interstate airplane flights. The upshot of all this is that the good of the community is a value we share with the seventeenth century residents of Salem, but we simply believe that they were factually wrong about the affect of witches upon that good.

Philosopher James Rachels presents another example of how the knowledge of certain facts may help us understand why it *seems* that other people have different values.[6] He points to the Eskimos' practice of infanticide (on primarily female babies). On the surface, this practice seems to show that the Eskimos have a radically different value of human life than we do. And because one's view of human life is so fundamental, it seems to follow from this that moral relativism is correct. Rachels does not agree. He explains that once one realizes that certain factual considerations have made the practice of infanticide a necessary evil for the Eskimos, one sees that the Eskimos' value of human life is not all that different from ours. Writes Rachels:

> But suppose we ask *why* the Eskimos do this. The explanation is not that they have less affection for their children or less respect for human life. An Eskimo family will always protect its babies if conditions permit. But they live in a harsh environment, where food is often in short supply. . . . Infant girls are readily disposed of because, first, in this society the males are the primary food providers—they are the hunters, according to the traditional division of labor—and it is obviously important to maintain a sufficient

number of food gatherers. But there is an important second reason as well. Because the hunters suffer a high casualty rate, the adult men who die prematurely far outnumber the women who die early. Thus if male and female infants survived in equal numbers, the female adult population would greatly outnumber the male adult population. Examining the available statistics, one writer concluded that "were it not for female infanticide . . . there would be approximately one-and-a-half times as many females in the average Eskimo local group as there are food-producing males."

> So among the Eskimos, infanticide does not signal a fundamentally different attitude toward children. Instead, it is a recognition that drastic measures are sometimes needed to ensure the family's survival. Even then, however, killing the baby is not the first option considered. Adoption is common; childless couples are especially happy to take a more fertile couple's "surplus." Killing is only the last resort. I emphasize this in order to show that the raw data of the anthropologists can be misleading; it can make the differences in values between cultures appear greater than they are. The Eskimos' values are not all that different from our values. It is only that life forces upon them choices that we do not have to make.[7]

This is not to say that the Eskimos are right or that we should not try to persuade them to believe that their practice is wrong. Rather, this example simply shows so-called moral differences may not really be moral differences at all after one carefully examines why a certain practice, such as female infanticide, is performed.

Consider again the issue of abortion. The conventional wisdom is that the moral and legal debate over abortion is a dispute between two factions that hold incommensurable value systems. But the conventional wisdom is mistaken, for these factions hold many values in common.

First, each side believes that all human persons possess certain inalienable rights regardless of whether their governments protect these rights. That is why both sides appeal to what each believes is a fundamental right. The pro-life advocate appeals to "life" whereas the pro-choice advocate appeals to "liberty" (or "choice"). Both believe that a constitutional regime, in order to be just, must uphold fundamental rights.

Second, each side believes that its position best exemplifies its opponents's fundamental value. The pro-choice advocate does not deny that "life" is a value, but argues that his position's appeal to human liberty is a necessary ingredient by which an individual can pursue the fullest and most complete life possible.

On the other hand, the pro-life advocate does not eschew "liberty." She believes that all human liberty is limited by another human person's right to life. For example, one has a right to freely pursue any goal one believes is consistent with one's happiness, such as attending a Los Angeles Lakers basketball game. One has, however, no right to freely pursue this goal at the expense of another's life or liberty, such as running over pedestrians with one's car so that one can get to the game on time. And, of course, the pro-life advocate argues that fetuses are persons with a full right to life. Because the act of abortion typically results in the death of the unborn, abortion, with few exceptions, is not morally justified, and for that reason ought to be made illegal.

The pro-choice advocate does not deny that human persons have a right to life. He just believes that this right to life is not extended to fetuses since they are not human persons. The pro-life advocate does not deny that people have the liberty to make choices that they believe are in their best interests. She just believes that this liberty does not entail the right to choose abortion since such a choice conflicts with the life, liberty, and interests of another human person (the fetus), which is defenseless, weak, and vulnerable, and has a natural claim upon its parents' care, both pre- and post-natally. Thus, when all is said and done, the debate over abortion is not really

about conflicting value systems. After all, imagine if a pro-life politician were to say the following in a campaign speech: "My party's platform affirms a woman's right to terminate her pregnancy if and only if it does not result in the death of her unborn child." Disagreement over such a plank would not be over the morality of killing persons; it would be over the metaphysical question of whether the unborn human is a person.[8]

d. Absurd consequences follow from moral relativism. First, if there are no objective moral norms that apply to all persons in all times and in all places, then certain moral judgments, such as the following, cannot be universally true: Mother Teresa was morally better than Adolf Hitler; rape is always wrong; and it is wrong to torture babies for fun. But to deny that these judgments are not universally true seems absurd. For there seem to be some moral judgments that are absolutely correct regardless of what cultures or individuals may think.

Second, if the relativist claims that morality is relative to the individual, what happens when individual moralities conflict? For example, suppose that Jeffrey Dahmer's morality permits him to cannibalize his neighbor, but his neighbor disagrees. What would the relativist suggest be done in this case, since, according to this form of relativism, nobody's morality is in principle superior to any other? In addition, if the moral life is no more than a reflection of people's individual tastes, preferences, and orientations, then we cannot tell young people that it is morally wrong to lie, steal, cheat, smoke, abuse drugs, kill their newborns, and drop out of school, even though these behaviors may be consistent with the students' own personal tastes, preferences and/or orientations.

Third, even if the relativist were to make the more modest claim that morality is not relative to the individual but to the individual's culture, that one is only obligated to follow the dictates of one's society, other problems follow.

(1) The cultural relativist's position is self-refuting. What does it mean for a position to be self-refuting? J.P. Moreland explains:

> When a statement fails to satisfy itself (i.e., to conform to its own criteria of validity or acceptability), it is self-refuting. . . . Consider some examples. "I cannot say a word in English" is self-refuting when uttered in English. "I do not exist" is self-refuting, for one must exist to utter it. The claim "there are no truths" is self-refuting. If it is false, then it is false. But if it is true, then it is false as well, for in that case there would be no truths, including the statement itself.[9]

How is cultural relativism self-refuting? The supporter of cultural relativism maintains that there are no objective and universal moral norms and for that reason everyone ought follow the moral norms of his or her own culture. But the cultural relativist is making an absolute and universal moral claim, namely, that everyone is morally obligated to follow the moral norms of his or her own culture. So, if this moral norm is absolute and universal, then cultural relativism is false. But if this moral norm is neither absolute nor universal, then cultural relativism is still false, for in that case I would not have a moral obligation to follow the moral norms of my culture.

(2) Since each of us belongs to a number of different "societies" or "cultures," which one of them should be followed when they conflict? For example, suppose a woman named "Sheena" is a resident of a liberal upscale neighborhood in Hollywood, California, attends a Christian church, and is a partner in a prestigious law firm. In her neighborhood, having an adulterous affair is considered "enlightened" and those who do not pursue such unions are considered repressed prudes. At her church, however, adultery is condemned as sinful, while at her law firm adultery is neither encouraged nor discouraged. Suppose further that Sheena chooses to commit adultery in the firm's back office with a fellow churchgoer, Donald, who resides in a conservative neighborhood in which adultery is condemned. The office, it turns out, is adjacent to the church as well as precisely half way between Sheena's neighborhood and Donald's neighborhood. It is not clear which society is morally relevant.

(3) There can be no moral progress or moral reformers. If morality is reducible to culture, then there can be no real moral progress. For the only way one can say that a culture is getting better, or progressing, is if there are objective moral norms that are not dependent on culture to which a society may draw closer. But if what is morally good is merely what one's culture says is morally good, then we can only say that cultural norms change, not that the society is progressing or getting better. Yet, it seems, for example, that the abolition of slavery and the establishment of civil rights of African Americans in the United States were instances of moral progress. In addition, there can be no true moral reformers if cultural relativism is true. Moreland writes:

> If [cultural] relativism is true, then it is impossible in principle to have a true moral reformer who changes a society's code and does not merely bring out what was already implicit in that code. For moral reformers, by definition, *change* a society's code by arguing that it is somehow morally inadequate. But if [cultural] relativism is true, an act is right if and only if it is in society's code; so the reformer is by definition immoral (since he adopts a set of values outside the society's code and attempts to change that code in keeping with these values). It is odd, to say the least, for someone to hold that every moral reformer who ever lived—Moses, Jesus, Gandhi, Martin Luther King—was immoral by definition. Any moral view which implies that is surely false.[10]

Thus, in order to remain consistent, the cultural relativist must deny that there can any real moral progress or any real moral reformers. For such judgments presuppose the existence of real objective and absolute moral norms.

2. Argument from Tolerance. Many people see relativism as necessary for promoting tolerance, nonjudgmentalism, and inclusiveness, for they think if you believe your moral position is correct and others' incorrect you are close-minded and intolerant. They usually base this premise on the well-known differences of opinion on morality between cultures and individuals. So, the moral relativist embraces the view that one should not judge other cultures and individuals, for to do so would be intolerant. There are at least four problems with this argument, all of which maintain that tolerance (rightly understood) and relativism are actually incompatible with each other.

a. Tolerance supports objective morality, not relativism. Ironically, the call to tolerance by relativists presupposes the existence of at least one nonrelative, universal, and objective norm: tolerance. Bioethicist Tom Beauchamp explains:

> If we interpret normative relativism as requiring tolerance of other views, the whole theory is imperiled by inconsistency. The proposition that we ought to tolerate the views of others, or that it is right not to interfere with others, is precluded by the very strictures of the theory. Such a proposition bears all the marks of a non-relative account of moral rightness, one based on, but not reducible to, the cross-cultural findings of anthropologists. . . . But if this moral principle [of tolerance] is recognized as valid, it can of course be employed as an instrument for criticizing such cultural practices as the denial of human rights to minorities and such beliefs as that of racial superiority. A moral commitment to tolerance of other practices and beliefs thus leads inexorably to the abandonment of normative relativism.[11]

Thus, if everyone ought to be tolerant, then tolerance is an objective moral norm. And, therefore, moral relativism is false. Also, tolerance presupposes that there is something good about being tolerant, such as being able to learn from others with whom one disagrees or to impart knowledge and wisdom to that person. But that presupposes objective moral values, namely, that knowledge and wisdom are good things. Moreover, tolerance presupposes that someone may be correct about his or her moral perspective. That is to say, it seems that part of the motivation for advocating tolerance is to encourage people to be open to the possibility that one may be able to gain truth and insight (including moral truth and insight) from another who may possess it. If that is the case, then there are objective moral truths that I can learn.

In addition, tolerance presupposes a moral judgment of another's viewpoint. That it to say, I can only be tolerant of those ideas that I think are mistaken. I am not tolerant of that with which I agree; I embrace it. And I am not tolerant of that for which I have no interest (e.g., European professional soccer); I merely have benign neglect for it. (That is, I don't care one way or another). Consider the following example. Suppose I tell a friend that I believe that homosexuality is immoral. And suppose my friend requests that I be tolerant toward homosexuals in my community. If I accept this advice, and choose to be civil, respectful, and gracious to gay men and women with whom I have contact, while at the same time judging their sexual practices as immoral, it seems that I would be truly tolerant. But suppose that someone says that my judging of homosexuality as immoral still makes me "intolerant." At that point, given my understanding of "tolerance," I have no idea what I am supposed to do. For if I change my view of homosexuality, and say either that it is not immoral or that I have no opinion (i.e., I have benign neglect), then I cannot be tolerant, for I can only be tolerant of that which I believe is wrong or mistaken. On the other hand, if judging another's position as wrong or mistaken makes one intolerant, then the person who judges my negative assessment of homosexuality is, by that person's own definition, intolerant. But that is absurd. For if "tolerance" means that one ought not to judge a view as morally wrong, then it seems to be consistent with either embracing the view or having benign neglect for it. If that is the case, then "tolerance" has lost its meaning and is simply a cover for trying to shame and coerce others not to publicly (and/or perhaps privately) disagree with one's controversial and disputed position on human sexuality. This, ironically, is an example of intolerance (as traditionally understood). So, it seems to me, that the appeal to tolerance, once we have a clear understanding of its meaning, is *inconsistent* with relativism.

b. Relativism is itself a closed-minded and intolerant position. After all, the relativist dogmatically asserts that there is no moral truth. To illustrate this, consider a dialogue (based loosely on a real-life exchange) between a high-school teacher and her student Elizabeth.[12] The teacher instructs her class, "Welcome, students. This is the first day of class, and so I want to lay down some ground rules. First, since no one has the truth about morality, you should be open-minded to the opinions of your fellow students." The teacher recognizes the raised hand of Elizabeth, who asks, "If nobody has the truth, isn't that a good reason for me not to listen to my fellow students? After all, if nobody has the truth, why should I waste my time listening to other people and their opinions? What's the point? Only if somebody has the truth does it make sense to be open-minded. Don't you agree?"

"No, I don't. Are you claiming to know the truth? Isn't that a bit arrogant and dogmatic?"

"Not at all. Rather, I think it's dogmatic, as well as arrogant, to assert that no single person on earth knows the truth. After all, have you met every person in the world and quizzed them exhaustively? If not, how can you make such a claim? Also, I believe it is actually the

opposite of arrogance to say that I will alter my opinions to fit the truth whenever and wherever I find it. And if I happen to think that I have good reason to believe I do know the truth and would like to share it with you, why wouldn't you listen to me? Why would you automatically discredit my opinion before it is even uttered? I thought we were supposed to listen to everyone's opinion."

"This should prove to be an interesting semester."

Another student blurts out, "Ain't that the truth," provoking the class to laughter.

c. Relativism is judgmental, exclusivist, and partisan. This may seem like an odd thing to say since the relativist would like you to think his viewpoint is nonjudgmental, inclusivist, and neutral when it comes to moral beliefs. But consider the following.

First, the relativist says that if you believe in objective moral truth, you are *wrong*. Hence, relativism is judgmental. Second, it follows from this that relativism is *excluding* your beliefs from the realm of legitimate options. Thus, relativism is exclusivist. And third, because relativism is exclusive, all nonrelativists are automatically not members of the "correct thinking" party. So, relativism is partisan.

Tolerance only makes sense within the framework of a moral order, for it is within such a framework that one can morally justify tolerating some things while not tolerating others. For tolerance without a moral framework, or absolute tolerance, leads to a dogmatic relativism, and thus to an intolerance of any viewpoint that does not embrace relativism. It is no wonder that in such a climate of "tolerance" any person who maintains that there is an objective moral order to which society ought to subscribe is greeted with ferocious hatred.

d. The "tolerance" of moral relativism either condones barbarism or is self-refuting. As I pointed out, some moral relativists embrace tolerance because they believe that such a posture is appropriate given the diversity of moral and cultural traditions in the world today. Humanist author Xiaorong Li points out the fallacy in this reasoning:

> But the existence of moral diversity does no more to justify that we ought to respect different moral values than the existence of disease, hunger, torture, slavery do to justify that we ought to value them. Empirical claims thus are not suitable as the basis for developing moral principles such as "Never judge other cultures" or "We ought to tolerate different values." . . .
>
> What if the respected or tolerated culture disrespects and advocates violence against individuals who dissent? When a girl fights to escape female genital circumcision or footbinding or arranged marriage, when a widow does not want to be burned to death to honor her dead husband, the relativist is obligated to "respect" the cultural or traditional customs from which the individuals are trying to escape. In so doing, the relativist is not merely disrespecting the individual but effectively endorsing the moral ground for torture, rape and murder. *On moral issues, ethical relativists cannot possibly remain neutral. They are committed either to the individual or to the dominant force within a culture.*
>
> Relativists have made explicit one central value—equal respect and tolerance of other ways of life, which they insist to be absolute and universal. *Ethical relativism is thus repudiated by itself.*[13]

CONCLUSION

Moral relativism is a philosophical failure. The two main arguments for moral relativism—the argument from disagreement and the argument from tolerance—are seriously flawed in numerous ways. Given the failure of moral relativism, it seems reasonable to believe that objective moral norms exist.

NOTES

1. Hadley Arkes' work, *First Things: An Inquiry Into the First Principles of Moral and Justice* (Princeton NJ: Princeton University Press, 1986), was instrumental in helping me to better understand the difference between the two statements.

2. For an overview of the abortion debate from different sides, see Louis P. Pojman and Francis J. Beckwith, eds., *The Abortion Controversy 25 Years After Roe v. Wade: A Reader,* 2nd ed. (Belmont, CA: Wadsworth, 1998).

3. See, for example, Louis P. Pojman, *Ethics: Discovering Right and Wrong,* 3rd ed. (Belmont, CA: Wadsworth, 1998). Pojman, a supporter of abortion rights, is a critic of moral relativism as well as a defender of moral objectivism. For his defense of the pro-choice position, see Pojman, "Abortion: A Defense of the Personhood Argument," in *The Abortion Controversy.*

4. Arkes, *First Things,* 149.

5. Ibid., 132.

6. See James Rachels, "A Critique of Ethical Relativism," in *Philosophy: The Quest for Truth,* ed. Louis P. Pojman (Belmont, CA: Wadsworth, 1989), 317–325.

7. Ibid., 322–323.

8. Sophisticated pro-choice advocates argue that fetuses are not human persons. And for this reason, fetuses do not have a right to life if their life hinders the liberty of a being who is a person (i.e., the pregnant woman). See H. Tristram Englehardt, Jr., "The Ontology of Abortion," *Ethics* 84 (1973–74); Michael Tooley, *Abortion and Infanticide* (New York: Oxford, 1983); Michael Tooley, "In Defense of Abortion and Infanticide," in *The Abortion Controversy;* Pojman, "Abortion: A Defense of the Personhood Argument," in *The Abortion Controversy;* and Mary Ann Warren, "On the Moral and Legal Status of Abortion," in *The Problem of Abortion,* 2nd ed., ed. Joel Feinberg (Belmont, CA: Wadsworth, 1984). For critiques of these and other views, see Francis J. Beckwith, *Politically Correct Death:*

Answering the Arguments for Abortion Rights (Grand Rapids MI: Baker, 1993); Francis J. Beckwith, *Abortion and the Sanctity of Human Life* (Joplin, MO: College Press, 2000); Patrick Lee, *Abortion and Unborn Human Life* (Washington, DC: The Catholic University of America Press, 1996); J. P. Moreland and Scott B. Rae, *Body and Soul: Human Nature and the Crisis in Ethics* (Downers Grove, IL: InterVarsity Press, 2000); Stephen Schwarz, *The Moral Question of Abortion* (Chicago: Loyola University Press, 1990); and Don Marquis, "Why Abortion is Immoral," *The Journal of Philosophy* 86 (April 1989).

9. J. P. Moreland, *Scaling the Secular City* (Grand Rapids MI: Baker, 1987), 92.
10. Ibid., 243.
11. Tom L. Beauchamp, *Philosophical Ethics: An Introduction to Moral Philosophy* (New York: McGraw-Hill, 1982), 42.
12. This dialogue is presented in slightly different form in Francis J. Beckwith and Gregory P. Koukl, *Relativism: Feet Firmly Planted in Mid-Air* (Grand Rapids MI: Baker, 1998), 74.
13. Xiaorang Li, "Postmodernism and Universal Human Rights: Why Theory and Reality Don't Mix," *Free Inquiry* 18.4 (fall 1998): 28.

Discussion Questions

1. How, according to Professor Beckwith, has moral relativism negatively affected the way in which we understand moral issues? Do you agree or disagree with this assessment? Explain and defend your answer.
2. Present and explain the first argument for moral relativism to which Professor Beckwith introduces us in his essay. Present and explain the four problems he sees with this argument. Do you agree or disagree with him? Explain and defend your answer.
3. Present and explain the second argument for moral relativism to which Professor Beckwith introduces us in his essay. Present and explain the four problems he sees with this argument. Do you agree or disagree with him? Explain and defend your answer.

You can locate InfoTrac-College Education articles about this chapter by accessing the InfoTrac-College Edition website (http://www.infotrac-college.com/wadsworth/). Using the InfoTrac-College Edition subject guide, enter the search terms relevant to this chapter, and then read abstracts for relevant articles.

SECTION B

Ethical Theory

Introduction to Section B

The field of ethics traditionally has been dominated by two types of ethical systems, that is, methods of reasoning that either tell us what is the correct moral decision in a given situation or explain why the moral judgment we have already made is correct or incorrect. *Utilitarian* systems of ethics say that moral decisions ought to be made because of their nonmoral consequences (e.g., more pleasure than pain or more benefit than harm for the greatest number), resulting from either the act itself (act utilitarianism) or obeying a general rule (rule utilitarianism). Although agreeing that results may play a part in ethical decision making, *deontological* systems say that moral decisions ought to be made on the basis of the intrinsic moral goodness or badness of the act in question. In order to better understand these types of systems, Professor Louis P. Pojman provides the following story:

> Suppose that you are on an island with a dying millionaire. As he lies dying, he asks you for one final favor. He entreats you, "I've dedicated my whole life to baseball and have gotten endless pleasure (and some pain) rooting for the New York Yankees for 50 years. Now that I am dying, I want to give all of my assets, $2 million, to the Yankees. Would you take this money (he indicates a box containing money in large bills) to New York and give it to the Yankees' owner, George Steinbrenner?" You agree to carry out his wish, at which point a huge smile of relief and gratitude breaks out on his face as he expires in your arms. Now on traveling to New York you see a newspaper advertisement placed by the World Hunger Relief Organization (whose integrity you do not doubt), pleading for $2 million to be used to save 100,000 people dying of starvation in East Africa. Not only will $2 million be used to save 100,000 lives, but it will also enable the purchase of certain kinds of technology and the kinds of fertilizers necessary to build a sustainable economy. You begin to consider your promise to the dying Yankees fan in the light of the advertisement. What should you do with the money?[1]

If you decide to give the money to the World Hunger Relief Organization you are siding with the utilitarians (at least, the *act* utilitarians), since they would conclude that the greatest good for the greatest number is achieved by donating the money to charity, and not following the millionaire's wishes. (Some *rule* utilitarians may not do this, for they may see a greater societal benefit in keeping a promise made to a dying person). On the other hand, if you decide to give the money to the Yankees' organization, you are siding with the deontologists, who maintain that truth-telling and promise-keeping are intrinsically good.

Immanuel Kant is the author of Chapter 3. Kant, a German philosopher of the eighteenth-century, was the quintessential deontologist, maintaining that certain moral absolutes could be arrived at by the employment of reason by means of what Kant called "the categorical imperative." Chapter 4 is authored by John Stuart Mill, a nineteenth-century British philosopher, who defended a form of utilitarianism. In Chapter 5, Susan Dimock provides a presentation of the natural law view of St. Thomas Aquinas. Thomas maintained that certain moral laws, grounded in the nature of God and his eternal laws, could be known by reflection on the nature and order of things. Although a deontologist like Kant, Aquinas, unlike Kant, believed that there are certain moral truths about human nature that we can know. Aquinas did not have a formula, like the categorical imperative, from which he derived certain moral rules. Rather, Aquinas's natural law view stems from a particular view of what constitutes the good of human life from which one can know certain moral truths. Virtue ethics is the topic of Chapter 6. Education professor William K. Kilpatrick argues that the traditional way of teaching ethics and morality—reasoning from theories to principles and applying them to moral dilemmas (such as the New York Yankees example above)—is highly contrived and should be supplemented, if not eclipsed, by virtue ethics (or character ethics), the instilling of ethics by studying the stories, lives, and examples of virtuous people found in history, fiction, and mythology. This is a view championed by former United States Secretary of Education, William J. Bennett, in his anthology *The Book of Virtues* (1993).

Keywords: ethical theory, utilitarianism, deontological ethics, natural law, virtue ethics, Kantian ethics, metaethics, philosophical ethics, moral philosophy.

NOTES

1. Louis P. Pojman, *Ethics: Discovering Right and Wrong* (Belmont, CA: Wadsworth, 1990), 73–74.

For Further Reading

Tom L. Beauchamp, *Philosophical Ethics: An Introduction to Moral Philosophy,* 2nd ed. (New York: McGraw-Hill, 1991).

J. Budziszewski, *Written on the Heart: The Case for Natural Law* (Downers Grove, IL: InterVarsity Press, 1987).

David K. Clark and Robert V. Rakestraw, eds., *Readings in Christian Ethics, Volume 1: Theory and Method* (Grand Rapids, MI: Baker, 1994).

John Finnis, *Natural Law and Natural Rights* (New York: Oxford University Press, 1980).

William K. Frankena, *Ethics,* 2nd ed. (Englewood Cliffs, NJ: Prentice-Hall, 1973).

Robert P. George, *In Defense of Natural Law* (New York: Oxford University Press, 1999).

Bernard Gert, *Morality: A Justification of the Moral Rules* (New York: Oxford University Press, 1988).

Russell Hittinger, *A Critique of the New Natural Law Theory* (Notre Dame, IN: University of Notre Dame Press, 1987).

Immanuel Kant, *The Foundations of the Metaphysic of Morals,* trans. Lewis White Beck (Indianapolis: Bobbs-Merrill, 1959).

John Stuart Mill, *Utilitarianism* (Indianapolis: Bobbs-Merrill, 1957).

Kai Nielsen, *Ethics Without God,* rev. ed. (Buffalo, NY: Prometheus, 1989).

Louis P. Pojman, ed., *Ethical Theory: Classical and Contemporary Readings,* 3rd ed. (Belmont, CA: Wadsworth, 1998).

————, ed., *Ethics: Discovering Right and Wrong,* 3rd ed. (Belmont, CA: Wadsworth, 1998).

James Rachels, *The Elements of Moral Philosophy,* (New York: Random House, 1986).

3   The Categorical Imperative

IMMANUEL KANT

Immanuel Kant (1724–1804) was a German philosopher who taught at the University of Koenigsberg. One of the most important philosophers in the history of Western thought, Kant is the author of numerous works including *The Critique of Pure Reason* (1781), a book that challenged the traditional way philosophers had thought we acquired knowledge. Kant argued that the mind and its categories significantly shaped our knowledge of "the world" to such an extent that Kant believed that causality, time, and space were not "out there" but in our minds. Kant is also the author of *Fundamental Principles of the Metaphysics of Ethics* (1785), from which the following selection is taken.

In this essay Kant argues that morality cannot be grounded in the contingent facts of human nature but on a rational principle that is universal and necessary. Although this may sound strange, it has a certain intuitive appeal. For example, suppose someone were to present the following contingent moral principle: "Each person has a moral right to do whatever he or she wants to do as long as he or she does not hurt anybody else." Kant would say that such a moral "principle" is no principle at all, for it has little if anything to do with moral justification. Consider the following example. If Bob killed his neighbor, Fred, because Fred was bald and Bob believed the bald should die, that would not constitute justification for killing Fred. However, what if, while Bob was plotting to kill him, Fred came to the same realization as Bob had and concluded that the bald, including himself, should die. Suppose that Fred goes ahead and kills himself for *the same reason* as Bob would have killed him if Fred had not beat him to it. Since the reason for the killing is the same, and the reason is unjustified, it cannot be that "each person has a moral right to do whatever he or she wants to do as long as he or she does not hurt anybody else." Thus, it is not, according to Kant's thinking, a real moral principle.

After a brief discussion of why moral law must be universal and necessary, Kant concerns himself with the "good will," arguing that because apparently good

---

Reprinted from Fundamental Principles of the Metaphysics of Ethics *(1785) T.K. Abbott, translator (London: Longmans, Green, and Co., 1934)*

behaviors (e.g., self-control) may be consistent with an evil act (e.g., a calm and collective thief), what is most important is a good will, that is, a will that wills the good for its own sake rather than for some end or purpose. Kant then goes on to argue that reason must guide the will. After presenting what he considers the three propositions of morality, Kant explains and defends the basis of his moral theory, the categorical imperative. In the final sections of his essay Kant provides four illustrations of the application of the categorical imperative as well as a second formulation of it, which includes a brief discussion of "the kingdom of ends."

PREFACE

AS MY CONCERN HERE is with moral philosophy, I limit the question suggested to this: Whether it is not of the utmost necessity to construct a pure moral philosophy, perfectly cleared of everything which is only empirical, and which belongs to anthropology? for that such a philosophy must be possible is evident from the common idea of duty and of the moral laws. Everyone must admit that if a law is to have moral force, *i.e.* to be the basis of an obligation, it must carry with it absolute necessity; that, for example, the precept, "Thou shall not lie," is not valid for men alone, as if other rational beings had no need to observe it; and so with all the other moral laws properly so called; that, therefore, the basis of obligation must not be sought in the nature of man, or in the circumstances in the world in which he is placed, but *a priori* simply in the conception of pure reason; and although any other precept which is founded on principles of mere experience may be in certain respects universal, yet in as far as it rests even in the least degree on an empirical basis, perhaps only as to a motive, such a precept, while it may be a practical rule, can never be called a moral law. . . .

THE GOOD WILL

Nothing can possibly be conceived in the world, or even out of it, which can be called good, without qualification, except a Good Will. Intelligence, wit, judgment, and the other *talents* of the mind, however they may be named, or courage, resolution, perseverance, as qualities of temperament, are undoubtedly good and desirable in many respects; but these gifts of nature may also become extremely bad and mischievous if the will which is to make use of them, and which, therefore, constitutes what is called *character*, is not good. It is the same with the *gifts of fortune*. Power, riches, honour, even health, and the general well-being and contentment with one's conditions which is called *happiness*, inspire pride, and often presumption, if there is not a good will to correct the influence of these on the mind, and with this also to rectify the whole principle of acting, and adapt it to its end. The sight of a being who is not adorned with a single feature of a pure and good will, enjoying unbroken prosperity, can never give pleasure to an impartial rational spectator. Thus a good will appears to constitute the indispensable condition even of being worthy of happiness.

There are even some qualities which are of service to this good will itself, and may facilitate its action, yet which have no intrinsic unconditional value, but always presuppose a good will, and this qualifies the esteem that we justly have for them, and does not permit us to regard them as absolutely good. Moderation in the affections and passions, self-control, and calm deliberation are not only good in many respects, but even seem to constitute part of the intrinsic worth of the person; but they are far from deserving to be called good without qualification, although they have been so unconditionally praised by the ancients. For without the principles of a good will, they may become extremely bad; and the coolness of a villain not only makes him far more dangerous, but also directly makes him more abominable in our eyes than he would have been without it.

A good will is good not because of what it performs or effects, not by its aptness for the attainment of some proposed end, but simply by virtue of the volition, that is, it is good in itself, and considered by itself to be esteemed much higher than all that can be brought about by it in favour of any inclination, nay, even of the sum-total of all inclinations. Even if it should happen that, owing to special disfavour of fortune, or the niggardly provision of a step-motherly nature, this will should wholly lack power to accomplish its purpose, if with its greatest efforts it should yet achieve nothing, and there should remain only the good will (not, to be sure, a mere wish, but the summoning of all means in our power), then, like a jewel, it would still shine by its own light, as a thing which has its whole value in itself. Its usefulness or fruitlessness can neither add to nor take away anything from this value. It would be, as it were, only the setting to enable us to handle it the more conveniently in common commerce, or to attract to it the attention of those who are not yet connoisseurs, but not to recommend it to true connoisseurs, or to determine its value.

WHY REASON WAS MADE TO GUIDE THE WILL

There is, however, something so strange in this idea of the absolute value of the mere will, in which no account is taken of its utility, that notwithstanding the thorough assent of even common reason to the idea, yet a suspicion must arise that it may perhaps really be the product of mere high-blown fancy, and that we may have misunderstood the purpose of nature

in assigning reason as the governor of the will. Therefore we will examine this idea from this point of view.

In the physical constitution of an organized being, that is, a being adapted suitably to the purposes of life, we assume it as a fundamental principle that no organ for any purpose will be found but what is also the fittest and best adapted for that purpose. Now in a being which has reason and a will, if the proper object of nature were its *conservatism,* its *welfare,* in a word, its *happiness,* then nature would have hit upon a very bad arrangement in selecting the reason of the creature to carry out this purpose. For all the actions which the creature has to perform with a view to this purpose, and the whole rule of its conduct, would be far more surely prescribed to it by instinct, and that end would have been attained thereby much more certainly than it ever can be by reason. Should reason have been communicated to this favoured creature over and above, it must only have served it to contemplate the happy constitution of its nature, to admire it, to congratulate itself thereon, and to feel thankful for it to the beneficent cause, but not that it should subject its desires to that weak and delusive guidance, and meddle bunglingly with the purpose of nature. In a word, nature would have taken care that reason should not break forth into *practical exercise,* nor have the presumption, with its weak insight, to think out for itself the plan of happiness, and of the means of attaining it. Nature would not only have taken on herself the choice of the ends, but also of the means, and with wise foresight would have entrusted both to instinct.

And, in fact, we find that the more a cultivated reason applies itself with deliberate purpose to the enjoyment of life and happiness, so much the more does the man fail of true satisfaction. And from this circumstance there arises in many, if they are candid enough to confess it, a certain degree of *misology,* that is, hatred of reason, especially in the case of those who are most experienced in the use of it, because after calculating all the advantages they derive, I do not say from the invention of all the arts of common luxury, but even from the sciences (which seem to them to be after all only a luxury of the understanding), they find that they have, in fact, only brought more trouble on their shoulders, rather than gained in happiness; and they end by envying, rather than despising, the more common stamp of men who keep closer to the guidance of mere instinct, and do not allow their reason much influence on their conduct. And this we must admit, that the judgment of those who would very much lower the lofty eulogies of the advantages which reason gives us in regard to the happiness and satisfaction of life, or who would even reduce them below zero, is by no means morose or ungrateful to the goodness with which the world is governed, but that there lies at the root of these judgments the idea that our existence has a different and far nobler end, for which, and not for happiness, reason is properly intended, and which must, therefore, be regarded as the supreme condition to which the private ends of man must, for the most part, be postponed.

For as reason is not competent to guide the will with certainty in regard to its objects and the satisfaction of all our wants (which it to some extent even multiplies), this being an end to which an implanted instinct would have led with much greater certainty; and since, nevertheless, reason is imparted to us as a practical faculty *i.e.* as one which is to have influence on the *will,* therefore, admitting that nature generally in the distribution of her capacities has adapted the means to the end, its true destination must be to produce a *will,* not merely good as a *means* to something else, but *good in itself,* for which reason was absolutely necessary. This will then, though not indeed the sole and complete good, must be the supreme good and the condition of every other, even of the desire of happiness. Under these circumstances, there is nothing inconsistent with the wisdom of nature in the fact that the cultivation of the rea-

son, which is requisite for the first and unconditional purpose, does in many ways interfere, at least in this life, with the attainment of the second, which is always conditional, namely, happiness. Nay, it may even reduce it to nothing, without nature thereby failing in her purpose. For reason recognizes the establishment of a good will as its highest practical destination, and in attaining this purpose is capable only of a satisfaction of its own proper kind, namely, that from the attainment of an end, which end again is determined by reason only, notwithstanding that this may involve many a disappointment to the ends of inclination.

THE FIRST PROPOSITION OF MORALITY [AN ACTION MUST BE DONE FROM A SENSE OF DUTY, IF IT IS TO HAVE MORAL WORTH]

We have then to develop the notion of a will which deserves to be highly esteemed for itself, and is good without a view to anything further, a notion which exists already in the sound natural understanding, requiring rather to be cleared up than to be taught, and which in estimating the value of our actions always takes the first place, and constitutes the condition of all the rest. In order to do this, we will take the notion of duty, which includes that of a good will, although implying certain subjective restrictions and hindrances. These, however, far from concealing it, or rendering it unrecognizable, rather bring it out by contrast, and make it shine forth so much the brighter.

I omit here all actions which are already recognized as inconsistent with duty although they may be useful for this or that purpose, for with these the question whether they are done *from duty* cannot arise at all, since they even conflict with it. I also set aside those actions which really conform to duty, but to which men have *no* direct *inclination,* performing them because they are impelled thereto by some other inclination.

For in this case we can readily distinguish whether the action which agrees with duty is done *from duty,* or from a selfish view. It is much harder to make this distinction when the action accords with duty, and the subject has besides a *direct* inclination to it. For example, it is always a matter of duty that a dealer should not overcharge an inexperienced purchaser; and wherever there is much commerce the prudent tradesman does not overcharge, but keeps a fixed price for everyone, so that a child buys of him as well as any other. Men are thus *honestly* served; but this is not enough to make us believe that the tradesman has so acted from duty and from principles of honesty: his own advantage required it; it is out of the question in this case to suppose that he might besides have a direct inclination in favour of the buyers, so that, as it were, from love he should give no advantage to one over another. Accordingly the action was done neither from duty nor from direct inclination, but merely with a selfish view.

On the other hand, it is a duty to maintain one's life; and, in addition, everyone has also a direct inclination to do so. But on this account the often anxious care which most men take for it has no intrinsic worth, and their maxim has no moral import. They preserve their life *as duty requires,* no doubt, but not *because duty requires.* On the other hand, if adversity and hopeless sorrow have completely taken away the relish for life; if the unfortunate one, strong in mind, indignant at his fate rather than desponding or dejected, wishes for death, and yet preserves his life without loving it— not from inclination or fear, but from duty— then his maxim has a moral worth.

To be beneficent when we can is a duty; and besides this, there are many minds so sympathetically constituted that, without any other motive of vanity or self-interest, they find a pleasure in spreading joy around them, and can take delight in the satisfaction of others so far as it is their own work. But I maintain that in such a case an action of this kind, however proper, however amiable it may be, has nevertheless no true moral worth, but is on a level with other inclinations, *e.g.* the inclination to honour, which, if it is happily directed to that which is in fact of public utility and accordant with duty, and consequently honourable, deserves praise and encouragement, but not esteem. For the maxim lacks the moral import, namely, that such actions be done *from duty,* not from inclination. Put the case that the mind of that philanthropist was clouded by sorrow of his own, extinguishing all sympathy with the lot of others, and that while he still has the power to benefit others in distress, he is not touched by their trouble because he is absorbed with his own; and now suppose that he tears himself out of this dead insensibility, and performs the action without any inclination to it, but simply from duty, then first has his action its genuine moral worth. Further still; if nature has put little sympathy in the heart of this or that man; if he, supposed to be an upright man, is by temperament cold and indifferent to the sufferings of others, perhaps because in respect of his own he is provided with the special gift of patience and fortitude, and supposes, or even requires, that others should have the same—and such a man would certainly not be the meanest product of nature—but if nature had not specially framed him for a philanthropist, would he not still find in himself a source from whence to give himself a far higher worth than that of a good-natured temperament? Unquestionably. It is just in this that the moral worth of the character is brought out which is incomparably the highest of all, namely that he is beneficent, not from inclination, but from duty.

To secure one's own happiness is a duty, at least indirectly; for discontent with one's condition, under a pressure of many anxieties and amidst unsatisfied wants, might easily become a great *temptation to transgression of duty.* But here again, without looking to duty, all men have already the strongest and most intimate inclination to happiness, because it is just in this idea that all inclinations are combined in one total. But the precept of happiness is often of such a sort that it greatly interferes with some inclinations, and yet a man cannot form any definite and certain conception of the sum of satisfaction of all of them which is called happiness. It is not then to be wondered at that a single inclination, definite both as to what it promises and as to the time within which it can be gratified, is often able to overcome such a fluctuating idea, and that a gouty patient, for instance, can choose to enjoy what he likes, and to suffer what he may, since, according to his calculation, on this occasion at least, he has [only] not sacrificed the enjoyment of the present moment to a possibly mistaken expectation of a happiness which is supposed to be found in health. But even in this case, if the general desire for happiness did not influence his will, and supposing that in his particular case health was not a necessary element in this calculation, there yet remains in this, as in all other cases, this law, namely, that he should promote his happiness not from inclination but from duty, and by this would his conduct first acquire true moral worth.

It is in this manner, undoubtedly, that we are to understand those passages of Scripture also in which we are commanded to love our neighbour, even our enemy. For love, as an affection, cannot be commanded, but beneficence for duty's sake may; even though we are not impelled to it by any inclination—nay, are even repelled by a natural and unconquerable aversion. This is *practical* love, and not *pathological* [passional or emotional—Ed.]—a love which is seated in the will, and not in the propensions of sense—in principles of action and not of tender sympathy; and it is this love alone which can be commanded.

THE SECOND PROPOSITION OF MORALITY

The second proposition is: That an action done from duty derives its moral worth, *not from the purpose* which is to be attained by it,

but from the maxim by which it is determined, and therefore does not depend on the realization of the object of the action, but merely on the *principle of volition* by which the action has taken place, without regard to any object of desire. It is clear from what precedes that the purposes which we may have in view in our actions, or their effects regarded as ends and springs of the will, cannot give to actions any unconditional or moral worth. In what, then, can their worth lie, if it is not to consist in the will and in reference to its expected effect? It cannot lie anywhere but in the *principle of the will* without regard to the ends which can be attained by the action. For the will stands between its *a priori principle,* which is formal, and its *a posteriori* spring, which is material, as between two roads, and as it must be determined by something, it follows that it must be determined by the formal principle of volition when an action is done from duty, in which case every material principle has been withdrawn from it.

THE THIRD PROPOSITION OF MORALITY

The third proposition, which is a consequence of the two preceding, I would express thus: *Duty is the necessity of acting from respect for the law.* I may have *inclination* for an object as the effect of my proposed action, but I cannot have *respect* for it, just for this reason, that it is an effect and not an energy of will. Similarly, I cannot have respect for inclination, whether my own or another's; I can at most, if my own, approve it; if another's, sometimes even love it; *i.e.* look on it as favourable to my own interest. It is only what is connected with my will as a principle, by no means as an effect—what does not subserve my inclination, but overpowers it, or at least in case of choice excludes it from its calculation—in other words, simply the law of itself, which can be an object of respect, and hence a command. Now an action done from duty must wholly exclude the influence of inclination, and with it every object of the will, so that nothing remains which can determine the will except objectively the *law,* and subjectively *pure respect* for this practical law, and consequently the maxim that I should follow this law even to the thwarting of all my inclinations.

Thus the moral worth of an action does not lie in the effect expected from it, nor in any principle of action which requires to borrow its motive from this expected effect. For all these effects—agreeableness of one's condition, and even the promotion of the happiness of others— could have been also brought about by other causes, so that for this there would have been no need of the will of a rational being; whereas it is in this alone that the supreme and unconditional good can be found. The pre-eminent good which we call moral can therefore consist in nothing else than *the conception of law* in itself, *which certainly is only possible in a rational being,* in so far as this conception, and not the expected effect, determines the will. This is a good which is already present in the person who acts accordingly, and we have not to wait for it to appear first in the result.

THE SUPREME PRINCIPLE OF MORALITY: THE CATEGORICAL IMPERATIVE

But what sort of law can that be, the conception of which must determine the will, even without paying any regard to the effect expected from it, in order that this will may be called good absolutely and without qualification? As I have deprived the will of every impulse which could arise to it from obedience to any law, there remains nothing but the universal conformity of its actions to law in general, which alone is to serve the will as a principle, *i.e.* I am never to act otherwise than so *that I could also will that my maxim should become a universal law.* Here, now, it is the simple conformity to law in general, without assuming any

particular law applicable to certain actions, that serves the will as its principle, and must so serve it, if duty is not to be a vain delusion and a chimerical notion. The common reason of men in its practical judgments perfectly coincides with this, and always has in view the principle here suggested. Let the question be, for example: May I when in distress make a promise with the intention not to keep it? I readily distinguish here between the two significations which the question may have: Whether it is prudent, or whether it is right, to make a false promise? The former may undoubtedly often be the case. I see clearly indeed that it is not enough to extricate myself from a present difficulty by means of this subterfuge, but it must be well considered whether there may not hereafter spring from this lie much greater inconvenience than that from which I now free myself, and as, with all my supposed *cunning,* the consequences cannot be so easily foreseen but that credit once lost may be much more injurious to me than any mischief which I seek to avoid at present, it should be considered whether it would not be more *prudent* to act herein according to a universal maxim, and to make it a habit to promise nothing except with the intention of keeping it. But it is soon clear to me that such a maxim will still only be based on the fear of consequences. Now it is a wholly different thing to be truthful from duty, and to be so from apprehension of injurious consequences. In the first case, the very notion of the action already implies a law for me; in the second case, I must first look about elsewhere to see what results may be combined with it which would affect myself. For to deviate from the principle of duty is beyond all doubt wicked; but to be unfaithful to my maxim of prudence may often be very advantageous to me, although to abide by it is certainly safer. The shortest way, however, and an unerring one, to discover the answer to this question whether a lying promise is consistent with duty, is to ask myself, Should I be content that my maxim (to extricate myself from difficulty by a false promise) should hold good as a universal law, for myself as well as for others? and should I be able to say to myself, "Every one may make a deceitful promise when he finds himself in a difficulty from which he cannot otherwise extricate himself"? Then I presently become aware that while I can will the lie, I can by no means will that lying should be a universal law. For with such a law there would be no promises at all, since it would be in vain to allege my intention in regard to my future actions to those who would not believe this allegation, or if they over-hastily did so, would pay me back in my own coin. Hence my maxim, as soon as it should be made a universal law, would necessarily destroy itself.

I do not, therefore, need any far-reaching penetration to discern what I have to do in order that my will may be morally good. Inexperienced in the course of the world, incapable of being prepared for all its contingencies, I only ask myself: Canst thou also will that thy maxim should be a universal law? If not, then it must be rejected, and that not because of a disadvantage accruing from myself or even to others, but because it cannot enter as a principle into a possible universal legislation, and reason extorts from me immediate respect for such legislation. I do not indeed as yet *discern* on what this respect is based (this the philosopher may inquire), but at least I understand this, that it is an estimation of the worth which far outweighs all worth of what is recommended by inclination, and that the necessity of acting from *pure* respect for the practical law is what constitutes duty, to which every other motive must give place, because it is the condition of a will being good *in itself,* and the worth of such a will is above everything.

Thus, then, without quitting the moral knowledge of common human reason, we have arrived at its principle. And although, no doubt, common men do not conceive it in such an abstract and universal form, yet they always have it really before their eyes, and use it as the standard of their decision. . . .

Nor could anything be more fatal to morality than that we should wish to derive it from examples. For every example of it that is set before me must be first itself tested by principles of morality, whether it is worthy to serve as an original example, *i.e.* as a pattern, but by no means can it authoritatively furnish the conception of morality. Even the Holy One of the Gospels must first be compared with our ideal of moral perfection before we can recognize Him as such; and so He says of Himself, "Why call ye Me [whom you see] good; none is good [the model of good] but God only [whom ye do not see]." But whence have we the conception of God as the supreme good? Simply from the *idea* of moral perfection, which reason frames *a priori,* and connects inseparably with the notion of a free will. Imitation finds no place at all in morality, and examples serve only for encouragement, *i.e.* they put beyond doubt the feasibility of what the law commands, they make visible that which the practical rule expresses more generally, but they can never authorize us to set aside the true original which lies in reason, and to guide ourselves by examples.

From what has been said, it is clear that all moral conceptions have their seat and origin completely *a priori* in the reason, and that, moreover, in the commonest reason just as truly as in that which is in the highest degree speculative; that they cannot be obtained by abstraction from any empirical, and therefore merely contingent knowledge; that it is just this purity of their origin that makes them worthy to serve as our supreme practical principle, and that just in proportion as we add anything empirical, we detract from their genuine influence, and from the absolute value of actions; that it is not only of the greatest necessity, in a purely speculative point of view, but is also of the greatest practical importance, to derive these notions and laws from pure reason, to present them pure and unmixed, and even to determine the compass of this practical or pure rational knowledge, *i.e.* to determine the whole faculty of pure practical reason; and, in doing so, we must not make its principles dependent on the particular nature of human reason, though in speculative philosophy this may be permitted, or may even at times be necessary; but since moral laws ought to hold good for every rational creature, we must derive them from the general concept of a rational being. In this way, although for its *application* to man morality has need of anthropology, yet, in the first instance, we must treat it independently as pure philosophy, *i.e.* as metaphysic, complete in itself (a thing which in such distinct branches of science is easily done); knowing well that unless we are in possession of this, it would not only be vain to determine the moral element of duty in right actions for purposes of speculative criticism, but it would be impossible to base morals on their genuine principles, even for common practical purposes, especially of moral instruction, so as to produce pure moral dispositions, and to engraft them on men's minds to the promotion of the greatest possible good in the world. . . .

THE RATIONAL GROUND OF THE CATEGORICAL IMPERATIVE

. . . the question, how the imperative of *morality* is possible, is undoubtedly one, the only one, demanding a solution, as this is not at all hypothetical, and the objective necessity which it presents cannot rest on any hypothesis, as is the case with the hypothetical imperatives. Only here we must never leave out of consideration that we *cannot* make out *by any example*, in other words empirically, whether there is such an imperative at all; but it is rather to be feared that all those which seem to be categorical may yet be at bottom hypothetical. For instance, when the precept is: Thou shalt not promise deceitfully; and it is assumed that the necessity of this is not a mere counsel to avoid some other evil, so that it should mean: Thou shalt not make a lying promise, lest if it become known thou shouldst destroy thy credit, but that an action of this kind must be regarded as evil in itself, so that the imperative of the prohibition is categorical; then we cannot show with certainty in any example that the will was determined merely by the law, without any other spring of action, although it may appear to be so. For it is always possible that fear of disgrace, perhaps also obscure dread of other dangers, may have a secret influence on the will. Who can prove by experience the nonexistence of a cause when all that experience tells us is that we do not perceive it? But in such a case the so-called moral imperative, which as such appears to be categorical and unconditional, would in reality be only a pragmatic precept, drawing our attention to our own interests, and merely teaching us to take these into consideration.

We shall therefore have to investigate *a priori* the possibility of a categorical imperative, as we have not in this case the advantage of its reality being given in experience, so that [the elucidation of] its possibility should be requisite only for its explanation, not for its establishment. In the meantime it may be discerned beforehand that the categorical imperative alone has the purport of a practical law: all the rest may indeed be called *principles* of the will but not laws, since whatever is only necessary for the attainment of some arbitrary purpose may be considered as in itself contingent, and we can at any time be free from the precept if we give up the purpose: on the contrary, the unconditional command leaves the will no liberty to choose the opposite; consequently it alone carries with it that necessity which we require in a law.

Secondly, in the case of this categorical imperative or law of morality, the difficulty (of discerning its possibility) is a very profound one. It is an *a priori* synthetical practical proposition; and as there is so much difficulty in discerning the possibility of speculative propositions of this kind, it may readily be supposed that the difficulty will be no less with the practical.

FIRST FORMULATION OF THE CATEGORICAL IMPERATIVE: UNIVERSAL LAW

In this problem we will first inquire whether the mere conception of a categorical imperative may not perhaps supply us also with the formula of it, containing the proposition which alone can be a categorical imperative; for even if we know the tenor of such an absolute command, yet how it is possible will require further special and laborious study, which we postpone to the last section.

When I conceive a hypothetical imperative, in general I do not know beforehand what it will contain until I am given the condition. But when I conceive a categorical imperative, I know at once what it contains. For as the imperative contains besides the law only the necessity that the maxims shall conform to this law, while the law contain no conditions restricting it, there remains nothing but the general statement that the maxim of the action should conform to a universal law, and it is this conformity alone that the imperative properly represents as necessary.

There is therefore but one categorical imperative, namely, this: *Act only on that maxim whereby thou canst at the same time will that it should become a universal law.*

Now if all imperatives of duty can be deduced from this one imperative as from their principle, then, although it should remain undecided whether what is called duty is not merely a vain notion, yet at least we shall be able to show what we understand by it and what this notion means.

Since the universality of the law according to which effects are produced constitutes what is properly called *nature* in the most general sense (as to form), that is the existence of

things so far as it is determined by general laws, the imperative of duty may be expressed thus: *Act as if the maxim of thy action were to become by thy will a universal law of nature.*

FOUR ILLUSTRATIONS

We will now enumerate a few duties, adopting the usual division of them into duties to ourselves and to others, and into perfect and imperfect duties.

1. A man reduced to despair by a series of misfortunes feels wearied of life, but is still so far in possession of his reason that he can ask himself whether it would not be contrary to his duty to himself to take his own life. Now he inquires whether the maxim of his action could become a universal law of nature. His maxim is: From self-love I adopt it as a principle to shorten my life when its longer duration is likely to bring more evil than satisfaction. It is asked then simply whether this principle founded on self-love can become a universal law of nature. Now we see at once that a system of nature of which it should be a law to destroy life by means of the very feeling whose special nature it is to impel to the improvement of life would contradict itself, and therefore could not exist as a system of nature; hence the maxim cannot possibly exist as a universal law of nature, and consequently would be wholly inconsistent with the supreme principle of all duty.

2. Another finds himself forced by necessity to borrow money. He knows that he will not be able to repay it, but sees also that nothing will be lent to him, unless he promises stoutly to repay it in a definite time. He desires to make this promise, but he has still so much conscience as to ask himself: Is it not unlawful and inconsistent with duty to get out of a difficulty in this way? Suppose, however, that he resolves to do so, then the maxim of his action would be expressed thus: When I think myself

in want of money, I will borrow money and promise to repay it, although I know that I never can do so. Now this principle of self-love or of one's own advantage may perhaps be consistent with my whole future welfare; but the question is, Is it right? I change then the suggestion of self-love into a universal law, and state the question thus: How would it be if my maxim were a universal law? Then I see at once that it could never hold as a universal law of nature, but would necessarily contradict itself. For supposing it to be a universal law that everyone when he thinks himself in a difficulty should be able to promise whatever he pleases, with the purpose of not keeping his promise, the promise itself would become impossible, as well as the end that one might have in view in it, since no one would consider that anything was promised to him, but would ridicule all such statements as vain pretenses.

3. A third finds in himself a talent which with the help of some culture might make him a useful man in many respects. But he finds himself in comfortable circumstances, and prefers to indulge in pleasure rather than to take pains in enlarging and improving his happy natural capacities. He asks, however, whether his maxim of neglect of his natural gifts, besides agreeing with his inclination to indulgence, agrees also with what is called duty. He sees then that a system of nature could indeed subsist with such a universal law although men (like the South Sea islanders) should let their talents rest, and resolve to devote their lives merely to idleness, amusement, and propagation of their species—in a word, to enjoyment; but he cannot possibly *will* that this should be a universal law of nature, or be implanted in us as such by a natural instinct. For, as a rational being, he necessarily wills that his faculties be developed, since they serve him, and have been given him, for all sorts of possible purposes.

4. A fourth, who is in prosperity, while he sees that others have to contend with great wretchedness and that he could help them,

thinks: What concern is it of mine? Let everyone be as happy as Heaven pleases, or as he can make himself; I will take nothing from him nor even envy him, only I do not wish to contribute anything to his welfare or to his assistance in distress! Now no doubt if such a mode of thinking were a universal law, the human race might very well subsist, and doubtless even better than in a state in which everyone talks of sympathy and good-will, or even takes care occasionally to put it into practice, but, on the other side, also cheats when he can, betrays the rights of men, or otherwise violates them. But although it is possible that a universal law of nature might exist in accordance with that maxim, it is impossible to *will* that such a principle should have the universal validity of a law of nature. For a will which resolved this would contradict itself, inasmuch as many cases might occur in which one would have need of the love and sympathy of others, and in which, by such a law of nature, sprung from his own will, he would deprive himself of all hope of the aid he desires.

These are a few of the many actual duties, or at least what we regard as such, which obviously fall into two classes on the one principle that we have laid down. We must be *able to will* that a maxim of our action should be a universal law. This is the canon of the moral appreciation of the action generally. Some actions are of such a character that their maxim cannot without contradiction be even *conceived* as a universal law of nature, far from it being possible that we should *will* that it *should* be so. In others this intrinsic impossibility is not found, but still it is impossible to *will* that their maxim should be raised to the universality of a law of nature, since such a will would contradict itself. It is easily seen that the former violate strict or rigorous (inflexible) duty; the latter only laxer (meritorious) duty. Thus it has been completely shown by these examples how all duties depend as regards the nature of the obligation (not the object of the action) on the same principle. . . .

SECOND FORMULATION OF THE CATEGORICAL IMPERATIVE: HUMANITY AS AN END IN ITSELF

Now I say: man and generally any rational being *exists* as an end in himself, *not merely as a means* to be arbitrarily used by this or that will, but in all his actions, whether they concern himself or other rational beings, must be always regarded at the same time as an end. All objects of the inclinations have only a conditional worth; for if the inclinations and the wants founded on them did not exist, then their object would be without value. But the inclinations themselves being sources of want are so far from having an absolute worth for which they should be desired, that, on the contrary, it must be the universal wish of every rational being to be wholly free from them. Thus the worth of any object which is *to be acquired* by our action is always conditional. Beings whose existence depends not on our will but on nature's, have nevertheless, if they are non-rational beings, only a relative value as means, and are therefore called *things;* rational beings, on the contrary, are called *persons,* because their very nature points them out as ends in themselves, that is as something which must not be used merely as means, and so far therefore restricts freedom of action (and is an object of respect). These, therefore, are not merely subjective ends whose existence has a worth *for us* as an effect of our action, but *objective ends,* that is things whose existence is an end in itself: an end moreover for which no other can be substituted, which they should subserve *merely* as means, for otherwise nothing whatever would possess *absolute worth;* but if all worth were conditioned and therefore contingent, then there would be no supreme practical principle of reason whatever.

If then there is a supreme practical principle or, in respect of the human will, a categorical imperative, it must be one which, being drawn from the conception of that which is necessarily an end for everyone because it is *an end in itself,* constitutes an *objective* principle of will, and can therefore serve as a universal practical law. The foundation of this principle is: *rational nature exists as an end in itself.* Man necessarily conceives his own existence as being so: so far then this is a *subjective* principle of human actions. But every other rational being regards its existence similarly, just on the same rational principle that holds for me: so that it is at the same time an objective principle, from which as a supreme practical law all laws of the will must be capable of being deduced. Accordingly the practical imperative will be as follows: *So act as to treat humanity, whether in thine own person or in that of any other, in every case as an end withal, never as means only.* . . .

. . . Looking back now on all previous attempts to discover the principle of morality, we need not wonder why they all failed. It was seen that man was bound to laws by duty, but it was not observed that the laws to which he is subject are *only those of his own giving,* though at the same time they are *universal,* and that he is only bound to act in conformity with his own will; a will, however, which is designed by nature to give universal laws. For when one has conceived man only as subject to a law (no matter what), then this law required some interest, either by way of attraction or constraint, since it did not originate as a law from *his own* will, but this will was according to a law obliged by *something else* to act in a certain manner. Now by this necessary consequence all the labour spent in finding a supreme principle of *duty* was irrevocably lost. For men never elicited duty, but only a necessity of acting from a certain interest. Whether this interest was private or otherwise, in any case the imperative must be conditional, and could not by any means be capable of being a moral command. I will therefore call this the principle of *Autonomy* of the will, in contrast with every other which I accordingly reckon as *Heteronomy.*

THE KINGDOM OF ENDS

The conception of every rational being as one which must consider itself as giving in all the maxims of its will universal laws, so as to judge itself and its actions from this point of view—this conception leads to another which depends on it and is very fruitful, namely, that of a *kingdom of ends*.

By a *kingdom* I understand the union of different rational beings in a system by common laws. Now since it is by laws that ends are determined as regards their universal validity, hence, if we abstract from the personal differences of rational beings, and likewise from all the content of their private ends, we shall be able to conceive all ends combined in a systematic whole (including both rational beings as ends in themselves, and also the special ends which each may propose to himself), that is to say, we can conceive a kingdom of ends, which on the preceding principles is possible.

For all rational beings come under the *law* that each of them must treat itself and all others *never merely as means,* but in every case *at the same time as ends in themselves.* Hence results a systematic union of rational beings by common objective laws, *i.e.* a kingdom which may be called a kingdom of ends, since what these laws have in view is just the relation of these beings to one another as ends and means. . . .

Discussion Questions

1. What does Kant mean by the good will? Do you agree with him that "nothing can possibly be conceived in the world, or even out of it, which can be called good, without qualification, except a Good Will"?
2. Do you think Kant's categorical imperative is similar to Jesus' Golden Rule, "Do unto others as you would have others do unto you"? Explain what you believe are the similarities and differences.
3. Do you agree with Kant that a moral rule can never be overriden by an apparently higher good? Provide examples and defend your answer.
4. Could one defend moral rules that are universal and necessary but allow for exemptions? For example, suppose one were to say it is a moral rule that "one ought never to kill another person without justification." Suppose one were to kill another person for a reason that the moral rule allows as a justification, for example, self-defense. Would such a moral rule, with an exemption, be consistent with Kant's criterion that a moral rule must be universal and necessary? Explain and defend your answer.
5. How does Kant define the categorical imperative? How does it fit into what he calls a *kingdom of ends*?
6. Do you agree with Kant that sentiments, inclinations, and emotions should play no part in moral decision making? Explain and defend your answer.

You can locate InfoTrac-College Education articles about this chapter by accessing the InfoTrac-College Edition website (http://www.infotrac-college.com/wadsworth/). Using the InfoTrac-College Edition subject guide, enter the search terms relevant to this chapter, and then read abstracts for relevant articles.

Utilitarianism   **4**

JOHN STUART MILL

John Stuart Mill (1806–1873), born in London, was one of the great philosophers of the nineteenth century. His influence on contemporary ethical theory, legal philosophy, and politics is extraordinary. His contributions also extend to logic, philosophy of religion, and philosophy of science. Elected to the British Parliament in 1865, Mill is the author of many works including *A System of Logic* (1843), *Utilitarianism* (1861), *On Liberty* (1859), and *The Subjection of Women* (1869).

In this selection Mill defends his moral theory of utilitarianism. In contrast to the views of Immanuel Kant (Chapter 3) and Thomas Aquinas (Chapter 5), Mill's moral theory does not maintain that there are certain necessary and universal moral laws or principles (though laws and principles may be useful), but rather, Mill affirms that right and wrong standards ought to be derived and judged based on the nonmoral consequences of one's acts and/or one's obedience to certain moral rules. In other words, an act or rule is judged right if performing or obeying it produces the best nonmoral consequences (e.g., more pleasure than pain for the greatest number, closer friendships, greater happiness, fewer personal conflicts). For example, from Kant's perspective lying is inherently wrong regardless of what bad consequences may occur as the result of not lying. However, for the utilitarian, if one's lie has good consequences, then one ought to lie. On the other hand, the utilitarian may conclude that even if lying in this particular circumstance may bring about a good consequence, refraining may be better because lying may lead to a habit of telling lies and that, in the long run, may have bad consequences (e.g., people do not trust me and it hurts my job opportunities and thus my happiness). So, ironically, the Kantian and the utilitarian may wind up at the same place, but for entirely different reasons.

In this essay Mill provides a definition of utilitarianism, arguing that his version of it makes a distinction between higher and lower pleasures, that pleasures differ in kind. (This is in reply to the thought of Jeremy Bentham [1748–1832], Mill's utilitarian predecessor, who argued that all pleasures were equal). After clarifying his version of utilitarianism, Mill goes on to discuss the question of what would count as proof of the correctness of the principle of utility.

Reprinted from Utilitarianism (1861), chapters 2 and 4.

WHAT UTILITARIANISM IS

. . . THE CREED WHICH ACCEPTS as the foundation of morals, Utility, or the Greatest Happiness Principle, holds that actions are right in proportion as they tend to promote happiness, wrong as they tend to produce the reverse of happiness. By happiness is intended pleasure, and the absence of pain; by unhappiness, pain, and the privation of pleasure. To give a clear view of the moral standard set up by the theory, much more requires to be said; in particular, what things it includes in the ideas of pain and pleasure; and to what extent this is left an open question. But these supplementary explanations do not affect the theory of life on which this theory of morality is grounded—namely, that pleasure, and freedom from pain, are the only things desirable as ends; and that all desirable things (which are as numerous in the utilitarian as in any other scheme) are desirable either for the pleasure inherent in themselves, or as a means to the promotion of pleasure and the prevention of pain.

Now, such a theory of life excites in many minds, and among them in some of the most estimable in feeling and purpose, inveterate dislike. To suppose that life has (as they express it) no higher end than pleasure—no better and nobler object of desire and pursuit—they designate as utterly mean and grovelling; as a doctrine worthy only of swine, to whom the followers of Epicurus were, at a very early period, contemptuously likened; and modern holders of the doctrine are occasionally made the subject of equally polite comparisons by its German, French, and English assailants.

When thus attacked, the Epicureans have always answered, that it is not they, but their accusers, who represent human nature in a degrading light; since the accusation supposes human beings to be capable of no pleasures except those of which swine are capable. If this supposition were true, the charge could not be gainsaid, but would then be no longer an imputation; for if the sources of pleasure were precisely the same to human beings and to swine, the rule of life which is good enough for the one would be good enough for the other. The comparison of the Epicurean life to that of beasts is felt as degrading, precisely because a beast's pleasures do not satisfy a human being's conception of happiness. Human beings have faculties more elevated than the animal appetites, and when once made conscious of them, do not regard anything as happiness which does not include their gratification. I do not, indeed, consider the Epicureans to have been by any means faultless in drawing out their scheme of consequences from the utilitarian principle. To do this in any sufficient manner, many Stoic, as well as Christian elements require to be included. But there is no known Epicurean theory of life which does not assign to the pleasures of the intellect, of the feelings and imagination, and of the moral sentiments, a much higher value as pleasures than to those of mere sensation. It must be admitted, however, that utilitarian writers in general have placed the superiority of mental over bodily pleasures chiefly in the greater permanency, safety, uncostliness, etc., of the former—that is, in their circumstantial advantages rather than in their intrinsic nature. And on all these points utilitarians have fully proved their case; but they might have taken the other, and, as it may be called, higher ground, with entire consistency. It is quite compatible with the principle of utility to recognise the fact, that some *kinds* of pleasure are more desirable and more valuable than others. It would be absurd that while, in estimating all other things, quality is considered as well as quantity, the estimation of pleasures should be supposed to depend on quantity alone.

If I am asked, what I mean by difference of quality in pleasures, or what makes one pleasure more valuable than another, merely as a pleasure, except its being greater in amount, there is but one possible answer. Of two pleasures, if there be one which all or almost all who have experience of both give a decided preference, irrespective of any feeling of moral obligation to prefer it, that is the more desirable pleasure. If one of the two is, by those who are competently acquainted with both, placed so far above the other that they prefer it, even though knowing it to be attended with a great amount of discontent, and would not resign it for any quantity of the other pleasure which their nature is capable of, we are justified in ascribing to the preferred enjoyment a superiority in quality, so far outweighing quantity as to render it, in comparison, of small account.

Now it is an unquestionable fact that those who are equally acquainted with, and equally capable of appreciating and enjoying, both, do give a most marked preference to the manner of existence which employs their higher faculties. Few human creatures would consent to be changed into any of the lower animals, for a promise of the fullest allowance of a beast's pleasures; no intelligent human being would consent to be a fool, no instructed person would be an ignoramus, no person of feeling and conscience would be selfish and base, even though they should be persuaded that the fool, the dunce, or the rascal is better satisfied with his lot than they are with theirs. They would not resign what they possess more than he for the most complete satisfaction of all the desires which they have in common with him. If they ever fancy they would, it is only in cases of unhappiness so extreme, that to escape from it they would exchange their lot for almost any other, however undesirable in their own eyes. A being of higher faculties requires more to make him happy, is capable probably of more acute suffering, and certainly accessible to it at more points, than one of an inferior type; but in spite of these liabilities, he can never really wish to sink into what he feels to be a lower grade of existence. We may give what explanation we please of this unwillingness; we may attribute it to pride, a name which is given indiscriminately to some of the most and to some of the least estimable feelings of which mankind are capable; we may refer it to the love of liberty and personal independence, an appeal to which was with the Stoics one of the most effective means for the inculcation of it; to the love of power, or to the love of excitement, both of which do really enter into and contribute to it: but its most appropriate appellation is a sense of dignity, which all human beings possess in one form or another, and in some, though by no means in exact, proportion to their higher faculties, and which is so essential a part of the happiness of those in whom it is strong, that nothing which conflicts with it could be, otherwise than momentarily, an object of desire to them. Whoever supposes that this preference takes place at a sacrifice of happiness—that the superior being, in anything like equal circumstances, is not happier than the inferior—confounds the two very different ideas, of happiness, and content. It is indisputable that the being whose capacities of enjoyment are low, has the greatest chance of having them fully satisfied; and a highly endowed being will always feel that any happiness which he can look for, as the world is constituted, is imperfect. But he can learn to bear its imperfections, if they are at all bearable; and they will not make him envy the being who is indeed unconscious of the imperfections, but only because he feels not at all the good which those imperfections qualify. It is better to be a human being dissatisfied than a pig satisfied; better to be Socrates dissatisfied than a fool satisfied. And if the fool, or the pig, are of a different opinion, it is because they only know their own side of the question. The other party to the comparison knows both sides.

It may be objected, that many who are capable of the higher pleasures, occasionally, under the influence of temptation, postpone them to the lower. But this is quite compatible with a full appreciation of the intrinsic superiority of the higher. Men often, from infirmity of character, make their election for the nearer good, though they know it to be the less valuable; and this is no less when the choice is between two bodily pleasures, than when it is between bodily and mental. They pursue sensual indulgences to the injury of health, though perfectly aware that health is the greater good. It may be further objected, that many who begin with youthful enthusiasm for everything noble, as they advance in years sink into indolence and selfishness. But I do not believe that those who undergo this very common change, voluntarily choose the lower description of pleasures in preference to the higher. I believe that before they devote themselves exclusively to the one, they have already become incapable of the other. Capacity for the nobler feelings is in most natures a very tender plant, easily killed, not only by hostile influences, but by mere want of sustenance; and in the majority of young persons it speedily dies away if the occupations to which their position in life has devoted them, and the society into which it has thrown them, are not favourable to keeping that higher capacity in exercise. Men lose their high aspirations as they lose their intellectual tastes, because they have not time or opportunity for indulging them; and they addict themselves to inferior pleasures, not because they deliberately prefer them, but because they are either the only ones to which they have access, or the only ones which they are any longer capable of enjoying. It may be questioned whether any one who has remained equally susceptible to both classes of pleasures, ever knowingly and calmly preferred the lower; though many, in all ages, have broken down in an ineffectual attempt to combine both.

From this verdict of the only competent judges, I apprehend there can be no appeal. On a question which is the best worth having of two pleasures, or which of two modes of existence is the most grateful to the feelings, apart from its moral attributes and from its consequences, the judgment of those who are qualified by knowledge of both, or, if they differ, that of the majority among them, must be admitted as final. And there needs to be the less hesitation to accept this judgment respecting the quality of pleasures, since there is no other tribunal to be referred to even on the question of quantity. What means are there of determining which is the acutest of two pains, or the intensest of two pleasurable sensations, except the general suffrage of those who are familiar with both? Neither pains nor pleasures are homogeneous, and pain is always heterogeneous with pleasure. What is there to decide whether a particular pleasure is worth purchasing at the cost of a particular pain, except the feelings and judgment of the experienced? When, therefore, those feelings and judgment declare the pleasures derived from the higher faculties to be preferable *in kind,* apart from the question of intensity, to those of which the animal nature, disjoined from the higher faculties, is susceptible, they are entitled on this subject to the same regard.

I have dwelt on this point, as being a necessary part of a perfectly just conception of Utility or Happiness, considered as the directive rule of human conduct. But it is by no means an indispensable condition to the acceptance of the utilitarian standard; for that standard is not the agent's own greatest happiness, but the greatest amount of happiness altogether; and if it may possibly be doubted whether a noble character is always the happier for its nobleness, there can be no doubt that it makes other people happier, and that the world in general is immensely a gainer by it. Utilitarianism, therefore, could only attain its end by the general cultivation of nobleness of character, even if each individual were only benefited by the nobleness of others, and his own, so far as happiness is concerned, were a sheer deduction from the benefit. But the bare enunciation of such an absurdity as this last, renders refutation superfluous.

According to the Greatest Happiness Principle, as above explained, the ultimate end, with reference to and for the sake of which all other things are desirable (whether we are considering our own good or that of other people), is an existence exempt as far as possible from pain, and as rich as possible in enjoyments, both in point of quantity and quality; the test of quality, and the rule for measuring it against quantity, being the preference felt by those who in their opportunities of experience, to which must be added their habits of self-consciousness and self-observation, are best furnished with the means of comparison. This, being, according to the utilitarian opinion, the end of human action, is necessarily also the standard of morality; which may accordingly be defined, the rules and precepts for human conduct, by the observance of which an existence such as has been described might be, to the greatest extent possible, secured to all mankind; and not to them only, but, so far as the nature of things admits, to the whole sentient creation. . . .

The objectors to utilitarianism cannot always be charged with representing it in a discreditable light. On the contrary, those among them who entertain anything like a just idea of its disinterested character, sometimes find fault with its standard as being too high for humanity. They say it is exacting too much to require that people shall always act from the inducement of promoting the general interests of society. But this is to mistake the very meaning of a standard of morals, and confound the rule of action with the motive of it. It is the business of ethics to tell us what are our duties, or by what test we may know them; but no system of ethics requires that the sole motive of all we do shall be a feeling of duty; on the contrary, ninety-nine hundredths of all our actions are done from other motives, and rightly so done, if the rule of duty does not condemn them. It is the more unjust to utilitarianism than this particular misapprehension should be made a ground of objection to it, inasmuch as utilitarian moralists have gone beyond almost all others in affirming that the motive has nothing to do with the morality of the action, though much with the worth of the agent. He who saves a fellow-creature from drowning does what is morally right, whether his motive be

duty, or the hope of being paid for his trouble; he who betrays the friend that trusts him, is guilty of a crime, even if his object be to serve another friend to whom he is under greater obligation. But to speak only of actions done from the motive of duty, and in direct obedience to principle: it is a misapprehension of the utilitarian mode of thought, to conceive it as implying that people should fix their minds upon so wide a generality as the world, or society at large. The great majority of good actions are intended not for the benefit of the world, but for that of individuals, of which the good of the world is made up; and the thoughts of the most virtuous man need not on these occasions travel beyond the particular persons concerned, except so far as is necessary to assure himself that in benefiting them he is not violating the rights, that is, the legitimate and authorized expectations, of any one else. The multiplication of happiness is, according to the utilitarian ethics, the object of virtue: the occasions on which any person (except one in a thousand) has it in his power to do this on an extended scale, in other words to be a public benefactor, are but exceptional; and on these occasions alone is he called on to consider public utility; in every other case, private utility, the interest or happiness of some few persons, is all he has to attend to. Those alone the influence of whose actions extends to society in general, need concern themselves habitually about so large an object. In the case of abstinences indeed—of things which people forbear to do from moral considerations, though the consequences in the particular case might be beneficial—it would be unworthy of an intelligent agent not to be consciously aware that the action is of a class which, if practised generally, would be generally injurious, and that this is the ground of the obligation to abstain from it. The amount of regard for the public interest implied in this recognition, is no greater than is demanded by every system of morals, for they all enjoin to abstain from whatever is manifestly pernicious to society. . . .

CHAPTER IV: OF WHAT SORT OF PROOF THE PRINCIPLE OF UTILITY IS SUSCEPTIBLE

It has already been remarked, that questions of ultimate ends do not admit of proof, in the ordinary acceptation of the term. To be incapable of proof by reasoning is common to all first principles; to the first premises of our knowledge, as well as to those of our conduct. But the former, being matters of fact, may be the subject of a direct appeal to the faculties which judge of fact—namely, our senses, and our internal consciousness. Can an appeal be made to the same faculties on questions of practical ends? Or by what other faculty is cognisance taken of them?

Questions about ends are, in other words, questions about what things are desirable. The utilitarian doctrine is, that happiness is desirable, and the only thing desirable, as an end; all other things being desirable as means to that end. What ought to be required of this doctrine—what conditions is it requisite that the doctrine should fulfil—to make good its claim to be believed?

The only proof capable of being given that an object is visible, is that people actually see it. The only proof that a sound is audible, is that people hear it: and so of the other sources of our experience. In like manner, I apprehend, the sole evidence it is possible to produce that anything is desirable, is that people do actually desire it. If the end which the utilitarian doctrine proposes to itself were not, in theory and in practice, acknowledged to be an end, nothing could ever convince any person that it was so. No reason can be given why the general happiness is desirable, except that each person, so far as he believes it to be attainable, desires his own happiness. This, however, being a fact, we have not only all the proof which the case admits of, but all which it is possible to require, that happiness is a good: that each person's happiness is a good to that person, and the general happiness, therefore, a good to the aggregate of all persons. Happiness has made out its title as *one* of the ends of conduct, and consequently one of the criteria of morality.

But it has not, by this alone, proved itself to be the sole criterion. To do that, it would seem, by the same rule, necessary to show, not only that people desire happiness, but that they never desire anything else. . . .

We have now, then, an answer to the question, of what sort of proof the principle of utility is susceptible. If the opinion which I have now stated is psychologically true—if human nature is so constituted as to desire nothing which is not either a part of happiness or a means of happiness, we can have no other proof, and we require no other, that these are the only things desirable. If so, happiness is the sole end of human action, and the promotion of it the test by which to judge of all human conduct; from whence it necessarily follows that it must be the criterion of morality, since a part is included in the whole.

And now to decide whether this is really so; whether mankind do desire nothing for itself but that which is a pleasure to them, or of which the absence is a pain; we have evidently arrived at a question of fact and experience, dependent, like all similar questions, upon evidence. It can only be determined by practised self-consciousness and self-observation, assisted by observation of others. I believe that these sources of evidence, impartially consulted, will declare that desiring a thing and finding it pleasant, aversion to it and thinking of it as painful, are phenomena entirely inseparable, or rather two parts of the same phenomenon; in strictness of language, two different modes of naming the same psychological fact: that to think of an object as desirable (unless for the sake of its consequences), and to think of it as pleasant, are one and the same thing; and that to desire anything, except in proportion as the idea of it is pleasant, is a physical and metaphysical impossibility.

Discussion Questions

1. How does Mill define and defend utilitarianism and how does he respond to the charge that it is merely a "doctrine only worthy of swine" since it says that pleasure is the only way to measure moral rightness? Explain the charge and why its defenders believe it counts against utilitarianism. Do you think Mill succeeds in his rebuttal? Why or why not? Explain and defend your answer.

2. Do you agree with Mill that morality is simply increasing pleasure and decreasing pain? If Mill is correct, then what would be wrong with the government stealing the organs of several hundred homeless people every year and giving those organs to great scientists, philosophers, and scholars, whose extended lives will result in greater discoveries, insights, and scholarship that will benefit billions of people (e.g., cure for cancer, peace of mind), and thus, increase pleasure and decrease pain? Can you think of a way in which Mill could condemn this organ stealing and at the same time remain true to his utilitarianism? If not, please explain.

3. How does Mill define "happiness"? Do you agree with his definition? Explain and defend your answer.

You can locate InfoTrac-College Education articles about this chapter by accessing the InfoTrac-College Edition website (http://www.infotrac-college.com/wadsworth/). Using the InfoTrac-College Edition subject guide, enter the search terms relevant to this chapter, and then read abstracts for relevant articles.

The Natural Law Theory of St. Thomas Aquinas 5

SUSAN DIMOCK

Susan Dimock is Associate Professor of Philosophy at York University (in Canada). She has published essays in a number of publications in different areas including applied ethics, political philosophy, and the philosophy of law. She is the editor of the book *Classic Readings and Issues in the Philosophy of Law* (2001).

In this essay Professor Dimock provides us with an exegesis of a portion of Thomas Aquinas's (ca. 1225–1274) writings on his natural law theory that appeared in his *Summa Theologica*. As Professor Dimock points out, Aquinas's view is more than simply an ethical theory, but is a moral philosophy that attempts to capture the essence and foundation of moral law as it is found in political and legal institutions as well as ordinary ethical judgments. For Aquinas, natural moral law must be the foundation of any legal or political regime if it is be a just regime. This

Reprinted by permission of author from Philosophy of Law, 6th ed., ed. Joel Feinberg and Jules Coleman (Belmont, CA: Wadsworth, 2000), 19–32.

may seem an odd way of thinking to some people today who maintain that some fundamental rights are intended to, and ought to, give citizens the liberty to do a moral wrong (as long as they do not "hurt" anybody). Aquinas would likely find this type of thinking to be incoherent, for from his perspective, one cannot have a *moral right* to do a *moral wrong,* because the law, if it is good law, must be based on natural moral law, that which is morally good. Now the law may *permit* people to do wrongs, as Aquinas clearly concedes, but not because they have a moral right to do them, but rather, because criminalization of such wrongs may lead to greater evils (e.g., having an excessive police state, large segments of the population resenting the coercion). So, the state must legislate and enforce what is morally good (e.g., laws against murder, robbery, and assault), but, depending on the society and its level of moral development, it cannot, indeed it should not, attempt to coerce every virtue and criminalize every vice.

Professor Dimock covers three areas of Aquinas's thought: (1) the essence of the law; (2) the various kinds of law (eternal, natural, human, and divine); and (3) Aquinas's legacy. With the exception of the last section, Professor Dimock quotes extensively from Aquinas' work, providing insightful commentary as well as showing the contemporary relevance of this medieval philosopher.

INTRODUCTION

IN THIS ESSAY I present the core of St. Thomas Aquinas's theory of law. The aim is to introduce students both to the details of Aquinas's particular theory of law, as well as to the features of his view that define what has come to be known as "the natural law" conception of law more generally. Though the essay is for the most part exegetical, some of the more important implications of the natural law position are raised for further thought and to pave the way for the study of alternative views that have been developed in the subsequent history of the philosophy of law.

One brief note about the structure of the essay will complete my introductory remarks: The essay tries as far as possible to present Aquinas's theory in his own words. Material taken directly from Aquinas appears in italic type throughout, with the origin of the quotation given in parentheses following the text. All of the material is taken from Aquinas's *Summa Theologica;* the translation from Latin

is that of the Fathers of the English Dominican Province.[1]

I. OF THE ESSENCE OF LAW

Aquinas begins his discussion of law with a consideration of the nature or essence of law in general. In this way he sets the tone and task of future jurisprudence or philosophy of law. What makes a particular rule or directive a law? What is it that all laws have in common and which gives them the force of law? This is the search for the nature of law as law. In the course of his discussion of this matter Aquinas offers the following "definition of law": law *is nothing else than an ordinance of reason for the common good, made by him who has the care of the community, and promulgated* (Question 90: Of the Essence of Law, Article 4 "Whether Promulgation is Essential to a Law?"). We shall do well to begin our discussion of Aquinas's philosophy of law with an explication of each of the four component parts of this definition.

I.1 Law Is an Ordinance of Reason:

Law is a rule and measure of acts whereby man is induced to act or is restrained from acting; for *lex* (law) is derived from *ligare* (to bind), because it binds one to act. Now the rule and measure of human acts is the reason, which is the first principle of human acts . . . since it belongs to the reason to direct to the end, which is the first principle in all matters of action, according to the Philosopher [Aristotle]. . . . Consequently it follows that the law is something pertaining to reason (Q.90, Article 1 "Whether Law Is Something Pertaining to Reason?").

In arguing that law is an ordinance of reason, Aquinas is appealing to "practical reason", which provides practical directions concerning how one ought to act, rather than to "speculative reason", which provides us with propositional knowledge of the way things are. Since law aims to direct actions, and practical reason governs how we ought to act, law falls within the scope of reason.

To understand how practical reason directs us to action, however, we must be able to specify an "end" at which our action aims (a goal or objective that we hope to achieve). Reason then directs us to take those steps that are necessary to the achievement of our end. Thus, to say that law is an ordinance of practical reason is to say that there must be some end at which is it is directed. Aquinas identifies that end as "the common good".

I.2 Law Has As Its End the Common Good:

[T]he law belongs to that which is a principle of human acts, because it is their rule and measure. Now as reason is a principle of human acts, so in reason itself there is something which is the principle in respect of all the rest; wherefore to this principle chiefly and mainly law must needs be referred. Now the first principle in practical matters, which are the object of the practical reason, is the last end; and the last end of human life is bliss or happiness . . . Consequently the law must needs regard principally the relationship to happiness. Moreover, since every part is ordained to the whole, as perfect to imperfect; and since one man is a part of the perfect community, the law must needs regard properly the relationship to universal happiness. Wherefore the Philosopher . . . says that we call those legal matters *just*, "which are adapted to produce and preserve happiness and its parts for the body politic," since the state is a perfect community, as he says in *Politics* i, I.[2]

. . . Consequently, since the law is chiefly ordained to the common good, any other precept in regard to some individual work must needs be devoid of the nature of law, save in so far as it regards the common good. Therefore every law is ordained to the common good (Q.90, Article 2 "Whether Law Is Always Directed to the Common Good?").

In this article Aquinas makes clear his belief that happiness is the final end of human action and the first principle of practical reason. In other words, the end of all we do, when we act in accordance with reason, is happiness. In so far as law is an ordinance of reason, it too must aim at happiness. But the happiness at which the law must be directed is not the happiness of any particular individual or privileged group (such as the rulers), but the happiness of the whole as the perfect community.

The insistence that law must be aimed at the common good serves a number of purposes in Aquinas's theory of law. Together with the insistence that law is an ordinance of reason, the requirement that law serve the common good denies the truth of a widely held maxim which had been adopted from the Roman jurists: "Whatever pleases the sovereign, has the force of law" [Ulpian, *Digest* i, ff.]. This maxim had not only been accepted by subsequent philosophers, but by the Christian church as well. Yet it seems to imply that the will of the sovereign, however arbitrary, is sufficient to make law. Thus, the aim of law might simply be the sovereign's personal good. This Aquinas denies. He argues that in making law the sovereign (of whom we will say more shortly) must aim not merely at his own good, but at the good of all.

The good of all, however, should not be understood to mean the individual good of those subject to the law aggregated in some way. It is not just any individual interests that the sovereign may seek to serve in making law, even if those interests are shared by the majority or even all of the subjects. Rather, to say that the law must serve the common good is to say that it must serve the interests that all have *as members of* the perfect community or body politic. To understand which interests these are, some brief comment on what Aquinas means by the perfect community is needed.

Drawing both on Aristotelian philosophy and Christian theology, Aquinas holds that only within political society can human beings achieve the happiness that is appropriate to them. This is so for a number of reasons. First, human beings are born without the natural advantages that brute animals have with respect to satisfying their physical needs. In order to live, a multitude of individuals is needed, each performing different tasks according to a division of labour and in keeping with their varying skills and talents. This diversity must be brought into unity or order through law, which governs economic activity within society. Moreover, human beings require political society not only to meet their biological needs, but also to satisfy their uniquely human intellectual and spiritual needs. For Aquinas believes that, just as we seek our own biological preservation and the success of our offspring, so too do we seek knowledge, culture and religious enlightenment. These goods are attainable only through the order that political society makes possible. The conditions of an orderly society, in so far as they make possible the fulfillment of our needs and the highest happiness we can achieve on earth, are thus goods that are truly common to all members of the community. It is the aim of law to secure these goods.

I.3 Law Is Made by Him Who Has the Care of the Community:

A law, properly speaking, regards first and foremost the order of the common good. Now to order anything to the common good belongs either to the whole people or to someone who is the viceregent of the whole people. And therefore the making of a law belongs either to the whole people or to a public personage who has the care of the whole people, since in all other matters the directing of anything to the end concerns him to whom the end belongs (Q.90, Article 3 "Whether the Reason of Any Man Is Competent to Make Laws?").

There are a number of issues raised in this article, which concerns who is authorized to make laws. The obvious answer from the text quoted is that, because the laws are to govern the whole people, they must be made by the whole people or by their representatives. Thus it may seem that Aquinas is committed either to democratic or representative government. This conclusion would be premature, however.

Rather, following both Aristotle and St. Augustine, Aquinas believes that the relationship of political authority, between the ruler and the ruled, is natural. There are some who are naturally fit to rule, and others who are naturally fit to follow the ruler's commands. Those who are most fit to rule are those in whom virtue is most perfect. They are to rule with the goal of providing the unity and order necessary for those ruled to achieve material, intellectual and moral/spiritual well-being.

Moreover, Aquinas believes that these natural political relations must contain a coercive component. Before the Fall, when all desired what was truly good, the ruler had only to lead by example and instruction; after the Fall, however, men could no longer be trusted to seek the true good or to pursue that good voluntarily. Thus, there came to be added to the ruler's authority the coercive power of making laws and compelling obedience through the threat of penalties for those who transgress the law. The power to punish—to deprive others of their life, liberty or property—was thus annexed to political rulers, and it was so, on Aquinas's view, by divine authorization. Indeed, within canon law it was held that "All power comes from God" (St. Paul's Epistle to the Romans).

That Aquinas is not an advocate of democratic governance may also be seen in his political writings[3], where he makes it clear that the form of legitimate government may be monarchical (rule by one), aristocratic or oligarchic (rule by a few), or timocratic or democratic (rule by the many or all). The modern notion that all legitimate government derives in some way from the will or consent of the governed is foreign to him. Indeed, for the most part Aquinas favours monarchy—though he recognizes that what form of government is best for a given political community depends upon the material circumstances and cultural/moral development of the community in question.

I.4 Law Must Be Promulgated:

[A] law is imposed on others by way of a rule and measure. Now a rule or measure is imposed by being applied to those who are to be ruled and measured by it. Wherefore, in order that a law obtain the binding force which is proper to a law, it must needs be applied to the men who have to be ruled by it. Such application is made by its being notified to them by promulgation. Wherefore promulgation is necessary for the law to obtain its force (Q.90, Article 4 "Whether Promulgation Is Essential to a Law?").

In this article Aquinas is making the seemingly common-sense observation that laws must be made public. According to this requirement, a secret law, or a law willed only in the heart of the ruler, would fail to be law. And one reason for this requirement is quite simple: People can use the law as a rule and measure for their conduct only if they know what the law enjoins or forbids them to do.

There is another reason to insist upon promulgation, however, which is normative rather than pragmatic. Aquinas believes (as we shall see) that there is a general obligation to obey just laws and that individuals may be punished for disobedience. This is the normative sense of "the binding force which is proper to a law". But both the obligation to obey the law and the permissibility of punishing those who violate it presuppose that the laws which people have an obligation to conform to can be known by them. It would surely be morally wrong to hold people responsible and punishable for violating laws they could not be aware of.

I.5 The Validity Conditions for Law:

Question 90, which we have been considering, lays out Aquinas's answer to the question: what is the essence of law? What must be true of any rule or directive if it is to be law? One way of thinking about this is to say that Aquinas has provided *validity conditions* for law. In order to be valid law, a practical directive must be an ordinance of reason; it must be issued by the person or group who holds law-making authority within the community; it must be directed toward the common good; and it must be promulgated. Any directive which fails to meet one or more of these conditions thereby fails to be valid law. . . .

II. OF THE VARIOUS KINDS OF LAW

In Question 91 Aquinas identifies four kinds of laws that are of interest to us. To fully understand Aquinas's theory of law, it is necessary to understand not only the essence of each kind of law here identified, but also the relations between them. One way of working through this somewhat difficult discussion of the various kinds of law is to ask the following five questions of each kind: (1) by whom is it made? (2) to whom is it directed, or whom does it bind? (3) to what end is it directed? (4) how is it promulgated? (5) is it a dictate of reason? In this way we can apply the conditions for valid law which Aquinas laid out in the previous question to better understand why the various kinds of law here discussed are, in fact, laws.

II.1 Eternal Law:

[A] law is nothing else but a dictate of practical reason emanating from the ruler who governs the perfect community. Now it is evident, granted that the world is ruled by divine providence . . . that the whole community of the universe is governed by divine reason. Wherefore the very Idea of the government of things in God the Ruler of the universe has the nature of a law. And since the divine reason's conception of things is not subject to time but is eternal, according to Proverbs viii. 23, therefore it is that this kind of law must be called eternal (Question 91: Of the Various Kinds of Law, Article 1 "Whether There Is an Eternal Law?"). . . .

It is sufficient, for those who do not accept the theological underpinnings of Aquinas's view, to think of eternal law as comprising all those scientific (physical, chemical, biological, psychological, etc.) "laws" by which the universe is ordered. It must be kept in mind by those who wish to take this route, however, that what we call scientific laws could not properly be considered laws by Aquinas were they not also expressions of the divine will. This is because for Aquinas a law must necessarily have a law-maker.

II.2 Natural Law:

[L]aw, being a rule and measure, can be in a person in two ways: in one way, as in him that rules and measures; in another way, as in that which is ruled and measured, since a thing is ruled and measured in so far as it partakes of the rule or measure. Wherefore, since all things subject to divine providence are ruled and measured by the eternal law . . . it is evident that all things partake somewhat of the eternal law, in so far as, namely, from its being

imprinted on them, they derive their respective inclinations to their proper acts and ends. Now among all others the rational creature is subject to divine providence in the most excellent way, in so far as it partakes of a share of providence, by being provident both for itself and others. Wherefore it has a share of the eternal reason, whereby it has a natural inclination to its proper act and end: and this participation of the eternal law in the rational creature is called the natural law. . . . [T]he light of natural reason, whereby we discern what is good and what is evil, which is the function of the natural law, is nothing else than an imprint on us of the divine light. It is therefore evident that the natural law is nothing else than the rational creature's participation of the eternal law (Q.91, Article 2 "Whether There Is in Us a Natural Law?").

This is a crucial article for understanding Aquinas's theory of law. Though God is once again the legislator of this law, and the natural law is a proper subset of the eternal law, it differs from the eternal law as binding only rational creatures. The idea is that, in virtue of having reason and free will, rational creatures are not bound merely to obey eternal law through instinct or inclination, as irrational creatures are bound, but may participate more fully and more perfectly in the law. Through "natural reason", which we have through divine creation, we are able to distinguish right from wrong. Through free will, we are able to choose what is right. In so far as we do so, we participate more fully in eternal law: rather than merely being led blindly to our proper end, we are able to choose that end and so make our compliance with the eternal law an act of self-direction as well. In this way the law comes to be in us as a rule and measure; it is no longer merely a rule and measure imposed upon us from an external source. "Although [the Gentiles] have no written law, yet they have the natural law, whereby each one knows, and is conscious of, what is good and what is evil" [Romans ii. 14]. When we order our own actions in accordance with what is good and shun what is evil, we follow the natural law and participate in the eternal law rather than being merely acted upon by that law. . . .

We turn now to the all-important question of the end to which natural law directs rational creatures. Aquinas provides the following discussion of this matter.

> [The precepts of the natural law are the self-evident first principles of practical reason.] Now . . . "good" is the first thing that falls under the apprehension of the practical reason, which is directed to action, since every agent acts for an end under the aspect of good. Consequently the first principle in the practical reason is one founded on the notion of good, viz., that *good is that which all things seek after*. Hence this is the first precept of law, that *good is to be done and ensued, and evil is to be avoided*. All other precepts of the natural law are based upon this, so that whatever the practical reason naturally apprehends as man's good (or evil) belongs to the precepts of the natural law as something to be done or avoided.
>
> Since, however, good has the nature of an end, and evil the nature of a contrary, hence it is that all those things to which man has a natural inclination are naturally apprehended by reason as being good and, consequently, as objects of pursuit, and their contraries as evil and objects of avoidance. Wherefore the order of the precepts of the natural law is according to the order of the natural inclinations. Because in man there is first of all an inclination to good in accor-dance with the nature which he has in common with all substances, inasmuch as every substance seeks the preservation of its own being, according to its nature; and by reason of this inclination, whatever is a means of preserving human life and of warding off its obstacles belongs to the natural law. Secondly, there is in man an inclination to things that pertain to him more specifically, according to that nature which he has in common with other animals; and in virtue of this inclination, those things are said to belong to natural law "which nature has taught to all animals," [Justinian, *Digest* I, tit.i] such as sexual intercourse, education of

offspring, and so forth. Thirdly, there is in man an inclination to good, according to the nature of his reason, which nature is proper to him; thus man has a natural inclination to know the truth about God and to live in society; and in this respect, whatever pertains to this inclination belongs to the natural law, for instance, to shun ignorance, to avoid offending those among whom one has to live, and other such things regarding the above inclination (Question 94: Of The Natural Law, Article 2 "Whether the Natural Law Contains Several Precepts, or Only One?").

There is a great deal that requires comment upon in this passage. The first is the understanding of practical reason upon which Aquinas is relying. At the basis of this form of reasoning are indemonstrable first principles. These are definitions, which are self-evident in the sense that if a person knows the meaning of the terms then they must immediately recognize the truth of the principle. The first principle of practical reason is: "Good is that which all things seek after." The first precept of natural law, drawn from this principle as a conclusion is: "Good is to be done, evil avoided." In this case it is an action-guiding principle, and the conclusion of reasoning from it will be a directive about what action one ought to take.

Before we can draw any conclusions about which specific actions we ought to undertake from our first principle, however, we need an intermediate proposition concerning what is good or evil. Thus we need something like "The education of offspring is good, because it satisfies our natural inclination to procreate and to live together in on-going societies." The conclusion is "Therefore, we ought to perform those actions necessary for the education of our children." In this way we proceed from the first precept of the natural law to specific conclusions about what we ought to do or what the natural law directs us to do.

This means that, in order to understand what the natural law demands of us, we must be able to identify what is good and what is evil, so that the former may be pursued and the latter avoided. Aquinas thinks that we can do this by examining human nature. In taking this tack Aquinas is adopting an "essentialist" view of human nature, claiming that there are some characteristics or inclinations which are essential to human beings, and that our good consists in acting in accordance with those characteristics and inclinations. He identifies in the passage quoted three principal sets of interests which are essential to our nature in the relevant sense: those we have as living creatures, such as the interest in self preservation; those we have as animals, such as the interest in procreation; and those we have as rational creatures, such as the interest in living in society and exercising our intellectual and spiritual capacities in the pursuit of knowledge. Once we have filled out such a view of what is essential to human flourishing, based on our fundamental nature, we can determine by practical reason what is good for us and what bad. In this way natural law is an ordinance of reason.

This kind of essentialism about human nature, which implies that our most important ends are predetermined and that at base we all have common interests, has come into disfavour in contemporary philosophy. But it is important to note that, even if one rejects this foundation for determining what is good, as a natural law theorist one must provide an alternative which has the following characteristic: it must provide an "objective" conception of the good. That is, whatever the good is, it must be good independently of our believing it is good. We shall return to this idea later.

This discussion provides the basis of an answer to the question: What is the end toward which the natural law directs us? The natural law directs us to the good, as determined by those interests which we all share in virtue of our nature as human beings, and away from evil, which are those things that are incompatible with human flourishing. Thus we might think of the natural law as containing the basic precepts of the correct moral code.

The natural law is known to men innately: in creating men as rational creatures God has implanted within them knowledge of the first principles of the natural law. Thus *we must say that the natural law, as to general principles, is the same for all, both as to rectitude [validity] and as to knowledge* (Q.94, Article 4 "Whether the Natural Law Is the Same in All Men?"). Both through natural inclinations and the divine light we are informed of our proper acts and ends.

But if the natural law directs us to our common good, to those things which allow us to flourish in accordance with our nature, and all action aims at what is good; and if, furthermore, all men know what the natural law commands, and are naturally inclined to follow it, how is it that we sometimes pursue evil? How is it that human societies differ as greatly in their basic organizations as they do around the world and at different times? And why is natural law alone not enough to govern human behavior: why do we need human laws as well? Aquinas recognizes that his account raises these and related questions, and he provides the following answer.

[T]o the natural law belongs [sic] those things to which a man is inclined naturally; and among these it is proper to man to be inclined to act according to reason. Now the process of reason is from the common [general] to the proper [specific], as stated in *Physics* i [Aristotle]. The speculative reason, however, is differently situated in this matter, from the prac-tical reason. For, since the speculative reason is busied chiefly with necessary things, which cannot be otherwise than they are, its proper conclusion, like the universal principles, contain the truth without fail. The practical reason, on the other hand, is busied with contingent matters, about which human actions are concerned; and consequently, although there is necessity in the general principles, the more we descend to matters of detail, the more frequently we encounter defects. . . . [I]n matters of action, truth or practical rectitude is not the same for all, as to matters of detail but only as to general principles, and where there is the same rectitude in matters of detail, it is not equally known to all.

. . . Thus it is right and true for all to act according to reason; and from this principle it follows as a proper conclusion, that goods entrusted to another should be restored to their owner. Now this is true for the majority of cases: but it may happen in a particular case that it would be injurious, and therefore unreasonable, to restore goods held in trust; for instance if they are claimed for the purpose of fighting against one's country. And this principle will be found to fail the more, according as we descend further into detail, e.g., if one were to say that goods held in trust should be restored with such and such a guarantee, or in such and such a way; because the greater the number of conditions added, the greater the number of ways in which the principle may fail, so that it is not right to restore or not to restore.

Consequently we must say that the natural law, as to general principles, is the same for all, both as to rectitude and as to knowledge. But as to certain matters of details, which are conclusions, as it were, of those general principles, it is the same for all in the majority of cases, both as to rectitude and as to knowledge; and yet in some few cases it may fail, both as to rectitude, by reason of certain obstacles . . . and as to knowledge, since in some the reason is perverted by passion, or evil habit, or an evil disposition of nature; thus formerly theft, although it is expressly contrary to the natural law, was not considered wrong among the Germans, as Julius Caesar relates *[De bello Gallico]* (Q.94, Article 4).

Here Aquinas offers three different reasons way human beings may fail to act according to the natural law, and why they might disagree about what is good (he will offer more reasons in what follows). The first two might be considered to arise from the same source, namely, the very general and indeterminate nature of natural law when it is applied to specific matters of human action. The first difficulty that

the general nature of natural law creates is that the conclusions which are drawn from it using practical reason are not universally valid. For instance, even though the natural law clearly proscribes violence, there are exceptions to this rule: in the case of self-defense, for example, or a just war, violence may be justified. Thus as we attempt to deduce more specific rules from the natural law, exceptions arise, general rules have to be modified to fit exceptional circumstances, and so on. Secondly, because natural law provides only very general rules, which must be applied to specific cases by fallible human beings, error is possible concerning the exact content of the natural law, even when it is being interpreted by good people. Finally, though the most basic demands of natural law are known to all through natural reason, reason is sometimes perverted or overwhelmed by passion and bad habits, as the example of the Germans sanctioning theft illustrates. Thus although it is our nature to follow reason, we sometimes are led to vice by impulses which run contrary to reason. Human law remedies these defects by giving determinate content to the law and by providing an additional motive to obey it: the fear of punishment.

II.3 Human Law:

[A] law is a dictate of the practical reason. . . . [I]t is from the precepts of the natural law, as from general and indemonstrable principles, that the human reasons needs to proceed to the more particular determination of certain matters. These particular determinations, devised by human reason, are called human laws, provided the other essential conditions of law be observed, as stated above (Q.90, Articles 2, 3 and 4). Wherefore Cicero says in his *Rhetoric* that "justice has it source in nature; thence certain things came into custom by reason of their utility; afterward these things which emanated from nature and were approved by custom were sanctioned by fear and reverence for the law" [Cicero, *De inventione rhetorica*, ii] (Q.91, Article 3 "Whether There Is a Human Law?").

Here the purpose of human law is to render determinate the precepts of the natural law, and make it known what is required in particular cases in light of a society's specific circumstances. Human law is needed to clarify the demands of natural law, not only because the natural law's generality and human moral failings give rise to problems in our knowing and applying the natural law, but also because the natural law is sometimes *underdetermined;* it can be fulfilled in a variety of ways, all equally good. Aquinas stresses this issue of underdetermination in the following passage.

But it must be noted that something may be derived from the natural law in two ways: first, as a conclusion from premises; secondly, by way of determination of certain generalities. The first way is like to that by which, in the sciences, demonstrated conclusions are drawn from the principles, while the second mode is likened to that whereby, in the arts, general forms are particularized as to details: thus the craftsman needs to determine the general form of a house to some particular shape. Some things are therefore derived from the general principles of the natural law by way of conclusions, e.g., that "one must not kill" may be derived as a conclusion from the principle that "one should do harm to no man"; while some are derived therefrom by way of determination, e.g., the law of nature has it that the evildoer should be punished; but that he be punished in this or that way is not directly by natural law but is a derived determination of it.

Accordingly, both modes of derivation are found in the human law. But those things which are derived in the first way are contained in human law, not as emanating therefrom exclusively, but having some force from the natural law also. But those things which are derived in the second way have no other force than that of human few (Q.95, Article 2 "Whether Every Human Law Is Derived from the Natural Law?").

This discussion indicates that the underdetermined nature of the natural law leaves open room for variations within legal codes in different communities. For while the most basic principles of all human legal codes must be derived deductively from natural law "as conclusions", and so must be the same for all communities, those human laws which are derived "by determination" allow societies to tailor their legal codes to fit their particular circumstances and needs. Thus we can have a diversity of positive (human) laws in different communities: when human laws are enacted as particularizations from general principles, it is sometimes possible that different communities will choose different particular laws to give content to the general principles, just as different communities will give different particular shapes to their houses, despite the fact that houses have a general form (walls and a roof designed to provide shelter from the elements).

In drawing this distinction between those human laws that are derived deductively from natural law, on the one hand, and those which are mere determinations, on the other, Aquinas marks an important division within the category of human laws. For those laws that fall into the first group have not only the status of human law but also of the natural law. As such, they must direct behaviour in accordance with the correct moral code. This has the implication that any violation of such laws is not only a legal offence but also an offense against morality, i.e., a sin or vice. Such offenses, we say, are *mala in se,* for they involve actions that would be wrong independently of and prior to being made illegal. Murder is a *mala in se* offense, for it is morally wrong quite independently of being legally prohibited. Those laws which are derived from natural law in the second way, however, and which have only the force of human law, lack this independent moral status. When the human law prohibits actions that are not themselves morally wrong, we call such offenses *mala prohibita*. They are legal offenses, but not moral offenses, and one who commits them is guilty of legal wrongdoing but not also of an independent sin or vice. Thus, for example, in many jurisdictions there is a legal prohibition against persons under a certain age driving a car. Let's suppose the age is 16 years. Now, no one would want to say that driving when under the age of 16 is independently immoral or vicious, though it is equally clearly illegal. And this law may well be justified as a law derived in the second way from natural law: for having such restrictions on the use of dangerous machines like cars serves the common good. Thus while *mala in se* offenses are universally and invariably wrong, their wrongness being deductively derived from natural law, the class of *mala prohibita* offenses contains room for considerable variation across different communities.

Let us return now to our more immediate topic, which concerns the many reasons why we need human law. As we saw in our previous discussion, it is not only the generality and underdetermined nature of the natural law that explains why it must be supplemented with human law. A different reason is to be found in the moral failings of human beings: for we sometimes fail to willingly follow the dictates of natural law.

> [M]an has a natural aptitude for virtue, but the perfection of virtue must be acquired by man by means of some kind of training . . . Now it is difficult to see how man could suffice for himself in the matter of this training, since the perfection of virtue consists chiefly in withdrawing man from undue pleasures, to which above all man is inclined, and especially the young, who are more capable of being trained. Consequently a man needs to receive this training from another, whereby to arrive at the perfection of virtue. And as to those young people who are inclined to acts of virtue, by their good natural disposition, or by custom, or rather by the gift of God, paternal training suffices, which is by admonitions. But since some are found to be depraved and prone to vice, and not easily amenable to words, it was necessary for such to be restrained from evil by force and fear, in order that, at least, they might desist from evil-doing and leave others in peace, and that they themselves, by being habituated in this way, might be brought to do willingly what hitherto they did from fear, and thus become virtuous. Now this kind of training which compels through fear of punishment is the discipline of laws. Therefore, in order that man might have peace and virtue, it is necessary for laws to be framed . . . (Question 95: Of Human Law, Article 1 "Whether It Was Useful for Laws to be Framed by Men?").

Aquinas speaks here of two additional reasons why human laws are needed. First, they provide an educative effect upon those who do not pursue virtue willingly. In this way they promote virtue. But they do so by coercion, by threat of force (punishment) and the fear that threat engenders. This may itself lead to virtue, for what one does in the beginning out of fear can become habitual; when one habitually refrains from evil and does as virtue requires, then one has become virtuous. And this leads to the second role for human law, especially as backed up by the threat of coercive sanctions: it deters those who would do evil from actually doing it, and thus serves the goals of peace, security and order. . . .

Despite the fact that human law is needed for these reasons as a supplement to the natural law, Aquinas believes that valid human law is derived from the natural law. This is so because he believes that human law must meet one further validity condition to be genuine law; it must be just. Now this requirement is really only relevant to human law, since the law given by God cannot be unjust. But because human law is made by people, who are fallible as well as susceptible to vice, it is possible that a lawmaker might try to make laws which are unjust. Aquinas denies that such are valid laws, on the grounds that human law must be derived from natural law (as an ordinance of reason), and so it cannot be unjust. Rules only have the binding force appropriate to law if they are just.

> As Augustine says, "that which is not just seems to be no law at all" *[De libero arbitrio];* wherefore the force of law depends on the extent of its justice. Now in human affairs a

thing is said to be just from being right according to the rule of reason. But the first rule of reason is the law of nature . . . Consequently, every human law has just so much of the nature of law as it is derived from the law of nature. But if in any point it deflects from the law of nature, it is no longer a law but a perversion of law (Q.95, Article 2 "Whether Every Human Law Is Derived from the Natural Law?").

What are we to say of Aquinas's insistence that human laws have the binding force of law only if they are just? This seems, in some ways, an extraordinary claim, given that we are all familiar with things that seem to be human laws but which are clearly unjust, e.g., the slave laws of the United States before the Civil War, or the Nazi laws in Germany which sent millions of Jews to the death camps. Aquinas does not deny that such directives have the form of law, but he insists nonetheless that they fail to be genuine laws, that they fail to have the binding force of law. They lack that force, and the status of law, because they fail to conform with the dictates of justice which are contained within the natural law which is an ordinance of right reason.

Human law has the nature of law in so far as it partakes of right reason; and it is clear that, in this respect, it is derived from the eternal law. But in so far as it deviates from reason, it is called an unjust law and has the nature, not of law, but of violence. Nevertheless even an unjust law, in so far as it retains some appearance of law, through being framed by one who is in power, is derived from the eternal law, since all power is from the Lord God, according to Romans xiii. I (Question 93, Article 3 "Whether Every Law Is Derived from the Eternal Law?").

To say that "unjust laws" fail to have the binding force of law we must consider briefly what Aquinas calls the power of law "to bind a man in conscience". This is the power of law to impose a moral obligation of obedience upon those to whom the law applies. In discussing this question, Aquinas directly deals with this obligation, as well as specifies in more detail his conception of justice.

Laws framed by man are either just or unjust. If they be just, they have the power of binding in conscience, from the eternal law whence they are derived, according to Proverbs viii. 15: "By Me kings reign, and lawgivers decree just things." Now laws are said to be just—from the end, when, to wit, they are ordained to the common good—and from their author, that is to say, when the law that is made does not exceed the power of the lawgiver—and from their form, when, to wit, burdens are laid on the subjects, according to an equality of proportion and with a view to the common good. For, since one man is a part of the community, each man, in all that he is and has, belongs to the community, just as a part, in all that it is, belongs to the whole; wherefore nature inflicts a loss on the part in order to save the whole, so that on this account such laws as these which impose proportionate burdens are just and binding in conscience and are legal laws.

On the other hand, laws may be unjust in two ways: first, by being contrary to human good, through being opposed to the things mentioned above—either in respect of the end, as when an authority imposes on his subjects burdensome laws, conducive, not to the common good, but rather to his own cupidity or vainglory; or in respect of the author, as when a man makes a law that goes beyond the power committed to him; or in the respect of form, as when burdens are imposed unequally on the community, although with a view to the common good. The like are acts of violence rather than laws, because, as Augustine says, "A law that is not just seems to be no law at all." Wherefore such laws do not bind in conscience, except perhaps in order to avoid scandal or disturbance, for which cause a man should even yield his right . . .

Secondly, laws may be unjust through being opposed to the divine good: such are the laws of tyrants inducing to idolatry or to anything else contrary to the divine law and laws of this kind must nowise be observed because, as stated in Acts v.29, "we ought to obey God rather than men" (Q.95, Article 4 "Whether Human Law Binds a Man in Conscience?"). . . .

. . . [Here] Aquinas gives some content to his conception of justice and its relation to law. He outlines various ways in which a law may fail to be just: it may aim at the good of the lawgiver only, rather than at the common good; it may exceed the authority of the lawgiver; it may impose disproportionate burdens upon some of the people; it may be contrary in its directives to the divine law as known through revelation. In each of these cases, the law denies to those who are governed what they are due. Thus they can demand as their due that the ruler make laws which are directed to the common good rather than to his personal glory; that they be allowed to worship God; that they be ruled only within the limits of proper authority; and that the ruler not impose disproportionate burdens upon some for the benefit of others. This last requirement may lend itself to misunderstanding, however, in light of Aquinas's insistence that justice concerns the relations between persons and demands an equality of some kind. For Aquinas is not advocating an egalitarian society or insisting that the benefits and burdens of society be distributed equally. Indeed, he believes that class divisions and even slavery are natural relations. But he does insist that justice demands that the burdens and benefits of society be distributed proportionately and in the service of the common good. This allows that unequal burdens can be placed upon some, when that is needed for the good of the whole. Thus, for example, we can demand that the young and strong provide military service in defense of the society, and in so doing impose a heavy burden upon them that is not shared by all, provided that it be necessary for the common good and they receive compensatory benefits from society in other areas.

In all of the cases of unjust laws that he considers, Aquinas declares that such laws lose their binding force. In all but the last case, we may disobey such laws, though we must not do so at the risk of causing "scandal and disturbance". Scandal and disturbance signify a break-down of the order which is the foundation of human society, a loss of peace and security, as would be found in a situation of massive civil unrest or civil war. This should not be risked, even if that requires obeying laws which are unjust in terms of the end author or form. The final case, however, involving laws which are contrary to divine law, such as a law requiring that everyone abstain from Christian worship would be, is different: we must not obey such laws, regardless of the consequences. . . .

To say that we all have an obligation to obey (just) laws raises a different question, however: does it require that in every instance we must obey the letter of the law, even if doing so would be ruinous or cause great hardship to the common good? This issue was thought by Aquinas to raise the question of whether those who are subject to law are competent to interpret it and perhaps decide, in a given case, that the real intentions of the lawgiver would be better served by an action which is contrary to the letter of the law. He answers that it is sometimes permissible for those subject to the law to interpret the intentions of the lawmaker and decide not to obey the letter of the law.

> [E]very law is directed to the common weal of men and derives the force and nature of law accordingly. Hence the Jurist says: "By no reason of law or favor of equity is it allowable for us to interpret harshly and render burdensome those useful measures which have been enacted for the welfare of man" [Ulpian, *Digest* i. 3]. Now it happens often that the observance of some point of law conduces to the common weal in the majority of instances, and yet, in some cases, is very hurtful. Since, then, the lawgiver cannot have in view every single case, he shapes the law according to what happens most frequently, by directing his attention to the common good. Wherefore, if a case arises wherein the observance of

that law would be hurtful to the general welfare, it should not be observed. For instance, suppose that in a besieged city it is an established law that the gates of the city are to be kept closed, this is good for public welfare as a general rule, but if it were to happen that the enemy are in pursuit of certain citizens who are defenders of the city, it would be a great loss to the city if the gates were not opened to them; and so in that case the gates ought to be opened, contrary to the letter of the law, in order to maintain the common weal, which the lawgiver had in view.

Nevertheless it must be noted that if the observance of the law according to the letter does not involve any sudden risk needing instance remedy, it is not competent for everyone to expound what is useful and what is not useful to the state; those alone can do this who are in authority and who, on account of suchlike cases, have the power to dispense from the laws. If, however, the peril be so sudden as not to allow of the delay involved by referring the matter to authority, the mere necessity brings with it a dispensation, since necessity knows no law (Q.96, Article 6 "Whether He Who Is Under a Law May Act Beside the Letter of the Law?").

Thus we find Aquinas recognizing that blind obedience to the letter of the law is not desirable. While we must avoid a situation wherein every person feels competent to judge the law and decide he shall obey it only as it serves his own interests, we must equally avoid the situation wherein great harm is done to the common good out of servile obedience to the law. In his example of the besieged city, Aquinas notes one case in which the law ought not to be obeyed. But there are others, readily imaginable: in case of a fire within the city, for example, the law also ought not to be obeyed. These are exceptions to the general rule, but they cannot themselves be written into the law, both because they are too numerous and too unforeseeable. To attempt to write all the possible exceptions into the law would make the law too complex to be useful as a general rule and measure for human action. Thus we must be content to use general laws, while recognizing that exceptional cases may arise in which obedience to the letter of the law must give way to the spirit of the law, which aims always at the common good.

As these articles make clear, Aquinas believes that one important purpose of human laws is to make men virtuous. . . .

Human law is limited, however, in the extent to which it can aim to make men fully virtuous. In the first place, there are many forms of vice that do not fall within the prohibitions of human law.

> Now human law is framed for a number of human beings, the majority of whom are not perfect in virtue. Wherefore human laws do not forbid all vices from which the virtuous abstain, but only the more grievous vices from which it is possible for the majority to abstain; and chiefly those that are to the hurt of others, without the prohibition of which human society could not be maintained: thus human law prohibits murder, theft, and such like (Q.96 Article 2 "Whether it Belongs to Human Law to Repress All Vices?").

Likewise, human law does not proscribe all virtues, but only those which are ordainable to the common good (Q.96, Article 3 "Whether Human Law Prescribes Acts of All the Virtues?"). This defect in human law is rectified, however, with the addition of the final type of law: divine law.

II.4 Divine Law:

> Besides the natural and the human law it was necessary for the directing of human conduct to have a divine law. And this for four reasons. First, because it is by law that man is directed how to perform his proper acts in view of his last end. And indeed, if man were ordained to no other end than that which is proportionate to his natural faculty, there would be no need for man to have any further direction on the part of his reason besides the natural law and human law which is derived from it. But since man is ordained to an end of eternal happiness which is inproportionate to man's natural faculty . . . therefore it was necessary that, besides the natural and the human law, man should be directed to his end by a law given by God.

Secondly, because, on account of the uncertainty of human judgment, especially on contingent and particular matters, different people form different judgments on human acts; whence also different and contrary laws result. In order, therefore, that man may know without any doubt what he ought to do and what he ought to avoid, it was necessary for man to be directed in his proper acts by a law given by God, for it is certain that such a law cannot err.

Thirdly, because man can make laws in those matters of which he is competent to judge. But man is not competent to judge of interior movements that are bidden, but only of exterior acts which appear; and yet for the perfection of virtue it is necessary for man to conduct himself aright in both kinds of acts. Consequently human law could not sufficiently curb and direct interior acts, and it was necessary for this purpose that a divine law should supervene.

Fourthly, because, as Augustine says, human law cannot punish or forbid all evil deeds; since while aiming at doing away with all evils, it would do away with many good things, and would hinder the advance of the common good, which is necessary for human intercourse [*De libero arbitrio* i, 5, 6]. In order, therefore, that no evil might remain unforbidden and unpunished, it was necessary for the divine law to supervene, whereby all sins are forbidden (Q.91, Article 3 "Whether There Was Any Need for a Divine Law?").

Divine law is directed to the common good of mankind as beings capable of salvation and eternal happiness. That is its end. It is promulgated in the words of divine revelation and the pronouncements of the Pope. Because men cannot know, by natural reason unassisted by divine revelation, what God demands of them in order to be worthy of eternal happiness, divine law is needed in addition to natural and human law. It is also needed because human law must confine its attentions to the actions of persons; since having good motives and not merely doing the right thing is also part of virtue, and law aims to make men virtuous, human law must be supplemented with divine law. Moreover, as Aquinas points out, if human law were to attempt to prohibit and punish all vices, many good things would become exceedingly difficult or impossible to achieve. For instance, suppose that the human law attempted to forbid backbiting gossip, on the grounds that it is vicious; in order to enforce such a law, the privacy and trust which is necessary between spouses, friends, co-workers and others would have to be severely restricted. Given that the price of enforcing such a law would certainly outweigh the benefits of it, such a sin as gossiping ought not to be made an object of human law but must be left to God to judge of and punish.

NATURAL LAW THEORY: AQUINAS'S LEGACY

Although Aquinas developed his theory of law within the context of a Christian world-view, much of what he says remains relevant within modern secular societies. And in many ways the issues he raised continue yet to dominate the philosophy of law. Furthermore, the natural law theory of which he is taken to be the founder still attracts thoughtful adherents today, both Thomistic and secular. What, then, is the natural law theory?

Though there are many differences dividing natural law theorists on a myriad of issues, the following is meant to capture the central tenets of the natural law position. First, natural law theorists typically accept from Aquinas some version of the claim that law is a rule and measure. In more modern parlance, law is a system of rules by which human beings are to direct their behavior. But they also accept from Aquinas the view that the system of rules is supposed to direct human behavior *aright*. What is distinctive to the natural law position is the insistence that the direction provided by the law must be toward ends that are rationally defensible or objectively good; law must direct behaviour toward the common good. It is this requirement, that all genuine law aims at what is truly good, not just for the ruler but also for the ruled, that sets natural law theory apart from a great many others.

The insistence that law has as its end the common good makes natural law theory teleological. Teleology is the view that some things (perhaps all) have an end or function proper to them, and that they cannot be fully understood without reference to that end or function. So, for example, we cannot fully understand the essence of a knife without reference to its end, which is to cut things. Now one need not be a teleologist about everything in order to be a natural law theorist. But one must be a teleologist about law itself. That is, one must believe that law has an end, which is truly good, and that all genuine law aims at that end; there is some end which law must serve, *qua* law. Stated in terms of functions, the natural law theorist is committed to the view that law has some function, which is objectively good, and we cannot fully understand law independently of that function. Now there have been many functions proposed as essential to law: the preservation of order, to assist us in achieving the good appropriate to our nature, to make us virtuous, and so on. It is important to keep in mind, however, that it is not only natural law theorists who may attribute an essential function to law; one might think that the purpose of law is just to ensure obedience to the sovereign, and yet not be a natural law theorist. One will only be offering a natural law position if the end or func-tion claimed to be essential to law must be objectively good. The important point to all of this is that if one does offer such a position then one makes moral conditions validity conditions of law.

To say that valid law must have a certain moral content in order to be valid is to say that we cannot identify something as genuine law by its form or structure alone; we must look also to its content to determine whether it is law. For Aquinas and most natural law theorists who have followed him, this requirement takes the form of providing necessary condi-tions of law: it is necessary, though not sufficient, for something to be a human or positive law that it be aimed at the common good and that it be just. That is, it is enough to make a law invalid that it aim at something which is contrary to the common good or that is unjust. Thus "an unjust law is no law at all" has come to be one of the defining tenets of the natural law position.

Because there is a necessary connection between genuine law and morality, one further conclusion is licensed. Not only do we have a prudential reason to obey the law namely to avoid punishment; but we also have a moral obligation to obey the law, which derives from its independent justification or objective rightness. While the former may hold even with respect to "unjust laws", the latter holds only because the law, as genuine law, enjoins what we already morally ought to do. This is so directly in the case of *mala in se* offenses, which we ought to refrain from because they are both immoral and illegal, and indirectly in the case of *mala prohibita* offenses, which we ought to refrain from because doing so serves the common good. As Aquinas makes clear, however, the moral obligation binds us to the spirit of the law and not merely to its letter.

This conception of crime as being not only illegal but also immoral leads us to the final noteworthy feature common amongst natural law theorists: they have usually been committed to a retributivist theory of punishment. Though the natural lawyer's defense of retributivism cannot be fully explained or justified here, it typically consists of a defense of the following claims. Because those who break the law thereby also commit a sin, they deserve punishment. Their moral culpability makes them fit subjects of retribution. This is in keeping with justice, moreover, because it is just that those who do wrong suffer harm: for due equality is served when good is returned for good, and evil for evil. Whether the natural law theorist must adopt a retributive theory of punishment is an interesting question that we cannot explore here; we must be content with simply noting that Aquinas himself accepted the connection between his theory of law and retributivism in punishment.

This concludes our brief discussion of natural law theory. Though I have attempted to identify those tenets that are most common to the natural law tradition, this account must surely be deemed inadequate even for that purpose: for the natural law tradition embodies a diversity and richness of views that make it impossible to capture in an essay such as this. I shall be content, however, if I have succeeded it presenting and explicating Aquinas's particular brand of natural law theory in sufficient detail to enable those who may be interested to pursue the many controversies which surround it. I have not been able to enter into those controversies here, nor have I been able to critically assess the many tenets that I have just sketched. I leave such commentary and criticism to the history of jurisprudence.[4]

NOTES

1. Published by Burns, Oates and Washbourne, Ltd., London, Publishers to the Holy See; 22 volumes, 1912–36.
2. When Aquinas refers to the "perfect community" he does not mean some ideal or utopian state, but rather he means only the whole community of individuals united in a particular way. A perfect community is one in which a multiplicity of individuals are brought together, their diverse activities coordinated and directed to the attainment of their common end.
3. See especially St. Thomas Aquinas, *De Regimine (On Kingship)* trans. G. B. Phelan and I. T. Eschmann (Toronto: PIMS, 1949).
4. I would like to thank David Braybrooke, who many years ago taught me that Aquinas has much to say even to a secular society. I would also like to thank Eric Cavallero for his many helpful comments on an earlier draft of this essay.

Discussion Questions

1. What does Thomas Aquinas mean by "law"? Explain and define the four component parts of his definition.
2. According to Aquinas, what are the four different types of law? Define each and explain how they relate to each other. That is, can one believe in natural moral law without accepting Aquinas's view of eternal law and divine law? Explain and defend your answer.
3. Define "natural law" in greater detail, explaining how Aquinas would arrive at certain moral truths based on it. Do you think he succeeds? Why or why not?
4. Do you agree with Aquinas that in order for a law to be just it must be based on natural moral law? Explain and defend you answer.
5. Does Aquinas believe that all moral truths must be reflected in human law? Explain and defend you answer.
6. At the Nuremberg Trials (the tribunals at which Nazis were prosecuted, and some convicted, for war crimes), Associate Justice Robert H. Jackson of the U.S. Supreme Court, Chief Counsel for the United States, argued for conviction on the grounds that the 11 million victims (including 6 million Jews) of the Nazi Holocaust still possessed a natural right to life even though the German government sanctioned their murders. If one were to abandon natural law thinking, how would one prosecute the Nazis for war crimes?

You can locate InfoTrac-College Education articles about this chapter by accessing the InfoTrac-College Edition website (http://www.infotrac-college.com/wadsworth/). Using the InfoTrac-College Edition subject guide, enter the search terms relevant to this chapter, and then read abstracts for relevant articles.

6   Vision and Virtue

WILLIAM K. KILPATRICK

William K. Kilpatrick is Professor of Education at Boston College, where he teaches courses in human development and moral education. He is a frequent lecturer to parent and university audiences and the author of several books, including *Why Johnny Can't Tell Right From Wrong: Moral Literacy and the Case for Character Education* (1992).

In this essay Professor Kilpatrick argues that the traditional way of teaching ethics and morality—reasoning from theories to principles and applying them to moral dilemmas (e.g., the way in which Kant's, Mill's and even Thomas Aquinas's views are sometimes taught)—is highly contrived and artificial and should be supplemented, if not eclipsed, by virtue ethics (or character ethics), the instilling of ethics by studying the stories, lives, and example of virtuous people found in history, fiction, and mythology. Why is it that we apparently do not have to reason by way of ethical principles to conclude instantly that Mother Teresa was a virtuous person whereas Adolf Hitler was wicked and evil? Why do our eyes well up with tears when we see the character of George Bailey (played by actor Jimmy Stewart in the film *It's a Wonderful Life*), who sacrificed so much for the floundering Bailey Building and Loan, accepting the generosity of countless friends on Christmas Eve only hours after he tried to take his own life? According to Professor Kilpatrick, it is because we recognize virtue, integrity, and character in others. Although ethical principles, ethical theories, and moral dilemmas have their place, the author believes that they are inadequate in teaching morality unless they are employed along with stories, myths, historical narratives, and tales that teach us profound and important lessons of virtue and vice. Virtue ethics does not merely teach one the right thing to do, but rather, the right person to be.

ONE WAY TO COUNTER moral illiteracy is to acquaint youngsters with stories and histories that can give them a common reference point and supply them with a stock of good examples. One of the early calls for returning stories to the curriculum was made by William Bennett in a speech before the Manhattan Institute:

Do we want our children to know what honesty means? Then we might teach them about Abe Lincoln walking three miles to return six cents and, conversely, about Aesop's shepherd boy who cried wolf.

Do we want our children to know what courage means? Then we might teach them about Joan of Arc, Horatius at the Bridge, Harriet Tubman and the Underground Railroad.

Do we want them to know about kindness and compassion, and their opposites? Then

Reprinted by permission from William K. Kilpatrick, *Why Johnny Can't Tell Right from Wrong: Moral Literacy and the Case for Character Education* (New York: Simon & Schuster, 1992), 129–43.

they should read *A Christmas Carol* and *The Diary of Anne Frank* and, later on, *King Lear.*

. . . Among the reasons Bennett puts forward in arguing for the primacy of stories are that "unlike courses in moral reasoning," they provide a stock of examples illustrating what we believe to be right and wrong," and that they "help anchor our children in their culture, its history and traditions. They give children a mooring." "This is necessary," he continues, "because morality, of course, is inextricably bound both to the individual conscience and the memory of society . . . We should teach these accounts of character to our children so that we may welcome them to a common world . . ."

Bennett is not liked in teachers colleges and schools of education. He wasn't liked when he was Secretary of Education, and the legacy he left makes him unpopular still. As education secretary he stood for all those things progressive educators thought they had gotten rid of once and for all. He wanted to reemphasize content—not just any content but the content of Western culture. And he wanted to return character education to the schools. His emphasis on stories of virtue and heroism was an affront to the . . . tradition that had dominated education for years. Furthermore, by slighting "moral reasoning," Bennett also managed to alienate the party of critical thinking. Educators reacted angrily. Bennett was accused of being simplistic, reactionary, and worst of all, dogmatic. William Damon of Brown University, himself the author of a book on moral development, wrote that "Bennett's aversion to conscious moral decision making is itself so misguided as to present a threat to the very democratic traditions that he professes to cherish. Habit without reflection is adaptive only in a totalitarian climate."

Yet Bennett's concern over character was not simply a conservative phenomenon. Liberals too were having second thoughts about a moral education that relied only on moral reasoning. In a 1988 speech that could easily have been mistaken for one of Bennett's, Derek Bok, the president of Harvard University, stated:

> Socrates sometimes talked as if knowledge alone would suffice to ensure virtuous behavior. He did not stress the value of early habituation, positive example and obedience to rules in giving students the desire and self-discipline to live up to their beliefs and to respect the basic norms of behavior essential to civilized communities.

Bok went on to call for "a broader effort to teach by habit, example and exhortation," and unlike Bennett, he was speaking not of the elementary or high school but of the university level.

Nevertheless, one still finds a resistance among educators toward the kind of stories Bennett recommends—stories that teach by example. I don't mean this in a conspiratorial sense. I find this reaction in student teachers who have never heard of Bennett. Moreover, as far as I know, no committee of educators ever came together to promulgate an antistory agenda. It has been more a matter of climate, and of what the climate would allow. In my conversations with teachers and would-be teachers, one of the most common themes I hear is their conviction that they simply don't have the right to tell students anything about right and wrong. Many have a similar attitude toward literature with a moral; they would also feel uneasy about letting a story do the telling for them. The most pejorative word in their vocabulary is "preach." But the loss of stories doesn't strike them as a serious loss. They seem to be convinced that whatever is of value in the old stories will be found out anyway. Some are Rousseauians and believe it will be found out through instinct; others subscribe to some version or other of critical thinking and believe it will be found out through reason.

The latter attitude is a legacy of the Enlightenment, but it is far more widespread now than it ever was in the eighteenth century. The argument then and now is as follows: Stories and myth may have been necessary to get the attention of ignorant farmers and fishermen, but intelligent people don't need to have their ethical principles wrapped in a pretty box; they are perfectly capable of grasping the essential point without being charmed by myths, and because they can reach their own conclusions, they are less susceptible to the harmful superstitions and narrow prejudices that may be embedded in stories. This attitude may be characterized as one of wanting to establish the moral of the story without the story. It does not intend to do away with morality but to make it more secure by disentangling it from a web of fictions. For example, during the Enlightenment the Bible came to be looked upon as an attempt to convey a set of advanced ethical ideas to primitive people who could understand them only if they were couched in story form. A man of the Enlightenment, however, could dispense with the stories and myths, mysteries and miracles, could dispense, for that matter, with a belief in God, and still retain the essence—the Christian ethic.

[Lawrence] Kohlberg's approach to moral education is in this tradition. His dilemmas are stories of a sort, but they are stories with the juice squeezed out of them. . . . They are simply there to present a dilemma. And this is the way Kohlberg wanted it. . . . The important thing is to understand the principles involved. Moreover, a real story with well-defined characters might play on a child's emotions and thus intrude on his or her thinking process.

But is it really possible to streamline morality in this way? Can we extract the ethical kernel and discard the rest? Or does something vital get lost in the process? As the noted short story writer Flannery O'Connor put it, "A story is a way to say something that can't be said any other way . . . You tell a story because a statement would be inadequate." In brief, can we have the moral of the story without the story? And if we can, how long can we hold it in our hands before it begins to dissolve?

The danger of such abstraction is that we quickly tend to forget the human element in morality. The utilitarian system of ethics that was a product of the English Enlightenment provides a good illustration of what can happen. It was a sort of debit-credit system of morality in which the rightness or wrongness of acts depended on their usefulness in maintaining a smoothly running social machine. Utilitarianism oiled the cogs of the Industrial Revolution by providing reasonable justifications for child labor, dangerous working conditions, long hours and low wages. For the sake of an abstraction—"the greatest happiness for the greatest number"—utilitarianism was willing to ignore the real human suffering created by the factory system.

Some of the most powerful attacks on that system can be found in the novels of Charles Dickens. Dickens brought home to his readers the human face of child labor and debtor's prison. And he did it in a way that was hard to ignore or shake off. Such graphic "reminders" may come to us through reading or they may come to us through personal experience, but without them, even the most intelligent and best-educated person will begin to lose sight of the fact that moral issues are human issues.

I use the words "lose sight of" advisedly. There is an important sense in which morality has a visual base—or, if you want, a visible base. In other words, there is a connection between virtue and vision. One has to see correctly before one can act correctly. This connection was taken quite seriously in the ancient world. Plato's most famous parable—the parable of the cave—explains moral confusion in terms of simple misdirected vision: the men in the cave are looking in the wrong direction. Likewise, the Bible prophets regarded moral blindness not only as a sin but as the root of a multitude of sins.

The reason why seeing is so important to the moral life is that many of the moral facts of life are apprehended through observation. Much of the moral law consists of axioms or premises about human beings and human conduct. And one does not arrive at premises by reasoning. You either see them or you don't.

The Declaration of Independence's assertion that some truths are "self-evident" is one example of this visual approach to right and wrong. The word "evident" means "present and plainly visible." Many of Abraham Lincoln's arguments were of the same order. When Southern slave owners claimed the same right as Northerners to bring their "property" into the new territories, Lincoln replied: "That is to say, inasmuch as you do not object to my taking my hog to Nebraska, therefore I must not object to your taking your slave. Now, I admit this is perfectly logical, if there is no difference between hogs and Negroes."

Lincoln's argument against slavery is not logical but definitional. It is a matter of plain sight that Negroes are persons. But even the most obvious moral facts can be denied or explained away once the imagination becomes captive to a distorted vision. The point is illustrated by a recent Woody Allen film, *Crimes and Misdemeanors*. The central character, Judah Rosenthal, who is both an ophthalmologist and a philanthropist, is faced with a dilemma: What should he do about his mistress? She has become possessive and neurotic and has started to do what mistresses are never supposed to do: she has begun to make phone calls to his office and to his home, thus threatening to completely ruin his life, a life that in many ways has been one of service. Judah seeks advice from two people: his brother Jack, who has ties to the underworld, and a rabbi, who tries to call Judah back to the vision of his childhood faith. The rabbi (who is nearly blind) advises Judah to end the relationship, even if it means exposure, and to ask his wife for forgiveness. Jack, on the other hand, having ascertained the woman's potential for doing damage and her unwillingness to listen to reason, advises Judah to "go on to the next [logical] step," and he offers to have her "taken care of." The interesting thing is that Jack's reasoning powers are just as good as the rabbi's; and based on his vision of the world, they make perfect sense. You simply don't take

the chance that a vindictive person will destroy your marriage and your career. And indeed, Jack finally wins the argument. In an imagined conversation, Judah tells the rabbi, "You live in the Kingdom of Heaven, Jack lives in the real world." The woman is "taken care of."

Jack's reasoning may be taken as an example of deranged rationality or—if you change your angle of vision—as the only smart thing to do. Certain moral principles make sense within the context of certain visions of life, but from within the context of other visions, they don't make much sense at all. From within the vision provided by the rabbi's faith, all lives are sacred; from Jack's viewpoint, some lives don't count.

Many of the moral principles we subscribe to seem reasonable to us only because they are embedded within a vision or world-view we hold to be true even though we might not think very often about it. In the same way, a moral transformation is often accompanied by a transformation of vision. Many ordinary people describe their moral improvement as the result of seeing things in a different light or seeing them for the first time. "I was blind but now I see" is more than a line from an old hymn; it is the way a great many people explain their moral growth.

If we can agree that morality is intimately bound up with vision, then we can see why stories are so important for our moral development, and why neglecting them is a serious mistake. This is because stories are one of the chief ways by which visions are conveyed (a vision, in turn, may be defined as a story about the way things are or the way the world works). Just as vision and morality are intimately connected, so are story and morality. Some contemporary philosophers of ethics—most notably, Alasdair MacIntyre—now maintain that the connection between narrative and morality is an essential one, not merely a useful one. The Ph.D. needs the story "part" just as much as the peasant. In other words, story and moral may be less separable than we have come to think. The question is not whether the moral principle needs to be sweetened with the sugar of the story but whether moral principles make any sense outside the human context of stories. For example, since I referred earlier to the Enlightenment habit of distilling out the Christian ethic from the Bible, consider how much sense the following principles make when they are forced to stand on their own:

- Do good to those that harm you.
- Turn the other cheek.
- Walk an extra mile.
- Blessed are the poor.
- Feed the hungry.

"Feed the hungry" seems to have the most compelling claim on us, but just how rational is it? Science doesn't tell us to feed the hungry. Moreover, feeding the hungry defeats the purpose of natural selection. Why not let them die and thus "decrease the surplus population" as Ebenezer Scrooge suggests? Fortunately, the storyteller in this case takes care to put the suggestion in the mouth of a disagreeable old man.

Of course, there are visions or stories or ways of looking at life other than the Christian one, from which these counsels would still make sense. On the other hand, from some points of view they are sheer nonsense. Nietzsche, one of the great geniuses of philosophy, had nothing but contempt for the Christian ethic.

In recent years a number of prominent psychologists and educators have turned their attention to stories. In *The Uses of Enchantment* (1975), child psychiatrist Bruno Bettelheim argued that fairy tales are a vital source of psychological and moral strength; their formative power, he said, had been seriously underestimated. Robert Coles of Harvard University followed in the 1980s with three books (*The Moral Life of Children, The Spiritual Life of Children,* and *The Call of Stories*) which detailed the indispensable role of stories in the

life of both children and adults. Another Harvard scholar, Jerome Bruner, whose earlier *The Process of Education* had helped stimulate interest in critical thinking, had, by the mid-eighties, begun to worry that "propositional thinking" had been emphasized at the expense of "narrative thinking"—literally, a way of thinking in stories. In *Actual Minds, Possible Worlds,* Bruner suggests that it is this narrative thought, much more than logical thought, that gives meaning to life.

A number of other psychologists had arrived at similar conclusions. Theodore Sarbin, Donald Spence, Paul Vitz, and others have emphasized the extent to which individuals interpret their own lives as stories or narratives. "Indeed," writes Vitz, "it is almost impossible not to think this way." According to these psychologists, it is such narrative plots more than anything else that guide our moral choices. Coles, in *The Moral Life of Children,* observes how the children he came to know through his work not only understood their own lives in a narrative way but were profoundly influenced in their decisions by the stories, often of a religious kind, they had learned.

By the mid-eighties a similar story had begun to unfold in the field of education. Under the leadership of Professor Kevin Ryan, Boston University's Center for the Advancement of Character and Ethics produced a number of position papers calling for a reemphasis on literature as a moral teacher and guide. Meanwhile, in *Teaching as Storytelling* and other books, Kieran Egan of Canada's Simon Fraser University was proposing that the foundations of all education are poetic and imaginative. Even logico-mathematical and rational forms of thinking grow out of imagination, and depend on it. Egan argues that storytelling should be the basic educational method because it corresponds with fundamental structures of the human mind. Like Paul Vitz, he suggests that it is nearly impossible not to think in story terms. "Most of the world's cultures and its great religions," he points out, "have at their sacred core a story, and we indeed have difficulty keeping our rational history from being constantly shaped into stories."

In short, scholars in several fields were belatedly discovering what Flannery O'Connor, with her writer's intuition, had noticed years before: "A story is a way to say something that can't be said any other way . . ."

This recent interest in stories should not, however, be interpreted as simply another Romantic reaction to rationalism. None of the people I have mentioned could be classified as Romanticists. Several of them (including Flannery O'Connor) freely acknowledge their indebtedness to Aristotle and Aquinas—to what might be called the "realist" tradition in philosophy. Although literature can be used as an escape, the best literature, as Jacques Barzun said, carries us back to reality. It involves us in the detail and particularity of other lives. And unlike the superficial encounters of the workaday world, a book shows us what other lives are like from the inside. Moral principles also take on a reality in stories that they lack in purely logical form. Stories restrain our tendency to indulge in abstract speculation about ethics. They make it a little harder for us to reduce people to factors in an equation.

I can illustrate the overall point by mentioning a recurrent phenomenon in my classes. I have noticed that when my students are presented with a Values Clarification strategy and then with a dramatic account of the same situation, they respond one way to the dilemma and another to the story. In the Values Clarification dilemma called "The Lifeboat Exercise," the class is asked to imagine that a ship has sunk and a lifeboat has been put out from it. The lifeboat is overcrowded and in danger of being swamped unless the load is lightened. The students are given a brief description of the passengers—a young couple and their child, an elderly brother and sister, a doctor, a bookkeeper, an athlete, an entertainer, and so on—and from this list they must decide whom to throw overboard. Consistent with current thinking, there are no right and wrong answers in this exercise. The idea is to generate discussion. And it works quite well. Students are typically excited by the lifeboat dilemma.

This scenario, of course, is similar to the situation that faced the crew and passengers of the *Titanic* when it struck an iceberg in the North Atlantic in 1912. But when the event is presented as a story rather than as a dilemma, the response evoked is not the same. For example, when students who have done the exercise are given the opportunity to view the film *A Night to Remember,* they react in a strikingly different way. I've watched classes struggle with the lifeboat dilemma, but the struggle is mainly an intellectual one like doing a crossword puzzle. The characters in the exercise, after all, are only hypothetical. They are counters to be moved around at will. We can't really identify with them, nor can we be inspired or repelled by them. They exist only for the sake of the exercise.

When they watch the film, however, these normally blasé college students behave differently. Many of them cry. They cry as quietly as possible, of course: even on the college level it is extremely important to maintain one's cool. But this is a fairly consistent reaction. I've observed it in several different classes over several years. They don't even have to see the whole film. About twenty minutes of excerpts will do the trick.

What does the story do that the exercise doesn't? Very simply, it moves them deeply and profoundly. This is what art is supposed to do.

If you have seen the film, you may recall some of the vivid sketches of the passengers on the dying ship as the situation becomes clear to them: Edith Evans, giving up a place on the last boat to Mrs. Brown, saying, "You go first; you have children waiting at home." Harvey Collyer pleading with his wife, "Go, Lottie! For God's sake, be brave and go! I'll get a seat in another boat." Mrs. Isidor Straus declining a place in the boats: "I've always stayed with my husband, so why should I leave him now?"

The story is full of scenes like this: Arthur Ryerson stripping off his life vest and giving it to his wife's maid; men struggling below-decks to keep the pumps going in the face of almost certain death; the ship's band playing ragtime and then hymns till the very end; the women in boat 6 insisting that it return to pick up survivors; the men clinging to the hull of an overturned boat, reciting the Lord's Prayer; the *Carpathia,* weaving in and out of ice floes, racing at breakneck speed to the rescue. But there are other images as well: the indolence and stupidity of the *California*'s crew who, only ten miles away, might have made all the difference, but did nothing; the man disguised in a woman's shawl; the panicked mob of men rushing a lifeboat; passengers in half-empty lifeboats refusing to go back to save the drowning.

The film doesn't leave the viewer much room for ethical maneuvering. It is quite clear who has acted well and who has not. And anyone who has seen it will come away hoping that if ever put to a similar test, he or she will be brave and not cowardly, will think of others rather than of self.

Not only does the film move us, it moves us in certain directions. It is definitive, not openended. We are not being asked to ponder a complex ethical dilemma; rather, we are being taught what is proper. There are codes of conduct: women and children first; duty to others before self. If there is a dilemma in the film, it does not concern the code itself. The only dilemma is the perennial one that engages each soul: conscience versus cowardice, faith versus despair.

This is not to say that the film was produced as a moral fable. It is, after all, a true story and a gripping one, the type of thing that almost demands cinematic expression—hardly a case of didacticism. In fact, if we were to level a charge of didacticism, it would have to be against "The Lifeboat Exercise." It is quite

obviously an artificially contrived teaching exercise. But this is didacticism with a difference. "The Lifeboat Exercise" belongs to the age of relativism, and consequently, it has nothing to teach. No code of conduct is being passed down; no models of good and bad behavior are shown. Whether it is actually a good or bad thing to throw someone overboard is up to the youngster to decide for himself. The exercise is designed to initiate the group into the world of "each man his own moral compass."

Of course, we are comparing two somewhat different things: a story, on the one hand, and a discussion exercise, on the other. The point is that the logic of relativism necessitates the second approach. The story of the *Titanic* was surely known to the developers of "The Lifeboat Exercise." Why didn't they use it? The most probable answer is the one we have alluded to: The story doesn't allow for the type of dialogue desired. It marshals its audience swiftly and powerfully to the side of certain values. We feel admiration for the radio operators who stay at their post. We feel pity and contempt for the handful of male passengers who sneak into lifeboats. There are not an infinite number of ways in which to respond to these scenes, as there might be to a piece of abstract art. Drama is not the right medium for creating a value-neutral climate. It exerts too much moral force.

Drama also forces us to see things afresh. We don't always notice the humanity of the person sitting next to us on the bus. It is often the case that human beings and human problems must be presented dramatically for us to see them truly. Robert Coles relates an interesting anecdote in this regard about Ruby Bridges, the child who first integrated the New Orleans schools. Ruby had seen A *Raisin in the Sun,* and expressed to Coles the wish that white people would see it: "If all the [white] people on the street [who were heckling her mercilessly] saw that movie, they might stop coming out to bother us." When Coles asked her why she thought that, she answered, "Because the people in the movies would work on them, and maybe they'd listen." Ruby knew that whites who saw her every day didn't really see her. Maybe the movie would make them see.

Admittedly, I have been mixing media rather freely here, and this raises a question. Films obviously have to do with seeing, but how about books? The paradoxical answer is that the storyteller's craft is not only a matter of telling but also of showing. This is why writing is so often compared to painting, and why beginning writers are urged to visualize what they want to say. So, even when a writer has a moral theme, his work—if he is a good writer—is more like the work of an artist than a moralist. For example, C.S. Lewis's immensely popular children's books have strong moral and religious themes, but they were not conceived out of a moral intent. "All my seven Narnian books," Lewis wrote in 1960, "and my three science fiction books, began with seeing pictures in my head. At first they were not a story, just pictures. *The Lion* [*The Lion, the Witch and the Wardrobe*] all began with a picture of a faun carrying an umbrella and parcels in a snowy wood."

Stories are essentially moving pictures. That is why they are so readily adaptable to the screen. And a well-made film, in turn, needs surprisingly little dialogue to make its point. When, in *A Night to Remember*, the shawl is torn away from the man's head, we do not have to be told anything. We *see* that his behavior is shameful; it is written on his face.

On the simplest level the moral force of a story or film is the force of example. It shows us examples of men and women acting well or trying to act well, or acting badly. The story points to these people and says in effect, "Act like this; don't act like that." Except that, of course, nothing of the kind is actually stated. It is a matter of showing. There is, for instance, a scene in *Anna Karenina* in which Levin sits by the side of his dying brother and simply holds

his hand for an hour, and then another hour. Tolstoy doesn't come out and say that this is what he ought to do, but the scene is presented in such a way that the reader knows that it is the right thing to do. It is, to use a phrase of Bruno Bettelheim's, "tangibly right."

"Do I have to draw you a picture?" That much used put-down implies that normally intelligent people can do without graphic illustration. But when it comes to moral matters, it may be that we do need the picture more than we think. The story suits our nature because we think more readily in pictures than in propositions. And when a proposition or principle has the power to move us to action it is often because it is backed up by a picture or image. Consider, for example, the enormous importance historians assign to a single book— *Uncle Tom's Cabin*—in galvanizing public sentiment against slavery. After the novel appeared, it was acted out on the stage in hundreds of cities. For the first time, vast numbers of Americans had a visible and dramatic image of the evils of slavery. Lincoln, on being introduced to author Harriet Beecher Stowe, greeted her with the words, "So this is the little lady who started the big war." In more recent times the nation's conscience has been quickened by photo images of civil rights workers marching arm in arm, kneeling in prayer, and under police attack. It is nice to think that moral progress is the result of better reasoning, but it is naive to ignore the role of the imagination in our moral life.

The more abstract our ethic, the less power it has to move us. Yet the progression of recent decades has been in the direction of increasing verbalization and abstraction, toward a reason dissociated from ordinary feelings and cut off from images that convey humanness to us. "At the core of every moral code," observed Walter Lippmann, "there is a picture of human nature." But the picture coming out of our schools increasingly resembles a blank canvas. The deep human sympathies—the kind we acquire from good literature—are missing.

Perhaps the best novelistic portrait of disconnected rationalism is that of Raskolnikov in *Crime and Punishment*. Raskolnikov has mastered the art of asking the question, "Why not?" What is wrong with killing a repulsive old woman? he asks himself. What is wrong with taking her money and using it for a worthy cause—namely, to pay for his own education? With that education, Raskolnikov eventually plans to bring his intellectual gifts to the service of mankind. It is good utilitarian logic.

In commenting on *Crime and Punishment*, William Barrett observes that in the days and weeks after the killing, "A single image breaks into this [Raskolnikov's] thinking." It is the image of his victim, and this image saves Raskolnikov's soul. Not an idea but an image. For Dostoevsky the value of each soul was a mystery that could never be calculated but only shown.

The same theme recurs in *The Brothers Karamazov*. At the very end of the book, Alyosha speaks to the youngsters who love him: "My dear children . . . You must know that there is nothing higher and stronger and more wholesome and useful for life in after years than some good memory, especially a memory connected with childhood, with home. People talk to you a great deal about your education, but some fine, sacred memory, preserved from childhood, is perhaps the best education. If a man carries many such memories with him into life, he is safe to the end of his days, and if we have only one good memory left in our hearts, even that may sometime be the means of saving us."

There is no point in trying to improve on this. Let us only observe that what Dostoevsky says of good memories is true also of good stories. Some of our "sacred" memories may find their source in stories.

We carry around in our heads many more of these images and memories than we realize. The picture of Narcissus by the pool is probably there for most of us; and the Prodigal Son and his forgiving father likely inhabit some corner of our imagination. Atticus Finch, Ebenezer Scrooge, Laura Ingalls Wilder, Anne Frank, David and Goliath, Abraham Lincoln, Peter and the servant girl: for most of us these names will call up an image, and the image will summon up a story. The story in turn may give us the power or resolve to struggle through a difficult situation or to overcome our own moral sluggishness. Or it may simply give us the power to see things clearly. Above all, the story allows us to make that human connection we are always in danger of forgetting.

Most cultures have recognized that morality, religion, story, and myth are bound together in some vital way, and that to sever the connection among them leaves us not with strong and independent ethical principles but with weak and unprotected ones. What "enlightened" thinkers in every age envision is some sort of progression from story to freestanding moral principles unencumbered by stories. But the actual progression never stops there. Once we lose sight of the human fact of principle, the way is clear for attacking the principles themselves as merely situational or relative. The final stage of the progression is moral nihilism and the appeal to raw self-interest. . . .

Discussion Questions

1. Why does Professor Kilpatrick believe that there is a danger in teaching moral principles abstractly by way of contrived dilemmas? What does he suggest we do to correct this problem?

2. What is the "Lifeboat Exercise" and why does Professor Kirkpatrick think that it does not adequately teach students about morality? How does he compare and contrast this

exercise with the film *A Night to Remember?* What point is he trying to make with this comparison and contrast?

3. Professor Kilpatrick makes the claim that "much of the moral law consists of axioms and premises about human beings and human conduct. You either see them or you don't." What does he mean by this and what examples does he cite in order to make his point? Do you agree with Professor Kilpatrick's claim? Why or why not? Explain and defend your answer.

4. Comparing Professor Kilpatrick's essay to the views you've read about in the previous three essays on ethical theory (Kant, Mill, and Dimock), do you think that Professor Kilpatrick's virtue ethics is consistent with or complements any or all of these three other views? Explain and defend your answer.

You can locate InfoTrac-College Education articles about this chapter by accessing the InfoTrac-College Edition website (http://www.infotrac-college.com/wadsworth/). Using the InfoTrac-College Edition subject guide, enter the search terms relevant to this chapter, and then read abstracts for relevant articles.

SECTION C

God and Morality

Introduction to Section C

Can one be good without God? This may sound like a simple question, but like so many philosophical queries, it is rich with possible interpretations and possible answers. Take, for example, the meaning of the words "good" and "morality." Some philosophers argue that moral claims are real, nonmaterial, and irreducible properties that persons may possess. So, for instance, if someone claims, "Mother Teresa is good," that person is claiming that Mother Teresa in fact has the property of "goodness," a property as real as her height or weight, though it is not physical and thus cannot be measured by a ruler or a scale. But this poses a problem for some metaphysical worldviews. For example, *materialism* holds that all that exists can be reduced to physical matter, that nonmaterial things such as souls, numbers, and morality do not actually exist. For if moral properties are real and are irreducibly nonmaterial, then the presence of moral properties in the universe, in the words of atheist philosopher J. L. Mackie, "constitute such an odd cluster of properties and relations that they are most unlikely to have arisen in the ordinary course of events without an all-powerful god to create them."[1] Given his commitment to materialism (and atheism), Mackie rejects the existence of moral properties. In this section's only piece (in Chapter 7, "Does Ethics Depend on God?: A Debate"), Professor Kai Nielsen, an atheist, believes that the existence of moral properties is highly implausible.

How then do thinkers such as Mackie and Nielsen defend morality? Some of them argue that morality is not "real" in the same sense that material things are real, but rather, morality is more like traffic signals or civil or criminal law: it serves a purpose in promoting human flourishing and can be rationally defended. That is, morality is a human construction, resulting from evolution, that "exists" to help sustain the human species. For example, philosopher Michael Ruse writes: "Considered as a rationally justifiable set of claims about an objective something, ethics is illusory. I appreciate that when somebody says, 'Love thy neighbor as thyself,' they think they are referring above and beyond themselves. . . . Never the less . . . such reference is truly without foundation. Morality is just an aid to survival and reproduction . . . and any deeper meaning is illusory."[2]

Other philosophers, such as Nielsen and John Rawls,[3] choose to set aside the question of the nature of morality, even though some of them, such as Nielsen, believe that it is implausible that moral properties exist. According to these thinkers, we start our moral reasoning from our "considered judgments," those values and beliefs about morality with which we find ourselves and that seem to be prima facie correct (e.g., "do good and avoid evil"; "killing persons without justification is wrong"). We then make moral judgments that are consistent with these considered judgments, perhaps adjusting the latter when the former provide us with new insights. For example, if we were to come across in our space travel an alien race of "persons" (e.g., Klingons or Romulans of Star Trek lore) that are not human beings, we would have to rethink and amend the meaning of our prohibition of killing persons without justification (a considered judgment) to include more than just human beings but the members of this alien race as well, for such beings would have the moral properties that make human beings valuable (another considered judgment). Thus, an adjustment in one of our moral rules would be required in order to retain the coherency of our moral point of view. This is an example of what Rawls and Professor Nielsen mean by "reflective equilibrium." So, for Nielsen and Rawls, whether or not moral properties exist, or whether or not such properties depend on God, is an issue that must be put aside. What is most important is whether our moral judgments fit together (or cohere) with our considered judgments.

Let's get back to our initial question: Can one be good without God? But, like the term "good," the question before us could be looked at in a number of different ways. For instance, the question may be asking whether a person can be good without believing in God. That seems to have a simple answer: Yes. For there are decent atheists who live exemplary personal lives, keep their promises, and treat their fellow human beings justly. On the other hand, there are some "believers in God" who are not good people, and sometimes perform evil deeds in the name of God.

However, what if in our initial question we are asking whether God's existence is necessary for morality. This would be different from asking whether atheists could be good people. For example, just as cooks are necessary for the existence of prepared food at a restaurant, God may be necessary for the existence of morality. So, just as one can enjoy well-prepared restaurant food without believing in the existence of cooks, one may live a morally good life without acknowledging that morality depends on God (if, of course, it in fact depends on him).

But now one may raise another question: Is morality merely the commands of God? Some say "yes." They are defenders of what is called *Divine Command Theory* (DCT). That is, moral rules ought to be obeyed because they are God's commands and God is the omnipotent Creator of the universe. In reply to DCT, some philosophers argue that it falls prey to a variation of a dilemma raised by Socrates in a question found in Plato's *Euthyphro*.[4] Is something good because God loves it, or does God love it because it is good?[5] This is called the *Euthyphro Dilemma*, because it seems that whichever option of the two one chooses, one chooses an undesirable answer. For if one answers the question by saying that something is good because God loves it, then "goodness" is merely the result of God's power and will and is thus arbitrary. In other words, if God says that child torture is right, it's right; but if God says that child torture is wrong, it's wrong. On the other hand, if one embraces the second horn of the dilemma—God loves it because it is good—then there is a standard of goodness outside of God to which even he is subject. But this would mean that God's commands are not the foundation of morality.

A moderate version of DCT, defended by philosopher Robert Adams, suggests one answer to this dilemma. He argues that God's command is a necessary, though not a sufficient condition, to obey God. (Just as being "female" is a necessary though not a sufficient condition for being a "sister," for the other necessary condition, "sibling," is missing). According to Adams, God's command must be consistent with a loving character, which Adams believes God has. Although he concedes that it is logically possible that God command what is wrong, "it is unthinkable that God should do so."[6] An analysis of whether or not Adams's or another version of DCT can withstand the critique of the Euthyphro Dilemma is outside the scope of this introduction. Nevertheless, the point is that DCT is alive and well despite the criticisms leveled against it.

Ironically, both participants in the debate reprinted in this section, Professor Nielsen and Professor J. P. Moreland, *reject* DCT, even though they disagree over the issue of whether ethics depend on God. Moreland, the theist in the debate, argues that ethics do depend on God, not because God issues moral commands and God is the all-powerful Creator of the universe, but rather, because God's nature (or character) is the ground of the moral law. That is, God's commands are good, not because God commands them, but because God is good. According to Moreland, God is not subject to a moral order outside of Himself, and neither are God's moral commands arbitrary. God's commands are issued by a perfect being who is the source of all goodness. Nielsen, the atheist in the debate, sees no need in trying to solve the Euthyphro Dilemma, for he argues that ethics do not need God, that one can be rationally justified in one's ethical system without God existing, believing in God, or basing morality on God's commands.

Keywords: theistic ethics, divine command theory, Euthyphro dilemma, religion and morality, biblical ethics, religious ethics, humanism, evolutionary ethics, reflective equilibrium, moral realism, moral constructivism.

NOTES

1. J. L. Mackie, *The Miracle of Theism* (Oxford: Clarendon Press, 1982), 115.
2. Michael Ruse, "Evolutionary Theory and Christian Ethics," in *The Darwinian Paradigm* (London: Routledge, 1989), 262, 268–69.
3. See John Rawls, "Kantian Constructivism in Moral Theory: The Dewey Lectures 1980," *Journal of Philosophy* 77 (1980).
4. See, for example, Bertrand Russell, *Why I Am Not A Christian* (New York: Simon & Schuster, 1957), 590.
5. Socrates' formulates it a bit differently: "Is the pious loved by the gods because it is pious, or is it pious because it is loved by the gods?" (Plato, *Euthyphro,* 10a. *The Collected Dialogues of Plato,* eds. Edith Hamilton and Huntington Cairns [Princeton, NJ: Princeton University Press, 1961]).
6. Robert Adams, "A Modified Divine Command Theory of Ethical Wrongness," in *Philosophy of Religion,* ed. Louis P. Pojman (Belmont, CA: Wadsworth, 1987), 528.

For Further Reading

Robert Adams, "A Modified Divine Command Theory of Ethical Wrongness," in *Philosophy of Religion*, ed. Louis P. Pojman (Belmont, CA: Wadsworth, 1987).

Francis J. Beckwith and Gregory P. Koukl, *Relativism: Feet Firmly Planted in Mid-Air* (Grand Rapids, MI: Baker, 1998), chapters 14 and 15.

Paul Copan, "Can Michael Martin Be a Moral Realist?: *Sic et Non*," *Philosophia Christi* Series 2, 1.2 (1999).

Paul Helm, ed., *The Divine Command Theory of Ethics* (New York: Oxford University Press, 1979).

Immanuel Kant, *Religion Within the Bounds of Reason Alone,* tr. T. M. Greene and H. H. Hudson (San Francisco: Harper & Row, 1960).

Michael Martin, "Atheism, Christian Theism, and Rape." From the Internet Infidels website 23 June 1997 (www.infidels.org/library/modern/michael_martin/rape.html).

———, *Atheism: A Philosophical Justification* (Philadelphia: Temple University Press, 1990), pp. 212–217.

George I. Mavrodes, "Religion and the Queerness of Morality," in *Rationality, Religious Belief and Moral Committment*, eds. Robert Audi and William J. Wainwright (Ithaca, NY: Cornell University Press, 1986).

Basil Mitchell, *Morality: Religious and Secular* (New York: Oxford University Press, 1980).

J. P. Moreland, *Scaling the Secular City* (Grand Rapids, MI: Baker, 1987), chapter 4.

J. P. Moreland and Kai Nielsen, *Does God Exist? The Great Debate* (Amherst, NY: Prometheus, 1993).

Richard J. Mouw, *The God Who Commands* (Notre Dame, IN: University of Notre Dame Press, 1990).

Kai Nielsen, *Ethics Without God,* rev. ed. (Buffalo, NY: Prometheus, 1989).

———, *God and the Grounding of Morality* (Ottawa: University of Ottawa Press, 1991).

D. Z. Phillips, ed., *Religion & Morality* (New York: St. Martin's Press, 1996).

Louis P. Pojman, "Ethics: Religious and Secular," *The Modern Schoolman* 70 (November 1992).

———, "A Critique of Contemporary Egalitarianism: A Christian Perspective," *Faith and Philosophy* 8:4 (October 1991).

Philip Quinn, *Divine Commands and Moral Requirements* (Oxford: Clarendon Press, 1978).

Does Ethics Depend on God?: A Debate   7

J. P. MORELAND AND KAI NIELSEN

J. P. Moreland is Professor of Philosophy, Talbot School of Theology, Biola University (La Mirada, California). A Christian philosopher, Professor Moreland is the author of many books including *Body & Soul* (2000), *Scaling the Secular City:*

Reprinted by the permission of the authors from J. P. Moreland and Kai Nielsen, *Does God Exist?: The Great Debate* (Amherst, NY: Prometheus Books, 1993), 98–135. Endnotes omitted.

A Defense of Christianity (1987), and *Christianity and the Nature of Science* (1989). Kai Nielsen is a Professor Emeritus of Philosophy at the University of Calgary as well as Adjunct Professor of Philosophy, Concordia University (Montreal). One of the leading atheist philosophers of the twentieth century, Professor Nielsen's books include *Philosophy and Atheism: A Defense of Atheism* (1985), *Ethics Without God,* 2nd ed. (1989), and *Why Be Moral?* (1989).

This selection is excerpted from a transcript of a debate on God's existence that took place at the University of Mississippi (Oxford) in 1988. Both Professor Nielsen and Professor Moreland define "God" as the God of classical theism, as found in the three great monotheistic religions, Christianity, Judaism, and Islam. Although Moreland uses the phrase "Christian theism," it is clear what he is defending is a view of God that may be embraced by members of the other two religious traditions.

Professor Nielsen argues that a sound ethical system does not need God in order to be sound. He first critiques Divine Command Theory (DCT), the view that what makes something right is that God commands it. He argues, for example, that it is wrong, "God or no God, to torture children just for the fun of it." Professor Nielsen then critiques the argument that religious moralities are superior to secular ones. He argues, among other things, that religious moralities are typically dependent on the truth of the religion in question. But if religious truth is implausible, as Professor Nielsen believes, then religious morality is less attractive than secular morality. He then goes on to discuss the question of whether life can having meaning if God does not exist, maintaining that there may be purposes *in* life but not a cosmic purpose *to* life. Concerning the foundation of morality, Professor Nielsen asserts that it need not be grounded in God, for it can be grounded in our considered judgments that fit into wide reflective equilibrium. (This is an idea found in the works of Rawls—see chapter 36). But even the theist, argues Nielsen, must too rely on his "considered convictions," and thus is in the same boat as the atheist. Nielsen then argues that a common refrain employed by some theists—you ought obey God's moral law if you don't want to fry in hell—is a deeply immoral reason to do the right thing.

Professor Moreland, like Professor Nielsen, rejects DCT. However, Moreland argues that the existence of morality is best explained by the *existence* of God, not His commands. That is, God's commands are good because *He is good*. His commands are not good because He *commands* them. Professor Moreland admits that he is not making a knock-down drag-out proof for God's existence from the existence of morality. But rather, what he is doing is very much like what a prosecuting attorney may do in a criminal case in which she is trying to demonstrate a defendant's guilt. Moreland is, in a sense, arguing that given the "fingerprints" that one finds on moral norms when one reflects on their nature, it seems that they are best explained as the result of the hand and mind of the God of theism. Although one may reject this conclusion, Professor Moreland maintains that it is difficult to conceive of a better alternative. In fact, he explains and critiques the two leading alternatives, *the immanent purpose view,* and *the optimistic humanist view.* Professor Moreland believes, that in comparison to theism, both these alternatives fail to explain the existence and nature of morality. This debate concludes with members of the audience asking questions of the participants.

[*KAI*] NIELSEN: WELL, THANK you very much for having me here. . . . .

Religious people frequently claim that to make sense of our lives and to define an objective basis of morality, we must believe in God. Is this so? And exactly what does this claim come to?

Now when I speak of "God" here, I intend to use the term in a traditional sense. If you simply mean by "God" *love,* then all atheists can be led gently into belief. I am not concerned here with those who use the term in such an eccentric sense. So when I speak of "God," I'm going to mean something that I think orthodox Christians, Jews, and believers in Islam all hold. So when I say it's necessary to believe in God to make adequate sense of morality or indeed to make any sense of morality, I mean by "God" the one infinite creator of all things, the one infinite, uncreated, eternal, personal reality transcendent to the world, who created all that exists other than Himself and sustains and protects all His creation. This in our culture is a very standard conception of God, and for good or for ill, that is roughly what I mean when I raise this question.

Now does the viability of moral beliefs depend on belief in God? This can be asked in at least two forms. The one form asks, or asserts rather, that to have any kind of coherent moral belief at all, one must presuppose the existence of God. Remember Martin Luther's famous remark, "There's no greater enemy of grace than the ethics of Aristotle." This tradition, I suppose, is more Protestant than Catholic, though it is surely not adhered to by all Protestants. Its famous contemporary formulators have been people like Emil Brunner or Karl Barth. But there is another form of religious ethics (I think a more moderate and plausible form) which says that any secular ethic is inadequate when compared with an ethic inspired or informed by theistic commitments. That form doesn't deny what is obvious anyway, that nonreligious people can be morally responsible, but it maintains that a through and through adequate account of morality would answer to the deepest needs that human beings have and that, this account maintains, would have to be an ethic with theistic commitments. Contemporary representatives of that rather more moderate view are Professor John Hick and my colleague Terence Penelhum.

About the first view first, namely, the belief that to have any kind of coherent moral belief at all, you must believe in God—believe, that is, in God in the sense or roughly the sense I defined—I think that just the reverse is true. I think, that is, that you cannot even have a coherent sense, if indeed it is a coherent sense, of God that the Judeo-Christian-Islamic traditions wish to have, at least as that has been developed, without at least some prior *moral understanding.* That, in short, to oversimplify, instead of morality requiring religion, the very possibility of even understanding the concept of God and in making a religious response presupposes some minimal moral understanding.

Now I just asserted that it is not the case that without God nothing matters. I'm not going to argue for that in this lecture. The basic line of argumentation for it, the sort of thing I've argued on numerous occasions, including in my *Ethics Without God,* is familiar enough. I suppose most of you are in some philosophy course, and I suppose you have read about theories of divine command morality. That is, moral theories which say that to know what is right, to know what is obligatory, even to know what is good, you have to know what God commands, God wills, God ordains. And *whatever* God wills and *whatever* God ordains, that establishes what is right and what is wrong. This is the divine command theory.

If that theory could be justifiably held, not in its modified forms, where it does not meet secular ethics head on and does not challenge in the above way secular ethics, but in its unmodified form, it could be a very powerful moral theory indeed. It would yield some decisive decision procedures in ethics. These modified forms may be adequate for other purposes, but not as a kind of response to a secular morality. It is, in its unmodified strong form, as you see in Emil Brunner, where you simply determine what is right by knowing what God wills, that you get a deep challenge to secularism. These accounts just assume that there is a God—it is just background assumption. That, they claim, settles what is right, no matter what it seems to human beings, no matter what our frail moral sense suggests. You must do it even if God orders you to kill your only son. If God orders you to do it, then it is right, no matter what He orders you to do. You would, no doubt, say He wouldn't give you such orders, but if He did, you would still conclude that it is the right thing to do because whatever is right and whatever is wrong is determined by what God wills. We don't have even to look at the content of His commands. You just have to know that they are His commands.

I want to say, to understate it, that that sort of ethic is clearly inadequate. It's wrong, God or no God, to torture little children just for the fun of it. What basis we have for making that confident moral claim is another thing, but we know, if we know anything, if we have any moral understanding at all, that that is wrong. And moreover, to understand what you're talking about, to understand that God, among other things, is a being worthy of worship and that God is said to be perfect, the perfect good, we need some logically prior understanding of those normative concepts. In order to understand that something is the perfect good, you have to understand what is good, and in order to understand that something is worthy of worship, you have to have at least some elementary criteria or understanding of what worthiness is, and that is *not* itself derived from God. Or to put the point more accurately, though rather more pedantically, though it may be derived in a causal sense— since everything comes from God—it is not derived in a justificatory or logical sense from God or a belief in God. Our understanding of these concepts is quite logically prior to any religious response.

This is the thing, if I develop it properly, as I do when I teach elementary ethics courses, that takes me about three classes. So I won't try it today. I'll just assert it, and if there are questions which come up in the discussion about this, I will respond to them. But what I want to do here today is examine what I take to be the more moderate sort of claim that doesn't say that an atheist has no moral understanding, which doesn't deny that there could be such things as secular moralities, but which contends they are inadequate when compared with a religious ethic. Again, let me remind you, I develop a critique of divine command theory as well as other religious moral theories in my *Ethics Without God* and *God and the Grounding of Morality*.

I want to take up the claim that argues, and sometimes with considerable force, that the best of religious moralities, though not all religious moralities, are far more worthy of acceptance than even the best of secular moralities. I say not all religious moralities, for, after all, there are brutal religious moralities and there are brutal secular moralities and there are stupid religious moralities and there are stupid secular moralities. But the best forms of religious moralities, the ones expressing most adequately the tradition or the common traditions of Judaism, Christianity, and Islam, the claim I wish to examine goes, are more adequate than any form of humanistic ethic. It is not that there can't be secular humanistic ethics, but the most adequate morality would be a religious morality. That is the sort of thing that I want critically to examine.

Many Christians argue this way, and from now on I'll just talk about Christians because I suppose most of you are Christians in this environment. (I have, by the way, no strong preference between Christianity and Judaism and Islam, but that's another issue. I suppose if I were shopping around, I'd rather be a Zen Buddhist than any of the above, but that's neither here nor there for this discussion. So let us just talk about Christians.)

Some Christians accept the fact that there are coherent secular moralities and that atheists can indeed be decent and principled people. They can even admit that secular moralities can have a justification of sorts, while still claiming that a morality informed by theistic commitments will be a much superior and more securely founded morality than any purely secular morality. What I want to do is argue that this claim is false.

Now I don't think this claim is *demonstrably* false in the way that I think the divine command theory is demonstrably false. I may, of course, be mistaken in thinking it is demonstrably false, but what I think goes on is the more moderate argument that you can give considerations, none of them decisive, for both views; I think, however, that considerations can be given that are cogent enough such that most people, if they reflect upon them very carefully in a cool hour, will come to say what I'm about to say. But I may, of course, be wrong in saying this. That is for you to make up your mind about in reflecting on the force of my arguments.

First, what grounds lead religious moralists to make such assertions? Why do they believe that a fully adequate religious morality would be a more adequate morality than any humanistic secular morality? Well, one of the claims, and an important one, is that religious moralities answer more deeply to our deepest human needs. This, of course, goes with a background assumption—an assumption I am perfectly comfortable with—that an adequate morality is a morality that will meet human needs. It will not be a morality so concerned with rights and duties that it will ignore the importance of meeting human needs.

They will make claims, diversely expressed, something like this: Human beings everywhere are religious animals, religious beings, in need of rituals and saving myths. Even if the reference to "saving myths" means that there is no

truth involved here, the claim might still be pressed. Moreover, myths could also be ways of indicating something which was true. But whether or not myths could be vehicles of truth or falsity, people need these big saving myths, the claim goes, with the framework beliefs that go with them. Without a belief in God and immortality, or at least a resurrection of the body (something that replaces immortality), our lives, the claim goes, will remain fragmented and meaningless and thus the deepest needs that we human beings have won't be answered.

A secular morality, they will say, can afford us no sense of providential care, while a Christian or Jewish or Islamic morality can. Recall that in the [Apostle's] Creed it speaks of "God the Father Almighty." God is a creator who is the source of care, protection, and moral guidance. We are, if our faith is strong, free of anxiety and fear. With a firm faith in God, we have the reassurance that if we will orient our will to God, we will be saved and that evil will not ultimately triumph and that our efforts will not be hopeless because the evil in the world is too much for us. In God we can find peace and a reassurance that all is not in vain.

Contrast this with how I have to respond, given my secular belief-system, when I reflect on the fact that 10,000 people will starve during the course of this day. (Just calculate, as you sit here, how many people will starve while I am giving this lecture.) All I can say about it, beyond expressing my anguish, is that we must work to halt this by struggling in a political-social way. While, if you're a believer, you could hate this, struggle against it just as much as I do, but you would also feel you have some awareness that somehow these struggles, especially when there is a sense of the struggles being defeated, are not in vain. In some ways that you as a religious person do not very well understand, it still is, appearances to the contrary notwithstanding, not all in vain. There's a kind of reassurance and peace religious people have—or so it is sometimes claimed—that no secular morality can offer. The Jew or the Christian or the Moslem can have a confident future-oriented view of the world, knowing that there is a purpose to life, that we are creatures of God, made for a purpose. There is, the belief goes, a purpose in which ultimately for all humankind there will be human liberation in a life of bliss. There is a hope there and a moral promise that no secular morality can match.

Now how should secularists and atheists respond to this? (I am, I should say parenthetically, something worse than this, for I am not only an atheist but a Marxian as well.) I will first tell you one response which I think is a bad one, and then I'll tell you what I think is a good response. The first one is not altogether bad, but it is question-begging and it smacks a bit of sour grapes.

It is the response I first heard when I took my Ph.D. at Duke. There was there a Freudian anthropologist who used to say about such things, "Look, we need to learn to stand on our feet as adults without behaving like children, relying on a father figure." Religious ethics, he contended, with its stress on providential care, infantalizes us. Instead of urging us to stand on our own feet as adult, autonomous, moral agents, it sets us on a search for a protective father figure.

I think myself that there is something in that, but only something. It is important to come to be able to stand on your feet, but after all, some religious people can—and do—learn to stand on their feet too. I mean, it's not just that God helps those who help themselves; but there is a sense within the Gospel tradition of both depending on God and being prepared to stand on your own feet too. So I think that that secular response, while having a grain of truth, is still a bit of sour grapes.

What do I think is important here? If I were arguing about the logic of divine commands— the first religious defense I mentioned—I would say to you, "Well, look, let's put aside all questions about whether God exists or doesn't exist. Let us argue that on another occasion. Let us just assume for the purposes of this discussion that God does exist and that the very concept of God is a coherent one. I want to still show you that even so the morality of divine commands won't work."

In the present argument about the comparative adequacy of a religious and purely secular morality, I don't think you can do that. And how you will go on here about a religious morality is not independent of what you believe about the truth-claims of religion. If you really believe that there is a God and that He has the attributes attributed to Him by the Christian tradition—I don't mean the most Neanderthal Christian traditions, but rather more like United Church Christian traditions in Canada or something like that—then there is considerable reason to take the religious morality as something added to the secular morality. It, moreover, plainly is something secular morality doesn't have. On the other hand, if you think, as I do, perhaps mistakenly, that belief in God is at its best problematic and deeply implausible, or if you thought like Kierkegaard that you had to crucify your intellect to believe in God, then the religious morality is going to be much less attractive. You can understand why people, if they have such an intellectual understanding of the world, would find it much less attractive. So the argument that is going on now, unlike philosophical arguments about divine command ethics, can't be made in independence of what you think about the reality of religious truth-claims. And that was not our present subject. But we need to recognize here that such arguments are relevant to the kind of argument that is going to be broached now.

To start the whole matter, suppose, just suppose, there are within religious traditions a lot of people who are sort of Barthian-Kierkegaardians. People, that is, who are extreme fideistic Christians. They are extremely skeptical about the possibility of establishing anything about religion by the use of rational argumentation or investigation. Let us for now ignore the question of whether they are right about this. And yet, like Pascal, Kierkegaard, and Hamann, they think that if you do not believe in God, then everything goes down and so you need at least the saving religious myths, even though they may be very implausible myths as I think they tend to be. They even tend to agree with the secularist about this. You need to believe this, they maintain, in order to make sense of morality or at least to make the deepest sense of morality. And so they are going to say it is because of this that we are going to believe, in spite of the fact that it seems very implausible.

Now here I think you have to make trade-offs. And here I think the secularist could make a rather strong comeback. He can argue, and argue persuasively, that there is a lot more to morality that is quite independent of religious orientation. He can point out that there is a lot that is important about morality that holds quite apart from religious belief.

Let me spend the rest of the lecture dealing with this. In the first place, there can be purposes *in* life even if there is no purpose *to* life. So, if God exists, you were made for a purpose. And that itself poses problems about your autonomy. Such matters caused a lot of trouble for the Christian tradition, especially in the Calvinist tradition. But maybe there is a way of resolving this. That, at any rate, is not the issue I want to pursue here. What I want to stress is the point there can be purposes *in* life, even though there is no purpose *to* life. You have lots of intentions, interests, aims, goals, things that you care about, that, God or no God, remain perfectly intact. If you love someone, whether there is a God or not, that love can go on. It remains intact. It might even be more intact, because if death ends it all, the love relationships between people in life are all the more precious because that is all there is in that respect. So that's perfectly intact, God or no God. Indeed, as I have just argued, it may even become more important.

If you have some life plan, if you want to be a doctor or a professor or a political radical, whatever you want to be, if there's something you want to do in this world, you can do that, God or no God. There are all those intentions, purposes, goals, and the like that you can figure out and find and can have. They are what John Rawls called *life plans*. You figure out what you want to do with your life. You can have all these purposes *in* life even though there is no purpose *to* life, so life doesn't become meaningless and pointless if you were not *made for* a purpose.

There can be small individual purposes, things like love, friendship, caring, knowledge, self-respect, pleasure in life. All of these things remain perfectly intact in a godless world. There can also be larger political and social purposes that you can struggle for. You can, in Camus's famous phrase, fight the plague, if you will. Even if you are skeptical about transforming the world, at least you can try to cut back some of the evil in the world, and sometimes you can succeed in some measure.

And all of this remains perfectly in place in a godless universe. You don't have to have a Kierkegaardian sense of sickness unto death where all worldly hopes are undermined because there is no purpose to life. There are these intact purposes in life, and they can be forged together in clusters to give you a coherent but still utterly secularist worldview. There are, that is, things that are worthwhile doing and having. It is worthwhile struggling to make a better world. Friendship, love, caring, all these things I mentioned remain intact in a godless world.

And morality in the terms of questions of justice and the like will still retain a point in a godless world. We need, in living together, a set of practices that work to adjudicate, in a fair way, conflicts of interests. That is in a simple way what justice is all about. We need a set of social practices which, when you get into a hassle with a colleague, let's say, or if one group gets in a hassle with another group, or suppose you and I get into a hassle about how long we're going to talk, we need some procedures rooted in social practices to fairly adjudicate those conflicts of interests. And those remain totally intact in a godless world. Justice hardly requires God.

Secondly, and rather more controversially, I think, a secularist can be a Kantian who can reflectively desire the kingdom of ends. What I mean by that big and rather pretentious phrase is that a secularist can believe that it's essential to morality that no person should be treated as a means only. This obtains for good people and bad people alike. The good of self-respect should be directed to everyone.

That conception is usually rooted in a religious worldview, but it needn't be. You can see if you reflect on the fact that probably one of our most fundamental goods as individuals is the good of self-respect. John Rawls took it to be the most fundamental of our primary social goods. But if I recognize this as a deep good for me, I also recognize that it's going to be a deep good for you. And while there are many differences between us, there is no relevant difference between us with respect to that. Moreover, if I judge this to be a fundamental good for me, I must, logically must, on pain of rejecting universalizability—that is, rejecting what is good for the goose is good for the gander—be prepared to recognize it for you too. So I can get to the good of self-respect on a purely secular basis, though it has come into our culture, of course, through a religious tradition. But validity is independent of origin.

It is worthwhile recalling that Kant developed this notion, though even as a very, very religious person, he justified his ethical beliefs on purely autonomous, nonreligious grounds. But it is no doubt true that he probably would never have come to have this belief in the kingdom of ends but for the fact that he grew up in a religious tradition. There is a thing called the genetic fallacy; in avoiding it we need to realize that the validity of a claim is independent of its origin. So even if things came out of our religious traditions, it doesn't mean that their present justification rests on these religious traditions.

We can also on a purely secular basis come to recognize things like the fact that human suffering is evil. And we can know that pain and suffering is bad if we can know anything at all, and we can come to recognize, without a recourse to God, that we have an obligation to relieve it.

There is a lot more to be said about this, but since I'm running out of time, let me shift to something else. The natural question to ask here is, "Yeah, so, Nielsen, you affirm all those things. You give expression to your deep moral commitment, but you, the bloody secularist that you are, need to explain to us on what basis, what foundation, do you make these affirmations. Aren't these just your personal preferences? Personal preferences you happen to hold, and if you had, after all, different personal preferences, you would have responded in different ways. Come clean. What foundations do you have?"

Well, I would say, like John Rawls and Norman Daniels, for those of you taking courses in ethics, that they rest on my considered judgments that I can fit into what I call wide reflective equilibrium. What do I mean by that big mouthful? I mean that it seems to me that we must start in ethics from considered judgments, like we start from evidence in empirical matters.

Suppose somebody—for example, that fellow over there—is drinking a coke. Whether I have good grounds for believing it to be true would rest on my being able to observe it and, if skeptical, to taste it and so forth and so on. Science isn't just a matter of this, but it is very fundamentally this. Suppose I am skeptical and the chap offers me a taste, but it isn't coke at all but colored water. I drink and just taste that it's in fact water. So I use my senses in a perfectly standard way to test an empirical claim. By the senses you have a way of testing these things. Just as sensory experience is to science, so in morality we start with considered judgments or, if you will, intuitions, where nothing funny epistemologically is built into such talk. They are not, that is, synthetic a *prioris* or any bizarre thing like that. So you start with considered judgments and then you try to get them into a coherent pattern with everything else you know, with the best theories of the function of morality in society, with the best theories we have about human nature, and so forth and so on. And you get this into a coherent package, and in the famous phrase of Otto Neurath, you rebuild the ship at sea. They are justified by putting them into a coherent pattern. And of course, in the process of doing that, some of them drop out.

But some of them won't drop out; not that there wouldn't be a logical possibility of their dropping out, but as a matter of brute fact, some of them will not, and by putting them into this coherent pattern, we will see their underlying rationale. Take something like "It is wrong to torture people." Some beliefs like that cut across cultures; they are not just "part of our tribe." To say it is wrong to torture people would probably never drop out in the reflective equilibrium. I can't realistically conceive of that ever dropping out. But in theory you could allow for the logical possibility of its dropping out. But that is not worrisome. It is *logically* possible that I might start to shrink right before you as well.

So you start with these considered judgments. You get them into a coherent packet with themselves and everything else we know; that's as much—indeed it's *the* only kind—of objectivity I think you can get in ethics. But I want to point out that the religious moralist is exactly in the same boat. He doesn't have any better or any worse objectivity. Because suppose he says, "We should love God," and then further suppose we ask the religious moralist, "Why love God? Why do, or try to do, the will of God? Why obey God's commands?" He basically would have to say, "Because God is the perfect good, and God with His perfect goodness reveals to us the great value of self-respect for people. He shows that people are of infinite precious worth." But even if you accept all this, you could go on to ask, "Why should you care? What difference does it make anyway whether people are of infinite precious worth?" Faced with such questioning, you will finally be pushed into a corner, where you say that "It is important to me that people be regarded as being of infinite worth because I just happen to care about people. It means something to me that people should be treated with respect."

So the religious moralist as well has to rely finally on his considered convictions. So if that is too subjective a ground—that is, grounding things in considered judgments in wide reflective equilibrium—then both the religious person and the secular person are in the same boat, though he [the religious person] has all these cosmological claims he might appeal to in backing his moral judgments. Nonetheless, you can ask, "Why pay attention to these cosmological claims?" "It simply," you might respond, "rests on a judgment about the importance of truth." "Why should you," Nietzsche asks, "pay attention to the truth?" You might say, "It is what you ought to do—you must simply pay attention to the truth." So there are these deep considered judgments that underlie our moral response, and which we justify by getting them into coherent patterns with everything else we know. That escapes a kind of relativism and subjectivity, though it doesn't give you an absolutism. If anybody is asking for any kind of form of absolutism, I think they're just kidding themselves. Critical modernity has knocked that out, and post-modernity doesn't even attempt to restore it. Absolutism belongs to a premodern view of the world.

Suppose somebody says, "Look, there's one thing you ignore. That simply is the fact that, after all, if there is a God and you don't do what He commands, you will fry in hell. This being so, you had better do what He commands so you won't fry in hell." I regard this as an utterly immoral response. It's just pure prudence masquerading as morality. You want to say, "Look, look, I want to do what is right so I won't burn." But that is hardly a good moral reason for doing anything. It is, as I said, a purely prudential reason, which says very little about the morality of someone that says it. Indeed, if anything, it reveals the person's immorality.

I'm not saying that all religious moralists or even most religious moralists appeal to it. I only say that if you try to resist the kind of argument I made by arguing in such a way, as even as good a philosopher as Peter Geach did once, that that is a despicable sort of answer. It simply substitutes prudence for morality.

Suppose somebody says, "All the same, there still are needs that a religious morality will answer to that no secular morality can." And that's true. But it also goes the other way around too. There are needs that a secular morality answers to that no religious morality can. And you have to make a kind of trade-off here. If there being a God really is highly implausible, I say, *if* because maybe it isn't, I haven't argued that in this lecture, though I do in the other one, then that poses problems for the religious moralist. If it is highly implausible to believe in God or immortality, then a secular ethic becomes very attractive, particularly if you consider the line of argument I've been giving you with its appeal to considered judgment in the wide reflective equilibrium. This is true because you can see how many of the things that are in a religious ethic, Nietzsche to the contrary notwithstanding, that remain intact in a secular ethic. However, there is Sartre's worry that too many remain intact in a humanist ethic.

However, suppose alternatively that a belief in God is very plausible, then, someone might add, the believer has an additional reason for being a moral person, for treating fellow human beings with equal respect. The additional reason is the fact that God created all

persons in His image as infinitely precious, destined to enjoy His fellowship forever. That, by a Jew or a Christian, can be added and that's a plus on the religious moralist side that the secular moralist doesn't have and can't have. And so then the question becomes, Which of these pluses count the most? But that judgment is not independent of your judgment about how plausible it is to believe in God.

But suppose that it isn't very plausible, just suppose. If that is so, one of the things that a secular morality can teach you is that you can give up a belief in God and immortality, but with that there will be a gain in moral integrity, and that is plainly not nothing. There is something to be said for a person who can hold steadily on a course without telling himself or herself fairy tales. Moral integrity, fraternity, and love of humankind are worth subscribing to without a thought to whether or not such virtues will be rewarded in heaven.

[J. P.] Moreland: To say something meaningful on this topic in fifteen minutes is roughly like trying to define the universe and give two examples. It's a difficult topic, and I'm not going to respond directly to a lot of the things Professor Nielsen said, since I was informed about this relatively late. Instead, I've got my own thoughts I'd like to share. Later I will interact with some of the things Professor Nielsen has said, and perhaps that will give you two different points of view on the subject about which you can ask questions.

To begin with, let me say that I do not hold to a Barthian-divine command theory. That is not my view. I part company with those theists who hold more extreme forms of voluntarism.

To push the boat off shore, let me begin by saying something about the genetic fallacy which Professor Nielsen mentioned. The genetic fallacy is the fallacy of faulting the rational justification of something because of where it came from. For example, it would be troublesome to me if you said that I can't know two and two is equal to four because I learned it from Mrs. Fred, my second grade teacher, and she was an evil person. That wouldn't be a very good argument to raise against my mathematical knowledge claim.

On the other hand, there are occasions where the origin of something does serve to count against it. Illustration: You're driving down a road, and you claim to see water in front of you. Your evidence for that would be experiences that you were having at the time, namely, experiences of a certain wetness down the road. However, we could have a relevant background theory to this claim that would tend to defeat it. Suppose that it happened to be in the desert, it was 95 degrees outside, and what was causing this to happen was light waves reflecting on the highway, and thus, you were experiencing a mirage. This background theory would give an alternate account of the causal origin of your experience of "water." This background theory would serve as a defeater. It would tend to defeat your claim that there really was water out there, and it would make more reasonable the belief that it was merely a mirage.

I think the very same thing is going on in the justification of morality. I don't know that Nielsen necessarily tried to do this, but many atheists say something like this: "Look, let's keep the world totally constant, remove nothing whatsoever, and then just assume God doesn't exist. Well, look here, God doesn't make any difference for morality."

Well, of course, if you stipulate by definition that you are going to hold the world constant and you're just not going to consider God, obviously, you've got two equivalent situations and appealing to God isn't going to make any difference. But this way of setting up the problem does not really bring into focus what most theists believe to be the relationship between God and morality. A better way to characterize the problem is to liken the atheist/theist debate about the nature and existence of morality to a situation where you are testing rival scientific hypotheses regarding a range of conceptual or empirical problems. Those of you who have had any study in confirmation theory know that if you have a range of phenomena to be explained, you try to determine which of two or more theories makes better sense or makes those phenomena more plausible, more reasonable, and less puzzling. That to me seems to be the proper way to characterize the difference between a secular and a theistic morality.

On an evolutionary secular scenario, this is basically the most plausible current background theory. Human beings are nothing special. The universe came from a Big Bang. It evolved to us through a blind process of chance and necessity. There is nothing intrinsically valuable about human beings in terms of having moral non-natural properties. The same processes that coughed up human beings coughed up amoebas; there is nothing special about being human. The view that being human is special is guilty of speciesism, an unjustifiable bias toward one's own species. The same process that coughed us up is eventually going to swallow us up, and in fact there is a good chance we will evolve toward higher forms of life sometime in the future. There is no point to history. There are no such things as non-natural properties or moral properties.

Now, the question that needs to be asked is this: In a universe of that sort, what possible reason could be given for why I should be moral? Keep in mind, the question Why I should be moral? is not asked from within the moral point of view. It's not saying, "Give me a moral reason for being moral." It is asking, "Why as a part of my rational life plan, when I'm trying to consider the rational way I wish to live, why should I include in that life plan the dictates of morality?"

Now, consider the following sentences: "Red is a color." "This ball is red." These are, at least, *prima facie* subject-predicate sentences. And they have ontological implications about the way the world is. If you believe that "Red is a color" is true, or that "This ball is red" is true, then you hold that there are certain entities which exist in the world, namely redness in this case, and perhaps what is called the second order, or higher order universal, color.

Similarly, consider the claims "Kindness is a virtue;" "Humans have value;" "Persons have value." Or, as Roderick Chisholm says, "Mercy as such is good." In spite of what Nielsen says, these are synthetic *a priori* propositions. They are standard subject-predicate propositions, where at least on the surface, it seems like, just as "Red is a color" commits one to the existence of red and color, "Kindness is a virtue" commits one to the existence of kindness and virtue. "Humans have value" commits one to the existence of there being such a thing as human nature, which is not merely a biological natural kind, but has moral properties as well, as David Wiggins has argued. "Mercy as such is good" commits one to non-natural properties that do exist and are part of the furniture of the universe.

Now the question for any view regarding the nature and justification of morality is this: Is that view adequate, and if so, what general metaphysical worldview must we embrace to render intelligible a particular conception of morality? Well, let me try to give you three answers to that question. As far as I can tell, the first one is not held by Nielsen. I think the second one is, and the third one would be a theistic answer.

The first answer I call the *immanent purpose view.* According to this view, the scientific account of the origin and nature of life is not all there is to the universe. In addition to natural properties, there are non-natural properties that exist as a part of reality. So there is such a thing as goodness. There are moral properties, value properties, and these things are, let's just say, Platonic forms. So why should I be moral? Well, because there are these things called moral properties that exist, and it's irrational to deny their existence.

What is the purpose of life? In this view the purpose of life involves trying to live for these intrinsically valuable states of affairs that can be realized in human life. For example, it's intrinsically valuable, according to the immanent purpose view, to have kindness, to achieve intellectual virtue and knowledge, to have wisdom, and so on. These would be states of affairs that are intrinsically valuable and worthwhile, and meaning in life comes from trying to embody these properties even though these properties themselves do not come from God. They're just there, that's all, part of the ultimate furniture of the universe.

I have several problems with this view. For one thing, to have these sorts of properties existing in a Godless universe would be odd and puzzling, to say the least. Now this isn't a knock-down argument, and I can only appeal to your basic intuitions on this question. But it does seem to me that to hold that moral properties, or non-natural properties, are modes of existence of an impersonal universe is less reasonable than seeing them as modes of existence of a personal universe.

The late J. L. Mackie, who in my opinion may be the best philosophical atheist of this century, agrees with me on this point. And he made the following statement: "Moral properties constitute so odd a cluster of properties and relations that they are most unlikely to have arisen in the ordinary course of events without an all-powerful god to create them." Mackie's solution is to just deny the existence of these properties. And he goes on to argue that all we can do is to create values subjectively; you just have to choose what you want to be.

Many atheists have agreed with that. They've said there is no essence to man ready-made for him; there are no moral properties in the universe. What you choose to do is what you find worthwhile. I think we're a bit closer to Nielsen's view at this point, and we'll touch on this alternative in just a moment. So first of all, in light of the immanent purpose view, it seems odd that these properties would exist.

Second, let's grant that they do exist. It is nonetheless odd that they would have anything whatsoever to do with human beings. Why would these moral properties ever refer to or supervene upon a short-lived little cluster of creatures that were a result of a blindness process on a tiny dot hurling through space?

Two scientists, Barrow and Tipler, recently wrote a book called *The Anthropic Cosmological Principle*. They believe that there are these moral properties and that there is something in the world which is intrinsically valuable. The thing that's intrinsically valuable, they claim, is an idealized form of DNA molecule that the evolutionary process will ultimately realize in the universe. All intermediate forms on the way to that idealized state are means to ends, not ends in themselves. So from amoebas to men, you have a means to the end of trying to realize what is really the good in itself; that's this idealized DNA molecule.

It does seem to me to be a bit anthropocentric for an advocate of the immanent purpose view to single out human beings in this process and say, "Oh my, isn't it interesting that the moral universe intersects with the physical universe at just the point where human beings emerged, or at least largely at the point where human beings emerged." I, for one, don't know why, if the evolutionary process continues to go on, we won't find other forms of life years down the road which will have more value than we have, and we will stand to them as primitive life forms stand to us. So it seems odd to me that these properties would ever uniquely supervene upon human beings in the first place, and it would be hard to justify the claim that all are of equal moral value.

Third, it seems to me odd in the immanent purpose view of human beings that people could have one of the necessary preconditions for being moral agents in the first place. I believe it is important to have freedom of the will in order for there to be such a thing as human moral action or moral responsibility. And by freedom of the will I mean what Thomas Reid called agent causality. This includes the notion of incompatibilism. I know

that perhaps some of you here disagree with this view, but I for one do not believe that freedom and determinism are compatable because, for one thing, compatibilism is really determinism under another name. It reduces to a form of determinism, and it only shifts the causal factors from those outside the "person" to those inside the "person." And this shift doesn't leave any room for a real agent to act responsibly."

If we are mere creatures of matter, or even if we have mental properties or events which interact via state-to-state causation, and this Platonic moral universe exists and supervenes upon humans, then the immanent purpose view still has this difficulty. It is hard to see how we could ever have the requisite freedom to be morally responsible. Physicalist Paul Churchland has made the following point: "The important point about the standard evolutionary story is that the human species and all of its features are the wholly physical outcome of a purely physical process. If this is the correct account of our origin, then there seems neither need nor room to fit any nonphysical substances or properties into our theoretical accounts of ourselves. We are creatures of matter." If we are creatures of matter, it seems difficult to me to make sense out of how I could have freedom of the will. And that, I claim, is a necessary precondition for me even taking upon myself the moral point of view.

For these and some other reasons I could mention, I find the immanent purpose view highly implausible and unlikely.

But there is a second view, and this is more in keeping with what I take Professor Nielsen to hold, at least it's in keeping with some of his writings. He may have changed his views. You can correct me if you have. I call this view *optimistic humanism*.

According to this view, there are no moral facts. There are no moral truths to be discovered in an old-fashioned correspondent sense of the word "truth." And we can't ground morality in any kind of sense of pure reason or rational deliberation without sentiment and without what he calls "wide reflective equilibrium." And remember, wide reflective equilibrium, as John Rawls uses it, is not just theory of epistemic justificafion; in other words, it's not just a theory of how we justify our beliefs. It is an ontological theory about what truth is. It is a coherence theory, not of justification only, but of truth. Reflective equilibrium *creates* our moral views; it does not merely justify them.

Now one problem with a coherence theory of truth is this: You can have two coherent webs of beliefs that are both internally consistent. One of these systems of beliefs can say that *p* is legitimate and the other one can entail that not-*p* is legitimate. And according to a coherency theory of truth, both *p* and not-*p* would be correct. The standard objection against coherent theories of truth is that it removes the connection between propositions and a full blown, realist, mind- or theory- or language-independent world. You can have more than one system that's internally consistent; one can imply *p* and the other not-*p*. And according to that view, we would be in the position of saying both were true.

I might add as well that it seems to me that optimistic humanism tends toward formal autonomy-based ethics. Stanley Hauerwas at Duke has argued against such an autonomy-based ethic, because it reduces to a minimalist ethic wherein the good is ultimately what I competently and autonomously choose for myself, provided, of course, that I do not harm or offend others. This may be a necessary condition for an act of mine to be moral, but it is not sufficient; that the good is what I choose for myself is too empty. It is too formal to get us very far, and what we really need is a substantive theory of the good life. We require a substantive vision of the moral life to give content to formal principles of morality. And in my opinion, this substantive vision of the moral life is embodied in Jesus of Nazareth. Christianity does not leave morality at the abstract level of principles. Moral virtue and vision is embodied in Jesus of Nazareth and others in the Scriptures. According to a Christian view of the world, virtue properties exist and can be instanced in persons, and virtues and vices can be epistemologically distinguished.

But the optimistic humanist view will have none of that. There are no irreducibly non-natural properties, and we have to engage in a coherence reflective equilibrium where we create values by coherence. We don't discover them.

Second, why is it that someone should choose the moral point of view? As Nielsen has said elsewhere, choosing to embrace the moral point of view, vis-à-vis some form of private personal egoism, is arbitrary and subjective. It is not a rational decision. One simply has to choose what kind of life he wants to live and make his choice.

Now consider what Nielsen claimed in his presentation. When he talked earlier, he said, "We have to choose our vision of life, and we can have plenty of things that we find worthwhile even if God does not exist." Of course, the kinds of things he mentioned were the kinds of things that most people already know within theism are reasonable, like friendship, pursuing love, and so on.

The radical nature of this thesis, however, is that if there is no moral truth to be discovered and if I have to simply choose the moral point of view because that type of life is what I find worthwhile for myself, then the decision is arbitrary, rationally speaking. And the difference between, say, Mother Teresa and Hitler is roughly the same as the difference between whether I want to be a trumpet player or a baseball player. There is no rational factor or truth of the matter at stake. There are no moral truths that can be discovered to adjudicate between the two choices. I have to just decide my form of life.

This type of thing has surfaced recently in a book by James Rachels called *The End of Life*. Rachels says that we don't need purpose in the sense of an over-arching objective purpose *to* life, but we can have purpose *in* life, as Nielsen says. And he means by that "subjective satisfaction," things that we find worthwhile to us. Now if this is true, what's the difference, let's say, between becoming a doctor and feeding the poor, and sitting around pinching heads off rats or being a Sisyphus and pushing a rock up and down a hill, or giving your time to flipping tiddlywinks? There is no difference since each of these options could be satisfying and worthwhile to someone.

Or consider the case of a person called the Texas Burn Victim. There was a man who was burned in Texas named Donald C. Donald C. was burned in an accident; he was rehabilitated; but he was confined to a wheelchair. He could lead a normal life, only he was not able to be a ladies' man and go to rodeos, activities which were satisfying to him. He wanted to commit suicide. And according to James Rachels, he should have been allowed to do just that.

Why should he have been allowed to commit suicide? Because his life no longer had any point to it. Why didn't it have any point? Because he could no longer do the things that were worthwhile from his point of view. Well, what was worthwhile from his point of view? Chasing women and going to rodeos.

Now it seems to me that it's possible to trivialize your own life by giving yourself to things that are inherently trivial. If a person wanted to be the best male prostitute he could be, and if that was his subjective choice of how he wanted to live his life—that was his vision of the good life, as it were—it doesn't seem to me that the optimistic humanist view provides a sufficiently robust framework for criticizing that type of choice. Because, after all, a person could find trivial actions worthwhile from his perspective, and, therefore, this person's actions would be just as morally significant as the deeds of someone like a Mother Teresa who gives herself to helping other people. Nielsen has said time and again, and he's right, that atheists can in fact do good moral things. But what I'm arguing is, What would be the

point? Why should I do these things if they are not satisfying to me or if they are not in my interests?

This is a serious problem. It does not occur within theism, but it does occur within the optimistic humanist version of atheism. If there is no human nature which has intrinsic moral value as Nielsen says elsewhere, the question can arise: "Here I am with my money. Why should I give it to help the poor instead of keeping it and having a little better life for myself?" Well, a response might be that doing morally virtuous acts is what it means to take the moral point of view. This means that you universalize your judgments, you treat others as ends in themselves and yourself as an end in itself, you seek to promote the good, and so on.

But the problem is, Why should I take the moral point of view? "Well, what if you were in his shoes?" the answer could come back. But you see, I'm not in his shoes. "Well, if you were in his shoes, you would want him to do the same to you." Yes, but the difficulty is, you're already operating from within the moral point of view, and my question is, Why should I adopt the moral point of view as a part of my rational life plan? That's the very thing at issue.

Furthermore, why should I care for future generations, or why should I give to help the poor? I happen to like mice. Why shouldn't I give my money to caring for mice instead of caring for the poor? Well, you might say, "Human beings have certain properties that make them more valuable than mice, let's say rationality." I don't know if Nielsen would make that response, but if someone did, there is a difficulty. Because, after all, some people are more rational than others. And does that mean that we ought to help feed, let's say, university professors, but not plumbers, because they have more of the property of rationality?

Well, one way to go at this is just to say it's egoistically better to adopt the moral point of view. After all, it's better to live in community with other people rather than live a nasty, brutish, short life, and so I give up some of my rights because it is in my self-interest to do so. I will be egoistically altruistic. I will do things for you out of an egoistic motivation and because of an egoistic justification.

Now, apart from the fact that this appears to be a contradiction to me—ethical egoism appears to contradict the moral point of view—this type of recommendation suffers from the very same objection that Nielsen himself has raised against the Christian notion of hell. He said if a person merely embraces God out of a desire to cover his cosmic rear end and to avoid getting flames on it, then he is guilty of egoism.

The very same thing seems to me to be true of someone who is saying, "Now I think I'll consider the moral point of view. Why should I adopt it? Well because it's in my best interest to do so. And in fact I will adopt the moral point of view except in those cases when it's not in my best interest to do so." It doesn't seem to me that optimistic humanism can offer a good reason why one ought not to do that, rationally speaking. The point is that on the optimistic humanist view, we now substitute subjective satisfaction for objective value and meaning.

I've offered two solutions. I don't have much time, so let me say a brief word about *Christian theism*. Christian theism is a background theory that makes the existence and knowability of morality more likely than does the background theory of atheism. Morality is more at home and less ad hoc in a theistic universe than in an atheistic universe. This is because God is a postulated entity who is Himself good. He has the property of goodness. Men are made in His image and to be a human being is to be a member of a natural kind that is not merely defined biologically, but is also defined in terms of moral properties. I have intrinsic value or worth as I reflect the intrinsic value of God and His worth.

Second, I believe that Christian theism helps explain the knowability of morality in a number of ways. I can't get into this much, perhaps in the question and answer period we can, but Christian theism helps make sense out of how my moral faculties could have come about in the first place. How is it that humans can have intuitional insight into the nature of morality. God has created us to know moral values.

In summary then, Nielsen says something like this: "The theists are on a ship, and they claim there's meaning in life on this ship because there's a point at the end of the voyage. We are going to help lepers on the shore. So along the way we've got meaning because there's a goal we're heading toward that's meaningful. And furthermore, there's meaning in life and there's morality because we are ends in ourselves, because we have goodness in us, moral properties which reflect the moral properties of our creator.

"Never mind about that," he says. "Let's suppose that we are on another ship and call it the Titanic. The ship isn't going anywhere, just as long as it doesn't crash in the next few hours; let's let it crash, say, seventy years from now. I can still find plenty of things that are worthwhile from my point of view. I can visit these people in the sick bay of the ship. I can read Plato in the library of the ship, and I can do all kinds of wonderful things."

Of course, the problem is, Why should I do these things as opposed to, say, pushing a rock around the boat or spending my time staring at mice in my cabin quarters? It doesn't seem to me that there would be much difference. Furthermore, why should I worry about the people on this ship instead of, say, the mosquitoes, the orangutans, or some other life form? I am not denying, by the way, that theism has within itself a theory of animal rights. It does. But I am denying that human beings are on the same moral plane as animals. In the optimistic humanist view, it is difficult to see how you could make such a distinction. . . .

Question: Dr. Nielsen, how would you respond to Dr. Moreland's statement about covering your cosmic theories?

Nielsen: We might ask, rather more earthly, how would I respond about covering my cosmic rear end?

I found Professor Moreland's remarks interesting. There's a million ways I would want to respond, but I will limit myself to one very brief way. As he himself recognized but then seemed to forget, there is a great difference between asking the question, Why should I be moral? and asking a *moral* question. A question like, Why should I be moral? is like asking, What's valuable about science? which is not itself a scientific question. Similarly when you ask, Why be moral? you can't give a moral reason or you beg the question. And so you have to give a nonmoral reason.

And exactly the same problem emerges for the religious moralist when we, as I pointed out and Moreland didn't respond to, ask exactly the same question of the religious moralist. Why should you pay attention to the commands of God? In both cases, once you're outside of morality, the only thing you can give is a kind of prudential answer. But for me it is tremendously important, and I think he misses this, to distinguish the questions you ask as a moral being from purely prudential questions that might be asked outside of morality—might, that is, be asked even when we are not resolved to act or reason in accordance with the moral point of view. This remains so even if becoming a moral being is *finally* just a matter, as I am inclined to believe, of one having to commit oneself here.

Finally, at a certain point, you have to commit yourself. I think the religious person and the secular person are in exactly the same boat. Once you've committed yourself, then the morality you adopt has a certain structure, and it's no longer just a matter of choice. There is nothing in my views, especially my views in the last fifteen years, which says that moral claims are just choices, like, say, for A. J. Ayer or Axel Hägerström. I said, like Rawls, that there is a set of considered judgments which are *our* considered judgments, not just mine but yours

as well. They're in our culture, though not just in our culture. We start with these considered judgments, and we try to justify them in wide reflective equilibrium. The ones we cannot get into such as equilibrium—that we cannot reflectively sustain—we reject.

By the way, neither Rawls nor I regard this as an ontological theory about what truth is. Rawls's book, a six-hundred-page book, if you look in the index, has no reference to truth. We completely put aside all metaethical and ontological questions about the logical status of values. They may have those nonnatural properties. Moreland talks about them, but I think that is highly implausible. They may be more like Mackie's understanding, who takes them to be projections of emotional states. Both Rawls and I just put those questions aside. We're concerned with the justification of moral beliefs, practices, and principles, so we don't try to say what truth is, whether there's moral truth or anything. We say here's a bunch of moral judgments that a culture shares and that I may or may not share. And we see whether those fit together with everything else we know and match with our considered convictions.

And I want to claim that's the most plausible kind of justification you can get in the domain of morality. Moreover, there is nothing subjective, nothing individualistic, about it. The analogy with being on a ship that has to sink has little point. We have to die. But that doesn't make our present moral arrangements less meaningful or less objective. To even think in terms of that analogy is already to be into a religious point of view. I'm not talking about a ship that has to sink. Presumably, that is just a way of saying we have to die. But I'm saying that here and now we are moral beings. And how are we moral beings supposed to interact with each other? How do we make sense of our lives together? How do we justify doing one thing rather than another? These things can correctly and reasonably be deliberated on without any reference to religion at all.

Consider again the genetic fallacy. I have a great appreciation for religious traditions. Certain of our moral beliefs come out of religious traditions. Moreover, they might have not come to us in just the way they do but for our religious traditions. I am not saying you take away belief in God and everything remains intact for moral belief. Nietzsche and Sartre are right about that. Everything else isn't intact. But a lot is intact. Moreover, some things that are lost may not be such a bad thing to lose. And there, as I have shown, are gains in a purely secular ethic.

And so that morality *came* from religion, so what? That I learned that I shouldn't urinate in public from my grandmother, so what? The question is, Is there a good reason not to urinate in public? And there probably is a good reason not to urinate in public, and that's why I don't urinate in public.

Moreland: Well, for one thing, I didn't use the genetic fallacy. I hope you're not claiming that I argued in that way.

Nielsen: No. But you talked about it.

Moreland: But my argument was not itself a genetic fallacy. Secondly, Rawls, whether he explicitly states truth in coherence terms or not, that's exactly what he means. In Section 4 of his *A Theory of Justice,* where he explicitly goes over his notion of reflective equilibrium, he likens his views on morality to the views of Thomas Kuhn and Nelson Goodman. For Rawls, issues of moral justification are similar to Goodman's notion of an internal metaphysical problem and to Kuhn's idea that rational justification is itself paradigm dependent.

Now if you read *The Structure of Scientific Revolutions,* to my knowledge Kuhn only mentions truth once in the whole book. So he doesn't use the word, but it is still possible to understand Kuhn as though he is talking about a coherence theory of what is real, or a coherence theory of truth, whether he uses the word

truth or not. And the same point could be made regarding Rawls. In terms of your understanding of reflective equilibrium, the very same thing seemed to be implied by what you were saying.

Nielsen: Just one thing about this. Rawls explicitly says that he sets aside for this purpose questions of moral truth altogether because the notion of moral truth is problematic. He can say what he needs to say about coherence and justification in ethics without making any commitments or assumptions about moral truth at all. I said this explicitly too. I don't say that it doesn't make any sense to say moral propositions are true. We are concerned with questions of justification. Because you see that there are difficulties with asserting that moral propositions are either true or false, we set such issues aside. We can say what we want about coherence without invoking a coherence theory of truth or any other theory of truth at all.

We could, of course, speak quite unproblematically of moral claims being true if all we meant in saying they were true was a rather emphatic way of reasserting them. (Philosophers call it the assertive redundancy theory of truth.) But if you mean something stronger, like there is a correspondence between moral sentences and reality, then we will have trouble. Suppose I say, "Snow is white." You know exactly what will establish the truth of that. Suppose I say, "Hitler was a vile man." It isn't quite so clear what that refers to. Still, perhaps it does refer to something. Maybe there are truth conditions for it. Rawls sets all those questions aside, and his appeal to Goodman is not an appeal to a coherence theory of *truth.* He explicitly says he will not give or appeal to any account of truth at all. It's very clear in his essays on Kantian constructivism. I take exactly the same turn. It should also be noted, in passing, that we should, as Alvin Goldman does, sharply distinguish between accounts of what truth is and epistemological questions about how we justify whether claims that so and so is true are reasonable. All kinds of confusions emerge if we do not keep these questions apart. Coherence, as Goldman points out, is plausible as a partial account of how we justify truth claims, but it has no plausibility at all as an account of what truth is.

Question: My question is to Dr. Moreland. How would you respond to Dr. Nielsen's statement that you said that any secular ethic is inadequate compared to a theistic ethic in the fact that I think he says that it is always morally wrong to torture little children even if God commanded it? Wouldn't you say it is unreasonable to say if God would ever command it, it would be okay to torture little children? Or would you say that if God commands it, it must be morally right?

Moreland: I'm not a divine command theorist, so I don't hold the view like Nielsen correctly imputed to Barth and certain strong Calvinists who hold to rather extreme forms of voluntarism. This view implies that morality is merely grounded in God's will as opposed to His nature. You can see this in Descartes and others, that God could have made seven times seventy equal to twenty if He'd wanted to, and He could have made mercy as such a vice. That's not my view.

I think God's will is ultimately expressed in keeping with His nature. Morality is ultimately grounded in the nature of God, not independently of God. There is a Euthyprotype argument that Bertrand Russell raised against theism—namely, that for the theist, morality is either arbitrarily grounded in God's will or it's grounded in something outside of God. But this is a false disjunction. I think the tertium quid is that morality can be grounded in God's own nature. We obey God because He is good and loving. Now, when I say that God is good, I'm not stating a tautology. Further, I would agree with Nielsen that you have to understand the meaning of "good" before you can ascribe it to God.

But so what? That only grants there is a certain epistemological or conceptual order to moral knowledge that's different from the metaphysical order regarding the existence of goodness itself. I might have to look at a road map of Chicago before I can know where Chicago is, so the road map might be first in the order of epistemology, but Chicago has to exist prior to the fact of the road map. Similarly, God's goodness would exist prior to the existence of finite, derived goodnesses, though conceptually or epistemologically, I might have to understand what "goodness" means before I would be able to make a judgment that God is good.

Question: Dr. Nielsen, are you an atheist because you can't find any concrete evidence for the existence of God?

Nielsen: The short answer to that is no. The reasons that I became an atheist are something that took years. They are very diverse. They are in part related to the fact that I don't think there is much plausibility connected with believing in the existence of God. Indeed, I believe that the very concept of God in developed versions of Judeo-Christianity is incoherent. Part of the reason I believe that belief in God is implausible is that without recourse to God, we can make perfectly good sense out of our moral life, find meaning in life, and at certain junctures give meaning to life. In this connection, there is another thing I would say vis-à-vis what Professor Moreland was saying. There can be larger purposes in life. I mean you can be a Marxist or a socialist or you could be all kinds of things. There can be larger purposes in life even if you're an atheist. I have lots of larger purposes. There are a bunch of connected things, things connected with what kind of a social world I would like to see us forge together, which are among the things which give meaning to my life.

The point about asking the question, "Why be moral?" is to point out that there is no way of showing that an individual who doesn't care about people or anything else and is willing to be a freeloader and an unprincipled jerk need not be acting irrationally or be making an intellectual mistake in so living his life. Kant thought that you could show that such a person was irrational, as distinct from saying what a religious person might say, "just sinful." My argument is I don't think you can show that. But some secular theorists think you can do just that, show that you, if you are through-and-through rational, will also be committed to the moral point of view. Kurt Baier is one such secular moralist and David Gauthier is another. But I do not think there is any such intrinsic link between morality and rationality. At a certain point, morality just requires commitment and subscription.

But I'm saying that once you're in morality, once you take a moral point of view, that is not a live option. Just like it's not an open question once you're doing science to ask why pay attention to a well-conducted experiment. You may override its results for some reason, but you at least have to start off by paying attention to a well-conducted experiment.

[Moderator]: We've time for one more question, I believe. . . . The question is essentially, Is one of the reasons secular people are moral is because God made the world the way it is to put a kind of moral inclination into people?

Moreland: Okay, let me sort out a couple of questions real quickly. One, my argument was not primarily the claim that religious people are more moral than nonreligious people; though in my opinion, it has been primarily religious people who have gone to Third World countries and taken care of the poor and needy. And there's a good book by Patrick Sherry called *Spirit, Saints, and Immortality,* where he makes a similar claim. He offers a causal argument from religious experience, that Christianity has produced more people who have done heroic, supererogatory, and

morally virtuous kinds of acts. Thus we must postulate some power or cause to explain this effect.

The real question I am trying to emphasize is this: How could there be such a thing as goodness and morality in the universe? In my opinion, a worldview is inadequate which implies that it is not irrational to be a moral monster or to be indifferent to the moral point of view by embracing, say, a rational life plan centered in some form of ethical egoism. What kind of universe makes most reasonable the existence of objective morality?

And to me you cannot get away from the truth question, and I don't think that Rawls, Quine, or Kuhn adequately deal with the importance of truth for rationality. Just shaking hands via reflective equilibrium and saying, "I don't want to deal with truth," or accepting some redundancy theory of truth, is simply not adequate. For example, Carl Kordig wrote a recent journal article saying Quine's theory was self-refuting, because you can ask him, Is your theory true and normatively rational?

Now in terms of how we know the specific content of morality, very roughly, I think you need to utilize insights of virtue theory, you need to adopt particularism as an epistemic strategy, and you also need to include some form of moral intuitionism.

Finally, if we step back from the issue of knowing the specific content of morality, and we consider the broader, transcendental question of how it could come about that human beings have normative, rational, truth-gathering faculties in general, as well as how humans came to have these faculties regarding moral knowledge in particular, then we have the makings of a design argument for God. It is this concept of rationality that, at once, justifies the claim that a moral egoist is irrational and provides an argument for God to ground the possibility of moral knowledge. Well, a lot could be said, but time is up. Thank you very much for having us.

Discussion Questions

1. Who do you think won the debate, Professor Moreland or Professor Nielsen? Explain and defend your judgment.

2. What are the reasons why both Professor Nielsen and Professor Moreland reject Divine Command Theory (DCT)? Define DCT and explain why you either agree or disagree with their rejection of it.

3. Professor Moreland maintains that there are three options concerning the foundation of morality. Explain and define these three options. What does Moreland believe are their strengths and weaknesses? Do you agree or disagree with his conclusion? Explain and defend your answer.

4. Do you agree or disagree with Professor Nielsen that God is not necessary for morality? Explain and defend your answer.

5. Do you agree or disagree with Professor Moreland that ethics depend on God? Explain and defend your answer.

6. Professor Nielsen maintains that there may be purposes *in* life but not a cosmic purpose *to* life. What does he mean by this and why is it a response to theism? What is Moreland's reply to this charge? Do you think it is adequate? Why or why not?

7. What does Professor Nielsen believe is the foundation of ethics? How does Professor Moreland reply? Who do you think is correct? Explain and defend your answer.

You can locate InfoTrac-College Education articles about this chapter by accessing the InfoTrac-College Edition website (http://www.infotrac-college.com/wadsworth/). Using the InfoTrac-College Edition subject guide, enter the search terms relevant to this chapter, and then read abstracts for relevant articles.

SECTION D

State Neutrality, Religion, and Morality

Introduction to Section D

It seems to have become popular in North American culture to assert that "you can't legislate morality," though people oftentimes apply this prescription selectively, depending on whose ox is being gored. For example, social conservatives are sometimes told they should not pass laws that would prohibit or severely regulate abortion, homosexual acts, or pornography, because "you can't legislate morality." Yet, those who make this suggestion to social conservatives oftentimes seek to prohibit or regulate many activities that apparently have a moral dimension to them, including "hate speech," public prayers that may offend nonbelievers, public judgments against sexual minorities, abstinence education, cigarette advertising, the Boy Scouts's ban on homosexuals, and organized protests at abortion clinics. On the other hand, the views of social conservatives—at least on issues such as abortion and homosexuality—seem to be linked to their religious traditions. This is why many liberals believe that if these conservative views are reflected in our legal framework, they would violate the Establishment Clause of the First Amendment of the United States Constitution, which reads: "Congress shall make no law respecting the establishment of religion. . . ."

Some have interpreted this to mean that the state should remain neutral on moral questions which are connected with people's fundamental beliefs about reality, such as one's view of God, the good, the meaning of life, or even when human life begins. (Whether or not those who authored this part of the Constitution would have agreed with such an interpretation is another matter all together, one that is outside the scope of this text). This seems to be the reasoning behind the U.S. Supreme Court's upholding of abortion rights in *Planned Parenthood v. Casey* (1992):

> Our law affords constitutional protection to personal decisions relating to marriage, procreation, family relationships, child rearing, and education. . . . These matters, involving the most intimate and personal choices a person may make in a lifetime, choices central to personal dignity and autonomy, are central to the liberty protected by the

Fourteenth Amendment. At the heart of liberty is the right to define one's own concept of existence, of meaning, of the universe, and of the mystery of human life. Beliefs about these matters could not define the attributes of personhood were they formed under compulsion by the State.[1]

In his dissenting opinion in *Webster v. Reproductive Health Services* (1989), Supreme Court Justice John Paul Stephens writes: "The Missouri Legislature [which said that human life begins at conception] may not inject its endorsement of a particular religious tradition in this debate, for the Establishment Clause does not allow public bodies to foment such disagreement."[2]

This section concerns an area of our public life in which morality, law, and religion intersect. The authors of the two essays in this section take differing views on the relationship between one's religiously grounded moral beliefs and whether one has a right to shape the law in a way that reflects those beliefs.

One side of the debate (a version of which is defended in Chapter 8 by Robert Audi) holds to a perspective that is often referred to as *Political Liberalism* (PL). PL is a family of views. It includes such diverse perspectives as democratic socialism and secular libertarianism (i.e., classical liberalism). Since there are numerous members of this family, some of which conflict with each other on many fronts, the view defended by Audi should not be viewed as the only version of PL.

Like most political liberals, Audi argues that the state should remain neutral on religious and/or metaphysical beliefs (though liberals disagree among themselves as to what counts as "neutral," "religious," or "metaphysical"), unless one can come up with good secular reasons for the state to embrace a policy that is consistent with, though not dependent on, one's religious and/or metaphysical beliefs. And because of this neutrality, the individual has the right, within the framework of a liberal democracy, to make choices, unencumbered by another's vision of the good life, based on her subjective preferences, which may include not only moral beliefs but philosophical and religious beliefs as well. Again, like most political liberals, Audi supports what is sometimes called the *secular* (or public) *reason* requirement: citizens should not support their public policy proposals by appealing to exclusively religious reasons if they are trying to limit the liberty of other citizens (though liberals disagree among themselves as to what counts as a public reason and/or whether these public reasons should be used to the exclusion of, or in conjunction with, religious reasons and motivations). Consequently, in order to participate in public discourse and/or to influence law and public policy, the religious person must be willing to provide reasons that are not theological or religious. Just as the state must remain neutral on matters of religion, the religious person must provide nonsectarian, or neutral, reasons for matters of state. Audi, like most political liberals, argues that his view is the best way to achieve a civil society in which freedom of religion is respected while at the same time allowing for a just legal framework by which citizens may make their case without resorting to idiosyncratic sectarian reasons that will likely alienate their fellow citizens

Those who disagree with PL (as represented in this text in Chapter 9 by Nicholas Wolterstorff) maintain that PL, far from being the best way to achieve a civil society, marginalizes the religious believer by requiring her to pretend as if her beliefs are not true as well as stacking the deck in favor of liberal positions on controversial issues, some of which are linked to points of view that some consider "religious" and "metaphysical."[3] And thus, the proponents of these liberal positions themselves violate their own call to state neutrality. In other words, liberal neutrality is not only a bad idea, it is probably not even possible to achieve in practice.

It seems that both the liberal and the antiliberal cases appeal to bedrock moral and political principles that resonate with a large segment of the North American population. This is why the debate over PL is one of the most important of our time.

> **Keywords:** political liberalism, state neutrality, jurisprudence, legislating morality, religion and politics, John Rawls, Ronald Dworkin, church and state, public reason, religious reason, secular reason, religion and public policy, religion and law, religious neutrality.

NOTES

1. *Planned Parenthood v. Casey,* 112 Sup. Ct. 2791, 2807 (1992).
2. *Webster v. Reproductive Services* (1989), as found in *The United States Law Week* 57, no. 50 (27 July 1989): 5044–45.
3. For philosophical and legal defenses of a broader definition of religion that includes secular and philosophical commitments in addition to traditional "religion," see Roy Clouser, *The Myth of Religious Neutrality* (Notre Dame, IN: University of Notre Dame Press, 1991); and Joel Incorvaia, "Teaching Transcendental Meditation in Public Schools: Defining Religion for Establishment Purposes," *San Diego Law Review* 6 (1978–79).

For Further Reading

Robert Audi, *Religious Commitment and Secular Reason* (New York: Cambridge University Press, 2000).

Robert Audi and Nicholas Wolterstorff, *Religion In the Public Square: The Place of Religious Conviction in Public Debate* (Lanham, MD: Rowman & Littlefield, 1997).

Francis J. Beckwith, "Is Statecraft Soulcraft?: Faith, Politics, and Legal Neutrality," in *Bioengagement,* ed. Nigel Cameron, Scott Daniels, and Barbara White (Grand Rapids, MI: Eerdmans, 2000).

Francis J. Beckwith and John P. Peppin, "Physician-Value Neutrality: A Critique," *Journal of Law, Medicine, and Ethics* 28.1 (spring 2000).

Francis Canavan, *The Pluralist Game: Pluralism, Liberalism, and the Moral Conscience* (Lanham, MD: Rowan & Littlefield, 1995).

Stephen L. Carter, *The Culture of Disbelief: How American Law and Politics Trivialize Religious Devotion* (New York: Basic Books, 1993).

Ronald Dworkin, *Life's Dominion: An Argument About Abortion, Euthanasia, and Freedom.* (New York: Alfred A. Knopf, 1993).

———, "Liberalism," in *A Matter of Principle* (Cambridge, MA: Harvard University Press, 1985).

———, "Neutrality, Equality, and Liberalism," *in Liberalism Reconsidered,* eds. Douglas MacLean and Claudia Mills (Totowa, NJ: Rowan and Allanheld, 1983).

John Finnis, "Public Reason, Abortion, and Cloning." *Valparaiso University Law Review* 32.2 (spring 1998).

Robert P. George, *Making Men Moral: Civil Liberties and Public Morality* (Oxford: Clarendon Press, 1993).

———, "Public Reason and Political Conflict: Abortion and Homosexuality," *Yale Law Journal* 106 (June 1997)

Stephen Macedo, *Liberal Virtues* (Oxford: Oxford University Press, 1990).

John Rawls, *Political Liberalism.* (New York: Columbia University Press, 1993).

———, "The Idea of Public Reason Revisited," *University of Chicago Law Review* 64 (summer 1997).

Joseph Raz, *The Morality of Freedom.* (Oxford: Oxford University Press, 1986)

George Sher, *Beyond Neutrality: Perfectionism and Politics* (New York: Cambridge University Press, 1997).

James P. Sterba, "Reconciling Public Reason and Religious Values," *Social Theory and Practice* 25.1 (spring 1999).

Paul J. Weithman, ed., *Religion and Contemporary Liberalism* (Notre Dame, IN: University of Notre Dame Press, 1997).

The Place of Religious Argument in a Free and Democratic Society

8

ROBERT AUDI

Robert Audi is the Charles J. Mach Distinguished Service Professor of Philosophy, University of Nebraska, Lincoln. He has published widely in many areas of philosophy including epistemology, philosophy of religion, political philosophy, and ethics. He is the editor of the *Cambridge Dictionary of Philosophy,* 2nd ed. (1999) as well as the author and/or editor of many other books including *Religious Commitment and Secular Reason* (2000), *Moral Knowledge and Ethical Character* (1997), and *The Structure of Justification* (1993)

In this essay Professor Audi explores the question of the role of religious arguments in the public square, especially as they are employed in debates over controversial moral issues that touch on public policy. Audi first defines the concept of a religious argument, offering criteria, each of which he believes is sufficient for calling an argument "religious." He then goes on to discuss the different roles that religious arguments may play in people's lives. From there Professor Audi makes a case for what he believes are the proper roles of religious arguments in ethics and politics. He maintains that in a liberal democracy there is a presumption in favor of individual liberty and autonomy, and that the role of the state is to allow people the most liberty possible without harming or

Reprinted by the permission from San Diego Law Review 30 *(fall 1993): 677–702.*

interfering with another's similar liberty. Thus, the person who seeks to restrict liberty has the burden to prove her case. Audi suggests several criteria that, if fulfilled, would meet this burden. He does maintain that in order for coercion in a liberal democracy to be justified it cannot *exclusively* be based on religious reasons, but rather, must be accompanied by secular reasons and secular motivation. He defines what he means by secular reasons and gives some examples of inappropriate government coercion based on religious reasons. Professor Audi briefly discusses the relationship between religious arguments and moral principles, and then makes some concluding remarks about the relationship between citizenship, rights, liberal democracy, and the moral life.

INTRODUCTION

WE ARE LIVING IN a period of increasing secularity in the industrialized world and increasing sectarianism in much of the less industrialized world. In the West, however, and particularly in the United States, secularization is by no means welcomed by all, and is feared and resented by many who consider themselves religious. In the United States, at least, the tradition of separation of church and state has contributed to secularization. But even a strong separationist tradition is neither necessary nor sufficient for secularization except in certain matters of law and public policy. Many aspects of society can be largely unaffected by separation of church and state. The domains of law and public policy are, of course, large areas of human life, and any major secularization in those domains is bound to have wider effects. Still, it is easy to exaggerate how much a reasonable separation of church and state must secularize a society that practices it. The degree of secularization of a society may be less a matter of its operative principles of separation than of the personal inclinations and the historical and cultural traditions of its people.

This Article presents a theory of how, from the point of view of normative sociopolitical philosophy, religious arguments may be properly used in a free and democratic society in a way that neither masks their religious character nor undermines a desirable separation. This task requires an account of what constitutes a religious argument. It also requires a basic catalogue of the uses religious arguments may have and attention to the main contexts in which they play a socially and politically significant role. In the course of clarifying the nature and proper role of religious arguments, I will articulate two general principles of separation of church and state and illustrate how a society that abides by them can realize religious as well as secular ideals.[1] My primary focus, however, will not be the most common preoccupation of church-state discussions, the relation of the state to religious institutions. Rather, my focus will be on the sociopolitical role of religious arguments and the explicit use of, or tacit reliance on, religious consideration as grounds for laws or public policies. These arguments may occur in a variety of contexts, and they can be as important in the conduct of individuals acting outside of governmental or religious institutions as they are in the official work of the church or the state.

I. THE CONCEPT OF A RELIGIOUS ARGUMENT

What is a religious, as opposed to a secular, argument? Frequent references to religious arguments suggest that the notion of a religious argument is well understood. However, apart from the examples people commonly have in mind—such as arguing from one of the Ten Commandments as a premise to a conclusion about how people should behave—the notion of a religious argument is frequently misunderstood. The question of what constitutes a religious argument turns out to be particularly difficult when we realize that an argument can be religious in a way that is important for church-state issues even when it does not explicitly appeal to any religious notion or doctrine.[2]

There are several criteria for a religious argument, each of them providing a condition that is sufficient (but not necessary) for an argument's being religious.

A. The Content Criterion

First, there is a content criterion: on this standard, an argument with essentially religious content (as opposed to, say, merely quoted religious statements) is religious. Paradigmatically, this is theistic content such as a reference to a divine command. There are also other cases, such as appeals to scripture, or to a religious leader, as a guide in human life. Full clarification of the concept of religious content would require nothing less than an analysis of the notion of a religion. For our purposes, it is sufficient to think in terms of theistic, especially monotheistic, religions like Christianity, Judaism, and Islam, which are highly representative of the challenges faced by a liberal democracy seeking to give proper weight, in civil and political life, to religious considerations.

We should also construe the relevant kind of religious content as substantive, for example as expressing divine commands. We are not concerned with noncommittal or accidental religious content, as where a speaker refers, without endorsement, to someone else's statement of a religious doctrine.[3] A more difficult case, which does concern us, is one in which legislators or other public officials argue for a position

on the ground that the vast majority of their constituents, for deep religious reasons, favor it. There are at least two subcases here: one in which the reference to the religious convictions of constituents is simply added information, perhaps to indicate the depth of the people's conviction, and the other in which the constituents being religious is given justificatory weight in the argument. In the latter but not the former case religious content is essential to the legislator's argument. Nonetheless, the latter is only a second-order religious argument; roughly, one in which a positive evaluation of a set of religious reasons, but no religious reason itself, is given a justificatory role.

In the former case, where religious reasons are simply taken as evidence of deep conviction, a church-state issue arises in a way that might lead some people to call the argument religious. Granting that one's constituents favoring something for religious reasons is not itself a religious as opposed to sociological fact, giving it weight as deeply felt because of those reasons raises questions about the appropriate role of religious considerations in a liberal democracy. Would one, for example, take political, or ethical, or aesthetic reasons as seriously? If not, would that be justifiable solely on sociopsychological grounds concerning what does or does not indicate depth of conviction? This Article is designed to help us in dealing with such issues in whatever kind of argument they may arise. Contentually religious arguments are the primary kind that people think of as religious and may be the sort that most often raise church-state issues. They are not, however, the only kind of religious argument. We must certainly consider others if we are to develop an adequate theory of the relation between religious considerations, for example, and the sociopolitical domain.

B. The Epistemic Criterion

The second criterion of religious argument is the epistemic criterion. By this standard, an argument is religious not because of what it says, but, roughly speaking, because of how it must be justified. Specifically, I propose to call an argument epistemically religious provided that (a) its premises, or (b) its conclusion, or (c) both, or (d) its premises warranting its conclusion, cannot be known, or at least justifiably accepted, apart from reliance on religious considerations, for example scripture or revelation.

Most epistemically religious arguments will also be theistic in content, but not all arguments with theistic or religious content need be epistemically religious. Consider, for instance, a poor argument for a sound, purely moral conclusion, say that one should try to render aid to neighbors in dire need. Let the premise be an approving attribution of a moral view to the Bible, for example the statement that according to Moses, God prohibited bearing false witness against one's neighbors. This attribution is not a statement of a moral view or otherwise evidentially sufficient for the conclusion, which is on a different though related topic-rendering aid to neighbors in need. Thus, this argument would not meet the proposed epistemic criterion. Specifically, the argument meets none of the basic conditions of the criterion. First, its premise, being only an attribution of a moral view and not itself a moral statement, does not warrant its conclusion, which is a moral statement. Second, the premise can not be, even on a religious basis, known or justifiedly believed to warrant it[4] (so on this score there is no knowledge of justification to be had). Third, the truth of the premise can be known on textual as opposed to religious grounds. Finally, the conclusion itself could, on the nonskeptical assumptions I am making, also be known or justifiably believed on secular moral grounds.

A major reason for the importance of singling out epistemically religious arguments is that it seems possible for an argument to be epistemically religious without having any religious content. It is hard to find uncontroversial examples, but even a controversial one will bring out the nature of an epistemically religious argument. Consider a version of the notorious genetic argument for the personhood of the zygote: because all the normal human genetic information is present in the zygote and will normally result in a clear case of a person at the end of a natural process (pregnancy), the zygote itself is a person. Now it might be contended that if this conclusion can be known or justifiably believed through these premises, it is on a religious basis (e.g., on the basis of grounds for the belief that God ensouls members of the human species at conception). A plausible counter to construing the genetic argument as epistemically religious is the contention that there may be a purely metaphysical argument for ensoulment or personhood at this stage. It is not clear, however, that any such metaphysical arguments are sound or have even been widely taken to be sound.[5]

A related source of examples derives from natural law. Consider the argument that since the natural end of intercourse is procreation, and contraception thwarts that end, contraception is wrong. It is not evident that these premises can be known or justifiably believed apart from theistic grounds. But even supposing that they can be, given a statistical or other naturalistic standard of what is natural, the premises arguably cannot warrant the conclusion except on assumptions that patterns in the natural order reveal divine intentions regarding how human life should be conducted. Unless thwarting the natural end of an act is contrary to divine intention, why should it be morally important? It is this sort of dependency on religious considerations that seems to many to underlie the typical natural law arguments for moral conclusions and hence to undermine their ostensibly naturalistic, or at least nontheistic, character.

C. The Motivational Criterion

Third, there is a motivational criterion, according to which an argument, as presented in a context, is religious provided an essential part of the person's motivation for presenting it is to accomplish a religious purpose (for example, to elicit obedience to God's will or to fulfill a religious obligation to one's church). There may be more than one such purpose, and the purposes may be causally or evidentially independent, as where each derives from respect for an independent religious authority or source such as text and religious experience. This is a different kind of criterion from the first two. To understand the difference, notice that "argument" has two main uses. First, the term may designate a linguistic process, roughly the offering of one or more propositions as reasons for another proposition. Second, the term may refer to an abstract product of such a process, roughly the essential content put forward in arguing. The motivational criterion is an illocutionary[6] one, a criterion for an argument as linguistically presented not a propositional criterion, one applicable to an argument construed as an abstract structure of propositions. A propositional criterion applies no matter who presents the argument; an illocutionary criterion is proponent-relative and contextual. Thus, strictly speaking, the motivational criterion applies primarily to reasoning processes and only derivatively to arguments as the abstract structures realized in those processes. But since arguments do their chief work when so realized, it is appropriate to treat the motivational criterion as applicable to them.

The content of a motivationally religious argument need not be religious. Perhaps the genetic argument is an example of this. Certain natural law arguments might also illustrate the point. And if some of them, at least, need not be epistemically religious, they could exemplify arguments that are motivationally religious, but neither contentually nor epistemically so.

D. The Historical Criterion

Fourth, there is a historical criterion. It is illocutionary, like the motivational standard, but looser. The idea is roughly this: an argument, as used on a particular occasion, is religious in the historical sense provided that, as used on that occasion, it genetically traces, explicitly or implicitly, by some mainly cognitive chain, such as a chain of beliefs, to one or more arguments that are religious in one of the above senses, or to one or more propositions that are either religious in content or epistemically dependent on a proposition that is religious in content. Consider the argument that because taking an innocent human life is wrong, suicide is wrong. Here we have an argument that seems to many to be persuasive in its own right. Yet, there is no question that on many occasions of its use the argument traces to, and derives some of its persuasive power from, religious ideas such as the idea that God gives life, and only God should take it away, at least apart from self-defense and punishment.

There are, as this example about the permissibility of suicide suggests, at least two interesting subcases of historically religious arguments. First, there are those that are persuasively autonomous, in the sense that their persuasive power does not depend on their historically religious character. Second, there are those that are persuasively dependent, in that some of their persuasive power derives, whether evidentially or otherwise, from one or more religious sources to which they are traceable. Since persuasive power may depend on the audience, an argument can be persuasive in one case and not another, or persuasively autonomous with one audience and persuasively dependent with another. Consider the argument that monogamous marriage should be the only legally permissible kind because the only normal marital relation is between females and males. This normative assumption might, in turn, be partly based, evidentially, or historically, or in both ways, on the idea that only parents, or potential parents, or at least people who can identify in a certain way with parents, of the same child or children, should marry. Either idea might be historically religious, tracing to religious injunctions about marriage as divinely ordained for men and women from the Garden of Eden onward. The latter idea, however, might be partly based on some religious view and partly founded on a supposed moral obligation of parents to rear their children and a supposed right of children to be reared by both of their parents. An argument can thus have a mixed lineage: deriving, evidentially, or historically, or in both ways, from both a religious and a moral basis.

Two further points are in order and are readily understood in relation to the apparent historical dependence of the innocent-life, anti-suicide argument or the life-as-a-divine-gift argument. First, I take an argument or proposition to be implicit in the background of another argument, on an occasion of the presentation of the latter, when the first argument or proposition is not articulated, but the latter argument as presented is based on at least one of the premises of the former as a ground, or would at least be taken to be so based by a reasonable interpreter in the context. Second, the genetic line need not go through the speaker's mind. It is enough if the argument as presented has a history that meets the condition of traceability to religious considerations. The relevant causal chain, moreover, can branch. A single argument offered on one occasion can trace back historically, as it can motivationally, to two or more sources that are causally or evidentially independent, or independent in both ways.

The notion of a historically religious argument is of interest largely because, in some cases, we cannot account for the plausibility of an argument without so conceiving it. It convinces, as it were, by its pedigree or its associations rather than by its evidential merits. For example, whether the aforementioned marriage argument has any persuasive force apart from its religious historical connections is debatable. Note, however, that even if it has none apart from those connections, its conclusion could still be supported by any number of powerful considerations. Yet, it is neither epistemically religious nor necessarily motivation-

ally religious. To say, then, that an argument is historically religious is not, even from a secular point of view, to imply an epistemic criticism of its conclusion. Of the four kinds of religious arguments, it is only those that are epistemically religious that depend on religious considerations for the justification of some essential element in them.

II. ROLES OF RELIGIOUS ARGUMENTS

Religious arguments can play an indefinite number of roles. Some of these roles are perfectly compatible, such as expressing oneself and guiding someone else. There is no hope of providing an exhaustive list, but some of the roles most important for an account of the question of the appropriate uses of religious arguments in a liberal democracy should be noted.

One role of religious arguments is expressive, not merely in the minimal sense of putting something forth, but in the sense of "self-revelatory": to set out one's perspective on an issue, to articulate one's feelings on a major event, to get something off one's chest, and the like. This point has a major implication. A society that protects free expression must protect the freedom to express one's religious views, even in contexts in which there are good reasons to offer a secular case for those views, as in certain public forums. Thus, any constraints we establish as reasonable for religious arguments must operate within these freedoms. The constraints will apply to the appropriate discretion in exercising our freedoms, rather than restrict our right to do so.[7]

A second, closely-related role of religious arguments is communicative, to get across to someone else one's deepest feelings or to show someone else where one is "coming from." This kind of communicative argumentation may also be expressive, and must be so in the wide sense of expressing something. Here, however, the aim of argument is not mainly to articulate one's own position, but to change the understanding of someone else. There will be times when one cannot convey one's special sense of an issue or one's distinctive approach to a topic without using religious arguments, at least implicitly. Even if I do not expect a religious argument to persuade you, I may want to offer it as an indication of how deeply I feel and of the sources of my views. Far from necessarily seeming dogmatic or insular, this practice might suggest some common ground between us, religious or secular.

Still another role of religious argument is persuasive, above all, to get people to agree with our view, or follow our prescriptions, or identify with us. Persuasion may often be best when one is communicative and self-revelatory, but it need not have either of those characteristics. There are at least two major cases. The first is persuading people who accept one's general religious view. The second is persuading those who are either nonreligious or religiously different from oneself. Often, in the second case, some arguments with religious conclusions are needed first by way of partial conversion. But persuasion may be achievable simply through getting the addressee to acknowledge the importance of one's conclusion if only because it is religious. In the former case, redirection is usually the main strategy (for instance showing others how a shared religious premise has lead to resisting a conclusion). In the latter, one must create enough common ground to support the conclusion.

A fourth role of religious argument is evidential, to offer supporting reasons for a view or course of action. It may be that only religious people will accept the reasons in question as good, but that is not the point. It would be quite wrong to omit this purpose of using religious argument. It is an important underpinning for many instances of religious argumentation by conscientious people. That they regard their arguments as good is important for how those arguments should be received, even by those who reject them.

Fifth, religious arguments may play an important heuristic role. For instance, by raising the question what God would command, or what the Gospels of the Psalms imply, religious arguments may stimulate the discovery of new truths. The value of this approach should not be underestimated. The appeal to God's intellect or will as a standard of knowledge or value can open up hypotheses and clarify assumptions that might otherwise be lost. And the great religious texts are inexhaustable sources of ideas, standards, and practical wisdom. To exclude their study from public education is neither good academic policy nor required by a reasonable separation of church and state.

All five roles can be played by religious arguments in sociopolitical contexts. Here we encounter a host of questions about what, from the point of view of both normative political philosophy and the ethics of citizenship, are their appropriate uses. Those questions are the main topic of Part III.

III. THE PROPER ROLES OF RELIGIOUS ARGUMENTS IN ETHICS AND POLITICS

Liberal democracies are free societies and are above all committed to preserving freedom, especially in religion. There are many conceptions of liberal democracy. At one end of the spectrum, perhaps unoccupied by any major historical figure in the liberal tradition, are minimalist, procedural conceptions. These simply provide for a framework in which democracy can operate, and they impose no constraints whatever on the social goals appropriate to a free and democratic society.[8] At the other end are rich substantive conceptions that also incorporate such goals as respect for persons and social flourishing, a notion which itself can be substantively developed to a greater or lesser degree. Although a detailed conception cannot be presented here, this

Article proceeds on the hypothesis that a major basis for determining how much substance is permissible is what might be called a fidelity to essential premises constraint: a liberal political theory should build into its vision of a just society enough substance to fulfill the theory's essential underlying ideals.

If the fidelity constraint is assumed, it seems reasonable for a liberal society to build into its structure as much in the way of substantive promotion of the good as is implied in the essential premises underlying the liberal political theory by which it lives. These are not necessarily premises actually appealed to by proponents, but rather those that must be common to all the sets of grounds sufficient to justify the sociopolitical vision. The relevant premises are defined, then, as those minimally required for justification, not those historically used for the purpose. Normally, these two categories substantially overlap, and if they did not the fidelity to premises idea would be less interesting. But the historical inspiration for a liberal democracy could in principle lack justificatory force, and the minimally justifying grounds could, in some historical circumstances, lack persuasive power.

To illustrate the fidelity to premises idea, suppose that justification of a liberal political theory as a basis for governing a society requires at least ideals of democracy, in a sense implying one vote for each person; autonomy, in the sense of self-determination; respect for persons, implying at least equal treatment before the law and a legal system nurturing self-respect; and material well-being. In that case, proponents of the liberal theory in question might reasonably require that a society take positive steps to protect and nurture these ideals.

Although such an approach would warrant something at least close to the five ideas of the good that John Rawls finds in justice as fairness,[9] the purpose of this Article does not require endorsing any specific list of goods as essential aims in a liberal democracy. It is easy to go too far here. Someone might, for exam-ple, require religious observances by all citizens. Notice also that if a liberal society chooses to justify its liberal theory solely on certain pragmatic grounds, such as maximizing preference satisfaction within a framework of social and political liberties, it may have to use a thinner notion of the good. If, however, a morally inspired liberal political theory is justified, a richer notion of the good might be objectively warranted, such as one that emphasizes enhancing freedom and capacity for actualization of one's human capacities. But this society, being unable to countenance the grounds of that theory, would not be justified, in practice, in building in that richer notion.

Even within a fidelity to essential premises conception of liberalism, there is an important distinction between grounds appropriate for a liberal society in justifying promotion of the goods it may endorse and grounds appropriate to justifying coercion. Here again I appeal to a general principle as a constraint. It seems to me that once autonomy is taken sufficiently seriously—as it will be not only by liberal political theorists but also by any sound moral theory—the way is open to view the justification of coercion in a framework that gives high priority to respect for the self-determination of persons. For purposes of sociopolitical philosophy, it may be fruitful to work from a surrogacy conception of justified coercion, especially in cases of governmental coercion. According to this view, coercing a person, S, for reason R, to perform an action A, in circumstances C, is fully justified if and only if at least the following three conditions hold in C: (a) S morally ought to A in C, for example to abstain from stealing from others (perhaps someone has a right, in the circumstances, against S that S A— certainly a feature of most cases in which a liberal democracy can reasonably coerce its citizens); (b) if fully rational and adequately informed about the situation, S would see that (a) holds and would, for reason R (say from a sense of how theft creates mistrust and chaos, or for some essentially related reason), perform A, or at least tend to A;[10] (c) A is both an "important" kind of action (as opposed to breaking a casual promise to meet for lunch at the usual place) and one that may be reasonably believed to affect someone else (and perhaps not of a highly personal kind at all).[11] Thus, it is permissible, on grounds of the general welfare, to coerce people to pay taxes only if they ought to do so in the circumstances, and would (if fully rational and adequately informed) be appropriately motivated by seeing that they ought to do so. By contrast, it is not permissible to coerce someone to give up, say, smoking, unless it significantly affects others. (It is not self-evident that each citizen has a right that other citizens pay their taxes, but this is at least arguable.)

As these examples suggest, the greater the coercion needing to be justified (say, in terms of how much liberty it undermines), the more important the behavior in question must be; and parentalism, for normal adults, is ruled out. According to this view, then, we may coerce people to do only what they would autonomously do if appropriately informed and fully rational.[12] This view explains why justified coercion is not resented by agents when they adequately understand its rationale, why some coercion is consonant with liberal democratic ideals of autonomy, and why the kind that is can be supported by citizens independently of what they happen to approve of politically, religiously, or, to a large extent, even morally.

If the perspective on liberal democracy I have sketched is correct, then it is easy to understand why in such a society the use of secular reason must in general be the main basis of sociopolitical decision. Indeed, if there is secular reason which is esoteric in a sense implying that a normal rational person lacks access to it, then a stronger requirement is needed; one might thus speak of public reason, as Rawls and others do. This seems to apply especially to decisions that result in coercion, whether through law or even through restrictive social

policies not backed by legal sanctions. If I am coerced on grounds that cannot motivate me, as a rational informed person, to do the thing in question, I cannot come to identify with the deed and will tend to resent having to do it. Even if the deed should be my obligation, still, where only esoteric knowledge—say, through revelation that only the initiated experience—can show that it is, I will tend to resent the coercion. And it is part of the underlying rationale of liberalism that we should not have to feel this kind of resentment—that we give up autonomy only where, no matter what our specific preferences or particular world view, we can be expected, given adequate rationality and sufficient information, to see that we would have so acted on our own.

One might think that the importance of secular reasons is derivative from that of public reasons. But this is not so. For one thing, a liberal democracy must make special efforts to prevent religious domination of one group by another. There are, in turn, at least two reasons for this. One is that the authority structure common in many religions can make a desire to dominate other groups natural and can provide a rationale for it. (What could be more important or beneficial to others than saving their souls?) Another reason is that the dictates of a religion often extend to the religious as well as the secular conduct of persons, so that if domination occurs it undermines even religious freedom. (To save people's souls they must not only cease performing evil deeds but worship appropriately.) Religious freedom is a kind quite properly given high priority by a liberal democracy. And, if religious considerations threaten it more than nonpublic influences in general, additional reasons exist for a liberal democracy to constrain the role of those considerations.

Another ground for denying that the importance of specifically secular reason is not derivative from that of public reason is connected with the authority which religious principles, directives, and traditions are commonly felt to have. Where religious convictions are a basis of a disagreement, it is, other things being equal, less likely that the disputants can achieve resolution or even peacefully agree to disagree. If God's will is felt to be clear, there may seem to be only one way to view the issue. This can apply as much to prima facie nonreligious problems such as physical health care as it does to specifically religious practices. Granted, a nonreligious source of conviction can also be felt to be infallible, and it may also be nonpublic. But not every nonpublic source of views and preferences poses the authority problem, or the special threat to religious freedom, that can arise from certain kinds of unconstrained religious convictions. Particularly when people believe that extreme measures, such as bravely fighting a holy war, carry an eternal reward, they tend to be ready to take them. Being ready to die, they may find it much easier to kill.

So far, I have been imagining coercion by laws or institutional policies. But in my view, the same sorts of considerations imply that individual as well as institutional conduct—the more common domain of discussions of religion and politics—should be constrained in a related way. More specifically, I believe that just as we separate church and state institutionally, we should, in certain aspects of our thinking and public conduct, separate religion from law and public policy matters, especially when it comes to passing restrictive laws. This separation in turn implies the need for motivational as well as rationale principles. If, for example, some group has religious reasons for favoring circumcision, they should not argue for a legal requirement of it without having evidentially adequate secular reasons for such a law. Nor should they offer secular reasons that are not evidentially convincing to them or, for that reason or any other, cognitively motivating, such as statistics about cervical cancer in women married to men who are not circumcised. To do this would be to allow these reasons to serve as—or even to use them as—secular rationalizations that cloak the underlying religious motivation for seeking the legislation.

In earlier work I have articulated two principles to express these constraints upon conscience. First, the principle of secular rationale says that one has a prima facie obligation not to advocate or support any law or public policy that restricts human conduct unless one has, and is willing to offer, adequate secular reason for this advocacy or support.[13] A secular reason is roughly one whose normative force does not evidentially depend on the existence of God or on theological considerations, or on the pronouncements of a person or institution qua religious authority.[14] The second, the principle of secular motivation, adds the idea that one also has a prima facie obligation to abstain from such advocacy or support unless one is sufficiently motivated by adequate secular reason.[15] This implies that some secular reason is motivationally sufficient, roughly in the sense that one would act on it even if, other things remaining equal, other reasons were eliminated.[16]

Since an argument can be epistemically, motivationally, or historically religious without being religious in content, one might fail to live up to at least the second of these principles even in offering arguments that on their face are neither religious nor fail to provide an adequate secular reason for their conclusion. It might be argued, for example, that some people, in presenting a genetic argument for the personhood of the zygote, are not sufficiently motivated by the secular considerations cited in their argument and would not find the argument convincing apart from underlying religious beliefs.

Application of the principle of secular motivation can be complicated because it may be difficult to tell whether a reason for doing or believing something is in fact motivating. This difficulty is especially likely to occur before the relevant event or long afterwards. But what the motivation principle (beyond the rationale principle) requires of conscientious citizens contemplating support of restrictive laws or policies is at most this: (a) an attempt to formulate all the significant reasons for each major option—itself often a very useful exercise; (b) where one or more reasons is religious, consideration of the motivational weight of each reason taken by itself as well as in the context of the others (if none is religious, the principle does not imply any need to go any further into motivation); and (c) an attempt to ascertain, by considering hypothetical situations and motivational or cognitive impulses or tendencies, whether each reason is motivationally sufficient. I should ask myself, for example, whether I would believe something if I did not accept a certain premise and whether a given reason taken by itself seems persuasive, in the sense of providing a sense of surety. At least one secular reason should emerge as such.

In short, my principles imply that one should ask of one's reasons certain evidential, historical, and hypothetical questions. One is entitled to use practical wisdom in deciding how much effort is reasonable to expend in a given case. Here as elsewhere in applying a standard, one can be conscientious but mistaken. For instance, I might be wrong, but not unreasonably so, in believing a reason to be secular. I might then be subject to no criticism, or at least none deriving from the rationale or motivation principles as opposed to purely evidential ones. An interesting case here would be one's being mistaken in just this way, but so disposed that if one did not believe, of what is in fact a religious reason, that it is secular, one would not be moved by it. This is a kind of second-order conformity to the motivation principle simultaneously with first-order failure to abide by it, and the former adherence would help to excuse the latter deviation.

Fortunately, if the motivation principle is widely accepted, and perhaps even if it is not, and one is in good communication with people who disagree on the issue at hand, one will likely get substantial help from them. Whenever religious reasons seem motivationally too strong, people who disagree should be expected to help one probe. Others may think of revealing questions about us that we ourselves overlook, or observe words or deeds that tell us something we did not realize about our own thinking or motivation.[17]

It could turn out that most people are not usually good at forming reasonable judgments regarding what reasons they have, much less which, if any, are motivating.[18] If this is how it does turn out, the effort to find out may be all the more needed; if I cannot tell what my reasons are, I should probably wonder whether I have any worthy of the name, and I am likely to make better decisions if I try to find some good reasons. If I cannot accurately tell which reasons motivate me and how much they do so, I cannot adequately understand myself or reasonably predict my own behavior.

The problem of ascertaining and weighing motivating reasons is not peculiar to my view. In assigning moral praise or responsibility, for instance, we need to know not just what was done, but for what reasons it was done. Acting in accordance with duty, but for a selfish reason, earns one no moral praise. In any case, if there are any important questions, such as the abortion issue, in which people can identify their main reasons and can form reasonable judgments regarding which reasons are motivating, that gives the principle of secular motivation an important job to do. Surely there are some such issues.

It is important to emphasize two points about the proposed principles. First, the principle of secular motivation provides that one may also have religious reasons and be motivated by them. Second, my use of such separationist principles by no means presupposes that religious reasons cannot be evidentially adequate. My principles also allow that religious reasons may be motivationally sufficient (though not motivationally necessary, since secular reasons could not then be motivationally sufficient—they would be unable to produce belief or action without the cooperation of religious elements). The principles even allow a person to judge the religious reasons to be more important than the secular ones, or be more strongly motivated by them, or both. The rationale and motivation principles do not rule out a major role for religious considerations, even in public political advocacy. They simply provide a measure of protection against their domination in contexts in which they should be constrained.

While my principles do not imply that religious reasons are never evidentially adequate, their evidential adequacy is not a presupposition of liberal democracy.[19] Neither is their evidential inadequacy. Indeed, it may be that the absence of both presuppositions is a negative foundation of liberal democracy. It would be inappropriate for a liberal theory to contain either epistemological claim. This point need not be a positive plank in even a fully articulated democratic constitution, but it is an important strand in much liberal democratic theory.[20]

Neither of my principles precludes just pointing out to people how their religious commitments imply some conclusion which one is pressing. Telling me that I have an antecedent religious ground for agreeing with you is not arguing from that ground, and it can be done without implying that the ground is evidentially cogent. It is a persuasive, not an evidential, use of an appeal to a reason. We might call it leveraging by reasons; it is using other people's reasons to move them, as opposed to offering our own. In leveraging, one need not imply that the cited ground is sufficient to give any warrant to the conclusion. But, if one believes it is not, one is probably being manipulative rather than respectfully persuasive, since one is inviting, or exploiting, weak reasoning. I believe, however, a sufficient secular basis for using this strategy is necessary. Even then, its use can invite unwarranted appeal to religious considerations, since it may tacitly endorse their unrestricted appropriateness to laws or public policy conclusions.

Despite these restrictions, religious arguments can, in certain ways, be quite properly used in all the roles I have mentioned—expressive, communicative, persuasive, evidential, and heuristic-whether in public policy contexts or others. My thesis is that their use should be constrained, not that they should be eliminated. The implicit secularization is restricted and may be quite circumscribed. Indeed, it is quite appropriate to a secular ethic to endorse a principle that religion should be taken seriously because doing so is an aspect of one's integrity as a person. This is in part because ideals and commitments should be taken seriously; doing so is important to being a mature and integrated person, and it might be considered to be implicit in the duty of self-improvement as understood by such moral philosophers as Kant and W. D. Ross. It is also in part true because morality proscribes hypocrisy, and it is hypocritical to profess a religion and pay mere lip service to it.

If secular ethics may encourage taking one's religion seriously, what about government's role in this respect? Since government should not prefer the religious as such, law and public policy may not differentially encourage religious practice. But they may encourage living up to one's ideals within the constraints of mutual respect and of separation of church and state. This allows, however, that governments may require or even encourage employers to grant leaves for self-development. Governments may even encourage employers and schools to set aside time to pursue ideals, say by declaring a holiday for reflection and stock taking. This kind of attitude might in effect lead to respect for religious holidays in a way that gives visible governmental concern for the religious. But that outcome is neither inevitable nor necessarily objectionable, and the aim of the policy need not be specifically religious.

The goals of governmental policy and the kinds of reasons appropriate to laws and sociopolitical policy are the main focus of separation of church and state. It is not reasonable to prohibit policies that are properly motivated, even if they foreseeably favor the religious or the nonreligious. However, there are special cases here, such as a vast effect that would significantly reduce the freedom of nonreligious minorities.[21] An example of a policy that might be secularly motivated but affect the freedom of nonreligious minorities would be the mandatory observance of the Sabbath by closing government offices, where this is done for the convenience of a majority religious group though not because it is religious, but because it represents a majority. The required placement of condom machines in all public restrooms, even if motivated by public health concerns, might affect the freedom of religious minorities (who object to public exposure of such things). Perhaps requiring all normal adults to donate blood in wartime or epidemic would be an example favoring the nonreligious and some of the religious over religious minorities who strongly oppose the practice. Each of these cases is different from the others, and they all come in variant forms too numerous to discuss here. With any such cases, a point may come at which secularly motivated legislation can have a religiously significant effect that makes the legislation objectionable on reasonable grounds of separation. But there is no simple criterion of ascertaining that point.

IV. RELIGIOUS ARGUMENTS AND MORAL PRINCIPLES

The restricted role I suggest for religious arguments is compatible with the idea that there can be religious knowledge in ethical and sociopolitical matters. I think, however, that liberal democracy is or at least should be committed to the conceptual and epistemic autonomy of ethics (in the broad sense in which ethics encompasses normative political philosophy). This commitment does not imply

affirming the ontic independence of ethics; it is above all a commitment to the possibility of knowledge or at least justified moral beliefs or attitudes and is neutral with respect to the possibility that such beliefs can be true apart from God's existence (an ontological matter). Just as one might understand a poem, and know its aesthetic merits without knowing who its author is (or even that it has one), one might understand and know the truth or at least justification of a moral principle without knowing who its author is, or even whether it has one. If I believe that God necessarily exists, and is indeed the ultimate ground of moral truths and a kind of condition for the existence of anything, I can still embrace liberal democracy and defend the full sociopolitical rights of atheists. But I doubt that I could readily endorse all this if I thought there was no nontheistic route even to moral justification.

For reasons already given, it seems that liberal democracy is also committed to the possibility of justifying, on a secular moral basis, any coercion necessary for maintaining civil life, even where the conduct subject to coercion is defended by a religious justification, as with some religiously rationalized persecutions of religious minorities. Here secular coercion may have a justification that, in a liberal democracy, overrides a sincere and articulate religious rationale for allowing the proscribed conduct. This sociopolitical ascendency of secular argument in justifying coercion does not, however, imply a commitment to its being epistemically better than all religious argument. Agreeing on the principles—and referees—of a game does not entail believing that, from a higher point of view, there can be no better game, or superior referees.[22] But at least as long as we consent to play the game, we are obligated to abide by its rules.[23]

Teachers of ethics, and indeed teachers in general, should presuppose the epistemic autonomy of ethics, even if in a noncognitivist version.[24] It is a further question whether specific moral principles, such as the principle that people should be allowed a high degree of free expression, must be presupposed by liberal democracy and teachers. I believe that some of them must be, if only because they reflect underlying premises of such a system, and the very name "liberal democracy" suggests the same conclusion. But it is arguable that only a pragmatic assumption to this effect is presupposed. The issue is whether liberal democracy must be in a sense morally constituted, as opposed to being grounded simply in instrumental considerations concerning the preference of the founding parties or the current citizens. I am not certain that it must be morally constituted, but I do feel sure that, even from the point of view of nonmoral values, it is best that a liberal democracy be morally constituted.

Everything I have said here is intended to be compatible with the existence of a religious grounding of ethics, and even of a religious grounding of moral knowledge—there can be epistemic overdetermination here. That is, there can be two routes that, from the point of view of knowledge and justification, are independent ways to reach moral principles. Moreover, on the assumption of at least a broadly Western theism, we can say this much: God would surely provide a route to moral truth along rational secular paths—as I think Aquinas, for one, believed God has done. Given how the world is—for instance, with so much evil that even many theists are tempted by the atheistic conclusion that such a realm could not have been created by God—it would seem cruel for God to do otherwise. Religious doubt, and certainly rejection of theism, would have to be accompanied, in reasonably reflective people, by moral nihilism, which would only compound the problem in ways there is no good reason to think God would wish to allow.[25]

Indeed, on the assumption that God is omniscient and omnibenevolent-all- knowing and all-good- any cogent argument, including an utterly nonreligious one, for a amoral principle is in effect a good argument for God's knowing that conclusion, and hence for urging or requiring conformity to it. How could God,

conceived as omniscient and omnibenevolent, not require or at least wish our conformity to a true moral principle? I should think, moreover, that in some cases good secular arguments for moral principles may be better reasons to believe those principles divinely enjoined than theological arguments for the principles, based on scripture or tradition. For the latter arguments seem more subject than the former to extraneous cultural influences, more vulnerable to misinterpretation of texts or their sheer corruption across time and translation, and more liable to bias stemming from political or other nonreligious aims. This turns one traditional view of the relation between ethics and religion on its head; it may be better to try to understand God through ethics than ethics through theology.

These considerations from philosophical theology suggest a positive approach. Ideally, the religious should try to achieve theo-ethical equilibrium, a rational integration between, on one side, religious deliverances and insights and, on the other, considerations drawn from secular thought and discussion. A seemingly moral conclusion that goes against scripture or well-established religious tradition should be scrutinized for error; a religious demand that appears to abridge moral rights should be studied for misinterpretation, errors of translation, or distortion of religious experience. Given the conception of God as omniscient, omnipotent, and omnibenevolent, the possibility of such equlibrium should surely be expected. A mature, conscientious theist who cannot reach it should be loath to stake too much on the unintegrated proposition.

It is possible that a person believes, on authority or revelation, that God commands a certain kind of action, yet has no understanding of why it should be divinely commanded or otherwise obligatory.[26] This might hold for persons of little education, particularly on matters where the available arguments, if there are any, are difficult to grasp. My principles do not deny such a person a right to act, even publicly, in favor of the commanded conduct. But, they also suggest an obligation to seek secular grounds for that conduct if it promotes any law of policy restricting freedom. On the other hand, if religious authorities are the source of the person's belief, we may certainly ask that the relevant people should themselves try to provide a readily intelligible secular rationale if they are promoting laws or public policies that restrict liberty. This may be what they would reasonably wish regarding their counterparts who promote practices incompatible with their own. The kind of commitment to secular reason that I propose may constrain the use of some religious arguments, but it can protect people against coercion or pressure brought by conflicting religious arguments from others.

If I have been right about the possibility, and indeed, the desirability, of a theo-ethical equilibrium for religious people who are citizens in a liberal democracy, then separation of church and state may seem far less of a detriment to the sociocultural influence of religion, or at least of traditional monotheistic religion, in proportion as the moral requirements of religion are properly understood in the light of the divine attributes. Not only should traditional theists expect there to be secular routes to moral truth; these same paths should also be secular routes to divine truth.[27]

V. RIGHTS, IDEALS, AND THE RANGE OF OUGHTS

My position as applied to individual conduct is above all one that lays out what we ought to do in something like an ideal case. It describes an aspect of civic virtue, not a limitation of civil (or other) rights. I have not meant to suggest that, for example, there is no right to base one's vote on a religious ground. But surely we can do better than guide our civic conduct merely within the constraints imposed by our rights. If ethics directs us merely to live within our rights, it gives us too minimal a guide for daily life.

One important way in which my position is highly consonant with theistic religion, and in particular with the Hebraic-Christian tradition, is its insistence that morality speaks to the heart and mind, not just to the hand and mouth; our thoughts, attitudes, and feelings can be morally criticizable or praiseworthy, as well as our words and deeds. And our deeds, however well they can be rationalized by the reasons we can offer for them, bespeak the reasons that motivate them. We are judged more by the reasons for which we act than by the reasons for which we could have acted. Loving one's neighbors as oneself implies appropriate motives as well as good deeds, and it is far more than extending them their rights of civic courtesy.

I must reiterate that in addition to expressing mainly ideals of citizenship as opposed to rights of citizens in a liberal democracy, the domain of application of my principles is primarily contexts of political advocacy and of public policy decision. The principles are addressed especially to citizens as voters and supporters of laws and public policy, to legislators in their official capacities, to judges in making and justifying decisions, and to administrators, especially government officials, laying down and interpreting policies. But the principles apply differently in different contexts. They apply less, for instance, in the classroom than in the statehouse, and less in private discussion than in corporate boardrooms.

There are, to be sure, various models of democracy, and some are highly permissive. I have been thinking of a liberal democracy, not just any system in which the people govern themselves. I am indeed particularly thinking of a constitutional democracy. My claim is that a substantially weaker separation of church and state than I have defended is not fully consonant with the ideals of liberal democracy, at least as it is best understood. I think that sound ethics itself dictates that, out of respect for others as free and dignified individuals, we should always have and be sufficiently motivated by adequate secular reasons for our positions on those matters of law or public policy in which our decisions might significantly restrict human freedom. If you are fully rational and I cannot convince you of my view by arguments framed in the concepts we share as rational beings, then even if mine is the majority view I should not coerce you. Perhaps the political system under which we live embodies a legal right for the majority to do so, for certain ranges of conduct; perhaps there is even a moral right to do so, given our mutual understanding of majority rule. But the principles I am suggesting still make a plausible claim on our allegiance. They require partial secularization of our advocacy, argumentation, and decisions, in certain contexts and for certain purposes. But they do not restrict our ultimate freedom of expression, and they leave us at liberty to fulfill our cherished religious ideals in all the ways compatible with a system in which those with differing ideals are equally free to pursue theirs.

Notes

1. The principles I shall generally presuppose are those stated in Robert Audi, The Separation of Church and State and the Obligations of Citizenship, 18 Phil. & Pub. Aff. 259 (1989) [hereinafter Audi, Separation]. For critical discussion of that article, see Paul J. Weithman, The Separation of Church and State: Some Questions for Professor Audi, 20 Phil. & Pub. Aff. 52 (1991). For my response to Professor Weithman, see Robert Audi, Religious Commitment and Secular Reason: A Reply to Professor Weithman, 20 Phil. & Pub. Aff. 66 (1991). Also highly relevant to this Article is Kent Greenawalt, Religious Convictions and Political Choice (Oxford University Press ed., 1988). I have discussed the theory of that book in Religion and the Ethics of Political Participation, 100 Ethics 386 (1990), and Professor Greenawalt has replied to me and others in Religious Convictions and Political Choice: Some Further Thoughts, 39 DePaul L. Rev. 4 (1990).

2. I follow the common and useful practice of using "church" generically to apply to any religious institution.

3. A sociological argument may be religious in content in the sense of having premises attributing religious beliefs to people; but here the attribution itself carries no religious commitment, and so it is not relevant to the notion we need here.

4. If the premise does not warrant the conclusion, it cannot be known through that premise. Presumably, in this example religious considerations also could not justify attributing a warranting relation, but that is not quite self-evident. Still, it would not be expected in a case like this, where the premise is largely irrelevant to the conclusion.

5. Here is a different example. Imagine an island society's discovering an inscription on the beach that reads: "Circumcise!" Someone might argue that this writing cannot be an accident. Hence, we should (prima facie) practice circumcision. Now arguably this conclusion cannot be known or justifiedly believed on ethical or medical grounds (at least for an adequately hygienic society). If it can be, it would likely be on grounds of just the sort of authority which only a deity could have. One might reply that the argument is enthymematic and has a suppressed religious premise, in which case it is religious in content; but to insist on that seems to me to import the likeliest defense of the argument into its content. The only obvious presupposition of this sort is something like this: We ought (prima facie) to heed a directive nonaccidentally found in nature.

6. "Illocutionary" means, roughly, 'in producing a locution.'

7. This point underlies my emphasis on setting forth prima facie normative principles, rather than restricting rights. See Audi, Separation, supra note 1.

8. For one kind of minimalist view—a neutrality conception—see Charles E. Larmore, Patterns of Moral Complexity (Cambridge University Press ed., 1987). I, too, embrace a neutrality condition, but one less strong than his.

9. These are "(1) the idea of goodness as rationality, (2) the idea of primary goods, (3) the

idea of permissible comprehensive conceptions of the good, (4) the idea of political virtues, and (5) the idea of the good of a well-ordered (political) society." See John Rawls, The Priority of Right and Ideas of the Good, 17 Phil. & Pub. Aff. 251 (1988). For related discussions see Thomas Nagel, Equality and Partiality (Oxford University Press ed., 1991); Michael J. Parry, Morality, Politics, and Law: A Bicentennial Essay (New York: Oxford University Press, 1988); Richard E. Flathman's essays in Toward a Liberalism (Cornell University Press ed., 1989); Richard W. Miller, Moral Differences (Princeton University Press ed., 1992). Perry is a critic of liberalism, Flathman a defender of it. For wide-ranging studies of Perry's views quite relevant to this Article, see Theodore Y. Blumoff, Disdain for the Lessons of History: Comments on Love and Power, 20 Cap. U. L. Rev. 159 (1991), and Edward B. Foley, Tillich and Camus, Talking Politics, 92 Colum. L. Rev. 954 (1992) (reviewing Michael J. Perry, Love & Power. The Role of Religion and Morality in American Politics (1991)).

10. The reason must be essentially related because otherwise the agent's hypothetical attitude will not be sufficiently connected with the coercive reason to warrant the coercion. A typical case would be this: where R is the state's reason, for example to protect other citizens, the related reason would be, say, to fulfill my duty not to harm others. Roughly, if the agent's reason is not R, it is something like a first-person version of R. It should also be noted that this approach does not imply that all moral obligation is discernible by reflection of this kind. It does seem appropriate, however, that the obligations grounding state rights of coercion should be discernible by such reflection. This is one reason to think that such obligations correspond to rights of citizens.

11. I assume here that a fully rational person with certain information about others has certain altruistic desires. If rationality is understood more narrowly, my formulation must be revised (unless we may assume, as I do not, that motivation to do something is entailed simply by a realization that it is one's moral obligation). The basic idea could, however, be largely preserved. I make a case for such desires in The Architecture of Reason, 62 Proc. & Addresses Am. Phil. Ass'n 227 (Supp. 1988).

12. This is so, at least, on the plausible assumption that fully rational persons can see their moral obligations. A further qualification is this: If purely rational considerations would convince a fully rational person to do certain religious deeds, such as worship God and follow certain religious principles, then they are not an appropriate basis of coercion. This is one reason the condition stated here is only necessary. Similar restrictions would apply to other possible domains in which a liberal society protects one's freedom to decline even what reason requires. Morality, I take it, is not such a domain, and some of its principles are essential to fully justifying liberalism.

13. See Audi, Separation, supra note 1, at 279–80.

14. An interesting question, put to me by Kent Greenawalt, is whether reasons presupposing atheism are ruled out as religious in the broad sense that they directly concern religion. I have not construed such reasons as religious, though the wording of my principles may allow including them, and certainly doing so may be appropriate to the overall spirit of my position. But these reasons are at least not religiously neutral and on that ground may be objectionable in certain ways in a liberal democracy. This allows, but does not entail, that there may be special church-state reasons to restrict their use. However, the two principles proposed here are not intended to exclude them.

15. Audi, Separation, supra note 1, at 284–86.

16. Two points are important. First, it may be common that this reason would in fact be sufficient only in the context of other elements, such as a general interest in civic duty, but it may still be sufficient as a specific reason for the conduct in question. Second, the person's believing the reason sufficient is neither necessary nor sufficient for its being so; but a justified false belief that it is so would have some excusatory force.

17. Weithman has questioned how feasible it is to try to follow the principle of secular rationale.

See Weithman, supra note 1. See also Lawrence B. Solum, Faith and Justice, 39 DePaul L. Rev. 1083, 1089–92 (1990). Also relevant is Paul J. Weithman, Liberalism and the Privitization of Religion: Three Theological Objections Considered, 22 J. Religious Ethics (forthcoming spring 1994). The above is only the beginning of a reply to such worries.

18. One might think that a person must have some motivating reason for a belief or action. But this is not so, if we distinguish reasons from causes or, more subtly, reasons for which one believes or acts from mere (explanatory) reasons why one does. Wishful thinking is a nonrational source of beliefs, and actions not performed intentionally need not be done for a reason.

19. The Declaration of Independence is one famous document supporting liberal democracy that seems to imply otherwise; but I am not certain that it must be so read, nor do I take it to be as authoritative on this matter as the work of John Stuart Mill.

20. An interesting problem arises here. Suppose one can have an objectively good secular argument for (a) God's existence and (b) His commanding our A -ing. One might then claim to have an (ultimately) secular reason for our A -ing. But notice that I characterize a secular reason as one whose justificatory force does not evidentially depend on God's existence or on theological considerations. So this argument would not qualify as providing a secular reason; it would evidentially depend on God's authority. Someone might protest that it does provide a secular route to moral knowledge, and that is all separation of church and state should demand. But although the route is open to any rational person, it may be questioned whether it is truly secular, since God is encountered (at least intellectually) on the way. Even apart from this, I think we need epistemically secular reasons for, and not merely epistemically secular routes to, the relevant conclusions. For (1) not all rational persons can be expected to take this route, even though it is open to them all if it is indeed objectively good. In any case, (2) one would still not have (unless through having other argu-

ments) a sufficient (purely) secular reason for one's belief or act, and thus would be speaking, or acting (for example, voting), in a primarily religious way; and (3) in practice, people of other religious persuasions would be uncomfortable. Even if they followed the same route in their arguments, they would not like having to travel through someone else's theology. That brings us to the question of the truth of the supposition: even if there are, from purely naturalistic premises, objectively justifiable arguments for God's existence, the arguments for His specific commands, especially in areas in which there is moral disagreement, are far from generally justificatory or purely naturalistic.

Granted, one's having what one reasonably, even if wrongly, takes to be good secular arguments for (a) and (b) is somewhat excusing (though that term is misleading because I do not deny a right to vote religiously). But the best ideal is still not met. Now is the best ideal one that is simply a sociopolitical ideal reasonable in a liberal democracy, or is it a moral ideal? The contrast may be artificial. If there is a sufficient moral case for liberal democracy, the best ideal can be argued to be moral. If not, it may not be moral; but there are principles about how to treat others in matters of coercion that are independent of liberal democracy and which support the rationale and motivation principles. Hence, there can be an independent moral case for them.

21. This paragraph has benefited from correspondence on the topic with Richard Arneson.

22. These among other points in this Article bear on the case made by Professor Larry Alexander to the effect that liberalism tends to assume that the epistemic credentials of religious claims are inferior to those of scientific claims. See Larry Alexander, Liberalism, Religion, and the Unity of Epistemology, 30 San Diego L. Rev. 763, 764 (1993).

23. I do not take consent to play to entail having consented to play; and the analogy to the consent of the governed is intended. I am not even implying "tacit consent" if that entails some act of consent, as opposed to having certain dispositions and behaving in certain ways.

24. In this case one would speak of, for example, justified moral attitudes rather than of moral knowledge or warranted moral belief. One might even be a skeptic and think that ethics is autonomous in a sense. Ethics has arguments independent of theology; they simply are not good enough, and hence there is no moral knowledge (or, for a stronger skeptic, even moral justification).

25. It might be objected that the same should hold for the evils themselves, or at least moral evils constituted by wrongdoing, that there must be a secular route to their elimination. Even if there is some plausibility to this conclusion, notice that it apparently presupposes that there is a secular route to moral principles. Otherwise free agents would not be overcoming evil or responsibly abstaining from it, but at best luckily avoiding its commission.

26. This possibility was put to me by Kent Greenawalt.

27. Of course, on one traditional theistic outlook there is a sense in which every contingent truth is divine, since God is at least responsible for the truth of all contingent propositions, by virtue of knowingly realizing the possible world in which they hold. But we may still distinguish—and must do so to understand the problem of evil—between those truths God willingly ordains and those He merely permits, for example, those describing evils that are necessary for a greater good.

Discussion Questions

1. Present and explain Professor Audi's criteria for an argument to be religious. Do you agree or disagree? Explain and defend your answer.
2. Why does Professor Audi believe that in a liberal democracy there should be a presumption in favor of individual liberty?
3. What does Professor Audi mean by theo-ethical equilibrium?
4. Explain and present Professor Audi's argument for the necessity of having secular reasons and motivation in shaping public policy and law in a liberal democracy.

You can locate InfoTrac-College Education articles about this chapter by accessing the InfoTrac-College Edition website (http://www.infotrac-college.com/wadsworth/). Using the InfoTrac-College Edition subject guide, enter the search terms relevant to this chapter, and then read abstracts for relevant articles.

Why We Should Reject What Liberalism Tells Us about Speaking and Acting in Public for Religious Reasons

9

NICHOLAS WOLTERSTORFF

Nicholas Wolterstorff is the Noah Porter Professor of Philosophical Theology, Yale Divinity School, Yale University. He has published in a number of areas of philosophy including philosophy of religion, epistemology, political philosophy, and

Reprinted by permission from Religion and Contemporary Liberalism, *ed., Paul J. Weithman (Notre Dame, IN: University of Notre Dame Press, 1997), 162–81.*

philosophy of education. His many books include *John Locke and the Ethics of Belief* (1996), *Educating for Responsible Action* (1980), and *Faith and Rationality* (1983).

·Professor Wolterstorff rejects PL's requirement that one must have secular (or public) reasons in order to legitimately shape public policy and law. He begins his essay with a brief overview of his own religious and political commitments as well as some clarifications about the scope, meaning, and influence of PL. Wolterstorff distinguishes two strands of liberalism. The first he calls the *political conception of justice*. Citing John Rawls' (see Chapter 36) and John Locke's views as examples (and pointing out their disagreements), Wolterstorff maintains that "the liberal tries to formulate a general criterion of political justice for a society whose members understand themselves as thus free and equal." The second strand, which he calls the *neutrality position,* consists of two components: (1) the *separation position,* "the government is to do nothing to advance or hinder religion," and (2) the *independent-basis position,* citizens "are neither to base their political debate in the public space, nor their political decisions, on their own particular religious convictions, nor on such religious convictions as they might all share." Professor Wolterstorff's essay focuses on the second component of the second strand, the independent-basis position. After an analysis of Locke's position, Wolterstorff concentrates his critique on Rawls, highlighting what he believes are significant flaws in Rawlsian liberalism. He then briefly critiques the separation position and concludes with some reflections on the relationship between religious reasons, public reasons, and political discourse.

§1. Psalm 72 in the Hebrew Bible and the Christian Old Testament opens as follows:

> Give the king your justice, O God,
>   and your righteousness to a king's son.
> May he judge your people with righteousness,
>   and your poor with justice.
> May the mountains yield prosperity for the
>   people,
>   and the hills, in righteousness.
> May he defend the cause of the poor of the
>   people,
>   give deliverance to the needy,
>   and crush the oppressor.

My own reflections on the moral and political significance of poverty have been decisively shaped by this and similar passages in the psalms, the prophets, and the gospels—all of which I accept as canonical scripture. I interpret what I read in these passages, about justice to the widows, the orphans, the aliens, and the poor, as implying that involuntary avoidable poverty is a violation of *rights*. Not, as such, a failure of charity on the part of the well-to-do—though such failure may well be involved. A violation of the rights of the poor, *qua* poor. What comes through, to my interpreting ear, is that to be a human being is to bear the unconditional natural right to fair and non-degrading access to the means of livelihood.

So far forth, this says nothing about the state. So let me add that in our society I see no option but for the state to function as the last-resort guarantor of this right. In other times and places it was different: The king was the last-resort guarantor, or the bishop. Should the state in our society not function as the last-resort guarantor of fair and non-degrading access to the means of livelihood, it is failing in its duty to secure justice.

My question in this paper is how I ought to espouse this religiously based view in public, and how I ought to act on it in the political domain, when so many of my fellow citizens accept neither the Christian nor the Hebrew Bible as canonical, and when so many of those who do accept these writings as canonical regard it as quaint and dangerous on my part to treat what they say about the moral and political significance of poverty as relevant to contemporary politics. You will understand, of course, that I am taking this particular case as an example of the general point: How should citizens espouse their religiously-based political views in the public space and act thereon?

The question arises for me because so many of my fellow citizens do not agree that the poor *qua* poor have rights. They believe that the poor *qua* poor are candidates for charity, not holders of rights. And they believe that the failure of the state to act as last-resort guarantor of fair and non-degrading access to the means of livelihood is not a failure on its part to secure justice, but a responsible refusal on its part to act as a charitable organization. If my views on these matters were universally shared by my fellow citizens, we would still have to discuss the difficult question of how best to secure the rights of the poor *qua* poor. But we wouldn't have to debate the moral and political significance of poverty. The only question in the region would be, how best to transmit our consensus to our children.

Of course, disagreement with my views on the moral and political significance of poverty is not only to be found among those of my fellow citizens who do not accept the Christian or Hebrew scriptures as canonical. It is also to be found among my fellow Christians. So there's work facing me on *two* fronts. Not only do I have to consider how to conduct my public, inter-community, discourse, but also how to conduct my intra-community discourse.

Within my own community, I will talk about the status of scripture, and about principles of scriptural interpretation, and about the exegesis of specific passages. Then I will move on to the Christian tradition, where I will highlight a large number of ringing passages about the rights of the poor *qua* poor. I will observe that the tradition was still alive in John Locke—where I, at least, would have expected it to be dead. (See his *Second Treatise*, § 135).[1] Along the way I will bring some live poor people into the room—so that their faces can be seen and their voices heard. Talk and argument about such matters, in the absence of faces and voices, is a frail reed. I'm sure I wouldn't succeed in persuading all of my fellow believers. But I think I would get some to come along— since many of them have formed their views in oblivion of scripture and tradition rather than on the basis thereof, while yet officially acknowledging their relevance.

§2. The most pervasive and influential answer to my question to be found on the American scene is that offered by political liberalism. I think that answer is mistaken. But given its popularity, it's with an analysis and appraisal of the liberal answer that we must begin.

Unfortunately, anyone who chooses to talk about liberalism faces the necessity of saying what is that about which he has chosen to talk. A shared understanding cannot be presupposed.

At the core of liberalism, as I shall be taking it, is a certain understanding of society and its members. The liberal regards the normal adult members of society as free and equal in the following way: *equally free* in that each has it in his or her power to act as moral agent; *equal* in that each has the inherent right, subject to appropriate qualifications, to pursue what he or she regards as good and obligatory; and *equal* also in that none bears a right by 'nature' which the others do not also bear.

With this understanding in hand, the liberal then focuses his attention on the political dimension of society. Here two strands of thought can be identified. In the first place, the liberal tries to formulate a general criterion of political justice for a society whose members understand themselves as thus free and equal— he tries to formulate, in Rawls' phrase, "a political conception of justice" for such a society. I speak, in this indefinite way, of the liberal as "trying to formulate a general criterion" for political justice, because, when it actually comes to the criterion offered, one finds considerable diversity among liberals. Classical liberals, such as John Locke, focused entirely on the rights of individuals in formulating their criterion of political justice. And as to the rights of individuals, they focused almost entirely on their *negative* rights—that is, on their right to freedom from interference in the pursuit of such goals, and the application of such principles, as they have chosen for themselves. But if we grant to John Rawls his wish to be regarded as a liberal, then we must regard classical liberalism as but one of many liberal options. For though Rawls also thinks entirely in terms of the rights of individuals, he most certainly does not hold that the formulation of a political conception of justice, for a society which regards its normal adult members as free and equal, can confine itself to the specification of negative rights. *Fairness* is what he regards as the appropriate principle.

I will be arguing that liberalism is unfair to at least certain kinds of religion. But before I get to that, let me put in a plea for fairness to liberalism. Many of the accusations which in recent years have been lobbed at liberalism are unfair. It is charged that liberalism denies the existence of moral agents other than individuals. That's unfair. Liberalism does not deny the existence of non-individual moral agents; it simply doesn't pay any attention to them in its theory. Ignoring is not denying. It is charged that liberalism denies that agents other than individuals have rights. That's also unfair. Liberalism does not deny the rights of entities other than human individuals; rather, in its theory it pays them no attention. It is charged that liberalism denies all but negative rights.

That's unfair. It's true that in its formulation of a political conception of justice, classical liberalism makes reference to no other rights than these; but it doesn't deny that there are others. And even that is not true for liberalisms such as Rawls'. It is charged that liberalism denies the existence of responsibilities and regards morality as consisting entirely of rights. That too is unfair. It's true that liberalism formulates its political conception of justice entirely in terms of rights; but that's fully compatible with holding that the moral life as a whole incorporates responsibilities along with rights. Indeed, any position other than that would be incoherent. It is charged that liberalism is "based on an atomistic, abstract, and ultimately incoherent concept of the self as the subject of rights."[2] Again, unfair. Liberalism says that the normal adult members of society are free and equal; it's entirely consistent with that to be as social and concrete in one's understanding of the self as one wishes. I don't doubt that liberalism encourages a *mentality* against which several of the above charges stick. But that, then, is the thing to say; not that to be a liberal just is to hold all these nasty positions. Let's be fair to liberalism!

I mentioned that two strands of thought can be identified in what the liberal says about the political dimension of society. Having identified the first, let me now move on to the second. Liberalism was born in the situation of a single society containing a diversity of religions, and was motivated by the conviction that there had to be a new and better way of relating the political dimension of society to that diversity than was then extant. The policy which liberalism advocated is regularly described as political toleration, or political neutrality. That's not an incorrect description. But it's important, for my purposes, to be a good deal more precise than that. Let me distinguish two aspects of the toleration, or neutrality, that the liberal advocates.

In the first place, definitive of liberalism, as I shall be taking it, is a certain view as to how government and its agents ought to treat the various religions to be found in society—when that society regards its normal adult members as free and equal. Call it the *separation* view. It would be possible to hold that government and its agents ought to treat all religions *impartially*. But that's not the liberal position. The liberal position is rather that government is to do nothing to advance or hinder any religion. The difference between the two positions can most easily be seen by taking note of the difference in result on the issue of state aid to schools. The impartiality position says that if the state aids any school, it must aid all schools, and aid them all equitably—no matter what their religious orientation. The separation position says that the state is to aid no school whose orientation is religious. The First Amendment in the United States Bill of Rights specifies that the government shall neither establish any religion nor infringe on the free exercise of any. That formulation is ambiguous as between the impartiality and the separation positions. Nonetheless, the U.S. Supreme Court, in its decisions over the past fifty years, has consistently interpreted the amendment as an affirmation of the separation position. It has ruled as if Jefferson's *wall of separation* metaphor had been incorporated into the constitution.[3]

It is also definitive of liberalism, as I shall be taking it, to embrace a certain view as to the proper basis of public political debate, and of political decision making, in a society which incorporates a diversity of religions—when that society regards its normal adult members as free and equal. The view is that those members are neither to base their political debate in the public space, nor their political decisions, on their own particular religious convictions, nor on such religious convictions as they might all share. When it comes to such activities, they are to allow their religious convictions to idle. They are to base their political debate in the public space, and their political decisions, on the principles yielded by some source *independent of* any and all of the religious perspectives

to be found in the society. To this, the liberal adds one important addendum: The source must be such that it is *fair* to insist that everybody base his or her public political discourse, and political decisions, on the principles yielded by that source. This addendum eliminates what would otherwise be obvious candidates for the political basis. A good many of the nationalisms of the contemporary world are rich and thick enough to serve as the basis of the political debates and decisions of the members of a society; in addition, they are often relatively independent of the religions to be found in the society. But rarely if ever will it be fair to insist that the life of the polity be based on some nationalism; for it never happens anymore that all the citizens of a single polity belong to the same nation, the same 'people.'

In this paper I will have nothing further to say about liberalism's understanding of the normal adult members of society as free and equal. Neither will I have anything further to say about the first of the two major strands which I identified within liberalism, namely, liberalism's attempt to formulate a criterion of political justice appropriate for a society which thus understands its normal adult members. I will focus entirely on the second strand. And of the two elements in that strand, liberalism's embrace of the *separation* position with respect to governmental action, and liberalism's embrace of the *independent-basis* position with respect to political debates and decisions, I will speak mostly about the second. For the sake of convenience, I shall call the second strand as a whole, with its two components, the *neutrality* postulate.

§3. Why does liberalism affirm the independent-basis position? That is, why does the liberal insist that, in a society which regards its normal adult members as free and equal, political debate in the public space be conducted on the basis of principles yielded by some source independent of all the religions in society, and why does he insist that political decisions be made on the basis of such independent principles?

An obvious question to ask at the outset is, what are we to understand as the scope of "political"? It's open to the liberal to carve out, within the sphere of what is ordinarily and loosely called "political," a sphere of the *truly political,* or of the *politically fundamental*—call it what you will—and to specify that he means his thesis to apply only to that inner sphere. Rawls does that; citizens in public are to appeal to the independent basis when dealing with matters of constitutional essentials and basic justice. But nothing that I have to say will depend on reaching precision on this point. And in any case, the dynamics of liberalism lead to a very expansive view on the matter. Rawls' willingness to limit the scope of his normative thesis to matters of constitutional essentials and basic justice is grounded on his conviction that though in principle *all* political debates in the public space, and all political decisions, ought to be conducted in accord with the thesis, it's much less *important* that we do so when we move beyond constitutional essentials and matters of basic justice. (The difficult but unavoidable question of what constitutes *public* space is also one which I cannot treat on this occasion.)

My question, once again, is why the liberal embraces the independent-basis position. What are his reasons? One reason which liberals have offered ever since the emergence of liberalism in the seventeenth century is that it's just too dangerous to let religious people debate political issues outside their own confessional circles, and to act politically, on the basis of their religious views. The only way to forestall religious wars is to get people to stop invoking God and to stop invoking canonical scriptures when arguing and determining politics—unless perchance the independent basis should yield various propositions about God, and should yield the conclusion that some canonical scripture is reliable on certain matters.

I must confess my inability to see any cogency in this reasoning. I think that if I had been living in the seventeenth century, I would

have found it cogent. But I live in the twentieth century. And so far as I can see, the slaughter, torture, and generalized brutality of our century has mainly been conducted in the name of one and another secularism: nationalisms of many sorts, communism, fascism, patriotisms of various sorts, economic hegemony. The common denominator is that human beings tend to kill and brutalize each other for what they care deeply about. In seventeenth-century Europe, human beings cared deeply about religion. In our century, most seem to have cared much more deeply about one and another secular cause. Liberalism's myopic preoccupation with religious wars is outdated.

The other side of the matter is also worth mentioning: Many of the movements in the modern world which have resulted in reforms and revolutions that the liberal admires have been deeply religious in their orientation: the abolitionist movement in nineteenth-century America, the civil rights movement in twentieth-century America, the resistance movements in fascist Germany, in communist Eastern Europe, and in apartheid South Africa. These movements are regularly analyzed by Western academics and intellectuals as if religion were nowhere in the picture.[4] The assumption, presumably, is that religion plays no explanatory role in human affairs; it's only an epiphenomenon. Thus does ideology shape scholarship! The truth is that even the *free and equal* doctrine, which lies at the very heart of liberalism, had religious roots—in Protestant dissent of the seventeenth century.[5]

However, thinkers in the liberal tradition have offered other and more substantial arguments for the independent-basis position than the argument that the offering of religious reasons in political debate is dangerous. Let me look briefly at Locke's main argument; and then, somewhat more expansively, at Rawls'.

§4. Locke's argumentation was epistemological—part and parcel of his general epistemology.[6] Though Locke had a good deal to say about awareness, or "perception," as he called it, this being what he identified as knowledge, the focus of his epistemology as a whole was on *belief,* and more specifically, on *entitlement* to believe. Doing what we ought to do, by way of the formation and maintenance of our beliefs, was what he mainly had his eye on. Belief is more important than knowledge, Locke says, because there's much more of it: Knowledge is short and scanty. And entitlement in beliefs is important because in many situations we are obligated to do better, by way of gaining true beliefs and eliminating false ones, than we would be doing if we just allowed beliefs to be formed in us haphazardly.

Accordingly, Locke set out to formulate a criterion for entitlement in beliefs. Not a *general* criterion for entitlement, however. Though much of Locke's rhetoric is universalistic, a number of passages, both in the *Essay concerning Human Understanding* and in the *Conduct of the Understanding,* make clear that Locke had no interest whatsoever in offering a criterion of entitlement applicable to all beliefs. He was concerned exclusively with situations of maximal concernment—"concernment" being his word. That is, he was concerned exclusively with situations in which one is obligated to do *the best* to find out the truth of the matter, and to believe in accord with the results of one's endeavor. His strategy was to articulate a practice of inquiry whose employment constitutes, in his judgment, doing the best. It follows that, on matters of maximal concernment, one is entitled to one's belief (or non-belief) if and only if one has employed the optimal practice, and one believes or refrains from believing in a manner appropriate to the results of the employment.

Locke sometimes describes this supposedly optimal practice as "listening to the voice of Reason." At other times he describes it as "getting to the things themselves." The point of the latter formulation is that, by employing the practice, one gets to the things themselves *instead of resting content with what people tell one about the things.* One circumvents tradition.

The essential elements of the practice are easily described. We can think of it as having three stages. With some proposition in mind concerning the matter in question, one first collects evidence concerning the truth or falsehood of the proposition, this evidence to consist of a non-skewed and sufficiently ample set of beliefs which are certain for one because their propositional content corresponds directly to facts of which one is (or was) aware. Secondly, by the exercise of one's reason one determines the probability of the proposition on that evidence. And lastly, one adopts a level of confidence in the proposition corresponding to its probability on that evidence. To employ this practice, says Locke, is to do the best.

Whether or not a matter is of maximal concernment to a person is a function of the whole contour of that person's obligations—with the consequence that which matters are matters of maximal concernment varies from person to person. Locke insisted on an extremely important limitation on this principle of variation, however. Matters of religion and morality are of maximal concernment to everybody. Accordingly, everybody is under obligation to employ the optimal practice on such matters.

Locke himself believed that by employing the practice we could arrive at a substantial set of beliefs about God; he furthermore believed that by employing the practice we could establish the reliability of the New Testament. Thus Locke was definitely not a proponent of secularism. His thought, rather, was that when it comes to forming beliefs on matters of religion and morality, it is our obligation, instead of appealing to the moral and religious traditions into which we have been inducted, to appeal to the deliverances of our generic human nature—to the yield of our human "hard wiring."

It just follows that when debating political matters, we are not entitled to appeal to our own particular religious tradition. It would be wrong to do so. It would be wrong to do so whether or not the matter was political. That's not to say that everything we have come to believe, by virtue of being inducted into some religious and ethical tradition, is off-limits in political debate. If, by employing that generically human, optimal, practice, one succeeds in arriving at some of the content of one's tradition, then one is entitled to appeal to that content in one's political debates. But one is then entitled to do so only because it's part of the yield of that generically human practice. Though religion is not necessarily excluded from the debate, everything other than *rational* religion most definitely is.

This Lockean defense of the independent-basis principle of liberalism was enormously influential in the centuries between him and us. Today, however, almost nobody accepts it—at least, almost nobody in academia. The defense rests directly on the epistemology of classically modern foundationalism. "We hold these truths to be self-evident." Constitutional assemblies making epistemological pronouncements! The intertwinement of traditional liberalism with classical foundationalism is there for all to see. But almost everybody today rejects classically modern foundationalism. I do so as well. With that rejection, the traditional defense of the independent-basis principle is rendered null and void.

No point in beating the dead horse—not on this occasion, anyway. Let me rather close our discussion of Locke by remarking that as long as the Lockean practice was widely thought to yield a substantial rational religion, along with rational evidence for the reliability of the Christian scriptures, American religious leaders were relatively content with liberalism. That was the situation throughout the nineteenth century. It was when skepticism on those scores began to spread—impelled especially, in my judgment, by the emergence of Darwinian evolutionary theory and the rise of biblical criticism—that tensions began to mount between religion and political liberalism.

§5. In his recent book, *Political Liberalism,*[7] John Rawls tacitly concedes the untenability of Locke's way of defending the independent-basis principle of liberalism. For he concedes the existence in our society of a plurality of significantly different religions with adherents who are *entitled* to their adherence. The test of entitlement does not pick out one from the diversity; nor can it serve as guide for newly devising a "rational" religion, or some "rational" secular perspective, which will then be the sole entitled member of the mix. "The political culture of a democratic society," he says, "is always marked by a diversity of opposing and irreconcilable religious, philosophical, and moral doctrines. Some of these are perfectly reasonable, and this diversity among reasonable doctrines political liberalism sees as the inevitable long-run result of the powers of human reason at work within the background of enduring free institutions" (3–4). It must be conceded that Rawls' *reasonableness* is not identical with what I mean by "entitlement." But in the course of his discussion it becomes clear, so I judge, that if "reasonable" in the above passage is interpreted as *entitled,* Rawls would happily affirm what would then be said.

How, then, does Rawls defend the independent-basis principle of liberalism? Locke held it to be a truth of the matter about normal adult human beings that they are free and equal. Though I did not explicate this part of his thought in my discussion above, Locke offered arguments for this position. He thought that societies which did not regard their normal adult members thus were mistaken—deeply mistaken. Rawls shies away from all such ontological claims. In their stead, he employs a *consensus populi* strategy.

In the contemporary world there are societies which regard their normal adult members as free and equal. Rawls thinks American society is such a society; he holds, so far as I can tell, that all constitutional democracies are such societies. So consider such societies. And attend then to the shared political culture of such societies; attend to the "political mind," as one might call it, of such societies. Identify the fundamental organizing ideas in those political minds. And then "elaborate" or "unfold" (27) those ideas into principles of justice capable of serving as the basis of deliberations and determinations concerning matters of constitutional essentials and basic justice. Of course the identification of those ideas, and the elaboration of those ideas into principles of justice, must not be whimsical or arbitrary. The principles one arrives at must be ones that one can reasonably expect all citizens of such societies to endorse *who use the light of our common human reason*. The principles must "win [their] support by addressing each citizen's reason" (143).

The principles of justice thus arrived at will be "freestanding" (10) with respect to all the comprehensive perspectives present in society. For they will not have been derived from any one of those perspectives, nor from any overlapping consensus among those perspectives. They will have been derived instead from the shared political culture of the society. However, if the society is to be at all stable and enduring, the comprehensive perspectives present within the society—or at least the reasonable ones among them—must each find the principles of justice acceptable from its own standpoint. Citizens must "within their comprehensive doctrines regard the political conception of justice as true, or as reasonable, whatever their view allows" (151). This is necessary if the society is to be stable and enduring and no one position is to enjoy a hegemony which stifles opposition by coercion or persuasion. But the source of the principles is to be independent of one and all comprehensive doctrines. The principles are to be *arrived at*—to repeat—by rational reflection on the political culture of constitutional democracies.

It is principles of justice thus arrived at that are to serve as the basis of political debate in the public space, and political decisions—at least on matters of constitutional essentials and basic justice. The "question the dominant tradition has tried to answer has no answer," says Rawls; "no comprehensive doctrine is appropriate as a political conception" (135). Not at least for democratic societies with constitutional regimes. In such a society, no one of the reasonable comprehensive doctrines can "secure the basis of social unity, nor can it provide the content of public reason on fundamental political questions" (134). One of the great merits of Rawls' discussion is that, under "comprehensive doctrines," he includes not only religions but comprehensive philosophies. No comprehensive vision—be it religious or not, be it of God and the good, or only of the good—no comprehensive vision can properly serve as the basis of public reason on fundamental political questions.

Rawls acknowledges that liberalism may well seem paradoxical at this point. Speaking on behalf of the objector, he asks:

> why should citizens in discussing and voting on the most fundamental political questions honor the limits of public reason? How can it be either reasonable or rational, when basic matters are at stake, for citizens to appeal only to a public conception of justice and not to the whole truth as they see it? Surely, the most fundamental questions should be settled by appealing to the most important truths, yet these may far transcend public reason! (216)

His answer is that it would be inconsistent with the society's understanding of its adult members as free and equal for the members to conduct their fundamental political debates and make their fundamental political decisions on any basis other than that of the consensus populi. Democracy, he says,

> implies . . . an equal share in the coercive political power that citizens exercise over one another by voting and in other ways. As reasonable and rational, and knowing that they affirm a diversity of reasonable religious and philosophical doctrines, they should be ready to explain the basis of their actions to one another in terms each could reasonably expect that others might endorse as consistent with their freedom and equality. Trying to meet this condition is one of the tests that

this ideal of democratic politics asks of us. Understanding how to conduct oneself as a democratic citizen includes understanding an ideal of public reason (217–18).[8]

§6. What Rawls tells me is that if I step outside my own religious community and enter the public debate about the treatment of the poor in our society, I must at no point appeal to my religious convictions. In my debates with others I must not cite them as reasons; in my political actions—in my voting, for example—I must not employ them as reasons. I must base my discourse and actions on the consensus populi—more precisely, on the results of analyzing the core ideas in the political consensus populi of constitutional democracies and elaborating those ideas into principles of justice—both the analysis and the elaboration having been conducted in such a way that one can reasonably expect all who use their common human reason to accept the principles of justice that emerge. When the coercive power of the state is involved, as ultimately it always is when political issues are under consideration, I would violate the equal freedom of my fellow citizens if I did not debate and act on the basis of reasons which I can reasonably expect at least the reasonable and rational among them to accept. And to fail to treat them as free and equal is out of accord with the consensus populi of the constitutional democracy of which I am a citizen.

May it be that I have interpreted Rawls more sternly than he intends? He does say, after all, that "the ideal of citizenship imposes a moral . . . duty . . . *to be able to explain* to one another on those fundamental political questions how the principles and policies they advocate and vote for can be supported by the political values of public reason" (219, my italics).[9] The ideal imposes a duty *to be able* to explain, not *to explain*. Possibly this is what Rawls has in mind. It's a position which has some plausibility with respect to one's own deliberations and decisions; it has none whatsoever, though, when it comes to the offering

of reasons in public. Suppose that the reasons I offer in the public square for the policies I favor and the actions I take are ones that it would be unreasonable of me to expect all my reasonable fellow citizens to accept—parochial religious reasons. There are consensus populi reasons which I am *able to offer* to the same end—in some sense or other of "able to." But I don't in fact offer those reasons. Perhaps I'm not interested in offering them; perhaps I'm not aware that I could offer them. I offer what I acknowledge to be parochial religious reasons. If there's an issue here of the violation of the equal freedom of my fellow citizens, surely it's the reasons which I *actually offer* that is the relevant phenomenon, not the reasons I *could have* offered. Consider an analogy from epistemology. If I hold a belief on the basis of reasons, then it's the reasons *on the basis of which* I actually hold the belief that determine its entitlement, not my possession of reasons on the basis of which I *could have* held it.

Or perhaps what Rawls has in mind is not just that I *be able* to offer reasons that I can reasonably expect all my reasonable fellow citizens to accept, but that I be *ready and able* to offer such reasons. That is suggested by this passage: "As reasonable and rational, and knowing that they affirm a diversity of reasonable religious and philosophical doctrines, they *should be ready to explain* the basis of their actions to one another in terms each could reasonably expect that others might endorse as consistent with their freedom and equality" (218; my italics). If this is what Rawls has in mind, it would be appropriate to ask what constitutes *readiness*. I'm ready and able to offer such reasons, but I don't in fact do so.

Appropriate, but not especially relevant. The relevant response is that I, as one who holds the views indicated at the beginning of this paper, would find myself silenced were I to accept even this qualified stricture. As I have indicated, my own views on the rights of the poor have been formed by reflecting on the scriptures which I accept as canonical. I am now told that if I want to present and debate those views in the political arena, I must find an entirely different basis. I must base them on the consensus populi, rationally analyzed. Either that, or be ready and able to appeal to base them on that. I see no hope whatsoever of success in that project. A large proportion of my fellow citizens deny that the poor have any such rights as I believe they have. Should someone extract principles of justice from the consensus populi which entail that the poor do have such rights as I believe they have, I would, on the basis of that entailment, conclude that her analysis was a *mis*-analysis. I cannot *appeal* to the consensus populi; the challenge facing me is to try to *reform* it.

The fact that I would find myself silenced will not seem to most people a decisive objection to Rawls' strictures! So let me move on to highlight other difficulties. The strategy Rawls proposes for arriving at the consensus which is necessary if his stricture is to be met has no chance whatsoever of succeeding. The stricture is that, with respect to fundamental political issues, we are to debate in the public arena and to act (or to be ready and able to debate and act), on the basis of principles of justice that we can reasonably expect all those of our fellow citizens who are reasonable and rational to accept. The strategy for obtaining those principles of justice is the analysis/elaboration strategy. Suppose, then, that someone has followed that strategy; she has analyzed our political mentality into its constituent ideas and has elaborated those ideas into principles of justice. I submit that no matter what those resultant principles of justice may be, the reasonable thing for her to expect is *not* that all reasonable people who use their common human reason will agree with her results, but that *not all* reasonable people will agree. It would be utterly *unreasonable* for her to expect anything else than disagreement. The contested fate of Rawls' own principles of justice is an illustrative case in point. There's no more hope that all those among us who are reasonable and rational will arrive, in the way

Rawls recommends, at consensus on principles of justice, than that we will all, in the foreseeable future, agree on some comprehensive philosophical or religious doctrine.

But what about the stricture itself, and Rawls' reason for it: Failure to satisfy the stricture represents failure to treat one's fellow citizens as free and equal? Well, in the first place, there's something very much like a fallacy of composition in Rawls' reasoning at this point. We must each stand ready to defend our political beliefs and actions, says Rawls, in terms that we can "reasonably expect that others might endorse as consistent with their freedom and equality" (218). So suppose it's true that, when conversing with Ryan, I must, to honor his freedom and equality, offer (or be ready to offer) reasons for my political beliefs and actions which I can reasonably expect him to endorse if he uses "our common human reason"; and suppose it's also true that, when conversing with Wendy, I must, to honor her freedom and equality, offer (or be ready to offer) reasons for my political beliefs and actions which I can reasonably expect her to endorse if she uses "our common human reason." It doesn't follow that the reasons I offer to Ryan must be the same as the reasons I offer to Wendy. To Ryan, I offer reasons that I hope he will find persuasive; to Wendy, I offer reasons that I hope she will find persuasive. They need not be the same reasons. They need not even be reasons that I myself accept! Ad hoc reasons would satisfy Rawls' stricture. Contrary to his assumption, the reasons don't have to be reasons for all comers.

But is it true—and this, finally, is the fundamental point—is it true that offering to Wendy reasons for my political views which I know or learn she doesn't accept, and which, accordingly, I cannot reasonably expect her to accept, is to violate her freedom and equality? And is it true that to vote, and otherwise act politically, on the basis of reasons which I do not expect all those affected to accept, is to violate their freedom and equality?

A distinction here is important. What's wrong with explaining to Wendy my religious reasons for thinking that involuntary avoidable impoverishment is a violation of rights, even though I don't expect her to accept those reasons? How does doing that violate her freedom and dignity? In no way whatsoever, so far as I can see. The 'silencing' component in Rawls' stricture—if that's the right interpretation—is just out of place. At most what he ought to say, as, so we have seen, perhaps he means to say, is that I should always have *additional* reasons available—reasons that I reasonably expect Wendy to accept.

But even this I fail to see. In our constitutional democracies we try to persuade each other on political issues, usually on an ad hoc basis: Offering to Republicans reasons that we think might appeal to them, if we can find such; offering to Democrats reasons that we think might appeal to them, if we can find such; offering to Christians reasons that we think might appeal to them, if we can find such; offering to America-firsters reasons that we think might appeal to them, if we can find such; and so forth. Rarely do we succeed in reaching consensus even among reasonable people of all these different stripes; but we try. Then, finally, we vote. Are we, in voting under these circumstances, all violating somebody's freedom and equality? On certain understandings of freedom and equality we probably are; "freedom" and "equality" are extraordinarily elastic terms. But it cannot be the case that we are violating those concepts of freedom and equality which are ingredients in the political culture of constitutional democracies, since it is characteristic of all constitutional democracies to take votes and act on the will of the majority.

A final point: In our society, the independent-basis principle of liberalism engenders a paradox. It's my own conviction that, when it comes to the political issue of poverty, I ought to act and vote on the basis of my religious convictions—that conviction being itself a religious conviction on my part. Should someone try to stop me from voting, and acting politically, on the basis of my religious convictions, that would violate the free exercise of my religion. Accordingly, if honoring the freedom and equality of citizens did require adherence to the independent-basis principle, then honoring the freedom and equality of citizens would also require non-adherence. Let it be added that I am not unique in my refusal on religious grounds to divide my life into secular and religious components.

In summary, the Rawlsian defense of the independent-basis principle of liberalism fares no better than the Lockean defense. Yet these, though not the only defenses of the principle, seem to me the best.

§7. It's worth briefly taking note of the fact that the other half of the neutrality postulate of liberalism, namely, the separation principle, also has consequences in our society which violate the freedom and equality of citizens. The state, in all contemporary constitutional democracies, funds a large part of the educational system. One can imagine a constitutional democracy in which that is not the case; in the contemporary world, however, it always is the case. The separation principle specifies, then, that such state-funding must not in any significant way aid any religion—nor any comprehensive non-religions perspective.

Now suppose there are parents present in society for whom it is a matter of religious conviction that their children receive a religiously integrated education. There are in fact such parents present in contemporary American society. Were the state to fund an educational program in accord with the religious convictions of those parents, it would, obviously, be aiding their religion, and thereby violating the separation principle. But if the state funds other schools but refuses to fund schools satisfactory to those parents, then those parents, in a perfectly obvious way, are discriminated against. If those parents are forbidden by law to establish schools which teach in accord with their convictions, then the discrimination is embodied in law. If they are not legally forbidden to establish such schools, then the discrimination is located in the economics of the matter. Were those parents to establish schools which teach in accord with their convictions, they would have to pay for those schools out of their own pockets while yet contributing to the general tax fund for schools. Obviously the free exercise of their religion is thereby infringed on—in a way in which that of others is not.

There's a common pattern to the liberal's impression that his independent-basis principle and his separation principle both deal fairly with religion—to his impression that the neutrality postulate honors the freedom and equality of the religious members of society as much as it does the non-religious members. That common pattern is this: The liberal assumes that requiring religious persons to debate and act politically for reasons other than religions reasons is not in violation of their *religious* convictions; likewise he assumes that an educational program which makes no reference to religion is not in violation of any parent's *religious* convictions. He assumes, in other words, that though religious people may not be in the *habit of* dividing their life into a religious component and a non-religious component, and though some might be *unhappy* doing so, nonetheless, their doing so would not be in violation of anybody's religion. But he's wrong about this. It's when we bring into the picture persons for whom it is a matter of religious conviction that they ought to strive for a religiously integrated existence—it's then, especially, though not only then, that the unfairness of liberalism to religion comes to light.

§8. My argument up to this point has been entirely at the level of ethical, political, and epistemological theory. Let me now be so bold as to engage in some social analysis. I understand Stephen Carter, in his recent book, *The Culture of Disbelief,*[10] to be pointing to a prominent feature of our actual civil and political society here in the United States. What he observes is that there is a strong impulse in very many Americans to disapprove of bringing religious conviction into discussions which take place in the public space—and it makes no difference whether those discussions be on political issues or others. "We are," says Carter, "one of the most religious nations on earth, in the sense that we have a deeply religious citizenry; but we are also perhaps the most zealous in guarding our public institutions against explicit religious influences. One result is that we often ask our citizens to split their public and private selves, telling them in effect that it is fine to be religious in private, but there is something askew when those private beliefs become the basis for public action" (8). This seems to me indubitably correct. There has been, in our country, a widespread embrace of the independent-basis thesis of liberalism—and more generally, of its neutrality postulate. There has been a silencing of religion in the public square.

What has rushed in to fill the void is not noble discussions about principles of justice which have been extracted in Rawlsian fashion from the consensus populi. For nobody *cares about* principles of justice thus obtained. What has rushed in to fill the void is mainly considerations of economic self-interest, of privatism, and of nationalism. These today dominate our discourse in the public square. For people do genuinely care about their own economic well-being, they do genuinely care about protecting their private lives, and many of them do genuinely care about their nation.

As a consequence, public discussion of political issues has been profoundly debased—assuming, as I do, that discussion of political issues purely in the flat secular terms of economic self-interest, of privatism, and of nationalism, is a debased discussion. Let alone not mentioning God, none of these even so much as alludes to anything at all transcendent. Indeed, of the three, only nationalism even so much as extends beyond the self; and it extends beyond egocentric self-ism only by introducing group self-ism into the picture. I do not regard the embrace of the neutrality postulate as the only cause of the debasement of public dialogue. The spread of capitalism, intensively and extensively, also bears responsibility,[11] as do the contemporary media. But apart from religion, what people in contemporary society care most deeply about is their pocketbooks, their privacy, and their nation. If the reigning ethos says that it is wrong to introduce religion into the public space, then it is these other concerns that people will appeal to. What else? In all the great religions of the world there are strands of conviction which tell us that pocketbook, privacy, and nation are not of first importance. In all of them there are strands of conviction which tell that, in the name of God, we must honor the other— even when that other is not only other than ourselves but other than a member of our nation. Silence religion, and the debasement represented by private and group egoism will follow.

Adherence to the neutrality postulate has a debasing effect on religion as well. What we are witnessing today on the American scene, as the utterly natural and predictable response of religious people to the silencing of religion in the public space, is outbursts of resentment. We had better expect such outbursts to continue. Many religious people feel profoundly that their voice is not being heard—as of course it isn't. But an outburst of resentment is very different from a reasoned and civil discussion. Yet how are religious communities supposed to develop a reasoned voice on political matters when the neutrality postulate is in full sway? In their churches and synagogues and mosques? Does anybody seriously believe that churches, synagogues, and mosques can possibly engage in reflection of a depth which could compete with the sustained reflection that takes place in the public academies of the land? The only thing that can compete with the academy is the academy. But when it comes to the academy, we must note that though no one raises an eyebrow when those who are committed to comprehensive utilitarianism use the resources of the public academy to work out the political implications of their view, a similar use of the resources of the public academy by Christians, Jews, or Muslims would raise an uproar. This is the effect of the liberal silencing of religion in the public square, coupled with the tag-end of the Enlightenment view, that while religion is irrational, utilitarianism and such like, though they may be mistaken, are eminently rational, and thus appropriate for the public academy. I think we must expect, in a society committed to the neutrality postulate, that religious people, *qua* religious, will by and large either have little to say on matters of politics, or little to say beyond simplistic sentiments expressed in tones of resentment. The system disadvantages serious religious reflection on political issues.

I think there's reason to believe that the fate of liberalism itself is threatened in a society shaped by the neutrality postulate of liberalism. I suggested that at the very heart of liberalism is the conviction that the normal adult members of society are free and equal. That conviction emerged slowly, haltingly, and in complicated ways, out of the seedbed of Christianity in the West. Now suppose one shares—as probably most people nowadays do—the epistemological despair which underlies Rawls' project. I mean, the despair of ever grounding that conviction in the deliverances of our generic human nature. If one rejects appeal to religion and anything similar, it is hard indeed to see what other source there could be for that conviction than the consensus populi. We Americans—or as Richard Rorty candidly and bluntly puts it, we liberal bourgeois democrats—we, as it so happens, just do believe that we are free and equal. Not that everybody is. Just that *we* are.

I think it is more than dubious that we all do believe this; Rawls seems to me to have an extraordinarily idealized picture of the political culture of modern constitutional democracies. But let that pass on this occasion; and notice that the consensus populi is a most peculiar source. Throughout my discussion I have been assuming that the consensus populi, if there is one, and if it is rich and thick enough, does qualify as the independent source that the liberal needs; and indeed it does, in a way. But it's a very odd source in the following way: If someone asks, *why* should I believe that all normal adult members of my society are free and equal, *what reason* is there for believing it, no answer is forthcoming. The liberal can observe that, as it just so happens, we all do believe this. But this *We-ism* is not an answer to the *why believe* question. When someone begins to wonder whether we are all free and equal— perhaps the hypocrisy of our own society on the issue raises the question in his mind, perhaps critical comments by someone from an alternative society raises the question, perhaps his own internal reflections do so—when someone begins to wonder, the observation, *"But we all do happen so to believe,"* is no answer.

Rorty's response is that no answer is needed. *We-ism* is sufficient. We all do happen to believe that the normal adult members of our society are free and equal; we like it this way; and that's the entirely satisfactory end of the matter. Rawls' strategy allows him more room to maneuver. It's open to him to say that if a person wants a reason, the place to look is to his or her own particular religion or comprehensive perspective. But if I'm right in my argument above, that the commitment of our society to the neutrality postulate has an inhibiting effect on serious reflection by religious communities on political issues, then it will be unlikely that the various religious communities will in fact develop their reasons with any depth and solidity. Liberalism saws off the branch on which it sits.

§9. Recently a group of Christians, organized as the Christian Environment Council, appeared in Washington D.C. Speaking to the national media and the congressional leadership, they spoke up in support of endangered species, declaring themselves opposed to "any Congressional action that would weaken, hamper, reduce or end the protection, recovery, and preservation of God's creatures, including their habitats, especially as accomplished under the Endangered Species Act." The heart of the reason they offered was that "according to the Scriptures, the earth is the Lord's and all that dwells within it (Psalm 24:1), and the Lord shows concern for every creature (Matthew 6:26)."

Liberalism, with its neutrality postulate, insists that such appeals as this must be silenced—or that those who present the appeal always have an additional, consensus populi, reason at the ready. To those organized as the Christian Environment Council it says: speak thus to each other in your own churches, if you wish; but when you come to Washington, speak, or be ready to speak, on an independent basis. I regard that silencing-injunction as without basis, and unfair to religion.[12] Besides which, I care about species; and I firmly believe that, over the long haul, endangered species are safer in the hands of those who ground their appeals in religion than in the hands of those who ground them in privatism, nationalism, or economism.

Instead of forbidding the Christian Environment Council to offer its religious reasons in the public space, why not invite them to continue saying with civility what they do believe for such reasons as they do in fact have for their beliefs—which in this case are religious reasons? Why not invite others to do the same? And why not invite and urge all of them then to listen to each other, genuinely to listen, changing their minds as they feel the force of the testimony and argumentation of others, in this way slowly coming to so much agreement as is necessary for the task at hand? In the case just mentioned, that will be a distinct service to the species endangered. And it will recognize, in the other human being, not only the worth of her humanity, and the worth of her membership in one's own people, but the worth of her convictional particularity. Why not let people say what they want, but insist that they say it with civility? Why not concern ourselves with the *virtues* of the conduct of the debate rather than with the *content* of the positions staked out in the debate? Why not let people act for whatever reasons they wish, provided their actions fall within the boundaries of the constitution?[13]

The agreement arrived at need not be agreement based on principles rich enough to settle *all substantial political issues whatsoever.* Sufficient if it be agreement *on the matter at hand.* It need not be agreement based on *principles shared by all alike.* Sufficient if all, each *on his or her own principles,* come to agreement on the matter at hand. It need not be agreement *for all time.* Sufficient if it be agreement for *today and tomorrow.* It need not be agreement that one can reasonably expect of *all human beings whatsoever.* Sufficient if it be agreement among *us.* It need not even be agreement among *each and every one* of us. Sufficient if it be the fairly-gained and fairly-executed agreement *of the majority* of us.

NOTES

1. I have done same of this intra-community argumentation in my essay, "Has the Cloak Become a Cage? Charity, Justice, and Economic Activity" in Robert Wuthnow, ed., *Rethinking Materialism: Perspectives on the Spiritual Dimension of Economic Behavior* (Grand Rapids, Mich.: Eerdmans Publishing Co., 1995), 145–68.
2. Jean Cohen and Andrew Arato, *Civil Society and Political Theory* (Cambridge, Mass.: MIT Press, 1992), 9.
3. An exception to this generalization is the recent *Virginia v. Rosenberger* decision. It remains to be seen whether this represents a change of direction.
4. See, for example, Chapter 1 of Cohen and Arato, *Civil Society and Political Theory,* which talks as if there were no churches in Eastern Europe at the time of the overthrow of communism!
5. A recent discussion of this point is David Richards, "Public Reason and Abolitionist Dissent," *Chicago-Kent Law Review* 69 (1994): 787–842. The irony, of course, is that a doctrine born out of religion should be turned by Rawls and cohorts against that which gave it birth!

6. The matters which follow are discussed much more amply in my recent *John Locke and the Ethics of Belief* (Cambridge: Cambridge University Press, 1996).
7. New York: Columbia University Press, 1993.
8. Cf. Ibid., 217: "when may citizens by their vote properly exercise their coercive political power over one another when fundamental questions are at stake? Or in the light of what principles and ideals must we exercise that power if our doing so is to be justifiable to others as free and equal? To this question political liberalism replies: our exercise of political power is proper and hence justifiable only when it is exercised in accordance with a constitution the essentials of which all citizens may reasonably be expected to endorse in the light of principles and ideals acceptable to them as reasonable and rational. This is the liberal principle of legitimacy. And since the exercise of political power itself must be legitimate, the ideal of citizenship imposes a moral, not a legal, duty—the duty of civility—to be able to explain to one another on those fundamental questions how the principles and policies they advocate and vote for can be supported by the political values of public reason."
9. *Cf.,*Ibid., "What public reason asks is that citizens *be able to explain* their vote to one another in terms of a reasonable balance of public political values" (243; italics added).
10. New York: Basic Books, 1993.
11. See my argument in "The Schools We Deserve," in Stanley Hauerwas and John H. Westerhoff, eds., *Schooling Christians* (Grand Rapids, Mich.: Eerdmans Publishing Co., 1992), 3–28.
12. It appears that Rawls agrees on this specific point, on the ground that "the status of the natural world and our proper relation to it is not a constitutional essential or a basic question of justice" (*Political Liberalism,* 246).
13. And what justifies the constitution—that all citizens accept it on the basis of their common human reason? Hardly. At the American constitutional convention, votes were taken! It's not likely that, if votes were taken today among the populace as a whole, our present Constitution would result. But so far, most of us agree that overturning it would be the greater evil.

Discussion Questions

1. How does Professor Wolterstorff distinguish the two strands of liberalism? Name and define each strand. Name and define the two components of the second strand. Do you think that Professor Wolterstorff has accurately defined liberalism? Explain and defend you answer.

2. Why does Professor Wolterstorff believe that Locke's version of the independent-basis position is different from Rawls' and why would religious people more comfortable with the former than with the latter?

3. Present and explain Professor Wolterstorff's critique of Rawls's version of the independent-basis position. Do you think his critique is adequate? Why or why not? Do you think that you could amend Rawls's position in a way that would be sensitive to Wolterstorff's concerns and yet remain "liberal"? Why or why not? Explain and defend your answer.

4. Why does Professor Wolterstorff believe that the neutrality position has bad consequences? Do you think that Wolterstorff is correct about these bad consequences, including the apparent unfairness to religious believers who strive for an integrated existence?

5. What does Professor Wolterstorff mean when he claims that PL has had a debasing effect on American culture? Do you agree or disagree with his assessment?

6. How do you think Rawls or Professor Audi (Chapter 8) would respond to Wolterstorff's question?: "Why not let people act for whatever reasons they wish, provided their actions fall within the boundaries of the constitution?"

You can locate InfoTrac-College Education articles about this chapter by accessing the InfoTrac-College Edition website (http://www.infotrac-college.com/wadsworth/). Using the InfoTrac-College Edition subject guide, enter the search terms relevant to this chapter, and then read abstracts for relevant articles.

Part II

Life and Death Issues

General Introduction to Part II

When, if ever, is it right to take one's own or another human being's life? Are there some human beings who are not human *persons*? Is experimentation on prenatal human beings morally justified? Is it right to clone a human being? These and other questions will be discussed by the authors in this section, when they confront the issues of abortion (Section A), euthanasia and physician-assisted suicide (Section B), creating and experimenting with life at the margins (Section C), and the death penalty (Section D).

The disputants in all these issues seem to presuppose a primary moral judgment: it is wrong to kill human persons without justification. Where they disagree is over two issues: (1) what constitutes circumstances which justify the killing of a human person; and (2) what is a human person. For instance, concerning (1), some ethicists argue that the death penalty is just retribution for the killing of another human person while others argue that killing persons in war is justified in order to defend one's nation against a non-provoked aggressor. On the issue of abortion, some pro-choice ethicists are willing to grant pro-lifers (those who oppose abortion) that the fetus is a human person, but they nevertheless argue that a pregnant woman still has a right to terminate her pregnancy, since the fetus has no right to use the pregnant woman's body against her will if she did not consent to the pregnancy, just as one has no claim upon a neighbor's kidney even if one needs it in order to live. Concerning (2), some ethicists argue that abortion and some cases of euthanasia are morally justified because the entity whose death results in either abortion (the fetus) or some cases of euthanasia, though genetically a human being, is not a human *person*. Others argue that both fetal tissue research as well as cloning are justified for precisely the same reason, for there is no person whose rights are being violated.

So, when reading and studying the issues and authors in this section, pay careful attention to the moral judgments on which they apparently agree and the reason (or reasons) why they disagree about the application of those moral judgments.

For Further Reading

Tom L. Beauchamp and James Childress, *Principles of Biomedical Ethics,* 4th ed. (New York: Oxford University Press, 1994).

Edwin R. Dubose, Ron Hamel, and Laurence J. O'Connell, eds., *A Matter of Principles?: Ferment in U.S. Bioethics,* (Valley Forge, PA: Trinity Press International, 1994).

Ronald Dworkin, *Life's Dominion: An Argument About Abortion, Euthanasia, and Freedom* (New York: Alfred A. Knopf, 1993).

Mark Foreman, *Christianity and Bioethics* (Joplin, MO: College Press, 1999).

Stanley Hauerwaus, *Suffering Presence* (Notre Dame, IN: University of Notre Dame Press, 1986).

J. P. Moreland and Scott B. Rae, *Body and Soul: Human Nature and the Crisis in Ethics* (Downers Grove, IL: InterVarsity Press, 2000).

Louis P. Pojman, ed., *Life and Death: A Reader in Moral Problems,* 2nd ed. (Belmont, CA: Wadsworth, 1998).

Louis Pojman, *Life and Death: Grappling with the Moral Dilemmas of Our Time,* 2nd ed. (Belmont, CA: Wadsworth, 1998).

President's Commission for the Study of Ethical Problems in Medicine and Biomedical and Behavioral Research, *Defining Death: Medical, Legal, and Ethical Issues in the Determination of Death* (Washington, DC: GPO, 1983).

Thomas Regan, ed., *Matters of Life and Death: New Introductory Essays in Moral Philosophy,* 3rd ed (New York: McGraw-Hill, 1993).

Scott B. Rae and Paul Cox, *Bioethics* (Grand Rapids, MI: Eerdmans, 1999).

Andrew Varga, *The Main Issues in Bioethics,* rev. ed. (New York: Paulist Press, 1984).

Robert M. Veatch, *Medical Ethics,* The Jones & Bartlett Series in Philosophy (Boston: Jones & Bartlett, 1993).

SECTION A

Abortion

Introduction to Section A

Abortion is probably the most controversial and most often discussed moral issue in North America today. The arguments for and against abortion rights are put forth in the political arena with greater vigor and rhetorical hostility than ever before. However, in comparison to the way the abortion debate is popularly portrayed, it is approached quite differently by philosophers and ethicists. In fact, most of the popular arguments for and against abortion rights one may hear on television and radio talk programs are logically fallacious.

A. Flawed Pro-choice Arguments: One argument often presented goes like this: If abortion is made illegal, then women will once again be harmed by unsafe and illegal abortions performed by back-alley butchers. But there is a serious problem with this argument's reasoning. If we are to accept the contention of *Roe v. Wade's* majority author Justice Harry Blackmun, this argument turns out to be question-begging, for Justice Blackmun argues that if the fetus is a human person then abortion is homicide and cannot be a Constitutional right.[1] In other words, the illegal abortion argument assumes as incorrect without reason the very point, if true, which would invalidate *Roe v. Wade,* namely, that the fetus is a human person. That is to say, only by assuming that the fetus is not a human person does the argument work. For if the fetus is a human person, this pro-choice argument is tantamount to saying that because people die or are harmed while killing other people (i.e., preborn people), the government should make it safe for them to do so. Consequently, only by begging the question as to status of the fetus does this pro-choice argument work. Even Professor Mary Anne Warren, an abortion rights supporter, clearly sees that the abortion rights defender cannot use this argument for support unless it is first shown that the fetus is not a human person. Warren writes that "the fact that restricting access to abortion has tragic side effects does not, in itself, show that the restrictions are unjustified, since murder is wrong regardless of the consequences of prohibiting it."[2]

This same critique can be applied to most other popular abortion rights arguments, such as those which appeal to the upsetting of the pregnant woman's career, the difficulty of childrearing, or the mother's poverty. In not one of these cases do we believe that the child's execution is justified after its birth. Thus, if we are to take Justice Blackmun seriously (as most supporters of abortion rights do), it is the status of the fetus which is the issue that must be addressed, not these other issues.

The argument from fetal viability is another popular argument that is used to defend abortion rights in the first two trimesters of pregnancy. Viability is the time at which the fetus can live outside its mother's womb (with or without the assistance of artificial life support). Some abortion-rights advocates have argued that since the fetus in the first two trimesters cannot survive independent of its mother, it is not a complete independent human life and hence not a human person. In arguing for increased state interest in fetal life after viability, Justice Blackmun makes use of the viability criterion in his dissenting opinion in *Webster v. Reproductive Health Services* (1989):

> The viability line reflects the biological facts and truths of fetal development; it marks the threshold moment prior to which a fetus cannot survive separate from the woman and cannot reasonably and objectively be regarded as a subject of rights or interests distinct from, or paramount to, those of the pregnant woman. At the same time, the viability standard takes account of the undeniable fact that as the fetus evolves into its postnatal form, and as it loses its dependence on the uterine environment, the State's interest in the fetus' potential human life, and in fostering a regard for human life in general, become compelling.[3]

Although some people employ this argument to defend fetal personhood at viability rather than merely a state's interest in potential human life as Blackmun argues, it nevertheless is a circular argument. Blackmun is claiming that the state has no interest in protecting fetal life until that life is able to live outside the womb. But why is this correct? Because, we are told, prior to being able to live outside the womb, the fetus has no interests or rights. But this is clearly a case of circular reasoning, for Blackmun is assuming (that the fetus has no interests or rights prior to viability) what he is trying to prove (that the fetus has no interests or rights prior to viability). This argument is no better than the one provided by the zealous Boston Celtic fan who argues that the Celtics are the best team because no team is better (which, of course, is the same as being the best team).[4]

B. Flawed Pro-life Arguments. In response to the pro-choice argument that abortion is justified because there are too many unwanted children, some pro-life advocates often cite statistics that they believe support the fact that there are a large number of childless couples wanting to adopt children.[5] There are several problems with this pro-life response. First, why should this point even matter? If there were no such couples, would abortion ipso facto become morally correct? If the unborn have an inherent right to life, a principle that is the foundation of the pro-life position, why should the absence or presence of a couple who wants a child make a difference? Second, a sophisticated pro-choice advocate would remain unconvinced, since, according to his position, a woman has a right to an abortion but has no obligation to make sure other people have the opportunity to adopt her child. Why should the pro-choice advocate accept pro-life assumptions? And third, it follows from these two points that the pro-life advocate's appeal to adoption puts him in the odd position of appearing to support the assumption of many pro-choice advocates that only if the fetus is wanted does it have value.

Another popular pro-life argument can be put this way: Since the unborn is a human being from the moment of conception, and since it is morally wrong in almost all circumstances to kill human beings, therefore, abortion is morally wrong in almost all circumstances. Although the pro-life advocate is not incorrect in asserting that the unborn is a human being in the genetic sense from the moment of conception,[6] it is not clear from the biological facts alone, without philosophical reflection, that the unborn is a human person and possesses the rights which are entailed by that status. In this section, authors Mary Anne Warren (Chapter 12) and Stephen D. Schwarz (Chapter 13) wrestle with this issue.

ABORTION AND THE LAW

The legal nature of the debate is often misunderstood. Arguing that the right to abortion is as constitutionally fundamental as the freedom religion or speech, Justice Blackmun, in *Roe v. Wade* (1973), divided pregnancy into trimesters. Aside from normal procedural guidelines to insure protection for the pregnant woman (e.g., an abortion must be safely performed by a licensed physician), Blackmun ruled that a state has no right to restrict abortion in the first 6 months of pregnancy (first 2 trimesters). Since, according to Blackmun, the state has a legitimate interest in pre-natal life, in the last trimester (after the fetus is viable) the state has a right though no obligation to restrict abortions to only those cases in which the mother's life or health is in danger. But this health exception for third trimester abortions, some have argued, is so broad in principle that *Roe* turns out to be a much more permissive decision than most people realize. In a decision which the Court considers a companion to *Roe,* it ruled that "health" must be taken in its broadest possible context, defined "in light of all factors—physical, emotional, psychological, familial, and the woman's age—relevant to the well being of the patient. All these factors relate to health."[7] This is why the U.S. Senate Judiciary Committee concluded in 1983 that "no significant legal barriers of any kind whatsoever exist today in the United States for a woman to obtain an abortion for any reason during any stage of her pregnancy."[8]

In *Webster v. Reproductive Health Services* (1989),[9] the Court reversed a lower-court decision and upheld a Missouri statute that contains several provisions, one of which forbids physicians to perform abortions after the fetus is 20 weeks old, except when the pregnant woman's life is in imminent danger. The statute requires a physician, if he believes that his pregnant patient seeking an abortion may be 20 weeks pregnant, to have her undergo a test in order to determine the fetus' gestational age. *Webster* modified *Roe* in at least two significant ways. First, it rejected *Roe's* trimester breakdown of pregnancy. Chief Justice William Rehnquist, who wrote the majority opinion in the 5 to 4 decision, argued that the trimester breakdown is not found in the Constitution and that the Court sees no reason why a state's interest in protecting prenatal life should arrive at the point of viability. Second, the Court in *Webster* ruled as constitutional the portion of the Missouri statute that prohibited the use of government funds for nontherapeutic abortions as well as the use of government employees to perform, and counsel women who seek to undergo such abortions. Although chipping away at the foundation of *Roe*, *Webster* did not overturn it.

In *Planned Parenthood v. Casey* (1992) the Supreme Court was asked to consider the constitutionality of five provisions of the Pennsylvania Abortion Control Act of 1982. This act requires that (1) "a woman seeking an abortion give her informed consent prior to the procedure, and specifies that she be provided with certain information at least 24 hours before the abortion is performed." (2) The act "mandates the informed consent of one parent for a minor to obtain an abortion, but provides a judicial bypass procedure." (3) It also "commands that, unless certain exceptions apply, a married woman seeking an abortion must sign a statement indicating that she has notified her husband." (4) However, the act allows for "a 'medical emergency' that will excuse compliance with forgoing requirements." (5) The act also imposes "certain reporting requirements on facilities providing abortion services."[10]

The Court upheld as constitutional four of the five provisions, rejecting the third one based on what it calls the *undue burden* standard. This is a departure from *Roe*. *Roe* affirms abortion as a fundamental constitutional right and thus makes any possible restrictions subject to strict scrutiny. In other words, possible restrictions in order to be valid must be essential to meeting a compelling state interest. For example, laws that forbid yelling "fire" in a crowded theater pass strict scrutiny when subject to the fundamental right of freedom of expression. But the *Casey* court, by subscribing to the undue burden standard, does not support the right to abortion as fundamental. Therefore, the states may restrict abortion by passing laws that may not withstand strict scrutiny but nevertheless do not result in an undue burden for the pregnant woman.

The *Casey* court upheld *Roe* as a precedent, despite the fact that it rejected *Roe*'s trimester framework, that a woman has a fundamental right to abortion, and *Roe*'s requirement that restrictions be subject to strict scrutiny. Perhaps this is why Chief Justice Rehnquist made the comment in his dissenting opinion in *Casey*: "*Roe* continues to exist, but only in the way a storefront on a western movie set exists: a mere facade to give the illusion of reality."[11]

Starting in 1996 then-President Bill Clinton vetoed several bills passed by the U.S. Congress to prohibit what anti-abortion activists call "partial-birth abortion." Also known as D & X (for dilation and extraction) abortion, this procedure is performed in some second-trimester and third-trimester abortions. Using ultrasound, the doctor grips the fetus's legs with forceps. The fetus is then pulled out through the birth canal and delivered with the exception of its head. While the head is in the womb the doctor penetrates the live fetus's skull with scissors, opens the scissors to enlarge the hole, and then inserts a catheter. The fetus's brain is vacuumed out, resulting in the skull's collapse. The doctor then completes the womb's evacuation by removing a dead fetus.

Although none of the congressional bills became law, thirty states, including Nebraska, passed similar laws that prohibited D & X abortions. However, in *Stenberg v. Carhart* (2000),[12] the Supreme Court, in a 5–4 decision, struck down Nebraska's ban on partial-birth abortion, on two grounds. (1) The law lacked an exception for the preservation of the mother's life and health, which *Casey* required of any restrictions on abortion. (2) Nebraska's ban imposed an undue burden on a woman's fundamental right to have an abortion. For the type of abortion performed in 95 percent of the cases between the 12th and 20th weeks of pregnancy, D & E abortion (dilation and evacuation), is similar to D & X abortion. So, the Court reasoned, if a ban on D& X abortions is legally permissible, then so is a ban on D & E abortions. But that would imperil the right to abortion. Hence Nebraska's ban imposes an undue burden on the pregnant woman, and thus violates the standard laid down in *Casey*. Nevertheless, it remains to be seen whether Congress and/or state legislatures will try to enact new laws that include both a health exception as well as a more narrow definition of D & X abortion.

Included in this text are abridged versions of the Supreme Court's two most important decisions on abortion rights, *Roe v. Wade* (Chapter 10) and *Casey v. Planned Parenthood* (Chapter 11). The former contains Justice Blackmun's majority opinion as well as Justice William Rehnquist's dissent while the latter contains the plurality opinion of Justices Sandra Day O'Connor, Anthony Kennedy, and David Souter as well as the dissenting opinion of Justice Antonin Scalia.

THE MORALITY OF ABORTION

Philosophers and ethicists have argued for and against abortion rights in primarily two ways: (1) from the moral status of the fetus, or (2) from the bodily rights of the pregnant woman.

A. Arguments from the Moral Status of the Fetus. Scientifically there is no doubt that the beginning of individual human life begins at conception and does not end until natural death. At the moment of conception, when sperm and ovum cease to exist as individual entities, a new being with its own genetic code comes into existence. No new genetic information is added to the individual from this moment until natural death. All that is needed for its development is food, water, air, and an environment conducive to its survival.

These facts are not denied by those who believe that abortion is morally justified at some point during pregnancy. What they argue is that the unborn entity, though a human being from conception, is not a person until some decisive moment after conception. Some argue that personhood does not arrive until brain waves are detected (40 to 43 days) or some other decisive moment (e.g., sentience, viability, self-awareness) either during or after pregnancy. Others, such as Warren (Chapter 12), define a person as a being who can do certain things, such as have consciousness, solve complex problems, and communicate, which would put the arrival of personhood quite possibly after birth. Traditional pro-lifers, such as Schwarz (Chapter 13), respond by maintaining that there are good reasons to continue to accept and no good reason to deny that human personhood begins at conception.

B. Arguments from Bodily Rights of the Pregnant Woman. Some abortion rights supporters, such as Judith Jarvis Thomson (Chapter 14), disagree that the abortion debate hinges on the moral status of the fetus. They argue that even if the unborn is a human person from conception or sometime early on in pregnancy, abortion is still morally justified. Thomson argues that the fetus's physical dependence on the pregnancy woman's body entails a conflict of rights if the pregnant woman did not consent to the pregnancy. Consequently, the fetus, regardless of whether it is fully a human person, cannot use another's body without her consent. Thus, a pregnant woman's removal of the fetus by abortion, though it will result in its death, is no more immoral than an adult person's refusal to donate her kidney, though this refusal may result in the death of the person who needs the kidney. In response to Thomson's argument as is an essay by Francis J. Beckwith (Chapter 15).

Keywords: abortion, fetus, embryo, women's rights, pro-life, pro-choice, *Roe v. Wade, Planned Parenthood v. Casey,* reproductive rights, personhood, abortion rights, anti-abortion, pro-abortion, *Stenberg v. Carhart*

NOTES

1. Blackmun writes: "The appellee and certain amici argue that the fetus is a 'person' within the language and meaning of the Fourteenth Amendment. In support of this, they outline at length and in detail the well-known facts of fetal development. If this suggestion of personhood is established, the appellant's case, of course, collapses, for the fetus' right to life would then be guaranteed specifically by the Amendment." (*Roe v. Wade* 410 U.S. 113, 157–58 [1973]).

2. Mary Anne Warren, "On the Moral and Legal Status of Abortion," in *The Moral Problem of Abortion,* 2nd ed., ed. Joel Feinberg (Belmont, CA: Wadsworth, 1984), 103.

3. *Webster v. Reproductive Health Services* U.S. 490 (1989), as found in *The United States Law Week* 57, no. 50 (27 July 1989): 5040.

4. Other flaws in the viability argument have been pointed out elsewhere. See, for example, Francis J. Beckwith, *Politically Correct Death: Answering the Arguments for Abortion Rights* (Grand Rapids, MI: Baker, 1993), 99–101; Stephen D. Schwarz, *The Moral Question of Abortion* (Chicago: Loyola University Press, 1990), 44–47; and Andrew Varga, *The Main Issues in Bioethics,* rev. ed. (New York: Paulist Press, 1984), 62–63.

5. See, for example, Dr. and Mrs. J. C. Willke, *Abortion: Questions and Answers,* rev. ed. (Cincinnati: Hayes Publishing, 1988), 305–313.

6. See Andre E. Hellegers, "Fetal Development," in *Biomedical Ethics,* eds. Thomas A. Mappes and Jane S. Zembaty (New York: McGraw-Hill, 1981), 405–409; and Beckwith, *Politically Correct Death,* 41–51.

7. *Doe v. Bolton* 410 U.S. 179, 192 (1973).

8. Report, Committee on the Judiciary, U.S. Senate, on Senate Resolution 3, 98th Congress, 98-149, 7 June 1983, 6.

9. *Webster v. Reproductive Health Services* U.S. 490 (1989).

10. *Planned Parenthood v. Casey*, nos. 91-744 and 91-902 (1992): I (Syllabus).
11. *Ibid.*, 12.
12. *Stenberg v. Carhart*, no. 99-830 (2000).

For Further Reading

Francis J. Beckwith, *Abortion and the Sanctity of Human Life* (Joplin, MO: College Press, 2000).

———, "Abortion, Personhood, and Bioethics: A Philosophical Reflection," *The Southern Baptist Journal of Theology* 6 (spring 2000).

———, *Politically Correct Death: Answering the Arguments for Abortion Rights* (Grand Rapids: Baker, 1993).

David Boonin-Vail, "Death Comes for the Violinist." *Social Theory and Practice* 23.3 (fall 1997).

Baruch Brody, *Abortion and the Sanctity of Human Life: A Philosophical View* (Cambridge, MA: M.I.T. Press, 1975).

Daniel Callahan, *Abortion: Law, Choice, and Morality* (New York: Macmillan, 1975).

Doris Gordon, "Abortion and Rights: Applying Libertarian Principles Correctly," *Studies in Prolife Feminism* 1.2 (spring 1995).

F. M. Kamm, *Creation and Abortion: A Study in Moral and Legal Philosophy* (New York: Oxford University Press, 1992).

Dennis J. Horan, Edward R. Grant, and Paige C. Cunningham, eds., *Abortion and the Constitution: Reversing* Roe v. Wade *Through the Courts* (Washington, DC: Georgetown University Press, 1987).

Patrick Lee, *Abortion and Unborn Human Life* (Washington, DC: The Catholic University of America Press, 1996).

Don Marquis, "Abortion," *The Encyclopedia of Philosophy Supplement,* ed. Donald M. Borchert (New York: Simon & Schuster Macmillan, 1996).

———. "Why Abortion Is Immoral," *The Journal of Philosophy* 86 (1989).

P. McInerny, "Does a Fetus Already Have a Future-Like-Ours?" *The Journal of Philosophy* 87 (1990).

A. Norcross, "Killing, Abortion, and Contraception: A Reply to Marquis" *The Journal of Philosophy* 87 (1990).

Louis P. Pojman and Francis J. Beckwith, eds., *The Abortion Controversy 25 Years After Roe v. Wade: A Reader,* 2nd ed. (Belmont, CA: Wadsworth, 1998).

Stephen D. Schwarz, *The Moral Question of Abortion* (Chicago: Loyola University Press, 1990).

Michael Tooley, *Abortion and Infanticide* (Oxford: Clarendon, 1983).

Abortion and the Law

Roe v. Wade (1973)*   10

U.S. SUPREME COURT

A resident of Texas, Jane Roe (a pseudonym for Norma McCorvey), claimed to have become pregnant after being gang raped, which later was found to be a false charge. The law in Texas, which had been essentially unchanged since 1856, stated that a woman can have an abortion only if it is necessary to save her life. Because her pregnancy was not life-threatening, Roe had to sue the state of Texas. The unmarried Roe, in 1970, filed a class action suit in federal court in Dallas. The court ruled that the Texas statute was overbroad, constitutionally vague, and infringed upon a woman's right to reproductive freedom. The case was appealed by the state of Texas to the U.S. Supreme Court. On January 22, 1973, the Court, in agreement with the federal court's opinion, ruled in *Roe v. Wade* that the Texas law was unconstitutional and that not only must all the states including Texas permit abortions in cases of rape but in all cases.

 The following are excerpts from two opinions in *Roe*. The first is the Court's majority opinion, written by Justice Harry Blackmun. The second is a dissenting opinion, written by Justice William Rehnquist, who is presently the Court's Chief Justice.

*Footnotes omitted and most citations removed and others edited.

MR. JUSTICE BLACKMUN DELIVERED the opinion of the Court . . .

The principal thrust of appellant's attack on the Texas statutes is that they improperly invade a right, said to be possessed by the pregnant woman, to choose to terminate her pregnancy. Appellant would discover this right in the concept of personal "liberty" embodied in the Fourteenth Amendment's Due Process Clause; or in personal, marital, familial, and sexual privacy said to be protected by the Bill of Rights or its penumbras, see *Griswold v. Connecticut*, (1965); *Eisenstadt v. Baird*, (1972); (White, J., concurring in result); or among those rights reserved to the people by the Ninth Amendment, *Griswold v. Connecticut* (Goldberg, J., concurring). Before addressing this claim, we feel it desirable briefly to survey, in several aspects, the history of abortion, for such insight as that history may afford us, and then to examine the state purposes and interests behind the criminal abortion laws.

It perhaps is not generally appreciated that the restrictive criminal abortion laws in effect in a majority of States today are of relatively recent vintage. Those laws, generally proscribing abortion or its attempt at any time during pregnancy except when necessary to preserve the pregnant woman's life, are not of ancient or even of common-law origin. Instead, they derive from statutory changes effected, for the most part, in the latter half of the 19th century.

ANCIENT ATTITUDES

These are not capable of precise determination. We are told that at the time of the Persian Empire abortifacients were known and that criminal abortions were severely punished. We are also told, however, that abortion was practiced in Greek times as well as in the Roman Era, and that "it was resorted to without scruple." The Ephesian, Soranos, often described as the greatest of the ancient gynecologists, appears to have been generally opposed to Rome's prevailing free abortion practices. He found it necessary to think first of the life of the mother, and he resorted to abortion when, upon this standard, he felt the procedure advisable. Greek and Roman law afforded little protection to the unborn. If abortion was prosecuted in some places, it seems to have been based on a concept of a violation of the father's right to his offspring. Ancient religion did not bar abortion.

THE HIPPOCRATIC OATH

What then of the famous Oath that has stood so long as the ethical guide of the medical profession and that bears the name of the great Greek (460(?)–377(?) B.C.), who has been described as the Father of Medicine, the "wisest and the greatest practitioner of his art," and the "most important and most complete medical personality of antiquity," who dominated the medical schools of his time, and who typified the sum of the medical knowledge of the past? The Oath varies somewhat according to the particular translation, but in any translation the content is clear: "I will give no deadly medicine to anyone if asked, nor suggest any such counsel; and in like manner I will not give to a woman a pessary to produce abortion," or "I will neither give a deadly drug to anybody if asked for it, nor will I make a suggestion to this effect. Similarly, I will not give to a woman an abortive remedy."

Although the Oath is not mentioned in any of the principal briefs in this case or in *Doe v. Bolton*, it represents the apex of the development of strict ethical concepts in medicine, and its influence endures to this day. Why did not the authority of Hippocrates dissuade abortion practice in his time and that of Rome? The late Dr. Edelstein provides us with a theory: The Oath was not uncontested even in Hippocrates' day; only the Pythagorean school of philosophers frowned upon the related act of suicide. Most Greek thinkers, on the other hand, commended abortion, at least prior to viability. See Plato, Republic, V, 461; Aristotle, Politics, VII, 1335b 25. For the Pythagoreans, however, it was a matter of dogma. For them the embryo was animate from the moment of conception, and abortion meant destruction of a living being. The abortion clause of the Oath, therefore, "echoes Pythagorean doctrines," and "[i]n no other stratum of Greek opinion were such views held or proposed in the same spirit of uncompromising austerity."

Dr. Edelstein then concludes that the Oath originated in a group representing only a small segment of Greek opinion and that it certainly was not accepted by all ancient physicians. He points out that medical writings down to Galen (A.D. 130–200) "give evidence of the violation of almost every one of its injunctions." But with the end of antiquity a decided change took place. Resistance against suicide and against abortion became common. The Oath came to be popular. The emerging teachings of Christianity were in agreement with the Pythagorean ethic. The Oath "became the nucleus of all medical ethics" and "was applauded as the embodiment of truth." Thus, suggests Dr. Edelstein, it is "a Pythagorean manifesto and not the expression of an absolute standard of medical conduct."

This, it seems to us, is a satisfactory and acceptable explanation of the Hippocratic Oath's apparent rigidity. It enables us to understand, in historical context, a long-accepted and revered statement of medical ethics.

THE COMMON LAW

It is undisputed that at common law, abortion performed before "quickening"—the first recognizable movement of the fetus in utero, appearing usually from the sixteenth to the eighteenth week of pregnancy—was not an indictable offense. The absence of a common-law crime for pre-quickening abortion appears to have developed from a confluence of earlier philosophical, theological, and civil and canon law concepts of when life begins. These disciplines variously approached the question in terms of the point at which the embryo or fetus became "formed" or recognizably human, or in terms of when a "person" came into being, that is, infused with a "soul" or "animated." A loose consensus evolved in early English law that these events occurred at some point between conception and live birth. This was "mediate animation" although Christian theology and the canon law came to fix the point of animation at 40 days for a male and 80 days for a female, a view that persisted until the 19th century, there was otherwise little agreement about the precise time of formation or animation. There was agreement, however, that prior to this point the fetus was to be regarded as part of the mother, and its destruction, therefore, was not homicide. Due to continued uncertainty about the precise time when animation occurred, to the lack of any empirical basis for the 40–80-day view, and perhaps to Aquinas' definition of movement as one of the first two principles of life, Brackton focused upon quickening as the critical point. The significance of quickening was echoed by later common-law scholars and found its way into the received common law in this country.

Whether abortion of a *quick* fetus was a felony at common law, or even a lesser crime, is still disputed. Brackton, writing early in the 13th century, thought it homicide. But the later and predominant view, following the great common-law scholars, has been that it was, at most, a lesser offense. In a frequently cited passage, Coke took the position that abortion of a woman "quick with childe" is "a great misprision and no murder." Blackstone followed, saying that while abortion after quickening had once been considered manslaughter (though not murder), "modern law" took a less severe view. A recent review of the common-law precedents argues, however, that those precedents contradict Coke and that even post-quickening abortion was never established as a common-law crime. This is of some importance because while most American courts ruled, in holding or dictum, that abortion of an unquickened fetus was not criminal under their received common law, others followed Coke in stating that abortion of a quick fetus was a "misprision," a term they translated to mean "misdemeanor." That their reliance on Coke on this aspect of the law was uncritical and, apparently in all reported cases dictum (due probably to the paucity of common-law prosecutions for post-quickening abortion), makes it now appear doubtful that abortion was ever firmly established as common-law crime even with respect to the destruction of a quick fetus. . . .

THE AMERICAN LAW

In this country, the law in effect in all but a few States until mid-19th century was the pre-existing English common law. Connecticut, the first State to enact abortion legislation, adopted in 1821 that part of Lord Ellenborough's Act that related to a woman "quick with child." The death penalty was not imposed. Abortion before quickening was made a crime in that State only in 1860. In 1828, New York enacted legislation that, in two respects, was to serve as a model for early antiabortion statutes. First, while barring destruction of an unquickened fetus as well as a quick fetus, it made the former only a misdemeanor, but the latter second-degree manslaughter. Second, it incorporated a concept of therapeutic abortion by providing that an abortion was excused if it "shall have been necessary to preserve the life of such mother or shall have been advised by two physicians to be necessary for such purpose." By 1840, when Texas had received the common law, only eight American States had statutes dealing with abortion. It was not until

after the War Between the States that legislation began generally to replace the common law. Most of these initial statutes dealt severely with abortion after quickening but were lenient with it before quickening. Most punished attempts equally with completed abortions. While many statutes included the exception for an abortion thought by one or more physicians to be necessary to save the mother's life, that provision soon disappeared and the typical law required that the procedure actually be necessary for that purpose.

Gradually, in the middle and late 19th century, the quickening distinction disappeared from the statutory law of most States and the degree of the offense and the penalties were increased. By the end of the 1950s, a large majority of the jurisdictions banned abortion, however and whenever performed, unless done to save or preserve the life of the mother. The exceptions, Alabama and the District of Columbia, permitted abortion to preserve the mother's health. Three States permitted abortions that were not "unlawfully" performed or that were not "without lawful justification," leaving interpretation of those standards to the courts. In the past several years, however, a trend toward liberalization of abortion statutes has resulted in adoption, by about one-third of the States, of less stringent laws, most of them patterned after the ALI Model Penal Code, §230.3.

It is thus apparent that at common law, at the time of the adoption of our Constitution, and throughout the major portion of the 19th century, abortion was viewed with less disfavor than under most American statutes currently in effect. Phrasing it another way, a woman enjoyed a substantially broader right to terminate a pregnancy than she does in most States today. At least with respect to the early stage of pregnancy and very possibly without such a limitation, the opportunity to make this choice was present in this country well into the 19th century. Even later the law continued for some time to treat less punitively an abortion procured in early pregnancy.

THE POSITION OF THE AMERICAN MEDICAL ASSOCIATION

The antiabortion mood prevalent in this country in the late 19th century was shared by the medical profession. Indeed, the attitude of the profession may have played a significant role in the enactment of stringent criminal abortion legislation during that period.

An AMA Committee on Criminal Abortion was appointed in May 1857. It presented its report, 12 Trans. of the Am. Med. Assn. 73–78 (1859), to the Twelfth Annual Meeting. That report observed that the Committee had been appointed to investigate criminal abortion "with a view to its general suppression." It deplored abortion and its frequency and it listed three causes of "this general demoralization":

> "The first of these causes is a widespread popular ignorance of the true character of the crime—a belief, even among mothers themselves, that the foetus is not alive till after the period of quickening.
>
> "The second of the agents alluded to is the fact that the profession themselves are frequently supposed careless of foetal life. . . .
>
> "The third reason of the frightful extent of this crime is found in the grave defects of our laws, both common and statute, as regards the independent and actual existence of the child before birth, as a living being. These errors, which are sufficient in most instances to prevent conviction, are based, and only based, upon mistaken and exploded medical dogmas. With strange inconsistency, the law fully acknowledges the foetus in utero and its inherent rights, for civil purposes; while personally and as criminally affected, it fails to recognize it, and to its life as yet denies all protection."

The Committee then offered, and the Association adopted, resolutions protesting "against such unwarrantable destruction of human life," calling upon state legislatures to revise their abortion laws, and requesting the cooperation of state medical societies "in pressing the subject."

In 1871 a long and vivid report was submitted by the Committee on Criminal Abortion. It ended with the observation, "We had to deal with human life. In a matter of less importance we could entertain no compromise. An honest judge on the bench would call things by their proper names. We could do no less." 22 Trans. of the Am. Med. Assn. 258 (1871). It proffered resolutions, adopted by the Association, recommending, among other things, that it "be unlawful and unprofessional for any physician to induce abortion or premature labor, without the concurrent opinion of at least one respectable consulting physician, and then always with a view to the safety of the child—if that be possible," and calling "the attention of the clergy of all denominations to the perverted views of morality entertained by a large class of females—aye, and men also, on this important question."

Except for periodic condemnation of the criminal abortionist, no further formal AMA action took place until 1967. In that year, the Committee on Human Reproduction urged the adoption of a stated policy of opposition to induced abortion, except when there is "documented medical evidence" of a threat to the health or life of the mother, or that the child "may be born with incapacitating physical deformity or mental deficiency," or that a pregnancy "resulting from legally established statutory or forcible rape or incest may constitute a threat to the mental or physical health of the patient," two other physicians "chosen because of their recognized professional competence have examined the patient and have concurred in writing," and the procedure "is performed in a hospital accredited by the Joint Commission on Accreditation of Hospitals." The providing of medical information by physicians to state legislatures in their consideration of legislation regarding therapeutic abortion was "to be considered consistent with the principles of ethics of the

American Medical Association." This recommendation was adopted by the House of Delegates. Proceedings of the AMA House of Delegates 40–51 (June 1967).

In 1970, after the introduction of a variety of proposed resolutions, and of a report from its Board of Trustees, a reference committee noted "polarization of the medical professional on this controversial issue"; division among those who had testified; a difference of opinion among AMA councils and committees; "the remarkable shift in testimony" in six months felt to be influenced "by the rapid changes in state laws and by the judicial decisions which tend to make abortion more freely available" and a feeling "that this trend will continue." On June 25, 1970, the House of Delegates adopted preambles and most of the resolutions proposed by the reference committee. The preambles emphasized "the best interests of the patient," "sound clinical judgment," and "informed patient consent," in contrast to "mere acquiescence to the patient's demand." The resolutions asserted that abortion is a medical procedure that should be performed by a licensed physician in an accredited hospital only after consultation with two other physicians and in conformity with state law, and that no party to the procedure should be required to violate personally held moral principles. Proceedings of the AMA House of Delegates 220 (June 1970). The AMA Judicial Council rendered a complementary opinion.

THE POSITION
OF THE AMERICAN PUBLIC
HEALTH ASSOCIATION

In October, 1970, the Executive Board of the APHA adopted Standards for Abortion Services. These were five in number:

a. Rapid and simple abortion referral must be readily available through state and local public health departments, medical societies, or other nonprofit organizations.

b. An important function of counseling should be to simplify and expedite the provision of abortion services; it should not delay the obtaining of these services.

c. Psychiatric consultation should not be mandatory. As in the case of other specialized medical services, psychiatric consultation should be sought for definite indications and not on a routine basis.

d. A wide range of individuals from appropriately trained, sympathetic volunteers to highly skilled physicians may qualify as abortion counselors.

e. Contraception and/or sterilization should be discussed with each abortion patient." Recommended Standards for Abortion Services, 61 Am. J. Pub. Health 396 (1971).

Among factors pertinent to life and health risks associated with abortion were three that "are recognized as important":

a. the skill of the physician,

b. the environment in which the abortion is performed, and above all

c. the duration of pregnancy, as determined by uterine size and confirmed by menstrual history."

It was said that "a well-equipped hospital" offers more protection "to cope with unforeseen difficulties than an office or clinic without such resources. . . . The factor of gestational age is of overriding importance." Thus, it was recommended that abortions in the second trimester and early abortions in the presence of existing medical complications be performed in hospitals as inpatient procedures. For pregnancies in the first trimester, abortion in the hospital with or without overnight stay "is probably the safest practice." An abortion in an extramural facility, however, is an acceptable alternative "provided arrangements exist in advance to admit patients promptly if unforeseen complications develop." Standards for an abortion facility were listed. It was said that at present abortions should be performed by physicians or osteopaths who are licensed to practice and who have "adequate training." . . .

Three reasons have been advanced to explain historically the enactment of criminal abortion laws in the 19th century and to justify their continued existence.

It has been argued occasionally that these laws were the product of a Victorian social concern to discourage illicit sexual conduct. Texas, however, does not advance this justification in the present case, and it appears that no court or commentator has taken the argument seriously. The appellants and *amici* contend, moreover, that this is not a proper state purpose at all and suggest that, if it were, the Texas statutes are overboard in protecting it since the law fails to distinguish between married and unwed mothers.

A second reason is concerned with abortion as a medical procedure. When most criminal abortion laws were first enacted, the procedure was a hazardous one for the woman. This was particularly true prior to the development of antisepsis. Antiseptic techniques, of course, were based on discoveries by Lister, Pasteur, and others first announced in 1867, but were not generally accepted and employed until about the turn of the century. Abortion mortality was high. Even after 1900, and perhaps until as late as the development of antibiotics in the 1940's standard modern techniques such as dilation and curettage were not nearly so safe as they are today. Thus, it has been argued that a State's real concern in enacting a criminal abortion law was to protect the pregnant woman, that is, to restrain her from submitting to a procedure that placed her life in serious jeopardy.

Modern medical techniques have altered this situation. Appellants and various *amici* refer to medical data indicating that abortion in early pregnancy, that is, prior to the end of the first trimester, although not without its risk, is now relatively safe. Mortality rates for women undergoing early abortions, where the procedure is legal, appear to be as low as or lower than the rates for normal childbirth. Consequently, any interest of the State in protecting the woman from an inherently hazardous procedure, except when it would be equally dangerous for her to forgo it, has largely disappeared. Of course, important state interests in the areas of health and medical standards do remain. The State has a legitimate interest in seeing to it that abortion, like any other medical procedure, is performed under circumstances that insure maximum safety for the patient. This interest obviously extends at least to the performing physician and his staff, to the facilities involved, to the availability of aftercare, and to adequate provision for any complication or emergency that might arise. The prevalence of high mortality rates at illegal "abortion mills" strengthens, rather than weakens, the State's interest in regulating the conditions under which abortions are performed. Moreover, the risk to the woman increases as her pregnancy continues. Thus, the State retains a definite interest in protecting the woman's own health and safety when an abortion is proposed at a late stage of pregnancy.

The third reason is the State's interest—some phrase it in terms of duty—in protecting prenatal life. Some of the argument for this justification rests on the theory that a new human life is present from the moment of conception. The State's interest and general obligation to protect life then extends, it is argued, to prenatal life. Only when the life of the pregnant mother herself is at stake, balanced against the life she carries within her, should the interest of the embryo or fetus not prevail. Logically, of course, a legitimate state interest in this area need not stand or fall on acceptance of the belief that life begins at conception or at some other point prior to live birth. In assessing the State's interest recognition may be given to the less rigid claim that as long as at least *potential* life is involved, the State may assert interests beyond the protection of the pregnant woman alone.

Parties challenging state abortion laws have sharply disputed in some courts the contention that a purpose of these laws, when enacted, was to protect prenatal life. Pointing to the absence of legislative history to support the contention, they claim that most state laws were designed solely to protect the woman. Because medical advances have lessened this concern, at least with respect to abortion in early pregnancy, they argue that with respect to such abortions the laws can no longer be justified by any state interest. There is some scholarly support for this view of original purpose. The few state courts called upon to interpret their laws in the late 19th and early 20th centuries did focus on the State's interest in protecting the woman's health rather than in preserving the embryo and fetus. Proponents of this view point out that in many States, including Texas, by statute or judicial interpretation, the pregnant woman herself could not be prosecuted for self-abortion or for cooperating in an abortion performed upon her by another. They claim that adoption of the "quickening" distinction through received common law and state statutes tacitly recognizes the greater health hazards inherent in late abortion and impliedly repudiates the theory that life begins at conception.

It is with these interests, and the weight to be attached to them, that this case is concerned.

The Constitution does not explicitly mention any right of privacy. In a line of decisions, however, going back perhaps as far as *Union Pacific R. Co. v. Botsford* (1891), the Court has recognized that a right of personal privacy, or a guarantee of certain areas or zones of privacy, does exist under the Constitution. In carrying contexts, the Court or individual Justices have, indeed, found at least the roots of that right in the First Amendment, in the Fourth and Fifth Amendments, in the penumbras of the Bill of Rights, in the Ninth Amendment, or in the concept of liberty guaranteed by the first section of the Fourteenth Amendment. These decisions make it clear that only personal rights that can be deemed "fundamental" or "implicit in the concept of ordered liberty," are included in this guarantee of personal privacy. They also make it clear that the right has some extension to activities relating to marriage, procreation, contraception, family relationships, and child rearing and education.

This right of privacy, whether it be founded in the Fourteenth Amendment's concept of personal liberty and restrictions upon state action, as we feel it is, or, as the District Court determined, in the Ninth Amendment's reservation of rights to the people, is broad enough to encompass a woman's decision whether or not to terminate her pregnancy. The detriment that the State would impose upon the pregnant woman by denying this choice altogether is apparent. Specific and direct harm medically diagnosable even in early pregnancy may be involved. Maternity, or additional offspring, may force upon the woman a distressful life and future. Psychological harm may be imminent. Mental and physical health may be taxed by child care. There is also the distress, for all concerned, associated with the unwanted child, and there is the problem of bringing a child into a family already unable, psychologically and otherwise, to care for it. In other cases, as in this one, the additional difficulties and continuing stigma of unwed motherhood may be involved. All these are factors the woman and her responsible physician necessarily will consider in consultation.

On the basis of elements such as these, appellant and some *amici* argue that the woman's right is absolute and that she is entitled to terminate her pregnancy at whatever time, in whatever way, and for whatever reason she alone chooses. With this we do not agree. Appellant's arguments that Texas either has no valid interest at all in regulating the abortion decision, or no interest strong enough to support any limitation upon the woman's sole determination, are unpersuasive. The Court's decisions recognizing a right of privacy also acknowledge that some state regulation in areas protected by that right is appropriate. As noted above, a State may properly assert important interests in safeguarding health, in maintaining medical standards, and in protecting potential life. At some point in pregnancy, these respective interests become sufficiently compelling to sustain regulation of the factors that govern the abortion decision. The privacy right involved, therefore, cannot be said to be absolute. In fact, it is not clear to us that the claim asserted by some *amici* that one has an unlimited right to do with one's body as one pleases bears a close relationship to the right of privacy previously articulated in the Court's decisions. The Court has refused to recognize an unlimited right of this kind in the past.

We, therefore, conclude that the right of personal privacy includes the abortion decision, but that this right is not unqualified and must be considered against important state interests in regulation.

We note that those federal and state courts that have recently considered abortion law challenges have reached the same conclusion.

Although the results are divided, most of these courts have agreed that the right of privacy, however based, is broad enough to cover the abortion decision; that the right, nonetheless, is not absolute and is subject to some limitations; and that at some point the state interests as to protection of health, medical standards, and prenatal life, become dominant. We agree with this approach.

Where certain "fundamental rights" are involved, the Court has held that regulation limiting these rights may be justified only by a "compelling state interest," and that legislative enactments must be narrowly drawn to express only the legitimate state interests at stake.

In the recent abortion cases, cited above, courts have recognized these principles. Those striking down state laws have generally scrutinized the State's interests in protecting health and potential life, and have concluded that neither interest justified broad limitations on the reasons for which a physician and his pregnant patient might decide that she should have an abortion in the early stages of pregnancy. Courts sustaining state laws have held that the State's determinations to protect health or prenatal life are dominant and constitutionally justifiable.

The District Court held that the appellee failed to meet his burden demonstrating that the Texas statute's infringement upon Roe's rights was necessary to support a compelling state interest, and that, although the appellee presented "several compelling justifications for state presence in the area of abortions," the statutes outstripped these justifications and swept "far beyond any areas of compelling state interest." Appellant and appellee both contest that holding. Appellant, as has been indicated, claims an absolute right that bars any state imposition of criminal penalties in the area. Appellee argues that the State's determination to recognize and protect prenatal life from and after conception constitutes a compelling state interest. As noted above, we do not agree fully with either formulation.

A. The appellee and certain *amici* argue that the fetus is a "person" within the language and meaning of the Fourteenth Amendment. In support of this, they outline at length and in detail the well-known facts of fetal development. If this suggestion of personhood is established, the appellant's case, of course, collapses, for the fetus' right to life would then be guaranteed specifically by the Amendment. The appellant conceded as much on re-argument. On the other hand, the appellee conceded on re-argument that no case could be cited that holds that a fetus is a person within the meaning of the Fourteenth Amendment.

The Constitution does not define "person" in so many words. Section 1 of the Fourteenth Amendment contains three references to "person." In nearly all these instances, the use of the word is such that it has application only postnatally. None indicates, with any assurance, that it has any possible prenatal application.

All this, together with our observation, *supra,* that throughout the major portion of the 19th century prevailing legal abortion practices were far freer than they are today, persuades us that the word "person," as used in the Fourteenth Amendment, does not include the unborn. This is in accord with the results reached in those few cases where the issue has been squarely presented. Indeed, our decision in *United States v. Vuitch* (1971), inferentially is to the same effect, for we there would not have indulged in statutory interpretation favorable to abortion in specified circumstances if the necessary consequence was the termination of life entitled to Fourteenth Amendment protection.

This conclusion, however, does not of itself fully answer the contentions raised by Texas, and we pass on to other considerations.

B. The pregnant woman cannot be isolated in her privacy. She carried an embryo and, later, a fetus, if one accepts the medical definitions of the developing young in the human uterus. See Dorland's Illustrated Medical Dictionary 478–479, 547 (24th ed. 1965). The situation therefore is inherently different from marital intimacy, or bedroom possession of obscene material, or marriage, or procreation, or education, with which *Eisenstadt* and *Griswold, Stanley, Loving, Skinner,* and *Pierce* and *Meyer* were respectively concerned. As we have intimated above, it is reasonable and appropriate for a State to decide that at some point in time another interest, that of health of the mother or that of potential human life, becomes significantly involved. The woman's privacy is no longer sole and any right of privacy she possesses must be measured accordingly.

Texas urges that, apart from the Fourteenth Amendment, life begins at conception and is present throughout pregnancy, and that, therefore, the State has a compelling interest in protecting that life from and after conception. We need not resolve the difficult question of when life begins. When those trained in the respective disciplines of medicine, philosophy, and theology are unable to arrive at any consensus, the judiciary, at this point in the development of man's knowledge, is not in a position to speculate as to the answer.

It should be sufficient to note briefly the wide divergence of thinking on this most sensitive and difficult question. There has always been strong support for the view that life does not begin until live birth. This was the belief of the Stoics. It appears to be the predominant, though not the unanimous, attitude of the Jewish faith. It may be taken to represent also the position of a large segment of the Protestant community, insofar as that can be ascertained; organized groups that have taken a formal position on the abortion issue have generally regarded abortion as a matter for the conscience of the individual and her family. As we have noted, the common law found greater significance in quickening. Physicians and their scientific colleagues have regarded that event with less interest and have tended to focus either upon conception, upon live birth, or upon the interim point at which the fetus becomes "viable," that is, potentially able to live outside the mother's womb, albeit with artificial aid. Viability is usually placed at about seven months (28 weeks) but may occur earlier, even at 24 weeks. The Aristotelian theory of "mediate animation," that held sway throughout the Middle Ages and the Renaissance in Europe, continued to be official Roman Catholic dogma until the 19th century, despite opposition to this "ensoulment" theory from those in the Church who would recognize the existence of life from the moment of conception. The latter is now, of course, the official belief of the Catholic Church. As one brief *amicus* discloses, this is a view strongly held by many non-Catholics as well, and by many physicians. Substantial problems for precise definition of this view are posed, however, by new embryological data that purport to indicate that conception is a "process" over time, rather than an event, and by new medical techniques such as menstrual extraction, the "morning-after" pill, implantation of embryos, artificial insemination, and even artificial wombs.

In areas other than criminal abortion, the law has been reluctant to endorse any theory that life, as we recognize it, begins before live birth or to accord legal rights to the unborn except in narrowly defined situations and except when the rights are contingent upon live birth. For example, the traditional rule of tort law denied recovery for prenatal injuries even though the child was born alive. That rule has been changed in almost every jurisdiction. In most States, recovery is said to be permitted only if the fetus was viable, or at least quick, when the injuries were sustained, though few courts have squarely so held. In a recent development, generally opposed by the commentators, some States permit the parents of a still-born child to maintain an action for wrongful death because of prenatal injuries. Such an action, however, would appear to be one to vindicate the parents' interest and is thus consistent with the view that the fetus, at most, represents only the potentiality of life. Similarly, unborn children have been recognized as acquiring rights or interests by way of inheritance or other devolution of property, and have been represented by guardians *ad litem*. Perfection of the interests involved, again, has generally been contingent upon live birth. In short, the unborn have never been recognized in the law as persons in the whole sense.

In view of all this, we do not agree that, by adopting one theory of life, Texas may override the rights of the pregnant woman that are at stake. We repeat, however, that the State does have an important and legitimate interest in preserving and protecting the health of the pregnant woman, whether she be a resident of the State or a nonresident who seeks medical consultation and treatment there, and that it has still *another* important and legitimate interest in protecting the potentiality of human

life. These interests are separate and distinct. Each grows in substantiality as the woman approaches term and, at a point during pregnancy, each becomes "compelling."

With respect to the State's important and legitimate interest in the health of the mother, the "compelling" point, in the light of present medical knowledge, is at approximately the end of the first trimester. This is so because of the now-established medical fact, referred to above, that until the end of the first trimester mortality in abortion may be less than mortality in normal childbirth. It follows that, from and after this point, a State may regulate the abortion procedure to the extent that the regulation reasonably relates to the preservation and protection of maternal health. Examples of permissible state regulation in this area are requirements as to the qualifications of the person who is to perform the abortion; as to the licensure of that person; as to the facility in which the procedure is to be performed, that is, whether it must be a hospital or may be a clinic or some other place of less-than-hospital status; as to the licensing of the facility; and the like.

This means, on the other hand, that, for the period of pregnancy prior to this "compelling" point, the attending physician, in consultation with his patient, is free to determine, without regulation by the State, that, in his medical judgment, the patient's pregnancy should be terminated. If that decision is reached, the judgment may be effectuated by an abortion free of interference by the State.

With respect to the State's important and legitimate interest in potential life, the "compelling" point is at viability. This is so because the fetus then presumably has the capability of meaningful life outside the mother's womb. State regulation protective of fetal life after viability thus has both logical and biological justifications. If the State is interested in protecting fetal life after viability, it may go so far as to proscribe abortion during that period, except when it is necessary to preserve the life or health of the mother.

To summarize and to repeat:

1. A state criminal abortion statute of the current Texas type, that excepts from criminality only a *lifesaving* procedure on behalf of the mother, without regard to pregnancy stage and without recognition of the other interests involved, is violative of the Due Process Clause of the Fourteenth Amendment.

a. For the stage prior to approximately the end of the first trimester, the abortion decision and its effectuation must be left to the medical judgment of the pregnant woman's attending physician.

b. For the stage subsequent to approximately the end of the first trimester, the State, in promoting its interest in the health of the mother, may, if it chooses, regulate the abortion procedure in ways that are reasonably related to maternal health.

c. For the stage subsequent to viability, the State in promoting its interest in the potentiality of human life may, if it chooses, regulate, and even proscribe, abortion except where it is necessary, in appropriate medical judgment, for the preservation of the life or health of the mother.

2. The State may define the term "physician" as it has been employed in the preceding paragraphs of this Part XI of this opinion, to mean only a physician currently licensed by the State, and may proscribe any abortion by a person who is not a physician as so defined.

In *Doe v. Bolton*, procedural requirements contained in one of the modern abortion statutes are considered. That opinion and this one, of course, are to be read together.

This holding, we feel, is consistent with the relative weights of the respective interests involved, with the lessons and examples of medical and legal history, with the lenity of the common law, and with the demands of the profound problems of the present day. The decision leaves the State free to place increasing restrictions on abortion as the period of pregnancy lengthens, so long as those restrictions are tailored to the recognized state interests. The decision vindicates the right of the physician to administer medical treatment according to his professional judgment up to the points where important state interests provide compelling justifications for intervention. Up to those points, the abortion decision in all its aspects is inherently, and primarily, a medical decision, and basic responsibility for it must rest with the physician. If an individual practitioner abuses the privilege of exercising proper medical judgment, the usual remedies, judicial and intra-professional, are available.

MR. JUSTICE REHNQUIST, DISSENTING.

The Court's opinion brings to the decision of this troubling question both extensive historical fact and a wealth of legal scholarship. While the opinion thus commands my respect, I find myself nonetheless in fundamental disagreement with those parts of it that invalidate the Texas statute in question, and therefore dissent.

The Court's opinion decides that a State may impose virtually no restriction on the performance of abortions during the first trimester of pregnancy. Our previous decisions indicate that a necessary predicate for such an opinion is a plaintiff who was in her first trimester of pregnancy at some time during the pendency of her lawsuit. While a party may vindicate his own constitutional rights, he may not seek vindication for the rights of others. The Court's statement of facts in this case makes clear, however, that the record in no way indicates the presence of such a plaintiff. We know only that plaintiff Roe at the time of filing her complaint was a pregnant woman; for aught that appears in this record, she may have been in her last trimester of pregnancy as of the date the complaint was filed.

Nothing in the Court's opinion indicates that Texas might not constitutionally apply its proscription of abortion as written to a woman in that stage of pregnancy. Nonetheless, the

Court uses her complaint against the Texas statute as a fulcrum for deciding that States may impose virtually no restrictions on medical abortions performed during the *first* trimester of pregnancy. In deciding such a hypothetical lawsuit, the Court departs from the longstanding admonition that it should never "formulate a rule of constitutional law broader than is required by the precise facts to which it is to be applied." *Liverpool, New York & Philadelphia S.S. Co. v. Commissioners of Emigration,* (1885).

Even if there were a plaintiff in this case capable of litigating the issue which the Court decides, I would reach a conclusion opposite to that reached by the Court. I have difficulty in concluding, as the Court does, that the right of "privacy" is involved in this case. Texas, by the statute here challenged, bars the performance of a medical abortion by a licensed physician on a plaintiff such as Roe. A transaction resulting in an operation such as this is not "private" in the ordinary usage of that word. Nor is the "privacy" that the Court finds here even a distant relative of the freedom from searches and seizures protected by the Fourth Amendment to the Constitution, which the Court has referred to as embodying a right to privacy. *Katz v. United States* (1967).

If the Court means by the term "privacy" no more than that the claim of a person to be free from unwanted state regulation of consensual transactions may be a form of "liberty" protected by the Fourteenth Amendment, there is no doubt that similar claims have been upheld in our earlier decisions on the basis of that liberty. I agree with the statement of Mr. Justice Stewart in his concurring opinion that the "liberty," against deprivation of which without due process the Fourteenth Amendment protects, embraces more than the rights found in the Bill of Rights. But that liberty is not guaranteed absolutely against deprivation, only against deprivation without due process of law. The test traditionally applied in the area

of social and economic legislation is whether or not a law such as that challenged has a rational relation to a valid state objective. The Due Process Clause of the Fourteenth Amendment undoubtedly does place a limit, albeit a broad one, on legislative power to enact laws such as this. If the Texas statute were to prohibit an abortion even where the mother's life is in jeopardy, I have little doubt that such a statute would lack a rational relation to a valid state objective under the test stated in *Williamson.* But the Court's sweeping invalidation of any restrictions on abortion during the first trimester is impossible to justify under that standard, and the conscious weighing of competing factors that the Court's opinion apparently substitutes for the established test is far more appropriate to a legislative judgment than to a judicial one.

The Court eschews the history of the Fourteenth Amendment in its reliance on the "compelling state interest" test. But the Court adds a new wrinkle to this test by transposing it from the legal considerations associated with the Equal Protection Clause of the Fourteenth Amendment to this case arising under the Due Process Clause of the Fourteenth Amendment. Unless I misapprehend the consequences of this transplanting of the "compelling state interest test," the Court's opinion will accomplish the seemingly impossible feat of leaving this area of the law more confused than it found it.

While the Court's opinion quotes from the dissent of Mr. Justice Holmes in *Lochner v. New York* (1905), the result it reaches is more closely attuned to the majority opinion of Mr. Justice Peckham in that case. As in *Lochner* and similar cases applying substantive due process standards to economic and social welfare legislation, the adoption of the compelling state interest standard will inevitably require this Court to examine the legislative policies and pass on the wisdom of these policies in the very process of deciding whether a particular state interest put forward may or may not be "compelling." The decision here to break pregnancy into three distinct terms and to outline the permissible restrictions the State may impose in each one, for example, partakes more of judicial legislation than it does of a determination of the intent of the drafters of the Fourteenth Amendment.

The fact that a majority of the States reflecting, after all, the majority sentiment in those States, have had restrictions on abortions for at least a century is a strong indication, it seems to me, that the asserted right to an abortion is not "so rooted in the traditions and conscience of our people as to be ranked as fundamental," *Snyder v. Massachusetts* (1934). Even today, when society's views on abortion are changing the very existence of the debate is evidence that the "right" to an abortion is not so universally accepted as the appellant would have us believe.

To reach its result, the Court necessarily has had to find within the scope of the Fourteenth Amendment a right that was apparently completely unknown to the drafters of the Amendment. As early as 1821, the first state law dealing directly with abortion was enacted by the Connecticut Legislature. Conn. Stat., Tit. 22 §§ 14, 16. By the time of the adoption of the Fourteenth Amendment in 1868, there were at least 36 laws enacted by state or territorial legislatures limiting abortion. While many State have amended or updated their laws, 21 of the law on the books in 1868 remain in effect today. Indeed, the Texas statute struck down today was, as the majority notes, first enacted in 1857 and "has remained substantially unchanged to the present time."

There apparently was no question concerning the validity of this provision or of any of the other state statutes when the Fourteenth Amendment was adopted. The only conclusion possible from this history is that the drafters did not intend to have the Fourteenth Amendment withdraw from the States the power to legislate with respect to this matter.

Discussion Questions

1. In *Roe*, on what basis did the U.S. Supreme Court reason that the right to abortion is a fundamental right? How did the Court's appeal to the history of abortion in Western law, especially American law, influence its decision?

2. The Court argued that since people are divided over the issue of fetal personhood, therefore, abortion should remain legal. Do you agree with this reasoning? If you do not, explain why. If you do, how would you respond to the pro-life reply that the Court's argument is an argument from ignorance? That is to say, if one *does not* know that one is killing a human person, isn't that a good reason *not to* proceed with the activity, just as it would be prudent not to blow up a building because you do not know whether or not someone is still inside it?

3. Briefly summarize Justice Rehnquist's dissent? Do you think that he adequately addresses Justice Blackmun's case? Why or why not?

You can locate InfoTrac-College Education articles about this chapter by accessing the InfoTrac-College Edition website (http://www.infotrac-college.com/wadsworth/). Using the InfoTrac-College Edition subject guide, enter the search terms relevant to this chapter, and then read abstracts for relevant articles.

Planned Parenthood v. Casey (1992)   **11**

U.S. SUPREME COURT*

Planned Parenthood v. Casey (1992) is an important Supreme Court decision because, although it upheld *Roe* as a legal precedent, it rejected *Roe's* trimester breakdown and its conclusion that abortion is a fundamental constitutional right. In *Casey* the Court was asked to consider the constitutionality of five provisions of the Pennsylvania Abortion Control Act of 1982: (1) a woman seeking an abortion must give her informed consent before the procedure and be provided with certain information at least 24 hours before the abortion is performed; (2) the informed consent of one parent must be obtained for a minor to undergo an abortion, but judicial bypass procedure is provided; (3) a married woman seeking an abortion must sign a statement indicating that she has notified her husband, unless certain exceptions apply (e.g., she is being abused by her husband); (4) a medical emergency will excuse compliance with the statute's requirements; and (5) abortion-providing facilities must comply with certain reporting requirements. The Court upheld as constitutional four of the five provisions, rejecting the third one based on what it calls the "undue burden" standard. That is to say, does the provision constitute a "substantial obstacle" for the woman seeking an abortion?

The following are excerpts from two opinions in *Casey*. The first represents the Court's opinion. It is written by Justices Sandra Day O'Connor, David Souter, and Anthony Kennedy. The second is Justice Antonin Scalia's dissent.

JUSTICE O'CONNOR, JUSTICE KENNEDY, AND JUSTICE SOUTER announced the judgment of the Court and delivered the opinion of the Court with respect to Parts I, II, III, V-A, V-C, and VI, an opinion with respect to Part V-E, in which Justice Stevens joins, and an opinion with respect to Parts IV, V-B, and V-D.

I

Liberty finds no refuge in a jurisprudence of doubt. Yet 19 years after our holding that the Constitution protects a woman's right to terminate her pregnancy in its early stages, *Roe v. Wade,* 410 U.S. 113 (1973), the definition of liberty is still questioned. Joining the respondents as *amicus curiae,* the United States, as it has done in five other cases in the last decade, again asks us to overrule *Roe.* See Brief for Respondents 104–117; Brief for United States as *Amicus Curiae* 8.

At issue in these cases are five provisions of the Pennsylvania Abortion Control Act of 1982 as amended in 1988 and 1989. 18 Pa. Cons. Stat. §§3203–3220 (1990). Relevant

---

Footnotes eliminated and some citations omitted and other citations edited.

portions of the Act are set forth in the appendix. The Act requires that a woman seeking an abortion give her informed consent prior to the abortion procedure, and specifies that she be provided with certain information at least 24 hours before the abortion is performed. §3205. For a minor to obtain an abortion, the Act requires the informed consent of one of her parents, but provides for a judicial bypass option if the minor does not wish to or cannot obtain a parent's consent. §3206. Another provision of the Act requires that, unless certain exceptions apply, a married woman seeking an abortion must sign a statement indicating that she has notified her husband of her intended abortion. §3209. The Act exempts compliance with these three requirements in the event of a "medical emergency," which is defined in §3203 of the Act. See §§3203, 3205(a), 3206(a), 3209(c). In addition to the above provisions regulating the performance of abortions, the Act imposes certain reporting requirements on facilities that provide abortion services. §§3207(b), 3214(a), 3214(f).

Before any of these provisions took effect, the petitioners, who are five abortion clinics and one physician representing himself as well as a class of physicians who provide abortion services, brought this suit seeking declaratory and injunctive relief. Each provision was challenged as unconstitutional on its face. The District Court entered a preliminary injunction against the enforcement of the regulations, and, after a 3-day bench trial, held all the provisions at issue here unconstitutional, entering a permanent injunction against Pennsylvania's enforcement of them. The Court of Appeals for the Third Circuit affirmed in part and reversed in part, upholding all of the regulations except for the husband notification requirement. We granted certiorari.

The Court of Appeals found it necessary to follow an elaborate course of reasoning even to identify the first premise to use to determine whether the statute enacted by Pennsylvania meets constitutional standards. And at oral argument in this Court, the attorney for the parties challenging the statute took the position that none of the enactments can be upheld without overruling *Roe v. Wade*. Tr. of Oral Arg. 5–6. We disagree with that analysis; but we acknowledge that our decisions after *Roe* cast doubt upon the meaning and reach of its holding. Further, the Chief Justice admits that he would overrule the central holding of *Roe* and adopt the rational relationship test as the sole criterion of constitutionality. State and federal courts as well as legislatures throughout the Union must have guidance as they seek to address this subject in conformance with the Constitution. Given these premises, we find it imperative to review once more the principles that define the rights of the woman and the legitimate authority of the State respecting the termination of pregnancies by abortion procedures.

After considering the fundamental constitutional questions resolved by *Roe,* principles of institutional integrity, and the rule of *stare decisis,* we are led to conclude this: the essential holding of *Roe v. Wade* should be retained and once again reaffirmed.

It must be stated at the outset and with clarity that *Roe*'s essential holding, the holding we affirm, has three parts. First is a recognition of the right of the woman to choose to have an abortion before viability and to obtain it without undue interference from the State. Before viability, the State's interests are not strong enough to support a prohibition of abortion or the imposition of a substantial obstacle to the woman's effective right to elect the procedure. Second is a confirmation of the State's power to restrict abortions after fetal viability, if the law contains exceptions for pregnancies which endanger a woman's life or health. And third is the principle that the State has legitimate interests from the outset of the pregnancy in protecting the health of the woman and the life of the fetus that may become a child. These principles do not contradict one another; and we adhere to each.

II

Constitutional protection of the woman's decision to terminate her pregnancy derives from the Due Process Clause of the Fourteenth Amendment. It declares that no State shall "deprive any person of life, liberty, or property, without due process of law." The controlling word in the case before us is "liberty." Although a literal reading of the Clause might suggest that it governs only the procedures by which a State may deprive persons of liberty, for at least 105 years, at least since *Mugler v. Kansas,* (1887), the Clause has been understood to contain a substantive component as well, one "barring certain government actions regardless of the fairness of the procedures used to implement them." *Daniels v. Williams,* (1986). As Justice Brandeis (joined by Justice Holmes) observed, "[d]espite arguments to the contrary which had seemed to me persuasive, it is settled that the due process clause of the Fourteenth Amendment applies to matters of substantive law as well as to matters of procedure. Thus all fundamental rights comprised within the term liberty are protected by the Federal Constitution from invasion by the States." *Whitney v. California,* (1927) (Brandeis, J., concurring). "[T]he guaranties of due process, though having their roots in Magna Carta's *'per legem terrae'* and considered as procedural safeguards 'against executive usurpation and tyranny,' have in this country 'become bulwarks also against arbitrary legislation.'" *Poe v. Ullman,* (1961).

The most familiar of the substantive liberties protected by the Fourteenth Amendment are those recognized by the Bill of Rights. We have held that the Due Process Clause of the Fourteenth Amendment incorporates most of the Bill of Rights against the States. See e.g., *Duncan v. Louisiana,* (1968). It is tempting, as a means of curbing the discretion of federal judges, to suppose that liberty encompasses no more than those rights already guaranteed to the individual against federal interference by the express provisions of the first eight amendments to the Constitution. See *Adamson v. California,* (1947) (Black, J., dissenting). But of course this Court has never accepted that view.

It is also tempting, for the same reason, to suppose that the Due Process Clause protects only those practices, defined at the most specific level, that were protected against government interference by other rules of law when the Fourteenth Amendment was ratified. But such a view would be inconsistent with our law. It is a promise of the Constitution that there is a realm of personal liberty which the government may not enter. We have vindicated this principle before. Marriage is mentioned nowhere in the Bill of Rights and interracial marriage was illegal in most States in the 19th century, but the Court was no doubt correct in finding it to be an aspect of liberty protected against state interference by the substantive component of the Due Process Clause in *Loving v. Virginia,* (1967) (relying, in an opinion for eight Justices, on the Due Process Clause). . . .

Neither the Bill of Rights nor the specific practices of States at the time of the adoption of the Fourteenth Amendment marks the outer limits of the substantive sphere of liberty which the Fourteenth Amendment protects. See U.S. Const., Amend. 9. As the second Justice Harlan recognized:

"[T]he full scope of the liberty guaranteed by the Due Process Clause cannot be found in or limited by the precise terms of the specific guarantees elsewhere provided in the Constitution. This 'liberty' is not a series of isolated points pricked out in terms of the taking of property; the freedom of speech, press, and religion; the right to keep and bear arms; the freedom from unreasonable searches and seizures; and so on. It is a rational continuum which, broadly speaking, includes a freedom from all substantial arbitrary impositions and purposeless restraints, . . . and which also recognizes, what a reasonable and sensitive judgment must, that certain interests require particularly careful scrutiny of the state needs asserted to justify their abridgment." *Poe v. Ullman,* (Harlan, J., dissenting from dismissal on jurisdictional grounds).

Justice Harlan wrote these words in addressing an issue the full Court did not reach in *Poe v. Ullman,* but the Court adopted his position four Terms later in *Griswold v. Connecticut, supra.* In Griswold, we held that the Constitution does not permit a State to forbid a married couple to use contraceptives. That same freedom was later guaranteed, under the Equal Protection Clause, for unmarried couples.

Constitutional protection was extended to the sale and distribution of contraceptives in *Carey v. Population Services International, supra.* It is settled now, as it was when the Court heard arguments in *Roe v. Wade,* that the Constitution places limits on a State's right to interfere with a person's most basic decisions about family and parenthood. . . .

The inescapable fact is that adjudication of substantive due process claims may call upon the Court in interpreting the Constitution to exercise that same capacity which by tradition courts always have exercised: reasoned judgment. Its boundaries are not susceptible of expression as a simple rule. That does not mean we are free to invalidate state policy choices with which we disagree; yet neither does it permit us to shrink from the duties of our office. As Justice Harlan observed:

"Due process has not been reduced to any formula; its content cannot be determined by reference to any code. The best that can be said is that through the course of this Court's decisions it has represented the balance which our Nation, built upon postulates of respect for the liberty of the individual, has struck between that liberty and the demands of organized society. If the supplying of content to this Constitutional concept has of necessity been a rational process, it certainly has not been one where judges have felt free to roam where unguided speculation might take them. The balance of which I speak is the balance struck by this country, having regard to what history teaches are the traditions from which it developed as well as the traditions from which it broke. That tradition is a living thing. A decision of this Court which radically departs from it could not long survive, while a decision which builds on what has survived is likely to be sound. No formula could serve as a substitute, in this area, for judgment and restraint." *Poe v. Ullman,* (Harlan, J., dissenting from dismissal on jurisdictional grounds).

Men and women of good conscience can disagree, and we suppose some always shall disagree, about the profound moral and spiritual implications of terminating a pregnancy, even in its earliest stage. Some of us as individuals find abortion offensive to our most basic principles of morality, but that cannot control our decision. Our obligation is to define the liberty of all, not to mandate our own moral code. The underlying constitutional issue is whether the State can resolve these philosophic questions in such a definitive way that a woman lacks all choice in the matter except perhaps in those rare circumstances in which the pregnancy is itself a danger to her own life or health, or is the result of rape or incest.

It is conventional constitutional doctrine that when reasonable people disagree the government can adopt one position or the other. That theorem, however, assumes a state of affairs in which the choice does not intrude upon a protected liberty. Thus, while some people might disagree about whether or not the flag should be saluted, or disagree about the proposition that it may not be defiled, we have ruled that a State may not compel or enforce one view or the other.

Our law affords constitutional protection to personal decisions relating to marriage, procreation, contraception, family relationships, child rearing, and education. Our cases recognize "the right of the individual, married or single, to be free from unwarranted governmental intrusion into matters so fundamentally affecting a person as the decision whether to bear or beget a child." *Eisenstadt v. Baird*. Our precedents "have respected the private realm of family life which the state cannot enter." *Prince v. Massachusetts,* (1944). These matters involving the most intimate and personal choices a person may make in a lifetime, choices central to personal dignity and autonomy, are central to the liberty protected by the Fourteenth Amendment. At the heart of liberty is the right to define one's own concept of existence, of meaning, of the universe, and of the mystery of human life. Beliefs about these matters could not define the attributes of personhood were they formed under compulsion of the State.

These considerations begin our analysis of the woman's interest in terminating her pregnancy but cannot end it, for this reason: though the abortion decision may originate within the zone of conscience and belief it is more than a philosophic exercise. Abortion is a unique act. It is an act fraught with consequences for others: for the woman who must live with the implications of her decision; for the persons who perform and assist in the procedure; for the spouse, family, and society which must confront the knowledge that these procedures exist, procedures some deem nothing short of an act of violence against innocent human life; and, depending on one's beliefs, for the life or potential life that is aborted. Though abortion is conduct, it does not follow that the State is entitled to proscribe it in all instances. That is because the liberty of the woman is at stake in a sense unique to the human condition and so unique to the law. The mother who carries a child to full term is subject to anxieties, to physical constraints, to pain that only she must bear. That these sacrifices have from the beginning of the human race been endured by woman with a pride that ennobles her in the eyes of others and gives to the infant a bond of love cannot alone be grounds for the State to insist she make the sacrifice. Her suffering is too intimate and personal for the State to insist, without more, upon its own vision of the woman's role, however dominant that vision has been in the course of our history and our culture. The destiny of the woman must be shaped to a large extent on her own conception of her spiritual imperatives and her place in society.

It should be recognized, moreover, that in some critical respects the abortion decision is of the same character as the decision to use contraception, to which *Griswold v. Connecticut, Eisenstadt v. Baird,* and *Carey v. Population Services International,* afford constitutional protection. We have no doubt as to the correctness of those decisions. They support the reasoning in *Roe* relating to the woman's liberty because they involve personal decisions concerning not only the meaning of procreation but also human responsibility and respect for it. As with abortion, reasonable people will have differences of opinion about these matters. One view is based on such reverence for the wonder of creation that any pregnancy ought to be welcomed and carried to full term no matter how difficult it will be to provide for the child and ensure its wellbeing. Another is that the inability to provide for the nurture and care of the infant is a cruelty to the child and an anguish to the parent. These are intimate views with infinite variations, and their deep, personal character underlay our decisions in *Griswold, Eisenstadt,* and *Carey.* The same concerns are present when the woman confronts the reality that, perhaps despite her attempts to avoid it, she has become pregnant.

It was this dimension of personal liberty that *Roe* sought to protect, and its holding invoked the reasoning and the tradition of the precedents we have discussed, granting protection to substantive liberties of the person. *Roe* was, of course, an extension of those cases and, as the decision itself indicated, the separate States could act in some degree to further their own legitimate interests in protecting prenatal life. The extent to which the legislatures of the States might act to outweigh the interests of the woman in choosing to terminate her pregnancy was a subject of debate both in *Roe* itself and in decisions following it.

While we appreciate the weight of the arguments made on behalf of the State in the case before us, arguments which in their ultimate formulation conclude that *Roe* should be overruled, the reservations any of us may have in reaffirming the central holding of *Roe* are outweighed by the explication of individual liberty we have given combined with the force of *stare decisis*. We turn now to that doctrine.

III

A

The obligation to follow precedent begins with necessity, and a contrary necessity marks its outer limit. With Cardozo, we recognize that no judicial system could do society's work if it eyed each issue afresh in every case that raised it. See B. Cardozo, The Nature of the Judicial Process (1921). Indeed, the very concept of the rule of law underlying our own Constitution requires such continuity over time that a respect for precedent is, by definition, indispensable. At the other extreme, a different necessity would make itself felt if a prior judicial ruling should come to be seen so

clearly as error that its enforcement was for that very reason doomed.

Even when the decision to overrule a prior case is not, as in the rare, latter instance, virtually foreordained, it is common wisdom that the rule of *stare decisis* is not an "inexorable command," and certainly it is not such in every constitutional case. . . . Rather, when this Court reexamines a prior holding, its judgment is customarily informed by a series of prudential and pragmatic considerations designed to test the consistency of overruling a prior decision with the ideal of the rule of law, and to gauge the respective costs of reaffirming and overruling a prior case. Thus, for example, we may ask whether the rule has proved to be intolerable simply in defying practical workability, *Swift & Co. v. Wickham*, (1965); whether the rule is subject to a kind of reliance that would lend a special hardship to the consequences of overruling and add inequity to the cost of repudiation, e.g., *United States v. Title Ins. & Trust Co.*, (1924); whether related principles of law have so far developed as to have left the old rule no more than a remnant of abandoned doctrine, see *Patterson v. McLean Credit Union*, (1989); or whether facts have so changed or come to be seen so differently, as to have robbed the old rule of significant application or justification.

So in this case we may inquire whether *Roe*'s central rule has been found unworkable; whether the rule's limitation on state power could be removed without serious inequity to those who have relied upon it or significant damage to the stability of the society governed by the rule in question; whether the law's growth in the intervening years has left *Roe*'s central rule a doctrinal anachronism discounted by society; and whether *Roe*'s premises of fact have so far changed in the ensuing two decades as to render its central holding somehow irrelevant or unjustifiable in dealing with the issue it addressed.

1

Although *Roe* has engendered opposition, it has in no sense proven "unworkable," representing as it does a simple limitation beyond which a state law is unenforceable. While *Roe* has, of course, required judicial assessment of state laws affecting the exercise of the choice guaranteed against government infringement, and although the need for such review will remain as a consequence of today's decision, the required determinations fall within judicial competence.

2

The inquiry into reliance counts the cost of a rule's repudiation as it would fall on those who have relied reasonably on the rule's continued application. Since the classic case for weighing reliance heavily in favor of following the earlier rule occurs in the commercial context, see *Payne v. Tennessee*, where advance planning of great precision is most obviously a necessity, it is no cause for surprise that some would find no reliance worthy of consideration in support of *Roe*.

While neither respondents nor their *amici* in so many words deny that the abortion right invites some reliance prior to its actual exercise, one can readily imagine an argument stressing the dissimilarity of this case to one involving property or contract. Abortion is customarily chosen as an unplanned response to the consequence of unplanned activity or to the failure of conventional birth control, and except on the assumption that no intercourse would have occurred but for *Roe*'s holding, such behavior may appear to justify no reliance claim. Even if reliance could be claimed on that unrealistic assumption, the argument might run, any reliance interest would be *de minimis*. This argument would be premised on the hypothesis that reproductive planning could take virtually immediate account of any sudden restoration of state authority to ban abortions.

To eliminate the issue of reliance that easily, however, one would need to limit cognizable reliance to specific instances of sexual activity. But to do this would be simply to refuse to face the fact that for two decades of economic and social developments, people have organized intimate relationships and made choices that define their views of themselves and their places in society, in reliance on the availability of abortion in the event that contraception should fail. The ability of women to participate equally in the economic and social life of the Nation has been facilitated by their ability to control their reproductive lives. The Constitution serves human values, and while the effect of reliance on *Roe* cannot be exactly measured, neither can the certain cost of overruling *Roe* for people who have ordered their thinking and living around that case be dismissed.

3

No evolution of legal principle has left *Roe*'s doctrinal footings weaker than they were in 1973. No development of constitutional law since the case was decided has implicitly or explicitly left *Roe* behind as a mere survivor of obsolete constitutional thinking.

It will be recognized, of course, that *Roe* stands at an intersection of two lines of decisions, but in whichever doctrinal category one reads the case, the result for present purposes will be the same. The *Roe* Court itself placed its holding in the succession of cases most prominently exemplified by *Griswold v. Connecticut*, (1965). When it is so seen, *Roe* is clearly in no jeopardy, since subsequent constitutional developments have neither disturbed, nor do they threaten to diminish, the scope of recognized protection accorded to the liberty relating to intimate relationships, the family, and decisions about whether or not to beget or bear a child. . . .

Roe, however, may be seen not only as an exemplar of *Griswold* liberty but as a rule (whether or not mistaken) of personal autonomy and bodily integrity, with doctrinal affinity to cases recognizing limits on governmental power to mandate medical treatment or to bar its rejection. If so, our cases since *Roe* accord with *Roe*'s view that a State's interest in the protection of life falls short of justifying any plenary override of individual liberty claims. . . .

Finally, one could classify *Roe* as *sui generis.* If the case is so viewed then there clearly has been no erosion of its central determination. The original holding resting on the concurrence of seven Members of the Court in 1973 was expressly affirmed by a majority of six in 1983, . . .

More recently, in *Webster v. Reproductive Health Services,* (1989), although two of the present authors questioned the trimester framework in a way consistent with our judgment today, (Rehnquist, C.J., joined by White, and Kennedy, JJ.) (O'Connor, J., concurring in part and concurring in judgment), a majority of the Court either decided to reaffirm or declined to address the constitutional validity of the central holding of *Roe.* (Rehnquist, C.J., joined by White and Kennedy, JJ.); (O'Connor, J., concurring in part and concurring in judgment); (Blackmun, J. joined by Brennan and Marshall, JJ., concurring in part and dissenting in part); (Stevens, J., concurring in part and dissenting in part).

Nor will courts building upon *Roe* be likely to hand down erroneous decisions as a consequence. Even on the assumption that the central holding of *Roe* was in error, that error would go only to the strength of the state interest in fetal protection, not to the recognition afforded by the Constitution to the woman's liberty. The latter aspect of the decision fits comfortably within the framework of the Court's prior decisions including *Skinner v. Oklahoma ex rel. Williamson,* (1942), *Griswold, Loving v. Virginia,* (1967), and *Eisen-*

stadt v. Baird, (1972), the holdings of which are "not a series of isolated points," but mark a "rational continuum." *Poe v. Ullman,* (1961) (Harlan, J., dissenting). As we described in *Carey v. Population Services International,* the liberty which encompasses those decisions

> "includes 'the interest in independence in making certain kinds of important decisions.' While the outer limits of this aspect of [protected liberty] have not been marked by the Court, it is clear that among the decisions that an individual may make without unjustified government interference are personal decisions 'relating to marriage, procreation, contraception, family relationships, and child rearing and education.' " (citations omitted).

The soundness of this prong of the *Roe* analysis is apparent from a consideration of the alternative. If indeed the woman's interest in deciding whether to bear and beget a child had not been recognized as in *Roe* the State might as readily restrict a woman's right to choose to carry a pregnancy to term as to terminate it, to further asserted state interests in population control, or eugenics, for example. Yet *Roe* has been sensibly relied upon to counter any such suggestions. . . . In any event, because *Roe*'s scope is confined by the fact of its concern with post-conception potential life, a concern otherwise likely to be implicated only by some forms of contraception protected independently under *Griswold* and later cases, any error in *Roe* is unlikely to have serious ramifications in future cases.

4

We have seen how time has overtaken some of *Roe*'s factual assumptions: advances in maternal health care allow for abortions safe to the mother later in pregnancy than was true in 1973, and advances in neonatal care have advanced viability to a point somewhat earlier. . . . But these facts go only to the scheme of time limits on the realization of competing interests, and the divergences from the factual premises of 1973 have no bearing on the validity of *Roe*'s central holding, that viability marks the earliest point at which the State's interest in fetal life is constitutionally adequate to justify a legislative ban on non-therapeutic abortions. The soundness or unsoundness of that constitutional judgment in no sense turns on whether viability occurs at approximately 28 weeks, as was usual at the time of *Roe,* at 23 to 24 weeks, as it sometimes does today, or at some moment even slightly earlier in pregnancy, as it may if fetal respiratory capacity can somehow be enhanced in the future. Whenever it may occur, the attainment of viability may continue to serve as the critical fact, just as it has done since *Roe* was decided; which is to say that no change in *Roe*'s factual underpinning has left its central holding obsolete, and none supports an argument for overruling it.

5

The sum of the precedential inquiry to this point shows *Roe*'s underpinnings unweakened in any way affecting its central holding. While it has engendered disapproval, it has not been unworkable. An entire generation has come of age free to assume *Roe*'s concept of liberty in defining the capacity of women to act in society, and to make reproductive decisions, no erosion of principle going to liberty or personal autonomy has left *Roe*'s central holding a doctrinal remnant; *Roe* portends no developments at odds with other precedent for the analysis of personal liberty; and no changes of fact have rendered viability more or less appropriate as the point at which the balance of interests tips. Within the bounds of normal *stare decisis* analysis, then, and subject to the considerations on which it customarily turns, the stronger argument is for affirming *Roe*'s central holding, with whatever degree of personal reluctance any of us may have, not for overruling it.

B

In a less significant case, *stare decisis* analysis could, and would, stop at the point we have reached. But the sustained and widespread debate *Roe* has provoked calls for some comparison between that case and others of comparable dimension that have responded to national controversies and taken on the impress of the controversies addressed. Only two such decisional lines from the past century present themselves for examination, and in each instance the result reached by the Court accorded with the principles we apply today.

The first example is that line of cases identified with *Lochner v. New York* (1905), which imposed substantive limitations on legislation limiting economic autonomy in favor of health and welfare regulation, adopting, in Justice Holmes' view, the theory of *laissez-faire*. (Holmes, J., dissenting). The *Lochner* decisions were exemplified by *Adkins v. Children's Hospital of D.C.* (1923), in which this Court held it to be an infringement of constitutionally protected liberty of contract to require the employers of adult women to satisfy minimum wage standards. Fourteen years later, *West Coast Hotel Co. v. Parrish* (1937), signaled the demise of *Lochner* by overruling *Adkins*. In the meantime, the Depression had come and, with it, the lesson that seemed unmistakable to most people by 1937, that the interpretation of contractual freedom protected in *Adkins* rested on fundamentally false factual assumptions about the capacity of a relatively unregulated market to satisfy minimal levels of human welfare. As Justice Jackson wrote of the constitutional crisis of 1937 shortly before he came on the bench, "The older world of *laissez faire* was recognized everywhere outside the Court to be dead." R. Jackson, The Struggle for Judicial Supremacy 85 (1941). The facts upon which the earlier case had premised a constitutional resolution of social controversy had proved to be untrue, and history's demonstration of their untruth not only justified but required the new choice of constitutional principle that *West Coast Hotel* announced. Of course, it was true that the Court lost something by its misperception, or its lack of prescience, and the Court-packing crisis only magnified the loss; but the clear demonstration that the facts of economic life were different from those previously assumed warranted the repudiation of the old law.

The second comparison that 20th century history invites is with the cases employing the separate-but-equal rule for applying the Fourteenth Amendment's equal protection guarantee. They began with *Plessy v. Ferguson*, (1896), holding that legislatively mandated racial segregation in public transportation works no denial of equal protection, rejecting the argument that racial separation enforced by the legal machinery of American society treats the black race as inferior. The *Plessy* Court considered "the underlying fallacy of the plaintiff's argument to consist in the assumption that the enforced separation of the two races stamps the colored race with a badge of inferiority. If this be so, it is not by reason of anything found in the act, but solely because the colored race chooses to put that construction upon it." Whether, as a matter of historical fact, the Justices in the *Plessy* majority believed this or not, this understanding of the implication of segregation was the stated justification for the Court's opinion. But this understanding of the facts and the rule it was stated to justify were repudiated in *Brown v. Board of Education* (1954). As one commentator observed, the question before the Court in *Brown* was "whether discrimination inheres in that segregation which is imposed by law in the twentieth century in certain specific states in the American Union. And that question has meaning and can find an answer only on the ground of history and of common knowledge about the facts of life in the times and places aforesaid." Black, The Lawfulness of the Segregation Decisions, 69 Yale L. J. 421, 427 (1960).

The Court in *Brown* addressed these facts of life by observing that whatever may have been the understanding in *Plessy*'s time of the power of segregation to stigmatize those who were segregated with a "badge of inferiority," it was clear by 1954 that legally sanctioned segregation had just such an effect, to the point that racially separate public educational facilities were deemed inherently unequal. Society's understanding of the facts upon which a constitutional ruling was sought in 1954 was thus fundamentally different from the basis claimed for the decision in 1896. While we think *Plessy* was wrong the day it was decided, we must also recognize that the *Plessy* Court's explanation for its decision was so clearly at odds with the facts apparent to the Court in 1954 that the decision to reexamine *Plessy* was on this ground alone not only justified but required.

West Coast Hotel and *Brown* each rested on facts, or an understanding of facts, changed from those which furnished the claimed justifications for the earlier constitutional resolutions. Each case was comprehensible as the Court's response to facts that the country could understand, or had come to understand already, but which the Court of an earlier day, as its own declarations disclosed, had not been able to perceive. As the decisions were thus comprehensible they were also defensible, not merely as the victories of one doctrinal school over another by dint of numbers (victories though they were), but as applications of constitutional principle to facts as they had not been seen by the Court before. In constitutional adjudication, as elsewhere in life, changed circumstances may impose new obligations, and the thoughtful part of the Nation could accept each decision to overrule a prior case as a response to the Court's constitutional duty.

Because the case before us presents no such occasion it could be seen as no such response. Because neither the factual underpinnings of *Roe*'s central holding nor our understanding of it has changed (and because no other indication of weakened precedent has been shown) the Court could not pretend to be reexamining the prior law with any justification beyond a present doctrinal disposition to come out differently from the Court of 1973. To overrule prior law for no other reason than that would run counter to the view repeated in our cases, that a decision to overrule should rest on some special reason over and above the belief that a prior case was wrongly decided. . . .

C

The examination of the conditions justifying the repudiation of *Adkins* by *West Coast Hotel* and *Plessy* by *Brown* is enough to suggest the terrible price that would have been paid if the Court had not overruled as it did. In the present case, however, as our analysis to this point makes clear, the terrible price would be paid for overruling. Our analysis would not be complete, however, without explaining why overruling *Roe*'s central holding would not only reach an unjustifiable result under principles of *stare decisis*, but would seriously weaken the Court's capacity to exercise the judicial power and to function as the Supreme Court of a Nation dedicated to the rule of law. To understand why this would be so it is necessary to understand the source of this Court's authority, the conditions necessary for its preservation, and its relationship to the country's understanding of itself as a constitutional Republic.

The root of American governmental power is revealed most clearly in the instance of the power conferred by the Constitution upon the Judiciary of the United States and specifically upon this Court. As Americans of each succeeding generation are rightly told, the Court cannot buy support for its decisions by spending money and, except to a minor degree, it cannot independently coerce obedience to its decrees. The Court's power lies, rather, in its legitimacy, a product of substance and perception that shows itself in the people's accep-

tance of the Judiciary as fit to determine what the Nation's law means and to declare what it demands.

The underlying substance of this legitimacy is of course the warrant for the Court's decisions in the Constitution and the lesser sources of legal principle on which the Court draws. That substance is expressed in the Court's opinions, and our contemporary understanding is such that a decision without principled justification would be no judicial act at all. But even when justification is furnished by apposite legal principle, something more is required. Because not every conscientious claim of principled justification will be accepted as such, the justification claimed must be beyond dispute. The Court must take care to speak and act in ways that allow people to accept its decisions on the terms the Court claims for them, as grounded truly in principle, not as compromises with social and political pressures having, as such, no bearing on the principled choices that the Court is obliged to make. Thus, the Court's legitimacy depends on making legally principled decisions under circumstances in which their principled character is sufficiently plausible to be accepted by the Nation.

The need for principled action to be perceived as such is implicated to some degree whenever this, or any other appellate court, overrules a prior case. This is not to say, of course, that this Court cannot give a perfectly satisfactory explanation in most cases. People understand that some of the Constitution's language is hard to fathom and that the Court's Justices are sometimes able to perceive significant facts or to understand principles of law that eluded their predecessors and that justify departures from existing decisions. However upsetting it may be to those most directly affected when one judicially derived rule replaces another, the country can accept some correction of error without necessarily questioning the legitimacy of the Court.

In two circumstances, however, the Court would almost certainly fail to receive the benefit of the doubt in overruling prior cases. There is, first, a point beyond which frequent overruling would overtax the country's belief in the Court's good faith. Despite the variety of reasons that may inform and justify a decision to overrule, we cannot forget that such a decision is usually perceived (and perceived correctly) as, at the least, a statement that a prior decision was wrong. There is a limit to the amount of error that can plausibly be imputed to prior courts. If that limit should be exceeded, disturbance of prior rulings would be taken as evidence that justifiable reexamination of principle had given way to drives for particular results in the short term. The legitimacy of the Court would fade with the frequency of its vacillation.

That first circumstance can be described as hypothetical; the second is to the point here and now. Where, in the performance of its judicial duties, the Court decides a case in such a way as to resolve the sort of intensely divisive controversy reflected in *Roe* and those rare, comparable cases, its decision has a dimension that the resolution of the normal case does not carry. It is the dimension present whenever the Court's interpretation of the Constitution calls the contending sides of a national controversy to end their national division by accepting a common mandate rooted in the Constitution.

The Court is not asked to do this very often, having thus addressed the Nation only twice in our lifetime, in the decisions of *Brown* and *Roe*. But when the Court does act in this way, its decision requires an equally rare precedential force to counter the inevitable efforts to overturn it and to thwart its implementation. Some of those efforts may be mere unprincipled emotional reactions; others may proceed from principles worthy of profound respect. But whatever the premises of opposition may be, only the most convincing justification under accepted standards of precedent could suffice to demonstrate that a later decision overruling the first was anything but a surrender to political pressure, and an unjusti-

fied repudiation of the principle on which the Court staked its authority in the first instance. So to overrule under fire in the absence of the most compelling reason to reexamine a watershed decision would subvert the Court's legitimacy beyond any serious question. . . .

The country's loss of confidence in the judiciary would be underscored by an equally certain and equally reasonable condemnation for another failing in overruling unnecessarily and under pressure. Some cost will be paid by anyone who approves or implements a constitutional decision where it is unpopular, or who refuses to work to undermine the decision or to force its reversal. The price may be criticism or ostracism or it may be violence. An extra price will be paid by those who themselves disapprove of the decision's results when viewed outside of constitutional terms, but who nevertheless struggle to accept it, because they respect the rule of law. To all those who will be so tested by following, the Court implicitly undertakes to remain steadfast, lest in the end a price be paid for nothing. The promise of constancy, once given, binds its maker for as long as the power to stand by the decision survives and the understanding of the issue has not changed so fundamentally as to render the commitment obsolete. From the obligation of this promise this Court cannot and should not assume any exemption when duty requires it to decide a case in conformance with the Constitution. A willing breach of it would be nothing less than a breach of faith, and no Court that broke its faith with the people could sensibly expect credit for principle in the decision by which it did that.

It is true that diminished legitimacy may be restored, but only slowly. Unlike the political branches, a Court thus weakened could not seek to regain its position with a new mandate from the voters, and even if the Court could somehow go to the polls, the loss of its principled character could not be retrieved by the casting of so many votes. Like the character of an individual, the legitimacy of the Court must be earned over time. So, indeed, must be the character of a Nation of people who aspire to live according to the rule of law. Their belief in themselves as such a people is not readily separable from their understanding of the Court invested with the authority to decide their constitutional cases and speak before all others for their constitutional ideals. If the Court's legitimacy should be undermined, then, so would the country be in its very ability to see itself through its constitutional ideals. The Court's concern with legitimacy is not for the sake of the Court but for the sake of the Nation to which it is responsible.

The Court's duty in the present case is clear. In 1973, it confronted the already divisive issue of governmental power to limit personal choice to undergo abortion, for which it provided a new resolution based on the due process guaranteed by the Fourteenth Amendment. Whether or not a new social consensus is developing on that issue, its divisiveness is no less today than in 1973, and pressure to overrule the decision, like pressure to retain it, has grown only more intense. A decision to overrule *Roe*'s essential holding under the existing circumstances would address error, if error there was, at the cost of both profound and unnecessary damage to the Court's legitimacy, and to the Nation's commitment to the rule of law. It is therefore imperative to adhere to the essence of *Roe*'s original decision, and we do so today.

IV

From what we have said so far it follows that it is a constitutional liberty of the woman to have some freedom to terminate her pregnancy. We conclude that the basic decision in *Roe* was based on a constitutional analysis which we cannot now repudiate. The woman's liberty is not so unlimited, however, that from the outset the State cannot show its concern for the life of the unborn, and at a later point in fetal development the State's interest in life has sufficient force so that the right of the woman to terminate the pregnancy can be restricted.

That brings us, of course, to the point where much criticism has been directed at *Roe*, a criticism that always inheres when the Court draws a specific rule from what in the Constitution is but a general standard. We conclude, however, that the urgent claims of the woman to retain the ultimate control over her destiny and her body, claims implicit in the meaning of liberty, require us to perform that function. Liberty must not be extinguished for want of a line that is clear. And it falls to us to give some real substance to the woman's liberty to determine whether to carry her pregnancy to full term.

We conclude the line should be drawn at viability, so that before that time the woman has a right to choose to terminate her pregnancy. We adhere to this principle for two reasons. First, as we have said, is the doctrine of *stare decisis*. Any judicial act of line-drawing may seem somewhat arbitrary, but *Roe* was a reasoned statement, elaborated with great care. We have twice reaffirmed it in the face of great opposition. . . . Although we must overrule those parts of *Thornburgh* and *Akron I* which, in our view, are inconsistent with *Roe*'s statement that the State has a legitimate interest in promoting the life or potential life of the unborn, the central premise of those cases represents an unbroken commitment by this Court to the essential holding of *Roe*. It is that premise which we reaffirm today.

The second reason is that the concept of viability, as we noted in *Roe,* is the time at which there is a realistic possibility of maintaining and nourishing a life outside the womb, so that the independent existence of the second life can in reason and all fairness be the object of state protection that now overrides the rights of the woman. Consistent with other constitutional norms, legislatures may draw lines which appear arbitrary without the necessity of offering a justification. But courts may not. We must justify the lines we draw.

And there is no line other than viability which is more workable. To be sure, as we have said, there may be some medical developments that affect the precise point of viability, but this is an imprecision within tolerable limits given that the medical community and all those who must apply its discoveries will continue to explore the matter. The viability line also has, as a practical matter, an element of fairness. In some broad sense it might be said that a woman who fails to act before viability has consented to the State's intervention on behalf of the developing child.

The woman's right to terminate her pregnancy before viability is the most central principle of *Roe v. Wade*. It is a rule of law and a component of liberty we cannot renounce.

On the other side of the equation is the interest of the State in the protection of potential life. The *Roe* Court recognized the State's "important and legitimate interest in protecting the potentiality of human life." The weight to be given this state interest, not the strength of the woman's interest, was the difficult question faced in *Roe*. We do not need to say whether each of us, had we been Members of the Court when the valuation of the State interest came before it as an original matter, would have concluded, as the *Roe* Court did, that its weight is insufficient to justify a ban on abortions prior to viability even when it is subject to certain exceptions. The matter is not before us in the first instance, and coming as it does after nearly 20 years of litigation in *Roe*'s wake we are satisfied that the immediate question is not the soundness of *Roe*'s resolution of the issue, but the precedential force that must be accorded to its holding. And we have concluded that the essential holding of *Roe* should be reaffirmed.

Yet it must be remembered that *Roe v. Wade* speaks with clarity in establishing not only the woman's liberty but also the State's "important and legitimate interest in potential life." That portion of the decision in *Roe* has been given too little acknowledgement and implementa-

tion by the Court in its subsequent cases. Those cases decided that any regulation touching upon the abortion decision must survive strict scrutiny, to be sustained only if drawn in narrow terms to further a compelling state interest. . . . Not all of the cases decided under that formulation can be reconciled with the holding in *Roe* itself that the State has legitimate interests in the health of the woman and in protecting the potential life within her. In resolving this tension, we choose to rely upon *Roe*, as against the later cases.

Roe established a trimester framework to govern abortion regulations. Under this elaborate but rigid construct, almost no regulation at all is permitted during the first trimester of pregnancy; regulations designed to protect the woman's health, but not to further the State's interest in potential life, are permitted during the second trimester and during the third trimester, when the fetus is viable, prohibitions are permitted provided the life or health of the mother is not at stake. Most of our cases since *Roe* have involved the application of rules derived from the trimester framework. . . .

The trimester framework no doubt was erected to ensure that the woman's right to choose not become so subordinate to the State's interest in promoting fetal life that her choice exists in theory but not in fact. We do not agree, however, that the trimester approach is necessary to accomplish this objective. A framework of this rigidity was unnecessary and in its later interpretation sometimes contradicted the State's permissible exercise of its powers.

Though the woman has a right to choose to terminate or continue her pregnancy before viability, it does not at all follow that the State is prohibited from taking steps to ensure that this choice is thoughtful and informed. Even in the earliest stages of pregnancy, the State may enact rules and regulations designed to encourage her to know that there are philosophic and social arguments of great weight that can be brought to bear in favor of continuing the pregnancy to full term and that there are procedures and institutions to allow adoption of unwanted children as well as a certain degree of state assistance if the mother chooses to raise the child herself. " '[T]he Constitution does not forbid a State or city, pursuant to democratic processes, from expressing a preference for normal childbirth.' " *Webster v. Reproductive Health Services,* (opinion of the Court) (quoting *Poelker v. Doe,* (1977)). It follows that States are free to enact laws to provide a reasonable framework for a woman to make a decision that has such profound and lasting meaning. This, too, we find consistent with *Roe*'s central premises, and indeed the inevitable consequence of our holding that the State has an interest in protecting the life of the unborn.

We reject the trimester framework, which we do not consider to be part of the essential holding of *Roe*. See *Webster v. Reproductive Health Services,* (opinion of Rehnquist, C.J.); (O'Connor, J., concurring in part and concurring in judgment) (describing the trimester framework as "problematic"). Measures aimed at ensuring that a women's choice contemplates the consequences for the fetus do not necessarily interfere with the right recognized in *Roe,* although those measures have been found to be inconsistent with the rigid trimester framework announced in that case. A logical reading of the central holding in *Roe* itself, and a necessary reconciliation of the liberty of the women and the interest of the State in promoting prenatal life, require, in our view, that we abandon the trimester framework as a rigid prohibition on all previability regulation aimed at the protection of fetal life. The trimester framework suffers from these basic flaws: in its formulation it misconceives the nature of the pregnant woman's interest; and in practice it undervalues the State's interest in potential life, as recognized in *Roe*.

As our jurisprudence relating to all liberties save perhaps abortion has recognized, not every law which makes a right more difficult to exercise is, *ipso facto,* an infringement of that right. An example clarifies the point. We have held that not every ballot access limitation amounts to an infringement of the right to vote. Rather, the States are granted substantial flexibility in establishing the framework within which voters choose the candidates for whom they wish to vote. *Anderson v. Celebrezze,* (1983); *Norman v. Reed,* (1992).

The abortion right is similar. Numerous forms of state regulation might have the incidental effect of increasing the cost or decreasing the availability of medical care, whether for abortion or any other medical procedure. The fact that a law which serves a valid purpose, one not designed to strike at the right itself, has the incidental effect of making it more difficult or more expensive to procure an abortion cannot be enough to invalidate it. Only where state regulation imposes an undue burden on a woman's ability to make this decision does the power of the State reach into the heart of the liberty protected by the Due Process Clause. . . .

For the most part, the Court's early abortion cases adhered to this view. In *Maher v. Roe* (1977), the Court explained: "*Roe* did not declare an unqualified 'constitutional right to an abortion,' as the District Court seemed to think. Rather, the right protects the woman from unduly burdensome interference with her freedom to decide whether to terminate her pregnancy." . . .

These considerations of the nature of the abortion right illustrate that it is an overstatement to describe it as a right to decide whether to have an abortion "without interference from the State," *Planned Parenthood of Central Mo. v. Danforth* (1976). All abortion regulations interfere to some degree with a woman's ability to decide whether to terminate her pregnancy. It is, as a consequence, not surprising that despite the protestations contained in the original *Roe* opinion to the effect that the Court was not recognizing an absolute right, the Court's experience applying the trimester framework has led to the striking down of some abortion regulations which in no real sense deprived women of the ultimate decision. Those decisions went too far because the right recognized by *Roe* is a right "to be free from unwarranted governmental intrusion into matters so fundamentally affecting a person as the decision whether to bear or beget a child." *Eisenstadt v. Baird.* Not all governmental intrusion is of necessity unwarranted; and that brings us to the other basic flaw in the trimester framework: even in *Roe*'s terms, in practice it undervalues the State's interest in the potential life within the woman.

Roe v. Wade was express in its recognition of the State's "important and legitimate interest[s] in preserving and protecting the health of the pregnant woman [and] in protecting the potentiality of human life." The trimester framework, however, does not fulfill *Roe*'s own promise that the State has an interest in protecting fetal life or potential life. *Roe* began the contradiction by using the trimester framework to forbid any regulation of abortion designed to advance that interest before viability. Before viability, *Roe* and subsequent cases treat all governmental attempts to influence a woman's decision on behalf of the potential life within her as unwarranted. This treatment is, in our judgment, incompatible with the recognition that there is a substantial state interest in potential life throughout pregnancy.

The very notion that the State has a substantial interest in potential life leads to the conclusion that not all regulations must be deemed unwarranted. Not all burdens on the right to decide whether to terminate a pregnancy will be undue. In our view, the undue burden standard is the appropriate means of reconciling the State's interest with the woman's constitutionally protected liberty.

The concept of an undue burden has been utilized by the Court as well as individual members of the Court, including two of us, in ways that could be considered inconsistent. . . .

Because we set forth a standard of general application to which we intend to adhere, it is important to clarify what is meant by an undue burden.

A finding of an undue burden is a shorthand for the conclusion that a state regulation has the purpose or effect of placing a substantial obstacle in the path of a woman seeking an abortion of a nonviable fetus. A statute with this purpose is invalid because the means chosen by the State to further the interest in potential life must be calculated to inform the woman's free choice, not hinder it. And a statute which, while furthering the interest in potential life or some other valid state interest, has the effect of placing a substantial obstacle in the path of a woman's choice cannot be considered a permissible means of serving its legitimate ends. To the extent that the opinions of the Court or of individual Justices use the undue burden standard in a manner that is inconsistent with this analysis, we set out what in our view should be the controlling standard. Cf. *McCleskey v. Zant,* (1991) (attempting to "define the doctrine of abuse of the writ with more precision" after acknowledging tension among earlier cases). In our considered judgment, an undue burden is an unconstitutional burden. See *Akron II,* (opinion of Kennedy, J.). Understood another way, we answer the question, left open in previous opinions discussing the undue burden formulation, whether a law designed to further the State's interest in fetal life which imposes an undue burden on the woman's decision before fetal viability could be constitutional.

Some guiding principles should emerge. What is at stake is the woman's right to make the ultimate decision, not a right to be insulated from all others in doing so. Regulations which do no more than create a structural mechanism by which the State, or the parent or guardian of a minor, may express profound respect for the life of the unborn are permitted, if they are not a substantial obstacle to the woman's exercise of the right to choose. Unless it has that effect on her right of choice, a state measure designed to persuade her to choose childbirth over abortion will be upheld if reasonably related to that goal. Regulations designed to foster the health of a woman seeking an abortion are valid if they do not constitute an undue burden.

Even when jurists reason from shared premises, some disagreement is inevitable. . . . That is to be expected in the application of any legal standard which must accommodate life's complexity. We do not expect it to be otherwise with respect to the undue burden standard. We give this summary:

(a) To protect the central right recognized by *Roe v. Wade* while at the same time accommodating the State's profound interest in potential life, we will employ the undue burden analysis as explained in this opinion. An undue burden exists, and therefore a provision of law is invalid, if its purpose or effect is to place a substantial obstacle in the path of a woman seeking an abortion before the fetus attains viability.

(b) We reject the rigid trimester framework of *Roe v. Wade*. To promote the State's profound interest in potential life, throughout pregnancy the State may take measures to ensure that the woman's choice is informed, and measures designed to advance this interest will not be invalidated as long as their purpose is to persuade the woman to choose childbirth over abortion. These measures must not be an undue burden on the right.

(c) As with any medical procedure, the State may enact regulations to further the health or safety of a woman seeking an abortion. Unnecessary health regulations that have the purpose or effect of presenting a substantial obstacle to a woman seeking an abortion impose an undue burden on the right.

(d) Our adoption of the undue burden analysis does not disturb the central holding of *Roe v. Wade,* and we reaffirm that holding.

Regardless of whether exceptions are made for particular circumstances, a State may not prohibit any woman from making the ultimate decision to terminate her pregnancy before viability.

(e) We also reaffirm Roe's holding that "subsequent to viability, the State in promoting its interest in the potentiality of human life may, if it chooses, regulate, and even proscribe, abortion except where it is necessary, in appropriate medical judgment, for the preservation of the life or health of the mother." *Roe v. Wade,* . . . .

JUSTICE SCALIA, WITH WHOM THE CHIEF JUSTICE, JUSTICE WHITE, AND JUSTICE THOMAS join, concurring in the judgment in part and dissenting in part.

My views on this matter are unchanged from those I set forth in my separate opinions in *Webster v. Reproductive Health Services,* (1989) and *Ohio v. Akron Center for Reproductive Health,* (1990) (*Akron II*). The States may, if they wish, permit abortion on demand, but the Constitution does not require them to do so. The permissibility of abortion, and the limitations upon it, are to be resolved like most important questions in our democracy: by citizens trying to persuade one another and then voting. As the Court acknowledges "where reasonable people disagree the government can adopt one position or the other." The Court is correct in adding the qualification that this "assumes a state of affairs in which the choice does not intrude upon a protected liberty,"—but the crucial part of that qualification is the penultimate word. A State's choice between two positions on which reasonable people can disagree is constitutional even when (as is often the case) it intrudes upon a "liberty" in the absolute sense. Laws against bigamy, for example—which entire societies of reasonable people disagree with—intrude upon men and women's liberty to marry and live with one another. But bigamy happens not to be a liberty specially "protected" by the Constitution.

That is, quite simply, the issue in this case: not whether the power of a woman to abort her unborn child is a "liberty" in the absolute sense; or even whether it is a liberty of great importance to many women. Of course it is both. The issue is whether it is a liberty protected by the Constitution of the United States. I am sure it is not. I reach that conclusion not because of anything so exalted as my views concerning the "concept of existence, of meaning, of the universe, and of the mystery of human life." Rather, I reach it for the same reason I reach the conclusion that bigamy is not constitutionally protected—because of two simple facts: (1) the Constitution says absolutely nothing about it, and (2) the long-standing traditions of American society have permitted it to be legally proscribed.

The Court destroys the proposition, evidently meant to represent my position, that "liberty" includes "only those practices, defined at the most specific level, that were protected against government interference by other rules of law when the Fourteenth Amendment was ratified" (citing *Michael H. v. Gerald D.*, (1989) (opinion of Scalia, J.). That is not, however, what *Michael H.* says: it merely observes that, in defining a "liberty," we may not disregard a specific, "relevant tradition protecting, or denying protection to, the asserted right." But the Court does not wish to be fettered by any such limitations on its preferences. The Court's statement that it is "tempting" to acknowledge the authoritativeness of tradition in order to "cur[b] the discretion of federal judges," is of course rhetoric rather than reality; no government official is "tempted" to place restraints upon his own freedom of action, which is why Lord Acton did not say "Power tends to purify." The Court's temptation is in the quite opposite and more natural direction—towards systematically eliminating checks upon its own power; and it succumbs.

Beyond that brief summary of the essence of my position, I will not swell the United States Reports with repetition of what I have said before; and applying the rational basis test, I would uphold the Pennsylvania statute in its entirety. I must, however, respond to a few of the more outrageous arguments in today's opinion, which it is beyond human nature to leave unanswered. I shall discuss each of them under a quotation from the Court's opinion to which they pertain.

The inescapable fact is that adjudication of substantive due process claims may call upon the Court in interpreting the Constitution to exercise that same capacity which by tradition courts always have exercised: reasoned judgment.

Assuming that the question before us is to be resolved at such a level of philosophical abstraction, in such isolation from the traditions of American society, as by simply applying "reasoned judgment," I do not see how that could possibly have produced the answer the Court arrived at in *Roe v. Wade* (1973). Today's opinion describes the methodology of *Roe,* quite accurately, as weighing against the woman's interest the State's "important and legitimate interest in protecting the potentiality of human life.' " (quoting *Roe*). But "reasoned judgment" does not begin by begging the question, as *Roe* and subsequent cases unquestionably did by assuming that what the State is protecting is the mere "potentiality of human life." . . . The whole argument of abortion opponents is that what the Court calls the fetus and what others call the unborn child *is a human life.* Thus whatever answer *Roe* came up with after conducting its "balancing" is bound to be wrong, unless it is correct that the human fetus is in some critical sense merely potentially human. There is of course no way to determine that as a legal matter; it is in fact a value judgment. Some societies have considered newborn children not yet human, or the incompetent elderly no longer so.

The authors of the joint opinion, of course, do not squarely contend that *Roe v. Wade* was a *correct* application of "reasoned judgment"; merely that it must be followed, because of *stare decisis*. But in their exhaustive discussion of all the factors that go into the determination of when *stare decisis* should be observed and when disregarded, they never mention "how wrong was the decision on its face?" Surely, if "[t]he Court's power lies . . . in its legitimacy, a product of substance and perception," the "substance" part of the equation demands that plain error be acknowledged and eliminated. *Roe* was plainly wrong—even on the Court's methodology of "reasoned judgment," and even more so (of course) if the proper criteria of text and tradition are applied.

The emptiness of the "reasoned judgment" that produced *Roe* is displayed in plain view by the fact that, after more than 19 years of effort by some of the brightest (and most determined) legal minds in the country, after more than 10 cases upholding abortion rights in this Court, and after dozens upon dozens of *amicus* briefs submitted in this and other cases, the best the Court can do to explain how it is that the word "liberty" *must* be thought to include the right to destroy human fetuses is to rattle off a collection of adjectives that simply decorate a value judgment and conceal a political choice. The right to abort, we are told, inheres in "liberty" because it is among "a person's most basic decisions;" it involves a "most intimate and personal choic[e]," it is "central to personal dignity and autonomy;" it "originate[s] within the zone of conscience and belief;" it is "too intimate and personal" for state interference; it reflects "intimate views" of a "deep, personal character;" it involves "intimate relationships," and notions of "personal autonomy and bodily integrity;" and it concerns a particularly " 'important decisio[n]' ". But it is obvious to anyone applying "reasoned judgment" that the same adjectives can be applied to many forms of conduct that this Court including one of the Justices in today's majority, see *Bowers v. Hardwick* (1986), has held are *not* entitled to constitu-

tional protection—because, like abortion, they are forms of conduct that have long been criminalized in American society. Those adjectives might be applied, for example, to homosexual sodomy, polygamy, adult incest, and suicide, all of which are equally "intimate" and "deep[ly] personal" decisions involving "personal autonomy and bodily integrity," and all of which can constitutionally be proscribed because it is our unquestionable constitutional tradition that they are proscribable. It is not reasoned judgment that supports the Court's decision; only personal predilection. Justice Curtis's warning is as timely today as it was 135 years ago:

> "[W]hen a strict interpretation of the Constitution, according to the fixed rules which govern the interpretation of laws, is abandoned, and the theoretical opinions of individuals are allowed to control its meaning, we have no longer a Constitution; we are under the government of individual men, who for the time being have power to declare what the Constitution is, according to their own views of what it ought to mean." *Dred Scott v. Sandford* (1857).

Liberty finds no refuge in a jurisprudence of doubt.

One might have feared to encounter this august and sonorous phrase in an opinion defending the real *Roe v. Wade,* rather than the revised version fabricated today by the authors of the joint opinion. The shortcomings of *Roe* did not include lack of clarity: Virtually all regulation of abortion before the third trimester was invalid. But to come across this phrase in the joint opinion—which calls upon federal district judges to apply an "undue burden" standard as doubtful in application as it is unprincipled in origin—is really more than one should have to bear.

The joint opinion frankly concedes that the amorphous concept of "undue burden" has been inconsistently applied by the Members of this Court in the few brief years since that "test" was first explicitly propounded by Justice

O'Connor in her dissent in *Akron I*. Because the three Justices now wish to "set forth a standard of general application," the joint opinion announces that "it is important to clarify what is meant by an undue burden." I certainly agree with that, but I do not agree that the joint opinion succeeds in the announced endeavor. To the contrary, its efforts at clarification make clear only that the standard is inherently manipulable and will prove hopelessly unworkable in practice.

The joint opinion explains that a state regulation imposes an "undue burden" if it "has the purpose or effect of placing a substantial obstacle in the path of a woman seeking an abortion of a nonviable fetus." An obstacle is "substantial," we are told, if it is "calculated[,] [not] to inform the woman's free choice, [but to] hinder it." This latter statement cannot possibly mean what it says. *Any* regulation of abortion that is intended to advance what the joint opinion concedes is the State's "substantial" interest in protecting unborn life will be "calculated [to] hinder" a decision to have an abortion. It thus seems more accurate to say that the joint opinion would uphold abortion regulations only if they do not *unduly* hinder the woman's decision. That, of course, brings us right back to square one: Defining an "undue burden" as an "undue hindrance" (or a "substantial obstacle") hardly "clarifies" the test. Consciously or not, the joint opinion's verbal shell game will conceal raw judicial policy choices concerning what is "appropriate" abortion legislation.

The ultimately standardless nature of the "undue burden" inquiry is a reflection of the underlying fact that the concept has no principled or coherent legal basis. As the Chief Justice points out [in his opinion; not published here] *Roe*'s strict scrutiny standard "at least had a recognized basis in constitutional law at the time *Roe* was decided," while "[t]he same cannot be said for the 'undue burden' standard, which is created largely out of whole cloth by the authors of the joint opinion."

The joint opinion is flatly wrong in asserting that "our jurisprudence relating to all liberties save perhaps abortion has recognized" the permissibility of laws that do not impose an "undue burden." It argues that the abortion right is similar to other rights in that a law "not designed to strike at the right itself, [but which] has the incidental effect of making it more difficult or more expensive to [exercise the right,]" is not invalid. I agree, indeed I have forcefully urged, that a law of general applicability which places only an incidental burden on a fundamental right does not infringe that right, see *R.A.V. v. St. Paul*, (1992); *Employment Division, Dept. of Human Resources of Ore. v. Smith* (1990), but that principle does not establish the quite different (and quite dangerous) proposition that a law which *directly* regulates a fundamental right will not be found to violate the Constitution unless it imposes an "undue burden." It is that, of course, which is at issue here: Pennsylvania has *consciously and directly* regulated conduct that our cases have held is constitutionally protected. The appropriate analogy, therefore, is that of a state law requiring purchasers of religious books to endure a 24-hour waiting period, or to pay a nominal additional tax of 1¢. The joint opinion cannot possibly be correct in suggesting that we would uphold such legislation on the ground that it does not impose a "substantial obstacle" to the exercise of First Amendment rights. The "undue burden" standard is not at all the generally applicable principle the joint opinion pretends it to be; rather, it is a unique concept created specially for this case, to preserve some judicial foothold in this ill-gotten territory. In claiming otherwise, the three Justices show their willingness to place all constitutional rights at risk in an effort to preserve what they deem the "central holding in *Roe*."

The rootless nature of the "undue burden" standard, a phrase plucked out of context from our earlier abortion decisions, is further reflected in the fact that the joint opinion finds it necessary expressly to repudiate the more narrow formulations used in Justice O'Connor's earlier opinions. Those opinions stated that a statute imposes an "undue burden" if it imposes *absolute* obstacles or *severe* limitations on the abortion decision," *Akron I.* . . . Those strong adjectives are conspicuously missing from the joint opinion, whose authors have for some unexplained reason now determined that a burden is "undue" if it merely imposes a "substantial" obstacle to abortion decisions. Justice O'Connor has also abandoned (again without explanation) the view she expressed in *Planned Parenthood Assn. of Kansas City, Mo., Inc. v. Ashcroft* (1983) (dissenting opinion), that a medical regulation which imposes an "undue burden" could nevertheless be upheld if it "reasonably relate[s] to the preservation and protection of maternal health" (citation and internal quotation marks omitted). In today's version, even health measures will be upheld only *"if they do not constitute an undue burden"* (emphasis added). Gone too is Justice O'Connor's statement that "the State possesses *compelling* interests in the protection of potential human life . . . throughout pregnancy" *Akron I* (emphasis added); instead, the state's interest in unborn human life is stealthily downgraded to a merely "substantial" or "profound" interest. (That had to be done, of course, since designating the interest as "compelling" throughout pregnancy would have been, shall we say, a "substantial obstacle" to the joint opinion's determined effort to reaffirm what it views as the "central holding" of *Roe*. . . . And "viability" is no longer the "arbitrary" dividing line previously decried by Justice O'Connor in *Akron I*; the Court now announces that "the attainment of viability may continue to serve as the critical fact." It is difficult to maintain the illusion that we are interpreting a Constitution rather than inventing one, when we amend its provisions so breezily.

Because the portion of the joint opinion adopting and describing the undue-burden test provides no more useful guidance than the empty phrases discussed above, one must turn to the 23 pages applying that standard to the present fads for further guidance. In evaluating Pennsylvania's abortion law, the joint opinion relies extensively on the factual findings of the District Court, and repeatedly qualifies its conclusions by noting that they are contingent upon the record developed in this case. Thus, the joint opinion would uphold the 24-hour waiting period contained in the Pennsylvania statute's informed consent provision, because "the record evidence shows that in the vast majority of cases, a 24-hour delay does not create any appreciable health risk." The three Justices therefore conclude that "on the record before us, . . . we are not convinced that the 24-hour waiting period constitutes an undue burden." The requirement that a doctor provide the information pertinent to informed consent would also be upheld because "there is no evidence on this record that [this requirement] would amount in practical terms to a substantial obstacle to a woman seeking an abortion." Similarly, the joint opinion would uphold the reporting requirements of the Act, because "there is no . . . showing on the record before us" that these requirements constitute a "substantial obstacle" to abortion decisions. But at the same time the opinion pointedly observes that these reporting requirements may increase the costs of abortions and that "at some point [that fact] could become a substantial obstacle." Most significantly, the joint opinion's conclusion that the spousal notice requirement of the Act, imposes an "undue burden" is based in large measure on the District Court's "detailed findings of fact," which the joint opinion sets out at great length.

I do not, of course, have any objection to the notion that, in applying legal principles, one should rely only upon the facts that are contained in the record or that are properly subject to judicial notice. But what is remarkable about the joint opinion's fact-intensive

analysis is that it does not result in any measurable clarification of the "undue burden"
standard. Rather, the approach of the joint
opinion is, for the most part, simply to highlight certain facts in the record that apparently
strike the three Justices as particularly significant in establishing (or refuting) the existence
of an undue burden; after describing these
facts, the opinion then simply announces that
the provision either does or does not impose a
"substantial obstacle" or an "undue burden."
. . . We do not know whether the same conclusions could have been reached on a different record, or in what respects the record
would have had to differ before an opposite
conclusion would have been appropriate. The
inherently standardless nature of this inquiry
invites the district judge to give effect to his
personal preferences about abortion. By finding and relying upon the right facts, he can
invalidate, it would seem, almost any abortion
restriction that strikes him as "undue"—
subject, of course, to the possibility of being
reversed by a Circuit Court or Supreme Court
that is as unconstrained in reviewing his decision as he was in making it.

To the extent I can discern *any* meaningful
content in the "undue burden" standard as
applied in the joint opinion, it appears to be
that a State may not regulate abortion in such
a way as to reduce significantly its incidence.
The joint opinion repeatedly emphasizes that
an important factor in the "undue burden"
analysis is whether the regulation "prevent[s] a
significant number of women from obtaining
an abortion;" whether a "significant number
of women . . . are likely to be deterred from
procuring an abortion;" and whether the regulation often "deters" women from seeking
abortions. We are not told, however, what
forms of "deterrence" are impermissible or
what degree of success in deterrence is too
much to be tolerated. If, for example, a State
required a woman to read a pamphlet describing, with illustrations, the facts of fetal development before she could obtain an abortion,

the effect of such legislation might be to
"deter" a "significant number of women"
from procuring abortions, thereby seemingly
allowing a district judge to invalidate it as an
undue burden. Thus, despite flowery rhetoric
about the State's "substantial" and "profound" interest in "potential human life," and
criticism of *Roe* for undervaluing that interest,
the joint opinion permits the State to pursue
that interest only so long as it is not too successful. As Justice Blackmun recognizes (with
evident hope), the "undue burden" standard
may ultimately require the invalidation of each
provision upheld today if it can be shown, on
a better record, that the State is too effectively
"express[ing] a preference for childbirth over
abortion." Reason finds no refuge in this
jurisprudence of confusion.

> While we appreciate the weight of the
> arguments . . . that *Roe* should be over-
> ruled, the reservations any of us may have
> in reaffirming the central holding of *Roe*
> are outweighed by the explication of indi-
> vidual liberty we have given combined
> with the force of *stare decisis.*

The Court's reliance upon *stare decisis* can
best be described as contrived. It insists upon
the necessity of adhering not to all of *Roe,* but
only to what it calls the "central holding." It
seems to me that *stare decisis* ought to be
applied even to the doctrine of *stare decisis,* and
I confess never to have heard of this new, keep-
what-you-want-and-throw-away-the-rest version. I wonder whether, as applied to *Marbury
v. Madison* (1803), for example, the new version of *stare decisis* would be satisfied if we
allowed courts to review the constitutionality
of only those statutes that (like the one in *Marbury*) pertain to the jurisdiction of the courts.

I am certainly not in a good position to dispute that the Court *has saved* the "central
holding" of *Roe,* since to do that effectively I
would have to know what the Court has saved,
which in turn would require me to understand
(as I do not) what the "undue burden" test

means. I must confess, however, that I have always thought, and I think a lot of other people have always thought, that the arbitrary trimester framework, which the Court today discards, was quite as central to *Roe* as the arbitrary viability test, which the Court today retains. It seems particularly ungrateful to carve the trimester framework out of the core of *Roe,* since its very rigidity (in sharp contrast to the utter indeterminability of the "undue burden" test) is probably the only reason the Court is able to say, in urging *stare decisis,* that Roe "has in no sense proven 'unworkable.' " I suppose the Court is entitled to call a "central holding" whatever it wants to call a "central holding"—which is, come to think of it, perhaps one of the difficulties with this modified version of *stare decisis.* I thought I might note, however, that the following portions of *Roe* have not been saved:

- Under *Roe,* requiring that a woman seeking an abortion be provided truthful information about abortion before giving informed written consent is unconstitutional, if the information is designed to influence her choice, *Thornburgh; Akron I.* Under the joint opinion's "undue burden" regime (as applied today, at least) such a requirement is constitutional.

- Under *Roe,* requiring that information be provided by a doctor, rather than by nonphysician counselors, is unconstitutional *Akron I.* Under the "undue burden" regime (as applied today, at least) it is not.

- Under *Roe,* requiring a 24-hour waiting period between the time the woman gives her informed consent and the time of the abortion is unconstitutional, *Akron I.* Under the "undue burden" regime (as applied today, at least) it is not.

- Under Roe, requiring detailed reports that include demographic data about

each woman who seeks an abortion and various information about each abortion is unconstitutional, *Thornburgh.* Under the "undue burden" regime (as applied today, at least) it generally is not.

Where, in the performance of its judicial duties, the Court decides a case in such a way as to resolve the sort of intensely divisive controversy reflected in *Roe* . . . , its decision has a dimension that the resolution of the normal case does not carry. It is the dimension present whenever the Court's interpretation of the Constitution calls the contending sides of a national controversy to end their national division by accepting a common mandate rooted in the Constitution.

The Court's description of the place of *Roe* in the social history of the United States is unrecognizable. Not only did Roe not, as the Court suggests, resolve the deeply divisive issue of abortion; it did more than anything else to nourish it, by elevating it to the national level where it is infinitely more difficult to resolve. National politics were not plagued by abortion protests, national abortion lobbying, or abortion marches on Congress, before *Roe v. Wade* was decided. Profound disagreement existed among our citizens over the issue—as it does over other issues, such as the death penalty—but that disagreement was being worked out at the state level. As with many other issues, the division of sentiment within each State was not as closely balanced as it was among the population of the Nation as a whole, meaning not only that more people would be satisfied with the results of state-by-state resolution, but also that those results would be more stable. Pre-*Roe,* moreover, political compromise was possible.

Roe's mandate for abortion on demand destroyed the compromises of the past, rendered compromise impossible for the future, and required the entire issue to be resolved uniformly, at the national level. At the same time, Roe created a vast new class of abortion

consumers and abortion proponents by eliminating the moral opprobrium that had
attached to the act. ("If the Constitution guarantees abortion, how can it be bad?"—not an
accurate line of thought, but a natural one.)
Many favor all of those developments, and it is
not for me to say that they are wrong. But to
portray *Roe* as the statesmanlike "settlement"
of a divisive issue, a jurisprudential Peace of
Westphalia that is worth preserving, is nothing
less than Orwellian. *Roe* fanned into life an
issue that has inflamed our national politics in
general, and has obscured with its smoke the
selection of Justices to this Court in particular,
ever since. And by keeping us in the abortion-
umpiring business, it is the perpetuation of
that disruption, rather than of any *pax Roeana,*
that the Court's new majority decrees.

> [T]o overrule under fire . . . would sub-
> vert the Court's legitimacy. . . .
> To all those who will be . . . tested by
> following, the Court implicitly under-
> takes to remain steadfast. . . . The
> promise of constancy, once given, binds its
> maker for as long as the power to stand by
> the decision survives and . . . the com-
> mitment [is not] obsolete. . . .
> [The American people's] belief in them-
> selves as . . . a people [who aspire to live
> according to the rule of law] is not readily
> separable from their understanding of the
> Court invested with the authority to
> decide their constitutional cases and speak
> before all others for their constitutional
> ideals. If the Court's legitimacy should be
> undermined, then, so would the country
> be in its very ability to see itself through
> its constitutional ideals.

The Imperial Judiciary lives. It is instructive to
compare this Nietzschean vision of us unelected,
life-tenured judges—leading a Volk who will be
"tested by following," and whose very "belief in
themselves" is mystically bound up in their
"understanding" of a Court that "speak[s]
before all others for their constitutional ideals"—
with the somewhat more modest role envisioned
for these lawyers by the Founders.

> "The judiciary . . . has . . . no direction
> either of the strength or of the wealth of the
> society, and can take no active resolution
> whatever. It may truly be said to have neither
> FORCE nor WILL but merely Judgment. . . ."
> The Federalist No. 78 (G. Wills ed. 1982).

Or, again, to compare this ecstasy of a
Supreme Court in which there is, especially on
controversial matters, no shadow of change or
hint of alteration ("There is a limit to the
amount of error that can plausibly be imputed
to prior courts,") with the more democratic
views of a more humble man:

> "[T]he candid citizen must confess that if the
> policy of the Government upon vital ques-
> tions affecting the whole people is to be irre-
> vocably fixed by decisions of the Supreme
> Court, . . . the people will have ceased to be
> their own rulers, having to that extent practi-
> cally resigned their Government into the
> hands of that eminent tribunal." A. Lincoln,
> First Inaugural Address (Mar. 4, 1861), . . .

It is particularly difficult, in the circumstances of the present decision, to sit still for
the Court's lengthy lecture upon the virtues of
"constancy," of "remain[ing] steadfast," and
adhering to "principle." Among the five Justices who purportedly adhere to *Roe,* at most
three agree upon the *principle* that constitutes
adherence (the joint opinion's "undue burden" standard) and that principle is inconsistent with *Roe.* To make matters worse two of
the three, in order thus to remain steadfast,
had to abandon previously stated positions. It
is beyond me how the Court expects these
accommodations to be accepted "as grounded
truly in principle, not as compromises with
social and political pressures having, as such,
no bearing on the principled choices that the
Court is obliged to make." The only principle
the Court "adheres" to, it seems to me, is the
principle that the Court must be seen as standing by *Roe.* That is not a principle of law
(which is what I thought the Court was talking
about), but a principle of *Realpolitik*—and a
wrong one at that.

I cannot agree with, indeed I am appalled by, the Court's suggestion that the decision whether to stand by an erroneous constitutional decision must be strongly influenced—*against* overruling, no less—by the substantial and continuing public opposition the decision has generated. The Court's judgment that any other course would "subvert the Court's legitimacy" must be another consequence of reading the error-filled history book that described the deeply divided country brought together by *Roe*. In my history book, the Court was covered with dishonor and deprived of legitimacy by *Dred Scott v. Sandford* (1857), an erroneous (and widely opposed) opinion that it did not abandon, rather than by *West Coast Hotel Co. v. Parrish* (1937), which produced the famous "switch in time" from the Court's erroneous (and widely opposed) constitutional opposition to the social measures of the New Deal. (Both *Dred Scott* and one line of the cases resisting the New Deal rested upon the concept of "substantive due process" that the Court praises and employs today. Indeed, *Dred Scott* was "very possibly the first application of substantive due process in the Supreme Court, the original precedent for *Lochner v. New York* and *Roe v. Wade*." D. Currie, The Constitution in the Supreme Court 271 (1985) (footnotes omitted).)

But whether it would "subvert the Court's legitimacy" or not, the notion that we would decide a case differently from the way we otherwise would have in order to show that we can stand firm against public disapproval is frightening. It is a bad enough idea, even in the head of someone like me, who believes that the text of the Constitution, and our traditions, say what they say and there is no fiddling with them. But when it is in the mind of a Court that believes the Constitution has an evolving meaning; that the Ninth Amendment's reference to "othe[r]" rights is not a disclaimer, but a charter for action; and that the function of this Court is to "speak before all others for [the people's] constitutional ideals" unrestrained by meaningful text or tra-

dition—then the notion that the Court must adhere to a decision for as long as the decision faces "great opposition" and the Court is "under fire" acquires a character of almost czarist arrogance. We are offended by these marchers who descend upon us, every year on the anniversary of *Roe,* to protest our saying that the Constitution requires what our society has never thought the Constitution requires. These people who refuse to be "tested by following" must be taught a lesson. We have no Cossacks, but at least we can stubbornly refuse to abandon an erroneous opinion that we might otherwise change—to show how little they intimidate us.

Of course, as the Chief Justice points out, we have been subjected to what the Court calls "political pressure" by *both* sides of this issue. Maybe today's decision not to overrule *Roe* will be seen as buckling to pressure from that direction. Instead of engaging in the hopeless task of predicting public perception—a job not for lawyers but for political campaign managers—the Justices should do what is legally right by asking two questions: (1) Was *Roe* correctly decided? (2) Has *Roe* succeeded in producing a settled body of law? If the answer to both questions is no, *Roe* should undoubtedly be overruled. In truth, I am as distressed as the Court is—and expressed my distress several years ago, see *Webster*—about the "political pressure" directed to the Court: the marches, the mail, the protests aimed at inducing us to change our opinions. How upsetting it is, that so many of our citizens (good people, not lawless ones, on both sides of this abortion issue, and on various sides of other issues as well) think that we Justices should properly take into account their views, as though we were engaged not in ascertaining an objective law but in determining some kind of social consensus. The Court would profit, I think, from giving less attention to the *fact* of this distressing phenomenon, and more attention to the *cause of* it. That cause permeates today's opinion: a new mode of constitutional adjudication that relies not upon text and traditional practice to determine the law, but upon what the Court calls "reasoned judgment," which turns out to be nothing but philosophical predilection and moral intuition. All manner of "liberties," the Court tells us, inhere in the Constitution and are enforceable by this Court—not just those mentioned in the text or established in the traditions of our society. Why even the Ninth Amendment—which says only that "[t]he enumeration in the Constitution of certain rights shall not be construed to deny or disparage others retained by the people"—is, despite our contrary understanding for almost 200 years, a literally boundless source of additional, unnamed, unhinted-at "rights," definable and enforceable by us, through "reasoned judgment."

What makes all this relevant to the bothersome application of "political pressure" against the Court are the twin facts that the American people love democracy and the American people are not fools. As long as the Court thought (and the people thought) that we Justices were doing essentially lawyers' work up here—reading text and discerning our society's traditional understanding of that text—the public pretty much left us alone. Texts and traditions are facts to study, not convictions to demonstrate about. But if in reality our process of constitutional adjudication consists primarily of making *value judgments,* if we can ignore a long and clear tradition clarifying an ambiguous text, as we did, for example, five days ago in declaring unconstitutional invocations and benedictions at public-high-school graduation ceremonies, *Lee v. Weisman* (1992); if, as I say, our pronouncement of constitutional law rests primarily on value judgments, then a free and intelligent people's attitude towards us can be expected to be (ought to be) quite different. The people know that their value judgments are quite as good as those taught in any law school—maybe better. If, indeed, the "liberties" protected by the Constitution are, as the Court says, undefined and unbounded, then the people *should* demonstrate, to protest that we do not implement *their* values instead of *ours.* Not only that, but confirmation hearings for new Justices should deteriorate into question-and-answer sessions in which Senators go through a list of their constituents' most favored and most disfavored alleged constitutional rights, and seek the nominee's commitment to support or oppose them. Value judgments, after all, should be voted on, not dictated; and if our Constitution has somehow accidentally committed them to the Supreme Court, at least we can have a sort of plebiscite each time a new nominee to that body is put forward.

Discussion Questions

1. In *Casey* Justices O'Connor, Kennedy, and Souter argue that *Roe* must be preserved as a precedent. On what basis do they draw this conclusion?

2. According to the Court, a law which attempts to limit a fundamental right must be able to withstand *strict scrutiny* whereas a law that attempts to limit a liberty must not pose an *undue burden.* How does the Court distinguish the strict scrutiny standard from the undue burden standard? How does this distinction apply to *Casey's* affect on *Roe?*

3. What is the basis of Justice Scalia's scathing dissent? Do you think his arguments are plausible? Why or why not?

You can locate InfoTrac-College Education articles about this chapter by accessing the InfoTrac-College Edition website (http://www.infotrac-college.com/wadsworth/). Using the InfoTrac-College Edition subject guide, enter the search terms relevant to this chapter, and then read abstracts for relevant articles.

SECTION A2

The Morality of Abortion

On the Moral and Legal Status of Abortion 12

MARY ANNE WARREN

Mary Anne Warren is Professor of Philosophy at San Francisco State University. She is the author of numerous works on moral philosophy, bioethics, and feminism, including two books, *Gendercide: The Implications of Sex Selection* (1985) and *The Nature of Woman* (1980).

In this article Professor Warren argues that though the fetus is a human being *in the genetic sense*, it is not a human being *in the moral sense*. That is to say, the fetus is a human being but not a human person. Professor Warren suggests five traits that are central to the concept of personhood. Although she admits a person may lack as many as two or even three of these traits, she does claim that any being that posseses none of these traits is not a person: (1) consciousness of events and objects internal and/or external to one's being as well as the capacity to feel pain, (2) a developed capacity for reasoning, (3) self-motivated activity that is relatively independent of external or genetic control, (4) the capacity to engage in complex communication, and (5) the presence of self-awareness and self-concepts. "Thus," according to Warren, "neither a fetus's resemblance to a person, or its potential for becoming a person provides any basis whatever for the claim that it has any significant right to life."

Reprinted by permission from The Monist, *vol. 57, no. 1 (1973).*

THE QUESTION WHICH WE MUST answer in order to produce a satisfactory solution to the problem of the moral status of abortion is this: How are we to define the moral community, the set of beings with full and equal moral rights, such that we can decide whether a human fetus is a member of this community or not? What sort of entity, exactly, has the inalienable rights to life, liberty, and the pursuit of happiness? Jefferson attributed these rights to all men, and it may or may not be fair to suggest that he intended to attribute them *only* to men. Perhaps he ought to have attributed them to all human beings. If so, then we arrive, first, at [John T.] Noonan's problem of defining what makes a being human, and, second, at the equally vital question which Noonan does not consider, namely, What reason is there for identifying the moral community with the set of all human beings, in whatever way we have chosen to define that term?

1. ON THE DEFINITION OF "HUMAN"

One reason why this vital second question is so frequently overlooked in the debate over the moral status of abortion is that the term "human" has two distinct, but not often distinguished, senses. This fact results in a slide of meaning, which serves to conceal the fallaciousness of the traditional argument that since (1) it is wrong to kill innocent human beings, and (2) fetuses are innocent human beings, then (3) it is wrong to kill fetuses. For if "human" is used in the same sense in both (1) and (2) then, whichever of the two senses is meant, one of these premises is question-begging. And if it is used in two different senses then of course the conclusion doesn't follow.

Thus, (1) is a self-evident moral truth,[1] and avoids begging the question about abortion, only if "human being" is used to mean something like "a full-fledged member of the moral community." (It may or may not also be meant to refer exclusively to members of the species *Homo sapiens*.) We may call this the *moral* sense of "human." It is not to be confused with what we will call the *genetic* sense, i.e., the sense in which *any* member of the species is a human being, and no member of any other species could be. If (1) is acceptable only if the moral sense is intended, (2) is non-question-begging only if what is intended is the genetic sense.

In "Deciding Who Is Human," Noonan argues for the classification of fetuses with human beings by pointing to the presence of the full genetic code, and the potential capacity for rational thought.[2] It is clear that what he needs to show, for his version of the traditional argument to be valid, is that fetuses are human in the moral sense, the sense in which it is analytically true that all human beings have full moral rights. But, in the absence of any argument showing that whatever is genetically human is also morally human, and he gives none, nothing more than genetic humanity can be demonstrated by the presence of the human genetic code. And, as we will see, the *potential* capacity for rational thought can at most show that an entity has the potential for *becoming* human in the moral sense.

2. DEFINING THE MORAL COMMUNITY

Can it be established that genetic humanity is sufficient for moral humanity? I think that there are very good reasons for not defining the moral community in this way. I would like to suggest an alternative way of defining the moral community, which I will argue for only to the extent of explaining why it is, or should be, self-evident. The suggestion is simply that the moral community consists of all and only *people*, rather than all and only human beings;[3] and probably the best way of demonstrating its self-evidence is by considering the concept of personhood, to see what sorts of entity are and are not persons, and what the decision that a being is or is not a person implies about its moral rights.

What characteristics entitle an entity to be considered a person? This is obviously not the place to attempt a complete analysis of the concept of personhood, but we do not need such a fully adequate analysis just to determine whether and why a fetus is or isn't a person. All we need is a rough and approximate list of the most basic criteria of personhood, and some idea of which, or how many, of these an entity must satisfy in order to properly be considered a person.

In searching for such criteria, it is useful to look beyond the set of people with whom we are acquainted, and ask how we would decide whether a totally alien being was a person or not. (For we have no right to assume that genetic humanity is necessary for personhood.) Imagine a space traveler who lands on an unknown planet and encounters a race of beings utterly unlike any he has ever seen or heard of. If he wants to be sure of behaving morally toward these beings, he has to somehow decide whether they are people, and hence have full moral rights, or whether they are the sort of thing which he need not feel guilty about treating as, for example, a source of food.

How should he go about making this decision? If he has some anthropological background, he might look for such things as religion, art, and the manufacturing of tools, weapons, or shelters, since these factors have been used to distinguish our human from our prehuman ancestors, in what seems to be closer to the moral than the genetic sense of "human." And no doubt he would be right to consider the presence of such factors as good evidence that the alien beings were people, and morally human. It would, however, be overly anthropocentric of him to take the absence of these things as adequate evidence that they were not, since we can imagine people who have progressed beyond, or evolved without ever developing, these cultural characteristics.

I suggest that the traits which are most central to the concept of personhood, or humanity in the moral sense, are, very roughly, the following:

1. consciousness (of objects and events external and/or internal to the being), and in particular the capacity to feel pain;
2. reasoning (the *developed* capacity to solve new and relatively complex problems);
3. self-motivated activity (activity which is relatively independent of either genetic or direct external control);
4. the capacity to communicate, by whatever means, messages of an indefinite variety of types, that is, not just with an indefinite number of possible contents, but on indefinitely many possible topics;
5. the presence of self-concepts, and self-awareness, either individual or racial, or both.

Admittedly, there are apt to be a great many problems involved in formulating precise definitions of these criteria, let alone in developing universally valid behavioral criteria for deciding when they apply. But I will assume that both we and our explorer know approximately what (1)–(5) mean, and that he is also able to determine whether or not they apply. How, then, should he use his findings to decide whether or not the alien beings are people? We needn't suppose that an entity must have *all* of these attributes to be properly considered a person; (1) and (2) alone may well be sufficient for personhood, and quite probably (1)–(3) are sufficient. Neither do we need to insist that any one of these criteria is *necessary* for personhood, although once again (1) and (2) look like fairly good candidates for necessary conditions, as does (3), if "activity" is construed so as to include the activity of reasoning.

All we need to claim, to demonstrate that a fetus is not a person, is that any being which satisfies *none* of (1)–(5) is certainly not a person. I consider this claim to be so obvious that I think anyone who denied it, and claimed that a being which satisfied none of (1)–(5) was a person all the same, would thereby demonstrate that he had no notion at all of what a person is—perhaps because he had confused the concept of a person with that of genetic humanity. If the opponents of abortion were to deny the appropriateness of these five criteria, I do not know what further arguments would convince them. We would probably have to admit that our conceptual schemes were indeed irreconcilably different, and that our dispute could not be settled objectively.

I do not expect this to happen, however, since I think that the concept of a person is one which is very nearly universal (to people), and that it is common to both pro-abortionists and anti-abortionists, even though neither group has fully realized the relevance of this concept to the resolution of their dispute. Furthermore, I think that on reflection even the antiabortionists ought to agree not only that (1)–(5) are central to the concept of personhood, but also that it is a part of this concept that all and only people have full moral rights. The concept of a person is in part a moral concept; once we have admitted that X is a person we have recognized, even if we have not agreed to respect, X's right to be treated as a member of the moral community. It is true that the claim that X is a *human being* is more commonly voiced as part of an appeal to treat X decently than is the claim that X is a person, but this is either because "human being" is here used in the sense which implies personhood, or because the genetic and moral senses of "human" have been confused.

Now if (1)–(5) are indeed the primary criteria of personhood, then it is clear that genetic humanity is neither necessary nor sufficient for establishing that an entity is a person. Some human beings are not people, and there may well be people who are not human beings. A man or woman whose consciousness has been permanently obliterated but who remains alive is a human being which is no longer a person; defective human beings, with no appreciable mental capacity, are not and presumably never will be people; and a fetus is a human being which is not yet a person, and which therefore cannot coherently be said to have full moral rights. Citizens of the next century should be prepared to recognize highly advanced, self-aware robots or computers, should such be developed, and intelligent inhabitants of other worlds, should such be found, as people in the fullest sense, and to respect their moral rights. But to ascribe full moral rights to an entity which is not a person is as absurd as to ascribe moral obligations and responsibilities to such an entity.

3. FETAL DEVELOPMENT AND THE RIGHT TO LIFE

Two problems arise in the application of these suggestions for the definition of the moral community to the determination of the precise moral status of a human fetus. Given that the paradigm example of a person is a normal adult human being, then (1) How like this paradigm, in particular how far advanced since conception, does a human being need to be before it begins to have a right to life by virtue, not of being fully a person as of yet, but of being *like* a person? and (2) To what extent, if any, does the fact that a fetus has the *potential* for becoming a person endow it with some of the same rights? Each of these questions requires some comment.

In answering the first question, we need not attempt a detailed consideration of the moral rights of organisms which are not developed enough, aware enough, intelligent enough, etc., to be considered people, but which resemble people in some respects. It does seem reasonable to suggest that the more like a person, in the relevant respects, a being is, the stronger is the case for regarding it as having a right to life, and indeed the stronger its right to life is. Thus we ought to take seriously the suggestion that, insofar as "the human individual develops biologically in a continuous fashion . . . the rights of a human person might develop in the same way."[4] But we must keep in mind that the attributes which are relevant in determining whether or not an entity is enough like a person to be regarded as having some of the same moral rights are no different from those which are relevant to determining whether or not it is fully a person—i.e., are no different from (1)–(5)—and that being genetically human, or having recognizably human facial and other physical features, or detectable brain activity, or the capacity to survive outside the uterus, are simply not among these relevant attributes.

Thus it is clear that even though a seven- or eight-month fetus has features which make it apt to arouse in us almost the same powerful protective instinct as is commonly aroused by a small infant, nevertheless it is not significantly more person-like than is a very small embryo. It is *somewhat* more person-like; it can apparently feel and respond to pain, and it may even have a rudimentary form of consciousness, insofar as its brain is quite active. Nevertheless, it seems safe to say that it is not fully conscious, in the way that an infant of a few months is, and that it cannot reason, or communicate messages of indefinitely many sorts, does not engage in self-motivated activity, and has no self-awareness. Thus, in the *relevant* respects, a fetus, even a fully developed one, is considerably less person-like than is the average mature mammal, indeed the average fish. And I think that a rational person must conclude that if the right to life of a fetus is to be based upon its resemblance to a person, then it cannot be

said to have any more right to life than, let us say, a newborn guppy (which also seems to be capable of feeling pain) and that a right of that magnitude could never override a woman's right to obtain an abortion, at any stage of her pregnancy.

There may, of course, be other arguments in favor of placing legal limits upon the stage of pregnancy in which an abortion may be performed. Given the relative safety of the new techniques of artificially inducing labor during the third trimester, the danger to the woman's life or health is no longer such an argument. Neither is the fact that people tend to respond to the thought of abortion in the later stages of pregnancy with emotional repulsion, since mere emotional responses cannot take the place of moral reasoning in determining what ought to be permitted. Nor, finally, is the frequently heard argument that legalizing abortion, especially late in the pregnancy, may erode the level of respect for human life, leading, perhaps, to an increase in unjustified euthanasia and other crimes. For this threat, if it is a threat, can be better met by educating people to the kinds of moral distinctions which we are making here than by limiting access to abortion (which limitation may, in its disregard for the rights of women, be just as damaging to the level of respect for human rights).

Thus, since the fact that even a fully developed fetus is not person-like enough to have any significant right to life on the basis of its person-likeness shows that no legal restrictions upon the stage of pregnancy in which an abortion may be performed can be justified on the grounds that we should protect the rights of the older fetus, and since there is no other apparent justification for such restrictions, we may conclude that they are entirely unjustified. Whether or not it would be *indecent* (whatever that means) for a woman in her seventh month to obtain an abortion just to avoid having to postpone a trip to Europe, it would not, in itself, be *immoral* and therefore it ought to be permitted.

4. POTENTIAL PERSONHOOD AND THE RIGHT TO LIFE

We have seen that a fetus does not resemble a person in any way which can support the claim that it has even some of the same rights. But what about its *potential*, the fact that if nurtured and allowed to develop naturally it will very probably become a person? Doesn't that alone give it at least some right to life? It is hard to deny that the fact that an entity is a potential person is a strong prima facie reason for not destroying it; but we need not conclude from this that a potential person has a right to life, by virtue of that potential. It may be that our feeling that it is better, other things being equal, not to destroy a potential person is better explained by the fact that potential people are still (felt to be) an invaluable resource, not to be lightly squandered. Surely, if every speck of dust were a potential person, we would be much less apt to conclude that every potential person has a right to become actual.

Still, we do not need to insist that a potential person has no right to life whatever. There may well be something immoral, and not just imprudent, about wantonly destroying potential people, when doing so isn't necessary to protect anyone's rights. But even if a potential person does have some prima facie right to life, such a right could not possibly outweigh the right of a woman to obtain an abortion, since the rights of any actual person invariably outweigh those of any potential person, whenever the two conflict. Since this may not be immediately obvious in the case of a human fetus, let us look at another case.

Suppose that our space explorer falls into the hands of an alien culture, whose scientists decide to create a few hundred thousand or more human beings, by breaking his body into its component cells, and using these to create fully developed human beings, with, of course, his genetic code. We may imagine that each of these newly created men will have all of the original man's abilities, skills, knowledge, and so on, and also have an individual self-concept, in short that each of them will be a bona fide (though hardly unique) person. Imagine that the whole project will take only seconds, and that its chances of success are extremely high, and that our explorer knows all of this, and also knows that these people will be treated fairly. I maintain that in such a situation he would have every right to escape if he could, and thus to deprive all of these potential people of their potential lives; for his right to life outweighs all of theirs together, in spite of the fact that they are all genetically human, all innocent, and all have a very high probability of becoming people very soon, if only he refrains from acting.

Indeed, I think he would have a right to escape even if it were not his life which the alien scientists planned to take, but only a year of his freedom, or, indeed, only a day. Nor would he be obligated to stay if he had gotten captured (thus bringing all these people potentials into existence) because of his own carelessness, or even if he had done so deliberately, knowing the consequences. Regardless of how he got captured, he is not morally obligated to remain in captivity for *any* period of time for the sake of permitting any number of potential people to come into actuality, so great is the margin by which one actual person's right to liberty outweighs whatever right to life even a hundred thousand potential people have. And it seems reasonable to conclude that the rights of a woman will outweigh by a similar margin whatever right to life a fetus may have by virtue of its potential personhood.

Thus, neither a fetus's resemblance to a person, nor its potential for becoming a person provides any basis whatever for the claim that it has any significant right to life. Consequently, a woman's right to protect her health, happiness, freedom, and even her life, by terminating an unwanted pregnancy, will always override whatever right to life it may be appropriate to ascribe to a fetus, even a fully developed one. And thus, in the absence of any overwhelming social need for every possible child, the laws which restrict the right to obtain an abortion, or limit the period of pregnancy during which an abortion may be performed, are a wholly unjustified violation of a woman's most basic moral and constitutional rights.

NOTES

1. Of course, the principle that it is (always) wrong to kill innocent human beings is in need of many other modifications, e.g., that it may be permissible to do so to save a greater number of other innocent human beings, but we may safely ignore these complications here.

2. John Noonan, "Deciding Who Is Human," *Natural Law Forum*, 13 (1968).

3. From here on, we will use "human" to mean genetically human, since the moral sense seems closely connected to, and perhaps derived from, the assumption that genetic humanity is sufficient for membership in the moral community.

4. Thomas L. Hayes, "A Biological View," *Commonweal*, 85 (March 17, 1967), 677–78; quoted by Daniel Callahan, in *Abortion: Law, Choice and Morality* (London: Macmillan & Co., 1970).

Discussion Questions

1. Professor Warren claims that there are two senses to the term "human." What are they? How does she reason from these two senses to a justification of abortion? And what does she mean when she says that there could be persons who are not human beings?

2. Some have argued that Professor Warren's position supports the moral justification of infanticide (the killing of infants), since by her criteria newborns, it would seem, are not persons. How do you think she would respond to this observation?

3. Briefly describe Professor Warren's five-part criterion for personhood. One objection raised against this criterion is that some beings, who we clearly recognize as persons such as the temporarily comatose, do not fulfill any part of the criterion. How do you think Warren would respond to this objection?

4. If Professor Warren is right that a fetus is a potential but not an actual person because some of its person-defining capacities have not been actualized, do you think this would mean that she believes that human beings who have lost person-defining abilities that have been actualized (e.g., the temporarily comatose, Alzheimer patients) are no longer persons?

You can locate InfoTrac-College Education articles about this chapter by accessing the InfoTrac-College Edition website (http://www.infotrac-college.com/wadsworth/). Using the InfoTrac-College Edition subject guide, enter the search terms relevant to this chapter, and then read abstracts for relevant articles.

13   Personhood Begins at Conception*

STEPHEN D. SCHWARZ

Stephen D. Schwarz is Professor of Philosophy at University of Rhode Island. He has authored a number of works in philosophy of religion, metaphysics, and moral philosophy, including the book *The Moral Question of Abortion* (1990).

Professor Schwarz defends the traditional pro-life position on abortion: since abortion entails the intentional killing of an innocent human person who exists from the moment of conception, abortion is unjustified homicide, and consequently, morally wrong, even if the pregnancy resulted from rape or incest. Although he believes that a woman has a right to terminate her pregnancy if continuing it will result in her death (what some call "the life of the mother" exception), he does not consider such termination an "abortion," since the intention is to save the life of the mother rather than to kill the fetus even though the procedure if performed before fetal viability will result in the fetus's death. Professor Schwarz responds to the position defended by Mary Anne Warren (see Chapter 12): the fetus is a human being but not a person. He argues that Professor Warren and others who defend similar arguments confuse *being a person* with *functioning as a person*. They mistakenly infer from the fetus's lack of certain functions that it is therefore not a person.

A THEORY ABOUT HUMAN BEINGS AND PERSONS

LET US NOW EXAMINE a theory that defends abortion on the grounds that the child in the womb, though undoubtedly a human being, is not a person, and that it is only the killing of persons that is intrinsically and seriously wrong. The theory consists of two major theses: First, that killing human beings is not wrong; second, that the child (in the womb and for a time after birth) is human but not a person. I shall argue that both of these theses are mistaken.

This theory recognizes that abortion is the deliberate killing of an innocent human being, but it denies this is wrong because it denies that it is wrong to deliberately kill human beings. What is wrong is killing human beings who are persons. Now, of course, many human beings are persons, for example, normal adult human beings, and it is wrong to kill them because they are persons. But small infants, such as newborn babies or babies in the womb, though they are undoubtedly human, are not, according to this theory, persons. And so it is not intrinsically wrong to kill them. That is, it is not wrong in itself, though it may be wrong

---

*Reprinted by permission from Stephen D. Schwarz, The Moral Question of Abortion *(Chicago: Loyola University Press, 1990), chapter 7. Endnotes removed.*

because of adverse consequences. A small child, therefore, has no right to life as a normal adult does, and if the child is unwanted, he may be killed.

Thus, the theory allows for abortion and infanticide alike. It rejects the typical pro-abortion lines, such as viability and birth. It agrees that there is no morally significant difference between "before" and "after." But instead of saying that killing a human being is *wrong* on both sides of such a line, it claims that it is *right* (or can be right) on both sides of the line.

Joseph Fletcher expresses this view when he remarks, "I would support the . . . position . . . that both abortion and infanticide can be justified if and when the good to be gained outweighs the evil—that neither abortion nor infanticide is as such immoral."

Michael Tooley has an essay entitled, "A Defense of Abortion and Infanticide." If the idea that killing babies is morally right is shocking to most people, Tooley replies in his essay that this is merely an emotional response, not a reasoned one. "The response, rather than appealing to carefully formulated moral principles, is primarily visceral," he says. And, "It is reasonable to suspect that one is dealing with a taboo rather than with a rational prohibition." His position is: "Since I do not believe human infants are persons, but only potential persons, and since I think that the destruction of potential persons is a morally neutral action, the correct conclusion seems to me to be that infanticide is in itself morally acceptable."

I want to show that the theories held by Fletcher, Tooley, and others are absolutely wrong. Infanticide and abortion are both morally wrong, as wrong as the deliberate killing of an older child or an adult, and thus our emotional response of shock and horror at killing babies is completely grounded in reason and moral principles. I want to show that a small child, after birth or still in the womb, is a person, as much a person as the rest of us; that the notion of person as used by these writers is a special one, a narrower concept, and

not the one that is crucial for morality. I want to make clear why the attempts to show that a small child is not a person are mistaken, and that all human beings as such are persons.

THE ARGUMENT OF MARY ANN WARREN

In an argument for this theory, Mary Ann Warren examines "the traditional argument that since (1) it is wrong to kill innocent human beings, and (2) fetuses are innocent human beings, then (3) it is wrong to kill fetuses." This argument, she claims, is "fallacious," because "the term 'human' has two distinct, but not often distinguished, senses." In premise one, human means person, or full-fledged member of the moral community, a being whom it is wrong to kill. In premise two, on the other hand, the term human refers merely to a member of the biological species human, as opposed, say, to a rabbit or an eagle. Warren's claim is that mere membership in a biological species is morally irrelevant and thus does not confer on the being in question a right to life.

"Yes, a fetus is biologically human (human in the genetic sense), but that does not make it the kind of being who has a right to life. It is only persons (those who are human in the moral sense) who have such a right. It is wrong to kill persons, and if a human being is not also a person he does not have a right to life, and it is, or often can be, morally right to destroy him." This, in essence, is Warren's argument.

Warren offers an analysis of what is a person, a full-fledged member of the moral community:

> I suggest that the traits which are most central to the concept of personhood, or humanity in the moral sense, are, very roughly, the following:
>
> 1. consciousness (of objects and events external and/or internal to the being), and in particular the capacity to feel pain;

2. reasoning (the developed capacity to solve new and relatively complex problems);

3. self-motivated activity (activity which is relatively independent of either genetic or direct external control);

4. the capacity to communicate, by whatever means, messages of an indefinite variety of types, that is, not just with an indefinite number of possible contents, but on indefinitely many possible topics;

5. the presence of self-concepts, and self-awareness, either individual or racial, or both.

This, she acknowledges, is not a full analysis of the concept of a person. It is not a list of necessary and sufficient conditions for being a person. But, she says, this does not matter.

> All we need to claim, to demonstrate that a fetus is not a person, is that any being which satisfies none of (1)–(5) is certainly not a person. I consider this claim to be so obvious that I think anyone who denied it, and claimed that a being which satisfied none of (1)–(5) was a person all the same, would thereby demonstrate that he had no notion at all of what a person is—perhaps because he had confused the concept of a person with that of genetic humanity.

We can now see Warren's argument for abortion in its entirety. A fetus is human in the genetic sense; that is morally irrelevant. A fetus is not human in the moral sense; he is not a person since he satisfies none of the criteria she has outlined. Not being a person, he has no right to life, and abortion is morally permissible. The same applies to the child after birth. "Killing a newborn infant isn't murder." Infanticide is wrong, according to Warren, only to the extent that the child is wanted, that there are couples who would like to adopt or keep him. "Thus, infanticide is wrong for reasons analogous to those which make it wrong to wantonly destroy natural resources, or great works of art."

But destroying natural resources or works of art is not always wrong, and certainly not wrong in the sense in which murder is wrong. Warren acknowledges this when she says, "It follows from my argument that when an unwanted or defective infant is born into a society which I cannot afford and/or is not willing to care for it, then its destruction is permissible."

BEING A PERSON AND FUNCTIONING AS A PERSON

The failure of Warren's argument can be seen in light of the distinction between being a person and functioning as a person. Consider Warren's five characteristics of a person: consciousness, reasoning, self-motivated activity, the capacity to communicate, and the presence of self-concepts. Imagine a person in a deep, dreamless sleep. She is not conscious, she cannot reason, etc.; she lacks all five of these traits. She is not functioning as a person; that is part of what being asleep means. But of course she is a person; she retains fully her status of being a person, and killing her while asleep is just as wrong as killing her while she is awake and functioning as a person.

Functioning as a person refers to all the activities proper to persons as persons, to thinking in the broadest sense. It includes reasoning, deciding, imagining, talking, experiencing love and beauty, remembering, intending, and much more. The term *function* does not refer here to bodily functions, but rather to those of the mind, though certain bodily functions, especially those of the brain, are necessary conditions for functioning as a person.

When Warren points out that a fetus satisfies none of the five traits she mentions, she shows only that a fetus does not function as a person, not that it lacks the being of a person, which is the crucial thing.

At this point several objections are likely to be raised: First, the sleeping person will soon wake up and function as a person, while the being in the womb will not.

In reply, neither the sleeping person nor the being in the womb now displays the qualities of a functioning person. Both will display them. It is only a matter of time. Why should the one count as a real person because the time is short, while the other does not, simply because in her case the time is longer?

Second, the sleeping adult was already self-conscious, had already solved some problems. Therefore, she has a history of functioning as a person. The child in the womb has no such history. Thus Tooley argues that "an organism cannot have a serious right to life [be a person] unless it either now possesses, or did possess at some time in the past, the concept of a self . . . [what is required for functioning as a person]." The human being sound asleep counts as a person because she once functioned as a person; the child never did, so she does not count as a person.

True, there is a difference with respect to past functioning, but the difference is not morally relevant. The reason the child never functioned as a person is because her capacity to do so is not yet sufficiently developed. It cannot be, for she is near the beginning of her existence, in the first phase of her life.

Imagine a case of two children. One is born comatose, and he will remain so until the age of nine. The other is healthy at birth, but as soon as she achieves the concept of a continuing self for a brief time, she, too, lapses into a coma, from which she will not emerge until she is nine. Can anyone seriously hold that the second child is a person with a right to life, while the first child is not? In one case, self-awareness will come only after nine years have elapsed, in the other, it will return. In both cases, self-awareness will grow and develop. Picture the two unconscious children lying side by side. Almost nine years have passed. Would it not be absurd to say that only one of them is a person, that there is some essential, morally relevant, difference between them? Imagine someone about to kill both of them. Consistent with his theory, Tooley would have

to say: "You may kill the first, for he is not a person. He is human only in the genetic sense, since he has no history of functioning as a person. You may not kill the second, since she does have such a history." If this distinction is absurd when applied to the two born human beings, is it any less absurd when applied to two human beings, one born (asleep in a bed), the other preborn (sleeping in the womb)?

In short, when it comes to functioning as a person, there is no moral difference between "did, but does not" (the sleeping adult) and "does not, but will" (the small child).

Third, a sleeping person has the capacity to function as a person and therefore counts as being a person, even though this capacity is not now actualized. In contrast a child in the womb lacks this capacity, so he does not count as being a person.

This is the most fundamental objection, and probably underlies the preceding two objections. In considering it, compare the following beings:

A. A normal adult, sound asleep, not conscious.

B. An adult in a coma from which he will emerge in, say, six months and function normally as a person.

C. A normal newborn baby.

D. A normal baby soon to be born.

E. A normal "well proportioned small scale baby" in the womb at seven weeks.

F. A normal embryo or zygote.

Case A, the normal adult sound asleep, is someone who has the being of a person, who is not now functioning as a person, and who clearly has the capacity to function as a person. I want to show now that all the other cases are essentially similar to this one. That is, if case A is a person—a full-fledged member of the moral community, a being with a right to life, whose value lies in his own being and dignity, and not merely in his significance for others (like the natural resources and works of art), a being whose willful destruction is murder—each of the other cases is a person as well.

The objection claims that the being in the womb lacks the capacity to function as a person. True, it lacks what I shall call the *present immediate capacity* to function, where responses may be immediately elicited. Such a capacity means the capability of functioning, where such a capability varies enormously among people, and normally develops and grows (as a result of learning and other experiences).

The capability of functioning as a person is grounded in the *basic inherent capacity* to function. This is proper to the being of a person and it has a physical basis, typically the brain and nervous system. It is a capacity that grows and develops as the child grows and develops.

This basic inherent capacity may be fully accessible, as in a normal sleeping adult. It then exists in its present immediate form. It may also exist in other forms where it is latent, as in reversible coma. I shall call this the latent-1 capacity, where the basic inherent capacity is present but temporarily damaged or blocked. In a small child, the basic inherent capacity is there but insufficiently developed for the child to function in the manner of a normal adult. I shall call this the latent-2 capacity.

Let me turn to the actual refutation of this objection. I will begin with cases A through E (replies 1 and 2), then case F (3), then abnormal or handicapped human beings (4).

(1) The beings on our list, A through E, differ only with respect to their present immediate capacity to function. They are all essentially similar with respect to their basic inherent capacity, and through this, their being as persons.

Thus the adult in a coma, case B, is not essentially different from the sleeping person in case A. Person B is in a deep, deep sleep; person A in a comparatively superficial sleep. Person B cannot be awakened easily; person A can be. Person B is in a very long sleep; person A is in a short sleep, say 8 hours. Both have the basic inherent capacity; in A it is present imme-

diate; in B it is latent-1. That is certainly not a morally relevant difference. If the status of persons is to be viewed in terms of capacity to function as a person, then surely a latent-1 capacity (temporarily blocked—person B) qualifies as much as a nonlatent capacity (present immediate—person A).

Consider now the newborn baby, case C. He too has the physical basis for functioning as a person (brain, nervous system, etc.). Only his overall development is insufficient for him to actually function on the level of the normal adult. He has a latent-2 capacity. Thus there is an essential similarity between cases B and C, the adult in a coma and the newborn baby. Neither has the present immediate capacity to function as a person. Both take longer than the sleeping adult (case A) to wake up from their slumber. But both have a latent capacity to function, because they both have the basic inherent capacity to function. In the case of B, the impossibility of eliciting an immediate response is due to an abnormality, which brought on the coma. In the other, case C, this is due to the fact that the being is not yet far enough along in his process of development. In both cases the basic inherent capacity is there, it is merely latent.

Cases C and D, babies just after birth and just before birth, are clearly the same in terms of their capacity to function as persons. Birth is, among other things, the beginning of vast new opportunities to develop the basic inherent capacity to function by seeing, hearing, touching, etc., a capacity that is equally present just before birth.

Case E, a baby at seven weeks, has "all the internal organs of the adult"; and "after the eighth week no further primordia will form; *everything* is already present that will be found in the full term baby." It is these "internal organs" and "primordia" that constitute the physical base of the basic inherent capacity to function as a person. They are substantially present in both the very young preborn child, at seven and eight weeks (case E), and the older preborn child (case D). Thus the cases D and E are essentially similar with respect to their basic inherent capacity, and because of this, their being as persons.

In brief, cases A through E are essentially similar. Cases B through E are similar in themselves (each represents a latent capacity); and, taken together, in comparison with A (present immediate capacity). There is no essentially difference among cases B through E. If a person whose lack of present immediate capacity to function is due to a disorder (as in case B) should be respected as a person, then surely a being whose lack of this capacity to function is due to insufficient development (cases C through E) should also be respected as a person. Both are beings with the potential to function as a person; and this they can only have if they have the basis for it, that is, the being of a person. Case B represents a latent-1 capacity, cases C through E, a latent-2 capacity; both are forms of the basic inherent capacity to function, proper to the nature of a person. If a latent-1 capacity (B) is a mark of a person, then surely a latent-2 capacity (C through E) is also a mark of a person. Both B and C through E represent beings who will have the capability to function as persons, who lack this capability now because of the condition of the working basis of this capability (brain, nervous system, etc.). In one, that condition is one of disorder or blockage, in the other, the lack of development proper to the age of the being in question.

(2) The essential similarity among the beings A through E is also established if they are imagined as the same being: a being in the womb developing from seven weeks to birth (E to C), then lapsing into a coma (B), then recovering (A). Thus if there is a person at the end (A), there is also that same person at the beginning (E). It is the same person going through various stages, representing first a latent-2 capacity, then a latent-1 capacity, and finally a present immediate capacity.

I am now a being capable of functioning as a person (present immediate capacity). Many years ago I was a small newborn baby, and before that a smaller child in my mother's womb. My capabilities have changed, they have increased as my basic inherent capacity to function as a person has developed; but I remain always *the same person,* the same essential being, the being who has these growing capabilities. If I am essentially a person now, I was essentially a person then, when I was a baby. The fact that my capabilities to function as a person have changed and grown does not alter the absolute continuity of my essential being, that of a person. In fact, this variation in capabilities presupposes the continuity of my being as a person. It is *as a person* that I develop my capabilities to function as a person. It is because I am a person that I have these capabilities, to whatever degree.

And so the basic reality is being as a person. This is what entails your right to life, the wrongness of killing you, the necessity of respecting you as a person, and not just as a desired commodity like a natural resource.

(3) Let us turn now to case F, the zygote or embryo. There are three considerations that show the essential similarity between this case and cases A through E.

First: The continuum argument applies here as well. The adult now sleeping is the same being who was once an embryo and a zygote. There is a direct continuity between the zygote at F and the child at E, through to the adult at A. If the being at the later stages should be given the respect due to persons, then that same being should also be given this respect when he is at an earlier stage.

Second: It may be objected that the zygote lacks "a well-developed physical substratum of consciousness"—that it lacks the actual physical basis (brain, nervous system, etc.) for the basic inherent capacity to function as a person. This is incorrect. The zygote does not lack this physical basis; it is merely that it is now in a primitive, undeveloped form. The zygote has the essential structure of this basis; a structure that will unfold, grow, develop, mature, which takes time. As Blechschmidt states, " . . . the fertilized ovum (zygote) is already a form of man. Indeed, it is already active. . . . All the organs of the developing organism are differentiation products of each unique (fertilized) human ovum." That is, the organs that form the physical basis for the more developed basic inherent capacity to function as a person (at various stages, E to A) are "differentiation products" of what is already present in the zygote. Thus the zygote has, in primitive form, the physical basis of his basic inherent capacity to function as a person. In the adult this same basis exists in developed form.

The zygote actually has the basic inherent capacity to function as a person because he has the essential physical structure for this. This structure is merely undeveloped:

> The zygotic self cannot actually breathe, but he *actually has* the undeveloped capacity for breathing. Nor can this zygotic self actually think and love as an adult does, but he *actually has* the undeveloped capacity for thinking and loving. And the human zygote could not actually have such undeveloped capacities unless he actually IS the kind of being that *has* such capacities. Just as it is obviously true that only a human being can have the *developed* capacities for thinking and loving, it should be obviously true that only a human being can have the *undeveloped* capacities for thinking and loving.

Elsewhere, Robert Joyce remarks:

> A person is not an individual with a *developed* capacity for reasoning, willing, desiring, and relating to others. A person is an individual with a *natural* capacity for these activities and relationships, whether this natural capacity is ever developed or not—i.e., whether he or she ever attains the functional capacity or not. Individuals of a rational, volitional, self-conscious nature may never attain or may lose the functional capacity for fulfilling this nature to any appreciable extent. But this inability to fulfill their nature does not negate or destroy the nature itself.

A being at the beginning of his development cannot be expected to possess what only that development can provide for him. He is already the being who will later function as a person, given time. The sleeping person is also a being who will later function as a person, only he will do it much sooner. What they each have now—a fully developed brain in one case, and a potential brain, that which will grow into a developed brain, in the other—is a basis for their capacity to function as persons. It is the same essential basis, one undeveloped, the other developed. It is merely a matter of degree; there is no difference in kind.

One must already *be* a human being in order to develop the human brain necessary for the present and immediate capacity to function as a person. As we noted earlier, *"only a human being can develop a human brain, a human brain cannot develop before a human exists."* "Human being" means of course "human person," the same being in different phases of his existence.

Third: Imagine a person J solving new and relatively complex problems (item 2 on Mary Ann Warren's list).

1. Person J *is doing* this.
2. Person K *has the capacity* to do this (like the sleeping person A on the list).
3. Person L *has the capacity to learn* to do this (to learn what is necessary for having this capacity; for example, a child in school).
4. Person M *has the capacity to acquire*, by natural development, what is necessary for the capacity to learn to do this.

What is true of person M applies to a newborn baby (C), or a baby about to be born (D), or a much younger baby, at seven weeks (E). It applies equally to that same being at a still earlier stage of her development, as a zygote (F).

There is a continuity here. If being a person is approached from the point of view of capacity to function as a person, then clearly persons K, L, and M are essentially alike. Each is removed by one or more steps from the person J, who is actually functioning as a person. None of these steps is of moral or metaphysical significance. In reverse order from M to J, there is, respectively, a capacity to acquire, a capacity to learn, and a capacity to do what the next being represents. If doing is to count for being a person, then surely the capacity to do, the capacity to learn to do, and the capacity to acquire what is needed to learn to do must also count.

This chain argument shows not only the essential similarity between the zygote (F) and the child at later stages (C through E) but also the essential similarity among the beings A through F.

We are now in a better position to understand the real significance of past functioning as a person, which is present in the adult (asleep or in a coma), and absent from the child. It is a sign that the being in question is a person. Because a certain being has functioned in the past, he must be a person. But if he has not, or we do not know it, it does not follow that he is not a person. Other indications must also be examined. In the case of a small baby, born or preborn, including the zygote stage of a baby's existence, there are three such indications.

One, the *continuum of being,* the identity of the person. The baby is now the same being, the same "self" that the child will be later on. "I was once a newborn baby and before that, a baby inside my mother." Since it is a human being's essential nature to be a person, this being—as a zygote, as a seven-week-old baby, as a newborn—is always a person.

Two, the *continuum of essential structure* for the basic inherent capacity to function as a person. The baby as a zygote has the essential physical structure that represents this capacity. Both in the primitive form of development and

in all later stages of development, there exists the same essential structure.

Three, the *continuum of capacities,* to acquire, learn, and do. The zygote has the capacity to acquire what is needed to learn to function as a person.

If a being is not now functioning as a person, is he a person? Two perspectives can be used in answering this question: present to past and present to future. An affirmative answer in either case suffices to indicate that the being in question is a person. Present to past: yes, he is a person because he functioned as a person in the past. Present to future: yes, he is a person because he will function as a person in the future, based on the three-fold continuum. The mistake of writers such as Tooley is to ignore the second of these.

(4) Let us turn, finally, to the case of abnormal, or handicapped, human beings. Does the analysis offered here—that the beings A through F are essentially similar with respect to their being as persons—apply equally to abnormal, or handicapped, human beings?

It certainly does. A handicapped person (physically, mentally, or both) has the same being of a person as the rest of us who are fortunate enough not to be so afflicted. He has, with this, the same dignity, the same rights as the rest of us. We must "do unto him" as we would want others to "do unto us" if we were afflicted with a handicap. Just as there is no morally relevant difference between a normal functioning person and a small child who cannot yet function as a person because of his lack of development, there is also no morally relevant difference between the normal functioning person and one incapable, or less capable, of doing so. Any one of us who now has the present immediate capacity to function as a person may lose it through a severe illness or accident. If that happened to you, you would still have the same status of being a person, the same dignity and rights of a person.

Even a very severely abnormal or handicapped human being has the basic inherent capacity to function as a person, which is a sign that he is a person. The abnormality represents a hindrance to the actual working of this capacity, to its manifestation in actual functioning. It does not imply the absence of this capacity, as in a nonperson.

The normal adult and child were selected for this analysis because it is in them that the essence of functioning as a person, or its usual absence because of (normal) lack of development, can most easily be seen and understood. Once recognized there, it applies equally to all persons, regardless of the degree to which they are able to accomplish it.

To conclude this part of the main argument: would Mary Ann Warren admit the adult sound asleep to the status of person? If not, she is saying it is acceptable to kill people in their sleep. Suppose she admits sleeping person A. She must then admit sleeping person B, the one in a longer, deeper sleep. The only differences are the length and nature of the sleep. In each case there is a being with a capacity to function as a person, who will, if not killed, wake up to exercise it. Clearly there is no morally relevant difference between them. This proves decisively that present immediate capacity to function as a person is not necessary to being a person. This is plainly true of the newborn baby C. Having then admitted B as a person, Warren is forced to admit C as well, for the two cases are essentially the same; no present immediate capacity to function as a person, the presence of latent capacity, rooted in the basic inherent capacity.

With this, Warren's whole argument is destroyed. For she herself claims that, in terms of their intrinsic nature, their being (as persons or nonpersons), the newborn baby (C) and the preborn baby (D through F) are morally on a par. Neither (her argument shows) can now function as a person. Both, I have shown, have the basic inherent capacity to function as persons. In all of these cases, there is the same being, with the same essential structure of a person, differing only with respect to the degree of development of the capacity to function as a person.

Views like those of Warren and Tooley do not reach the crucial point: the fact that a human being functions as a person or has the present and immediate capacity to do so, is not the ground for his dignity, preciousness, and right to life; rather, that decisive ground is the fact of his *being* a person.

THE REALITY OF THE PERSON SEEN THROUGH LOVE

Imagine a person you deeply love in a coma from which he will emerge in about thirty weeks, perfectly normal. Apply Warren's five criteria. He fails them all. He is not conscious, he cannot reason, he is incapable of self-motivated activity, he cannot communicate, he has no self-concepts or awareness of himself. This doesn't mean he is not a person; that he has no right to life of his own; that he could be killed if no one cared. He is just as real, just as precious, just as much a full person as if he were now capable of functioning as a person. It is just as important and necessary to respect him and care for him as if he were awake.

The child in the womb is in a comparable state, only his "sleep" is normal and is not preceded by a phase where he is able to function as a person. He is also unseen. But none of these makes a morally relevant difference. If one person in "deep sleep" (inability to function as a person) is to be respected and cared for, then the other person should be cared for and respected as well.

THE DISTINCTION APPLIED TO SOME PRO-ABORTION VIEWS

Given our understanding of the distinction between being a person and functioning as a person, we can now come to a better understanding of some of the things put forward by defenders of abortion.

1. Drawing Lines. We examined ten suggested places to draw the line between what is supposed to be merely a *preparation* for a person and the actual person. Every line proved false. In each case the same fully real person is clearly present in both sides of it. No line marks any real difference with regard to *being* a person; the person is there before as well as after. But many of these lines do have a bearing on *functioning* as a person. Thus a baby after birth interacts with others in a way not possible before birth. A baby who has reached sentience has developed an important dimension of his capacity to function as a person. And the presence of a functioning brain marks a significant milestone in the child's development as a functioning person. If these lines seem to have any plausibility, it is because one has in mind functioning as a person. But the plausibility evaporates when one realizes that the crucial thing is not functioning as a person, but being a person.

2. The Agnostic Position. Realizing that these lines do not work, some people say that it is simply not known when a human person begins to exist. What should be said is, rather, that it is not known when *functioning* as a person begins, for there is indeed no single place on the continuum of human life at which this begins. It is a gradual development. But the *being* of the person is there all along. And the development is what it is because the being of the person is there all the way through: it is the person's development. Agnosticism regarding functioning as a person should not lead to agnosticism regarding being a person.

3. The Gradualist Position. False when applied to the *being* of a person, the gradualist position is absolutely valid when applied to *functioning* as a person. That is indeed a matter of degree. We gradually develop our basic capacity to think and to communicate.

4. The Notion of Potential Person. False when applied to *being* a person, the notion of potential person has a validity when applied to *functioning* as a person. If by "person" we mean "functioning person," for example, a normal adult making a complex decision or reading a book, then clearly a child in the womb, or just born, or even at age one, is only potentially such a person. A baby is a potential functioning person; but he is that only because he has the actual being of a person.

HUMAN IS NOT MERELY A BIOLOGICAL CATEGORY

The theory advanced by writers such as Fletcher, Tooley, and Warren holds that killing babies is permissible because they are not persons; whereas, in fact, they are nonfunctioning persons. A functioning person is one who either is now actually functioning as a person, or has the present immediate capacity to do so. What the theory holds is that only functioning persons (and those who were once such persons) are truly persons. It may, therefore, be called the *functioning-person theory*.

Advocates of the functioning-person theory hold that it is not in itself wrong to kill human beings; that this can only be wrong when the being in question is a "person," as defined by the theory (one who has the present immediate capacity to function as a person, or has had it in the past). Such advocates hold that the single fact that a being is human does not constitute any reason for not deliberately killing it. Hence, they say, killing babies, born or preborn, is not in itself wrong. *If* it is ever wrong, it is so because these babies are wanted and would be missed by adults. The thesis, as Tooley puts it, is that "membership in a biological species is not morally significant *in itself*." In the words of Singer, "Whether a being is or is not a member of our species is, in itself no more relevant to the wrongness of killing it than whether it is or is not a member of our race." Warren says that being human in the genetic sense does not give the being in question a right to life.

The thrust of this is to drive a wedge between two categories of beings—persons and human beings—and to hold that it is the former, not the latter, that is of moral significance. There are two fundamental and disastrous errors in this approach. The first concerns the category of persons, and consists in equating this term with functioning persons (present or past), thereby excluding babies who have not yet developed the present immediate capacity to function as persons. The second error, closely related to the first, is to dismiss the category of human being as not (in itself) morally significant.

Proponents of the functioning-person theory are quite right in maintaining that there is a distinction between persons and human beings. They point out that there could be persons who are not human beings, for example, creatures on distant planets who can think, make decisions, feel gratitude, and so forth. They would certainly be persons, without being human beings. In the Christian faith, angels are persons, but not human beings. So, not all persons are necessarily human beings. But, I shall maintain, all human beings are persons (though not necessarily functioning persons). Being human is not necessary to being a person (there could be others), but it is sufficient, for all human beings are persons.

The fundamental error here is the notion that human is a mere biological category, that it designates simply one of many zoological species. If this were so, if the difference between human and other species were like the difference between, say, cats and dogs, or tigers and bears, then of course it would be morally irrelevant. But human—though it may be viewed as a zoological species, and compared to other species in the study of anatomy and physiology—is not simply a biological category. It is rather a mode of being a person.

Human designates, in its most significant meaning, a type of being whose nature it is to be a person. A person is a being who has the basic inherent capacity to function as a person, regardless of how developed this capacity is, or whether or not it is blocked, as in severe senility. We respect and value human beings, not because they are a certain biological species, but because they are persons; because it is the nature of a human being to be a person. All human beings are persons, even if they can no longer function as persons (severe senility), or cannot yet function as persons (small babies), or cannot now function as persons (sound asleep or under anesthesia or in a coma).

The theory is correct when it says that it is persons who are of moral significance; and that persons need not be human persons (they may be martians or angels). The error is to fail to recognize that humans are persons. Being human is a mode of existence of persons. So we should respect human beings—all human beings, regardless of race, degree of intelligence, degree of bodily health, degree of development as functioning persons—because they are persons.

"Do unto others as you would have them do unto you." Surely the class of others is not limited to functioning persons. It includes all human beings; perhaps others as well, but at least all human beings. "Do unto others" must include, very specifically, the lame, the retarded, the weak. It must include those no longer able to function as persons, as well as those not yet able to do so.

When we love another person, it is the *total human being* that we love, not just his or her rationality, or that which makes him or her capable of functioning as a person. We love their individual mode of being, expressed in many ways, such as gestures, facial features, tone of voice, expressions in the eyes, etc. These are, of course, in one respect, bodily features. This does not render them merely biological in the sense dismissed by Singer,

Tooley, and others. They are dimensions of the total human person.

The present immediate capacity to function as a person is not essential to this fundamental reality, the total human being. When a loved one is under anesthesia, he is still fully that person, the total human being. More than that, part of the beauty, the charm, the lovableness of a small child is that he is *only a child,* not yet matured, not yet (fully) capable of functioning as a person. The total human being in such a case does not even require the present capacity to function as a person.

Warren, Tooley, and Singer fall into the trap of seeing "human" as a mere biological category because of an earlier, and more fundamental, error: confusing person and functioning person (present or past), indeed, grouping the two together. For if it is assumed that "person" equals "functioning person," and if a small child is not a (fully) functioning person, it follows that the child is not a person. If the child is not a human *person,* "human" can then refer only to a biological species. Once one strips the child of his status as a person (on the grounds that he cannot now function as a person), what is there left except his being a member of a biological species? Separated from the notion of person, the notion of "human" is indeed only a biological species, and as such morally irrelevant.

The fallacy is, then, the separation of human and person, the failure to see that humans are precisely *human persons.* Humans are human persons, where "persons" includes nonfunctioning persons as well as functioning persons.

THE NOTION OF POTENTIAL PERSON

In arguing for this thesis that abortion is morally right, Tooley goes to great lengths to show that potential persons do not have a serious right to life. "There appears to be little hope of defending a conservative view [i.e.,

that abortion is wrong] unless it can be shown that the destruction of potential persons is intrinsically wrong, and seriously so."

On the contrary, abortion is wrong because it destroys an actual person. The assumption that the being in the womb is merely a potential person is typical of the functioning-person theory. Thus Warren speaks of the "fetus" as a "potential person"; and of "its potential for becoming a person." She denies that the latter "provides any basis whatever for the claims that it has any significant right to life."

What is potential about the child in the womb is not her *being* as a person, but rather her *functioning* as a person. That functioning is potential in the sense that she now has only a latent capacity to function, and not yet a present immediate capacity, because her basic inherent capacity has not yet had a chance to develop sufficiently.

The child in the womb is not, as the functioning-person theory maintains, a potential person, but rather a *potentially functioning actual person.* To be a potentially functioning person already ensures that the baby is a person, an actual, real, full person, for a potentially functioning person must necessarily be a person.

In the words of Joyce, "A one celled person at conception is not a potential person, but an actual person with great potential for development and self-expression. That single-celled individual is just as actually a person as you and I."

I submit that there is no such thing as a potential person. The ovum and the sperm are preparations for a new person. Each of them is not that person in potential form, because it is not that person at all. There is a radical break between sperm/ovum and the new person in the zygotic state. The transition from "potential x" to "actual x" always involves a continuity. Thus a medical student is recognized as a potential doctor because when the student *becomes* a doctor this will have happened within a continuity involving the same person. In contrast, as Joyce puts it, "sperm and ovum

. . . do not, even together, become a new human life, because they do not survive beyond conception."

"The sperm and the ovum," Joyce says, "are not potential [personal] life; rather they are potential *causes* of individual human life."

THE ACHIEVEMENT VIEW

The *functioning-person theory* implies a certain elitism, something that may be called the *achievement view,* namely, that only human beings who have achieved a certain degree of development of the present immediate capacity to function as persons count as real persons. Thus Mary Ann Warren, Michael Tooley, and Peter Singer dismiss infants as nonpersons simply on the grounds that they have not yet achieved the status of functioning persons. But why hold that against them? That they have not achieved this status is perfectly normal, and could not be otherwise; for they have not yet reached that stage in their development over time when such a capacity is normal. The achievement view is a clear example of discrimination: "You don't count as a real person, for you have not yet achieved the degree of development necessary for the present immediate capacity to function as a person."

The functioning-person theory is presented as if it were the product of careful, rational, philosophical analysis, a contribution to clear thinking. It gains this appearance largely from the element of truth it contains: that the concepts of "person" and "human being" are not identical, for there could be nonhuman persons. This hides its true nature, that it is in fact a form of elitism, leading to discrimination of the worst sort. For the theory implies that only some persons count; those who have achieved the status of functioning persons.

"At what point in its development does a fetus become a person?" (Or, when does it become human, meaning a person, since it is obviously human in the biological sense all along.) This whole question is misplaced. For there is a person, a human being, all along. It is only a matter of degree of development of the basic inherent capacity to function as a person. What we can now see, with new clarity, is that this question assumes the achievement view, indeed expresses it, and would collapse without it. Translated, the question reads: "How much must a human being achieve in the way of attaining the capability of functioning as a person in order to count as a person, that is, a being whose life we must respect?" The answer is clear: nothing. No achievement is necessary, and to demand it is elitism and discrimination. What is required is *being,* not achievement: being a person, having the nature of a person, regardless of how far along the achievement scale one has progressed.

It is wrong for a white to demand that real persons be white in order to count as persons. Blacks are equally persons, though they are "different." So too, it is wrong for a functioning person to demand that real persons be capable of functioning as persons. Small babies, incapable of this—or less capable—are equally persons, though they are "different." Being white is not a special achievement that blacks have failed to reach. Having the capability of functioning as a person, while it is an achievement, is equally irrelevant, morally. To demand it as a condition for membership in the class of persons is equally unjust and discriminatory.

It is wrong to discriminate against anyone who has not yet achieved the status of a functioning person. It is equally wrong to discriminate against anyone who is *no longer* capable of functioning because of severe senility. Likewise, it is wrong to discriminate against anyone who cannot now function, whether or not he ever could function in the past and whether or not he will be able to function in the future.

In the present context, in which we are analyzing a theory that raises—as a serious issue— the question of which human beings may be killed and which may not, it is not a matter of discrimination in merely a general sense, but something very specific, and particularly odious: It is a discrimination that takes advantage of a person's inability to function as a person and uses that against them as a pretext for killing them. The effect of adopting the functioning-person theory would be to legitimize this taking advantage of a person's lack of ability. This is sheer "might over right," power and ability over frailty and (natural) disability. Those who have power and ability exercise it over those who do not—infants whom their theory can rule out as non-persons. I submit that, quite generally, it is wrong for those who have the advantage of power and ability to take advantage of it over those who do not and to discriminate against them on the basis of this advantage. Let me express this in terms of the following moral principle:

It is always wrong for persons who have power and ability to take advantage of their status by discriminating against persons who are powerless, especially in order to kill them.

And, as a corollary: *it is always wrong to take advantage of anyone's inability to function as a person by acts of discrimination that would deny that individual the full respect that is due to every person.*

This principle and its corollary apply not only to actions but also to rules and theories that would legitimatize such actions. Any theory that calls for or allows such discrimination is itself an immoral theory. (This is not a moral judgment on those who propose the theory, but strictly a judgment on the theory itself, in terms of its content and its logical consequences.) The functioning-person theory legitimizes the deliberate killing of small babies merely because they have not reached a sufficient level of development as predetermined by the theory. This is immoral.

MULTIPLE DEFINITIONS OF FUNCTIONING PERSON

The *functioning-person theory* wants to divide humanity into two separate categories: "persons" and "mere human beings," who are nonpersons. I have argued that this is a false division, that all human beings are persons, and that "person" does not mean "functioning person" but includes those with a merely latent capacity to function.

The falsity of the view that "person" means "functioning person" can also be shown in another way—that is, by carefully examining the notion of functioning person with respect to the definition provided by the advocates of the functioning-person theory. What is this definition? What characteristics must a being have in order to be classified as a person? A survey of the current literature on this topic reveals a bewildering array of suggestions, some brief, some detailed, some at variance with others. Let us look at some examples:

Mary Ann Warren proposes consciousness, reasoning, self-motivated activity, the capacity to communicate, the presence of self-concepts and self-awareness as the characteristics of a person.

Peter Singer offers a definition of "person" that "selects two crucial characteristics . . . as the core of the concept": rationality and self-consciousness.

Joseph Fletcher proposes "a list of criteria or indicators" of "humanness" (by which he means personhood). They include minimum intelligence ("Any individual of the species *homo sapiens* who falls below an I.Q. grade of 40 . . . is questionably a person; below the mark of 20, not a person. . . . The *ratio* . . . is what makes a person of the *vita* [life]."), self-awareness, self-control, a sense of time, the capacity to relate to others, and curiosity.

Michael Tooley, in his 1973 paper, "A Defense of Abortion and Infanticide," offers this list: (1) The capacity to envisage a future for oneself, and to have desires about one's future states. (2) The capacity to have a concept of a self, the concept of a continuing subject of experiences and other mental states. (3) Being a self. (4) Self-consciousness. (5) The capacity for self-consciousness.

In his book *Abortion and Infanticide*, Tooley observes, "There is a very general agreement [among writers on this topic] that something is not a person unless it is, in some sense, capable of consciousness." Further, that "many people . . . felt that mere consciousness is not itself sufficient to make something appear, and several proposals have been advanced as to what additional properties are required." He then gives a list of some of "the more important suggestions" for these additional properties. Fifteen are mentioned, many of them similar to those listed above. Among the others are: (1) The capacity to experience pleasure and/or pain. (2) The capacity to have desires. (3) The capacity to use language.

Tooley devotes a major portion of his book to his own proposal for defining a person. His perspective is that of "a right to continued existence." His thesis is, "An individual cannot have a right to continued existence unless there is at least one time at which it possesses the concept of a continuing self or mental substance."

A few pages later he says "that some *psychological continuity* is required" for one to be a person; and that "there must also be *recognition of the continuity* by the enduring mental substance in question [the person]." Putting them together, it seems that Tooley's criteria for being a person (as listed in his book) are: (1) being conscious, (2) possessing the concept of a continuing self or mental substance (at least at one time), (3) recognition of one's psychological continuity over time.

Which of these definitions, or sets of indicators or criteria, or combinations of them, is the correct one for the concept of a person? Which features are necessary for being a person? Which ones are sufficient? Which ones are both necessary and sufficient? This problem is further complicated by the fact that the authors cited here offer conflicting views about the features to be used in defining the concept of person. Thus, *rationality* is affirmed by Warren and Singer, and denied by Tooley in his book. It seems to be affirmed by Fletcher ("minimum intelligence"). *Self-consciousness* is affirmed by Warren, Singer, and Fletcher, and by Tooley in three of his articles. It is later

denied by Tooley in his book. *Being an agent* or having self-control is affirmed by Fletcher ("control of existence"), denied by Tooley.

Which criteria are to be employed is one problem. But there is another, equally serious problem. Given a criterion or feature that is to be employed in defining the concept of person, how much of it is necessary? How much is sufficient? Mary Ann Warren, for example, in listing reasoning as one of the features, says it must be "the *developed* capacity to solve new and relatively complex problems." That seems to be a tall order! Why wouldn't reasoning as the capacity to solve elementary problems be sufficient? In any case, how complex must the problems be? Or, more generally, what kinds of reasoning are to be required? And how extensive must the ability to reason be?

All, or virtually all, of these characteristics exist in degrees. Some people have more self-control, others less. Self-consciousness awakens gradually in a child. If it is to be counted as part of the definition of a person, how developed must it be? Parallel questions apply to the rest of the items on these lists.

There is still a further problem. Even if we knew which features were essential to being a person, and also how much development was necessary, even then we would have the problem of measuring the features and their degree of development. Given a small born baby, how do we know how much self consciousness the baby has? And suppose a child has a given feature but cannot display it? How are we to exclude such a possibility, so that we don't label the child a nonperson who is, in fact, a person? In a lengthy section of his book, Tooley tries to grapple with the problem of measurement, by examining a complexity of scientific evidence about "neurophysical development." But such evidence, even if it were adequate, could only be indirect, in that it measures the physical requirements for functioning as a person and not the functioning itself, for example, having self-consciousness. Needless to say, Tooley does not solve the problem.

The conclusion to be drawn from this is the following: There is no one correct definition of "person," in the sense of functioning person. It is not that there is a correct definition but no one has yet found it. There are many definitions, and a given being will be a person under one of them, and not under another. It is similar to the term *capable*. Is a given person capable? Yes, for some things, or to a certain degree; no, for other things, or to a greater degree. There are many definitions of capable, and the attempt to find the one true definition would obviously be misguided. If "person" is to be defined in terms of "capable of functioning," the same thing applies. There can be no one correct definition of person as a functioning person, because "functioning person" means precisely: one who has the present immediate capacity to function. And functioning as a person means a wide variety of things, each to varying degrees, as the above sample of proposals amply demonstrates.

This wide variety, representing the plurality and complexity of what it means to function as a person, involves two fundamental dimensions.

One is *gradual development*. The attainment of the status of functioning as a person is something that a human being develops gradually. During growth and development, both in the womb and after birth, the child gradually acquires more and more of the features discussed here, and each of them to greater and greater degrees. There is no one moment, or even a short period of time (such as a week), where one could draw a line and say, "Before that there is no functioning person, after that, there is." Thus even if we had an adequate definition, consisting of features A through Z, that makes someone a functioning person, it would still be impossible to divide humanity into two groups: human persons and human non-persons. Whatever definition there is, a human being grows into the features that comprise it.

Consider self-consciousness: A human being is somewhat self-conscious at an early stage in life, a bit more later, still more at a later stage, and so on. The point is not that we do not know when these stages occur, or just what degree of self-consciousness is involved during each of them. The point is that self-consciousness is itself a matter of degree. And so a set of defining characteristics of the person, even if we had one, would have to be in terms of more or less. "Person" (in this context) means "functioning person," and a being that exemplifies more of A through Z, or exemplifies them to a greater degree, would have more capabilities of functioning as a person. There can be no definition of person that picks out certain beings and excludes others; there can only be various features (such as self-consciousness) that different human beings exemplify to varying degrees.

The plurality and complexity of what it means to function as a person involves a second dimension, *relativity to context;* that is, how we construe the term person when it is used to designate "functioning person" varies from case to case. Suppose, for example, that in order to be legally binding, a document must be signed with two persons present as witnesses. Here a degree of functioning as a person is required that far exceeds the level attained by, say, a child of three. A three-year-old would hardly be an appropriate witness for the signing of a will. So the degree of attainment of present capacity to function as a person that we have in mind, and require, for someone to be called a person varies according to the situation, and is determined by our needs and interests.

There is no such thing as the definition of the term *functioning person* because the features that constitute any definition vary across the spectrum of gradual development, and the spectrum of context. Hence, the definition itself varies; there is no one meaning of functioning person. This shows that the whole attempt by Warren, Singer, Fletcher, Tooley, and others, to define the person is fundamentally misguided.

In her paper, "Abortion and the Concept of a Person," Jane English reaches what is in part the same conclusion: in part, because she fails to distinguish between being a person and functioning as a person. Her thesis is that there is no such thing as the correct definition of a person. She offers a refutation of the view that "the concept of a person can be captured in a straitjacket of necessary and/or sufficient conditions," which is what would be required for an adequate definition of a person. "Rather," she claims, " 'person' is a cluster of features, of which rationality, having a self-concept . . . are only part." Thus, "People typically exhibit rationality . . . but someone who was irrational would not thereby fail to qualify as a person." Her conclusion, in the first part of her paper, is that "our concept of a person is not sharp or decisive enough to bear the weight of a solution to the abortion controversy. To use it to solve that problem is to clarify *obscurum peri obscurius* [the obscure by the more obscure]."

When this is applied to the concept of functioning person, it is valid and of great significance. When, as in her paper, it is applied to the concept of being a person—and used as a reason for justifying some abortions—it is a serious mistake. The analysis offered by English is excellent, but she draws the wrong conclusion. What her analysis shows is that *functioning person* cannot be adequately defined. Nothing follows from this regarding *being a person,* especially not the conclusion that the being in the womb is not a person.

PRACTICAL CONSEQUENCES

Consider again the fact that the meaning of *functioning person* is relative to context. When occasions such as validly witnessing the signing of legal documents arise, then a division of humanity into two groups is justified. Here the requirement of a particular level of achievement for functioning as a person is appropriate. But when it is a matter of deciding who will be respected as a real person, and who will be dismissed as a nonperson and treated as a being who may be killed, the requirement of a particular level of achievement for functioning as a person is another matter entirely. Specifically, if it is in the interests of some people to kill a certain class of human beings, they can simply define them as nonpersons, on the grounds that they have not attained [or no longer retain] a particular level of achievement as functioning persons. Abortion is an obvious example. When there is a strong predisposition on the part of some people to destroy a child, there is an interest that can obviously be used to draw a line in the scale of gradual development of the capacity to function as a person, designed specifically to exclude the child that one wants to get rid of. That line may come at birth, or it may come after birth, as in Tooley's analysis, which would justify infanticide as well.

Since there is no one correct definition of person when that term designates "functioning person"; and since functioning as a person is something that develops gradually, any division of human beings into two classes, persons (who are to be respected) and nonpersons (who may be killed) must be based on a decision. This will be a decision based on interests, and where the interest is "getting rid of," any person falling into that unlucky class can be labeled a non-person and killed with impunity.

Preborn children are a striking example of this, but they are not alone. Parents who decide that their newborn child does not have a meaningful life because of a handicap, or who do not want to be burdened with the extra care that a child needs, can turn to the functioning-person theory, and use the achievement view inherent in it, to define their baby as a nonperson, in order to justify killing him.

When it is personal interests, utilizing the theory of the achievement view, rather than a person's inherent nature, that determines the morality of killing human beings, then ultimately no one is safe. For the functioning-person theory that underlies the achievement view can easily be formulated as excluding not only those who have not yet achieved functioning as a person (as in Tooley), but also those who no longer can function as persons in a particular, specified way. Thus if a person were to suffer a terrible accident that left him in a severely debilitated state, he could be classified as a nonperson and killed by those who wanted to get rid of him.

Ultimately, it would be a matter of power. Those in power could decide the level of achievement necessary for being counted as a person, and whether it would be only a matter of "not yet" or also a matter of "no longer." This is, of course, what we see in the case of abortion. Doctors kill babies, and not the other way around, because doctors have power, babies do not. This applies in an immediate and obvious way to the physical level. In general, the physically strong have the power to crush the physically weak. That is nothing new. What is new is the attempt to legitimize this by a theory: the functioning-person theory with its attendant achievement view. The effect of this is that those in power can decide who will, and who will not, count as a person, depending on whether or not the human being in question had attained (or retained) the requisite achievement.

"Might over right" is truly frightening. When it is raw physical might, with no pretense to moral legitimacy, it is frightening enough. When a claim to moral legitimacy is added, it becomes even more frightening. Murder is perpetrated without even being recognized as murder. The results of the functioning-person theory and achievement view is that, if adopted, they would provide precisely such a pretense of moral legitimacy to murder.

THE DIGNITY OF THE HUMAN PERSON

The true alternative to might over right is reverence for the dignity of each person as a person; because he or she has the being of a person.

The important reality of the dignity of the human person can be seen, and taken seriously, in many ways, especially when that dignity is denied or under attack. Slavery, child abuse, sexual molestation, and rape are among some of the more striking examples. Or, a person with a physical handicap is severely beaten by someone who takes advantage of that handicap. Another is the wrongness of taking advantage of a person's inability to function as a person, either because he is not now capable of doing so, or no longer capable, or not yet capable. This is perfectly parallel to the injustice of taking advantage of a person's physical inabilities. Persons are persons, they have the dignity of a person, whether they have these abilities or not. To take advantage of a person's inabilities is to affront his dignity. It is an antithesis to the reverence due to his dignity as a person.

It is wrong to kill a child in the womb, or a newborn baby, on the grounds that he has not yet reached a sufficient degree of functioning as a person. The same applies to a severely retarded child who probably never will achieve a certain normal level of functioning as a person. He has the same human nature, he is equally a person, he has the same dignity as a person fortunate enough to be normal. As always, it is his being as a person that counts, not his capabilities for functioning as a person.

It is the achievement view that constitutes the principal denial of this. In one case (the normal child), it denies his personhood, his dignity, because he has not yet achieved the required level of functioning as a person. In another case (the severely retarded child), it denies his personhood, his dignity, because he will never achieve the required level of functioning. But who says he must? Nobody has the right to set such standards, and impose them on others, especially at the price of their lives.

The normal person deserves our reverence, our respect for his dignity, not because he is normal, not because of actual or potential achievements in functioning as a person, but simply because he is a person. And the non-normal person is equally a person, and deserves equal reverence. If you were to become a victim of a disease or accident that left you severely retarded, incapacitated, you would want your dignity respected just as before. You would still be yourself, the same person, hence a person, hence a being with the dignity of a person. Exactly the same applies to the severely retarded child, and to the preborn child, who is in many respects similar in his capabilities.

Reverence is the most fundamental response due to another person in his dignity; it is not the whole of it. Love is the fulfillment and the highest form of this response. Each in its own way is an antithesis to using a person as a mere means, as in rape, enslavement, and other ways, and to the attitude of "get rid of it" so often displayed in the context of abortion. Each is also an antithesis to the achievement view and its odious discrimination between those who have achieved, and therefore count, and those who have not achieved, and therefore don't count, and thus may be destroyed.

The reality of love as the deepest response to another in his dignity manifests itself in the attitude and work of Mother Theresa of Calcutta. The story is told of a man whom she found abandoned in the gutter of a street. She picked him up, brought him to her home, cared for him in love for the few remaining days (or hours) of his life. He responded by saying, "I have lived like an animal in the street, but I will die like an angel, loved and cared for."

Discussion Questions

1. Mary Anne Warren suggests a five-part criterion to distinguish human beings in the genetic sense with human beings in the moral sense. How does Professor Schwarz respond to this distinction? What does he mean when he says that Professor Warren and others confuse being a person with functioning as a person? Do you consider his argument compelling? Why or why not?

2. What imaginary story does Professor Schwarz tell in order to show that "when it comes to functioning as a person, there is no moral difference between 'did, but does not' (the sleeping adult) and 'does not, but will' (the small child)"? Do you consider the story an adequate argument to support Professor Schwarz's position? Why or why not?

3. One objection to Professor Schwarz's position goes something like this: if one's potential for personal function makes one a person (as Schwarz's position appears to be saying), then could not a candidate for the U.S. Presidency (that is, a *potential* president) claim that he is an *actual* president because of his potential? How do you think Professor Schwarz would respond to this? Is it in accurate portrayal of his argument? Why or why not?

You can locate InfoTrac-College Education articles about this chapter by accessing the InfoTrac-College Edition website (http://www.infotrac-college.com/wadsworth/). Using the InfoTrac-College Edition subject guide, enter the search terms relevant to this chapter, and then read abstracts for relevant articles.

A Defense of Abortion   **14**

JUDITH JARVIS THOMSON

Judith Jarvis Thomson is Professor Emeritus of Philosophy at Massachusetts Institute of Technology and the author of several books and articles in moral and political philosophy, including *Rights, Restitution, and Risk* (1986). She has served as a president of the American Philosophical Association.

In the following essay Professor Thomson argues that even if the fetus is a human person throughout most of a woman's pregnancy, a woman still has a right to an abortion. She employs a number of stories to make her point, including the case of the famous unconscious violinist who needs your kidneys for nine months. The Society of Music Lovers kidnaps you and then hooks you up to the violinist. Do you have the right to pull the plug on the violinist and withdraw your help even if it results in the violinist's death? Thomson answers yes. She argues from this fictional case that just as you have the right to unplug yourself from the violinist if you did not consent to have your kidneys used to preserve his life, the pregnant woman has a right to have an abortion if she did not consent to become pregnant and permit her body to be used to preserve the life of another (the fetus). However, Thomson does believe that there are times at which it would be a good thing for a woman not to have an abortion.

MOST OPPOSITION TO ABORTION relies on the premise that the fetus is a human being, a person, from the moment of conception. The premise is argued for, but, as I think, not well. Take, for example, the most common argument. We are asked to notice that the development of a human being from conception through birth into childhood is continuous; then it is said that to draw a line, to choose a point in this development and say "before this point the thing is not a person, after this point it is a person" is to make an arbitrary choice, a choice for which in the nature of things no good reason can be given. It is concluded that the fetus is, or anyway that we had better say it is, a person from the moment of conception.

But this conclusion does not follow. Similar things might be said about the development of an acorn into an oak tree, and it does not follow that acorns are oak trees, or that we had better say they are. Arguments of this form are sometimes called "slippery slope arguments"—the phrase is perhaps self-explanatory—and it is dismaying that opponents of abortion rely on them so heavily and uncritically.

I am inclined to agree, however, that the prospects for "drawing a line" in the development of the fetus look dim. I am inclined to think also that we shall probably have to agree that the fetus has already become a human person well before birth. Indeed, it comes as a surprise when one first learns how early in its

Reprinted by permission of Princeton University Press from Philosophy and Public Affairs, *vol. 1, no. 1 (1971).*
Endnotes removed.

life it begins to acquire human characteristics. By the tenth week, for example, it already has a face, arms and legs, fingers and toes; it has internal organs, and brain activity is detectable. On the other hand, I think that the premise is false, that the fetus is not a person from the moment of conception. A newly fertilized ovum, a newly implanted clump of cells, is no more a person than an acorn is an oak tree. But I shall not discuss any of this. For it seems to me to be of great interest to ask what happens if, for the sake of argument, we allow the premise. How, precisely, are we supposed to get from there to the conclusion that abortion is morally impermissible? Opponents of abortion commonly spend most of their time establishing that the fetus is a person, and hardly any time explaining the step from there to the impermissibility of abortion. Perhaps they think the step too simple and obvious to require much comment. Or perhaps instead they are simply being economical in argument. Many of those who defend abortion rely on the premise that the fetus is not a person, but only a bit of tissue that will become a person at birth; and why pay out more arguments than you have to? Whatever the explanation, I suggest that the step they take is neither easy nor obvious, that it calls for closer examination than it is commonly given, and that when we do give it this closer examination we shall feel inclined to reject it.

I propose, then, that we grant that the fetus is a person from the moment of conception. How does the argument go from here? Something like this, I take it. Every person has a right to life. So the fetus has a right to life. No doubt the mother has a right to decide what shall happen in and to her body; everyone would grant that. But surely a person's right to life is stronger and more stringent than the mother's right to decide what happens in and to her body, and so outweighs it. So the fetus may not be killed; an abortion may not be performed.

It sounds plausible. But now let me ask you to imagine this. You wake up in the morning and find yourself back to back in bed with an unconscious violinist. A famous unconscious violinist. He has been found to have a fatal kidney ailment, and the Society of Music Lovers has canvassed all the available medical records and found that you alone have the right blood type to help. They have therefore kidnapped you, and last night the violinist's circulatory system was plugged into yours, so that your kidneys can be used to extract poisons from his blood as well as your own. The director of the hospital now tells you, "Look, we're sorry the Society of Music Lovers did this to you—we would never have permitted it if we had known. But still, they did it, and the violinist is now plugged into you. To unplug you would be to kill him. But never mind, it's only for nine months. By then he will have recovered from his ailment, and can safely be unplugged from you." Is it morally incumbent on you to accede to this situation? No doubt it would be very nice of you if you did, a great kindness. But do you *have* to accede to it? What if it were not nine months, but nine years? Or longer still? What if the director of the hospital says, "Tough luck, I agree, but you've now got to stay in bed, with the violinist plugged into you, for the rest of your life. Because remember this. All persons have a right to life, and violinists are persons. Granted you have a right to decide what happens in and to your body, but a person's right to life outweighs your right to decide what happens in and to your body. So you cannot ever be unplugged from him." I imagine you would regard this as outrageous, which suggests that something really is wrong with that plausible-sounding argument I mentioned a moment ago.

In this case, of course, you were kidnapped; you didn't volunteer for the operation that plugged the violinist into your kidneys. Can those who oppose abortion on the ground I mentioned make an exception for a pregnancy due to rape? Certainly. They can say that persons have a right to life only if they didn't come into existence because of rape; or they can say that all persons have a right to life, but that some have less of a right to life than others, in particular, that those who came into existence because of rape have less. But these statements have a rather unpleasant sound. Surely the question of whether you have a right to life at all, or how much of it you have, shouldn't turn on the question of whether or not you are the product of a rape. And in fact the people who oppose abortion on the ground I mentioned do not make this distinction, and hence do not make an exception in case of rape.

Nor do they make an exception for a case in which the mother has to spend the nine months of her pregnancy in bed. They would agree that would be a great pity, and hard on the mother, but all the same all persons have a right to life, the fetus is a person, and so on. I suspect, in fact, that they would not make an exception for a case in which, miraculously enough, the pregnancy went on for nine years, or even the rest of the mother's life.

Some won't even make an exception for a case in which continuation of the pregnancy is likely to shorten the mother's life; they regard abortion as impermissible even to save the mother's life. Such cases are nowadays very rare, and many opponents of abortion do not accept this extreme view. All the same, it is a good place to begin: a number of points of interest come out in respect to it.

1. Let us call the view that abortion is impermissible even to save the mother's life "the extreme view." I want to suggest first that it does not issue from the argument I mentioned earlier without the addition of some fairly powerful premises. Suppose a woman has become pregnant, and now learns that she has a cardiac condition such that she will die if she carries the baby to term. What may be done for her? The fetus—being a person—has a right to life, but as the mother is a person too, so has she a right to life. Presumably they have an equal right to life. How is it supposed to come out that an abortion may not be performed? If mother and child have an equal right to life, shouldn't we perhaps flip a coin? Or should we add to the mother's right to life her right to decide what happens in and to her body, which everybody seems to be ready to grant—the sum of her rights now outweighing the fetus' right to life?

The most familiar argument here is the following. We are told that performing the abortion would be directly killing the child, whereas doing nothing would not be killing the mother, but only letting her die. Moreover, in killing the child, one would be killing an innocent person, for the child has committed no crime, and is not aiming at his mother's death. And then there are a variety of ways in which this might be continued. (1) But as directly killing an innocent person is always and absolutely impermissible, an abortion may not be performed. Or, (2) as directly killing an innocent person is murder, and murder is always and absolutely impermissible, an abortion may not be performed. Or, (3) as one's duty to refrain from directly killing an innocent person is more stringent than one's duty to keep a person from dying, an abortion may not be performed. Or, (4) if one's only options are directly killing an innocent person or letting a person die, one must prefer letting the person die, and thus an abortion may not be performed.

Some people seem to have thought that these are not further premises which must be added if the conclusion is to be reached, but that they follow from the very fact that an innocent person has a right to life. But this seems to me to be a mistake, and perhaps the simplest way to show this is to bring out that while we must certainly grant that innocent persons have a right to life, the theses in (1) through (4) are all false. Take (2), for example. If directly killing an innocent person is murder, and thus is impermissible, then the mother's directly killing the innocent person inside her is murder, and thus is impermissible. But it cannot seriously be thought to be murder if the mother performs an abortion on herself to save her life. It cannot seriously be said that she must refrain, that she must sit passively by and wait for her death. Let us look again at the case of you and the violinist. There you are, in bed with the violinist, and the director of the hospital says to you, "It's all most distressing, and I deeply sympathize, but you see this is putting an additional strain on your kidneys, and you'll be dead within the month. But you *have* to stay where you are all the same. Because unplugging you would be directly killing an innocent violinist, and that's murder, and that's impermissible." If anything in the world is true, it is that you do not commit murder, you do not do what is impermissible, if you reach around your back and unplug yourself from that violinist to save your life.

The main focus of attention in writings on abortion has been on what a third party may or may not do in answer to a request from a woman for an abortion. This is in a way understandable. Things being as they are, there isn't much a woman can safely do to abort herself. So the question asked is what a third party may do, and what the mother may do, if it is mentioned at all, is deduced, almost as an afterthought, from what it is concluded that third parties may do. But it seems to me that to treat the matter in this way is to refuse to grant to the mother that very status of person which is so firmly insisted on for the fetus. For we cannot simply read off what a person may do from what a third party may do. Suppose you find yourself trapped in a tiny house with a growing child. I mean a very tiny house, and a rapidly growing child—you are already up against the wall of the house and in a few minutes you'll be crushed to death. The child on the other hand won't be crushed to death; if nothing is done to stop him from growing he'll be hurt, but in the end he'll simply burst open the house and walk out a free man. Now I could well understand it if a bystander were to say, "There's nothing we can do for you. We can-

not choose between your life and his, we cannot be the ones to decide who is to live, we cannot intervene." But it cannot be concluded that you too can do nothing, that you cannot attack it to save your life. However innocent the child may be, you do not have to wait passively while it crushes you to death. Perhaps a pregnant woman is vaguely felt to have the status of house, to which we don't allow the right of self-defense. But if the woman houses the child, it should be remembered that she is a person who houses it.

I should perhaps stop to say explicitly that I am not claiming that people have a right to do anything whatever to save their lives. I think, rather, that there are drastic limits to the right of self-defense. If someone threatens you with death unless you torture someone else to death, I think you have not the right, even to save your life, to do so. But the case under consideration here is very different. In our case there are only two people involved, one whose life is threatened, and one who threatens it. Both are innocent: the one who is threatened is not threatened because of any fault, the one who threatens does not threaten because of any fault. For this reason we may feel that we bystanders cannot intervene. But the person threatened can.

In sum, a woman surely can defend her life against the threat to it posed by the unborn child, even if doing so involves its death. And this shows not merely that the theses in (1) through (4) are false; it shows also that the extreme view of abortion is false, and so we need not canvass any other possible ways of arriving at it from the argument I mentioned at the outset.

2. The extreme view could of course be weakened to say that while abortion is permissible to save the mother's life, it may not be performed by a third party, but only by the mother herself. But this cannot be right either. For what we have to keep in mind is that the mother and the unborn child are not like two tenants in a small house which has, by an unfortunate mistake, been rented to both: the mother *owns* the house. The fact that she does adds to the offensiveness of deducing that the mother can do nothing from the supposition that third parties can do nothing. But it does more than this: it casts a bright light on the supposition that third parties can do nothing. Certainly it lets us see that a third party who says "I cannot choose between you" is fooling himself if he thinks this is impartiality. If Jones has found and fastened on a certain coat, which he needs to keep him from freezing, but which Smith also needs to keep him from freezing, then it is not impartiality that says "I cannot choose between you" when Smith owns the coat. Women have said again and again "This body is *my* body!" and they have reason to feel angry, reason to feel that it has been like shouting into the wind. Smith, after all, is hardly likely to bless us if we say to him, "Of course it's your coat, anybody would grant that it is. But no one may choose between you and Jones who is to have it."

We should really ask what it is that says "no one may choose" in the face of the fact that the body that houses the child is the mother's body. It may be simply a failure to appreciate this fact. But it may be something more interesting, namely the sense that one has a right to refuse to lay hands on people, even where it would be just and fair to do so, even where justice seems to require that somebody do so. Thus justice might call for somebody to get Smith's coat back from Jones, and yet you have a right to refuse to be the one to lay hands on Jones, a right to refuse to do physical violence to him. This, I think, must be granted. But then what should be said is not "no one may choose," but only "*I* cannot choose," and indeed not even this, but "*I* will not *act*," leaving it open that somebody else can or should, and in particular that anyone in a position of authority, with the job of securing people's rights, both can and should. So this is no difficulty. I have not been arguing that any

given third party must accede to the mother's request that he perform an abortion to save her life, but only that he may.

I suppose that in some views of human life the mother's body is only on loan to her, the loan not being one which gives her any prior claim to it. One who held this view might well think it impartiality to say "I cannot choose." But I shall simply ignore this possibility. My own view is that if a human being has any just, prior claim to anything at all, he has a just, prior claim to his own body. And perhaps this needn't be argued for here anyway, since, as I mentioned, the arguments against abortion we are looking at do grant that the woman has a right to decide what happens in and to her body.

But although they do grant it, I have tried to show that they do not take seriously what is done in granting it. I suggest the same thing will reappear even more clearly when we turn away from cases in which the mother's life is at stake, and attend, as I propose we now do, to the vastly more common cases in which a woman wants an abortion for some less weighty reason than preserving her own life.

3. Where the mother's life is not at stake, the argument I mentioned at the outset seems to have a much stronger pull. "Everyone has a right to life, so the unborn person has a right to life." And isn't the child's right to life weightier than anything other than the mother's own right to life, which she might put forward as a ground for an abortion?

This argument treats the right to life as if it were unproblematic. It is not, and this seems to me to be precisely the source of the mistake.

For we should now, at long last, ask what it comes to, to have a right to life. In some views having a right to life includes having a right to be given at least the bare minimum one needs for continued life. But suppose that what in fact is the bare minimum a man needs for continued life is something he has no right at all to be given? If I am sick unto death, and the only thing that will save my life is the touch of

Henry Fonda's cool hand on my fevered brow, then all the same, I have no right to be given the touch of Henry Fonda's cool hand on my fevered brow. It would be frightfully nice of him to fly in from the West Coast to provide it. It would be less nice, though no doubt well meant, if my friends flew out to the West Coast and carried Henry Fonda back with them. But I have no right at all against anybody that he should do this for me. Or again, to return to the story I told earlier, the fact that for continued life that violinist needs the continued use of your kidneys does not establish that he has a right to be given the continuous use of your kidneys. He certainly has no right against you that *you* should give him continued use of your kidneys. For nobody has any right to use your kidneys unless you give him such a right; and nobody has the right against you that you shall give him this right—if you do allow him to go on using your kidneys this is a kindness on your part, and not something he can claim from you as his due. Nor has he any right against anybody else that *they* should give him continued use of your kidneys. Certainly he had no right against the Society of Music Lovers that they should plug him into you in the first place. And if you now start to unplug yourself, having learned that you will otherwise have to spend nine years in bed with him, there is nobody in the world who must try to prevent you, in order to see to it that he is given something he has a right to be given.

Some people are rather stricter about the right to life. In their view it does not include the right to be given anything, but amounts to, and only to, the right not to be killed by anybody. But here a related difficulty arises. If everybody is to refrain from killing that violinist, then everybody must refrain from doing a great many different sorts of things. Everybody must refrain from slitting his throat, everybody must refrain from shooting him— and everybody must refrain from unplugging you from him. But does he have a right against everybody that they shall refrain from unplug-

ging you from him? To refrain from doing this is to allow him to use your kidneys. It could be argued that he has a right against us that *we* should allow him to continue to use your kidneys. That is, while he had no right against us that we should give him the use of your kidneys, it might be argued that he anyway has a right against us that we shall not now intervene and deprive him of the use of your kidneys. I shall come back to third-party interventions later. But certainly the violinist has no right against you that *you* shall allow him to continue to use your kidneys. As I said, if you do allow him to use them, it is a kindness on your part, and not something you owe him.

The difficulty I point to here is not peculiar to the right to life. It reappears in connection with all the other natural rights; and it is something which an adequate account of rights must deal with. For present purposes it is enough just to draw attention to it. But I would stress that I am not arguing that people do not have a right to life—quite to the contrary, it seems to me that the primary control we must place on the acceptability of an account of rights is that it should turn out in that account to be a truth that all persons have a right to life. I am arguing only that having a right to life does not guarantee having either a right to be given the use of or a right to be allowed continued use of another person's body—even if one needs it for life itself. So the right to life will not serve the opponents of abortion in the very simple and clear way in which they seem to have thought it would.

4. There is another way to bring out the difficulty. In the most ordinary sort of case, to deprive someone of what he has a right to is to treat him unjustly. Suppose a boy and his small brother are jointly given a box of chocolates for Christmas. If the older boy takes the box and refuses to give his brother any of the chocolates, he is unjust to him, for the brother has been given a right to half of them. But suppose that, having learned that otherwise it means nine years in bed with that violinist, you unplug yourself from him. You surely are not being unjust to him, for you gave him no right to use your kidneys, and no one else can have given him any such right. But we have to notice that in unplugging yourself, you are killing him; and violinists, like everybody else, have a right to life, and thus in the view we were considering just now, the right not to be killed. So here you do what he supposedly has a right you shall not do, but you do not act unjustly to him in doing it.

The emendation which may be made at this point is this: the right to life consists not in the right not to be killed, but rather in the right not to be killed unjustly. This runs a risk of circularity, but never mind: it would enable us to square the fact that the violinist has a right to life with the fact that you do not act unjustly toward him in unplugging yourself, thereby killing him. For if you do not kill him unjustly, you do not violate his right to life, and so it is no wonder you do him no injustice.

But if this emendation is accepted, the gap in the argument against abortion stares us plainly in the face: it is by no means enough to show that the fetus is a person, and to remind us that all persons have a right to life—we need to be shown also that killing the fetus violates its right to life, i.e., that abortion is unjust killing. And is it?

I suppose we may take it as a datum that in a case of pregnancy due to rape the mother has not given the unborn person a right to the use of her body for food and shelter. Indeed, in what pregnancy could it be supposed that the mother has given the unborn person such a right? It is not as if there were unborn persons drifting about the world, to whom a woman who wants a child says "I invite you in."

But it might be argued that there are other ways one can have acquired a right to the use of another person's body than by having been invited to use it by that person. Suppose a woman voluntarily indulges in intercourse, knowing of the chance it will issue in pregnancy, and then she does become pregnant; is she not in part responsible for the presence, in fact the very existence, of the unborn person inside her? No doubt she did not invite it in. But doesn't her partial responsibility for its being there itself give it a right to the use of her body? If so, then her aborting it would be more like the boy's taking away the chocolates, and less like your unplugging yourself from the violinist—doing so would be depriving it of what it does have a right to, and thus would be doing it an injustice.

And then, too, it might be asked whether or not she can kill it even to save her own life: If she voluntarily called it into existence, how can she now kill it, even in self-defense?

The first thing to be said about this is that it is something new. Opponents of abortion have been so concerned to make out the independence of the fetus, in order to establish that it has a right to life, just as its mother does, that they have tended to overlook the possible support they might gain from making out that the fetus is *dependent* on the mother, in order to establish that she has a special kind of responsibility for it, a responsibility that gives it rights against her which are not possessed by any independent person—such as an ailing violinist who is a stranger to her.

On the other hand, this argument would give the unborn person a right to its mother's body only if her pregnancy resulted from a voluntary act, undertaken in full knowledge of the chance a pregnancy might result from it. It would leave out entirely the unborn person whose existence is due to rape. Pending the availability of some further argument, then, we would be left with the conclusion that unborn persons whose existence is due to rape have no right to the use of their mothers' bodies, and thus that aborting them is not depriving them of anything that they have a right to and hence is not unjust killing.

And we should also notice that it is not at all plain that this argument really does go even as far as it purports to. For there are cases and cases, and the details make a difference. If the room is stuffy, and I therefore open a window to air it, and a burglar climbs in, it would be absurd to say, "Ah, now he can stay, she's given him a right to the use of her house—for she is partially responsible for his presence there, having voluntarily done what enabled him to get in, in full knowledge that there are such things as burglars, and that burglars burgle." It would be still more absurd to say this if I had had bars installed outside my windows, precisely to prevent burglars from getting in, and a burglar got in only because of a defect in the bars. It remains equally absurd if we imagine it is not a burglar who climbs in, but an innocent person who blunders or falls in. Again, suppose it were like this: people-seeds drift about in the air like pollen, and if you open your windows, one may drift in and take root in your carpets or upholstery. You don't want children, so you fix up your windows with fine mesh screens, the very best you can buy. As can happen, however, and on very, very rare occasions does happen, one of the screens is defective; and a seed drifts in and takes root. Does the person-plant who now develops have a right to the use of your house? Surely not—despite the fact that you voluntarily opened your windows, you knowingly kept carpets and upholstered furniture, and you knew that screens were sometimes defective. Someone may argue that you are responsible for its rooting, that it does have a right to your house, because after all you *could* have lived out your life with bare floors and furniture, or with sealed windows and doors. But this won't do—for by the same token anyone can avoid a pregnancy due to rape by having a hysterectomy, or anyway by never leaving home without a (reliable!) army.

It seems to me that the argument we are looking at can establish at most that there are some cases in which the unborn person has a right to the use of its mother's body, and therefore some cases in which abortion is unjust killing. There is room for much discussion and argument as to precisely which, if any.

But I think she should sidestep this issue and leave it open, for at any rate the argument certainly does not establish that all abortion is unjust killing.

5. There is room for yet another argument here, however. We surely must all grant that there may be cases in which it would be morally indecent to detach a person from your body at the cost of his life. Suppose you learn that what the violinist needs is not nine years of your life, but only one hour: all you need do to save his life is to spend one hour in that bed with him. Suppose also that letting him use your kidneys for that one hour would not affect your health in the slightest. Admittedly you were kidnapped. Admittedly you did not give anyone permission to plug him into you. Nevertheless it seems to me plain you *ought* to allow him to use your kidneys for that hour— that it would be indecent to refuse.

Again, suppose pregnancy lasted only an hour, and constituted no threat to life or health. And suppose that a woman becomes pregnant as a result of rape. Admittedly she did not voluntarily do anything to bring about the existence of a child. Admittedly she did nothing at all which would give the unborn person a right to the use of her body. All the same it might well be said, as in the newly emended violinist story, that she *ought* to allow it to remain for that hour— that it would be indecent in her to refuse.

Now some people are inclined to use the term "right" in such a way that it follows from the fact that you ought to allow a person to use your body for the hour he needs, that he has a right to use your body for the hour he needs, even though he has not been given that right by any person or act. They may say that it follows also that if you refuse, you act unjustly toward him. This use of the term is perhaps so common that it cannot be called wrong; nevertheless it seems to me to be an unfortunate loosening of what we would do better to keep a tight rein on. Suppose that box of chocolates I mentioned earlier had not been given to both boys jointly, but was given only to the older boy. There he sits, stolidly eating his way through the box, his small brother watching enviously. Here we are likely to say "You ought not to be so mean. You ought to give your brother some of those chocolates." My own view is that it just does not follow from the truth of this that the brother has any right to any of the chocolates. If the boy refuses to give his brother any, he is greedy, stingy, callous—but not unjust. I suppose that the people I have in mind will say it does follow that the brother has a right to some of the chocolates and that the boy does act unjustly if he refuses to give his brother any. But the effect of saying this is to obscure what should be kept distinct, namely the difference between the boy's refusal in this case and the boy's refusal in the earlier case, in which the box was given to both boys jointly, and in which the small brother thus had what was from any point of view clear title to half.

A further objection to so using the term "right" that from the fact that A ought to do a thing for B, it follows that B has a right against A that A do it for him, is that it is going to make the question of whether or not a man has a right to a thing turn on how easy it is to provide him with it; and this seems not merely unfortunate, but morally unacceptable. Take the case of Henry Fonda again. I said earlier that I had no right to the touch of his cool hand on my fevered brow, even though I needed it to save my life. I said it would be frightfully nice of him to fly in from the West Coast to provide me with it, but that I had no right against him that he should do so. But suppose he isn't on the West Coast. Suppose he has only to walk across the room, place a hand briefly on my brow—and, lo, my life is saved. Then surely he ought to do it, it would be indecent to refuse. Is it to be said, "Ah, well, it follows that in this case she has a right to the touch of his hand on her brow, and so it would be an injustice in him to refuse"? So that I have a right to it when it is easy for him to provide it, though no right when it's hard?

It's rather a shocking idea that anyone's rights should fade away and disappear as it gets harder and harder to accord them to him.

So my own view is that even though you ought to let the violinist use your kidneys for the one hour he needs, we should not conclude that he has a right to do so—we should say that if you refuse, you are, like the boy who owns all the chocolates and will give none away, self-centered and callous, indecent in fact, but not unjust. And similarly, that even supposing a case in which a woman pregnant due to rape ought to allow the unborn person to use her body for the hour he needs, we should not conclude that he has a right to do so; we should conclude that she is self-centered, callous, indecent, but not unjust, if she refuses. The complaints are no less grave; they are just different. However, there is no need to insist on this point. If anyone does wish to deduce "he has a right" from "you ought," then all the same he must surely grant that there are cases in which it is not morally required of you that you allow that violinist to use your kidneys, and in which he does not have a right to use them, and in which you do not do him an injustice if you refuse. And so also for mother and unborn child. Except in such cases as the unborn person has a right to demand it—and we were leaving open the possibility that there may be such cases—nobody is morally required to make large sacrifices, of health, of all other interests and concerns, of all other duties and commitments, for nine years, or even for nine months, in order to keep another person alive.

6. We have in fact to distinguish between two kinds of Samaritan: the Good Samaritan and what we might call the Minimally Decent Samaritan. The story of the Good Samaritan, you will remember, goes like this:

> A certain man went down from Jerusalem to Jericho, and fell among thieves, which stripped him of his raiment, and wounded him, and departed, leaving him half dead.

And by chance there came down a certain priest that way and when he saw him, he passed by on the other side.

And likewise a Levite, when he was at the place, came and looked on him, and passed by on the other side.

But a certain Samaritan, as he journeyed, came where he was; and when he saw him he had compassion on him.

And went to him, and bound up his wounds, pouring in oil and wine, and set him on his own beast, and brought him to an inn, and took care of him.

And on the morrow, when he departed, he took out two pence, and gave them to the host, and said unto him, "Take care of him; and whatsoever thou spendest more, when I come again, I will repay thee."

(Luke 10:30–35)

The Good Samaritan went out of his way, at some cost to himself, to help one in need of it. We are not told what the options were, that is, whether or not the priest and the Levite could have helped by doing less than the Good Samaritan did, but assuming they could have, then the fact they did nothing at all shows they were not even Minimally Decent Samaritans, not because they were not Samaritans, but because they were not even minimally decent.

These things are a matter of degree, of course, but there is a difference, and it comes out perhaps most clearly in the story of Kitty Genovese, who, as you will remember, was murdered while thirty-eight people watched or listened, and did nothing at all to help her. A Good Samaritan would have rushed out to give direct assistance against the murderer. Or perhaps we had better allow that it would have been a Splendid Samaritan who did this, on the ground that it would have involved a risk of death for himself. But the thirty-eight not only did not do this, they did not even trouble to pick up a phone to call the police. Minimally Decent Samaritanism would call for doing at least that, and their not having done it was monstrous.

After telling the story of the Good Samaritan, Jesus said, "Go, and do thou likewise." Perhaps he meant that we are morally required to act as the Good Samaritan did. Perhaps he was urging people to do more than is morally required of them. At all events it seems plain that it was not morally required of any of the thirty-eight that he rush out to give direct assistance at the risk of his own life, and that it is not morally required of anyone that he give long stretches of his life—nine years or nine months—to sustaining the life of a person who has no special right (we were leaving open the possibility of this) to demand it.

Indeed, with one rather striking class of exceptions, no one in any country in the world is *legally* required to do anywhere near as much as this for anyone else. The class of exceptions is obvious. My main concern here is not the state of the law in respect to abortion, but it is worth drawing attention to the fact that in no state in this country is any man compelled by law to be even a Minimally Decent Samaritan to any person; there is no law under which charges could be brought against the thirty-eight who stood by while Kitty Genovese died. By contrast, in most states in this country women are compelled by law to be not merely Minimally Decent Samaritans, but Good Samaritans to unborn persons inside them. This doesn't by itself settle anything one way or the other, because it may well be argued that there should be laws in this country—as there are in many European countries—compelling at least Minimally Decent Samaritanism. But it does show that there is a gross injustice in the existing state of the law and it shows also that the groups currently working against liberalization of abortion laws, in fact working toward having it declared unconstitutional for a state to permit abortion, had better start working for the adoption of Good Samaritan law generally, or earn the charge that they are acting in bad faith.

I should think, myself, that Minimally Decent Samaritan laws would be one thing, Good Samaritan laws quite another, and in fact highly improper. But we are not here concerned with the law. What we should ask is not whether anybody should be compelled by law to be a Good Samaritan, but whether we must accede to a situation in which somebody is being compelled—by nature, perhaps—to be a Good Samaritan. We have, in other words, to look now at third-party interventions. I have been arguing that no person is morally required to make large sacrifices to sustain the life of another who has no right to demand them, and this even where the sacrifices do not include life itself; we are not morally required to be Good Samaritans or anyway Very Good Samaritans to one another. But what if a man cannot extricate himself from such a situation? What if he appeals to us to extricate him? It seems to me plain that there are cases in which we can, cases in which a Good Samaritan would extricate him. There you are, you were kidnapped, and nine years in bed with that violinist lie ahead of you. You have your own life to lead. You are sorry, but you simply cannot see giving up so much of your life to the sustaining of his. You cannot extricate yourself, and ask us to do so. I should have thought that—in light of his having no right to the use of your body—it was obvious that we do not have to accede to your being forced to give up so much. We can do what you ask. There is no injustice to the violinist in our doing so.

7. Following the thread of the opponents of abortion, I have throughout been speaking of the fetus merely as a person, and what I have been asking is whether or not the argument we began with, which proceeds only from the fetus' being a person, really does establish its conclusion. I have argued that it does not.

But of course there are arguments and arguments, and it may be said that I have simply fastened on the wrong one. It may be said that what is important is not merely the fact that the fetus is a person, but that it is a person for whom the woman has a special kind of responsibility issuing from the fact that she is its mother. And it might be argued that all my analogies are therefore irrelevant—for you do not have that special kind of responsibility for that violinist, Henry Fonda does not have that special kind of responsibility for me. And our attention might be drawn to the fact that men and women both are compelled by law to provide support for their children.

I have in effect dealt (briefly) with this argument in section 4 above; but a (still briefer) recapitulation now may be in order. Surely we do not have any such "special responsibility" for a person unless we have assumed it, explicitly or implicitly. If a set of parents do not try to prevent pregnancy, do not obtain an abortion, and then at the time of birth of the child do not put it out for adoption, but rather take it home with them, then they have assumed responsibility for it, they have given it rights, and they cannot now withdraw support from it at the cost of its life because they now find it difficult to go on providing for it. But if they have taken all reasonable precautions against having a child, they do not simply by virtue of their biological relationship to the child who comes into existence have a special responsibility for it. They may wish to assume responsibility for it, or they may not wish to. And I am suggesting that if assuming responsibility for it would require large sacrifices, then they may refuse. A Good Samaritan would not refuse—or anyway, a Splendid Samaritan, if the sacrifices that had to be made were enormous. But then so would a Good Samaritan assume responsibility for that violinist; so would Henry Fonda, if he is a Good Samaritan, fly in from the West Coast and assume responsibility for me.

8. My argument will be found unsatisfactory on two counts by many of those who want to regard abortion as morally permissible. First, while I do argue that abortion is not impermissible, I do not argue that it is always permissible. There may well be cases in which carrying the child to term requires only Minimally Decent Samaritanism of the mother, and this is a standard we must not fall below. I am inclined to think it a merit of my account precisely that it does *not* give a general yes or a general no. It allows and supports our sense that, for example, a sick and desperately frightened fourteen-year-old schoolgirl, pregnant due to rape, may *of course* choose abortion, and that any law which rules this out is an insane law. And it also allows for and supports our sense that in other cases resort to abortion is even positively indecent. It would be indecent in the woman to request an abortion, and indecent in a doctor to perform it, if she is in her seventh month, and wants the abortion just to avoid the nuisance of postponing a trip abroad. The very fact that the arguments I have been drawing attention to treat all cases of abortion, or even all cases of abortion in which the mother's life is not at stake, as morally on a par ought to have made them suspect at the outset.

Secondly, while I am arguing for the permissibility of abortion in some cases, I am not arguing for the right to secure the death of the unborn child. It is easy to confuse these two things in that up to a certain point in the life of the fetus it is not able to survive outside the mother's body; hence removing it from her body guarantees its death. But they are importantly different. I have argued that you are not morally required to spend nine months in bed, sustaining the life of that violinist, but to say this is by no means to say that if, when you unplug yourself, there is a miracle and he survives, you then have a right to turn round and slit his throat. You may detach yourself even if this costs him his life; you have no right to be guaranteed his death, by some other means, if unplugging yourself does not kill him. There are some people who will feel dissatisfied by this feature of my argument. A woman may be utterly devastated by the thought of a child, a bit of herself, put out for adoption and never seen or heard of again. She may therefore want not merely that the child be detached from her, but more, that it die. Some opponents of abortion are inclined to regard this as beneath contempt—thereby showing insensitivity to what is surely a powerful source of despair. All the same, I agree that the desire for the child's death is not one which anybody may gratify, should it turn out to be possible to detach the child alive.

At this place, however, it should be remembered that we have only been pretending throughout that the fetus is a human being from the moment of conception. A very early abortion is surely not the killing of a person, and so is not dealt with by anything I have said here.

Discussion Questions

1. Present and explain Thomson's argument for the permissibility of abortion. Do you think that she is correct in comparing the violinist case with pregnancy? What if any problems do you see with this analogy?
2. Some people, such as Harvard Law Professor Laurence Tribe, argue that the Supreme Court should have used Thomson's argument in *Roe v. Wade,* rather than conceding that the constitutional question of abortion hinged on fetal personhood. If you were a member of the Supreme Court, how would you incorporate Tribe's suggestion? And how would you address the question of fetal personhood in your rewritten decision?

3. Some people argue that Thomson's argument seems applicable only to pregnancy resulting from rape, where the sex was not voluntary. If you do not agree because you believe
it applies in other cases, explain and defend your position. If you agree that Thomson's
argument does apply exclusively to cases of rape, why does it not apply to cases where
sex is voluntary?

You can locate InfoTrac-College Education articles about this chapter by accessing the InfoTrac-College
Edition website (http://www.infotrac-college.com/wadsworth/). Using the InfoTrac-College Edition
subject guide, enter the search terms relevant to this chapter, and then read abstracts for relevant articles.

Arguments from Bodily Rights   15

FRANCIS J. BECKWITH

Francis J. Beckwith is Associate Professor of Philosophy, Culture, and Law, Trinity
Graduate School, Trinity International University, where he also holds adjunct
appointments in both Trinity Evangelical Divinity School and Trinity Law School.
Some of his books include *Politically Correct Death: Answering the Arguments for
Abortion Rights* (1993); *The Abortion Controversy 25 Years After Roe v. Wade: A
Reader,* 2nd ed. (1998); and *Abortion and the Sanctity of Human Life* (2000).

   In this essay Beckwith contends that Judith Jarvis Thomson's argument is flawed
for several reasons: (1) it assumes that moral obligations must be voluntary in order
to have moral weight, (2) it denies special obligations to family members, (3) it
denies *prima facie* rights of children, including the unborn, to their parents' goods,
(4) it ignores the distinction between killing and withholding treatment, (5) it does
not take into consideration legal precedent, and (6) it seems in at least three ways
inconsistent with the radical feminism espoused by many of the argument's
proponents: (i) its use of the burden of pregnancy, (ii) its appeal to libertarian
principles, and (iii) its macho view of bodily control.

SOME ABORTION-RIGHTS ADVOCATES do not see
the status of the unborn as the decisive factor
in whether or not abortion is morally justified.
They argue that the unborn's presence in the
pregnant woman's body entails a conflict of
rights if the pregnant woman does not want to
be pregnant. Therefore, the unborn, regardless
of whether it is fully human and has a full right

Reprinted, with revisions, by permission of the author, from Francis J. Beckwith, Politically Correct Death:
Answering the Arguments for Abortion Rights *(Grand Rapids, MI: Baker, 1993), chapter 7.*

to life, cannot use the body of another against her will. Hence, a pregnant woman's removal of an unborn entity from her body, even though it will probably result in that entity's death, is no more immoral than an ordinary person's refusal to donate his kidney to another in need of one, even though this refusal will probably result in the death of the prospective recipient. In this essay we will discuss such arguments from rights.

The most famous and influential argument from rights is the one presented by philosopher Judith Jarvis Thomson.

ARGUMENT FROM UNPLUGGING THE VIOLINIST

Thomson presents a philosophically sophisticated version of the argument from a woman's right to control her body.[1] Thomson argues that even if the unborn entity is a person with a right to life, this does not mean that a woman must be forced to use her bodily organs to sustain its life. Just as one does not have a right to use another's kidney if one's kidney has failed, the unborn entity, although having a basic right to life, does not have a right to life so strong that it outweighs the pregnant woman's right to personal bodily autonomy.

Presentation of the Argument

This argument is called "the argument from unplugging the violinist" because of a story Thomson uses to illustrate her position:

> You wake up in the morning and find yourself back to back in bed with an unconscious violinist. A famous unconscious violinist. He has been found to have a fatal kidney ailment, and the Society of Music Lovers has canvassed all the available medical records and found that you alone have the right blood type to help. They have therefore kidnapped you, and last night the violinist's circulatory system was plugged into yours, so that your kidneys can be used to extract poisons from his blood as

well as your own. The director of the hospital now tells you, "Look, we're sorry the Society of Music Lovers did this to you—we would never have permitted it if we had known. But still, they did it, and the violinist now is plugged into you. To unplug you would be to kill him. But never mind, it's only for nine months. By then he will have recovered from his ailment, and can safely be unplugged from you." Is it morally incumbent on you to accede to this situation? No doubt it would be very nice of you if you did, a great kindness. But do you *have* to accede to it? What if it were not nine months, but nine years? Or still longer? What if the director of the hospital says, "Tough luck, I agree, but you've now got to stay in bed, with the violinist plugged into you, for the rest of your life. Because remember this. All persons have a right to life, and violinists are persons. Granted you have a right to decide what happens in and to your body, but a person's right to life outweighs your right to decide what happens in and to your body. So you cannot ever be unplugged from him." I imagine that you would regard this as outrageous."[2]

Thomson concludes that she is "only arguing that having a right to life does not guarantee having either a right to be given the use of or a right to be allowed continued use of another person's body even if one needs it for life itself."[3] Thomson anticipates several objections to her argument, and in the process of responding to them further clarifies it. It is not important, however, that we go over these clarifications now, for some are not germane to the pro-life position I am defending in this essay,[4] and the remaining will be dealt with in the following critique. In any event, it should not be ignored by the pro-life advocate that Thomson's argument makes some important observations which have gone virtually unnoticed by the pro-life movement. In defending the relevance of her story, Thomson points out that it is "of great interest to ask what happens if, for the sake of argument, we allow the premise [that the unborn are fully human or persons]. How, precisely, are we supposed to get from there to the conclusion that abortion is morally impermissible?[5] Thomson's argument poses a special difficulty because she believes that since pregnancy constitutes an infringement on the pregnant woman's personal rights by the unborn entity, the ordinary abortion, although it results in the death of an innocent human person, is not prima facie wrong.

A CRITIQUE OF THOMSON'S ARGUMENT

There are at least nine problems with Thomson's argument. These problems can be put into three categories: ethical, legal, and ideological.

ETHICAL PROBLEMS WITH THOMSON'S ARGUMENT

1. Thomson assumes volunteerism. By using the story as a paradigm for all relationships, thus implying that moral obligations must be voluntarily accepted in order to have moral force, Thomson mistakenly infers that all true moral obligations to one's offspring are voluntary. But consider the following story. Suppose a couple has a sexual encounter that is fully protected by several forms of birth control short of surgical abortion (condom, the Pill, IUD), but nevertheless results in conception. Instead of getting an abortion, the mother of the conceptus decides to bring it to term, although the father is unaware of this decision. After the birth of the child, the mother pleads with the father for child support. Because he refuses, she takes legal action. Although he took every precaution to avoid fatherhood, thus showing that he did not wish to accept such a status, according to nearly all child-support laws in the United States he would still be obligated to pay support *precisely because* of his relationship to this child.[6] As Michael Levin points out, "All child-support laws make the

parental body an indirect resource for the child. If the father is a construction worker, the state will intervene unless some of his calories he expends lifting equipment go to providing food for his children."[7]

But this obligatory relationship is not based strictly on biology, for this would make sperm donors morally responsible for children conceived by their seed. Rather, the father's responsibility for his offspring stems from the fact that he engaged in an act, sexual intercourse, that he fully realized could result in the creation of another human being, although he took every precaution to avoid such a result. This is not an unusual way to frame moral obligations, for we hold drunk people whose driving results in manslaughter responsible for their actions, even if they did not intend to kill someone prior to becoming intoxicated. Such special obligations, although not directly undertaken voluntarily, are necessary in any civilized culture in order to preserve the rights of the vulnerable, the weak, and the young, who can offer very little in exchange for the rights bestowed upon them by the strong, the powerful, and the post-uterine in Thomson's moral universe of the social contract. Thus, Thomson is wrong, in addition to ignoring the *natural* relationship between sexual intercourse and human reproduction,[8] when she claims that if a couple has "taken all reasonable precautions against having a child, they do not by virtue of their biological relationship to the child who comes into existence have a special responsibility for it." "Surely we do not have any such 'special responsibility' for a person unless we have assumed it, explicitly or implicitly."[9] Hence, instead of providing reasons for rejecting any special responsibilities for one's offspring, Thomson simply dismisses the concept altogether.

2. Thomson's argument is fatal to family morality. It follows from the first criticism that Thomson's volunteerism is fatal to family morality which has as one of its central beliefs that an individual has special and filial obliga-tions to his offspring and family that he does not have to other persons. Although Thomson may not consider such a fatality as being all that terrible, since she may accept the feminist dogma that the traditional family is "oppres-sive" to women, a great number of ordinary men and women, who have found joy, happi-ness, and love in family life, find Thomson's volunteerism to be counterintuitive. Philoso-pher Christina Sommers has come to a similar conclusion:

> For it [the volunteerist thesis] means that there is no such thing as filial duty per se, no such thing as the special duty of mother to child, and generally no such thing as morality of special family or kinship relations. All of which is contrary to what people think. For most people think that we do owe special debts to our parents even though we have not voluntarily assumed our obligations to them. Most people think that what we owe to our children does not have its origin in any vol-untary undertaking, explicit or implicit, that we have made to them. And "preanalytically," many people believe that we owe special con-sideration to our siblings even at times when we may not *feel* very friendly to them. . . . The idea that to be committed to an individ-ual is to have made a voluntarily implicit or explicit commitment to that individual is gen-erally fatal to family morality. For it looks upon the network of felt obligation and expectation that binds family members as a sociological phenomenon that is without pre-sumptive moral force. The social critics who hold this view of family obligation usually are aware that promoting it in public policy must further the disintegration of the traditional family as an institution. But whether they deplore the disintegration or welcome it, they are bound in principle to abet it.[10]

3. A case can be made that the unborn does have a prima facie right to her mother's body. Assuming that there is such a thing as a special filial obligation, a principle that does not have to be voluntarily accepted in order to have moral force, it is not obvious that the unborn entity in ordinary circumstances (that is, with the exception of when the mother's life is in significant danger) does not have a natural prima facie claim to her mother's body. There are several reasons to suppose that the unborn entity does have such a natural claim.

a. Unlike Thomson's violinist, who is artifi-cially attached to another person in order to save his life and is therefore not naturally dependent on any particular human being, the unborn entity is a human being who by her very nature is dependent on her mother, for this is how human beings are at this stage of their development.

b. This period of a human being's natural development occurs in the womb. This is the journey which we all must take and is a neces-sary condition for any human being's post-uterine existence. And this fact alone brings out the most glaring difference between the violinist and the unborn: the womb is the unborn's natural environment, whereas being artificially hooked up to a stranger is not the natural environment for the violinist. It would seem, then, that the unborn has a prima facie natural claim upon her mother's body.

c. This same entity, when she becomes a newborn, has a natural claim upon her parents to care for her, regardless of whether her par-ents wanted her (see the story of the irrespon-sible father). This is why we prosecute child abusers, people who throw their babies in trash cans, and parents who abandon their children. Although it should not be ignored that preg-nancy and childbirth entail certain emotional, physical, and financial sacrifices on the part of the pregnant woman, these sacrifices are also endemic of parenthood in general (which ordi-narily lasts much longer than nine months), and do not seem to justify the execution of troublesome infants and younger children whose existence entails a natural claim to cer-tain financial and bodily goods that are under the ownership of their parents. If the unborn entity is fully human, as Thomson is willing to grant, why should the unborn's natural prima facie claim to her parents' goods differ before birth? Of course, a court will not force a parent to donate a kidney to her dying offspring, but this sort of dependence on the parent's body is highly unusual and is not part of the ordinary obligations associated with the natural process of human development, just as in the case of the violinist's artificial dependency on the reluctant music lover.

As Schwartz points out: "So, the very thing that makes it plausible to say that the person in bed with the violinist has no duty to sustain him, namely, that he is a stranger unnaturally hooked up to him, is precisely what is absent in the case of the mother and her child." That is to say, the mother "does have an obligation to take care of her child, to sustain her, to protect her, and especially, to let her live in the only place where she can now be protected, nourished, and allowed to grow, namely the womb."[11]

If Thomson responds to this argument by saying that birth is the threshold at which parents become fully responsible, then she has begged the question, for her argument was supposed to show us why there is no parental responsibility before birth. That is to say, Thomson cannot appeal to birth as the decisive moment at which parents become responsible in order to prove that birth is the time at which parents become responsible.

It is evident that Thomson's violinist illustration undermines the deep natural bond between mother and child by making it seem no different from that between two strangers artificially hooked up to each other so that one can "steal" the service of the other's kidneys. Never has something so human, so natural, so beautiful, and so wonderfully demanding of our human creativity and love been reduced to such a brutal caricature.

I am not saying that the unborn entity has an absolute natural claim to her mother's body, but simply that she has a prima facie natural claim. For one can easily imagine a situation in

which this natural claim is outweighed by other important prima facie values, such as when a pregnancy significantly endangers the mother's life. Since the continuation of such a pregnancy would most likely entail the death of both mother and child, and since it is better that one human should live rather than two die, terminating such a pregnancy via abortion is morally justified.

Someone may respond to the three criticisms by agreeing that Thomson's illustration may not apply in cases of ordinary sexual intercourse, but only in cases in which pregnancy results from rape or incest, although it should be noted that Thomson herself does not press this argument. She writes: "Surely the question of whether you have a right to life at all, or how much of it you have, shouldn't turn on the question of whether or not you are the product of rape."[12]

But those who do press the rape argument may choose to argue in the following way. Just as the sperm donor is not responsible for how his sperm is used or what results from its use (e.g., it may be stolen, or an unmarried woman may purchase it, inseminate herself, and give birth to a child), the raped woman, who did not voluntarily engage in intercourse, cannot be held responsible for the unborn human who is living inside her.

But there is a problem with this analogy: The sperm donor's relinquishing of responsibility does not result in the death of a human person. The following story should help to illustrate the differences and similarities between these two cases.

Suppose that the sperm donated by the sperm donor was stolen by an unscrupulous physician and inseminated into a woman. Although he is not morally responsible for the child that results from such an insemination, the donor is nevertheless forced by an unjust court to pay a large monthly sum for child support, a sum so large that it may drive him into serious debt, maybe even bankruptcy. This would be similar to the woman who became pregnant as a result of rape. She was unjustly violated and is supporting a human being against her will at an emotional and financial cost. Is it morally right for the sperm donor to kill the child he is supporting in order to allegedly right the wrong that has been committed against him? Not at all, because such an act would be murder. Now if we assume, as does Thomson, that the raped woman is carrying a being who is fully human (or "a person"), her killing of the unborn entity by abortion, except if the pregnancy has a strong possibility of endangering her life, would be as unjust as the sperm donor killing the child he is unjustly forced to support. As the victimized man may rightly refuse to pay the child support, the raped woman may rightly refuse to bring up her child after the pregnancy has come to term. She can choose to put the child up for adoption. But in both cases, the killing of the child is not morally justified. Although neither the sperm donor nor the rape victim may have the same special obligation to their biological offspring as does the couple who voluntarily engaged in intercourse with no direct intention to produce a child, it seems that the more general obligation not to directly kill another human person does apply.

4. Thomson ignores the fact that abortion is indeed killing and not merely the withholding of treatment. Thomson makes an excellent point: namely, there are times when withholding and/or withdrawing medical treatment is morally justified. For instance, I am not morally obligated to donate my kidney to Fred, my next-door neighbor, simply because he needs a kidney in order to live. In other words, I am not obligated to risk my life so that Fred may live a few years longer. Fred should not expect that of me. If, however, I donate one of my kidneys to Fred, I will have acted above and beyond the call of duty, since I will have performed a supererogatory moral act. But this case is not analogous to pregnancy and abortion.

Levin argues that there is an essential difference between abortion and the unplugging of the violinist. In the case of the violinist (as well as my relationship to Fred's welfare), "the person who withdraws [or withholds] his assistance is not completely responsible for the dependency on him of the person who is about to die, while the mother is completely responsible for the dependency of her fetus on her. When one is completely responsible for dependence, refusal to continue to aid is indeed killing." For example, "if a woman brings a newborn home from the hospital, puts it in its crib and refuses to feed it until it has starved to death, it would be absurd to say that she simply refused to assist it and had done nothing for which she should be criminally liable."[13] In other words, just as the withholding of food kills the child after birth, in the case of abortion, the abortion kills the child. In neither case is there any ailment from which the child suffers and for which highly invasive medical treatment, with the cooperation of another's bodily organs, is necessary in order to cure this ailment and save the child's life.

Or consider the following case, which can be applied to the case of pregnancy resulting from rape or incest. Suppose a person returns home after work to find a baby at his doorstep. Suppose that no one else is able to take care of the child, but this person has only to take care of the child for nine months (after that time a couple will adopt the child). Imagine that this person, because of the child's presence, will have some bouts with morning sickness, water retention, and other minor ailments. If we assume with Thomson that the unborn child is as much a person as you or I, would "withholding treatment" from this child and its subsequent death be justified on the basis that the homeowner was only "withholding treatment" of a child he did not ask for in order to benefit himself? Is any person, born or unborn, obligated to sacrifice his life because his death would benefit another person? Consequently, there is no doubt that such "withholding" of treatment (and it seems totally false to call ordinary shelter and sustenance "treatment") is indeed murder.

But is it even accurate to refer to abortion as the "withholding of support or treatment"? Professors Schwarz and R. K. Tacelli make the important point that although "a woman who has an abortion is indeed 'withholding support' from her unborn child . . . abortion is far more than that. It is the active killing of a human person—by burning him, by crushing him, by dismembering him."[14] Euphemistically calling abortion the "withholding of support or treatment" makes about as much sense as calling suffocating someone with a pillow the withdrawing of oxygen.

In summary, I agree with Professor Brody when he concludes that "Thomson has not established the truth of her claim about abortion, primarily because she has not sufficiently attended to the distinction between our duty to save X's life and our duty not to take it." But "once one attends to that distinction, it would seem that the mother, in order to regain control over her body, has no right to abort the fetus from the point at which it becomes a human being."[15]

LEGAL PROBLEMS WITH THOMSON'S ARGUMENT

There are at least two legal problems with Thomson's argument: one has to do with tort law, and the other has to do with parental responsibility and child-welfare law.

1. Thomson's argument ignores tort law. Judge John T. Noonan of the U.S. Ninth Circuit Court of Appeals points out that "while Thomson focuses on this fantasy [the violinist story], she ignores a real case from which American tort law has generalized."[16]

> On a January night in Minnesota, a cattle buyer, Orlando Depue, asked a family of farmers, the Flateaus, with whom he had dined, if he could remain overnight at their house. The Flateaus refused and, although Depue was sick and had fainted, put him out of the house into the cold night. Imposing liability on the Flateaus for Depue's loss of his frostbitten fingers, the court said: "In the case at bar defendants were under no contract obligation to minister to plaintiff in his distress; but humanity demanded they do so, if they understood and appreciated his condition. . . . The law as well as humanity required that he not be exposed in his helpless condition to the merciless elements." Depue was a guest for supper although not a guest after supper. The American Law Institute, generalizing, has said that it makes no difference whether the person is a guest or a trespasser. He has the privilege of staying. His host has the duty not to injure him or put him into an environment where he becomes nonviable. The obligation arises when one "understands and appreciates" the condition of the other.[17]

Noonan concludes that "although the analogy is not exact, the case is much closer to the mother's situation than the case imagined by Thomson; and the emotional response of the Minnesota judges seems to be a truer reflection of what humanity requires."[18]

2. Thomson's argument ignores family law. Thomson's argument is inconsistent with the body of well-established family law, which presupposes parental responsibility of a child's welfare. And, of course, assuming as Thomson does that the unborn are fully human, this body of law would also apply to parents' responsibility for their unborn children. According to legal scholars Dennis J. Horan and Burke J. Balche, "All 50 states, the District of Columbia, American Samoa, Guam, and the U.S. Virgin Islands have child abuse and neglect statutes which provide for the protection of a child who does not receive needed medical care." They further state that "a review of cases makes it clear that these statutes are properly applied to secure emergency medical treatment and sustenance (food or water, whether given orally or through intravenous or nasogastric tube) for children when parents, with or without the acquiescence of physicians, refuse to provide it."[19] Evidently, "pulling the plug" on a perfectly healthy unborn entity, assuming that it is a human person, would clearly violate these statutes.

For example, in a case in New York, the court ruled that the parents' actions constituted neglect when they failed to provide medical care to a child with leukemia: "The parent . . . may not deprive a child of life-saving treatment, however well-intentioned. Even when the parents' decision to decline necessary treatment is based on constitutional grounds, such as religious beliefs, it must yield to the State's interests, as parens patriae, in protecting the health and welfare of the child."[20] The fact of the matter is that the "courts have uniformly held that a parent has the legal responsibility of furnishing his dependent child with adequate food and medical care."[21]

It is evident then that child-protection laws reflect our deepest moral intuitions about parental responsibility and the utter helplessness of infants and small children. And without these moral scruples—which are undoubtedly undermined by "brave new notions" of a socially contracted "voluntaristic" family (Thomson's view)—the protection of children and the natural bonds and filial obligations that are an integral part of ordinary family life will become a thing of the past. This seems too high a price for bodily autonomy.

IDEOLOGICAL PROBLEMS WITH THE USE OF THOMSON'S ARGUMENT

There are at least three ideological problems in the use of Thomson's argument by others. The latter two problems are usually found in the books, speeches, articles, or papers, of those in the feminist and/or abortion-rights movements who sometimes uncritically use Thomson's argument or ones similar to it. In fact, Thomson may very well agree with most or all of the following critique.

1. Inconsistent use of the burden of pregnancy. Thomson has to paint pregnancy in the most horrific of terms in order to make her argument seem plausible. Dr. Bernard Nathanson, an obstetrician/ gynecologist and former abortion provider, objects "strenuously to Thomson's portrayal of pregnancy as a nine-month involuntary imprisonment in bed. This casts an unfair and wrongheaded prejudice against the consideration of the state of pregnancy and skews the argument." Nathanson points out that "pregnancy is not a 'sickness.' Few pregnant women are bedridden and many, emotionally and physically, have never felt better. For these it is a stimulating experience, even for mothers who originally did not 'want' to be pregnant." Unlike the person who is plugged into Thomson's violinist, "alpha [the unborn entity] does not hurt the mother by being 'plugged in,' . . . except in the case of well-defined medical indications." And "in those few cases where pregnancy *is* a medical penalty, it is a penalty lasting nine months."[22]

Compare and contrast Thomson's portrayal of pregnancy with the fact that researchers have recently discovered that many people believe that a pregnant woman cannot work as effectively as a nonpregnant woman who is employed to do the same job in the same workplace. This has upset a number of feminists, and rightfully so. They argue that a pregnant woman is not incapacitated or ill, but can work just as effectively as a nonpregnant woman.[23] But why then do feminists who use Thomson's argument argue, when it comes to abortion, that pregnancy is similar to being bedridden and hooked up to a violinist for nine months? When it comes to equality in the workplace (with which I agree with the feminists) there is no problem. But in the case of morally justifying abortion rights, pregnancy is painted in the most horrific of terms. Although not logically fatal to the abortion-rights position, this sort of double-mindedness is not conducive to good moral reasoning.

2. The libertarian principles underlying Thomson's case are inconsistent with the state-mandated agenda of radical feminism.

If Thomson's illustration works at all, it works contrary to the statist principles of radical feminism (of course, a libertarian feminist need not be fazed by this objection). Levin points out that "while appeal to an absolute right to the disposition of one's body coheres well with other strongly libertarian positions (laissez-faire in the marketplace, parental autonomy in education of their children, freedom of private association), this appeal is most commonly made by feminists who are antilibertarian on just about every other issue." For example, "feminists who advocate state-mandated quotas, state-mandated comparable worth pay scales, the censorship of 'sexist' textbooks in the public schools, laws against 'sexually harassing speech' and legal limitations on private association excluding homosexuals, will go on to advocate abortion on the basis of an absolute libertarianism at odds with every one of those policies."[24] Although this criticism is ad hominem, as was the previous one, it serves to underscore the important political fact that many abortion-rights advocates are more than willing to hold and earnestly defend contrary principles for the sake of legally mandating their ideological agenda.

3. Thomson's argument implies a macho view of bodily control, a view inconsistent with true feminism.

Some have pointed out that Thomson's argument and/or reasoning behind it is actually quite antifeminist. In response to a similar argument from a woman's right to control her own body, one feminist publication asks, "What kind of control are we talking about? A control that allows for violence against another human being is a macho, oppressive kind of control. Women rightly object when others try to have that kind of control over them, and the movement for women's rights asserts the moral right of women to be free from the control of others." After all, "abortion involves violence against a small, weak and dependent child. It is macho control, the very kind the feminist movement most eloquently opposes in other contexts."[25]

Celia Wolf-Devine observes that "abortion has something . . . in common with the behavior ecofeminists and pacifist feminists take to be characteristically masculine; it shows a willingness to use violence in order to take control. The fetus is destroyed by being pulled apart by suction, cut in pieces, or poisoned." Wolf-Devine goes on to point out that "in terms of social thought . . . it is the masculine models which are most frequently employed in thinking about abortion. If masculine thought is naturally hierarchical and oriented toward power and control, then the interests of the fetus (who has no power) would naturally be suppressed in favor of the interests of the mother. But to the extent that feminist social thought is egalitarian, the question must be raised of why the mother's interests should prevail over the child's. . . . Feminist thought about abortion has . . . been deeply pervaded by the individualism which they so ardently criticize."[26]

NOTES

1. Judith Jarvis Thomson, "A Defense of Abortion," in *The Problem of Abortion*, 2nd ed., ed. Joel Feinberg (Belmont, CA: Wadsworth, 1984), pp. 173–187. This article was originally published in *Philosophy and Public Affairs* 1 (1971): 47–66.
2. Thomson, "A Defense of Abortion," pp. 174–175.
3. Ibid., p. 180.
4. For example, in clarifying her own view, Thomson criticizes the absolutist position on abortion that it is morally impermissible to have an abortion even if the life of the mother is in significant danger. Needless to say, I

agree with Thomson that this view is seriously flawed.

5. Thomson, "A Defense of Abortion," p. 174.

6. See *In the Best Interest of the Child: A Guide to State Child Support and Paternity Laws,* eds. Carolyn Royce Kastner and Lawrence R. Young (n.p.: Child Support Enforcement Beneficial Laws Project, National Conference of State Legislatures, 1981).

7. Michael Levin, review of *Life in the Balance* by Robert Wennberg, *Constitutional Commentary* 3 (Summer 1986): 511.

8. The lengths to which Thomson will go in order to deny the *natural* relationship between sex, reproduction, and filial obligations is evident in her use of the following analogy: "If the room is stuffy, and I therefore open a window to air it, and a burglar climbs in, it would be absurd to say, 'Ah, now he can stay, she's given him a right to use her house—for she is partially responsible for his presence there, having voluntarily done what enabled him to get in, in full knowledge that there are such things as burglars, and that burglars burgle'" (Thomson, "A Defense of Abortion," p. 182). Since there is no *natural* dependency between burglar and homeowner, as there is between child and parent, Thomson's analogy is way off the mark. Burglars *don't belong* in other people's homes, whereas preborn children belong in *no other place except* their mother's womb.

9. Ibid., p. 186.

10. Christina Sommers, "Philosophers Against the Family," in *Vice and Virtue in Everyday Life: Readings in Ethics,* eds. Christina Sommers and Fred Sommers (San Diego, CA: Harcourt Brace Jovanovich, 1989), p. 744–745.

11. Stephen D. Schwarz, *The Moral Question of Abortion* (Chicago: Loyola University Press, 1990), p. 118.

12. Thomson, "A Defense of Abortion," p. 175.

13. Michael Levin, *Feminism and Freedom* (New Brunswick, NJ: Transaction, 1987), pp. 288–289.

14. Stephen D. Schwarz and R.K. Tacelli, "Abortion and Some Philosophers: A Critical Examination," *Public Affairs Quarterly* 3 (April 1989): 85.

15. Baruch Brody, *Abortion and the Sanctity of Human Life: A Philosophical View* (Cambridge, MA: M.I.T. Press, 1975), p. 30.

16. John T. Noonan, "How to Argue About Abortion," in *Morality in Practice,* 2nd ed., ed. James P. Sterba (Belmont, CA: Wadsworth, 1988), p. 150.

17. Ibid.

18. Ibid.

19. Dennis J. Horan and Burke J. Balch, *Infant Doe and Baby Jane Doe: Medical Treatment of the Handicapped Newborn,* Studies in Law & Medicine Series (Chicago: Americans United for Life, 1985), p. 2.

20. *In re Storar,* 53 N.Y. 2d 363, 380–381, 420 N.E. 2d 64, 73, 438 N.Y.S. 2d 266, 275 (1981), as quoted in Ibid., pp. 2–3.

21. Horan and Balch, *Infant Doe,* pp. 3–4.

22. Bernard Nathanson, M.D., *Aborting America* (New York: Doubleday, 1979), p. 220.

23. Michelle Healy, "At Work: Maternity Bias," *USA Today* (July 30, 1990): 1A. Conducted by researcher Hal Grueutal of State University of New York, Albany, this survey found that 41 percent of those interviewed (133 women and 122 men at eight businesses in the Northeast) "said they think pregnancy hurts a woman's job performance."

24. Levin, review of *Life in the Balance,* pp. 507–508.

25. n.a., *Sound Advice for All Prolife Activists and Candidates Who Wish to Include a Concern for Women's Rights in Their Prolife Advocacy: Feminists for Life Debate Handbook* (Kansas City, MO: Feminists for Life of American, n.d.), pp. 15–16.

26. Celia Wolf-Devine, "Abortion and the 'Feminine Voice'," *Public Affairs Quarterly* 3 (July 1989): 86, 87.

Discussion Questions

1. How does Professor Beckwith argue philosophically and legally against Professor Thomson's position? Do you think he is successful? Why or why not?
2. Professor Beckwith does not believe that Professor Thomson's argument applies to the case of a woman becoming pregnant due to rape. Do you think that Beckwith is correct in his assessment? Do you think the analogies he uses are successful when arguing for this position?
3. At what three points does Professor Beckwith believe that Thomson's argument is inconsistent with radical feminism? How does he argue for this position? Do you think he is correct? Why or why not?

You can locate InfoTrac-College Education articles about this chapter by accessing the InfoTrac-College Edition website (http://www.infotrac-college.com/wadsworth/). Using the InfoTrac-College Edition subject guide, enter the search terms relevant to this chapter, and then read abstracts for relevant articles.

Euthanasia and Physician-Assisted Suicide

Introduction to Section B

The Hippocratic Oath, a minority viewpoint at the time of its origin in the fourth century B.C., would later become the guiding ethical light of Western medicine for nearly twenty centuries. One section of it, which deals with physician-assisted suicide and euthanasia, reads:

> I will not give poison to anyone though asked to do so, nor will I suggest such a plan. . . . But in purity and in holiness I will guard my life and my art.[1]

Within recent years there has come a serious challenge to the Hippocratic tradition. There are a number of reasons for this challenge. Some scholars say it is because there has been a philosophical shift in Western medicine from the Judeo-Christian view that human life is a gift of God and thus inherently sacred (which is consistent with the Hippocratic Oath though it preceded Christianity by nearly 400 years) to a more secular view which sees the physician as the facilitator of the patient's autonomous choices (which may include physician-assisted suicide) based on the patient's own personal religious and philosophical views.[2]

Other scholars, though not entirely in disagreement with this assessment, see the rise of advanced medical technologies, especially those used to sustain life almost indefinitely, as making the greatest contribution to the waning influence of the Hippocratic Oath. "People can be kept alive against their wishes or in states of pain and other forms of suffering, such as loss of control, fatigue, depression, hopelessness. It is also possible to keep people alive who are in a coma or a persistent vegetative state. . . . In cases like these, the use of medical technologies raises questions about the moral appropriateness of death."[3] Involved in such cases are the following major life-sustaining interventions:

1. Cardiopulmonary resuscitation (CPR): This refers to a range of interventions that restore heartbeat and maintain blood flow and breathing following a cardiac or respiratory arrest, for example, mouth-to-mouth resuscitation and electric shock to restore the heart to its normal pacing.

2. Mechanical ventilation: The use of a machine to assist in breathing and in regulating the exchange of gases in the blood.

3. Renal dialysis: An artificial method of sustaining the chemical balance of the blood when the kidneys have failed.

4. Antibiotics: A number of drugs used to protect a patient from various types of life-threatening infections.

5. Nutritional support and hydration: This refers to artificial methods of providing nourishment and fluids. This usually involves the insertion of a feeding tube, which delivers nutrition directly into the digestive tract or intravenous feeding, which delivers nourishment into the bloodstream. . . .[4]

The traditional view, consistent with the Hippocratic Oath, maintains that it is always morally wrong for a physician intentionally to kill an innocent human being, but that sometimes it is morally permissible to allow a patient to die by withdrawing or withholding treatment (*withdrawing treatment* is ending treatment which has already begun whereas *withholding treatment* is not beginning the treatment at all). Recently a more radical view, espoused by groups such as The Hemlock Society and the Society for the Right to Die, has made some headway with the medical profession as well as the general public. This view maintains that physician-assisted suicide for some terminally-ill patients is morally justified.

On June 4, 1990, Dr. Jack Kevorkian, a Michigan pathologist made headlines nationwide with the use of his "suicide machine" on a fifty-four-year-old Oregon woman, Janet Adkins. Janet, who had been diagnosed with Alzheimer's disease a year earlier, had begun to experience the symptoms of the disease three years prior to her death. Alzheimer's disease is an irreversible degeneration of brain cells that results in dementia, chronic and increasing memory loss, and, eventually, death. In a 1968 Volkswagen van, Dr. Kevorkian attached Janet to his machine, which consisted of three bottles and an intravenous tube. When the button was pushed, the contents of each bottle was released into Janet. One bottle held saline solution, the second induced sleep and contained thiopental sodium, and the last held potassium chloride, which caused her heart to stop beating.

Calling his practice "medicide,"[5] Dr. Kevorkian engaged in a form of euthanasia which is rarely, if ever, approved by medical ethicists. Nevertheless, his actions have brought to the forefront the moral question of whether euthanasia of any sort is ever justified. The word *euthanasia* comes from two Greek words, *eu* and *thanatos,* which translated literally means "good death" or "happy death." Today euthanasia is defined as an act that brings about the death of a terminally ill person who is either suffering tremendously and/or is near death. Death is brought about either by actively causing the patient's death, such as by giving a lethal injection or removing oxygen from the patient's room, or by passively causing the patient's death, such as by withdrawing or withholding treatment which is perceived as useless. The former is known as *active euthanasia* while the latter is known as *passive euthanasia*. In passive euthanasia the *intent* is not to kill but simply to relieve the patient of an unnecessary burden and to permit nature to take its course.

In decisions concerning the withdrawing or withholding of treatment, many ethicists argue that intentions are an integral part in judging the morality of the act. For example, if a man receiving chemotherapy which will extend his life only a few months chooses to withdraw treatment for the sake of not undergoing the physical pain, then he has chosen passive euthanasia, for his intention is not to die but to relieve pain (with the help of pain-killers when the cancer gets more severe), although the decision to withdraw treatment will most certainly hasten death. On the other hand, suppose another man in a similar situation requests a lethal injection in addition to withdrawing treatment. In this case, he has chosen death, and hence has chosen active euthanasia, for he intends to end his life prematurely rather than merely to relieve pain.

The difference between the first man and the second man is a difference between choosing life without pain (although the cancer will eventually kill the first man) and choosing death (i.e., it is the lethal injection and *not* the cancer that kills the second man). Although not all so-called cases of passive and active euthanasia are as clear-cut, the above clearly shows to most peoples' satisfaction that there is a fundamental moral difference between passive and active euthanasia.

The view of the American Medical Association is based on this distinction. Consider the statement endorsed by the AMA's house of delegates on December 4, 1973:

> The intentional termination of life of one human being by another—mercy killing—is contrary to that for which the medical profession stands and is contrary to the policy of the American Medical Association.
>
> The cessation of the employment of extraordinary means to prolong the life of the body when there is irrefutable evidence that biological death is imminent is the decision of the patient and/or his immediate family. The advice and judgment of the physician should be freely available to the patient and/or his immediate family.[6]

In 1982 the AMA's judicial council endorsed the following guidelines, which differ slightly from and are more detailed than the 1973 statement on euthanasia:

> In the making of decisions for the treatment of seriously deformed newborns or persons who are severely deteriorated victims of injury, illness or advanced age, the primary consideration should be what is best for the individual patient and not the avoidance of a burden to the family or to society. Quality of life is a factor to be considered in determining what is best for the individual. Life should be cherished despite disabilities and handicaps, except when prolongation would be inhumane and unconscionable. Under these circumstances, withholding or removing life supporting means is ethical provided that the normal care given an individual who is ill is not discontinued. The social commitment of the physician is to prolong life and relieve suffering. Where the observance of one conflicts with the other, the physician, patient, and/or family of the patient have discretion to resolve the conflict.
>
> For humane reasons, with informed consent a physician may do what is medically necessary to alleviate severe pain, or cease or omit treatment to let a terminally ill patient die, but should not intentionally cause death. In determining whether the administration of potentially life-prolonging medical treatment is in the best interest of the patient,

the physician should consider what the possibility is for extending life under humane and comfortable conditions and what are the wishes and attitudes of the family or those who have responsibility for the custody of the patient.

Where a terminally ill patient's coma is beyond doubt irreversible and there are adequate safeguards to confirm the accuracy of the diagnosis, all means of life support may be discontinued. If death does not occur when life support systems are discontinued, the comfort and dignity of the patient should be maintained.[7]

Philosopher James Rachels disagrees with both the 1973 and 1982 AMA statements. In Chapter 18, Rachels argues that there is no difference between active and passive euthanasia. He also argues that what makes life worth living is not merely biological life, but biographical life (one's hopes, life experiences, dreams, pursuits, interests, etc.). Thus, if one's biographical life has ended, we have no right to prevent a person from ending his or her biological life. Paul Chamberlain responds to Rachels in Chapter 19 by defending the active/passive distinction as well as arguing that physician-assisted suicide is not morally permissible.

Ethicists who accept the passive/active distinction see each type of euthanasia as being either voluntary, involuntary, or nonvoluntary. *Voluntary* euthanasia occurs when a fully informed competent patient freely *consents* either to withdraw/withhold treatment (passive euthanasia) or to intentionally hasten death by any number of means, such as a lethal injection (active euthanasia). Euthanasia is *involuntary* when it is forced upon a patient (whether it is passive or active) *against* his or her request not to be euthanized. *Nonvoluntary* euthanasia is performed on a patient (whether it is passive or active) *without* but not against his or her request not to be euthanized. For example, a PVS patient is taken off life support by her physician even though the physician was given no prior indication by the patient (such as through a living will) of what her wishes might be concerning the withdrawing/withholding of treatment. Hence, there are six types of euthanasia: (1) voluntary active euthanasia; (2) voluntary passive euthanasia; (3) nonvoluntary passive euthanasia; (4) nonvoluntary active euthanasia; (5) involuntary passive euthanasia; and (6) involuntary active euthanasia. Although types (1) and (2) are defended by medical ethicists in North America (though many more of them defend [2] than [1]), with (2) being the only type supported by the A.M.A., there are a few proponents of types (3), (4), and (5) (with very few defending [5]), whereas type (6) is associated by most people with the Nazi euthanasia programs.

The first part of this section (The Law and Euthanasia) contains two contributions, Chapters 16 and 17. They are abridged opinions from U.S. Supreme Court cases *Cruzan v. Harmon* (1991) and *Washington v. Glucksberg* (1997). The court ruled in both decisions that there is no constitutional right to suicide (as there is a constitutional right to abortion), though in *Cruzan* it ruled that there is a constitutional right to withdraw or withhold life-sustaining treatment. But, as Chief Justice William Rehnquist points out in his opinion in *Glucksberg,* the fact that there is no constitutional right to suicide does not prevent the individual states from passing laws that *permit* some form of physician-assisted suicide or euthanasia. However, with the exception of a 1994 Oregon ballot initiative, the Death With Dignity Act, which legalized physician-assisted suicide, every time the issue has been put to a vote in either legislatures or referenda, physician-assisted suicide has been defeated. States in which physician-assisted suicide has been voted down include Washington, California, Iowa, and Rhode Island.

In addition to the essays by Rachels and Chamberlain, the second part of this section (Morality of Euthanasia) contains two other articles. The first (Chapter 20), written by physician Timothy Quill, originally appeared in 1991 in *The New England Journal of Medicine*. In this piece Dr. Quill defends his decision to give a patient diagnosed with leukemia a prescription for barbiturates, though knowing full well that she will commit suicide by taking an overdose in order to avoid dying of leukemia. In response to Dr. Quill (Chapter 21), psychiatrist Patricia Wesley argues that Dr. Quill's use of euphemisms in telling his story avoids confronting the important issue of physician responsibility to a despondent patient who is most likely suffering from clinical depression.

> **Key words:** physician-assisted suicide, euthanasia, medical futility, personhood, active euthanasia, passive euthanasia, living will, DNR order, burdensome care, ordinary care, extraordinary care, law of double effect, suicide, Jack Kevorkian, Hemlock Society, University Faculty for Life, end of life issues, bioethics, medical ethics, *Washington v. Glucksberg, Quill v. Vacco, Compassion in Dying v. Washington,* Karen Ann Quinlan, right to die, Dutch euthanasia.

NOTES

1. As quoted in Nigel M. de S. Cameron, *The New Medicine: Life and Death after Hippocrates* (Wheaton, IL: Crossway, 1991), 25.
2. This is the view of Cameron in *Ibid* and Stanley Hauerwaus, *Suffering Presence: Theological Reflections on Medicine, the Mentally Handicapped, and the Church* (Notre Dame, IN: University of Notre Dame Press, 1986).
3. J.P Moreland and Norman L. Geisler, *The Life and Death Debate: Moral Issues of Our Time* (New York: Praeger, 1990), 63.
4. Ibid., 63–64.
5. Jack Kevorkian, *Prescription: Medicide: The Goodness of Planned Death* (Buffalo, NY: Prometheus Books, 1991).
6. As quoted in James Rachels, "Active and Passive Euthanasia," in *Ethical Theory and Social Issues: Historical Texts and Contemporary Readings,* ed. David Theo Goldberg (New York: Holt, Rinehart and Winston, 1989), 411–412.
7. From selections from "Opinions of the Judicial Council of the American Medical Association," John Burkhart, chairman, American Medical Association, Chicago (1982) at 9–10, as published in President's Commission for the Study of Ethical Problems in Medicine and Biomedical and Behavioral Research, *Deciding to Forgo Life-Sustaining Treatment: A Report on the Ethical, Medical, and Legal Issues of Treatment Decisions* (Washington, DC: GPO, 1983), 299–300.

For Further Reading

Nigel M. de S. Cameron, *The New Medicine: Life and Death after Hippocrates* (Wheaton, IL: Crossway, 1991).

Paul Chamberlain, *Final Wishes: A Cautionary Tale on Death, Dignity & Physician-Assisted Suicide* (Downers Grove, IL: InterVarsity Press, 2000).

Timothy J. Demy and Gary P. Stewart, eds., *Suicide: A Christian Response* (Grand Rapids, MI: Kregel, 1998).

Ronald Dworkin, "Do We Have a Right to Die?," in *Freedom's Law: The Moral Reading of the American Constitution* by Ronald Dworkin (Cambridge, MA: Harvard University Press, 1996).

Dennis J. Horan and David Mall, eds., *Death, Dying and Euthanasia* (Frederick, MD: University Publications of America, 1980).

Jack Kevorkian, "A Fail-Safe Model for Justifiable Medically Assisted Suicide," *American Journal of Forensic Psychiatry* 13.1 (1992).

————, *Prescription: Medicide: The Goodness of Planned Death* (Buffalo, NY: Prometheus Books, 1991).

J. P. Moreland and Scott B. Rae, *Body & Soul: Human Nature and the Crisis in Ethics* (Downers Grove, IL: InterVarsity Press, 2000).

President's Commission for the Study of Ethical Problems in Medicine and Biomedical and Behavioral Research, *Deciding to Forego Life-Sustaining Treatment* (Washington, DC: GPO, 1983).

James Rachels, *The End of Life* (Oxford: Oxford University Press, 1986).

Paul Ramsey, *The Patient as Person* (New Haven, CT: Yale University Press, 1970).

David Schiedermayer, *Putting the Soul Back in Medicine: Reflections on Compassion and Ethics* (Grand Rapids, MI: Baker, 1994).

Peter Singer, *Rethinking Life and Death: The Collapse of Our Traditional Ethics* (New York: St. Martin's Press, 1995).

Robert Wennberg, *Terminal Choices: Euthanasia, Suicide, and the Right to Die* (Grand Rapids, MI: Eerdmans, 1989).

Michael Uhlman, ed., *Last Rights?: Assisted Suicide and Euthanasia Debated* (Grand Rapids, MI: Eerdmans/Washington, DC: Ethics & Public Policy Center, 1998).

SECTION B1

The Law and Euthanasia

Cruzan v. Harmon (1991)   16

U.S. SUPREME COURT*

As a result of an accident on January 11, 1983, Nancy Beth Cruzan entered a persistent vegetative state (PVS), being fed through a tube inserted in her stomach. A PVS patient has lower brain functions (that is, the brain stem may be the only part

Footnotes omitted and most citations deleted or edited.

of the brain that is functioning, the part that controls many normal bodily functions such as respiration and heartbeat) but no higher brain functions (that is, the cerebral cortex may not be functioning, the part of the brain whose function is associated with thought, intellect, and personality). Nancy Cruzan, like most PVS patients, was not hooked up to a machine, but was cared for by others in many ways (clothed, cleaned, fed via a tube, etc.). In this state she was awake but not aware, though she had been observed grimacing perhaps in recognition of ordinary painful stimuli and/or in response to sound. Nancy's parents asked her doctors to remove the feeding tube so that she could die. The case went to court. First a state trial court ruled in favor of withdrawal, saying that the feeding tube was "heroically invasive" or burdensome. But the Missouri Supreme Court overturned the trial court's opinion, declaring: "We choose to err on the side of life." The U.S. Supreme Court, in *Cruzan v. Harmon* (1990), agreed with the state supreme court, concluding that if Nancy had a living will requesting the withdrawal of food and water, then termination would have been justified. Interestingly enough, several months later the Cruzans obtained more evidence that a lower court believed constituted a living will and which was within the U.S. Supreme Court's parameters. In December 1990, physicians withdrew Nancy's feeding tubes. She died of starvation and dehydration several days later. The following is an abridged version of the majority opinion from *Cruzan v. Harmon*, authored by Chief Justice William Rehnquist.

PETITIONER NANCY BETH CRUZAN was rendered incompetent as a result of severe injuries sustained during an automobile accident. Co-petitioners Lester and Joyce Cruzan, Nancy's parents and co-guardians, sought a court order directing the withdrawal of their daughter's artificial feeding and hydration equipment after it became apparent that she had virtually no chance of recovering her cognitive faculties. The Supreme Court of Missouri held that because there was no clear and convincing evidence of Nancy's desire to have life-sustaining treatment withdrawn under such circumstances, her parents lacked authority to effectuate such a request. . . .

After it had become apparent that Nancy Cruzan had virtually no chance of regaining her mental faculties her parents asked hospital employees to terminate the artificial nutrition and hydration procedures. All agree that such a removal would cause her death. The employees refused to honor the request without court approval. The parents then sought and received authorization from the state trial court for termination. The court found that a person in Nancy's condition had a fundamental right under the State and Federal Constitutions to refuse or direct the withdrawal of "death prolonging procedures." The court also found that Nancy's "expressed thoughts at age 25 in somewhat serious conversation with a housemate friend that if sick or injured she would not wish to continue her life unless she could live at least halfway normally" suggests that given her present condition she would not wish to continue on with her nutrition and hydration.

The Supreme Court of Missouri reversed by a divided vote. The court recognized a right to refuse treatment embodied in the common-law doctrine of informed consent, but expressed skepticism about the application of that doctrine in the circumstances of this case. . . . The court also declined to read a broad right of privacy into the State Constitution which would "support the right of a person to refuse medical treatment in every circumstance," and expressed doubt as to whether such a right existed under the United States Constitution. It then decided that the Missouri Living Will statute embodied a state policy strongly favoring the preservation of life. The court found that Cruzan's statements to her roommate regarding her desire to live or die under certain conditions were "unreliable for the purpose of determining her intent," "and thus insufficient to support the co-guardians' claim to exercise substituted judgment on Nancy's behalf." . . .

We granted *certiorari* to consider the question of whether Cruzan has a right under the United States Constitution which would require the hospital to withdraw life-sustaining treatment from her under these circumstances.

At common law, even the touching of one person by another without consent and without legal justification was a battery.

The logical corollary of the doctrine of informed consent is that the patient generally possesses the right not to consent, that is, to refuse treatment. Until about 15 years ago and the seminal decision in *In re Quinlan,* 70 N.J. 10, the number of right-to-refuse-treatment decisions were relatively few. . . . More recently, however, with the advance of medical technology capable of sustaining life well past the point where natural forces would have brought certain death in earlier times, cases involving the right to refuse life-sustaining treatment have burgeoned. . . .

As these cases demonstrate, the common-law doctrine of informed consent is viewed as generally encompassing the right of a competent individual to refuse medical treatment. Beyond that, these decisions demonstrate both similarity and diversity in their approach to decision of what all agree is a perplexing question with unusually strong moral and ethical overtones. State courts have available to them for decision a number of sources—state constitutions, statutes, and common law—which are not available to us.

In this Court, the question is simply and starkly whether the United States Constitution prohibits Missouri from choosing the rule of decision which it did. This is the first case in which we have been squarely presented with the issue of whether the United States Constitution grants what is in common parlance referred to as a "right to die."

The 14th Amendment provides that no state shall "deprive any person of life, liberty, or property, without due process of law." The principle that a competent person has a constitutionally protected liberty interest in refusing unwanted medical treatment may be inferred from our prior decisions. . . .

Just this term, in the course of holding that a state's procedures for administering antipsychotic medication to prisoners were sufficient to satisfy due process concerns, we recognized that prisoners possess "a significant liberty interest in avoiding the unwanted administration of antipsychotic drugs under the Due Process Clause of the 14th Amendment." *Washington v. Harper* (1990) . . .

But determining that a person has a "liberty interest" under the Due Process Clause does not end the inquiry; "whether respondent's constitutional rights have been violated must be determined by balancing his liberty interests against the relevant state interests."

Petitioners insist that under the general holdings of our cases, the forced administration of life-sustaining medical treatment, and even of artificially delivered food and water essential to life, would implicate a competent person's liberty interest. Although we think the logic of the cases discussed above would embrace such a liberty interest, the dramatic consequences involved in refusal of such treatment would inform the inquiry as to whether the deprivation of that interest is constitutionally permissible. But for purposes of this case, we assume that the United States Constitution would grant a competent person a constitutionally protected right to refuse life-saving hydration and nutrition.

Petitioners go on to assert that an incompetent person should possess the same right in this respect as is possessed by a competent person. . . .

The difficulty with petitioners' claim is that in a sense it begs the question: an incompetent person is not able to make an informed and voluntary choice to exercise a hypothetical right to refuse treatment or any other right. Such a "right" must be exercised for her, if at all, by some sort of surrogate. Here, Missouri has in effect recognized that under certain circumstances a surrogate may act for the patient in electing to have hydration and nutrition withdrawn in such a way as to cause death, but it has established a procedural safeguard to assure that the action of the surrogate conforms as best it may to the wishes expressed by the patient while competent.

Missouri requires that evidence of the incompetent's wishes as to the withdrawal of treatment be proved by clear and convincing evidence. The question, then, is whether the United States Constitution forbids the establishment of this procedural requirement by the state. We hold that it does not.

Whether or not Missouri's clear and convincing evidence requirement comports with the United States Constitution depends in part on what interests the state may properly seek to protect in this situation. Missouri relies on its interest in the protection and preservation of human life, and there can be no gainsaying this interest. As a general matter, the states—indeed, all civilized nations—demonstrate their commitment to life by treating homicide as serious crime. Moreover, the majority of states in this country have laws imposing criminal penalties on one who assists another to commit suicide. We do not think a state is required to remain neutral in the face of an informed and voluntary decision by a physically able adult to starve to death.

But in the context presented here, a state has more particular interests at stake. The choice between life and death is a deeply personal decision of obvious and overwhelming finality. We believe Missouri may legitimately seek to safeguard the personal element of this choice through the imposition of heightened evidentiary requirements. It cannot be disputed that the Due Process Clause protects an interest in life as well as an interest in refusing life-sustaining medical treatment. Not all incompetent patients will have loved ones available to serve as surrogate decision makers. . . .

In our view, Missouri has permissibly sought to advance these interests through the adoption of a "clear and convincing" standard of proof to govern such proceedings. . . .

In sum, we conclude that a state may apply a clear and convincing evidence standard in proceedings where a guardian seeks to discontinue nutrition and hydration of a person diagnosed to be in a persistent vegetative state. . . .

The Supreme Court of Missouri held that in this case the testimony adduced at trial did not amount to clear and convincing proof of the patient's desire to have hydration and nutrition withdrawn.

No doubt is engendered by anything in this record but that Nancy Cruzan's mother and father are loving and caring parents. If the state were required by the United States Constitution to repose a right of "substituted judgment" with anyone, the Cruzans would surely qualify. But we do not think the Due Process Clause requires the state to repose judgment on these matters with anyone but the patient herself. Close family members may have a strong feeling—a feeling not at all ignoble or unworthy, but not entirely disinterested, either—that they do not wish to witness the continuation of the life of a loved one which they regard as hopeless, meaningless and even degrading. But there is no automatic assurance that the view of close family members will necessarily be the same as the patient's would have been had she been confronted with the prospect of her situation while competent. All of the reasons previously discussed for allowing

Missouri to require clear and convincing evidence of the patient's wishes lead us to conclude that the state may choose to defer only to those wishes, rather than confide the decision to close family members.

Discussion Questions

1. How did the U.S. Supreme Court justify its claim that Nancy Cruzan has a right under the U.S. Constitution to require the hospital to withdraw from her life-sustaining treatment? Why then did the Court reject her parents' wishes to require the hospital to withdraw food and water?
2. Why did the Court reject the testimony of Nancy Cruzan's housemate who claimed that Nancy had told her a year before the accident that "she would not want to live should she face life as a 'vegetable,' and other observations to the same?"
3. The Court would have allowed Nancy Cruzan's parents to require the hospital to withdraw food and water if Nancy had made that request in a living will. On what legal basis did the Court justify this conclusion?

You can locate InfoTrac-College Education articles about this chapter by accessing the InfoTrac-College Edition website (http://www.infotrac-college.com/wadsworth/). Using the InfoTrac-College Edition subject guide, enter the search terms relevant to this chapter, and then read abstracts for relevant articles.

Washington v. Glucksberg (1997)   17

U.S. SUPREME COURT*

In 1991, the citizens of the state of Washington, through a statewide referendum, reaffirmed their state's long-time prohibition of assisted suicide. But the pro-euthanasia organization Compassion in Dying sued the state and won in two federal courts, with both courts saying that the law violated the Fourteenth Amendment of the U.S. Constitution. In 1994, in *Compassion in Dying v. Washington,* Judge Barbara Rothstein of the U.S. District Court in Seattle struck

---

Footnotes omitted and most citations deleted or edited.

down the state's ban on physician-assisted suicide, employing a line from the U.S. Supreme Court's *Casey v. Planned Parenthood* (Chapter 11): "Like the abortion decision, the decision of a terminally ill person to end his or her life 'involves the most intimate and personal choices a person can make in a lifetime,' and constitutes a 'choice central to personal dignity and autonomy.' " In a 1996 appeal by the state of Washington, Judge Stephen Reinhardt of the Ninth Circuit Court of Appeals affirmed not only a constitutional "right to die," but also called the state's motivation for banning physician-assisted suicide "cruel": "Not only is the state's interest in preventing such individuals from hastening their deaths of comparatively little weight, but its insistence on frustrating their wishes seems cruel indeed." However, in 1997, in *Washington v. Glucksberg* (Compassion in Dying had been replaced by Dr. Harold Glucksberg as the principal party), the Supreme Court in a 9–0 decision overturned Judge Reinhardt's ruling.

The following are abridged versions of some of the justices' opinions in *Washington v. Glucksberg*. The first is penned by Chief Justice William Rehnquist (who is joined in his opinion by Justices Sandra Day O'Connor, Antonin Scalia, Anthony M. Kennedy, and Clarence Thomas). He begins by providing a brief history of suicide law from the common law through the mid-1990s. Justice Rehnquist argues that any constitutional evaluation of suicide must start with our legal and cultural beliefs and traditions. And clearly, there is an overwhelming consensus against legalizing suicide. He recognizes the constraints on personal liberty that have resulted from technologies that can prolong a person's life. But, he maintains, that the right to withdraw life-sustaining treatments (affirmed in *Cruzan*—Chapter 16) is sufficient to accommodate our technological progress as well as to recognize the state's legitimate interest in protecting human life, an interest that is grounded in our "history, tradition, and practice." The Chief Justice rejects the claim by the lower courts that *Cruzan*, coupled with the alleged autonomy rights affirmed in *Casey* (Chapter 11), establish a constitutional right to suicide. He also points out that the lower courts did not take into serious consideration the possibility of the harm and prejudice to vulnerable people (e.g., the handicapped, the elderly, the terminally ill) that may result from legalizing suicide. He cites as an example the practice of euthanasia in the Netherlands.

The concurring opinions of Justices David Souter and Stephen Breyer are included as well. The reader should pay particular attention to Justice Souter's remarks, for even though he agrees with the court's judgment, he seems to believe (contra Rehnquist) that the Fourteenth Amendment allows for the possibility that a future court may find a right to suicide in the Constitution.

[CHIEF JUSTICE REHNQUIST DELIVERED THE OPINION OF THE COURT]

The question presented in this case is whether Washington's prohibition against "caus[ing]" or "aid[ing]" a suicide offends the Fourteenth Amendment to the United States Constitution. We hold that it does not. . . .

We begin, as we do in all due-process cases, by examining our nation's history, legal traditions, and practices. In almost every state—

indeed, in almost every western democracy—it is a crime to assist a suicide. The states' assisted-suicide bans are not innovations. Rather, they are longstanding expressions of the states' commitment to the protection and preservation of all human life. Indeed, opposition to and condemnation of suicide—and, therefore, of assisting suicide—are consistent and enduring themes of our philosophical, legal, and cultural heritages.

More specifically, for over 700 years, the Anglo-American common-law tradition has punished or otherwise disapproved of both suicide and assisting suicide. In the thirteenth century, Henry de Bracton, one of the first legal treatise writers, observed that "[j]ust as a man may commit felony by slaying another so may he do so by slaying himself." The real and personal property of one who killed himself to avoid conviction and punishment for a crime were forfeit to the king; however, thought Bracton, "if a man slays himself in weariness of life or because he is unwilling to endure further bodily pain . . . [only] his movable goods [were] confiscated." Thus, "[t]he principle that suicide of a sane person, for whatever reason, was a punishable felony was . . . introduced into English common law." Centuries later, Sir William Blackstone, whose *Commentaries on the Laws of England* not only provided a definitive summary of the common law but was also a primary legal authority for eighteenth- and nineteenth-century American lawyers, referred to suicide as "self-murder" and "the pretended heroism, but real cowardice, of the Stoic philosophers, who destroyed themselves to avoid those ills which they had not the fortitude to endure. . . ." Blackstone emphasized that "the law has . . . ranked [suicide] among the highest crimes," although, anticipating later developments, he conceded that the harsh and shameful punishments imposed for suicide "borde[r] a little upon severity."

For the most part, the early American colonies adopted the common-law approach.

For example, the legislators of the Providence Plantations, which would later become Rhode Island, declared, in 1647, that "[s]elf murder is by all agreed to be the most unnatural, and it is by this present Assembly declared, to be that, wherein he that doth it, kills himself out of a premeditated hatred against his own life or other humor: . . . his goods and chattels are the king's custom, but not his debts nor lands; but in case he be an infant, a lunatic, mad or distracted man, he forfeits nothing." Virginia also required ignominious burial for suicides, and their estates were forfeit to the crown.

Over time, however, the American colonies abolished these harsh common-law penalties. William Penn abandoned the criminal forfeiture sanction in Pennsylvania in 1701, and the other colonies (and later, the other states) eventually followed this example. Zephaniah Swift, who would later become chief justice of Connecticut, wrote in 1796 that

[t]here can be no act more contemptible, than to attempt to punish an offender for a crime, by exercising a mean act of revenge upon lifeless clay, that is insensible of the punishment. There can be no greater cruelty, than the inflicting [of] a punishment, as the forfeiture of goods, which must fall solely on the innocent offspring of the offender. . . . [Suicide] is so abhorrent to the feelings of mankind, and that strong love of life which is implanted in the human heart, that it cannot be so frequently committed, as to become dangerous to society. There can of course be no necessity of any punishment.

This statement makes it clear, however, that the movement away from the common law's harsh sanctions did not represent an acceptance of suicide; rather, as Chief Justice Swift observed, this change reflected the growing consensus that it was unfair to punish the suicide's family for his wrongdoing. Nonetheless, although states moved away from Blackstone's treatment of suicide, courts continued to condemn it as a grave public wrong.

That suicide remained a grievous, though non-felonious, wrong is confirmed by the fact that colonial and early state legislatures and courts did not retreat from prohibiting assisting suicide. Swift, in his early nineteenth-century treatise on the laws of Connecticut, stated that "[i]f one counsels another to commit suicide, and the other by reason of the advice kills himself, the advisor is guilty of murder as principal." This was the well-established common-law view, as was the similar principle that the consent of a homicide victim is "wholly immaterial to the guilt of the person who cause[d] [his death]." And the prohibitions against assisting suicide never contained exceptions for those who were near death. Rather, "[t]he life of those to whom life ha[d] become a burden—of those who [were] hopelessly diseased or fatally wounded—nay, even the lives of criminals condemned to death, [were] under the protection of law, equally as the lives of those who [were] in the full tide of life's enjoyment, and anxious to continue to live." *Blackburn v. State,* (1872).

The earliest American statute explicitly to outlaw assisting suicide was enacted in New York in 1828, and many of the new states and territories followed New York's example. Between 1857 and 1865, a New York commission led by Dudley Field drafted a criminal code that prohibited "aiding" a suicide and, specifically, "furnish[ing] another person with any deadly weapon or poisonous drug, knowing that such person intends to use such weapon or drug in taking his own life." By the time the Fourteenth Amendment was ratified, it was a crime in most states to assist a suicide. The Field Penal Code was adopted in the Dakota Territory in 1877, in New York in 1881, and its language served as a model for several other western states' statutes in the late nineteenth and early twentieth centuries. California, for example, codified its assisted-suicide prohibition in 1874, using language similar to the Field Code's. In this century, the Model Penal Code also prohibited "aiding" suicide,

prompting many states to enact or revise their assisted-suicide bans. The code's drafters observed that "the interests in the sanctity of life that are represented by the criminal homicide laws are threatened by one who expresses a willingness to participate in taking the life of another, even though the act may be accomplished with the consent, or at the request, of the suicide victim."

Though deeply rooted, the states' assisted-suicide bans have in recent years been reexamined and, generally, reaffirmed. Because of advances in medicine and technology, Americans today are increasingly likely to die in institutions, from chronic illnesses. Public concern and democratic action are therefore sharply focused on how best to protect dignity and independence at the end of life, with the result that there have been many significant changes in state laws and in the attitudes these laws reflect. Many states, for example, now permit "living wills," surrogate health-care decision-making, and the withdrawal or refusal of life-sustaining medical treatment. At the same time, however, voters and legislators continue for the most part to reaffirm their states' prohibitions on assisting suicide.

The Washington statute at issue in this case was enacted in 1975 as part of a revision of that state's criminal code. Four years later, Washington passed its Natural Death Act, which specifically stated that the "withholding or withdrawal of life-sustaining treatment . . . shall not, for any purpose, constitute a suicide" and that "[n]othing in this chapter shall be construed to condone, authorize, or approve mercy killing. . . ." In 1991, Washington voters rejected a ballot initiative which, had it passed, would have permitted a form of physician-assisted suicide. Washington then added a provision to the Natural Death Act expressly excluding physician-assisted suicide.

California voters rejected an assisted-suicide initiative similar to Washington's in 1993. On the other hand, in 1994, voters in Oregon enacted, also through ballot initiative, that state's Death With Dignity Act, which legalized physician-assisted suicide for competent, terminally ill adults. Since the Oregon vote, many proposals to legalize assisted suicide have been and continue to be introduced in the states' legislatures, but none has been enacted. And just last year, Iowa and Rhode Island joined the overwhelming majority of states explicitly prohibiting assisted suicide. Also, on April 30, 1997, President Clinton signed the Federal Assisted Suicide Funding Restriction Act of 1997, which prohibits the use of federal funds in support of physician-assisted suicide.

Thus, the states are currently engaged in serious, thoughtful examinations of physician-assisted suicide and other similar issues. For example, New York State's Task Force on Life and the Law—an ongoing, blue-ribbon commission composed of doctors, ethicists, lawyers, religious leaders, and interested laymen—was convened in 1984 and commissioned with "a broad mandate to recommend public policy on issues raised by medical advances." Over the past decade, the Task Force has recommended laws relating to end-of-life decisions, surrogate pregnancy, and organ donation. After studying physician-assisted suicide, however, the Task Force unanimously concluded that "[l]egalizing assisted suicide and euthanasia would pose profound risks to many individuals who are ill and vulnerable. . . . [T]he potential dangers of this dramatic change in public policy would outweigh any benefit that might be achieved." New York State Task Force, *When Death Is Sought: Assisted Suicide and Euthanasia in the Medical Context* (May 1994).

Attitudes toward suicide itself have changed since Bracton, but our laws have consistently condemned, and continue to prohibit, assisting suicide. Despite changes in medical technology and notwithstanding an increased emphasis on the importance of end-of-life decision-making, we have not retreated from this prohibition. Against this backdrop of history, tradition, and practice, we now turn to respondents' constitutional claim.

II

The Due Process Clause guarantees more than fair process, and the "liberty" it protects includes more than the absence of physical restraint. The clause also provides heightened protection against government interference with certain fundamental rights and liberty interests. In a long line of cases, we have held that, in addition to the specific freedoms protected by the Bill of Rights, the "liberty" specially protected by the Due Process Clause includes the rights to marry *Loving v. Virginia* (1967); to have children, *Skinner v. Oklahoma ex rel. Williamson* (1942); to direct the education and upbringing of one's children, *Meyer v. Nebraska* (1923); *Pierce v. Society of Sisters* (1925); to marital privacy, *Griswold v. Connecticut* (1965); to use contraception, (*id.; Eisenstadt v. Baird* (1972); to bodily integrity, *Rochin v. California* (1952); and to abortion, *Planned Parenthood v. Casey* (1992). We have also assumed, and strongly suggested, that the Due Process Clause protects the traditional right to refuse unwanted lifesaving medical treatment. *Cruzan v. Director, Mo. Dept. of Health,* (1990).

But we "ha[ve] always been reluctant to expand the concept of substantive due process because guideposts for responsible decision-making in this unchartered area are scarce and open ended." *Collins v. Harker Heights,* (1992). By extending constitutional protection to an asserted right or liberty interest, we, to a great extent, place the matter outside the arena of public debate and legislative action. We must therefore "exercise the utmost care whenever we are asked to break new ground in this field" (*id.*), lest the liberty protected by the Due Process Clause be subtly transformed into the policy preferences of the members of this Court.

Our established method of substantive-due-process analysis has two primary features: First, we have regularly observed that the Due Process Clause specially protects those fundamental rights and liberties which are, objectively, "deeply rooted in this nation's history and tradition." *Moore v. East Cleveland,* (1977). Second, we have required in substantive-due-process cases a "careful description" of the asserted fundamental liberty interest. Our nation's history, legal traditions, and practices thus provide the crucial "guideposts for responsible decision-making" that direct and restrain our exposition of the Due Process Clause. As we stated recently in *Flores,* the Fourteenth Amendment "forbids the government to infringe . . . 'fundamental' liberty interests *at all,* no matter what process is provided, unless the infringement is narrowly tailored to serve a compelling state interest." *Reno v. Flores,* (1993).

Justice Souter, relying on Justice Harlan's dissenting opinion in *Poe v. Ullman,* would largely abandon this restrained methodology, and instead ask "whether [Washington's] statute sets up one of those 'arbitrary impositions' or 'purposeless restraints' at odds with the Due Process Clause of the Fourteenth Amendment." In our view, however, the development of this Court's substantive-due-process jurisprudence, described briefly above, has been a process whereby the outlines of the "liberty" specially protected by the Fourteenth Amendment—never fully clarified, to be sure, and perhaps not capable of being fully clarified—have at least been carefully refined by concrete examples involving fundamental rights found to be deeply rooted in our legal tradition. This approach tends to rein in the subjective elements that are necessarily present in due-process judicial review. In addition, by establishing a threshold requirement—that a challenged state action implicate a fundamental right—before requiring more than a reasonable relation to a legitimate state interest to justify the action, it avoids the need for complex balancing of competing interests in every case.

Turning to the claim at issue here, the Court of Appeals stated that "[p]roperly analyzed, the first issue to be resolved is whether there is a liberty interest in determining the time and manner of one's death," or in other words, "[i]s there a right to die?" Similarly, respondents assert a "liberty to choose how to die" and a right to "control of one's final days," and describe the asserted liberty as "the right to choose a humane, dignified death," and "the liberty to shape death." As noted above, we have a tradition of carefully formulating the interest at stake in substantive-due-process cases. For example, although *Cruzan* is often described as a "right to die" case, we were, in fact, more precise: we assumed that the Constitution granted competent persons a "constitutionally protected right to refuse life-saving hydration and nutrition." The Washington statute at issue in this case prohibits "aid[ing] another person to attempt suicide," and, thus, the question before us is whether the "liberty" specially protected by the Due Process Clause includes a right to commit suicide which itself includes a right to assistance in doing so.

We now inquire whether this asserted right has any place in our nation's traditions. Here . . . we are confronted with a consistent and almost universal tradition that has long rejected the asserted right, and continues explicitly to reject it today, even for terminally ill, mentally competent adults. To hold for respondents, we would have to reverse centuries of legal doctrine and practice, and strike down the considered policy choice of almost every state.

Respondents contend, however, that the liberty interest they assert *is* consistent with this Court's substantive-due-process line of cases, if not with this nation's history and practice. Pointing to *Casey* and *Cruzan,* respondents read our jurisprudence in this area as reflecting a general tradition of "self sovereignty," and as teaching that the "liberty" protected by the Due Process Clause includes "basic and intimate exercises of personal autonomy." According to respondents, our liberty jurisprudence, and the broad, individualistic principles it reflects, protects the "liberty of competent, terminally ill adults to make end-of-life decisions free of undue governmental interference." The question presented in this case, however, is whether the protections of the Due Process Clause include a right to commit suicide with another's assistance. With this "careful description" of respondents' claim in mind, we turn to *Casey* and *Cruzan*.

In *Cruzan*, we considered whether Nancy Beth Cruzan, who had been severely injured in an automobile accident and was in a persistive vegetative state, "ha[d] a right under the United States Constitution which would require the hospital to withdraw life-sustaining treatment" at her parents' request. We began with the observation that "[a]t common law, even the touching of one person by another without consent and without legal justification was a battery." We then discussed the related rule that "informed consent is generally required for medical treatment." After reviewing a long line of relevant state cases, we concluded that "the common-law doctrine of informed consent is viewed as generally encompassing the right of a competent individual to refuse medical treatment." Next, we reviewed our own cases on the subject, and stated that "[t]he principle that a competent person has a constitutionally protected liberty interest in refusing unwanted medical treatment may be inferred from our prior decisions." Therefore, "for purposes of [that] case, we assume[d] that the United States Constitution would grant a competent person a constitutionally protected right to refuse lifesaving hydration and nutrition." We concluded that, notwithstanding this right, the Constitution permitted Missouri to require clear and convincing evidence of an incompetent patient's wishes concerning the withdrawal of life-sustaining treatment.

Respondents contend that in *Cruzan* we "acknowledged that competent, dying persons have the right to direct the removal of life-sustaining medical treatment and thus hasten death," and that "the constitutional principle behind recognizing the patient's liberty to direct the withdrawal of artificial life support applies at least as strongly to the choice to hasten impending death by consuming lethal medication." Similarly, the Court of Appeals concluded that "*Cruzan*, by recognizing a liberty interest that includes the refusal of artificial provision of life-sustaining food and water, necessarily recognize[d] a liberty interest in hastening one's own death."

The right assumed in *Cruzan*, however, was not simply deduced from abstract concepts of personal autonomy. Given the common-law rule that forced medication was a battery, and the long legal tradition protecting the decision to refuse unwanted medical treatment, our assumption was entirely consistent with this nation's history and constitutional traditions. The decision to commit suicide with the assistance of another may be just as personal and profound as the decision to refuse unwanted medical treatment, but it has never enjoyed similar legal protection. Indeed, the two acts are widely and reasonably regarded as quite distinct. In *Cruzan* itself, we recognized that most states outlawed assisted suicide—and even more do today—and we certainly gave no intimation that the right to refuse unwanted medical treatment could be somehow transmuted into a right to assistance in committing suicide.

Respondents also rely on *Casey*. There, the Court's opinion concluded that "the essential holding of *Roe v. Wade* should be retained and once again reaffirmed." We held, first, that a woman has a right, before her fetus is viable, to an abortion "without undue interference from the state"; second, that states may restrict post-viability abortions, so long as exceptions are made to protect a woman's life and health; and third, that the state has legitimate interests throughout a pregnancy in protecting the health of the woman and the life of the unborn child. In reaching this conclusion, the opinion discussed in some detail this Court's substantive-due-process tradition of interpreting the Due Process Clause to protect certain fundamental rights and "personal decisions relating to marriage, procreation, contraception, family relationships, child rearing, and education," and noted that many of those rights and liberties "involv[e] the most intimate and personal choices a person may make in a lifetime."

The Court of Appeals, like the District Court, found *Casey* " 'highly instructive' " and " 'almost prescriptive' " for determining " 'what liberty interest may inhere in a terminally ill person's choice to commit suicide' ":

> Like the decision of whether or not to have an abortion, the decision how and when to die is one of "the most intimate and personal choices a person may make in a lifetime," a choice "central to personal dignity and autonomy."

Similarly, respondents emphasize the statement in *Casey* that:

> At the heart of liberty is the right to define one's own concept of existence, of meaning, of the universe, and of the mystery of human life. Beliefs about these matters could not define the attributes of personhood were they formed under compulsion of the State.

By choosing this language, the Court's opinion in *Casey* described, in a general way and in light of our prior cases, those personal activities and decisions that this Court has identified as so deeply rooted in our history and traditions, or so fundamental to our concept of constitutionally ordered liberty, that they are protected by the Fourteenth Amendment. The opinion moved from the recognition that liberty necessarily includes freedom of conscience and belief about ultimate considerations to the observation that "though the abortion decision may originate within the zone of conscience and belief, it is *more than a philosophic exercise*." (emphasis added). That many of the rights and liberties protected by the Due Process Clause sound in personal autonomy does not warrant the sweeping conclusion that any and all important, intimate, and personal decisions are so protected, and *Casey* did not suggest otherwise.

The history of the law's treatment of assisted suicide in this country has been and continues to be one of the rejection of nearly all efforts to permit it. That being the case, our decisions lead us to conclude that the asserted "right" to assistance in committing suicide is not a fundamental liberty interest protected by the Due Process Clause. The Constitution also requires, however, that Washington's assisted-suicide ban be rationally related to legitimate government interests. This requirement is unquestionably met here. . . . Washington's assisted-suicide ban implicates a number of state interests.

First, Washington has an "unqualified interest in the preservation of human life." *Cruzan*. The state's prohibition on assisted suicide, like all homicide laws, both reflects and advances its commitment to this interest. This interest is symbolic and aspirational as well as practical:

> "While suicide is no longer prohibited or penalized, the ban against assisted suicide and euthanasia shores up the notion of limits in human relationships. It reflects the gravity with which we view the decision to take one's own life or the life of another, and our reluctance to encourage or promote these decisions." New York Task Force.

Respondents admit that "[t]he state has a real interest in preserving the lives of those who can still contribute to society and enjoy life." The Court of Appeals also recognized Washington's interest in protecting life, but held that the "weight" of this interest depends on the "medical condition and the wishes of the person whose life is at stake." Washington, however, has rejected this sliding-scale approach and, through its assisted-suicide ban, insists that all persons' lives, from beginning to end, regardless of physical or mental condition, are under the full protection of the law. As we have previously affirmed, the states "may properly decline to make judgments about the 'quality' of life that a particular individual may enjoy." *Cruzan*. This remains true, as *Cruzan* makes clear, even for those who are near death.

Relatedly, all admit that suicide is a serious public-health problem, especially among persons in otherwise vulnerable groups. The state has an interest in preventing suicide, and in studying, identifying, and treating its causes.

Those who attempt suicide—terminally ill or not—often suffer from depression or other mental disorders. Research indicates, however, that many people who request physician-assisted suicide withdraw that request if their depression and pain are treated. The New York Task Force, however, expressed its concern that, because depression is difficult to diagnose, physicians and medical professionals often fail to respond adequately to seriously ill patients' needs. Thus, legal physician-assisted suicide could make it more difficult for the state to protect depressed or mentally ill persons, or those who are suffering from untreated pain, from suicidal impulses.

The state also has an interest in protecting the integrity and ethics of the medical profession. In contrast to the Court of Appeals' conclusion that "the integrity of the medical profession would [not] be threatened in any way by [physician-assisted suicide]," the American Medical Association, like many other medical and physicians' groups, has concluded that "[p]hysician-assisted suicide is fundamentally incompatible with the physician's role as healer." American Medical Association, Code of Ethics §2.211 (1994). And physician-assisted suicide could, it is argued, undermine the trust that is essential to the doctor-patient relationship by blurring the time-honored line between healing and harming.

Next, the state has an interest in protecting vulnerable groups—including the poor, the elderly, and disabled persons—from abuse, neglect, and mistakes. The Court of Appeals dismissed the state's concern that disadvantaged persons might be pressured into physician-assisted suicide as "ludicrous on its face." We have recognized, however, the real risk of subtle coercion and undue influence in end-of-life situations. *Cruzan*. Similarly, the New York Task Force warned that "[l]egalizing physician-assisted suicide would pose profound risks to many individuals who are ill and vulnerable. . . . The risk of harm is greatest for the many individuals in our society whose autonomy and well being are already compromised by poverty, lack of access to good medical care, advanced age, or membership in a stigmatized social group." If physician-assisted suicide were permitted, many might resort to it to spare their families the substantial financial burden of end-of-life healthcare costs.

The state's interest here goes beyond protecting the vulnerable from coercion; it extends to protecting disabled and terminally ill people from prejudice, negative and inaccurate stereotypes, and "societal indifference." The state's assisted-suicide ban reflects and reinforces its policy that the lives of terminally ill, disabled, and elderly people must be no less valued than the lives of the young and healthy, and that a seriously disabled person's suicidal impulses should be interpreted and treated the same way as anyone else's.

Finally, the state may fear that permitting assisted suicide will start it down the path to voluntary and perhaps even involuntary euthanasia. The Court of Appeals struck down Washington's assisted-suicide ban only "as applied to competent, terminally ill adults who wish to hasten their deaths by obtaining medication prescribed by their doctors." Washington insists, however, that the impact of the court's decision will not and cannot be so limited. If suicide is protected as a matter of constitutional right, it is argued, "every man and woman in the United States must enjoy it." The Court of Appeals' decision, and its expansive reasoning, provide ample support for the state's concerns. The court noted, for example, that the "decision of a duly appointed surrogate decision-maker is for all legal purposes the decision of the patient himself"; that "in some instances, the patient may be unable to self-administer the drugs and . . . administration by the physician . . . may be the only way the patient may be able to receive them"; and that not only physicians, but also family members and loved ones, will inevitably participate in assisting suicide. Thus, it turns out that what is couched as a limited right to "physician-assisted suicide" is likely, in effect, a much broader license, which could prove extremely difficult to police and contain. Washington's ban on assisting suicide prevents such erosion.

This concern is further supported by evidence about the practice of euthanasia in the Netherlands. The Dutch government's own study revealed that in 1990, there were 2,300 cases of voluntary euthanasia (defined as "the deliberate termination of another's life at his request"), 400 cases of assisted suicide, and more than 1,000 cases of euthanasia without an explicit request. In addition to these latter 1,000 cases, the study found an additional 4,941 cases where physicians administered lethal morphine overdoses without the patients' explicit consent. This study suggests that, despite the existence of various reporting procedures, euthanasia in the Netherlands has not been limited to competent, terminally ill adults who are enduring physical suffering, and that regulation of the practice may not have prevented abuses in cases involving vulnerable persons, including severely disabled neonates and elderly persons suffering from dementia. The New York Task Force, citing the Dutch experience, observed that "assisted suicide and euthanasia are closely linked," and concluded that the "risk of . . . abuse is neither speculative nor distant." Washington, like most other states, reasonably ensures against this risk by banning, rather than regulating, assisting suicide.

We need not weigh exactly the relative strengths of these various interests. They are unquestionably important and legitimate, and

Washington's ban on assisted suicide is at least reasonably related to their promotion and protection. We therefore hold that Wash. Rev. Code §9A.36.060(1) (1994) does not violate the Fourteenth Amendment, either on its face or "as applied to competent, terminally ill adults who wish to hasten their deaths by obtaining medication prescribed by their doctors."

Throughout the nation, Americans are engaged in an earnest and profound debate about the morality, legality, and practicality of physician-assisted suicide. Our holding permits this debate to continue, as it should in a democratic society. The decision of the en banc Court of Appeals is reversed, and the case is remanded for further proceedings consistent with this opinion.

It is so ordered. . . .

Justice Souter, concurring in the judgment

The state has put forward several interests to justify the Washington law as applied to physicians treating terminally ill patients, even those competent to make responsible choices: protecting life generally, discouraging suicide even if knowing and voluntary, and protecting terminally ill patients from involuntary suicide and euthanasia, both voluntary and non-voluntary.

It is not necessary to discuss the exact strengths of the first two claims of justification in the present circumstances, for the third is dispositive for me. That third justification is different from the first two, for it addresses specific features of respondents' claim, and it opposes that claim not with a moral judgment contrary to respondents', but with a recognized state interest in the protection of non-responsible individuals and those who do not stand in relation either to death or to their physicians as do the patients whom respondents describe.

The state claims interests in protecting patients from mistakenly and involuntarily deciding to end their lives, and in guarding against both voluntary and involuntary euthanasia. Leaving aside any difficulties in coming to a clear concept of imminent death, mistaken decisions may result from inadequate palliative care or a terminal prognosis that turns out to be error; coercion and abuse may stem from the large medical bills that family members cannot bear or unreimbursed hospitals decline to shoulder. Voluntary and involuntary euthanasia may result once doctors are authorized to prescribe lethal medication in the first instance, for they might find it pointless to distinguish between patients who administer their own fatal drugs and those who wish not to, and their compassion for those who suffer may obscure the distinction between those who ask for death and those who may be unable to request it. The argument is that a progression would occur, obscuring the line between the ill and the dying, and between the responsible and the unduly influenced, until ultimately doctors and perhaps others would abuse a limited freedom to aid suicides by yielding to the impulse to end another's suffering under conditions going beyond the narrow limits the respondents propose. The state thus argues, essentially, that respondents' claim is not as narrow as it sounds, simply because no recognition of the interest they assert could be limited to vindicating those interests and affecting no others. The state says that the claim, in practical effect, would entail consequences that the state could, without doubt, legitimately act to prevent.

The mere assertion that the terminally sick might be pressured into suicide decisions by close friends and family members would not alone be very telling. Of course that is possible, not only because the costs of care might be more than family members could bear but simply because they might naturally wish to see an end of suffering for someone they love. But one of the points of restricting any right of assistance to physicians would be to condition the right on an exercise of judgment by someone qualified to assess the patient's responsible capacity and detect the influence of those outside the medical relationship.

The state, however, goes further, to argue that dependence on the vigilance of physicians will not be enough. First, the lines proposed here (particularly the requirement of a knowing and voluntary decision by the patient) would be more difficult to draw than the lines that have limited other recently recognized due-process rights. Limiting a state from prosecuting use of artificial contraceptives by married couples posed no practical threat to the state's capacity to regulate contraceptives in other ways that were assumed at the time of *Poe* to be legitimate; the trimester measurements of *Roe* and the viability determination of *Casey* were easy to make with a real degree of certainty. But the knowing and responsible mind is harder to assess.

Second, this difficulty could become the greater by combining with another fact within the realm of plausibility, that physicians simply would not be assiduous to preserve the line. They have compassion, and those who would be willing to assist in suicide at all might be the most susceptible to the wishes of a patient, whether the patient were technically quite responsible or not. Physicians, and their hospitals, have their own financial incentives, too, in this new age of managed care. Whether acting from compassion or under some other influence, a physician who would provide a drug for a patient to administer might well go the further step of administering the drug himself; so, the barrier between assisted suicide and euthanasia could become porous, and the line between voluntary and involuntary euthanasia as well. The case for the slippery slope is fairly made out here, not because recognizing one due-process right would leave a court with no principled basis to avoid recognizing another, but because there is a plausible case that the right claimed would not be readily containable by reference to facts about the mind that are matters of difficult judgment, or by gatekeepers who are subject to temptation, noble or not.

Respondents propose an answer to all this, the answer of state regulation with teeth. Legislation proposed in several states, for example, would authorize physician-assisted suicide but require two qualified physicians to confirm the patient's diagnosis, prognosis, and competence; and would mandate that the patient make repeated requests witnessed by at least two others over a specified time span; and would impose reporting requirements and criminal penalties for various acts of coercion.

But at least at this moment there are reasons for caution in predicting the effectiveness of the teeth proposed. Respondents' proposals, as it turns out, sound much like the guidelines now in place in the Netherlands, the only place where experience with physician-assisted suicide and euthanasia has yielded empirical evidence about how such regulations might affect actual practice. Dutch physicians must engage in consultation before proceeding, and must decide whether the patient's decision is voluntary, well considered, and stable, whether the request to die is enduring and made more than once, and whether the patient's future will involve unacceptable suffering. There is, however, a substantial dispute today about what the Dutch experience shows. Some commentators marshall evidence that the Dutch guidelines have in practice failed to protect patients from involuntary euthanasia and have been violated with impunity. This evidence is contested. The day may come when we can say with some assurance which side is right, but for now it is the substantiality of the factual disagreement, and the alternatives for resolving it, that matter. They are, for me, dispositive of the due-process claim at this time.

I take it that the basic concept of judicial review with its possible displacement of legislative judgment bars any finding that a legislature has acted arbitrarily when the following conditions are met: there is a serious factual controversy over the feasibility of recognizing the claimed right without at the same time making it impossible for the state to engage in an undoubtedly legitimate exercise of power; facts necessary to resolve the controversy are not readily ascertainable through the judicial process; but they are more readily subject to discovery through legislative fact-finding and experimentation. It is assumed in this case, and must be, that a state's interest in protecting those unable to make responsible decisions and those who make no decisions at all entitles the state to bar aid to any but a knowing and responsible person intending suicide, and to prohibit euthanasia. How, and how far, a state should act in that interest are judgments for the state, but the legitimacy of its action to deny a physician the option to aid any but the knowing and responsible is beyond question.

The capacity of the state to protect the others if respondents were to prevail is, however, subject to some genuine question, underscored by the responsible disagreement over the basic facts of the Dutch experience. This factual controversy is not open to a judicial resolution with any substantial degree of assurance at this time. It is not, of course, that any controversy about the factual predicate of a due-process claim disqualifies a court from resolving it. Courts can recognize captiousness, and most factual issues can be settled in a trial court. At this point, however, the factual issue at the heart of this case does not appear to be one of those. The principal enquiry at the moment is into the Dutch experience, and I question whether an independent front-line investigation into the facts of a foreign country's legal administration can be soundly undertaken through American courtroom litigation. While an extensive literature on any subject can raise the hopes for judicial understanding, the literature on this subject is only nascent. Since there is little experience directly bearing on the issue, the most that can be said is that whichever way the Court might rule today, events could overtake its assumptions, as experimentation in some jurisdictions confirmed or discredited the concerns about progression from assisted suicide to euthanasia.

Legislatures, on the other hand, have superior opportunities to obtain the facts necessary for a judgment about the present controversy. Not only do they have more flexible mechanisms for fact-finding than the judiciary, but their mechanisms include the power to experiment, moving forward and pulling back as facts emerge within their own jurisdictions. There is, indeed, good reason to suppose that in the absence of a judgment for respondents here, just such experimentation will be attempted in some of the states.

I do not decide here what the significance might be of legislative foot-dragging in ascertaining the facts going to the state's argument that the right in question could not be confined as claimed. Sometimes a court may be bound to act regardless of the institutional preferability of the political branches as forums for addressing constitutional claims. Now, it is enough to say that our examination of legislative reasonableness should consider the fact that the legislature of the State of Washington is no more obviously at fault than this Court is in being uncertain about what would happen if respondents prevailed today. We therefore have a clear question about which institution, a legislature or a court, is relatively more competent to deal with an emerging issue as to which facts currently unknown could be dispositive. The answer has to be, for the reasons already stated, that the legislative process is to be preferred. There is a closely related further reason as well.

One must bear in mind that the nature of the right claimed, if recognized as one constitutionally required, would differ in no essential way from other constitutional rights guaranteed by enumeration or derived from some more definite textual source than "due process." An unenumerated right should not therefore be recognized, with the effect of displacing the legislative ordering of things, without the assurance that its recognition would prove as durable as the recognition of those other rights differently derived. To recognize a right of lesser promise would simply create a constitutional regime too uncertain to bring with it the expectation of finality that is one of this Court's central obligations in making constitutional decisions.

Legislatures, however, are not so constrained. The experimentation that should be out of the question in constitutional adjudication displacing legislative judgments is entirely proper, as well as highly desirable, when the legislative power addresses an emerging issue like assisted suicide. The Court should accordingly stay its hand to allow reasonable legislative consideration. While I do not decide for all time that respondents' claim should not be recognized, I acknowledge the legislative institutional competence as the better one to deal with that claim at this time. . . .

JUSTICE BREYER, CONCURRING IN THE JUDGMENTS:

I concur in the judgments. I shall briefly explain how I differ from the Court.

I agree with the Court in *Vacco v. Quill* that the articulated state interests justify the distinction drawn between physician-assisted suicide and withdrawal of life support. I also agree with the Court that the critical question in both of the cases before us is whether "the 'liberty' specially protected by the Due Process Clause includes a right" of the sort that the respondents assert. I do not agree, however, with the Court's formulation of that claimed "liberty" interest. The Court describes it as a "right to commit suicide with another's assistance." But I would not reject the respondents' claim without considering a different formulation, for which our legal tradition may provide greater support. That formulation would use words roughly like a "right to die with dignity." But irrespective of the exact words used, at its core would lie personal control over the manner of death, professional medical assistance, and the avoidance of unnecessary and severe physical suffering—combined.

As Justice Souter points out, Justice Harlan's dissenting opinion in *Poe v. Ullman* offers some support for such a claim. In that opinion, Justice Harlan referred to the "liberty" that the Fourteenth Amendment protects as including "a freedom from all substantial arbitrary impositions and purposeless restraints" and also as recognizing that "certain interests require particularly careful scrutiny of the state needs asserted to justify their abridgment." The "certain interests" to which Justice Harlan referred may well be similar (perhaps identical) to the rights, liberties, or interests that the Court today, as in the past, regards as "fundamental."

Justice Harlan concluded that marital privacy was such a "special interest." He found in the Constitution a right of "privacy of the home"—with the home, the bedroom, and "intimate details of the marital relation" at its heart—by examining the protection that the law had earlier provided for related, but not identical, interests described by such words as "privacy," "home," and "family." The respondents here essentially ask us to do the same. They argue that one can find a "right to die with dignity" by examining the protection the law has provided for related, but not identical, interests relating to personal dignity, medical treatment, and freedom from state-inflicted pain.

I do not believe, however, that this Court need or now should decide whether or not such a right is "fundamental." That is because, in my view, the avoidance of severe physical pain (connected with death) would have to comprise an essential part of any successful claim and because . . . , the laws before us do not force a dying person to undergo that kind

of pain. Rather, the laws of New York and of Washington do not prohibit doctors from providing patients with drugs sufficient to control pain despite the risk that those drugs themselves will kill. And under these circumstances the laws of New York and Washington would overcome any remaining significant interests and would be justified, regardless.

Medical technology, we are repeatedly told, makes the administration of pain-relieving drugs sufficient, except for a very few individuals for whom the ineffectiveness of pain-control medicines can mean, not pain, but the need for sedation which can end in a coma. We are also told that there are many instances in which patients do not receive the palliative care that, in principle, is available, but that is so for institutional reasons or inadequacies or obstacles, which would seem possible to overcome, and which do not include a prohibitive set of laws.

This legal circumstance means that the state laws before us do not infringe directly upon the (assumed) central interest (what I have called the core of the interest in dying with dignity) as, by way of contrast, the state anti-contraceptive laws at issue in *Poe* did interfere with the central interest there at stake—by bringing the state's police powers to bear upon the marital bedroom.

Were the legal circumstances different—for example, were state law to prevent the provision of palliative care, including the administration of drugs as needed to avoid pain at the end of life—then the law's impact upon serious and otherwise unavoidable physical pain (accompanying death) would be more directly at issue. And as Justice O'Connor suggests [in her opinion; not republished here], the Court might have to revisit its conclusions in these cases.

Discussion Questions

1. Present the main components of Chief Justice Rehnquist's opinion. When combined, how are they employed to support his conclusion that there is no constitutional right to die?

2. According to Justice Rehnquist, what role does the common law and our other legal and cultural traditions play in discovering whether there is a right to die?

3. Present and explain the reasons why Justice Rehnquist believes that the lower federal courts were mistaken in citing *Cruzan* and *Casey* as supporting a constitutional right to die. Do you agree or disagree with him? Explain and defend your answer.

4. Why does Justice Rehnquist believe that the Fourteenth Amendment's Due Process Clause cannot be extended to include a constitutional right to die even thought it had already been employed in supporting a right to abortion as well as a right to refuse medical treatment? In this regard, how does Justice Souter's opinion differ from Justice Rehnquist's?

5. How does the experience of the Dutch factor into Justice Rehnquist's view that the state has an interest in prohibiting assisted suicide?

6. Do you think that the opinion of Justice Breyer adds something to the court's judgment that is lacking in Justice Rehnquist's opinion? Explain and defend your answer.

You can locate InfoTrac-College Education articles about this chapter by accessing the InfoTrac-College Edition website (http://www.infotrac-college.com/wadsworth/). Using the InfoTrac-College Edition subject guide, enter the search terms relevant to this chapter, and then read abstracts for relevant articles.

Morality of Euthanasia

18   A Defense of Active Euthanasia

JAMES RACHELS

James Rachels, Professor of Philosophy at the University of Alabama, Birmingham, is the author of numerous scholarly articles in ethics and moral philosophy. Among his published books are *The End of Life: Euthanasia and Morality* (1986) and *The Right Thing to Do: Basic Readings in Moral Philosophy* (1989).

In this essay Professor Rachels maintains that active euthanasia is morally justified in some circumstances. First, he argues that a patient who has mere *biological life* and has lost his *biographical life* has a right to commit suicide. Professor Rachels believes that what makes life worth living is not mere biological life, but one's biographical life, one's hopes, life experiences, dreams, pursuits, interests, etc. Thus, if one's biographical life has ended, we have no right to prevent a person from ending his or her biological life. Professor Rachels also argues that there is no essential moral difference between active (killing) and passive (letting-die) euthanasia. But then, he concludes, if passive euthanasia is morally acceptable, and there is no moral difference between passive and active euthanasia, then active euthanasia must also be morally acceptable. He defends this position by employing the fictional story of Jones and Smith, in which both seem to be guilty of committing morally equivalent acts (i.e., each murders his six-year-old cousin), though Jones merely "let the boy die" whereas Smith "killed the boy."

Reprinted by permission from "Active and Passive Euthanasia," New England Journal of Medicine *292 (January 9, 1975); and* The End of Life *(New York: Oxford University Press, 1986).*

THE TRADITIONAL VIEW

CONSIDER THE RECENT CASE of Hans Florian and his wife. They had been married for thirty-three years when he shot her dead. She was a victim of Alzheimer's disease, which attacks the brain, and for which there is no known cause or cure. The effects of the disease are devastating. The deterioration of the brain can be traced through several stages, as the victim loses all semblance of human personality.

Soon after the onset of the disease, Mrs. Florian began to lose the ability to do simple chores and, at the same time, began to develop abnormal fears. She could not drive or write, and would panic when her husband would leave the room. As the disease progressed, he would have to feed her by forcing her mouth open, and he would bathe her and change her clothes several times each day as she soiled them. Then her vocabulary shrank to two words: "fire" and "pain", screamed in her native German. Finally, she had to be placed in a nursing home for her own safety. Although her condition was irreversible, it was not "terminal"—she could have lived on, in this deranged state, indefinitely.

Was it wrong for Hans Florian to have killed his wife? He explained that he killed her because, being seventeen years older, he did not want to die first and leave her alone. Legally, of course, he had no right to do it. Under American law, he could have been found guilty of murder in the first degree—although no charges were brought, because the Florida grand jury refused to indict him. (As we shall see, juries often react this way in such cases.) But, legal questions aside, was his act *immoral*?

We may certainly feel sympathy for Hans Florian; he faced a terrible situation, and acted from honourable motives. Nevertheless, according to the dominant moral tradition of our culture, what he did was indefensible. He intentionally killed an innocent human being, and, according to our tradition, that is always wrong. This tradition is largely the product of Christian teaching. Christianity says, of course, that every human being is made in the image of God, and so all human life is sacred. Killing a person, even one so pitiable as Mrs. Florian, is therefore an offence against the Creator.

Most people in the Western world accept some such perspective as this. Even those who imagine themselves to have rejected this way of thinking continue, more often than not, to be influenced by it—it is not easy to shrug off the values of the culture in which one has been raised and educated. Thus, even those who reject the old theological ideas may continue to accept their secular equivalents—if one no longer believes that human life is "sacred", then one can at least believe that human life is "intrinsically valuable" or that "every human life has a special dignity and worth". And, on the strength of this, one may continue to doubt whether Mr. Florian acted correctly.

The traditional view is not, however, a simple view. Through the centuries various thinkers have contributed to its development, and a complex account of the morality of killing has resulted. This account appeals to a series of distinctions that, taken together, define a class of actions said to be absolutely forbidden. In deciding whether a particular killing is permissible, the method is to apply the distinctions to determine whether the act falls into the forbidden class.

Some of these distinctions have to do with the status of the victim: for example, the distinction between human and non-human is held to be crucial. At the heart of the traditional doctrine is the idea that the protection of *human* life—all human life—is immensely important. If one is human, and alive, then according to the traditional view one's life is sacred. At the same time, *non-human* life is given relatively little importance. So, in general, killing people is said to be gravely wrong, while killing other animals requires almost no justification at all.

But this does not mean that killing people can never be justified. Sometimes it is justified, and here it matters a great deal whether the human in question is "innocent". Capital punishment and killing in war are traditionally sanctioned, on the grounds that the people who are killed are not innocent. It is the killing of the *innocent*, such as Mrs. Florian, that is prohibited.

Other traditional distinctions focus on other qualities of the act; for example, it matters whether the killing would be *intentional*. (Like "innocent", "intentional" is something of a technical term, whose meaning we will have occasion to examine later.) It is *the intentional killing of innocent humans* that is absolutely forbidden.

But perhaps the most interesting of the traditional distinctions is between *killing people* and merely *letting people die*. On the traditional view, even though killing innocent people is forbidden, letting them die is sometimes permitted. This is especially important in considering what may or may not be done in medical treatment. The point is that we are not always required to use every available resource to prolong life, even if it is the life of an innocent human. When extraordinary means are required to keep someone alive, those means may be omitted. (The use of *ordinary* treatments is morally mandatory, but *extraordinary* treatments are optional—this is another of the distinctions the traditional view finds so important.)

The traditional theory must be taken seriously; not only has its influence been enormous, but from a philosophical point of view it is the only fully worked-out, systematically elaborated theory of the subject we have. Its development has been one of the great intellectual achievements of Western culture, accomplished by thinkers of great ingenuity and high moral purpose. However, I shall be mainly interested in the question of whether this theory is *true*—granted that it has history and tradition on its side, still we may ask whether there is good reason for a rational person to accept it.

If the traditional theory is not true, then in our society many decisions concerning life and death are being made on unsound grounds, and the law concerning such matters is badly in need of reform. I believe that the traditional view is mistaken at almost every point. The maze of distinctions on which it is based cannot withstand analysis. Much of this essay is a defence of that judgement.

AN ALTERNATIVE VIEW

To replace the traditional view, I offer a different way of looking at such matters. The alternative view begins by pointing out that there is a deep difference between *having a life* and merely *being alive*. The point of the moral rule against killing is not to keep "innocent humans" alive. Being alive, in the biological sense, is relatively unimportant. One's *life*, by contrast, is immensely important; it is the sum of one's aspirations, decisions, activities, projects, and human relationships. The point of the rule against killing is the protection of *lives* and the interests that some beings, including ourselves, have in virtue of the fact that we are subjects of lives. Only by paying careful attention to the concept of a life can we understand the value of life and the evil of death.

The details of this account are strikingly different from the traditional approach. The distinction between human and non-human turns out to be less important than has been assumed. From a moral point of view, it is the protection of lives that is important, and so, because most humans have lives, killing them is objectionable. However, some unfortunate humans, such as Mrs. Florian, do not have lives, even though they are alive; and so killing *them* is a morally different matter. Moreover, some nonhuman animals also have lives, and so consistency requires that they also be protected by the rule against killing.

. . . And, I will argue, the distinction between killing and letting die is morally insignificant as well: the fact that one act is an act of killing (for example, "mercy-killing") while another act is an act of "merely" letting someone die (for example, "pulling the plug" of a life-sustaining medical device) is not in itself a reason for thinking one act morally better than the other.

The upshot is that this view is much simpler than the traditional view, in that not nearly so many things are considered important. In deciding questions of life and death, the crucial question is: Is a *life,* in the biographical sense, being destroyed or otherwise adversely affected? If not, the rule against killing offers no objection. The species of the subject of the life, and the means that are used, as well as the intention with which the act is done, are all more or less irrelevant.

As one might suspect, the implication for Mrs. Florian is different from the implication of the traditional view. Although this unfortunate woman was still alive, that fact has little significance. The critical fact is that, when her husband shot her, her life was already over. He was not destroying her life; it had already been destroyed by Alzheimer's disease. Thus he was not behaving immorally.

This approach assumes a certain conception of morality. The traditional theory is often presented in theological terms, but its partisans emphasize that the religious trappings are not necessary. It is meant to be a moral view, not a religious dogma, binding on moral agents regardless of their theological convictions or lack of them. My approach is secular in this sense, plus another. It sees being moral, not as a matter of faithfulness to abstract rules or divine laws, but as a matter of doing what is best for those who are affected by our conduct. If we should not kill, it is because in killing we are *harming someone.* That is the reason killing is wrong. The rule against killing has as its point the protection of the victims.

If this seems a truism, remember Mrs. Florian. This conception leads directly to the conclusion that her husband did no wrong. She

was not harmed by her husband's killing her—indeed, if anything, it seems more likely that she was helped. But on the traditional view, this has little importance. Mrs. Florian was an innocent human, and so she could not intentionally be killed. Against the background of the traditional view, the alternative approach emerges not as a truism but as a radical idea. . . .

THE CONCEPT OF A LIFE

Generally speaking, death is a misfortune for the person who dies because it puts an end to his life. Like many philosophical theses, this is more complicated than it first appears. Death is a misfortune, not because it puts an end to one's *being alive* (in the biological sense), but because it ends one's *life* (in the biographical sense). To explain the thesis—to show how the termination of one's life can be a bad thing—we need to examine some aspects of what it means to have a life.

COMPLETE AND INCOMPLETE LIVES

The contingencies of human existence determine the general shape of our lives. Because we are born physically weak and without knowledge or skills, the first part of our lives is a process of growth, learning, and general maturation. Because we will not live much longer than seventy-five years, and because in the last years we will decline mentally and physically, the projects and activities that will fill our lives cannot be planned for much longer than that. The forms of life within human society are adjusted to these dimensions: families care for children while they are small and are acquiring a basic understanding of the world; schools continue the educational process; careers last about forty years; and people normally retire some time between sixty and seventy.

A life can, therefore, be complete or incomplete; it can run its course, or be cut short. Bertrand Russell lived an extraordinarily full life. Born in 1872, he lived ninety-seven years, during which time he was twice married and raised a family; he travelled the world and enjoyed the friendship of such as George Bernard Shaw, H. G. Wells, and Ludwig Wittgenstein; he published seventy-one books and pamphlets, including many that made fundamental contributions to human thought, and was awarded the Nobel Prize; and he was internationally famous as a political and moral propagandist. Compare this with the life of another philosopher, Frank P. Ramsey, who died in 1930 at the age of twenty-six. Ramsey's life had hardly begun; he had achieved only a little of what he could have achieved. The two deaths were, therefore, very different. Ramsey's death was a tragedy, while Russell's death was only the occasion for solemn reflection on a life well lived.

The tragedy of Ramsey's death was threefold. First, there was the sense of *incompleteness*. It was as though a story was only half-told; we had the beginning, and intimations of the middle, but no idea of what the ending might be. Second, there was the sense of futility connected with the fact that Ramsey's life to that point had been *training* him for something that now could not take place. He had been educated and studied philosophy and the foundations of mathematics; prepared now for fundamental work in these fields, he died before he could do it. And third, there was the sense of unfulfilled promise: Ramsey *could have* done great things; but death prevented it. None of this could be said of Russell, whose life was complete, and so Russell's death was not comparably tragic.

This does not mean that Russell's death was not a bad thing in its own way, but we must be careful in describing how it was bad. Even Russell's personal friends, saddened by his passing, must have realized that his life was rich, successful, and in some important sense complete. If there was anything bad about the death, it is because we are able to view a life as in principle open-ended, as always having further possibilities that still might be realized, if only it could go on. There were still desires that Russell could have satisfied; there were still ambitions he might have accomplished. These thoughts make sense of seeing evil even in this death.

Our equanimity about his death, however, is due to our conception of life as bounded by the natural human contingencies. If those contingencies were different, our conception of a life's possibilities would be different. In reality, the possibilities for Russell's life had been exhausted by age and the feebleness it brings; thus thought about what he still might have done are largely fanciful. But suppose people lived to be a hundred and fifty, and at ninety-seven Russell was still vigorous and only half-done with the tasks he could naturally expect to accomplish. Then his death would be as tragic as Ramsey's; but then, too, our conception of what a life can contain would be changed, and so the reasons for judging the death tragic would be changed.

THE STAGES OF A LIFE

The stages of a life are not isolated or self-contained parts. They bear relations to one another that must be understood if any part of the life is to be understood.

We cannot understand what a medical student is doing, for example, if we do not appreciate the way in which her present activity is preparation for the stages of her life which will come later. She wants to be a doctor, and live the kind of life that doctors have: apart from that, her present activity makes no sense. (Thus death at an early age renders this part of the life *pointless*.)

Moreover, the *evaluation* of one stage of a life may require reference to what came before. To be a doorkeeper, with a small but steady income sufficient to pay the rent on a modest apartment, might be a laudable achievement for one who previously was a homeless drunk; but for one who was a vice-president of the United States, caught taking bribes, the same existence might be a sign of failure and disgrace. (This is of course a fictitious example, since we know this is not what happens to American vice-presidents caught taking bribes.)

Thus the fact that people have memories, and are able to contemplate their futures, is important in explaining why they are able to have lives. Without these capacities, one could not see one's present condition as part of a larger, temporally extended existence; and one could have neither regrets nor aspirations.

Consider the plight of someone in whom the connections of memory have been severed. A striking example of this is described by Oliver Sacks, a professor of neurology at the Albert Einstein School of Medicine. Sacks has a patient, whom he calls Jimmie R., suffering from Korsakov's syndrome, which is associated with brain damage produced by alcohol. Jimmie remembers his life vividly up to 1945, when he was nineteen years old. After that, he remembers nothing. He is a bright, alert man who will talk to you intelligently when you are introduced; but two minutes later he will not remember having met you before and the conversation will start again. (Dr. Sacks has been "re-meeting" him regularly for nine years.) He believes he is still nineteen and that it is still 1945; but this is not because he is deluded in the way of someone who thinks he is Napoleon. He is rational enough; he simply has no memory of anything that has happened between then and now. When shown himself in the mirror he panics and thinks something terrible has happened to his face. Soon, though, he forgets having seen the mirror and the worry disappears.

Of course, Jimmie cannot have a normal life because he cannot do any of the things that constitute a life—he cannot relate normally to other people, hold a job, or even take care of his basic needs by shopping for food. (He is cared for in an institution.) But his lack of memory deprives him of a life in a deeper sense: without memory, he cannot conceive of his present state as connected with any other part of himself; plans, even intentional actions become impossible in any but a truncated sense. Without these connections, even the simplest feelings and attitudes lose their objects and meaning. Sacks recorded this conversation with Jimmie:

> "How do you feel?"
> "How do I feel," he repeated and scratched his head.
> "I cannot say I feel ill. But I cannot say I feel well. I cannot say I feel anything at all."
> "Are you miserable?" I continued.
> "Can't say I am."
> "Do you enjoy life?"
> "I can't say I do . . ."
> "You don't enjoy life," I repeated, hesitating somewhat. "How then *do* you feel about life?"
> "I can't say I feel anything at all."
> "You feel alive though?"
> " 'Feel alive' . . . Not really. I haven't felt alive for a very long time."

After nine years of trying to deal with this case, Dr. Sacks's own conclusion is continuing bafflement about " . . . whether, indeed, one [can] speak of an 'existence,' given so absolute a privation of memory or continuity". We can, of course, speak of an "existence"—Jimmie R. exists. But Dr. Sacks's point is clear enough. Without the continuity that memory makes possible, a life, in any but the most rudimentary sense, is unattainable.

MULTIPLE LIVES

We sometimes speak of a person's having more than one life: a bigamist may be said to "lead two lives". This is not merely an idle way of speaking; it has a point. Lives are characterized by sets of interconnected projects, concerns, and relationships. A person may be said to "lead two lives" when there are two such sets, held rigidly separate, with little or no interaction between elements of the sets. The bigamist has two sets of relationships which must be kept absolutely apart—it is important that the members of one household not even know of the other's existence. Thus it is natural to speak of him as going back and forth between two lives.

Similarly, someone who moves to a distant city to start a new profession may be said to take up "a new life". Suppose a woman who was a prostitute in Miami moves to Los Angeles to become the proprietor of a clothing shop. She will spend her time on an entirely new set of activities, she will have a new set of friends—everything will be different. Like the bigamist, she may not even want her friends in Los Angeles to know about her life in Miami. Hence, a new life.

On some occasions, the effect of physical injury is to leave a patient alive and able to lead a life, but not the same life he had before. The famous "Texas burn case", often discussed in the literature of medical ethics, is a case of this type. In 1973 a young man known as "Donald C." was horribly burned over 68 percent of his body by an exploding gas line, and left blind, crippled, without fingers, and deformed in other ways as well. He was kept alive in the hospital for two years by a series of extraordinary and painful treatments; but all these treatments were against his will. Wanting to die, he continually demanded to be removed from the protective environment of the hospital. The doctors refused. He attempted to commit suicide, but was physically unable to bring it off. Finally, to justify keeping him in the hospital against his wishes, a psychiatrist was brought in to examine him, in the expectation that he would testify that Donald was incompetent. But, after interviewing him, the psychiatrist refused to do that, pronouncing—to the surprise of the physicians—that the patient was perfectly rational. So the young man was given the right to leave the hospital. But then, in a dramatic reversal, he changed his mind, and he is still alive today.

Now what could be said in defence of the judgement that this man's desire to die was rational? I believe focusing on the notion of his *life* (in the biographical sense) points us in the right direction. He was, among other things, a rodeo performer, a pilot, and what used to be called a 'ladies' man'. His life was not the life of a scholar or a solitary dreamer. What his injury had done, from his point of view, was to destroy his ability to lead the life that made him the distinctive individual he was. There could be no more rodeos, no more aeroplanes, no more dancing with the ladies, and a lot more. Donald's position was that if he could not lead *that* life, he didn't want to live.

Donald's physicians, in resisting his demand to die, argued in effect that he could take up a different sort of life, and that this different life might come to have some value for him. That is what he eventually did. The physicians may naturally think that these later developments vindicate their refusal to let Donald die, but Donald himself disagrees. Nine years after his ordeal, he appeared before a group of medical students to insist, with some bitterness, that the doctors had been wrong to refuse his demand. Although one may feel some sympathy with the doctors' view, it isn't hard to see Donald's point. We may applaud the courage he eventually showed in making a new life for himself, but we shouldn't miss noticing that his old life was gone. That is why his despair was not merely a temporary hysterical reaction to his situation.

The Temporal Boundaries of a Life

L. C. Morris was a 63-year-old Miami man who was shot in the head one night in 1970 when police mistook him for a roof-top sniper. The damage to his brain was extensive, but he did not die. He lived on, after a fashion, in a nursing home, where for more than three years he was fed through a tube running to his stomach and periodically turned to prevent bedsores. His body had private attendants round the clock; the cost of maintaining it alive was $2,600 per month. The emotional cost to Mrs. Morris cannot be calculated. Under the strain of daily visits to see him, her health deteriorated and she too had to be hospitalized. When told in 1972 that her husband might live for two more years, she replied, "He died back in 1970. We know that."

At the same time that Mr. Morris was in his coma, Miguel Martinez was also lying unconscious in a hospital. Martinez, a well-known Spanish athlete, had been injured in a soccer game in 1964 and remained in a coma until he died eight years later. When he died, his family announced, "Miguel died at the age of 34 after having lived 26 years."

Mrs. Morris's statement that her husband died in 1970 was simply false. The Martinez's melodramatic statement was paradoxical. Yet it is easy to see the point in both cases. The *lives* of these two men were over when they entered the comas, even though both remained alive for some time longer. Both families realized that being alive, in the absence of having a life, was not very important. . . .

ACTIVE AND PASSIVE EUTHANASIA

. . . The distinction between active and passive euthanasia is thought to be crucial for medical ethics. The idea is that it is permissible, at least in some cases, to withhold treatment and allow a patient to die, but it is never permissible to take any direct action designed to kill the patient. This doctrine seems to be accepted by most doctors, and it is endorsed in a statement adopted by the House of Delegates of the American Medical Association on December 4, 1973:

The intentional termination of the life of one human being by another—mercy killing—is contrary to that for which the medical profession stands and is contrary to the policy of the American Medical Association.

The cessation of the employment of extraordinary means to prolong the life of the body when there is irrefutable evidence that biological death is imminent is the decision of the patient and/or his immediate family. The advice and judgment of the physician should be freely available to the patient and/or his immediate family.

However, a strong case can be made against this doctrine. In what follows I will set out some of the relevant arguments, and urge doctors to reconsider their views on this matter.

To begin with a familiar type of situation, a patient who is dying of incurable cancer of the throat is in terrible pain, which can no longer be satisfactorily alleviated. He is certain to die within a few days, even if present treatment is continued, but he does not want to go on living for those days since the pain is unbearable. So he asks the doctor for an end to it, and his family joins in the request.

Suppose the doctor agrees to withhold treatment, as the conventional doctrine says he may. The justification for his doing so is that the patient is in terrible agony, and since he is going to die anyway, it would be wrong to prolong his suffering needlessly. But now notice this. If one simply withholds treatment, it may take the patient longer to die, and so he may suffer more than he would if more direct action were taken and a lethal injection given. This fact provides strong reason for thinking that, once the initial decision not to prolong his agony has been made, active euthanasia is actually preferable to passive euthanasia, rather than the reverse. To say otherwise is to endorse the option that leads to more suffering rather than less, and is contrary to the humanitarian impulse that prompts the decision not to prolong his life in the first place.

Part of my point is that the process of being "allowed to die" can be relatively slow and painful, whereas being given a lethal injection is relatively quick and painless. Let me give a different sort of example. In the United States about one in 600 babies is born with Down's syndrome. Most of these babies are otherwise healthy—that is, with only the usual pediatric care, they will proceed to an otherwise normal infancy. Some, however, are born with congenital defects such as intestinal obstructions that require operations if they are to live. Sometimes, the parents and the doctor will decide not to operate, and let the infant die. Anthony Shaw describes what happens then:

> . . . When surgery is denied [the doctor] must try to keep the infant from suffering while natural forces sap the baby's life away. As a surgeon whose natural inclination is to use the scalpel to fight off death, standing by and watching a salvageable baby die is the most emotionally exhausting experience I know. It is easy at a conference, in a theoretical discussion, to decide that such infants should be allowed to die. It is altogether *different* to stand by in the nursery and watch as dehydration and infection wither a tiny being over hours and days. This is a terrible for me and the hospital staff—much more so than for the parents who never set foot in the nursery.[1]

I can understand why some people are opposed to all euthanasia, and insist that such infants must be allowed to live. I think I can also understand why other people favor destroying these babies quickly and painlessly. But why should anyone favor letting "dehydration and infection wither a tiny being over hours and days"? The doctrine that says that a baby may be allowed to dehydrate and wither, but may not be given an injection that would end its life without suffering, seems so patently cruel as to require no further refutation. The strong language is not intended to offend, but only to put the point in the clearest possible way.

My second argument is that the conventional doctrine leads to decisions concerning life and death made on irrelevant grounds.

Consider again the case of the infants with Down's syndrome who need operations for congenital defects unrelated to the syndrome to live. Sometimes, there is no operation, and the baby dies, but when there is no such defect, the baby lives on. Now, an operation such as that to remove an intestinal obstruction is not prohibitively difficult. The reason why such operations are not performed in these cases is, clearly, that the child has Down's syndrome and the parents and doctor judge that because of that fact it is better for the child to die.

But notice that this situation is absurd, no matter what view one takes of the lives and potentials of such babies. If the life of such an infant is worth preserving, what does it matter if it needs a simple operation? Or, if one thinks it better that such a baby should not live on, what difference does it make that it happens to have an unobstructed intestinal tract? In either case, the matter of life and death is being decided on irrelevant grounds. It is the Down's syndrome, and not the intestines, that is the issue. The matter should be decided, if at all, on that basis, and not be allowed to depend on the essentially irrelevant question of whether the intestinal tract is blocked.

What makes this situation possible, of course, is the idea that when there is an intestinal blockage, one can "let the baby die," but when there is no such defect there is nothing that can be done, for one must not "kill" it. The fact that this idea leads to such results as deciding life or death on irrelevant grounds is another good reason why the doctrine should be rejected.

One reason why so many people think that there is an important moral difference between active and passive euthanasia is that they think killing someone is morally worse than letting someone die. But is it? Is killing, in itself, worse than letting die? To investigate this issue, two cases may be considered that are exactly alike except that one involves killing whereas the other involves letting someone die. Then, it can be asked whether this difference makes any difference to the moral assessments.

It is important that the cases be exactly alike, except for this one difference, since otherwise one cannot be confident that it is this difference and not some other that accounts for any variation in the assessments of the two cases. So, let us consider this pair of cases:

In the first, Smith stands to gain a large inheritance if anything should happen to his six-year-old cousin. One evening while the child is taking bath, Smith sneaks into the bathroom and drowns the child, and then arranges things so that it will look like an accident.

In the second, Jones also stands to gain if anything should happen to his six-year-old cousin. Like Smith, Jones sneaks in planning to drown the child in his bath. However, just as he enters the bathroom Jones sees the child slip and hit his head, and fall face down in the water. Jones is delighted; he stands by, ready to push the child's head back under if it is necessary, but it is not necessary. With only a little thrashing about, the child drowns all by himself, "accidentally," as Jones watches and does nothing.

Now Smith killed the child, whereas Jones "merely" let the child die. That is the only difference between them. Did either man behave better, from a moral point of view? If the difference between killing and letting die were in itself a morally important matter, one should say that Jones's behavior was less reprehensible than Smith's. But does one really want to say that? I think not. In the first place, both men acted from the same motive, personal gain, and both had exactly the same end in view when they acted. It may be inferred from Smith's conduct that he is a bad man, although that judgment may be withdrawn or modified if certain further facts are learned about him—for example, that he is mentally deranged. But would not the very same thing be inferred about Jones from his conduct? And would not the same further considerations also be relevant to any modification of this judgment? Moreover, suppose Jones pleaded, in his own defense, "After all, I didn't do anything except just stand there and

watch the child drown. I didn't kill him; I only let him die." Again, if letting die were in itself less bad than killing, this defense should have at least some weight. But it does not. Such a "defense" can only be regarded as a grotesque perversion of moral reasoning. Morally speaking, it is no defense at all.

Now, it may be pointed out, quite properly, that the cases of euthanasia with which doctors are concerned are not like this at all. They do not involve personal gain or the destruction of normal healthy children. Doctors are concerned only with cases in which the patient's life is of no further use to him, or in which the patient's life has become or will soon become a terrible burden. However, the point is the same in these cases: the bare difference between killing and letting die does not, in itself, make a moral difference. If a doctor lets a patient die, for humane reasons, he is in the same moral position as if he had given the patient a lethal injection for humane reasons. If his decision was wrong—if, for example, the patient's illness was in fact curable—the decision would be equally regrettable no matter which method was used to carry it out. And if the doctor's decision was the right one, the method used is not in itself important.

The AMA policy statement isolates the crucial issue very well; the crucial issue is "the intentional termination of the life of one human being by another." But after identifying this issue, and forbidding "mercy killing," the statement goes on to deny that the cessation of treatment is the intentional termination of a life. This is where the mistake comes in, for what is the cessation of treatment, in these circumstances, if it is not "the intentional termination of the life of one human being by another"? Of course, it is exactly that, and if it were not, there would be no point to it.

Many people will find this judgment hard to accept. One reason, I think, is that it is very easy to conflate the question of whether killing is, in itself, worse than letting die, with the very different question of whether most actual cases of killing are more reprehensible than most actual cases of letting die. Most actual cases of killing are clearly terrible (think, for example, of all the murders reported in the newspapers), and one hears of such cases every day. On the other hand, one hardly ever hears of a case of letting die, except for the actions of doctors who are motivated by humanitarian reasons. So one learns to think of killing in a much worse light than of letting die. But this does not mean that there is something about killing that makes it in itself worse than letting die, for it is not the bare difference between killing and letting die that makes the difference in these cases. Rather, the other factors—the murderer's motive of personal gain, for example, contrasted with the doctor's humanitarian motivation—account for different reactions to the different cases.

I have argued that killing is not in itself any worse than letting die; if my contention is right, it follows that active euthanasia is not any worse than passive euthanasia. What arguments can be given on the other side? The most common, I believe, is the following:

"The important difference between active and passive euthanasia is that, in passive euthanasia, the doctor does not do anything to bring about the patient's death. The doctor does nothing, and the patient dies of whatever ills already afflict him. In active euthanasia, however, the doctor does something to bring about the patient's death: he kills him. The doctor who gives the patient with cancer a lethal injection has himself caused his patient's death; whereas if he merely ceases treatment, the cancer is the cause of the death."

A number of points need to be made here. The first is that it is not exactly correct to say that in passive euthanasia the doctor does nothing, for he does do one thing that is very important: he lets the patient die. "Letting someone die" is certainly different, in some respects, from other types of action—mainly in that it is a kind of action that one may perform by way of not performing certain other actions.

For example, one may let a patient die by way of not giving medication, just as one may insult someone by way of not shaking his hand. But for any purpose of moral assessment, it is a type of action nonetheless. The decision to let a patient die is subject to moral appraisal in the same way that a decision to kill him would be subject to moral appraisal; it may be assessed as wise or unwise, compassionate or sadistic, right or wrong. If a doctor deliberately let a patient die who was suffering from a routinely curable illness, the doctor would certainly be to blame if he had needlessly killed the patient. Charges against him would then be appropriate. If so, it would be no defense at all for him to insist that he didn't "do anything." He would have done something very serious indeed, for he let his patient die.

Fixing the cause of death may be very important from a legal point of view, for it may determine whether criminal charges are brought against the doctor. But I do not think that this notion can be used to show a moral difference between active and passive euthanasia. The reason why it is considered bad to be the cause of someone's death is that death is regarded as a great evil—and so it is. However, if it has been decided that euthanasia—even passive euthanasia—is desirable in a given case, it has also been decided that in this instance death is no greater an evil than the patient's continued existence. And if this is true, the usual reason for not wanting to be the cause of someone's death simply does not apply.

Finally, doctors may think that all of this is only of academic interest—the sort of thing that philosophers may worry about but that has no practical bearing on their own work. After all, doctors must be concerned about the legal consequences of what they do, and active euthanasia is clearly forbidden by the law. But even so, doctors should also be concerned with the fact that the law is forcing upon them a moral doctrine that may well be indefensible, and has a considerable effect on their practices. Of course, most doctors are not now in the position of being coerced in this matter, for they do not regard themselves as merely going along with what the law requires. Rather, in statements such as the AMA policy statement that I have quoted, they are endorsing this doctrine as a central point of medical ethics. In that statement, active euthanasia is condemned not merely as illegal but as "contrary to that for which the medical profession stands," whereas passive euthanasia is approved. However, the preceding considerations suggest that there is really no moral difference between the two, considered in themselves (there may be important moral differences in some cases in their *consequences,* but, as I pointed out, these differences may make active euthanasia, and not passive euthanasia, the morally preferable option). So whereas doctors may have to discriminate between active and passive euthanasia to satisfy the law, they should not do any more than that. In particular, they should not give the distinction any added authority and weight by writing it into official statements of medical ethics.

NOTE

1. A. Shaw, "Doctor, Do We Have a Choice?" *The New York Times Magazine,* January 30, 1972, p. 54.

Discussion Questions

1. How does Professor Rachels distinguish between biographical and biological life? Why does he believe that biographical life is more important than biological life? And how does this distinction, according to Professor Rachels, justify active euthanasia? Do you agree with this? Why or why not?

2. Briefly tell the story of Jones and Smith. Why does Professor Rachels believe that this tale shows that there is no moral distinction between passive and active euthanasia? Do you agree that there is no distinction between active and passive euthanasia? Explain and defend your answer.

3. Imagine if a distraught teenager wants to commit suicide because he believes his biographical life has ended, that is, his girlfriend has broken up with him and he has bad acne. Given the apparent subjective nature of what constitutes a biographically significant life, on what grounds could Professor Rachels argue that the teenager is morally wrong in committing suicide? If Professor Rachels says that it is an inappropriate choice for a human person to make, then isn't it possible that patients who want to end their biological lives because of what they perceive as the end of their biographical lives are making an inappropriate choice? How do you think Rachels would respond to this inquiry?

You can locate InfoTrac-College Education articles about this chapter by accessing the InfoTrac-College Edition website (http://www.infotrac-college.com/wadsworth/). Using the InfoTrac-College Edition subject guide, enter the search terms relevant to this chapter, and then read abstracts for relevant articles.

19   A Case Against Physician-Assisted Suicide

PAUL CHAMBERLAIN

Paul Chamberlain has taught Ethics and Political Philosophy at Trinity Western University for 10 years and continues to hold the position of Adjunct Professor of Philosophy there. He is also the Executive Director for Canada of Ravi Zacharias International Ministries. His areas of scholarly interest are bioethics, political philosophy, and philosophy of religion. Among his books are *Can We Be Good Without God?* (1996) and *Final Wishes* (2000).

The following summary was provided by the author:

In this article I set out and respond to six arguments for legalizing physician-assisted suicide (hereafter PAS) that have become prominent in recent times. I contend that ultimately, none of them is successful. The six arguments are: firstly, that the right of everyone to personal autonomy or self-determination requires the right to PAS; secondly, that there is no moral distinction between killing and letting die in similar circumstances; thirdly, that a slippery slope to other unwanted practices from legalizing PAS can be contained through a proper set of safeguards; fourthly, that by not legalizing PAS we end up treating suffering humans worse than we treat suffering animals; fifthly, that assisted suicides are happening whether PAS is legal or not—some are botched, and that we only cause more harm than good by keeping this practice illegal; and sixthly, that PAS should be legal if a majority of people want it to be legal.

I argue that the critical question to be asked of PAS is what the effects would be of legalizing it on the people most directly affected by it. I then set out three kinds of harm, almost sure to follow from legalizing this procedure. I also argue that there are morally significant differences between killing and letting die, that due to the nature of PAS there is good reason to believe that it is a practice that would be virtually impossible to contain, that our treatment of animals does not provide an adequate analogy for determining proper treatment of human beings, and that both the botched suicide and the democratic arguments rest on flawed principles.

CONSIDER THE CASE OF Sue Rodriguez, a Canadian victim of ALS who fought a very public campaign to have the right to receive a physician-assisted suicide legalized in Canada. After hearing of the Supreme Court's 1994 decision to deny her request by a vote of 5 to 4, these were her words: "A year ago when I was first diagnosed, I was quite agile. Today I can barely walk. I want to ask you gentlemen, if I cannot give consent to my own death, whose body is this? Who owns my life?"[1]

To put it bluntly, the effects of ALS are devastating. It is a progressive, fatal, neuromuscular disease that destroys nerves that control all

---

This essay was commissioned exclusively for publication in this text. It is published by permission of its author.

voluntary muscles. When they aren't being used the muscles die. In most cases, over a period of 2 to 5 years, the body of someone who has this illness becomes completely debilitated even though the mind remains clear. Was it wrong for the Supreme Court to deny Sue Rodriguez her request to receive a physician-assisted suicide (hereafter PAS)? Was she wrong to request it? We may certainly feel sympathy for her and others like her. They face tragic situations. The real question, however, is whether there is a moral obligation on the part of society to grant people like Sue Rodriguez the right to request and receive a PAS when they believe their suffering is too great and no longer want to endure it.

A number of arguments in favor of legalizing PAS have risen to prominence. My purpose in this article is to respond to six of these. Before proceeding further, however, it is important to clarify precisely what the term PAS means. It does not refer to the practice of a suffering person refusing medical care. In any case, the right to refuse medical treatment is already legal and available in most, if not all, jurisdictions. A PAS occurs when a physician provides the means, method, or both to a suffering person who has decided to end her life.

PERSONAL AUTONOMY

Perhaps the most fundamental argument put forward for legalizing PAS is the argument from the right to personal autonomy or self-determination. It usually goes something like this: There are people who are suffering beyond what they wish to endure and who want to end their suffering gently and peacefully. What right does anyone have to deny this wish to people in such tragic situations? They are asking for nothing more than the freedom to end their suffering in a gentle and peaceful way. Who are we to force them to go on suffering when they do not wish to?[2]

I say this is the most fundamental argument in favor of legalizing PAS because at the end of the day, even when supporters of PAS are willing to concede other points in this debate, they will usually continue to insist that the right to individual autonomy requires that people should be given the choice to receive a PAS if they want it. This right is said to overpower all opposing arguments and concerns. It, in fact, is the argument Sue Rodriguez was alluding to in her statement to the Justices of the Supreme Court. If she was not able to choose the time of her own death, then whose body was it? Surely, her body and her life were hers. If not hers, then whose? But if so, then how can we deny that the choice of when and how to end her life must also be hers?

This line of reasoning has great appeal to most Westerners, and especially to those with a strong Libertarian bent. But the critical question is what this argument, based on personal autonomy, proves. Not as much as it first appears. The fact is that many people want to do many things. Some are good, some are bad, and of course there is a whole range in between. Would anyone seriously suggest that we give anyone and everyone complete liberty to perform any action at all just so long as they *want* to perform it? What about the person who enjoys drinking and driving, or stealing from elderly people? These people *want* to do these things.

With only a little thought it becomes clear that it is never enough, even for the most ardent Libertarian, to simply ask whether a person wants to do something when deciding whether or not to make an activity legal. One of the most basic principles of liberty set out in a class on Political Philosophy is that individual choice must be limited if political liberty is to be meaningful at all. Without limits, might becomes right, the strongest rule, all liberty is threatened or destroyed, and chaos follows. Legal restrictions are required in order to secure and protect civil liberty. What is sometimes forgotten, however, is that any legal restriction is a restriction on someone's choice whether it concerns driving habits, zoning laws, breaking and entering, or anything else.

But perhaps we should pursue the question further. Why, exactly, do we restrict some people's choices? Why not let people do whatever they want to do? At least part of the answer is that some of our actions bring harm to others, and the rights of those others not to be harmed by our actions justify such restrictions. In other words, we restrict some choices not merely because someone here or there thinks a particular action is immoral or unpleasant—that is seldom argued as sufficient reason to make something illegal. Rather, certain actions harm others, or can reasonably be expected to harm others, and that is why there are laws against all sorts of things that people would like to do.

But what is the point for PAS? Surely if there ever were a purely private act that brought no harm to others, the act of a physician assisting a patient in ending her life behind the closed doors of a hospital room or private home would be it.

But is this characterization of PAS accurate? There is reason to believe that it is overly optimistic. It misses the critical distinction between a private act on the one hand and a public policy change on the other, which is really at issue here. Legalizing PAS entails changing a public policy, writing a new law to replace a former one. The new law would have to set out what is now legal and available, for whom, under exactly what conditions, and so on. As such, it would affect far more people than merely those wanting this new liberty. It would affect everyone whose life circumstances fit the conditions set out in the new law. Whenever we change public policy we must at the very least show that the new policy will not harm those directly affected by it and preferably that it will bring about more good to them than the previous policy. This, of course, requires that we analyze the effects of

the new public policy, which of course means that a simple appeal to individual choice or autonomy as *the reason* for implementing any new public policy, including this one, is grossly inadequate.

The relevant question then is what the effects would be of changing public policy to give people the right to use the medical profession to help end their lives. What possible harm could come from it? What burden might be imposed on others who are affected by this new public policy? To see what burden there may be, think carefully of the plight of a person who is elderly, terminally ill, or disabled. Here she is, in the midst of the stress, trauma, and discouragement that comes from facing a terminal illness or a disability. Or perhaps she is a paraplegic or a quadriplegic from a serious accident, living with the fact that she is now a burden and an expense to others—to family, to loved ones, and to caregivers. She needs constant care. She's now become a high-maintenance person. She needs trips to the doctor, the pharmacy, the hospital, and may even need help to be fed or use the toilet. She knows this is causing stress and strain on her loved ones—they're giving up time with family and friends to care for her. They do their best not to show it, but an elderly or disabled person is not stupid. Occasionally she catches a look of stress on someone's face and wishes she didn't have to be such a burden. She requires as much care as a one- or two-year old child but the difference is that the child has the rest of its life to return the favor.

But that's not all. A person in this position is no longer making the contribution she used to and consequently doesn't often feel needed, something we all long to be. She has lost the ability to earn an income and is dependent on others for almost everything. She occasionally finds herself asking what happened to her dignity and to her sense of self-worth. At times she feels useless. How could she not? This is her life.

Consider the significance for people in these tragic circumstances, of our legalizing PAS. They would be offered the choice to die, and we may wonder what could possibly be wrong with giving them this choice. They don't have to exercise it but can if they wish. Isn't that the point of giving them a choice?

It is worth noting, however, that contrary to the way we often speak, giving people more choices is not always, invariably, doing them a favor. Some choices are burdensome. The choice the unlucky CEO has to make of which 500 employees to lay off is a burden as is the one that the political leader has to make of whether or not to send troops into battle, knowing that people will probably die either way. Who among us has not considered a difficult choice facing someone else and uttered the words, "Now there's a choice I'm glad I don't have to make"? Experience teaches us that some choices are burdens, not favors.

And the choice we will have given to the elderly, terminally ill, and the disabled by legalizing PAS will almost certainly impose a devastating burden upon them. By giving them the choice to die, we will have also unwittingly placed upon these vulnerable people the added burden of having to justify their own continued existence, if not to others, at least to themselves, and this at a time when they feel useless, discouraged, and a burden to others. The world will have changed for them because from now on, their own existence is a choice they must make and can be called upon to justify. People like this can be asked why, when other people are choosing PAS, giving up their medical equipment for others, and ending the burden and expense on family and society, *they* would like to live on, as of course, the vast majority will.

Consider the words of Peter Kyne, a neuropsychiatrist and palliative-care specialist, commenting on the effects which legalizing PAS will have upon vulnerable people.

> I know for a fact that people who are dependent upon others, almost universally feel grief and pain over the burden they are to their families. The sense of obligation to exit the situation, if it becomes a legal possibility, will be overwhelming.[3]

This is the harm that could come to these vulnerable citizens by legalizing PAS. Furthermore, discussions one hears from time to time of a possible *duty to die* or of the potential benefit of harvesting organs for others, which could follow from legalizing PAS, would only add to the pressure people may feel of having to justify their own continued existence.[4]

Our present laws prohibiting PAS are pillars of protection for vulnerable people. At present, they know they will be kept alive by default. No decision to live need be made because the issue never comes up. No justification is necessary for why one ought to live on or deserves to live on. No discussion with others, or even within one's own mind, is needed. Once PAS is legalized, all that changes.

But couldn't we construct safeguards to protect vulnerable people if PAS is legalized? Couldn't we carefully craft the law in just such a way that we could prevent this abuse? One wonders what kind of safeguards could be developed which would protect elderly and terminally ill people from an inner sense of obligation to choose PAS. The most commonly suggested safeguards are that the person must be terminally ill or experiencing unbearable suffering with no hope of relief, that the request for an assisted suicide must be in writing, that at least two physicians need to be involved and that the request for suicide must be persistent over time and be revocable.[5] It is hard to see how any of these could prevent dependent, vulnerable people from feeling an inner sense of obligation to stop being a burden to their families or caregivers. The problem is not with safeguards. It is that safeguards simply are not designed to prevent this kind of abuse. It is hard to imagine what could, apart from laws making PAS illegal and, hence, not open to discussion.

There is a second form of harm to vulnerable people that could result from legalizing

PAS: the possibility of misdiagnoses leading patients who may not even be terminally ill but who think they are, to request and receive a PAS. Every physician knows that medicine is not an exact science and the possibility of physicians misdiagnosing their patients is very real. It happens, and because it happens it allows for the possibility that a physician may actually help end the life of the "wrong person" if PAS were an available option. What makes this especially serious is that most requests for suicide come immediately upon patients being diagnosed with a terminal illness or after serious accidents when people are told they are now paraplegics or quadriplegics. Who wouldn't be highly vulnerable at a time like this? Devastating news has a way of destroying a person's will to live. Herbert Hendin, director of the American Foundation for Suicide Prevention, has written that "in our society right now, even without physicians available to help people die, more individuals, particularly elderly people kill themselves because they fear and *mistakenly* believe they have cancer, than those who kill themselves and actually have cancer."[6]

Hendin also writes that preoccupation with suicide is greater among those awaiting the results of tests for HIV antibodies than among those who already know they are HIV positive.[7] These people leave their doctors' offices deeply distressed, worried that they have cancer or AIDS or at least wondering if they might. There is nothing they can do but wait for the test results. Every bruise or stomach pain makes them wonder all over again if they are deathly ill, and yet if there is a misdiagnosis, they aren't seriously ill at all. The laws prohibiting PAS are there to protect people such as these. The very possibility that a physician could help a healthy but misdiagnosed and deeply distressed person die is reason enough not to eliminate these pillars of protection. This is why we should seriously question whether a physician's assistance to help end one's life should be available to people who have just heard devastating news.

This is the same form of argumentation as is often put forward by opponents of capital punishment, namely that the practice of executing criminals creates the possibility of executing an innocent person. This has always been an important consideration in the capital punishment debate and for good reason. Whatever we may think on that issue, over the years innocent people have been executed for crimes they never committed. Others, in countries where capital punishment is not practiced, have been released from life sentences when their innocence has become known. There is little doubt that a similar thing will happen if we legalize PAS.

The third kind of harm almost sure to result from legalizing PAS is that carrying out this practice would entail making a discriminatory value judgment about certain human lives, and in the process, would violate the principle of human equality. This principle asserts that all human life is to be valued equally and that we ought not to select one group for poorer treatment than another unless there is some overriding moral justification, for example, the poorer treatment we give to criminals for their crimes. It rules out practices such as slavery by asserting that the fact that people are members of a certain class or race does not justify valuing them lower or treating them worse than other humans. Their humanity requires that they be valued and treated with the same respect given to other human beings in similar circumstances. How then, would legalization of PAS entail a discriminatory value judgment and violate this principle?

To see how it would do so, consider precisely who the proponents of legalization have in mind as the beneficiaries of this practice. Who would PAS be for if it were legalized? Would it be for all of us? No, it would not. It would be for those who are elderly, terminally ill, and perhaps for certain disabled people. Compassion, we are told, requires that we give people in these conditions the option of ending their suffering with suicide assistance. After all, if we were one of them, in their position, we may well want that option for ourselves so we should do for them what we would want done for ourselves.[8]

This sounds compelling until we consider how we might respond if the person who wanted to die were *not* elderly or terminally ill or disabled but rather were able-bodied, healthy, or young. Should a person like this be given suicide assistance to end her life of suffering? "Of course not!" comes the instant reply. "These people need our help in difficult times. They need hope. They need the best suicide prevention measures we can bring them. They have so much to live for."[9] But if compassion requires we give suicide assistance to the elderly, terminally ill, or disabled when they want to end their lives, then where is our compassion for these able-bodied people who also want to die because of their own painful circumstances? They, too, see their lives as hopeless, as not worth living and want to end them. They, too, are experiencing suffering which they regard as intolerable. If compassion requires us to offer suicide assistance in one case, why not in the other? Let us not forget that if we were in the place of the thirty-year-old able-bodied suicidal person, we would equally want the choice to die.

It looks very much like we have made a value judgment about the worth of lives that are disabled, terminally ill, or elderly. Both the able-bodied and healthy on one hand and the disabled, elderly, and terminally ill on the other, are suffering, feel life is hopeless, and want assistance in dying. However, legalizing PAS with safeguards, which every proponent of legalizations calls for, will mean that we've decided that while able-bodied, healthy life is worth fighting for, even to the extent of overriding individual autonomy, disabled, elderly, or terminally ill life is not, at least not to the same degree. Somehow, compassion and the right to personal autonomy will have required that we grant suicide assistance to people in this group but not to the other one. It's hard

to avoid the conclusion that however passionate our statements to the contrary, disabled, elderly, and terminally ill human life is valued less, or at least considered less worth fighting for, than able-bodied, healthy life.

KILLING VERSUS LETTING DIE: MORALLY EQUIVALENT?

A second common argument in favor of legalizing PAS is that there is no moral difference between killing a person and letting that person die in similar circumstances. In other words, there is no reason to prefer one over the other as a matter of principle. If you believe one of these is morally permissible in a certain circumstance, then you should view the other as also permissible in that circumstance since they are morally equivalent[10] This argument is usually stated by pointing out that at the present time people who are being kept alive by ventilators, respirators, or other life-support systems may ask to be removed from these systems. They can legally receive a physician's help to end their life of suffering by "pulling the plug." What is more, these patients need a physician's help to do this. Without that help their death could involve painful and needless problems. Physicians shut off life-support systems and administer medication to render the patient unconscious so that death will be painless and humane.

The moral equivalence argument is that it makes no sense for a physician to do all of this but then refuse to help another patient die who likewise is suffering, but simply has no life-support system to shut off. Morally, it is inconsistent. In both cases, a person is suffering, is wishing to end life, and needs a doctor's help to do so. Furthermore, in both cases the result is the same. The person's life of suffering is over. Even the motives behind the action are said to be the same, namely to help the person die. The only difference is that in one case there is a switch to shut off while in the other, the only "switch" is a lethal injection. To make a moral distinction between these two actions is seen to be meaningless, philosophical hairsplitting.

This argument has been responded to by Sullivan, Moreland, Beauchamp, and others and I do not need to repeat their responses, but let us note what has happened.[11] The similarities between certain cases of killing and letting die are stressed, and the conclusion is drawn that because of these similarities, these two kinds of actions are morally equivalent.

Two comments should be made. First, in emphasizing the similarities, the one key difference that really counts is being overlooked, namely, that when a person is killed by a physician, she dies as the direct result of the actions of the physician. On the other hand, when a person is allowed to die, she does not die as the result of the physician's actions, but rather as the result of whatever condition she happens to have. It is the condition, not the physician, which kills. To overlook this difference, simply because of the other similarities, is to overlook the one factor that actually constitutes the difference between killing and letting die, a difference that is highly significant in making moral judgments.

Secondly, the proponent of the moral-equivalency argument errs on the last similarity, namely, the motives. It is not necessarily true that the motives are the same in cases of killing and letting die. In cases of killing, the motives are clear—to end the life of the person. When a physician shuts off a respirator, however, the motives may well be merely to end attempts to heal and let nature take its course, or let God's will be done. It is simply a mistake to say the motives are always the same. This is important because motives and intentions behind our actions are highly significant in assessing both their morality and legality. It is the difference between one motorist who intentionally steers his car into a group of pedestrians, killing them, and another whose vehicle also careens into the pedestrians but only because his brakes malfunctioned and he could not avoid them. In both cases the pedestrians are dead but, both morally and legally, we assess the actions of the drivers vastly differently.

Most will agree that there are cases in which we are morally justified in letting a person die. In fact, the mere recognition that we all will die someday and that it is futile to try to prevent death forever leads us to accept the fact that when further medical treatment will only prolong the dying process, and increase human suffering, then there is no obligation to give that treatment. Whether there are also arguments for going the next step and giving a lethal injection to people, in other words killing people who would not otherwise die at that time from the conditions they have, is precisely the question at issue. To simply identify the similarities between killing and letting die, and on this basis assert that there is no moral difference between them, is not adequate.

THERE IS NO SLIPPERY SLOPE

The next argument in favor of legalizing PAS is actually a response to one put forward by the opponents of legalization. The argument against legalizing PAS is that it is a practice that, if made legal, would be difficult, maybe impossible, to contain. Legalizing this practice today would lead to practices we all agree would be wrong and unfortunate, such as PAS for teenagers and for people who are not even terminally ill but just emotionally depressed, people being euthanized with no request, and infanticide.

The response by proponents of legalization is that this slippery-slope argument is wrongheaded. Admittedly, liberties can be, and occasionally are, abused, goes the response. Some drivers ignore the speed limit and a few pilots disobey the instructions of the air-traffic controller, but the possibility of abuse of any liberty does not automatically constitute a reason to destroy that liberty. Instead, we look for ways of dealing with the abuses, of containing them, and in this way guarding our liberties. The possibility of abuses following from legalizing PAS is not said to be a reason to destroy that liberty either. We can contain these abuses by carefully crafting a law with a set of safeguards, conditions which must be met anytime a PAS is administered, just as we do with all our other liberties. Certain safeguards such as the ones mentioned above are then suggested.[12]

Is this an adequate response to the slippery-slope argument. Can potential abuses be sufficiently contained such that they do not constitute an argument against legalizing PAS? Is this kind of argument wrong-headed as the proponents of legalization assert? It is true that certain forms of the slippery-slope argument are illegitimate. Most any practice or action can be abused and the possibility of abuse does not necessarily constitute an argument against every practice. But not all cases are alike. They differ in the seriousness of the potential abuses, the likelihood of these abuses happening, the numbers and kinds of people affected by them, and so on. This all means that there are also different kinds of slippery-slope arguments and some are legitimate and should be taken seriously. In the case of PAS, it is widely agreed that the potential abuses from legalizing it are serious and that the people affected by them are highly vulnerable. The only question remaining concerns the likelihood of these abuses happening, and there is good reason to believe that due to the nature of PAS, the likelihood would be high. It is a practice that would be exceedingly difficult, maybe impossible, to contain. There are two reasons for this.

First of all, in some cases, including PAS, one action does more than simply *invite* the question of pursuing the next action, or *desensitize* people to the seriousness of the next action. Rather, in certain cases, the reasons we set out for doing one thing actually *justify* other actions that we have not yet begun to pursue and may not even be thinking of at the time. This makes a slippery slope virtually inevitable, or unstoppable.

In 1991, a fifty-year-old woman in the Netherlands, who was physically healthy but seriously depressed, sought a PAS from her psychiatrist and received one, in violation of the existing legal safeguards. The physician, Dr. Chabot, went to court because of his illegal administering of a PAS and was eventually exonerated. Although we may wonder how he could have been acquitted when he so clearly and indisputably violated the guidelines, the more important question may be how he could possibly have been convicted. After all, the woman was suffering grievously. She had an abusive alcoholic husband and two sons. Both had died, one through suicide.[13] The woman had decided that her suffering was too great and that she did not want to endure it any longer, just as the principle upon which the right to a PAS is based says. It states that any person who believes her suffering is too great and no longer wants to endure it should have the right to request and receive a PAS. So she asked for a PAS and got it. Why wouldn't she? The only difference was that her suffering was psychological rather than physical. We may think this is an important difference but she, her doctor, his lawyer, and ultimately the court did not. In fact, Dr. Chabot's lawyer's very words after the verdict were that the court decision showed that intolerable *psychological* suffering was no different than intolerable *physical* suffering. The fact that this was not the intention of the law permitting PAS or of those who initially argued for it is precisely the point.

The safeguards intended to prevent the move down the slippery slope to other unwanted practices could not stop that slide because the law making PAS legal rested on the principle that the individual has the right to choose. That is the point of the principle on which PAS is based and it is always the most fundamental reason given for why the practice ought to be legalized. The safeguards, in this case, conflicted with the fundamental principle of personal autonomy and so they, the safeguards, were struck down and rewritten. Courts simply did what courts do. They applied principles and legal precedents consistently.

If this principle were enacted into law, one wonders how we could deny a PAS to a twenty-five-year-old anorexic woman who requests it, as one did in the Netherlands not long ago. She received it. Or the request of the fifty-year-old depressed woman mentioned above? Or any other young person who is physically healthy but deeply depressed and wants to end his suffering with an assisted suicide? The principle says that it is he, the one suffering, who decides whether or not his suffering is too great and that he wants an assisted suicide.

What will we tell this person? That his suffering is not bad enough? How could we know that? What arrogance on our part to tell him that. Or will we tell him that his suffering is the wrong kind of suffering? On what basis would we say that? Or will we say that PAS was not intended for him or for the kind of suffering he is experiencing? What does he care? You and I may say all these things and really believe them but the courts won't because they will do what courts do—they will interpret principles and precedents consistently. The very reasons for the original principle unwittingly become reasons for granting an assisted suicide to people far beyond those it was originally intended for.

Herbert Hendin, after researching the history of PAS in the Netherlands, has written that what was intended as an unfortunate necessity in exceptional cases has become a routine way of dealing with serious or terminal illnesses so that doctors are often the first to suggest euthanasia to terminally ill patients.[14] In his words, "Virtually every guideline set up by the Dutch—a voluntary, well-considered, persistent request; intolerable suffering that cannot be relieved; consultation; and reporting of cases—has failed to protect patients or has been modified or violated."[15]

The second reason for thinking that PAS would be impossible to contain concerns the incentives which exist to move down the slope rather than up it. These are *incentives,* not reasons or arguments, and they function largely at the subconscious level. There is an economic incentive, which cash-strapped governments everywhere feel, to reduce spending, and health-care spending is a large part of most government budgets. Estimates are that somewhere between 30 and 70 percent of all health-care dollars are spent on people in the last 60 to 90 days of their lives. It does not take a great deal of figuring to imagine the savings to cash-strapped governments looking for ways to cut debts and deficits, if even 10 to 20 percent of these people would end their lives before the 60 to 90 days began.

Then, there is the family incentive. Those who have gone through the pain of seeing a loved one suffer from a terminal illness or a long-term debilitating disease or a serious accident will know that care-giving family members experience grave burdens and inconveniences. It requires time and energy and is a constant emotional drain. It means visits to the hospital, doctor's office, pharmacy, and so on. It might mean bathing and toileting the loved one. The most saintly person in that situation can be forgiven for having the occasional thought that it would be nice if it were over. Who could blame them for sometimes wishing the burden could be lifted? These subconscious incentives, both economic and family, are on the side of moving down the slope, not up, making it even more likely that this will be the direction in which we move.

ANIMALS

A fourth and increasingly common argument in favor of legalizing PAS is that by not legalizing it, we end up treating suffering humans worse than we treat suffering animals. When animals in our society suffer greatly, we put them out of their misery. We do not let them linger on and on. Furthermore, we do this because torturing them or letting them linger in their misery would be *inhumane* treatment. But consider the plight of a suffering human in this same society if PAS remains illegal. Whereas an animal's life of suffering will be ended, some humans will have no option but to linger on and on in their suffering even when they go so far as to ask us to end it for them. If animals deserve to be treated with compassion in their suffering, don't humans deserve at least that much?

What can be said to this line of reasoning? Could it be that our moral principles are causing us to deny humans the basic compassion we readily give to animals? On the other hand, could there be reasons why proper treatment of animals does not provide a correct analogy for how we ought to treat humans? Are there considerations to be taken into account when dealing with humans that do not apply to animals?

Imagine homicide detectives being called to a home in a society where people were free to end human suffering just as we now end animal suffering. In this home the detectives find a dead person and another person who quickly says to them, "He asked me to do it. He decided life was too great a burden and no longer wanted to live." How are the detectives ever going to begin that investigation? The only person who could confirm or deny this explanation is dead.

This detective example gets at the reasons we have laws prohibiting one person from helping another person die when we do not have the same prohibitions against putting animals down. That is the argument at issue here, that because we end the lives of suffering animals, we should do the same for suffering people. This case highlights at least two reasons why this argument is not persuasive.

First, we prohibit people from helping other people die to protect us all from being murdered by someone who then uses this "he-asked-me-to-do-it" defense. After all, as noted above, the only person who could confirm or deny that he had, indeed, asked him to do it is now dead and unavailable for further com-

ment. Consider the implications of giving lawyers this defense for clients accused of murder. If such a defense were available, lawyers would use it whenever possible, not because they are bad, sleazy lawyers, but precisely because they are good lawyers. It is their job to use every legal means at their disposal to defend their clients and to whatever degree they used this defense, legal protection for all of us would diminish. To allow one group of people, namely physicians, to help other people die would make this legal defense available to members of at least this one group.

Second, our laws against helping others die even when they want us to, are there to protect suicidal people from being helped in making the worst decision of their lives in the midst of serious depression and suffering. Suicidal people need our help to get them through these very difficult periods in their lives. They need protection from people who just might be willing to "help" them make this grave mistake. The point is that there are reasons for not allowing us to help other people die, which do not apply to animals. The fact that we put animals down does not necessarily mean we ought to do the same for humans. We need more reasons for helping suffering humans die than simply the fact that we help suffering animals die.

But is this detective example really like PAS for a suffering person? Couldn't we carefully craft a law permitting PAS requiring that the person's suffering and wish to die be verified? Couldn't the law require that physicians and not merely friends be involved, and so on?

The important question here is whether safeguards could be counted on to provide the same level of protection from abuse as an outright prohibition against PAS. Not only are they continually subject to change as we have noted, but adherence to them also needs somehow to be verified. Due to the nature of medical practice and the private relationship between physicians and their patients, this is not always a simple matter. One prominent physician described the difficulty this way in his submission to a senate subcommittee holding hearings on the matter,

> I believe that every safeguard that could be created has weaknesses and is open to failure. We know that what doctors do and say to patients is done behind closed doors and is between the doctor and the patient. In the case of euthanasia, the only witness that could testify that safeguards were or were not followed would be dead. The other witness to the safeguards would be unlikely to testify against him or herself. Legislative safeguards of physician-assisted suicide protect the doctor against prosecution, not the patient or the public. I believe that it is my duty as a physician, and a duty of my profession, to tell the public how difficult it would be to monitor and police any safeguards.[16]

This statement points out the extreme limitations of safeguards. To allow physicians to help other human beings die when they ask for such help would be to destroy the pillars of protection for those who have illnesses, disabilities, or who for any other reason become suicidal, and replace them with a set of shifting safeguards and a legal system with a new "he-asked-me-to-do-it" defense in its arsenal.

BOTCHED SUICIDES

The botched suicide argument in favor of legalizing PAS is akin to what is sometimes termed the back-alley argument for abortion. This argument for abortion is that whether it is legal or not, abortions will occur, some will be performed by amateurs, and women will be harmed or even die. Therefore, to protect these women, we should make abortion legal and bring this practice out into the open where we can regulate it and make it more humane.

The botched suicide argument similarly is that assisted suicides are happening and will continue whether PAS is legal or not. The assistance is not always given by a physician.

Often it is friends helping friends die. The method may be morphine gained illegally and administered poorly, or a plastic bag, or a pillow, or any other instrument that a person might use to help a friend die. Many of these attempts are botched, often with horrific results. In the light of these facts, surely it would be better, whether we agree with PAS or not, to legalize it and bring it out into the open as well, where we could regulate it and make it more humane.[17]

This argument is unique in that, unlike other arguments for PAS, it does not try to prove that PAS is good or right, only that it is inevitable and that we will only cause more harm by trying to stop it. Furthermore, it has intuitive force because it appears to recognize reality and deal with it. But is this argument sound? Perhaps we should ask whether or not we would be willing or should be willing to be consistent with the principle this argument is based on. The underlying principle upon which it appears to rest is that the fact that someone violates a law and is harmed in the process is a good reason to change that law and make the forbidden practice legal. That way no one would ever have to do it in secret anymore. It would be out in the open, regulated, and safe.

What if we were to apply this principle to other illegal actions? It's a simple way to test any principle to see whether or not it should be followed. I once read of a would-be thief who broke into a store during the night through the heating ducts and began making his way toward the merchandise area. Soon the ducts were too small and as he was sliding through, he got stuck, unable to move either in or out. He began to suffocate and nearly died before the surprised business owner arrived in the morning, heard groans, and called for help. Should we then legalize breaking and entering because, legal or not, it is happening and people are being harmed in the process? Obviously not.

But aren't there differences between a case like this and PAS? Yes, there are differences—there always are. No two cases in any analogy are ever identical nor are they totally dissimilar. There are always similarities and differences between any two things and the question which must be asked of any analogy is whether the things being compared are similar at the relevant points for the purpose of the comparison. Indeed there are differences between the case of the would-be burglar and PAS, but not relevant differences. PAS, and breaking and entering are both illegal, the laws against both are sometimes violated, and in both cases people sometimes get hurt in the process of violating them. These are the facts which this botched-suicide argument pinpoints about PAS as the reason it should be legalized. Hence, these are the relevant facts in our comparison. All the other differences don't matter. They're profoundly irrelevant because the principle this argument assumes does not pertain to them. Applying this principle consistently would mean legalizing a host of presently illegal actions people sometimes perform and get hurt as they do.

Where there are good reasons for any law, then the fact that someone violates the law and is harmed in the process is never enough reason to change that law, whether it be a law against breaking and entering, drug trafficking, murder, rape, or PAS. Interestingly, the flip-side of this is also true. If there are no good reasons for making or keeping something illegal, then we don't even need the botched suicide argument to set aside that law. It shouldn't have been there in the first place. As far as I can tell, the botched suicide argument serves no useful purpose. It is either unpersuasive or unnecessary.

THE DEMOCRATIC ARGUMENT

One final argument for PAS should be addressed. It is that regardless of the reasons any of us may have for holding one view or the other on questions like this, we ought not to cast our vote either way, or attempt to implement our moral views on these issues without carefully considering the wishes of the people of our society. After all, it is their country and they will have to live with whatever decisions are made. Various polls and surveys are then pointed to as indicators of the people's wishes, and on PAS the results often indicate that a majority of people want this service to be available. Given that this is the case, opponents of legalization are told that although they have a right to hold their views on this topic or any other, they do not have a right to force their views on citizens who disagree with them. It is simply wrong, we are told, for a minority of people who do not want this service, to impose their moral values on the populace at large. It is wrong for them to deny the majority a particular service or liberty which it wants to enjoy.

To some, this argument from the nature of democracy seems like the trump card in the PAS debate. After all, we all have our views but at the end of the day shouldn't the people themselves be able to decide their own fate in matters of morality and social policy? If the majority don't have this right, then who does? Surely not a minority that simply holds a different view than the majority.

How are we to evaluate this line of reasoning? It has a ring of credibility to the ears of anyone living in a democratic society where, by definition, the majority rules. Elected officials cast votes on the social issues of the day with an eye to the next election.

Two comments should be made about this argument. The first is that the will of the people is more difficult to discern than it first appears. Not only is it fickle and changing at the best of times, but the surveys and polls reporting it may yield different results depending upon the knowledge of the people questioned and the wording of the question. The pollster who asks, "Are you in favor of death with dignity for patients in unbearable suffering with no hope of relief?" will garner a different response than the one who asks, "Do you think physicians should ever kill their patients?" This is why a great deal of intense negotiation regularly goes into the process of determining the wording of plebiscites and referenda wherever they are held. And yet the results of polls and surveys on PAS are routinely held up as sure-fire indicators of the will of the people. This difficulty, of determining the will of the people, is of particular significance with an issue like PAS due to its emotional nature and the vastly different levels of knowledge people have about it.

Secondly, assuming we can know the wishes of the people, we must ask whether we are prepared to say that this is a reliable method for deciding these issues? If so, there are far-reaching implications. Not long ago, in Western democracies, a majority of citizens were opposed to women voting. Should we conclude from this fact that at that time it was right and good that women were not permitted to vote? More specifically, are we willing to say that it was right because a majority of people opposed it?

There was also a time in many Western democracies when a majority of citizens believed it was right for black people to be regarded as property and used as slaves. Polls would have registered majority support for this practice as well. In fact, a large part of the economy of some countries had become dependent upon the institution of slavery and when it was attacked by its opponents, its defenders predicted dire consequences that were sure to follow if it were abolished. Are we seriously willing to say that because the majority supported the practice of slavery, it was good and right at that time to round up people in Africa, herd them into stench-filled ships, transport them to another country, sell as property those who survived the trip over, and treat them as such for the rest of their lives?

To be fair, I must point out that I have never met any proponent of legalization of PAS who also believed that slavery was good or right in its day. It is virtually unanimously considered a shameful blight on our history. But that is precisely the point of this response to the democratic argument for PAS. If the proper method of deciding morality or even of what should become legalized is to follow the will of the majority, then, like it or not, we will have no choice but to admit that slavery was at one time morally justified. After all, a majority favored it. If the people at that time had the right to choose their own fate in matters of moral and social policy, and the minority had no right to impose its views on the majority, then we simply have no choice but to admit that this heinous treatment of slaves was good and right at that time. But since we do not agree that slavery was morally justified, even though the majority favored it, we should drop this way of deciding moral questions and admit that looking to the will of the people does not always lead to truth on them. We have already admitted it for the issue of slavery.

The questions we ought to ask about PAS are the same ones which ought to have been asked about slavery. What will be the effect of legalizing this practice on those most directly affected by it and upon society as a whole? If legalizing PAS would impose a devastating burden on the entire classes of the elderly, terminally ill, and disabled, and would risk the possibility that misdiagnosed patients who are not even seriously ill might receive assisted suicides, then the fact that the majority desires it and that it is only a minority that is affected negatively by this practice in no way makes it morally justified to legalize.

In summary, if I am correct in my evaluations of these arguments for legalizing PAS, then those who favor its legalization will have to seek other arguments if they wish to make their case successful.

NOTES

1. From the CBS news program "Sixty Minutes." This segment, featuring Sue Rodrigues, aired November 20, 1994, and was entitled "Whose Life Is It Anyway?"

2. Hodge's argument here, that the right to personal autonomy requires the legalization of PAS, is possibly the most common and fundamental contention supporting PAS. My experience has been that even when supporters of PAS are willing to concede numerous other points in this debate, they will continue to insist that the right to individual autonomy requires that people should be given the choice to die if they want it. For an analysis of the meaning of individual autonomy in society, see philosopher and lawyer John Warwick Montgomery, "Human Dignity in Birth and Death: A Question of Values," *Christian Legal Journal 2*, no. 3 (1993): 17–23. He argues that the very fact that each individual has the same inherent worth as each other individual creates a built-in restraint on our choices and actions. He applies this principle to a number of issues, including suicide. See Ronald Dworkin, *Life's Dominion: An Argument About Abortion, Euthanasia and Individual Freedom* (New York: Vantage Books, 1994), for a fuller statement of the argument from autonomy in favor of assisted suicide. This argument is also made by Russel Ogden in "The Right to Die: A Policy Proposal for Euthanasia and Aid in Dying," *Canadian Public Policy* 20, no. 1 (1994): 2–3. For a critique of this argument see Paul Chamberlain, "Physician-Assisted Suicide: Should We or Shouldn't We?" *The Scholaris* 1, no. 4 (1995): 1–6.

3. This statement was made to me in a personal conversation in 1995 with Dr. Peter Kyne, a neuropsychiatrist and palliative-care expert in Vancouver, British Columbia. Yale Kamisar also says that if euthanasia became a socially approved option, there could be "subtle pressure to request it" (in Hendin, *Seduced by Death*, p. 214). See also *When Death Is Sought*, a study carried out and published by the New York State Task Force on Life and the Law, convened by governor Mario Cuomo, published in May 1994. The unanimous recommendations of the task force were that New York laws prohibiting assisted suicide and euthanasia should not be changed. One of the reasons given was that these practices "would be profoundly dangerous for many individuals who are ill and vulnerable." According to the task force, the "risks would be most severe for those who are elderly, poor, socially disadvantaged, or without access to good medical care" (p. ix).

4. See philosopher Margaret P. Battin, "Age-Rationing and the Distribution of Health Care: Is There a Duty to Die?" in *The Moral Life,* eds. Steven Luper-Foy and Curtis Brown (Toronto: Harcourt Brace, 1992), pp. 313–24. In this article Battin assumes a Rawlsian basis for rights and obligations in society and asserts that on this basis, while individuals would not have their lives "discontinued" while in full health, people who are irreversibly ill or of advanced age would have no automatic right to medical care. She says that at a certain point in their illness or age there would be a "disenfranchisement from care and the expectation that it is time to die" (p. 323). Wesley J. Smith gives a helpful summary of the issue in his book *Forced Exit* (New York: Random House, 1997), pp. 163–79. He includes a quote from former Colorado governor Richard Lamm, who said that old people "have a duty to die and get out of the way" (p. 172).

5. For the view that safeguards could effectively prevent a slippery slope see Peter Singer, *Practical Ethics* (Cambridge: Cambridge University Press, 1979), pp. 128–29, 140–46. Singer sets out a number of safeguards that have been suggested by voluntary euthanasia societies around the world. Patrick Nowell-Smith in "The Right to Die," in *Contemporary Moral Issues,* ed. Wesley Cragg (Toronto: McGraw-Hill Ryerson, 1992), pp. 7–15, also argues that most serious abuses of legalizing PAS can be "all but eliminated" through proper safeguards. For an opposing view on the effectiveness of safeguards see Barry A. Bostrom, "Euthanasia in the Netherlands: A Model for the United States?" *Issues in Law and Medicine* 4, no. 4 (1989): 471–75. Pointing to the Netherlands as an example, Bostrom describes the changing

guidelines from 1973 to 1986 to demonstrate that euthanasia has become more widely practiced and for different reasons than at first intended. For another critique of the effectiveness of safeguards, see Herbert Hendin, *Seduced by Death,* 2nd ed. (New York: W. W. Norton, 1998), p. 136. He argues that it is impossible to regulate PAS. In his words, "Virtually every guideline set up by the Dutch—a voluntary, well-considered, persistent request; intolerable suffering that cannot be relieved; consultation; and reporting of cases—has failed to protect patients or has been modified or violated."

6. Dr. Herbert Hendin, director of The American Foundation for Suicide Prevention, in the first edition of his book *Seduced by Death* (New York: W. W. Norton, 1997), p. 181, cites various studies to show that suicides are being committed today by people who mistakenly believe they have cancer. It is my contention that misdiagnoses lead to this type of mistaken belief about one's health.

7. Hendin, Herbert. *Seduced by Death* 1st ed. (New York: W. W. Norton, 1997), p. 181.

8. This assertion was made repeatedly by Dr. Faye Girsch, the Executive Director of the Hemlock Society, in a series of public forums in which we participated at six Canadian universities in October, 1997. Virtually every proponent of PAS whom I've ever interacted with seriously on this issue has also voiced this same contention.

9. This exact response was made to me in a public forum when I put this question to a proponent of legalization in June 1995.

10. From *Ethical Issues Relating to Life and Death,* edited by John Ladd, pp. 146–161. Copyright © 1979 Oxford University Press, Inc. Reprinted by permission.

11. The argument that there is no meaningful moral distinction between killing and letting die in similar circumstances is made forcefully by James Rachels in "Euthanasia, Killing, and Letting Die," in *Ethical Issues Relating to Life and Death,* ed. John Ladd (Oxford: Oxford University Press, 1979), pp. 146–61. In this article, Rachels introduces his famous "Smith and Jones" example to illustrate that killing and letting die are equally reprehensible if the surrounding circumstances are the same. Furthermore, Peter Singer argues in *Rethinking Life and Death* (New York: St. Martin's, 1994), pp. 155–56, that patients would very likely benefit if the distinction between killing and letting die were dropped. A well-known response to Rachels has been made by Thomas D. Sullivan in "Active and Passive Euthanasia: An Impertinent Distinction?" *Human Life Review* 3, no. 3 (1977): 40–46. Two other critiques of Rachels's position are made by J. P. Moreland in "James Rachels and the Active Euthanasia Debate," reprinted in *Do the Right Thing,* ed. Francis J. Beckwith (Sudbury, MA.: Jones and Bartlett, 1996), pp. 239–46, and by Tom L. Beauchamp in "A Reply to Rachels on Active and Passive Euthanasia," reprinted in *Contemporary Moral Problems,* ed. James E. White (New York: West, 1991), pp. 107–15.

12. Hendin, Herbert. *Seduced by Death,* 2nd ed. (New York: W. W. Norton, 1998), p. 136. Peter Singer has set out a number of safeguards that have been suggested by right-to-die societies around the world. These include 1) the patient being diagnosed by two doctors as suffering from an incurable illness expected to cause severe distress or the loss of rational faculties; 2) at least 30 days before the proposed act of euthanasia, and in the presence of two independent witnesses, the patient makes a written request for euthanasia in the event of the situation described in #1 occurring; 3) allowing only a doctor to administer euthanasia and making sure that the patient still wished the declaration to be acted upon; and 4) the patient's declaration could be revoked at any time.

13. "Killing the Psychic Pain," *Time,* July 4, 1994, p. 55. This case was explored by Herbert Hendin, who traveled to the Netherlands and interviewed Dr. Chabot, the psychiatrist who administered the physician-assisted suicide. In *Seduced by Death,* 2nd ed., pp. 63–64, 76–87, Hendin provides a more complete description of the process leading to her death. See also Wesley Smith, *Forced Exit,* pp. 104–5, for another description of the case.

14. From *Seduced by Death,* 1st ed., by Dr. Herbert Hendin (New York: W. W. Norton, 1997), p. 182.

15. From *Seduced by Death*, 2nd ed., by Dr. Herbert Hendin (New York: W. W. Norton, 1998), p. 136.

16. This was part of a presentation made by Dr. Jim Lane, the President of the British Columbia Medical Association, before a Canadian Senate Subcommittee which was conducting hearings on euthanasia and physician-assisted suicide, 26–9–1994 (14:26).

17. This argument is made by Russel Ogden in "When the Sick Request Death: Palliative Care and Euthanasia—A Continuum of Care?" *Journal of Palliative Care* 10, no. 2 (1994): 82–85. In this article Ogden includes a few accounts of botched suicide attempts that he discovered in his research in the AIDS community. For a critique of the botched-suicide argument, see physician H. Robert Pankratz, "The Person in Community: An Examination of Euthanasia," pp. 16–17. This was part of a brief to the Canadian Senate Committee on Euthanasia and Assisted Suicide presented by Canadian Physicians for Life on August 29, 1994.

Discussion Questions

1. Present and explain the autonomy and anti–slippery-slope arguments for physician-assisted suicide to which Professor Chamberlain responds. Briefly explain each of Chamberlain's responses. Do they succeed? Why or why not?

2. Present and explain in detail Professor Chamberlain's response to Professor Rachels's case against the active/passive distinction. What role does *motive* have in his response? Do you think Professor Chamberlain has adequately responded to the argument? Why or why not? How do you think Rachels would respond to Chamberlain's rebuttal?

3. Present and explain the second three arguments for physician-assisted suicide to which Professor Chamberlain responds (i.e., the arguments from animal suffering, botched suicides, and democracy). Briefly explain each of Chamberlain's responses. Do they succeed? Why or why not?

You can locate InfoTrac-College Education articles about this chapter by accessing the InfoTrac-College Edition website (http://www.infotrac-college.com/wadsworth/). Using the InfoTrac-College Edition subject guide, enter the search terms relevant to this chapter, and then read abstracts for relevant articles.

20   Death and Dignity: A Case of Individualized Decision Making

TIMOTHY E. QUILL

Timothy E. Quill is Professor of Medicine at the University of Rochester Medical Center. He has published a number of articles as well as the book, *Death and Dignity: Making Choices and Taking Charge* (1993).

In this essay Dr. Quill tells the story of Diane, a patient of his who had been diagnosed with leukemia. Diane, who had overcome a number of obstacles throughout her life including vaginal cancer, depression, and alcoholism, chose not to undergo treatment that has a 25 percent success rate. Although the choice to refuse treatment is morally uncontroversial in most cases, it was his fulfilling of one of Diane's other requests that is morally problematic and caused Dr. Quill, in his own words, to explore the boundaries of the "spiritual, legal, professional, and personal." Several months before her death Diane told Dr. Quill that if toward the end of the illness she could no longer control herself and her dignity in her time remaining, she would want to die. In other words, Diane was requesting physician-assisted suicide. In order to facilitate her request, Dr. Quill told Diane that information was available from the Hemlock Society, a pro-suicide activist group. Consistent with the society's protocol for suicide, Diane asked Dr. Quill for barbiturates for sleep. Knowing the real reason why she made the request, he wrote the prescription. Several months later, after having called friends and family to say farewell, Diane killed herself with an overdose of barbiturates. However, in order to avoid criminal investigation, Dr. Quill told the medical examiner that she died from "acute leukemia."

DIANE WAS FEELING TIRED and had a rash. A common scenario, though there was something subliminally worrisome that prompted me to check her blood count. Her hematocrit was 22, and the white-cell count was 4.3 with some metamyelocytes and unusual white cells. I wanted it to be viral, trying to deny what was staring me in the face. Perhaps in a repeated count it would disappear. I called Diane and told her it might be more serious than I had initially thought—that the test needed to be repeated and that if she felt worse, we might have to move quickly. When she pressed for the possibilities, I reluctantly opened the door for leukemia. Hearing the word seemed to make it exist. "Oh, shit!" she said. "Don't tell me that." Oh, shit! I thought, I wish I didn't have to.

Diane was no ordinary person (although no one I have ever come to know has been really ordinary). She was raised in an alcoholic family and had felt alone for much of her life. She had vaginal cancer as a young woman. Through much of her adult life, she had struggled with

Reprinted by permission from New England Journal of Medicine *324 (March 7, 1991).*

depression and her own alcoholism. I had come to know, respect, and admire her over the previous eight years as she confronted these problems and gradually overcame them. She was an incredibly clear, at times brutally honest, thinker and communicator. As she took control of her life, she developed a strong sense of independence and confidence. In the previous 3½ years, her hard work had paid off. She was completely abstinent from alcohol, she had established much deeper connections with her husband, college-age son, and several friends, and her business and her artistic work were blossoming. She felt she was really living fully for the first time.

Not surprisingly, the repeated blood count was abnormal, and detailed examination of the peripheral-blood smear showed myelocytes. I advised her to come into the hospital, explaining that we needed to do a bone marrow biopsy and make some decisions relatively rapidly. She came to the hospital knowing what we would find. She was terrified, angry, and sad. Although we knew the odds, we both clung to the thread of possibility that it might be something else.

The bone marrow confirmed the worst: acute myelomonocytic leukemia. In the face of this tragedy, we looked for signs of hope. This is an area of medicine in which technological intervention has been successful, with cures 25 percent of the time—long-term cures. As I probed the costs of these cures, I heard about induction chemotherapy (three weeks in the hospital, prolonged neutropenia, probable infectious complications, and hair loss; 75 percent of patients respond, 25 percent do not). For the survivors, this is followed by consolidation chemotherapy (with similar side effects; another 25 percent die, for a net survival of 50 percent). Those still alive, to have a reasonable chance of long-term survival, then need bone marrow transplantation (hospitalization for two months and whole-body irradiation, with complete killing of the bone marrow, infectious complications, and the possibility for graft-versus-host disease—with a survival of approximately 50 percent, or 25 percent of the original group). Though hematologists may argue over the exact percentages, they don't argue about the outcome of no treatment—certain death in days, weeks, or at most a few months.

Believing that delay was dangerous, our oncologist broke the news to Diane and began making plans to insert a Hickman catheter and begin induction chemotherapy that afternoon. When I saw her shortly thereafter, she was enraged at this presumption that she would want treatment, and devastated by the finality of the diagnosis. All she wanted to do was go home and be with her family. She had no further questions about treatment and in fact had decided that she wanted none. Together we lamented her tragedy and the unfairness of life. Before she left, I felt the need to be sure that she and her husband understood that there was some risk in delay, that the problem was not going to go away, and that we needed to keep considering the options over the next several days. We agreed to meet in two days.

She returned in two days with her husband and son. They had talked extensively about the problem and the options. She remained very clear about her wish not to undergo chemotherapy and to live whatever time she had left outside the hospital. As we explored her thinking further, it became clear that she was convinced she would die during the period of treatment and would suffer unspeakably in the process (from hospitalization, from lack of control over her body, from the side effects of chemotherapy, and from pain and anguish). Although I could offer support and my best effort to minimize her suffering if she chose treatment, there was no way I could say any of this would not occur. In fact, the last four patients with acute leukemia at our hospital had died very painful deaths in the hospital during various stages of treatment (a fact I did not share with her). Her family wished she would choose treatment but sadly accepted her decision. She articulated very clearly that it was she who would be experiencing all the side effects of treatment and that odds of 25 percent were not good enough for her to undergo so toxic a course of therapy, given her expectations of chemotherapy and hospitalization and the absence of a closely matched bone marrow donor. I had her repeat her understanding of the treatment, the odds, and what to expect if there were no treatment. I clarified a few misunderstandings, but she had a remarkable grasp of the options and implications.

I have been a longtime advocate of active, informed patient choice of treatment or nontreatment and of a patient's right to die with as much control and dignity as possible. Yet there was something about her giving up a 25 percent chance of long-term survival in favor of almost certain death that disturbed me. I had seen Diane fight and use her considerable inner resources to overcome alcoholism and depression, and I half expected her to change her mind over the next week. Since the window of time in which effective treatment can be initiated is rather narrow, we met several times that week. We obtained a second hematology consultation and talked at length about the meaning and implications of treatment and nontreatment. She talked to a psychologist she had seen in the past. I gradually understood the decision from her perspective and became convinced that it was the right decision for her. We arranged for home hospice care (although at that time Diane felt reasonably well, was active, and looked healthy), left the door open for her to change her mind, and tried to anticipate how to keep her comfortable in the time she had left.

Just as I was adjusting to her decision, she opened up another area that would stretch me profoundly. It was extraordinarily important to Diane to maintain control of herself and her own dignity during the time remaining to her. When this was no longer possible, she clearly wanted to die. As a former director of a hospice program, I know how to use pain medicines to keep patients comfortable and lessen suffering. I explained the philosophy of comfort care, which I strongly believe in. Although Diane understood and appreciated this, she had known of people lingering in what was called relative comfort, and she wanted no part of it. When the time came, she wanted to take her life in the least painful way possible. Knowing of her desire for independence and her decision to stay in control, I thought this request made perfect sense. I acknowledged and explored this wish but also thought that it was out of the realm of currently accepted medical practice and that it was more than I could offer or promise. In our discussion, it became clear that preoccupation with her fear of a lingering death would interfere with Diane's getting the most out of the time she had left until she found a safe way to ensure her death. I feared the effects of a violent death on her family, the consequences of an ineffective suicide that would leave her lingering in precisely the state she dreaded so much, and the possibility that a family member would be forced to assist her, with all the legal and personal repercussions that would follow. She discussed this at length with her family. They believed that they should respect her choice. With this in mind, I told Diane that information was available from the Hemlock Society that might be helpful to her.

A week later she phoned me with a request for barbiturates for sleep. Since I knew that this was an essential ingredient in a Hemlock Society suicide, I asked her to come to the office to talk things over. She was more than wiling to protect me by participating in a superficial conversation about her insomnia, but it was important to me to know how she planned to use the drugs and to be sure that she was not in despair or overwhelmed in a way that might color her judgment. In our discussion, it was apparent that she was having trouble sleeping, but it was also evident that the security of having enough barbiturates available to commit suicide when and if the time came would leave her secure enough to live fully and concentrate on the present. It was clear that she was not despondent and that in fact she was making deep, personal connections with her family and close friends. I made sure that she knew how to use the barbiturates for sleep, and also that she knew the amount needed to commit suicide. We agreed to meet regularly, and she promised to meet with me before taking her life, to ensure that all other avenues had been exhausted. I wrote the prescription with an uneasy feeling about the boundaries I was exploring—spiritual, legal, professional, and personal. Yet I also felt strongly that I was setting her free to get the most out of the time she had left, and to maintain dignity and control on her own terms until her death.

The next several months were very intense and important for Diane. Her son stayed home from college, and they were able to be with one another and say much that had not been said earlier. Her husband did his work at home so that he and Diane could spend more time together. She spent time with her closest friends. I had her come into the hospital for a conference with our residents, at which she illustrated in a most profound and personal way the importance of informed decision making, the right to refuse treatment, and the extraordinarily personal effects of illness and interaction with the medical system. There were emotional and physical hardships as well. She had periods of intense sadness and anger. Several times she became very weak, but she received transfusions as an outpatient and responded with marked improvement of symptoms. She had two serious infections that responded surprisingly well to empirical courses of oral antibiotics. After three tumultuous months, there were two weeks of relative calm and well-being, and fantasies of a miracle began to surface.

Unfortunately, we had no miracle. Bone pain, weakness, fatigue, and fevers began to dominate her life. Although the hospice workers, family members, and I tried our best to minimize the suffering and promote comfort, it was clear that the end was approaching. Diane's immediate future held what she feared the most—increasing discomfort, dependence, and hard choices between pain and sedation. She called up her closest friends and asked them to come over to say goodbye, telling them that she would be even more terrified to stay and suffer. In our tearful goodbye, she promised a reunion in the future at her favorite spot on the edge of Lake Geneva, with dragons swimming in the sunset.

Two days later her husband called to say that Diane had died. She had said her final goodbyes to her husband and son that morning, and asked them to leave her alone for an hour. After an hour, which must have seemed an eternity, they found her on the couch, lying very still and covered by her favorite shawl. There was no sign of struggle. She seemed to be at peace. They called me for advice about how to proceed. When I arrived at their house, Diane indeed seemed peaceful. Her husband and son were quiet. We talked about what a remarkable person she had been. They seemed to have no doubts about the course she had chosen or about their cooperation, although the unfairness of her illness and the finality of her death were overwhelming to us all.

I called the medical examiner to inform him that a hospice patient had died. When asked about the cause of death, I said, "acute leukemia." He said that was fine and that we should call a funeral director. Although acute leukemia was the truth, it was not the whole story. Yet any mention of suicide would have given rise to a police investigation and probably brought the arrival of an ambulance crew for resuscitation. Diane would have become a "coroner's case," and the decision to perform an autopsy would have been made at the discretion of the medical examiner. The family or I could have been subject to criminal prosecution, and I to professional review, for our roles in support of Diane's choices. Although I truly believe that the family and I gave her the best care possible, allowing her to define her limits and directions as much as possible, I am not sure the law, society, or the medical profession would agree. So I said "acute leukemia" to protect all of us, to protect Diane from an invasion into her past and her body, and to continue to shield society from the knowledge of the degree of suffering that people often undergo in the process of dying. Suffering can be lessened to some extent, but in no way eliminated or made benign, by the careful intervention of a competent, caring physician, given current social constraints.

Diane taught me about the range of help I can provide if I know people well and if I allow them to say what they really want. She taught me about life, death, and honesty and about taking charge and facing tragedy squarely when it strikes. She taught me that I can take small risks for people that I really know and care about. Although I did not assist in her suicide directly, I helped indirectly to make it possible, successful, and relatively painless.

Although I know we have measures to help control pain and lessen suffering, to think that people do not suffer in the process of dying is an illusion. Prolonged dying can occasionally be peaceful, but more often the role of the physician and family is limited to lessening but not eliminating severe suffering.

I wonder how many families and physicians secretly help patients over the edge into death in the face of such severe suffering. I wonder how many severely ill or dying patients secretly take their lives, dying alone in despair. I wonder whether the image of Diane's final aloneness will persist in the minds of her family, or if they will remember more the intense, meaningful months they had together before she died. I wonder whether Diane struggled in that last hour, and whether the Hemlock Society's way of death by suicide is the most benign. I wonder why Diane, who gave so much to so many of us, had to be alone for the last hour of her life. I wonder whether I will see Diane again, on the shore of Lake Geneva at sunset, with dragons swimming on the horizon.

Discussion Questions

1. Do you think it was morally right for Dr. Quill to lie to the medical examiner as to the true cause of Diane's death? Please explain and defend your answer.
2. Can you present and explain Dr. Quill's moral justification for assisting in Diane's suicide. Do you find this justification compelling? Why or why not?
3. Assuming Dr. Quill was morally justified in assisting with Diane's suicide, would he still be morally justified if Diane's chance of recovering from leukemia after undergoing treatment was 80 percent rather than 25 percent? Explain and defend your answer.

 You can locate InfoTrac-College Education articles about this chapter by accessing the InfoTrac-College Edition website (http://www.infotrac-college.com/wadsworth/). Using the InfoTrac-College Edition subject guide, enter the search terms relevant to this chapter, and then read abstracts for relevant articles.

Dying Safely: An Analysis of "A Case of Individualized Decision Making" by Timothy E. Quill, M.D.

21

PATRICIA WESLEY

Patricia Wesley practices psychiatry in New York City. For many years she was a Clinical Professor of Psychiatry at the Yale University School of Medicine.

Dr. Wesley raises some serious moral and professional questions about the justification of Dr. Timothy Quill's assistance in the suicide of his patient, Diane (Chapter 20). In this essay Dr. Wesley, employing her accomplished skills in literary analysis and psychiatry, asks us to read Dr. Quill's story "between the lines," to ask critical questions as to why Dr. Quill didn't make further inquiries about his patient's personal and medical background in order to better understand her reaction to being diagnosed with leukemia, to reflect on how Dr. Quill used euphemisms and emotive language to capture the reader's sympathy, and to notice how Dr. Quill's philosophical presuppositions about the morality of active euthanasia, and physician-assisted suicide in particular, influenced the interaction with his patient. Dr. Wesley maintains that despite Dr. Quill's claim of neutrality and respecting his patient's autonomy, he was a powerful actor in pushing Diane to commit suicide: "With his help, Diane dies a politically correct death, accompanied to her grave by all the rhetoric of patient autonomy and medical egalitarianism that litters our intellectual landscape today, and that so often distracts us from the difficult task of knowing, if we are lucky, the depths of human willing and acting, and of trying to preserve life while we do."

A RABBINICAL DICTUM HAS it that we should 'place fences around the law.' The idea that restraints and prohibitions should be in place to prevent us from reaching, or at least impede our progress toward, the point of absolute and damning transgression. There should at least be safety rails around the abyss. Perhaps the best that our culture can provide are signposts warning against the danger ahead.[1]

I wrote the prescription with an uneasy feeling about the boundaries I was exploring— spiritual, legal, professional, and personal.[2]

Tenderness leads to the gas chamber.[3]

Doctors like to tell stories. Sometimes the story is a brief clinical vignette one physician shares with another over coffee in the nurses' station. Sometimes the story is a literary masterpiece by a renowned physician-artist such as William Carlos Williams, Anton Chekhov, or Walker Percy. And sometimes doctors tell stories designed to revolutionize the heart and soul of medical practice. Such a story, "Death and Dignity: A Case of Individualized Decision Making," appeared in the March 7, 1991, issue of *The New England Journal of Medicine*.[4] Author Timothy E. Quill, M.D., a

Published by permission from Issues in Law & Medicine 8, 4 (1993): 467–485. *This is a revised version of Professor Wesley's keynote address at the first annual meeting of the University Faculty for Life, Georgetown University, Washington, D.C. (8–10 June 1991).*

Rochester, New York, internist, tells us about his patient Diane, who developed acute leukemia, refused treatment for it, and ultimately asked for and got his aid in killing herself.[5] This story is no simple clinical anecdote, however. While never directly saying so, Dr. Quill offers it as evidence that under certain circumstances, like those in which he and Diane found themselves, physician-assisted suicide can be clinically and ethically "right," and our laws should be changed to permit it.[6]

This text invites examination precisely because of its revolutionary agenda. Yet this story is so disarmingly simple and moving, and its surface so smooth and opaque, that our inquiry seems to be barred. The euthanasia project is hidden here behind the mask of plain narrative and attractive metaphor. How can we get up close for a clear look at this encounter between Diane and Dr. Quill?

Any text speaks to us on many levels. Astute readers note *how* the author writes as well as *what* he writes about. Close attention is paid to such formal elements as language, tone of voice, point of view, genre, plot, and figures of speech. We note patterns in the narrative action. Who says or does what to whom, when? In addition to reading on the lines, readers should attend to the white space between the lines. What is not being said? Are there paradoxes or gaps in a seemingly unified text that, once explicated, can lead us to a more complete understanding of the story? What is the author trying to persuade us about? Are there contradictions in such authorial claims on us that might qualify our assent? In what social and cultural context does the text appear? What audience is it designed to reach? Who publishes it, and why? No work of art is ever simply the product of its time and place; nonetheless, attention to these more external factors provides another perspective for apprehending the text in its fullness.

Patients also tell physicians stories, to which physicians listen, although not always as patiently as they should. The patient's account of a developing illness is still the threshold at which the physician enters the patient's life. One group of specialists who are particularly likely to hear such stories are psychodynamically oriented psychiatrists. They use some of the same techniques to understand their patients' stories that a reader uses to understand a novel or a short story. Of course, no live patient is equivalent to a written text, or vice versa. Nonetheless, similar techniques of listening *do* characterize these two human activities. Let me first describe how the psychiatrist listens. Then, let us "listen" to Dr. Quill's story in the same way, and perhaps find a way into its interior.

At the beginning, the psychiatrist will hear the patient's story as it is told but, equally important, will note *how* the patient tells his story. What kind of language does the patient use, in what tone of voice and manner? Is the patient glib, humorous, vague, dramatic, or sarcastic? Is his mood anxious, angry, or sad? Discrepancies between what is said and the affect accompanying it are also noted; for example, the psychiatrist would be puzzled that whenever a particular patient says he's angry, he smiles or speaks so softly that he cannot be heard.

What the patient doesn't say is important, too; the doctor/listener would observe that an elderly widow mentioned almost casually a few weeks ago that a much-loved, previously much-mentioned pet cat died, but since then she has said nothing further about this loss or her reactions to it.

Of particular interest are contradictions between what the patient says he wants and how he goes about getting it. For example, a patient may announce that he is bound and determined to succeed in the same family business his father failed at, yet repeatedly makes easily avoidable errors in management that bring the business to the brink of bankruptcy.

From a more historical perspective, the psychiatrist would want to know when a depression developed and what life events preceded it. Did the patient end a love affair, or make an important scientific discovery that brought acclaim? Did a decision to divorce follow a year or so after the death of a child in a car accident in which one of the parents was the driver? Did a loss of self-esteem follow the diagnosis of a serious illness? An investigation of the historical antecedents, near or remote, of any life event can often be illuminating.

Very crucially, the psychiatrist would try to help the patient become aware of how past experiences, from early childhood, adolescence, and adulthood, shape current reactions and decisions. When and in what human context did the patient develop certain views about herself? How might those views protect against the remembering of old traumas or the resurgence of old needs in new situations? Sometimes, even the patient may not be fully aware of how such views can influence current choices. As we will explore later in more detail, did Diane's view that she must be independent and in control, no matter what the cost, impair her ability to fully assess all her options as she faced a life-threatening illness?

For the psychiatrist to be of help to the patient, he must construct a safe, structured, and rule-bound therapeutic setting, in which the patient can articulate, perhaps for the first time, wishes, hopes, and fears from both past and present life dramas. The psychiatrist must attend not only to the patient, but to himself and his interaction with the patient as well. Psychiatric residents are admonished to keep the following question always in mind: Why is *this* patient saying *this* to *me* at *this* time? Does the patient want me to see her in a certain way, feel certain things about, or with, her? Is the patient trying to please me, enrage me, make me an ally or a judge, or test me in some way? Is the patient asking a question by enfolding it in a seemingly simple statement, one that might make "perfect sense," to use Dr. Quill's characterization of Diane's stated intention to take her own life?

The psychiatrist must also be constantly aware of how his own values and personality can shape what he says to the patient and how, in turn, this can influence the story the patient tells. Patients tend to tell stories they know, or imagine they know, their doctors like to hear.

The famous American psychiatrist Harry Stack Sullivan captured the complexities of the psychiatrist's tasks in his concept of the "participant-observer."[7] As he warned on many occasions, it is no easy job to simultaneously participate and observe. The psychiatrist, or any other doctor who listens to a patient, must resonate, judiciously, to the appeal and power of the story the patient tells. At the same time, she must meticulously avoid re-enacting past traumas, or joining in self-deluding scenarios, with the patient—especially those involving unlikely posthumous reunions along the shores of certain European bodies of water. The difficult balance required here is to remain inside *and* outside the story, empathic toward, but not misidentified with, the patient and the tale he tells.

To be such a listener and such a questioner, the physician must appreciate the complexity, ambiguity, and multiplicity in all human desire and action and in every human life, lived or told. However much we may speculate about their psychodynamic origins, or know about their neurophysiological correlates, human character and behavior remain resilient mysteries. Unhappily—and happily—no human being can ever be completely understood by someone else, even when the someone else is a skilled psychiatric professional. This is a chilly reminder of our essential aloneness, but it is also a helpful reminder to be chary about ever claiming, as Dr. Quill does, that we can know someone else "well."

When we, doctors and patients alike, acknowledge that we do not know, and can never know in any final sense, all the motivations for any human action, then we have paradoxically secured the only foundation for knowing what *can* be known, incomplete and tentative as that may be. We should be listening and asking questions, but we cannot expect any "right" answers or be assured, as Dr. Quill is, that our decisions or those of our patients are the "right" ones. The fences against euthanasia are there to remind us that when so much is unknown, we need to be aware of the dangers of false certainty. Even dragons cannot live in that abyss.

With this background in place, let us begin our confrontation of this most seductive text, "A Case of Individualized Decision Making."[8] As we do, keep in mind that we have no direct, unmediated knowledge about "Diane" herself, as she was in life or in death, or about her actual interactions with Dr. Quill. We know her only through the filter of Dr. Quill's narrative. Absent actual clinical contact, we have no way of knowing if the questions I will raise about her psychological make-up were at all relevant to the actual person this account is based on. Too, either Dr. Quill himself or Diane's psychologist may have raised these questions with her, and others even far more pertinent.

What follows, then, is not so much a review of Dr. Quill's actual treatment of Diane as it is a critique of Dr. Quill's text and the rhetorical use he wishes to make of it. Dr. Quill wants us to believe that *what he tells us* about Diane and about his interactions with her constitutes sufficient evidence to support his claim that, at least in certain circumstances, physician-assisted suicide can be good medicine. Therefore, we are justified in taking this text itself as the object of our inquiry. What is the nature of the evidence it offers, and should we be persuaded by it?

Dr. Quill's account warrants scrutiny for a number of reasons. It is such an engaging and pretty story! We are made privy to an engrossing medical drama, in which Diane develops acute leukemia, refuses any specific treatment for it, and eventually requests and receives her physician's aid in taking her own life in the final—*presumably* final—days of her illness.

Diane is an interesting and feisty woman, and Dr. Quill is a tenderhearted doctor who actually listens to and talks to his patients!

This story also deserves our attention because of where it was published. *The New England Journal of Medicine* is certainly the most respected medical journal in the United States and arguably in the world. Place of publication alone influenced how this report was received, and granted to assisted suicide a medical elitist cachet it might not otherwise have had. If you want to start the euthanasia train rolling, as at least some of medicine's best and brightest do, there is no better station to leave from than the editorial offices of *The New England Journal of Medicine*. Given its distinguished birthplace, this account is exactly what the Society for the Right to Die would love to hand out to voters considering the decriminalization of euthanasia. Dr. Kevorkian, with his rusty van and his macabre machinery, is one thing;[9] Dr. Quill and his dragons are quite another and deserve confrontation precisely because of the genteel but deadly power they wield.

The text awaits us.

Did Diane make an informed decision when she refused specific treatment for leukemia? Based on what we are told about her, and if we focus purely on her cognitive capacity, there is little question that she did. Diane is presented as an intelligent, intact woman, apparently free of any dementia or major mental illness that would impair her grasp of reality or her judgment. Moreover, Dr. Quill worked hard with her to be sure that she understood her illness and her options.

There is, however, another aspect of informed decision making that rarely gets the attention it deserves and certainly does not in Dr. Quill's story. All human willing and acting is imbued with complexities and ambiguities that can baffle our best efforts to sort them out. In life's drama, it is often not so easy to decide who does what to whom, when. Who is the actor, and who the acted-upon? Can we ever be sure we have teased apart the many densely intertwined strands of human motivation? Nowhere are these questions more relevant than in the human interaction between physician and patient. How do these questions play out with Diane and her doctors?

The skeptical reader spots the first gap in this seemingly seamless story in this passage:

> Believing that delay was dangerous, our oncologist broke the news to Diane and began to make plans to insert a Hickman catheter and begin induction chemotherapy that afternoon. When I saw her shortly thereafter, she was enraged at his presumption that she would want treatment, and devastated by the finality of the diagnosis. All she wanted to do was go home and be with her family. She had no further questions about treatment and in fact had decided that she wanted none. Together we lamented her tragedy and the unfairness of life.[10]

We are unsure here what news the oncologist broke to Diane—was it confirmation of the diagnosis, information about treatment, or both? Nonetheless, as the sequence of events is described, Diane makes her decision against treatment immediately after talking to the oncologist. By the time Dr. Quill sees her, her mind is already made up. Mutual lamentations about the unfairness of life can wait. What in heaven's name transpired between Diane and the oncologist during their meeting? We have no details, but we do know there was some clinical urgency about beginning treatment. Given this, was the oncologist possibly a bit pressing or peremptory with Diane? I do not raise this possibility to be critical of the oncologist; for all we know, he was the paragon of sensitivity. Nonetheless, physicians have an understandable, and even defensible, tendency to take action in urgent situations. The cost may be that physicians appear pushy and arrogant and may evoke the patient's stormy "NO!" If people do not like the message, they may shoot the messenger; and if they do not like the way the messenger delivers the message, they may

erase it, or they may reach some premature decision about it. Did something like this occur between Diane and the oncologist?

Often in discussions about patient decision making, the patient is presented as though she were an isolated individual, in a hermetically sealed room, getting information from a user-friendly computerized learning program. Unfortunately, and fortunately, that is not the case. The patient receives data in the context of a particular physician-patient relationship at a particular moment in time. Hopefully, the physician will temper the need to act with respect for the patient's ability to process the news that must be conveyed, but as in every profession, ideal and actual do not always meet. Medicine is a hands-on activity, and an "affect-on" activity as well. The affect—and the stress—can be found on both sides of the equation.

Here's the second series of gaps: Diane's rage at the oncologist, the fact that she had no further questions, and the rapidity of her decision against treatment. Why was she *so* mad, and why no further questions in a personal situation rife with questions of all sorts? Why the rush? Were there other, less obvious reasons for Diane's rage? Justified or not, did her rage at the oncologist influence her decision about treatment? Diane might have profited from a suggestion at this point that it's risky to make a life-and-death decision when one is in a rage. Anger is no friend of clear thinking and careful judgment.

Patients can and often do see their doctors as authority figures or parental stand-ins and may react to them in some ways similar to how they reacted to their own parents.[11] Indeed, some physicians have encouraged this view of themselves as presumably beneficent authorities as the only viable ethical basis for medical practice.[12] Doctor, like mother, knows best! Such an asymmetry in the doctor-patient relationship is not necessarily as evil as its critics charge, or as altruistic as its proponents believe, nor is it the only way or even the predominant way in which patients view their physicians. However, such tendencies do exist, particularly when a patient, like Diane, is facing a newly diagnosed, life-threatening illness. In such circumstances, when adult capacities to control fear and master stress are severely tested, patients tend to return to earlier models of interaction with others. They may wish for a benign and comforting authority who will tell them what to do and against whom they may then rebel. When people are seriously ill, the professional upon whose skill life depends becomes very important in many ways, some of them quite rational and some of them quite ancient.

We know very little about Diane, except that she was raised in an alcoholic family, had felt alone for much of her life, and had overcome her own alcoholism and depression.[13] Could this personal background have affected how Diane reacted to her illness and her doctors? Could it have shaped how she reached her decision to forgo treatment and ultimately end her own life?

While adult children of alcoholics have received much attention in the popular culture, and from researchers in the field of alcohol studies, there still is no scientific consensus on how parental alcoholism affects children. Some investigators have concluded that these children are at high risk for psychological and social problems;[14] others have concluded that no definitive conclusions can be drawn.[15] Still others have identified "resilient" offspring of alcoholic parents, who demonstrate good adaptation.[16]

Moreover, parental alcoholism and its alleged impact on children is not a unitary phenomenon; many variables affect how any particular child fares, including the severity and duration of parental alcoholism, the degree of conflict in the marital couple, the presence of violence in the home, the gender of the child vis-a-vis the affected parent, and the availability of alternative support systems.[17]

Given the complexity of these findings, any questions about how Diane might have been affected by her alcoholic family are tentative, especially since we know so little about her and her parents. Nonetheless, Dr. Quill's text virtually invites us to raise certain questions about this connection, precisely because he mentions nothing about it.

Throughout Dr. Quill's report, Diane's need to be "in control" is alluded to over and over again.[18] The wish to be responsible is an admirable trait of a mature individual; it makes "perfect sense," as Dr. Quill notes. However, at times we must surrender some control and tolerate a certain degree of dependence on others. Serious illness is such an occasion. Diane does accept some limited treatment from Dr. Quill, but her fear of losing that valued self-control and becoming dependent on others in a hospital setting is one of her reasons for refusing more aggressive therapy for her leukemia. Such reasoning may be fully compatible with Diane's adult character style, but since it may have carried such a high price tag, we can also wonder about its origins in a more distant, and possibly more traumatic, childhood past as well.

Mental health professionals who treat adult children of alcoholics note that such individuals must always be "in control" and often cannot acknowledge their own needs or trust others to meet them when necessary. For example, Timmen Cermak and Stephanie Brown state:

> Our observations of the issues and dynamics that characterize group meetings [with adult children of alcoholics] could be condensed into one word, 'control.' Conflicts involving issues of control were pervasive and often were the context within which other issues concerning trust, acknowledgment of personal needs, responsibility, and feelings arose. . . . The concern with control was often the most significant source of anxiety.

* * *

The other side of the issue of control—feelings of deprivation, depression, loss, and intense dependency needs—are well-disguised and hidden. The intense emphasis on control is a rigid defense to protect against acknowledging the overwhelming threat of that underlying neediness.[19]

Granting that further research is needed to confirm their clinical impressions, Cermak and Brown hypothesize as follows:

> Our experience to date does suggest the existence of a recognizable pattern of conflicts carried by the children of alcoholics into their adult lives. . . . Members recalled instructions from the non-alcoholic parent to help keep the family peace. . . . Those instructions result in the offspring's growing up in an atmosphere of arbitrariness and changing limits. . . . A unique poignancy seems to exist in the secondary gain that the adult children of alcoholics receive from their sense of control. Primarily, it is a gain in their sense of self-worth, which is greatly enhanced by feelings of having matters in control.[20]

Parents who are alcoholic may be unpredictable and unreliable; their actions toward their children may come out of the blue, without rhyme or reason. Was this Diane's experience? Did Diane's leukemia seem like a bolt from the blue? Did her oncologist's well-intentioned but perhaps too-quick decision to proceed with treatment seem like a replay of her parents' possibly unpredictable behavior and elicit her stormy "No" to try to regain control and predictability? When Diane was a child and got sick, how was she cared for? Did her parents muster their resources and do so properly—certainly a possibility—or was she neglected, humiliated, or made to feel alone? If Diane did have some unfortunate experiences with illness in the past, these may make her wary now about trusting Dr. Quill's assurances that he will do everything he can to alleviate her pain and discomfort during treatment or during her last days.

There is much in Dr. Quill's account to suggest that Diane's need to be in control was adaptive for her. Nonetheless, adaptive traits can have an origin in earlier trauma, as well as in autonomous ego capacities. We do not know if the observations made by Cermak and Brown, and others, about the adult children of alcoholics are at all applicable to Diane. Each patient can only be understood as an individual, with a unique history. Moreover, no adult decision can be explained away by possible—and here, quite hypothetical—childhood antecedents. However, each of us does begin life dependent on the adults around us for sheer survival; how those adults meet those needs early on shapes how much we trust others to meet similar needs later on.

This does not suggest that patients should blindly trust their physicians. It does suggest that physicians will enhance their patients' adult participation in their own medical care when they remember that old fears can affect how patients respond to new stressors.

Moving to the more recent past, we note that Diane had vaginal cancer as a young woman, although we are told nothing further about its etiology or treatment. Did this more recent experience echo in the conversations Diane had with herself and her doctors as she confronted a second malignancy? How was she treated then? Was she left with some disfigurement or dysfunction in a part of her body vital to her self-esteem? If her earlier treatment involved modalities other than surgery, could she secretly believe that it contributed to the development of her second malignancy, or that they were linked in some other way? How might such a belief affect her treatment decisions at this point?

According to Dr. Quill's history, Diane struggled with depression throughout most of her adult life.[21] If this depression was secondary to serious alcohol abuse, abstinence may have cured it. He presents little evidence that Diane was clinically depressed. Dr. Quill queries himself on this a number of times, as when he notes that she "was not in despair or overwhelmed"[22] or that she "was not despondent."[23] Nonetheless, Diane does have a history of chronic depression; could it be recurring? Moreover, serious physical illness can be accompanied by depression, either because of the impact of the patho-physiological processes on the central nervous system, or because of the psychological meaning of the illness to the afflicted person, or both.

Was Diane's refusal of treatment in itself a suicidal act, stemming from a depressive personality style, if not from an overt symptomatic depression? People can do highly self-destructive things without being overtly depressed; such individuals probably make up the majority of psychotherapy patients in any psychiatrist's practice. There are the noisy and public suicides, like jumps off a bridge, and there are the quiet and private suicides, like the single-car accidents in good weather, where determining if the death was intended is most difficult.

People with depressive tendencies often feel guilty and self-recriminatory and may seek punishments or limitations of various kinds.[24] Diane was "convinced" that she would die during treatment for her leukemia.[25] Why? True enough, the chances for cure are dicey, at best, but why is she "convinced" she won't make it? Like the word *control,* the word *conviction* also haunts this narrative. Did Diane become convinced she would die because she saw herself as deserving of punishment for some crime, real or fantasied? Did she feel that she did not deserve to survive a second bout with cancer? Skepticism about her treatment refusal is bolstered by the fact that in my experience, at least, very few patients forgo initial treatment for a *newly diagnosed,* nonterminal malignancy.

What role might Dr. Quill have played in Diane's conviction that she was doomed? Did his knowledge of those four patients who died painful deaths from similar disorders make it harder for him to keep in mind those who were cured? Was he thus less likely to probe Diane's conviction that she would perish, and did he instead mirror it with his own conviction that it was the "right" decision for her to refuse treatment?

There are no easy answers or neat resolutions to these questions. Childhood experience, personal history, and less than fully conscious motivation can influence any human decision, including the decision to accept a recommended treatment. It is all too easy to assume that the patient is acting rationally when he agrees with his physician and can only be acting irrationally when he disagrees.

Despite these salutary cautions, these questions about Diane emerge from the very text Dr. Quill offers as evidence that her decision to refuse treatment and to commit suicide was a fully conscious, autonomous human preference, not essentially different from a preference for country-western over classical. Indeed, Dr. Quill appeals to this type of characterization of Diane's wishes and actions to justify his own actions concerning her.[26] Dr. Quill wants us to leave his theater feeling reassured that no ambiguous plots or silent fears lurk in Diane's drama, at least.

But we remain troubled. The gaps in Dr. Quill's story challenge the simplistic notion that the psychological processes involved in patient choices are readily or completely apprehensible within the current emphasis, approaching obsession, on patient rationality and autonomy. The heart has reasons the ACLU knows nothing about.

When day is done and all the questions asked, it is the patient who decides to accept or reject treatment. That right is recognized in our law,[27] even though it has sometimes been ignored in the more paternalistic type of medical practice. Respecting a patient's right to decide about treatment does not necessarily mean, however, that we should become convinced that the decision is "right," as Dr. Quill did, despite his early reservations.

In this case, there was some chance that treatment would be effective and virtual certainty that no treatment would prove fatal.[28] The patient was initially in good enough physical condition to tolerate aggressive therapy and was not already terminally ill.[29] Too, Diane doesn't sound like someone who would pass up a good fight. Given all this, we are suspicious that much more is going on with the patient than Dr. Quill reveals and possibly more than Diane realized. Some blunt comments might be in order, such as: "While I respect your right to make decisions about your own medical care, I still have some reservations and questions about the decision you've made. I'm not convinced it is the right one, and I wonder if you might have some questions too, even now."

In medicine today, physicians are encouraged to be empathic towards patients, ascertain and respect their values, and support their choices.[30] There is much good in such an emphasis, but applied in a stereotyped fashion, without asking "Why?" "How come?" and "What makes you think that?" nothing can be more dangerous. The model of the beneficent, paternalistic physician, making choices in the patient's "best interest," was certainly not value-free. It had its own costly side effect, namely, the creation of passive and infantilized patients who end up bitterly disappointed and unable to trust any physician when magical expectations cannot be met. However, it is frighteningly naive to assume that when our guide to medical practice is "doing what the patient wants," we will escape the imposition of the physician's values on the clinical encounter. Personal values can be sequestered in the question not asked, or the gentle challenge not posed, when both should have been.

Now let us turn to the far more controversial part of this story, Diane's suicidal wishes and Dr. Quill's series of responses to them. Far from being the neutral reflector and facilitator of Diane's desires that he believes himself to be, Dr. Quill in fact powerfully and directly shapes those desires.

> Just as I was adjusting to her decision, she opened up another area that would stretch me profoundly. It was extraordinarily important to Diane to maintain control of herself and her own dignity during the time remaining to her. When this was no longer possible, she clearly wanted to die. As a former director of a hospice program, I know how to use pain medicines to keep patients comfortable and lessen suffering. I explained the philosophy of comfort care, which I strongly believe in. Although Diane understood and appreciated this, she had known of people lingering in what was called relative comfort, and she wanted no part of it. When the time came, she wanted to take her life in the least painful way possible. Knowing of her desire for independence and her decision to stay in control, I thought this request made perfect sense.[31]

Note here again the icon words—control, dignity, and independence. Is this the new rhetoric of self-murder? Bear in mind that Diane's suicidal wishes came at a time when she was "reasonably well, was active, and looked healthy"[32] and when Dr. Quill was arranging supportive care, while still leaving "the door open for her to change her mind"[33] about treatment. Given what he was trying to accomplish, should Diane's statement just make "perfect sense" to Dr. Quill?

On one level, Diane's request for aid in killing herself does make some sense. Dr. Quill describes her as someone who wants to call the shots for many reasons, including the troubling one that she felt alone for much of her life;[34] perhaps someone like this sees little option but to be in lonely control at the end as well. Hearing of Diane's suicidal intentions, the skeptic might remember that advice I told you about earlier. Why is *this* patient saying *this* to *me* at *this* time? Is she asking a question in the guise of making a statement? Is a trial balloon being launched, some testing being done? Is Diane asking her doctor: When I become more ill, more dependent, and when I no longer have that control I prize so much—and that I suspect *you* prize so much—will you still see me as a person of value? What if I changed my mind and pursued treatment, with the need for hospital confinement and care by others, would you still see me as worthwhile even when I might seem worthless to myself?

At first, Dr. Quill keeps up the fences that might have made a fuller exploration of these hypotheses possible when he tells Diane that such assistance is more than he can give her. Then he wavers, takes down the fences, and clears the path to death: "In our discussion, it became clear that preoccupation with her fears of a lingering death would interfere with Diane's getting the most of the time she had left until she found a safe way to ensure her death."[35] If you feel a chill as you read this passage, it probably comes from the oxymoron "safe . . . death." Since when is death safe? This is classic doublespeak and reminiscent of the pro-abortion doublespeak that the only safe way to avoid being an unplanned child is to be destroyed before you're born.[36]

It is not clear if Diane actually threatened to take her own life by "violent means" or "force" a family member to kill her, or if these are solely Dr. Quill's fears. If Diane made these comments, then Dr. Quill allowed himself to be blackmailed when he gave in to them. No physician is responsible for every action a competent patient might take or persuade others to take. It is ironic that Dr. Quill, who so wants to enhance Diane's control, in effect takes control away from her by his own action. What might have happened if Dr. Quill had said, "I would be sorry to see you do that, or enlist someone else to do it, but I do not control you or everything you do. I have said I will not help you end your own life, and if I flip-flop on that now because of your threats, you'd never believe anything else I say, and you shouldn't." Such a statement would recognize Diane as the prime actor in her own play. Sometimes a "No" is a big relief to patients testing the waters and seeing just how tough their doctors can be when the going gets tough. Instead, Dr. Quill responds with a referral to the Hemlock Society.[37]

Those who favor assisted suicide and euthanasia often discuss the patient as though she were an isolated actor, totally divorced from any interpersonal or historical context.

This is how Dr. Quill wants us to see Diane. He reassures us that he was only helping her to say and do what she "really wanted" and would do anyway, with or without his help. Dr. Quill wants us to see him as a kind of minimalist mirror or valueless facilitator of Diane's wishes. A close reading of the sequence of events indicates otherwise.

While this may be changing because of recent public discussion about euthanasia, it is still unlikely that most internists know what the Hemlock Society is, much less refer their seriously ill patients to it. More importantly, it is not clear that Diane had ever heard of the Hemlock Society—until Dr. Quill told her about it. In making this referral and describing it as "helpful,"[38] Dr. Quill once again powerfully shaped the clinical interaction between himself and his patient.

It is not a neutral act to refer a patient contemplating suicide to the Hemlock Society. It is putting a loaded gun into the hands of a desperate person. It renders utterly incoherent to us, as possibly it did to Diane, Dr. Quill's claim that he had left the door open for her to change her mind.[39] You cannot have it both ways, Dr. Quill! The Hemlock Society is about closing doors, not keeping them open.

What other messages might Diane have heard in this referral? Did she feel she had a physician who respected her as an autonomous person? Or did she feel that she had a doctor who shared her belief—forged in the heat of a troubled past—that if you cannot be fully independent, you are better off dead? Remember that Diane was in the midst of a profound crisis. In such circumstances any suggestion by the physician carries tremendous impact, often far more than the physician intends. When human beings are in such straits, they will grasp at anything that offers a way out. This anxious seeking for quick resolution, while understandable, must be mitigated and resisted by the physician. At the very least, doctors must be careful about any suggestions they might make, especially when their side effect is death. Would the endgame have been different if Dr. Quill had referred Diane to a self-help support group of cancer patients instead of the Hemlock Society?

Physicians' values affect how they deliver medical care and what they will or will not do for patients. Those who oppose assisted suicide are often reminded that they are imposing their own personal values and ignoring those of the dying patient who requests aid in committing suicide.[40] It seems that all those pesky "values" belong only to those of us who want to keep the fences intact, while those who favor taking them down costume themselves with the cloak of gray neutrality. Dr. Quill's own account shows how false this simplistic dichotomy is. In providing Diane with a referral to the Hemlock Society, he interjects his own values into the clinical situation, just as his article disingenuously promotes the values of the Hemlock Society.

Dr. Quill knew that barbiturates are "an essential ingredient" in a Hemlock Society suicide.[41] If so, Dr. Quill's own act of referring Diane to the Hemlock Society brings him onto center stage to play a direct and material role in Diane's death. It is not a neutral act to advise a suicidal person how many barbiturate capsules are needed for sleep and how many are needed to commit suicide, and then provide the lethal quantity.

Throughout his story, and like many another skilled penman before him, Dr. Quill wants us to believe that he effaced himself as an actor, both in the story he lived and in the story he tells us. Diane is presented as someone who determined her own tragic fate, free of the imprisonment of medical paternalism and what Derek Humphry might call outmoded ideas about the sanctity of life. Closely observed, Dr. Quill's text itself reveals that he was a powerful actor in his story. With his help, Diane dies a politically correct death, accompanied to her grave by all the rhetoric of patient autonomy and medical egalitarianism that litters our intellectual landscape today, and that distracts us from the difficult task of knowing the depths of human willing and acting and of trying to preserve life while we do.

After Diane decides to take her own life, she and Dr. Quill meet for a final good-bye, in which she promises "a reunion in the future at her favorite spot on the edge of Lake Geneva, with dragons swimming in the sunset."[42] After her death, Dr. Quill mirrors her fantasy and wonders whether he "will see Diane again, on the shore of Lake Geneva at sunset, with dragons swimming on the horizon."[43]

This is a beautiful image. On one level we can hardly blame Dr. Quill for employing all the evocative metaphors he can to make his case. However, like all figurative language, this image is essentially a beautiful mistake, a transfer of elements from one realm of reference into another, where they literally do not belong. Does this shared image of a mystical afterlife, complete with mythical animals, signal a mistaken transfer between doctor and patient as well? Did Dr. Quill become so misidentified with Diane that he erased that disengagement so crucial in the doctor-patient relationship? Such disengagement might have permitted him to ask those literal and blunt questions that may have been needed but may not have been asked. Shared fantasies about dragons swimming in Lake Geneva do not make Diane's death less violent or less final, or lessen Dr. Quill's complicity in it. Charming figures of speech do not make her grave less of a grave.

If we follow them, Dr. Quill and his colleagues who promote assisted suicide will lead us not to the sunny shores of Lake Geneva, but rather into a very dark forest indeed, where we will wish we'd had those fences and warnings that Richard John Neuhaus told us to keep up. Dr. Quill's lakes and forests look sunny and bright in the daytime. Some in medicine and law find them alluring pieces of real estate. But anyone who grew up in the country knows that lakes can be deeper than they appear and that forests are inviting but dangerous places. Night falls quickly, and we can lose our way, and ourselves. Those fences will come in handy.

NOTES

1. Richard J. Neuhaus, *The Way They Were, the Way We Are: Bioethics and the Holocaust,* First Things, Mar. 1990, at 31, 34.

2. Timothy E. Quill, *Death and Dignity: A Case of Individualized Decision Making,* 324 New Eng. J. Med. 6791, 693 (1991).

3. Walker Percy, The Thanatos Syndrome 36 (1987).

4. Quill, *supra* note 2, at 691.

5. *See id.* at 693.

6. Dr. Quill has since directly advocated the legalization of physician-assisted suicide. *See* Timothy E. Quill et al., *Care of the Hopelessly Ill: Proposed Clinical Criteria for Physician-Assisted Suicide,* 327 New Eng. J. Med. 1380(1992).

7. *See* Harry S. Sullivan, The Psychiatric Interview 18–24 (Helen S. Perry & Mary L. Gawal, eds., 1954). *See also,* Donald P. Spence, Narrative Truth and Historical Truth 41 (1982). Spence identifies similarities between reading a text and listening to a patient in psychoanalysis, but also warns of the dangers in such similarities. In listening to the analysand's free associations, the analyst may impose narrative coherence and continuity where none exists, thereby distorting the very data (the patient's verbal productions) upon which interpretive hypotheses will be based. Moreover, the psychoanalytic concepts the analyst uses shape not only how the analyst listens, but also what the patient says. Thus, the analyst finds his hypotheses confirmed but, unaware of how the dice are loaded, believes that he is making "discoveries." Spence's masterful critique of psychoanalytic clinical theory reminds us that any communication between a doctor and a patient is not just a two-way street, but a complex tangle of verbal and cognitive traffic with the potential for many wrong exits and dead end streets. To some extent, the same cautions apply when we "listen" to a written text. In that case, however, we have a physical object (words printed on bound pieces of paper) that is relatively immutable and accessible to a more or less broad pubic. These facts impose some welcome constraints on textual criticism that are not present in the far more ambiguous oral milieu of the psychoanalytic situation, or in any doctor-patient exchange.

8. Quill, *supra* note 2, at 692.

9. *See* Lisa Belkin, *Doctor Tells of First Death Using His Suicide Device,* N.Y. Times, June 6, 1990, at A1 (describing how a woman, aided by Dr. Jack Kevorkian, committed suicide in an old Volkswagen van).

10. Quill, *supra* note 2, at 692.

11. Jay Katz, The Silent World of Doctor and Patient 142–47 (1984).

12. *See id.* at 2, 27.

13. Quill, *supra* note 2, at 691–92.

14. *See* M. Russell et al., Children of Alcoholics 17 (1985).

15. *See* Jeannette L. Johnson & Jon E. Rolf, *When Children Change: Research Perspectives on Children of Alcoholics, in* Alcohol and the Family 163 (R. Lorraine Collins et al., eds., 1990).

16. *See* Emmy E. Warner, *Resilient Offspring of Alcoholics: A Longitudinal Study from Birth to Age 18,* 47 J. Stud. on Alcohol 34, 39 (1986).

17. Johnson & Rolf, *supra* note 15, at 175.

18. Quill, *supra* note 2, at 692, 693.

19. Timmen L. Cermak & Stephanie Brown, *Interactional Group Therapy with the Adult Children of Alcoholics,* 32 Int'l. J. Group Psychotherapy 375, 377–78, 380 (1982).

20. *Id.* at 385–86.

21. Quill, *supra* note 2, at 692.

22. *Id.,* at 693.

23. *Id.*

24. American Psychiatric Association, Diagnostic and Statistical Manual of Mental Disorders 218–19 (3d ed. rev. 1987).

25. Quill, *supra* note 2, at 692.

26. *Id.* at 692, 693.

27. *See, e.g.,* Union Pac. Ry. Co. v. Botsford, 141 U.S. 250, 251 (1891) ("No right is held more sacred, or is more carefully guarded, by the common law, than the right of every individual to the possession and control of his own person, free from all restraint or interference of others, unless by clear and unquestionable authority of law"); Wall v. Brim, 138 F.2d 478, 481 (5th Cir. 1943) ("The law is well settled that an operation cannot be performed without the patient's consent . . . .");

Bouvia v. Superior Court, 225 Cal. Rptr. 197, 300 (Ct. App. 1986) ("[A] patient has the right to refuse *any* medical treatment, even that which may save or prolong her life"); Natanson v. Kline, 350 P.2d 1093, 1104 (Kan. 1960) ("[E]ach man is considered to be master of his own body, and he may, if he be of sound mind, expressly prohibit the performance of life-saving surgery, or other medical treatment"); *In re* Long Island Jewish Medical Ctr., 557 N.Y.S.2d 239, 242 (Sup. Ct. 1990) ("It is well-settled law in this, and most other jurisdictions, that a competent adult has a common law right to refuse medical treatment"); Scott v. Bradford, 606 P.2d 554, 558 (Okla. 1979) ("A patient's right to make up his mind whether to undergo treatment should not be delegated to the local medical group").

28. Quill, *supra* note 2, at 692.

29. *See id.* By "terminally ill," I mean suffering from an illness that will cause death within days or weeks, even if all appropriate treatment and supportive medical interventions are applied, including "artificially administered" food and water.

30. *See* Sidney H. Wanzer et al., *The Physician's Responsibility Toward Hopelessly Ill Patients: A Second Look,* 320 New Eng. J. Med. 844, 845 (1989).

31. Quill, *supra* note 2, at 693.

32. *Id.* at 692.

33. *Id.*

34. *Id.*

35. *Id.* at 693.

36. *See* Daniel Callahan, Abortion, Law, Choice, and Morality 451–60 (1970) (criticizing the assertion that one should abort a potential human being in the interests of that human being).

37. Quill, *supra* note 2, at 693.

38. *Id.*

39. *Id.* at 692.

40. A professor of nursing ethics at the University of California School of Nursing in San Francisco has written:

Recently I had the clinical experience of caring for a dying patient who clearly said one week before she died, 'kill me.' She understood completely what she was asking for and the consequences of her request. I felt that we failed her and were less than faithful to her when we denied this request. It seemed to me that, while we had said directly and indirectly all along that she was in charge, when it came to that moment, we said, No, we are in charge, and we won't do what you ask because it is not in our best interest.

Anne I. Davis, *Should Physicians Perform Euthanasia?* Am Med. News, Jan. 7, 1991, at 15.

41. Quill, *supra* note 2, at 693.

42. *Id.*

43. *Id.* at 694.

Discussion Questions

1. What does Dr. Wesley mean when she says that we should "read between the lines" when reading Dr. Quill's report of his interaction with Diane? Provide some examples from Dr. Quill's essay of what she means.

2. Dr. Wesley claims that Dr. Quill, far from being neutral on the issue of physician-assisted suicide, was a powerful actor in influencing Diane's decision to commit suicide. How does she draw this conclusion? Do you agree with her assessment? Why or why not? Explain your answer.

3. If you were Dr. Quill, how would you respond to Dr. Wesley's critique? Explain and defend your answer. If you appeal to the autonomy of the patient in support of your decision, reply in detail to Dr. Wesley's claim that Diane may not have been truly autonomous?

You can locate InfoTrac-College Education articles about this chapter by accessing the InfoTrac-College Edition website (http://www.infotrac-college.com/wadsworth/). Using the InfoTrac-College Edition subject guide, enter the search terms relevant to this chapter, and then read abstracts for relevant articles.

SECTION C

Creating and Experimenting with Life at the Margins

Introduction to Section C

There are a number of issues in the field of bioethics that deal with "life at the margins." Among these issues are fetal tissue transplantation and human cloning. They are like abortion and euthanasia insofar as they touch on questions of who and what we are. But unlike those two issues, fetal tissue transplantation and human cloning offer possibilities for curing diseases and extending the human life span, both in quality and quantity, as well as altering the means of human reproduction that would have appeared to most of us only several years ago as ideas more at home in a Star Trek episode than as topics of serious scientific and ethical discussion. But things have changed.

FETAL TISSUE TRANSPLANTATION

The use of fetal brain cells has shown some promise in improving the condition of some Parkinson's disease patients in whom the cells have been implanted. Consider the example of Don Nelson, a fifty-two-year-old victim of Parkinson's disease, in whom surgeons at the University of Colorado Medical Center (on November 10, 1988) implanted the brain cells of a fetus. Soon after the surgery, Nelson noted improved walking and speaking ability. Should the technology be perfected on Parkinson's patients, "it shows promise for application to a number of other degenerative diseases such as Alzheimer's disease, Huntington's Chorea, and spinal cord or other neural injuries. In addition, the use of fetal liver cells shows promise for treating bone marrow diseases and blood disorders, and fetal pancreatic cells have been shown to help treat diabetes."[1]

The ethical questions this research raises are numerous. Consider the following. If the fetus is not a human person, as abortion rights supporters contend, why not encourage continued experimentation and research on the fetus so that those of us who *are* human persons can be helped? Why should we not permit women to purposely become pregnant so that we can use their fetal tissue for helping patients such as Mr. Nelson? But if the fetus is at least a *potential person* who is a human being, as almost all abortion rights supporters affirm, does the fetus not have *some* right not to be treated as a thing we can take apart and on which we can experiment without any restrictions whatsoever? If fetal tissue transplantation becomes even more promising, will this not sway pregnant women ambivalent about undergoing abortion in the direction of abortion, since they will know that it is possible that some good for another person (such as Mr. Nelson) may come from their tragic decision? Will the pressure for fetal tissue transplantation provide a financial incentive for abortion clinics to sell fetal tissue either legally or on the black market? These and other questions will be the focus of the first two essays in this section. The author of the first essay (Chapter 22), John Robertson, opposes nearly any restriction on fetal tissue transplantation, except if the restriction is intended to protect women from possible economic exploitation. He supports federal funding with a few caveats. In the second essay (Chapter 23), Scott B. Rae argues that it is morally wrong to use fetal tissue for experimentation or transplantation if the fetus's death did not result from a spontaneous abortion.

Another issue that is similar to fetal experimentation and transplantation is embryo research. In fall 1993, the National Institutes for Health's (NIH) Human Embryo Research Panel was commissioned to make recommendations as to what types of research on the embryo prior to implantation and outside the woman's uterus (ex utero) are appropriate or inappropriate for federal funding. The main ethical concern for the Panel was the moral permissibility of the creation of human embryos for the sole purpose of experimenting on them. After hearing thousands of hours of testimony by experts on all sides of the debate, the Panel concluded, in its Final Report, that some research was acceptable for federal support, some warranted additional review, and some was unacceptable. The Panel based its conclusions on ethical considerations as well as concern for promoting research that results in human benefit. Although the Panel asserted that "it conducted its deliberations in terms that were independent of a particular religious or philosophical perspective," it nevertheless supported federal funding of research on the preimplanted embryo on the basis that "it does not have the same moral status as infants and children" since it lacks "developmental individuation . . . . the lack of the possibility of sentience and most other qualities considered relevant to the moral status of persons, and the very high rate of natural mortality at this state" (i.e., the large number of preimplantation embryos that die before implantation).[2] However, the Panel did forbid federal funding of research on embryos after the 14th day after conception, since around that time the embryo acquires the primitive streak, "an advancing groove that develops along the midline of the embryonic disc. . . . A milestone in embryo development, the primitive streak establishes and reveals the embryo's head-tale and left-right orientations."[3]

Although there are no essays in this section that are dedicated exclusively to the topic of embryo research, many of the questions raised by the authors in the essays on fetal transplantation and experimentation as well as cloning apply to the issue of embryo research as well. For example, Leon Kass (Chapter 24), as part of his case against cloning, touches on embryo research and the moral reasoning of those who support it.

HUMAN CLONING

In early 1997, Dr. Ian Wilmut, a Scottish scientist, made headlines when he presented to the world, Dolly, a sheep he cloned from a six-year-old ewe. Three and one-half years earlier, Drs. Jerry Hall and Robert Stillman cloned a human embryo by successfully splitting one human embryo into two. Although this occurs naturally in the case of identical twins, Hall and Stillman were the first to replicate this process artificially.

Many of us are acquainted with the concept of cloning because of popular films like *Multiplicity* and *The Boys From Brazil,* but many of us do not know exactly what cloning is. When a scientist refers to "cloning," he may be speaking of one of two procedures: (1) embryo cloning; or (2) somatic cell nuclear transfer (SCNT) cloning.

1. Embryo Cloning. This is the type of cloning performed by Hall and Stillman. It has been successfully used with animals for many years. Hall and Stillman began with what is called "in-vitro fertilization" or IVF: in a laboratory they produced in a petri dish human embryos by taking ova and fertilizing them with male sperm. Rae goes on to explain the process: "The embryos they used in their experiments had been fertilized by two sperm instead of one, making them abnormal embryos and destined to die within a week. This cloning process would be no different if the embryo were properly fertilized and had a normal chance at becoming a baby if implanted."[4] Hart and Stillman produced defective embryos rather than normal ones because they did not intend for either the clones or the defective embryos to develop into babies.[5] They just wanted to see if they could artificially clone a human embryo.

In order to induce cloning, the following procedure was conducted. After the ovum was fertilized, the embryo divided in two, which is what occurs in normal development. The scientists then removed the zona pellucida, "the coating that contains enzymes that promote cell division that is necessary for growth and development." The two cells were then separated. Because development cannot continue unless the zona pellucida is replaced, Hall and Stillman "used an artificial zona pellucida to recoat the two embryonic cells, enabling development to continue. As the cells [grow] they [formed] genetically identical embryos, a laboratory equivalent to what occurs naturally in the body when identical twins are conceived."[6] But because the embryos were defective, they perished after six days.[7]

2. SCNT Cloning. This is the type of cloning that produced Dolly the sheep. Because sheep, like human beings, are mammals, it is probable that in the future, perhaps the near future, scientists will be able to clone human beings by this method.

The DNA of every cell in the human body, except for the sperm and ovum, contains the genetic material that in theory is capable of producing an identical clone of the body from which the cell is taken. But since the cells are programmed to perform certain functions (i.e., liver cells perform different functions than brain cells), and since all other functions are dormant, conception has to be replicated for a new and genetically identical human being to come into existence. This is accomplished by extracting the nucleus of a cell from a human body, fusing that cell with an ovum that has had its nucleus removed, and then electrically stimulating this fused entity. This is what occurred in the case of Dolly. But, according to molecule biologist Dr. Raymond Bohlin, "[t]he process was inefficient. Out of 277 cell fusions, twenty-nine began growing in vitro. All twenty-nine were implanted in receptive ewes, thirteen became pregnant, and only one lamb was born as a result. This is a success rate of only 3.4 percent. In nature, somewhere between 33 and 50 percent of all fertilized eggs develop fully into newborns."[8]

If SCNT cloning is performed on a human, a resulting clone will always be younger than her twin, unlike the adult clones of the character played by actor Michael Keaton in the film *Multiplicity*. So, if a 24-year-old woman clones herself, her cloned twin will always be 24 years her younger.

In this section, two different positions on cloning are represented. In Chapter 24, physician and ethicist Leon Kass argues that all human cloning should be banned. In Chapter 25 legal scholar Shannon H. Smith calls for the lifting of all bans on cloning, because "the potential for good . . . is too compelling."[9]

> **Key words:** fetal tissue transplantation, cloning, reproductive technology, embryo experimentation, NIH Panel on Fetal Tissue Transplantation Research, bioethics, pre-embryo, invitro fertilization, assisted reproduction, human genome project, genetics and ethics, DNA, Uniform Anatomical Gift Act, NIH Embryo Research Panel, stem cell research, somatic cell nuclear transfer, embryo cloning.

NOTES

1. Scott B. Rae, "Spare Parts from the Unborn?: The Ethics of Fetal Tissue Transplantation," *Christian Research Journal* 14 (fall 1991): 29. Portions of this article are reprinted in this text as Chapter 23.
2. National Institutes of Health, *Final Report of the Human Embryo Research Panel* (27 September 1994): 2–3. For a response to the panel's findings, see The Ramsey Colloquium, "The Inhuman Use of Human Beings: A Statement on Embryo Research," *First Things: A Monthly Journal of Religion and Public Life* no. 49 (January 1995).
3. From the glossary of *Final Report of the Human Embryo Research Panel,* 107.
4. Scott B. Rae, *Brave New Families: Biblical Ethics and Reproductive Technologies* (Grand Rapids, MI: Baker, 1996), 172–73.
5. Connie Cass, "Spotlight thrust on scientists who cloned human embryos," *Las Vegas Review-Journal* (October 23, 1993): 1A, 2A.
6. See Rae, *Brave New Families,* 173.
7. Rae's description of the technical procedure is taken from Philip Elmer-Dewitt, "Cloning: Where Do We Draw the Line?," *Time* (November 8, 1993): 67.
8. Raymond G. Bohlin, "The Little Lamb that Made a Monkey of Us All," (March 7, 1997), available online at: www.probe.org/docs/lambclon.html.
9. Shannon H. Smith, "Ignorance Is Bliss: Why a Ban on Human Cloning is Unacceptable," *Health-Matrix: Journal of Law-Medicine* 9 (summer 1999): 334. Portions of this article are reprinted in this text as Chapter 26.

For Further Reading

James Bopp and James Burtchaell, "Fetal Tissue Transplantation: The Fetus as Medical Commodity," *This World* 26 (summer 1989).
James F. Childress, "Deliberations of the Human Fetal Tissue Transplantation Research Panel," in *Biomedical Politics,* ed. Kathi E. Hanna (Washington, DC: National Academy Press, 1991).

Alan Fine, "The Ethics of Fetal Tissue Transplants." From *The Hastings Center Report* 18 (June/July 1988).

Henry T. Greely, et. al., "The Ethical Use of Human Fetal Tissue in Medicine," *New England Journal of Medicine* 320 (April 20, 1989).

Dianne N. Irving, "'New Age' Embryology Text Books: 'Pre-Embryo,' 'Pregnancy' and Abortion Counseling; Implications for Fetal Research," *Linacre Quarterly* (May 1994).

J. P. Moreland and Scott B. Rae, *Body & Soul: Human Nature and the Crisis in Ethics* (Downers Grove, IL: InterVarsity Press, 2000).

National Bioethics Advisory Commission, *Cloning Human Beings, Vol. 1: Report and Recommendations of the National Bioethics Advisory Commission* (9 June 1997). This can be obtained free of charge from the NBAC in Rockville, Maryland.

National Institutes of Health, *Final Report of the Human Embryo Research Panel* (27 September 1994). This can obtained free of charge from the NIH in Washington, D.C.

Martha Nussbaum and Cass R. Sunstein, eds., *Clones and Clones: Facts and Fantasies About Human Cloning* (New York: W.W. Norton, 1998).

Gregory E. Pence, ed., *Flesh of My Flesh: The Ethics of Cloning Humans: A Reader* (Lanham, MD: Rowman & Littlefield, 1998).

Paul Ramsey, *The Ethics of Fetal Research* (New Haven, CT: Yale University Press, 1975).

The Ramsey Colloquium, "The Inhuman Use of Human Beings: A Statement on Embryo Research," *First Things: A Monthly Journal of Religion and Public Life* no. 49 (January 1995).

John A. Robertson, "Fetal Tissue Transplants," *Washington University Law Quarterly* 66 (1988).

Valparaiso University Law Review 32.2 (spring 1998). This entire issue is dedicated to the legal, moral, and religious questions raised by cloning. Some of the authors in this issue include John Finnis, Geri J. Yonover, Robert F. Blomquist, Catharine Cookson, Clarke D. Forsythe, Michael J. McDaniel, Gilbert Meilander, and Thomas A. Shannon.

LeRoy Walters, "Ethical Issues in Experimentation on the Human Fetus," *Journal of Religious Ethics* 2 (spring 1974).

Mildred Washington, "Fetal Research: A Survey of State Law," *Congressional Research Service Report for Congress* (March 8, 1988).

22   Rights, Symbolism, and Public Policy on Fetal Tissue Transplants

JOHN A. ROBERTSON

John A. Robertson is Baker & Botts Professor of Law, University of Texas School of Law in Austin, Texas. He was a member of the NIH Panel on Fetal Tissue Transplantation Research. He has published widely in the areas of bioethics, law, and public policy, including articles in *The Hastings Center Report* and *Washington University Law Quarterly*. He is author of the book, *Children of Choice: Freedom and the New Reproductive Technologies* (1994).

Reprinted by permission from The Hastings Center Report *18 (December 1988). This essay has been edited for this book.*

In this essay Professor Robertson defends a liberal view of fetal tissue transplants, arguing that it is morally justified to use fetal tissue for transplantation even if the fetus's death did result from an elective non-therapeutic abortion. He begins his essay with a clarification of the issues surrounding fetal tissue transplantation. He then moves on to respond to two arguments brought up by those who oppose the use of fetal tissue from elective abortions: (1) using such fetal tissue involves moral complicity in the abortion, and (2) using such fetal tissue will result in legitimizing, entrenching, and encouraging abortion. In order to articulate his position more clearly, Professor Robertson presents hypothetical scenarios that concern the use of tissue in different situations (e.g., a woman becoming pregnant with the intent of donating the fetal tissue, a woman donating the fetal tissue after she discovers she is pregnant). He then goes on to discuss recruiting unrelated fetal tissue donors, the woman's right to dispose of fetal tissue, the consent process and abortion, commercialization of fetal tissue, federal funding, and legal bans on fetal tissue transplants. He concludes that "ethical concerns should not bar research with fetal tissue transplants as a therapy for serious illness." Other than protecting women from possible economic exploitation, he opposes nearly any restriction on fetal tissue transplantation and supports, with a few caveats, federal funding.

CLARIFYING THE ISSUES

AS WITH MANY ISSUES in bioethics, careful analysis will help elucidate the normative conflict, showing both areas of agreement and irreducible conflict. An essential distinction in the fetal tissue controversy is between procuring tissue from family planning abortions and procuring tissue from abortions performed expressly to provide tissue for transplant. Although opponents of fetal tissue transplants have often conflated the two, tissue from family planning abortions may be used without implying approval of abortions to produce tissue. Indeed, with ample tissue available from family planning abortions, the latter scenario may never occur.

A second important distinction is that between retrieving tissue for transplant from dead and from live fetuses. Only the use of tissue from dead fetuses is at issue. Researchers are not proposing to maintain non-viable fetuses ex utero to procure tissue, or to take tissue from them before they are dead, practices that current regulations and law prohibit.[1]

A third set of issues concern tissue procurement procedures. If fetal tissue transplants do occur, questions about the timing, substance, and process of consent must be addressed, as well as the role of nonprofit and for-profit agencies in retrieving and distributing fetal tissue. As with solid organ transplantation, effective tissue procurement may occur without buying and selling fetal tissue.

At present there are few legal barriers to research or therapeutic use of donated fetal tissue for transplant. The Uniform Anatomical Gift Act (UAGA) in all states treats fetal remains like other cadaveric remains and allows next of kin to donate the tissue, though a few states have laws banning experimental use of aborted fetuses.[2] Federal regulations for fetal research, enacted in 1976 after careful study by the National Commission for the Protection of Human Subjects of Biomedical and Behavioral Research, permit research activities "involving the dead fetus, mascerated fetal material, or cells, tissue, or organs excised from a dead fetus . . . in accordance with any applicable state or local laws regarding such activities."[3]

The most immediate public policy question is whether these rules should be changed to prohibit experimental or therapeutic fetal tissue transplants, as the most extreme opponents urge. A second public policy issue is whether federal funding of fetal tissue research should occur. A third set of policy issues concerns the circumstances and procedures by which fetal tissue will be retrieved.

TISSUE FROM FAMILY PLANNING ABORTIONS

Fetal tissue transplant research for Parkinson's disease, diabetes, and other disorders will use tissue retrieved from the one and a half million abortions performed annually in the United States to end unwanted pregnancies. Nearly 80 percent of induced abortions are performed between the sixth and eleventh weeks of gestation, at which time neural and other tissue is sufficiently developed to be retrieved and transplanted.[4] Abortions performed at fourteen to sixteen weeks provide pancreatic tissue used in diabetes research, but it may prove possible to use pancreases retrieved earlier.[5]

No need now or in the foreseeable future exists to have a family member conceive and abort to produce fetal tissue. The neural tissue to be transplanted in Parkinson's disease lacks antigenicity, thus obviating the need for a close match between donor and recipient. Fetal pancreas is more antigenetic, but processing can reduce this, also making family connection less important.

The key question is whether women who abort to end unwanted pregnancies may donate the aborted fetuses for use in medical research or therapy by persons who have no connection with or influence on the decision to terminate the pregnancy. One's views on abortion need not determine one's answer to this question, because the abortion and subsequent transplant use are clearly separated. But some opposed to abortion object that transplanting fetal tissue involves complicity in an immoral act and will legitimate and even encourage abortion. Analysis of these concerns will show that they are insufficient to justify a public policy that bans or refuses to fund research or therapy with fetal tissue from induced abortion.

COMPLICITY IN ABORTION

Even proponents of the complicity argument recognize that not all situations of subsequent benefit make one morally complicitous in a prior evil act. For example, James Burtchaell claims that complicity occurs not merely from partaking of benefit but only when one enters into a "supportive alliance" with the underlying evil that makes the benefit possible. He distinguishes "a neutral or even an opponent and an ally" of the underlying evil by "the way in which one does or does not hold oneself apart from the enterprise and its purposes."[6]

On this analysis, a researcher using fetal tissue from an elective abortion is not necessarily an accomplice with the abortionist and woman choosing abortion. The researcher and recipient have no role in the abortion process. They will not have requested it, and may have no knowledge of who performed the abortion or where it occurred since a third-party intermediary will procure the tissue. They may be morally opposed to abortion, and surely are not compromised because they choose to salvage some good from an abortion that will occur regardless of their research or therapeutic goals.

A useful analogy is transplant of organs and tissue from homicide victims. Families of murder victims are often asked to donate organs and bodies for research, therapy, and education. If they consent, organ procurement agencies retrieve the organs and distribute them to recipients. No one would seriously argue that the surgeon who transplants the victim's kidneys, heart, liver, or corneas, or the recipient of the organs, becomes an accomplice in the homicide that made the organs available, even if aware of the source. Nor is the medical student who uses the cadaver of a murder victim to study anatomy.

If organs from murder victims may be used without complicity in the murder that makes the organs available, then fetal remains could also be used without complicity in the abortion. Burtchaell's approach to the problem of complicity assumes that researchers necessarily applaud the underlying act of abortion. But one may benefit from another's evil act without applauding or approving of that evil. X may disapprove of Y's murder of Z, even though X gains an inheritance or a promotion as a result. Indeed, one might even question Burtchaell's assumption that X becomes an accomplice in Y's prior act if he subsequently applauds it. Applauding Y's murder of Z might be insensitive or callous. But that alone would not make one morally responsible for, complicitous in, the murder that has already occurred. In any event, the willingness to derive benefit from another's wrongful death does not create complicity in that death because the beneficiary played no role in causing it.

The complicity argument against use of aborted fetuses often draws an analogy to a perceived reluctance to use the results of unethical medical research carried out by the Nazis. Burtchaell and others have claimed that it would make us retroactively accomplices in the Nazi horrors to use the results of their unethical and lethal research.[7] This ignores, however, the clear separation between the perpetrator and beneficiary of the immoral act that breaks the chain of moral complicity for that act.

Thus one could rely on Nazi-generated data while decrying the horrendous acts of Nazi doctors that produced the data. Nor would it necessarily dishonor those unfortunate victims. Indeed, it could reasonably be viewed as retrospectively honoring them by saving others. The Jewish doctors who made systematic studies of starvation in the Warsaw ghetto to reap some good from the evil being done to their brethren were not accomplices in that evil, nor are doctors and patients who now benefit from their studies.[8]

If the complicity claim is doubtful when the underlying immorality of the act is clear, as with Nazi-produced data or transplants from murder victims, it is considerably weakened when the act making the benefit possible is legal and its immorality vigorously debated, as is the case with abortion. Even persons opposed to abortion might agree that perceptions of complicity should not determine public policy on fetal tissue transplants.

LEGITIMIZING, ENTRENCHING, AND ENCOURAGING ABORTION

A second objection is that salvaging tissue for transplant from aborted fetuses will make abortion less morally offensive and more easily tolerated both by individual pregnant women and by society, and perhaps transform it into a morally positive act. This will encourage abortions that would not otherwise occur, and dilute support for reversing the legal acceptability of abortion, in effect creating complicity in future abortions.[9]

But the feared impact on abortion practices and attitudes is highly speculative, particularly at a time when few fetal transplants have occurred. The main motivation for abortion is the desire to avoid the burdens of an unwanted pregnancy. The fact that fetal remains may be donated for transplant will continue to be of little significance in the total array of factors that lead a woman to abort a pregnancy.

Having decided to abort, a woman may feel better if she then donates the fetal remains. But this does not show that tissue donation will lead to a termination decision that would not otherwise have occurred, particularly if the decision to abort is made before the opportunity to donate the remains is offered. Perhaps a few more abortions will occur because of the general knowledge that tissue can be donated for transplant, but it is highly unlikely that donation—as opposed to contraceptive practices and sex education—will contribute significantly to the rate of abortion.[10]

Nor does the use of fetal remains for transplant mean that a public otherwise ready to outlaw abortion would refrain from doing so. Legal acceptance of abortion flows from the wide disagreement that exists over early fetal status. If a majority agreed that fetuses should be respected as persons despite the burdens placed on pregnant women, such possible secondary benefits of induced abortion as fetal tissue transplants would not prevent a change in the legality of abortion.

Indeed, one could make the same argument against organ transplants from homicide, suicide, and accident victims. The willingness to use their organs might be seen to encourage or legitimate such deaths, or at least make it harder to enact lower speed limits, seatbelt, gun control, and drunk driving laws to prevent them. After all, the need to prevent murder, suicide, and fatal accidents becomes less pressing if some good to others might come from use of victims' organs for transplant. In either case, the connection is too tenuous and speculative to ban organ or fetal tissue transplants.

In sum, fetal tissue transplants are practically and morally separate from decisions to end unwanted pregnancy. Given that abortion is legal and occurring on a large scale, the willingness to use resulting tissue for transplant neither creates complicity in past abortions nor appears significantly to encourage more future abortions. Such ethical concerns and speculations are not sufficient, given the possible

good to others, to justify banning use of fetal tissue for research or therapy.

ABORTING TO OBTAIN TISSUE FOR TRANSPLANT

Central to the argument for transplanting fetal tissue from family planning abortions has been the assumption that the abortion occurs independently of the need for tissue, and that permitting such transplants does not also entail pregnancy and abortion to produce fetal tissue.

But successful tissue transplants may create the need to abort to produce fetal tissue in two future situations. One situation would arise if histocompatibility between the fetus and recipient were necessary for effective fetal transplants. Female relatives, spouses, or even unrelated persons might then seek to conceive to provide properly matched fetal tissue for transplant.

The second situation would arise if fetal transplants were so successful that demand far outstripped supply, such as might occur if the treatment were advantageous to most patients with Parkinson's disease and diabetes, or if the number of surgical family planning abortions decreased. Pressure on supply might also occur if tissue from several aborted fetuses were needed to produce one viable transplant.

The hypothetical possibility of such situations is not a sufficient reason to ban all tissue transplants from family planning abortions. But should such abortions be banned if the imagined situations occurred? Most commentators assume that conception and abortion for tissue procurement is so clearly unethical that the prospect hardly merits discussion.[11] Accordingly, they would ban all tissue transplants from related persons and deny the donor the right to designate the recipient of a fetal tissue transplant.

Analysis will show, however, that the question is more ethically complicated than generally assumed, and should not be the driving force in setting policy for tissue transplants from family planning abortions.

A HYPOTHETICAL SITUATION

Consider first the situation where a woman pregnant with her husband's child learns that tissue from her fetus could cure severe neurologic disease in herself or a close relative, such as her husband, child, parent, father or mother-in-law, sibling, or brother or sister-in-law. May she ethically abort the pregnancy to obtain tissue for transplant to the relative? Or may a woman not yet pregnant, conceive a fetus that she will then abort to provide tissue for transplant to herself or to her relative?

To focus analysis on fetal welfare, assume in each case that no other viable tissue source exists, and that the advanced state of neurologic disease has become a major tragedy for the patient and family. The woman has broached the question of abortion to obtain tissue without any direct pressure or inducements from the family or others. Her husband accepts an abortion for transplant purposes if she is willing, but exerts no pressure on her to abort.

The woman is already pregnant. If the woman is already pregnant, the question is whether a first trimester fetus that would otherwise have been carried to term may be sacrificed to procure tissue for transplant to the woman herself or to a sick family member. The answer depends on the value placed on early fetuses and on the acceptable reasons for abortion. One may distinguish between fetuses that have developed the neurologic and cognitive capacity for sentience and interests in themselves, and those so neurologically immature that they cannot experience harm.[12] While aborting fetuses at that earlier stage prevents them from achieving their potential, it does not harm or wrong them, since they are insufficiently developed to experience harm.[13]

Although aborting the fetus at that early stage does not wrong the fetus, it may impose symbolic costs measurable in terms of the reduced respect for human life generally that a willingness to abort early fetuses connotes. Still, the abortion may be ethically acceptable if the good sought sufficiently outweighs the symbolic devaluation of life that occurs when fetuses that cannot be harmed in their own right are aborted. Many persons find that the burdens of unwanted pregnancy outweigh the symbolic devaluation of human life. Others would require a more compelling reason for abortion, such as protecting the mother's life or health, avoiding the birth of a handicapped child, or avoiding the burdens of a pregnancy due to rape or incest.

By comparison, abortion to obtain tissue to save one's own life or the life of a close relative seems equally, if not more compelling. If abortion in the case of an unwanted pregnancy is deemed permissible, surely abortion to obtain tissue to save another person's life is. Indeed, aborting to obtain tissue would seem as compelling as the most stringent reasons for permitting abortion. In fact, many would find this motive more compelling than the desire to end an unwanted pregnancy.

Of course, aborting a wanted pregnancy to prevent severe neurologic disease in oneself or a close relative will hardly be done joyfully, and will place the mother in an excruciating dilemma. A fetus that could be carried to term will have to be sacrificed to save a parent, spouse, sibling, or child who already exists. Such a tragic choice will induce fear and trembling, and engender loss or grief whatever the decision. Yet one cannot say that the choice to abort is ethically impermissible. There is no sound ethical basis for prohibiting *this* sacrifice of the fetus when its sacrifice to end an unwanted pregnancy or pursue other goals is permitted.

Public attitudes toward a woman aborting an otherwise wanted pregnancy to benefit a family member would most likely reflect attitudes toward abortion generally. Those who are against abortion in all circumstances will object to abortions done to treat severe neurologic disease in the mother or in a family member. Similarly, persons who accept family planning abortions should have no objection to abortion to procure tissue for transplant, since fetal status is no more compelling and the interest of the woman in controlling her body and reproductive capacity is similar.

Since neither group forms a majority, however, persons who object to family planning abortions but accept abortions necessary to protect the mother's health, in cases of rape or incest, or to prevent the birth of a handicapped child will determine whether a majority of people approve.[14] It is conceivable that many persons in this swing group would find abortion to produce tissue for transplant to a family member to be acceptable. The benefit of alleviating severe neurologic disease is arguably as great as the benefits in the cases they accept as justifiable abortion, and more compelling than abortions done for family planning purposes.

Conceiving and aborting for transplant purposes. What is the objection, then, when a woman not yet pregnant seeks to conceive in order to abort and provide tissue for transplant?

In terms of fetal welfare, no greater harm occurs to the fetus conceived to be aborted, as long as the abortion occurs at a stage at which the fetus is insufficiently developed to experience harm, such as during the first trimester. Of course, such deliberate creation may have greater symbolic significance, because it denotes a willingness to use fetuses as a means or object to serve other ends. However, aborting when already pregnant to procure tissue for transplant (or aborting for the more customary reasons) also denotes a willingness to use the fetus as a means to other ends.

As long as abortion of an existing pregnancy for transplant purposes is ethically accepted, conceiving in order to abort and procure tissue for transplant should also be ethically acceptable when necessary to alleviate great suffering in others.[15] People could reasonably find that the additional symbolic devaluation is negligible, or in any case, insufficient to outweigh the

substantial gain to transplant recipients that deliberate creation provides.

Many people, no doubt, will resist this conclusion, even if they accept abortion to procure tissue when the woman is already pregnant. Whether rational or not, they assign moral or symbolic significance to deliberate creation, and are less ready to sanction such a practice. Others who accept abortion for tissue procurement when the woman is already pregnant will find an insufficient difference in deliberate creation to outweigh the resulting good. Public acceptability of such a practice thus depends on how the swing group that views abortion as acceptable only for very stringent reasons views the fact of deliberate creation for the purpose of abortion. If it would accept abortion to produce tissue when the pregnancy is unplanned, it might accept conception to produce fetal tissue as well.

In sum, deliberate creation of fetuses to be aborted for tissue procurement is more ethically complex, and more defensible, than its current widespread dismissal would suggest. Such a practice is, of course, not in itself desirable, but in a specific situation of strong personal or familial need may be more justified than previously thought. In any case, the fear that fetal tissue transplant will lead to abortions performed solely to obtain tissue for transplant should not prevent use of tissue from abortions not performed for that purpose.

RECRUITING UNRELATED FETAL TISSUE DONORS

The strongest case for conception and abortion to produce fetal tissue—if the need arose—is to save oneself or a close relative from death or serious harm. But many patients in need would lack a female relative willing to donate. May unrelated women be recruited for this purpose?

If the hypothetical need arose, a strong case for unrelated fetal tissue donors can be made. If a relative may provide tissue, why not a stranger who chooses to do so altruistically? At this point concerns about fetal status become less important, and the focus shifts toward the welfare of the donor. But the physical effects of pregnancy and abortion to produce fetal tissue are roughly comparable to the effects of kidney or bone marrow donation, though somewhat less since general anesthesia will not be involved. While few unrelated persons now act as kidney donors, there is a national registry for unrelated bone marrow donors. Even if fetal tissue donation were psychologically more complicated, the risks to the woman would appear to be within the boundaries of autonomous choice.

Some persons might object that this will turn women into "fetal tissue farms," thus denigrating their inherent worth as persons. This charge could also be made against any living donor, whether of kidney, bone marrow, blood, sperm, or egg. Insofar as persons donate body parts, they may be viewed as mere tissue or organ producers. Indeed, women who bear children are always in danger of being viewed as "breeders." But such views oversimplify the complex emotional reality of organ and tissue donation and of human reproduction. The risk of misperception does not justify barring women from freely choosing to be fetal tissue donors.

Special attention should be given to consent procedures that will protect the woman from coercion or undue pressure by prospective recipients and their families, just as occurs with living related kidney and marrow donors. Waiting periods, consent advisors and monitors, and other devices to guarantee free, informed consent are clearly justified.[16]

THE WOMAN'S RIGHT TO DISPOSE OF FETAL TISSUE

The UAGA and federal research regulations give the mother the right to make or withhold donations of fetal remains for research or ther-

apy, subject to objection by the father.[17] Yet some ethicists claim that the decision to abort disqualifies the mother from playing any role in disposition of fetal remains.[18] If accepted, this argument would lead either to procuring fetal tissue without parental consent or to a total ban on fetal transplants. But the argument is mistaken on two grounds.

Its major premise is that the person disposing of cadaveric remains acts as a guardian or proxy for the deceased. Since the woman has chosen to kill the fetus by abortion, she is no longer qualified to act as proxy. But this premise is seriously flawed. Deceased persons or fetuses no longer have interests to be protected, as the notion of proxy implies. Control of human remains is assigned to next of kin because of their own interests and feelings about how cadaveric remains are treated, not because they are best situated to implement the deceased's prior wishes concerning disposition of his cadaver. The latter concern is particularly inappropriate in the case of an aborted fetus, which could have had no specific wishes concerning disposition of its remains.

A second mistake is the assumption that a woman has no interest in what happens to the fetus that she chooses to abort. As a product of her body and potential heir that she has for her own compelling reasons chosen to abort, she may care deeply about whether fetal remains are contributed to research or therapy to help others. Given that interest, there is good reason to respect her wishes, as current law does. Indeed, in cases of conflict between her and the father over disposition, one could argue that her interests control because the fetus was removed from her body.

An alternative policy requiring that fetal remains be used without parental consent or not at all is unacceptable. American public policy has vigorously rejected routine salvage of body parts without family consent as a way to increase the supply of organs for transplant.[19] Even presumed consent, which would take organs unless the family actually objects, has been largely rejected.[20] Depriving the mother (and father who agrees to the abortion) of the power to veto fetal tissue transplants would single out fetal tissue for transplant use without family consent. Such a radical change in tissue procurement practice is not needed to satisfy the demand for fetal tissue. It serves only to punish women who abort.

The alternative would be to ban fetal tissue transplants altogether. But this solution burns the house to roast the pig, in effect banning tissue transplants because the parent is not permitted to consent. As we have seen, however, a ban on all fetal transplants is not justified.

In short, the ethical case for denying the woman who aborts dispositional control of fetal remains is not persuasive. She cannot insist that fetal remains be used for transplant because no donor has the right to require that intended donees accept anatomical gifts, but she should retain the existing legal right to veto use of fetal remains for transplant research or therapy. Her consent to donation of fetal tissue should be routinely sought.

THE CONSENT PROCESS AND ABORTION

If the woman retains the right to determine whether fetal tissue is used for research or therapy, the main ethical concern is to assure that her choice about tissue donation and the abortion is free and informed. A clear separation of the two decisions will assure that tissue donation is not a prerequisite to performance of the abortion. Also, it will prevent the prospect of donating fetal remains from influencing the decision to abort, a preferable policy when sufficient tissue from family planning abortions is available.

To that end, the request to donate fetal tissue should be made only after the woman has consented to the abortion.[21] The alternative of waiting until the abortion has been performed would add little protection and not be practical. In addition, the person requesting consent to tissue donation and performing the abortion should not be the person using the donated tissue in research or therapy, a constraint widely followed in cadaveric organ procurement.

Federal regulations governing fetal research also state that "no procedural changes which may cause greater than minimal risk to the fetus or pregnant woman will be introduced into the procedure for terminating the pregnancy solely in the interest of the activity."[22] While this policy is partially intended to protect fetuses from later or more painful abortions, it also aims to protect women from prolonging pregnancy or undergoing more onerous abortion procedures to obtain tissue.

Some changes in abortion procedures to enhance tissue procurement pose little additional risk and should be permitted. For example, reductions in the amount of suction, use of a larger bore needle, and ultrasound-guided placement of the suction instrument in evacuation abortions would, without increasing risk, facilitate tissue retrieval by preventing masceration of the fetus.

More problematic would be changes such as substitution of prostaglandin-induced labor and delivery or hysterotomy for less risky methods, or postponement of abortion too late in the first trimester or to the second trimester. Apart from her desire to facilitate tissue donation, these changes would not appear to be in the woman's interest.

Asking a woman who is aborting to take on these extra burdens can be ethically justified only if necessary to obtain viable tissue. Because sufficient fetal tissue may now be obtained without increasing the burdens of abortion, the current federal regulations are sound.

A different policy should be considered if changes in timing or method of abortion became necessary to procure viable tissue for transplant. If the need were clearly shown, there is no objection in principle to asking a woman to assume some additional burdens for the sake of tissue procurement. If the woman is already pregnant and determined to have an abortion, the additional risks of postponing the abortion a few weeks or even changing to a prostaglandin abortion would be well within the range of risks that persons may voluntarily choose to benefit others. However, special procedures to protect the woman's autonomy would be in order.

COMMERCIALIZATION OF FETAL TISSUE

In addition to ethical concerns about fetal and maternal welfare, opponents of fetal tissue transplants have raised the specter of fetal tissue procurement leading to a commercial market in abortions and in fetal tissue.

Paying money to women to abort, or to donate once they abort, is generally perceived as damaging to human dignity, as would be commercial buying and selling of fetal tissue. Such market transactions risk exploiting women and their reproductive capacity and may denigrate the human dignity of aborted fetuses by treating them as market commodities.[23]

Most commentators and advisory bodies that have considered fetal tissue transplants recommend that market transactions in abortions and fetal tissue be prohibited.[24] The National Organ Transplant Act of 1984, which bans the payment of "valuable consideration" for the donation or distribution of solid organs, was amended in 1988 to ban sales of fetal organs and "subparts thereof."[25] Also, several states prohibit the sale of fetal tissue and organs.[26]

At present such policies are easily supported, for they would have little impact on the supply of fetal tissue. There is no reason to think that women who abort unwanted pregnancies would not donate fetal tissue altruistically. Indeed, many women who abort are likely to donate fetal remains in the hope that some additional good might result from the abortion. Paying them to donate—buying their aborted fetuses—is thus unnecessary.

But what if altruistic donations did not produce a sufficient supply of fetal tissue for transplant, or the need for histocompatible tissue required hiring women to be impregnated to produce a sufficient supply of fetal tissue? Would such payments be unethical? Should current legal policy still be maintained? Answering those questions would require balancing the risks of exploiting woman and the symbolic costs of perceived commodification against the benefits to needy patients and the rights of women to determine use of their reproductive capacity.

No doubt many people would object to hiring women to become pregnant and abort. However, if pregnancy and abortion to produce fetal tissue is ethically defensible, then money payments in some circumstances may also be defensible, given obligations of beneficence and respect for persons, the lack of alternative tissue sources, and social practices in which some tissue donors are paid.[27] Legal policy might then be reconsidered to permit payments when essential to save the life or protect the health of transplant recipients who lack other alternatives. However, resolution of this difficult issue should await the actual occurrence of the need to pay to obtain fetal tissue for transplant. In the meantime, research and therapy with fetal tissue should proceed without payments to women to abort or to donate fetal tissue.

Current bans on buying and selling fetal tissue do not—and should not—prohibit making reasonable payments to recover the costs of retrieving fetal tissue. The law and ethics of organ procurement allow for payment of costs incurred in the acquisition of organs.[28] Organ donor families, for example, are not asked to pay for the costs of maintaining brain-dead cadavers or for surgically removing the organs that they donate. The same principle should apply to fetal tissue donations. Two related issues concern paying the donor's abortion expenses and paying other tissue retrieval costs.

Paying abortion expenses. Paying the cost of the abortion should occur only in those instances in which the abortion is performed solely to obtain tissue for transplant—a mere hypothetical possibility at present. In that case, paying for the abortion is not a fee to donate tissue, but payment of the costs of acquiring the donated tissue, comparable to paying the cost of the nephrectomy that makes a kidney donation possible. Other out-of-pocket costs incurred by the donor could also be reimbursed without violating federal law or ethical constraints.

In contrast, when the abortion is performed for reasons unrelated to tissue procurement, paying abortion expenses amounts to paying the women to donate the tissue. This payment would constitute a sale of fetal tissue and should not be permitted if fetal tissue sales are prohibited.[29] The willingness of most women to donate without a fee should make payment of abortion expenses unnecessary.

Retrieval costs and for-profit agencies. In the past researchers have obtained fetal tissue through informal contacts with physicians doing abortions, often in the same institution. More recently, agencies that retrieve tissue from abortion facilities and distribute it to researchers have developed. In some cases for-profit firms that specialize in processing the tissue for transplant may enter the field.

What role will money payments play in the operation of retrieval agencies? Under existing law tissue procurement agencies will be unable to pay women to donate fetal tissue. However, they should be free to pay the costs of personnel directly involved in retrieval, whether employees of the procurement agency or of the facility performing the abortion. For example, a tissue retrieval agency may reimburse the abortion clinic for using its space and staff to obtain consent for tissue donations and to retrieve tissue from aborted fetuses.[30]

In distributing fetal tissue to researchers and physicians, retrieval agencies should be able to recoup the expenses of procuring the tissue, including overhead and other operating expenses of the agency itself. Such payment is consistent with heart and kidney transplant recipients (or their payors) paying for the analogous costs of organ procurement.

If the retrieval agency is a for-profit enterprise, some profit margin should also be recognized in the amount it charges the recipient of the tissue. While some persons might argue that allowing any profit amounts to a sale of fetal tissue that risks treating it as a market commodity, those who organize resources and invest capital to provide viable fetal tissue for transplant are performing a useful social activity. Fears about treating donors and fetuses as commodities might justify policies against buying tissue from donors and abortion facilities. But they should not prevent giving for-profit firms the incentives necessary to organize the resources required to obtain fetal tissue altruistically. Such a practice would be consistent with the role of for-profit physicians, hospitals, drug companies, and air transport services in organ transplantation.

FEDERAL FUNDING

While existing federal regulations permit transplant research with tissue from aborted fetuses when state law permits, the question of whether the federal government should fund fetal tissue research nevertheless remains. A special panel was recently convened by the National Institutes of Health to advise the Assistant Secretary for Health on whether intramural and extramural research programs involving fetal tissue transplants should be supported.[31] The panel gave a positive recommendation, with restrictions on tissue procurement comparable to the existing federal regulations, but its approval does not guarantee that federal research funding will occur?[32]

Because funding decisions ordinarily do not infringe constitutional rights, the government is not obligated to fund fetal tissue research (or therapy), no matter how desirable it appears.[33] However, the arguments strongly favor supporting such research. Of overriding importance is the potential benefit to thousands of patients suffering from severe disease. Federal funding will also allow the government to play a more active oversight role than if it leaves the field entirely to private funding, as occurred with in vitro fertilization research.[34]

The arguments against federal research funding come from right-to-life groups that would remove the federal government entirely from any financial support of abortion in the United States. Research funding, however, does not subsidize the abortions making the tissue available. Nor, as we have seen, does it place an imprimatur of legitimacy on abortion, or encourage to any great extent abortions that would not otherwise have occurred.

If the politics of abortion lead to withdrawal of direct government funding of research with tissue from family planning abortions, the government should not penalize institutions that conduct such research with nonfederal funds by denying them other research assistance. The symbolic gains of refusing to fund other medical research in institutions doing nonfederally funded research with aborted fetuses are too few to justify the burden on researchers. Clearly at that point the link to abortion is too attenuated to claim complicity in or encouragement of it.

These same issues will be refought if fetal tissue transplants became a proven therapy for Parkinson's disease, diabetes, or other disorders. While the government is not constitutionally obligated to fund a given therapy, the case for federal funding of treatment is even stronger than for funding of research, because the benefits to patients are clearer. A policy of denying Medicare or Medicaid funding for safe and effective fetal tissue transplants would deprive needy patients of essential therapies simply to avoid speculative concerns about complicity and encouragement of abortion. A more prudent approach would be to fund all therapies that meet the general funding standards for these programs. Alternatively, the government's funding policies should distinguish between therapies dependent on tissue retrieved from family planning abortions and those dependent on tissue from abortions performed to provide tissue for transplant.

LEGAL BANS ON FETAL TISSUE TRANSPLANTS

While the UAGA in every state permits the mother to donate fetal tissue for transplant research and therapy, eight states ban the experimental use of dead aborted fetuses.[35] None of these laws distinguish tissue from family planning abortions and abortions performed solely to obtain fetal tissue. Six of the eight states ban experimental but not unexperimental use of aborted fetuses. None ban similar uses of other cadaveric tissue, including cadavers that resulted from homicide.[36]

As a policy matter, the case for a legal ban on all research uses of dead fetal tissue is weak. Given that the use of fetal remains from lawful abortions is at issue, such laws are difficult to sustain. They purport to show the state's respect for prenatal life, but they do it in such an irrational way that they are clearly vulnerable to constitutional attack on several grounds, including vagueness, irrationality, and interference with the right to abort and the recipient's right to medical care.[37] A case invalidating the Louisiana law will be a potent precedent in future attacks on these laws.[38]

Even laws that prohibited intrafamilial donations or donor designation of recipients, which aim to prevent women from conceiving and aborting to produce fetal tissue, would be vulnerable if such practices were necessary to provide transplants to sick patients.[39] If the woman is already pregnant, such laws would prevent her from aborting to provide tissue. If not yet pregnant, they would arguably interfere with marital and procreative privacy or the recipient's right to life and medical care. A state's interest in preventing women from becoming "tissue farms," from abusing the reproductive process, or from being pressured to donate would not justify intrusion on such fundamental rights when the patient had no other alternative.[40]

SYMBOLIC AND RIGHTS-BASED CONCERNS

Ethical concerns should not bar research with fetal tissue transplants as a therapy for serious illness. Although many persons have ethical reservations about abortion, a wide range of opinion would likely support many research uses of fetal tissue, particularly when the abortions occur for reasons other than tissue procurement.

The use of fetal tissue inevitably implicates the strong feelings that abortion engenders. The disparate issues raised, however, can be treated separately, so that ethical concerns and the politics of abortion do not impede the progress of important research. For example, transplants with fetal tissue from family planning abortions do not necessarily entail approval of pregnancy and abortion undertaken to produce tissue for transplant. Nor will recognizing the woman's right to donate fetal tissue cause fetuses to be bought and sold, or women to be paid to abort.

In the final analysis, fetal tissue transplants raise symbolic questions as well as questions of rights. The symbolic issues raised by fetal tissue transplants cut in many directions. Sorting out symbolic and rights-based concerns will help to respect both important ethical values and the need for progress in medical science.

NOTES

1. 45 CFR 46.209; John A. Robertson, "Relaxing the Death Standard for Pediatric Organ Donations," in *Organ Substitution Technology: Ethical, Legal, and Public Policy Issues* (Boulder, CO: Press, 1988), 69–77.
2. John A. Robertson, "Fetal Tissue Transplants," *Washington University Law Quarterly* 66:3 (November 1988).
3. 45 CFR 46.210.
4. Stanley K. Henshaw *et al.*, "A Portrait of American Women Who Obtain Abortions," *Family Planning Perspectives* 17:2 (1985), 90–96.
5. Kevin Lafferty, Statement to the Fetal Tissue Transplantation Research Panel, NIH, Sept. 15, 1988.
6. James Burtchaell, "Case Study: University Policy on Experimental Use of Aborted Fetal Tissue," *IRB: A Review of Human Subjects Research* 10:4 (July/August 1988), 7–11.
7. Burtchaell, "Case Study," 10; Phillip Shabecoff, "Head of E.P.A. Bars Nazi Data in Study in Gas," *New York Times,* March 23, 1988, 1.
8. Leonard Tushnet, *The Uses of Adversity: Studies of Starvation in the Warsaw Ghetto* (New York: Thomas Yoseloff, 1966); "Minnesota Scientist Plans to Publish a Nazi Study," *New York Times,* May 12, 1988, 9.
9. Tamar Lewin, "Medical Use of Fetal Tissue Spurs New Abortion Debate," *New York Times,* Aug. 16, 1987, A1.
10. John A. Robertson, "Fetal Tissue Transplants."
11. Mary B. Mahowald, Jerry Silver, and Robert A. Ratcheson, "The Ethical Options in Transplanting Fetal Tissue," *Hastings Center Report* 17:2 (February 1987), 9–15; Mark Danis, "Fetal Tissue Transplants: Restricting Recipient Designation," *Hastings Law Journal* 39:5 (July 1988), 1079–1107.
12. Clifford Grobstein, *Science and the Unborn* (New York: Basic Books, 1988).
13. John A. Robertson, "Gestational Burdens and Fetal Status: A Defense of *Roe v. Wade,*" *American Journal of Law and Medicine* 13:2/3 (1988), 189–212; John Bigelow and Robert Pargetter, "Morality, Potential Persons, and Abortion," *American Philosophical Quarterly* 25 (1988), 173–81.

14. See, for example, "America's Abortion Dilemma," *Newsweek*, January 14, 1985, 22–26.

15. John A. Robertson, "Embryos, Families, and Procreative Liberty: The Legal Structure of the New Reproduction," *Southern California Law Review* 59 (1986), 939–1041.

16. John A. Robertson, "Taking Consent Seriously: IRB Interventions in the Consent Process," *IRB: A Review of Human Subjects Research* 4:5 (May 1982), 1–5.

17. Uniform Anatomical Gift Act, 8A U.L.A. 15–16 (West 1983 and Supp. 1987) (Table of Jurisdictions Wherein Act Has Been Adopted); 45 CFR 46.207(b).

18. Burtchaell, "Case Study," 8; Mary B. Mahowald, "Placing Wedges Along a Slippery Slope: Use of Fetal Neural Tissue for Transplantation," *Clinical Research* 36 (1988), 220–23.

19. John A. Robertson, "Supply and Distribution of Hearts for Transplantation: Legal, Ethical, and Policy Issues," *Circulation* 75 (1987), 77–88.

20. Robertson, "Supply and Distribution"; Department of Health and Human Services, *Organ Transplantation: Issues and Recommendations. Report of the Task Force on Organ Transplantation*, April 1986, 30.

21. 45 CFR 46.206(a).

22. 45 CFR 46.206(a)(4).

23. Margaret Radin, "Market Inalienability," *Harvard Law Review* 100 (1987), 1849–1931; Thomas H. Murray, "Gifts of the Body and the Needs of Strangers," *Hastings Center Report* 17:2 (April 1987), 30–38.

24. Alan Fine, "The Ethics of Fetal Tissue Transplants: *Hastings Center Report* 18:3 (June 1988): 5–8. Mahowald, Silver, and Ratcheson, "The Ethical Options."

25. 42 U.S.C.A. No. 247e (West Supp. 1985).

26. 28, Ark. Stat. Ann. §82-459 (Supp. 1985); Ill. Stat. Ann. ch. 38, §81.54(7) (Smith-Hurd 1983); La. Civ. Code Ann.art. 9:122 (Supp. 1987); Ohio Rev. Code Ann. §2919.14 (Page 1985); Okla. Stat. tit. 63, §1-753 (1987); Fla. Stat. Ann. §873.05 (West Supp. 1987); Mass. Gen. Laws Ann. ch. 112, §1593 (19640); Me. Rev. Stat. Ann. Tit. 22, §1593 (1964); Mich. Comp. Laws Ann. §333.2690 (West); Minn.Stat.Ann. §145.422 (West Supp. 1986);

N.D. Cent. Code §14-022-02 (1981); Nev. Rev. Stat. §451.015 (1985); R.I. Gen. Laws §11-54-1(f) (Supp. 1987); Tenn. Code Ann. §39-4-208 (Supp. 1987); Tex. Penal Code Ann. §42.10,48.02 (Vernon 1974 and Supp. 1988); Wyo. Stat. §35-6-115 (1986); 18 Pa. Cons. Stat. 3216 (Purdon 1983). See also "Note, Regulating the Sale of Human Organs," *Virginia Law Review* 71 (1985), 1015–38.

27. John A. Robertson," Technology and Motherhood: Legal and Ethical Issues in Human Egg Donation," *Case Western Reserve Law Review* 39:1 (1988) (forthcoming).

28. National Organ Transplant Act, 42 U.S.C.A. 274e (West Supp. 1985).

29. National Organ Transplant Act.

30. National Organ Transplant Act.

31. G. Kolata, "Federal Agency Bars Implanting of Fetal Tissue," *New York Times*, April 16, 1988, 1.

32. "Fetal Tissue 'Acceptable' for Research," *Washington Post*, September 17, 1988, 1; Barbara Culliton, "White House Wants Fetal Research Ban," *Science* (Sept. 16, 1988), 1423.

33. *McCrae v. Harris*, 448 U.S. 297 (1980); *Beal v. Doe*, 432 U.S. 438 (1977); *Poelher v. Doe*, 432 U.S. 519 (1977) (*per curiam*).

34. John Fletcher and Kenneth Ryan, "Federal Regulations for Fetal Research: A Case for Reform," *Law, Medicine, and Health Care* 15:3 (Fall 1987), 126–28.

35. 37. Ark. Stat. Arm. §82-438 (Supp. 1985); Ariz. Rev. Stat. Ann. §36-2302 (1986); Ind. Code Ann. §35-1-58.5-6 (West 1986); Ill. Ann. Stat. ch. 38, §81-54(7) (Smith-Hurd 1983); La. Rev. Stat. Ann. §1299.35.13 (West 1986); Ohio Rev. Code Ann. §2919.14 (Page 1985); Okla. Stat. tit. 63, §1-735; N.M. Stat. Ann. §§24-9A-3, 24-9A-3, 24-9A-5 (1986).

36. A Missouri law bans use of fetal tissue produced for transplant purposes, but not fetal tissue from family planning abortions. Missouri HB No. 1479 (1988).

37. Robertson, "Fetal Tissue Transplants"; "Note: State Prohibition of Fetal Experimentation and the Fundamental Right of Privacy." *Columbia Law Review* 88 (1988), 1073–1109.

38. *Margaret S. v. Edwards*, 794 F.2d 944 (5th 1986).

39. Robertson, "Fetal Tissue Transplants."

40. Danis, "Fetal Tissue Transplants."

Discussion Questions

1. Briefly summarize the "complicity in abortion" as well as the "legitimizing, entrenching, and encouraging abortion" arguments against fetal transplantation. Present and explain Professor Robertson's responses to these arguments. Do you agree or disagree with his reasoning? Explain and defend your answer.

2. What is Professor Robertson's position on a woman intentionally becoming pregnant in order to donate fetal tissue to a relative or a nonrelative? How does he defend his position? Do you agree or disagree with his reasoning? Explain and defend your answer.

3. Many opponents of transplantation of fetal tissue from elective abortions argue that the woman has no parental right to dispose of the tissue as she wishes since she is the one who killed "her child." How does Professor Robertson respond to this argument? Do you find his case compelling? Why or why not?

4. Present and explain Professor Robertson's position on the commercialization of fetal tissue.

5. Present and explain Professor Robertson's position on the federal funding of fetal tissue transplantation.

You can locate InfoTrac-College Education articles about this chapter by accessing the InfoTrac-College Edition website (http://www.infotrac-college.com/wadsworth/). Using the InfoTrac-College Edition subject guide, enter the search terms relevant to this chapter, and then read abstracts for relevant articles.

23   Spare Parts from the Unborn?: The Ethics of Fetal Tissue Transplantation

SCOTT B. RAE

Scott B. Rae is Associate Professor of Biblical Studies and Christian Ethics at Talbot School of Theology, Biola University (La Mirada, California). He has contributed to a number of scholarly journals as well as authoring the books *The Ethics of Surrogate Motherhood: Brave New Families?* (1994) and *Body & Soul: Human Nature and the Crisis in Ethics* (2000).

In this essay Professor Rae maintains that it is morally wrong to use fetal tissue for experimentation if the fetus's death did not result from a spontaneous abortion, that is, a miscarriage. Professor Rae points out that proponents of using fetal tissue from elective abortions either imply or claim that their position is within the framework of the Uniform Anatomical Gift Act (UAGA), arguing that the dead fetus is parallel to the adult cadaver as an organ donor. Professor Rae claims that it

Reprinted by permission from Christian Research Journal *(fall 1991). This essay has been edited for this text.*

is *not* parallel to adult organ transplants, because (1) the fetus's death is not accidental but caused intentionally, (2) it is impossible to receive valid consent from the donor (fetus) or proxy (the mother), (3) the fetus is both donor and donation, and (4) the gift (the fetus) cannot at the same time be both worthless (under *Roe v. Wade*) and priceless (as an organ donation). Professor Rae also argues that proposed restrictions, such as banning financial inducements, are unenforceable, that fetal tissue donation will enhance abortion's image (which he considers a negative development), and there are possibilities for serious abuse. He concludes with recommending an alternative: use only fetal tissue from spontaneous abortions and ectopic pregnancies (tubal pregnancies where abortion is necessary to save the mother's life).

THE ETHICS OF FETAL TISSUE TRANSPLANTS

As WE CONSIDER THE ethical issues pertaining to fetal tissue transplants, three primary positions have emerged. The first not only justifies the use of the tissue from induced abortion; it also permits the conceiving woman to specify the person who receives the donated tissue. Thus, one may conceive *solely* for tissue donation (normally for a family member or relative), and even recruit unrelated women to conceive in order to donate the tissue.[1]

The idea of conceiving life solely to terminate it and use the remains strikes most people as morally repugnant since the fetus is overtly used as a means and not an end, treated as a thing and not a person or potential person. For example, a Southern California family recently acknowledged publicly that the mother had conceived solely to provide a bone marrow match for her teenage daughter suffering from leukemia.[2] There were significant ethical concerns raised, even though there was no intent at any point to terminate the pregnancy. The child would grow up to enjoy a normal life irrespective of donor compatibility. The strong reaction in a case where the pregnancy will continue helps one understand the discomfort many feel over terminating a pregnancy for the purpose of donating tissue. Even if one

granted that the fetus may not have full personhood from the point of conception (an assumption that is clearly inconsistent with a biblical medical ethic), it would still have some interests and be entitled to certain protections under the law. It cannot be argued that the fetus is morally neutral in the same way an organ or a piece of tissue is. The fetus is at least a *potential* person not to be treated merely as a piece of tissue that is exclusively the property of the woman. To legitimate the use of fetal tissue to this degree makes a powerful statement that life in the womb can be used without any consideration for its *potential* to become a fully human being—let alone its *already realized* status, according to the pro-life position, as fully human.

The second position also justifies the use of the tissue, but prohibits the right of the conceiving mother to donate the tissue to whom she pleases. This is essentially the position recommended by the NIH Panel in their December 1988 report.

The third position prohibits the use of all fetal tissue obtained from induced abortions. Since abortion done for family planning purposes cannot in any sense be considered good, the use of fetal tissue obtained from abortion is morally tainted. In addition, this position points out the difficulty with which lines are drawn that restrict the use of the tissue, and argues that there is nothing to prevent one from ending up with the commercialization of organs and human tissue.[3]

ARGUMENTS AGAINST FETAL TISSUE TRANSPLANTS FROM ELECTIVE ABORTION

Not Parallel to Adult Organ Transplants

Advocates of fetal tissue transplants either assume or explicitly invoke the framework of the Uniform Anatomical Gift Act (UAGA). The UAGA has governed adult organ transplants for some time, and recently—with the rise of fetal tissue transplant technology—the law was expanded to include the fetus as an organ donor. The relevant part of the UAGA framework is the parallel between the dead fetus and the adult cadaver as an organ donor.

In a recent article in *Christianity Today*, Dr. Billy Arant, Jr., of the University of Texas Southwestern Medical Center, makes this parallel when he compares the debate on fetal tissue transplants to the earlier debate on organ donations in general: "The ethical and moral concerns raised during the early years when human organ transplantation was considered experimental were not very different from the ones heard today regarding the use of fetal tissue."[4] Later he asks, "Where, then, is the difference in using tissue obtained from human fetuses to restore health or extend life, especially if the tissue is obtained from fetuses aborted spontaneously—which will occur unpredictably in many pregnancies—just as accidental deaths provide a source of donor organs?"[5] This is precisely the parallel that is appropriate, and there is no moral difficulty with using the tissue from spontaneous abortions. However, most fetal tissue used in transplants comes from induced, not spontaneous, abortions. There are enormous differences between fetal tissue transplants from induced abortions and adult organ transplantations from accidental deaths; these render this parallel highly invalid. The use of the tissue from induced abortion is inconsistent with the UAGA framework, since:

(1) The death of the fetus is intentionally caused, not accidental. Though a small amount of fetal tissue from miscarriages and ectopic pregnancies is useful for transplants, the great majority of fetal tissue becomes available when a woman agrees to end her pregnancy *intentionally,* thus killing the developing fetus. This is hardly the same as when organs are recovered from someone killed in a tragic accident, LeRoy Walters, the Chairman of the Ethical and Legal Issues of the NIH Panel, said in 1974 (when only experimentation with the fetus, not tissue transplants, was being deliberated): "Ought one to make experimental use of the products of an abortion system, when one would object on ethical grounds to many or most of the abortions performed within that system? If a particular hospital became the beneficiary of an organized homicide system which provided a fresh supply of cadavers, one would be justified in raising questions about the moral appropriateness of the hospital's continuing cooperation with the suppliers."[6]

A better parallel might be a banker who regards the drug trade as morally wrong, yet agrees to accept drug money at his bank in order to finance low income housing for the community. This banker would be involved in complicity with the drug trade, even though he is not involved with the actual sale of narcotics.

(2) Valid consent is impossible. To date, fetal tissue transplants have been treated as any other organ transplants under the UAGA, thus requiring consent of next of kin. The mother cannot give morally legitimate consent, since she initiated the termination of the pregnancy. Elimination of consent, however, would further turn the unborn child into an object;

it would be inconsistent with the fact that, biologically, the developing fetus does not represent the woman's tissue.

The UAGA and the NIH Panel both fail to recognize the difference between normal organ transplants and the use of fetal tissue. In the case of fetal tissue, the mother is presumed to be the one who gives consent to the use of the tissue for the transplant (or for some other form of experimentation). According to the normal understanding of proxy consent, her role assumes that she is acting in the best interest of the unborn child. Yet, she is *also* the one who has initiated the termination of the pregnancy. The late ethicist Paul Ramsey concluded that it is morally outrageous and a charade to give the woman who aborts any right to proxy consent for the donation of or experimentation on the aborted fetus's body parts.[7] James Bopp and Father James Burtchaell conclude in their dissent from the NIH Panel Report, "We can think of no sound precedent for putting a living human into the power of such an estranged person, not for his or her own welfare, but for the 'interests' of the one in power."

Ironically, some who support fetal tissue transplants have argued that the aborted fetus would have "desired" to help those suffering from diseases that the tissue would benefit. This idea of fetal desire was first put forth in the attempt to justify research on living, nonviable fetuses. Case Western University ethicist Mary Mahowald and her team use this concept to justify not only fetal experiments but also tissue transplants, and appeal to Catholic ethicist Richard McCormick's concept that children, as members of the moral community, have a responsibility to be subjects in research that will benefit that community. (However, McCormick was arguing for the obligation of *children*, not *fetuses*, as research subjects.) When Mahowald and associates make this appeal, they are caught between affirming that the fetus has a responsibility as part of the moral community, and excluding it from the

same community since it has no recognized right to life.[8]

One may object to the need for consent in the first place, if the fetus is not considered a person. Yet this fails to recognize why fetal tissue is so valuable: *precisely because it is human.* Biologically, the fetus is much more than an organ or a piece of tissue. It is a developing human being with *at least* the potential for full personhood and thus *at least* the potential for full membership in the moral community from the time of conception. (It is not necessary here to argue that the fetus has full personhood from the time of conception, only that its potential to assume personhood makes it qualitatively different from an organ or other piece of tissue. Though the only logical point during pregnancy in which to recognize the full personhood of the unborn child is at conception, one does not need to press this point in order to oppose fetal tissue transplants.) Since abortion is taking innocent human life, all use of fetal tissue for experiments and treatment is ethically troubling—it is doing evil to accomplish good. The notion of the fetus as the source of biological "spare parts" is uncomfortably reminiscent of Aldous Huxley's *Brave New World.*[9]

(3) There is an equation of the donor and the donation of the tissue. A more significant problem is encountered when one considers that the fetus is simultaneously both a *donation* and a *donor.* It is difficult to see how a fetus can be called a donor under the UAGA in parallel to an adult organ donor, if the personhood of the fetus is discounted. The fetus is a victim rather than a willing donor. When the donation of fetal tissue is described as a gift from the fetus as a donor, only miscarriages and ectopic pregnancies can stand on a moral basis, since these fetuses were only *unable,* and not *unwelcome,* to join the human community.[10]

This is not a parallel to surrogate motherhood, where the mother is viewed as the donor and the tissue as the donation. Mahowald and associates equate the "moral problems thus raised [in fetal tissue transplants] to those that may occur in surrogate motherhood." However, they earlier acknowledge that "with fetal tissue transplantation (as with transplantation in general), a bad effect (loss of an organ or tissue) is suffered for the sake of the recipient, and there is no similarly bad effect in surrogacy." Their suggestion then that the parallel with surrogate motherhood helps provide some of the guidelines for fetal tissue transplantation ignores the obvious discontinuity, that the death of the fetus results from the transplants. This is hardly only a "bad effect," it is the destruction of the fetus.[11]

(4) The "gift" of the tissue transplant cannot be both priceless and worthless at the same time. The use of the term "gift" is, to say the least, inappropriate when induced abortion is the means by which the gift is made available. If the fetus has no value, how can the tissue be legitimately called a gift and the fetus a donor? Few seem prepared to reject the UAGA framework to govern the use of fetal tissue. Yet the inadequacy of the language to describe the "gift" of a fetus reflects a strange ambivalence about the nature of the fetus.

Kathleen Nolan of the Hastings Center describes the alternative if the UAGA framework is rejected: "If we reject the framework of the UAGA, we seem doomed to accept arguments that implicitly or explicitly equate fetuses with things or beings that they are not—among them kidneys, tumors and discarded surgical specimens. Yet biologically, the fetus is not a tissue or an organ but a body, and morally, the fetus is a developing being and potential member of the human community. Fetal remains accordingly ought to evoke emotions and protections beyond those given tumorous tissue or unwanted organs."[12]

PROPOSED RESTRICTIONS ARE UNENFORCEABLE

Given the growing public awareness of medical technology and the increasing benefits that will be made available, *keeping the two distinct acts of consent (abortion and tissue donation) separate is virtually impossible*. All of the proposed guidelines treat this as one of the non-negotiable aspects of the transplants. It would not be difficult to imagine that, given separate consent forms, coercion to donate tissue would enter in, in view of potential transplant benefits, the likely scarcity of available tissue as the technology develops, and the vulnerability of women anticipating an abortion.

Given the potentially lucrative market for the transplants, keeping *financial inducements* from entering in would be difficult, and impossible to enforce. For example, Hana Biologics, one of the firms testifying before the NIH Panel, estimates the total market for using the fetal pancreatic tissue to treat diabetes amounts to approximately six billion dollars annually.[13] This obviously has the potential to become very big business.

Abortion clinics stand to reap a substantial increase in revenue simply from the small amount (on average, $25 per organ, multiplied by the hundreds of thousands of abortions performed annually) that the nonprofit acquisition organizations offer. The financial incentives to "recruit" fetal tissue donors would be significant. Moreover, there are numerous noncash inducements that are difficult to detect and impossible to adequately police that would be especially appealing to poor and minority women. For example, the clinic could offer a "discount" on the abortion procedure itself or promise to provide future medical care for a specified time following the donation of the tissue. With the anticipated profitability of the industry once the technology can alleviate a larger number of diseases, there will be increasing pressures to "share the wealth" produced by these transplants.

A recent California court decision may set a precedent that will make it more difficult to prevent women from obtaining compensation for the donation of fetal tissue. In Moore v. Regents of the University of California, an appeals court reversed a lower court decision, ruling that a person does have a property interest in his or her own cells.[14] In treatment for leukemia, doctors at the UCLA Medical Center removed the spleen of a Mr. Moore, and discovered that they could manufacture a cell line from that tissue that was effective in slowing certain types of leukemia. The medical center then sought out a commercial arrangement with a pharmaceutical company to market the cell line. When asked for his consent, Moore refused and sued the University for his share of any profit resulting from the cell line. Though the court did not rule on his right to compensation, they did hold that individuals have a property interest in their own cells, and thus a right to control what becomes of their tissues. One can see how this could open the door not only to financial inducements but to a *right* to compensation for fetal tissue donation.

This potentially lucrative market will make it increasingly difficult to enforce another of the proponents' guidelines, *the separation of the transplant physician/researcher and the one who performs the abortion*. This is a key distinction for transplant proponents, even for those who are against abortion in most cases, who assume that the morality of abortion and transplants can be separated. Yet, clearly, the means as well as the end have moral significance.

For the best medical results there would need to be an institutional, symbiotic relationship with the abortion industry, thereby making the separation of abortion and tissue procurement very difficult. This partnership will also make it more complicated to isolate the timing and method of abortion from what is

necessary to procure the best possible tissue. Mahowald and associates already propose that pregnancies be prolonged and the method of abortion be modified, if necessary, in order to procure the most fresh, and thus the most useful tissue.[15] In addition, some acknowledge the legitimate possibility of tissue being removed from live, nonviable fetuses.

REDEEMING ABORTION?

Fetal tissue transplants from induced abortions will serve to enhance abortion's image—to many it will at least seem morally neutral. At a minimum, donating tissue would offer relief from some of the guilt that many women feel when electing abortion, thus alleviating some of the ambivalence that usually accompanies it. Though our society tragically permits abortion, most do not view abortion itself as good. Even the most vocal pro-choice advocates acknowledge that it is the *right to choose* that is good, not the act of terminating a pregnancy itself.

The prospect of donating tissue is not likely to dramatically increase abortions unless the pregnant mother is allowed to designate who receives the tissue. But it would certainly *contribute* to the decision to abort and might push some women "over the line." The routine retrieval of the tissue would no doubt make the unborn's death seem less tragic. Nolan puts it this way: "Enhancing abortion's image could thus be expected to undermine efforts to make it as little needed and little used a procedure as possible."[16]

Even some tissue transplant advocates acknowledge that they may create a greater incentive to abortion, or may lead women to decide for abortion who would not otherwise.[17] This argument against the transplants distinguishes between abortion and the freedom to choose abortion. Many pro-choice advocates are increasingly uncomfortable with the number of abortions performed in this country. Many see the increased effectiveness of contraception as good because it prevents the occurrence of the trauma and tragedy of surgical abortion. Even support for RU 486 (the "abortion pill," currently sold in much of Europe and the Third World, but not available in the United States) is based on this same notion. Thus, anything that would increase surgical abortions can hardly be considered good by anyone. Though our society recognizes the *legality* of abortion, we have rarely seen fit to actively *encourage* it.

Research shows great ambivalence toward abortion among women considering it.[18] There is usually intense anxiety during the final 24 hours before the abortion is performed. Studies of pregnant women choosing abortion show that between one-third and 40 percent change their minds at least once, and around 30 percent do not finally make up their mind until just prior to the procedure. Thus, it is likely that the prospect of solace over the guilt that usually accompanies abortion will enter into the complex set of factors that are involved in the decision to abort. The possibility of "redeeming abortion" throws a powerful human motivation into the already complex situation that will affect those one-third to 40 percent who change their minds during the process. Bopp and Burtchaell, in their dissent from the NIH Panel Report, state, "It is willful fantasy to imagine that young pregnant women estranged from their families and their sexual partners, and torn by the knowledge that they are with child, will not be powerfully relieved at the prospect that the sad act of violence they are reluctant to accept can now have redemptive value."

One wonders if government sponsorship of fetal tissue transplants would have the same legitimizing influence on abortion that Roe v. Wade did. Though the justices in that decision clearly did not want to make a decision on the personhood of the fetus, it can be argued that by allowing abortion they did make a powerful statement that has "trickled down" to a significant part of society.

POSSIBILITIES FOR ABUSE

Some of the abuses that the proponents' regulations are designed to prohibit are already being seriously proposed by more radical proponents. These primarily deal with recipient designation of the tissue. Though the "slide down the slippery slope" can likely be stopped in the short term, given the promise of the technology, it is doubtful that long-term pressures can be resisted to allow women to conceive in order to abort and thus donate the tissue. As interest groups—many of whom testified before the NIH Panel—become more dependent on this tissue, further complicating the ability of society to stop the descent down the slippery slope before it reaches a place that only the most extreme proponents advocate.

There are thus possibilities for abuse about which even the more moderate advocates are wary. Already there have been people not simply *willing* but eager to conceive just to donate the tissue.[19] Fetal tissue is currently being used to make cosmetics in Sweden, and fetal kidneys from Brazil and India are being sold in West Germany to physicians for transplant.[20] It is true that most advocates recommend some laws or voluntary guidelines to keep such abuses from taking place. These may be adequate for the short run, but there are no guarantees that these kinds of abuses can be prevented in the long run as the process becomes more acceptable. This opposition to the transplants is not "burning down the barn to roast the pig," but rather, stopping the descent down the slippery slope at the top. It is naive to think that the long-run pressure can be resisted, given the powerful incentives to donate the tissue that the advances in medical science promise to provide.

A VALID ALTERNATIVE

One viable alternative is the combination of the use of tissue from spontaneous abortions and ectopic pregnancies for both transplants *and* the development of cell cultures from the most promising tissue. This is already being done for diabetes. Also, the development of neuroblastoma cells shows promise for treating Parkinson's disease. The American Paralysis Association's statement to the NIH Panel encouraged adequate funding to develop tissue cloning that will bypass the need for the fetus per se.

My opposition to fetal tissue transplants from induced abortion is essentially that of the British Medical Association in their interim guidelines.[21] The first of these guidelines is the most relevant for this section: "Tissue may be obtained only from dead foetuses [*sic*] resulting from therapeutic or spontaneous abortion." These guidelines reflect the statement of the Council of Europe, adopted in September, 1986. As of July, 1989, however, the British government had adopted the recommendation of the later Polkinghorne Report that fetal tissue transplants from induced abortions be allowed. Interestingly, the Committee suggested that the fetus does have the same moral status as a human being from the fourteenth day after conception. In contradiction to this, they denied that there is any inherent immorality involved in using the tissue from an induced abortion. If the fetus has such full personhood, the arguments favoring abortion as well as fetal tissue transplants are very difficult to maintain.

I wish there were not ethical difficulties with fetal tissue transplants, since they hold promise for treating various diseases. Because of the moral tensions involved, I support the continuation of the moratorium on research and transplants of fetal tissue from induced abortions. One hopes for the day when cell culture technology will have advanced to the point where fetal tissue from induced abortions. One hopes for the day when cell culture technology will have advanced to the point where fetal tissue from induced abortions will no longer be needed to achieve the same benefits.

NOTES

1. This position appears in the writing of John A. Robertson in two principal articles: "Fetal Tissue Transplants," *Washington University Law Quarterly* 66 (1988):443–98; and "Rights, Symbolism, and Public Policy in Fetal Tissue Transplants," *Hastings Center Report* 18 (December 1988): 5–12.

2. The intent of the family to conceive solely for the bone marrow donor is underscored by the fact that the father underwent surgery to reverse a vasectomy six months prior to conception of the child who will be the donor. See *Orange County Register*, Sect. B, 31 August 1990. The bone marrow transplant was performed in May, 1991.

3. This position is represented by James Bopp, Esq. and Father James Burtchaell in their dissent from the majority opinion of the NIH Panel.

4. Billy S. Arant, Jr., "Why the Government Should Lift the Moratorium," *Christianity Today*, 19 November 1990, 28.

5. *Ibid.*

6. LeRoy Walters, "Ethical Issues in Experimentation on the Human Fetus," *Journal of Religious Ethics* 2 (Spring 1974): 41, 48.

7. Paul Ramsey, *The Ethics of Fetal Research* (New Haven: Yale University Press, 1975): 89.

8. This point is made by Kathleen Nolan, "Genug Ist Genug: A Fetus Is Not a Kidney," *Hastings Center Report* 18 (Dec. 1988): 14. The reference to Mahowald and team is taken from Mary B. Mahowald, Jerry Silver, and Robert A. Ratcheson, "The Ethical Options in Transplanting Fetal Tissue," *Hastings Center Report* 17 (February 1987): 9–15.

9. Stuart Newman, "Statement on Proposed Uses of Human Fetal Tissue," *Panel Report*, vol. 2, D207.

10. Nolan, 18.

11. Mahowald, et al., 12, 15.

12. Nolan, 16.

13. Karen Southwick, "Fetal Tissue Market Draws Profits, Rebuke," *Health Week*, 12 October 1987, 1.

14. *Moore v. Regents of the University of California*, California Court of Appeal, 249 Cal.

Rptr. 494 (1988). Review granted by California Supreme Court, 252 Cal. Rptr. 816
(10 November 1988).

15. Mahowald, et al., 7–15.

16. Nolan, 17.

17. Concern that the use of fetal tissue for transplantation in such cases could become an
incentive for abortion thus appears well
grounded. Alan Fine, "The Ethics of Fetal
Tissue Transplants," *Hastings Center Report*
18 (June/July 1988): 6.

18. Michael Bracken, Lorraine Klerman, and
Mary Ann Bracken, "Abortion, Adoption
or Motherhood: An Empirical Study of
Decision-Making During Pregnancy," *American Journal of Obstetrics and Gynecology* 130
(1978): 256–57.

19. Tamar Lewin, "Medical Use of Fetal Tissue
Spurs New Abortion Debate," *New York
Times,* 16 August 1987, 1.

20. Debra McKenzie, "Third World Kidneys for
Sale," *New Scientist,* 28 March 1985, 7;
"Embryos to Lipsticks?" *New Scientist,*
10 October 1985, 21.

21. See David Dickson, "Fetal Tissue Transplants
Win U.K. Approval," *Science* 245 (4 August
1989):464–65.

Discussion Questions

1. Present and explain the four reasons why Professor Rae does not think the dead fetus is
   parallel to the adult cadaver as organ donor. Do you agree with his reasoning? Why or
   why not? Explain and defend your answer.

2. What are some of the abuses Professor Rae believes will occur if fetal tissue from elective abortions is allowed to be used for medical research? Do you agree with his concerns? Explain and defend your answer.

3. If the current law concerning fetal personhood *(Roe v. Wade)* states that fetuses are nonpersons, why should we worry about Professor Rae's concerns if so much good for actual
   persons may be able to come from fetal tissue research? If you disagree with Professor
   Rae, do you think there should be *any* restrictions on the use of fetal tissue? Explain and
   defend your answer. If you agree with Professor Rae, explain and defend his alternative
   to using fetuses who have died as a result of elective abortions.

4. Why does Professor Rae hold that one does not have to be pro-life on abortion in order
   to oppose the transplantation of fetal tissue from elective abortions?

You can locate InfoTrac-College Education articles about this chapter by accessing the InfoTrac-College
Edition website (http://www.infotrac-college.com/wadsworth/). Using the InfoTrac-College Edition
subject guide, enter the search terms relevant to this chapter, and then read abstracts for relevant articles.

The Wisdom of Repugnance

24

LEON KASS

Leon Kass is the Addie Clark Harding Professor in the Committee of Social Thought and the College of the University of Chicago. Among his books are *The Hungry Soul: Eating and the Perfecting of Our Nature* (1994) and *Toward a More Natural Science: Biology and Human Affairs* (1988).

Professor Kass, in this essay, argues that human cloning should be declared "unethical in itself and dangerous in its likely consequences." He believes that people's initial repugnance toward the practice of human cloning is the result of an inarticulate moral wisdom that should be taken seriously. After some initial comments about cloning and government regulation, Professor Kass argues that even though there is strong opposition to cloning, "cloning turns out to be the perfect embodiment of the ruling opinions of our new age." For the moral principles of the sexual revolution that are already widely accepted concerning human copulation and reproduction (e.g., personal autonomy) may be appropriately extended to include human cloning. But Kass does not want to allow human cloning. So, he marshals a case that maintains that the visceral opposition to cloning is evidence that the moral principles of the sexual revolution are wrong. This is why he argues that the three contexts in which human cloning is discussed—technological, liberal, and meliorist—"all quintessentially American and all perfectly fine in their places, are sorely wanting as approaches to human procreation." He moves on to discuss the profundity of sex and the perversities of cloning. He then replies to some objections to his case. He concludes by calling for an absolute ban against human cloning.

I. INTRODUCTION

OUR HABIT OF DELIGHTING IN news of scientific and technological breakthroughs has been sorely challenged by the birth announcement of a sheep named Dolly. Though Dolly shares with previous sheep the "softest clothing, woolly, bright," William Blake's question, "Little Lamb, who made thee?"[1] has for her a radically different answer: Dolly was, quite literally, made. She is the work not of nature or nature's God but of man, an Englishman, Ian Wilmut, and his fellow scientists. What's more, Dolly came into being not only asexually—ironically, just like "He [who] calls Himself a Lamb"[2]—but also as the genetically identical copy (and the perfect incarnation of the form or blueprint) of a mature ewe, of whom she is a clone. This long-awaited yet not quite expected success in cloning a mammal raised immediately the prospect—and the specter—of cloning human beings: "I a child, and thou a lamb,"[3]

Reprinted by permission from Valparaiso University Law Review *32.2 (spring 1998), 679–705. An earlier version of this article was published in* The New Republic *(June 2, 1997).*

despite our differences, have always been equal candidates for creative making, only now, by means of cloning, we may both spring from the hand of man playing at being God.

After an initial flurry of expert comment and public consternation, with opinion polls showing overwhelming opposition to cloning human beings, President Clinton ordered a ban on all federal support for human cloning research (even though none was being supported) and charged the National Bioethics Advisory Commission (NBAC or Commission) to report in ninety days on the ethics of human cloning research. The Commission (an eighteen-member panel, evenly balanced between scientists and non-scientists, appointed by the President and reporting to the National Science and Technology Council) invited testimony from scientists, religious thinkers, and bioethicists, as well as from the general public. In its report, issued in June, 1997, the Commission concluded that attempting to clone a human being was "at this time . . . morally unacceptable"; recommended continuing the President's moratorium on the use of federal funds to support the cloning of humans; and called for federal legislation to prohibit anyone from attempting (during the next three to five years) to create a child through cloning.[4]

Even before the Commission reported, Congress was poised to act. Bills to prohibit the use of federal funds for human cloning research have been introduced in the House of Representatives[5] and the Senate[6]; and one bill, in the House, would make it illegal "for any person to use a human somatic cell for the process of producing a human clone."[7] A fateful decision is at hand. To clone or not to clone a human being is no longer an academic question.

II. TAKING CLONING SERIOUSLY, THEN AND NOW

Cloning first came to public attention roughly thirty years ago, following the successful asexual production, in England, of a clutch of tadpole clones by the technique of nuclear transplantation. The individual largely responsible for bringing the prospect and promise of human cloning to public notice was Joshua Lederberg, a Nobel Laureate geneticist and a man of large vision. In 1966, Lederberg wrote a remarkable article in *The American Naturalist* detailing the eugenic advantages of human cloning and other forms of genetic engineering, and the following year he devoted a column in *The Washington Post,* where he wrote regularly on science and society, to the prospect of human cloning.[8] He suggested that cloning could help us overcome the unpredictable variety that still rules human reproduction and allow us to benefit from perpetuating superior genetic endowments. These writings sparked a small public debate in which I became a participant. At the time a young researcher in molecular biology at the National Institutes of Health (NIH), I wrote a reply to the *Post,* arguing against Lederberg's amoral treatment of this morally weighty subject and insisting on the urgency of confronting a series of questions and objections, culminating in the suggestion that "the programmed reproduction of man will, in fact, dehumanize him."[9]

Much has happened in the intervening years. It has become harder, not easier, to discern the true meaning of human cloning. We have in some sense been softened up to the idea—through movies, cartoons, jokes, and intermittent commentary in the mass media, some serious, most lighthearted. We have become accustomed to new practices in human reproduction: not just *in vitro* fertilization (IVF), but also embryo manipulation, embryo donation, and surrogate pregnancy. Animal biotechnology has yielded transgenic animals and a burgeoning science of genetic engineering, easily and soon to be transferable to humans.

Even more important, changes in the broader culture make it now vastly more difficult to express a common and respectful understanding of sexuality, procreation, nascent life, family, and the meaning of motherhood, fatherhood, and the links between the generations. Twenty-five years ago, abortion was still largely illegal and thought to be immoral, the sexual revolution (made possible by the extra-marital use of the pill) was still in its infancy, and few had yet heard about the reproductive rights of single women, homosexual men, and lesbians. (Never mind shameless memoirs about one's own incest!) Then one could argue, without embarrassment, that the new technologies of human reproduction—babies without sex—and their confounding of normal kin relations (who is the mother: the egg donor, the surrogate who carries and delivers, or the one who rears?) would "undermine[ ] the justification and support which biological parenthood gives to the monogamous marriage."[10] Today, defenders of stable, monogamous marriage risk charges of giving offense to those adults who are living in "new family forms" or to those children who, even without the benefit of assisted reproduction, have acquired either three or four parents or one or none at all. Today, one must even apologize for voicing opinions that twenty-five years ago were nearly universally regarded as the core of our culture's wisdom on these matters. In a world whose once-given natural boundaries are blurred by technological change and whose moral boundaries are seemingly up for grabs, it is much more difficult to make persuasive the still-compelling case against cloning human beings. As Raskolnikov put it, "man gets used to everything—the beast!"[11]

Indeed, perhaps the most depressing feature of the discussions that immediately followed the news about Dolly was their ironical tone, their genial cynicism, their moral fatigue: *An Udder Way of Making Lambs,*[12] *Who Will Cash in on Breakthrough in Cloning?,*[13] and *Is Cloning a Baaad Idea?*[14] Gone from the scene are the wise and courageous voices of Theodosius Dobzhansky (genetics), Hans Jonas (philosophy), and Paul Ramsey (theology) who, only twenty-five years ago, all made powerful moral arguments against ever cloning a human being.[15] We are now too sophisticated for such argumentation; we wouldn't be caught in public with a strong moral stance, never mind an absolutist one. We are all, or almost all, post-modernists now.

Cloning turns out to be the perfect embodiment of the ruling opinions of our new age. Thanks to the sexual revolution, we are able to deny in practice, and increasingly in thought, the inherent procreative teleology of sexuality itself. But, if sex has no intrinsic connection to generating babies, babies need have no necessary connection to sex. Thanks to feminism and the gay rights movement, we are increasingly encouraged to treat the natural heterosexual difference and its preeminence as a matter of "cultural construction." But if male and female are not normatively complementary and generatively significant, babies need not come from male and female complementarity. Thanks to the prominence and acceptability of divorce and out-of-wedlock births, stable, monogamous marriage as the ideal home for procreation is no longer the agreed-upon cultural norm. For this new dispensation, the clone is the ideal emblem: the ultimate "single-parent child."

Thanks to our belief that all children should be *wanted* children (the more high-minded principle we use to justify contraception and abortion), sooner or later only those children who fulfill our wants will be fully acceptable. Through cloning, we can work our wants and wills on the very identity of our children, exercising control as never before. Thanks to modern notions of individualism and the rate of cultural change, we see ourselves not as linked to ancestors and defined by traditions, but as projects for our own self-creation, not only as self-made men but also man-made selves; and self-cloning is simply an extension of such rootless and narcissistic self-re-creation.

Unwilling to acknowledge our debt to the past and unwilling to embrace the uncertainties and the limitations of the future, we have a false relation to both: cloning personifies our desire fully to control the future, while being subject to no controls ourselves. Enchanted and enslaved by the glamour of technology, we have lost our awe and wonder before the deep mysteries of nature and of life. We cheerfully take our own beginnings in our hands and, like the last man, we blink.

Part of the blame for our complacency lies, sadly, with the field of bioethics itself, and its claim to expertise in these moral matters. Bioethics was founded by people who understood that the new biology touched and threatened the deepest matters of our humanity: bodily integrity, identity and individuality, lineage and kinship, freedom and self-command, eros and aspiration, and the relations and strivings of body and soul. With its capture by analytic philosophy, however, and its inevitable routinization and professionalization, the field has by and large come to content itself with analyzing moral arguments, reacting to new technological developments, and taking on emerging issues of public policy, all performed with a naive faith that the evils we fear can all be avoided by compassion, regulation, and a respect for autonomy. Bioethics has made some major contributions in the protection of human subjects and in other areas where personal freedom is threatened; but its practitioners, with few exceptions, have turned the big human questions into pretty thin gruel.

One reason for this is that the piecemeal formation of public policy tends to grind down large questions of morals into small questions of procedure. Many of the country's leading bioethicists have served on national commissions or state task forces and advisory boards, where, understandably, they have found utilitarianism to be the only ethical vocabulary acceptable to all participants in discussing issues of law, regulation, and public policy. As many of these commissions have been either officially under the aegis of NIH or the Health and Human Services Department, or otherwise dominated by powerful voices for scientific progress, the ethicists have for the most part been content, after some "values clarifica-tion" and wringing of hands, to pronounce their blessings upon the inevitable. Indeed, it is the bioethicists, not the scientists, who are now the most articulate defenders of human cloning: the two witnesses testifying before the NBAC in favor of cloning human beings were bioethicists,[16] eager to rebut what they regard as the irrational concerns of those of us in opposition. We have come to expect from the "experts" an accommodationist ethic that will rubber-stamp all biomedical innovation, in the mistaken belief that all other goods must bow down before the gods of better health and scientific advance. Regrettably, as we shall see near the end of this Article, the report of the present Commission, though better than its predecessors, is finally not an exception.

If we are to correct our moral myopia, we must first of all persuade ourselves not to be complacent about what is at issue here. Human cloning, though it is in some respects continuous with previous reproductive technologies, also represents something radically new, in itself and in its easily foreseeable consequences. The stakes are very high indeed. I exaggerate, but in the direction of the truth, when I insist that we are faced with having to decide nothing less than whether human procreation is going to remain human, whether children are going to be made rather than begotten, whether it is a good thing, humanly speaking, to say yes in principle to the road which leads (at best) to the dehumanized rationality of *Brave New World*.[17] This is not business as usual, to be fretted about for a while but finally to be given our seal of approval. We must rise to the occasion and make our judgments as if the future of our humanity hangs in the balance. For so it does.

III. THE STATE OF THE ART

If we should not underestimate the significance of human cloning, neither should we exaggerate its imminence or misunderstand just what is involved. The procedure is conceptually simple. The nucleus of a mature but unfertilized egg is removed and replaced with a nucleus obtained from a specialized cell of an adult (or fetal) organism (in Dolly's case, the donor nucleus came from mammary gland epithelium). Because almost all the hereditary material of a cell is contained within its nucleus, the renucleated egg and the individual into which this egg develops are genetically identical to the organism that was the source of the transferred nucleus. An unlimited number of genetically identical individuals—clones—could be produced by nuclear transfer. In principle, any person, male or female, newborn or adult, could be cloned, and in any quantity. With laboratory cultivation and storage of tissues, cells outliving their sources make it possible even to clone the dead.

The technical stumbling block, overcome by Wilmut and his colleagues, was to find a means of reprogramming the state of the DNA in the donor cells, reversing its differentiated expression and restoring its full totipotency, so that it could again direct the entire process of producing a mature organism. Now that this problem has been solved, we should expect a rush to develop cloning for other animals, especially livestock, in order to propagate in perpetuity the champion meat or milk producers. Though exactly how soon someone will succeed in cloning a human being is anybody's guess, Wilmut's technique, almost certainly applicable to humans, makes *attempting* the feat an imminent possibility.

Yet some cautions are in order, and some possible misconceptions need correcting. For a start, cloning is not Xeroxing. As has been reassuringly reiterated, the clone of Mel Gibson, though his genetic double, would enter the world hairless, toothless, and peeing in his diapers, just like any other human infant. Moreover, the success rate, at least at first, will probably not be very high: the British scientists transferred 277 adult nuclei into enucleated sheep eggs, and implanted twenty-nine clonal embryos, but they achieved the birth of only one live lamb clone. For this reason, among others, it is unlikely that, at least for now, the practice would be very popular, and there is no immediate worry of mass-scale production of multicopies. The need of repeated surgery to obtain eggs and, more crucially, of numerous borrowed wombs for implantation will surely limit use, as will the expense; besides, almost everyone who is able will doubtless prefer nature's sexier way of conceiving.

Still, for the tens of thousands of people already sustaining over 200 assisted-reproduction clinics in the United States and already availing themselves of IVF, intracytoplasmic sperm injection, and other techniques of assisted reproduction, cloning would be an option with virtually no added fuss (especially when the success rate improves). Should commercial interests develop in "nucleus-banking," as they have in sperm-banking; should famous athletes or other celebrities decide to market their DNA the way they now market their autographs and just about everything else; should techniques of embryo and germline genetic testing and manipulation arrive as anticipated, increasing the use of laboratory assistance in order to obtain "better" babies—should all this come to pass, then cloning, if it is permitted, could become more than a marginal practice simply on the basis of free reproductive choice, even without any social encouragement to upgrade the gene pool or to replicate superior types. Moreover, if laboratory research on human cloning proceeds, even without any intention to produce cloned humans, the existence of cloned human embryos in the laboratory, created to begin with only for research purposes, would surely pave the way for later baby-making implantations.

In anticipation of human cloning, apologists and proponents have already made clear possible uses of the perfected technology, ranging from the sentimental and compassionate to the grandiose. They include: providing a child for an infertile couple; "replacing" a beloved spouse or child who is dying or has died; avoiding the risk of genetic disease; permitting reproduction for homosexual men and lesbians who want nothing sexual to do with the opposite sex; securing a genetically identical source of organs or tissues perfectly suitable for transplantation; getting a child with a genotype of one's own choosing, not excluding oneself; replicating individuals of great genius, talent, or beauty—having a child who really could "be like Mike"; and creating large sets of genetically identical humans suitable for research on, for instance, the question of nature versus nurture, or for special missions in peace and war (not excluding espionage), in which using identical humans would be an advantage. Most people who envision the cloning of human beings, of course, want none of these scenarios. That they cannot say why is not surprising. What is surprising, and welcome, is that, in our cynical age, they are saying anything at all.

IV. THE WISDOM OF REPUGNANCE

"Offensive." "Grotesque." "Revolting." "Repugnant." "Repulsive." These are the words most commonly heard regarding the prospect of human cloning. Such reactions come both from the man or woman in the street and from intellectuals, from believers and atheists, from humanists and scientists. Even Dolly's creator has said he "would find it offensive"[18] to clone a human being.

People are repelled by many aspects of human cloning. They recoil from the prospect of the mass production of human beings, with large clones of look-alikes, compromised in their individuality; the idea of father-son or mother-daughter twins; the bizarre prospects of a woman giving birth to and rearing a genetic copy of herself, her spouse, or even her deceased father or mother; the grotesqueness of conceiving a child as an exact replacement

for another who has died; the utilitarian creation of embryonic genetic duplicates of oneself, to be frozen away or created when necessary, in case of need for homologous tissues or organs for transplantation; the narcissism of those who would clone themselves and the arrogance of others who think they know who deserves to be cloned or which genotype any child-to-be should be thrilled to receive; the Frankensteinian hubris to create human life and increasingly to control its destiny; man playing God. Almost no one finds any of the suggested reasons for human cloning compelling; almost everyone anticipates its possible misuses and abuses. Moreover, many people feel oppressed by the sense that there is probably nothing we can do to prevent it from happening. This makes the prospect all the more revolting.

Revulsion is not an argument; and some of yesterday's repugnances are today calmly accepted—though, one must add, not always for the better. In crucial cases, however, repugnance is the emotional expression of deep wisdom, beyond reason's power fully to articulate it. Can anyone really give an argument fully adequate to the horror which is father-daughter incest (even with consent), or having sex with animals, or mutilating a corpse, or eating human flesh, or even just (just!) raping or murdering another human being? Would anybody's failure to give full rational justification for his or her revulsion at these practices make that revulsion ethically suspect? Not at all. On the contrary, we are suspicious of those who think that they can rationalize away our horror, say, by trying to explain the enormity of incest with arguments only about the genetic risks of inbreeding.

Our repugnance at human cloning belongs in this category. We are repelled by the prospect of cloning human beings not because of the strangeness or novelty of the undertaking, but because we intuit and feel, immediately and without argument, the violation of things that we rightfully hold dear. Repugnance, here as elsewhere, revolts against the excesses of human willfulness, warning us not to transgress what is unspeakably profound. Indeed, in this age in which everything is held to be permissible so long as it is freely done, in which our given human nature no longer commands respect, in which our bodies are regarded as mere instruments of our autonomous rational wills, repugnance may be the only voice left that speaks up to defend the central core of our humanity. Shallow are the souls that have forgotten how to shudder.

The goods protected by repugnance are generally overlooked by our customary ways of approaching all new biomedical technologies. The way we evaluate cloning ethically will in fact be shaped by how we characterize it descriptively, by the context into which we place it, and by the perspective from which we view it. The first task for ethics is proper description. And here is where our failure begins.

Typically, cloning is discussed in one or more of three familiar contexts, which one might call the technological, the liberal, and the meliorist. Under the first, cloning will be seen as an extension of existing techniques for assisting reproduction and determining the genetic makeup of children. Like them, cloning is to be regarded as a neutral technique, with no inherent meaning or goodness, but subject to multiple uses, some good, some bad. The morality of cloning thus depends absolutely on the goodness or badness of the motives and intentions of the cloners: as one bioethicist defender of cloning puts it, "The ethics . . . must be judged [only] by the way . . . the parents nurture and rear their resulting child and whether they bestow the same love and affection on a child brought into existence by a technique of assisted reproduction as they would on a child born in the usual way."[19]

The liberal (or libertarian or liberationist) perspective sets cloning in the context of rights, freedoms, and personal empowerment. Cloning is just a new option for exercising an individual's right to reproduce or to have the kind of child that he or she wants. Alternatively, cloning enhances our liberation (especially women's liberation) from the confines of nature, the vagaries of chance, or the necessity for sexual mating. Indeed, it liberates women from the need for men altogether, for the process requires only eggs, nuclei, and (for the time being) uteri—plus, of course, a healthy dose of our (allegedly "masculine") manipulative science that likes to do all these things to Mother Nature and nature's mothers. For those who hold this outlook, the only moral restraints on cloning are adequately informed consent and the avoidance of bodily harm. If no one is cloned without her consent, and if the clonant is not physically damaged, then the liberal conditions for licit, hence moral, conduct are met. Worries that go beyond violating the will or maiming the body are dismissed as "symbolic"—which is to say, "unreal."

The meliorist perspective embraces valetudinarians and also eugenicists. The latter were formerly more vocal in these discussions, but they are now generally happy to see their goals advanced under the less threatening banners of freedom and technological growth. These people see in cloning a new prospect for improving human beings—minimally, by ensuring the perpetuation of healthy individuals by avoiding the risks of genetic disease inherent in the lottery of sex, and maximally, by producing "optimum babies," preserving outstanding genetic material, and (with the help of soon-to-come techniques for precise genetic engineering) enhancing inborn human capacities on many fronts. Here the morality of cloning as a means is justified solely by the excellence of the end, that is, by the outstanding traits or individuals cloned—beauty, or brawn, or brains.

These three approaches, all quintessentially American and all perfectly fine in their places, are sorely wanting as approaches to human procreation. It is, to say the least, grossly distorting to view the wondrous mysteries of birth, renewal, and individuality, and the deep meaning of parent-child relations, largely through the lens of our reductive science and its potent technologies. Similarly, considering reproduction (and the intimate relations of family life!) primarily under the political-legal, adversarial, and individualistic notion of rights can only undermine the private yet fundamentally social, cooperative, and duty-laden character of child-bearing, child-rearing, and their bond to the covenant of marriage. Seeking to escape entirely from nature (in order to satisfy a natural desire or natural right to reproduce!) is self-contradictory in theory and self-alienating in practice. For we are erotic beings only because we are embodied beings, and not merely intellects and wills unfortunately imprisoned in our bodies. And, though health and fitness are clearly great goods, there is something deeply disquieting in looking on our prospective children as artful products perfectible by genetic engineering, increasingly held to our willfully imposed designs, specifications, and margins of tolerable error.

The technical, liberal, and meliorist approaches all ignore the deeper anthropological, social, and, indeed, ontological meanings of bringing forth new life. To this more fitting and profound point of view, cloning shows itself to be a major alteration, indeed, a major violation, of our given nature as embodied, gendered, and engendering beings—and of the social relations built on this natural ground. Once this perspective is recognized, the ethical judgment on cloning can no longer be reduced to a matter of motives and intentions, rights and freedoms, benefits and harms, or even means and ends. It must be regarded primarily as a matter of meaning: Is cloning a fulfillment of human begetting and belonging? Or is cloning rather, as I contend, their pollution and perversion? To pollution and perversion, the fitting response can only be horror and revulsion; and conversely, generalized horror and revulsion are *prima facie* evidence of foulness and violation. The burden of moral argument must fall entirely on those who want to declare the widespread repugnances of humankind to be mere timidity or superstition.

Yet repugnance need not stand naked before the bar of reason. The wisdom of our horror at human cloning can be partially articulated, even if this is finally one of those instances about which the heart has its reasons that reason cannot entirely know.

V. THE PROFUNDITY OF SEX

To see cloning in its proper context, we must begin not, as I did before, with laboratory technique, but with the anthropology—natural and social—of sexual reproduction. Sexual reproduction—by which I mean the generation of new life from (exactly) two complementary elements, one female, one male, (usually) through coitus—is established (if that is the right term) not by human decision, culture, or tradition, but by nature; it is the natural way of all mammalian reproduction. By nature, each child has two complementary biological progenitors. Each child thus stems from and unites exactly two lineages. In natural generation, moreover, the precise genetic constitution of the resulting offspring is determined by a combination of nature and chance, not by human design: each human child shares the common natural human species genotype, each child is genetically (equally) kin to each (both) parent(s), yet each child is also genetically unique.

These biological truths about our origins foretell deep truths about our identity and about our human condition altogether. Every one of us is at once equally human, equally enmeshed in a particular familial nexus of origin, and equally individuated in our trajectory from birth to death—and, if all goes well, equally capable (despite our mortality) of participating, with a complementary other, in the very same renewal of such human possibility through procreation. Though less momentous than our common humanity, our genetic individuality is not humanly trivial. It shows itself forth in our distinctive appearance through which we are everywhere recognized; it is revealed in our "signature" marks of fingerprints and our self-recognizing immune system; it symbolizes and foreshadows exactly the unique, never-to-be repeated character of each human life.

Human societies virtually everywhere have structured child-rearing responsibilities and systems of identity and relationship on the bases of these deep natural facts of begetting. The mysterious yet ubiquitous natural "love of one's own" is everywhere culturally exploited, to make sure that children are not just produced but well cared for and to create for everyone clear ties of meaning, belonging, and obligation. But it is wrong to treat such naturally rooted social practices as mere cultural constructs (like left- or right-driving, or like burying or cremating the dead) that we can alter with little human cost. What would kinship be without its clear natural grounding? And what would identity be without kinship? We must resist those who have begun to refer to sexual reproduction as the "traditional method of reproduction,"[20] who would have us regard as merely traditional, and by implication arbitrary, what is in truth not only natural but most certainly profound.

Asexual reproduction, which produces "single-parent" offspring, is a radical departure from the natural human way, confounding all normal understandings of father, mother, sibling, grandparent, etc., and all moral relations tied thereto. It becomes even more of a radical departure when the resulting offspring is a clone derived not from an embryo, but from a mature adult to whom it would be an identical twin; and when the process occurs not by natural accident (as in natural twinning), but by deliberate human design and manipulation; and when the child's (or children's) genetic constitution is pre-selected by the parent(s) (or scientists). Accordingly, as we will see, cloning is vulnerable to three kinds of concerns and objections, related to these three points: cloning threatens confusion of identity and

individuality, even in small-scale cloning; cloning represents a giant step (though not the first one) toward transforming procreation into manufacture, that is, toward the increasing depersonalization of the process of generation and, increasingly, toward the "production" of human children as artifacts, products of human will and design (what others have called the problem of "commodification" of new life); and cloning—like other forms of eugenic engineering of the next generation—represents a form of despotism of the cloners over the cloned, and thus (even in benevolent cases) represents a blatant violation of the inner meaning of parent-child relations, of what it means to have a child, of what it means to say "yes" to our own demise and "replacement."

Before turning to these specific ethical objections, let me test my claim of the profundity of the natural way by taking up a challenge recently posed by a friend. What if the given natural human way of reproduction were asexual, and we now had to deal with a new technological innovation—artificially induced sexual dimorphism and the fusing of complementary gametes—whose inventors argued that sexual reproduction promised all sorts of advantages, including hybrid vigor and the creation of greatly increased individuality? Would one then be forced to defend natural asexuality because it was natural? Could one claim that it carried deep human meaning?

The response to this challenge broaches the ontological meaning of sexual reproduction. For it is impossible, I submit, for there to have been human life—or even higher forms of animal life—in the absence of sexuality and sexual reproduction. We find asexual reproduction only in the lowest forms of life: bacteria, algae, fungi, some lower invertebrates. Sexuality brings with it a new and enriched relationship to the world. Only sexual animals can seek and find complementary others with whom to pursue a goal that transcends their own existence. For a sexual being, the world is no longer an indifferent and largely homogeneous *otherness*, in part edible, in part dangerous. It also contains some very special and related and complementary beings, of the same kind but of opposite sex, toward whom one reaches out with special interest and intensity. In higher birds and mammals, the outward gaze keeps a lookout not only for food and predators, but also for prospective mates; the beholding of the many splendored world is suffused with desire for union, the animal antecedent of human eros and the germ of sociality. Not by accident is the human animal both the sexiest animal—whose females do not go into heat but are receptive throughout the estrous cycle and whose males must therefore have greater sexual appetite and energy in order to reproduce successfully—and also the most aspiring, the most social, the most open, and the most intelligent animal.

The soul-elevating power of sexuality is, at bottom, rooted in its strange connection to mortality, which it simultaneously accepts and tries to overcome. Asexual reproduction may be seen as a continuation of the activity of self-preservation. When one organism buds or divides to become two, the original being is (doubly) preserved, and nothing dies. Sexuality, by contrast, means perishability and serves replacement; the two that come together to generate one soon will die. Sexual desire, in human beings as in animals, thus serves an end that is partly hidden from, and finally at odds with, the self-serving individual. Whether we know it or not, when we are sexually active, we are voting with our genitalia for our own demise. The salmon swimming upstream to spawn and die tell the universal story: sex is bound up with death, to which it holds a partial answer in procreation.

The salmon and the other animals evince this truth blindly. Only the human being can understand what it means. As we learn so powerfully from the story of the Garden of Eden, our humanization is coincident with sexual self-consciousness, with the recognition of our sexual nakedness and all that it implies: shame at our needy incompleteness, unruly self-division, and finitude; awe before the eternal; hope in the self-transcending possibilities of children and a relationship to the divine. In the sexually self-conscious animal, sexual desire can become eros, lust can become love. Sexual desire humanly regarded is thus sublimated into erotic longing for wholeness, completion, and immortality, which drives us knowingly into the embrace and its generative fruit—as well as into all the higher human possibilities of deed, speech, and song.

Through children, a good common to both husband and wife, male and female achieve some genuine unification (beyond the mere sexual "union," which fails to do so). The two become one through sharing generous (not needy) love for this third being as good. Flesh of their flesh, the child is the parents' own commingled being externalized and given a separate and persisting existence. Unification is enhanced also by their commingled work of rearing, providing an opening to the future beyond the grave, carrying not only our seed but also our names, our ways and our hopes that they will surpass us in goodness and happiness, children are a testament to the possibility of transcendence. Gender duality and sexual desire, which first draws our love toward and outside of ourselves, finally provide for the partial overcoming of the confinement and limitation of perishable embodiment altogether.

Human procreation, in sum, is thus not simply an activity of our rational wills. It is a more complete activity precisely because it engages us bodily, erotically, and spiritually, as well as rationally. There is wisdom in the mystery of nature that has joined the pleasure of sex, the inarticulate longing for union, the communication of the loving embrace, and the deep-seated and only partly articulate desire for children in the very activity by which we continue the chain of human existence and participate in the renewal of human possibility. Whether or not we know it, the severing of procreation from sex, love, and intimacy is inherently dehumanizing, no matter how good the product.

We are now ready for the more specific objections to cloning.

VI. THE PERVERSITIES OF CLONING

First, an important if formal objection: any attempt to clone a human being would constitute an unethical experiment upon the resulting child-to-be. As the animal experiments (frog and sheep) indicate, there are grave risks of mishaps and deformities. Moreover, because of what cloning means, one cannot presume a future cloned child's consent to be a clone, even a healthy one. Thus, ethically speaking, we cannot even get to know whether human cloning is feasible.

I understand, of course, the philosophical difficulty of trying to compare a life with defects against nonexistence. Several bioethicists, proud of their philosophical cleverness, use this conundrum to embarrass claims that one can injure a child in its conception, precisely because it is only thanks to that complained-of conception that the child is alive to complain. But common sense tells us that we have no reason to fear such philosophisms. For we surely know that people can harm and even maim children in the very act of conceiving them, say, by paternal transmission of the AIDS virus, maternal transmission of heroin dependence, or, arguably, even by bringing them into being as bastards or with no capacity or willingness to look after them properly. And we believe that to do this intentionally, or even negligently, is inexcusable and clearly unethical.

The objection about the impossibility of presuming consent may even go beyond the obvious and sufficient point that a clonant, were he subsequently to be asked, could rightly resent having been made a clone. At issue are not just benefits and harms, but doubts about the very independence needed to give proper (even retroactive) consent, that is, not just the capacity to choose but the disposition and ability to choose freely and well. It is not at all clear to what extent a clone will truly be a moral agent. For, as we shall see, in the very act of cloning and of rearing him as a clone, his makers subvert the cloned child's independence, beginning with that aspect that comes from knowing that one was an unbidden surprise, a gift, to the world rather than the designed result of someone's artful project.

Cloning creates serious issues of identity and individuality. The cloned person may experience concerns about his distinctive identity not only because he will be in genotype and appearance identical to another human being, but, in this case, because he may also be twin to the person who is his "father" or "mother"—if one can still call them that. What would be the psychic burdens of being the "child" or "parent" of your twin? The cloned individual, moreover, will be saddled with a genotype that has already lived. He will not be fully a surprise to the world. People are likely always to compare his performances in life with that of his alter ego. True, his nurture and circumstance in life will be different; genotype is not exactly destiny. Still, one must also expect parental and other efforts to shape this new life after the original—or at least to view the child with the original version always firmly in mind. Why else did they clone from the star basketball player, mathematician, and beauty queen—or even dear old Dad—in the first place?

Since the birth of Dolly, there has been a fair amount of doublespeak on this matter of genetic identity. Experts have rushed in to reassure the public that the clone would in no way be the same person, or have any confusions about his or her identity: as previously noted, they are pleased to point out that the clone of Mel Gibson would not be Mel Gibson. Fair enough. But one is shortchanging the truth by emphasizing the additional importance of the intrauterine environment, rearing, and social setting: genotype obviously matters plenty. That, after all, is the only reason to clone, whether human beings or sheep. The odds that clones of Wilt Chamberlain will play in the NBA are, I submit, infinitely greater than they are for clones of Robert Reich.

Curiously, this conclusion is supported, inadvertently, by the one ethical sticking point insisted on by friends of cloning: no cloning without the donor's consent. Though an orthodox liberal objection, it is in fact quite puzzling when it comes from people (such as Ruth Macklin[21]) who also insist that genotype is not identity or individuality, and who deny that a child could reasonably complain about being made a genetic copy. If the clone of Mel Gibson would not be Mel Gibson, why should Mel Gibson have grounds to object that someone had been made his clone? We already allow researchers to use blood and tissue samples for research purposes of no benefit to their sources: my falling hair, my expectorations, my urine, and even my biopsied tissues are "not me" and not mine. Courts have held that the profit gained from uses to which scientists put my discarded tissues do not legally belong to me.[22] Why, then, no cloning without consent—not including, I assume, no cloning from the body of someone who just died? What harm is done the donor, if genotype is "not me"? Truth to tell, the only powerful justification for objecting is that genotype really does have something to do with identity, and everybody knows it. If not, on what basis could Michael Jordan object that someone cloned "him," say, from cells taken from a "lost," scraped-off piece of his skin? The insistence on donor consent unwittingly reveals the problem of identity in all cloning.

Genetic distinctiveness not only symbolizes the uniqueness of each human life and the independence of its parents that each human child rightfully attains; it can also be an important support for living a worthy and dignified life. Such arguments apply with great force to any large-scale replication of human individu-als. But they are sufficient, in my view, to rebut even the first attempts to clone a human being. One must never forget that these are human beings upon whom our eugenic or merely playful fantasies are to be enacted.

Troubled psychic identity (distinctiveness), based on all-too-evident genetic identity (sameness), will be made much worse by the utter confusion of social identity and kinship ties. For, as already noted, cloning radically confounds lineage and social relations, for "offspring" as for "parents." As bioethicist James Nelson has pointed out, a female child cloned from her "mother" might develop a desire for a relationship to her "father," and might understandably seek out the father of her "mother," who is after all also her biological twin sister.[23] Would "grandpa," who thought his paternal duties concluded, be pleased to discover that the clonant looked to him for paternal attention and support?

Social identity and social ties of relationship and responsibility are widely connected to, and supported by, biological kinship. Social taboos on incest (and adultery) everywhere serve to keep clear who is related to whom (and especially which child belongs to which parents), as well as to avoid confounding the social identity of parent-and-child (or brother-and-sister) with the social identity of lovers, spouses, and co-parents. True, social identity is altered by adoption (but as a matter of the best interest of already living children: we do not deliberately produce children for adoption). True, artificial insemination and IVF with donor sperm, or whole embryo donation, are in some way forms of "prenatal adoption"—a not altogether unproblematic practice. Even here, though, there is in each case (as in all sexual reproduction) a known male source of sperm and a known single female source of egg—a genetic father and a genetic mother—should anyone care to know (as adopted children often do) who is genetically related to whom.

In the case of cloning, however, there is but one "parent." The usually sad situation of the "single-parent child" is here deliberately planned, and with a vengeance. In the case of self-cloning, the "offspring" is, in addition, one's twin; and so the dreaded result of incest—to be parent to one's sibling—is here bought about deliberately, albeit without any act of coitus. Moreover, all other relationships will be confounded. What will father, grandfather, aunt, cousin, sister mean? Who will bear what ties and what burdens? What sort of social entity will someone have with one whole side—"father's" or "mother's"—necessarily excluded? It is no answer to say that our society, with its high incidence of divorce, remarriage, adoption, extramarital childbearing, and the rest, already confounds lineage and confuses kinship and responsibility for children (and everyone else), unless one also wants to argue that this is, for its children, a preferable state of affairs.

Human cloning would also represent a giant step toward turning begetting into making, procreation into manufacture (literally, something "handmade"), a process already begun with IVF and genetic testing of embryos. With cloning, not only is the process in hand, but the total genetic blueprint of the cloned individual is selected and determined by the human artisans. To be sure, subsequent development will take place according to natural processes; and the resulting children will still be recognizably human. But we here would be taking a major step into making man himself simply another one of the man-made things. Human nature becomes merely the last part of nature to succumb to the technological project, which turns all of nature into raw material human disposal, to be homogenized by our rationalized technique according to the subjective prejudices of the day.

How does begetting differ from making? In natural procreation, human beings come together, complementarily male and female, to give existence to another being who is formed, exactly as we were, *by what we are:* living, hence perishable, hence aspiringly erotic, human

beings. In clonal reproduction, by contrast, and in the more advanced forms of manufacture to which it leads, we give existence to a being not by what we are but by what we intend and design. As with any product of our making, no matter how excellent, the artificer stands above it, not as an equal but as a superior, transcending it by his will and creative prowess. Scientists who clone animals make it perfectly clear that they are engaged in instrumental making; the animals are, from the start, designed as means to serve rational human purposes. In human cloning, scientists and prospective "parents" would be adopting the same technocratic mentality to human children: human children would be their artifacts.

Such an arrangement is profoundly dehumanizing, no matter how good the product. Mass-scale cloning of the same individual makes the point vividly, but the violation of human equality, freedom, and dignity are present even in a single planned clone. And procreation dehumanized into manufacture is further degraded by commodification, a virtually inescapable result of allowing baby-making to proceed under the banner of commerce. Genetic and reproductive biotechnology companies are already growth industries, but they will go into commercial orbit once the Human Genome Project nears completion. Supply will create enormous demand. Even before the capacity for human cloning arrives, established companies will have invested in the harvesting of eggs from ovaries obtained at autopsy or through ovarian surgery, practiced embryonic genetic alteration, and initiated the stockpiling of prospective donor tissues. Through the rental of surrogate-womb services, and through the buying and selling of tissues and embryos, priced according to the merit of the donor, the commodification of nascent human life will be unstoppable.

Finally, and perhaps most important, the practice of human cloning by nuclear transfer—like other anticipated forms of genetic engineering of the next generation—would enshrine and aggravate a profound and mischievous misunderstanding of the meaning of having children and of the parent-child relationship. When a couple now chooses to procreate, the partners are saying yes to the emergence of new life in its novelty, saying yes not only to having a child but also, tacitly, to having whatever child this child turns out to be. In accepting our finitude and opening ourselves to our replacement, we are tacitly confessing the limits of our control. In this ubiquitous way of nature, embracing the future by procreating means precisely that we are relinquishing our grip, in the very activity of taking up our own share in what we hope will be the immortality of human life and the human species. This means that our children are not *our* children: they are not our property, not our possessions. Neither are they supposed to live our lives for us, or anyone else's lives but their own. To be sure, we seek to guide them on their way, imparting to them not just life but nurturing, love, and a way of life; to be sure, they bear our hopes that they will live fine and flourishing lives, enabling us in small measure to transcend our own limitations. Still, their genetic distinctiveness and independence are the natural foreshadowing of the deep truth that they have their own and never-before-enacted life to live. They are sprung from a past, but they take an uncharted course into the future.

Much harm is already done by parents who try to live vicariously through their children. Children are sometimes compelled to fulfill the broken dreams of unhappy parents; John Doe, Jr. or the III is under the burden of having to live up to his forebear's name. Still, if most parents have hopes for their children, cloning parents will have expectations. In cloning, such overbearing parents take at the start a decisive step which contradicts the entire meaning of the open and forward-looking nature of parent-child relations. The child is given a genotype that has already lived, with full expectation that this blueprint of a past life ought to be controlling of the life that is to come. Cloning is inherently despotic, for it seeks to make one's children (or someone else's children) after one's own image (or an image of one's choosing) and their future according to one's will. In some cases, the despotism may be mild and benevolent. In other cases, it will be mischievous and downright tyrannical. But despotism—the control of another through one's will—it inevitably will be.

VII. MEETING SOME OBJECTIONS

The defenders of cloning, of course, are not wittingly friends of despotism. Indeed, they regard themselves mainly as friends of freedom: the freedom of individuals to reproduce, and the freedom of scientists and inventors to discover and devise and to foster "progress" in genetic knowledge and technique. They want large-scale cloning only for animals, but they wish to preserve cloning as a human option for exercising our "right to reproduce"—our right to have children, and children with "desirable genes." As law professor John Robertson points out, under our "right to reproduce," we already practice early forms of unnatural, artificial, and extra-marital reproduction, and we already practice early forms of eugenic choice.[24] For this reason, he argues, cloning is no big deal.

We have here a perfect example of the logic of the slippery slope, and the slippery way in which it already works in this area. Only a few years ago, slippery slope arguments were used to oppose artificial insemination and IVF using unrelated sperm donors. Principles used to justify these practices, it was said, will be used to justify more artificial and more eugenic practices, including cloning. Not so, the defenders retorted, because we can make the necessary distinctions. And now, without even a gesture at making the necessary distinctions, the continuity of practice is held by itself to be justificatory.

The principle of reproductive freedom as currently enunciated by the proponents of cloning logically embraces the ethical acceptability of sliding down the entire rest of the slope—to producing children ectogenetically from sperm to term (should it become feasible) and to producing children whose entire genetic makeup will be the product of parental eugenic planning and choice. If reproductive freedom means the right to have a child of one's own choosing, by whatever means, it knows and accepts no limits.

But, far from being legitimated by a "right to reproduce," the emergence of techniques of assisted reproduction and genetic engineering should compel us to reconsider the meaning and limits of such a putative right. In truth, a "right to reproduce" has always been a peculiar and problematic notion. Rights generally belong to individuals, but this is a right which (before cloning) no one can exercise alone. Does the right then inhere only in couples? Only in married couples? Is it a (woman's) right to carry or deliver or a right (of one or more parents) to nurture and rear? Is it a right to have your own biological child? Is it a right only to attempt reproduction, or a right also to succeed? Is it a right to acquire the baby of one's choice?

The assertion of a negative "right to reproduce" certainly makes sense when it claims protection against state interference with procreative liberty, say, through a program of compulsory sterilization. But surely it cannot be the basis of a tort claim against nature, to be made good by technology, should free efforts at natural procreation fail. Some insist that the right to reproduce embraces also the right against state interference with the free use of all technological means to obtain a child. Yet such a position cannot be sustained: for reasons having to do with the means employed, any community may rightfully prohibit surrogate pregnancy, or polygamy, or the sale of babies to infertile couples, without violating anyone's basic human "right to reproduce."

When the exercise of a previously innocuous freedom now involves or impinges on troublesome practices that the original freedom never was intended to reach, the general presumption of liberty needs to be reconsidered.

We do indeed already practice negative eugenic selection, through genetic screening and prenatal diagnosis. Yet our practices are governed by a norm of health. We seek to prevent the birth of children who suffer from known (serious) genetic diseases. When and if gene therapy becomes possible, such diseases could then be treated, *in utero* or even before implantation—I have no ethical objection in principle to such a practice (though I have some practical worries), precisely because it serves the medical goal of healing existing individuals. But therapy, to be therapy, implies not only an existing "patient," it also implies a norm of health. In this respect, even germline gene "therapy," though practiced not on a human being but on egg and sperm, is less radical than cloning, which is in no way therapeutic. But once one blurs the distinction between health promotion and genetic enhancement, between so-called negative and positive eugenics, one opens the door to all future eugenic designs. "[T]o make sure that a child will be healthy and have good chances in life": this is Robertson's principle,[25] and owing to its latter clause it is an utterly elastic principle, with no boundaries. Being over eight feet tall will likely produce some very good chances in life, and so will having the looks of Marilyn Monroe, and so will a genius-level intelligence.

Proponents want us to believe that there are legitimate uses of cloning that can be distinguished from illegitimate uses, but by their own principles no such limits can be found. (Nor could any such limits be enforced in practice.) Reproductive freedom, as they understand it, is governed solely by the subjective wishes of the parents-to-be (plus the avoidance of bodily harm to the child). The sentimentally appealing case of the childless married couple is, on these grounds, indistinguishable from the case of an individual (married or not) who would like to clone someone famous or talented, living or dead. Further, the principle here endorsed justifies not only cloning but, indeed, all future artificial attempts to create (manufacture) "perfect" babies.

A concrete example will show how, in practice no less than in principle, the so-called innocent case will merge with, or even turn into, the more troubling ones. In practice, the eager parents-to-be will necessarily be subject to the tyranny of expertise. Consider an infertile married couple, she lacking eggs or he lacking sperm, that wants a child of their (genetic) own, and propose to clone either husband or wife. The scientist-physician (who is also co-owner of the cloning company) points out the likely difficulties—a cloned child is not really their (genetic) child, but the child of only *one* of them; this imbalance may produce strains on the marriage; the child might suffer identity confusion; there is a risk of perpetuating the cause of sterility; and so on—and he also points out the advantages of choosing a donor nucleus. Far better than a child of their own would be a child of their own choosing. Touting his own expertise in selecting healthy and talented donors, the doctor presents the couple with his latest catalog containing the pictures, the health records, and the accomplishments of his stable of cloning donors, samples of whose tissues are in his deep freeze. Why not, dearly beloved, a more perfect baby?

The "perfect baby," of course, is the project not of the infertility doctors, but of the eugenic scientists and their supporters. For them, the paramount right is not the so-called right to reproduce, but what biologist Bentley Glass called, a quarter of a century ago, "the right of every child to be born with a sound physical and mental constitution, based on a sound genotype . . . [that is,] the inalienable right to a sound heritage."[26] But to secure this right, and to achieve the requisite quality control over new human life, human concep-tion and gestation will need to be brought fully into the bright light of the laboratory, beneath which it can be fertilized, nourished, pruned, weeded, watched, inspected, prodded, pinched, cajoled, injected, tested, rated, graded, approved, stamped, wrapped, sealed, and delivered. There is no other way to produce the perfect baby.

Yet we are urged by proponents of cloning to forget about the science fiction scenarios of laboratory manufacture and multiple-copied clones, and to focus only on the homely cases of infertile couples exercising their reproductive rights. But why, if the single cases are so innocent, should multiplying their performance be so off-putting? (Similarly, why do others object to people making money off this practice, if the practice itself is perfectly acceptable?) When we follow the sound ethical principle of universalizing our choice—"would it be right if everyone cloned a Wilt Chamberlain (with his consent, of course)? Would it be right if everyone decided to practice asexual reproduction?"—we discover what is wrong with these seemingly innocent cases. The so-called science fiction cases make vivid the meaning of what looks to us, mistakenly, to be benign.

Though I recognize certain continuities between cloning and, say, IVF, I believe that cloning differs in essential and important ways. But those who disagree should be reminded that the "continuity" argument cuts both ways. Sometimes we establish bad precedents and discover that they were bad only when we follow their inexorable logic to places we never meant to go. Can the defenders of cloning show us today how, on their principles, we will be able to see producing babies ("perfect babies") entirely in the laboratory or exercising full control over their genotypes (including so-called enhancement) as ethically different, in any essential way, from present forms of assisted reproduction? Or are they willing to admit, despite their attachment to the principle of continuity, that the complete obliteration of "mother" or "father," the complete depersonalization of procreation, the complete manufacture of human beings, and the complete genetic control of one generation over the next would be ethically problematic and essentially different from current forms of assisted reproduction? If so, where and how will they draw the line, and why? I draw it at cloning, for all the reasons given.

VIII. BAN THE CLONING OF HUMANS

What, then, should we do? We should declare that human cloning is unethical in itself and dangerous in its likely consequences. In so doing, we shall have the backing of the overwhelming majority of our fellow Americans, and of the human race, and (I believe) of most practicing scientists. Next, we should do all that we can to prevent the cloning of human beings. We should do this by means of an international legal ban if possible, and by a unilateral national ban, at a minimum. Scientists may secretly undertake to violate such a law, but they will be deterred by not being able to stand up proudly to claim the credit for their technological bravado and success. Such a ban on clonal baby-making, moreover, will not harm the progress of basic genetic science and technology. On the contrary, it will reassure the public that scientists are happy to proceed without violating the deep ethical norms and intuitions of the human community.

This still leaves the vexed question about laboratory research using early embryonic human clones, specially created only for such research purposes, with no intention to implant them into a uterus. There is no question that such research holds great promise for gaining fundamental knowledge about normal (and abnormal) differentiation, and for developing tissue lines for transplantation that might be used, say, in treating leukemia or in repairing brain or spinal cord injuries—to mention just a few of the conceivable benefits.

Still, unrestricted clonal embryo research will surely make the production of living human clones much more likely. Once the genies put the cloned embryos into the bottles, who can strictly control where they go (especially in the absence of legal prohibitions against implanting them to produce a child)?

I appreciate the potentially great gains in scientific knowledge and medical treatment available from embryo research, especially with cloned embryos. At the same time, I have serious reservations about creating human embryos for the sole purpose of experimentation. There is something deeply repugnant and fundamentally transgressive about such a utilitarian treatment of prospective human life. This total, shameless exploitation is worse, in my opinion, than the "mere" destruction of nascent life. But I see no added objections, as a matter of principle, to creating and using *cloned* early embryos for research purposes, beyond the objections that I might raise to doing so with embryos produced sexually.

And yet, as a matter of policy and prudence, any opponent of the manufacture of cloned humans must, I think, in the end oppose also the creating of cloned human embryos. Frozen embryonic clones (belonging to whom?) can be shuttled around without detection. Commercial ventures in human cloning will be developed without adequate oversight. In order to build a fence around the law, prudence dictates that one oppose—for this reason alone—all production of cloned human embryos, even for research purposes. We should allow all cloning research on animals to go forward, but the only safe trench that we can dig across the slippery slope, I suspect, is to insist on the inviolable distinction between animal and human cloning.

Some readers, and certainly most scientists, will not accept such prudent restraints, because they desire the benefits of research. They will prefer, even in fear and trembling, to allow human embryo cloning research to go forward.

Very well. Let us test them. If the scientists want to be taken seriously on ethical grounds, they must at the very least agree that embryonic research may proceed if and only if it is preceded by an absolute and effective ban on all attempts to implant into a uterus a cloned human embryo (cloned from an adult) to produce a living child. Absolutely no permission for the former without the latter.

The NBAC's recommendations regarding these matters were a step in the right direction, but a step made limpingly and, finally, without adequate support. To its credit, the Commission has indeed called for federal legislation to prevent anyone from attempting to create a child through cloning; this was, frankly, more than I expected. But the *moral basis* for the Commission's opposition to cloning is, sadly, much less than expected and needed, and the ban it urges is to be only temporary. Trying to clone a human being, says the Commission, is "morally unacceptable" "*at this time*" because the technique has not yet been perfected to the point of safe usage.[27] In other words, once it becomes readily feasible to clone a human being, with little risk of bodily harm to the resulting child, the Commission has offered not one agreed-upon reason to object. Indeed, anticipating such improvements in technique, the Commission insists that "it is critical" that any legislative ban on baby-making through cloning should "include a sunset clause to ensure that Congress will review the issue after a specified time period (three to five years) in order to decide whether the prohibition continues to be needed."[28] Although it identifies other ethical concerns (beyond the issue of safety), this blue-ribbon ethics commission takes no stand on any of them! It says only that these issues "require much more widespread and careful public deliberation *before this technology may be used*"[29]—N.B. not to decide *whether* it should be used. Relativistically, it wants to insure only that such ethical and social issues be regularly reviewed "in light of public understandings at that time."[30] This is

hardly the sort of principled opposition to cloning that could be made the basis of any lasting prohibition.

Almost as worrisome, the report is silent on the vexed question of creating cloned human embryos for use in research. Silence is, of course, not an endorsement, but neither is it opposition. Given the currently existing ban on the use of federal funds for any research that involves creating human embryos for experimentation, the Commission may have preferred to avoid needless controversy by addressing this issue. Besides, those commissioners (no doubt a big majority) who favor proceeding with cloned embryo research have in fact gained their goal precisely by silence. For both the moratorium on federal funding and the legislative ban called for by the Commission are confined *solely* to attempts to *create a child* through cloning. The Commission knows well how vigorously and rapidly embryo research is progressing in the private sector, and it surely understands that its silence on the subject—and Congress'—means that the creation of human embryonic clones will proceed, and is perhaps already proceeding, in private or commercial laboratories. Indeed, the report expects and tacitly welcomes such human embryo research: for by what other means will we arrive at the expected improvements in human cloning technology that would require the recommended periodic reconsideration of any legislative ban?

In the end, the report of the Commission turns out to be a moral and (despite its best efforts) a practical failure. Morally, this ethics commission has waffled on the main ethical question, by refusing to declare the production of human clones unethical (or ethical). Practically, the moratorium and ban on baby-making that the Commission calls for, while welcome as temporary restraints, have not been given the justification needed to provide a solid and lasting protection against the production of cloned human beings. To the contrary, the Commission's weak ethical stance may be said to undermine even its limited call for restraint. Do we really need a federal law solely to protect unborn babies from bodily harm?

Opponents of cloning need therefore to be vigilant. They should press for legislation to *permanently* prohibit baby-making through cloning, and they should take steps to make such a prohibition effective.

The proposal for such a legislative ban is without American precedent, at least in technological matters, though the British and others have banned the cloning of human beings, and we ourselves ban incest, polygamy, and other forms of "reproductive freedom." Needless to say, working out the details of such a ban, especially a global one, would be tricky, what with the need to develop appropriate sanctions for violators. Perhaps such a ban will prove ineffective; perhaps it will eventually be shown to have been a mistake. But it would at least place the burden of practical proof where it belongs: on the proponents of this horror, requiring them to show very clearly what great social or medical good can be had only by the cloning of human beings.

We Americans have lived by, and prospered under, a rosy optimism about scientific and technological progress. The technological imperative—if it can be done, it must be done—has probably served us well, though we should admit that there is no accurate method for weighing benefits and harms. Even when, as in the cases of environmental pollution, urban decay, or the lingering deaths that are the unintended by-products of medical success, we recognize the unwelcome outcomes of technological advance, we remain confident in our ability to fix all the "bad" consequences—usually by means of still newer and better technologies. How successful we can continue to be in such post hoc repairing is at least an open question. But there is very good reason for shifting the paradigm around, at least regarding those technological interventions into the human body and mind that will surely effect fundamental (and likely irreversible) changes in human nature, basic human relationships, and what it means to be a human being. Here, we surely should not be willing to risk everything in the naive hope that, should things go wrong, we can later set them right.

The President's call for a moratorium on human cloning has given us an important opportunity. In a truly unprecedented way, we can strike a blow for the human control of the technological project, for wisdom, prudence, and human dignity. The prospect of human cloning, so repulsive to contemplate, is the occasion for deciding whether we shall be slaves of unregulated progress, and ultimately its artifacts, or whether we shall remain free human beings who guide our technique toward the enhancement of human dignity. If we are to seize the occasion, we must, as the late Paul Ramsey wrote,

> raise the ethical questions with a serious and not a frivolous conscience. A man of frivolous conscience announces that there are ethical quandaries ahead that we must urgently consider before the future catches up with us. By this he often means that we need to devise a new ethics that will provide the rationalization for doing in the future what men are bound to do because of new actions and interventions science will have made possible. In contrast, a man of serious conscience means to say in raising urgent ethical questions that there may be some things that men should never do. The good things that men do can be made complete only by the things they refuse to do.[31]

Notes

1. William Blake, *The Lamb, in* An Oxford Anthology of English Poems 535 (1956).
2. *Id.*
3. *Id.*
4. National Bioethics Advisory Commission, Cloning Human Beings, Report and Recommendations of the National Bioethics Advisory Commission iii–iv (1997) [hereinafter NBAC Report].

5. *See, e.g.,* H.R. 922, 105th Cong. (1997); H.R. 923, 105th Cong. (1997).

6. *See, e.g.,* S. 368, 105th Cong. (1997).

7. H.R. 923.

8. *See* Joshua Lederberg, *Experimental Genetics and Human Evolution,* 100 AM. NATURALIST 519 (1996); Joshua Lederberg, *Unpredictable Variety Still Rules Human Reproduction,* WASH. POST, Sept. 30, 1967, at A17.

9. Leon R. Kass, *Genetic Tampering,* WASH. POST, Nov. 3, 1967, at A20. *See also* Leon R. Kass, *Making Babies—The New Biology and the 'Old' Morality,* PUB. INTEREST, Winter 1972, at 18 [hereinafter Kass, *Making Babies*].

10. Kass, *Making Babies, supra* note 9, at 50.

11. FYODOR DOSTOYEVSKY, CRIME AND PUNISHMENT 44 (David Magarshack trans., Penguin Books 1966).

12. Colin Stewart, *Nuclear Transplantation: An Udder Way of Making Lambs,* 385 NATURE 769 (1997).

13. Robert Langreth & Michael Waldholz, *Who Will Cash in on Breakthrough in Cloning?,* WALL ST. J., Feb. 25, 1997, at B1.

14. Amanda Vogt, *Is Cloning a Baaad Idea?,* CHI. TRIB., Mar. 4, 1997, (Kidnews), at 3.

15. *See, e.g.,* HANS JONAS, *Biological Engineering—A Preview, in* PHILOSOPHICAL ESSAYS: FROM ANCIENT CREED TO TECHNOLOGICAL MAN 153–63 (1974); PAUL RAMSEY, *Shall We Clone a Man?, in* FABRICATED MAN: THE ETHICS OF GENETIC CONTROL 60–103 (1970).

16. *See* Ruth Macklin, *Possible Benefits of Cloning Humans,* BIOLAW, June 1997, at S130 [hereinafter Macklin, BIOLAW]; Ruth Macklin, *Possible Benefits of Cloning Humans* (visited Mar. 18, 1998) <http://www.all.org/nbac/970313b.htm> (testimony presented before the National Bioethics Advisory Commission, Washington, D.C., Mar. 14, 1997). *See also* John A. Robertson, *A Ban on Cloning and Cloning Research Is Unjustified,* BIOLAW, June 1997, at S133 [hereinafter Robertson, BIOLAW]; John A. Robertson, *A Ban on Cloning and Cloning Research Is Unjustified* (visited Mar. 18, 1998) <http://www.all.org/nbac/970313b.htm> (testimony presented before the National Bioethics Advisory Commission, Washington, D.C., Mar. 14, 1997).

17. ALDOUS HUXLEY, BRAVE NEW WORLD (1946).

18. Dave Anderson, *Sports of the Times: Could Jordan Be Cloned? Not Exactly,* N.Y. TIMES, Feb. 28, 1997, at B7.

19. *See* Macklin, BIOLAW, *supra* note 16, at S132.

20. Robertson, BIOLAW, *supra* note 16, at S134.

21. *See* Macklin, BIOLAW, *supra* note 16, at S131. "One incontestable ethical requirement is that no adult person should be cloned without his or her consent." *Id.*

22. *See, e.g.,* Moore v. Regents of the University of California, 793 P.2d 479 (Cal. 1990).

23. *See* James Lindemann Nelson, *Cloning, Families, and the Reproduction of Persons,* BIOLAW, June 1997, at S144; James Lindemann Nelson, *Cloning, Families, and the Reproduction of Persons,* 32 VAL. U. L. REV. 715 (1998); James Lindemann Nelson, *Cloning, Families, and the Reproduction of Persons* (visited Apr. 18, 1998) <http://www.all.org/nbac/970313b.htm> (testimony presented before the National Bioethics Advisory Commission, Washington, D.C., Mar. 14, 1997).

24. Robertson, BIOLAW, *supra* note 16, at S134–37.

25. *Id.* at S137.

26. Bentley Glass, *Science: Endless Horizons or Golden Age?* 171 SCI. 23, 28 (1971). In this presidential address to the American Association for the Advancement of Science, Glass continues: "No parents will in that future time have a right to burden society with a malformed or mentally incompetent child." *Id.*

27. NBAC REPORT, *supra* note 4, at iii, 82, 108 (emphasis added).

28. *Id.* at iv, 109.

29. *Id.* at iii (emphasis added).

30. *Id.* at iv, 109.

31. RAMSEY, *supra* note 15, at 122–23 (footnote omitted).

Discussion Questions

1. What does Professor Kass mean by the "wisdom of repugnance"? Do you agree or disagree? Explain and defend your answer.

2. Professor Kass claims that cultural changes over the last three decades of the twentieth century have made it "vastly more difficult to express a common and respectful understanding of sexuality, procreation, nascent life, family, and the meaning of motherhood, fatherhood and the links between the generations." Do you think that Kass is correct? What cultural changes is he talking about? Do you agree with Kass that these cultural changes were generally a bad thing? Explain and defend your answers.

3. According to Professor Kass, what are the three contexts in which cloning is discussed and why does he think they "are sorely wanting as approaches to human procreation"? Do you agree or disagree with him? Explain and defend your answer.

4. What does Professor Kass mean by the profundity of sex? Do you agree or disagree with him? Explain and defend your answer.

5. What does Professor Kass believe are some of the perversities of cloning? Do you think that he is correct about any of these "perversities"? Explain and defend your answer.

6. Professor Kass presents some objections to his case against human cloning. What are they and how does he respond to them? Do you think his responses are adequate? Why or why not?

You can locate InfoTrac-College Education articles about this chapter by accessing the InfoTrac-College Edition website (http://www.infotrac-college.com/wadsworth/). Using the InfoTrac-College Edition subject guide, enter the search terms relevant to this chapter, and then read abstracts for relevant articles.

Ignorance Is Not Bliss: Why a Ban on Human Cloning Is Unacceptable   25

SHANNON H. SMITH

Shannon H. Smith is a practicing attorney. She earned her J.D. from Case Western University School of Law where she did research on cloning and the law.

In her essay Ms. Smith makes an argument against laws that prohibit the cloning of human beings. She first covers some of the American and international regulations on human cloning that were proposed at the end of the 1990s, many of which are in force today. Ms. Smith then analyzes some of the legal issues involved in cloning human beings. She first discusses the question of cloning for reproductive purposes, pointing out that the U.S. Supreme Court's decisions that upheld reproductive freedom (e.g., *Griswold v. Connecticut* [1965], *Eisenstadt v.*

Reprinted by permission from Health Matrix: Journal of Law-Medicine *9 (summer 1999): 317–34. This essay has been edited for this text.*

Baird [1972], and *Planned Parenthood v. Casey* [1992]) may be broad enough to encompass reproductive technologies including cloning, though she does make the observation that the right to privacy and reproductive choice are not absolute. For "a state may have the power to regulate cloning for reproductive purposes . . . due to its quasi-sovereign interests in protecting the health, safety, and welfare of its citizens." Ms. Smith then moves on to discuss two different types of cloning for non-reproductive purposes: cloning entire human beings and cloning less than a whole person. She tries to find analogies from existing bioethical issues in order to come to an ethical and legal understanding about these types of cloning. For example, concerning the cloning of less than a whole person, Ms. Smith raises the question of whether it would be right to clone a human being but to remove some of its brain cells while it is in its embryo stage, so that it cannot have the capacity for sentience or consciousness. She argues that such a "human being" would be like an anencephalic child, a being who lacks a cerebral hemisphere and from whom organs can be procured ethically prior to its death (a least according to the American Medical Association's Council on Ethical and Judicial Affairs). Given that, why can't we make human clones without cerebral hemispheres and harvest their organs? She concludes that the attempt to ban cloning is the result of ignorance and science fiction fantasies (e.g., *Brave New World, Boys From Brazil*). In addition, because of its potential for good, "the United States should not rush to ban cloning."

I. PROPOSED REGULATIONS ON HUMAN CLONING

CURRENTLY, THERE ARE NUMEROUS state and federal proposals for regulating the cloning of human beings. Most attempt an outright ban on human cloning or the use of government funds for cloning humans. President Clinton, in a press conference on March 4, 1997, announced the prohibition of federal funding for cloning human beings. Stating that "human cloning would have to raise deep concerns, given our most cherished concepts of faith and humanity." Clinton issued a directive that "no federal agency may support, fund, or undertake such activity." He also called for a voluntary moratorium, in the entire scientific and medical community, on attempts to clone human beings through privately funded projects. Believing that a voluntary moratorium is not sufficient, many state

and federal legislators have proposed bills specifically banning the cloning of humans regardless of the funding source. Additionally, a couple of states have passed laws creating state advisory boards on the issue, similar to the President's National Bioethics Advisory Commission, to investigate the technology and provide legislative recommendations.

Another source of possible government regulation of human cloning endeavors is likely to come from the Food and Drug Administration (FDA). The acting FDA Commissioner, Michael A. Friedman, stated in an interview on January 20, 1998, that the FDA has the authority to regulate any human cloning research. The FDA asserts authority under the Food, Drug, and Cosmetic Act because the "kinds of manipulations involved in human cloning present(s) 'serious health and safety issues."[1] As of the date of this writing, however, the FDA has not specifically indicated where in the Act it finds the authority to regulate human cloning efforts, especially those of privately funded research.

Additionally, the concept of cloning humans is under attack on an international level. Several countries including Spain, Britain, Germany, Denmark, and Australia have enacted national legislation banning any aspect of human cloning. On January 12, 1998, the Council of Europe enacted an international treaty that would also ban the cloning of human beings in response to the recent scientific developments in the field of mammal cloning. Building on the provisions of the Convention on Human Rights and Biomedicine, the Council of Europe followed standards which formed "clear barriers against the misuse of human embryos." Thus, the treaty prohibits any intervention which socks to create a human being genetically identical to another human, whether living or dead. To date, twenty-four of the Council's member countries, but none of the non-member invitees, have signed the agreement. The treaty will become effective when five countries, including four member countries, have ratified the agreement. It is difficult to speculate exactly when, if ever, the treaty will become effective because there is no set procedure for the signing countries to follow. Each individual country must follow and complete its own political process for ratifying an international treaty.

II. ANALYSIS OF THE LEGAL ISSUES INVOLVED IN CLONING HUMAN BEINGS

A. *Cloning for Reproductive Purposes*

The United States Supreme Court first recognized the right to procreative liberty as an extension of the right to privacy in the landmark case Griswold v. Connecticut. The Griswold court, focusing on a married couple's right to privacy in family planning, held that the decision whether or not to bear a child was protected under the constitutional right to privacy. In 1972, however, the Court extended this right to individuals in Eisenstadt v. Baird which states that, "(if) the right of privacy means anything, it is the right of the individual, married or single, to be free from unwarranted governmental intrusion into matters so fundamentally affecting a person as the decision whether to bear or beget a child. This "recognized protection accorded to the liberty relating to intimate relationships, the family, and decisions about whether or not to beget or bear a child," was recently reaffirmed by the Court in Planned Parenthood v. Casey.[2]

Although the Supreme Court's rulings in Griswold and Eisenstadt were issued before the advent of most assisted reproductive technologies, the decisions are so broad as to arguably encompass these assisted reproductive technologies. In fact, a federal district court has interpreted the right to make procreative decisions to include the right of an infertile couple to undergo medically assisted reproduction, including the use of in vitro fertilization and a donated embryo.[3] The Supreme Court, however, denied certiorari in the case. Absent a decision by the Court addressing assisted reproductive technologies, it is unclear whether the choice to create a child through cloning would be viewed in the same light as the fundamental right to procreative liberty. Since cloning for reproductive purposes, via somatic cell nuclear transfer, would involve bringing a child into the world, "it is quite possible that one could characterize it as a form of procreation, for which the courts have carved out large areas of special protection."[4]

The reproductive right relevant to human cloning is a negative right, that is the right to use assisted reproductive technologies without fear of government interference. This right can be included in the concept of reproductive freedom even when it is not the only means of having a child via assisted reproductive technologies. Whereas the right to reproductive freedom has traditionally been thought of as the right to choose between various methods of preventing pregnancy, the right to reproductive freedom arguably includes the right to take affirmative steps, through the use of assisted reproductive technologies, to become pregnant. Arguably, when infertile individuals have a choice between different methods of medically assisted reproduction, human cloning would be favored because it replicates a particular individual's genome. Thus, for individuals looking to have a child genetically related to them, cloning, if successful, would be a viable alternative even when it is not the only means for those individuals to have a child through medical assistance.

Additionally, the right to reproductive freedom is generally understood to cover some element of choice about the kind, and number, of children a person will have. In the case of choosing cloning for reproductive purposes over other assisted reproductive technologies, the interest in question is not simply reproduction itself, but a more specific interest in choosing what kind of child to have. Unfortunately, not all individuals have the choice to decide between different methods of assisted reproduction. The case for permitting cloning as a means of reproduction is strongest, therefore, when it would be the only way for an individual to procreate while retaining a biological tie to the child.

The Supreme Court has not left the right to privacy and reproductive freedom unchecked, however. The Court has held that individual states can regulate or limit reproductive rights, but only if there is a compelling state interest in doing so.[5] If cloning is held to be within a constitutionally protected fundamental right, included in reproductive freedom and the right to privacy originally outlined in Griswold, any attempt by the states to regulate the technology would be tested against the strictest scrutiny of the judicial system. In order to pass constitutional muster, a state's

legislation "prohibiting the ability to clone or prohibiting (cloning) research would have to further a compelling interest in the least restrictive manner possible in order to survive this standard of review."[6]

A state may have the power to regulate cloning for reproductive purposes based on its role as parens patriac,[7] due to its quasi-sovereign interests in protecting the health, safety, and welfare of its citizens. Thus, a state may assert the power to regulate cloning based on its concern for the health and safety of the cloned child during the process. The advent of cloning, however, would not necessitate an expansion of the power states currently assert over assisted reproductive technologies. Human cloning, consistent with other reproductive technologies, would arguably be regulated under a state's statutory provisions aimed at protecting the health and safety of its citizens with respect to obtaining medical treatment (in addition to State Medical Board standards that are applicable). While there may be debate as to the moral and ethical differences between current technology and cloning, the science of cloning is actually taken from various techniques used in currently practiced forms of assisted reproduction and medical science. Therefore, the nature of the science involved in cloning is not so diverse from other reproductive technologies to require an expansion of a state's power to protect the parties involved.

B. Cloning for Non-Reproductive Purposes

There are a number of individuals who argue in favor of cloning humans for non-reproductive purposes. Among the purposes discussed for which human cloning could have a pronounced effect are disease research and prevention as well as organ and tissue supply. Currently. molecular and cellular biologists use cloning technology to create cell lines for research that have had an enormous effect on medicine in recent history.[8] One of the most attractive potential applications of non-reproductive cloning, however, is to increase the supply of organs and tissues for transplantation.

1. Cloning Entire Human Beings

Human cloning could solve the problem of finding a transplant donor who is an acceptable organ or tissue match, and as a result could drastically reduce the risk of transplant rejection by the host. In fact, prior to the discovery of immunosupressive drugs to help combat the rejection of a transplanted organ by a host, donation from one identical twin to another had, by far, the highest probability and rate of success. By cloning humans for organ or tissue donation, we would be creating a " 'delayed' genetic twin,"[9] dramatically increasing the probability of a successful transplant.

As with cloning for reproductive purposes, cloning humans for organ and tissue donors raises serious legal and ethical issues. The concept has been criticized on the ground that it treats the delayed genetic twin as simply a means for benefiting another, not as a loved and valued child for its own sake. In a well-publicized case from 1990, the parents of a nineteen-year-old suffering with leukemia chose to have another child in hopes of obtaining a source for a bone marrow transplant. The Ayalas, a California couple, jumped through medical hoops to conceive a daughter, and a successful match for their nineteen-year-old's bone marrow. Around the same time, another couple from Indiana chose to immediately attempt to have another child in order to provide fetal stem cells to their newborn, who had been diagnosed with Fanconi's anemia. The first fetus miscarried, but the mother waited a month and got pregnant again. When this child was born, she was an unsuitable donor. Twelve weeks later, the mother was pregnant again, this time with a child who turned out to be compatible. In both cases, each of these families argue that whether or not the child they conceived turned out to be a possible donor (as was the case for the Indiana

couple), they would value and love the child for itself, and treat it as they would any member of their family.

It is not just the newspaper headlines and magazine articles that report on cases like these noted above. Several cases have been decided in the courts on whether a child will be allowed to donate needed organs or tissue to a sibling.[10] While these cases deal primarily with existing children, not the concept of conceiving a child for donation purposes, the moral and legal arguments are similar. It is important to note, however, that the lack of case law on situations such as the Ayala's does imply that there is a definite difference between subjecting an existing child to donation and creating one for that purpose. Arguably, the fact that legal action has not been filed against families like the Ayalas demonstrates that the government (in its parens patriae role) does not feel there is a sufficient reason to press criminal charges in these situations. Thus, in cases like the Ayala's, the fundamental right to privacy and reproductive freedom appears to make it legally acceptable for the couple to conceive a child for donation purposes. If cloning is held protected under procreative liberty, cloning for proposes of having a child that is an acceptable organ donor would fall under that protection as well.

The idea of parents being allowed to consent to donation between naturally occurring identical twins has been addressed in the courts. In Hart v. Brown,[11] the Superior Court of Connecticut allowed the parents of identical seven-year-old twins to consent to the donation of a kidney from one twin to the other who was in the hospital waiting for a transplant. Noting that the kidney was a necessity for continued life to one twin, and that the risks of the operation to both twins were negligible, the court acknowledged the preference for isografts, "one-egg twin graft(s) from one to another."[12]

Isografts, because the twin carries the same genetic material, do not present the problems with rejection that even parental homografts involve. Therefore, cloning a human and creating a delayed genetic twin would truly be the best way to ensure the acceptance of an organ outside of naturally occurring identical twins, because it would provide an isograft where nature had not done so. It has been argued that the "availability of human cloning for this purpose would amount to a form of insurance policy to enable treatment of certain kinds of medical needs."[13]

Additionally, it has been held that a parent may consent on behalf of a minor child for the child to donate bone marrow to a sibling when doing so would be in the minor's best interest.[14] The court in Curran v. Bosze stated that critical factors for determining what would be in the best interest of a minor child are:

(1) the consenting parent is informed of the risks and benefits inherent in the bone marrow-harvesting procedure to the child; (2) there must be emotional support available to the child from the persons who are responsible for the care of the child; and (3) there must be an existing close relationship between the donor and recipient.[15]

Many courts equate an "existing close relationship" with the "substantial benefit" to the donor in determining what is in the donor's best interests.[16] In order to find an existing close relationship, however, there must necessarily be an existing donor, who has had the opportunity (and time) to form a close bond with the recipient. Creating a child, or clone, for the purposes of being an organ donor does not implicate the need to find an existing relationship for a finding of benefit to the donor. The relationship that will exist between the donor and donee siblings will only be formed after the donor gives the needed organ to save the donee's life.

There is additional authority in case law to support the idea that even "nontheraputic operations can be legally permitted on a minor as long as the parents or other guardians consent to the procedure."[17] In Bonner v. Moran,

the court determined that the parents of a fifteen-year-old boy could consent to his skin grafting in order to donate the tissue to his severely burned cousin.[18] In a time when skin homografting-transferring was a new procedure, the court stated that knowing exactly what was involved required a "mature mind." Because of this requirement, parental consent was necessary.[19] Interestingly, Bonner allows for donation by a minor to a relative who is not a sibling when there is parental consent. In light of this fact, there is a much stronger argument for donation by a sibling with parental consent, or delayed genetic twin in the case of cloning, due to the increase in success rates of isografts, along with the increased "benefit" to the donor in the long-term by having saved her sibling's life.

2. Cloning Less Than a Whole Person

Some have argued for the proposition of cloning less than a whole person to solve situations where the needed organ may be vital to the donor's life, such as a heart. For instance, Carol Kahn argues that after cell differentiation, "some of the brain cells of the embryo or fetus would be removed so that it could then be grown as a brain-dead body for spare parts for its earlier twin."[20] Thus, a "body clone" would be analogous to an anencephalic newborn[21] or presentient fetus,[22] neither of whom can arguably be harmed because of their lack of capacity for consciousness. "(I)f one pushes what is already science fiction quite a bit further . . . the ability to clone and grow in an artificial environment only the particular life-saving organ a person needed for transplantation," would not be that difficult to imagine.[23]

The issue of anencephalic newborns as organ donors does offer some useful comparisons to cloning less than an entire person. Some courts have held that these children are not "dead."[24] However, the condition is invariably fatal, with more than ninety-five percent of those who survive birth dying within one week.[25] In the United States, the Uniform Anatomical Gift Act (UAGA) requires that an individual be declared dead before organs can be procured.[26] The definition of death, according to the Uniform Determination of Death Act (UDDA), is either (1) the irreversible cessation of heart rate and respiration, or (2) total brain death. Since anencephalics are capable of maintaining both a heart beat and respiration without medical assistance, they do not meet the traditional cardio-respiratory medical definition of death. Additionally, because most anencephalics have active brain stems, they do not fit into the definition of whole brain death. It is likely that the problems with defining death under the traditional cardio-respiratory cessation standard would also arise with body clones. While they could be created requiring medical respiratory assistance, body clones would need to have a functioning heart in order to survive and keep the rest of the organs viable. The whole brain definition of death, however, could resolve any debate because body clones would be created without any part of a brain.

Since anencephalic infants lack cerebral hemispheres, it is commonly believed that they are incapable of sensing pain, or developing any sort of cognitive process. Because of this fact, along with the severe shortage of neonatal organ donors, the American Medical Association Council on Ethical and Judicial Affairs (CEJA), revised its position on the removal of organs from anencephalic neonates in June of 1994, finding that "(w)hile respect for life is a value of utmost importance, it is not clear what implications that value has for the treatment of anencephalic neonates."[27] As a result, CEJA stated that it was ethically permissible to consider the anencephalic infant a limited exception to the "dead donor rule."[28]

In following CEJA's opinion,[29] it is ethically acceptable to procure organs from anencephalics prior to their "death" as long as parental consent is obtained, and certain safeguards are followed. In fact, the Council stated that the value of life "is not an absolute value in the sense of overriding all other values. Rather, it must be balanced with other important social values, including, as in this case, the fundamental social value of saving lives."[30] Therefore, if it is ethically permissible to procure organs from anencephalics, would it not also be permissible to procure organs from a clone that is created in much the same medical state as an anencephalic? Arguably, the social value of saving lives would be better served, and substantially outweigh the value of the donor's life according to CEJA's balancing test, by creating an identical organ match, instead of procuring an organ from a non-related donor.

Currently, in order for organs to be preserved for transplant, the donor's cardiopulmonary system must be kept functioning until the organs can be removed. This can involve hours, or possibly days, of artificial respiratory assistance before the organs are matched and an accepting recipient is located. In such a case, is there a difference between keeping a person's body going, without brain activity, for the purpose of harvesting organs, and creating a body in theoretically the same state for the same purpose? While most people would likely find this practice appalling, there are many practical arguments for allowing the technique. Currently, over 64,000 of them are awaiting transplants in the United States.[31] Additionally, if the science of cloning is allowed to proceed, the technology could one day be perfected to the point where scientists are able to clone specific needed parts. In such a scenario, the science of cloning would then have moved into a more morally and ethically permissible state where children or body clones are not the most effective way of procuring a needed organ. Unfortunately, if the technology is prohibited at its current early stage of development, society will never know the full potential, or be able to reap the full benefits, of cloning human beings.

III. CONCLUSIONS

The constantly increasing number of proposed laws, inspired by the rush to prohibit the morally unacceptable and regulate the unknown, are especially troublesome. The bills do not suffer from the problem of unconstitutional vagueness since the activity they ban, cloning, is explicitly described. The problem arises from the fact that cloning is described in different ways in different legislation. This could lead to definitional problems "similar to those encountered in the fetal research laws as new variations of the technology are developed that may not exactly fit into the current cloning definition."[32]

In addition, the bills present differing definitions about what constitutes an embryo, thus taking the cloning issue into the "when does life begin?" debate most often associated with abortion. (Not to mention that the language of the bills tread dangerously close to prohibiting currently acceptable reproductive technologies and research studies.) Arguably, cloning for reproductive purposes would not change current laws addressing the issue. The point of life for a clone would not necessarily be different than that currently associated with children produced by other assisted reproductive technologies, such as in vitro fertilization and artificial insemination. Additionally, the cloning of specific organs would not implicate the issue of "life" because a living person would not be created, only the needed part.

Finally, there is no consistency between bills or states as to who would be prohibited from cloning. In most cases, the legislation generally prohibits cloning, without reference to whether the scientists and the people seeking the ability to be cloned are both targets. Some states, however, have drafted more recent legislation that do state, and attempt to direct, the penalties of breaking the proposed law.[33] Inconsistency, however, will likely only confuse individuals or scientists about the state of the law between jurisdictions. It will also produce a situation where individuals may be "shopping" for facilities in states with laws amenable to their desire for cloning. In such a situation, these individuals may not receive the best care, due to long-distance travel to and from the cloning facility and the possible lack of local emergency care in case of complications.

A large part of the rush to legislate cloning can be attributed to two things: (1) a fear of the unknown, and (2) ignorance as to the science involved in cloning. Fiction, such as the novels, *Brave New World* and *The Boys from Brazil,* depicts cloning as a source of creating inhuman people, and bringing back the dead. In fact, one of the most common fallacies associated with cloning is that it would be a means of recreating exemplary or evil people, thus allowing scientists to create a basketball team full of Michael Jordans, a science lab full of Albert Einsteins, or an army of Adolf Hitlers. Although genes do provide the building blocks for individuals, and cloning would necessarily replicate an individual's genes, the idea that cloning could be used to re-create evil, or even exemplary people simply has no scientific basis.[34] Environment plays an enormous role in the development of children. The exposure and experiences a child receives will vary between different cultures, socio-economic classes, religions, decades, and countless other environmental factors.

The United States should not rush to ban human cloning technology. While there may be legitimate arguments and cause for concern regarding the need to regulate the procedure in order to ensure that the highest quality of medical standards are met, a ban is not in the best interest of society as a whole. Cloning could create new alternatives in reproductive technology, help decrease the need for organ donors (not to mention the reduction in host rejection), and open the scientific and medical world to possibilities that have not even been contemplated. A ban, as currently contemplated by the U.S. Congress as well as many state legislatures, would effectively close the door to this technology forever. The potential for good, as one cloning advocate argues,[35] is too compelling.

NOTES

1. Eisenstadt v. Baird, 405 U.S. 438, 453 (1972) (describing the case where a Boston University professor appealed his conviction of violating Massachusetts law, which made it a felony to provide contraceptives to unmarried persons, for giving a single woman contraceptive foam after his lecture to students on contraception).

2. 505 U.S. 833, 112 S.Ct. 2791, 2810 (1992) (describing the case where abortion clinics and physicians challenged the constitutionality of the 1988 and 1989 amendments to the Pennsylvania abortion statute on due process grounds).

3. See Lifchez v. Hartigan, 735 F. Supp. 1361 (N.D. Ill.) (holding that a ban on research of contraceptives was unconstitutional because it impermissibly infringed upon a woman's right to privacy), aff'd sub nom. Scholberg v. Lifchez, 914 F.2d 260 (7th Cir. 1990), cert. denied, 498 U.S. 1069 (1991).

4. Nat'l Bioethics Advisory Comm'n, 1 Cloning Human Beings 1, 92 (1997) (stating that "it is necessary to examine whether the choice to create a child via somatic cell nuclear transfer cloning would be viewed as a fundamental liberty").

5. See Bowers v. Hardwick, 478 U.S. 186 (1986) (stating that a State has to prove that there is a compelling interest in regulating a fundamental right and that the regulation must be the most "narrowly drawn means of achieving that end," while finding that no such fundamental right extends to homosexuals who engage in sexual relations, based on the majority's view that such acts are immoral). See generally Webster v. Reproductive Health Services, 492 U.S. 490 (1989) (upholding a Missouri statute prohibiting the use of public funds, employees, and facilities for the purpose of encouraging, assisting, or performing abortions not necessary to save a woman's life, based on the premise that life begins at conception).

6. Lori B. Andrews, Cloning Human Beings: The Current and Future Legal Status of Cloning, in 2 Cloning Human Beings, supra note 4, F1, F37 (looking into the legal aspects of future and current challenges to human cloning and what potential standards states may face when creating laws).

7. "Refers traditionally to role of state as sovereign and guardian of persons under legal disability, such as juveniles or the insane." Black's Law Dictionary 1114 (6th ed. 1990).

8. See NBAC, supra note 4, at 14 (discussing the use of cloning technology as the mainstay of recombinant DNA technology which has lead to the production of insulin for diabetic treatment and maintenance, tissue plasminogen activator (tPA) that dissolves blood clots after heart attacks, and erythropoietin (EPO) that treats anemia associated with dialysis for kidney disease).

9. See id. at 3 (defining a "delayed" genetic twin as "a new individual genetically identical to an existing (or previously existing) person").

10. Compare Strunk v. Strunk, 445 S.W.2d 145 (Ky. 1969) (permitting a kidney to be removed from a twenty-seven-year-old incompetent for transplantation into his brother who was suffering from a fatal kidney disease); Hart v. Brown, 289 A.2d 386 (Conn. Super. Ct. 1972) (permitting parents of seven-year-old twins to give consent to the donation of a kidney by one identical twin child to the other); Little v. Little, 576 S.W.2d 493 (Tex. App. 1979) (allowing the mother of a 14-year-old incompetent to give consent to the donation of a kidney to a younger sibling); with In re Guardianship of Pescinski, 226 N.W.2d 180 (Wis. 1975) (refusing to authorize the donation of a kidney by an incompetent adult to his sister); Curran v. Bosze, 566 N.E.2d 1319 (Ill. 1990) (refusing to require three-and-one-half- year-old twins to undergo a bone marrow-harvesting procedure to determine if they were acceptable matches for a half-brother suffering from

leukemia), In re Richardson, 284 So.2d 185 (La. Ct. App. 1973) (refusing to adopt the doctrine of substituted judgment, thereby refusing to authorize the donation of a kidney by a seventeen-year-old incompetent boy to his sister, even though parental consent existed).

11. 289 A.2d at 386.

12. Id. at 388.

13. Dan W. Brock. An Assessment of the Ethical Issues Pro and Con, in 2 cloning human Beings, supra note 4, 2t E8 (exploring the moral implications of cloning solely for organ donation and transplantation).

14. See Curran v. Bosze, 566 N.E.2d at 1331 (holding that minors could not be required to donate bone marrow over the objections of their mother, where it was not in the children's best interest).

15. Id. at 1343 (discussing the criteria the court used to determine whether it is in the best interest of a minor to donate bone marrow to a sibling).

16. See Strunk v. Strunk, 445 S.W.2d 145, 146–147 (Ky. 1969) (describing how the dependent relationship between the incompetent brother and the donee brother has greater substantial benefit if the donation takes place than if it does not); see also In re Guardianship of Pescinski, 226 N.W.2d 180, 182 (Wis. 1975) (explaining that there must be a showing of real consent by, or a benefit to, an incompetent adult before the court will permit the incompetent adult to donate a kidney to a sibling); Little v. Little, 576 S.W.2d 493, 498–500 (Tex. App. 1979) (describing how the existing close relationship between donor sister and donee brother resulted in substantial benefit to both); Hart v. Brown, 289 A.2d 386, 391 (Conn. Super. Ct. 1972) (noting that it would be beneficial to a donor sibling to give her identical twin sister a kidney, thus saving her sister's life); Curran v. Bosze, 566 N.E.2d 1343 (discussing the types of benefits to a child who donates bone marrow to a sibling).

17. Hart v. Brown, 289 A.2d at 386, 390 (Conn. 1972) (citing Bonner v. Moran, 126 F.2d at 121(D.C. Cir. 1941)) (involving the consent necessary to permit skin grafting from a 15-year old to his cousin).

18. 126 F.2d at 121 (deciding that consent of the parent is necessary when a child is to undergo a surgical operation for the benefit of another and requires a mature mind to understand what the child has done).

19. Id. at 123 (stating that the appreciation of the nature and consequences of a complex surgical procedure requires more than that of a child's limited understanding and therefore requires a surgeon to gain consent of the parent or guardian prior to operating on a child).

20. Brock, supra note 13, at E8 (referencing Carol Kahn, can we Achieve Immortality?: The Ethics of Cloning and Other Life Extension Technologies, Free Inquiry, Spring 1989, 2 & 14, 15.

21. Anencephaly is a birth defect in which the child typically is born with only a brain stem, but otherwise lacks a human brain and most of the skull. According to the Medical Task Force on Anencephaly, a diagnosis of anencephaly is only proper when four criteria are present: "(1) A large portion of the skull is absent; (2) The scalp, which extends to the margin of the bone, is absent over the skull defect; (3) Hemorrhagic, fibrotic tissue is exposed because of defects in the skull and scalp; (and) (4) Recognizable cerebral hemispheres are absent." David A. Stumpf et al., The Infant with Anencephaly, 322 New Eng. J. Med. 669, 670 (1990).

22. A fetus, who is not yet alert, cognizant, or able to have conscious thought.

23. Brock, supra note 13, at E8 (considering the future of cloning as a method of obtaining organs for transplantation).

24. See In re T.A.C.P., 609 So.2d 588, 595 (Fla. 1992) (holding that an anencephalic newborn is not considered dead for purposes of organ donation solely by reason of its congenital deformity).

25. See National Conference on Birth Death and Law, Report on Conference, 29 Jurimetrics J. 403, 422 (Lori B. Andrews et al., eds. 1989) (discussing the "difficulty of finding sufficient organs for transplantation in young children" and the possibility of using anencephalic children as organ donors).

26. Uniform Anatomical Gift Act S1(1), 8A U.L.A. 29 (1993) (establishing that organs may be procured only after the death of the donor).

27. Council on Ethical and Judicial Affairs, Am. Med. Ass'n, The Use of Anencephalic Neonates as Organ Donors, 273 JAMA 1614, 1616 (1995) (stating that the reasoning for the "dead donor rule" may not apply with regard to anencephalic neonates).

28. See id. at 1618 (stating that the lack of and inability to ever experience consciousness qualifies anencephalic neonates as potential donors as a limited exception to the "dead donor rule").

29. Council on Ethical and Judicial Affairs, American Medical Association, Code of Med. Ethics: Current Opinions with Annotations 33 (1996) (outlining formal opinion 2.162 describing anencephaly and when organs may be retrieved from such infants and used for transplant).

30. Council on Ethical and Judicial Affairs, Am. Med. Ass'n, supra note 27, at 1616.

31. LifeBanc Fact Sheet (Jan. 1999) (stating statistics of organ transplant demand and availability compiled by LifeBanc, the organ procurement agency for Northeast Ohio).

32. Andrews, supra note 6, at F22 (pointing out definitional problems that go with legislating a new area in science and technology, where laws governing the same subject can be interpreted in vastly different ways).

33. See, e.g., H.R. 2235, 90th Leg., 1997–98 Reg. Sess. (Ill. 1997) (creating the Human Cloning Prohibition Act and stating that violating the Act would be a Class 4 felony); S. 1243, 90th Leg., 1997–98 Reg. Sess. (Ill. 1997) (creating the Human Cloning Act prohibiting a person from purchasing or selling an ovum, zygote, embryo, or fetus for the purpose of cloning a human being, and stating that violating the Act would be a Class 4 felony); S. 2877, 221st Leg., 1997–98 Reg. Sess. (N.Y. 1997) (amending the penal law to make cloning a Class D felony, and conspiracy to clone, a Class E felony); A.B. 5383, 221st Leg., 1997 Reg. Sess. (N.Y. 1997) (prohibiting the extracting of the nucleus from any unfertilized human egg and infusing into such egg DNA from any other cell, and creating a new crime of cloning as a Class D felony); A.B. 9116, 221st Leg., 1997 Reg. Sess. (N.Y. 1997) (prohibiting a "person" from cloning a human being and establishing civil penalties for doing so); A.B. 9183, 221st Leg., 1997 Reg. Sess. (N.Y. 1997) (prohibiting all persons and other entities from engaging in, participating in, or financing human cloning and stating that violations of the bill constitute a felony and grounds for license revocation); and S. 5993, 221st Leg., 1997 Reg. Sess. (N.Y. 1997) (establishing a civil penalty for cloning human beings).

34. See NBAC, supra note 4, at 2 (explaining that genes are the building blocks of each individual, but it is the interaction of genes, environment, and learning that make each individual unique); see also John A. Robertson, The Question of Human Cloning, Hastings Center Rep., Mar. - Apr. 1994, at 6, 11 (stating that "because phenotype and genotype do diverge, and because the environment in which the child will be raised will be different from that of his (parent), the child will still have a unique individuality").

35. See A Ban on Cloning and Cloning Research is Unjustified, 1997 2 Biolaw (Univ. Pub. Am.) No. 6, 2t S:135, S:139 (arguing that the good uses for cloning technology should not be stymied by a ban that is based upon "vague and highly speculative fears").

Discussion Questions

1. Why does Ms. Smith maintain that human cloning for reproductive purposes may be thought of as an extension of the right to reproductive freedom supported by some U.S. Supreme Court decisions?

2. Do you think that there are good reasons for the state to forbid the cloning of human beings, or do you think, like Ms. Smith, that cloning probably falls under "reproductive freedom" and thus ought not to be banned?

3. What are some of the ethical and legal issues raised in the cloning of entire human beings?

4. What are some of the ethical and legal issues raised in the cloning of less than a whole person? Do you think there is a moral difference between intentionally bringing anencephelic children into existence for the purpose of using their organs and using the organs of anencephelic children who came to be that way accidentally? Explain and defend your answer.

5. Do you agree or disagree with Ms. Smith that the United States should not rush to ban cloning? Explain and defend your answer.

You can locate InfoTrac-College Education articles about this chapter by accessing the InfoTrac-College Edition website (http://www.infotrac-college.com/wadsworth/). Using the InfoTrac-College Edition subject guide, enter the search terms relevant to this chapter, and then read abstracts for relevant articles.

SECTION D

The Death Penalty

Introduction to Section D

Whenever an innocent person is brutally murdered, many of us feel within ourselves a righteous anger, a demand for justice rising up. Some people believe that the only just punishment for such a killing is the death penalty, or what is sometimes called, capital punishment. Those who defend this notion are called *retentionists,* for they believe that the death penalty should be retained and not abolished. In this section, Louis P. Pojman represents the retentionist position (Chapter 26). Others disagree. They believe that the death penalty is not a just punishment, even for first degree murder. They believe that life imprisonment without the possibility of parole is adequate. They are called *abolitionists,* for they believe that capital punishment should be abolished. Hugo Adam Bedau represents the abolitionist position in Chapter 27 of this section.

Both sides of the moral question believe that they are upholding the sanctity of human life. Death penalty proponents maintain that executing a murderer correctly speaks to the gravity of the crime, that unjustly stripped the right to life from another human. Opponents of the death penalty contend that when the state executes a murderer, it violates the very sanctity of life it is claiming to uphold.

Although today we think of capital punishment as applying only to war criminals and a special class of first degree murderers, people have not always thought so. The Old Testament portion of the Bible lists a number of crimes punishable by the death penalty, including murder, sorcery, kidnapping, worshiping of false gods, and disobedience to parents by children. Other cultures, and historical epochs, have employed the death penalty for a variety of reasons. Writes philosopher Louis P. Pojman:

> In the seventh century B.C., Draco's Athenian code prescribed the death penalty even for stealing fruit salad. Later Athenians were executed for idleness and for making misleading political speeches. Socrates was executed on the charges of corrupting youth by putting dangerous ideas into their minds and for not believing in the gods. The criminal code of the Holy Roman Empire and later Europe punished sorcery, arson, blasphemy, sodomy, and counterfeiting by burning at the stake. In England during the Tudor and Stuart dynasties 50 offenses were subject to capital punishment, and in 1819,

233 capital offenses were listed, including poaching and pick-pocketing of twelve pence or more. In North Carolina in 1837 the death penalty was required for rape, stealing bank notes, slave-stealing, sodomy, burning of a public building, robbery, concealing a slave with the intent to free him, and bigamy.[1]

The United States has not followed other industrialized nations that have eliminated the death penalty from their criminal law. For a time, however, the death penalty was prohibited in the U.S. In *Furman v. Georgia* (1972), the U.S. Supreme Court prohibited capital punishment on procedural grounds, though two of the justices who voted with the majority opined that the death penalty should never be employed for the punishment of any crime because it violates the Eighth Amendment, which bans "cruel and unusual punishments." But four years later, in *Gregg v. Georgia* (1976), the Court reinstated the death penalty, for a majority was convinced that the procedural flaws that were lacking four years earlier had been eliminated.

There are two different types of theories employed in the contemporary debate over the death penalty. The first type of theory is *retributivist*. Supporters of this type of theory maintain that it is justified for the state to employ the death penalty because it is just retribution for the crime. That is, the gravity of the offense demands that the criminal be punished proportionate to the crime he or she commits. Thus, if you willingly and with forethought take another's life unjustly, you have forfeited your right to life and thus are subject to the death penalty. One finds this notion in the Bible where we are told that "thou shalt give life for life, eye for eye, tooth for tooth, hand for hand, foot for foot, burning for burning, wound for wound, stripe for stripe" (Ex. 21:23b–25). This is called the *lex talionis,* which literally means "law of the claw." Immanuel Kant's defense of the death penalty is considered the classic philosophical presentation of this position.[2] Defenses of retributivism are typically deontological (see Chapters 3 and 5), for they emphasize doing the right thing because it is the right thing to do rather than because of some end it may achieve. So, for the retributivist, the justification of the death penalty is backward looking. That is, it is employed to punish an evil that has already occurred rather than to influence others so that they may not commit crimes in the future.

The second type are *deterrent* theories. As one would guess, supporters of deterrence tend to be utilitarian in their ethics (see Chapter 4) and thus focus on the forward looking features of capital punishment. That is, if instituting the death penalty in our criminal justice system is likely to deter or prevent future crimes, then, according to the supporter of deterrence, it is morally justified. In his essay, Louis Pojman employs versions of both retributivist and deterrent arguments in his case for the death penalty. In his rejection of capital punishment, Hugo Bedau critiques both retributivist and deterrent cases for the death penalty.

Although a vast majority of Americans and both major political parties (Democrat and Republican) support the death penalty, there is a small group of activists consisting largely of academics, literary figures, artists, religious leaders, civil rights spokespersons, and some elected officials who oppose it. Some of them oppose it for purely moral reasons, for instance, the death penalty is barbaric and thus inherently wrong. Others, especially some Roman Catholics, also oppose the death penalty for moral reasons, but they do so because they see their opposition to it as part of a "seamless garment" of support for the dignity of human life. Hence, they oppose both abortion and the death penalty. There are others who believe that the death penalty is not unjust in principle, but that it has not been fairly and justly administered: the poor and minorities (especially blacks) have received a disproportionate number of death sentences.

For some years now these voices, though prominent in the 1960s through the 1980s, have been largely silent in the American political scene. However, two events in 2000 have reopened the debate over the death penalty and have brought these voices back to the forefront of American political discourse. The first event concerned the state of Illinois's capital punishment system. Because it was discovered that there had been a number of wrongful convictions in that state, Governor George Ryan placed a moratorium on executions until an official investigation has been conducted.

The second event in 2000 was the release of a report by James S. Liebman, Simon H. Rifkind Professor of Law at Columbia Law School: *A Broken System: Error Rates in Capital Cases 1973–1995* (online at http://207.153.244.129 or www.TheJustice-Project.org). In his report, Professor Liebman concludes, among other things, that "nationally, during the 23-year study period [1973–1995], the overall rate of prejudicial error in the American capital punishment system was 68 percent. In other words, courts found serious reversible error in nearly 7 of every 10 of the thousands of capital sentences that were fully reviewed during the period."[3]

There were, as one would expect, immediate replies to Professor Liebman's study, including an op-ed piece in *The New York Times* by political scientist James Q. Wilson. Wilson argues, among other things, that "no one has shown that innocent people are being executed. The argument against the death penalty cannot, on the evidence we now have, rest on the likelihood of serious error. It can only rest, I think, on moral grounds. Is death an excessive penalty for any offense? I think not, but those who disagree should make their arguments on the morality of execution clear and not rely on arguments about appeals, costs, and the tiny chance that someday somebody innocent will be killed."[4]

In the end, Professor Wilson is probably correct about the nature of the debate over the death penalty. It is either morally wrong or it isn't morally wrong. If it isn't, then it should be administered justly and fairly. But if it is morally wrong, then no matter how "fairly" it is administered, it is impermissible and should be prohibited by law.

> **Key words:** death penalty, capital punishment, retributivism, deterrence, lex talionis, sanctity of life, seamless garment, crime and punishment, the Justice Project, *Furman v. Georgia, Gregg v. Georgia.*

NOTES

1. From Louis Pojman's introductory comments to the part, "The Death Penalty," in *Life and Death: A Reader in Moral Problems,* ed. Louis P. Pojman (Boston: Jones & Bartlett, 1993), 332.
2. See Immanuel Kant, *The Philosophy of Law,* Part II, trans. W. Hastie (Edinburgh: Clark, 1887), 194–98.

3. James S. Leibman, *A Broken System: Error Rates in Capital Cases 1973–1995,* online at http://207.153.244.129 or www.TheJusticeProject.org (as of 26 July 2000).
4. James Q. Wilson, "What Death-Penalty Errors?," *The New York Times* (10 July 2000).

For Further Reading

Hugo A. Bedau, ed., *The Death Penalty in America: Current Controversies,* reprint edition (New York: Oxford University Press, 1998).

Hugo A. Bedau and Chester M. Pierce, eds., *Capital Punishment in the United States* (New York: AMS Press, 1976).

Walter Berns, *For Capital Punishment: The Inevitably of Caprice and Mistake* (New York: Norton, 1974).

Rudolph Gerber and Patrick McAnany, eds., *Contemporary Punishment* (Notre Dame, IN: University of Notre Dame Press, 1972).

James S. Leibman, *A Broken System: Error Rates in Capital Cases 1973–1995,* online at http://207.153.244.129 or www.TheJusticeProject.org (as of 26 July 2000).

Karl Menninger, *The Crime of Punishment* (New York: Viking Press, 1968).

Jeffrie Murphy, ed., *Punishment and Rehabilitation,* 3rd ed. (Belmont, CA: Wadsworth, 1995).

Louis P. Pojman and Jeffrey Reiman, *The Death Penalty: For and Against* (Lanham, MD: Rowman & Littlefield, 1998).

Tom Sorell, *Moral Theory and Capital Punishment* (Oxford: Blackwell, 1987).

Bonnie Szumski, Lynn Hall, and Susan Bursell, eds., *The Death Penalty: Opposing Viewpoints* (St. Paul, MN: Greenhaven Press, 1986).

Ernest Van den Haag and John P. Conrad, *The Death Penalty: A Debate* (New York: Plenum Press, 1983).

26   The Case for Capital Punishment

LOUIS P. POJMAN

Louis P. Pojman is Professor of Philosophy at the United States Military Academy in West Point, New York. He has published widely in the areas of philosophy of religion, epistemology, ethics, and political philosophy. Among his many books are *Ethical Theory: Classical and Contemporary Readings,* 3rd ed. (1998), *Ethics: Discovering Right and Wrong,* 3rd ed. (1998), and *The Death Penalty: For and Against* (1998).

In this essay Professor Pojman makes a case for the moral, as well as legal, permissibility of the death penalty. He supports his case by employing two arguments:

Reprinted by permission of the author from Philosophy: The Quest for Truth, *3rd ed., ed. Louis P. Pojman (Belmont, CA: Wadsworth, 1996).*

a retribitivist argument and a deterrence argument. First, Pojman argues that everyone has a right to life, but if you take another's life intentionally and with malice of forethought, you forfeit your right to life. He calls himself a "moderate retributivist" because he "might well allow mercy to enter the picture earlier." For example, "if society is secure, it might well opt to show mercy and not execute murderers." Second, Professor Pojman maintains that it is difficult to prove whether or not the death penalty deters future murders. Given that absence of information, society ought to err on the side of the innocent. That is, since it is possible that the death penalty may deter the killing of some innocent persons, the death penalty is justified. Pojman concludes with responses to three objections to the death penalty: (1) "capital punishment is a morally unacceptable thirst for revenge"; (2) the death penalty "is to be rejected because of human fallibility in convicting innocent parties and sentencing them to death"; and (3) Capital punishment "constitutes a denial of the wrongdoer's essential dignity as a human being."

IN THIS PAPER, I ARGUE that there are moral reasons to apply the death penalty to those who commit first-degree murder. I use both retributivist and a type of deterrence argument to support my position. At the end of the paper, I meet three important objections to the use of the death penalty.

A classic expression of the retributivist position on capital punishment is Kant's statement that if an offender "has committed murder, he must *die*. In this case, no possible substitute can satisfy justice. For there is no *parallel* between death and even the most miserable life, so that there is no equality of crime and retribution unless the perpetrator is judicially put to death (at all events without any maltreatment which might make humanity an object of horror in the person of the sufferer)."

Kant illustrates his doctrine of exact retribution:

> Even if a civil society were to dissolve itself with the consent of all its members (for example, if a people who inhabited an island decided to separate and disperse to other parts of the world), the last murderer in prison would first have to be executed in order that each should receive his just deserts and that the people should not bear the guilt of a capital crime through failing to insist on

> its punishment; for if they do not do so, they can be regarded as accomplices in the public violation of justice. (*The Metaphysics of Morals,* p. 156)

For Kant, the death penalty was a conclusion of the argument for justice, just recompense to the victim and just punishment to the offender. As a person of dignity the victim deserves to have his offender harmed in proportion to the gravity of the crime and as a person of high worth and responsibility, the offender shows himself deserving of capital punishment.

Let us expand on the retributivist argument. Each person has a right to life. But criminal C violates an innocent victim V's right to life by threatening it or by killing V. The threat to V constitutes a grave offense, but taking V's life constitutes a capital offense. C deserves to be put to death for his offense.

But the abolitionist responds, "No, putting C to death only compounds evil. If killing is an evil, then the State actually doubles the evil by executing the murderer. The State violates C's right to life."

But the abolitionist is mistaken on two counts. First, the State does not violate C's right to life. C has already forfeited any right he had to life in murdering V. The right to life is not an absolute right that can never be overridden. It is a serious prima facie right that can be jettisoned only by a more weighty moral reason. In this case, the violating of V's right is sufficient reason for overriding C's right to life. Secondly, while killing C may be an evil, it is a lesser of evils and may be justified. Not to right a wrong, not to punish the criminal, may be a worse evil than harming him.

I said that the criminal *forfeits* his or her right to life by deliberately murdering his victim. But forfeiture does not tell the whole story. Not only does he forfeit his life, but he positively deserves his punishment. If he has committed a capital offense, he deserves a capital punishment. If first-degree murder is on the level of the worst types of crimes, as we think it is, then we are justified in imposing the worst type of punishments on the murderer. Death would seem to be the fitting punishment—anything less would seem to lessen the seriousness of the offense.

Of course, we know of worse crimes than murder—torturing a victim over a long period of time and driving him insane is worse than murdering him. It might well be that society should torture the torturer and the rapist (it would be too repulsive to rape him). *Lex talionis* with a vengeance! For most of us, death seems an adequate punishment for the worst types of crimes—though strictly speaking it may not be anywhere near to the proportion of suffering or evil done by the criminal. How could we punish Hitler in proportion to the gravity of his offense? There are limits to punishment. Nothing more than death seems right. The question is whether something less than death would do as well—say long-term prison sentences?

A moderate retributivist (like myself) might well allow mercy to enter the picture earlier. If society is secure, it might well opt to show mercy and not execute murderers. It may be that utilitarian reasons enter into the calculation. Retributivism may be mitigated by utilitarian considerations. Not because the criminal doesn't deserve the death penalty but because a secure society isn't threatened as a whole by occasional murders, heinous though they be. In a secure society (Scandinavian or Swiss societies, with crime rates a tiny fraction of that of the United States, come to mind) capital offenses are not tearing away at the very fabric of the social order.

The utilitarian argument for capital punishment is that it deters would-be offenders from committing first-degree murder. The evidence for this is very weak. There is a lack of evidence that capital punishment deters, but this should not be construed as evidence for the lack of deterrence. There is no such evidence for non-deterrence. We simply don't know. Statistics are hard to read, though common sense would seem to give some credence to the idea. Arthur Lewis, a British member of Parliament, was converted from abolitionism to supporting the death penalty. Here is an account of his change of mind:

> One reason that has stuck in my mind, and which has proved to me beyond question, is that there was once a professional burglar in [my] constituency who consistently boasted of the fact that he had spent about one-third of his life in prison. . . . He said to me, "I am a professional burglar. Before we go out on a job we plan it down to every detail. Before we go into the boozer to have a drink we say, 'Don't forget, no shooters' "—shooters being guns. He adds "We did our job and didn't have shooters because at that time there was capital punishment. Our wives, girlfriends and our mums said, 'Whatever you do, do not carry a shooter because if you are caught you might be topped.' If you do away with capital punishment they will all be carrying shooters."[1]

However, it is difficult to know how widespread such reasoning is. Perhaps it is mainly confined to a certain class of professional burglars or middle-class people who are tempted to kill their enemies. We simply don't know

	CP works	**CP doesn't work**
We bet on CP	a. We win: some murderers die and some innocents are saved.	b. We lose: some murderers die for no purpose.
We bet vs. CP	c. We lose: murderers live and some innocents die needlessly.	d. We win: murderers live and the lives of others are unaffected.

how much capital punishment deters or whether the deterrence is negligible.

John Stuart Mill admitted that capital punishment does not inspire terror in hardened criminals, but it may well make an impression on prospective murderers. "As for what is called the failure of the death punishment, who is able to judge of that? We partly know who those are whom it has not deterred; but who is there who knows whom it has deterred, or how many human beings it has saved who would have lived to be murderers if that awful association had not been thrown round the idea of murder from their earliest infancy."[2]

In this regard the best argument for capital punishment is Ernest van den Haag's best-bet argument.[3] Ernest van den Haag has argued that even though we don't know for certain whether the death penalty deters or prevents other murders, we should bet that it does. Actually, due to our ignorance, any social policy we take is a gamble. Not to choose capital punishment for first-degree murder is as much a bet that capital punishment doesn't deter as choosing the policy is a bet that it does. There is a significant difference in the betting, however, in that to bet against capital punishment is to bet against the innocent, while to bet for it is to bet against the murderer and for the innocent.

Suppose that we choose a policy of capital punishment for capital crimes. In this case we are betting that the death of some murderers will be more than compensated by the lives of some innocents not being murdered (either by these murderers or others who would have murdered—for example, Lewis' burglar). If we're right, we have saved the lives of the innocent. If we're wrong, unfortunately, we've

sacrificed the lives of some murderers. But say we choose not to have a social policy of capital punishment. If capital punishment doesn't work as a deterrent, we've come out ahead, but if it does, then we've missed an opportunity to save innocent lives. If we value the saving of innocent lives more highly than the loss of the guilty, then it is rational to bet on a policy of capital punishment. The reasoning for this is shown in the table at the top of the page (CP stands for capital punishment).

Suppose that we estimate that the utility value of a murderer's life is 5 and that the value of an innocent's life is 10 (it's at least twice the value of the murderer's life). The sums work out this way:

A murderer saved	+5
A murderer executed	−5
An innocent saved	+10
An innocent murdered	−10

Suppose that for each execution only two innocent lives are spared. Then the sums read as follows:

a. −5 + 20 = +15

b. −5

c. +5 − 10 = −15

d. +5

If all the possibilities are roughly equal, we can sum the results like this:

If we bet on CP, we get (a) and (b), or +10

If we bet against CP, we get (c) and (d), or −10

So it turns out that it is a good bet to execute convicted murderers. It is a bad bet to choose to abolish the death penalty. We unnecessarily put the innocent at risk.

Even if we value the utility of an innocent life only slightly more than that of the murderers, it is still rational to execute convicted murderers. As van den Haag writes, "Though we have no proof of the positive deterrence of the penalty, we also have no proof of zero or negative effectiveness. I believe we have no right to risk additional future victims of murder for the sake of sparing convicted murderers; on the contrary, our moral obligation is to risk the possible ineffectiveness of executions."[4]

OBJECTIONS TO CAPITAL PUNISHMENT

Objection 1: Capital punishment is a morally unacceptable thirst for revenge. As former British Prime Minister Edward Heath put it, "The real point which is emphasized to me by many constituents is that even if the death penalty is not a deterrent, murderers deserve to die. This is the question of revenge. Again, this will be a matter of moral judgment for each of us. I do not believe in revenge. If I were to become the victim of terrorists, I would not wish them to be hanged or killed in any other way for revenge. All that would do is deepen the bitterness which already tragically exists in the conflicts we experience in society, particularly in Northern Ireland."[5]

Response: Retributivism is not to be equated with revenge, although the motifs are often intermixed in practice. Revenge is a personal response to someone for an injury. Retribution is an impartial and impersonal response to an offender for an offense done against someone. It is not possible to want revenge for the harm of someone whom you are indifferent to. Revenge always involves personal concern for the victim. Retribution is not personal but based on objective factors—the criminal has deliberately harmed an innocent party and so

deserves to be punished—whether I wish it or not. I would agree that I or my son or daughter *deserve* to be punished for our crimes—but I don't wish any vengeance on myself or my son or daughter.

Furthermore, while revenge often leads us to exact more suffering from the offender than the offense warrants, retribution stipulates that the offender be punished in proportion to the gravity of the offense. In this sense, the *lex talionis* ("an eye for an eye, a tooth for a tooth, a life for a life") that we find in the Old Testament is actually a progressive rule, where retribution replaces revenge as the mode of punishment. It says that there are limits to what one can do to the offender. Revenge demands a life for an eye or a tooth, but Moses gives a rule that exacts a penalty equal to the harm done by the offender.

Objection 2: Capital punishment is to be rejected because of human fallibility in convicting innocent parties and sentencing them to death. While some compensation is available to those unjustly imprisoned, the death sentence is irrevocable. We can't compensate the dead. As John Maxton, a member of the British Parliament, puts it, "If we allow one innocent person to be executed, morally we are committing the same, or, in some ways, a worse crime than the person who committed the murder."[6]

Response: Maxton is incorrect in saying that mistaken judicial execution is morally the same or worse than murder, for in a murder there is a deliberate intention to kill the innocent, whereas in wrongful capital punishment there is no such intention.

The fact that we can err in applying the death penalty should give us pause and cause us to build an appeals process into the judicial system. Such a process is already in the American and British legal systems. The fact that occasional error may be made, regrettable though this is, is not a sufficient reason for us to refuse to use the death penalty, if on balance it serves a just and useful function.

Objection 3: The death penalty constitutes a denial of the wrongdoer's essential dignity as a human being. No matter how bad a person becomes, no matter how terrible his deed, we must never cease to regard him as an end in himself, as someone with inherent dignity. Capital punishment violates that dignity. As Thurgood Marshall wrote in *Gregg* vs. *Georgia,*

> The Eighth Amendment demands more than that a challenged punishment can be acceptable to contemporary society. To be sustained under the Eighth Amendment, the death penalty must [comport] with the basic concept of human dignity at the core of the Amendment; the objective in imposing it must be [consistent] with our respect for the dignity of [other] men. Under these standards, the taking of life "because the wrongdoer deserves it" surely must fail, for such a punishment has as its very basis the total denial of the wrongdoer's dignity and worth. The death penalty, unnecessary to promote the goal of deterrence or to further any legitimate notion of retribution, is an excessive penalty forbidden by the Eighth and Fourteenth Amendments (United States Supreme Court, 428 U.S. 153 [1976]).

Margaret Falls argues eloquently that treating people as moral agents prohibits us from executing them. "Holding an offender responsible necessarily includes demanding that she respond as only moral agents can: by reevaluating her behavior. If the punishment meted out makes reflective response to it impossible, then it is not a demand for response as a moral agent. Death is not a punishment to which reflective moral response is possible. . . . Death terminates the possibility of moral reform."[7]

Response: Actually, rather than being a violation of the wrongdoer's dignity, capital punishment may constitute a recognition of human dignity. As we noted in discussing Kant's view of retribution, the use of capital punishment respects the worth of the victim in calling for an equal punishment to be exacted from the offender, and it respects the dignity of the offender in treating him as a free agent who must be respected for his decisions and who must bear the cost of his acts as a responsible agent.

First, it respects the worth of the victim. Columnist Mike Royko bluntly put it this way:

> When I think of the thousands of inhabitants of Death Rows in the hundreds of prisons in this country, I don't react the way the kindly souls do—with revulsion that the state would take these lives. My reaction is: What's taking us so long? Let's get that electrical current flowing. Drop the pellets now!
>
> Whenever I argue this with friends who have opposite views, they say that I don't have enough regard for that most marvelous of miracles—human life.
>
> Just the opposite: It's because I have so much regard for human life that I favor capital punishment. Murder is the most terrible crime there is. Anything less than the death penalty is an insult to the victim and society. It says, in effect, that we don't value the victim's life enough to punish the killer fully.[8]

It is just because the *victim's* life is sacred that the death penalty is a fitting punishment for first-degree murder.

Secondly, it's just because the murderer is an autonomous, free agent, that we regard his act of murder as his own and hold him responsible for it. Not to hold him responsible for his crime is to treat him as less than autonomous. Just as we praise and reward people in proportion to the merit of their good deeds, so we blame and punish them in proportion to the evil of their bad deeds. If there is evidence that the offender did not act freely, we would mitigate his sentence. But if he did act of his own free will, he bears the responsibility for his actions and deserves to be punished accordingly.

To Meg Falls' argument that the death penalty makes moral reform impossible, two things must be said: (1) It's false and (2) it's not an argument for the complete abolition of capital punishment.

(1) It's false. The criminal may be given to repent of his or her offense before execution. It is hard to know when the murderer has truly repented and has been rehabilitated—faking it is in his self-interest—but even if he does repent, the heinousness of the deed remains and he should receive his just deserts.

(2) Even if some offenders are suitably rehabilitated, and even if we have a policy of showing mercy to those who give strong evidence of having been morally reformed, many criminals may be and probably are incurable—given our present means for rehabilitation and moral reform. At present, rehabilitation programs are not very successful.

I have not argued for an absolute duty to execute first-degree murderers. The principle that the guilty should suffer in proportion to the harm they caused, and that this sometimes entails the death penalty, is not absolute. I can be overridden by mercy. But it must be a judicious expression of mercy, serving the public good.

No doubt we should work toward the day when capital punishment is no longer necessary, when the murder rate becomes a tiny fraction of what it is today, when a civilized society can safely incarcerate the relatively few violent criminals in its midst, and where moral reform of the criminal is a reality. I for one regret the use of the death penalty. I am against capital punishment. I would vote for its abolition in an instant if only one condition were met—that those contemplating murder would set an example for me. Otherwise, it is better that the murderer perish than that innocent victims be cut down by the murderer's knife or bullet.

NOTES

1. British *Parliamentary Debates* fifth series, vol 23, issue 1243, House of Commons, 11 May 1982. Quoted in Tom Sorell, *Moral Theory and Capital Punishment* (Blackwell, 1987), p. 36.
2. *Parliamentary Debates,* third series, 21 April 1868. Reprinted in Peter Singer, ed., *Applied Ethics* (Oxford University Press), pp. 97–104.
3. Ernest van den Haag, "On Deterrence and the Death Penalty," *Ethics, 78* (July 1968).
4. Op. cit.
5. British *Parliamentary Debates,* 1982 quoted in Sorell, op. cit., p. 43.
6. Op. cit., p. 47.
7. Margaret Falls, "Against the Death Penalty: A Christian Stance in a Secular World" in the *Christian Century,* December 10, 1986, pp. 1118, 1119.
8. Mike Royko, *Chicago Sun-Times,* September 1983.

Discussion Questions

1. Present and explain Professor Pojman's retributivist argument for the death penalty. Do you agree or disagree with it? Explain and defend your answer.
2. Present and explain Professor Pojman's deterrence argument for the death penalty. Do you agree or disagree with it? Explain and defend your answer.
3. Present and explain the three objections to the death penalty that Professor Pojman addresses. How does Pojman respond to these objections? Do you think he succeeds? Explain and defend your answer.
4. Why does Pojman believe that it may be prudent in some societies to let mercy enter the picture and prohibit the death penalty, even if it is morally justified? Present and explain his reasoning. Do you agree or disagree with it? Explain and defend your answer.

You can locate InfoTrac-College Education articles about this chapter by accessing the InfoTrac-College Edition website (http://www.infotrac-college.com/wadsworth/). Using the InfoTrac-College Edition subject guide, enter the search terms relevant to this chapter, and then read abstracts for relevant articles.

The Death Penalty Is Not Morally Permissible   27

HUGO ADAM BEDAU

Hugo Adam Bedau is Professor of Philosophy at Tufts University in Boston. A former president of the American League to Abolish Capital Punishment, Professor Bedau is an important intellectual figure in the movement to abolish the death penalty. He is the author of *The Courts, the Constitution, and Capital Punishment* (1977) and editor of *The Death Penalty in America* (1982).

In this essay, Professor Bedau argues for the abolishment of the death penalty. He first critiques the argument that capital punishment is analogous to self-defense. He teases out this analogy and maintains that killing in self-defense is only justified if it is necessary to, or an unintended consequence of, resisting an aggressor when the loss of life is imminent. But if there is a non-lethal alternative and/or loss of life is not imminent, then killing an aggressor is not justified. Thus, criminals should receive punishment that is adequate to protect society. Bedau then argues that since neither the retributive nor the deterrence arguments work, and because long prison sentences seem to work just as well as the death penalty, capital punishment goes beyond what is necessary to protect society. He argues that the "life for life" ethic (*lex talionis*) plays virtually no part in actual criminal law and that a literal interpretation of it is barbaric. Bedau also argues that the death penalty is administered arbitrarily and capriciously, for the poor and minorities (especially blacks) have received a disproportionate number of death sentences. This "cheapens and degrades," rather than enhances, "human life."

CAPITAL PUNISHMENT AND SOCIAL DEFENSE

The Analogy with Self-Defense

CAPITAL PUNISHMENT, IT IS sometimes said, is to the body politic what self-defense is to the individual. If the latter is not morally wrong, how can the former be morally wrong? In order to assess the strength of this analogy, we need first to inspect the morality of self-defense.

Except for absolute pacifists, who believe it is morally wrong to use violence even to defend themselves or others from unprovoked and undeserved aggression, most of us believe that it is not morally wrong and may even be our moral duty to use violence to prevent aggression directed either against ourselves or against innocent third parties. The law has long granted persons the right to defend themselves against the unjust aggressions of others, even to the extent of using lethal force to kill a would-be assailant. It is very difficult

Reprinted by permission from Matters of Life and Death, *2nd ed., ed. Tom Regan (New York: McGraw-Hill, 1986). Endnotes omitted.*

to think of any convincing argument that would show it is never rational to risk the death of another in order to prevent death or grave injury to oneself. Certainly self-interest dictates the legitimacy of self-defense. So does concern for the well-being of others. So also does justice. If it is unfair for one person to inflict violence on another, then it is hard to see how morality could require the victim to acquiesce in the attempt by another to hurt him or her, rather than to resist it, even if that resistance involves or risks injury to the assailant.

The foregoing account assumes that the person acting in self-defense is innocent of any provocation of the assailant. It also assumes that there is no alternative to victimization except resistance. In actual life, both assumptions—especially the second—are often false, because there may be a third alternative: escape, or removing oneself from the scene of danger and imminent aggression. Hence, the law imposes on us the "duty to retreat." Before we use violence to resist aggression, we must try to get out of the way, lest unnecessary violence be used to resist aggression. Now suppose that unjust aggression is imminent, and there is no path open for escape. How much violence may justifiably be used to ward off aggression? The answer is: No more violence than is necessary to prevent the aggressive assault. Violence beyond that is unnecessary and therefore unjustified. We may restate the principle governing the use of violence in self-defense in terms of the use of "deadly force" by the police in the discharge of their duties. The rule is this: Use of deadly force is justified only to prevent loss of life in immediate jeopardy where a lesser use of force cannot reasonably be expected to save the life that is threatened.

In real life, violence in self-defense in excess of the minimum necessary to prevent aggression, even though it is not justifiable, is often excusable. One cannot always tell what will suffice to deter or prevent becoming a victim, and so the law looks with a certain tolerance upon the frightened and innocent would-be victim who in self-protection turns upon a vicious assailant and inflicts a fatal injury even though a lesser injury would have been sufficient. What is not justified is deliberately using far more violence than is necessary to prevent becoming a victim. It is the deliberate, not the impulsive or the unintentional use of violence that is relevant to the death-penalty controversy, since the death penalty is enacted into law and carried out in each case only after ample time to weigh alternatives. Notice that we are assuming that the act of self-defense is to protect one's person or that of a third party. The reasoning outlined here does not extend to the defense of one's property. Shooting a thief to prevent one's automobile from being stolen cannot be excused or justified in the way that shooting an assailant charging with a knife pointed at one's face can be. In terms of the concept of "deadly force," our criterion is that deadly force is never justified to prevent crimes against property or other violent crimes not immediately threatening the life of an innocent person.

The rationale for self-defense as set out above illustrates two moral principles of great importance to our discussion. . . . One is that if a life is to be risked, then it is better that it be the life of someone who is guilty (in our context, the initial assailant) rather than the life of someone who is not (the innocent potential victim). It is not fair to expect the innocent prospective victim to run the added risk of severe injury or death in order to avoid using violence in self-defense to the extent of possibly killing his assailant. It is only fair that the guilty aggressor run the risk.

The other principle is that taking life deliberately is not justified so long as there is any feasible alternative. One does not expect miracles, of course, but in theory, if shooting a burglar through the foot will stop the burglary and enable one to call the police for help, then there is no reason to shoot to kill. Likewise, if the burglar is unarmed, there is no reason to shoot at all. In actual life, of course, burglars are likely to be shot at by aroused household-ers because one does not know whether they are armed, and prudence may dictate the assumption that they are. Even so, although the burglar has no right to commit a felony against a person or a person's property, the attempt to do so does not give the chosen vic-tim the right to respond in whatever way one pleases, and then to excuse or justify such con-duct on the ground that one was "only acting in self-defense." In these ways the law shows a tacit regard for the life of even a felon and dis-courages the use of unnecessary violence even by the innocent; morality can hardly do less.

Preventing versus Deterring Crime

The analogy between capital punishment and self-defense requires us to face squarely the empirical questions surrounding the preven-tive and deterrent effects of the death penalty. Executing a murderer in the name of punish-ment can be seen as a crime-*preventive* measure just to the extent it is reasonable to believe that if the murderer had not been executed he or she would have committed other crimes (including, but not necessarily confined to, murder). Executing a murderer can be seen as a crime *deterrent* just to the extent it is reason-able to believe that by the example of the exe-cution other persons would be frightened off from committing murder. Any punishment can be a crime preventive without being a crime deterrent, just as it can be a deterrent without being a preventive. It can also be both or nei-ther. Prevention and deterrence are theoreti-cally independent because they operate by dif-ferent methods. Crimes can be prevented by taking guns out of the hands of criminals, by putting criminals behind bars, by alerting the public to be less careless and less prone to vic-timization, and so forth. Crimes can be deterred only by making would-be criminals frightened of being arrested, convicted, and punished for crimes—that is, making persons overcome their desire to commit crimes by a

stronger desire to avoid the risk of being caught and punished.

The Death Penalty as a Crime Preventive

Capital punishment is unusual among penalties because its preventive effects limit its deterrent effects. The death penalty can never deter the executed person from further crimes. At most, it can prevent a person from committing them. Popular discussions of the death penalty are frequently confused because they so often assume that the death penalty is a perfect and infallible deterrent so far as the executed crim-inal is concerned, whereas nothing of the sort is true. What is even more important, it is also wrong to think that in every execution the death penalty has proved to be an infallible crime preventive. What is obviously true is that once an offender has been executed, it is phys-ically impossible for that person to commit any further crimes, since the punishment is totally incapacitative. But incapacitation is not identi-cal with prevention. Prevention by means of incapacitation occurs only if the executed criminal would have committed other crimes if he or she had not been executed and had been punished only in some less incapacitative way (e.g., by imprisonment).

What evidence is there that the incapacita-tive effects of the death penalty are an effective crime preventive? From the study of imprison-ment, parole, release records, this much is clear: If the murderers and other criminals who have been executed are like the murderers who were convicted but not executed, then (1) exe-cuting all convicted murderers would have prevented many crimes, but not many murders (less than one convicted murderer in five hun-dred commits another murder); and (2) con-victed murderers, whether inside prison or outside after release, have at least as good a record of no further criminal activity as any other class of convicted felon.

These facts show that the general public tends to overrate the danger and threat to public safety constituted by the failure to execute every murderer who is caught and convicted. While it would be quite wrong to say that there is no risk such criminals will repeat their crimes—or similar ones—if they are not executed, it would be equally erroneous to say that by executing every convicted murderer many horrible crimes will he prevented. All we know is that a few such crimes will never be committed; we do not know how many or by whom they would have been committed. (Obviously, if we did know we would have tried to prevent them!) This is the nub of the problem. There is no way to know in advance which if any of the incarcerated or released murderers will kill again. It is useful in this connection to remember that the only way to guarantee that no horrible crimes ever occur is to execute *everyone* who might conceivably commit such a crime. Similarly, the only way to guarantee that no convicted murderer ever commits another murder is to execute them all. No modern society has ever done this, and for two hundred years ours has been moving steadily in the opposite direction.

These considerations show that our society has implicitly adopted an attitude toward the risk of murder rather like the attitude it has adopted toward the risk of fatality from other sources, such as automobile accidents, lung cancer, or drowning. Since no one knows when or where or upon whom any of these lethal events will fall, it would be too great an invasion of freedom to undertake the severe restrictions that alone would suffice to prevent any such deaths from occurring. It is better to take the risks and keep our freedom than to try to eliminate the risks altogether and lose our freedom in the process. Hence, we have lifeguards at the beach, but swimming is not totally prohibited; smokers are warned, but cigarettes are still legally sold; pedestrians may be given the right of way in a crosswalk, but marginally competent drivers are still allowed to operate motor vehicles. Some risk is therefore imposed on the innocent; in the name of

our right to freedom, our other rights are not protected by society at all costs.

The Death Penalty as a Crime Deterrent

Determining whether the death penalty is an effective deterrent is even more difficult than determining its effectiveness as a crime preventive. In general, our knowledge about how penalties deter crimes and whether in fact they do—whom they deter, from which crimes, and under what conditions—is distressingly inexact. Most people nevertheless are convinced that punishments do deter, and that the more severe a punishment is the better it will deter. For half a century, social scientists have studied the questions whether the death penalty is a deterrent and whether it is a better deterrent than the alternative of imprisonment. Their verdict, while not unanimous, is nearly so. Whatever may be true about the deterrence of lesser crimes by other penalties, the deterrence achieved by the death penalty for murder is not measurably any greater than the deterrence achieved by long-term imprisonment. In the nature of the case, the evidence is quite indirect. No one can identify for certain any crimes that did not occur because the would-be offender was deterred by the threat of the death penalty and could not have been deterred by a less severe threat. Likewise, no one can identify any crimes that did occur because the offender was not deterred by the threat of prison even though he would have been deterred by the threat of death. Nevertheless, such evidence as we have fails to show that the more severe penalty (death) is really a better deterrent than the less severe penalty (imprisonment) for such crimes as murder.

If the conclusion stated above is correct, and the death penalty and long-term imprisonment are equally effective (or ineffective) as deterrents to murder, then the argument for the death penalty on grounds of deterrence is seriously weakened. One of the moral principles identified earlier now comes into play. It is the principle that unless there is a good reason for choosing a more rather than a less severe punishment for a crime, the less severe penalty is to be preferred. This principle obviously commends itself to anyone who values human life and who concedes that, all other things being equal, less pain and suffering is always better than more. Human life is valued in part to the degree that it is free of pain, suffering, misery, and frustration, and in particular to the extent that it is free of such experiences when they serve no purpose. If the death penalty is not a more effective deterrent than imprisonment, then its greater severity is gratuitous, purposeless suffering and deprivation. Accordingly, we must reject it in favor of some less severe alternative, unless we can identify some more weighty moral principle that the death penalty protects better than any less severe mode of punishment does. Whether there is any such principle is unclear.

A Cost/Benefit Analysis of the Death Penalty

A full study of the costs and benefits involved in the practice of capital punishment would not be confined solely to the question of whether it is a better deterrent or preventive of murder than imprisonment. Any thorough-going utilitarian approach to the death-penalty controversy would need to examine carefully other costs and benefits as well, because maximizing the balance of all the social benefits over all the social costs is the sole criterion of right and wrong according to utilitarianism. . . . Let us consider, therefore, some of the other costs and benefits to be calculated. Clinical psychologists have presented evidence to suggest that the death penalty actually incites some persons of unstable mind to murder others, either because they are afraid to take their own lives and hope that society will punish them for murder by putting them to death, or because they fancy that they, too, are killing with justification analogously to the lawful and presumably justified killing involved in capital punishment. If such

evidence is sound, capital punishment can serve as a counterpreventive or even an incitement to murder; such incited murders become part of its social cost. Imprisonment, however, has not been known to incite any murders or other crimes of violence in a comparable fashion. (A possible exception might be found in the imprisonment of terrorists, which has inspired other terrorists to take hostages as part of a scheme to force the authorities to release their imprisoned comrades.) The risks of executing the innocent are also part of the social cost. The historical record is replete with innocent persons arrested, indicted, convicted, sentenced, and occasionally legally executed for crimes they did not commit. This is quite apart from the guilty persons unfairly convicted, sentenced to death, and executed on the strength of perjured testimony, fraudulent evidence, subornation of jurors, and other violations of the civil rights and liberties of the accused. Nor is this all. The high costs of a capital trial and of the inevitable appeals, the costly methods of custody most prisons adopt for convicts on "death row," are among the straightforward economic costs that the death penalty incurs. Conducting a valid cost/benefit analysis of capital punishment is extremely difficult, and it is impossible to predict exactly what such a study would show. Nevertheless, based on such evidence as we do have, it is quite possible that a study of this sort would favor abolition of all death penalties rather than their retention.

What If Executions Did Deter?

From the moral point of view, it is quite important to determine what one should think about capital punishment if the evidence were clearly to show that the death penalty is a distinctly superior method of social defense by comparison with less severe alternatives. Kantian moralists . . . would have no use for such knowledge, because their entire case for the morality of the death penalty rests on the way it is thought to provide just retribution, not on the way it is thought to provide social defense. For a utilitarian, however, such knowledge would be conclusive. Those who follow Locke's reasoning would also be gratified, because they defend the morality of the death penalty both on the ground that it is retributively just and on the ground that it provides needed social defense.

What about the opponents of the death penalty, however? To oppose the death penalty in the face of incontestable evidence that it is an effective method of social defense violates the moral principle that where grave risks are to be run, it is better that they be run by the guilty than by the innocent. Consider in this connection an imaginary world in which by executing the murderer his victim is invariably restored to life, whole and intact, as though the murder had never occurred. In such a miraculous world, it is hard to see how anyone could oppose the death penalty on moral grounds. Why shouldn't a murderer die if that will infallibly bring the victim back to life? What could possibly be morally wrong with taking the murderer's life under such conditions? The death penalty would now be an instrument of perfect restitution, and it would give a new and better meaning to *lex talionis,* "a life for a life." The whole idea is fanciful, of course, but it shows as nothing else can how opposition to the death penalty cannot be both moral and wholly unconditional. If opposition to the death penalty is to be morally responsible, then it must be conceded that there are conditions (however unlikely) under which that opposition should cease.

But even if the death penalty were known to be a uniquely effective social defense, we could still imagine conditions under which it would be reasonable to oppose it. Suppose that in addition to being a slightly better preventive and deterrent than imprisonment, executions also have a slight incitive effect (so that for every ten murders an execution prevents or deters, it also incites another murder). Suppose also that the administration of criminal justice

in capital cases is inefficient, unequal, and tends to secure convictions and death sentences only for murderers who least "deserve" to be sentenced to death (including some death sentences and a few executions of the innocent). Under such conditions, it would still be reasonable to oppose the death penalty, because on the facts supposed more (or not fewer) innocent lives are being threatened and lost by using the death penalty than would be risked by abolishing it. It is important to remember throughout our evaluation of the deterrence controversy that we cannot ever apply the principle . . . that advises us to risk the lives of the guilty in order to save the lives of the innocent. Instead, the most we can do is weigh the risk for the general public against the execution of those who are *found* guilty by an imperfect system of criminal justice. These hypothetical factual assumptions illustrate the contingencies upon which the morality of opposition to the death penalty rests. And not only the morality of opposition; the morality of any defense of the death penalty rests on the same contingencies. This should help us understand why, in resolving the morality of capital punishment one way or the other, it is so important to know, as well as we can, whether the death penalty really does deter, prevent, or incite crime, whether the innocent really are ever executed, and how likely is the occurrence of these things in the future.

How Many Guilty Lives Is One Innocent Life Worth?

The great unanswered question that utilitarians must face concerns the level of social defense that executions should be expected to achieve before it is justifiable to carry them out. Consider three possible situations: (1) At the level of a hundred executions per year, each additional execution of a convicted murderer reduces the number of murder victims by ten. (2) Executing every convicted murderer reduces the number of murders to 5,000 victims annually, whereas executing only one out of ten reduces the number to 5,001. (3) Executing every convicted murderer reduces the murder rate no more than does executing one in a hundred and no more than does a random pattern of executions.

Many people contemplating situation (1) would regard this as a reasonable trade-off: The execution of each further guilty person saves the lives of ten innocent ones. (In fact, situation (1) or something like it may be taken as a description of what most of those who defend the death penalty on grounds of social defense believe is true.) But suppose that, instead of saving 10 lives, the number dropped to 0.5, i.e., one victim avoided for each two additional executions. Would that be a reasonable price to pay? We are on the road toward the situation described in situation (2), where a drastic 90 percent reduction in the number of persons executed causes the level of social defense to drop by only 0.0002 percent. Would it be worth it to execute so many more murderers at the cost of such a slight decrease in social defense? How many guilty lives is one innocent life worth? (Only those who think that guilty lives are *worthless* can avoid facing this problem.) In situation (3), of course, there is no basis for executing all convicted murderers, since there is no gain in social defense to show for each additional execution after the first out of each hundred has been executed. How, then, should we determine which out of each hundred convicted murderers is the unlucky one to be put to death?

It may be possible, under a complete and thoroughgoing cost/benefit analysis of the death penalty, to answer such questions. But an appeal merely to the moral principle that if lives are to be risked then let it be the lives of the guilty rather than of the innocent will not suffice. (We have already noticed . . . that this abstract principle is of little use in the actual administration of criminal justice, because the police and the courts do not deal with the guilty as such but only with those *judged* guilty.) Nor will it suffice to agree that society deserves all the crime prevention and deterrence it can get as a result of inflicting severe punishments. These principles are consistent with too many different policies. They are too vague by themselves to resolve the choice on grounds of social defense when confronted with hypothetical situations like those proposed above.

Since no adequate cost/benefit analysis of the death penalty exists, there is no way to resolve these questions from that standpoint at this time. Moreover, it can be argued that we cannot have such an analysis without already establishing in some way or other the relative value of innocent lives versus guilty lives. Far from being a product of cost/benefit analysis, a comparative evaluation of lives would have to be available to us before we undertook any such analysis. Without it, no cost/benefit analysis can get off the ground. Finally, it must be noted that our knowledge at present does not approximate to anything like the situation described above in (1). On the contrary, from the evidence we do have it seems we achieve about the same deterrent and preventive effects whether we punish murder by death or by imprisonment. . . . Therefore, something like the situation in (2) or in (3) may be correct. If so, this shows that the choice between the two policies of capital punishment and life imprisonment for murder will probably have to be made on some basis other than social defense; on that basis alone, the two policies are equivalent and therefore equally acceptable.

CAPITAL PUNISHMENT AND RETRIBUTIVE JUSTICE

As we have noticed earlier in several contexts, there are two leading principles of retributive justice relevant to the capital punishment controversy. One is the principle that crimes should be punished. The other is the principle that the severity of a punishment should be proportional to the gravity of the offense. They are moral principles of recognized weight. No discussion of the morality of punishment would be complete without taking them into account. Leaving aside all questions of social defense, how strong a case for capital punishment can be made on their basis? How reliable and persuasive are these principles themselves?

Crime Must Be Punished

Given the general rationale for punishment sketched earlier . . ., there cannot be any dispute over this principle. In embracing it, of course, we are not automatically making a fetish of "law and order," in the sense that we would be if we thought that the most important single thing to do with social resources is to punish crimes. In addition, this principle need not be in dispute between proponents and opponents of the death penalty. Only those who completely oppose punishment for murder and other erstwhile capital crimes would appear to disregard this principle. Even defenders of the death penalty must admit that putting a convicted murderer in prison for years is a punishment of that criminal. The principle that crime must be punished is neutral to our controversy, because both sides acknowledge it.

It is the other principle of retributive justice that seems to be a decisive one. Under the principle of retaliation, *lex talionis,* it must always have seemed that murderers ought to be put to death. Proponents of the death penalty, with rare exceptions, have insisted on this point, and it seems that even opponents of the death penalty must give it grudging assent. The strategy of opponents of the death penalty is to argue either that (1) this principle is not really a principle of justice after all, or that (2) to the extent it is, it does not require death for murderers, or that (3) in any case it is not the only principle of punitive justice. As we shall see, all these objections have merit.

Is Murder Alone to Be Punished by Death?

Let us recall, first, that not even the Biblical world limited the death penalty to the punishment of murder. Many other nonhomicidal crimes also carried this penalty (e.g., kidnapping, witchcraft, cursing one's parents). In our own nation's recent history, persons have been executed for aggravated assault, rape, kidnapping, armed robbery, sabotage, and espionage. It is not possible to defend *any* of these executions (not to mention some of the more bizarre capital statutes, like the one in Georgia that used to provide an optional death penalty for desecration of a grave) on grounds of just retribution. This entails that either such executions are not justified or that they are justified on some ground other than retribution. In actual practice, few if any defenders of the death penalty have ever been willing to rest their case entirely on the moral principle of just retribution as formulated in terms of "a life for a life." (Kant seems to have been a conspicuous exception.) Most defenders of the death penalty have implied by their willingness to use executions to defend not only life but limb and property as well, that they did not place much value on the lives of criminals when compared to the value of both lives and things belonging to innocent citizens.

Are All Murders to Be Punished by Death?

European civilization for several centuries has tended to limit the variety of criminal homicides punishable by death. Even Kant took a casual attitude toward a mother's killing of her illegitimate child. ("A child born into the world outside marriage is outside the law . . ., and consequently it is also outside the protection of the law.") In our society, the development nearly two hundred years ago of the distinction between first- and second-degree murder was an attempt to narrow the class of criminal homicides deserving the death penalty. Yet those dead owing to manslaughter, or to any kind of unintentional, accidental, unpremeditated, unavoidable, unmalicious killing are just as dead as the victims of the most ghastly murder. Both the law in practice and moral reflection show how difficult it is to identify all and only the criminal homicides that are appropriately punished by death (assuming that any are). Individual judges and juries differ in the conclusions they reach. The history of capital punishment for homicides reveals continual efforts, uniformly unsuccessful, to identify before the fact those homicides for which the slayer should die. Sixty years ago, Benjamin Cardozo, then a justice of the United States Supreme Court, said of the distinction between degrees of murder that it was

> . . . so obscure that no jury hearing it for the first time can fairly be expected to assimilate and understand it. I am not at all sure that I understand it myself after trying to apply it for many years and after diligent study of what has been written in the books. Upon the basis of this fine distinction with its obscure and mystifying psychology, scores of men have gone to their death.

Similar skepticism has been expressed on the reliability and rationality of death-penalty statutes that give the trial court the discretion ot sentence to prison or to death. As Justice John Marshall Harlan of the Supreme Court observed more than a decade ago,

> Those who have come to grips with the hard task of actually attempting to draft means of channeling capital sentencing discretion have confirmed the lesson taught by history. . . . To identify before the fact those characteristics of criminal homicide and their perpetrators which call for the death penalty, and to express these characteristics in language which can be fairly understood and applied by the sentencing authority, appear to be tasks which are beyond present human ability.

The abstract principle that the punishment of death best fits the crime of murder turns out to be extremely difficult to interpret and apply.

If we look at the matter from the standpoint of the actual practice of criminal justice, we can only conclude that "a life for a life" plays little or no role whatever. Plea bargaining (in which a person charged with a crime pleads guilty in exchange for a less severe sentence than he might have received if his case went to trial and he was found guilty), even where murder is concerned, is widespread. Studies of criminal justice reveal that what the courts (trial or appellate) in a given jurisdiction decide on a given day is first-degree murder suitably punished by death could just as well be decided in a neighboring jurisdiction on another day either as second-degree murder or as first-degree murder but without the death penalty. The factors that influence prosecutors in determining the charge under which they will prosecute go far beyond the simple principle of "a life for a life." Cynics, of course, will say that these facts show that our society does not care about justice. To put it succinctly, either justice in punishment does not consist of retribution, because there are other principles of justice; or there are other moral considerations besides justice that must be honored; or retributive justice is not adequately expressed in the idea of "a life for a life"; or justice in the criminal justice system is beyond our reach.

Is Death Sufficiently Retributive?

Those who advocate capital punishment for murder on retributive grounds must face the objection that, on their own principles, the death penalty in some cases is morally inadequate. How could death in the electric chair or the gas chamber or before a firing squad or on a gallows suffice as just retribution, given the savage, brutal, wanton character of so many murders? How can retributive justice be served by anything less than equally savage methods of execution? From a retributive point of view, the oft-heard exclamation, "Death is too good for him!" has a certain truth. Are defenders of the death penalty willing to embrace this consequence of their own doctrine?

If they were, they would be stooping to the methods and thus to the squalor of the murderer. Where the quality of the crime sets the limits of just methods of punishment, as it will if we attempt to give exact and literal implementation to *lex talionis,* society will find itself descending to the cruelties and savagery that criminals employ. What is worse, society would be deliberately authorizing such acts, in the cool light of reason, and not (as is often true of vicious criminals) impulsively or in hatred and anger or with an insane or unbalanced mind. Moral restraints, in short, prohibit us from trying to make executions perfectly retributive. Once we grant that such restraints are proper, it is unreasonable to insist that the principle of "a life for a life" nevertheless by itself justifies the execution of murderers.

Other considerations take us in a different direction. Few murders, outside television and movie scripts, involve anything like an execution. An execution, after all, begins with a solemn pronouncement of the death sentence from a judge; this is followed by long detention in maximum security awaiting the date of execution, during which various complex and protracted appeals will be pursued; after this there is a clemency hearing before the governor, and then "the last mile" to the execution chamber itself. As the French writer Albert Camus once remarked,

> For there to be an equivalence, the death penalty would have to punish a criminal who had warned his victim of the date at which he would inflict a horrible death on him and who, from that moment onward, had confined him at his mercy for months. Such a monster is not encountered in private life.

Differential Severity Does Not Require Executions

What, then, emerges from our examination of retributive justice and the death penalty? If retributive justice is thought to consist in *lex talionis,* all one can say is that this principle has never exercised more than a crude and indirect effect on the actual punishments meted out by society. Other principles interfere with a literal

and single-minded application of this one. Some homicides seem improperly punished by death at all; others would require methods of execution too horrible to inflict; in still other cases any possible execution is too deliberate and monstrous given the nature of the motivation culminating in the murder. In any case, proponents of the death penalty rarely confine themselves to reliance on nothing but this principle of just retribution, since they rarely confine themselves to supporting the death penalty only for all murders.

But retributive justice need not be thought of as consisting in *lex talionis.* One may reject that principle as too crude and still embrace the retributive principle that the severity of punishments should be graded according to the gravity of the offense. Even though one need not claim that life imprisonment (or any kind of punishment other than death) "fits" the crime of murder, one can claim that this punishment is the proper one for murder. To do this, the schedule of punishments accepted by society must be arranged so that this mode of imprisonment is the most severe penalty used. Opponents of the death penalty need not reject this principle of retributive justice, even though they must reject a literal *lex talionis.*

Equal Justice and Capital Punishment

During the past generation, the strongest practical objection to the death penalty has been the inequities with which it has been applied. As the late Supreme Court Justice William O. Douglas once observed, "One searches our chronicles in vain for the execution of any member of the affluent strata of this society." One does not search our chronicles in vain for the crime of murder committed by the affluent. All the sociological evidence points to the conclusion that the death penalty is the poor man's justice; hence the slogan, "Those without the capital get the punishment." The death penalty is also racially sensitive. Every study of the death penalty for rape (unconstitutional only since 1977) has confirmed that black male rapists (especially where the victim is a white female) are far more likely to be sentenced to death and executed than white male rapists. Convicted black murderers are more likely to end up on "death row" than are others, and the killers of whites (whether white or nonwhite) are more likely to be sentenced to death than are the killers of nonwhites.

Let us suppose that the factual basis for such a criticism is sound. What follows for the morality of capital punishment? Many defenders of the death penalty have been quick to point out that since there is nothing intrinsic about the crime of murder or rape dictating that only the poor or only racial-minority males will commit it, and since there is nothing overtly racist about the statutes that authorize the death penalty for murder or rape, capital punishment itself is hardly at fault if in practice it falls with unfair impact on the poor and the black. There is, in short, nothing in the death penalty that requires it to be applied unfairly and with arbitrary or discriminatory results. It is at worst a fault in the system of administering criminal justice. (Some, who dispute the facts cited above, would deny even this.) There is an adequate remedy—execute more whites, women, and affluent murderers.

Presumably, both proponents and opponents of capital punishment would concede that it is a fundamental dictate of justice that a punishment should not be unfairly—inequitably or unevenly—enforced and applied. They should also be able to agree that when the punishment in question is the extremely severe one of death, then the requirement to be fair in using such a punishment becomes even more stringent. There should be no dispute in the death penalty controversy over these principles of justice. The dispute begins as soon as one attempts to connect the principles with the actual use of this punishment.

In this country, many critics of the death penalty have argued, we would long ago have got rid of it entirely if it had been a condition of its use that it be applied equally and fairly. In the words of the attorneys who argued against the death penalty in the Supreme Court during 1972, "It is a freakish aberration, a random extreme act of violence, visibly arbitrary and discriminatory—a penalty reserved for unusual application because, if it were usually used, it would affront universally shared standards of public decency." It is difficult to dispute this judgment, when one considers that there have been in the United States during the past fifty years about half a million criminal homicides but only about 3,900 executions (all but 33 of which were of men).

We can look at these statistics in another way to illustrate the same point. If we could be assured that the nearly 4,000 persons executed were the worst of the bad, repeated offenders incapable of safe incarceration, much less of rehabilitation, the most dangerous murderers in captivity—the ones who had killed more than once and were likely to kill again, and the least likely to be confined in prison without chronic danger to other inmates and the staff—then one might accept half a million murders and a few thousand executions with a sense that rough justice had been done. But the truth is otherwise. Persons are sentenced to death and executed not because they have been found to be uncontrollably violent or hopelessly poor confinement and release risks. Instead, they are executed because they have a poor defense (inexperienced or overworked counsel) at trial; they have no funds to bring sympathetic witnesses to court; they are transients or strangers in the community where they are tried; the prosecuting attorney wants the publicity that goes with "sending a killer to the chair"; there are no funds for an appeal or for a transcript of the trial record; they are members of a despised racial or political minority. In short, the actual study of why particular persons have been sentenced to death and executed does not show any careful winnowing of the worst from the bad. It shows that the executed were usually the unlucky victims of prejudice and discrimination, the losers in an arbitrary lottery that could just as well have spared them, the victims of the disadvantages that almost always go with poverty. A system like this does not enhance human life; it cheapens and degrades it. However heinous murder and other crimes are, the system of capital punishment does not compensate for or erase those crimes. It only tends to add new injuries of its own to the catalogue of human brutality.

CONCLUSION

Our discussion of the death penalty from the moral point of view shows that there is no one moral principle the validity of which is paramount and that decisively favors one side of the controversy. Rather, we have seen how it is possible to argue either for or against the death penalty, and in each case to be appealing to moral principles that derive from the worth, value, or dignity of human life. We have also seen how it is impossible to connect any of these abstract principles with the actual practice of capital punishment witout a close study of sociological, psychological, and economic factors. By themselves, the moral principles that are relevant are too abstract and uncertain in application to be of much help. Without the guidance of such principles, of course, the facts (who gets executed, and why) are of little use, either.

My own view of the controversy is that, given the moral principles we have identified in the course of our discussion (including the overriding value of human life), and given all the facts about capital punishment, the balance of reasons favors abolition of the death penalty. The alternative to capital punishment that I favor, as things currently stand, is long-term imprisonment. Such a punishment is retributive and can be made appropriately severe to reflect the gravity of the crime. It gives adequate (though hardly perfect) protection to the public. It is free of the worst defect to which the death penalty is liable: execution of the innocent. It tacitly acknowledges that there is no way for a criminal, alive or dead, to make complete amends for murder or other grave crimes against the person. Last but not least, it has symbolic significance. The death penalty, more than any other kind of killing, is done by officials in the name of society and on its behalf. Yet each of us has a hand in such killings. Unless they are absolutely necessary they cannot be justified. Thus, abolishing the death penalty represents extending the hand of life even to those who by their crimes have "forfeited" any right to live. It is a tacit admission that we must abandon the folly and pretense of attempting to secure perfect justice in an imperfect world.

Searching for an epigram suitable for our times, in which governments have waged war and suppressed internal dissent by using methods that can only be described as savage and criminal, Camus was prompted to admonish: "Let us be neither victims nor executioners." Perhaps better than any other, this exhortation points the way between forbidden extremes if we are to respect the humanity in each of us.

Discussion Questions

1. Present and explain why Professor Bedau believes that the analogy between the death penalty and self-defense actually works in favor of the abolition of capital punishment. Explain why you agree or disagree with Bedau's argument.
2. Present and explain the reasons why Professor Bedau does not believe that the retributivist argument works. Why does he believe that a literal interpretation of the "life for life" ethic fails? Do you agree or disagree? Explain and defend your answer.

3. Present and explain the reasons why Professor Bedau does not believe that the deterrence argument works. How do you think he would respond to Professor Pojman's defense of the deterrence argument (Chapter 26)? Explain and defend your answer.

4. Why does Professor Bedau maintain that the death penalty is arbitrarily and capriciously administered? Do you agree or disagree? Explain and defend your position.

You can locate InfoTrac-College Education articles about this chapter by accessing the InfoTrac-College Edition website (http://www.infotrac-college.com/wadsworth/). Using the InfoTrac-College Edition subject guide, enter the search terms relevant to this chapter, and then read abstracts for relevant articles.

Part III

Issues of Social Justice and Personal Liberty

General Introduction to Part III

The following is from a *Wall Street Journal* editorial (December 13, 1993):

> Mrs. Schnell is a 50-year-old divorced woman who works part time. In October the state of Wisconsin found that she had engaged in sexual and religious discrimination by taking out the following ad in a local newspaper: *Apartment for rent, 1 bedroom, electric included, mature Christian handyman.*
>
> Initially, Mrs. Schnell was contacted by the Milwaukee Fair Housing Council, a nonprofit organization. The Council said she had discriminated because her ad suggested that a "handyman" or male was preferred. And "Christian" implied that non-Christians wouldn't be welcome. . . . The Council offered to drop the case if Mrs. Schnell paid a $50 fine and $500 in attorney's fees.
>
> She refused, claiming she hadn't intended to discriminate. She says she merely wanted a tenant who could help her remodel her 100-year-old house in exchange for a lower rent. As a Christian, she also felt an obligation to help other Christians first. She never asked the religion of the emotionally disturbed man she ended up accepting as her tenant. . . .
>
> After Mrs. Schnell refused to settle with the Fair Housing Council, the next time she heard about her ad was last year, when she was notified that the Fair Housing Council had indeed filed a complaint with the state, as it is somehow empowered to do. After the state's Equal Rights Division found her guilty, she learned the fines and fees would total $8,000. She fears she may have to take out a second mortgage on her house if she loses her appeal to the local circuit court.

This real-life story raises some very important questions, such as the following. Does the state have a right to employ its concepts of fairness and justice (nondiscrimination) in such a way that Mrs. Schnell is forced to use her property only if it is consistent with the state's concepts, or is such coercion a violation of Mrs. Schnell's personal liberty, privacy rights, and property rights? This sort of question brings out deeper philosophical questions about the nature of justice, fairness, liberty, privacy rights, and property rights as well as the role of the state and the "public good" in deciding such matters. Of course, it seems correct to many people, especially those who have suffered because of bigotry and prejudice, that laws against discrimination based on race, ethnicity, or gender are just laws, even if the state coerces businesses and property owners to act consistently with them. Yet, the thought of the middle-aged Mrs. Schnell being harassed by government lawyers seems just as disturbing as a black man being denied employment by local bigots. In order to resolve this apparent tension, one must carefully explore the philosophical assumptions that lurk behind it.

This part of our text deals with issues that touch on these philosophical assumptions: Affirmative Action (Section A), Economic and Social Justice (Section B), Censorship and Freedom of Expression (Section C), and Homosexuality (Section D)

For Further Reading

Hadley Arkes, *First Things: An Inquiry into the First Principles of Morals and Justice* (Princeton, NJ: Princeton University Press, 1986).

Ronald Dworkin, *Taking Rights Seriously* (Cambridge, MA: Harvard University Press, 1977).

John Locke, *Two Treatises on Government,* a critical edition with an introduction and apparatus criticus by Peter Laslett, rev. ed. (New York: Cambridge University Press, 1963).

Karl Marx, *The Communist Manifesto,* ed. Frederic L. Bender (New York: W. W. Norton, 1988).

Michael Novak, *The Spirit of Democratic Capitalism* (New York: A Touchstone Book, 1982).

Robert Nozick, *Anarchy, State, and Utopia* (New York: Basic Books, 1974).

Susan Moller Okin, *Justice, Gender, and the Family* (New York: Basic Books, 1989).

John Rawls, *A Theory of Justice* (Cambridge, MA: Belnap Press of the Harvard University Press, 1971).

Murray Rothbard, *For a New Liberty* (New York: Macmillan, 1973).

Jean-Jacques Rousseau, *The Social Contract* (London: Everyman's Library, 1947).

Michael Sandel, *Liberalism and the Limits of Justice,* 2nd ed. (Cambridge: Cambridge University Press, 1998).

Leo Strauss, *Natural Right and History* (Chicago: University of Chicago Press, 1950).

SECTION A

Affirmative Action

Introduction to Section A

A vast majority of Californians who went to the polls on November 5, 1996, voted "yes" on one of the most important ballot questions pertaining to civil rights, the California Civil Rights Initiative (CCRI). It's purpose was to eliminate most forms of affirmative action practiced by the state of California as well as its local governments. A portion of CCRI reads:

> Neither the State of California nor any of its political subdivisions or agents shall use race, sex, color, ethnicity, or national origin as a criterion for either discriminating against, or granting preferential treatment to, any individual or group in the operation of the State's system of public employment, public education or public contracting.

Supporters of the initiative maintain that CCRI is consistent with the central purpose of the American Civil Rights Movement: equal opportunity for all citizens without regard to race, ethnicity, or gender. To defend this, they cite a section of the 1964 Civil Rights Act that affirms that no employer is required to "grant preferential treatment to any individual or group on account of any imbalance which may exist" between the number of employees in such groups and "the total number or percentage of persons of such race, color, religion, sex, or national origin in any community, State, section, or other area."[1]

Also, supporters of the initiative point out that the Congressmen who sponsored the Civil Rights Act of 1964, as well as the leadership of the civil rights movement, denied the equation of support for this legislation (and general support of civil rights) with support for affirmative action or preferential treatment programs. Take for example the following:

> Title VII does not require an employer to achieve any sort of racial balance in his work-force by giving preferential treatment to any individual or group.[2] (Senator Hubert H. Humphrey)
>
> [Title VII] specifically prohibit[s] the Attorney General, or any agency of the government, from requiring employment to be on the basis of racial or religious quotas. Under [this provision] an employer with only white employees could continue to have the best qualified persons even if they were all white.[3] (Senator Harrison A. Williams)

Our association has never been in favor of a quota system. We believe the quota system is unfair whether it is used for [blacks] or against [blacks]. . . . [We] feel people ought to be hired because of their ability, irrespective of their color. . . . We want equality, equality of opportunity and employment on the basis of ability.[4] (Roy Wilkins, then-Executive Director of the NAACP)

Opponents of CCRI, on the other hand, defend preferential treatment by pointing out that the elimination of discriminatory laws did not result in the completely unsegregated and just society for which the civil rights movement had hoped. This is why in 1965 President Johnson issued Executive Order 11246. It required the Department of Labor to offer government contracts with construction companies on the basis of the ownership's race. It was argued that such a policy is necessary in order to remedy the oppression that resulted in centuries of the loathsome practice of racial discrimination. In 1967 President Johnson issued Executive Order 11375 so that affirmative action would be extended to women. In time affirmative action benefits were extended to Native Americans, Asians, Hispanics, and people with handicaps. Although at that time affirmative action was interpreted by most to mean *weak affirmative action* (entailing equal opportunity, active recruitment of minorities, using race or gender as a tie breaker, etc.), eventually it evolved into *strong affirmative action* (entailing certain results of racial proportionality based on numerical quotas, goals, and timetables) since it was apparent to many supporters of affirmative action that the weak version of it was not producing the results they expected. (Weak and strong affirmative action will be looked at more closely below).

In his 1965 commencement address at Howard University, President Johnson made a moral defense of affirmative action by employing a now famous analogy:

But freedom is not enough. You do not wipe away the scars of centuries by saying: Now you are free to go where you want, and do as you desire, and choose the leaders you please.

You do not take a person who, for years, has been hobbled by chains and liberate him, bring him to the starting line of a race and then say, "you are free to compete with all the others," and still justly believe that you have been completely fair.

Thus it is not enough just to open the gates of opportunity. All our citizens must have the ability to walk through those gates.

This is the next and more profound stage of the battle for civil rights. We seek not just freedom of opportunity. We seek not just legal equity but human ability, not just equality as a right and a theory but equality as a fact and equality as a result.[5]

According to the champions of affirmative action, white males largely dominate and control a network of social institutions—for example, banks, universities, corporations, governments—that is the hub of authority and power in our culture. This disproportionate representation, it is argued, is the result of a long history of discrimination in America against minorities and women. Therefore, these institutions must undergo radical changes so that justice and fairness may be truly achieved. This can only be accomplished, according to affirmative action supporters, by preferential treatment programs with goals, timetables, and diversity hiring programs.

Although the term "affirmative action" is well known and well used, it is not often defined with much clarity. After all, affirmative action programs take a variety of forms in a diversity of employment and educational settings. Nevertheless, some commentators see affirmative action programs as falling into one of two broad categories. The first, *weak affirmative action,* is the use of "such measures as the elimination of segregation, widespread advertisement to groups not previously represented in certain privileged positions, special scholarships for the disadvantaged classes (e.g., all the poor), using underrepresentation or a history of past discrimination as a tie breaker when candidates are relatively equal, and the like."[6] Weak affirmative action puts an emphasis on *equal opportunity* rather than equal results. For example, an employer should, in seeking new employees, cast as wide a net as possible so as not to unintentionally bypass minority and female applicants. However, when it comes to evaluating all the candidates for the position, the employer should ignore the race or gender of the applicant (except perhaps in the case of a tie or close call). If weak affirmative action is used and it happens to result in the disproportionate hiring of members of a certain group in comparison to the percentage of the general population (e.g., 78 percent of the general population is white while 95 percent of the employees are white), according to the proponent of this type of affirmative action, it makes no sense to call this result "unfair" or "unjust," for the employer had cast a wide net, treated everyone equally, and did not take race, ethnicity or gender into consideration for the purpose of excluding minorities and women.

Strong affirmative action, on the other hand, "involves more positive steps to eliminate past injustice, such as reverse discrimination, hiring candidates on the basis of race or gender in order to reach equal or near equal results, proportionate representation in each area of society."[7] In other words, strong affirmative action puts an emphasis on equal results that fit some goal, pattern, or diversity plan that ought to be achieved.

Some thinkers have called for the elimination of affirmative action based on race, ethnicity, and gender, and replacing it with policies that target those who are truly disadvantaged regardless of race, ethnicity, or gender.[8] The rationale for such programs is that they will help those who are truly needy and who lack many opportunities due to poverty and poor schooling. Because these programs would not be based on race, ethnicity or gender, the male and female children of Eddie Murphy, Bill Cosby, and Clarence Thomas would not be able to use their minority status, as they can now do so, to gain special privileges, such as minority scholarships and set-asides, while the children of white poor Appalachian parents are given no help whatsoever. However, since a larger percentage of minorities (including blacks) than whites are in need, minorities would receive the bulk of benefits dispensed by these new affirmative action programs.

There are different ways in which affirmative action is defended. Some people stress the *backward looking* feature of affirmative action. That is to say, the purpose of affirmative action is to remedy or compensate for past wrongs. Those who stress this feature tend to think of affirmative action as a policy grounded in some form of deontological ethics (Chapter 3 and 5). Others stress the *forward looking* feature of affirmative action. They do not necessarily view affirmative action as a remedy for past injustice, but rather, they see it as a tool by which society (or a business or an educational institution) sees to it that its goods do not line up with divisions along ethnic and gender lines. Forward-looking policies are usually both deontological and utilitarian (Chapter 4). For the supporters of such policies tend to appeal both to consequences, that is, these policies will likely result in the greatest happiness for the greatest number, as well as to notions of goodness and justice, that is, these policies will likely result in a society that is more fair or more just irrespective of decreases or increases of happiness.

Preferential treatment programs are defended in this section by Tom Beauchamp in Chapter 31 and Richard Wasserstrom in Chapter 29. There are two critiques of preferential treatment in this section, one in Chapter 30 by Louis P. Pojman and another in Chapter 32 by Thomas Sowell. A recent U.S. Supreme Court decision on affirmative action is covered in Chapter 28 (*Adarand v. Pena* [1995]). Although the court has allowed certain strong affirmative action programs in the past (e.g., see *Fullilove v. Klutznick* [1980]), it is not clear that the jurisprudence one finds in *Adarand* would have allowed them today (despite the fact that the author of the Court's controlling opinion in *Adarand,* Justice Sandra Day O'Connor, seems to think otherwise).

> **Key words:** Diversity, fair representation, affirmative action, preferential treatment, timetables, quotas, preferences, California Civil Rights Initiative, race norming, reparations, disproportionate representation, reverse discrimination, Bakke, *Adarand v. Pena, United Steelworkers of America, AFL-CIO-CLC v. Weber, Fullilove v. Klutznick.*

NOTES

1. From provision 703(j) of Title VII of the Civil Rights Act of 1964.
2. Humphrey (110 *Congressional Quarterly* 12723), as quoted in Nicholas Capaldi, *Out of Order: Affirmative Action and the Crisis of Doctrinaire Liberalism* (Buffalo, NY: Prometheus, 1985), 28. In 1968, Humphrey evidently had a change of heart: " 'without regard to race, creed, or color.' This is still what we seek in the long run. But in the short run, now, in this situation, we have learned that we have to pay attention to race and color . . . . affirmative action . . . must take account of race. . . . Someday—hopefully soon—we really will be able to drop all the nonsense about race, and deal with each other just as equals and as persons. But first we have some bad history to overcome" (Hubert Humphrey, *Beyond Civil Rights* [New York: Random House, 1968], 140, 144, as quoted in Capaldi, *Out of Order,* 142).
3. Williams (110 *Congressional Quarterly* 1433), as quoted in Capaldi, *Out of Order,* 28.
4. Quoted in Louis P. Pojman, "The Moral Status of Affirmative Action," *Public Affairs Quarterly* 6 (April 1992): 184, which quoted from William Bradford Reynolds, "Affirmative Action Is Unjust," in *Social Justice,* eds. D. Bender and B. Lenore (St. Paul, MN, 1984), 23.
5. Lyndon Baines Johnson, "To Fulfill These Rights: Commencement Address at Howard University," in *Affirmative Action: Social Justice or Reverse Discrimination?,* eds. Francis J. Beckwith and Todd E. Jones (Amherst, NY: Prometheus Books, 1997), 57.
6. Pojman, "The Moral Status of Affirmative Action," 183.
7. Ibid.
8. See, for example, Dinesh D'Souza, "Final Thoughts on Political Correctness: Some Proposals," in *Are You Politically Correct?: Debating America's Cultural Standards,* eds. Francis J. Beckwith and Michael E. Bauman (Buffalo, NY: Prometheus, 1993), 252–254.

For Further Reading

Francis J. Beckwith and James Harris, *Race-Based Affirmative Action: A Debate,* Crossroads Monograph Series in Faith and Public Policy (Wynnewood, PA: Crossroads, 1997).

Francis J. Beckwith and Todd Jones, eds., *Affirmative Action: Social Justice or Reverse Discrimination?* (Amherst, NY: Prometheus Books, 1997).

Francis J. Beckwith, "The 'No One Deserves His or Her Talents' Argument for Affirmative Action," *Social Theory and Practice* 25.1 (spring 1999).

Derrick Bell, Jr., "*Bakke,* Minority Admissions, and the Usual Price of Racial Remedies," *California Law Review* 67 (January 1979).

Norman E. Bowie, ed. *Equal Opportunity* (Boulder, CO: Westview, 1988).

Nicholas Capaldi, *Out of Order: Affirmative Action and the Crisis of Doctrinaire Liberalism* (Buffalo, NY: Prometheus, 1985).

Stephen Carter, *Reflections of an Affirmative Action Baby* (New York: Basic Books, 1991).

Joseph G. Conti and Brad Stetson, *Challenging the Civil Rights Establishment: Profiles of a New Black Vanguard* (Westport, CT: Praeger, 1993).

Ronald Dworkin, "Why Bakke Has No Case," *New York Review of Books* (November 10, 1977).

D. T. Goldberg, ed. *Anatomy of Racism* (Minneapolis: University of Minnesota Press, 1988).

Barry Gross, *Discrimination in Reverse: Is Turnabout Fair Play?* (New York: State University of New York Press, 1978).

Frederick R. Lynch, *Invisible Victims: White Males and the Crisis of Affirmative Action* (New York: Greenwood, 1989).

H. Remick, *Comparable Worth and Wage Discrimination* (Philadelphia, PA: Temple University Press, 1985).

Thomas Sowell, *Civil Rights: Rhetoric or Reality?* (New York: William Morrow, 1984).

Steven Yates, *Civil Wrongs: What Went Wrong with Affirmative Action* (San Francisco, CA: Institute for Contemporary Studies, 1994).

28   Adarand v. Pena (1995)

U.S. SUPREME COURT

This chapter consists of the opinions of three Justices from the case of *Adarand v. Pena:* Justice Sandra Day O'Connor, Justice Clarence Thomas, and Justice John Paul Stevens. This case concerned a lawsuit brought by Adarand Construction against Frederico Pena, Secretary of Transportation. The construction company argued that the federal government's policy of awarding highway construction contracts to disadvantaged businesses is unconstitutional. The Supreme Court reversed a lower court ruling (which sided with the government) and remanded to the lower court for further proceedings consistent with its controlling opinion.

Most citations omitted.

The first opinion, authored by Justice O'Connor, is the controlling one in the case. As she argued in her dissent in *Metro Broadcasting, Inc. v. FCC* (1990), O'Connor concludes in *Adarand* that strict scrutiny review is "the appropriate standard of review for federal *and* state and local affirmative action programs" That is, unless a government's affirmative action policy serves a compelling state interest and can be narrowly tailored to further that interest, the racial classifications employed in the policy are suspect. The policy under analysis in this case, according to O'Connor, does not meet this burden. She argues that her *Adarand* opinion is consistent with prior Supreme Court rulings, and that the Court's *Metro* "decision was an anomaly based on the false premise that the Constitution protected *groups* rather than *individuals*." In essence, her controlling opinion overruled *Metro*.

Justice Thomas, in his concurring opinion in *Adarand,* brings his natural law jurisprudence to bear on the question of affirmative action (for more on natural law, see Chapter 5). Even though Justice Stevens (in a footnote not reprinted here) calls Thomas's reasoning "extreme," it is reasoning that touches on a fundamental question of principle: what is it about racial discrimination that makes it wrong and thus ought to be proscribed by law? It is a philosophical question that forces one to *morally justify* one's legal principle without recourse to the comfort of legal categories. Thomas's case in *Adarand* is two-pronged. First, he makes an in-principle case against affirmative action: if racial discrimination is in-principle immoral, then it cannot be employed in any policies, even if those polices are intended for good (e.g., eradicating a caste system). In the second-prong of his case, Thomas argues that because racial discrimination is immoral, it is likely to result in other evils, even though these results are *not* the basis to think it is wrong.

In his dissent in *Adarand,* Justice Stevens argues that O'Connor's understanding of the Court's prior cases on affirmative action is flawed and that she does not address important differences between federal and state and local affirmative action policies, something on which the Court had in prior rulings spent much "time, effort, and paper." In addition, Stevens makes the point that O'Connor failed "to distinguish between government actions designed to *help* minority groups and those designed to *hurt* them" So, for Stevens, if a particular affirmative action policy benefits members of a minority group but results in a slight burden to some majority group members, such a policy may be constitutionally justified, for, in Stevens's words, "there is no moral or constitutional equivalence between a policy that is designed to perpetuate a caste system and one that seeks to eradicate racial subordination. Invidious discrimination is an engine of oppression, subjugating a disfavored group to enhance or maintain the power of the majority."

JUSTICE O'CONNOR ANNOUNCED THE judgment of the Court and delivered an opinion with respect to Parts I, II, III-A, III-B, III-D, and IV, which is for the Court except insofar as it might be inconsistent with the views expressed in Justice SCALIA's concurrence, and an opinion with respect to Part III-C in which Justice KENNEDY joins.

Petitioner Adarand Constructors, Inc., claims that the Federal Government's practice of giving general contractors on Government projects a financial incentive to hire subcontractors controlled by "socially and economically disadvantaged individuals," and in particular, the Government's use of race- based presumptions in identifying such individuals, violates the equal protection component of the Fifth Amendment's Due Process Clause. The Court of Appeals rejected Adarand's claim. We conclude, however, that courts should analyze cases of this kind under a different standard of review than the one the Court of Appeals applied. We therefore vacate the Court of Appeals' judgment and remand the case for further proceedings.

I

In 1989, the Central Federal Lands Highway Division (CFLHD), which is part of the United States Department of Transportation (DOT), awarded the prime contract for a highway construction project in Colorado to Mountain Gravel & Construction Company. Mountain Gravel then solicited bids from subcontractors for the guardrail portion of the contract. Adarand, a Colorado-based highway construction company specializing in guardrail work, submitted the low bid. Gonzales Construction Company also submitted a bid.

The prime contract's terms provide that Mountain Gravel would receive additional compensation if it hired subcontractors certified as small businesses controlled by "socially and economically disadvantaged individuals," Gonzales is certified as such a business; Adarand is not. Mountain Gravel awarded the subcontract to Gonzales, despite Adarand's low bid, and Mountain Gravel's Chief Estimator has submitted an affidavit stating that Mountain Gravel would have accepted Adarand's bid, had it not been for the additional payment it received by hiring Gonzales instead. Federal law requires that a subcon-

tracting clause similar to the one used here must appear in most federal agency contracts, and it also requires the clause to state that "[it]he contractor shall presume that socially and economically disadvantaged individuals include Black Americans, Hispanic Americans, Native Americans, Asian Pacific Americans, and other minorities, or any other individual found to be disadvantaged by the [Small Business] Administration pursuant to section 8(a) of the Small Business Act." Adarand claims that the presumption set forth in that statute discriminates on the basis of race in violation of the Federal Government's Fifth Amendment obligation not to deny anyone equal protection of the laws.

These fairly straightforward facts implicate a complex scheme of federal statutes and regulations, to which we now turn. The Small Business Act (Act), . . . declares it to be "the policy of the United States that small business concerns, [and] small business concerns owned and controlled by socially and economically disadvantaged individuals, . . . shall have the maximum practicable opportunity to participate in the performance of contracts let by any Federal agency." The Act defines "socially disadvantaged individuals" as "those who have been subjected to racial or ethnic prejudice or cultural bias because of their identity as a member of a group without regard to their individual qualities," and it defines "economically disadvantaged individuals" as "those socially disadvantaged individuals whose ability to compete in the free enterprise system has been impaired due to diminished capital and credit opportunities as compared to others in the same business area who are not socially disadvantaged."

In furtherance of the policy . . . , the Act establishes "[t]he Government-wide goal for participation by small business concerns owned and controlled by socially and economically disadvantaged individuals" at "not less than 5 percent of the total value of all prime contract and subcontract awards for each fiscal year." It also requires the head of each federal agency to set agency-specific goals for participation by businesses controlled by socially and economically disadvantaged individuals.

The Small Business Administration (SBA) has implemented these statutory directives in a variety of ways, two of which are relevant here. One is the "8(a) program," which is available to small businesses controlled by socially and economically disadvantaged individuals as the SBA has defined those terms. The 8(a) program confers a wide range of benefits on participating businesses, one of which is automatic eligibility for subcontractor compensation provisions of the kind at issue in this case, (conferring presumptive eligibility on anyone "found to be disadvantaged . . . pursuant to section 8(a) of the Small Business Act"). To participate in the 8(a) program, a business must be "small," as defined in 13 CFR § 124.102 (1994); and it must be 51% owned by individuals who qualify as "socially and economically disadvantaged." The SBA presumes that black, Hispanic, Asian Pacific, Subcontinent Asian, and Native Americans, as well as "members of other groups designated from time to time by SBA," are "socially disadvantaged." It also allows any individual not a member of a listed group to prove social disadvantage "on the basis of clear and convincing evidence," as described in § 124.105(c). Social disadvantage is not enough to establish eligibility, however; SBA also requires each 8(a) program participant to prove "economic disadvantage" according to the criteria set forth in § 124.106(a).

The other SBA program relevant to this case is the "8(d) subcontracting program," which unlike the 8(a) program is limited to eligibility for subcontracting provisions like the one at issue here. In determining eligibility, the SBA presumes social disadvantage based on membership in certain minority groups, just as in the 8(a) program, and again appears to require an individualized, although "less restrictive," showing of economic disadvantage. A different set of regulations, however, says that members of minority groups wishing to participate in the 8(d) subcontracting program are entitled to a race-based presumption of social and economic disadvantage. We are left with some uncertainty as to whether participation in the 8(d) subcontracting program requires an individualized showing of economic disadvantage. In any event, in both the 8(a) and the 8(d) programs, the presumptions of disadvantage are rebuttable if a third party comes forward with evidence suggesting that the participant is not, in fact, either economically or socially disadvantaged.

The contract giving rise to the dispute in this case came about as a result of the Surface Transportation and Uniform Relocation Assistance Act of 1987, a DOT appropriations measure. Section 106(c)(1) of STURAA provides that "not less than 10 percent" of the appropriated funds "shall be expended with small business concerns owned and controlled by socially and economically disadvantaged individuals." STURAA adopts the Small Business Act's definition of "socially and economically disadvantaged individual," including the applicable race-based presumptions, and adds that "women shall be presumed to be socially and economically disadvantaged individuals for purposes of this subsection." STURAA also requires the Secretary of Transportation to establish "minimum uniform criteria for State governments to use in certifying whether a concern qualifies for purposes of this subsection." The Secretary has done so in 49 CFR pt. 23, subpt. D (1994). Those regulations say that the certifying authority should presume both social and economic disadvantage (i,e., eligibility to participate) if the applicant belongs to certain racial groups, or is a woman. As with the SBA programs, third parties may come forward with evidence in an effort to rebut the presumption of disadvantage for a particular business.

The operative clause in the contract in this case reads as follows:

*209 Subcontracting. This subsection is supplemented to include a Disadvantaged Business Enterprise (DBE) Development and Subcontracting Provision as follows:

Monetary compensation is offered for awarding subcontracts to small business concerns owned and controlled by socially and economically disadvantaged individuals. . . .

A small business concern will be considered a DBE after it has been certified as such by the U.S. Small Business Administration or any State Highway Agency. Certification by other Government agencies, 4 counties, or cities may be acceptable on an individual basis provided the Contracting Officer has determined the certifying agency has an acceptable and viable DBE certification program. If the Contractor requests payment under this provision, the Contractor shall furnish the engineer with acceptable evidence of the subcontractor(s) DBE certification and shall furnish one certified copy of the executed subcontract(s).

. . . . .

The Contractor will be paid an amount computed as follows:

1. If a subcontract is awarded to one DBE, 10 percent of the final amount of the approved DBE subcontract, not to exceed 1.5 percent of the original contract amount.

2. If subcontracts are awarded to two or more DBEs, 10 percent of the final amount of the approved DBE subcontracts, not to exceed 2 percent of the original contract amount." App. 24–26.

To benefit from this clause, Mountain Gravel had to hire a subcontractor who had been certified as a small disadvantaged business by the SBA, a state highway agency, or some other certifying authority acceptable to the contracting officer. Any of the three routes to such certification described above—SBA's 8(a) or 8(d) program, or certification by a State under the DOT regulations—would meet that requirement. The record does not reveal how Gonzales obtained its certification as a small disadvantaged business.

After losing the guardrail subcontract to Gonzales, Adarand filed suit against various federal officials in the United States District Court for the District of Colorado, claiming that the race-based presumptions involved in the use of subcontracting compensation clauses violate Adarand's right to equal protection. The District Court granted the Government's motion for summary judgment. The Court of Appeals for the Tenth Circuit affirmed. It understood our decision in Fullilove v. Klutznick, (1980), to have adopted "a lenient standard, resembling intermediate scrutiny, in assessing" the constitutionality of federal race-based action. Applying that "lenient standard," as further developed in Metro Broadcasting, Inc. v. FCC, (1990), the Court of Appeals upheld the use of subcontractor compensation clauses. We granted certiorari.

II

[1][2] Adarand, in addition to its general prayer for "such other and further relief as to the Court seems just and equitable," specifically seeks declaratory and injunctive relief against any future use of subcontractor compensation clauses. Before reaching the merits of Adarand's challenge, we must consider whether Adarand has standing to seek forward-looking relief. Adarand's allegation that it has lost a contract in the past because of a subcontractor compensation clause of course entitles it to

seek damages for the loss of that contract (we express no view, however, as to whether sovereign immunity would bar such relief on these facts). But as we explained in Los Angeles v. Lyons, (1983), the fact of past injury, "white presumably affording [the plaintiff] standing to claim damages . . . , does nothing to establish a real and immediate threat that he would again" suffer similar injury in the future."

[3] If Adarand is to maintain its claim for forward-looking relief, our cases require it to allege that the use of subcontractor compensation clauses in the future constitutes "an invasion of a legally protected interest which is (a) concrete and particularized, and (b) actual or imminent, not conjectural or hypothetical." Lujan v. Defenders of Wildlife, (1992) (footnote, citations, and internal quotation marks omitted). Adarand's claim that the Government's use of subcontractor compensation clauses denies it equal protection of the laws of course alleges an invasion of a legally protected interest, and it does so in a manner that is "particularized" as to Adarand. We note that, contrary to respondents' suggestion, Adarand need not demonstrate that it has been, or will be, the low bidder on a Government contract. The injury in cases of this kind is that a "discriminatory classification prevent[s] the plaintiff from competing on an equal footing." Northeastern Fla. Chapter, Associated Gen. Contractors of America v. Jacksonville, (1993). The aggrieved party "need not allege that he would have obtained the benefit but for the barrier in order to establish standing."

It is less clear, however, that the future use of subcontractor compensation clauses will cause Adarand "imminent" injury. We said in Lujan that "[a]lthough 'imminence' is concededly a somewhat elastic concept, it cannot be stretched beyond its purpose, which is to ensure that the alleged injury is not too speculative for Article III purposes—that the injury is 'certainly impending.' " We therefore must ask whether Adarand has made an adequate showing that

sometime in the relatively near future it will bid on another Government contract that offers financial incentives to a prime contractor for hiring disadvantaged subcontractors.

We conclude that Adarand has satisfied this requirement. Adarand's general manager said in a deposition that his company bids on every guardrail project in Colorado. According to documents produced in discovery, the CFLHD let 14 prime contracts in Colorado that included guardrail work between 1983 and 1990. Two of those contracts do not present the kind of injury Adarand alleges here. In one, the prime contractor did not subcontract out the guardrail work; in another, the prime contractor was itself a disadvantaged business, and in such cases the contract generally does not include a subcontractor compensation clause. Thus, statistics from the years 1983 through 1990 indicate that the CFLHD lets on average 1 1/2 contracts per year that could injure Adarand in the manner it alleges here. Nothing in the record suggests that the CFLHD has altered the frequency with which it lets contracts that include guardrail work. And the record indicates that Adarand often must compete for contracts against companies certified as small disadvantaged businesses. Because the evidence in this case indicates that the CFLHD is likely to let contracts involving guardrail work that contain a subcontractor compensation clause at least once per year in Colorado, that Adarand is very likely to bid on each such contract, and that Adarand often must compete for such contracts against small disadvantaged businesses, we are satisfied that Adarand has standing to bring this lawsuit.

III

[4] Respondents urge that "[t]he Subcontracting Compensation Clause program is . . . a program based on disadvantage, not on race," and thus that it is subject only to "the most relaxed judicial scrutiny." To the extent that

the statutes and regulations involved in this case are race neutral, we agree. Respondents concede, however, that "the race-based rebuttable presumption used in some certification determinations under the Subcontracting Compensation Clause" is subject to some heightened level of scrutiny. The parties disagree as to what that level should be. (We note, incidentally, that this case concerns only classifications based explicitly on race, and presents none of the additional difficulties posed by laws that, although facially race neutral, result in racially disproportionate impact and are motivated by a racially discriminatory purpose. See generally Arlington Heights v. Metropolitan Housing Development Corp., (1977); Washington v. Davis, (1976).)

Adarand's claim arises under the Fifth Amendment to the Constitution, which provides that "No person shall . . . be deprived of life, liberty, or property, without due process of law." Although this Court has always understood that Clause to provide some measure of protection against arbitrary treatment by the Federal Government, it is not as explicit a guarantee of equal treatment as the Fourteenth Amendment, which provides that "No State shall . . . deny to any person within its jurisdiction the equal protection of the laws". Our cases have accorded varying degrees of significance to the difference in the language of those two Clauses. We think it necessary to revisit the issue here.

A

Through the 1940's, this Court had routinely taken the view in non-race-related cases that, "[u]nlike the Fourteenth Amendment, the Fifth contains no equal protection clause and it provides no guaranty against discriminatory legislation by Congress." Detroit Bank v. United States, (1943); see also, e.g., Helvering v. Lerner Stores Corp., (1941); LaBelle Iron Works v. United States, (1921) ("Reference is made to cases decided under the equal protection clause of the Fourteenth Amendment . . . ; but clearly they are not in point. The Fifth Amendment has no equal protection clause"). When the Court first faced a Fifth Amendment equal protection challenge to a federal racial classification, it adopted a similar approach, with most unfortunate results. In Hirabayashi v. United States, (1943), the Court considered a curfew applicable only to persons of Japanese ancestry. The Court observed—correctly—that "[d]istinctions between citizens solely because of their ancestry are by their very nature odious to a free people whose institutions are founded upon the doctrine of equality," and that "racial discriminations are in most circumstances irrelevant and therefore prohibited." But it also cited Detroit Bank for the proposition that the Fifth Amendment "restrains only such discriminatory legislation by Congress as amounts to a denial of due process," and upheld the curfew because "circumstances within the knowledge of those charged with the responsibility for maintaining the national defense afforded a rational basis for the decision which they made."

Eighteen months later, the Court again approved wartime measures directed at persons of Japanese ancestry. Korematsu v. United States, (1944), concerned an order that completely excluded such persons from particular areas. The Court did not address the view, expressed in cases like Hirabayashi and Detroit Bank, that the Federal Government's obligation to provide equal protection differs significantly from that of the States. Instead, it began by noting that "all legal restrictions which curtail the civil rights of a single racial group are immediately suspect . . . [and] courts must subject them to the most rigid scrutiny." That promising dictum might be read to undermine the view that the Federal Government is under a lesser obligation to avoid injurious racial classifications than are the States. . . . But in spite of the "most rigid scrutiny" standard it had just set forth, the Court then inexplicably relied on "the principles we announced in the Hirabayashi case," to conclude that, although "exclusion from the area in which one's home is located is a far greater deprivation than constant confinement to the home from 8 p.m. to 6 a.m.," the racially discriminatory order was nonetheless within the Federal Government's power.

In Bolling v. Sharpe, (1954), the Court for the first time explicitly questioned the existence of any difference between the obligations of the Federal Government and the States to avoid racial classifications. Bolling did note that "[t]he 'equal protection of the laws' is a more explicit safeguard of prohibited unfairness than 'due process of law,'" But Bolling then concluded that, "[i]n view of [the] decision that the Constitution prohibits the states from maintaining racially segregated public schools, it would be unthinkable that the same Constitution would impose a lesser duty on the Federal Government."

Bolling's facts concerned school desegregation, but its reasoning was not so limited. The Court's observations that "[d]istinctions between citizens solely because of their ancestry are by their very nature odious," Hirabayashi, supra, 320 U.S., at 100, 63 S. Ct., at 1385, and that "all legal restrictions which curtail the civil rights of a single racial group are immediately suspect," Korematsu, supra, 323 U.S., at 216, 65 S.Ct., at 194, carry no less force in the context of federal action than in the context of action by the States— indeed, they first appeared in cases concerning action by the Federal Government. Bolling relied on those observations, and reiterated " 'that the Constitution of the United States, in its present form, forbids, so far as civil and political rights are concerned, discrimination by the General Government, or by the States, against any citizen because of his race,'" (quoting Gibson v. Mississippi, (1896)). The Court's application of that general principle to the case before it, and the resulting imposition on the Federal Government of an obligation equivalent to that of the States, followed as a matter of course.

Later cases in contexts other than school desegregation did not distinguish between the duties of the States and the Federal Government to avoid racial classifications. Consider, for example, the following passage from McLaughlin v. Florida, a 1964 case that struck down a race-based state law: "[W]e deal here with a classification based upon the race of the participants, which must be viewed in light of the historical fact that the central purpose of the Fourteenth Amendment was to eliminate racial discrimination emanating from official sources in the States. This strong policy renders racial classifications 'constitutionally suspect,' Boiling v. Sharpe, and subject to the 'most rigid scrutiny,' Korematsu v. United States, and 'in most circumstances irrelevant' to any constitutionally acceptable legislative purpose, Hirabayashi v. United States, 1385]."

McLaughlin's reliance on cases involving federal action for the standards applicable to a case involving state legislation suggests that the Court understood the standards for federal and state racial classifications to be the same.

Cases decided after McLaughlin continued to treat the equal protection obligations imposed by the Fifth and the Fourteenth Amendments as indistinguishable: one commentator observed that "[i]n case after case, fifth amendment equal protection problems are discussed on the assumption that fourteenth amendment precedents are controlling." Karst, The Fifth Amendment's Guarantee of Equal Protection, 55 N.C.L.Rev. 541, 554 (1977). Loving v. Virginia, (1967), which struck down a race-based state law, cited Korematsu for the proposition that "the Equal Protection Clause demands that racial classifications . . . be subjected to the 'most rigid scrutiny.'" The various opinions in Frontiero v. Richardson, (1973), which concerned sex discrimination by the Federal Government, took their equal protection standard of review from Reed v. Reed, (1971), a case that invalidated sex discrimination by a State, without mentioning any possibility of a difference between the standards applicable to state and federal action. Thus, in 1975, the Court stated explicitly that "[t]his Court's approach to Fifth Amendment equal protection claims has always been precisely the same as to equal protection claims under the Fourteenth Amendment." Weinberger v. Wiesenfeld. . . .

B

Most of the cases discussed above involved classifications burdening groups that have suffered discrimination in our society. In 1978, the Court confronted the question whether race-based governmental action designed to benefit such groups should also be subject to "the most rigid scrutiny." Regents of Univ. of Cal. v. Bakke, 750, involved an equal protection challenge to a state-run medical school's practice of reserving a number of spaces in its entering class for minority students. The petitioners argued that "strict scrutiny" should apply only to "classifications that disadvantage 'discrete and insular minorities.' " (citing United States v. Carolene Products Co., (1938)). Bakke did not produce an opinion for the Court, but Justice Powell's opinion announcing the Court's judgment rejected the argument. In a passage joined by Justice White, Justice Powell wrote that "[t]he guarantee of equal protection cannot mean one thing when applied to one individual and something else when applied to a person of another color." He concluded that "[r]acial and ethnic distinctions of any sort are inherently suspect and thus call for the most exacting judicial examination." On the other hand, four Justices in Bakke would have applied a less stringent standard of review to racial classifications "designed to further remedial purposes," (Brennan, White, Marshall, and Blackmun, JJ., concurring in judgment in part and dissenting in part). And four Justices thought the case should be decided on statutory grounds. (STEVENS, J., joined by Burger, C.J., and Stewart and REHNQUIST, JJ., concurring in judgment in part and dissenting in part).

Two years after Bakke, the Court faced another challenge to remedial race-based action, this time involving action undertaken by the Federal Government. In Fullilove v. Klutznick, (1980), the Court upheld Congress' inclusion of a 10% set-aside for minority-owned businesses in the Public Works Employment Act of 1977. As in Bakke, there was no opinion for the Court. Chief Justice Burger, in an opinion joined by Justices White and Powell, observed that "[a]ny preference based on racial or ethnic criteria must necessarily receive a most searching examination to make sure that it does not conflict with constitutional guarantees." That opinion, however, "d[id] not adopt, either expressly or implicitly, the formulas of analysis articulated in such cases as [Bakke]." It employed instead a two-part test which asked, first, "whether the objectives of th[e] legislation are within the power of Congress," and second, "whether the limited use of racial and ethnic criteria, in the context presented, is a constitutionally permissible means for achieving the congressional objectives." It then upheld the program under that test, adding at the end of the opinion that the program also "would survive judicial review under either 'test' articulated in the several Bakke opinions." Justice Powell wrote separately to express his view that the plurality opinion had essentially applied "strict scrutiny" as described in his Bakke opinion—i.e., it had determined that the set-aside was "a necessary means of advancing a compelling governmental interest"—and had done so correctly, (concurring opinion). Justice Stewart (joined by then-Justice REHNQUIST) dissented, arguing that the Constitution required the Federal Government to meet the same strict standard as the States when enacting racial classifications, and that the program before the Court failed that standard. Justice STEVENS also dissented, arguing that "[r]acial classifications are simply too pernicious to permit any but the most exact connection between justification and classification," and that the program before the Court could not be characterized "as a 'narrowly tailored' remedial measure." Justice Marshall (joined by Justices Brennan and Blackmun) concurred in the judgment, reiterating the view of four Justices in Bakke that any race-based governmental action designed to "remed[y] the present effects of past racial discrimination" should be upheld if it was "substantially related" to the achievement of an "important governmental objective"—i.e., such action should be subjected only to what we now call "intermediate scrutiny."

In Wygant v. Jackson Bd. of Ed., (1986), the Court considered a Fourteenth Amendment challenge to another form of remedial racial classification. The issue in Wygant was whether a school board could adopt race-based preferences in determining which teachers to lay off. Justice Powell's plurality opinion observed that "the level of scrutiny does not change merely because the challenged classification operates against a group that historically has not been subject to governmental discrimination," and stated the two-part inquiry as "whether the layoff provision is supported by a compelling state purpose and whether the means chosen to accomplish that purpose are narrowly tailored." In other words, "racial classifications of any sort must be subjected to 'strict scrutiny.'" (O'CONNOR, J., concurring in part and concurring in judgment). The plurality then concluded that the school board's interest in "providing minority role models for its minority students, as an attempt to alleviate the effects of societal discrimination," was not a compelling interest that could justify the use of a racial classification. It added that "[s]ocietal discrimination, without more, is too amorphous a basis for imposing a racially classified remedy," and insisted instead that "a public employer . . . must ensure that, before it embarks on an affirmative-action program, it has convincing evidence that remedial action is warranted. That is, it must have sufficient evidence to justify the conclusion that there has been prior discrimination." Justice White con-

curred only in the judgment, although he agreed that the school board's asserted interests could not, "singly or together, justify this racially discriminatory layoff policy." Four Justices dissented, three of whom again argued for intermediate scrutiny of remedial race-based government action. (Marshall, J., joined by Brennan and Blackmun, JJ., dissenting).

The Court's failure to produce a majority opinion in Bakke, Fullilove, and Wygant left unresolved the proper analysis for remedial race-based governmental action. . . . Lower courts found this lack of guidance unsettling. . . .

The Court resolved the issue, at least in part, in 1989. Richmond v. J.A. Croson Co., (1989), concerned a city's determination that 30% of its contracting work should go to minority-owned businesses. A majority of the Court in Croson held that "the standard of review under the Equal Protection Clause is not dependent on the race of those burdened or benefited by a particular classification," and that the single standard of review for racial classifications should be "strict scrutiny." (opinion of O'CONNOR, J., joined by REHNQUIST, C.J., and White and KENNEDY, JJ.); (SCALIA, J., concurring in judgment) ("I agree . . . with Justice O'CONNOR's conclusion that strict scrutiny must be applied to all governmental classification by race"). As to the classification before the Court, the plurality agreed that "a state or local subdivision . . . has the authority to eradicate the effects of private discrimination within its own legislative jurisdiction," but the Court thought that the city had not acted with "a 'strong basis in evidence for its conclusion that remedial action was necessary,'" at 725 (majority opinion) (quoting Wygant, (plurality opinion)). The Court also thought it "obvious that [the] program is not narrowly tailored to remedy the effects of prior discrimination."

With Croson, the Court finally agreed that the Fourteenth Amendment requires strict scrutiny of all race-based action by state and local governments. But Croson of course had no occasion to declare what standard of review the Fifth Amendment requires for such action taken by the Federal Government. Croson observed simply that the Court's "treatment of an exercise of congressional power in Fullilove cannot be dispositive here," because Croson's facts did not implicate Congress' broad power under § 5 of the Fourteenth Amendment. . . . On the other hand, the Court subsequently indicated that Croson had at least some bearing on federal race-based action when it vacated a decision upholding such action and remanded for further consideration in light of Croson. . . . Thus, some uncertainty persisted with respect to the standard of review for federal racial classifications. . . .

Despite lingering uncertainty in the details, however, the Court's cases through Croson had established three general propositions with respect to governmental racial classifications. First, skepticism: " 'Any preference based on racial or ethnic criteria must necessarily receive a most searching examination,' " Wygant, (plurality opinion of Powell, J.); Second, consistency: "[T]he standard of review under the Equal Protection Clause is not dependent on the race of those burdened or benefited by a particular classification," Croson, (plurality opinion); And third, congruence: "Equal protection analysis in the Fifth Amendment area is the same as that under the Fourteenth Amendment," Buckley v. Valeo, Taken together, these three propositions lead to the conclusion that any person, of whatever race, has the right to demand that any governmental actor subject to the Constitution justify any racial classification subjecting that person to unequal treatment under the strictest judicial scrutiny. Justice Powell's defense of this conclusion bears repeating here:

"If it is the individual who is entitled to judicial protection against classifications based upon his racial or ethnic background because such distinctions impinge upon personal rights, rather than the individual only because of his membership in a particular group, then constitutional standards may be applied consistently. Political judgments regarding the necessity for the particular classification may be weighed in the constitutional balance, [Korematsu], but the standard of justification will remain constant. This is as it should be, since those political judgments are the product of rough compromise struck by contending groups within the democratic process. When they touch upon an individual's race or ethnic background, he is entitled to a judicial determination that the burden he is asked to bear on that basis is precisely tailored to serve a compelling governmental interest. The Constitution guarantees that right to every person regardless of his background. Shelley v. Kraemer, 334 U.S. [1, 22, 68 S.Ct. 836, 846, 92 L.Ed, 1161 (1948)]." Bakke, (opinion of Powell, J.) (footnote omitted).

[In 1990], however, the Court took a surprising turn. Metro Broadcasting, Inc. v. FCC, involved a Fifth Amendment challenge to two race-based policies of the Federal Communications Commission (FCC). In Metro Broadcasting, the Court repudiated the long-held notion that "it would be unthinkable that the same Constitution would impose a lesser duty on the Federal Government" than it does on a State to afford equal protection of the laws, Bolling. It did so by holding that "benign" federal racial classifications need only satisfy intermediate scrutiny, even though Croson had recently concluded that such classifications enacted by a State must satisfy strict scrutiny. "[B]enign" federal racial classifications, the Court said, "—even if those measures are not 'remedial' in the sense of being designed to compensate victims of past governmental or societal discrimination—are constitutionally permissible to the extent that they serve important governmental objectives within the power of Congress and are substantially related to achievement of those objectives." The Court did not explain how to tell whether a racial classification should be deemed "benign," other than to express "confiden[ce] that an 'examination of the legislative scheme and its history' will separate benign measures from other types of racial classifications."

Applying this test, the Court first noted that the FCC policies at issue did not serve us a remedy for past discrimination. Proceeding on the assumption that the policies were nonetheless "benign," it concluded that they served the "important governmental objective" of "enhancing broadcast diversity," and that they were "substantially related" to that objective, It therefore upheld the policies.

By adopting intermediate scrutiny as the standard of review for congressionally mandated "benign" racial classifications, Metro Broadcasting departed from prior cases in two significant respects. First, it turned its back on Croson's explanation of why strict scrutiny of all governmental racial classifications is essential:

> "Absent searching judicial inquiry into the justification for such race-based measures, there is simply no way of determining what classifications are 'benign' or 'remedial' and what classifications are in fact motivated by illegitimate notions of racial inferiority or simple racial politics. Indeed, the purpose of strict scrutiny is to 'smoke out' illegitimate uses of race by assuring that the legislative body is pursuing a goal important enough to warrant use of a highly suspect tool. The test also ensures that the means chosen 'fit' this compelling goal so closely that there is little or no possibility that the motive for the classification was illegitimate racial prejudice or stereotype." Croson, (plurality opinion of O'CONNOR, J.).

We adhere to that view today, despite the surface appeal of holding "benign" racial classifications to a lower standard, because "it may not always be clear that a so-called preference is in fact benign," Bakke, (opinion of Powell, J.). . . .

Second, Metro Broadcasting squarely rejected one of the three propositions established by the Court's earlier equal protection cases, namely, congruence between the standards applicable to federal and state racial classifications, and in so doing also undermined the other two—skepticism of all racial classifications and consistency of treatment irrespective of the race of the burdened or benefited group. Under Metro Broadcasting, certain racial classifications ("benign" ones enacted by the Federal Government) should be treated less skeptically than others; and the race of the benefited group is critical to the determination of which standard of review to apply. Metro Broadcasting was thus a significant departure from much of what had come before it.

[5][6] The three propositions undermined by Metro Broadcasting all derive from the basic principle that the Fifth and Fourteenth Amendments to the Constitution protect persons, not groups. It follows from that principle that all governmental action based on race—a group classification long recognized as "in most circumstances irrelevant and therefore prohibited," Hirabayashi,—should be subjected to detailed judicial inquiry to ensure that the personal right to equal protection of the laws has not been infringed. These ideas have long been central to this Court's understanding of equal protection, and holding "benign" state and federal racial classifications to different standards does not square with them. "[A] free people whose institutions are founded upon the doctrine of equality," ibid., should tolerate no retreat from the principle that government may treat people differently because of their race only for the most compelling reasons. Accordingly, we hold today that all racial classifications, imposed by whatever federal, state, or local governmental actor, must be analyzed by a reviewing court under strict scrutiny. In other words, such classifications are constitutional only if they are narrowly tailored measures that further compelling governmental interests. To the extent

that Metro Broadcasting is inconsistent with that holding, it is overruled.

In dissent, Justice STEVENS criticizes us for "deliver[ing] a disconcerting lecture about the evils of governmental racial classifications." With respect, we believe his criticisms reflect a serious misunderstanding of our opinion.

Justice STEVENS concurs in our view that courts should take a skeptical view of all governmental racial classifications. He also allows that "[n]othing is inherently wrong with applying a single standard to fundamentally different situations, as long as that standard takes relevant differences into account." What he fails to recognize is that strict scrutiny does take "relevant differences" into account— indeed, that is its fundamental purpose. The point of carefully examining the interest asserted by the government in support of a racial classification, and the evidence offered to show that the classification is needed, is precisely to distinguish legitimate from illegitimate uses of race in governmental decision-making. And Justice STEVENS concedes that "some cases may be difficult to classify," all the more reason, in our view, to examine all racial classifications carefully. Strict scrutiny does not "trea[t] dissimilar race-based decisions as though they were equally objectionable," to the contrary, it evaluates carefully all governmental race-based decisions in order to decide which are constitutionally objectionable and which are not. By requiring strict scrutiny of racial classifications, we require courts to make sure that a governmental classification based on race, which "so seldom provide[s] a relevant basis for disparate treatment," Fullilove, (STEVENS, J., dissenting), is legitimate, before permitting unequal treatment based on race to proceed.

Justice STEVENS chides us for our "supposed inability to differentiate between 'invidious' and 'benign' discrimination," because it is in his view sufficient that "people understand the difference between good intentions and bad." But, as we have just explained, the point of strict scrutiny is to "differentiate between" permissible and impermissible governmental use of race. And Justice STEVENS himself has already explained in his dissent in Fullilove why "good intentions" alone are not enough to sustain a supposedly "benign" racial classification: "[E]ven though it is not the actual predicate for this legislation, a statute of this kind inevitably is perceived by many as resting on an assumption that those who are granted this special preference are less qualified in some respect that is identified purely by their race. Because that perception—especially when fostered by the Congress of the United States—can only exacerbate rather than reduce racial prejudice, it will delay the time when race will become a truly irrelevant, or at least insignificant, factor. Unless Congress clearly articulates the need and basis for a racial classification, and also tailors the classification to its justification, the Court should not uphold this kind of statute." Fullilove, (dissenting opinion) (emphasis added; footnote omitted).

Perhaps it is not the standard of strict scrutiny itself, but our use of the concepts of "consistency" and "congruence" in conjunction with it, that leads Justice STEVENS to dissent. According to Justice STEVENS, our view of consistency "equate[s] remedial preferences with invidious discrimination." and ignores the difference between "an engine of oppression" and an effort "to foster equality in society," or, more colorfully, "between a 'No Trespassing' sign and a welcome mat." It does nothing of the kind. The principle of consistency simply means that whenever the government treats any person unequally because of his or her race, that person has suffered an injury that falls squarely within the language and spirit of the Constitution's guarantee of equal protection. It says nothing about the ultimate validity of any particular law; that determination is the job of the court applying strict scrutiny. The principle of consistency explains the circumstances in which the injury requiring strict scrutiny occurs. The application of strict scrutiny, in turn, determines whether a compelling governmental interest justifies the infliction of that injury.

Consistency does recognize that any individual suffers an injury when he or she is disadvantaged by the government because of his or her race, whatever that race maybe. This Court clearly stated that principle in Croson, Justice STEVENS does not explain how his views square with Croson, or with the long line of cases understanding equal protection as a personal right.

Justice STEVENS also claims that we have ignored any difference between federal and state legislatures. But requiring that Congress, like the States, enact racial classifications only when doing so is necessary to further a "compelling interest" does not contravene any principle of appropriate respect for a coequal branch of the Government. It is true that various Members of this Court have taken different views of the authority § 5 of the Fourteenth Amendment confers upon Congress to deal with the problem of racial discrimination, and the extent to which courts should defer to Congress' exercise of that authority. We need not, and do not, address these differences today. For now, it is enough to observe that Justice STEVENS' suggestion that any Member of this Court has repudiated in this case his or her previously expressed views on the subject, is incorrect.

C

"Although adherence to precedent is not rigidly required in constitutional cases, any departure from the doctrine of stare decisis demands special justification." Arizona v. Rumsey, (1984). In deciding whether this case presents such justification, we recall Justice Frankfurter's admonition that "stare decisis is a principle of policy and not a mechanical formula of adherence to the latest decision, however recent and questionable, when such adherence involves collision with a prior doc-

trine more embracing in its scope, intrinsically sounder, and verified by experience." Helvering v. Hallock, (1940). Remaining true to an "intrinsically sounder" doctrine established in prior cases better serves the values of stare decisis than would following a more recently decided case inconsistent with the decisions that came before it; the latter course would simply compound the recent error and would likely make the unjustified break from previously established doctrine complete. In such a situation, "special justification" exists to depart from the recently decided case.

As we have explained, Metro Broadcasting undermined important principles of this Court's equal protection jurisprudence, established in a line of cases stretching back over 50 years. Those principles together stood for an "embracing" and "intrinsically soun[d]" understanding of equal protection "verified by experience," namely, that the Constitution imposes upon federal, state, and local governmental actors the same obligation to respect the personal right to equal protection of the laws. This case therefore presents precisely the situation described by Justice Frankfurter in Helvering: We cannot adhere to our most recent decision without colliding with an accepted and established doctrine. We also note that Metro Broadcasting's application of different standards of review to federal and state racial classifications has been consistently criticized by commentators. . . .

Our past practice in similar situations supports our action today. [The Court presents a number at C2505 it overruled in the past; they are omitted from this text]

It is worth pointing out the difference between the applications of stare decisis in this case and in Planned Parenthood of Southeastern Pa. v. Casey, (1992). Casey explained how considerations of stare decisis inform the decision whether to overrule a long-established precedent that has become integrated into the fabric of the law. Overruling precedent of that kind naturally may have consequences for "the ideal of the rule of law." In addition, such precedent is likely to have engendered substantial reliance, as was true in Casey itself. ("[F]or two decades of economic and social developments, people have organized intimate relationships and made choices that define their views of themselves and their places in society, in reliance on the availability of abortion in the event that contraception should fail"). But in this case, as we have explained, we do not face a precedent of that kind, because Metro Broadcasting itself departed from our prior cases—and did so quite recently. By refusing to follow Metro Broadcasting, then, we do not depart from the fabric of the law; we restore it. We also note that reliance on a case that has recently departed from precedent is likely to be minimal, particularly where, as here, the rule set forth in that case is unlikely to affect primary conduct in any event. . . .

Justice STEVENS takes us to task for what he perceives to be an erroneous application of the doctrine of stare decisis. But again, he misunderstands our position. We have acknowledged that, after Croson, "some uncertainty persisted with respect to the standard of review for federal racial classifications," and we therefore do not say that we "merely restor[e] the status quo ante" today. But as we have described, we think that well-settled legal principles pointed toward a conclusion different from that reached in Metro Broadcasting, and we therefore disagree with Justice STEVENS that "the law at the time of that decision was entirely open to the result the Court reached." We also disagree with Justice STEVENS that Justice Stewart's dissenting opinion in Fullilove supports his "novelty" argument, see post, at 2128, and n. 13. Justice Stewart said that "[u]nder our Constitution, any official action that treats a person differently on account of his race or ethnic origin is inherently suspect and presumptively invalid," and that " '[e]qual protection analysis in the Fifth Amendment area is the same as that under the Fourteenth Amendment.' " Fullilove, He took

the view that "[t]he hostility of the Constitution to racial classifications by government has been manifested in many cases decided by this Court," and that "our cases have made clear that the Constitution is wholly neutral in forbidding such racial discrimination, whatever the race may be of those who are its victims." Justice Stewart gave no indication that he thought he was addressing a "novel" proposition. Rather, he relied on the fact that the text of the Fourteenth Amendment extends its guarantee to "persons," and on cases like Buckley, Loving, McLaughlin, Bolling, Hirabayashi, and Korematsu, see Fullilove, as do we today. There is nothing new about the notion that Congress, like the States, may treat people differently because of their race only for compelling reasons.

"The real problem," Justice Frankfurter explained, "is whether a principle shall prevail over its later misapplications." Helvering. Metro Broadcasting's untenable distinction between state and federal racial classifications lacks support in our precedent, and undermines the fundamental principle of equal protection as a personal right. In this case, as between that principle and "its later misapplications," the principle must prevail.

D

[7] Our action today makes explicit what Justice Powell thought implicit in the Fullilove lead opinion: Federal racial classifications, like those of a State, must serve a compelling governmental interest, and must be narrowly tailored to further that interest. . . .

Of course, it follows that to the extent (if any) that Fullilove held federal racial classifications to be subject to a less rigorous standard, it is no longer controlling. But we need not decide today whether the program upheld in Fullilove would survive strict scrutiny as our more recent cases have defined it.

Some have questioned the importance of debating the proper standard of review of race-based legislation. . . . But we agree with Justice STEVENS that, "[b]ecause racial characteristics so seldom provide a relevant basis for disparate treatment, and because classifications based on race are potentially so harmful to the entire body politic, it is especially important that the reasons for any such classification be clearly identified and unquestionably legitimate," and that "[r]acial classifications are simply too pernicious to permit any but the most exact connection between justification and classification." Fullilove, (dissenting opinion) (footnotes omitted). We think that requiring strict scrutiny is the best way to ensure that courts will consistently give racial classifications that kind of detailed examination, both as to ends and as to means. Korematsu demonstrates vividly that even "the most rigid scrutiny" can sometimes fail to detect an illegitimate racial classification, ... Any retreat from the most searching judicial inquiry can only increase the risk of another such error occurring in the future.

[8] Finally, we wish to dispel the notion that strict scrutiny is "strict in theory, but fatal in fact." Fullilove, (Marshall, J., concurring in judgment). The unhappy persistence of both the practice and the lingering effects of racial discrimination against minority groups in this country is an unfortunate reality, and government is not disqualified from acting in response to it. As recently as 1987, for example, every Justice of this Court agreed that the Alabama Department of Public Safety's "pervasive, systematic, and obstinate discriminatory conduct" justified a narrowly tailored race-based remedy. See United States v. Paradise. . . . When race-based action is necessary to further a compelling interest, such action is within constitutional constraints if it satisfies the "narrow tailoring" test this Court has set out in previous cases.

IV

[9] Because our decision today alters the playing field in some important respects, we think it best to remand the case to the lower courts for further consideration in light of the principles we have announced. The Court of Appeals, following Metro Broadcasting and Fullilove, analyzed the case in terms of intermediate scrutiny. It upheld the challenged statutes and regulations because it found them to be "narrowly tailored to achieve [their] significant governmental purpose of providing subcontracting opportunities for small disadvantaged business enterprises." The Court of Appeals did not decide the question whether the interests served by the use of subcontractor compensation clauses are properly described as "compelling." It also did not address the question of narrow tailoring in terms of our strict scrutiny cases, by asking, for example, whether there was "any consideration of the use of race-neutral means to increase minority business participation" in government contracting, Croson, or whether the program was appropriately limited such that it "will not last longer than the discriminatory effects it is designed to eliminate," Fullilove, (Powell, J., concurring).

Moreover, unresolved questions remain concerning the details of the complex regulatory regimes implicated by the use of subcontractor compensation clauses. For example, the SBA's 8(a) program requires an individualized inquiry into the economic disadvantage of every participant, whereas the DOT's regulations implementing STURAA § 106(c) do not require certifying authorities to make such individualized inquiries. And the regulations seem unclear as to whether 8(d) subcontractors must make individualized showings, or instead whether the race-based presumption applies both to social and economic disadvantage. . . . We also note an apparent discrepancy between the definitions of which socially disadvantaged individuals qualify as economically disadvantaged for the 8(a) and 8(d) programs; the former requires a showing that such individuals' ability to compete has been impaired "as compared to others in the same or similar line of business who are not socially disadvantaged," while the latter requires that showing only "as compared to others in the same or similar line of business," The question whether any of the ways in which the Government uses subcontractor compensation clauses can survive strict scrutiny, and any relevance distinctions such as these may have to that question, should be addressed in the first instance by the lower courts.

Accordingly, the judgment of the Court of Appeals is vacated, and the case is remanded for further proceedings consistent with this opinion.

It is so ordered.

Justice THOMAS, concurring in part and concurring in the judgment.

I agree with the majority's conclusion that strict scrutiny applies to all government classifications based on race. I write separately, however, to express my disagreement with the premise underlying Justice STEVENS' and Justice GINSBURG's dissents: that there is a racial paternalism exception to the principle of equal protection. I believe that there is a "moral [and] constitutional equivalence," (STEVENS, J., dissenting), between laws designed to subjugate a race and those that distribute benefits on the basis of race in order to foster some current notion of equality. Government cannot make us equal; it can only recognize, respect, and protect us as equal before the law.

That these programs may have been motivated, in part, by good intentions cannot provide refuge from the principle that under our Constitution, the government may not make distinctions on the basis of race. As far as the Constitution is concerned, it is irrelevant whether a government's racial classifications are drawn by those who wish to oppress a race or by those who have a sincere desire to help those thought to be disadvantaged. There can be no doubt that the paternalism that appears to lie at the heart of this program is at war with the principle of inherent equality that underlies and infuses our Constitution. See Declaration of Independence ("We hold these truths to be self-evident, that all men are created equal, that they are endowed by their Creator with certain unalienable Rights, that among these are Life, Liberty, and the pursuit of Happiness").

These programs not only raise grave constitutional questions, they also undermine the moral basis of the equal protection principle. Purchased at the price of immeasurable human suffering, the equal protection principle reflects our Nation's understanding that such classifications ultimately have a destructive impact on the individual and our society. Unquestionably, "[i]nvidious [racial] discrimination is an engine of oppression," (STEVENS, J., dissenting). It is also true that "[r]emedial" racial preferences may reflect "a desire to foster equality in society." But there can be no doubt that racial paternalism and its unintended consequences can be as poisonous and pernicious as any other form of discrimination. So-called "benign" discrimination teaches many that because of chronic and apparently immutable handicaps, minorities cannot compete with them without their patronizing indulgence. Inevitably, such programs engender attitudes of superiority or, alternatively, provoke resentment among those who believe that they have been wronged by the government's use of race. These programs stamp minorities with a badge of inferiority and may cause them to develop dependencies or to adopt an attitude that they are "entitled" to preferences. Indeed, Justice STEVENS once recognized the real harms stemming from seemingly "benign" discrimination. See Fullilove v. Klutznick, (1980) (STEVENS, J., dissenting) (noting that "remedial" race legislation "is perceived by many as resting on an assumption that those who are granted this special preference are less qualified in some respect that is identified purely by their race").

In my mind, government-sponsored racial discrimination based on benign prejudice is just as noxious as discrimination inspired by malicious prejudice. In each instance, it is racial discrimination, plain and simple.

Justice STEVENS, with whom Justice GINSBURG joins, dissenting.

Instead of deciding this case in accordance with controlling precedent, the Court today delivers a disconcerting lecture about the evils of governmental racial classifications. For its text the Court has selected three propositions, represented by the bywords "skepticism," "consistency," and "congruence." I shall comment on each of these propositions, then add a few words about stare decisis, and finally explain why I believe this Court has a duty to affirm the judgment of the Court of Appeals.

I

The Court's concept of skepticism is, at least in principle, a good statement of law and of common sense. Undoubtedly, a court should be wary of a governmental decision that relies upon a racial classification. "Because racial characteristics so seldom provide a relevant basis for disparate treatment, and because classifications based on race are potentially so harmful to the entire body politic," a reviewing court must satisfy itself that the reasons for any such classification are "clearly identified and unquestionably legitimate." Fullilove v. Klutznick, (STEVENS, J., dissenting). This principle is explicit in Chief Justice Burger's opinion, in Justice Powell's concurrence, and in my dissent in Fullilove. I welcome its renewed endorsement by the Court today. But, as the opinions in Fullilove demonstrate, substantial agreement on the standard to be applied in deciding difficult cases does not necessarily lead to agreement on how those cases actually should or will be resolved. In my judgment, because uniform standards are often anything but uniform, we should evaluate the Court's comments on "consistency," "congruence," and stare decisis with the same type of skepticism that the Court advocates for the underlying issue.

II

The Court's concept of "consistency" assumes that there is no significant difference between a decision by the majority to impose a special burden on the members of a minority race and a decision by the majority to provide a benefit to certain members of that minority notwithstanding its incidental burden on some members of the majority. In my opinion that assumption is untenable. There is no moral or constitutional equivalence between a policy that is designed to perpetuate a caste system and one that seeks to eradicate racial subordination. Invidious discrimination is an engine of opression, subjugating a disfavored group to enhance or maintain the power of the majority. Remedial race-based preferences reflect the opposite impulse: a desire to foster equality in society. No sensible conception of the Government's constitutional obligation to "govern impartially," Hampton v. Mow Sun Wong, (1976), should ignore this distinction.

To illustrate the point, consider our cases addressing the Federal Government's discrimination against Japanese-Americans during World War II, Hirabayashi v. United States, (1943), and Korematsu v. United States, (1944). The discrimination at issue in those cases was invidious because the Government imposed special burdens—a curfew and exclusion from certain areas on the West Coast—on the members of a minority class defined by racial and ethnic characteristics. Members of the same racially defined class exhibited exceptional heroism in the service of our country during that war. Now suppose Congress decided to reward that service with a federal program that gave all Japanese-American veterans an extraordinary preference in Government employment. . . . If Congress had done so, the same racial characteristics that motivated the discriminatory burdens in Hirabayashi and Korematsu would have defined the preferred class of veterans. Nevertheless, "consistency" surely would not require us to describe the incidental burden on everyone else in the country as "odious" or "invidious" as those terms were used in those cases. We should reject a concept of "consistency" that would view the special preferences that the National Government has provided to Native Americans since 1834 as comparable to the official discrimination against African-Americans that was prevalent for much of our history.

The consistency that the Court espouses would disregard the difference between a "No Trespassing" sign and a welcome mat. It would treat a Dixiecrat Senator's decision to vote against Thurgood Marshall's confirmation in order to keep African-Americans off the Supreme Court as on a par with President Johnson's evaluation of his nominee's race as a positive factor. It would equate a law that made black citizens ineligible for military service with a program aimed at recruiting black soldiers. An attempt by the majority to exclude members of a minority race from a regulated market is fundamentally different from a subsidy that enables a relatively small group of newcomers to enter that market. An interest in "consistency" does not justify treating differences as though they were similarities.

The Court's explanation for treating dissimilar race-based decisions as though they were equally objectionable is a supposed inability to differentiate between "invidious" and "benign" discrimination. But the term "affirmative action" is common and well understood. Its presence in everyday parlance shows that people understand the difference between good intentions and bad. As with any legal concept, some cases may be difficult to classify, but our equal protection jurisprudence has identified a critical difference between state action that imposes burdens on a disfavored few and state action that benefits the few "in spite of" its adverse effects on the many.

Indeed, our jurisprudence has made the standard to be applied in cases of invidious discrimination turn on whether the discrimina-

tion is "intentional," or whether, by contrast, it merely has a discriminatory "effect." Washington v. Davis, (1976). Surely this distinction is at least as subtle, and at least as difficult to apply, as the usually obvious distinction between a measure intended to benefit members of a particular minority race and a measure intended to burden a minority race. A state actor inclined to subvert the Constitution might easily hide bad intentions in the guise of unintended "effects"; but I should think it far more difficult to enact a law intending to preserve the majority's hegemony while casting it plausibly in the guise of affirmative action for minorities.

Nothing is inherently wrong with applying a single standard to fundamentally different situations, as long as that standard takes relevant differences into account. For example, if the Court in all equal protection cases were to insist that differential treatment be justified by relevant characteristics of the members of the favored and disfavored classes that provide a legitimate basis for disparate treatment, such a standard would treat dissimilar cases differently while still recognizing that there is, after all, only one Equal Protection Clause. . . . Under such a standard, subsidies for disadvantaged businesses may be constitutional though special taxes on such businesses would be invalid. But a single standard that purports to equate remedial preferences with invidious discrimination cannot be defended in the name of "equal protection."

Moreover, the Court may find that its new "consistency" approach to race-based classifications is difficult to square with its insistence upon rigidly separate categories for discrimination against different classes of individuals. For example, as the law currently stands, the Court will apply "intermediate scrutiny" to cases of invidious gender discrimination and "strict scrutiny" to cases of invidious race discrimination, while applying the same standard for benign classifications as for invidious ones. If this remains the law, then today's lecture about "consistency" will produce the anomalous result that the Government can more easily enact affirmative-action programs to remedy discrimination against women than it can enact affirmative-action programs to remedy discrimination against African-Americans—even though the primary purpose of the Equal Protection Clause was to end discrimination against the former slaves. . . . When a court becomes preoccupied with abstract standards, it risks sacrificing common sense at the altar of formal consistency.

As a matter of constitutional and democratic principle, a decision by representatives of the majority to discriminate against the members of a minority race is fundamentally different from those same representatives' decision to impose incidental costs on the majority of their constituents in order to provide a benefit to a disadvantaged minority. Indeed, as I have previously argued, the former is virtually always repugnant to the principles of a free and democratic society, whereas the latter is, in some circumstances, entirely consistent with the ideal of equality. Wygant v. Jackson Bd. of Ed., (1986) (STEVENS, J., dissenting). By insisting on a doctrinaire notion of "consistency" in the standard applicable to all race-based governmental actions, the Court obscures this essential dichotomy.

III

The Court's concept of "congruence" assumes that there is no significant difference between a decision by the Congress of the United States to adopt an affirmative-action program and such a decision by a State or a municipality. In my opinion that assumption is untenable. It ignores important practical and legal differences between federal and state or local decision makers.

These differences have been identified repeatedly and consistently both in opinions of the Court and in separate opinions authored by Members of today's majority. Thus, in Metro Broadcasting, Inc. v. FCC, (1990), in which we upheld a federal program designed to foster racial diversity in broadcasting, we identified the special "institutional competence" of our National Legislature. "It is of overriding significance in these cases," we were careful to emphasize, "that the FCC's minority ownership programs have been specifically approved—indeed, mandated—by Congress." We recalled the several opinions in Fullilove that admonished this Court to " 'approach our task with appropriate deference to the Congress, a co-equal branch charged by the Constitution with the power to "provide for the . . . general Welfare of the United States" and "to enforce, by appropriate legislation," the equal protection guarantees of the Fourteenth Amendment.' . . . " We recalled that the opinions of Chief Justice Burger and Justice Powell in Fullilove had "explained that deference was appropriate in light of Congress' institutional competence as the National Legislature, as well as Congress' powers under the Commerce Clause, the Spending Clause, and the Civil War Amendments."

The majority in Metro Broadcasting and the plurality in Fullilove were not alone in relying upon a critical distinction between federal and state programs. In his separate opinion in Richmond v. J.A. Croson Co., (1989), Justice SCALIA discussed the basis for this distinction. He observed that "it is one thing to permit racially based conduct by the Federal Government—whose legislative powers concerning matters of race were explicitly enhanced by the Fourteenth Amendment, and quite another to permit it by the precise entities against whose conduct in matters of race that Amendment was specifically directed, 1." Continuing, Justice SCALIA explained why a "sound distinction between federal and state (or local) action based on race rests not only upon the substance of the Civil War Amendments, but upon social reality and governmental theory."

"What the record shows, in other words, is that racial discrimination against any group finds a more ready expression at the state and local than at the federal level. To the children of the Founding Fathers, this should come as no surprise. An acute awareness of the heightened danger of oppression from political factions in small, rather than large, political units dates to the very beginning of our national history. See G. Wood, The Creation of the American Republic, 1776–1787, pp. 499–506 (1969). As James Madison observed in support of the proposed Constitution's enhancement of national powers:

" 'The smaller the society, the fewer probably will be the distinct parties and interests composing it; the fewer the distinct parties and interests, the more frequently will a majority be found of the same party; and the smaller the number of individuals composing a majority, and the smaller the compass within which they are placed, the more easily will they concert and execute their plan of oppression. Extend the sphere and you take in a greater variety of parties and interests; you make it less probable that a majority of the whole will have a common motive to invade the rights of other citizens; or if such a common motive exists, it will be more difficult for all who feel it to discover their own strength and to act in unison with each other.' The Federalist No. 10, pp. 82–84 (C. Rossiter ed. 1961)."

In her plurality opinion in Croson, Justice O'CONNOR also emphasized the importance of this distinction when she responded to the city's argument that Fullilove was controlling. She wrote:

"What appellant ignores is that Congress, unlike any State or political subdivision, has a specific constitutional mandate to enforce the dictates of the Fourteenth Amendment. The power to 'enforce' may at times also include the power to define situations which Congress determines threaten principles of equality and to adopt prophylactic rules to deal with those situations. The Civil War Amendments themselves worked a dramatic change

in the balance between congressional and state power over matters of race."

An additional reason for giving greater deference to the National Legislature than to a local lawmaking body is that federal affirmative-action programs represent the will of our entire Nation's elected representatives, whereas a state or local program may have an impact on nonresident entities who played no part in the decision to enact it. Thus, in the state or local context, individuals who were unable to vote for the local representatives who enacted a race-conscious program may nonetheless feel the effects of that program. This difference recalls the goals of the Commerce Clause, which permits Congress to legislate on certain matters of national importance while denying power to the States in this area for fear of undue impact upon out-of-state residents.

Ironically, after all of the time, effort, and paper this Court has expended in differentiating between federal and state affirmative action, the majority today virtually ignores the issue. It provides not a word of direct explanation for its sudden and enormous departure from the reasoning in past cases. Such silence, however, cannot erase the difference between Congress' institutional competence and constitutional authority to overcome historic racial subjugation and the States' lesser power to do so.

Presumably, the majority is now satisfied that its theory of "congruence" between the substantive rights provided by the Fifth and Fourteenth Amendments disposes of the objection based upon divided constitutional powers. But it is one thing to say (as no one seems to dispute) that the Fifth Amendment encompasses a general guarantee of equal protection as broad as that contained within the Fourteenth Amendment. It is another thing entirely to say that Congress' institutional competence and constitutional authority entitles it to no greater deference when it enacts a program designed to foster equality than the deference due a state legislature. The latter is an extraordinary proposition; and, as the foregoing discussion demonstrates, our precedents have rejected it explicitly and repeatedly.

Our opinion in Metro Broadcasting relied on several constitutional provisions to justify the greater deference we owe to Congress when it acts with respect to private individuals. In the programs challenged in this case, Congress has acted both with respect to private individuals and, as in Fullilove, with respect to the States themselves. When Congress does this, it draws its power directly from § 5 of the Fourteenth Amendment. That section reads. "The Congress shall have power to enforce, by appropriate legislation, the provisions of this article." One of the "provisions of this article" that Congress is thus empowered to enforce reads: "No State shall make or enforce any law which shall abridge the privileges or immunities of citizens of the United States; nor shall any State deprive any person of life, liberty, or property, without due process of law; nor deny to any person within its jurisdiction the equal protection of the laws." The Fourteenth Amendment directly empowers Congress at the same time it expressly limits the States. This is no accident. It represents our Nation's consensus, achieved after hard experience throughout our sorry history of race relations, that the Federal Government must be the primary defender of racial minorities against the States, some of which may be inclined to oppress such minorities. A rule of "congruence" that ignores a purposeful "incongruity" so fundamental to our system of government is unacceptable.

In my judgment, the Court's novel doctrine of "congruence" is seriously misguided. Congressional deliberations about a matter as important as affirmative action should be accorded far greater deference than those of a State or municipality.

IV

The Court's concept of stare decisis treats some of the language we have used in explaining our decisions as though it were more important than our actual holdings. In my opinion that treatment is incorrect.

This is the third time in the Court's entire history that it has considered the constitutionality of a federal affirmative-action program. On each of the two prior occasions, the first in 1980, Fullilove v. Klutznick, and the second in 1990, Metro Broadcasting, Inc. v. FCC, the Court upheld the program. Today the Court explicitly overrules Metro Broadcasting (at least in part), and undermines Fullilove by recasting the standard on which it rested and by calling even its holding into question. By way of explanation, Justice O'CONNOR advises the federal agencies and private parties that have made countless decisions in reliance on those cases that "we do not depart from the fabric of the law; we restore it." A skeptical observer might ask whether this pronouncement is a faithful application of the doctrine of stare decisis. A brief comment on each of the two ailing cases may provide the answer.

In the Court's view, our decision in Metro Broadcasting was inconsistent with the rule announced in Richmond v. J.A. Croson Co., (1989). But two decisive distinctions separate those two cases. First, Metro Broadcasting involved a federal program, whereas Croson involved a city ordinance. Metro Broadcasting thus drew primary support from Fullilove, which predated Croson and which Croson distinguished on the grounds of the federal-state dichotomy that the majority today discredits. Although Members of today's majority trumpeted the importance of that distinction in Croson, they now reject it in the name of "congruence." It is therefore quite wrong for the Court to suggest today that overruling Metro Broadcasting merely restores the status quo ante, for the law at the time of that decision was entirely open to the result the Court reached. Today's decision is an unjustified departure from settled law.

Second, Metro Broadcasting's holding rested on more than its application of "intermediate scrutiny." Indeed, I have always believed that, labels notwithstanding, the Federal Communications Commission (FCC) program we upheld in that case would have satisfied any of our various standards in affirmative-action cases—including the one the majority fashions today. What truly distinguishes Metro Broadcasting from our other affirmative-action precedents is the distinctive goal of the federal program in that case. Instead of merely seeking to remedy past discrimination, the FCC program was intended to achieve future benefits in the form of broadcast diversity. Reliance on race as a legitimate means of achieving diversity was first endorsed by Justice Powell in Regents of Univ. of Cal. v. Bakke, (1978). Later, in Wygant v. Jackson Bd. of (1986), I also argued that race is not always irrelevant to governmental decision-making, in response, Justice O'CONNOR correctly noted that, although the school board had relied on an interest in providing black teachers to serve as role models for black students, that interest "should not be confused with the very different goal of promoting racial diversity among the faculty." She then added that, because the school board had not relied on an interest in diversity, it was not "necessary to discuss the magnitude of that interest or its applicability in this case."

Thus, prior to Metro Broadcasting, the interest in diversity had been mentioned in a few opinions, but it is perfectly clear that the Court had not yet decided whether thatinterest had sufficient magnitude to justify a racial classification. Metro Broadcasting, of course, answered that question in the affirmative. The majority today overrules Metro Broadcasting only insofar as it is "inconsistent with [the] holding" that strict scrutiny applies to "benign" racial classifications promulgated by the Federal Government. The proposition that fostering diversity may provide a sufficient interest to justify such a program is not inconsistent with the Court's holding today—indeed, the question is not remotely presented

in this case—and I do not take the Court's opinion to diminish that aspect of our decision in Metro Broadcasting.

The Court's suggestion that it may he necessary in the future to overrule Fullilove in order to restore the fabric of the law, is even more disingenuous than its treatment of Metro Broadcasting. For the Court endorses the "strict scrutiny" standard that Justice Powell applied in Bakke, and acknowledges that he applied that standard in Fullilove as well. Moreover, Chief Justice Burger also expressly concluded that the program we considered in Fullilove was valid under any of the tests articulated in Bakke, which of course included Justice Powell's. The Court thus adopts a standard applied in Fullilove at the same time it questions that case's continued vitality and accuses it of departing from prior law. I continue to believe that the Fullilove case was incorrectly decided, but neither my dissent nor that filed by Justice Stewart, contained any suggestion that the issue the Court was resolving had been decided before. As was true of Metro Broadcasting, the Court in Fullilove decided an important, novel, and difficult question. Providing a different answer to a similar question today cannot fairly be characterized as merely "restoring" previously settled law.

V

The Court's holding in Fullilove surely governs the result in this case. The Public Works Employment Act of 1977, which this Court upheld in Fullilove, is different in several critical respects from the portions of the Small Business Act (SBA), challenged in this case. Each of those differences makes the current program designed to provide assistance to DBE's significantly less objectionable than the 1977 categorical grant of $400 million in exchange for a 10% set-aside in public contracts to "a class of investors defined solely by racial characteristics." Fullilove, (STEVENS, J., dissenting). In no meaningful respect is the current scheme more objectionable than the 1977 Act. Thus, if the 1977 Act was constitutional, then so must be the SBA and STURAA. Indeed, even if my dissenting views in Fullilove had prevailed, this program would be valid.

Unlike the 1977 Act, the present statutory scheme does not make race the sole criterion of eligibility for participation in the program. Race does give rise to a rebuttable presumption of social disadvantage which, at least under STURAA, gives rise to a second rebuttable presumption of economic disadvantage. But a small business may qualify as a DBE, by showing that it is both socially and economically disadvantaged, even if it receives neither of these presumptions. Thus, the current preference is more inclusive than the 1977 Act because it does not make race a necessary qualification.

More importantly, race is not a sufficient qualification. Whereas a millionaire with a long history of financial successes, who was a member of numerous social clubs and trade associations, would have qualified for a preference under the 1977 Act merely because he was an Asian-American or an African-American, see Fullilove, (STEVENS, J., dissenting), neither the SBA nor STURAA creates any such anomaly. The DBE program excludes members of minority races who are not, in fact, socially or economically disadvantaged. The presumption of social disadvantage reflects the unfortunate fact that irrational racial prejudice—along with its lingering effects—still survives. The presumption of economic disadvantage embodies a recognition that success in the private sector of the economy is often attributable, in part, to social skills and relationships. Unlike the 1977 set-asides, the current preference is designed to overcome the social and economic disadvantages that are often associated with racial characteristics. If, in a particular case, these disadvantages are not present, the presump-

tions can be rebutted. The program is thus designed to allow race to play a part in the decisional process only when there is a meaningful basis for assuming its relevance. In this connection, I think it is particularly significant that the current program targets the negotiation of subcontracts between private firms. The 1977 Act applied entirely to the award of public contracts, an area of the economy in which social relationships should be irrelevant and in which proper supervision of government contracting officers should preclude any discrimination against particular bidders on account of their race. In this case, in contrast, the program seeks to overcome barriers of prejudice between private parties—specifically, between general contractors and subcontractors. The SBA and STURAA embody Congress' recognition that such barriers may actually handicap minority firms seeking business as subcontractors from established leaders in the industry that have a history of doing business with their golfing partners. Indeed, minority subcontractors may face more obstacles than direct, intentional racial prejudice: They may face particular barriers simply because they are more likely to be new in the business and less likely to know others in the business. Given such difficulties, Congress could reasonably find that a minority subcontractor is less likely to receive favors from the entrenched businesspersons who award subcontracts only to people with whom—or with whose friends—they have an existing relationship. This program, then, if in part a remedy for past discrimination, is most importantly a forward-looking response to practical problems faced by minority subcontractors.

The current program contains another forward-looking component that the 1977 set-asides did not share. Section 8(a) of the SBA provides for periodic review of the status of DBE's, and DBE status can be challenged by a competitor at any time under any of the routes to certification. Such review prevents ineligible firms from taking part in the program solely because of their minority ownership, even when those firms were once disadvantaged but have since become successful. The emphasis on review also indicates the Administration's anticipation that after their presumed disadvantages have been overcome, firms will "graduate" into a status in which they will be able to compete for business, including prime contracts, on an equal basis. As with other phases of the statutory policy of encouraging the formation and growth of small business enterprises, this program is intended to facilitate entry and increase competition in the free market.

Significantly, the current program, unlike the 1977 set-aside, does not establish any requirement—numerical or otherwise—that a general contractor must hire DBE subcontractors. The program we upheld in Fullilove required that 10% of the federal grant for every federally funded project be expended on minority business enterprises. In contrast, the current program contains no quota. Although it provides monetary incentives to general contractors to hire DBE subcontractors, it does not require them to hire DBE's, and they do not lose their contracts if they fail to do so. The importance of this incentive to general contractors (who always seek to offer the lowest bid) should not be underestimated; but the preference here is far less rigid, and thus more narrowly tailored, than the 1977 Act.

Finally, the record shows a dramatic contrast between the sparse deliberations that preceded the 1977 Act, and the extensive hearings conducted in several Congresses before the current program was developed. However we might evaluate the benefits and costs—both fiscal and social—of this or any other affirmative-action program, our obligation to give deference to Congress' policy choices is much more demanding in this case than it was in Fullilove. If the 1977 program of race-based set-asides satisfied the strict scrutiny dictated by Justice Powell's vision of the Constitution—a vision the Court expressly endorses today—it must follow as night follows the day that the Court of Appeals' judgment upholding this more carefully crafted program should be affirmed.

VI

My skeptical scrutiny of the Court's opinion leaves me in dissent. The majority's concept of "consistency" ignores a difference, fundamental to the idea of equal protection, between oppression and assistance. The majority's concept of "congruence" ignores a difference, fundamental to our constitutional system, between the Federal Government and the States. And the majority's concept of stare decisis ignores the force of binding precedent. I would affirm the judgment of the Court of Appeals.

Discussion Questions

1. Briefly summarize the facts in this case including the parties involved and what each is claiming.
2. Present and explain Justice O'Connor's case for reversing the lower court ruling. What does she mean by strict scrutiny, and why does she think that the government's policy must meet that level of review if it is to be considered constitutional?
3. Present and explain the reasons why Justice O'Connor believes that her opinion is consistent with prior affirmative action cases. Why does she think that the *Metro* case is inconsistent with those prior cases? How does Justice Stevens in his dissent reply to

O'Connor's reliance on these prior cases? Do you find his rebuttal convincing? Why or why not? Explain and defend your answer.

4. Why does Justice Stevens believe that "consistency" on the use of race is not always fair or just? Do you agree or disagree? Explain and defend your answer. How does Justice Thomas's opinion respond to Justice Stevens's argument?

5. Why does Justice Stevens maintain that Justice O'Connor does not adequately distinguish between federal, local, and state affirmative action policies?

6. What are the two prongs of Justice Thomas's opinion? Present and explain them. Do you agree or disagree with his opinion? Explain and defend your answer.

7. How does Justice O'Connor reply to Justice Stevens's criticism of her opinion? Present and explain her reply. Do you think that she succeeds? Why or why not? Explain and defend you answer.

You can locate InfoTrac-College Education articles about this chapter by accessing the InfoTrac-College Edition website (http://www.infotrac-college.com/wadsworth/). Using the InfoTrac-College Edition subject guide, enter the search terms relevant to this chapter, and then read abstracts for relevant articles.

A1

The Moral Justification of Affirmative Action

---

29   **A Defense of Programs of Preferential Treatment**

RICHARD WASSERSTROM

Richard Wasserstrom is Professor of Philosophy at the University of California at Santa Cruz. He has written extensively in professional journals in the areas of ethics and social philosophy. Among his books are *War and Morality* (1970) and *Philosophy and Social Issues* (1980).

In this essay Professor Wasserstrom presents a moral defense of the type of affirmative action which calls for preferential treatment for groups (e.g., blacks, Hispanics, women) whose members have suffered discrimination. Although he admits that he is not attempting to establish that preferential treatment programs are right and desirable, he is arguing that two of the arguments proposed by those who oppose preferential treatment do not work. The first argument is the argument from *intellectual inconsistency:* proponents of preferential treatment "programs are guilty of intellectual inconsistency," since they propose to use criteria (race and sex), in order to help minorities, which they condemn when used by bigots *against* minorities. Professor Wasserstrom responds to this argument by saying what made and makes discrimination against minorities wrong is that it denies them positions of social and political power in society; that is not happening to nonminorities when a job or an academic admission is given to a minority due to a preferential treatment program. The second argument is the argument from *an individual's*

Reprinted by permission from National Forum: The Phi Kappa Phi Journal *58 (winter 1978). This originally appeared as Part II of "Racism, Sexism, and Preferential Treatment," 24 U.C.L.A. Law Review 581 (1977).*

qualifications: "preferential treatment programs are wrong because they take race or sex into account rather than the only thing that does matter—that is, an individual's qualifications." Professor Wasserstrom provides three responses: (1) in jobs of substantial power and authority there is no serious "qualification requirement"; (2) if qualification is the same as "good consequences for the employer," then one must accept preferential treatment programs if they result in good consequences; and (3) nobody deserves or is entitled to a position simply because they are "qualified."

MANY JUSTIFICATIONS OF PROGRAMS of preferential treatment depend upon the claim that in one respect or another such programs have good consequences or that they are effective means by which to bring about one desirable end, e.g., an integrated, equalitarian society. I mean by "programs of preferential treatment" to refer to programs such as those at issue in the *Bakke* case—programs which set aside a certain number of places (for example, in a law school) as to which members of minority groups (for example, persons who are nonwhite or female) who possess certain minimum qualifications (in terms of grades and test scores) may be preferred for admission to those places over some members of the majority group who possess higher qualifications (in terms of grades and test scores).

Many criticisms of programs of preferential treatment claim that such programs, even if effective, are unjustifiable because they are in some important sense unfair or unjust. In this paper I present a limited defense of such programs by showing that two of the chief arguments offered for the unfairness or injustice of these programs do not work in the way or to the degree supposed by critics of these programs.

The first argument is this. Opponents of preferential treatment programs sometimes assert that proponents of these programs are guilty of intellectual inconsistency, if not racism or sexism. For, as is now readily acknowledged, at times past employers, universities, and many other social institutions did have racial or sexual quotas (when they did not practice overt racial or sexual exclusion), and many of those who were most concerned to bring about the eradication of those racial quotas are now untroubled by the new programs which reinstitute them. And this, it claimed, is inconsistent. If it was wrong to take race or sex into account when blacks and women were the objects of racial and sexual policies and practices of exclusion, then it is wrong to take race or sex into account when the objects of the policies have their race or sex reversed. Simple considerations of intellectual consistency—of what it means to give racism or sexism as a reason for condemning these social policies and practices—require that what was a good reason then is still a good reason now.

The problem with this argument is that despite appearances, there is no inconsistency involved in holding both views. Even if contemporary preferential treatment programs which contain quotas are wrong, they are not wrong for the reasons that made quotas against blacks and women pernicious. The reason why is that the social realities do make an enormous difference. The fundamental evil of programs that discriminated against blacks or women was that these programs were a part of a larger social universe which systematically maintained a network of institutions which unjustifiably concentrated power, authority, and goods in the hands of white male individuals, and which systematically consigned blacks and women to subordinate positions in the society.

Whatever may be wrong with today's affirmative action programs and quota systems, it should be clear that the evil, if any, is just not the same. Racial and sexual minorities do not constitute the dominant social group. Nor is the conception of who is a fully developed member of the moral and social community one of an individual who is either female or black. Quotas which prefer women or blacks do not add to an already relatively overabundant supply of resources and opportunities at the disposal of members of these groups in the way in which the quotas of the past did maintain and augment the overabundant supply of resources and opportunities already available to white males.

The same point can be made in a somewhat different way. Sometimes people say that what was wrong, for example, with the system of racial discrimination in the South was that it took an irrelevant characteristic, namely race, and used it systematically to allocate social benefits and burdens of various sorts. The defect was the irrelevance of the characteristic used—race—for that meant that individuals ended up being treated in a manner that was arbitrary and capricious.

I do not think that was the central flaw at all. Take, for instance, the most hideous of the practices, human slavery. The primary thing that was wrong with the institution was not that the particular individuals who were assigned the place of slaves were assigned there arbitrarily because the assignment was made in virtue of an irrelevant characteristic, their race. Rather, it seems to me that the primary thing that was and is wrong with slavery is the practice itself—the fact of some individuals being able to own other individuals and all that goes with that practice. It would not matter by what criterion individuals were assigned; human slavery would still be wrong. And the same can be said for most if not all of the other discrete practices and institutions which comprised the system of racial discrimination even after human slavery was abolished. The practices

were unjustifiable—they were oppressive—and they would have been so no matter how the assignment of victims had been made. What made it worse, still, was that the institutions and the supporting ideology all interlocked to create a system of human oppression whose effects on those living under it were as devastating as they were unjustifiable.

Again, if there is anything wrong with the programs of preferential treatment that have begun to flourish within the past ten years, it should be evident that the social realities in respect to the distribution of resources and opportunities make the difference. Apart from everything else, there is simply no way in which all of these programs taken together could plausibly be viewed as capable of relegating white males to the kind of genuinely oppressive status characteristically bestowed upon women and blacks by the dominant social institutions and ideology.

The second objection is that preferential treatment programs are wrong because they take race or sex into account rather than the only thing that does matter—that is, an individual's qualification. What all such programs have in common and what makes them all objectionable, so this argument goes, is that they ignore the persons who are more qualified by bestowing a preference on those who are less qualified in virtue of their being black or female.

There are, I think, a number of things wrong with this objection based on qualifications, and not the least of them is that we do not live in a society in which there is even the serious pretense of a qualification requirement for many jobs of substantial power and authority. Would anyone claim, for example, that the persons who comprise the judiciary are there because they are the most qualified lawyers or the most qualified persons to be judges? Would anyone claim that Henry Ford II is the head of the Ford Motor Company because he is the most qualified person for the job? Part of what is wrong with even talking about qualifications and merit is that the argument derives some of its force from the erroneous notion that we would have a meritocracy were it not for programs of preferential treatment. In fact, the higher one goes in terms of prestige, power and the like, the less qualifications seem ever to be decisive. It is only for certain jobs and certain places that qualifications are used to do more than establish the possession of certain minimum competencies.

But difficulties such as these to one side, there are theoretical difficulties as well which cut much more deeply into the argument about qualifications. To begin with, it is important to see that there is a serious inconsistency present if the person who favors "pure qualifications" does so on the ground that the most qualified ought to be selected because this promotes maximum efficiency. Let us suppose that the argument is that if we have the most qualified performing the relevant tasks we will get those tasks done in the most economical and efficient manner. There is nothing wrong in principle with arguments based upon the good consequences that will flow from maintaining a social practice in a certain way. But it is inconsistent for the opponent of preferential treatment to attach much weight to qualifications on this ground, because it was an analogous appeal to the good consequences that the opponent of preferential treatment thought was wrong in the first place. That is to say, if the chief thing to be said in favor of strict qualifications and preferring the most qualified is that it is the most efficient way of getting things done, then we are right back to an assessment of the different consequences that will flow from different programs, and we are far removed from the considerations of justice or fairness that were thought to weigh so heavily against these programs.

It is important to note, too, that qualifications—at least in the educational context—are often not connected at all closely with any plausible conception of social effectiveness. To admit the most qualified students to law school, for example—given the way qualifications are now determined—is primarily to admit those who have the greatest chance of scoring the highest grades at law school. This says little about efficiency except perhaps that these students are the easiest for the faculty to teach. However, since we know so little about what constitutes being a good, or even successful lawyer, and even less about the correlation between being a very good law student and being a very good lawyer, we can hardly claim very confidently that the legal system will operate more efficiently if we admit only the most qualified students to law school.

To be at all decisive, the argument for qualifications must be that those who are the most qualified deserve to receive the benefits (the job, the place in law school, etc.) because they are the most qualified. The introduction of the concept of desert now makes it an objection as to justice or fairness of the sort promised by the original criticism of the programs. But now the problem is that there is no reason to think that there is any strong sense of "desert" in which it is correct that the most qualified deserve anything.

Let us consider more closely one case, that of preferential treatment in respect to admission to college or graduate school. There is a logical gap in the inference from the claim that a person is most qualified to perform a task, e.g., to be a good student, to the conclusion that he or she deserves to be admitted as a student. Of course, those who deserve to be admitted should be admitted. But why do the most qualified deserve anything? There is simply no necessary connection between academic merit (in the sense of being most qualified) and deserving to be a member of a student body. Suppose, for instance, that there is only one tennis court in the community. Is it clear that the two best tennis players ought to be the ones permitted to use it? Why not those who were there first? Or those who will enjoy playing the most? Or those who are the worst and, therefore, need the greatest opportunity to practice? Or those who have the chance to play least frequently?

We might, of course, have a rule that says that the best tennis players get to use the court before the others. Under such a rule the best players would deserve the court more than the poorer ones. But that is just to push the inquiry back one stage. Is there any reason to think that we ought to have a rule giving good tennis players such a preference? Indeed, the arguments that might be given for or against such a rule are many and varied. And few if any of the arguments that might support the rule would depend upon a connection between ability and desert.

Someone might reply, however, that the most able students deserve to be admitted to the university because all of their earlier schooling was a kind of competition, with university admission being the prize awarded to the winners. They deserve to be admitted because that is what the rule of the competition provides. In addition, it might be argued, it would be unfair now to exclude them in favor of others, given the reasonable expectations they developed about the way in which their industry and performance would be rewarded. Minority-admission programs, which inevitably prefer some who are less qualified over some who are more qualified, all possess this flaw.

There are several problems with this argument. The most substantial of them is that it is an empirically implausible picture of our social world. Most of what are regarded as the decisive characteristics for higher education have a great deal to do with things over which the individual has neither control nor responsibility; such things as home environment, socio-economic class of parents, and, of course, the quality of the primary and secondary schools attended. Since individuals do not deserve having had any of these things vis-à-vis other individuals, they do not, for the most part, deserve their qualifications. And since they do not deserve their abilities they do not in any strong

sense deserve to be admitted because of their abilities.

To be sure, if there has been a rule which connects, say, performance at high school with admission to college, then there is a weak sense in which those who do well at high school deserve, for that reason alone, to be admitted to college. In addition, if persons have built up or relied upon their reasonable expectations concerning performance and admission, they have a claim to be admitted on this ground as well. But it is certainly not obvious that these claims of desert are any stronger or more compelling than the competing claims based upon the needs of or advantages to women or blacks from programs of preferential treatment. And as I have indicated, all rule-based claims of desert are very weak unless and until the rule which creates the claim is itself shown to be a justified one. Unless one has a strong preference for the status quo, and unless one can defend that preference, the practice within a system of allocating places in a certain way does not go very far at all in showing that this is the right or the just way to allocate those places in the future.

A proponent of programs of preferential treatment is not at all committed to the view that qualifications ought to be wholly irrelevant. He or she can agree that, given the existing structure of any institution, there is probably some minimal set of qualifications without which one cannot participate meaningfully within the institution. In addition, it can be granted that the qualifications of those involved will affect the way the institution works and the way it affects others in the society. And the consequences will vary depending upon the particular institution. But all of this only establishes that qualifications, in this sense, are relevant, not that they are decisive. This is wholly consistent with the claim that race or sex should today also be relevant when it comes to matters such as admission to college or law school. And that is all that any preferential treatment program—even one with the kind of quota used in the *Bakke* case—has ever tried to do.

I have not attempted to establish that programs of preferential treatment are right and desirable. There are empirical issues concerning the consequences of these programs that I have not discussed, and certainly not settled. Nor, for that matter, have I considered the argument that justice may permit, if not require, these programs as a way to provide compensation or reparation for injuries suffered in the recent as well as distant past, or as a way to remove benefits that are undeservedly enjoyed by those of the dominant group. What I have tried to do is show that it is wrong to think that programs of preferential treatment are objectionable in the centrally important sense in which many past and present discriminatory features of our society have been and are racist and sexist. The social realities as to power and opportunity do make a fundamental difference. It is also wrong to think that programs of preferential treatment could, therefore, plausibly rest both on the view that such programs are not unfair to white males (except in the weak, rule-dependent sense described above) and on the view that it is unfair to continue the present set of unjust—often racist and sexist—institutions that comprise the social reality. And the case for these programs could rest as well on the proposition that, given the distribution of power and influence in the United States today, such programs may reasonably be viewed as potentially valuable, effective means by which to achieve admirable and significant social ideals of equality and integration.

Discussion Questions

1. Professor Wasserstrom points out that opponents of preferential treatment claim that the supporters of preferential treatment are guilty of "intellectual inconsistency." How does Professor Wasserstrom attempt to refute this claim? Do you think he succeeds? Why or why not? Explain and defend your answer.

2. How does Professor Wasserstrom respond to the second argument against preferential treatment: "preferential treatment programs are wrong because they take race or sex into account rather than the only thing that does matter—that is, an individual's qualifications."? Do you think his response is convincing? Do you find his analogy with tennis to be a sound one? Explain and defend your answers.

3. Do you agree with Professor Wasserstrom's claim that there is no necessary connection between desert and qualifications? Explain and defend your answer.

You can locate InfoTrac-College Education articles about this chapter by accessing the InfoTrac-College Edition website (http://www.infotrac-college.com/wadsworth/). Using the InfoTrac-College Edition subject guide, enter the search terms relevant to this chapter, and then read abstracts for relevant articles.

30   The Moral Status of Affirmative Action

LOUIS P. POJMAN

Louis P. Pojman is Professor of Philosophy at the United States Military Academy in West Point, New York. He has published widely in the areas of philosophy of religion, epistemology, ethics, and political philosophy. Among his many books are *Ethical Theory: Classical and Contemporary Readings,* 3rd ed. (1998), *Ethics: Discovering Right and Wrong,* 3rd ed. (1998), and *The Abortion Controversy 25 Years After Roe v. Wade: A Reader,* 2nd ed. (1998).

In this essay Professor Pojman makes a distinction between weak and strong versions of affirmative action and then argues that strong affirmative action is not morally justified. He defines *weak affirmative action* as the employment of "such measures as the elimination of segregation, widespread advertisement to groups not previously represented in certain privileged positions, special scholarships for the disadvantaged classes (e.g., all the poor), using underrepresentation or a history of past discrimination as a tie breaker when candidates are relatively equal, and the like." On the other hand, *strong affirmative action* "involves more positive steps to eliminate past injustice, such as reverse discrimination, hiring candidates on the basis of race or gender in order to reach equal or near equal results, proportionate representation in each area of society." In order to support his position, Professor Pojman critiques seven arguments for affirmative action and provides seven arguments against affirmative action. The seven arguments for affirmative action are: (1) the need for role models; (2) the need for breaking the stereotypes; (3) the equal results argument; (4) the compensation argument; (5) the argument based on compensation from those who innocently benefited from past injustice; (6) the diversity argument; and (7) the anti-meritocratic (desert) argument to justify reverse discrimination: "no one deserves his or her talents." The seven arguments against affirmative action are: (1) affirmative action requires discrimination against a different group; (2) affirmative action perpetuates victimization syndrome; (3) affirmative action encourages mediocrity and incompetence; (4) affirmative action policies unjustly shift the burden of proof; (5) an argument from merit; (6) the slippery slope argument; and (7) the argument from the mounting evidence against the success of affirmative action.

A ruler who appoints any man to an office, when there is in his dominion another man better qualified for it, sins against God and against the State.

—The *Koran*

[Affirmative Action] is the meagerest recompense for centuries of unrelieved oppression.

—quoted by Shelby Steele as the justification for Affirmative Action

Reprinted by permission from Public Affairs Quarterly *6 (April 1992). This essay has been edited for this text.*

HARDLY A WEEK GOES by but that the subject of Affirmative Action does not come up. Whether in the guise of reverse discrimination, preferential hiring, nontraditional casting, quotas, goals and time tables, minority scholarships, or race-norming, the issue confronts us as a terribly perplexing problem. Last summer's Actor's Equity debacle over the casting of the British actor, Jonathan Pryce, as a Eurasian in *Miss Saigon;* Assistant Secretary of Education Michael Williams' judgment that Minority Scholarships are unconstitutional; the "Civil Rights Bill of 1991," reversing recent decisions of the Supreme Court which constrain preferential hiring practices; the demand that Harvard Law School hire a black female professor; grade stipends for black students at Pennsylvania State University and other schools; the revelations of race norming in state employment agencies; as well as debates over quotas, under-utilization guidelines, and diversity in employment; all testify to the importance of this subject for contemporary society.

There is something salutary as well as terribly tragic inherent in this problem. The salutary aspect is the fact that our society has shown itself committed to eliminating unjust discrimination. Even in the heart of Dixie there is a recognition of the injustice of racial discrimination. Both sides of the affirmative action debate have good will and appeal to moral principles. Both sides are attempting to bring about a better society, one which is color blind, but they differ profoundly on the morally proper means to accomplish that goal.

And this is just the tragedy of the situation: good people on both sides of the issue are ready to tear each other to pieces over a problem that has no easy or obvious solution. And so the voices become shrill and the rhetoric hyperbolic. The same spirit which divides the pro-choice movement from the right to life movement on abortion divides liberal pro-Affirmative Action advocates from liberal anti-Affirmative Action advocates. This problem, more than any other, threatens to destroy the traditional liberal consensus in our society. I have seen family members and close friends who until recently fought on the same side of the barricades against racial injustice divide in enmity over this issue. The anti-affirmative liberals ("liberals who've been mugged") have tended towards a form of neo-conservatism and the pro-affirmative liberals have tended to side with the radical left to form the "politically correct ideology" movement.

In this paper I will confine myself primarily to Affirmative Action policies with regard to race, but much of what I say can be applied to the areas of gender and ethnic minorities.

I. DEFINITIONS

First let me define my terms:

Discrimination is simply judging one thing to differ from another on the basis of some criterion. "Discrimination" is essentially a good quality, having reference to our ability to make distinctions. As rational and moral agents we need to make proper distinctions. To be rational is to discriminate between good and bad arguments, and to think morally is to discriminate between reasons based on valid principles and those based on invalid ones. What needs to be distinguished is the difference between rational and moral discrimination, on the one hand, and irrational and immoral discrimination, on the other hand.

Prejudice is a discrimination based on irrelevant grounds. It may simply be an attitude which never surfaces in action, or it may cause prejudicial actions. A prejudicial discrimination in action is immoral if it denies someone a fair deal. So discrimination on the basis of race or sex where these are not relevant for job performance is unfair. Likewise, one may act prejudicially in applying a relevant criterion on insufficient grounds, as in the case where I apply the criterion of being a hard worker but then assume, on insufficient evidence; that the black man who applies for the job is not a hard worker.

There is a difference between *prejudice* and *bias*. Bias signifies a tendency towards one thing rather than another where the evidence is incomplete or based on non-moral factors. For example, you may have a bias towards blondes and I towards red-heads. But prejudice is an attitude (or action) where unfairness is present—where one *should* know or do better, as in the case where I give people jobs simply because they are red-heads. Bias implies ignorance or incomplete knowledge, whereas prejudice is deeper, involving a moral failure— usually a failure to pay attention to the evidence. But note that calling people racist or sexist without good evidence is also an act of prejudice. I call this form of prejudice "defamism," for it unfairly defames the victim. It is a contemporary version of McCarthyism.

Equal Opportunity is offering everyone a fair chance at the best positions that society has at its disposal. Only native aptitude and effort should be decisive in the outcome, not factors of race, sex or special favors.

Affirmative Action is the effort to rectify the injustice of the past by special policies. Put this way, it is Janus-faced or ambiguous, having both a backward-looking and a forward-looking feature. The backward-looking feature is its attempt to correct and compensate for past injustice. This aspect of Affirmative Action is strictly deontological. The forward-looking feature is its implicit ideal of a society free from prejudice; this is both deontological and utilitarian.

When we look at a social problem from a backward-looking perspective we need to determine who has committed or benefited from a wrongful or prejudicial act and to determine who deserves compensation for that act.

When we look at a social problem from a forward-looking perspective we need to determine what a just society (one free from prejudice) would look like and how to obtain that kind of society. The forward-looking aspect of Affirmative Action is paradoxically race-conscious, since it uses race to bring about a society which is not race-conscious, which is color-blind (in the morally relevant sense of this term).

It is also useful to distinguish two versions of Affirmative Action. *Weak Affirmative Action* involves such measures as the elimination of segregation (namely the idea of "separate but equal"), widespread advertisement to groups not previously represented in certain privileged positions, special scholarships for the disadvantaged classes (e.g., all the poor), using underrepresentation or a history of past discrimination as a tie breaker when candidates are relatively equal, and the like.

Strong Affirmative Action involves more positive steps to eliminate past injustice, such as reverse discrimination, hiring candidates on the basis of race and gender in order to reach equal or near equal results, proportionate representation in each area of society. . . .

[II.] ARGUMENTS FOR AFFIRMATIVE ACTION

Let us now survey the main arguments typically cited in the debate over Affirmative Action. I will briefly discuss seven arguments on each side of the issue.

1. Need for Role Models

This argument is straightforward. We all have need for role models, and it helps to know that others like us can be successful. We learn and are encouraged to strive for excellence by emulating our heroes and role models.

However, it is doubtful whether role models of one's own racial or sexual type are necessary for success. One of my heroes was Gandhi, an Indian Hindu, another was my grade school science teacher, one Miss DeVoe, and another was Martin Luther King. More important than having role models of one's own type is having genuinely good people, of whatever race or gender, to emulate. Furthermore, even if it is of some help to people with low self-esteem to gain encouragement from seeing others of their particular kind in leadership roles, it is doubtful whether this need is a sufficient condition to justify preferential hiring or reverse discrimination. What good is a role model who is inferior to other professors or business personnel? Excellence will rise to the top in a system of fair opportunity. Natural development of role models will come more slowly and more surely. Proponents of preferential policies simply lack the patience to let history take its own course.

2. *The Need of Breaking the Stereotypes*

Society may simply need to know that there are talented blacks and women, so that it does not automatically assign them lesser respect or status. We need to have unjustified stereotype beliefs replaced with more accurate ones about the talents of blacks and women. So we need to engage in preferential hiring of qualified minorities even when they are not the most qualified.

Again, the response is that hiring the less qualified is neither fair to those better qualified who are passed over nor an effective way of removing inaccurate stereotypes. If competence is accepted as the criterion for hiring, then it is unjust to override it for purposes of social engineering. Furthermore, if blacks or women are known to hold high positions simply because of reverse discrimination, then they will still lack the respect due to those of their rank. In New York City there is a saying among doctors, "Never go to a black physician under 40," referring to the fact that AA has affected the medical system during the past fifteen years. The police use "Quota Cops" and "Welfare Sergeants" to refer to those hired without passing the standardized tests. (In 1985 180 black and Hispanic policemen, who had failed a promotion test, were promoted anyway to the rank of sergeant.) The destruction of false stereotypes will come naturally as qualified blacks rise naturally in fair competition (or if it does not—then the stereotypes may be justified). Reverse discrimination sends the message home that the stereotypes are deserved—otherwise, why do these minorities need so much extra help?

3. *Equal Results Argument*

Some philosophers and social scientists hold that human nature is roughly identical, so that on a fair playing field the same proportion from every race and gender and ethnic group would attain to the highest positions in every area of endeavor. It would follow that any inequality of results itself is evidence for inequality of opportunity. John Arthur, in discussing an intelligence test, Test 21, puts the case this way.

> History is important when considering governmental rules like Test 21 because low scores by blacks can be traced in large measure to the legacy of slavery and racism: segregation, poor schooling, exclusion from trade unions, malnutrition, and poverty have all played their roles. Unless one assumes that blacks are naturally less able to pass the test, the conclusion must be that the results are themselves socially and legally constructed, not a mere given for which law and society can claim no responsibility.
>
> The conclusion seems to be that genuine equality eventually requires equal results. Obviously blacks have been treated unequally throughout US history, and just as obviously the economic and psychological effects of that inequality linger to this day, showing up in lower income and poorer performance in school and on tests than whites achieve. Since we have no reason to believe that differences in performance can be explained by factors other than history, equal results are a good benchmark by which to measure progress made toward genuine equality.[1]

The result of a just society should be equal numbers in proportion to each group in the work force.

However, Arthur fails even to consider studies that suggest that there are innate differences between races, sexes, and groups. If there are genetic differences in intelligence and temperament within families, why should we not expect such differences between racial groups and the two genders? Why should the evidence for this be completely discounted?

Perhaps some race or one gender is more intelligent in one way than another. At present we have only limited knowledge about genetic differences, but what we do have suggests some difference besides the obvious physiological traits.[2] The proper use of this evidence is not to promote discriminatory policies but to be *open* to the possibility that innate difference may have led to an overrepresentation of certain groups in certain areas of endeavor. It seems that on average blacks have genetic endowments favoring them in the development of skills necessary for excellence in basketball.

Furthermore, on Arthur's logic, we should take aggressive AA against Asians and Jews since they are over-represented in science, technology, and medicine. So that each group receives its fair share, we should ensure that 12% of the philosophers in the United States are Black, reduce the percentage of Jews from an estimated 15% to 2%—firing about 1,300 Jewish philosophers. The fact that Asians are producing 50% of Ph.D.'s in science and math and blacks less than 1% clearly shows, on this reasoning, that we are providing special secret advantages to Asians.

But why does society have to enter into this results game in the first place? Why do we have to decide whether all difference is environmental or genetic? Perhaps we should simply admit that we lack sufficient evidence to pronounce on these issues with any certainty—but if so, should we not be more modest in insisting on equal results? Here is a thought experiment. Take two families of different racial groups, Green and Blue. The Greens decide to have only two children, to spend all their resources on them, to give them the best edu-

cation. The two Green kids respond well and end up with achievement test scores in the 99th percentile. The Blues fail to practice family planning. They have 15 children. They can only afford 2 children, but lack of ability or whatever prevents them from keeping their family down. Now they need help for their large family. Why does society have to step in and help them? Society did not force them to have 15 children. Suppose that the achievement test scores of the 15 children fall below the 25th percentile. They cannot compete with the Greens. But now enters AA. It says that it is society's fault that the Blue children are not as able as the Greens and that the Greens must pay extra taxes to enable the Blues to compete. No restraints are put on the Blues regarding family size. This seems unfair to the Greens. Should the Green children be made to bear responsibility for the consequences of the Blues' voluntary behavior?

My point is simply that Arthur needs to cast his net wider and recognize that demographics and childbearing and -rearing practices are crucial factors in achievement. People have to take some responsibility for their actions. The equal results argument (or axiom) misses a greater part of the picture.

4. The Compensation Argument

The argument goes like this: blacks have been wronged and severely harmed by whites. Therefore white society should compensate blacks for the injury caused them. Reverse discrimination in terms of preferential hiring, contracts, and scholarships is a fitting way to compensate for the past wrongs.

This argument actually involves a distorted notion of compensation. Normally, we think of compensation as owed by a specific person *A* to another person *B* whom *A* has wronged in a specific way *C*. For example, if I have stolen your car and used it for a period of time to make business profits that would have gone to you, it is not enough that I return your car. I must pay you an amount reflecting your loss and my ability to pay. If I have only made $5,000 and only have $10,000 in assets, it would not be possible for you to collect $20,000 in damages—even though that is the amount of loss you have incurred.

Sometimes compensation is extended to groups of people who have been unjustly harmed by the greater society. For example, the United States government has compensated the Japanese-Americans who were interned during the Second World War, and the West German government has paid reparations to the survivors of Nazi concentration camps. But here a specific people have been identified who were wronged in an identifiable way by the government of the nation in question.

On the face of it the demand by blacks for compensation does not fit the usual pattern. Perhaps Southern States with Jim Crow laws could be accused of unjustly harming blacks, but it is hard to see that the United States government was involved in doing so. Furthermore, it is not clear that all blacks were harmed in the same way or whether some were *unjustly* harmed or harmed more than poor whites and others (e.g., short people). Finally, even if identifiable blacks were harmed by identifiable social practices, it is not clear that most forms of Affirmative Action are appropriate to restore the situation. The usual practice of a financial payment seems more appropriate than giving a high level job to someone unqualified or only minimally qualified, who, speculatively, might have been better qualified had he not been subject to racial discrimination. If John is the star tailback of our college team with a promising professional future and I accidentally (but culpably) drive my pick-up truck over his legs, and so cripple him, John may be due compensation, but he is not due the tailback spot on the football team.

Still, there may be something intuitively compelling about compensating members of an oppressed group who are minimally qualified. Suppose that the Hatfields and the

McCoys are enemy clans and some youths from the Hatfields go over and steal diamonds and gold from the McCoys, distributing it within the Hatfield economy. Even though we do not know which Hatfield youths did the stealing, we would want to restore the wealth, as far as possible, to the McCoys. One way might be to tax the Hatfields, but another might be to give preferential treatment in terms of scholarships and training programs and hiring to the McCoys.[3]

This is perhaps the strongest argument for Affirmative Action, and it may well justify some weak versions of AA, but it is doubtful whether it is sufficient to justify strong versions with quotas and goals and time tables in skilled positions. There are at least two reasons for this. First, we have no way of knowing how many people of group G would have been at competence level L had the world been different. Secondly, the normal criterion of competence is a strong prima facie consideration when the most important positions are at stake. There are two reasons for this: (1) society has given people expectations that if they attain certain levels of excellence they will be awarded appropriately and (2) filling the most important positions with the best qualified is the best way to insure efficiency in job-related areas and in society in general. These reasons are not absolutes. They can be overridden. But there is a strong presumption in their favor so that a burden of proof rests with those who would override them.

At this point we get into the problem of whether innocent non-blacks should have to pay a penalty in terms of preferential hiring of blacks. We turn to that argument.

5. Compensation from Those Who Innocently Benefited from Past Injustice

White males as innocent beneficiaries of unjust discrimination of blacks and women have no grounds for complaint when society seeks to rectify the tilted field. White males may be innocent of oppressing blacks and minorities (and women), but they have unjustly benefited from that oppression or discrimination. So it is perfectly proper that less qualified women and blacks be hired before them.

The operative principle is: He who knowingly and willingly benefits from a wrong must help pay for the wrong. Judith Jarvis Thomson puts it this way. "Many [white males] have been direct beneficiaries of policies which have down-graded blacks and women . . . and even those who did not directly benefit . . . had, at any rate, the advantage in the competition which comes of the confidence in one's full membership [in the community], and of one's right being recognized as a matter of course."[4] That is, white males obtain advantages in self-respect and self-confidence deriving from a racist system which denies these to blacks and women.

Objection. As I noted in the previous section, compensation is normally individual and specific. If *A* harms *B* regarding *x*, *B* has a right to compensation from *A* in regards to *x*. If *A* steals *B*'s car and wrecks it, *A* has an obligation to compensate *B* for the stolen car, but *A*'s son has no obligation to compensate *B*. Furthermore, if *A* dies or disappears, *B* has no moral right to claim that society compensate him for the stolen car—though if he has insurance, he can make such a claim to the insurance company. Sometimes a wrong cannot be compensated, and we just have to make the best of an imperfect world.

Suppose my parents, divining that I would grow up to have an unsurpassable desire to be a basketball player, bought an expensive growth hormone for me. Unfortunately, a neighbor stole it and gave it to little Lew Alcindor, who gained the extra 18 inches—my 18 inches—and shot up to an enviable 7 feet 2 inches. Alias Kareem Abdul Jabbar, he excelled in basketball, as I would have done had I had my proper dose.

Do I have a right to the millions of dollars that Jabbar made as a professional basketball player—the unjustly innocent beneficiary of my growth hormone? I have a right to something from the neighbor who stole the hormone, and it might be kind of Jabbar to give me free tickets to the Laker basketball games, and perhaps I should be remembered in his will. As far as I can see, however, he does not *owe* me anything, either legally or morally.

Suppose further that Lew Alcindor and I are in high school together and we are both qualified to play basketball, only he is far better than I. Do I deserve to start in his position because I would have been as good as he is had someone not cheated me as a child? Again, I think not. But if being the lucky beneficiary of wrong-doing does not entail that Alcindor (or the coach) owes me anything in regards to basketball, why should it be a reason to engage in preferential hiring in academic positions or highly coveted jobs? If minimal qualifications are not adequate to override excellence in basketball, even when the minimality is a consequence of wrongdoing, why should they be adequate in other areas?

6. The Diversity Argument

It is important that we learn to live in a pluralistic world, learning to get along with those of other races and cultures, so we should have fully integrated schools and employment situations. Diversity is an important symbol and educative device. Thus preferential treatment is warranted to perform this role in society.

But, again, while we can admit the value of diversity, it hardly seems adequate to override considerations of merit and efficiency. Diversity for diversity's sake is moral promiscuity, since it obfuscates rational distinctions, and unless those hired are highly qualified the diversity factor threatens to become a fetish. At least at the higher levels of business and the professions, competence far outweighs considerations of diversity. I do not care whether the group of surgeons operating on me reflect racial or gender balance, but I do care that they are highly qualified. And likewise with air-plane pilots, military leaders, business executives, and, may I say it, teachers and professors. Moreover, there are other ways of learning about other cultures besides engaging in reverse discrimination.

7. Anti-Meritocratic (Desert) Argument to Justify Reverse Discrimination: "No One Deserves His Talents"

According to this argument, the competent do not deserve their intelligence, their superior character, their industriousness, or their discipline; therefore they have no right to the best positions in society; therefore society is not unjust in giving these positions to less (but still minimally) qualified blacks and women. In one form this argument holds that since no one deserves anything, society may use any criteria it pleases to distribute goods. The criterion most often designated is social utility. Versions of this argument are found in the writings of John Arthur, John Rawls, Bernard Boxill, Michael Kinsley, Ronald Dworkin, and Richard Wasserstrom. Rawls writes, "No one deserves his place in the distribution of native endowments, any more than one deserves one's initial starting place in society. The assertion that a man deserves the superior character that enables him to make the effort to cultivate his abilities is equally problematic; for his character depends in large part upon fortunate family and social circumstances for which he can claim no credit. The notion of desert seems not to apply to these cases."[5] Michael Kinsley is even more adamant:

> Opponents of affirmative action are hung up on a distinction that seems more profoundly irrelevant: treating individuals versus treating groups. What is the moral difference between dispensing favors to people on their "merits" as individuals and passing out society's benefits on the basis of group identification?
>
> Group identifications like race and sex are, of course, immutable. They have nothing to do with a person's moral worth. But the same is true of most of what comes under the label "merit." The tools you need for getting ahead in a meritocratic society—not all of them but most: talent, education, instilled cultural values such as ambition—are distributed just as arbitrarily as skin color. They are fate. The notion that people somehow "deserve" the advantages of these characteristics in a way they don't "deserve" the advantage of their race is powerful, but illogical.[6]

It will help to put the argument in outline form.

1. Society may award jobs and positions as it sees fit as long as individuals have no claim to these positions.
2. To have a claim to something means that one has earned it or deserves it.
3. But no one has earned or deserves his intelligence, talent, education, or cultural values which produce superior qualifications.
4. If a person does not deserve what produces something, he does not deserve its products.
5. Therefore better qualified people do not deserve their qualifications.
6. Therefore, society may override their qualifications in awarding jobs and positions as it sees fit (for social utility or to compensate for previous wrongs).

So it is permissible if a minimally qualified black or woman is admitted to law or medical school ahead of a white male with excellent credentials or if a less qualified person from an "underutilized" group gets a professorship ahead of a far better qualified white male. Sufficiency and underutilization together outweigh excellence.

Objection. Premise 4 is false. To see this, reflect that just because I do not deserve the money that I have been given as a gift (for instance) does not mean that I am not entitled to what I get with that money. If you and

I both get a gift of $100 and I bury mine in the sand for 5 years while you invest yours wisely and double its value at the end of five years, I cannot complain that you should split the increase 50/50 since neither of us deserved the original gift. If we accept the notion of responsibility at all, we must hold that persons deserve the fruits of their labor and conscious choices. Of course, we might want to distinguish moral from legal desert and argue that, morally speaking, effort is more important than outcome, whereas, legally speaking, outcome may be more important. Nevertheless, there are good reasons in terms of efficiency, motivation, and rough justice for holding a strong prima facie principle of giving scarce high positions to those most competent.

The attack on moral desert is perhaps the most radical move that egalitarians like Rawls and company have made against meritocracy, but the ramifications of their attack are far reaching. The following are some of its implications. Since I do not deserve my two good eyes or two good kidneys, the social engineers may take one of each from me to give to those needing an eye or a kidney—even if they have damaged their organs by their own voluntary actions. Since no one deserves anything, we do not deserve pay for our labors or praise for a job well done or first prize in the race we win. The notion of moral responsibility vanishes in a system of levelling.

But there is no good reason to accept the argument against desert. We do act freely and, as such, we are responsible for our actions. We deserve the fruits of our labor, reward for our noble feats and punishment for our misbehavior.

We have considered seven arguments for Affirmative Action and have found no compelling case for Strong AA and only one plausible argument (a version of the compensation argument) for Weak AA. We must now turn to the arguments against Affirmative Action to see whether they fare any better.[7]

[III.] ARGUMENTS AGAINST AFFIRMATIVE ACTION

1. Affirmative Action Requires Discrimination against a Different Group

Weak Affirmative Action weakly discriminates against new minorities, mostly innocent young white males, and Strong Affirmative Action strongly discriminates against these new minorities. As I argued in II.5, this discrimination is unwarranted, since, even if some compensation to blacks were indicated, it would be unfair to make innocent white males bear the whole brunt of the payments. In fact, it is poor white youth who become the new pariahs on the job market. The children of the wealthy have no trouble getting into the best private grammar schools and, on the basis of superior early education, into the best universities, graduate schools, managerial and professional positions. Affirmative Action simply shifts injustice, setting blacks and women against young white males, especially ethnic and poor white males. It does little to rectify the goal of providing equal opportunity to all. If the goal is a society where everyone has a fair chance, then it would be better to concentrate on support for families and early education and decide the matter of university admissions and job hiring on the basis of traditional standards of competence.

2. Affirmative Action Perpetuates the Victimization Syndrome

Shelby Steele admits that Affirmative Action may seem "the meagerest recompense for centuries of unrelieved oppression" and that it helps promote diversity. At the same time, though, notes Steele, Affirmative Action reinforces the spirit of victimization by telling blacks that they can gain more by emphasizing their suffering, degradation and helplessness than by discipline and work. This message holds the danger of blacks becoming permanently handicapped by a need for special treatment. It also sends to society at large the message that blacks cannot make it on their own.

Leon Wieseltier sums up the problem this way.

> The memory of oppression is a pillar and a strut of the identity of every people oppressed. It is no ordinary marker of difference. It is unusually stiffening. It instructs the individual and the group about what to expect of the world, imparts an isolating sense of aptness. . . . Don't be fooled, it teaches, there is only repetition. For that reason, the collective memory of an oppressed people is not only a treasure but a trap.
>
> In the memory of oppression, oppression outlives itself. The scar does the work of the wound. That is the real tragedy: that injustice retains the power to distort long after it has ceased to be real. It is a posthumous victory for the oppressors, when pain becomes a tradition. And yet the atrocities of the past must never be forgotten. This is the unfairly difficult dilemma of the newly emancipated and the newly enfranchised: an honorable life is not possible if they remember too little and a normal life is not possible if they remember too much.[8]

With the eye of recollection, which does not "remember too much," Steele recommends a policy which offers "educational and economic development of disadvantaged people regardless of race and the eradication from our society—through close monitoring and severe sanctions—of racial and gender discrimination."[9]

3. Affirmative Action Encourages Mediocrity and Incompetence

Last Spring Jesse Jackson joined protesters at Harvard Law School in demanding that the Law School faculty hire black women. Jackson dismissed Dean of the Law School, Robert C. Clark's standard of choosing the best qualified person for the job as "Cultural anemia." "We cannot just define who is qualified in the most narrow vertical academic terms," he said. "Most people in the world are yellow, brown, black, poor, non-Christian and don't speak English, and they can't wait for some White male with archaic rules to appraise them."[10] It might be noted that if Jackson is correct about the depth of cultural decadence at Harvard, blacks might be well advised to form and support their own more vital law schools and leave places like Harvard to their archaism.

At several universities, the administration has forced departments to hire members of minorities even when far superior candidates were available. Shortly after obtaining my Ph.D. in the late 70's I was mistakenly identified as a black philosopher (I had a civil rights record and was once a black studies major) and was flown to a major university, only to be rejected for a more qualified candidate when it discovered that I was white.

Stories of the bad effects of Affirmative Action abound. The philosopher Sidney Hook writes that "At one Ivy League university, representatives of the Regional HEW demanded an explanation of why there were no women or minority students in the Graduate Department of Religious Studies. They were told that a reading knowledge of Hebrew and Greek was presupposed. Whereupon the representatives of HEW advised orally: 'Then end those old fashioned programs that require irrelevant languages. And start up programs on relevant things which minority group students can study without learning languages.' "[11]

Nicholas Capaldi notes that the staff of HEW itself was one-half women, three-fifths members of minorities, and one-half black—a clear case of racial over-representation.

In 1972 officials at Stanford University discovered a proposal for the government to monitor curriculum in higher education: the "Summary Statement . . . Sex Discrimination Proposed HEW Regulation to Effectuate Title IX of the Education Amendment of 1972" to "establish and use internal procedure for reviewing curricula, designed both to ensure that they do not reflect discrimination on the basis of sex and to resolve complaints concerning allegations of such discrimination, pursuant to procedural standards to be prescribed by the Director of the office of Civil Rights." Fortunately, Secretary of HEW Caspar Weinberger, when alerted to the intrusion, assured Stanford University that he would never approve of it.[12]

Government programs of enforced preferential treatment tend to appeal to the lowest possible common denominator. Witness the 1974 HEW Revised Order No. 14 on Affirmative Action expectations for preferential hiring: "Neither minorities nor female employees should be required to possess higher qualifications than those of the lowest qualified incumbents."

Furthermore, no tests may be given to candidates unless it is *proved* to be relevant to the job.

> No standard or criteria which have, by intent or effect, worked to exclude women or minorities as a class can be utilized, unless the institution can demonstrate the necessity of such standard to the performance of the job in question.
>
> Whenever a validity study is called for . . . the user should include . . . an investigation of suitable alternative selection procedures and suitable alternative methods of using the selection procedure which have as little adverse impact as possible. . . . Whenever the user is shown an alternative selection procedure with evidence of less adverse impact and substantial evidence of validity for the same job in similar circumstances, the user should investigate it to determine the appropriateness of using or validating it in accord with these guidelines.[13]

At the same time Americans are wondering why standards in our country are falling and the Japanese are getting ahead. Affirmative Action with its twin idols, Sufficiency and Diversity, is the enemy of excellence. I will develop this thought below (IV.6).

4. *Affirmative Action Policies Unjustly Shift the Burden of Proof*

Affirmative Action legislation tends to place the burden of proof on the employer who does not have an "adequate" representation of "underutilized" groups in his work force. He is guilty until proven innocent. I have already recounted how in the mid-eighties the Supreme Court shifted the burden of proof back onto the plaintiff, while Congress is now attempting to shift the burden back to the employer. Those in favor of deeming disproportional representation "guilty until proven innocent" argue that it is easy for employers to discriminate against minorities by various subterfuges, and I agree that steps should be taken to monitor against prejudicial treatment. But being prejudiced against employers is not the way to attain a just solution to discrimination. The principle: innocent until proven guilty, applies to employers as well as criminals. Indeed, it is clearly special pleading to reject this basic principle of Anglo-American law in this case of discrimination while adhering to it everywhere else.

5. *An Argument from Merit*

Traditionally, we have believed that the highest positions in society should be awarded to those who are best qualified—as the Koran states in the quotation at the beginning of this paper. Rewarding excellence both seems just to the individuals in the competition and makes for efficiency. Note that one of the most successful acts of integration, the recruitment of Jackie Robinson in the late 40s, was done in just this way, according to merit. If Robinson had been brought into the major league as a mediocre player or had batted .200 he would have been scorned and sent back to the minors where he belonged.

Merit is not an absolute value. There are times when it may be overridden for social goals, but there is a strong prima facie reason for awarding positions on its basis, and it should enjoy a weighty presumption in our social practices.

In a celebrated article Ronald Dworkin says that "Bakke had no case" because society did not owe Bakke anything. That may be, but then why does it owe anyone anything? Dworkin puts the matter in Utility terms, but if that is the case, society may owe Bakke a place at the University of California/Davis, for it seems a reasonable rule-utilitarian principle that achievement should be rewarded in society. We generally want the best to have the best positions, the best qualified candidate to win the political office, the most brilliant and competent scientist to be chosen for the most challenging research project, the best qualified pilots to become commercial pilots, only the best soldiers to become generals. Only when little is at stake do we weaken the standards and content ourselves with sufficiency (rather than excellence)—there are plenty of jobs where "sufficiency" rather than excellence is required. Perhaps we now feel that medicine or law or university professorships are so routine that they can be performed by minimally qualified people—in which case AA has a place.

But note, no one is calling for quotas or proportional representation of *underutilized* groups in the National Basketball Association where blacks make up 80% of the players. But if merit and merit alone reigns in sports, should it not be valued at least as much in education and industry?

6. The Slippery Slope

Even if Strong AA or Reverse Discrimination could meet the other objections, it would face a tough question: once you embark on this project, how do you limit it? Who should be excluded from reverse discrimination? Asians and Jews are overrepresented, so if we give blacks positive quotas, should we place negative quotas to these other groups? Since white males, "WMs," are a minority which is suffering from reverse discrimination, will we need a

New Affirmative Action policy in the 21st century to compensate for the discrimination against WMs in the late 20th century?

Furthermore, Affirmative Action has stigmatized the *young* white male. Assuming that we accept reverse discrimination, the fair way to make sacrifices would be to retire *older* white males who are more likely to have benefited from a favored status. Probably the least guilty of any harm to minority groups is the young white male—usually a liberal who has been required to bear the brunt of ages of past injustice. Justice Brennan's announcement that the Civil Rights Act did not apply to discrimination against whites shows how the clearest language can be bent to serve the ideology of the moment).[14]

7. The Mounting Evidence against the Success of Affirmative Action

Thomas Sowell of the Hoover Institute has shown in his book *Preferential Policies: An International Perspective* that preferential hiring almost never solves social problems. It generally builds in mediocrity or incompetence and causes deep resentment. It is a short term solution which lacks serious grounding in social realities.

For instance, Sowell cites some disturbing statistics on education. Although twice as many blacks as Asian students took the nationwide Scholastic Aptitude Test in 1983, approximately fifteen times as many Asian students scored above 700 (out of a possible 800) on the mathematics half of the SAT. The percentage of Asians who scored above 700 in math was also more than six times higher than the percentage of American Indians and more than ten times higher than that of Mexican Americans—as well as more than double the percentage of whites. As Sowell points out, in all countries studied, "intergroup performance disparities are huge."

> There are dozens of American colleges and universities where the median combined verbal SAT score and mathematics SAT score total

1200 or above. As of 1983 there were less than 600 black students in the entire US with combined SAT scores of 1200. This meant that, despite widespread attempts to get a black student "representation" comparable to the black percentage of the population (about 11%), there were not enough black students in the entire country for the Ivy League alone to have such a "representation" without going beyond this pool—even if the entire pool went to the eight Ivy League colleges.[15]

Often it is claimed that a cultural bias is the cause of the poor performance of blacks on SAT (or IQ tests), but Sowell shows that these test scores are actually a better predictor of college performance for blacks than for Asians and whites. He also shows the harmfulness of the effect on blacks of preferential acceptance. At the University of California, Berkeley, where the freshman class closely reflects the actual ethnic distribution of California high school students, more than 70% of blacks fail to graduate. All 312 black students entering Berkeley in 1987 were admitted under "Affirmative Action" criteria rather than by meeting standard academic criteria. So were 480 out of 507 Hispanic students. In 1986 the median SAT score for blacks at Berkeley was 952, for Mexican Americans 1014, for American Indians 1082 and for Asian Americans 1254. (The average SAT for all students was 1181.)

The result of this mismatching is that blacks who might do well if they went to a second tier or third tier school where their test scores would indicate they belong, actually are harmed by preferential treatment. They cannot compete in the institutions where high abilities are necessary.

Sowell also points out that Affirmative Action policies have mainly assisted the middle class black, those who have suffered least from discrimination. "Black couples in which both husband and wife are college-educated overtook white couples of the same description back in the early 1970's and continued to at least hold their own in the 1980's."

Sowell's conclusion is that similar patterns of results obtained from India to the USA wherever preferential policies exist. "In education, preferential admissions policies have led to high attrition rates and substandard performances for those preferred students . . . who survived to graduate." In all countries the preferred tended to concentrate in less difficult subjects which lead to less remunerative careers. "In the employment market, both blacks and untouchables at the higher levels have advanced substantially while those at the lower levels show no such advancement and even some signs of retrogression. These patterns are also broadly consistent with patterns found in countries in which majorities have created preferences for themselves. . . ."

The tendency has been to focus at the high level end of education and employment rather than on the lower level of family structure and early education. But if we really want to help the worst off improve, we need to concentrate on the family and early education. It is foolish to expect equal results when we begin with grossly unequal starting points—and discriminating against young white males is no more just than discriminating against women, blacks or anyone else.

CONCLUSION

Let me sum up. The goal of the Civil Rights movement and of moral people everywhere has been equal opportunity. The question is: how best to get there. Civil Rights legislation removed the legal barriers to equal opportunity, but did not tackle the deeper causes that produced differential results. Weak Affirmative Action aims at encouraging minorities in striving for the highest positions without unduly jeopardizing the rights of majorities, but the problem of Weak Affirmative Action is that it easily slides into Strong Affirmative Action where quotas, "goals," and equal results are forced into groups, thus promoting mediocrity, inefficiency, and resentment. Furthermore, Affirmative Action aims at the higher levels of society—universities and skilled jobs—yet if we want to improve our society, the best way to do it is to concentrate on families, children, early education, and the like. Affirmative Action is, on the one hand, too much, too soon and on the other hand, too little, too late.

Martin Luther said that humanity is like a man mounting a horse who always tends to fall off on the other side of the horse. This seems to be the case with Affirmative Action. Attempting to redress the discriminatory iniquities of our history, our well-intentioned social engineers engage in new forms of discriminatory iniquity and thereby think that they have successfully mounted the horse of racial harmony. They have only fallen off on the other side of the issue.[16]

NOTES

1. John Arthur, *The Unfinished Constitution* (Belmont, CA, 1990), p. 238.
2. See Phillip E. Vernon's excellent summary of the literature in *Intelligence: Heredity and Environment* (New York, 1979) and Yves Christen "Sex Differences in the Human Brain" in Nicholas Davidson (ed.) *Gender Sanity* (Lanham, 1989) and T. Bouchard, *et al.,* "Sources of Human Psychological Differences: The Minnesota Studies of Twins Reared Apart," *Science,* vol. 250 (1990).
3. See Michael Levin, "Is Racial Discrimination Special?" *Policy Review,* Fall issue (1982).
4. Judith Jarvis Thomson, "Preferential Hiring" in Marshall Cohen, Thomas Nagel and Thomas Scanlon (eds.) *Equality and Preferential Treatment* (Princeton, 1977).
5. John Rawls, *A Theory of Justice* (Cambridge, 1971), p. 104; See Richard Wasserstrom "A Defense of Programs of Preferential Treatment," *National Forum* (Phi Kappa Phi Journal), vol. 58 (1978). See also Bernard Boxill, "The Morality of Preferential Hiring," *Philosophy and Public Affairs,* vol. 7 (1978).

6. Michael Kinsley, "Equal Lack of Opportunity," *Harper's,* June issue (1983).
7. There is one other argument which I have omitted. It is from precedence and has been stated by Judith Jarvis Thomson in the article cited earlier:

   "Suppose two candidates for a civil service job have equally good test scores, but there is only one job available. We could decide between them by coin-tossing. But in fact we do allow for declaring for *A* straightaway, where *A* is a veteran, and *B* is not. It may be that *B* is a non-veteran through no fault of his own . . . Yet the fact is that *B* is not a veteran and *A* is. On the assumption that the veteran has served his country, the country owes him something. And it is plain that giving him preference is not an unjust way in which part of that debt of gratitude can be paid" (p. 379f).

   The two forms of preferential hiring are analogous. Veteran's preference is justified as a way of paying a debt of gratitude, preferential hiring is a way of paying a debt of compensation. In both cases innocent parties bear the burden of the community's debt, but it is justified.

   My response to this argument is that veterans should not be hired in place of better qualified candidates, but that benefits like the GI scholarships are part of the contract with veterans who serve their country in the armed services. The notion of compensation only applies to individuals who have been injured by identifiable entities. So the analogy between veterans and minority groups seems weak.
8. Quoted in Jim Sleeper, *The Closest of Strangers* (New York, 1990), p. 209.
9. Shelby Steele, "A Negative Vote on Affirmative Action," *New York Times,* May 13, 1990 issue.
10. *New York Times,* May 10, 1990 issue.
11. Nicholas Capaldi, *Out of Order: Affirmative Action and the Crisis of Doctrinaire Liberalism* (Buffalo, NY: Prometheus, 1985), p. 85.
12. *Ibid.,* p. 95.
13. *Ibid.*

14. The extreme form of this New Speak is incarnate in the Politically Correct Movement ("PC" ideology) where a new orthodoxy has emerged, condemning white, European culture and seeing African culture as the new savior of us all. Perhaps the clearest example of this is Paula Rothenberg's book *Racism and Sexism* (New York, 1987) which asserts that there is no such thing as black racism; only whites are capable of racism (p. 6). Ms. Rothenberg's book has been scheduled as required reading for all freshmen at the University of Texas. See Joseph Salemi, "Lone Star Academic Politics," no. 87 (1990).

15. Thomas Sowell, *Preferential Policies: An International Perspective* (New York: Morrow, 1990), p. 108.

16. I am indebted to Jim Landesman, Michael Levin, and Abigail Rosenthal for comments on a previous draft of this paper. I am also indebted to Nicholas Capaldi's *Out of Order* for first making me aware of the extent of the problem of Affirmative Action.

Discussion Questions

1. Present and explain the seven arguments for affirmative action which Professor Pojman critiques. Are there any aspects of his critiques with which you disagree and which you believe are flawed? Explain and defend your answer.
2. Present and explain the seven arguments against affirmative action which Professor Pojman supports. Are there any aspects of these arguments with which you disagree and which you believe are flawed? Explain and defend your answer.
3. Are there any arguments which Professor Pojman may have failed to mention which you believe either support or count against the morality of affirmative action? Explain and defend your answer.

 You can locate InfoTrac-College Education articles about this chapter by accessing the InfoTrac-College Edition website (http://www.infotrac-college.com/wadsworth/). Using the InfoTrac-College Edition subject guide, enter the search terms relevant to this chapter, and then read abstracts for relevant articles.

31   The Justification of Reverse Discrimination

TOM BEAUCHAMP

Tom Beauchamp is Professor of Philosophy at Georgetown University (Washington, D.C.) as well as Senior Research Scholar at Georgetown's Kennedy Institute of Ethics. One of America's leading ethicists, he is the author of numerous

Reprinted by permission from Ethical Theory and Business, *3rd ed., ed. Tom Beauchamp (Princeton, NJ: Prentice-Hall, 1988).*

scholarly articles as well as books including *Principles of Biomedical Ethics,* 4th ed. (1993) and *Case Studies in Business Society, and Ethics,* 4th ed. (1997)

In this essay Professor Beauchamp argues that some forms of reverse discrimination and preferential treatment are morally justified. Although he admits that reverse discrimination is prima facia unethical (just as taking a human life is prima facia unethical), there may be situations in which certain moral principles and values justify reverse discrimination, just as there may be some situations in which certain moral principles and values justify taking a human life, such as in a just war or self-defense. Professor Beauchamp defends his position on two grounds: (1) there is overwhelming and wide-ranging statistical evidence, as well as testimonial evidence, that there is and has been unjust discrimination against minorities and women which cannot be overcome by weak affirmative action or equal opportunity policies, but only by policies which provide preferential treatment to members of discriminated groups with specified goals and timetables; (2) corporate interests as well as the public good are well-served by goals and quotas. Professor Beauchamp provides testimonial and statistical evidence to support this. Even though there are counter-considerations against preferential treatment, they are "not strong enough to overcome the even more powerful case against" them.

DURING THE PAST TWO decades, government and corporate policies aimed at hiring women and racial minorities by setting numerical goals have been sharply criticized on grounds that they discriminate in reverse, often against more qualified white males. My objective in this paper is to defend such policies. I agree with those critics who maintain that some policies have created situations of injustice. However, I do not agree with the presumption that when policies with numerical goals create *injustices* they are necessarily *unjustified*. Equal opportunity is but one principle of justice, and justice is but one demand of ethics. We need also to take account of principles of just compensation (compensatory justice) and the public interest (utility).

A policy can create or perpetuate injustices, such as violations of principles of equal opportunity, and yet be justified by other reasons. It would, for example, be an injustice in one respect for a bank to fire one of two branch managers with identical professional creden-tials while retaining the other; yet the financial condition of the bank or compensation owed the retained person might provide compelling reasons that justify the action. An established seniority system might justifiably be used to decide such a matter; indeed, a devoted employee with long service might be retained in preference to a younger person with better credentials and higher productivity. In some circumstances, when implementing schemes of hiring, promoting, and firing, equal opportunity and the blinded evaluations of persons will have to yield on the scales of justice to the weight of other principles.

I shall use this general line of argument in defense of numerical targets, goals, quotas, and timetables. I contend that goals and even quotas are congenial to management, not hostile to business, as academic and government agency officials generally seem to presume. I also believe that business' long-range interest and the public interest are best served by preferential hiring, advancement, and layoff policies.

TWO POLAR POSITIONS

The U.S. Supreme Court and numerous scholars in ethics and legal theory have struggled with these problems of principle and balance in combatting discrimination, at least since President Lyndon Johnson's 1965 executive order that announced a toughened federal initiative by requiring specific goals and timetables for equal employment opportunity. This struggle has led to two primary competing schools of thought on the justifiability of preferential programs.

The first school locates justice in the claim that we are all entitled to an equal opportunity and to constitutional guarantees of equal protection in a color-blind, nonsexist society. An entitlement of this sort is an entitlement that only individuals possess. Civil rights laws therefore should offer protection not to aggregate groups but only to specific individuals who have been demonstrably victimized by racial, sexual, religious, or other forms of discrimination. Hiring goals, timetables, and quotas violate these laws as well as our moral sense of justice, because they create new victims of discrimination. The U.S. Department of Justice has spearheaded this view in recent years, but it has found adherents in many quarters as well.

The second school believes that mandated goals and enforced hiring measures are essential to ensure fairness in hiring and to achieve meaningful results in the attempt to eradicate discrimination. This group believes it is too onerous to require the actual identification of individual victims of discrimination—an assignment that is generally impossible because of secrecy (and sometimes even unintentional discrimination). Even the victims may not know they are victims. As the editors of the *New York Times* put it, finding actual victims as the means of ending discrimination would be the "project of a century and [would] leave most victims of discrimination with only empty legal rights. [Many] are still victims of the myths of racial superiority that once infused

the law itself." The *Times* joined the Supreme Court in calling for the "adequate remedy" of "race-conscious relief" in the form of goals and timetables to the extent necessary to achieve the end of a nondiscriminatory society.[1] The second group thus tends to see the first group as construing "equal opportunity" and "civil rights" so narrowly that those affected by discrimination can receive no practical aid in overcoming the phenomenon of prejudice. That is, the noble ideal of equal opportunity is viewed as but a theoretical postulate that has no practical application in the real world under the first group's policies.

These two groups are perhaps not as far apart as they appear at first glance. Edwin Meese, Attorney General during the Reagan administration and the most publicly visible proponent of the first viewpoint in recent memory, dismissed the seemingly enormous gulf between his views and those of the U.S. Supreme Court—which has endorsed the second viewpoint—by saying that the Court *accepted* his views that racial preferences are wrong and merely "carved out various exceptions to that general rule, even while affirming the rule itself." There is something to be said for Meese's bold statement (although I think not quite what he intended): The second group need not disagree with the first group if legal enforcement were adequate to identify discriminatory treatment and to protect its victims. If we lived in such a society, then the second group could easily agree that the first group's policies are preferable for that society.

But there are two reasons why no member of the second group will agree to this solution at the present time. First, there is the unresolved issue whether those in contemporary society who have been advantaged by *past* discrimination deserve their advantages, and thus whether classes such as blacks and women deserve some of those advantages. This thorny issue is surpassed in importance, however, by the second reason, which is whether *present,* ongoing discrimination can be successfully, comprehensively, and fairly combatted by identifying and prosecuting the violators. I do not believe that the form of enforcement so essential to the first group's position is possible. But I do believe that the enforcement of goals and quotas is both possible and necessary. Two reasons now to be discussed lead me to the conclusion that the second position is preferable to the first.

THE DATA ON DISCRIMINATION

My argument rests on the hypothesis that invidious discrimination that affects hiring and promotion is present in our society—not everywhere, of course, but pervasively. Such a claim requires empirical evidence; and like almost any broad generalization, the evidence is not entirely conclusive. However, I believe the claim can be adequately substantiated, as some representative samples of available data indicate.

Statistical imbalances in hiring and admission and promotion are often discounted because so many variables can be hypothesized to explain why, for nondiscriminatory reasons, an imbalance exists. We can all think of plausible nondiscriminatory reasons why almost half of the graduate students in the United States are women but the tenured Arts and Sciences graduate faculties often hover around 5 to 10 percent women—and in some of the most prestigious schools, even lower. Occasionally we are able to discover firm evidence supporting the claim that such skewed statistics are not random but are the result of discrimination. Quantities of such discriminatory findings, in turn, raise questions about the real reasons for suspicious statistics in those cases where we have not been able to determine these reasons.

An impressive body of statistics constituting prima facie evidence of discrimination has been assembled in recent years indicating that women with identical credentials are promoted at almost exactly one-half the rate of their male counterparts; that 69 percent or more of the white-collar positions in the United States are presently held by women, but only 10 percent or so of the management positions are held by women (and again their pay is significantly lower); that 8.7 percent of all professionals in the private business sector are Orientals, but they comprise only 1.3 percent of management; that in the population as a whole in the United States 3 out of 7 employees hold white-collar positions, but only 1 of 7 blacks holds such a position (and these positions are clustered in professions that have the fewest jobs to offer in top-paying positions); and that numerous major U.S. corporations have settled discrimination suits out of court for hundreds of millions of dollars.[2]

Such statistics are far from decisive indicators of discrimination. But further evidence concerning the reasons for the statistics can sometimes be discovered to prove a discriminatory influence.[3] Other facts support the general conclusion that racist and sexist biases have a powerful influence in the marketplace. For example, from 1965 to 1975 the number of blacks in college doubled, but from 1975 to 1985 it leveled off without increase. The number of blacks making more than $25,000 in constant-dollar salary also doubled from 1965 to 1975, but dropped from 1975 to 1985.[4] There is a ready reason for both statistics. Both the Grier Partnership and the Urban League produced separate studies completed in 1985 that show striking disparities in the employment levels of college-trained blacks and whites in the job market in Washington, D.C.—one of the best markets for blacks. Both studies found that college-trained blacks find far more frustration in landing a position and that discrimination is a major underlying factor.[5]

Another example of prevailing biases in marketplace transactions is found in real estate rentals and sales. In a 1985 statement, Lucius McKelvey, president of a large Cleveland real estate firm, publicly proclaimed what numerous real estate agents had already privately reported: "You'd be surprised at the number of professional people, white-collar people, who ask us to discriminate—it's discouraging." Surveys have shown that blacks face an 85 percent probability of encountering discrimination in rental housing and almost 50 percent in buying a house.[6]

These studies and dozens that replicate their findings indicate that we live in a discriminatory society whose laws will make little difference in practice unless the laws are tough and are gauged to change the practices and underlying attitudes. The law cannot wait for evidence of abuse confined to demonstrable individual victims without permitting the continuation of present injustices.

PROBLEMS OF PROOF AND INTENTION

The central problems of proof and enforcement in individual cases can best be captured in taking a particular case that illustrates the difficulty in determining whether discrimination—especially intentional discrimination—is occurring.

In December 1974 a decision was reached by the Commission against Discrimination of the Executive Department of the State of Massachusetts regarding a case at Smith College; the two complainants were women who were denied tenure and dismissed by the English Department.[7] The women claimed sex discrimination and based their case on the following: (1) Women at the full professor level in the college declined from 54 percent in 1958 to 21 percent in 1972 and in the English Department from 57 percent in 1960 to 11 percent in 1972. These statistics compare unfavorably at all levels with data from Mt. Holyoke, a comparable institution (since both have an all-female student body and are located in western Massachusetts). (2) Thirteen of the department's fifteen associate and full professorships at Smith belonged to men. (3) The two tenured women had obtained

tenure under "distinctly peculiar experiences," including a stipulation that one be only part-time and that the other not be promoted when given tenure. (4) The department's faculty members conceded that tenure standards were applied subjectively, were vague, and lacked the kind of precision that would avoid discriminatory application. (5) The women denied tenure were at no time given advance warning that their work was deficient. Rather, they were given favorable evaluations of their teaching and were encouraged to believe that they would receive tenure. (6) Some of the stated reasons for the dismissals were later demonstrated to be rationalizations, and one letter from a senior member to the tenure and promotion committee contradicted his own appraisal of teaching ability filed with the department. (7) The court accepted expert testimony that any deficiencies in the women candidates were also found in male candidates promoted and given tenure in the same period and that the women's positive credentials were at least as good as the men's.[8]

The commissioner's opinion found that "the Complainants properly used statistics to demonstrate that the Respondents' practices operate with a discriminatory effect." Citing *Parham v. Southwestern Bell Telephone Co.*, the commissioner argued that "in such cases extreme statistics may establish discrimination as a matter of law, without additional supportive evidence." But in this case the commissioner found abundant additional evidence in the form of the "historical absence of women," "word-of-mouth recruitment policies" that operate discriminatorily, and a number of "subtle and not so subtle, societal patterns" existing at Smith.[9] On December 30, 1974, the commissioner ordered the two women reinstated with tenure and ordered the department to submit an affirmative action program within sixty days.

There is little in the way of clinching proof that the members of the English Department held discriminatory attitudes. Yet so consistent a pattern of *apparently* discriminatory results must be regarded, according to this decision, as de facto discrimination. The commissioner's ruling and other laws explicitly state that "intent or lack thereof is of no consequence." If a procedure constitutes discriminatory treatment, then the parties discriminated against must be recompensed. If irresistible statistics and other sociological evidence of "social exclusion" and "subtle societal patterns" provide compelling evidence that quotas, goals, or strong court-backed measures are necessary to overcome the discriminatory pattern (as the Respondents' testimony in the case indicates),[10] I find this fact sufficient to justify the measures.

In early 1985 the U.S. Supreme Court came down with perhaps its clearest example of this general point in the case of *Alexander v. Choate*. The Court held unanimously—against the U.S. Justice Department and the state of Tennessee—that states may be held guilty of discriminating against the handicapped because such discrimination is "most often the product not of invidious animus, but rather of thoughtlessness and indifference—of benign neglect." The Court rightly held that discrimination would be "difficult if not impossible to ban if only *intentional* acts of discrimination qualified as discrimination."[11]

PROBLEMS OF ENFORCEMENT

The protective camouflage surrounding discriminatory attitudes makes enforcement difficult in both the particular case and in the general case of monitoring nondiscriminatory guidelines. This problem is lessened by having specific goals and quotas, which are easier to meet and to enforce. In this section, I want to present two cases that show how difficult—indeed meaningless—enforcement can be in the absence of specified goals and tough-minded control.

The January 1975 Report of the United States Commission on Civil Rights contains a section of "compliance reviews" of various universities.[12] The commissioners reviewed four major campuses in the United States: Harvard, University of Michigan, University of Washington, and Berkeley. They concluded that there has been a pattern of inadequate compliance reviews, inordinate delays, and inexcusable failures to take enforcement action where there were clear violations of the executive order regulations.[13]

Consider the example of the "case history of compliance contracts at the University of California at Berkeley. When the Office for Civil Rights (OCR) of HHS determined to investigate Berkeley (April 1971), after several complaints, including a class action sex discrimination complaint, the university refused to permit access to its personnel files and refused to permit the interviewing of faculty members without an administrator present. Both refusals are, as the report points out, "direct violations of the Executive order's equal opportunity clause," under which Berkeley held contracts. A year and a half later, after negotiations and more complaints, the university was instructed to develop a written affirmative action plan to correct" documented deficiencies" of "pervasive discrimination." The plan was to include target goals and timetables wherever job underutilization had been identified.[14]

In January 1973 the university submitted a draft affirmative action plan that was judged "totally unacceptable." Throughout 1973 Berkeley received "extensive technical assistance" from the government to aid it in developing a better plan. No such plan emerged, and OCR at the end of the year began to question "the university's commitment to comply with the executive order." The university submitted other unacceptable plans, and finally in March 1974 a conciliation document was reached. However, the document was vague and the university and OCR continued for years to be in disagreement on the meaning of key provisions.

Berkeley is an instructive case study, because it was at the time among the most concerned institutions in the United States over issues of race and civil rights. If it and the other three universities studied by the Commission on Civil Rights have troubled histories in installing and monitoring antidiscrimination laws, one can imagine the problems found elsewhere. Consider, as a revealing example of far more egregious resistance, what is perhaps the most important Supreme Court case on the issues of quotas and reverse discrimination: the case of *Local 28 v. Equal Employment Opportunity Commission,* generally known as *Sheet Metal Workers.*[15] Although this case was decided in 1986, the discriminatory actions of Local 28 of the Sheet Metal Workers International had been in and out of court since 1963. The record, says the Supreme Court, was one of complete "foot-dragging resistance" to the idea of hiring from minority groups into the apprenticeship training programs that supply workers for construction in the New York City metropolitan area. In 1964 the New York Commission for Human Rights investigated the union and concluded that it excluded nonwhites through an impenetrable barrier of hiring by discriminatory selection. The state Supreme Court concurred and issued a "cease and desist" order. The union ignored it. Eventually, in a 1975 trial, the U.S. District Court found a record "replete with instances of bad faith" and ordered a "remedial racial goal" of 29 percent nonwhite membership (based on the percentage of nonwhites in the local labor pool). Another court then found that the union had "consistently and egregiously violated" the law of the land (Title 7, in particular). In 1982 and 1983 court fines and civil contempt proceedings were issued. In 1981, virtually nothing had been done to modify the discriminatory hiring practices after twenty-two years of struggle.

The Supreme Court held that one need not produce "identified victims" of discrimination and that goals such as the 29 percent quota are justified when "an employer or a labor union has been engaged in persistent or egregious discrimination, or where necessary to dissipate the lingering effects of pervasive discrimination." I find the latter clause particularly suitable. Goals and quotas are needed where there are lingering effects of pervasive preference for particular groups (e.g., white male graduates of certain schools) or discriminatory attitudes that control hiring. Otherwise, goals and quotas are not needed, and no one should invoke them. But if these problems are not restricted to a few isolated cases involving Sheet Metal Workers Unions or Departments of English, then it makes sense to see goals and quotas as a basic tool for eradicating discriminatory practices.

The Supreme Court points out that the present laws in the United States were enacted by Congress to prevent "pervasive and systematic discrimination in employment." No one should expect that practices like those of the Sheet Metal Workers can easily be removed by exhortations or by finding "identified victims." The stronger the resistance, the tougher the rules must be.

I might add, however, that the Supreme Court has not said, nor have I, that there cannot be a case of reverse discrimination in which a white male has unjustifiably been excluded from consideration for employment and has a right to compensation. Certainly *unwarranted* discrimination in reverse is no better than unwarranted discrimination in forward speed. But the following should also be considered: There is an important distinction between real reverse discrimination and merely apparent reverse discrimination. Sometimes persons who appear to be displacing better applicants will be hired or admitted—on a quota basis, for example, but the appearance may be the result of discriminatory perceptions of the person's qualifications. In this case there will appear to be reverse discrimination, and this impression will be reinforced by knowledge that quotas were used. However, the allegation of reverse discrimination will be mistaken. On other occasions there will be genuine reverse discrimination, and on many occasions it will be impossible to determine whether this consequence occurs.

I have argued that real and not merely apparent reverse discrimination is justified. But it is justified only as a means to the end of ensuring nondiscriminatory treatment of all persons. If the use of goals and quotas functioned as a vindictive tool (and, let us suppose, the end of nondiscrimination had already been achieved), then no reverse discriminatory effects would be justified.

WHY CORPORATIONS SHOULD WELCOME GOALS AND QUOTAS

Little has been said thus far about the relevance of these arguments to employment in business, largely because we have been concentrating on public policy affecting all institutions. In conclusion, I turn to corporate policy, which I believe would be aided by the use of goals and targets in the late 1980s and early 1990s. Here I shall discuss only policies voluntarily adopted by corporations—that is, voluntary programs using target goals and quotas. These programs stand in contrast to agency-ordered objectives featured in some previous examples.

Because of this shift to voluntary programs, my argument may seem a trivial addition to the problems mentioned above; a corporation can either accept or reject a program at its discretion. However, the issue of voluntary goals and quotas is far from trivial, for two reasons. First, the Justice Department has sought in recent years to ban voluntary corporate programs using goals and quotas, on grounds that these policies result in reverse discrimination. Many corporations and municipalities have resisted these government moves, and some have flatly refused to ease their affirmative action goals. Second, I believe that the active good will of corporations will prove to be more important than any other development (with the possible exception of activity in the U.S. Supreme Court) in ending discrimination and prejudice in the American workplace; and the workplace more than any other environment will serve as the melting pot of American society.

I offer four reasons why it is in the interest of responsible businesses to use aggressive plans involving goals and quotas. The judgment that such plans are fair and justified—as I have argued previously—could be appended as a reason, but it is not the type of reason needed in the present context.

(1) First, to the extent that a corporation either discriminates or fails to look at the full range of qualified persons in the market, to that extent it will eventually wind up with a larger percentage of second-best employees. Corporations continue to report that they find fewer qualified workers for available positions than they formerly did, and that they have profited from rules of nonracial, nonsexist hiring.[16] Hal Johnson, a senior vice-president at Travelers Companies, projects that, "In 1990 more of the work force is going to be minorities—Hispanics, blacks—and women. The companies that started building bridges back in the 1970s will be all right. Those that didn't won't."[17] The free market has its own way of eroding color and sexual barriers in the search for the best talent. No one would argue, for example, that baseball has poorer talent for dropping its color barrier. To find that talent in its best form, bridges had to be built that extended far into, for example, the population of Puerto Rico. Businesses will be analogously improved if they extend their boundaries and provide the proper training programs. Bill McEwen of Monsanto Corporation and spokesperson for the National Association of Manufacturers notes that this extension not only will happen but has been happening at NAM companies for twenty years:

> We have been utilizing affirmative action plans for over 20 years. We were brought into it kicking and screaming. But over the past

20 years we've learned that there's a reservoir of talent out there, of minorities and women that we hadn't been using before. We found that it works.[18]

Some corporations have found it difficult to find and keep these talented persons and therefore have developed incentives and special benefits, such as job-sharing, home work, flextime, extended maternity leave, and day-care centers in order to keep them. These companies include Gannett, General Foods, General Motors, IBM, Lotus Development, Mellon Bank, Mutual Life, Peat Marwick Mitchell, and Procter & Gamble.[19]

(2) A second reason is that pulling the foundations from beneath affirmative action hiring would open old sores, especially for municipalities and corporations who over a period of years have developed target goals and quotas either through a consent-decree process with courts or direct negotiations with representatives of minority groups such as PUSH and the NAACP. These plans—which now cover over 20 million Americans employed by federal contractors alone—have been agonizingly difficult to develop in some cases and would be disintegrated by the principle that goals and timetables are impermissible. Removal might also stigmatize a business by signalling to minority groups a return to old patterns of discrimination.[20]

(3) Third, the risk of reverse discrimination suits would be minimized, not maximized, by the use of goals and quotas. This paradox has been explained by Peter Robertson of Organizational Resource Counselors:

In a recent survey of chief executive officers by the management consulting firm for which I work, 95 percent indicated that they will use numbers as a management tool to measure corporate progress whether the government requires them or not. However, once the government requirements are gone, there would be a risk of so-called "reverse discrimination" suits alleging that employers have gone too far with affirmative action.[21]

Thus, government programs and court decisions that *allow* voluntary goals and quotas actually protect good-faith employers rather than undermining them. As Robertson points out, the president of the National Association of Manufacturers, Alexander Trowbridge, has been making exactly that point to affiliate manufacturers. It has also been reported that many corporations enthusiastically greeted the 1986 and 1987 pro-affirmative-action decisions in the U.S. Supreme Court, because they feared that if the Justice Department's argument had been victorious, then employers would have been exposed to reverse discrimination suits by white males because of the plans corporations already had in effect.[22]

(4) Finally, the editors of *Business Week* have offered the following general reason in favor of voluntary and negotiated goals and quotas: "over the years business and regulators have worked out rules and procedures for affirmative action, including numerical yardsticks for sizing up progress, that both sides understand. It has worked and should be left alone."[23] The reason why it has worked is intrinsic to a businesslike approach to problems: Managers set goals and timetables for almost everything they hope to achieve—from profits to salary bonuses. From a manager's point of view, setting goals and timetables is simply a basic way of measuring progress. One survey of 200 major American corporations found that over 75 percent already use "voluntary internal numerical objectives to assess [equal employment opportunity] performance."[24] A side benefit of the use of such numerical objectives is to create a ready defense of one's practices for government investigators, unions, or minority group representatives who inquire into the company's historical record. Many corporations have also promoted their record through public reports and recruiting brochures. Such reports and brochures have been developed, for example, by Schering-Plough, Philip Morris, Exxon, AT&T, IBM, Westinghouse, and Chemical Bank.[25]

CONCLUSION

Early in this paper I acknowledged that all racial and sexual discrimination, including reverse discrimination, is prima facie immoral, because a basic principle of justice creates a duty to abstain from such treatment of persons. But no absolute duty is created come what may. The thesis I have defended is that considerations of compensatory justice, equal opportunity, and utility are *conjointly* of sufficient weight to neutralize and overcome the quite proper presumption of immorality in the case of some policies productive of reverse discrimination.

My conclusion is premised on balancing several moral principles as well as on empirical judgments about the actual state of discrimination in American society. With some basic changes, the presumption might turn in a different direction, and thus my claims are contingent on the social circumstances. Moreover, I agree with critics of the position I have defended that the introduction of preferential treatment on a large scale might in some measure produce economic advantages to some who do not deserve them, protracted court battles, jockeying for favored position by other minorities, congressional lobbying by power groups, a lowering of admission and work standards in vital institutions, reduced social and economic efficiency, increased racial hostility, and continued suspicion that well-placed women and minority group members received their positions purely on the basis of quotas. Conjointly these reasons constitute a strong case against policies that use numerical goals and quotas in hiring, promotion, firing, and layoffs. However, this powerful case is not strong enough to overcome the even more powerful case against it.

NOTES

1. "Their Right to Remedy, Affirmed," *New York Times*, July 3, 1986, p. A30.

2. See the data and comments in the following sources: Kenneth M. Davidson, Ruth B. Ginsburg, and Herma H. Kay, eds., *Sex-Based Discrimination: Text, Cases and Materials* (Minneapolis: West Publishing Company, 1974), esp. Ch. 3. Hereafter *Sex-Based Discrimination;* Irene Pave, "A Woman's Place Is at GE, Federal Express, P&G. . . ," *Business Week*, June 23, 1986, pp. 75–76; Winifred Yu, "Asian Americans Charge Prejudice Slows Climb to Management Rank," *Wall Street Journal*, September 11, 1985, p. 35.

3. From *Discrimination Against Women: Congressional Hearings on Equal Rights in Education and Employment*, ed. Catharine R. Stimpson (New York: R. R. Bowker, 1973), 505–506.

4. See Juan Williams, "The Vast Gap Between Black and White Visions of Reality" and "Blacks Don't See It the Way Whites Do," *Washington Post*, March 31, 1985, pp. K1, K4.

5. As reported by Rudolf A. Pyatt, Jr., "Significant Job Studies," *Washington Post*, April 30, 1985, pp. D1–D2.

6. See "Business Bulletin," *Wall Street Journal*, February 28, 1985, p. 1.

7. *Maurianne Adams and Mary Schroeder v. Smith College*, Massachusetts Commission Against Discrimination, Nos. 72-S-53, 72-S-54 (December 30, 1974). Hereafter *The Smith College Case.*

8. 433 F.2d 421, 426 (8 cir. 1970).

9. *The Smith College Case*, pp. 23, 26.

10. Ibid., pp. 26–27.

11. As reported by and quoted in Al Kamen, "Justices Attack Inadvertent Bias," *Washington Post*, January 10, 1985, p. A4.

12. *The Federal Civil Rights Enforcement Effort—1974*, 2: p. 276.

13. Ibid., p. 281.

14. Ibid., all the following text references are from pp. 281–286.

15. *Local 28 v. Equal Employment Opportunity Commission*, U.S. 84-1656. All the following quotations are from this case.

16. See Pave, "A Woman's Place," p. 76.

17. As quoted in Walter Kiechel, "Living with Human Resources," *Fortune*, August 18, 1986, p. 100.

18. AS quoted in Peter Perl, "Rulings Provide Hiring Direction: Employers Welcome Move," *Washington Post,* July 3, 1986, pp. A1, A11.

19. See Alex Taylor, "Why Women Managers Are Bailing Out," *Fortune,* August 18, 1986, pp. 16–23 (cover story).

20. See Mary Thornton, "Justice Dept. Stance on Hiring Goals Resisted," *Washington Post,* May 25, 1985, p. A2; Linda Williams, "Minorities Find Pacts with Corporations Are Hard to Come By and Enforce," *Wall Street Journal,* August 23, 1985, p. 13; and Perl, "Rulings Provide Hiring Direction," pp. A1, A11.

21. Peter C. Robertson, "Why Bosses Like to Be Told to Hire Minorities," *Washington Post,* November 10, 1985, pp. D1–D2.

22. Perl, "Rulings Provide Hiring Direction," p. 1; Al Kamen, "Justice Dept, Surrenders in War on Hiring Goals," *Washington Post,* March 28, 1987, p. A4.

23. Editorial, "Don't Scuttle Affirmative Action," *Business Week,* April 5, 1985, p. 174.

24. Robertson, "Why Bosses Like to Be Told," p. 2.

25. Ibid.

Discussion Questions

1. Briefly summarize Professor Beauchamp's case for preferential treatment programs. What are the two grounds on which he bases his position? Present and explain each ground. Why does he believe that discrimination is pervasive and cannot be overcome except by preferential treatment programs? Do you consider his case persuasive? Why or why not?

2. What does Professor Beauchamp mean when he says that discrimination is prima facie immoral and that the burden of proof is on the person who supports preferential treatment programs? Explain his position. Do you agree or disagree with him? Explain and defend your position.

3. Why does Professor Beauchamp think that a policy of equal opportunity—that protection should not be provided to groups but only individuals who have been discriminated against—will not work? Explain his position. Do you consider his case persuasive? Why or why not?

You can locate InfoTrac-College Education articles about this chapter by accessing the InfoTrac-College Edition website (http://www.infotrac-college.com/wadsworth/). Using the InfoTrac-College Edition subject guide, enter the search terms relevant to this chapter, and then read abstracts for relevant articles.

From Equal Opportunity to "Affirmative Action"   32

THOMAS SOWELL

Thomas Sowell is a Senior Fellow at the Hoover Institution, Stanford University. He has been a professor of economics at a number of leading universities and colleges in America. He is the author of numerous articles and books including *The Economics and Politics and Race* (1983) and *Inside American Education* (1993).

In this essay Dr. Sowell challenges much of the reasoning found in Professor Beauchamp's article (Chapter 31), which attempted to prove pervasive discrimination against minorities and women on the basis of strong statistical disparities and then on that basis concluded that strong affirmative action programs are morally justified. Although he does not deny that discrimination exists, Dr. Sowell argues that one cannot prove that it is all-pervasive simply on the basis of statistical differences between racial, ethnic, and gender groups in society. He provides evidence to show that age, cultural differences, and other factors do a much better job (at least just as well a job) of accounting for disparities as does discrimination. He then goes on to make the controversial argument (by citing a number of statistical findings) that the Civil Rights Movement and subsequent affirmative action policies have helped to advance highly qualified minorities but have resulted in harm to lower class minorities. Dr. Sowell concludes by showing how statistics are manipulated in order to "prove" discrimination even if there is no concrete evidence.

THE VERY MEANING OF the phrase "civil rights" has changed greatly since the *Brown* decision in 1954, or since the Civil Rights Act of 1964. Initially, civil rights meant, quite simply, that all individuals should be treated the same under the law, regardless of their race, religion, sex or other such social categories. For blacks, especially, this would have represented a dramatic improvement in those states where law and public policy mandated racially separate institutions and highly discriminatory treatment.

Many Americans who supported the initial thrust of civil rights, as represented by the *Brown v. Board of Education* decision and the Civil Rights Act of 1964, later felt betrayed as the original concept of equal individual *opportunity* evolved toward the concept of equal group *results*. The idea that statistical differences in results were weighty presumptive evidence of discriminatory processes was not initially an explicit part of civil rights law. But neither was it merely an inexplicable perversion, as many critics seem to think, for it followed logically from the civil rights *vision*.

If the causes of intergroup differences can be dichotomized into discrimination and innate ability, then non-racists and non-sexists must

Reprinted by permission from Thomas Sowell, Civil Rights: Rhetoric or Reality? *(New York: William Morrow, 1984), 42–60. This essay has been edited for this text.*

expect equal results from non-discrimination. Conversely, the persistence of highly disparate results must indicate that discrimination continues to be pervasive among recalcitrant employers, culturally biased tests, hypocritical educational institutions, etc. The early leaders and supporters of the civil rights movement did not advocate such corollaries, and many explicitly repudiated them, especially during the congressional debates that preceded passage of the Civil Rights Act of 1964.[1] But the corollaries were implicit in the vision—and in the long run that proved to be more decisive than the positions taken by the original leaders in the cause of civil rights. In the face of crying injustices, many Americans accepted a vision that promised to further a noble cause, without quibbling over its assumptions or verbal formulations. But visions have a momentum of their own, and those who accept their assumptions have entailed their corollaries, however surprised they may be when these corollaries emerge historically.

"Equal opportunity" laws and policies require that individuals be judged on their qualifications as individuals, *without regard* to race, sex, age, etc. "Affirmative action" requires that they be judged *with regard* to such group membership, receiving preferential or compensatory treatment in some cases to achieve a more proportional "representation" in various institutions and occupations. . . .

Those who carry the civil rights vision to its ultimate conclusion see no great difference between promoting equality of opportunity and equality of results. If there are not equal results among groups presumed to have equal genetic potential, then some inequality of opportunity must have intervened somewhere, and the question of precisely where is less important than the remedy of restoring the less fortunate to their just position. The fatal flaw in this kind of thinking is that there are many reasons, besides genes and discrimination, why groups differ in their economic performances and rewards. Groups differ by large amounts demographically, culturally, and geographically—and all of these differences have profound effects on incomes and occupations.

Age differences are quite large. Blacks are a decade younger than the Japanese. Jews are a quarter of a century older than Puerto Ricans. Polish Americans are twice as old as American Indians.[2] These represent major differences in the quantity of work experience, in an economy where income differences between age brackets are even greater than black-white income differences.[3] Even if the various racial and ethnic groups were identical in every other respect, their age differences alone would prevent their being equally represented in occupations requiring experience or higher education. Their very different age distributions likewise prevent their being equally represented in colleges, jails, homes for the elderly, the armed forces, sports and numerous other institutions and activities that tend to have more people from one age bracket than from another.

Cultural difference add to the age differences. . . . [Half] of all Mexican American wives were married in their teens, while only 10 percent of Japanese American wives married that young.[4] Such very different patterns imply not only different values but also very different future opportunities. Those who marry and begin having children earlier face more restricted options for future education and less geographic mobility for seeking their best career opportunities. Even among those young people who go on to colleges and universities, their opportunities to prepare themselves for the better paid professions are severely limited by their previous educational choices and performances, as well as by their selections of fields of study in the colleges and universities. All of these things vary enormously from one group to another.

For example, mathematics preparation and performance differ greatly from one ethnic group to another and between men and women. A study of high school students in northern California showed that four-fifths of

Asian youngsters were enrolled in the sequence of mathematics courses that culminate in calculus, while only one-fifth of black youngsters were enrolled in such courses. Moreover, even among those who began this sequence in geometry, the percentage that persisted all the way through to calculus was several times higher among the Asian students.[5] Sex differences in mathematics preparation are comparably large. Among both black and white freshmen at the University of Maryland, the men had had four years of mathematics in high school more than twice as often as the women.[6]

Mathematics is of decisive importance for many more professions than that of mathematician. Whole ranges of fields of study and work are off-limits to those without the necessary mathematical foundation. Physicists, chemists, statisticians, and engineers are only some of the more obvious occupations. In some colleges, one cannot even be an undergraduate economics major without having had calculus, and to go on to graduate school and become a professional economist requires much more mathematics, as well as statistical analysis. Even in fields where mathematics is not an absolute prerequisite, its presence or absence makes a major difference in one's ability to rise in the profession. Mathematics is becoming an important factor in the social sciences and is even beginning to invade some of the humanities. To be mathematically illiterate is to carry an increasing burden into an increasing number of occupations. Even the ability to pass a civil service examination for modest clerical jobs is helped or hindered by one's facility in mathematics.

It is hardly surprising that test scores reflect these group differences in mathematics preparation. Nationwide results on the Scholastic Aptitude Test (SAT) for college applicants show Asians and whites consistently scoring higher on the quantitative test than Hispanics or blacks, and men scoring higher than women.[7] Nor are these differences merely the result of socioeconomic "disadvantage" caused by "society." Black, Mexican American, and American Indian youngsters from families with incomes of $50,000 and up score lower than Asians from families whose incomes are just $6,000 and under.[8] Moreover, Asians as a group score higher than whites as a group on the quantitative portion of the SAT and the Japanese in Japan specialize in mathematics, science and engineering to a far greater extent than do American students in the United States.[9] Cultural differences are real, and cannot be talked away by using pejorative terms such as "stereotypes" or "racism."

The racial, ethnic, and sex differences in mathematics that begin in high school (or earlier) continue on through to the Ph.D. level, affecting career choices and economic rewards. Hispanic Ph.D.'s outnumber Asian Ph.D.'s in the United States by three-to-one in history, but the Asians outnumber the Hispanics by ten-to-one in chemistry.[10] More than half of all Asian Ph.D.'s are in mathematics, science or engineering, and more than half the Asians who teach college teach in those fields. By contrast, more than half of all black doctorates are in the field of education, a notoriously undemanding and less remunerative field. So are half the doctorates received by American Indians, not one of whom received a Ph.D. in either mathematics or physics in 1980.[11] Female Ph.D.'s are in quantitatively-based fields only half as frequently as male Ph.D.'s.[12]

Important as mathematics is in itself, it is also a symptom of broader and deeper disparities in educational choices and performances in general. Those groups with smaller quantities of education tend also to have lower qualities of education, and these disparities follow them all the way through their educational careers and into the job market. The children of lower income racial and ethnic groups typically score lower on tests all through school and attend lower quality colleges when they go to college at all, as well as majoring in the easier courses in fields with the least economic promise. How much of this is due to the home environment and how much to the deficiencies of the public schools in their neighborhoods is a large question that cannot be answered here. But what is clear is that what is called the "same" education, measured in years of schooling, is not even remotely the same in reality.

The civil rights vision relies heavily on statistical "disparities" in income and employment between members of different groups to support its sweeping claims of rampant discrimination. The U.S. Civil Rights Commission, for example, considers itself to be "controlling for those factors"[13] when it examines people of the same age with the same number of years of schooling—resolutely ignoring the substance of that schooling.

Age and education do not begin to exhaust the differences between groups. They are simply more readily quantitative than some other differences. The geographic distributions of groups also vary greatly, with Mexican Americans being concentrated in the southwest, Puerto Ricans in the northeast, half of blacks in the south, and most Asians in California and Hawaii. Differences in income between the states are also larger than black-white income differences, so that these distributional differences affect national income differences. A number of past studies, for example, have shown black and Puerto Rican incomes to be very similar nationally, but blacks generally earn higher incomes than Puerto Ricans in New York and other places where Puerto Ricans are concentrated.[14] Their incomes nationally have shown up in the studies as similar, because there are very few Puerto Ricans living in low-income southern states.

One of the most important causes of differences in income and employment is the way people work—some diligently, carefully, persistently, cooperatively, and without requiring much supervision or warnings about absenteeism, tardiness, or drinking, and others requiring much such concern over such matters. Not only are such things inherently diffi-

cult to quantify; any suggestion that such differences even exist is sure to bring forth a storm of condemnation. In short, the civil rights vision has been hermetically sealed off from any such evidence. Both historical and contemporary observations on intergroup differences in work habits, discipline, reliability, sobriety, cleanliness, or cooperative attitude—anywhere in the world—or automatically dismissed as evidence only of the bias or bigotry of the observers. "Stereotypes" is the magic word that makes thinking about such things unnecessary. Yet despite this closed circle of reasoning that surrounds the civil rights vision, there is some evidence that cannot disposed of in that way.

Self-employed farmers, for example, do not depend for their rewards on the biases of employers or the stereotypes of observers. Yet self-employed farmers of different ethnicity have fared very differently on the same land, even in earlier pre-mechanization times, when the principal input was the farmer's own labor. German farmers, for example, had more prosperous farms than other farmers in colonial America[15]—and were more prosperous than Irish farmers in eighteenth-century Ireland,[16] as well as more prosperous than Brazilian farmers in Brazil,[17] Mexican farmers in Mexico,[18] Russian farmers in Russia,[19] and Chilean farmers in Chile.[20] We may ignore the forbidden testimony from these countries as to how hard the German farmers worked, how frugally they lived, or how sober they were. Still, the results speak for themselves.

That Jews earn far higher incomes than Hispanics in the United States might be taken as evidence that anti-Hispanic bias is stronger than anti-Semitism—if one followed the logic of the civil rights vision. But this explanation is considerably weakened by the greater prosperity of Jews than Hispanics in *Hispanic countries* throughout Latin America.[21] Again, even if one dismisses out of hand all the observers who see great differences in the way these two groups work, study, or save, major tangible differences in economic performance remain that cannot be explained in terms of the civil rights vision.

One of the commonly used indices of inter-group economic differences is family income. Yet families are of different sizes from group to group, reflecting differences in the incidence of broken homes. Female headed households are several times more common among blacks than among whites, and in both groups these are the lowest income families. Moreover, the proportion of people working differs greatly from group to group. More than three-fifths of all Japanese American families have multiple income earners while only about a third of Puerto Rican families do. Nor is this a purely socioeconomic phenomenon. Blacks have similar incomes to Puerto Ricans, but the proportion of black families with a woman working is nearly three times that among Puerto Ricans.[22]

None of this disproves the existence of discrimination, nor is that its purpose. What is at issue is whether statistical differences mean discrimination, or whether there are innumerable demographic, cultural, and geographic differences that make this crucial automatic inference highly questionable.

EFFECTS VERSUS HOPES

Thus far, we have not even considered the actual effects of the incentives and constraints created by affirmative action policies—as distinguished from the rationales, hopes or claims made for these policies. Because these policies are invoked on behalf of the most disadvantaged groups, and the most disadvantaged classes within these groups, it is especially important to scrutinize the factual record of what has happened to the economic position of such people under both equal opportunity and affirmative policies.

Before crediting either political policy with economic gains, it is worth considering what trends were already under way before they were instituted. Much has been made of the number of blacks in high-level occupations before and after the Civil Rights Act of 1964. What has been almost totally ignored is the historical *trend* of black representation in such occupations before the Act was passed. In the period from 1954 to 1964, for example, the number of blacks in professional, technical, and similar high-level positions more than doubled.[23] In other kinds of occupations, the advance of blacks was even greater during the 1940s—when there was little or no civil rights policy—than during the 1950s when the civil rights revolution was in its heyday.[24]

The rise in the number of blacks in professional and technical occupations in the two years from 1964 to 1966 (after the Civil Rights Act) was in fact *less* than in the one year from 1961 to 1962 (before the Civil Rights Act).[25] If one takes into account the growing black population by looking at percentages instead of absolute numbers, it becomes even clearer that the Civil Rights Act of 1964 represented no acceleration in trends that had been going on for many years. The percentage of employed blacks who were professional and technical workers rose less in the five years following the Civil Rights Act of 1964 than in the five years preceding it. The percentage of employed blacks who were managers and administrators was the same in 1967 as in 1964—and in 1960. Nor did the institution of "goals and timetables" at the end of 1971 mark any acceleration in the long trend of rising black representation in these occupations. True, there was an appreciable increase in the percentage of blacks in professional and technical fields from 1971 to 1972, but almost entirely offset by a reduction in the percentage of blacks who were managers and administrators.[26]

The history of Asians and Hispanics likewise shows long-term upward trends that began years before the Civil Rights Act of 1964 and were not noticeably accelerated by the Act or by later "affirmative action" policies. The income of Mexican Americans rose relative to that of non-Hispanic whites between 1959 and 1969 (after the Civil Rights Act), but no more so than from 1949 to 1959 (before the Act).[27] Chinese and Japanese Americans overtook other Americans in income by 1959—five years before the Civil Rights Act.

Ignoring trends already in progress for years makes before-and-after comparisons completely misleading. Yet that is precisely the approach of supporters of the civil rights vision, who proceed as if "before" was a static situation. Yet the notion that the Civil Rights Act and "affirmative action" have had a dramatic impact on the economic progress of minorities has become part of the folklore of the land, established primarily through repetition and vehemence, rather than evidence.

The evidence of the *political* impact of civil rights changes in the 1960s is far more clear-cut. The number of black elected officials, especially in the South, increased many-fold in a relatively few years, including blacks elected to public office in some places for the first time since the Reconstruction era after the Civil War. Perhaps even more important, white elected officials in the South had to change both their policies and their rhetoric to accommodate the new political reality that blacks could vote.

What is truly surprising—and relatively ignored—is the economic impact of affirmative action on the disadvantaged, for whom it is most insistently invoked. The relative position of disadvantaged individuals within the groups singled out for preferential treatment has generally *declined* under affirmative action. This is particularly clear in data for individuals, as distinguished from families.

Family income data have too many pitfalls to be taken at face value. There are, for example, significant variations in what constitutes a family, both from time to time and from group to group. But since many people insist on using such data, these statistics cannot be passed over in silence. In 1969, *before* the federal imposition of numerical "goals and timetables," Puerto Rican family income was 63 percent of the national average. By 1977, it was down to 50 percent. In 1969, Mexican American family income was 76 percent of the national average. By 1977 it was down to 73 percent. Black family income fell from 62 percent of the national average to 60 percent over the same span.[28]

There are many complex factors behind these numbers. The point here is simply that they do not support the civil rights vision. A finer breakdown of the data for blacks shows the most disadvantaged families—the female-headed, with no husband present—to be not only the poorest and with the slowest increase in money income during the 1970s (a decline in *real* income) but also with money incomes increasing even more slowly than among white, female-headed families. By contrast, black husband-wife families had money incomes that were rising faster than that of their white counterparts.[29] It is part of a more general pattern of the most disadvantaged falling farther behind during the affirmative action era, while the already advantaged forged ahead.

Individual data tell the same story, even more clearly. Those blacks with less education and less job experience—the truly disadvantaged—have been falling farther and farther behind their white counterparts under affirmative action, during the very same years when blacks with more education and more job experience have been advancing economically, both absolutely and relative to their white counterparts. First, the disadvantaged: Black male high school dropouts with less than six years of work experience earned 79 percent of the income of white male high school dropouts with less than six years of work experience in 1967 (before affirmative action quotas) and this *fell* to 69 percent by 1978 (after affirmative action quotas). Over these very same years, the income of black males who had completed college and had more than six years of work experience *rose* from 75 percent of the income of their white counterparts to 98 percent.[30] Some economic trends can be explained in terms of general conditions in the economy, but such diametrically opposite trends during the very same span of years obviously cannot.

There is additional evidence that the advantaged have benefited under affirmative action while the disadvantaged have fallen behind. Black faculty members with numerous publications and Ph.D.'s from top-rated institutions earned more than white faculty members with the same high qualifications, but black faculty members who lacked a doctorate or publications earned less than whites with the same low qualifications.[31] The pattern of diametrically opposite trends in economic well-being among advantaged and disadvantaged blacks is also shown by the general internal distribution of income among blacks. The top fifth of blacks have absorbed a growing proportion of all income received by blacks, while each of the bottom three fifths has received declining shares.[32] Black college-educated couples with husband and wife working had by 1980 achieved incomes higher then white couples of the same description.[33] Meanwhile, at the other end of the spectrum, the black female-headed household was receiving only 62 percent of the income of white, female-headed households—down from 70 percent in 1970.[34]

None of this is easily reconcilable with the civil rights vision's all-purpose explanation, racism and discrimination. To explain such diametrically opposite trends within the black community on the basis of whites' behavior would require us to believe that racism and discrimination were growing and declining at the same time. It is much more reconcilable with ordinary economic analysis.

Affirmative action hiring pressures make it costly to have no minority employees, but continuing affirmative action pressures at the promotion and discharge phases also make it costly to have minority employees who do not work out well. The net effect is to increase the demand for highly qualified minority employees while decreasing the demand for less qualified minority employees or for those without a sufficient track record to reassure employers.

Those who are most vocal about the need for affirmative action are of course the more articulate minority members—the advantaged who speak in the name of the disadvantaged. Their position on the issue may accord with their own personal experience, as well as their own self-interest. But that cannot dismiss the growing evidence that it is precisely the disadvantaged who suffer from affirmative action.

BY THE NUMBERS

Averages versus Variance

One of the remarkable aspects of affirmative action is that, while numbers—and *assumptions* about numbers—abound, proponents of the program are almost never challenged to produce positive numerical evidence for its effectiveness or to support their statistical presuppositions. The mere fact that some group is *x* percent of the population but only *y* percent of the employees is taken as weighty presumption of employer discrimination. There are serious statistical problems with this approach, quite aside from substantial group differences in age, education, and cultural values.

Even in a random world of identical things, to say that something happens a certain way *on the average* is not to say that it happens that way *every time*. But affirmative action deals with averages almost as if there were no variance. If Hispanics are 8 percent of the carpenters in a given town, it does not follow that *every* employer of carpenters in that town would have 8 percent Hispanics if there were no discrimination. Even if carpenters were assigned to employers by drawing lots (or by some other random process), there would be *variance* in the proportion of Hispanic carpenters from one employer to another. To convict those employers with fewer Hispanics of discrimination in hiring would be to make statistical variance a federal offense.

To illustrate the point, we can consider some process where racial, sexual, or ideological factors do not enter, such as the flipping of a coin. There is no reason to expect a persistent preponderance of heads over tails (or vice versa) on the *average,* but there is also no reason to expect exactly half heads and half tails every time we flip a coin a few times. That is, *variance* will exist.

To illustrate the effect of statistical variance, a coin was flipped ten times and then this experiment was repeated ten times. Here are the results.

Heads	3	4	3	4	6	7	2	4	5	3
Tails	7	6	7	6	4	3	8	6	5	7

At one extreme, there were seven heads and three tails, and at the other extreme eight tails and two heads. Statistics not only have averages, they have variance.

Translate this into employment decisions. Imagine that you are the employer who ends up with eight employees from one group and two from another, even though both groups are the same size and no different in qualifications, and even though you have been unbiased in selecting. Try explaining to EEOC and the courts that you ended up with four times as many employees from one group by random chance! You may be convicted of discrimination, even if you have only been guilty of statistical variance.

Of course some employers are biased, just as some coins are biased because of the way their weight is distributed on the design. This particular coin might have been biased; over all, it came up heads 41 percent of the time and tails 59 percent. But even if the coin was biased toward tails, it still came up heads seven times out of ten in one set of flips. If an employer were similarly biased in *favor* of a particular group, he could still be convicted of discrimination *against* that very group, if they ended up with less than half the "representation" of some other group.

No one needs to assume that this particular coin was unbiased or even that the results were accurately reported. Anyone can collect ten people and have them flip a coin ten times, to see the statistical variance for himself. Frivolous as this might seem, the results have deadly serious implications for the way people are convicted of violating federal laws, regulations, and guidelines. It might be especially instructive if this little experiment were performed by editorial writers for publications that fervently support affirmative action, or by clerks of the Supreme Court.

Even when conclusions are based only on differences that statisticians call "statistically significant," this by no means eliminates the basic problem. What is statistically significant depends upon the probability that such a result would have happened by random chance. A common litmus test used by statisticians is whether the event would occur more than 5 times out of a hundred by random chance. Applying this common test of statistical significance to affirmative action means that even in the most extreme case imaginable—zero discrimination and zero difference among racial, ethnic, and other groups—the EEOC could still run 10,000 employers' records through a computer and come up with about 500 "discriminators."

The illustration chosen is in fact too favorable to the proponents of affirmative action, because it shows the probability of incorrectly calling an employer a discriminator when there is only *one* group in question that might be discriminated against. Affirmative action has a number of groups whose statistical employment patterns can lead to charges of discrimination. To escape a false charge of discrimination, an employer must avoid being in the fatal 5 percent for *all* the groups in question simultaneously. That becomes progressively harder when there are more groups.

While there is a 95 percent chance for a nondiscriminatory employer to escape when there is only one group, this falls to 86 percent when there are three separate groups and to 73 percent when there are six.[35] That is, even in a world of zero discrimination and zero differences among groups, more than one-fourth of all employers would be called "discriminators" by this common test of statistical significance, when there are six separate groups in question.

What this means is that the courts have sanctioned a procedure which insures that large-scale statistical "discrimination" will exist forever, regardless of what the actual facts may be. They have made statistical variance a federal offense.[36]

Shopping for Discrimination

Often the very same raw data point to different conclusions at different levels of aggregation. For example, statistics have shown that black faculty members earn less than white faculty members, but as these data are broken down by field of specialization, by number of publications, by possession (or nonpossession) of a Ph.D. and by the ranking of the institution that issued it, then the black-white income difference not only shrinks but disappears, and in some fields reverses—with black faculty earning more than white faculty with the same characteristics.[37] For those who accept statistics as proof of discrimination, how much discrimination there is, and in what direction, depends upon how finely these data are broken down.

There is no "objective" or "scientific" way to decide at what level of aggregation to stop breaking the data down into finer categories. Nor have the laws or the courts specified in advance what will and will not be the accepted way to break down the statistics. Any individual or organization contemplating a lawsuit against an employer can arrange that employer's statistics in any number of possible ways and then go shopping among the possibilities for the one that will present the employment pattern in the worst light. This is a very effective strategy in a society in which groups differ enormously in their characteristics and choices, while the prevailing vision makes deviations from a random distribution evidence against the employer.

A discrimination case can depend entirely on what level of statistical breakdown the judge accepts, for different groups will be represented—or "underrepresented"—differently according to how precisely occupations and qualifications are defined. While there were more black than Asian American "social scientists" receiving a Ph.D. in 1980, when social scientists were broken down further, there were nearly three times as many Asian as black *economists*.[38] While male recipients of Ph.D.'s in the social sciences outnumbered female recipients of Ph.D.'s by slightly less than two-to-one in 1980, men outnumbered women by more than four-to-one among doctorates in economics and by ten-to-one among doctorates in econometrics.[39] What is the employer hiring: social scientists, economists or econometricians? He may in fact be looking for an econometrician specializing in international trade—and there may be no statistics available on that. Nor can anyone infer the proportion of women or minority members available in that specialty from their distribution in broader categories, for the distribution changes at every level of aggregation.

The same principle applies in other fields as well. A computer manufacturer who is looking for an engineer is not looking for the same kind of engineer as a company that builds bridges. Nor is there the slightest reason to expect all groups to be distributed the same in these sub-specialties as they are among engineers in general. Even within a narrow occupational range such as mathematical specialists, blacks outnumber Asian Americans in gross numbers but Asian Americans outnumber blacks more than two-to-one among statisticians.[40]

When comparing any employer's work force with the available labor pool to determine "underrepresentation," everything depends on how that labor pool is defined—at what level of aggregation. Those who wish to argue for discrimination generally prefer broad, loose, heterogeneous categories. The concept of a "qualified" worker aids that approach. When the barely qualified is treated as being the same as the most highly skilled and experienced, it is the same as staying at a very general level of aggregation. Anything that creates or widens the disparity between what the job requires and how the categories are defined increases the potential for statistical "discrimination."

An employer may be guilty or innocent according to what level of statistical aggregation a judge accepts, after the plaintiffs have shopped around among the many possibilities. But that is only part of the problem. A more fundamental problem is that *the burden of proof is on the accused* to prove his innocence, once suspicious numbers have been found. Shopping around for suspicious numbers is by no means difficult, especially for a federal agency, given statistical variance, multiple groups, multiple occupations, and wide-ranging differences in the characteristics and choices of the groups themselves.

Statistical aggregation is a major factor not only in courts of law but also in the court of public opinion. Many statistics from a very general level of aggregation are repeatedly presented in the media as demonstrating pervasive discrimination. The finer breakdowns are more likely to appear in specialized scholarly journals, read by a relative handful of people. Yet these finer breakdowns of statistics often tell a drastically different story, not only for black-white differences and male-female differences but for other groups as well.

For example, American Indian males earn significantly less than white males, and Asian males earn significantly more. Yet, as one holds a wide range of variables constant, these income differences shrink to the vanishing point. Asian Americans, for example, are distributed geographically in a very different pattern from whites. Asians are concentrated in higher income states, in more urban areas, and

have more education. When all of this is held constant, their income advantage vanishes.[41] By the same token, when various demographic and cultural variables—notably proficiency in the English language—are held constant, the income disadvantages of Hispanic and American Indian males also disappear.[42]

It can hardly be expected that discrimination lawsuits and discrimination as a political issue will be correspondingly reduced any time soon. The methods by which it is measured in the courts and in politics insures that it will be a continuing source of controversy.

Poverty and huge intergroup differences in income are serious matters, whether or not discrimination is the cause—and whether or not affirmative action is the cure. Yet any attempt to deal with these very real disadvantages must first cut through the fog generated by a vision more powerful than its evidence—and, in fact, a vision shaping what courts will accept as evidence.

NOTES

1. U.S. Equal Employment Opportunity Commission, *Legislative History of Titles VII and XI of Civil Rights At of 1964* (Washington, D.C.: U.S. Government Printing Office, no date) pp. 1007–08, 1014, 3005, 3006, 3013, 3160, and *passim.*

2. Thomas Sowell, *Markets and Minorities* (New York: Basic Books, 1981), p. 11.

3. U.S. Bureau of the Census, *Social Indicators, 1976* (Washington, D.C.: U.S. Government Printing Office, 1977), pp. 454–456.

4. Peter Uhlenberg, "Demographic Correlates of Group Achievement: Contrasting Patterns of Mexican-Americans and Japanese-Americans," *Race, Creed, Color, or National Origin,* ed. Robert K. Yin (Itasca, Illinois: F. E. Peacock Publishers, 1973), p. 91.

5. Lucy W. Sells, "Leverage for Equal Opportunity Through Mastery of Mathematics," *Women and Minorities in Science,* ed. Sheila M. Humphreys (Boulder, Colorado: Westview Press, 1982), pp. 12, 16.

6. Ibid., p. 11.

7. College Entrance Examination Board, *Profiles, College-Bound Seniors, 1981* (New York: College Entrance Examination Board, 1982), pp. 12, 22, 41, 51, 60, 65.

8. Ibid., pp. 27, 36, 46, 55.

9. Ibid., pp. 60, 79; Alexander Randall, "East Meets West," *Science,* November 1981, p. 72.

10. National Research Council, *Science, Engineering, and Humanities Doctorates in the United States* (Washington, D.C.: National Academy of Sciences, 1980), pp. 13, 39.

11. National Research Council, *Summary Report: 1980 Doctorate Recipients from United States Universities* (Washington, D.C.: National Academy Press, 1981), pp. 26, 29.

12. Sue E. Berryman,"Trends in and Causes of Minority and Female Representation Among Science and Mathematics Doctorates," mimeographed, The Rand Corporation, 1983, p. 13.

13. U.S. Commission on Civil Rights, *Unemployment and Underemployment Among Blacks, Hispanics, and Women* (Washington, D.C.: U.S. Commission on Civil Rights, 1982), p. 58.

14. Thomas Sowell, *Ethnic America* (New York: Basic Books, 1981), p. 222.

15. J. C. Furnas, *The Americans* (New York: G. P. Putnam's Sons, 1969), p. 86; Daniel Boorstin, *The Americans* (New York: Random House, 1958), Vol. I, p. 225.

16. Arthur Young, *A Tour in Ireland* (Shannon, Ireland: Irish University Press, 1970), Vol. I, pp. 377–379.

17. Thomas H. Holloway, *Immigrants on the Land* (Chapel Hill, N.C.: University of North Carolina Press, 1980), p. 151.

18. Harry Leonard Sawatzky, *They Sought a Country* (Berkeley: University of California Press, 1971), pp. 129, 244. Apparently Germans prospered in Honduras as well. Ibid., pp. 361, 365.

19. Hattie Plum Williams, *The Czar's Germans* (Lincoln, Nebraska: American Historical Society of Germans from Russia, 1975), pp. 135, 159.

20. Carl Solberg, *Immigration and Nationalism* (Austin: University of Texas Press, 1970), pp. 27, 40.

21. Judith Laikin Elkin, *Jews of the Latin American Republics* (Chapel Hill, N.C.: University of North Carolina Press, 1980), pp. 214–237. See also Robert Weisbrot, *The Jews of Argentina* (Philadelphia: The Jewish Publication Society of America, 1979), pp. 175–184.

22. Thomas Sowell, *Ethnic America,* p. 238.

23. Daniel P. Moynihan, "Employment, Income, and the Ordeal of the Negro Family," *Daedalus,* Fall 1965, p. 752.

24. Daniel O. Price, *Changing Characteristics of the Negro Population* (Washington, D.C.: U.S. Government Printing Office, 1969), pp. 117, 118.

25. *Employment and Training Report of the President, 1981* (Washington, D.C.: U.S. Government Printing Office, 1981), p. 150.

26. Ibid., p. 151.

27. Thomas Sowell, *Ethnic America,* p. 260.

28. Thomas Sowell, *The Economics and Politics of Race* (New York: William Morrow, 1983), p. 187.

29. U.S. Bureau of the Census, *Social Indicators III* (Washington, D.C.: U.S. Government Printing Office, 1980), p. 485.

30. Finis Welch, "Affirmative Action and Its Enforcement," *American Economic Review,* May 1981, p. 132.

31. Thomas Sowell, *Affirmative Action Reconsidered* (Washington, D.C.: American Enterprise Institute, 1975), pp. 16–22.

32. Martin Kilson, "Black Social Classes and Intergenerational Policy," *The Public Interest,* Summer 1981, p. 63.

33. U.S. Bureau of the Census, *Current Population Reports,* Series P-20, No. 366 (Washington, D.C.: U.S. Government Printing Office, 1981), pp. 182, 184.

34. U.S. Bureau of the Census, *Current Population Reports,* Series P-60, No. 80, p. 37; Ibid., Series P-60, No. 132, pp. 41–42.

35. The probability that a non-discriminatory employer will escape a false charge of discrimination is 95 percent, when the standard of "statistical significance" is that his employment pattern would not occur more than 5 times out of 100 by random chance. But the probability of escaping the same false charge for three separate groups simultaneously is

$(.95)^3$ or about 86 percent. When there are six separate groups, the probability is $(.95)^6$ or about 73 percent. Not all groups are separate; women and the aged, for example, overlap racial and ethnic groups. This complicates the calculation without changing the basic principle.

36. The greater ease of "proving" discrimination statistically, when there are multiple groups, multiple jobs, and substantial demographic, cultural and other differences between groups, may either take the form of finding more "discriminators" at a given level of statistical significance (5 percent, for example) or using a more stringent standard of statistical significance (1 percent, for example) to produce a more impressive-looking case against a smaller number of "discriminators."

37. Thomas Sowell, *Affirmative Action Reconsidered* (Washington, D.C.: American Enterprise Institute, 1975), pp. 16–22.

38. Commission on Human Resources, National Research Council, *Summary Report: 1980 Doctorate Recipients from United States Universities* (National Academy Press, 1981), p. 27.

39. Ibid., p. 25.

40. U.S. Bureau of the Census, *Current Population Reports,* Series P-23, No. 120 (Washington, D.C.: U.S. Government Printing Office, 1982), p. 5.

41. Barry R. Chiswick, "An Analysis of the Earnings and Employment of Asian-American Men," *Journal of Labor Economics,* April 1983, pp. 197–214.

42. Walter McManus, William Gould and Finis Welch, "Earnings of Hispanic Men: The Role of English Language Performance," Ibid., pp. 101–130; Gary D. Sandefur, "Minority Group Status and the Wages of White, Black, and Indian Males," *Social Science Research,* March 1983, pp. 44–68.

Discussion Questions

1. Dr. Sowell argues that one cannot prove that discrimination is all-pervasive simply on the basis of statistical differences between racial, ethnic, and gender groups in society. What evidence does he provide to support his claim that age, cultural differences, and other factors do a much better job (at least just as well a job) of accounting for disparities as does discrimination? Do you consider his case persuasive? Why or why not?

2. How does Dr. Sowell attempt to demonstrate his claim that the Civil Rights Movement and subsequent affirmative action policies have helped to advance highly qualified minorities but have resulted in harm to lower class minorities? What statistics does he cite in order to support his claim? Do you consider his case persuasive? Why or why not?

3. In the last section of his essay, Dr. Sowell argues that statistics are manipulated in order to "prove" discrimination even when there is no concrete evidence. How does he attempt to demonstrate this? What does he mean when he claims that current anti-discrimination policies make statistical variance a federal offense? Do you agree or disagree with Dr. Sowell's reasoning? Explain and defend and your position.

You can locate InfoTrac-College Education articles about this chapter by accessing the InfoTrac-College Edition website (http://www.infotrac-college.com/wadsworth/). Using the InfoTrac-College Edition subject guide, enter the search terms relevant to this chapter, and then read abstracts for relevant articles.

SECTION B

Economic and Social Justice

Introduction to Section B

In a September 23, 1993, address to a joint session of Congress and the nation, then-President Bill Clinton defended his Health Security Plan by appealing to a number of principles, some of which apply to the issue debated in this section, *economic and social justice*. Consider the following comments from the President's speech:

> [The principle of security] speaks to the human misery, to the costs, to the anxiety we hear about every day—all of us—when people talk about their problems with the present [health care] system. Security means that those who do not now have health care will have it; and for those who have it, it will never be taken away. We must achieve that security as soon as possible.
>
> Under our plan, every American would receive a health care security card that will guarantee a comprehensive package of benefits over the course of an entire lifetime, roughly comparable to the benefits package offered by most Fortune 500 companies. This health care security card will offer this package of benefits in a way that can never be taken away. . . .
>
> With this card, if you lose your job or you switch jobs, you're covered. If you leave your job to start a small business, you're covered. If you're an early retiree, you're covered. If someone in your family, unfortunately, had an illness that qualifies as a preexisting condition, you're still covered. If you get sick or a member of your family gets sick, even if it's a life threatening illness, you're covered. And if your insurance company tries to drop you for any reason, you will still be covered, because that will be illegal. . . .
>
> And now, it is our turn to strike a blow for freedom in this country. The freedom of Americans to live without fear that their own nation's health care system won't be there for them when they need it.[1]

Although the former President and the First Lady (Hillary Rodham Clinton) courageously took on the enormous task of reforming our health care system, their plan failed to make it through Congress. No one doubts that they should be applauded for their efforts, but a government program of universal health coverage raises some important philosophical questions concerning the meaning of *distributive justice:* What is the proper role of government in people's lives? What is the nature of private property? Do citizens have a right to receive certain positive benefits (such as health care) from their government? In other words, the former President's health care plan raises questions about the meaning and application of such concepts as *liberty, justice,* and *ownership.*

There are a number of social philosophers, such as John Rawls (Chapter 33) who would probably defend some type of universal health care plan as morally justifiable, since they agree with President Clinton that Americans can only truly exercise *liberty* when they are "without fear that their own nation's health care system won't be there for them when they need it." That is, these philosophers believe that the principle of *justice* trumps property rights so that benefits (in this case, health care) can be distributed fairly to all, and consequently, will lead to the greatest liberty for the greatest number.

On the other hand, there are others social philosophers, such as Murray N. Rothbard (Chapter 34), who would see the Clinton plan as a violation of private property rights and personal liberty and is therefore unjust. That is to say, some social philosophers do not agree with the former President's claim that a government-mandated universal health care plan will "strike a blow for freedom in this country," but rather, they argue that such a plan limits freedom since it entails the government confiscating the fairly acquired assets of employers and citizens so that the government can redistribute these assets to those to whom these assets are not entitled. It also requires all citizens to participate in the system without the consent of each individual who is forced to participate in it. Social philosophers who hold to this position see *property rights* and personal *liberty* as the means by which one evaluates the *justice* of an act. Thus, the Clinton health care plan is unjust since it violates property rights as well as personal liberty.

Of course, the philosophical dispute over distributive justice is much bigger than the issue of health care, but that issue, since it is paramount on the minds of most North Americans, serves as an excellent way to introduce the dispute. Other issues, such as public education, welfare, food stamps, and government funding of public and private works, also raise the same questions about the meaning of distributive justice.

Another perspective on the issue comes from some feminist political philosophers, who are concerned about the influence of traditional family and gender roles on the fair distribution of power in society, which, of course, has an influence on the distribution of capital. Professor Susan Moller Okin (Chapter 35) argues that contemporary theories of social justice, such as those held by Rawls, and Rothbard, have not sufficiently addressed the issue of how we are to assess whether a family structure meets the requirement of justice. She believes that there are a number of reasons for this, but the primary one is that virtually all contemporary political and legal theorists assume that the family is "nonpolitical." Moller Okin provides three reasons why such an assumption is not justified.

NOTE

1. President Bill Clinton, "Address of the President to the Joint Session of Congress (September 22, 1993)," in *The President's Health Security Plan: The Complete Draft and Final Reports of the White House Domestic Policy Council* (New York: Random House, 1993), 108–109, 125.

Key words: welfare rights, equality, libertarianism, socialism, free market, capitalism, social justice, democracy, property rights, wealth redistribution, Karl Marx, Adam Smith, Ludwig Von Mises, John Locke, John Rawls, justice and gender, feminism, distributive justice, John Maynard Keynes

For Further Reading

Bruce Ackerman, *Social Justice and the Liberal State* (New Haven: Yale University Press, 1980).

Ronald Dworkin, *Taking Rights Seriously* (Cambridge, MA: Harvard University Press, 1977).

William A. Galston, *Justice and the Human Good* (Chicago: University of Chicago Press, 1980).

Alison Jaggar, "On Sexual Equality," in *Sex Equality,* ed. Jane English (Englewood Cliffs, NJ: Prentice-Hall, 1977).

John Kekes, *Against Liberalism* (Ithaca, NY: Cornell University Press, 1997).

David Kelley, *A Life of One's Own: Individual Rights and the Welfare State* (Washington, DC: The Cato Institute, 1998).

Michael Levin, *Feminism and Freedom* (New Brunswick, NJ: Transaction Books, 1987).

Tibor Machan, ed., *The Libertarian Alternative* (Chicago: Nelson-Hall, 1974).

Jan Narveson, The *Libertarian Idea* (Philadelphia: Temple University Press, 1988).

Kai Nielsen, *Equality and Liberty: A Defense of Radical Egalitarianism* (Totowa, NJ: Rowman and Littlefield, 1985).

Michael Novak, *The Spirit of Democratic Capitalism* (New York: A Touchstone Book, 1982).

Robert Nozick, *Anarchy, State, and Utopia* (New York: Basic Books, 1974).

Susan Moller Okin, *Justice, Gender, and the Family* (New York: Basic Books, 1989).

John Rawls, *A Theory of Justice* (Cambridge, MA: Belnap Press of the Harvard University Press, 1971).

Jeffrey Reiman, "The Fallacy of Libertarian Capitalism," *Ethics* (October 1981).

Murray Rothbard, *For a New Liberty* (New York: Macmillan, 1973).

James Sterba, *The Demands of Justice* (Notre Dame, IN: University of Notre Dame Press, 1980).

33   A Theory of Justice

JOHN RAWLS

John Rawls is Professor Emeritus of Philosophy at Harvard University. One of the foremost political philosophers of the twentieth-century, he is the author of numerous scholarly articles as well as the book which has become a contemporary classic, *A Theory of Justice* (1971). He is also the author of *Political Liberalism* (1993).

In this essay, Professor Rawls defends a theory of justice which most commentators have argued is consistent with the ideas of the liberal wing of the Democratic Party in the United States. In order to establish the rationality of this view, Professor Rawls asks us to use our imagination and pretend that each of us is behind a "veil of ignorance," that is, that we are unaware of our natural talents, age, appearance, social status, financial fortune or lack thereof, class, race, gender, etc. He then asks us to consider what principles of justice we would choose behind this veil of ignorance. Because there would be no bias behind the veil of ignorance (since no one would know who one really is or what one really has), Professor Rawls argues that the principles of justice arrived at by agreement behind this veil are most likely to be truly just and rational. He suggests two principles, the first being: "each person is to have an equal right to the most extensive basic liberty compatible with a similar liberty for others." The second principle is: "social and economic inequalities are to be arranged so that they are both (a) to the greatest benefit of the least advantaged, and (b) attached to offices and positions open to all under conditions of fair equality of opportunity. . . ." Professor Rawls then explains how these principles apply in society and government.

I SHALL BEGIN BY CONSIDERING the role of the principles of justice. Let us assume, to fix ideas, that a society is a more or less self-sufficient association of persons who in their relations to one another recognize certain rules of conduct as binding and who for the most part act in accordance with them. Suppose further that these rules specify a system of cooperation designed to advance the good of those taking part in it. Then, although a society is a cooperative venture for mutual advantage, it is typically marked by a conflict as well as by an identity of interests. There is an identity of interests since social cooperation makes possible a better life for all than any would have if each were to live solely by his own efforts. There is a conflict of interests since persons are not indifferent as to how the greater benefits produced by their collaboration are distributed, for in order to pursue their ends they each prefer a larger to a lesser share. A set of principles is required for choosing among the various social arrangements which determine this division of advantages and for underwriting an agreement on

Reprinted by permission from John Rawls, A Theory of Justice *(Cambridge, MA: Harvard University Press, 1971).*

the proper distributive shares. These principles are the principles of social justice: they provide a way of assigning rights and duties in the basic institutions of society and they define the appropriate distribution of the benefits and burdens of social cooperation. . . .

Men disagree about which principles should define the basic terms of their association. Yet we may still say, despite this disagreement, that they each have a conception of justice. That is, they understand the need for, and they are prepared to affirm, a characteristic set of principles for assigning basic rights and duties and for determining what they take to be the proper distribution of the benefits and burdens of social cooperation. Thus it seems natural to think of the concept of justice as distinct from the various conceptions of justice and as being specified by the role which these different sets of principles, these different conceptions, have in common. Those who hold different conceptions of justice can, then, still agree that institutions are just when no arbitrary distinctions are made between persons in the assigning of basic rights and duties and when the rules determine a proper balance between competing claims to the advantages of social life. . . .

Some measure of agreement in conceptions of justice is, however, not the only prerequisite for a viable human community. There are other fundamental social problems, in particular those of coordination, efficiency, and stability. Thus the plans of individuals need to be fitted together so that their activities are compatible with one another and they can all be carried through without anyone's legitimate expectations being severely disappointed. Moreover, the execution of these plans should lead to the achievement of social ends in ways that are efficient and consistent with justice. And finally the scheme of social cooperation must be stable; it must be more or less regularly complied with and its basic rules willingly acted upon; and when infractions occur, stabilizing forces should exist that prevent further violations and tend to restore the arrangement. Now it is evi-

dent that these three problems are connected with that of justice. In the absence of a certain measure of agreement on what is just and unjust, it is clearly more difficult for individuals to coordinate their plans efficiently in order to insure that mutually beneficial arrangements are maintained. Distrust and resentment corrode the ties of civility, and suspicion and hostility tempt men to act in ways they would otherwise avoid. So while the distinctive role of conceptions of justice is to specify basic rights and duties and to determine the appropriate distributive shares, the way in which a conception does this is bound to affect the problems of efficiency, coordination, and stability. We cannot, in general, assess a conception of justice by its distributive role alone, however useful this role may be in identifying the concept of justice. We must take into account its wider connections; for even though justice has a certain priority, being the most important virtue of institutions, it is still true that, other things equal, one conception of justice is preferable to another when its broader consequences are more desirable. . . .

For us the primary subject of justice is the basic structure of society, or more exactly, the way in which the major social institutions distribute fundamental rights and duties and determine the division of advantages from social cooperation. By major institutions I understand the political constitution and the principal economic and social arrangements. Thus the legal protection of freedom of thought and liberty of conscience, competitive markets, private property in the means of production, and the monogamous family are examples of major social institutions. Taken together as one scheme, the major institutions define men's rights and duties and influence their life-prospects, what they can expect to be and how well they can hope to do. The basic structure is the primary subject of justice because its effects are so profound and present from the start. The intuitive notion here is that this structure contains various social positions and that men born into different positions have different expectations of life determined, in part, by the political system as well as by economic and social circumstances. In this way the institutions of society favor certain starting places over others. These are especially deep inequalities. Not only are they pervasive, but they affect men's initial chances in life; yet they cannot possibly be justified by an appeal to the notions of merit or desert. It is these inequalities, presumably inevitable in the basic structure of any society, to which the principles of social justice must in the first instance apply. These principles then regulate the choice of a political constitution and the main elements of the economic and social system. The justice of a social scheme depends essentially on how fundamental rights and duties are assigned and on the economic opportunities and social conditions in the various sectors of society. . . .

My aim is to present a conception of justice which generalizes and carries to a higher level of abstraction the familiar theory of the social contract as found, say, in Locke, Rousseau, and Kant. In order to do this we are not to think of the original contract as one to enter a particular society or to set up a particular form of government. Rather, the guiding idea is that the principles of justice for the basic structure of society are the object of the original agreement. They are the principles that free and rational persons concerned to further their own interests would accept in an initial position of equality as defining the fundamental terms of their association. These principles are to regulate all further agreements; they specify the kinds of social cooperation that can be entered into and the forms of government that can be established. This way of regarding the principles of justice I shall call justice as fairness.

Thus we are to imagine that those who engage in social cooperation choose together, in one joint act, the principles which are to assign basic rights and duties and to determine the division of social benefits. Men are to decide in advance how they are to regulate

their claims against one another and what is to be the foundation charter of their society. Just as each person must decide by rational reflection what constitutes his good, that is, the system of ends which it is rational for him to pursue, so a group of persons must decide once and for all what is to count among them as just and unjust. The choice which rational men would make in this hypothetical situation of equal liberty, assuming for the present that this choice problem has a solution, determines the principles of justice.

In justice as fairness the original position of equality corresponds to the state of nature in the traditional theory of the social contract. This original position is not, of course, thought of as an actual historical state of affairs, much less as a primitive condition of culture. It is understood as a purely hypothetical situation characterized so as to lead to a certain conception of justice. Among the essential features of this situation is that no one knows his place in society, his class position or social status, nor does any one know his fortune in the distribution of natural assets and abilities, his intelligence, strength, and the like. I shall even assume that the parties do not know their conceptions of the good or their special psychological propensities. The principles of justice are chosen behind a veil of ignorance. This ensures that no one is advantaged or disadvantaged in the choice of principles by the outcome of natural chance or the contingency of social circumstances. Since all are similarly situated and no one is able to design principles to favor his particular condition, the principles of justice are the result of a fair agreement or bargain. For given the circumstances of the original position, the symmetry of everyone's relations to each other, this initial situation is fair between individuals as moral persons, that is, as rational beings with their own ends and capable, I shall assume, of a sense of justice. The original position is, one might say, the appropriate initial status quo, and thus the fundamental agreements reached in it are fair. This explains the propriety of the name "justice as fairness": it conveys the idea that the principles of justice are agreed to in an initial situation that is fair. . . .

Justice as fairness begins, as I have said, with one of the most general of all choices which persons might make together, namely, with the choice of the first principles of a conception of justice which is to regulate all subsequent criticism and reform of institutions. Then, having chosen a conception of justice, we can suppose that they are to choose a constitution and a legislature to enact laws, and so on, all in accordance with the principles of justice initially agreed upon. Our social situation is just if it is such that by this sequence of hypothetical agreements we would have contracted into the general system of rules which defines it. Moreover, assuming that the original position does determine a set of principles (that is, that a particular conception of justice would be chosen), it will then be true that whenever social institutions satisfy these principles those engaged in them can say to one another that they are cooperating on terms to which they would agree if they were free and equal persons whose relations with respect to one another were fair. They could all view their arrangements as meeting the stipulations which they would acknowledge in an initial situation that embodies widely accepted and reasonable constraints on the choice of principles. The general recognition of this fact would provide the basis for a public acceptance of the corresponding principles of justice. No society can, of course, be a scheme of cooperation which men enter voluntarily in a literal sense; each person finds himself placed at birth in some particular position in some particular society, and the nature of this position materially affects his life prospects. Yet a society satisfying the principles of justice as fairness comes as close as a society can to being a voluntary scheme, for it meets the principles which free and equal persons would assent to under circumstances that are fair. In this sense its members are autonomous and the obligations they recognize self-imposed.

One feature of justice as fairness is to think of the parties in the initial situation as rational and mutually disinterested. This does not mean that the parties are egoists, that is, individuals with only certain kinds of interests, say in wealth, prestige, and domination. But they are conceived as not taking an interest in one another's interests. They are to presume that even their spiritual aims may be opposed, in the way that the aims of those of different religions may be opposed. Moreover, the concept of rationality must be interpreted as far as possible in the narrow sense, standard in economic theory, of taking the most effective means to given ends. . . .

In working out the conception of justice as fairness one main task clearly is to determine which principles of justice would be chosen in the original position. To do this we must describe this situation in some detail and formulate with care the problem of choice which it presents. . . . It may be observed, however, that once the principles of justice are thought of as arising from an original agreement in a situation of equality, it is an open question whether the principle of utility would be acknowledged. Offhand it hardly seems likely that persons who view themselves as equals, entitled to press their claims upon one another, would agree to a principle which may require lesser life prospects for some simply for the sake of a greater sum of advantages enjoyed by others. Since each desires to protect his interests, his capacity to advance his conception of the good, no one has a reason to acquiesce in an enduring loss for himself in order to bring about a greater net balance of satisfaction. In the absence of strong and lasting benevolent impulses, a rational man would not accept a basic structure merely because it maximized the algebraic sum of advantages irrespective of its permanent effects on his own basic rights and interests. Thus it seems that the principle of utility is incompatible with the conception of social cooperation among equals for mutual advantage. It appears to be inconsistent with the idea of reciprocity implicit in the notion of a well-ordered society. . . .

I shall maintain instead that the person in the initial situation would choose two rather different principles: the first requires equality in the assignment of basic rights and duties, while the second holds that social and economic inequalities, for example inequalities of wealth and authority, are just only if they result in compensating benefits for everyone, and in particular for the least advantaged members of society. These principles rule out justifying institutions on the grounds that the hardships of some are offset by a greater good in the aggregate. It may be expedient but it is not just that some should have less in order that others may prosper. But there is no injustice in the greater benefits earned by a few provided that the situation of persons not so fortunate is thereby improved. The intuitive idea is that since everyone's well-being depends upon a scheme of cooperation without which no one could have a satisfactory life, the division of advantages should be such as to draw forth the willing cooperation of others when some workable scheme is a necessary condition of the welfare of all. Once we decide to look for a conception of justice that nullifies the accidents of natural endowment and the contingencies of social circumstance as counters in quest for political and economic advantage, we are led to these principles. They express the result of leaving aside those aspects of the social world that seem arbitrary from a moral point of view. . . .

Justice as fairness is an example of what I have called a contract theory. The merit of the contract terminology is that it conveys the idea that principles of justice may be conceived as principles that would be chosen by rational persons, and that in this way conceptions of justice may be explained and justified. . . . Furthermore, principles of justice deal with conflicting claims upon the advantages won by social cooperation; they apply to the relations among several persons or groups. The word "contract" suggests this plurality as well as the condition that the appropriate division of advantages must be in accordance with principles acceptable to all parties. The condition of publicity for principles of justice is also connoted by the contract phraseology. Thus, if these principles are the outcome of an agreement, citizens have a knowledge of the principles that others follow. . . .

I have said that the original position is the appropriate initial status quo which insures that the fundamental agreements reached in it are fair. This fact yields the name "justice as fairness." It is clear, then, that I want to say that one conception of justice is more reasonable than another, or justifiable with respect to it, if rational persons in the initial situation would choose its principles over those of the other for the role of justice. Conceptions of justice are to be ranked by their acceptability to persons so circumstanced. Understood in this way the question of justification is settled by working out a problem of deliberation: we have to ascertain which principles it would be rational to adopt given the contractual situation. This connects the theory of justice with the theory of rational choice. . . .

One should not be misled . . . by the somewhat unusual conditions which characterize the original position. The idea here is simply to make vivid to ourselves the restrictions that it seems reasonable to impose on arguments for principles of justice, and therefore on these principles themselves. Thus it seems reasonable and generally acceptable that no one should be advantaged or disadvantaged by natural fortune or social circumstances in the choice of principles. It also seems widely agreed that it should be impossible to tailor principles to the circumstances of one's own case. We should insure further that particular inclinations and aspirations, and persons' conceptions of their good do not affect the principles adopted. The aim is to rule out those principles that it would be rational to propose for acceptance, however little the chance of success, only if one knew certain things that are irrelevant from the standpoint of justice. For example, if a man knew that he was wealthy, he might find it rational to advance the principle that various taxes for welfare measures be counted unjust; if he knew that he was poor, he would most likely propose the contrary principle. To represent the desired restrictions one imagines a situation in which everyone is deprived of this sort of information. One excludes the knowledge of those contingencies which sets men at odds and allows them to be guided by their prejudices. In this manner the veil of ignorance is arrived at in a natural way. This concept should cause no difficulty if we keep in mind the constraints on arguments that it is meant to express. At any time we can enter the original position, so to speak, simply by following a certain procedure, namely, by arguing for principles of justice in accordance with these restrictions.

It seems reasonable to suppose that the parties in the original position are equal. That is, all have the same rights in the procedure for choosing principles; each can make proposals, submit reasons for their acceptance, and so on. Obviously the purpose of these conditions is to represent equality between human beings as moral persons, as creatures having a conception of their good and capable of a sense of justice. The basis of equality is taken to be similarity in these two respects. Systems of ends are not ranked in value; and each man is presumed to have the requisite ability to understand and to act upon whatever principles are adopted. Together with the veil of ignorance, these conditions define the principles of justice as those which rational persons concerned to advance their interests would consent to as equals when none are known to be advantaged or disadvantaged by social and natural contingencies.

There is, however, another side to justifying a particular description of the original position. This is to see if the principles which would be chosen match our considered convictions of justice or extend them in an acceptable way. We can note whether applying these principles would lead us to make the same judgments about the basic structure of society which we now make intuitively and in which we have the greatest confidence; or whether, in cases where our present judgments are in doubt and given with hesitation, these principles offer a resolution which we can affirm on reflection. There are questions which we feel sure must be answered in a certain way. For example, we are confident that religious intolerance and racial discrimination are unjust. We think that we have examined these things with care and have reached what we believe is an impartial judgment not likely to be distorted by an excessive attention to our own interests. These convictions are provisional fixed points which we presume any conception of justice must fit. But we have much less assurance as to what is the correct distribution of wealth and authority. Here we may be looking for a way to remove our doubts. We can check an interpretation of the initial situation, then, by the capacity of its principles to accommodate our firmest convictions and to provide guidance where guidance is needed. . . .

I shall now state in a provisional form the two principles of justice that I believe would be chosen in the original position. . . .

The first statement of the two principles reads as follows.

First: each person is to have an equal right to the most extensive basic liberty compatible with a similar liberty for others.

Second: social and economic inequalities are to be arranged so that they are both (a) reasonably expected to be to everyone's advantage, and (b) attached to positions and offices open to all. . . .

By way of general comment, these principles primarily apply, as I have said, to the basic structure of society. They are to govern the assignment of rights and duties and to regulate the distribution of social and economic advantages.

As their formulation suggests, these principles presuppose that the social structure can be divided into two more or less distinct parts, the first principle applying to the one, the second to the other. They distinguish between those aspects of the social system that define and secure the equal liberties of citizenship and those that specify and establish social and economic inequalities. The basic liberties of citizens are, roughly speaking, political liberty (the right to vote and to be eligible for public office) together with freedom of speech and assembly; liberty of conscience and freedom of thought; freedom of the person along with the right to hold (personal) property; and freedom from arbitrary arrest and seizure as defined by the concept of the rule of law. These liberties are all required to be equal by the first principle, since citizens of a just society are to have the same basic rights.

The second principle applies, in the first approximation, to the distribution of income and wealth and to the design of organizations that make use of differences in authority and responsibility, or chains of command. While the distribution of wealth and income need not be equal, it must be to everyone's advantage, and at the same time, positions of authority and offices of command must be accessible to all. One applies the second principle by holding positions open, and then, subject to this constraint, arranges social and economic inequalities so that everyone benefits.

These principles are to be arranged in a serial order with the first principle prior to the second. This ordering means that a departure from the institutions of equal liberty required by the first principle cannot be justified by, or compensated for, by greater social and economic advantages. The distribution of wealth and income, and the hierarchies of authority, must be consistent with both the liberties of equal citizenship and equality of opportunity.

Suppose that the basic structure of society distributes certain primary goods, that is, things that every rational man is presumed to want. These goods normally have a use whatever a person's rational plan of life. For simplicity, assume that the chief primary goods at the disposition of society are rights and liberties, powers and opportunities, income and wealth. . . . These are the social primary goods. Other primary goods such as health and vigor, intelligence and imagination, are natural goods; although their possession is influenced by the basic structure, they are not so directly under its control. Imagine, then a hypothetical initial arrangement in which all the social primary goods are equally distributed: everyone has similar rights and duties, and income and wealth are evenly shared. This state of affairs provides a benchmark for judging improvements. If certain inequalities of wealth and organizational powers would make everyone better off than in this hypothetical starting situation, then they accord with the general conception.

Now it is possible, at least theoretically, that by giving up some of their fundamental liberties men are sufficiently compensated by the resulting social and economic gains. The general conception of justice imposes no restrictions on what sort of inequalities are permissible; it only requires that everyone's position be improved. We need not suppose anything so drastic as consenting to a condition of slavery. Imagine instead that men forego certain political rights when the economic returns are significant and their capacity to influence the course of policy by the exercise of these rights would be marginal in any case. It is this kind of exchange which the two principles as stated rule out; being arranged in serial order they do not permit exchanges between basic liberties and economic and social gains. The serial ordering of principles expresses an underlying preference among primary social goods. When this preference is rational so likewise is the choice of these principles in this order. . . .

The fact that the two principles apply to institutions has certain consequences. Several points illustrate this. First of all, the rights and liberties referred to by these principles are those which are defined by the public rules of the basic structure. Whether men are free is determined by the rights and duties established by the major institutions of society. Liberty is a certain pattern of social forms. The first principle simply requires that certain sorts of rules, those defining basic liberties, apply to everyone equally and that they allow the most extensive liberty compatible with a like liberty for all. The only reason for circumscribing the rights defining liberty and making men's freedom less extensive than it might otherwise be is that these equal rights as institutionally defined would interfere with one another. . . .

Now the second principle insists that each person benefit from permissible inequalities in the basic structure. This means that it must be reasonable for each relevant representative man defined by this structure, when he views it as a going concern, to prefer his prospects with the inequality to his prospects without it. One is not allowed to justify differences in income or organizational powers on the ground that the disadvantages of those in one position are outweighed by the greater advantages of those in another. Much less can infringements of liberty be counterbalanced in this way. Applied to the basic structure, the principle of utility would have us maximize the sum of expectations of representative men (weighted by the number of persons they represent, on the classical view); and this would permit us to compensate for the losses of some by the gains of others. Instead, the two principles require that everyone benefit from economic and social inequalities. It is obvious, however, that there are indefinitely many ways in which all may be advantaged when the initial arrangement of equality is taken as a benchmark. How then are we to choose among these possibilities? The principles must be specified so that they yield a determinate conclusion. I now turn to this problem. . . .

In a basic structure with n relevant representatives, first maximize the welfare of the worst-off representative man; second, for equal welfare of the worst-off representative, maximize the welfare of the second worst-off representative man, and so on until the last case which is, for equal welfare of all the preceding $n-1$ representatives, maximize the welfare of the best-off representative man. We may think of this as the lexical difference principle. However, I shall always use the difference principle in the simpler form. And therefore. . . .

> the second principle is to read as follows. Social and economic inequalities are to be arranged so that they are both (a) to the greatest benefit of the least advantaged and (b) attached to offices and positions open to all under conditions of fair equality of opportunity. . . .

The idea of the original position is to set up a fair procedure so that any principles agreed to will be just. The aim is to use the notion of pure procedural justice as a basis of theory. Somehow we must nullify the effects of specific contingencies which put men at odds and tempt them to exploit social and natural circumstances to their own advantage. Now in order to do this I assume that the parties are situated behind a veil of ignorance. They do not know how the various alternatives will affect their own particular case and they are obliged to evaluate principles solely on the basis of general considerations.

It is assumed, then, that the parties do not know certain kinds of particular facts. First of all, no one knows his place in society, his class position or social status; nor does he know his fortune in the distribution of natural assets and abilities, his intelligence and strength, and the like. Nor, again, does anyone know his conception of the good, the particulars of his rational plan of life, or even the special features of his psychology such as his aversion to risk or liability to optimism or pessimism. More than this, I assume that the parties do not know the particular circumstances of their own society. That is, they do not know its economic or political situation, or the level of civilization and culture it has been able to achieve. The persons in the original position have no information as to which generation they belong. . . . In order to carry through the idea of the original position, the parties must not know the contingencies that set them in opposition. They must choose principles the consequences of which they are prepared to live with whatever generation they turn out to belong to.

As far as possible, then, the only particular facts which the parties know is that their society is subject to the circumstances of justice and whatever this implies. It is taken for granted, however, that they know the general facts about human society. They understand political affairs and the principles of economic theory; they know the basis of social organization and the laws of human psychology. Indeed, the parties are presumed to know whatever general facts affect the choice of the principles of justice. There are no limitations on general information, that is, on general laws and theories, since conceptions of justice must be adjusted to the characteristics of the systems of social cooperation which they are to regulate, and there is no reason to rule out these facts. . . .

The original position is not to be thought of as a general assembly which includes at one moment everyone who will live at some time; or, much less, as an assembly of everyone who could live at some time. It is not a gathering of all actual or possible persons. To conceive of the original position in either of these ways is to stretch fantasy too far; the conception would cease to be a natural guide to intuition. In any case, it is important that the original position be interpreted so that one can at any time adopt its perspective. It must make no difference when one takes up its viewpoint, or who does so; the restrictions must be such that the same principles are always chosen. The veil of ignorance is a key condition in meeting this requirement. It insures not only that the information available is relevant, but that it is at all times the same. . . .

Thus there follows the very important consequence that the parties have no basis for bargaining in the usual sense. No one knows his situation in society nor his natural assets, and therefore no one is in a position to tailor principles to his advantage. We might imagine that one of the contractees threatens to hold out unless the others agree to principles favorable to him. But how does one know which principles are especially in his interests? . . .

I have assumed throughout that the persons in the original position are rational. In choosing between principles each tries as best he can to advance his interests. But I have also assumed that the parties do not know their conception of the good. This means that while they know that they have some rational plan of life, they do not know the details of this plan, the particular ends and interest which it is calculated to promote. How, then, can they decide which conceptions of justice are most to their advantage? Or must we suppose that they are reduced to mere guessing? To meet this difficulty, I postulate that . . . they assume that they would prefer more primary social goods rather than less. Of course, it may turn out, once the veil of ignorance is removed, that some of them for religious or other reasons may not, in fact, want more of these goods.

But from the standpoint of the original position, it is rational for the parties to suppose that they do want a larger share, since in any case they are not compelled to accept more if they do not wish to, nor does a person suffer from a greater liberty. Thus even though the parties are deprived of information about their particular ends, they have enough knowledge to rank the alternatives. They know that in general they must try to protect their liberties, widen their opportunities, and enlarge their means for promoting their aims whatever these are. . . .

The assumption of mutually disinterested rationality, then, comes to this: the persons in the original position try to acknowledge principles which advance their system of ends as far as possible. They do this by attempting to win for themselves the highest index of primary social goods, since this enables them to promote their conception of the good most effectively whatever it turns out to be. The parties do not seek to confer benefits or to impose injuries on one another; they are not moved by affection or rancor. Nor do they try to gain relative to each other; they are not envious or vain. . . .

It seems clear . . . that the two principles are at least a plausible conception of justice. The question, though, is how one is to argue for them more systematically. Now there are several things to do. One can work out their consequences for institutions and note their implications for fundamental social policy. In this way they are tested by a comparison with our considered judgments of justice. . . . But one can also try to find arguments in their favor that are decisive from the standpoint of the original position. In order to see how this might be done, it is useful as a heuristic device to think of the two principles and the maximin rule for choice under uncertainty. This is evident from the fact that the two principles are those a person would choose for the design of a society in which his enemy is to assign him his place. The maximin rule tells us to rank alternatives by their worst possible outcomes: we are to adopt the alternative the worst outcome of which is superior to the worst outcomes of the others. . . . The term "maximin" means the *maximum minimorum;* and the rule directs our attention to the worst that can happen under any proposed course of action, and to decide in the light of that. . . .

The veil of ignorance excludes all but the vaguest knowledge of likelihoods. The parties have no basis for determining the probable nature of their society, or their place in it. Thus they have strong reasons for being wary of probability calculations if any other course is open to them. They must also take into account the fact that their choice of principles should seem reasonable to others, in particular their descendants, whose rights will be deeply affected by it. . . .

In this section my aim is to use the conditions of publicity and finality to give some of the main arguments for the two principles of justice. I shall rely upon the fact that for an agreement to be valid, the parties must be able to honor it under all relevant and foreseeable circumstances. There must be a rational assurance that one can carry through. The arguments I shall adduce fit under the heuristic schema suggested by the reasons for following the maximin rule. That is, they help to show that the two principles are an adequate minimum conception of justice in a situation of great uncertainty. Any further advantages that might be won by the principle of utility, or whatever, are highly problematical, whereas the hardships if things turn out badly are intolerable. It is at this point that the concept of a contract has a definite role: it suggests the condition of publicity and sets limits upon what can be agreed to. Thus justice as fairness uses the concept of contract to a greater extent than the discussion so far might suggest.

The first confirming ground for the two principles can be explained in terms of what I earlier referred to as the strains of commitment. I said . . . that the parties have a capacity for justice in the sense that they can be assured that their undertaking is not in vain. Assuming that they have taken everything into account, including the general facts of moral psychology, they can rely on one another to adhere to the principles adopted. Thus they consider the strains of commitment. They cannot enter into agreements that may have consequences they cannot accept. They will avoid those that they can adhere to only with great difficulty. Since the original agreement is final and made in perpetuity, there is no second chance. In view of the serious nature of the possible consequences, the question of the burden of commitment is especially acute. A person is choosing once and for all the standards which are to govern his life prospects. Moreover, when we enter an agreement we must be able to honor it even should the worst possibilities prove to be the case. Otherwise we have not acted in good faith. Thus the parties must weigh with care whether they will be able to stick by their commitment in all circumstances. Of course, in answering this question they have only a general knowledge of human psychology to go on. But this information is enough to tell which conception of justice involves the greater stress.

In this respect the two principles of justice have a definite advantage. Not only do the parties protect their basic rights but they insure themselves against the worst eventualities. They run no chance of having to acquiesce in a loss of freedom over the course of their life for the sake of a greater good enjoyed by others, an undertaking that in actual circumstances they might not be able to keep. . . . The principle of utility seems to require a greater identification with the interests of others than the two principles of justice. Thus the latter will be a more stable conception to the extent that this identification is difficult to achieve. When the two principles are satisfied, each person's liberties are secured and there is a sense defined by the difference principle in which everyone is benefited by social cooperation. Therefore we can explain the acceptance of the social system and the principles it satisfies by the psychological law that persons tend to love, cherish, and support whatever affirms their own good. Since everyone's good is affirmed, all acquire inclinations to uphold the scheme.

When the principle of utility is satisfied, however, there is no such assurance that everyone benefits. Allegiance to the social system may demand that some should forgo advantages for the sake of the greater good of the whole. Thus the scheme will not be stable unless those who must make sacrifices strongly identify with interests broader than their own. . . .

A desirable feature of a conception of justice is that it should publicly express men's respect for one another. In this way they insure a sense of their own value. Now the two principles

achieve this end. For when society follows these principles, everyone's good is included in a scheme of mutual benefit and this public affirmation in institutions of each man's endeavors supports men's self-esteem. The establishment of equal liberty and the operation of the difference principle are bound to have this effect. The two principles are equivalent, as I have remarked, to an undertaking to regard the distribution of natural abilities as a collective asset so that the more fortunate are to benefit only in ways that help those who have lost out. . . .

It is evident that some sort of framework is needed to simplify the application of the two principles of justice. For consider three kinds of judgments that a citizen has to make. First of all, he must judge the justice of legislation and social policies. But he also knows that his opinions will not always coincide with those of others, since men's judgments and beliefs are likely to differ especially when their interests are engaged. Therefore secondly, a citizen must decide which constitutional arrangements are just for reconciling conflicting opinions of justice. We may think of the political process as a machine which makes social decisions when the views of representatives and their constituents are fed into it. A citizen will regard some ways of designing this machine as more just than others. So a complete conception of justice is not only able to assess laws and policies but it can also rank procedures for selecting which political opinion is to be enacted into law. There is still a third problem. The citizen accepts a certain constitution as just, and he thinks that certain traditional procedures are appropriate, for example, the procedure of majority rule duly circumscribed. Yet since the political process is at best one of imperfect procedural justice, he must ascertain when the enactments of the majority are to be complied with and when they can be rejected as no longer binding. In short, he must be able to determine the grounds and limits of political duty and obligation. Thus a theory of justice has to deal with at least three types of questions, and this indicates that it may be useful to think of the principles as applied in a several-stage sequence. . . .

Thus I suppose that after the parties have adopted the principles of justice in the original position, they move to a constitutional convention. Here they are to decide upon the justice of political forms and choose a constitution; they are delegates, so to speak, to such a convention. Subject to the constraints of the principles of justice already chosen, they are to design a system for the constitutional powers of government and the basic rights of citizens. It is at this stage that they weigh the justice of procedures for coping with diverse political views. Since the appropriate conception of justice has been agreed upon, the veil of ignorance is partially lifted. The persons in the convention have, of course, no information about particular individuals; they do not know their own social position, their place in the distribution of natural attributes, or their conception of the good. But in addition to an understanding of the principles of social theory, they now know the relevant general facts about their society, that is, its natural circumstances and resources, its level of economic advance and political culture, and so on. They are no longer limited to the information implicit in the circumstances of justice. Given their theoretical knowledge and the appropriate general facts about their society, they are to choose the most effective just constitution, the constitution that satisfies the principles of justice and is best calculated to lead to just and effective legislation. . . .

The liberties of equal citizenship must be incorporated into and protected by the constitution. These liberties include those of liberty of conscience and freedom of thought, liberty of the person, and equal political rights. The political system, which I assume to be some form of constitutional democracy, would not be a just procedure if it did not embody these liberties.

Clearly any feasible political procedure may yield an unjust outcome. In fact, there is no scheme of procedural political rules which guarantees that unjust legislation will not be enacted. In the case of a constitutional regime, or indeed of any political form, the ideal of perfect procedural justice cannot be realized. The best attainable scheme is one of imperfect procedural justice. Nevertheless some schemes have a greater tendency than others to result in unjust laws. . . .

Now the question whether legislation is just or unjust, especially in connection with economic and social policies, is commonly subject to reasonable differences of opinion. In these cases judgment frequently depends upon speculative political and economic doctrines and upon social theory generally. Often the best that we can say of a law or policy is that it is at least not clearly unjust. The application of the difference principle in a precise way normally requires more information than we can expect to have and, in any case, more than the application of the first principle. It is often perfectly plain and evident when the equal liberties are violated. These violations are not only unjust but can be clearly seen to be unjust: the injustice is manifest in the public structure of institutions. But this state of affairs is comparatively rare with social and economic policies regulated by the difference principle.

I imagine then a division of labor between stages in which each deals with different questions of social justice. This division roughly corresponds to the two parts of the basic structure. The first principle of equal liberty is the primary standard for the constitutional convention. Its main requirements are that the fundamental liberties of the person and liberty of conscience and freedom of thought be protected and that the political process as a whole be a just procedure. Thus the constitution establishes a secure common status of equal citizenship and realizes political justice. The second principle comes into play at the stage of the legislature. It dictates that social and economic policies be aimed at maximizing the long-term expectations of the least advantaged under conditions of fair equality of opportunity, subject to the equal liberties being maintained. At this point the full range of general economic and social facts is brought to bear. The second part of the basic structure contains the distinctions and hierarchies of political, economic, and social forms which are necessary for efficient and mutually beneficial social cooperation. Thus the priority of the first principle of justice to the second is reflected in the priority of the constitutional convention to the legislative stage.

The last stage is that of the application of rules to particular cases by judges and administrators, and the following of rules by citizens generally. At this stage everyone has complete access to all the facts. No limits on knowledge remain since the full system of rules has now been adopted and applies to persons in virtue of their characteristics and circumstances. . . .

The availability of knowledge in the four-stage sequence is roughly as follows. Let us distinguish between three kinds of facts: the first principles of social theory (and other theories when relevant) and their consequences; general facts about society, such as its size and level of economic advance, its institutional structure and natural environment, and so on; and finally, particular facts about individuals such as their social position, natural attributes, and peculiar interests. In the original position the only particular facts known to the parties are those that can be inferred from the circumstances of justice. While they know the first principles of social theory, the course of history is closed to them; they have no information about how often society has taken this or that form, or which kinds of societies presently exist. In the next stages, however, the general facts about their society are made available to them but not the particularities of their own condition. Limitations on knowledge can be relaxed since the principles of justice are already chosen. The flow of information is

determined at each stage by what is required in order to apply these principles intelligently to the kind of question of justice at hand, while at the same time any knowledge that is likely to give rise to bias and distortion and to set men against one another is ruled out. The notion of the rational and impartial application of principles defines the kind of knowledge that is admissible. At the last stage, clearly, there are no reasons for the veil of ignorance in any form, and all restrictions are lifted.

It is essential to keep in mind that the four-stage sequence is a device for applying the principles of justice. This scheme is part of the theory of justice as fairness and not an account of how constitutional conventions and legislatures actually proceed. It sets out a series of points of view from which the different problems of justice are to be settled, each point of view inheriting the constraints adopted at the preceding stages. Thus a just constitution is one that rational delegates subject to the restrictions of the second stage would adopt for their society. And similarly just laws and policies are those that would be enacted at the legislative stage. Of course, this test is often indeterminate; it is not always clear which of several constitutions, or economic and social arrangements, would be chosen. But when this is so, justice is to that extent likewise indeterminate. Institutions within the permitted range are equally just, meaning that they could be chosen; they are compatible with all the constraints of the theory. Thus on many questions of social and economic policy we must fall back upon a notion of quasi-pure procedural justice: laws and policies are just provided that they lie within the allowed range, and the legislature, in ways authorized by a just constitution, has in fact enacted them. This indeterminacy in the theory of justice is not in itself a defect. It is what we should expect. Justice as fairness will prove a worthwhile theory if it defines the range of justice more in accordance with our considered judgments than do existing theories, and if it singles out with greater sharpness the graver wrongs a society should avoid. . . .

Political justice has two aspects arising from the fact that a just constitution is a case of imperfect procedural justice. First, the constitution is to be a just procedure satisfying the requirements of equal liberty; and second, it is to be framed so that of all the feasible just arrangements, it is the one more likely than any other to result in a just and effective system of legislation. The justice of the constitution is to be assessed under both headings in the light of what circumstances permit, these assessments being made from the standpoint of the constitutional convention.

The principle of equal liberty, when applied to the political procedure defined by the constitution, I shall refer to as the principle of (equal) participation. It requires that all citizens are to have an equal right to take part in, and to determine the outcome of, the constitutional process that establishes the laws with which they are to comply. Justice as fairness begins with the idea that where common principles are necessary and to everyone's advantage, they are to be worked out from the viewpoint of a suitably defined initial situation of equality in which each person is fairly represented. The principle of participation transfers this notion from the original position to the constitution as the highest-order system of social rules for making rules. If the state is to exercise a final and coercive authority over a certain territory, and if it is in this way to affect permanently men's prospects in life, then the constitutional process should preserve the equal representation of the original position to the degree that this is practicable. . . .

All sane adults, with certain generally recognized exceptions, have the right to take part in political affairs, and the precept one elector one vote is honored as far as possible. Elections are fair and free, and regularly held. Sporadic and unpredictable tests of public sentiment by plebiscite or other means, or at such times as may suit the convenience of those in office, do not suffice for a representative regime. There are firm constitutional protections for certain liberties, particularly freedom of speech and assembly, and liberty to form political associations. The principle of loyal opposition is recognized, the clash of political beliefs, and of the interests and attitudes that are likely to influence them, are accepted as a normal condition of human life. . . .

The principle of participation also holds that all citizens are to have an equal access, at least in the formal sense, to public office. Each is eligible to join political parties, to run for elective positions, and to hold places of authority. To be sure, there may be qualifications of age, residency, and so on. But these are to be reasonably related to the tasks of office; presumably these restrictions are in the common interest and do not discriminate unfairly among persons or groups in the sense that they fall evenly on everyone in the normal course of life.

The second point concerning equal political liberty is its extent. How broadly are these liberties to be defined? Offhand it is not clear what extent means here. Each of the political liberties can be more or less widely defined. Somewhat arbitrarily, but nevertheless in accordance with tradition, I shall assume that the main variation in the extent of equal political liberty lies in the degree to which the constitution is majoritarian. The definition of the other liberties I take to be more or less fixed. Thus the most extensive political liberty is established by a constitution that uses the procedure of so-called bare majority rule (the procedure in which a minority can neither override nor check a majority) for all significant political decisions unimpeded by any constitutional constraints. Whenever the constitution limits the scope and authority of majorities, either by requiring a greater plurality for certain types of measures, or by a bill of rights restricting the powers of the legislature, and the like, equal political liberty is less extensive. . . .

Turning now to the worth of political liberty, the constitution must take steps to enhance the value of the equal rights of participation for all members of society. It must underwrite a fair opportunity to take part in and to influence the political process. . . . Ideally, those similarly endowed and motivated should have roughly the same chance of attaining positions of political authority irrespective of their economic and social class. But how is this fair value of these liberties to be secured?

Compensating steps must . . . be taken to preserve the fair value for all of the equal political liberties. A variety of devices can be used. For example, in a society allowing private ownership of the means of production, property and wealth must be kept widely distributed and government monies provided on a regular basis to encourage free public discussion. In addition, political parties are to be made independent from private economic interests by allotting them sufficient tax revenues to play their part in the constitutional scheme. . . .

What is necessary is that political parties be autonomous with respect to private demands, that is, demands not expressed in the public forum and argued for openly by reference to a conception of the public good. If society does not bear the costs of organization, and party funds need to be solicited from the more advantaged social and economic interests, the pleadings of these groups are bound to receive excessive attention. And this is all the more likely when the less favored members of society, having been effectively prevented by their lack of means from exercising their fair degree of influence, withdraw into apathy and resentment.

Historically one of the main defects of constitutional government has bean the failure to insure the fair value of political liberty. The necessary corrective steps have not been taken, indeed, they never seem to have been seriously entertained. Disparities in the distribution of property and wealth that far exceed what is compatible with political equality have generally been tolerated by the legal system. Public resources have not been devoted to maintaining the institutions required for the fair value of political liberty. Essentially the fault lies in the fact that the democratic political process is at best regulated rivalry; it does not even in theory have the desirable properties that price theory ascribes to truly competitive markets. Moreover, the effects of injustices in the political system are much more grave and long lasting than market imperfections. Political power rapidly accumulates and becomes unequal; and making use of the coercive apparatus of the state and its law, those who gain the advantage can often assure themselves of a favored position. Thus inequities in the economic and social system may soon undermine whatever political equality might have existed under fortunate historical conditions. Universal suffrage is an insufficient counterpoise; for when parties and elections are financed not by public funds but by private contributions, the political forum is so constrained by the wishes of the dominant interests that the basic measures needed to establish just constitutional rule are seldom properly presented. . . .

An economic system regulates what things are produced and by what means, who receives them and in return for which contributions, and how large a fraction of social resources is devoted to saving and to the provision of public goods. Ideally all of these matters should be arranged in ways that satisfy the two principles of justice. But we have to ask whether this is possible and what in particular these principles require. . . .

A . . . feature of the public sector is the proportion of total social resources devoted to public goods. . . . A public good has two characteristic features, indivisibility and publicness. That is, there are many individuals, a public so to speak, who want more or less of this good, but if they are to enjoy it at all must each enjoy the same amount. The quantity produced cannot be divided up as private goods can and purchased by individuals according to their preferences for more and less. . . .

Where the public is large and includes many individuals, there is a temptation for each person to try to avoid doing his share. This is because whatever one man does his action will not significantly affect the amount produced. He regards the collective action of others as already given one way or the other. If the public good is produced his enjoyment of it is not decreased by his not making a contribution. If it is not produced his action would not have changed the situation anyway. A citizen receives the same protection from foreign invasion regardless of whether he has paid his taxes. Therefore in the polar case trade and voluntary agreements cannot be expected to develop.

It follows that arranging for and financing public goods must be taken over by the state and some binding rule requiring payment must be enforced. Even if all citizens were willing to pay their share, they would presumably do so only when they are assured that others will pay theirs as well. Thus once citizens have agreed to act collectively and not as isolated individuals taking the actions of the others as given, there is still the task of tying down the agreement. The sense of justice leads us to promote just schemes and to do our share in them when we believe that others, or sufficiently many of them, will do theirs. But in normal circumstances a reasonable assurance in this regard can only be given if there is a binding rule effectively enforced. Assuming that the public good is to everyone's advantage, and one that all would agree to arrange for, the use of coercion is perfectly rational from each man's point of view. Many of the traditional activities of government, insofar as they can be justified, can be accounted for in this way.

I should like to conclude with a few comments about the extent to which economic arrangements may rely upon a system of markets in which prices are freely determined by supply and demand. Several cases need to be distinguished. All regimes will normally use the market to ration out the consumption

goods actually produced. Any other procedure is administratively cumbersome, and rationing and other devices will be resorted to only in special cases. But in a free market system the output of commodities is also guided as to kind and quantity by the preferences of households as shown by their purchases on the market. Goods fetching a greater than normal profit will be produced in larger amounts until the excess is reduced. In a socialist regime planners' preferences or collective decisions often have a larger part in determining the direction of production. Both private-property and socialist systems normally allow for the free choice of occupation and of one's place of work. It is only under command systems of either kind that this freedom is overtly interfered with.

Finally, a basic feature is the extent to which the market is used to decide the rate of saving and the direction of investment, as well as the fraction of national wealth devoted to conservation and to the elimination of irremediable injuries to the welfare of future generations. Here there are a number of possibilities. A collective decision may determine the rate of saving while the direction of investment is left largely to individual firms competing for funds. In both a private-property as well as in a socialist society great concern may be expressed for preventing irreversible damages and for husbanding natural resources and preserving the environment. But again either one may do rather badly.

It is evident, then, that there is no essential tie between the use of free markets and private ownership of the instruments of production. The idea that competitive prices under normal conditions are just or fair goes back at least to medieval times. While the notion that a market economy is in some sense the best scheme has been most carefully investigated by so-called bourgeois economists, this connection is a historical contingency in that, theoretically at least, a socialist regime can avail itself of the advantages of this system. One of these advantages is efficiency. Under certain conditions competitive prices select the goods to be produced and allocate resources to their production in such a manner that there is no way to improve upon either the choice of productive methods by firms, or the distribution of goods that arises from the purchases of households. There exists no rearrangement of the resulting economic configuration that makes one household better off (in view of its preferences) without making another worse off. No further mutually advantageous trades are possible; nor are there any feasible productive processes that will yield more of some desired commodity without requiring a cutback in another. For if this were not so, the situation of some individuals could be made more advantageous without a loss for anyone else. The theory of general equilibrium explains how, given the appropriate conditions, the information supplied by prices leads economic agents to act in ways that sum up to achieve this outcome. Perfect competition is a perfect procedure with respect to efficiency. Of course, the requisite conditions are highly special ones and they are seldom if ever fully satisfied in the real world. Moreover, market failures and imperfections are often serious, and compensating adjustments must be made by the allocation branch. . . . Monopolistic restrictions, lack of information, external economies and diseconomies, and the like must be recognized and corrected. And the market fails altogether in the case of public goods. . . .

A further and more significant advantage of a market system is that, given the requisite background institutions, it is consistent with equal liberties and fair equality of opportunity. Citizens have a free choice of careers and occupations. There is no reason at all for the forced and central direction of labor. Indeed, in the absence of some differences in earnings as these arise in a competitive scheme, it is hard to see how, under ordinary circumstances anyway, certain aspects of a command society inconsistent with liberty can be avoided. Moreover, a system of markets decentralizes the exercise of economic power. Whatever the internal nature of firms, whether they are privately or state owned, or whether they are run by entrepreneurs or by managers elected by workers, they take the prices of outputs and inputs as given and draw up their plans accordingly. When markets are truly competitive, firms do not engage in price wars or other contests for market power. In conformity with political decisions reached democratically, the government regulates the economic climate by adjusting certain elements under its control, such as the overall amount of investment, the rate of interest, and the quantity of money, and so on. There is no necessity for comprehensive direct planning. Individual households and firms are free to make their decisions independently, subject to the general conditions of the economy. . . .

The main problem of distributive justice is the choice of a social system. The principles of justice apply to the basic structure and regulate how its major institutions are combined into one scheme. Now, as we have seen, the idea of justice as fairness is to use the notion of pure procedural justice to handle the contingencies of particular situations. The social system is to be designed so that the resulting distribution is just however things turn out. To achieve this end it is necessary to set the social and economic process within the surroundings of suitable political and legal institutions. Without an appropriate scheme of these background institutions the outcome of the distributive process will not be just.

I shall give a brief description of these supporting institutions as they might exist in a properly organized democratic state that allows private ownership of capital and natural resources. . . .

First of all, I assume that the basic structure is regulated by a just constitution that secures the liberties of equal citizenship (as described in the preceding chapter). Liberty of conscience and freedom of thought are taken for granted, and the fair value of political liberty is maintained. The political process is conducted, as far as circumstances permit, as a just procedure for choosing between governments and for enacting just legislation. I assume also that there is fair (as opposed to formal) equality of opportunity. This means that in addition to maintaining the usual kinds of social overhead capital, the government tries to insure equal chances of education and culture for persons similarly endowed and motivated either by subsidizing private schools or by establishing a public school system. It also enforces and underwrites equality of opportunity in economic activities and in the free choice of occupation. This is achieved by policing the conduct of firms and private associations and by preventing the establishment of monopolistic restrictions and barriers to the more desirable positions. Finally, the government guarantees a social minimum either by family allowances and special payments for sickness and employment, or more systematically by such devices as a graded income supplement (a so-called negative income tax).

In establishing these background institutions the government may be thought of as divided into four branches. Each branch consists of various agencies, or activities thereof, charged with preserving certain social and economic conditions. These divisions do not overlap with the usual organization of government but are to be understood as different functions. The allocation branch, for example, is to keep the price system workably competitive and to prevent the formation of unreasonable market power. Such power does not exist as long as markets cannot be made more competitive consistent with the requirements of efficiency and the facts of geography and the preferences of households. The allocation branch is also charged with identifying and correcting, say by suitable taxes and subsidies and by changes in the definition of property rights, the more obvious departures from efficiency caused by the failure of prices to measure accurately social benefits and costs. To this end

suitable taxes and subsidies may be used, or the scope and definition of property rights may be revised. The stabilization branch, on the other hand, strives to bring about reasonably full employment in the sense that those who want work can find it and the free choice of occupation and the deployment of finance are supported by strong effective demand. These two branches together are to maintain the efficiency of the market economy generally.

The social minimum is the responsibility of the transfer branch. . . . The essential idea is that the workings of this branch take needs into account and assign them an appropriate weight with respect to other claims. A competitive price system gives no consideration to needs and therefore it cannot be the sole device of distribution. There must be a division of labor between the parts of the social system in answering to the common sense precepts of justice. Different institutions meet different claims. Competitive markets properly regulated secure free choice of occupation and lead to an efficient use of resources and allocation of commodities to households. They set a weight on the conventional precepts associated with wages and earning, whereas the transfer branch guarantees a certain level of well-being and honors the claims of need. . . .

It is clear that the justice of distributive shares depends on the background institutions and how they allocate total income, wages and other income plus transfers. There is with reason strong objection to the competitive determination of total income, since this ignores the claims of need and an appropriate standard of life. From the standpoint of the legislative stage it is rational to insure oneself and one's descendants against these contingencies of the market. Indeed, the difference principle presumably requires this. But once a suitable minimum is provided by transfers, it may be perfectly fair that the rest of total income be settled by the price system, assuming that it is moderately efficient and free from monopolistic restrictions, and unreasonable externalities have been eliminated. Moreover, this way of dealing with the claims of need would appear to be more effective than trying to regulate income by minimum wage standards, and the like. It is better to assign to each branch only such tasks as are compatible with one another. Since the market is not suited to answer the claims of need, these should be met by a separate arrangement. Whether the principles of justice are satisfied, then, turns on whether the total income of the least advantaged (wages plus transfers) is such as to maximize their long-run expectations (consistent with the constraints of equal liberty and fair equality of opportunity).

Finally, there is a distribution branch. Its task is to preserve an approximate justice in distributive shares by means of taxation and the necessary adjustments in the rights of property. Two aspects of this branch may be distinguished. First of all, it imposes a number of inheritance and gift taxes, and sets restrictions on the rights of bequest. The purpose of these levies and regulations is not to raise revenue (release resources to government) but gradually and continually to correct the distribution of wealth and to prevent concentrations of power detrimental to the fair value of political liberty and fair equality of opportunity. . . .

The unequal inheritance of wealth is no more inherently unjust than the unequal inheritance of intelligence. It is true that the former is presumably more easily subject to social control; but the essential thing is that as far as possible inequalities founded on either should satisfy the difference principle. Thus inheritance is permissible provided that the resulting inequalities are to the advantage of the least fortunate and compatible with liberty and fair equality of opportunity. As earlier defined, fair equality of opportunity means a certain set of institutions that assures similar chances of education and culture for persons similarly motivated and keeps positions and offices open to all on the basis of qualities and efforts reasonably related to the relevant duties

and tasks. It is these institutions that are put in jeopardy when inequalities of wealth exceed a certain limit; and political liberty likewise tends to lose its value, and representative government to become such in appearance only. The taxes and enactments of the distribution branch are to prevent this limit from being exceeded. Naturally, where this limit lies is a matter of political judgment guided by theory, good sense, and plain hunch, at least within a wide range. On this sort of question the theory of justice has nothing specific to say. Its aim is to formulate the principles that are to regulate the background institutions.

The second part of the distribution branch is a scheme of taxation to raise the revenues that justice requires. Social resources must be released to the government so that it can provide for the public goods and make the transfer payments necessary to satisfy the difference principle. This problem belongs to the distribution branch since the burden of taxation is to be justly shared and it aims at establishing just arrangements. Leaving aside many complications, it is worth noting that a proportional expenditure tax may be part of the best tax scheme. For one thing, it is preferable to an income tax (of any kind) at the level of common sense precepts of justice, since it imposes a levy according to how much a person takes out of the common store of goods and not according to how much he contributes (assuming here that income is fairly earned). Again, a proportional tax on total consumption (for each year say) can contain the usual exemptions for dependents, and so on; and it treats everyone in a uniform way (still assuming that income is fairly earned). It may be better, therefore, to use progressive rates only when they are necessary, and so to forestall accumulations of property and power likely to undermine the corresponding institutions. Following this rule might help to signal an important distinction in questions of policy. And if proportional taxes should also prove more efficient, say because they interfere less with incentives, this might make the case for them decisive if a feasible scheme could be worked out. . . .

The two parts of the distribution branch derive from the two principles of justice. The taxation of inheritance and income at progressive rates (when necessary), and the legal definition of property rights, are to secure the institutions of equal liberty in a property-owning democracy and the fair value of the rights they establish. Proportional expenditure (or income) taxes are to provide revenue for public goods, the transfer branch and the establishment of fair equality of opportunity in education, and the like, so as to carry out the second principle. No mention has been made at any point of the traditional criteria of taxation such as that taxes are to be levied according to benefits received or the ability to pay. . . .

So far I have assumed that the aim of the branches of government is to establish a democratic regime in which land and capital are widely though not presumably equally held. Society is not so divided that one fairly small sector controls the preponderance of productive resources. When this is achieved and distributive shares satisfy the principles of justice, many socialist criticisms of the market economy are met. But it is clear that, in theory anyway, a liberal socialist regime can also answer to the two principles of justice. We have only to suppose that the means of production are publicly owned and that firms are managed by workers' councils say, or by agents appointed by them. Collective decisions made democratically under the constitution determine the general features of the economy, such as the rate of saving and the proportion of society's production devoted to essential public goods. Given the resulting economic environment, firms regulated by market forces conduct themselves much as before. Although the background institutions will take a different form, especially in the case of the distribution branch, there is no reason in principle why just distributive shares cannot be achieved. The theory of justice does not itself favor either form of regime. As we have seen, the decision as to which system is best for a given people depends upon their circumstances, institutions, and historical traditions. . . .

Discussion Questions

1. Define and explain what Professor Rawls means by "the original position?" Why does he believe that it is the fairest and most rational way to arrive at principles of justice? Do you agree or disagree with his assessment? Explain and defend your answer.

2. What are the principles of justice at which Professor Rawls arrives? Do you agree or disagree with these principles and how Rawls arrived at them? Explain and defend your answer.

3. In the second half of his essay Professor Rawls explains how the principles of justice may help us to make decisions about public policy questions such as economic policy, taxation, free-markets, social welfare, minimum wage, etc. Present and explain at least two examples of public policies to which Professor Rawls applies the principles of justice. Explain why you agree or disagree as to whether such applications are, or can be, successful.

You can locate InfoTrac-College Education articles about this chapter by accessing the InfoTrac-College Edition website (http://www.infotrac-college.com/wadsworth/). Using the InfoTrac-College Edition subject guide, enter the search terms relevant to this chapter, and then read abstracts for relevant articles.

34 Property, Exchange, and Libertarianism

MURRAY N. ROTHBARD

Murray N. Rothbard, prior to his death in 1995, was the S. J. Hall Professor of Economics at the University of Nevada, Las Vegas. One of the intellectual founders of the contemporary libertarian movement and arguably the leading spokesperson for Austrian Economics, Professor Rothbard was the author of numerous scholarly and popular articles. Among his books are *For a New Liberty* (1973) and his two volume magnum opus, *Man, Economy, and State* (1962).

In this essay Professor Rothbard defends the political and economic philosophy of *libertarianism* (a view held by members of the Libertarian Party as well as the libertarian wing of the Republican Party in the United States), covering four issues: (1) property rights, (2) society and the individual, (3) free exchange and free contract, and (4) property rights and "human rights." In support of property rights—the right of the individual to own property—Professor Rothbard first dispenses with emotivism and utilitarianism (Chapter 4) as ways to ground these rights, but argues that "natural law" (or natural right) provides an adequate philosophical grounding. He argues that human persons have a natural right to self-ownership as well as a right to private property. In response to the claim that individuals owe something to "society," or that society is to blame for crime and other ills, Professor Rothbard argues that "society" as such does not exist as an independent "person" or "identity" and that when people blame society they are blaming everyone *but* the perpetrator, which is absurd. He goes on to argue that people have a right to freely exchange what they own and to freely contract for goods and service. Professor Rothbard concludes by arguing that, contrary to what liberals generally think, there can be no "human rights" or personal liberty without property rights.

PROPERTY RIGHTS

IF THE CENTRAL AXIOM OF the libertarian creed is nonaggression against anyone's person and property, how is this axiom arrived at? What is its groundwork or support? Here, libertarians, past and present, have differed considerably. Roughly, there are three broad types of foundation for the libertarian axiom, corresponding to three kinds of ethical philosophy: the emotivist, the utilitarian, and the natural rights viewpoint. The emotivists assert that they take liberty or nonaggression as their premise purely on subjective, emotional grounds. While their own intense emotion might seem a valid basis for their own political philosophy, this can scarcely serve to convince anyone else. By ultimately taking themselves outside the realm of rational discourse, the emotivists thereby insure the lack of general success of their own cherished doctrine.

Reprinted by permission from Murray N. Rothbard, For a New Liberty *(New York: Macmillan, 1973).*

The utilitarians declare, from their study of the consequences of liberty as opposed to alternative systems, that liberty will lead more surely to widely approved goals: harmony, peace, prosperity, etc. Now no one disputes that relative consequences should be studied in assessing the merits or demerits of respective creeds. But there are many problems in confining ourselves to a utilitarian ethic. For one thing, utilitarianism assumes that we can weight alternatives, and decide upon policies, on the basis of their good or bad *consequences*. But if it is legitimate to apply value judgments to the *consequences* of X, why is it not equally legitimate to apply such judgments to *X itself*? May there not be something about an act itself which, in its very nature, can be considered good or evil?

Another problem with the utilitarian is that he will rarely adopt a principle as an absolute and consistent yardstick to apply to the varied concrete situations of the real world. He will only use a principle, at best, as a vague guideline or aspiration, as a *tendency* which he may choose to override at any time. This was the major defect of the nineteenth-century English Radicals, who had adopted the laissez-faire view of the eighteenth-century liberals but had substituted a supposedly "scientific" utilitarianism for the supposedly "mystical" concept of natural rights as the groundwork for that philosophy. Hence the nineteenth-century laissez-faire liberals came to use laissez-faire as a vague tendency rather than as an unblemished yardstick, and therefore, increasingly and fatally compromised the libertarian creed. To say that a utilitarian cannot be "trusted" to maintain libertarian principle in every specific application may sound harsh, but it puts the case fairly. A notable contemporary example is the free market economist Professor Milton Friedman who, like his classical economics forebears, holds to freedom as against state intervention as a general tendency, but in practice allows a myriad of damaging exceptions, exceptions which serve to vitiate the principle

almost completely, notably in the fields of police and military affairs, education, taxation, welfare, "neighborhood effects," antitrust laws, and money and banking.

Let us consider a stark example: Suppose a society which fervently considers all redheads to be agents of the Devil and therefore to be executed whenever found. Let us further assume that only a small number of redheads exist in any generation—so few as to be statistically insignificant. The utilitarian-libertarian might well reason: "While the murder of isolated redheads is deplorable, the executions are small in number; the vast majority of the public, as non-redheads, achieves enormous psychic satisfaction from the public execution of redheads. The social cost is negligible, the social, psychic benefit to the rest of society is great; therefore, it is right and proper for society to execute the redheads." The natural-rights libertarian, overwhelmingly concerned as he is for the *justice* of the act, will react in horror and staunchly and unequivocally oppose the executions as totally unjustified murder and aggression upon nonaggressive persons. The *consequence* of stopping the murders—depriving the bulk of society of great psychic pleasure—would not influence such a libertarian, the "absolutist" libertarian, in the slightest. Dedicated to justice and to logical consistency, the natural-rights libertarian cheerfully admits to being "doctrinaire," to being, in short, an unabashed follower of his own doctrines.

Let us turn then to the natural-rights basis for the libertarian creed, a basis which, in one form or another, has been adopted by most of the libertarians, past and resent. "Natural rights" is the cornerstone of a political philosophy which, in turn is embedded in a greater structure of "natural law." Natural law theory rests on the insight that we live in a world of more than one—in fact, a vast number—of entities, and that each entity has distinct and specific properties, a distinct "nature," which can be investigated by man's reason, by his sense perception and mental faculties. Copper has a distinct nature and behaves in a certain way, and so does iron, salt, etc. The species man, therefore, has a specifiable nature, as does the world around him and the ways of interaction between them. To put it with undue brevity, the activity of each inorganic and organic entity is determined by its own nature and by the nature of the other entities with which it comes in contact. Specifically, while the behavior of plants and at least the lower animals is determined by their biological nature or perhaps by their "instincts," the nature of man is such that each individual person must, in order to act, choose his own ends and employ his own means in order to attain them. Possessing no automatic instincts, each man must learn about himself and the world, use his mind to select values, learn about cause and effect, and act purposively to maintain himself and advance his life. Since men can think, feel, evaluate, and act only as individuals, it becomes vitally necessary for each man's survival and prosperity that he be free to learn, choose, develop his faculties, and act upon his knowledge and values. This is the necessary path of human nature; to interfere with and cripple this process by using violence goes profoundly against what is necessary by man's nature for his life and prosperity. Violent interference with a man's learning and choices is therefore profoundly "antihuman"; it violates the natural law of man's needs.

Individualists have always been accused by their enemies of being "atomistic"—of postulating that each individual lives in a kind of vacuum, thinking and choosing without relation to anyone else in society. This, however, is an authoritarian straw man; few, if any, individualists have ever been "atomists." On the contrary, it is evident that individuals always learn from each other, cooperate and interact with each other; and that this, too, is required for man's survival. But the point is that each individual makes the final choice of which influences to adopt and which to reject, or of which

to adopt first and which afterwards. The libertarian welcomes the process of voluntary exchange and cooperation between freely acting individuals; what he abhors is the use of violence to cripple such voluntary cooperation and force someone to choose and act in ways different from what his own mind dictates.

The most viable method of elaborating the natural rights statement of the libertarian position is to divide it into parts, and to begin with the basic axiom of the "right to self-ownership." The right to self-ownership asserts the absolute right of each man, by virtue of his (or her) being a human being, to "own" his or her own body; that is, to control that body free of coercive interference. Since each individual must think, learn, value, and choose his or her ends and means in order to survive and flourish, the right to self-ownership gives man the right to perform these vital activities without being hampered and restricted by coercive molestation.

Consider, too, the consequences of denying each man the right to own his own person. There are then only two alternatives: either (1) a certain class of people, A, have the right to own another class, B; or (2) everyone has the right to own his own equal quotal share of everyone else. The first alternative implies that while Class A deserves the rights of being human, Class B is in reality subhuman and therefore deserves no such rights. But since they *are* indeed human beings, the first alternative contradicts itself in denying natural human rights to one set of humans. Moreover, as we shall see, allowing Class A to own Class B means that the former is allowed to exploit, and therefore to live parasitically, *at the expense* of the latter. But this parasitism itself violates the basic economic requirement for life: production and exchange.

The second alternative, what we might call "participatory communalism" or "communism," holds that every man should have the right to own his equal quotal share of everyone else. If there are two billion people in the world, then everyone has the right to own one two-billionth of every other person. In the first place, we can state that this ideal rests on an absurdity: proclaiming that every man is entitled to own a part of everyone else, yet is not entitled *to own himself*. Secondly, we can picture the viability of such a world: a world in which *no* man is free to take *any* action whatever without prior approval or indeed command by *everyone* else in society. It should be clear that in that sort of "communist" world, no one would be able to do anything, and the human race would quickly perish. But if a world of zero self-ownership and one hundred percent other ownership spells death for the human race, then any steps in that direction also contravene the natural law of what is best for man and his life on earth.

Finally, however, the participatory communist world *cannot* be put into practice. For it is physically impossible for everyone to keep continual tabs on everyone else, and thereby to exercise his equal quotal share of partial ownership over every other man. In practice, then, the concept of universal and equal other-ownership is utopian and impossible, and supervision and therefore control and ownership of others necessarily devolves upon a specialist group of people, who thereby become a ruling class. Hence, in practice, any attempt at communist rule will automatically become class rule, and we would be back at our first alternative.

The libertarian therefore rejects these alternatives and concludes by adopting as his primary axiom the universal right of self-ownership, a right held by everyone by virtue of being a human being. A more difficult task is to settle on a theory of property in nonhuman objects, in the things of this earth. It is comparatively easy to recognize the practice when someone is aggressing against the property right of another's person: If A assaults B, he is violating the property right of B in his own body. But with nonhuman objects the problem is more complex. If, for example, we see X seizing a watch in the possession of Y, we cannot automatically assume that X is aggressing against Y's right of property in the watch; for may not X have been the original, "true" owner of the watch who can therefore be said to be repossessing his own legitimate property? In order to decide, we need a theory of justice in property, a theory that will tell us whether X or Y or indeed someone else is the legitimate owner.

A great many libertarians, mostly those in the right wing of the libertarian spectrum, attempt to resolve the problem by asserting that whoever the existing government decrees has the property title should be considered the just owner of the property. At this point, we have not yet delved deeply into the nature of government, but the anomaly here should be glaring enough: it is surely odd to find a group eternally suspicious of virtually any and all functions of government suddenly leaving it to government to define and apply the precious concept of property, the base and groundwork of the entire social order. It is particularly the utilitarian laissez-fairists who believe it most feasible to begin the new libertarian world by confirming all existing property titles; that is, property titles and rights as decreed by the very government that is condemned as a chronic aggressor.

Let us illustrate with a hypothetical example. Suppose that libertarian agitation and pressure has escalated to such a point that the government and its various branches are ready to abdicate. But they engineer a cunning ruse. Just before the government of New York State abdicates it passes a law turning over the entire territorial area of New York to become the private property of the Rockefeller family. The Massachusetts legislature does the same for the Kennedy family. And so on for each state. The government could then abdicate and decree the abolition of taxes and coercive legislation, but the victorious libertarians would now be confronted with a dilemma. Do they recognize the new property titles as legitimately private property? The utilitarians, who have no theory of justice in property rights, would, if they were consistent with their acceptance of given property titles as decreed by government, have to accept a new social order in which 50 new satraps would be collecting taxes in the form of unilaterally imposed "rent." The point is that *only* natural-rights libertarians, only those libertarians who have a theory of justice in property titles that does not depend on government decree, could be in a position to scoff at the new rulers' claims to have private property in the territory of the country, and to rebuff these claims as invalid. As the great nineteenth-century liberal Lord Acton saw clearly, the natural law provides the only sure ground for a continuing critique of governmental laws and decrees.[1] What, specifically, the natural rights position on property titles may be is the question to which we now turn.

We have established each individual's right to self-ownership, to a property right in his own body and person. But people are not floating wraiths; they are not self-subsistent entities; they can only survive and flourish by grappling with the earth around them. They must, for example, *stand* on land areas; they must also, in order to survive and maintain themselves, transform the resources given by nature into "consumer goods," into objects more suitable for their use and consumption. Food must be grown and eaten; minerals must be mined and then transformed into capital and then useful consumer goods, etc. Man, in other words, must own not only his own person, but also material objects for his control and use. How, then, should the property titles in these objects be allocated?

Let us take, as our first example, a sculptor fashioning a work of art out of clay and other materials; and let us waive, for the moment, the question of original property rights in the clay and the sculptor's tools. The question then becomes: *who* owns the work of art as it emerges from the sculptor's fashioning? It is, in fact, the sculptor's "creation," not in the sense that he has created matter, but in the sense that he has transformed nature-given matter—the clay—into another form dictated by his own ideas and fashioned by his own hands and energy. Surely, it is a rare person who, with the case put thus, would say that the sculptor does *not* have the property right in his own product. Surely, if every man has the right to own his own body, and if he must grapple with the material objects of the world in order to survive, then the sculptor has the right to own the product he has made, by his energy and effort, a veritable *extension* of his own personality. He has placed the stamp of his person upon the raw material, by "mixing his labor" with the clay, in the phrase of the great property theorist John Locke. And the product transformed by his own energy has become the material embodiment of the sculptor's ideas and vision. John Locke put the case this way:

> . . . every man has a *property* in his own *person*. This nobody has any right to but himself. The *labour* of his body and the *work* of his hands, we may say, are properly his. Whatsoever, then, he removes out of the state that nature hath provided and left it in, he hath mixed his labour with it, and joined it to something that is his own, and thereby makes it his property. It being by him removed from the common state nature placed it in, it hath by this labour something annexed to it that excludes the common right of other men. For this labour being the unquestionable property of the labourer, no man but he can have a right to what that is once joined to . . .[2]

As in the case of the ownership of people's bodies, we again have three logical alternatives: (1) either the transformer, or "creator," has the property right in his creation; or (2) another man or set of men have the right in that creation, i.e., have the right to appropriate it by force without the sculptor's consent; or (3)—the "communal" solution—every individual in the world has an equal, quotal share in the ownership of the sculpture. Again, put baldly, there are very few who would not concede the monstrous injustice of confiscating the sculptor's property, either by one or more others, or on behalf of the world as a whole. By what right do they do so? By what right do they appropriate to themselves the product of the creator's mind and energy? In this clear-cut case, the right of the creator to own what he has mixed his person and labor with would be generally conceded. (Once again, as in the case of communal ownership of persons, the world communal solution would, in practice, be reduced to an oligarchy of a *few* other expropriating the creator's work in the *name* of "world public" ownership.)

The main point, however, is that the case of the sculptor is not qualitatively different from *all* cases of "production." The man or men who had extracted the clay from the ground and had sold it to the sculptor may not be as "creative" as the sculptor, but they too are "producers," they too have mixed their ideas and their technological know-how with the nature-given soil to emerge with a useful product. They, too, are "producers," and they too have mixed their labor with natural materials to transform those materials into more useful goods and services. These persons, too, are entitled to the ownership of their products. Where then does the process begin? Again, let us turn to Locke:

> He that is nourished by the acorns he picked up under an oak, or the apples he gathered from the trees in the wood, has certainly appropriated them to himself. Nobody can deny but the nourishment is his. I ask then, when did they begin to be his? When he digested? or when he ate? or when he boiled? or when he brought them home? or when he picked them up? and 'tis plain, if the first gathering made them not his, nothing else could. That labour put a distinction between them and common. That added something got them more than Nature, the common mother of all, had done, and so they became his private right. And will any one say he had no right to those acorns or apples he thus appropriated because he had not the consent of all mankind to make them his? Was it a robbery thus to assume to himself what

belonged to all in common? If such a consent as that was necessary, man had starved, notwithstanding the plenty God had given him. . . . Thus, the grass my horse has bit, the turfs my servant has cut, and the ore I have digged in my place, where I have a right to them in common with others, become my property without the assignation or consent of any body. The labour that was mine, removing them out of that common state they were in, hath fixed my property in them.

> By making an explicit consent of every commoner necessary to any one's appropriating to himself any part of what is given in common, children or servants could not cut the meat which their father or master had provided for them in common without assigning to every one his peculiar part. Though the water running in the fountain be every one's, yet who can doubt but that in the pitcher is his only who drew it out? His labour hath taken it out of the hands of Nature where it was common . . . and hath thereby appropriated it to himself.

> Thus the law of reason makes the deer that Indian's who killed it; 'tis allowed to be his goods who hath bestowed his labour upon it, though, before, it was the common right of every one. And amongst those who are counted the civilized part of mankind . . . this original law of nature for the beginning of property, in what was before common, still takes place, and by virtue thereof, what fish any one catches in the ocean, that great and still remaining common of mankind; or what ambergris any one takes up here is by the labour that removes it out of that common state nature left it in, made his property who takes that pains about it.[3]

If every man owns his own person and therefore his own labor, and if by extension he owns whatever property he has "created" or gathered out of the previously unused, unowned, "state of nature," then what of the last great question: the right to own or control the earth *itself*? In short, if the gatherer has the right to own the acorns or berries he picks, or the farmer the right to own his crop of wheat or peaches, *who* has the right to own the land on which these things have grown? It is at this point that Henry George and his followers, who have gone all the way so far with the libertarians, leave the track and deny the individual's right to own the piece of land itself, the ground on which these activities have taken place. The Georgists argue that, while every man should own the goods which he produces or creates, since Nature or God created the land itself, no individual has the right to assume ownership of that land. Yet, if the land is to be used at all as a resource in any sort of efficient manner, it must be owned or controlled by *someone* or some group, and we are again faced with our three alternatives: either the land belongs to the first user, the man who first brings it into production; or it begins to the world as a whole, with every individual owning a quotal part of every acre of land. George's option for the last solution hardly solves his moral problem: if the land itself should belong to God or Nature, then why is it more moral for every acre in the world to be owned by the world as a whole, than to concede individual ownership? In practice, again, it is obviously impossible for every person in the world to exercise effective ownership of his four-billionth portion (if the world population is, say, four billion) of every piece of the world's land surface. In practice, of course, a small oligarchy would do the controlling and owning, and not the world as a whole.

But apart from these difficulties in the Georgist position, the natural-rights justification for the ownership of ground land is the same as the justification for the original ownership of all other property. For, as we have seen, no producer *really* "creates" matter; he takes nature-given matter and transforms it by his labor energy in accordance with his ideas and vision. But *this* is precisely what the pioneer—the "homesteader"—does when he brings previously unused land into his own private ownership. Just as the man who makes steel out of iron ore transforms that ore out of his knowhow and with his energy, and just as the man who takes the iron out of the ground does the same, so does the homesteader who clears, fences, cultivates or builds upon the land. The homesteader, too, has transformed the character of the nature-given soil by his labor and his personality. The homesteader is just as legitimately the owner of the property as the sculptor or the manufacturer; he is just as much a "producer" as the others.

Furthermore, if the original land is nature- or God-given then so are the people's talents, health, and beauty. And just as all these attributes are given to specific individuals and not to "society," so then are land and natural resources. All of these resources are given to individuals and not to "society," which is an abstraction that does not actually exist. There is no existing entity called "society"; there are only interacting individuals. To say that "society" should own land or any other property in common, then, must mean that a group of oligarchs—in practice, government bureaucrats—should own the property, and at the expense of expropriating the creator or the homesteader who had originally brought this product into existence.

Moreover, no one can produce *anything* without the cooperation of original land, if only as standing room. No man can produce or create anything by his labor alone; he must have the cooperation of land and other natural raw materials.

Man comes into the world with just himself and the world around him—the land and natural resources given him by nature. He takes these resources and transforms them by his labor and mind and energy into goods more useful to man. Therefore, if an individual cannot own original land, neither can he in the full sense own any of the fruits of his labor. The farmer cannot own his wheat crop if he cannot own the land on which the wheat grows. Now that his labor has been inextricably mixed with the land, he cannot be deprived of one without being deprived of the other.

Moreover, if a producer is *not* entitled to the fruits of his labor, who is? It is difficult to see why a newborn Pakistani baby should have a moral claim to a quotal share of ownership of a piece of Iowa land that someone has just transformed into a wheatfield—and vice versa of course for an Iowan baby and a Pakistani farm. Land in its original state is unused and unowned. Georgists and other land communalists may claim that the whole world population *really* "owns" it, but if no one has yet used it, it is in the real sense owned and controlled by no one. The pioneer, the homesteader, the first user and transformer of this land, is the man who first brings this simple valueless thing into production and social use. It is difficult to see the morality of depriving him of ownership in favor of people who have never gotten within a thousand miles of the land, and who may not even know of the existence of the property over which they are supposed to have a claim.

The moral, natural rights issue involved here is even clearer if we consider the case of animals. Animals are "economic land," since they are original nature-given resources. Yet will anyone deny full title to a horse to the man who finds and domesticates it—is this any different from the acorns and berries that are generally conceded to the gatherer? Yet in land, too, some homesteader takes the previously "wild," undomesticated land, and "tames" it by putting it to productive use. Mixing his labor with land sites should give him just as clear a title as in the case of animals. As Locke declared, "As much land as a man tills, plants, improves, cultivates, and can use the product of, so much is his property. He by his labour does, as it were, enclose it from the common."[4]

The libertarian theory of property was eloquently summed up by two nineteenth-century laissez-faire French economists:

If man acquires rights over things, it is because he is at once active, intelligent and free; by his activity he spreads over external nature; by his intelligence he governs it, and bends it to his use; by his liberty, he establishes between himself and it the relation of cause and effect and makes it his own. . . .

Where is there, in a civilized country, a clod of earth, a leaf, which does not bear this impress of the personality of man? In the town, we are surrounded by the works of man; we walk upon a level pavement or a beaten road; it is man who made healthy the formerly muddy soil, who took from the side of a far-away hill the flint or stone which covers it. We live in houses; it is man who has dug the stone from the quarry, who has hewn it, who has planed the woods; it is the thought of man which has arranged the materials properly and made a building of what was before rock and wood. And in the country, the action of man is still everywhere present; men have cultivated the soil and generations of laborers have mellowed and enriched it; the works of man have dammed the rivers and created fertility where the waters had brought only desolation. . . . Everywhere a powerful hand is divined which has moulded matter, and an intelligent will which has adapted it . . . to the satisfaction of the wants of one same being. Nature has recognized her master, and man feels that he is at home in nature. Nature has been *appropriated* by him for his use; she has become his *own;* she is his *property.* This property is legitimate; it constitutes a right as sacred for man as is the free exercise of his faculties. It is his because it has come entirely from himself, and is in no way anything but an emanation from his being. Before him, there was scarcely anything but matter; since him, and by him, there is interchangeable wealth, that is to say, articles having acquired a value by some industry, by manufacture, by handling, by extraction, or simply by transportation. From the picture of a great master, which is perhaps of all material production that in which matter plays the smallest part, to the pail of water which the carrier draws from the river and takes to the consumer, wealth, whatever it may be, acquires its value only by communicated qualities, and these qualities are part of human activity, intelligence, strength. The producer has left a fragment of his own person in the thing which has thus become valuable, and may hence be regarded as a prolongation of the faculties of man acting upon external nature. As a flee being he belongs to himself; now the cause, that is to say, the productive force is himself; the effect, that is to say, the wealth produced, is still himself. Who shall dare contest his title of ownership so clearly marked by the seal of his personality? . . .

It is then, to the human being, the creator of all wealth, that we must come back . . . it is by labor that man impresses his personality on matter. It is labor which cultivates the earth and makes of an unoccupied waste an appropriated field; it is labor which makes of an untrodden forest a regularly ordered wood; it is labor, or rather, a series of labors often executed by a very numerous succession of workmen, which brings hemp from seed, thread from hemp, cloth from thread, clothing from cloth; which transforms the shapeless pyrite, picked up in the mine, into an elegant bronze which adorns some public place, and repeats to an entire people the thought of an artist. . . .

Property, made manifest by labor, participates in the rights of the person whose emanation it is; like him, it is inviolable so long as it does not extend so far as to come into collision with another right; like him, it is individual, because it has origin in the independence of the individual, and because, when several persons have cooperated in its formation, the latest possessor has purchased with a value, the fruit of his personal labor, the work of all the fellow-laborers who have preceded him; this is what is usually the case with manufactured articles. When property has passed, by sale or by inheritance, from one hand to another, its conditions have not changed; it is still the fruit of human liberty manifested by labor, and the holder has the rights as the producer who took possession of it by right.[5]

SOCIETY AND THE INDIVIDUAL

We have talked at length of individual rights; but what, it may be asked, of the "rights of society"? Don't they supersede the rights of the mere individual? The libertarian, however, is an individualist; he believes that one of the prime errors in social theory is to treat "society" as if it were an actual existing entity. "Society" is sometimes treated as a superior or quasi-divine figure with overriding "rights" of its own; at other times as an existing evil which can be blamed for all the ills of the world. The individualist holds that only individuals exist, think, feel, choose, and act; and that "society" is not a living entity but simply a label for a set of interacting individuals. Treating society as a thing that chooses and acts, then, serves to obscure the real forces at work. If, in a small community, ten people band together to rob and expropriate three others, then this is clearly and evidently a case of a group of individuals acting in concert against another group. In this situation, if the ten people presumed to refer to themselves as "society" acting in "its" interest, the rationale would be laughed out of court; even the ten robbers would probably be too shamefaced to use this sort of argument. But let their size increase, and this kind of obfuscation becomes rife and succeeds in duping the public.

The fallacious use of a collective noun like "nation," similar in this respect to "society," has been trenchantly pointed out by the historian Parker T. Moon:

When one uses the simple monosyllable "France" one thinks of France as a unit, an entity. When . . . we say "France sent *her* troops to conquer Tunis"—we impute not only unity but personality to the country. The very words conceal the facts and make international relations a glamorous drama in which personalized nations are the actors, and all too easily we forget the flesh-and-blood men and women who are the true actors . . . if we had no such word as "France" . . . then we should more accurately describe the Tunis expedition in some such way as this: "A few of these thirty-eight million persons sent thirty thousand others to conquer Tunis." This way of putting the fact immediately suggests a question, or rather a series of questions. Who were the "few"? Why did they send the thirty thousand to Tunis? And why did these obey? Empire-building is done not by "nations," but by men. The problem before us is to discover the men, the active, interested minorities in each nation, who are directly interested in imperialism and then to analyze the reasons why the majorities pay the expense and fight the wars necessitated by imperialist expansion.[6]

The individualist view of "society" has been summed up in the phrase: *"Society" is everyone but yourself.* Put thus bluntly, this analysis can be used to consider those cases where "society" is treated, not only as a superhero with super-rights, but as a supervillain on whose shoulders massive blame is placed. Consider the typical view that not the individual criminal, but "society," is responsible for his crime. Take, for example, the case where Smith robs or murders Jones. The "old-fashioned" view is that Smith is responsible for his act. The modern liberal counters that "society" is responsible. This sounds both sophisticated and humanitarian, until we apply the individualist perspective. Then we see that what liberals are *really* saying is that *everyone but* Smith, including of course the victim Jones, is responsible for the crime. Put this baldly, almost everyone would recognize the absurdity of this position. But conjuring up the fictive entity "society" obfuscates this process. As the sociologist Arnold W. Green puts it: "It would follow, then, that if society is responsible for crime, and criminals are not responsible for crime, only those members of society who do not commit crime can be held responsible for crime. Nonsense this obvious can be circumvented only by conjuring up society as devil, as evil being apart from people and what they do."[7]

The great American libertarian writer Frank Chodorov stressed this view of society when he wrote that "Society Are People."

Society is a collective concept and nothing else; it is a convenience for designating a number of people. So, too, is family or crowd or gang, or any other name we give to an agglomeration of persons. Society . . . is not an extra "person"; if the census totals a hundred million, that's all there are, not one more, for there cannot be any accretion to Society except by procreation. The concept of Society as a metaphysical person falls flat when we observe that Society disappears when the component parts disperse; as in the case of a "ghost town" or of a civilization we learn about by the artifacts they left behind. When the individuals disappear so does the whole. The whole has no separate existence. Using the collective noun with a singular verb leads into a trap of the imagination; we are prone to personalize the collectivity and to think of it as having a body and a psyche of its own.[8]

FREE EXCHANGE AND FREE CONTRACT

The central core of the libertarian creed, then, is to establish the absolute right to private property of every man: first, in his own body, and second, in the previously unused natural resources which he first transforms by his labor. These two axioms, the right of self-ownership and the right to "homestead," establish the complete set of principles of the libertarian system. The entire libertarian doctrine then becomes the spinning out and the application of all the implications of this central doctrine. For example, a man, X, owns his own person and labor, and the farm he clears on which he grows wheat. Another man, Y, owns the fish he catches; A third man, Z, owns the cabbages he has grown and the land under it. But if a man owns anything, he then has the right to *give away* or *exchange* these property titles to someone else, after which point the other person also has absolute property title. From this corollary right to private property stems the basic justification for free contract and for the free-market economy. Thus, if X grows wheat, he may and probably will agree to exchange some of that wheat for some of the fish caught by Y or for some of the cabbages grown by Z. With both X and Y making voluntary agreements to exchange property titles (or Y and Z, or X and Z) the property then becomes with equal legitimacy the property of the other person. If X exchanges wheat for Y's fish, then that fish becomes X's property to do with as he wishes, and the wheat becomes Y's property in precisely the same way.

Further, a man may exchange not only the tangible objects he owns but also his own labor, which of course he owns as well. Thus, Z may sell his labor services of teaching farmer X's children in return for some of the farmer's produce.

It so happens that the free-market economy, and the specialization and division of labor it implies, is by far the most productive form of economy known to man, and has been responsible for industrialization and for the modern economy on which civilization has been built. This is a fortunate utilitarian result of the free market, but it is not, to the libertarian, the *prime* reason for his support of this system. That prime reason is moral, and is rooted in the natural rights defense of private property we have developed above. Even if a society of despotism and systematic invasion of rights could be shown to be more productive than what Adam Smith called "the system of natural liberty," the libertarian would support this system. Fortunately, as in so many other areas, the utilitarian and the moral, natural rights and general prosperity, go hand in hand.

The developed-market economy, as complex as the system appears to be on the surface, is nothing more than a vast network of voluntary and mutually agreed-upon two-person exchanges such as we have shown to occur between wheat and cabbage farmers, or between the farmer and the teacher. Thus, when I buy a newspaper for a dime, a mutually beneficial two-person exchange takes place: I transfer my ownership of the dime to the news dealer and he transfer ownership of the paper to me. We do this because, under the division of labor, I calculate that the paper is worth more to me than the dime, while the news dealer prefers the dime to keeping the paper. Or, when I teach at a university, I estimate that I prefer my salary to not expending my labor of teaching, while the university authorities calculate that they prefer gaining my teaching services to not paying me the money. If the newsdealer insisted on charging 50¢ for the paper, I might well decide that it isn't worth the price; similarly, if I should insist on triple my present salary, the university might well decide to dispense with my services.

Many people are willing to concede the justice and propriety of property rights and the free-market economy, to concede that the farmer should be able to charge whatever his wheat will bring from consumers or the worker to reap whatever others are willing to pay for his services. But they balk at one point: inheritance. If Willie Stargell is ten times as good and "productive" a ball player as Joe Jack, they are willing to concede the justice of Stargell's earning ten times the amount; but what, they ask, if the justification for someone whose only merit is being born a Rockefeller inheriting far more wealth than someone born a Rothbard? The libertarian answer is to concentrate *not* on the recipient, the child Rockefeller or the child Rothbard, but to concentrate on the *giver,* the man who bestows the inheritance. For if Smith and Jones and Stargell have the right to their labor and property and to exchange the titles to this property for the similar property of others, they also have the right to *give* their property to whomever they wish. And of course most such gifts consist of the gifts of the property owners to their children—in short, inheritance. If Willie Stargell owns his labor and the money he earns from it, then he has the right to give that money to the baby Stargell.

In the developed free-market economy, then, the farmer exchanges the wheat for money; the wheat is bought by the miller who processes and transforms the wheat into flour; the miller sells the flour to the baker who produces bread; the baker sells the bread to the wholesaler, who in turn sells it to the retailer, who finally sells it to the consumer. And at each step of the way, the producer may hire the labor services of the workers in exchange for money. How "money" enters the equation is a complex process; but it should be clear that *conceptually* the use of money is equivalent to any single or group of useful commodities that are exchanged for the wheat, flour, etc. Instead of money, the commodity exchanged could be cloth, iron, or whatever. At each step of the way, mutually beneficial exchanges of property titles are agreed upon and transacted.

We are now in the position to see how the libertarian defines the concept of "freedom" or "liberty." Freedom is a condition in which a person's ownership rights in his own body and his legitimate material property are *not* invaded, are not aggressed against. A man who steals another man's property is invading and restricting the victim's freedom, as does the man who beats another over the head. Freedom and unrestricted property right go hand in hand. On the other hand, to the libertarian, "crime" is an act of aggression against a man's property right, either in his own person or his materially owned objects. Crime is an invasion, by the use of violence, against a man's property and therefore against his liberty. "Slavery"—the opposite of freedom—is a condition in which the slave has little or no right of self-ownership; his person and his produce are systematically expropriated by his master by the use of violence.

The libertarian, then, is clearly an individualist but *not* an egalitarian. The only "equality" he would advocate is the equal right of every man to the property in his own person, to the property in the unused resources he "homesteads," and to the property of others he has acquired either through voluntary exchange or gift.

PROPERTY RIGHTS AND "HUMAN RIGHTS"

Liberals will generally concede the right of every individual to his "personal liberty," to his freedom to think, speak, write, and engage in such personal "exchanges" as sexual activity between "consenting adults." In short, the liberal attempts to uphold the individual's right to the ownership of his own body, but then denies his right to "property," i.e., to the ownership of material objects. Hence, the typical liberal dichotomy between "human rights," which he upholds, and "property rights," which he rejects. Yet the two, according to the libertarian, are inextricably intertwined; they stand or fall together.

Take, for example, the liberal socialist who advocates government ownership of all the "means of production" while upholding the "human" right of freedom of speech or press. How is this "human" right to be exercised if the individuals constituting the public are denied their right to ownership of property? If, for example, the government owns all the newsprint and all the printing shops, how is the right to a free press to be exercised? If the government owns all the newsprint, it then necessarily has the right and the power to allocate that newsprint, and someone's "right to a free press" becomes a mockery if the government decides not to allocate newsprint in his direction. And since the government must allocate scarce newsprint in *some* way, the right to a free press of, say, minorities or "subversive" antisocialists will get short shrift indeed. The same is true for the "right to free speech" if the government owns all the assembly halls, and therefore allocates those halls as it sees fit. Or, for example, if the government of Soviet Russia, being atheistic, decides not to allocate many scarce resources to the production of matzohs, for Orthodox Jews the "freedom of religion" becomes a mockery; but again, the Soviet government can always rebut that

Orthodox Jews are a small minority and that capital equipment should not be diverted to matzoh production.

The basic flaw in the liberal separation of "human rights" and "property rights" is that people are treated as ethereal abstractions. If a man has the right to self-ownership, to the control of his life, then in the real world he must also have the right to sustain his life by grappling with and transforming resources; he must be able to own the ground and the resources on which he stands and which he must use. In short, to sustain his "human right"—or his property rights in his own person—he must also have the property right in the material world, in the objects which he produces. Property rights *are* human rights, and are essential to the human rights which liberals attempt to maintain. The human right of a free press depends upon the human right of private property in newsprint.

In fact, there *are* no human rights that are separable from property rights. The human right of free speech is simply the property right to hire an assembly hall from the owners, or to own one oneself; the human right of a free press is the property right to buy materials and then print leaflets or books and to sell them to those who are willing to buy. There is no extra "right of free speech" or free press beyond the property rights we can enumerate in any given case. And furthermore, discovering and identifying the property rights involved will resolve any apparent conflicts of rights that may crop up.

Consider, for example, the classic example where liberals generally concede that a person's "right of freedom of speech" must be curbed in the name of the "public interest": Justice Holmes' famous dictum that no one has the right to cry "fire" falsely in a crowded theater. Holmes and his followers have used the illustration again and again to prove the supposed necessity for all rights to be relative and tentative rather than precise and absolute.

But the problem here is *not* that rights cannot be pushed too far, but that the whole case is discussed in terms of a vague and woolly "freedom of speech" rather than in terms of the rights of private property. Suppose we analyze the problem under the aspect of property rights. The fellow who brings on a riot by falsely shouting "fire" in a crowded theater is, necessarily, either the owner of the theater (or the owner's agent) or a paying patron. If he is the owner, then he has committed fraud on his customers. He has taken their money in exchange for a promise to put on a movie or play; and now, instead, he disrupts the show by falsely shouting "fire" and breaking up the performance. He has thus welshed on his contractual obligation, and has thereby stolen the property—the money—of his patrons and has violated their property rights.

Suppose, on the other hand, that the shouter is a patron and not the owner. In that case, he is violating the property right of the owner—as well as of the other guests to their paid-for performance. As a guest, he has gained access to the property on certain terms, including an obligation not to violate the owner's property or to disrupt the performance the owner is putting on. His malicious act, therefore, violates the property rights of the theater owner and of all the other patrons.

There is no need, therefore, for individual rights to be restricted in the case of the false shouter of "fire." The rights of the individual are *still* absolute; but they are *property* rights. The fellow who maliciously cried "fire" in a crowded theater is indeed a criminal, but *not* because his so-called "right of free speech" must be pragmatically restricted on behalf of the "public good"; he is a criminal because he has clearly and obviously violated the property rights of another person.

NOTES

1. See Gertrude Himmelfarb, *Lord Acton: A Study in Conscience and Politics* (Chicago: Phoenix Books, 1962), pp. 204–05. Compare also John Wild, *Plato's Modern Enemies*

and the Theory of Natural Law (Chicago: University of Chicago Press, 1953), p. 176.

2. John Locke, *An Essay Concerning the True Original, Extent and End of Civil Government,* in E. Barker, ed., *Social Contract* (New York: Oxford University Press, 1948), pp. 17–18.

3. Locke, *Civil Government,* pp. 18–19. While Locke was a brilliant property theorist, we are not claiming that he developed and applied his theory with anything like complete consistency.

4. Locke, *Civil Government,* p. 20.

5. Leon Wolowski and Émile Levasseur, "Property," in *Lalor's Cyclopedia of Political Science . . .* (Chicago: M. B. Cary & Co., 1884), III, 392–93.

6. Parker Thomas Moon, *Imperialism and World Politics* (New York: Macmillan, 1930), p. 58.

7. Arnold W. Green, "The Reified Villain," *Social Research* (Winter, 1968), p. 656.

8. Frank Chodorov, *The Rise and Fall of Society* (New York: Devin-Adair, 1959), pp. 29–30.

Discussion Questions

1. Why does Professor Rothbard believe that utilitarianism and emotivism are inadequate in grounding property rights?

2. Central to Professor Rothbard's philosophy is the view that self-ownership and ownership of property are natural rights. How does he argue for this position? How does he morally justify the acquisition and ownership of natural resources and land by individuals? Present and explain his position. Do you find Professor Rothbard's case persuasive? Explain and defend your answer.

3. Why does Professor Rothbard believe that one cannot have personal liberty (or "human rights") without property rights? Do you find his case persuasive? Explain and defend your answer.

4. Compare and contrast Professor Rothbard's view of natural law (or natural rights) with Thomas Aquinas's view (Chapter 5). Do you think Aquinas would find Rothbard's view objectionable? Why or why not? Explain and defend your answers.

You can locate InfoTrac-College Education articles about this chapter by accessing the InfoTrac-College Edition website (http://www.infotrac-college.com/wadsworth/). Using the InfoTrac-College Edition subject guide, enter the search terms relevant to this chapter, and then read abstracts for relevant articles.

35   Justice, Gender, and the Family

SUSAN MOLLER OKIN

Susan Moller Okin is Professor of Political Science and Director of the Ethics in Society Program at Stanford University. She is the author of numerous works in social and political philosophy, including the books *Justice, Gender, and the Family* (1989) and *Women in Western Political Thought* (1979).

In this essay Professor Okin argues that the "traditional family" and the cultural assumptions entailed by it are inherently unjust. She defines the traditional family as father, mother, and children, in which the father is the primary income resource and the mother is the chief caretaker of the home and children. The reason why these roles exist, according Okin, has nothing to do with their being essential to each gender (e.g., women are naturally better at nurturing children). Rather, they are a social construction. That is, gender role differences are largely socially produced. Professor Okin calls this "the social construction of gender." Consequently, if the traditional gender roles are socially constructed, and if they are unjust, then gender roles that are just can be socially constructed as well. Even though our society prides itself on its democratic values, Professor Okin maintains that there are "substantial inequalities between the sexes in our society today." She argues that such inequalities are the result of our culture's acceptance of the traditional family. Professor Okin believes that contemporary views of social justice (see the previous two chapters) have not adequately addressed the issue of what constitutes a just family structure. Although there are a number of reasons for this, she believes, the primary reason is that most works of contemporary political and legal theory do not discuss the family because it is assumed that the family is "nonpolitical." She gives three reasons why this is unacceptable.

WE AS A SOCIETY pride ourselves on our democratic values. We don't believe people should be constrained by innate differences from being able to achieve desired positions of influence or to improve their well-being; equality of opportunity is our professed aim. The Preamble to our Constitution stresses the importance of justice, as well as the general welfare and the blessings of liberty. The Pledge of Allegiance asserts that our republic preserves "liberty and justice for all."

Yet substantial inequalities between the sexes still exist in our society. In economic terms, full-time working women (after some very recent improvement) earn on average 71 percent of the earnings of full-time working men. One-half of poor and three-fifths of chronically poor households with dependent

Reprinted by permission from Susan Moller Okin, Justice, Gender, and the Family *(New York: Basic Books, 1989).*

children are maintained by a single female parent. The poverty rate for elderly women is nearly twice that for elderly men.[1] On the political front, [women are disproportionally unrepresented in the Congress and the courts]. . . . Underlying and intertwined with all these inequalities is the unequal distribution of the unpaid labor of the family.

An equal sharing between the sexes of family responsibilities, especially child care, is "the great revolution that has not happened."[2] Women, including mothers of young children, are, of course, working outside the household far more than their mothers did. And the small proportion of women who reach high-level positions in politics, business, and the professions command a vastly disproportionate amount of space in the media, compared with the millions of women who work at low-paying, dead-end jobs, the millions who do part-time work with its lack of benefits, and the millions of others who stay home performing for no pay what is frequently not even acknowledged as work. Certainly, the fact that women are doing more paid work does not imply that they are more equal. It is often said that we are living in a postfeminist era. This claim, due in part to the distorted emphasis on women who have "made it," is false, no matter which of its meanings is intended. It is certainly not true that feminism has been vanquished, and equally untrue that it is no longer needed because its aims have been fulfilled. Until there is justice within the family, women will not be able to gain equality in politics, at work, or in any other sphere.

. . . [T]he typical current practices of family life, structured to a large extent by gender, are not just. Both the expectation and the experience of the division of labor by sex make women vulnerable. . . . [A] cycle of power relations and decisions pervades both family and workplace, each reinforcing the inequalities between the sexes that already exist within the other. Not only women, but children of both sexes, too, are often made vulnerable by

gender-structured marriage. One-quarter of children in the United States now live in families with only one parent—in almost 90 percent of cases, the mother. Contrary to common perceptions—in which the situation of never-married mothers looms largest—65 percent of single-parent families are a result of marital separation or divorce.[3] Recent research in a number of states has shown that, in the average case, the standard of living of divorced women and the children who live with them plummets after divorce, whereas the economic situation of divorced men tends to be better than when they were married.

A central source of injustice for women these days is that the law, most noticeably in the event of divorce, treats more or less as equals those whom custom, workplace discrimination, and the still conventional division of labor within the family have made very unequal. Central to this socially created inequality are two commonly made but inconsistent presumptions: that women are primarily responsible for the rearing of children; and that serious and committed members of the work force (regardless of class) do not have primary responsibility, or even shared responsibility, for the rearing of children. The old assumption of the workplace, still implicit, is that workers have wives at home. It is built not only into the structure and expectations of the workplace but into the other crucial social institutions, such as schools, which make no attempt to take account, in their scheduled hours or vacations, of the fact that parents are likely to hold jobs.

Now, of course, many wage workers do not have wives at home. Often, they *are* wives and mothers, or single, separated, or divorced mothers of small children. But neither the family nor the workplace has taken much account of this fact. Employed wives still do by far the greatest proportion of unpaid family work, such as child care and housework. Women are far more likely to take time out of the workplace or to work part-time because of family responsibilities than are their husbands or male partners. And they are much more likely to move because of their husbands' employment needs or opportunities than their own. All these tendencies, which are due to a number of factors, including the sex segregation and discrimination of the workplace itself, tend to be cyclical in their effects: wives advance more slowly than their husbands at work and thus gain less seniority, and the discrepancy between their wages increases over time. Then, because both the power structure of the family and what is regarded as consensual "rational" family decision making reflect the fact that the husband usually earns more, it will become even less likely as time goes on that the unpaid work of the family will be shared between the spouses. Thus the cycle of inequality is perpetuated. Often hidden from view within a marriage, it is in the increasingly likely event of marital breakdown that the socially constructed inequality of married women is at its most visible.

This is what I mean when I say that gender-structured marriage *makes* women vulnerable. These are not matters of natural necessity, as some people would believe. Surely nothing in our natures dictates that men should not be equal participants in the rearing of their children. Nothing in the nature of work makes it impossible to adjust it to the fact that people are parents as well as workers. That these things have not happened is part of the historically, socially constructed differentiation between the sexes that feminists have come to call *gender*. We live in a society that has over the years regarded the innate characteristic of sex as one of the clearest legitimizers of different rights and restrictions, both formal and informal. While the legal sanctions that uphold male dominance have begun to be eroded in the past century, and more rapidly in the last twenty years, the heavy weight of tradition, combined with the effects of socialization, still works powerfully to reinforce sex roles that are commonly regarded as of unequal prestige and

worth. The sexual division of labor has not only been a fundamental part of the marriage contract, but so deeply influences us in our formative years that feminists of both sexes who try to reject it can find themselves struggling against it with varying degrees of ambivalence. Based on this linch-pin, "gender"—by which I mean *the deeply entrenched institutionalization of sexual difference*—still permeates our society.

THE CONSTRUCTION OF GENDER

Due to feminism and feminist theory, gender is coming to be recognized as a social factor of major importance. Indeed, the new meaning of the word reflects the fact that so much of what has traditionally been thought of as sexual difference is now considered by many to be largely socially produced.[4] Feminist scholars from many disciplines and with radically different points of view have contributed to the enterprise of making gender fully visible and comprehensible. At one end of the spectrum are those whose explanations of the subordination of women focus primarily on biological difference as causal in the construction of gender,[5] and at the other hand are those who argue that biological difference may not even lie at the core of the social construction that is gender[6]; the views of the vast majority of feminists fall between these extremes. The rejection of biological determinism and the corresponding emphasis on gender as a social construction characterize most current feminist scholarship. Of particular relevance is work in psychology, where scholars have investigated the importance of female primary parenting in the formation of our gendered identities,[7] and in history and anthropology,[8] where emphasis has been placed on the historical and cultural variability of gender. Some feminists have been criticized for developing theories of gender that do not take sufficient account of differences *among* women, especially race, class, religion, and ethnicity.[9] While such critiques should always inform our research and improve our arguments, it would be a mistake to allow them to detract our attention from gender itself as a factor of significance. Many injustices are experienced by women *as women,* whatever the differences among them and whatever other injustices they also suffer from. The past and present gendered nature of the family, and the ideology that surrounds it, affects virtually all women, whether or not they live or ever lived in traditional families. Recognizing this is not to deny or de-emphasize the fact that gender may affect different subgroups of women to a different extent and in different ways.

The potential significance of feminist discoveries and conclusions about gender for issues of social justice cannot be overemphasized. They undermine centuries of argument that started with the notion that not only the distinct differentiation of women and men but the domination of women by men, being natural, was therefore inevitable and not even to be considered in discussions of justice. . . . [D]espite the fact that such notions cannot stand up to rational scrutiny, they not only still survive but flourish in influential places.

During the same two decades in which feminists have been intensely thinking, researching, analyzing, disagreeing about, and rethinking the subject of gender, our political and legal institutions have been increasingly faced with issues concerning the injustices of gender and their effects. These issues are being decided within a fundamentally patriarchal system, founded in a tradition in which "individuals" were assumed to be male heads of households. Not surprisingly, the system has demonstrated a limited capacity for determining what is just, in many cases involving gender. Sex discrimination, sexual harassment, abortion, pregnancy in the workplace, parental leave, child care, and surrogate mothering have all become major and well-publicized issues of public policy, engaging both courts and legislatures. Issues of family justice, in particular—from child custody and terms of divorce to physical and sexual abuse of wives and children—have become increasingly visible and pressing, and are commanding increasing attention from the police and court systems. There is clearly a major "justice crisis" in contemporary society arising from issues of gender.

THEORIES OF JUSTICE AND THE NEGLECT OF GENDER

During these same two decades, there has been a great resurgence of theories of social justice. Political theory, which had been sparse for a period before the late 1960s except as an important branch of intellectual history, has become a flourishing field, with social justice as its central concern. Yet, remarkably, major contemporary theorists of justice have almost without exception ignored the situation I have just described. They have displayed little interest in or knowledge of the findings of feminism. They have largely bypassed the fact that the society to which their theories are supposed to pertain is heavily and deeply affected by gender, and faces difficult issues of justice stemming from its gendered past and present assumptions. Since theories of justice are centrally concerned with whether, how, and why persons should be treated differently from one another, this neglect seems inexplicable. These theories are *about* which initial or acquired characteristics or positions in society legitimize differential treatment of persons by social institutions, laws, and customs. They are *about* how and whether and to what extent beginnings should affect outcomes. The division of humanity into two sexes seems to provide an obvious subject for such inquiries. But, as we shall see, this does not strike most contemporary theorists of justice, and their theories suffer in both coherence and relevance because of it. . . .

Why is it that when we turn to contemporary theories of justice, we do not find illuminating and positive contributions to this question? How can theories of justice that are ostensibly about people in general neglect women, gender, and all the inequalities between the sexes? One reason is that most theorists *assume,* though they do not discuss, the traditional, gender-structured family. Another is that they often employ gender-neutral language in a false, hollow way. Let us examine [just the first point].

The Hidden Gender-Structured Family

In the past, political theorists often used to distinguish clearly between "private" domestic life and the "public" life of politics and the marketplace, claiming explicitly that the two spheres operated in accordance with different principles. They separated out the family from what they deemed the subject matter of politics, and they made closely related, explicit claims about the nature of women and the appropriateness of excluding them from civil and political life. Men, the subjects of the theories, were able to make the transition back and forth from domestic to public life with ease, largely because of the functions performed by women in the family.[10] When we turn to contemporary theories of justice, superficial appearances can easily lead to the impression that they are inclusive of women. In fact, they continue the same "separate spheres" tradition, by ignoring the family, its division of labor, and the related economic dependency and restricted opportunities of most women. The judgment that the family is "nonpolitical" is implicit in the fact that it is simply not discussed in most works of political theory today. In one way or another, as will become clear in the chapters that follow, almost all current theorists continue to assume that the "individual" who is the basic subject of their theories is the male head of a fairly traditional household. Thus the application of principles of justice to relations between the sexes, or within the household, is frequently, though tacitly, ruled out from the start. In the most influential of all twentieth-century theories of justice, that of John Rawls, family life is not only assumed, but is assumed to be just—and yet the prevalent gendered division of labor within the family is neglected, along with the associated distribution of power, responsibility, and privilege. . . .

Moreover, this stance is typical of contemporary theories of justice. They persist, despite the wealth of feminist challenges to their assumptions, in their refusal even to discuss the family and its gender structure, much less to recognize the family as a political institution of primary importance. . . . For gender is one aspect of social life about which clearly, in the United States in the latter part of the twentieth century, there are no shared understandings.

What is the basis of my claim that the family, while neglected, is *assumed* by theorists of justice? One obvious indication is that they take mature, independent human beings as the subjects of their theories without any mention of how they got to be that way. We know, of course, that human beings develop and mature only as a result of a great deal of attention and hard work, by far the greater part of it done by women. But when theorists of justice talk about "work," they mean paid work performed in the marketplace. They must be assuming that women, in the gender-structured family, continue to do their unpaid work of nurturing and socializing the young and providing a haven of intimate relations—otherwise there would be no moral subjects for them to theorize about. But these activities apparently take place outside the scope of their theories. Typically, the family itself is not examined in the light of whatever standard of justice the theorist arrives at.[11]

The continued neglect of the family by theorists of justice flies in the face of a great deal of persuasive feminist argument. . . . Scholars have clearly revealed the interconnections between the gender structure inside and outside the family and the extent to which the personal is political. They have shown that the assignment of primary parenting to women is crucial, both in forming the gendered identities of men and women and in influencing their respective choices and opportunities in life. Yet, so far, the simultaneous assumption and neglect of the family has allowed the impact of these arguments to go unnoticed in major theories of justice. . . .

GENDER AS AN ISSUE OF JUSTICE

For three major reasons, this state of affairs is unacceptable. The first is the obvious point that women must be fully included in any satisfactory theory of justice. The second is that equality of opportunity, not only for women but for children of both sexes, is seriously undermined by the current gender injustices of our society. And the third reason is that, as has already been suggested, the family—currently the linchpin of the gender structure—must be just if we are to have a just society, since it is within the family that we first come to have that sense of ourselves and our relations with others that is at the root of moral development.

Counting Women In

When we turn to the great tradition of Western political thought with questions about the justice of the treatment of the sexes in mind, it is to little avail. Bold feminists like Mary Astell, Mary Wollstonecraft, William Thompson, Harriet Taylor, and George Bernard Shaw have occasionally challenged the tradition, often using its own premises and arguments to overturn its explicit or implicit justification of the inequality of women. But John Stuart Mill is a rare exception to the rule that those who hold central positions in the tradition almost never question the justice of the subordination of

women.[12] This phenomenon is undoubtedly due in part to the fact that Aristotle, whose theory of justice has been so influential, relegated women to a sphere of "household justice"—populated by persons who are not fundamentally equal to the free men who participate in political justice, but inferiors whose natural function is to serve those who are more fully human. The liberal tradition, despite its supposed foundation of individual rights and human equality, is more Aristotelian in this respect than is generally acknowledged.[13] In one way or another, almost all liberal theorists have assumed that the "individual" who is the basic subject of the theories is the male head of a patriarchal household.[14] Thus they have not usually considered applying the principles of justice to women or to relations between the sexes.

When we turn to contemporary theories of justice, however, we expect to find more illuminating and positive contributions to the subject of gender and justice. As the omission of the family and the falseness of their gender-neutral language suggest, however, mainstream contemporary theories of justice do not address the subject any better than those of the past. Theories of justice that apply to only half of us simply won't do; the inclusiveness falsely implied by the current use of gender-neutral terms must become real. Theories of justice must apply to all of us, and to all of human life, instead of *assuming* silently that half of us take care of whole areas of life that are considered outside the scope of social justice. In a just society, the structure and practices of families must afford women the same opportunities as men to develop their capacities, to participate in political power, to influence social choices, and to be economically as well as physically secure.

Unfortunately, much feminist intellectual energy in the 1980s has gone into the claim that "justice" and "rights" are masculinist ways of thinking about morality that feminists should eschew or radically revise, advocating a morality of care.[15] The emphasis is misplaced, I think, for several reasons. First, what is by now a vast literature on the subject shows that the evidence for differences in women's and men's ways of thinking about moral issues is not (at least yet) very clear; neither is the evidence about the source of whatever differences there might be.[16] It may well turn out that any differences can be readily explained in terms of roles, including female primary parenting, that are socially determined and therefore alterable. There is certainly no evidence—nor could there be, in such a gender-structured society—for concluding that women are somehow naturally more inclined toward contextuality and away from universalism in their moral thinking, a false concept that unfortunately reinforced the old stereotypes that justify separate spheres. The capacity of reactionary forces to capitalize on the "different moralities" strain in feminism is particularly evident in Pope John Paul II's recent Apostolic Letter, "On the Dignity of Women," in which he refers to women's special capacity to care for others in arguing for confining them to motherhood or celibacy.[17]

Second, . . . I think the distinction between an ethic of justice and an ethic of care has been overdrawn. The best theorizing about justice, I argue, has integral to it the notions of care and empathy, of thinking of the interests and well-being of others who may be very different from ourselves. It is, therefore, misleading to draw a dichotomy as though they were two contrasting ethics. The best theorizing about justice is not some abstract "view from nowhere," but results from the carefully attentive consideration of *everyone's* point of view. This means, of course, that the best theorizing about justice is not good enough if it does not, or cannot readily be adapted to, include women and their points of view as fully as men and their points of view.

Gender and Equality of Opportunity

The family is a crucial determinant of our opportunities in life, of what we "become." It has frequently been acknowledged by those concerned with real equality of opportunity that the family presents a problem.[18] But though they have discerned a serious problem, these theorists have underestimated it because they have seen only half of it. They have seen that the disparity among families in terms of the physical and emotional environment, motivation, and material advantages they can give their children has a tremendous effect upon children's opportunities in life. We are not born as isolated, equal individuals in our society, but into family situations; some in the social middle, some poor and homeless, and some superaffluent; some to a single or soon-to-be-separated parent, some to parents whose marriage is fraught with conflict, some to parents who will stay together in love and happiness. Any claims that equal opportunity exists are therefore completely unfounded. Decades of neglect of the poor, especially of poor black and Hispanic households . . . have brought us farther from the principles of equal opportunity. To come close to them would require, for example, a high and uniform standard of public education and the provision of equal social services—including health care, employment training, job opportunities, drug rehabilitation, and decent housing—for all who need them. In addition to redistributive taxation, only massive reallocations of resources from the military to social services could make these things possible.

But even if all these disparities were somehow eliminated, we would still not attain equal opportunity for all. This is because what has not been recognized as an equal opportunity problem, except in feminist literature and circles, is the disparity *within* the family, the fact that its gender structure is itself a major obstacle to equality of opportunity. This is very important in itself, since one of the factors with most influence on our opportunities in life is the social significance attributed to our sex. The opportunities of girls and women are centrally affected by the structure and practices of family life, particularly by the fact that women are almost invariably primary parents. What nonfeminists who see in the family an obstacle to equal opportunity have *not* seen is that the extent to which a family is gender-structured can make the sex we belong to a relatively insignificant aspect of our identity and our life prospects or an all-pervading one. This is because so much of the social construction of gender takes place in the family, and particularly in the institution of female parenting.

Moreover, especially in recent years, with the increased rates of single motherhood, separation, and divorce, the inequalities between the sexes have *compounded* the first part of the problem. The disparity among families has grown largely because of the impoverishment of many women and children after separation or divorce. The division of labor in the typical family leaves most women far less capable than men of supporting themselves, and this disparity is accentuated by the fact that children of separated or divorced parents usually live with their mothers. The inadequacy—and frequent nonpayment—of child support has become recognized as a major social problem. Thus the inequalities of gender are now directly harming many children of both sexes as well as women themselves. Enhancing equal opportunity for women, important as it is in itself, is also a crucial way of improving the opportunities of many of the most disadvantaged children.

As there is a connection among the parts of this problem, so is there a connection among some of the solutions: much of what needs to be done to end the inequalities of gender, and to work in the direction of ending gender itself, will also help to equalize opportunity from one family to another. Subsidized, high-quality day care is obviously one such thing; another is the adaptation of the workplace to the needs of parents. . . .

The Family as a School of Justice

One of the things that theorists who have argued that families need not or cannot be just, or who have simply neglected them, have failed to explain is how, within a formative social environment that is *not* founded upon principles of justice, children can learn to develop that sense of justice they will require as citizens of a just society. Rather than being one among many co-equal institutions of a just society, a just family is its essential foundation.

It may seem uncontroversial, even obvious, that families must be just because of the vast influence they have on the moral development of children. But this is clearly not the case. . . . [U]nless the first and most formative example of adult interaction usually experienced by children is one of justice and reciprocity, rather than one of domination and manipulation or of unequal altruism and one-sided self-sacrifice, and unless they themselves are treated with concern and respect, they are likely to be considerably hindered in becoming people who are guided by principles of justice. Moreover, . . . the sharing of roles by men and women, rather than the division of roles between them, would have a further positive impact because of the experience of *being* a physical and psychological nurturer—whether of a child or of another adult—would increase that capacity to identify with and fully comprehend the viewpoints of others that is important to a sense of justice. In a society that minimized gender this would be more likely to be the experience of all of us.

Almost every person in our society starts life in a family of some sort or other. Fewer of these families now fit the usual, though by no means universal, standard of previous generations, that is, wageworking father, homemaking mother, and children. More families these days are headed by a single parent; lesbian and gay parenting is no longer so rare; many children have two wage-working parents, and receive at least some of their early care outside the home. While its forms are varied, the family in which a child is raised, especially in the earliest years, is clearly a crucial place for early moral development and for the formation of our basic attitudes to others. It is, potentially, a place where we can *learn* to be just. It is especially important for the development of a sense of justice that grows from sharing the experiences of others and becoming aware of the points of view of others who are different in some respects from ourselves, but with whom we clearly have some interests in common.

The importance of the family for the moral development of individuals was far more often recognized by political theorists of the past than it is by those of the present. Hegel, Rousseau, Tocqueville, Mill, and Dewey are obvious examples that come to mind. Rousseau, for example, shocked by Plato's proposal to abolish the family, says that it is

> as though there were no need for a natural base on which to form conventional ties; as though the love of one's nearest were not the principle of the love one owes the state; as though it were not by means of the small fatherland which is the family that the heart attaches itself to the large one.[19]

Defenders of both autocratic and democratic regimes have recognized the political importance of different family forms for the formation of citizens. On the one hand, the nineteenth-century monarchist Louis de Bonald argued against the divorce reforms of the French Revolution, which he claimed had weakened the patriarchal family, on the grounds that "in order to keep the state out of the hands of the people, it is necessary to keep the family out of the hands of women and children."[20] Taking this same line of thought in the opposite direction, the U.S. Supreme Court decided in 1879 in *Reynolds v. Nebraska* that familial patriarchy fostered despotism and was therefore intolerable. Denying Mormon men the freedom to practice polygamy, the Court asserted that it was an offense "subversive of good order" that "leads to the patriarchal principles, . . . [and] when applied to large communities, fetters the people in sta-

tionary despotism, while that principle cannot long exist in connection with monogamy."[21]

However, while de Bonald was consistent in his adherence to an hierarchical family structure as necessary for an undemocratic political system, the Supreme Court was by no means consistent in promoting an egalitarian family as an essential underpinning for political democracy. For in other decisions of the same period—such as *Bradwell v. Illinois,* the famous 1872 case that upheld the exclusion of women from the practice of law—the Court rejected women's claims to legal equality, in the name of a thoroughly patriarchal, though monogamous, family that was held to require the dependence of women and their exclusion from civil and political life.[22] While bigamy was considered patriarchal, and as such a threat to republican, democratic government, the refusal to allow a married woman to employ her talents and to make use of her qualifications to earn an independent living was not considered patriarchal. It was so far from being a threat to the civil order, in fact, that it was deemed necessary for it, and as such was ordained by both God and nature. Clearly, in both *Reynolds* and *Bradwell,* "state authorities enforced family forms preferred by those in power and justified as necessary to stability and order."[23] The Court noticed the despotic potential of polygamy, but was blind to the despotic potential of patriarchal monogamy. This was perfectly acceptable to them as a training ground for citizens.

Most theorists of the past who stressed the importance of the family and its practices for the wider world of moral and political life by no means insisted on congruence between the structures or practices of the family and those of the outside world. Though concerned with moral development, they bifurcated public from private life to such an extent that they had no trouble reconciling inegalitarian, sometimes admittedly unjust, relations founded upon sentiment within the family with a more just, even egalitarian, social structure outside the family. Rousseau, Hegel, Tocqueville—all thought the family was centrally important for the development of morality in citizens, but all defended the hierarchy of the marital structure while spurning such a degree of hierarchy in institutions and practices outside the household. Preferring instead to rely on love, altruism, and generosity as the basis for family relations, none of these theorists argued for *just* family structures as necessary for socializing children into citizenship in a just society.

The position that justice within the family is irrelevant to the development of just citizens was not plausible even when only men were citizens. John Stuart Mill, in *The Subjection of Women,* takes an impassioned stand against it. He argues that the inequality of women within the family is deeply subversive of justice in general in the wider social world, because it subverts the moral potential of men. Mill's first answer to the question, "For whose good are all these changes in women's rights to be undertaken?" is: "the advantage of having the most universal and pervading of all human relations regulated by justice instead of injustice." Making marriage a relationship of equals, he argues, would transform this central part of daily life from "a school of despotism" into "a school of moral cultivation."[24] He goes on to discuss, in the strongest of terms, the noxious effect of growing up in a family not regulated by justice. Consider, he says, "the self-worship, the unjust self-preference," nourished in a boy growing up in a household in which "by the mere fact of being born a male he is by right the superior of all and every one of an entire half of the human race." Mill concludes that the example set by perpetuating a marital structure "contradictory to the first principles of social justice" must have such "a perverting influence" that it is hard even to imagine the good effects of changing it. All other attempts to educate people to respect and practice justice, Mill claims, will be superficial "as long as the citadel of the enemy is not attacked." Mill felt as much hope for what the

family might be as he felt despair at what it was not. "The family, justly constituted, would be the real school of the virtues of freedom," primary among which was "justice, . . . grounded as before on equal, but now also on sympathetic association."[25] Mill both saw clearly and had the courage to address what so many other political philosophers either could not see, or saw and turned away from.

Despite the strength and fervor of his advocacy of women's rights, however, Mill's idea of a just family structure falls far short of that of many feminists even of his own time, including his wife, Harriet Taylor. In spite of the fact that Mill recognized both the empowering effect of earnings on one's position in the family and the limiting effect of domestic responsibility on women's opportunities, he balked at questioning the traditional division of labor between the sexes. For him, a woman's choice of marriage was parallel to a man's choice of a profession: unless and until she had fulfilled her obligations to her husband and children, she should not undertake anything else. But clearly, however equal the legal rights of husbands and wives, this position largely undermines Mill's own insistence upon the importance of marital equality for a just society. His acceptance of the traditional division of labor, without making any provision for wives who were thereby made economically dependent upon their husbands, largely undermines his insistence upon family justice as the necessary foundation for social justice.

Thus even those political theorists of the past who have perceived the family as an important school of moral development have rarely acknowledged the need for congruence between the family and the wide social order, which suggests that families themselves need to be just. Even when they have, as with Mill, they have been unwilling to push hard on the traditional division of labor within the family in the name of justice or equality.

Contemporary theorists of justice, with few exceptions, have paid little or no attention to the question of moral development—of how we are to *become* just. Most of them seem to think, to adapt slightly Hobbes's notable phrase, that just men spring like mushrooms from the earth.[26] Not surprisingly, then, it is far less often acknowledged in recent than in past theories that the family is important for moral development, and especially for instilling a sense of justice. As I have already noted, many theorists pay no attention at all to either the family or gender. In the rare case that the issue of justice within the family is given any sustained attention, the family is not viewed as a potential school of social justice.[27] In the rare case that a theorist pays any sustained attention to the development of a sense of justice or morality, little if any attention is likely to be paid to the family.[28] Even in the rare event that theorists pay considerably attention to the family *as* the first major locus of moral socialization, they do not refer to the fact that families are almost all still thoroughly gender-structured institutions.[29]

Among major contemporary theorists of justice, John Rawls alone treats the family seriously as the earliest school of moral development. He argues that a just, well-ordered society will be stable only if its members continue to develop a sense of justice. And he argues that families play a fundamental role in the stages by which this sense of justice is acquired. From the parents' love for their child, which comes to be reciprocated, comes the child's "sense of his own value and the desire to become the sort of person that they are."[30] The family, too, is the first of that series of "associations" in which we participate, from which we acquire the capacity, crucial for a sense of justice, to see things from the perspectives of others. . . . This capacity—the capacity for empathy—is essential for maintaining a sense of justice of the Rawlsian kind. For the perspective that is necessary for maintaining a sense of justice is not that of the egoistic or disembodied self, or of the dominant few who overdetermine "our" traditions or

"shared understandings," or (to use Nagel's term) of "the view from nowhere," but rather the perspective of every person in the society for whom the principles of justice are being arrived at. . . . The problem with Rawls's rare and interesting discussion of moral development is that it rests on the unexplained *assumption* that family institutions are just. If gendered family institutions are *not* just, but are, rather, a relic of caste or feudal societies in which responsibilities, roles, and resources are distributed, not in accordance with the principles of justice he arrives at or with any other commonly respected values, but in accordance with innate differences that are imbued with enormous social significance, then Rawls's theory of moral development would seem to be built on uncertain ground. This problem is exacerbated by suggestions in some of Rawls's most recent work that families are "private institutions," to which it is not appropriate to apply standards of justice. But if families are to help form just individuals and citizens, surely they must be *just families*.

In a just society, the structure and practices of families must give women the same opportunities as men to develop their capacities, to participate in political power and influence social choices, and to be economically secure. But in addition to this, families must be just because of the vast influence that they have on the moral development of children. The family is the primary institution of formative and moral development. And the structure and practices of the family must parallel those of the larger society if the sense of justice is to be fostered and maintained. While many theorists of justice, both past and present, appear to have denied the importance of at least one of these factors, my own view is that both are absolutely crucial. A society that is committed to equal respect for all of its members, and to justice in social distributions of benefits and responsibilities, can neither neglect the family nor accept family structures and practices that violate these norms, as do current gender-based structures and practices. It is essential that children who are to develop into adults with a strong sense of justice and commitment to just institutions spend their earliest and most formative years in an environment in which they are loved and nurtured, *and* in which principles of justice are abided by and respected. What is a child of either sex to learn about fairness in the average household with two full-time working parents, where the mother does, at the very least, twice as much family work as the father? What is a child to learn about the value of nurturing and domestic work in a home with a traditional division of labor in which the father either subtly or not so subtly uses the fact that he is the wage earner to "pull rank" on or to abuse his wife? What is a child to learn about responsibility for others in a family in which, after many years of arranging her life around the needs of her husband and children, a woman is faced with having to provide for herself and her children but is totally ill-equipped for the task by the life she agreed to lead, has led, and expected to go on leading? . . .

NOTES

1. U.S. Department of Labor, *Employment and Earnings: July 1987* (Washington, D.C.: Government Printing Office, 1987); Ruth Sidel, *Women and Children Last: The Plight of Poor Women in Affluent America* (New York: Viking, 1986), pp. xvi, 158. See also David T. Ellwood, *Poor Support: Poverty in the American Family* (New York: Basic Books, 1988), pp. 84–85, on the chronicity of poverty in single-parent households. . . .

2. Shirley Williams, in Williams and Elizabeth Holtzman, "Women in the Political World: Observations," *Daedalus* 116, no. 4 (Fall 1987): 30.

3. Twenty-three percent of single parents have never been married and 12 percent are widowed. (U.S. Bureau of the Census, Current Population Reports, *Household and Family Characteristics: March 1987* [Washington,

D.C.: Government Printing Office, 1987], p. 79). In 1987, 6.8 percent of children under eighteen were living with a never-married parent. ("Study Shows Growing Gap Between Rich and Poor," *New York Times,* March 23, 1989, p. A24).The proportions for the total population are very different from those for black families, of whom in 1984 half of those with adult members under thirty-five years of age were maintained by single, female parents, three-quarters of whom were never married. (Frank Levy, *Dollars and Dreams: The Changing American Income Distribution* [New York: Russell Sage, 1987], p. 156).

4. As Joan Scott has pointed out, *gender* was until recently used only as a grammatical term. See "Gender: A Useful Category of Historical Analysis," in Joan Wallach Scott, *Gender and the Politics of History* (New York: Columbia University Press, 1988), p. 28, citing Fowler's *Dictionary of Modern English Usage.*

5. Among Anglo-American feminists see, for example, Mary Daly, *Gyn/Ecology: The Metaethics of Radical Feminism* (Boston: Beacon Press, 1978); Susan Griffin, *Woman and Nature: The Roaring Inside Her* (New York: Harper & Row, 1978). For a good, succinct discussion of radical feminist biological determinism, see Alison Jaggar, *Feminist Politics and Human Nature* (Totowa, N.J.: Rowman and Allanheld, 1983).

6. See, for example, Sylvia Yanagisako and Jane Collier, "The Mode of Reproduction in Anthropology," in *Theoretical Perspectives on Sexual Difference,* ed. Deborah Rhode (New Haven: Yale University Press, in press).

7. Nancy Chodorow, *The Reproduction of Mothering: Psychoanalysis and the Sociology of Gender* (Berkeley: University of California Press, 1978); Dorothy Dinnerstein, *The Mermaid and the Minotaur: Sexual Arrangements and Human Malaise* (New York: Harper & Row, 1976). . . .

8. Linda Nichols, *Gender and History* (New York: Columbia University Press, 1986); Michelle Z. Rosaldo, "The Use and Abuse of Anthropology," *Signs* 5, no. 3 (1980); Joan Wallach Scott, *Gender and the Politics of*

History (New York: Columbia University Press, 1986).

9. For such critiques, see Bell Hooks, *Ain't I a Woman: black women and feminism* (Boston: South End Press, 1981), and *Feminist Theory: from margin to center* (Boston: South End Press, 1984); Elizabeth V. Spelman, *Inessential Woman: Problems of Exclusion in Feminist Thought* (Boston: Beacon Press, 1989).

10. There is now an abundant literature on the subject of women, their exclusion from non-domestic life, and the reasons given to justify it, in Western political theory. See, for example, Lorenne J. Clark and Lynda Lange, eds., *The Sexism of Social and Political Thought* (Toronto: University of Toronto Press, 1979); Jean Bethke Elshtain, *Public Man, Private Woman: Woman in Social and Political Thought* (Princeton: Princeton University Press, 1981); Genevieve Lloyd, *The Man of Reason: "Male" and "Female" in Western Philosophy* (Minneapolis: University of Minnesota Press, 1984); Mary O'Brien, *The Politics of Reproduction* (London: Routledge & Kegan Paul, 1981); Susan Moller Okin, *Women in Western Political Thought* (Princeton: Princeton University Press, 1979); Carole Pateman, "Feminist Critiques of the Public/Private Dichotomy," in *Public and Private in Social Life,* ed. S. Benn and G. Gaus (London: Croom Helm, 1983); Carole Pateman and Elizabeth Gross, eds., *Feminist Challenges: Social and Political Theory* (Boston: Northeastern University Press, 1987); Carol Pateman, *The Sexual Contract* (Stanford: Stanford University Press, 1988); Carole Pateman and Mary L. Shanley, eds., *Feminist Critiques of Political Theory* (Oxford: Polity Press, in press).

11. This is commented on and questioned by Francis Schrag, "Justice and the Family," *Inquiry* 19 (1976): 200 and Michael Walzer, *Spheres of Justice* (New York: Basic Books, 1983), chap. 9.

12. I have analyzed some of the ways in which theorists in the tradition avoided considering the justice of gender in "Are Our Theories of Justice Gender-Neutral?" in *The Moral Foundations of Civil Rights,* ed. Robert Fullinwider and Claudia Mills (Totowa, N.J.: Rowman and Littlefield, 1986).

13. See Judith Hicks Stiehm, "The Unit of Political Analysis: Our Aristotelian Hangover," in *Discovering Reality: Feminist Perspectives on Epistemology, Metaphysics, Methodology, and Philosophy of Science,* ed. Sandra Harding and Merrill B. Hintikka (Dordrecht, Holland: Reidel, 1983).

14. See Carole Pateman and Theresa Brennan, " 'Mere Auxiliaries to the Commonwealth': Women and the Origins of Liberalism," *Political Studies* 27, no. 2 (June 1979); also Susan Moller Okin, "Women and the Making of the Sentimental Family," *Philosophy and Public Affairs* 11, no. 1 (Winter 1982). This issue is treated at much greater length in Pateman, *The Sexual Contract.*

15. This claim, originating in the moral development literature, has significantly influenced recent feminist moral and political theory. Two central books are Carol Gilligan, *In a Different Voice* (Cambridge: Harvard University Press, 1982); and Nel Noddings, *Caring: A Feminine Approach to Ethics and Moral Education* (Berkeley: University of California Press, 1984). For the influence of Gilligan's work on feminist theory, see, for example, Seyla Benhabib, "The Generalized and the Concrete Other: The Kohlberg-Gilligan Controversy and Feminist Theory," in *Feminism as Critique,* ed. Benhabib and Drucilla Cornell (Minneapolis: University of Minnesota Press, 1987); Lawrence Blum, "Gilligan and Kohlberg: Implications for Moral Theory," *Ethics* 98, no. 3 (1988); and Eva Kittay and Diana Meyers, eds., *Women and Moral Theory* (Totowa, N.J.: Rowman and Allenheld, 1986). For a valuable alternative approach to the issues, and an excellent selective list of references to what has now become a vast literature, see Owen Flanagan and Kathryn Jackson, "Justice, Care and Gender: The Kohlberg-Gilligan Debate Revisited," *Ethics* 97, no. 3 (1987).

16. See, for example, John M. Broughton, "Women's Rationality and Men's Virtues: A Critique of Gender Dualism in Gilligan's Theory of Moral Development," *Social Research* 50, no. 3 (1983); Owen Flanagan,

Varieties of Moral Personality: Ethics and Psychological Realism (Cambridge: Harvard University Press, forthcoming), ch. 8; Catherine G. Greeno and Eleanor E. Maccoby, "How Different Is the 'Different Voice'?" and Gilligan's reply, *Signs* 11, no. 2 (1986); Debra Nails, "Social-Scientific Sexism: Gilligan's Mismeasure of man," *Social Research* 50, no. 3 (1983); Joan Tronto, " 'Women's Morality': Beyond Gender Difference to a Theory of Care," *Signs* 12, no. 4 (1987); Lawrence J. Walker, "Sex Differences in the Development of a Moral Reasoning: A Critical Review," *Child Development* 55 (1984).

17. See extracts from the Apostolic Letter in *New York Times,* October 1, 1988, pp. A1 and 6. On the reinforcement of the old stereotypes in general, see Susan Moller Okin, "Thinking like a Woman," in Rhode, ed., *Theoretical Perspectives.*

18. See esp. James Fishkin, *Justice, Equal Opportunity and the Family* (New Haven: Yale University Press, 1983); Derek L. Phillips, *Toward a Just Social Order* (Princeton, N.J.: Princeton University Press, 1986), esp. 346–49; John Rawls, *A Theory of Justice* (Cambridge, Mass.: Harvard University Press, 1971), pp. 74, 300–301, 511–12.

19. Jean-Jacques Rousseau, *Emile: or On Education,* trans. Allan Bloom (New York: Basic Books, 1979), p. 363.

20. Louis de Bonald, in *Archives Parlementaires,* 2e série (Paris, 1869), vol. 15, p. 612; cited and translated by Roderick Phillips, "Women and Family Breakdown in Eighteenth-Century France: Rouen 1780–1800," *Social History* 2 (1976): 217.

21. *Reynolds v. Nebraska,* 98 U.S. 145 (1879), 164, 166.

22. *Bradwell v. Illinois,* 83 U.S. 130 (1872).

23. Martha Minow, "We, the Family: Constitutional Rights and American Families," *The American Journal of History* 74, no. 3 (1987): 969, discussing *Reynolds* and other nineteenth-century cases.

24. John Stuart Mill, *The Subjection of Women* (1869), in *Collected Works,* ed. J. M. Robson (Toronto: University of Toronto Press, 1984), vol. 21, pp. 324, 293–95. At the time Mill wrote, women had no political rights and coverture deprived married women of most legal rights, too. He challenges all this in his essay.

25. Mill, *Subjection of Women,* pp. 324–25, 294–95.

26. Hobbes writes of "men . . . as if but even now sprung out of the earth . . . like mushrooms." "Philosophical Rudiments Concerning Government and Society," in *The English Works of Thomas Hobbes,* ed. Sir William Molesworth (London: John Bohn, 1966), vol. 2, p. 109.

27. For example, Walzer, *Spheres of Justice,* chap. 9, "Kinship and Love."

28. See Alan Gewirth, *Reason and Morality* (Chicago: University of Chicago Press, 1978). He discusses moral development from time to time, but places families within the broad category of "voluntary associations" and does not discuss gender roles within them.

29. This is the case with both Rawls's *Theory of Justice* and Phillips's sociologically oriented *Toward a Just Social Order,* as discussed above.

30. Rawls, *Theory,* p. 465.

Discussion Questions

1. What does Professor Okin mean by the "construction of gender"? Do you agree with her view of gender? Why or why not? Explain and defend your answer.

2. Professor Okin maintains that the traditional family and marriage (or "gendered structure of the family") are major obstacles to justice for women. What does she mean by this and how does she defend it?

3. Professor Okin claims that contemporary political and legal theorists do not discuss the justice of family structures. How does she defend this claim? Present and explain the three reasons why she thinks the current state of political and legal theory is unacceptable.

4. How does Professor Okin suggest that principles of justice should be used in judging family structures as just or unjust?

5. How does Professor Okin defend her assertion that there are "substantial inequalities between the sexes in our society today"? How does she think these inequalities have come about? Consult Thomas Sowell's essay (Chapter 32). Do you think that Sowell's analysis of the use of statistics and discrimination claims in the affirmative action debate can be applied to Okin's case for gender inequality? Why or why not?

6. Professor Okin maintains that the traditional family teaches children injustice. How does she defend this position? Do you agree with her? Why or why not? Explain and defend your answer.

7. How do you think that the other two authors in this section, especially Rawls (who Okin singles out), would reply to Okin's charges against contemporary political and legal theory?

You can locate InfoTrac-College Education articles about this chapter by accessing the InfoTrac-College Edition website (http://www.infotrac-college.com/wadsworth/). Using the InfoTrac-College Edition subject guide, enter the search terms relevant to this chapter, and then read abstracts for relevant articles.

SECTION C

Censorship and Freedom of Expression

Introduction to Section C

Although the First Amendment of the U.S. Constitution states that "Congress shall make no law . . . abridging the freedom of speech, or the press," it is clear that it is not absolute. For one cannot with impunity in the name of the First Amendment, for example, engage in slander, malice, sexual harassment, or the writing of fraudulent checks. Consequently, the question of whether the government has a right to censor obscene materials cannot be dismissed by merely appealing to the First Amendment as an absolute prohibition of censorship.

When I was a full-time faculty member at the University of Nevada (Las Vegas), I used to teach a course called "Contemporary Moral Issues." In that course we usually discussed the issue of censorship and pornography. In order to provoke my students to understand the moral and social conflicts that the issue entails, I made the following challenge to them:

> Every year the university library celebrates "Banned Book Month" by putting in glass cases books people have banned or tried to ban throughout American history, such as *Catcher in the Rye, The Adventures of Huckleberry Finn,* and *Tropic of Cancer.* Under each book is an index card on which is a brief history of the banning or attempted banning of the book and the reason or reasons why people did not want the book sold and/or permitted in their public or school library. Notice that all the books in the cases are classics that no intelligent person would want banned. The message is clear: people who favor censorship of any sort are idiots. But I have a feeling that the library would have a much more difficult time with its absolutism against censorship if one of you did the following. In fact, I challenge you to do this, if you have the guts. During "Banned Book Week" go to an adult bookstore and purchase the raunchiest hardcore pornographic magazine you can find, maybe with a catchy title like "Anal Sex Orgasm." Then take that magazine to a local public or school library and try to donate it. My guess is that the library staff will look at you as if you were crazy, and then politely say, "No thank you." Now take that same magazine to the university library and ask to see the person

in charge of the banned book cases. Present this person with the magazine and tell her that she should put it in the glass case since it is now a banned book. I have no doubt, like her colleagues at the public or school library, she will politely say, "No thank you." At that point you should demand your own glass case for books banned from the "Banned Book Month" case. You should promptly leave before she calls security.

No student took my challenge. But the point is clear. The issue of censorship and obscenity cannot be easily resolved by appealing to classic works that have been banned in the past as evidence that censorship is always a bad thing. For it seems obvious to many people that there are certain photographs, films, internet web sites, speech (e.g., harassing hate speech) and even literature that are so obscene that they have no place in either public or university libraries or even in the marketplace. On the hand, many people who oppose the censorship of any materials, even obscene ones, appeal to the First Amendment to the Constitution. They argue that those who want to restrict or ban speech, the press, or expression—which would include pornography—must first prove that the materials in question will pose a clear and present danger and/or significant harm to society and/or individuals. This is the position of philosopher Fred R. Berger, who argues, among other things, in Chapter 41 that the censor has the burden of providing convincing reasons to interfere with someone's consumption of pornography. On the other hand, in Chapter 40, legal scholar Robert H. Bork believes that this burden has been met and that government restriction of some forms of obscenity may be justified on the basis of the harm it may cause for the civic culture that makes good communities and good governments possible.

Due to the easy access to pornography afforded by the rapid growth of the Internet and cable television, the issue of obscenity and whether the government should be permitted to censor it is one of the most hotly contested issues of our day. Yet, even before the present technologies were in vogue, the executive branch of the United States government had attempted to address the issue. It formed two commissions. The first commission came to a more liberal conclusion in its final report (*Report of the Commission on Obscenity and Pornography* [1970]) and the second came to a more conservative conclusion (*Final Report of the Attorney General's Commission on Pornography* [1986]). The 1986 commission's legal review of the First Amendment, obscenity, and censorship is the topic of Chapter 36. It concludes that censorship of obscenity (which includes many but not all forms of pornography) is consistent with the First Amendment. This is supported by a number of U.S. Supreme Court decisions. According to the Court in *Miller v. California* (1973), something is obscene if it fulfills three conditions, and therefore can legally be banned. The commission for the most part agrees with the Court.

Recently, however, the Supreme Court has struck down attempts by the U.S. Congress to regulate the content of the Internet as well as cable television. However, it has upheld local ordinances that ban public nudity. In 1997, in *American Library Association v. U.S. Department of Justice* and *Reno v. American Civil Liberties Union*, the Court struck down, in a 9–0 decision, the Communication Decency Act. It "declared unconstitutional a federal law calling it a crime to send or display indecent material on line in a way available to minors. . . . The court held that speech on the Internet is entitled to the highest level of First Amendment protection, similar to the protection the Court gives to books and newspapers."[1] In 2000, in *United States v. Playboy,* the Court in a 5–4 decision struck down section 505 of the Telecommunications Act of 1996. It required cable television operators either to block or completely scramble obscene material, or to limit its broadcasting to the hours between 10 PM and 6 AM so that households that have not ordered the obscene channels, and who may have children with daytime access to the television, will not receive scrambled channels in which there is signal bleed. (This occurs when some audio and visual "bleeds" through despite the scrambling). Because section 504 of the Act already requires cable companies to inform their customers that they may receive, upon request, total blockage or complete scrambling 24 hours a day, and because 504, a regulation less restrictive than 505, can achieve the government's objective without regulating the content of the broadcast, the Court declared section 505 unconstitutional. Also in 2000, in *City of Erie v. "Kandyland,"* the court upheld an Erie, Pennsylvania, ordinance that prohibited public nudity. Since the ordinance prohibited conduct rather than speech, it passed constitutional muster. This is consistent with an earlier ruling the court made in *Barnes v. Glen Theatre* (1991).

Within the past several years, some feminists have come out strongly in support of laws that restrict pornography. Instead of arguing in the way that traditional opponents to pornography have argued (e.g., the material is obscene and sexually immoral), some feminists contend that pornography is an activity that abuses and exploits women by violating their dignity as well as aiding and abetting a climate in society which results in the rape and unjust discrimination of women. Chapter 37 contains a city ordinance drafted by feminist anti-pornography activists, Professor Catherine MacKinnon and Andrea Dworkin. A similar ordinance was struck down by the U.S. Supreme Court in *American Booksellers v. Hudnut* (1986). The authors of the essay in chapter 38, Professors Lisa Duggan, Nan Hunter, and Carole Vance, contend among other things that feminist anti-pornography legislation is hopelessly vague and ambiguous, paints all pornography with a broad brush, and plays into the hands of conservatives who have an anti-feminist agenda. Chapter 39, authored by Professor MacKinnon, defends the anti-pornography legislation, maintaining that the First Amendment allows for such restrictions. In addition, in reply to Duggan, Hunter, and Vance, she summarizes some of the testimonies and findings of the hearings that took place in conjunction with the ordinances proposed or passed in a number of major cities in the United States.

The issue of censorship and freedom of expression goes well beyond pornography and obscenity. For it sometimes touches on questions of government-funded artistic work, political and religious speech as well as so-called "hate speech." However, in this section the focus will be on obscenity and whether it is protected speech, and if citizens and governments have a right to restrict obscene expression.

It is clear that freedom of expression is a liberty integral to sustaining a society that strives to be just, fair, and good. However, what happens when the exercise of that liberty appears to some to undermine, or make less likely that we will achieve, the moral goals to which our society strives? Is there a greater harm in censoring the expression than permitting it? And if that is the case, is it correct to say that people therefore have a right to do wrong, or should we say that government censorship is a wrong that is worse than the bad expression? Can there ever be a form of expression so vile and obscene that permitting it is far worse than prohibiting the freedom to express it? As yon read the essays in this section keep these questions in mind.

> **Key words:** obscenity, pornography, censorship, freedom of speech, freedom of expression, right to privacy, protected speech, Internet pornography, First Amendment, *Hustler Magazine v. Falwell,* law and morality, Internet porn, *Miller v. California, Roth v. the United States, American Booksellers v. Hudnut.*

NOTE

1. American Library Association web site: www.ala.org/alaorg/oif/1stcases.html#2 (23 July 2000).

For Further Reading

Fred Berger, *Freedom of Expression* (Belmont, CA: Wadsworth, 1980).

Varda Burstyn, ed., *Women Against Censorship* (Vancouver: Groundwood Books/Douglas & McIntyre, 1985).

David Copp and Susan L. Wendell, eds., *Pornography and Censorship* (Buffalo, NY: Prometheus, 1983).

Dinesh D'Souza, "The New Censorship," in his *Illiberal Education: The Politics of Race and Sex on Campus* (New York: The Free Press, 1991), chapter 5.

Final Report of the Attorney General's Commission on Pornography (Nashville, TN: Rutledge Hill Press, 1986).

Stanley Fish, *There's No Such Thing as Free Speech, and It's a Good Thing, Too* (New York: Oxford University Press, 1994).

Robert P. George, *Making Men Moral: Civil Liberties and Public Morality* (New York: Oxford University Press, 1993).

H. H. Hart, ed., *Censorship: For and Against* (New York: Hart Publishing, 1971).

Nat Hentoff, *Free Speech for Me, But Not For Thee: How the American Left and Right Censor Each Other* (New York: HarperCollins, 1992).

Catharine MacKinnon, *Only Words* (Cambridge, MA: Harvard University Press, 1993).

Richard Perry and Patricia Williams, "Freedom from Hate Speech," in *Debating P.C.,* ed. Paul Berman (New York: Dell, 1992), 225–230.

Report of the Commission on Obscenity and Pornography (New York: Bantam Books, 1970).

The Constraints of the First Amendment   36

ATTORNEY GENERAL'S COMMISSION ON PORNOGRAPHY

The Attorney General's Commission was formed in 1985 by President Ronald Reagan's Administration. In 1986 the Commission published a report, from which the following essay is excerpted.

   In the following essay, the Attorney General's Commission is concerned with the foremost legal objection to regulating pornography: it violates the First Amendment right to freedom of expression. Although the First Amendment states that "Congress shall make no law . . . abridging the freedom of speech, or the press," it is clear that it is no absolute. For one cannot with impunity in the name of the First Amendment, for example, engage in slander, libel, sexual harassment, or the writing of fraudulent checks. However, the question before the commission was: Does the First Amendment allow the restriction of pornographic materials? After reviewing the court cases concerning this question, the commission concluded that pornography can be restricted without violating the First Amendment if the material under scrutiny is legally obscene (as in *Roth,* 1956). Something is obscene, according to the U.S. Supreme Court in *Miller v. California* (1973), if it fulfills three conditions. The commission reviews these conditions and then draws the conclusion that the court was for the most part correct. The commission also makes some observations about different interpretations of the meaning of the First Amendment, arguing in one place that some pornography may not be a First Amendment concern since the amendment was intended to protect cognitive expression and this type of pornography has none, for it is merely a masturbatory tool. The commission sums up its case by responding to the objection that any restrictions on obscenity, even if legally justified, can lead to abuse. It believes that such a concern, though legitimate, lacks evidence.

THE PRESUMPTIVE RELEVANCE OF THE FIRST AMENDMENT

THE SUBJECT OF PORNOGRAPHY is not coextensive with the subject of sex. Definitionally, pornography requires a portrayal, whether spoken, written, printed, photographed, sculpted, or drawn, and this essential feature of pornography necessarily implicates constitutional concerns that would not otherwise exist. The First Amendment to the Constitution of the United States provides quite simply that

Reprinted by permission from Final Report of the Attorney General's Commission on Pornography *(Nashville, TN: Rutledge Hill Press, 1986).*

"Congress shall make no law . . . abridging the freedom of speech, or of the press." Long-standing judicial interpretations make it now clear that this mandate is, because of the Fourteenth Amendment, applicable to the states as well, and make it equally clear that the restrictions of the First Amendment are applicable to any form of governmental action, and not merely to statutes enacted by a legislative body.

To the extent, therefore, that regulation of pornography constitutes an abridgment of the freedom of speech, or an abridgment of the freedom of the press, it is at least presumptively unconstitutional. And even if some or all forms of regulation of pornography are seen ultimately not to constitute abridgments of the freedom of speech or the freedom of the press, the fact remains that the Constitution treats speaking and printing as special, and thus the regulation of anything spoken or printed must be examined with extraordinary care. For even when some forms of regulation of what is spoken or printed are not abridgments of the freedom of speech, or abridgments of the freedom of the press, such regulations are closer to constituting abridgments than other forms of governmental action. If nothing else, the barriers between permissible restrictions on what is said or printed and unconstitutional abridgments must be scrupulously guarded.

Thus, we start with the presumption that the First Amendment is germane to our inquiry, and we start as well with the presumption that, both as citizens and as governmental officials who have sworn an oath to uphold and defend the Constitution, we have independent responsibilities to consider constitutional issues in our deliberations and in our conclusions. Although we are not free to take actions that relevant Supreme Court interpretations of the Constitution tell us we cannot take, we do not consider Supreme Court opinions as relieving us of our own constitutional responsibilities. The view that constitutional concerns are only for the Supreme Court, or only for courts in general, is simply fallacious,

and we do no service to the Constitution by adopting the view that the Constitution is someone else's responsibility. It is our responsibility, and we have treated it as such both in this Report and throughout our deliberation.

THE FIRST AMENDMENT, THE SUPREME COURT, AND THE REGULATION OF OBSCENITY

Although both speaking and printing are what the First Amendment is all about, closer examination reveals that the First Amendment cannot plausibly be taken to protect, or even to be relevant to, every act of speaking or writing. Government may plainly sanction the written acts of writing checks backed by insufficient funds, filing income tax returns that understate income or overstate deductions, and describing securities and consumer products in false or misleading terms. In none of these cases would First Amendment defenses even be taken seriously. The same can be said about sanctions against spoken acts such as lying while under oath, or committing most acts of criminal conspiracy. Although urging the public to rise up and overthrow the government is protected by the First Amendment, urging your brother to kill your father so that you can split the insurance money has never been considered the kind of spoken activity with which the First Amendment is concerned. Providing information to the public about the misdeeds of their political leaders is central to the First Amendment, but providing information to one's friends about the combination to the vault at the local bank is not a First Amendment matter at all.

The regulation of pornography, in light of the constraints of the First Amendment must thus be considered against this background—that not every use of words, pictures, or a printing press automatically triggers protection by the First Amendment. Indeed, as the examples above demonstrate, many uses of words, pictures, or a printing press do not even raise First

Amendment concerns. As Justice Holmes stated the matter in 1919, "the First Amendment . . . cannot have been, and obviously was not, intended to give immunity for every possible use of language." As described in Chapter 2, both the states and the federal government have long regulated the trade in sexually explicit materials under the label of "obscenity" regulation. And until 1957, obscenity regulation was treated as one of those forms of regulation that was totally unrelated to the concerns or the constraints of the First Amendment. If the aim of the state or federal regulation was the control of obscenity, then the First Amendment did not restrict government action, without regard to what particular materials might be deemed obscene and thus prohibited. When, throughout the first half of this century, states would determine to be obscene such works as Theodore Dreiser's *An American Tragedy,* or D. H. Lawrence's *Lady Chatterley's Lover,* or Erskine Caldwell's *God's Little Acre,* or Radclyffe Hall's *The Well of Loneliness,* the First Amendment was not taken to constitute a significant barrier to such actions.

In 1957, however, in *Roth v. United States,* the Supreme Court confronted squarely the tension between the regulation of what was alleged to be obscene and the constraints of the First Amendment. After *Roth,* it is not simply the form of regulation that immunizes a prosecution from the First Amendment. The Court made clear in *Roth,* and even clearer in subsequent cases, that the simple designation of a prosecution as one for obscenity does not cause the First Amendment considerations to drop out. If the particular materials prosecuted are themselves protected by the First Amendment, the prosecution is impermissible. After *Roth* mere labels could not be used to justify restricting the protected, and mere labels could not justify circumventing the protections of the First Amendment.

But the Supreme Court also made clear in *Roth* that some materials were themselves outside of the coverage of the First Amendment, and that obscenity, carefully delineated, could be considered as "utterly without redeeming social importance." As a result, the Court concluded, obscene materials were not the kind of speech or press included within the First Amendment, and could thus be regulated without the kind of overwhelming evidence of harm that would be necessary if materials of this variety were included within the scope of the First Amendment. But to the Court in *Roth,* that scope was limited to material containing *ideas.* All ideas, even the unorthodox, even the controversial, and even the hateful, were within the scope of the First Amendment. But if there were no ideas with "even the slightest redeeming social importance," then such material could be taken to be not speech in the relevant sense at all, and therefore outside of the realm of the First Amendment.

The general *Roth* approach to obscenity regulation has been adhered to ever since 1957, and remains still today the foundation of the somewhat more complex but nevertheless fundamentally similar treatment of obscenity by the Supreme Court. This treatment involves two major principles. The first, reiterated repeatedly and explained most thoroughly in *Paris Adult Theatre I v. Slaton,* is the principle that legal obscenity is treated as being either not speech at all, or at least not the kind of speech that is within the purview of any of the diverse aims and principles of the First Amendment. As a result, legal obscenity may be regulated by the states and by the federal government without having to meet the especially stringent standards of justification, often generalized as a "clear and present danger," and occasionally as a "compelling interest," that would be applicable to speech, including a great deal of sexually oriented or sexually explicit speech, that is within the aims and principles of the First Amendment. Instead, legal obscenity may constitutionally be regulated as long as there exists merely a "rational basis" for the regulation, a standard undoubtedly drastically less stringent than the standard of "clear and present danger" or "compelling interest."

That legal obscenity *may* be regulated by the states and the federal government pursuant to *Roth* and *Paris* does not, of course, mean that the states *must* regulate it, or even that they necessarily *should* regulate it. It is in the nature of our constitutional system that most of what the Constitution does is to establish structures and to set up outer boundaries of permissible regulation, without in any way addressing what ought to be done within these outer boundaries. There is no doubt, for example, that the speed limits on the highways could be significantly reduced without offending the Constitution, that states could eliminate all penalties for burglary without violating the Constitution, and that the highest marginal income tax rate could be increased from fifty percent to ninety percent without creating a valid constitutional challenge. None of these proposals seems a particularly good idea, and that is precisely the point—that the fact that an action is constitutional does not mean that it is wise. Thus, although the regulation of obscenity is, as a result of *Roth, Paris,* and many other cases, constitutionally permissible, this does not answer the question whether such regulation is desirable. Wisdom or desirability are not primarily constitutional questions.

Thus the first major principle is the constitutional permissibility of the regulation of obscenity. The second major principle is that the *definition* of what is obscene, as well as the determination of what in particular cases is obscene, is itself a matter of constitutional law. If the underpinnings of the exclusion of obscenity from the scope of the First Amendment are that obscenity is not what the First Amendment is all about, then special care must be taken to ensure that materials, including materials dealing with sex, that are within what the First Amendment is all about are not subject to restriction. Although what is on the unprotected side of the line between the legally obscene and constitutionally protected speech is not protected by the First Amendment, the location of the line itself is a consti-

tutional matter. That obscenity may be regulated consistent with the First Amendment does not mean that anything that is perceived by people or by legislatures as obscene may be so regulated.

As a result, the definition of obscenity is largely a question of constitutional law, and the current constitutionally permissible definition is found in another 1973 case, *Miller v. California.* According to *Miller,* material is obscene if all three of the following conditions are met:

1. The average person, applying contemporary community standards, would find that the work, taken as a whole, appeals to a prurient interest [in sex]; and

2. The work depicts or describes, in a patently offensive way, sexual conduct specifically defined by the applicable state [or federal] law; and

3. The work, taken as a whole, lacks serious literary, artistic, political, or scientific value.

It is not our function in this Report to provide an exposition of the law of obscenity. In a later part of this Report we do provide a much more detailed treatment of the current state of the law that we hope will be useful to those with a need to consider some of the details of obscenity law. But we do not wish our avoidance of extensive description of the law here to imply that the law is simple. Virtually every word or phrase in the *Miller* test has been the subject of extensive litigation and substantial commentary in the legal literature. The result of this is that there is now a large body of explanation and clarification of concepts such as "taken as a whole," "prurient interest," "patently offensive," "serious value," and "contemporary community standards." Moreover, there are many constitutionally mandated aspects of obscenity law that are not derived directly from the definition of obscenity. For example, no person may be prosecuted for an obscenity offense unless it can be shown that the person had knowledge of the general contents, character, and nature of the materials involved, for if the law were otherwise booksellers and others would avoid stocking anything even slightly sexually oriented for fear of being prosecuted on account of materials the content of which they were unaware. The procedures surrounding the initiation of a prosecution, including search and seizure, are also limited by constitutional considerations designed to prevent what would in effect be total suppression prior to a judicial determination of obscenity. And the entire subject of child pornography, which we discuss in Chapters 4 and 11, is governed by different principles and substantially different legal standards.

The constitutionally-based definition of obscenity is enforced not only by requiring that that definition be used in obscenity trials, but also, and more importantly, by close judicial scrutiny of materials determined to be obscene. This scrutiny, at both trial and appellate levels, is designed to ensure that nonobscene material is not erroneously determined to be obscene. The leading case here is the 1974 unanimous Supreme Court decision in *Jenkins v. Georgia,* which involved a conviction in Georgia of the Hollywood picture *Carnal Knowledge.* In reversing the conviction, the Supreme Court made clear that regardless of what the local community standards of that community may have been, the First Amendment prohibited *any* community, regardless of its standards, from finding that a motion picture such as this appealed to the prurient interest or was patently offensive. Thus, although appeal to the prurient interest and patent offensiveness are to be determined in the first instance by reference to local standards, it is clear after *Jenkins* that the range of local variation that the Supreme Court will permit consistent with the First Amendment is in fact quite limited.

In the final analysis, the effect of *Miller, Jenkins,* and a large number of other Supreme Court and lower court cases is to limit obscenity prosecutions to "hard core" material devoid of anything except the most explicit and offensive representations of sex. As we explained in our Introduction to this part, we believe that the late Justice Stewart was more perceptive than he has been given credit for having been in saying of hard-core pornography that he knew it when he saw it. Now that we have seen much of it, we are all confident that we too know it when we see it, but we also know that others have used this and other terms to encompass a range of materials wider than that which the Supreme Court permits to be restricted, and wider than that which most of us think ought to be restricted. But it should be plain both from the law, and from inspection of the kinds of material that the law has allowed to be prosecuted, that only the most thoroughly explicit materials, overwhelmingly devoted to patently offensive and explicit representations, and unmitigated by any significant amount of anything else, can be and are in fact determined to be legally obscene.

IS THE SUPREME COURT RIGHT?

We cannot ignore our own obligations not to recommend what we believe to be unconstitutional. Numerous people, in both oral and written evidence, have urged upon us the view that the Supreme Court's approach is a mistaken interpretation of the First Amendment. They have argued that we should conclude that any criminal prosecution based on the distribution to consenting adults of sexually explicit material, no matter how offensive to some, and no matter how hard-core, and no matter how devoid of literary, artistic, political, or scientific value, is impermissible under the First Amendment.

We have taken these arguments seriously. In light of the facts that the Supreme Court did not in *Roth* or since unanimously conclude that obscenity is outside the coverage of the First Amendment, and that its 1973 rulings were all decided by a scant 5–4 majority on this issue, there is no doubt that the issue was debatable within the Supreme Court, and thus could hardly be without difficulty. Moreover, we recognize that the bulk of scholarly comment is of the opinion that the Supreme Court's resolution of and basic approach to the First Amendment issues is incorrect. With dissent existing even within the Supreme Court, and with disagreement with the Supreme Court majority's approach predominant among legal scholars, we could hardly ignore the possibility that the Supreme Court might be wrong on this issue, and that we would wish to find protected that which the Supreme Court found unprotected.

There are both less and more plausible challenges to the Supreme Court's approach to obscenity. Among the least plausible, and usually more rhetorical device than serious argument, is the view that the First Amendment is in some way an "absolute," protecting, quite simply, all speech. Even Justices Black and Douglas, commonly taken to be "absolutists," would hardly have protected all spoken or written acts under the First Amendment, and on closer inspection of all those accused of or confessing to "absolutism" would at the very least apply their absolutism to a range of spoken or written acts smaller than the universe of all spoken, written, or pictorial acts. This is not to deny that under the views of many, including Black and Douglas, what is now considered obscene should be within the universe of what is absolutely protected. But "absolutism" in unadulterated form seems largely a strawman, and we see no need to use it as a way of avoiding difficult questions.

Much more plausible is the view not that the First Amendment protects all spoken, written, or pictorial acts, but that all spoken, written, or pictorial acts are at least in some way covered, even if not ultimately protected, by the First Amendment. That is, even if the government may regulate some such acts, it may never do so unless it has a reason substantially better than the reasons that normally are sufficient to justify governmental action. Whether this heightened standard of justification is described as a "clear and present danger," or "compelling interest," or some standard less stringent than those, the view is still that regulating any spoken, written, or pictorial act requires a particularly good reason. And when applied to the regulation of obscenity, so the argument goes, the reasons supplied and the empirical evidence offered remain too speculative to meet this especially high burden of justification.

Other views accept the fact that not all spoken, written, or pictorial acts need meet this especially high burden of justification. Only those acts that in some way relate to the purposes or principles of the First Amendment are covered, but, it is argued, even the hardest-core pornographic item is within the First Amendment's coverage. To some this is because both the distribution and use of such items are significant aspects of self-expression. And while not all acts of self-expression are covered by the First Amendment, acts of self-expression that take the form of books, magazines, and films are, according to the argument, so covered. These, it is argued, are the traditional media of communication, and when those media are used to express a different world view, or even merely to achieve sexual satisfaction, they remain the kinds of things towards which the First Amendment is directed. As a result, regulation of the process by which an alternative sexual vision is communicated, or regulation of the process by which people use the traditional media of communication to experience and to understand a different sexual vision, is as much a part of the First Amendment as communicating and experiencing different visions about, for example, politics or morals. A variant on this last argument, which takes obscenity to be within the range of First Amendment coverage admittedly smaller than the universe of communicative acts, looks not so much to the act or to the communication but instead to the government's reasons for regulating. If, so the argument goes, government's action in restricting is based on its reaction to a particular point of view, then the action is impermissible. Because it is the purpose of the First Amendment to allow all points of view to be expressed, an attempt by government to treat one point of view less favorably than another is unconstitutional for that reason alone, no matter how dangerous, offensive, or otherwise reprehensible the disfavored point of view may be.

We have heard witnesses articulate these various views intelligently and forcefully, and we have read more extensive versions of these arguments. They are not implausible by any means, but in the final analysis we remain unpersuaded that the fundamental direction of *Roth* and *Paris* is misguided. Indeed, we are confident that it is correct. Although we do not subscribe to the view that only political speech is covered by the First Amendment, we do not believe that a totally expansive approach is reasonable for society or conducive to preserving the particular values embodied in the First Amendment. The special power of the First Amendment ought, in our opinion, to be reserved for the conveying of arguments and information in a way that surpasses some admittedly low threshold of cognitive appeal, whether that appeal be emotive, intellectual, aesthetic, or informational. We have no doubt that this low threshold will be surpassed by a wide range of sexually explicit material conveying unpopular ideas about sex in a manner that is offensive to most people, and we accept that this is properly part of a vision of the First Amendment that is designed substantially to protect unpopular ways of saying unpopular things. But we also have little doubt that most of what we have seen that to us qualifies as hard-core material falls below this minimal threshold of cognitive or similar appeal. Lines are of course not always easy to draw, but we

find it difficult to understand how much of the material we have seen can be considered to be even remotely related to an exchange of views in the marketplace of ideas, to an attempt to articulate a point of view, to an attempt to persuade, or to an attempt seriously to convey through literary or artistic means a different vision of humanity or of the world. We do not deny that in a different context and presented in a different way, material as explicit as that which we have seen could be said to contain at least some of all of these characteristics. But we also have no doubt that these goals are remote from the goals of virtually all distributors or users of this material, and we also have no doubt that these values are present in most standard pornographic items to an extraordinarily limited degree.

In light of this, we are of the opinion that not only society at large but the First Amendment itself suffers if the essential appeal of the First Amendment is dissipated on arguments related to material so tenuously associated with any of the purposes or principles of the First Amendment. We believe it necessary that the plausibility of the First Amendment be protected, and we believe it equally necessary for this society to ensure that the First Amendment retains the strength it must have when it is most needed. This strength cannot reside exclusively in the courts, but must reside as well in widespread acceptance of the importance of the First Amendment. We fear that this acceptance is jeopardized when the First Amendment too often becomes the rhetorical device by which the commercial trade in materials directed virtually exclusively to sexual arousal is defended. There is a risk that in that process public willingness to defend and to accept the First Amendment will be lost, and the likely losers will be those who would speak out harshly, provocatively, and often offensively against the prevailing order, including the prevailing order with respect to sex. The manner of presentation and distribution of most standard pornography confirms the view that at bottom the predominant use of such material is as a masturbatory aid. We do not say that there is anything necessarily wrong with that for that reason. But once the predominant use, and the appeal to that predominant use, becomes apparent, what emerges is that much of what this material involves is not so much a portrayal of sex, or discussion of sex, but simply sex itself. As sex itself, the arguments for or against restriction are serious, but they are arguments properly removed from the First Amendment questions that surround primarily materials whose overwhelming use is not as a short-term masturbatory aid. Whether the state should, for example, prohibit masturbation in certain establishments that are open to the public is a question that some would wish to debate, but it is certainly not a First Amendment question. Similarly, the extent to which sex itself is and under what circumstances constitutionally protected is again an interesting and important constitutional question, but it is not usefully seen as a First Amendment question.

We recognize, of course, that using a picture of sex as a masturbatory aid is different from the simple act of masturbation, or any other form of sex. The very fact that pictures and words are used compels us to take First Amendment arguments more seriously than would be the case if the debate were about prostitution. Still, when we look at the standard pornographic item in its standard context of distribution and use, we find it difficult to avoid the conclusion that this material is so far removed from any of the central purposes of the First Amendment, and so close to so much of the rest of the sex industry, that including such material within the coverage of the First Amendment seems highly attenuated.

Like any other act, the act of making, distributing, and using pornographic items contains and sends messages. For government to act against some of these items on account of the messages involved may appear as problematic under the First Amendment, but to hold that such governmental action violates the

First Amendment is to preclude government from taking action in every case in which government fears that the restricted action will be copied, or proliferate because of its acceptance. Government may prosecute scofflaws because it fears the message that laws ought to be violated, and it may restrict the use of certain products in part because it does not wish the message that the product is desirable to be widely disseminated in perhaps its most effective form. So too with reference to the kind of material with which we deal here. If we are correct in our conclusion that this material is far removed from the cognitive, emotive, aesthetic, informational, persuasive, or intellectual core of the First Amendment, we are satisfied that a governmental desire to restrict the material for the messages its use sends out does not bring the material any closer to the center.

We thus conclude not that obscenity regulation creates no First Amendment concerns, nor even that the Supreme Court's approach is necessarily correct. But we do believe the Supreme Court's approach is most likely correct, and we believe as well that arguments against the Supreme Court's approach are becoming increasingly attenuated as we focus on the kind of material commonly sold in "adults only" establishments in this country. We may be wrong, but most of us can see no good reason at the moment for substituting a less persuasive approach for the Supreme Court's more persuasive one.

THE RISKS OF ABUSE

Although we are satisfied that there is a category of material so overwhelmingly preoccupied with sexual explicitness, and so overwhelming devoid of anything else, that its regulation does no violence to the principles underlying the First Amendment, we recognize that this cannot be the end of the First Amendment analysis. We must evaluate the possibility that in practice materials other than these will be restricted, and that the effect therefore will be the restriction of materials that are substantially closer to what the First Amendment ought to protect than the items in fact aimed at by the *Miller* definition of obscenity. We must also evaluate what is commonly referred to as the "chilling effect," the possibility that, even absent actual restriction, creators of material that is not in fact legally obscene will refrain from those creative activities, or will steer further to the safe side of the line, for fear that their protected works will mistakenly be deemed obscene. And finally we must evaluate whether the fact or restriction of obscene material will act, symbolically, to foster a "censorship mentality" that will in less immediate ways encourage or lead to various restrictions, in other contexts, of material which ought not in a free society be restricted. We have heard in one form or another from numerous organizations of publishers, booksellers, actors, and librarians, as well as from a number of individual book and magazine publishers. Although most have urged general anticensorship sentiments upon us, their oral and written submissions have failed to provide us with evidence to support claims of excess suppression in the name of obscenity laws, and indeed the evidence is to the contrary. The president of the Association of American Publishers testified that to his knowledge none of his members had even been threatened with enforcement of the criminal law against obscenity, and the American Library Association could find no record of any prosecution of a librarian on obscenity charges. Other groups of people involved in publishing, bookselling, or theatrical organizations relied exclusively on examples of excess censorship from periods of time no more recent than the 1940s. And still others were even less helpful, telling us, for example, that censorship was impermissible because "This is the United States, not the Soviet Union." We know that, but we know as well that difficult issues do not become easy by the use of inflammatory rhetoric. We wish that

many of these people or groups had been able to provide concrete examples to support their fears of excess censorship.

Throughout recent and not so recent history, excess censorship, although not necessarily prevalent, can hardly be said not to have occurred. As a result we have not been content to rest on the hollowness of the assertions of many of those who have reminded us of this theme. If there is a problem, we have our own obligations to identify it, even if witnesses before us have been unable to do so. Yet when we do our own researches, we discover that, with few exceptions, the period from 1974 to the present is marked by strikingly few actual or threatened prosecutions of material that is plainly not legally obscene. We do not say that there have been none. Attempted and unsuccessful actions against the film *Caligula* by the United States Custom Service, against *Playboy* magazine in Atlanta and several other places, and against some other plainly nonobscene publications indicate that mistakes can be made. But since 1974 such mistakes have been extremely rare, and the mistakes have all been remedied at some point in the process. While we wish there would be no mistakes, we are confident that application of *Miller* has been overwhelmingly limited to materials that would satisfy everyone's definition of "hard core."

Even without successful or seriously threatened prosecutions, it still may be the case that the very possibility of such an action deters filmmakers, photographers, and writers from exercising their creative abilities to the fullest. Once it appears that the likelihood of actual or seriously threatened prosecutions is almost completely illusory, however, we are in a quandary about how to respond to these claims of "chilling." We are in no position to deny the reality of someone's fears, but in almost every case those fears are unfounded. Where, as here, the fears seem to be fears of phantom dangers, we are hard pressed to say that the law is mistaken. It is those who are afraid who are mistaken. At least for the past ten years, not one remotely serious author, photographer, or filmmaker has had anything real to fear from the obscenity laws. The line between what is legally obscene and what is not is now so far away from their work that even substantially mistaken applications of current law would leave these individuals untouched. In light of that, we do not see their fears, however real to them, as a sufficient reason now to reconsider our views about the extent of First Amendment protection.

Much more serious, much more real, and much less in our control, is the extent to which nongovernmental or governmental but non-prohibitory actions may substantially influence what is published and what is not. What television scriptwriters write is in reality controlled by what television producers will buy, which is in turn controlled by what sponsors will sponsor and what viewers will view. Screen-writers may be effectively censored by the extent to which producers or studios desire to gain an "R" rating rather than an "X," or a "PG" rather than "R," or an "R" rather than a "PG." Book and magazine writers and publishers are restricted by what stores are willing to sell, and stores are restricted by what people are willing to buy. Writers of textbooks are in a sense censored by what school districts are willing to buy, authors are censored by what both bookstores and librarians are willing to offer, and librarians are censored by what boards of trustees are willing to tolerate.

In all of these settings there have been excesses. But every one of these settings involves some inevitable choice based on content. We think it unfortunate when *Catcher in the Rye* is unavailable in a high school library, but none of us would criticize the decision to keep *Lady Chatterley's Lover,* plainly protected by the First Amendment, out of the junior high schools.

We regret that legitimate bookstores have been pressured to remove from their shelves legitimate and serious discussions of sexuality, but none of us would presume to tell a Catholic bookseller that in choosing books he should not discriminate against books favoring abortion. Motion picture studios are unable to support an infinite number of screenwriters, and their choice to support those who write about families rather than homosexuality, for instance, is not only permissible, but is indeed itself protected by the First Amendment.

Where there have been excesses, and we do not ignore the extent to which the number of those excesses seems to be increasing, they seem often attributable to the plainly mistaken notion that the idea of "community standards" is a carte blanche to communities to determine entirely for themselves what is obscene. As we have tried once again to make clear in this report, nothing could be further from the truth. Apart from this, however, the excesses that have been reported to us are excesses that can only remotely be attributed to the obscenity laws. In a world of choice and of scarce resources, every one of these excesses could take place even were there no obscenity laws at all. In a world without obscenity law, television producers, motion picture studios, public library trustees, boards of education, convenience stores, and bookstores could still all choose to avoid any mention or discussion of sex entirely. And in a world without obscenity laws, all of these institutions and others could and would still make censorious choices based on their own views about politics, morals, religion, or science. Thus, the link between obscenity law and the excess narrowness, at times, of the choices made by private industry as well as government is far from direct.

Although the link is not direct, we are in no position to deny that there may be some psychological connection between obscenity laws and their enforcement and a general perception that nongovernmental restriction of anything dealing with sex is justifiable. We find the connection unjustifiable, but that is not to say that it may not exist in the world. But just as vigorous and vocal enforcement of robbery laws may create the environment in which vigilantes feel justified in punishing offenders outside the legal process, so too may obscenity law create an environment in which discussions of sexuality are effectively stifled. But we cannot ignore the extent to which much of this stifling, to the extent it exists, is no more than the exercise by citizens of their First Amendment rights to buy what they want to buy, and the exercise by others of First Amendment rights to sell or make what they wish. Choices are not always exercised wisely, but the leap from some unwise choices to the unconstitutionality of criminal laws only remotely related to those unwise choices is too big a leap for us to make.

Discussion Questions

1. What are some of the examples the commission cites in order to show that the First Amendment is not absolute? Do you think it makes its point? Why or why not?
2. How does the commission differentiate between pornography and obscenity? Why is not all obscenity pornography and all pornography obscenity? Explain.
3. What is the importance of the U.S. Supreme Court's decision *Roth v. United States* (1957)? How did it change the way the law dealt with the issue of pornography and censorship?
4. According to the commission, what are the two major principles in justifying regulation of obscenity? Present and explain each principle. How does the commission defend each?
5. What is the U.S. Supreme Court's view on the right of the government to restrict pornography? Present and explain the court's three-part standard to determine obscenity as found in *Miller v. California* (1973). Do you agree or disagree with the court? Explain and defend your answer.
6. Why does the commission believe that those who claim that restricting pornography will lead to abuse are wrong? Explain and present their case. Do you agree or disagree? Explain and defend your answer.

You can locate InfoTrac-College Education articles about this chapter by accessing the InfoTrac-College Edition website (http://www.infotrac-college.com/wadsworth/). Using the InfoTrac-College Edition subject guide, enter the search terms relevant to this chapter, and then read abstracts for relevant articles.

The Minneapolis and Indianapolis Anti-Pornography/ Civil Rights Ordinances

37

The following are anti-pornography ordinances proposed and passed in 1984. Helping draft these ordinances were feminist scholars, professor Catharine MacKinnon and Andrea Dworkin. The Indianapolis ordinance was struck down by the Court of Appeals, summarily affirmed by the U.S. Supreme Court, as unconstitutional in *American Booksellers v. Hudnut* (1986).

These ordinances are important because they are the focus of chapters 38 and 39. Because of that, there will be no study questions at the end of this chapter. The study questions at the end of chapters 38 and 39 should suffice.

Minneapolis Ordinance, 1984

AN ORDINANCE of the
CITY OF MINNEAPOLIS

1st Reading: 1-27-84
 Ref. to: Task Force on Pornography &
  GOVT OPS Comm.
Public Hearing: 6-20-84

Council Members Hoyt, Sayles Belton, White, and Scallon present the following ordinance:

Amending Title 7, Chapter 139 of the Minneapolis Code of Ordinances relating to Civil Rights: In General.

The City Council of the City of Minneapolis do ordain as follows:

Section 1. That Section 139.10 of the above-entitled ordinance be amended to read as follows:

139.10 Findings, declaration of policy and purpose.

(a) Findings. The council finds that discrimination in employment, labor union membership, housing accommodations, property rights, education, public accommodations and public services based on race, color, creed, religion, ancestry, national origin, sex, including sexual harassment AND PORNOGRAPHY, affectional preference, disability, age, marital status, or status with regard to public assistance or in housing accommodations based on familial status adversely affects the health, welfare, peace and safety of the community. Such discriminatory practices degrade individuals, foster intolerance and hate, and create and intensify unemployment, sub-standard housing, under-education, ill health, lawlessness and poverty, thereby injuring the public welfare.

(1) SPECIAL FINDINGS ON PORNOGRAPHY: THE COUNCIL FINDS THAT PORNOGRAPHY CONTRIBUTES TO CREATING AND MAINTAINING SEX AS A BASIS FOR DISCRIMINATION. PORNOGRAPHY IS A SYSTEMATIC PRACTICE OF EXPLOITATION AND SUBORDINATION BASED ON SEX WHICH DIFFERENTIALLY HARMS WOMEN. THIS HARM INCLUDES DEHUMANIZATION, SEXUAL EXPLOITATION, PHYSICAL INJURY, INTIMIDATION, AND INFERIORITY PRESENTED AS ENTERTAINMENT. THE BIGOTRY AND CONTEMPT IT ENCOURAGES, WITH THE ACTS OF AGGRESSION IT PROMOTES, DIMINISH OPPORTUNITIES FOR EQUALITY OF RIGHTS IN EMPLOYMENT, EDUCATION, PROPERTY, PUBLIC ACCOMMODATIONS AND PUBLIC SERVICES; PROMOTE RAPE, BATTERY AND PROSTITUTION AND INHIBIT JUST ENFORCEMENT OF LAWS AGAINST THESE ACTS; CONTRIBUTE SIGNIFICANTLY TO RESTRICTING WOMEN IN PARTICULAR FROM FULL EXERCISE OF CITIZENSHIP AND PARTICIPATION IN NEIGHBORHOODS AND OTHER CIVIL LIFE, DAMAGE RELATIONS BETWEEN THE SEXES; AND UNDERMINE WOMEN'S EQUAL EXERCISE OF RIGHTS TO SPEECH

AND ACTION GUARANTEED TO ALL CITIZENS UNDER THE CONSTITUTIONS AND LAWS OF THE UNITED STATES AND THE STATE OF MINNESOTA.

(b) <u>Declaration of policy and purpose.</u> It is the public policy of the City of Minneapolis and the purpose of this title:

(1) To recognize and declare that the opportunity to obtain employment, labor union membership, housing accommodations, property rights, education, public accommodations and public services without discrimination based on race, color, creed, religion, ancestry, national origin, sex, including sexual harassment AND PORNOGRAPHY, affectional preference, disability, age, marital status, or status with regard to public assistance or to obtain housing accommodations without discrimination based on familial status is a civil right;

(2) To prevent and prohibit all discriminatory practices based on race, color, creed, religion, ancestry, national origin, sex, including sexual harassment AND PORNOGRAPHY, affectional preference, disability, age, marital status, or status with regard to public assistance with respect to employment, labor union membership, housing accommodations, property rights, education, public accommodations or public services;

(3) To prevent and prohibit all discriminatory practices based on familial status with respect to housing accommodations;

(4) TO PREVENT AND PROHIBIT ALL DISCRIMINATORY PRACTICES OF SEXUAL SUBORDINATION OR INEQUALITY THROUGH PORNOGRAPHY;

(5) To protect all persons from unfounded charges of discriminatory practices;

(6) To eliminate existing and the development of any ghettos in the community; and

(7) To effectuate the foregoing policy by means of public information and education, mediation and conciliation, and enforcement.

Section 2. That Section 139.20 of the above-entitled ordinance be amended by adding thereto a new subsection (gg) to read as follows:

(gg) <u>Pornography.</u> Pornography is a form of discrimination on the basis of sex.

(1) Pornography is the graphic sexually explicit subordination of women, whether in pictures or in words, that also includes one or more of the following:

   (i) women are presented as sexual objects who enjoy pain or humiliation; or

   (ii) women are presented as sexual objects who experience sexual pleasure in being raped; or

   (iii) women are presented as sexual objects tied up or cut up or mutilated or bruised or physically hurt; or

   (iv) women are presented as sexual objects for domination, conquest, violation, exploitation, possession or use, through postures or positions of submission or servility or display; or

   (v) women are presented being penetrated by inanimate objects or animals; or

   (vi) women are presented in scenarios of degradation, injury, torture, dismembered or truncated or severed or fragmented into body parts, shown as filthy or inferior, bleeding, bruised, or hurt in a context that makes these conditions sexual.

(2) The use of men, children, or transsexuals in the place of women in (1) (i–iv) above is pornography for purposes of subsections (l)–(p) of this statute.

Section 3. That section 139.40 of the above-entitled ordinance be amended by adding thereto new subsections (l), (m), (n), (o), (p), (q), and (r) to read as follows:

(l) <u>Coercion into pornographic performances.</u> Any person, including transsexual, who is coerced, intimidated, or fraudulently induced (hereinafter "coerced") into performing for pornography shall have a claim against the maker(s), seller(s), exhibitor(s) or distributor(s) of said pornography which may date from any appearance or sale of any product(s) of such performance(s), for damages and for the elimination of the products of the performance(s) from the public view.

Proof of one or more of the following facts or conditions may or may not be admissible but shall not, without more, conclusively negate a finding of coercion:

(i) that the person is a woman; or

(ii) that the person is or has been a prostitute; or

(iii) that the person has attained the age of majority; or

(iv) that the person is connected by blood or marriage to anyone involved in or related to the making of the pornography; or

(v) that the person has previously had, or been thought to have had, sexual relations with anyone, including anyone involved in or related to the making of the pornography; or

(vi) that the person has previously posed for sexually explicit pictures for or with anyone, including anyone involved in or related to the making of the pornography at issue; or

(vii) that anyone else, including a spouse or other relative, has given permission on the person's behalf; or

(viii) that the person actually consented to a use of the performance that is altered into pornography; or

(ix) that the person knew that the purpose of the acts or events in question was to make pornography; or

(x) that the person showed no resistance or appeared to cooperate actively in the photographic sessions or in the sexual events that produced the pornography; or

(xi) that the person signed a contract, or made statements affirming a willingness to cooperate in the production of pornography; or

(xii) that no physical force, threats, or weapons were used in the pornographic sessions or in the sexual events recorded in the pornography; or

(xiii) that the person was paid or otherwise compensated.

(m) <u>Discrimination by trafficking in pornography.</u> The production, sale, exhibition, or distribution of pornography is sex discrimination by means of trafficking in pornography. Any woman has a claim hereunder as a woman acting against the subordination of women. Any man or transsexual who alleges injury by pornography in the way women are injured by it shall also have a claim.

(1) City, state, and federally funded public libraries or private and public university and college libraries shall not be construed to be trafficking in pornography.

(2) The formation of private clubs or associations for purposes of trafficking in pornography shall be considered a conspiracy to violate civil rights.

(3) This section shall not be construed to make isolated passage(s) or isolated part(s) actionable.

(n) <u>Forcing pornography on a person.</u> Any woman, man, child, or transsexual who has pornography forced on him/her in any place of employment, in education, in a home, or in any public place has a claim against the perpetrator and/or institution.

(o) <u>Assault or physical attack due to pornography.</u> Any woman, man, child, or transsexual who is assaulted, physically attacked or injured in a way that is directly caused by specific pornography has a claim for damages against the perpetrator(s), maker(s), distributor(s), seller(s), and/or exhibitor(s), and for an injunction against the specific pornography's further exhibition, distribution, or sale. No damages shall be assessed (A) against maker(s) for pornography made, (B) against distributor(s) for pornography distributed, (C) against seller(s) for pornography sold, or (D) against exhibitors for pornography exhibited prior to the enforcement date of this act.

(p) <u>Defenses.</u>

(1) Where the materials which are the subject matter of a claim under subsections (l), (m), (n), or (o) of this section are pornography, it shall not be a defense that the defendant did not know or intend that the materials were pornography or sex discrimination.

(2) It shall be a defense to a claim for damages under subsections (m) & (l), or the sale, distribution, or exhibition part of (o), that the respondent did not know, or should not reasonably have known, that the materials are pornography.

(3) It shall be a defense to a claim under section (m) that the materials complained of are those covered only by section 139.20(gg) (1)(iv).

(q) <u>Severability.</u> Should any part(s) of this ordinance be found legally invalid, the remaining part(s) remain valid. Should any part(s) of this ordinance be found legally invalid as applied in a particular way or to a particular case or category of cases, that part(s) remains valid as applied in other ways or to other cases or categories of cases, unless the remaining application would clearly frustrate the Council's intent in adopting this ordinance.

(r) <u>Enforcement dates.</u>

(1) Enforcement under (m) or the second sentence of (o) shall be suspended until January 1, 1985, to permit training, public education and voluntary compliance.

(2) No liability shall attach under (m) or as provided in the second sentence of (o) until January 1, 1985. Liability under all other sections of this act shall attach as of the date of passage.

RECORD OF COUNCIL VOTE

Council Member	Aye	Nay	Council Member	Aye	Nay
Dziedzic	X		Scallon	X	
O'Brien		X	Niemiec		X
Hilary	X		Cramer		X
White	X		Schulstad		X
Coyle	X		Hoyt	X	
Carlson		X	Pres. Rainville		X
Sayles Belton	X				

PASSED: July 13, 1984
VETOED: July 13, 1984

Indianapolis Ordinance, 1984

CODE OF INDIANAPOLIS
and MARION COUNTY, INDIANA

Chapter 16
HUMAN RELATIONS; EQUAL
OPPORTUNITY[1]

Sec. 16–1. Findings, policies and purposes.
(a) *Findings*. The city-county council hereby
makes the following findings:

(1) The council finds that the practice of
denying equal opportunities in
employment, education, access to and
use of public accommodations, and
acquisition of real estate based on race,
color, religion, ancestry, national origin,
handicap, or sex is contrary to the
principles of freedom and equality of
opportunity and is a burden to the
objectives of the policies contained
herein and shall be considered
discriminatory practices.

(2) Pornography is a discriminatory practice
based on sex which denies women equal
opportunities in society. Pornography is
central in creating and maintaining sex as
a basis for discrimination. Pornography is
a systematic practice of exploitation and
subordination based on sex which
differentially harms women. The bigotry
and contempt it promotes, with the acts
of aggression it fosters, harm women's
opportunities for equality of rights in
employment, education, access to and
use of public accommodations, and
acquisition of real property; promote
rape, battery, child abuse, kidnaping and
prostitution and inhibit just enforcement
of laws against such acts; and contribute

significantly to restricting women in
particular from full exercise of citizenship
and participation in public life, including
in neighborhoods.

(b) It is the purpose of this chapter to carry
out the following policies of the City of Indianapolis and Marion County:

(1) To provide equal employment
opportunity in all city and county jobs
without regard to race, color, religion,
handicap, national origin, ancestry, age,
sex, disabled veteran, or Vietnam era
veteran status;

(2) To encourage the hiring of the
handicapped in both the public and the
private sectors and to provide equal
access to the handicapped to public
accommodations;

(3) To utilize minority-owned businesses,
securing goods and services for the city
and county in a dollar amount equal to
at least (10) per cent of monies spent by
the City of Indianapolis and Marion
County;

(4) To utilize women-owned businesses and
encourage the utilization of women in
construction and industry;

(5) To protect employers, labor
organizations, employment agencies,
property owners, real estate brokers,
builders, lending institutions,
governmental and educational agencies
and other persons from unfounded
charges of discrimination;

(6) To provide all citizens of the City of
Indianapolis and Marion County equal
opportunity for education, employment,
access to public accommodations
without regard to race, religion, color,
handicap, sex, national origin, ancestry,
age, or disabled veteran or Vietnam era
veteran status;

(7) To provide all citizens of the City of
Indianapolis and Marion County equal

[1]*This is an edited version of the civil-rights law of the City of
Indianapolis and Marion County. All language relating
specifically to pornography is underlined. Spelling has been
corrected.*

opportunity for acquisition through purchase or rental of real property including, but not limited to, housing without regard to race, sex, religion or national origin; and

(8) To prevent and prohibit all discriminatory practices of sexual subordination or inequality through pornography.

Sec. 16–2. Nondiscrimination clauses.

(1) Every contract to which one of the parties is the city or the county, or any board, department or office of either the city or county, including franchises granted to public utilities, shall contain a provision requiring the governmental contractor and subcontractors not to discriminate against any employee or applicant for employment in the performance of the contract, with respect to hire, tenure, terms, conditions or privileges of employment, or any matter directly or indirectly related to employment, because of race, sex, religion, color, national origin, ancestry, age, handicap, disabled veteran status and Vietnam era veteran status. Breach of this provision may be regarded as a material breach of the contract.

(2) All applications, postings, announcements, and advertisements recruiting applicants for employment with the city or county shall conspicuously post in the bottom margin of such recruiting bids a clause as follows: "An Affirmative Action Equal Employment Opportunity Employer."

Sec. 16–3. Definitions.

As used in this chapter, the following terms shall have the meanings ascribed to them in this section:

. . .

(d) *Board* shall mean the equal opportunity advisory board.

(e) *Complainant* shall mean any person who signs a complaint on his/her own behalf alleging that he/she has been aggrieved by a discriminatory practice.

(f) *Complaint* shall mean a written grievance filed with the office of equal opportunity, either by a complainant or by the board or office, which meets all the requirements of sections 16–18 and 16–19.

(g) *Discriminatory practice* shall mean and include the following:

(1) The exclusion from or failure or refusal to extend to any person equal opportunities or any difference in the treatment of any person by reason of race, sex, religion, color, national origin or ancestry, handicap, age, disabled veteran or Vietnam era veteran status.

(2) The exclusion from or failure or refusal to extend to any person equal opportunities or any difference in the treatment of any person, because the person filed a complaint alleging a violation of this chapter, testified in a hearing before any members of the board or otherwise cooperated with the office or board in the performance of its duties and functions under this chapter, or requested assistance from the board in connection with any alleged discriminatory practice, whether or not such discriminatory practice was in violation of this chapter.

(3) In the case of a real estate broker or real estate salesperson or agent, acting in such a capacity in the ordinary course of his/her business or occupation, who does any of the following:

a. Any attempt to prevent, dissuade or discourage any prospective purchaser, lessee or tenant of real estate because of the race, sex, religion or national origin of:

1. Students, pupils or faculty of any school or school district;

2. Owners or occupants, or prospective owners or occupants, of real estate in any neighborhood or on any street or block; provided, however, this clause shall not be construed to prohibit disclosure in response to inquiry by any prospective purchaser, lessee or tenant of:

   (i) Information reasonably believed to be accurate regarding such race, sex, religion or national origin; or

   (ii) The honest professional opinion or belief of the broker, salesperson or agent regarding factors which may affect the value or desirability of property available for purchase or lease.

b. Any solicitation, promotion or attempt to influence or induce any owner to sell, lease or list for sale or lease any real estate, which solicitation, promotion or attempted inducement includes representations concerning:

   1. Race, sex, religion or national origin or present, prospective or possible purchasers or occupants of real estate in any area, neighborhoods or particular street or block;

   2. Present, prospective or possible neighborhood unrest, tension or change in the race, sex, religion or national origin of occupants or prospective occupants of real estate in any neighborhood or any street or block;

   3. Present, prospective or possible decline in market value of any real estate by reason of the present, prospective or possible entry into any neighborhood, street or block or persons of a particular race, sex, religion or national origin;

   4. Present, prospective or possible decline in the quality of education offered in any school or school district by reason of any change in the race, sex, religion or national origin of the students, pupils or faculty of such school or district.

(4) Trafficking in pornography: The production, sale, exhibition, or distribution of pornography.

   a. City, state, and federally funded public libraries or private and public university and college libraries in which pornography is available for study, including on open shelves, shall not be construed to be trafficking in pornography, but special display presentations of pornography in said places is sex discrimination.

   b. The formation of private clubs or associations for purposes of trafficking in pornography is illegal and shall be considered a conspiracy to violate the civil rights of women.

   c. This paragraph (4) shall not be construed to make isolated passages or isolated parts actionable.

(5) Coercion into pornographic performance: Coercing, intimidating or fraudulently inducing any person, including a man, child or transsexual into performing for pornography, which injury may date from any appearance or sale of any products of such performance.

   a. Proof of the following facts or conditions shall not constitute a defense:

      1. That the person is a woman; or

      2. That the person is or has been a prostitute; or

3. That the person has attained the age of majority; or

4. That the person is connected by blood or marriage to anyone involved in or related to the making of the pornography; or

5. That the person has previously had, or been though to have had, sexual relations with anyone, including anyone involved in or related to the making of the pornography; or

6. That the person has previously posed for sexually explicit pictures for or with anyone, including anyone involved in or related to the making of the pornography at issue; or

7. That anyone else, including a spouse or other relative, has given permission on the person's behalf; or

8. That the person actually consented to a use of the performance that is changed into pornography; or

9. That the person knew that the purpose of the acts or events in question was to make pornography; or

10. That the person demonstrated no resistance or appeared to cooperate actively in the photographic sessions or in the sexual events that produced the pornography; or

11. That the person signed a contract, or made statements affirming a willingness to cooperate in the production of pornography; or

12. That no physical force, threats, or weapons were used in the making of the pornography; or

13. That the person was paid or otherwise compensated.

(6) Forcing pornography on a person: The forcing of pornography on any woman, man, child or transsexual in any place of employment, in education, in a home, or in any public place.

(7) Assault or physical attack due to pornography: The assault, physical attack, or injury of any woman, man, child, or transsexual in a way that is directly caused by specific pornography.

(8) Defenses: Where the materials which are the subject matter of a complaint under paragraphs (4), (5), or (7) of this subsection (g) are pornography, it shall not be a defense that the respondent did not know or intend that the materials were pornography or sex discrimination; provided, however, that in the cases under paragraph (g)(4) of section 16–3 or against a seller, exhibitor or distributor under paragraph (g)(7) of section 16–3, no damages or compensation for losses shall be recoverable unless the complainant proves that the respondent knew or had reason to know that the materials were pornography. Provided, further, that it shall be a defense to a complaint under paragraph (g)(4) of section 16–3 that the materials complained of are those covered only by paragraph (q)(6) of section 16–3.

. . .

(n) *Office* shall mean the office of equal opportunity created by this chapter.

. . .

(p) *Person* shall mean and include one or more individuals, partnerships, associations, organizations, cooperatives, legal representatives, trustees, trustees in bankruptcy, receivers, governmental agencies and other organized groups of persons.

(q) *Pornography* shall mean the graphic sexually explicit subordination of women, whether in pictures or in words, that also includes one or more of the following:

(1) Women are presented as sexual objects who enjoy pain or humiliation; or

(2) Women are presented as sexual objects who experience sexual pleasure in being raped; or

(3) Women are presented as sexual objects tied up or cut up or mutilated or bruised or physically hurt, or as dismembered or truncated or fragmented or severed into body parts; or

(4) Women are presented being penetrated by objects or animals; or

(5) Women are presented in scenarios of degradation, injury, abasement, torture, shown as filthy or inferior, bleeding, bruised, or hurt in a context that makes these conditions sexual; [or]

(6) Women are presented as sexual objects for domination, conquest, violation, exploitation, possession, or use, or through postures or positions of servility or submission or display. The use of men, children, or transsexual in the place of women in paragraphs (1) through (6) above shall also constitute pornography under this section.

. . .

(v) *Respondent* shall mean one or more persons against whom a complaint is filed under this chapter, and who the complaint alleges has committed or is committing a discriminatory practice.

Sec. 16–4. Office of equal opportunity—Created; purpose.

There is hereby created a section of the legal division of the department of administration entitled the office of equal opportunity. This office and its board are empowered as provided in this chapter to carry out the public policy of the state as stated in section 2 of the Indiana Civil Rights Act, within the territorial boundaries of Marion County.

Sec. 16–5. Same—Composition of office; functions.

The office shall be directed by a chief officer who shall also be the affirmative action officer for the city and county. The chief officer shall be appointed by and serve at the pleasure of the mayor and shall be responsible for performing the following functions:

(1) To monitor internal employment practices [specified] . . .

(2) To monitor contract compliance as follows: [specified] . . .

(3) To receive, investigate and adjudicate community complaints as specified in sections 16–18 through 16–28.

Section 16–6. Same—General powers and duties.

In addition to the functions previously mentioned in section 16–5, the office shall have the following powers and duties.

(1) To gather and distribute information for the purpose of improving human relations and removing inequities to protected groups in the areas of housing, recreation, education, employment, law enforcement, vocational guidance and related matters.

(2) To assist other governmental and private agencies, groups and individuals in reducing community tensions and preventing conflicts between persons of different racial, ethnic and religious groups.

(3) To discourage persons from engaging in discriminatory practices through informal methods of persuasion and conciliation and through programs of public information and education.

(4) To furnish technical assistance upon request to persons to assist them in eliminating discriminatory practices or otherwise implementing the policy and purposes of the Indiana Civil Rights Act.

(5) To make such general investigations, studies and surveys as the office shall deem necessary for the performance of its duties.

(6) To prepare and submit at least annually a report of its activities to the mayor and to the public, which report shall describe the investigations and proceedings conducted by the office, the outcome thereof and the progress and the achievements of the office and the community toward elimination of discriminatory practices.

(7) To cooperate with the Indiana State Civil rights Commission, any appropriate federal, state or local agencies, and with private organizations, individuals and neighborhood associations in order to effectuate the purposes of this chapter and to further compliance with federal, state and local laws and ordinances prohibiting discriminatory practices.

(8) To perform any other duties assigned by ordinance or the mayor.

Sec. 16–7. Equal opportunity advisory board—Created; purpose.

There is hereby created an equal opportunity advisory board empowered as provided in this chapter to carry out the public policy of the state as stated in section 2 of the Indiana Civil Rights Act, within the territorial boundaries of Marion County.

Sec. 16–8. Same—Composition of board; appointment and terms of members.

. . .

Sec. 16–13. Complaint adjudication; territorial application.

This chapter shall apply within the territorial limits of the consolidated city and within the territorial limits of the county, with respect to any discriminatory practice occurring with such territorial limits and which relates to:

(1) Acquisition of real estate; or

(2) Employment; or

(3) Education controlled by any public board or agency; or

(4) Publication accommodations; or

(5) <u>Pornography.</u>

Sec. 16–14. Unlawful acts other than discriminatory practices; penalty.

(a) It shall be unlawful for any person to discharge, expel or otherwise discriminate against any other person because that person:

(1) Has filed a complaint alleging a violation of section 16–15;

(2) Has testified in a hearing before the board or any committee thereof;

(3) Has otherwise cooperated with the board or office in the performance of their duties and functions;

(4) Has requested assistance from the board or office in connection with any alleged discriminatory practice, whether or not the discriminatory practice was in violation of section 16–15.

(b) It shall be unlawful for any person willfully to file a complaint alleging a violation of section 16–15 with knowledge that the complaint is false in any material respect.

(c) Any person who violates any of the provisions of this section shall, upon conviction, be subject to fine in an amount not less than ten dollars ($10.00) nor more than three hundred dollars ($300.00); provided, however, no such fine shall be imposed upon any person against whom the board or office has proceedings under this chapter with respect to any violation of subsection (a), which violation is also a discriminatory practice. Any proceeding to impose a penalty under this section shall be commenced within six (6) months after the date the violation occurred.

Sec. 16–15. Discriminatory practices declared unlawful.

Each discriminatory practice as defined in section 16–3 shall be considered unlawful unless it is specifically exempted by this chapter.

Sec6. 16–16. Persons and activities to which sections 16–14 and 16–15 do not apply.

(a) Sections 16–14 and 16–15 shall not apply to employment performed for the consolidated city and department or agency thereof, or any employment performed for the county or agency thereof which is represented by the corporation counsel pursuant to IC 18-4-7-5.

(b) Subject to the provision of section 16–3(g)(4), the provisions of sections 16–14 and 16–15 shall not include any not-for-profit corporation or association organized exclusively for fraternal or religious purposes, nor any school, education, charitable or religious institution owned or conducted by, or affiliated with, a church or religious institution, nor any exclusively social club, corporation or association that is not organized for profit and is not in fact open to the general public.

(c) Sections 16–14 and 16–15 shall not apply to the rental of rooms in a boardinghouse or rooming house or single-family residential unit; provided, however, the owner of the building unit actually maintains and occupies a unit or room in the building as his/her residence and, at the time of the rental the owner intends to continue to so occupy the unit or room therein for an indefinite period subsequent to the rental.

(d) The following shall not be discrimination on the basis of sex:

(1) For any person to maintain separate restrooms or dressing rooms for the exclusive use of either sex;

(2) For an employer to hire and employ employees; for an employment agency to classify or refer for employment any individual; for a labor organization to classify its membership or to classify or refer for employment any individual; or for an employer, labor organization or joint labor-management committee, controlling apprenticeship or other training or retraining programs, to admit or employ any individual in any such program; on the basis of sex in those certain instances where sex is a bona fide occupational qualification reasonably necessary to the normal operation of that particular business or enterprise.

Sec. 16–17. Grounds for complaint; persons who may file; persons against whom complaint may be made.

(a) A complaint charging that any person has engaged in or is engaging in a discriminatory practice prohibited by sections 16–14 and/or 16–15 may be filed with the office by any person claiming to be aggrieved by the practice, or by one or more members of the board of employees of the office who have reasonable cause to believe that a violation of sections 16–14 and 16–15 has occurred, in any of the following circumstances:

(1) In the case of the acquisition of real estate, against the owner of the real estate, a real estate broker, real estate salesperson or agent, or a lending institution or appraiser;

(2) In the case of education, against the governing board of any public school district which operates schools within the territorial limits of the consolidated city or of the county;

(3) In the case of a public accommodation, against the owner or person in charge of any such establishment, or both;

(4) In the case of a public facility, against the governmental body which operates or has jurisdiction over the facility;

(5) In the case of employment, against any employer, employment agency or labor organization;

(6) In the cases of trafficking in pornography, coercion into pornographic performances, and assaults or physical attack due to pornography (as provided in section 16–3(g)(7) against the perpetrator(s), maker(s), seller(s), exhibitor(s), or distributor(s).[)]

(7) In the case of forcing pornography on a person, against the perpetrator(s) and/or institution.

(b) In the case of trafficking in pornography, any woman may file a complaint as a woman acting against the subordination of women and any man, child, or transsexual may file a complaint but must prove injury in the same way that a woman is injured in order to obtain relief under this chapter.

(c) In the case of assault or physical attack due to pornography, compensation for losses or an award of damages shall not be assessed against:

(1) Maker(s), for pornography made,

(2) Distributor(s), for pornography distributed,

(3) Seller(s), for pornography sold, or

(4) Exhibitor(s) for pornography exhibited, prior to the effective date of this act.

Sec. 16–18. Contents of complaint.

To be acceptable by the office, a complaint shall be sufficiently complete so as to reflect properly the full name and address of the complainant or other aggrieved person or persons; the full name and address of the person against whom the complaint is made; the alleged discriminatory practice and a statement of particulars thereof; the date or dates of the alleged discriminatory practice; if the alleged discriminatory practice is of a continuing nature, the dates between which the continuing discriminatory practices are alleged to have occurred; a statement as to any other action, civil or criminal, instituted before any other administrative agency, commission, department or court, whether state or federal, based upon the same grievance alleged in the complaint, with a statement as to the status or disposition of any such other action; and in the case of alleged employment discrimination a statement that the employer employs six (6) or more employees in the territorial jurisdiction of the office.

Sec. 16–19. Execution and verification of complaint.

The original complaint shall be signed and verified before a notary public or other person duly authorized by law to administer oaths and take acknowledgments. Notarial services shall be furnished by the office without charge.

Sec. 16–20. Timeliness of complaint.

No complaint shall be valid unless filed within ninety (90) calendar days from the date of occurrence of the alleged discriminatory practice or, in the case of a continuing discriminatory practice, during the time of the occurrence of the alleged practice; but not more than ninety (90) calendar days from the date of the most recent alleged discriminatory act.

Sec. 16–21. Referral of complaint to Indiana State Civil Rights Commission.

The chief officer may, in his/her discretion, prior to scheduling of the complaint for hearing under section 16–26, refer any complaint to the Indiana State Civil Rights Commission for proceedings in accordance with the Indiana Civil Rights Act.

Sec. 16–22. Receipt of complaint from Indiana State Civil Rights Commission.

The office is hereby authorized to receive any complaint referred to it by the Indiana State Civil Rights Commission pursuant to section 11a of the Indiana State Civil Rights Act, and to take such action with respect to any such complaint as is authorized or required in the case of a complaint filed under section 16–17.

Sec. 16–23. Service of complaint on respondent; answer.

The chief officer shall cause a copy of the complaint to be served by certified mail upon the respondent, who may file a written response to the complaint at any time prior to the close of proceedings with respect thereto, except as otherwise provided in section 16–26. The complaint and any response received shall not be made public by the chief officer, the board or any member thereof or any agent or employee of the office, unless and until a public hearing is scheduled thereon as provided in section 16–26.

Sec. 16–24. Investigation and conciliation.

(1) *Investigation.* Within ten (10) working days after the receipt of a complaint filed pursuant to this chapter, the chief officer shall initiate an investigation of the alleged discriminatory practice charged in the complaint. All such investigations shall be made by the office at the direction of the chief officer and may include informal conferences or discussions with any part to the complaint for the purpose of obtaining additional information or attempting to resolve or eliminate the alleged discriminatory practice by conciliation or persuasion. The office shall have the authority to initiate discovery, including but not limited to interrogatories, request for production of documents and subpoenas, on approval of the chief officer at any time within ten (10) working days after filing of a complaint. Any request by the office to compel discovery may be by appropriate petition to the Marion County circuit or superior courts.

(2) *Report of investigation; determination by panel.* Unless the complaint has been satisfactorily resolved prior thereto, the chief officer shall, within thirty (30) working days after the date of filing of a complaint pursuant to section 16–17, report the results of the investigation made pursuant to subsection (1) to a panel of three (3) members of the board designated by the chairperson or vice-chairperson or pursuant to the rules of the board, which panel shall not include any member of the board who initiated the complaint, who might have participated in the investigation of the complaint, or who is a member of the complaint adjudication committee. The chief officer shall make a recommendation as to whether there is reasonable cause to believe that the respondent has violated sections 16–14 and/or 16–15. The chairperson, vice-chairperson or such other member of the panel so designated may, for good cause shown, extend the time for making such report. Such extension thereof shall be evidenced in writing, and the office shall serve a copy of the extension on both the complainant and the respondent. The panel shall then determine by majority vote whether reasonable cause exists to believe that any respondent has violated sections 16–14 and/or 16–15. In making such a determination, the panel shall consider only the complaint, the response, if any, and the chief officer's report; provided, however, the panel may request the chief officer to make a supplemental investigation and report with respect to any matter which it deems material to such determination.

(3) *Action when violation found.* If the panel, pursuant to subsection (2), determines that reasonable cause exists to believe that any respondent has violated sections 16–14 and/or 16–15, it may direct the chief officer to endeavor to eliminate the alleged discriminatory practice through a conciliation conference. At least one

panel member shall be present at any conciliation conference at which both the complainant and respondent are present or represented. If the complaint is satisfactorily resolved through conciliation, the terms of any agreement reached or undertaking given by any party shall be reduced to writing and signed by the complainant, respondent and the chief officer. Any disagreement between the respondent and the chief officer in regard to the terms or conditions of a proposed conciliation agreement may be referred to the panel which considered the complaint, and the decision of the panel with respect to such terms or conditions shall be final for purposes of conciliation proceedings under this subsection, but shall not be binding upon the respondent without his written consent thereto. No action taken or statement made in connection with any proceedings under this subsection, and no written conciliation agreement or any of the terms thereof, shall be made public by the board or any member thereof, or any agent or employee of the officer, without the written consent of the parties, nor shall any such action, statement or agreement be admissible in evidence in any subsequent proceedings; provided, however, the board or officer may institute legal proceedings under this chapter for enforcement of any written agreement or undertaking executed in accordance with this subsection.

Sec. 16–25. Complaint adjudication committee; duties.

A complaint adjudication committee is hereby established. The committee shall be composed of seven (7) members of the board. The committee shall meet for the purpose of holding public hearings on citizen's complaints, which shall be at such times as its members deem necessary.

Sec. 16–26. Hearings, findings and recommendations when conciliation not effected.

(a) *Hearing to be held; notice.* If a complaint filed pursuant to this article has not been satisfactorily resolved within a reasonable time through informal proceedings pursuant to section 16–24, or if the panel investigating the complaint determines that a conciliation conference is inappropriate under the circumstances surrounding the complaint, the complaint adjudication committee may hold a public hearing thereon upon not less than ten (10) working days' written notice to the complainant or other aggrieved person, and to the respondent. If the respondent has not previously filed a written response to the complaint, he/she may file such response and serve a copy thereof upon the complainant and the office not later than five (5) working days prior to the date of the hearing.

(b) *Powers; rights of parties at hearing.* In connection with a hearing held pursuant to subsection (a), the complaint adjudication committee shall have power, upon any matter pertinent to the complaint or response thereto, to subpoena witnesses and compel their attendance; to require the production of pertinent books, papers or other documents; and to administer oaths. The complainant shall have the right to be represented by the chief officer or any attorney of his/her choice. The respondent shall have the right to be represented by an attorney or any other person of his/her choice. The complainant and respondent shall have the right to appear in person at the hearing, to be represented by an attorney or any other person, to subpoena and compel the attendance of witnesses, and to examine and cross-examine witnesses. The complaint adjudication committee may adopt appropriate rules for the issuance of subpoenas and the conduct of hearings under this section. The complaint adjudication committee and the board shall have the power to enforce discovery and subpoenas by appropriate petition to the Marion County circuit or superior courts.

(c) *Statement of evidence; exceptions; arguments.* Within thirty (30) working days from the close of the hearing, the complaint adjudication committee shall prepare a report containing written recommended findings of fact and conclusions and file such report with the office. A copy of the report shall be furnished to the complainant and respondent, each of whom shall have an opportunity to submit written exceptions within such time as the rules of the complaint adjudication committee shall permit. The complaint adjudication committee may, in its discretion, upon notice to each interested party hear further evidence or argument upon the issues presented by the report and exceptions, if any.

(d) *Findings of fact; sustaining or dismissing complaint.* If, upon the preponderance of the evidence, the committee shall be of the opinion that any respondent has engaged or is engaging in a discriminatory practice in violation of the chapter, it shall state its findings of fact and conclusions and serve a copy thereof upon the complainant and the respondent. In addition, the committee may cause to be served on the respondent an order requiring the respondent to cease and desist from the unlawful discriminatory practice and requiring such person to take further affirmative action as will effectuate the purposes of this chapter, including but not limited to the power to restore complainant's losses incurred as a result of discriminatory treatment, as the committee may deem necessary to assure justice; to require the posting of notice setting forth the public policy of Marion County concerning equal opportunity and respondent's compliance with said policy in places of public accommodations; to require proof of compliance to be filed by respondent at periodic intervals; to require a person who has been found to be in violation of this chapter and who is licensed by a city or county agency authorized to grant a license, to show cause to the licensing agency why his license should not be revoked or suspended. If, upon the preponderance of the evidence, the committee shall be of the opinion that any respondent has not engaged in a discriminatory practice in violation of this chapter it shall state its findings of fact and conclusions and serve a copy thereof upon the complainant and the respondent, and dismiss the complaint. Findings and conclusions made by the committee shall be based solely upon the record of the evidence presented at the hearing.

(e) *Appeal to the board.* Within thirty (30) working days after the issuance of findings and conclusions by the committee, either the complainant or the respondent may file a written appeal of the decision of the committee to the board; however, in the event that the committee requires the respondent to correct or eliminate a discriminatory practice within a time period less than thirty (30) working days, then that respondent must file his/her appeal within that time period. After considering the record of the evidence presented at the hearing and the findings and conclusions of the committee, the board may affirm the decision of the committee and adopt the findings and conclusions of the committee, or it may affirm the decision of the committee and make supplemental findings and conclusions of its own, or it may reverse the decision of the committee and made findings of fact and conclusions to support its decision. The board may also adopt, modify or reverse any relief ordered by the committee. The board must take any of the above actions within thirty (30) working days after the appeal is filed.

(f) *Members of Board who are ineligible to participate.* No member of the board who initiated a complaint under this chapter or who participated in the investigation thereof shall participate in any hearing or determination under this section as a member of either a hearing panel, the complaint adjudication committee or of the board.

(g) *Applicability of state law; judicial review.* Except as otherwise specifically provided in this section or in rules adopted by the board or the complaint adjudication committee under this chapter, the applicable provisions of the Administrative Adjudication Act, IC 4-22-1, shall govern the conduct of hearings and determinations under this section, and findings of the board hereunder shall be subject to judicial review as provided in that act.

Sec. 16–27. Court Enforcement.

(a) *Institution of action.* In any case where the board or the committee has found that a respondent has engaged in or is engaging in a discriminatory practice in violation of sections 16–14 and/or 16–15, and such respondent has failed to correct or eliminate such discriminatory practice within the time limit prescribed by the board or the committee and the time limit for appeal to the board has elapsed, the board may file in its own name in the Marion County circuit or superior courts a complaint against the respondent for the enforcement of seciton 16–26. Such complaint may request such temporary or permanent injunctive relief as may be appropriate and such additional affirmative relief or orders as will effectuate the purposes of this chapter and as may be equitable, within the powers and jurisdiction of the court.

(b) *Record of hearing; evidentiary value.* In any action filed pursuant to this seciton, the board may file with the court a record of the hearing held by the complaint adjudication committee pursuant to section 16–26, which record shall be certified by the secretary of the board as a true, correct and complete record of the proceedings upon which the findings of the complaint adjudication committee and/or the board were based. The court may, in its discretion, admit any evidence contained in the record as evidence in the action filed under subsection (a), to the extent such evidence would be admissible in court under the rules of evidence if the witness or witnesses were present in court, without limitation upon the right of any party to offer such additional evidence as may be pertinent to the issues and as the court shall, in its discretion, permit.

(c) *Temporary judicial relief upon filing of complaint.* Upon the filing of a complaint pursuant to seciton 16–17 by a person claiming to be aggrieved, the chief officer, in the name of the board and in accordance with such procedures as the board shall establish by rule, may seek temporary orders for injunctions in the Marion County circuit or superior courts to prevent irreparable harm to the complainant, pending resolution of the complaint by the office, complaint adjudication committee and the board.

(d) *Enforcement of conciliating agreements.* If the board determines that any party to a conciliation agreement approved by the chief officer under seciton 16–24 has failed or refused to comply with the terms of the agreement, it may file a complaint in the name of the board in the Marion County circuit or superior courts seeking an appropriate decree for the enforcement of the agreement.

(e) *Trial de novo upon finding of sex discrimination related to pornography.* In complaints involving discrimination through pornography, judicial review shall be de novo. Notwithstanding any other provision to the contrary, whenever the board or committee has found that a respondent has engaged in or is engaging in one of the discriminatory practices set forth in paragraph (g)(4) of section 16–3 or as against a seller, exhibitor or distributor under paragraph (g)(7) of section 16–3, the board shall, within ten (10) days after making such finding, file in its own name in the Marion County circuit or superior court an action for declaratory and/or injunctive relief. The board shall have the burden of proving that the actions of the respondent were in violation of this chapter.

Provided, however, that in any complaint under paragraph (g)(4) of section 16–3 or against a seller, exhibitor or distributor under paragraph (g)(7) of section 16–3 no temporary or permanent injunction shall issue prior to a final judicial determination that said activities of respondent do constitute a discriminatory practice under this chapter. Provided further, that no temporary or permanent injunction under paragraph (g)(4) of section 16–3 or against a seller, exhibitor or distributor under paragraph (g)(7) of section 16–3 shall extend beyond such material(s) that, having been described with reasonable specificity by the

injunction, have been determined to be validly proscribed under the chapter.

Sec. 16–28. Other remedies.
Nothing in this chapter shall affect any person's right to pursue any and all rights and remedies available in any other local, state or federal forum.

You can locate InfoTrac-College Education articles about this chapter by accessing the InfoTrac-College Edition website (http://www.infotrac-college.com/wadsworth/). Using the InfoTrac-College Edition subject guide, enter the search terms relevant to this chapter, and then read abstracts for relevant articles.

38   Feminist Antipornography Legislation: A Critical Analysis

LISA DUGGAN, NAN D. HUNTER, AND CAROLE VANCE

Lisa Duggan is Assistant Professor of History and American Studies, New York University. She has published a number of scholarly works on feminism and social philosophy, including the book *Our Monica, Ourselves, the Clinton Affair, and the National Interest* (2001). Nan D. Hunter is Professor of Law at Brooklyn Law School as well as founder and former director of the American Civil Liberties Union Lesbian and Gay Rights Project and AIDS Project. She has had articles published in such journals as *New York University Law Review* and *Harvard Civil Rights-Civil Liberties Law Review.* She is the author (with Lisa Duggan) of *Sex Wars: Sexual Dissent and Political Culture* (1995). Carole S. Vance is an anthropologist at Columbia University, New York City. She is the Director of the Program for the Study of Sexuality, Gender, Health, and Human Rights (a post-doctoral residency program funded by the Rockefeller Foundation) and Director of the Program in Medical Anthropology. Dr. Vance has published widely about sexual theory; science, sexuality, gender, and health; and policy controversies about sexual

Reprinted by permission from Women Against Censorship, *ed. Varda Burstyn (Vancouver: Groundwood Books/Douglas & McIntyre, 1985).*

expression and imagery. Dr. Vance is the editor of *Pleasure and Danger: Exploring Female Sexuality,* 2nd ed. (1992).

Professors Duggan, Hunter, and Vance challenge the antipornography position defended by Professor MacKinnon (in Chapter 39) and the versions of which have been proposed as civil law in the cities of Minneapolis and Indianapolis. Professor MacKinnon's proposal has also found support in the U.S. Congress. The authors of this essay argue that the proposed legislation, though put forth in defense of feminist vales, is antifeminist, for it contributes to the antifeminist crusade of conservatives and traditionalists. After presenting a brief history of the legislation, the authors expose what they believe is its central flaw: it is hopelessly vague and ambiguous, prohibiting nearly anything that is sexually explicit, though its supporters contend that they are trying to prohibit only materials that are violent, sexist, and sexually explicit. The authors also contend that Professor MacKinnon's proposal (which she created with feminist activist Andrea Dworkin) paints with a broad brush, interpreting pornographic depictions in only one way, degrading to women. They conclude by warning of the dangers of applying this antipornography legislation. They also question whether pornography is responsible for any more harm to women than much of the nonprohibited activity which is sexist and has been around for a much longer time.

IN THE UNITED STATES, after two decades of increasing community tolerance for dissenting or disturbing sexual or political materials, there is now growing momentum for retrenchment. In an atmosphere of increased conservatism, evidenced by a wave of book banning and anti-gay harassment, support for new repressive legislation of various kinds—from an Oklahoma law forbidding school teachers from advocating homosexuality to new antipornography laws passed in Minneapolis and Indianapolis—is growing.

The antipornography laws have mixed roots of support, however. Though they are popular with the conservative constituencies that traditionally favor legal restrictions on sexual expression of all kinds, they were drafted and endorsed by antipornography feminists who oppose traditional obscenity and censorship laws. The model law of this type, which is now being widely copied, was drawn up in the politically progressive city of Minneapolis by two radical feminists, author Andrea Dworkin and attorney Catharine MacKinnon. It was passed by the city council there, but vetoed by the mayor. A similar law was also passed in Indianapolis, but later declared unconstitutional in federal court, a ruling that the city will appeal. Other versions of the legislation are being considered in numerous cities, and Pennsylvania senator Arlen Specter has introduced legislation modeled on parts of the Dworkin-MacKinnon bill in the U.S. Congress.

Dworkin, MacKinnon and their feminist supporters believe that the new antipornography laws are not censorship laws. They also claim that the legislative effort behind them is based on feminist support. Both of these claims are dubious at best. Though the new laws are civil laws that allow individuals to sue the makers, sellers, distributors or exhibitors of pornography, and not criminal laws leading to arrest and imprisonment, their censoring impact would be substantially as severe as criminal obscenity laws. Materials could be removed from public availability by court injunction, and publishers and booksellers could be subject to potentially endless legal harassment. Passage of the laws was therefore achieved with the support of right-wing elements who expect the new laws to accomplish what censorship efforts are meant to accomplish. Ironically, many antifeminist conservatives backed these laws, while many feminists opposed them. In Indianapolis, the law was supported by extreme right-wing religious fundamentalists, including members of the Moral Majority, while there was *no* local feminist support. In other cities, traditional procensorship forces have expressed interest in the new approach to banning sexually explicit materials. Meanwhile, anticensorship feminists have become alarmed at these new developments and are seeking to galvanize feminist opposition to the new antipornography legislative strategy pioneered in Minneapolis.

One is tempted to ask in astonishment, how can this be happening? How can feminists be entrusting the patriarchal state with the task of legally distinguishing between permissible and impermissible sexual images? But in fact this new development is not as surprising as it at first seems. . . . [P]ornography has come to be seen as a central cause of women's oppression by a significant number of feminists. Some even argue that pornography is the root of virtually all forms of exploitation and discrimination against women. It is a short step from such a belief to the conviction that laws against pornography can end the inequality of the sexes. But this analysis takes feminists very close—indeed far too close—to measures that will ultimately support conservative, antisex, procensorship forces in American society, for it is with these forces that women have forged alliances in passing such legislation.

The first feminist-inspired antipornography law was passed in Minneapolis in 1983. Local legislators had been frustrated when their zoning restrictions on porn shops were struck down in the courts. Public hearings were held to discuss a new zoning ordinance. The Neighborhood Pornography Task Force of South and South Central Minneapolis invited Andrea Dworkin and Catharine MacKinnon, who were teaching a course on pornography at the University of Minnesota, to testify. They proposed an alternative that, they claimed, would completely eliminate, rather than merely regulate pornography. They suggested that pornography be defined as a form of sex discrimination, and that an amendment to the city's civil rights law be passed to proscribe it. City officials hired Dworkin and MacKinnon to develop their new approach and to organize another series of public hearings.

The initial debate over the legislation in Minneapolis was intense, and opinion was divided within nearly every political grouping. In contrast, the public hearings held before the city council were tightly controlled and carefully orchestrated; speakers invited by Dworkin and MacKinnon—sexual abuse victims, counselors, educators and social scientists—testified about the harm pornography does women. (Dworkin and MacKinnon's agenda was the compilation of a legislative record that would help the law stand up to its inevitable court challenges.) The legislation passed, supported by antipornography feminists, neighborhood groups concerned about the effects of porn shops on residential areas, and conservatives opposed to the availability of sexually explicit materials for "moral" reasons.

In Indianapolis, the alignment of forces was different. For the previous two years, conservative antipornography groups had grown in strength and public visibility, but they had been frustrated in their efforts. The police department could not convert its obscenity arrests into convictions; the city's zoning law was also tied up in court challenges. Then Mayor William Hudnutt III, a Republican and a Presbyterian minister, learned of the Minneapolis law. Mayor Hudnutt thought Minneapolis's approach to restricting pornography might be the solution to the Indianapolis problems. Beulah Coughenour, a conservative Republican stop-ERA activist, was recruited to sponsor the legislation in the city-county council.

Coughenour engaged MacKinnon as consultant to the city—Dworkin was not hired, but then, Dworkin's passionate radical feminist rhetoric would not have gone over well in Indianapolis. MacKinnon worked with the Indianapolis city prosecutor (a well-known anti-vice zealot), the city's legal department and Coughenour on the legislation. The law received the support of neighborhood groups, the Citizens for Decency and the Coalition for a Clean Community. There were no crowds of feminist supporters—in fact, there were no feminist supporters at all. The only feminists to make public statements opposed the legislation, which was nevertheless passed in a council meeting packed with 300 religious fundamentalists. All 24 Republicans voted for its passage; all five Democrats opposed it to no avail.

A group of publishers and booksellers challenged the law in Federal District Court, where they won the first round. This legal setback for the ordinance may cause some other cities considering similar legislation to hold off until the final resolution of the appeal of the Indianapolis decision; meanwhile, however, mutated versions of the Dworkin-MacKinnon bill have begun to appear. A version of the law introduced in Suffolk County on Long Island in New York emphasized its conservative potential— pornography was said to cause "sodomy" and "disruption" of the family unit, in addition to rape, incest, exploitation and other acts "inimical to the public good." In Suffolk, the law was put forward by a conservative, anti-ERA male legislator who wishes to "restore ladies to what they used to be." The Suffolk County bill clearly illustrates the repressive, antifeminist potential of the new antipornography legislation. The appearance of a federal bill, together with the possibility of a new, Reagan-appointed commission to study new antipornography legislation, indicates how widespread the repressive effects of the ordinances may become.

Yet it is true that some of the U.S. laws have been proposed and supported by antipornography feminists. This is therefore a critical moment in the feminist debate over sexual politics. As anticensorship feminists work to develop alternatives to antipornography campaigns, we also need to examine carefully the new laws and expose their underlying assumptions. We need to know why these laws, for all their apparent feminist rhetoric, actually appeal to conservative antifeminist forces, and why feminists should be preparing to move in a different direction.

DEFINITIONS: THE CENTRAL FLAW

The antipornography ordinances passed in Minneapolis and Indianapolis were framed as amendments to municipal civil rights laws. They provide for complaints to be filed against pornography in the same manner that complaints are filed against employment discrimination. If enforced, these laws would make illegal public or private availability (except in libraries) of any materials deemed pornographic.

Such material could be the object of a lawsuit on several grounds. The ordinance would penalize four kinds of behavior associated with pornography: its production, sale, exhibition or distribution ("trafficking"); coercion into pornographic performance; forcing pornography on a person; and assault or physical attack due to pornography. . . .

Although proponents claim that the Minneapolis and Indianapolis ordinances represent a new way to regulate pornography, the strategy is still laden with our culture's old, repressive approach to sexuality. The implementation of such laws hinges on the definition of pornography as interpreted by the court. The definition provided in the Minneapolis legislation is vague, leaving critical phrases such as "the sexually explicit subordination of women," "postures of sexual submission" and "whores by nature" to the interpretation of the citizen who files a complaint and to the civil court judge who hears the case. The legislation does not prohibit just the images of gross sexual violence that most supporters claim to be its target, but instead drifts toward covering an increasingly wide range of sexually explicit material.

The most problematic feature of this approach, then, is a conceptual flaw embedded in the law itself. Supporters of this type of legislation say that the target of their efforts is misogynist, sexually explicit and violent representation, whether in pictures or words. Indeed, the feminist antipornography movement is fueled by women's anger at the most repugnant of pornography. But a close examination of the wording of the model legislative text, and examples of purportedly actionable material offered by proponents of the legislation in court briefs suggest that the law is actually aimed at a range of material considerably broader than what proponents claim is their target. The discrepancies between the law's explicit and implicit aims have been almost invisible to us, because these distortions are very similar to distortions about sexuality in the culture as a whole. The legislation and supporting texts deserve close reading. Hidden beneath illogical transformations, nonsequiturs, and highly permeable definitions are familiar sexual scripts drawn from mainstream, sexist culture that potentially could have very negative consequences for women.

The Venn diagram [on the next page] illustrates the three areas targeted by the law, and represents a scheme that classifies words or images that have any of three characteristics: violence, sexual explicitness or sexism.

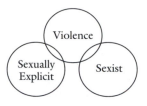

Clearly, a text or an image might have only one characteristic. Material can be violent but not sexually explicit or sexist: for example, a war movie in which both men and women suffer injury or death without regard to or because of their gender. Material can be sexist but not sexually explicit and violent. A vast number of materials from mainstream media—television, popular novels, magazines, newspapers—come to mind, all of which depict either distraught housewives or the "happy sexism" of the idealized family, with mom self-sacrificing, other-directed and content. Finally, material can be sexually explicit but not violent or sexist: for example the freely chosen sexual behavior depicted in sex education films or women's own explicit writing about sexuality.

As the diagram illustrates, areas can also intersect, reflecting a range of combinations of the three characteristics. Images can be violent and sexually explicit without being sexist—for example, a narrative about a rape in a men's prison, or a documentary about the effect of a rape on a woman. The latter example illustrates the importance of context in evaluating whether material that is sexually explicit and violent is also sexist. The intent of the maker, the context of the film and the perception of the viewer together render a depiction of a rape sympathetic, harrowing, even educational, rather than sensational, victim-blaming and laudatory.

Another possible overlap is between material that is violent and sexist but not sexually explicit. Films or books that describe violence directed against women by men in a way that clearly shows gender antagonism and inequality, and sometimes strong sexual tension, but no sexual explicitness fall into this category—for example, the popular genre of slasher films in which women are stalked, terrified and killed by men, or accounts of mass murder of women, fueled by male rage. Finally, a third point of overlap arises when material is sexually explicit and sexist without being violent—that is, when sex is consensual but still reflects themes of male superiority and female abjectness. Some sex education materials could be included in this category, as well as a great deal of regular pornography.

The remaining domain, the inner core, is one in which the material is simultaneously violent, sexually explicit and sexist—for example, an image of a naked woman being slashed by a knife-wielding rapist. The Minneapolis law, however, does not by any means confine itself to this material.

To be actionable under the law as pornography, material must be judged by the courts to be "the sexually explicit subordination of women, graphically depicted whether in pictures or in words that also includes at least one or more" of nine criteria. Of these, only four involve the intersection of violence, sexual explicitness and sexism, and then only arguably. . . . Even in these cases, many questions remain about whether images with all three characteristics do in fact cause violence against women. . . . And the task of evaluating material that is ostensibly the target of these criteria becomes complicated—indeed, hopeless—because most of the clauses that contain these criteria mix actions or qualities of violence with those that are not particularly associated with violence.

The section that comes closest to the stated purpose of the legislation is clause (iii): "women are presented as sexual objects who experience sexual pleasure in being raped." This clause is intended to cover depictions of rape that are sexually explicit and sexist; the act of rape itself signifies the violence. But other clauses are not so clearcut, because the list of characteristics often mixes signs or byproducts of violence with phenomena that are unrelated or irrelevant to judging violence. We might be willing to agree that clause (ii)—"women are presented as sexual objects who enjoy pain"—signifies the conjunction of all three characteristics, with violence the presumed cause of pain, but the presence of the words "and humiliation" at the end of the clause is problematic. Humiliation may be offensive or disagreeable, but it does not necessarily imply violence.

A similar problem occurs with clause (iv): "women are presented as sexual objects tied up or cut up or mutilated or bruised or physically hurt." All these except the first, "tied up," generally occur as a result of violence. "Tied up," if part of consensual sex, is not violent and, for some practitioners, not particularly sexist. Women who are tied up may be participants in nonviolent sex play involving bondage, a theme in both heterosexual and lesbian pornography. (See, for example *The Joy of Sex* and *Coming to Power*.) Clause (ix) contains another mixed list, in which "injury," "torture, "bleeding," "bruised" and "hurt" are combined with words such as "degradation" and "shown as filthy and inferior," neither of which is violent. Depending on the presentation, "filthy" and "inferior" may constitute sexually explicit sexism, although not violence. "Degradation" is a sufficiently inclusive term to cover most acts of which a viewer disapproves.

Several other clauses have little to do with violence at all; they refer to material that is sexually explicit and sexist, thus falling outside the triad of characteristics at which the legislation is supposedly aimed. For example, movies in which "women are presented as dehumanized sexual objects, things, or commodities" may be infuriating and offensive to feminists, but they are not violent.

Finally, some clauses describe material that is neither violent nor necessarily sexist. Clause (v), "women . . . in postures of sexual submission or sexual servility, including by inviting penetration," and clause (viii), "women . . . being penetrated by objects or animals," are sexually explicit, but not violent and not obviously sexist unless one believes that penetration—whether heterosexual, lesbian, or autoerotic masturbation—is indicative of gender inequality and female oppression. Similarly problematic are clauses that invoke representations of "women . . . as whores by nature" and "women's body parts . . . such that women are reduced to those parts."

Texts filed in support of the Indianapolis law show how broadly it could be applied. In the amicus brief filed on behalf of Linda Marchiano ("Linda Lovelace," the female lead in *Deep Throat*) in Indianapolis, Catharine MacKinnon offered *Deep Throat* as an example of the kind of pornography covered by the law. *Deep Throat* served a complicated function in this brief, because the movie, supporters of the ordinance argue, would be actionable on two counts: coercion into pornographic performance, because Marchiano alleges that she was coerced into making the movie; and trafficking in pornography, because the content of the film falls within one of the categories in the Indianapolis ordinance's definition—that which prohibits presenting women as sexual objects "through postures or positions of servility or submission or display." Proponents of the law have counted on women's repugnance at allegations of coerced sexual acts to spill over and discredit the sexual acts themselves in this movie.

The aspects of *Deep Throat* that MacKinnon considered to be indicative of "sexual subordination" are of particular interest, since any movie that depicted similar acts could be banned under the law. MacKinnon explained in her brief that the film "subordinates women by using women . . . sexually, specifically as eager servicing receptacles for male genitalia and ejaculate. The majority of the film presents 'Linda Lovelace' in, minimally, postures of sexual submission and/or servility." In its brief, the City of Indianapolis concurred: "In the film *Deep Throat* a woman is being shown as being ever eager for oral penetration by a series of men's penises, often on her hands and knees. There are repeated scenes in which her genitalia are graphically displayed and she is shown as enjoying men ejaculating on her face."

These descriptions are very revealing, since they suggest that multiple partners, group sex and oral sex subordinate women and hence are sexist. The notion that the female character is "used" by men suggests that it is improbable that a woman would engage in fellatio of her own accord. *Deep Throat* does draw on several sexist conventions common in advertising and the entire visual culture—the woman as object of the male gaze, and the assumption of heterosexuality, for example. But it is hardly an unending paean to male dominance, since the movie contains many contrary themes. In it, the main female character is shown as both actively seeking her own pleasure and as trying to please men; a secondary female character is shown as actually directing encounters with multiple male partners. Both briefs described a movie quite different from the one viewers see.

At its heart, this analysis implies that heterosexual sex itself is sexist; that women do not engage in it of their own volition; and that behavior pleasurable to men is repugnant to women. In some contexts, for example, the representation of fellatio and multiple partners can be sexist, but are we willing to concede that they always are? If not, then what is proposed as actionable under the Indianapolis law includes merely sexually explicit representation (the traditional target of obscenity laws), which proponents of the legislation vociferously insist they are not interested in attacking.

Some other examples offered through exhibits submitted with the City of Indianapolis brief and also introduced in the public hearing further illustrate this point. Many of the exhibits are depictions of sadomasochism. The court briefs treat SM material as depicting violence and aggression, not consensual sex, in spite of avowals to the contrary by many SM practitioners. With this legislation, then, a major question for feminists that has only begun to develop would be closed for discussion. Instead, a simplistic reduction has been advanced as the definitive feminist position. The description of the material in the briefs focused on submissive women and implied male domination, highlighting the similarity proponents would like to find between all SM narratives and male/female inequality. The actual exhibits, however, illustrated plots and power relationships far more diverse than the descriptions provided by MacKinnon and the City of Indianapolis would suggest, including SM between women and female dominant/male submissive SM. For example, the Indianapolis brief stated that in the magazine *The Bitch Goddesses,* "women are shown in torture chambers with their nude body parts being tortured by their 'master' for 'even the slightest offense'. . . . The magazine shows a woman in a scenario of torture." But the brief failed to mention that the dominants in this magazine are all female, with one exception. This kind of discrepancy characterized many examples offered in the briefs.

This is not to say that such representations do not raise questions for feminists. The current lively discussion about lesbian SM clearly demonstrates that this issue is still unresolved. But in the Indianapolis briefs all SM material was assumed to be male dominant/female submissive, thereby squeezing a nonconforming reality into prepackaged, inadequate—and therefore dangerous—categories. This legislation would virtually eliminate all SM pornography by recasting it as violent, thereby attacking a sexual minority while masquerading as an attempt to end violence against women.

Analysis of clauses in the Minneapolis ordinance and several examples offered in court briefs filed in connection with the Indianapolis ordinance show that the law targets material that is sexually explicit and sexist, but ignores material that is violent and sexist, violent and sexually explicit, only violent or only sexist.

Certain troubling questions arise here, for if one claims, as some antipornography activists do, that there is a direct relationship between images and behavior, why should images of violence against women or scenarios of sexism in general not be similarly proscribed? Why is sexual explicitness singled out as the cause of women's oppression? For proponents to exempt violent and sexist images, or even sexist images, from regulation is inconsistent, especially since they are so pervasive.

Even more difficulties arise from the vagueness of certain terms crucial in interpreting the ordinances. The term "subordination" is especially important, since pornography is defined as the "sexually explicit subordination of women." The authors of this legislation intend it to modify each of the clauses, and they appear to believe that it provides a definition of sexism that each example must meet. The term is never defined in the legislation, yet the Indianapolis brief, for example, suggests that the average viewer, on the basis of "his or her common understanding of what it means for one person to subordinate another" should be able to decide what is pornographic. But what kind of sexually explicit acts place a woman in an inferior status? To some, *any* graphic sexual act violates women's dignity and therefore subordinates them. To others, consensual heterosexual lovemaking within the boundaries of procreation and marriage is acceptable, but heterosexual acts that do not have reproduction as their aim lower women's status and hence subordinate them. Still others accept a wide range of nonprocreative, perhaps even nonmarital, heterosexuality but draw the line at lesbian sex, which they view as degrading.

The term "sex object" is also problematic. The City of Indianapolis's brief maintains that "the term sexual object, often shortened to sex object, has enjoyed a wide popularity in mainstream American culture in the past fifteen years, and is used to denote the objectification of a person on the basis of their sex or sex appeal. . . . People know what it means to disregard all aspects of personhood but sex, to reduce a person to a thing used for sex." But, indeed, people do not agree on this point. The definition of "sex object" is far from clear or uniform. For example, some feminist and liberal cultural critics have used the term to mean sex that occurs without strong emotional ties and experience. More conservative critics maintain that any detachment of women's sexuality from procreation, marriage and the family objectifies it, removing it from its "natural" web of associations and context. Unredeemed and unprotected by domesticity and family, women—and their sexuality—become things used by men. In both these views, women are never sexually autonomous agents who direct and enjoy their sexuality for their own purposes, but rather are victims. In the same vein, other problematic terms include "inviting penetration," "whores by nature" and "positions of display."

Through close analysis of the proposed legislation one sees how vague the boundaries of the definitions that contain the inner core of the Venn diagram really are. Their dissolution does not happen equally at all points, but only at some: the inner core begins to include sexually explicit and sexist material, and finally expands to include purely sexually explicit material. Thus "sexually explicit" becomes identified and equated with "violent" with no further definition or explanation.

It is also striking that so many feminists have failed to notice that the laws (as well as examples of actionable material) cover so much diverse work, not just that small and symbolic epicenter where many forms of opposition to women converge. It suggests that for us, as well as for others; sexuality remains a difficult area.

We have no clearly developed framework in which to think about sex equivalent to the frameworks that are available for thinking about race, gender and class issues. Consequently, in sex, as in few other areas of human behavior, unexamined and unjustifiable prejudice passes itself off as considered opinion about what is desirable and normal. And finally, sex arouses considerable anxiety, stemming from both the meeting with individual difference and from the prospect—suggested by feminists themselves—that sexual behavior is constructed socially and is not simply natural.

The law takes advantage of everyone's relative ignorance and anxious ambivalence about sex, distorting and oversimplifying what confronts us in building a sexual politic. For example, antipornography feminists draw on several feminist theories about the role of violent, aggressive or sexist representations. The first is relatively straightforward: that these images trigger men into action. The second suggests that violent images act more subtly, to socialize men to act in sexist or violent ways by making this behavior seem commonplace and more acceptable, if not expected. The third assumption is that violent, sexually explicit or even sexist images are offensive to women, assaulting their sensibilities and sense of self. Although we have all used metaphor to exhort women to action or illustrate a point, antipornography proponents have frequently used these conventions of speech as if they were literal statements of fact. But these metaphors have gotten out of hand, as Julie Abraham has noted, for they fail to recognize that the assault committed by the wife beater is quite different from the visual "assault" of a sexist ad on TV. The nature of the difference is still being clarified in a complex debate within feminism that must continue; this law cuts off speculation, settling on a causal relationship between image and action that is starkly simple, if unpersuasive.

This metaphor also paves the way for reclassifying images that are merely sexist as also violent and aggressive. Thus, it is no accident that the briefs supporting the legislation first invoke violent images and rapidly move to include sexist and sexually explicit images without noting that they are different. The equation is made more easy by the constant shifts back to examples of depictions of real violence, almost to draw attention away from the sexually explicit or sexist material that in fact would be affected by the laws.

Most important, what underlies this legislation and the success of its analysis in blurring and exceeding boundaries is an appeal to a very traditional view of sex: sex is degrading to women. By this logic, any illustrations or descriptions of explicit sexual acts that involve women are in themselves affronts to women's dignity. In its brief, the City of Indianapolis was quite specific about this point: "The harms caused by pornography are by no means limited to acts of physical aggression. The mere existence of pornography in society degrades and demeans all women." Embedded in this view are several other familiar themes: that sex is degrading to women, but not to men; that men are raving beasts; that sex is dangerous for women; that sexuality is male, not female; that women are victims, not sexual actors; that men inflict "it" on women; that penetration is submission; that heterosexual sexuality, rather than the institution of heterosexuality, is sexist.

These assumptions, in part intended, in part unintended, lead us back to the traditional target of obscenity law: sexually explicit material. What initially appeared novel, then, is really the reappearance of a traditional theme. It's ironic that a feminist position on pornography incorporates most of the myths about sexuality that feminism has struggled to displace.

THE DANGERS OF APPLICATION

The Minneapolis and Indianapolis ordinances embody a political view that holds pornography to be a central force in "creating and maintaining" the oppression of women. This view appears in summary form in the legislative findings section at the beginning of the Minneapolis bill, which describes a chain reaction of misogynistic acts generated by pornography. The legislation is based on the interweaving of several themes: that pornography constructs the meaning of sexuality for women and, as well, leads to discrete acts of violence against women; that sexuality is the primary cause of women's oppression; that explicitly sexual images, even if not violent or coerced, have the power to subordinate women; and that women's own accounts of force have been silenced because, as a universal and timeless rule, society credits pornographic constructions rather than women's experiences. Taking the silencing contention a step further, advocates of the ordinance effectively assume that women have been so conditioned by the pornographic world view that if their own experiences of the sexual acts identified in the definition are not subordinating, then they must simply be victims of false consciousness.

The heart of the ordinance is the "trafficking" section, which would allow almost anyone to seek the removal of any materials falling within the law's definition of pornography. Ordinance defenders strenuously protest that the issue is not censorship because the state, as such, is not authorized to initiate criminal prosecutions. But the prospect of having to defend a potentially infinite number of privately filed complaints creates at least as much of a chilling effect against pornographic or sexual speech as does a criminal law. And as long as representatives of the state—in this case, judges—have ultimate say over the interpretation, the distinction between this ordinance and "real" censorship will not hold.

In addition, three major problems should dissuade feminists from supporting this kind of law: first, the sexual images in question do not cause more harm than other aspects of misogynist culture; second, sexually explicit speech, even in male-dominated society, serves positive social functions for women; and third, the passage and enforcement of antipornography laws such as those supported in Minneapolis and Indianapolis are more likely to impede, rather than advance, feminist goals.

Ordinance proponents contend that pornography does cause violence because it conditions male sexual response to images of violence and thus provokes violence against women. The strongest research they offer is based on psychology experiments that employ films depicting a rape scene, toward the end of which the woman is shown to be enjoying the attack. The ordinances, by contrast, cover a much broader range of materials than this one specific heterosexual rape scenario. Further, the studies ordinance supporters cite do not support the theory that pornography causes violence against women. . . .

In addition, the argument that pornography itself plays a major role in the general oppression of women contradicts the evidence of history. It need hardly be said that pornography did not lead to the burning of witches or the English common law treatment of women as chattel property. If anything functioned then as the prime communication medium for woman-hating, it was probably religion. Nor can pornography be blamed for the enactment of laws from at least the eighteenth century that allowed a husband to rape or beat his wife with impunity. In any period, the causes of women's oppression have been many and complex, drawing on the fundamental social and economic structures of society. Ordinance proponents offer little evidence to explain how the mass production of pornography—a relatively recent phenomenon—could have become so potent a causative agent so quickly.

The silencing of women is another example of the harm attributed to pornography. Yet if this argument were correct, one would expect that as the social visibility of pornography has increased, the tendency to credit women's accounts of rape would have decreased. In fact, although the treatment of women complainants in rape cases is far from perfect, the last 15 years of work by the women's movement has resulted in marked improvements. In many places, the corroboration requirement has now been abolished; cross-examination of victims as to past sexual experiences has been prohibited; and a number of police forces have developed specially trained units and procedures to improve the handling of sexual assault cases. The presence of rape fantasies in pornography may in part reflect a backlash against these women's movement advances, but to argue that most people routinely disbelieve women who file charges of rape belittles the real improvements made in social consciousness and law.

The third type of harm suggested by the ordinance backers is a kind of libel: the maliciously false characterization of women as a group of sexual masochists. Like libel, the City of Indianapolis brief argues pornography is "a lie [which] once loosed" cannot be effectively rebutted by debate and further speech.

To claim that all pornography as defined by the ordinance is a lie is a false analogy. If truth is a defence to charges of libel, then surely depictions of consensual sex cannot be thought of as equivalent to a falsehood. For example, some women (and men) do enjoy being tied up or displaying themselves. The declaration by fiat that even sadomasochism is a "lie" about sexuality reflects an arrogance and moralism that feminists should combat, not engage in. When mutually desired sexual experiences are depicted, pornography is not "libelous." . . .

These laws, which would increase the state's regulation of sexual images, present many dangers for women. Although the ordinances draw much of their feminist support from women's anger at the market for images of sexual violence, they are aimed not at violence, but at sexual explicitness. Far-right elements recognize the possibility of using the full potential of the ordinances to enforce their sexually conservative world view, and have supported them for that reason. Feminists should therefore look carefully at the test of these "model" laws in order to understand why many believe them to be a useful tool in *anti*feminist moral crusades.

The proposed ordinances are also dangerous because they seek to embody in law an analysis of the role of sexuality and sexual images in the oppression of women with which even all feminists do not agree. Underlying virtually every section of the proposed laws there is an assumption that sexuality is a realm of unremitting, unequaled victimization for women. Pornography appears as the monster that made this so. The ordinances' authors seek to impose their analysis by putting state power behind it. But this analysis is not the only feminist perspective on sexuality. Feminist theorists have also argued that the sexual terrain, however power-laden, is actively contested. Women are agents, and not merely victims, who make decisions and act on them, and who desire, seek out and enjoy sexuality.

Discussion Questions

1. Why do the authors believe that Dworkin-MacKinnon type legislation is ultimately antifeminist and lends support to conservative elements is society who do not agree with feminist goals?

2. What do the authors believe is the central flaw in the Dworkin-MacKinnon proposal? Present and explain their position. Do you agree or disagree with their assessment? Explain and defend your answer.

3. Why do the authors believe that the Dworkin-MacKinnon proposal is mistaken in thinking that all pornography is degrading to women? Provide some of the examples they use while presenting and explaining their answer. Do you agree or disagree with their view? Explain and defend your answer.

4. The authors question whether pornography is responsible for any more harm to women than much of the nonprohibited activity which is sexist and has been around for a much longer time. Explain what they mean by this. Do you agree or disagree with their position? Explain and defend your answer.

You can locate InfoTrac-College Education articles about this chapter by accessing the InfoTrac-College Edition website (http://www.infotrac-college.com/wadsworth/). Using the InfoTrac-College Edition subject guide, enter the search terms relevant to this chapter, and then read abstracts for relevant articles.

39   The Sexual Politics of the First Amendment

CATHARINE MACKINNON

Catharine MacKinnon is Professor of Law at the University of Michigan Law School in Ann Arbor, Michigan. She is known for her application of feminist theory to American jurisprudence, especially in the areas of sexual harassment and pornography. She has contributed to many scholarly journals and anthologies, and has produced several books, including *Only Words* (1993) and *Feminism Unmodified* (1987).

In this essay Professor MacKinnon contends that the use of the First Amendment to defend pornography is illegitimate, because pornography abuses women as well as promotes a climate in society that results in rape. Professor MacKinnon is arguing against those she calls the First Amendment absolutists and who, in her opinion, use the Constitution to maintain their power and dominance over women. She maintains that, in order to move toward a society in which men and women are equal, legislation must be paased allowing women to file civil suits against pornographers, since pornography, she believes, violates the civil rights of women. In defending her position, Professor MacKinnon draws an analogy between the *Dred Scott v. Sandford* (1856) decision, in which the U.S. Supreme Court asserted that black slaves were mere property, and the Supreme Court's decision that struck down an anti-pornography ordinance she and Andrea Dworkin had helped draft (*American Booksellers v. Hudnut* [1986]): it reduced women to mere speech just as *Dred Scott* had reduced blacks to mere property.

In the second part of this essay Professor MacKinnon responds to her critics by summarizing some of the testimonies and findings of the hearings that took place in conjunction with the ordinances proposed or passed in a number of major cities in the United States. The purpose of this section is to respond to the charge by the authors of chapter 38 who claim that it is questionable that pornography is responsible for any more harm to women than much of the non-prohibited activity which is sexist and has been around for a much longer time.

Reprinted by permission from Catharine A. MacKinnon, Feminism Unmodified *(Cambridge, MA: Harvard University Press, 1987) and Catharine A. MacKinnon, "The Roar on the Other Side of Silence," in* In Harm's Way: The Pornography Civil Rights Hearings, *eds. Catharine A. MacKinnon and Andrea Dworkin (Cambridge, MA: Harvard University Press), 3–24. Most footnotes omitted.*

[The Dred Scott case] was a law to be cited, a lesson to be learned, judicial vigor to be emulated, political imprudence to be regretted, but most of all, as time passed—it was an embarrassment—the Court's highly visible skeleton in a transparent closet.

–Don E. Ferrenbacher, *The Dred Scott Case: Its Significance in American Law and Politics*

Frankfurter is said to have remarked that Dred Scott was never mentioned by the Supreme Court any more than ropes and scaffolds were mentioned by a family that had lost one of its number to the hangman.

–Bruce Catton, in John A. Garraty, ed., *Quarrels That Have Shaped the Constitution*

The Constitution of the United States, contrary to any impression you may have received, is a piece of paper with words written on it. Because it is old, it is considered a document. When it is interpreted by particular people under particular conditions, it becomes a text. Because it is backed up by the power of the state, it is a law.

Feminism, by contrast, springs from the impulse to self-respect in every woman. From this have come some fairly elegant things: a metaphysics of mind, a theory of knowledge, an approach to ethics, and a concept of social action. Aspiring to the point of view of all women on social life as a whole, feminism has expressed itself as a political movement for civil equality.

Looking at the Constitution through the lens of feminism, initially one sees exclusion of women from the Constitution. This is simply to say that we had no voice in the constituting document of this state. From that one can suppose that those who did constitute it may not have had the realities of our situation in mind.

Next one notices that the Constitution as interpreted is structured around what can generically be called the public, or state action.

This constituting document pervasively assumes that those guarantees of freedoms that must be secured to citizens begin where law begins, with the public order. This posture is exalted as "negative liberty"[1] and is a cornerstone of the liberal state. You notice this from the feminist standpoint because women are oppressed socially, prior to law, without express state acts, often in intimate contexts. For women this structure means that those domains in which women are distinctly subordinated are assumed by the Constitution to be the domain of freedom.

Finally, combining these first two observations, one sees that women are not given affirmative access to those rights we need most. Equality, for example. Equality, in the words of Andrea Dworkin, was tacked on to the Constitution with spit and a prayer. And, let me also say, late.

If we apply these observations to the First Amendment, our exclusion means that the First Amendment was conceived by white men from the point of view of their social position. Some of them owned slaves; most of them owned women.[2] They wrote it to guarantee their freedom to keep something they felt at risk of losing. Namely—and this gets to my next point—speech which they did not want to lose through state action. They wrote the First Amendment so their speech would not be threatened by this powerful instrument they were creating, the federal government. You recall it reads, "Congress shall make no law abridging . . . the freedom of speech." They were *creating* that body. They were worried that it would abridge something they *did have*. You can tell that they had speech, because what they said was written down: it became a document, it has been interpreted, it is the law of the state.

By contrast with those who wrote the First Amendment so they could keep what they had, those who didn't have it didn't get it. Those whose speech was silenced prior to law, prior to any operation of the state's prohibition of it, were not secured freedom of speech. Their speech was not regarded as something that had to be—and this gets to my next point—affirmatively guaranteed. Looking at the history of the First Amendment from this perspective, reprehensible examples of state attempts to suppress speech exist. But they constitute a history of comparative privilege in contrast with the history of silence of those whose speech has ever been able to exist for the state even to contemplate abridging it.

A few affirmative guarantees of access to speech do exist. The *Red Lion* decision is one, although it may be slated for extinction.[3] Because certain avenues of speech are inherently restricted—for instance, there are only so many broadcast frequencies—according to the *Red Lion* doctrine of fairness in access to broadcast media, some people's access has to be restricted in the interest of providing access to all. In other words, the speech of those who could buy up all the speech there is, is restricted. Conceptually, this doctrine works exactly like affirmative action. The speech of those who might be the only ones there, is not there, so that others' can be.

With a few exceptions like that we find no guarantees of access to speech. Take, for example, literacy. Even after it became clear that the Constitution applied to the states, nobody argued that the segregation of schools that created inferior conditions of access to literacy for Blacks violated their First Amendment rights. Or the slave codes that made it a crime to teach a slave to read and write or to advocate their freedom. Some of those folks who struggled for civil rights for Black people must have thought of this, but I never heard their lawyers argue it. If access to the means of speech is effectively socially precluded on the basis of race or class or gender, freedom from state burdens on speech does not meaningfully guarantee the freedom to speak.

The First Amendment absolutism, the view that speech must be absolutely protected, is not the law of the First Amendment. It is the conscience, the superego of the First Amendment, the implicit standard from which all deviations must be justified. It is also an advocacy position typically presented in debate as if it were legal fact. Consider for example that First Amendment bog, the distinction between speech and conduct. Most conduct is expressive as well as active; words are as often tantamount to acts as they are vehicles for removed cerebration. Case law knows this.[4] But the first question, the great divide, the beginning and the end, is still the absolutist question, "Is it speech or isn't it?"

First Amendment absolutism was forged in the crucible of obscenity litigation. Probably its most inspired expositions, its most passionate defenses, are to be found in Justice Douglas's dissents in obscenity cases.[5] This is not coincidence. Believe him when he says that pornography is at the core of the First Amendment. Absolutism has developed through obscenity litigation, I think, because pornography's protection fits perfectly with the power relations embedded in the First Amendment structure and jurisprudence from the start. Pornography is exactly that speech of men that silences the speech of women. I take it seriously when Justice Douglas speaking on pornography and others preaching absolutism say that pornography has to be protected speech or else free expression will not mean what it has always meant in this country.

I must also say that the First Amendment has become a sexual fetish through years of absolutist writing in the melodrama mode in *Playboy* in particular. You know those superheated articles where freedom of speech is extolled and its imminent repression is invoked. Behaviorally, *Playboy*'s consumers are reading about the First Amendment, masturbating to the women, reading about the First Amendment, masturbating to the women, reading about the First Amendment, masturbating to the women. It makes subliminal seduction look subtle. What is conveyed is not only that using women is as legitimate as thinking about the Constitution, but also that if you don't support these views about the Constitution, you won't be able to use these women.

This general approach affects even religious groups. I love to go speaking against pornography when the sponsors dig up some religious types, thinking they will make me look bad because they will agree with me. Then the ministers come on and say, "This is the first time we've ever agreed with the ACLU about anything . . . why, what she's advocating would *violate the First Amendment*." This isn't their view universally, I guess, but it has been my experience repeatedly, and I have personally never had a minister support me on the air. One of them finally explained it. The First Amendment, he said, also guarantees the freedom of religion. So this is not only what we already know: regardless of one's politics and one's moral views, one is into using women largely. It is also that, consistent with this, First Amendment absolutism resonates historically in the context of the long-term collaboration in misogyny between church and state. Don't let them tell you they're "separate" in that.

In pursuit of absolute freedom of speech, the ACLU has been a major institution in defending, and now I describe their behavior, the Nazis, the Klan, and the pornographers. I am waiting for them to add the antiabortionists, including the expressive conduct of their violence. Think about one of their favorite metaphors, a capitalist metaphor, the marketplace of ideas. Think about whether the speech of the Nazis has historically enhanced the speech of the Jews. Has the speech of the Klan expanded the speech of Blacks? Has the so-called speech of the pornographers enlarged the speech of women? In this context, apply to what they call the marketplace of ideas the question we were asked to consider in the keynote speech by Winona LaDuke: Is there a relationship between our poverty in speech and their wealth?

As many of you know, Andrea Dworkin and I, with a lot of others, have been working to establish a law that recognizes pornography as a violation of the civil rights of women in particular. It recognizes that pornography is a form of sex discrimination. Recently, in a fairly unprecedented display of contempt, the U.S. Supreme Court found that the Indianapolis version of our law violates the First Amendment.[6] On a direct appeal, the Supreme Court invalidated a local ordinance by summary affirmance—no arguments, no briefs on the merits, no victims, no opinion, not so much as a single line of citation to controlling precedent. One is entitled to think that they would have put one there if they had had one.

The Court of Appeals opinion they affirmed[7] expressly concedes that pornography violates women in all the ways Indianapolis found it did. The opinion never questioned that pornography is sex discrimination. Interesting enough, the Seventh Circuit, in an opinion by Judge Frank Easterbrook, conceded the issue of objective causation. The only problem was, the harm didn't matter as much as the materials mattered. They are valuable. So the law that prohibited the harm the materials caused was held to be content-based and impermissible discrimination on the basis of viewpoint.

This is a law that gives victims a civil action when they are coerced into pornography, when pornography is forced upon them, when they are assaulted because of specific pornography, and when they are subordinated through the trafficking of pornography. Some of us thought that sex discrimination and sexual abuse were against public policy. We defined pornography as the sexually explicit subordination of women through pictures or words that also includes presentations of women being sexually abused. There is a list of the specific acts of sexual abuse. The law covers men, too. We were so careful that practices whose abusiveness some people publicly question—for example, submission, servility, and display—are not covered by the trafficking provision. So we're talking rape, torture, pain, humiliation: we're talking violence against women turned into sex.

Now we are told that pornography, which, granted, does the harm we say it does, this pornography as we define it is protected speech. It has speech value. You can tell it has value as speech because it is so effective in doing the harm that it does.[8] (The passion of this rendition is mine, but the opinion really does say this.) The more harm, the more protection. This is now apparently the law of the First Amendment, at least where harm to women is the rationale. Judge LaDoris Cordell spoke earlier about the different legal standards for high-value and low-value speech, a doctrine that feminists who oppose pornography have always been averse to. But at least it is now clear that whatever the value of pornography is—and it is universally conceded to be low—the value of women is lower.

It is a matter of real interest to me exactly what the viewpoint element in our law is, according to Easterbrook's opinion. My best guess is that our law takes the point of view that women do not enjoy and deserve rape, and he saw that as just one point of view among many. Where do you suppose he got that idea? Another possible rendering is that our law takes the position that women should not be subordinated to men on the basis of sex, that women are or should be equal, and he regards relief to that end as the enforcement of a prohibited view.

Just what is and is not valuable, is and is not a viewpoint, is and is not against public policy was made even clearer the day after the summary affirmance. In the *Renton* case the Supreme Court revealed the conditions under which pornography can be restricted: it can be zoned away beyond the city limits.[9] It can be regulated this way on the basis of its "sec-ondary effects"—which are, guess what, property values. But it cannot be regulated on the basis of its primary effects on the bodies of the women who had to be ground up to make it.

Do you think it makes any difference to the woman who is coerced into pornography or who has just hit the end of this society's chances for women that the product of her exploitation is sold on the other side of the tracks? Does it matter to the molested child or the rape victim that the offender who used the pornography to get himself up or to plan what he would do or to decide what "type" to do it to had to drive across town to get it? It *does* matter to the women who live or work in the neighborhoods into which pornography is zoned. They pay in increased street harassment, in an atmosphere of terror and contempt for what other neighborhoods gain in keeping their property values up.

Reading the two decisions together, you see the Court doing what it has always done with pornography: making it available in private while decrying it in public. Pretending to be tough on pornography's effects, the *Renton* case still *gives it a place to exist.* Although obscenity is supposed to have such little value that it is not considered speech at all, *Renton* exposes the real bottom line of the First Amendment: the pornography stays. Anyone who doesn't think absolutism has made any progress, check that.

Why is it that obscenity law can exist and our trafficking provision cannot? Why can the law against child pornography exist and not our law against coercion? Why aren't obscenity and child pornography laws viewpoint laws? Obscenity, as Justice Brennan pointed out in his dissent in *Renton,* expresses a viewpoint: sexual mores should be more relaxed, and if they were, sex would look like pornography. Child pornography also presents a viewpoint: sex between adults and children is liberating, fulfilling, fun, and natural for the child. If one is concerned about the government taking a point of view through law, the laws against these things express the state's opposition to these viewpoints, to the extent of making them crimes to express. Why is a time-place-manner distinction all right in *Renton,* and not our forcing provision, which is kind of time-and-place-like and does not provide actions against the pornographers at all? Why is it all right to make across-the-board, content-based distinctions like obscenity and child pornography, but not our trafficking provision, not our coercion provision?

When do you see a viewpoint as a viewpoint? When you don't agree with it. When is a viewpoint not a viewpoint? When it's yours.[10] What is and is not a viewpoint, much less a prohibited one, is a matter of individual values and social consensus. The reason Judge Easterbrook saw a viewpoint in our law was because he disagrees with it. (I don't mean to personify it, because it isn't at all personal; I mean it *is* him, personally, but it isn't him only or only him, as a person.) There is real social disagreement as to whether women are or should be subordinated to men. Especially in sex.

His approach obscured the fact that our law is not content-based at all; it is harm-based. A harm is an act, an activity. It is not just a mental event. Coercion is not an image. Force is not a representation. Assault is not a symbol. Trafficking is not simply advocacy. Subordination is an activity, not just a point of view. The problem is, pornography is both theory and practice, both a metaphor for and a means of the subordination of women. The Seventh Circuit allowed the fact that pornography has a theory to obscure the fact that it is a practice, the fact that it is a metaphor to obscure the fact that it is also a means.

I don't want you to misunderstand what I am about to say. Our law comes nowhere near anybody's speech rights,[11] and the literatures of other inequalities do not relate to those inequalities in the same way pornography relates to sexism. But I risk your misunderstanding on both of these points in order to

say that there have been serious movements of liberation in this world. This is by contrast with liberal movements. In serious movements for human freedom, speech is serious, both the attempt to get some for those who do not have any and the recognition that the so-called speech of the other side is a form of the practice of the other side. In union struggles, yellow-dog presses are attacked. Abolitionists attacked slave presses. The monarchist press was not tolerated by the revolutionaries who founded this country. When the White Circle League published a racist pamphlet, it was found to violate a criminal law against libeling groups. After World War II the Nazi press was restricted in Germany by law under the aegis of the Allies. Nicaragua considers it "immoral" and contrary to the progress of education and the cultural development of the people to publish, distribute, circulate, exhibit, transmit, or sell materials that, among other things, "stimulate viciousness," "lower human dignity," or to "use women as sexual or commercial objects."

The analogy Norma Ramos mentioned between the fight against pornography to sex equality and the fight against segregation to race equality makes the analogy between the Indianapolis case and *Brown v. Board of Education* evocative to me also. But I think we may be at an even prior point. The Supreme Court just told us that it is a constitutional right to traffic in our flesh, so long as it is done through pictures and words, and a legislature may not give us access to court to contest it. The Indianapolis case is the *Dred Scott* of the women's movement. The Supreme Court told Dred Scott, to the Constitution, you are property. It told women, to the Constitution, you are speech. The struggle against pornography is an abolitionist struggle to establish that just as buying and selling human beings never was anyone's property right, buying and selling women and children is no one's civil liberty.

NOTES

1. Isaiah Berlin distinguishes negative from positive freedom. Negative freedom asks the question, "what is the area within which the subject— a person or group of persons—is or should be left to do or be what [he] is able to do or be, without interference from other persons?" Positive freedom asks the question, "what, or who, is the source of control or interference that can determine someone to do, or be, this rather than that?" "Two Concepts of Liberty," in *Four Essays on Liberty* 121–22 (1970). Is it not obvious that if one group is granted the positive freedom to do whatever they want to another group, to determine that the second group will be and do this rather than that, that no amount of negative freedom guaranteed to the second group will make it the equal of the first? The negative state is thus incapable of effective guarantees of rights in any but a just society, which is the society in which they are needed the least.

2. The analysis here is indebted to Andrea Dworkin, "For Men, Freedom of Speech, For Women, Silence Please" in *Take Back the Night: Women on Pornography* 255–58 (Laura Lederer ed. 1982).

3. Red Lion Broadcasting Co. v. F.C.C., 395 U.S. 367 (1969). In F.C.C. v. League of Women Voters, 468 U.S. 364 (1984), the Supreme Court hints that it would be receptive to a challenge to the fairness doctrine on the basis that it impedes rather than furthers the values of the First Amendment, 376 n. 11,378 n. 12.

4. The best examples are the laws against treason, bribery, conspiracy, threats, blackmail, and libel. Acts can also be expression, but are not necessarily protected as such.

5. Roth v. U.S., 354 U.S. 476,508–14 ("The first amendment, in prohibitions in terms absolute" at 514); Memoirs v. Massachusetts, 383 U.S. 413, 424–33 (concurring); Miller v. California, 413 U.S. 15, 37–47; Paris Adult Theatres v. Slaton, 413 U.S. 49, 70–73 (1973).

6. 106 S. Ct. 1172 (1986).

7. American Booksellers v. Hudnut, 771 F.2d 323 (7th Cir. 1985), *aff'd* 106 S. Ct. 1172 (1986).

8. 771 F.2d at 329.

9. Renton v. Playtime Theatres, 106 S.Ct. 925 (1986).

10. Laws against rape also express the view that sexual subordination is impermissible, and this is not considered repressive of thought, although presumably some thought is involved.

11. An erection is not a thought either, unless one thinks with one's penis.

A Roar on the Other Side of Silence

CATHARINE MACKINNON

Women speak in public for the first time in history of the harms done to them through pornography. Their first-person accounts stand against the pervasive sexual violation of women and children that is allowed to be done in private and is not allowed to be criticized in public.

Pornography and its apologists largely set the terms of public discussion over pornography's role in social life. Public, available, effectively legal, pornography has stature: it is visible, credible, and legitimated. At the same time, its influence and damaging effects are denied as nonexistent, indeterminate, or merely academic, contrary to all the evidence. Its victims have had no stature at all. These first-person accounts have changed the terms of this discussion by opening a space to speak for the real authorities on pornography: the casualties of its making and use. Against a background of claims that the victims and the harms done to them do not exist, must not be believed, and should not be given a legal hearing, the harms of pornography stood exposed and took shape as potential legal injuries. These hearings were the moment when the voices of those victimized through pornography broke the public surface. Their publication gives the public unmediated and unrestricted access to this direct evidence for the first time. The authority of their experience makes the harm of pornography undeniable: it harmed them.

In late 1983, legislators in Minneapolis initiated this process by employing Andrea Dworkin and me to write a law for the city that we had conceived on pornography as a human rights violation. Other jurisdictions followed, including Indianapolis, Los Angeles County, and the Commonwealth of Massachusetts, each seeking to adapt our civil rights approach to local concerns. All these laws recognized the concrete violations of civil rights done through pornography as practices of sex discrimination and gave the survivors access to civil court for relief through a law they could use themselves. The hearings that resulted from the introduction of the legislation gave pornography's survivors a forum, an audience, and a concrete opportunity to affect their world. Grasping the real chance that rights might be given to them, seeing that their participation could make a difference to the conditions of their lives, these women and men became prepared to run the risks of this political expression. The consequences anticipated at that time included public humiliation and shame, shunning and ostracism, loss of employment, threats, harassment, and physical assault.

The act of introducing the antipornography civil rights ordinances into the legislative arena gave pornography's victims back some measure of the dignity and hope that the pornography, with its pervasive social and legal support, takes away. The ordinances, in formulating pornography's harms as human rights deprivations, captured a denigrated reality of women's experience in a legal form that affirmed that to be treated in these ways violates a human being; it does not simply reveal and define what a woman is. As ending these violations and holding their perpetrators accountable became imaginable for the first time, and women participated directly in making the rules that govern their lives, the disgrace of being socially female—fit only for sexual use, unfit for human life—was exposed as a pimp's invention. In these hearings, women were citizens.

The first-person testimony, contextualized by expert witnesses as representative rather than unique or isolated, documented the material harm pornography does in the real world, showing the view that pornography is harmless fantasy to be as false as it is cliched. Women used for sex so that pornography can be made of them against their will—from Linda "Lovelace" forced to fellate men so *Deep Throat* could be made to a young girl sold as sex to *Hustler's* "Beaverhunt" to Valerie Harper's face on another woman's naked body on a T-shirt—refute the assumption promoted by the pornography industry that women are in pornography because they want to be there. The information provided by these witnesses also underlines the simplest fact to the visual materials: to be made, the acts in them had to be *done to someone*. A few who have escaped the sex factories describe the forms of force required.

Woman after woman used by consumers of pornography recounts its causal role in her sexual violation by a man close to her. A husband forces pornography on his wife and uses it to pressure her into sex acts she does not want. A father threatens his children with pornography so they will keep silent about what he shows them is being done, audibly, to their mother at night. A brother holds up pornography magazines as his friends gang-rape his sister, making her assume the poses in the materials, turning her as they turn the pages. A woman's boyfriend becomes aroused by watching other women being used in pornography and forces sexual access. A gay man inflicts the abusive sex learned through using pornography on is male lover, who tolerates it because he learned from pornography that a man's violence is the price of his love.

Although intimate settings provide privileged access for these acts, such violations occur throughout social life. White male motorists, spewing racist bile, rape a Native American woman at a highway rest stop in reenactment of a pornographic video game. Working men plaster women's crotches on the walls of workplaces. Therapists force pornography on clients. Pimps use pornography to train and trap child prostitutes. Men who buy and use women and children for sex bring pornography to show those prostituted what the men want them to do. Pornography is made of prostituted children to threaten them with exposure to keep them in prostitution. Serial sexual murderers use pornography to prepare and impel them to rape and kill.

Grounded in these realities, the ordinance that produced and resulted from the hearings provides civil access to court to prove the abuse and the role of pornography in it in each situation. The ordinance, with local variations, provides a cause of action to individuals who are coerced into pornography, forced to consume pornography, defamed by being used in pornography without consent, assaulted due to specific pornography, or subordinated as a member of a sex-based group through traffic in pornography as legally defined. The chance to prove in court the harmful role of pornography in each situation is what pornography's

victims have sought. This, to date, is what they have been denied.

The opponents of the civil rights laws against pornography were amply represented in the hearings. They did not openly defend pornography as such, or address the harms the witnesses document even to deny them. They treated the survivors as if they were not there or did not matter. That those victimized by pornography are lying or expendable is the upshot of the First Amendment defense of pornography that the opponents presented, preceding as if the "speech" of violation matters over the violation of the violated. Some opponents adopted the view that any factual disputes over the harm should not be resolved in court—in other words, that whatever harm may exist can be debated so long as the debate is endless, but the harm can never be stopped. As the Massachusetts hearing shows, the issue of whether pornography is harmful matters to pornography's defenders only as long as it is considered impossible to demonstrate that harm. Once it is judicially established that pornography does the harms made actionable in this law—as it was established in the litigation on the ordinance in 1985[12]—the ordinance's opponents lose interest in the question.

Addressed not at all by the opposition in the hearings is whether or not the practices of pornography made actionable by the ordinance are properly conceptualized as sex-based discrimination. Like the conclusion that pornography causes harm, the conclusion on the nature of that harm is based on evidence, on fact; these hearings provide those facts. As an analytic mater, although many people are shown to be victimized, actually and potentially, if even one woman, man, or child is victimized *because of their sex*, as a member of a group defined by sex, that person is discriminated against on the basis of sex; those who testified to their experiences in the hearings incontestably were hurt as members of their gender. Their specifically, differentially, and uncontestedly sex-based injuries ground the state's interest in equality that is vindicated by the ordinance.

The hearings show the ordinance in practice: it produced them. The hearings also present case after case of precisely the kinds of evidence the ordinance would introduce into court if it were enacted into law. These are the people who need to use it, who have nothing to use without it. The hearings empowered individuals to speak in public, provided a forum for them to confront their abusers, to prove their violations, and to secure accountability and relief, as the ordinance would in court. The hearings present witnesses to acts of abuse and injury—acts, not ideas, like those acts the ordinance would redress in court. In the hearings, the industry of exploitation and violence that produced these acts is connected inextricably with them, as it would also have to be in civil court proceedings. The hearings challenged the same concentration of non-governmental power that the ordinance would challenge in court, empowering the government no more than the hearings did. The hearings used the legislative process for the ends to which it is given to citizens to use, as the ordinance would use the civil judicial process to its designed purposes of conflict resolution and rectification of injury. As the ordinance would in court, the hearings brought pornography out of a half-lit underground into the public light of day. The hearings freed previously suppressed speech. So would the ordinance. Neither the ordinance nor the hearings have anything in common with censorship.

Until these hearings, the public discussion of pornography has been impoverished and deprived by often inaccurate or incomplete reports of victims' accounts and experts' views. Media reports of victims' testimony at the time of the hearings themselves were often cursory, distorted, or nonexistent. Some reports by journalists covering the Minneapolis hearings were rewritten by editors to conform the testimony to the story of pornography's harmlessness that they wanted told. Of this process,

one Minneapolis reporter assigned to cover those hearings told me, in reference to the reports she filed, "I have never been so censored in my life." Thus weakened, the victim testimony became easier to stigmatize as emotional and to dismiss as exceptional. Its representativeness has been further undermined by selective or misleading reports of expert testimony on scientific studies. . . . This body of scholarship predicts that the precise kinds of consequences *will* happen from exposure to pornography that the survivors report *did* happen in their own experience. In making the whole record available, this book shows these two kinds of evidence documenting the same harm in two different ways.

These hearings contribute other neglected or otherwise inaccessible information to the public discussion over the civil rights ordinance against pornography. For example, the allegation that opposing points of view were excluded from the hearings by the bills' proponents is refuted by the hearings on their face. Opponent after opponent of the civil rights of women, mostly liberals, parade through these pages, testifying ad nauseam. The hearings also go some distance toward refuting the now ubiquitous fabrication that locates the engine of the civil rights antipornography ordinances in an "unusual coalition of radical feminists and conservative women politicians."[13] This invention originated in a false report in *The New York Times* that Charlee Hoyt, one of the bill's original sponsors in Minneapolis, opposed the Equal Rights Amendment. The *Times* published a correction affirming Hoyt's constant support of ERA, but the lie about the ordinance's alliance with the right stuck, always changing ground but always growing.[14] The same *Times* article stated that the Indianapolis ordinance was passed with "the support of the Rev. Greg Dixon, a former Moral Majority official," who "packed Council hearings to lobby for passage of the proposed ordinance." Neither Rev. Dixon nor his followers appear to have spoken at the Indianapolis hearings. Enough votes for passage (the bill passed 24 to 5) existed prior to the meeting at which these individuals sat in the audience. No one has said that Rev. Dixon or his group had any other contact with the process. Thus it was that the outcome of a legislative vote came to be attributed to the presence of some who came to watch as others cast it.

Taint through innuendo has substituted for fact and analysis in much reporting and discussion of the ordinance. As the hearings document, of all the sponsors of the bill in all the cities in which it has been introduced, only one—Beulah Coughenour of Indianapolis—has been conservative. Work on one bill with an independent individual is hardly an alliance with a political wing. And exactly what is sinister about women uniting with women across conventional political lines against a form of abuse whose politics are sexual has remained unspecified by the critics.

The hearings correct such widely distorted facts simply by showing the sponsors and supporters of the ordinance in action, illustrating its progressive politics. The ordinance's two original sponsors in Minneapolis appear: Van White, a liberal Democratic African American man, and Charlee Hoyt, a liberal Republican white woman. (Sharon Sayles Belton, the Democratic African American woman who is now mayor of Minneapolis, sponsored the reintroduced ordinance after the first veto.) The grass-roots groups who inspired the Minneapolis ordinance by requesting help in their fight against pornographers' invasion of their neighborhoods testify in support of it. These same groups later supported the Indianapolis ordinance when it was challenged in court. Battered women's groups, rape crisis center workers and advocates, organizations of survivors of sexual abuse in childhood, and groups of former prostitutes present unanimous evidence from their experience in favor of the ordinance. They, too, supported it against later legal challenge. The large, ethnically diverse Los Angeles County Commission on Women that sponsored and supported the ordinance chaired the hearings there.

The progression of hearings reveals that opposition to the ordinance became better organized over time, its strategy refined. In the Los Angeles hearing on April 22, 1985, in which the pro-pimp lobby remained as always centered in the American Civil Liberties Union, the woman card was first played. There, a tiny, noisy elite of women who defend pornography professionally contrast with survivor after survivor whom they talk past and disregard—a division of a few women from all women subsequently magnified by a gleeful press. There, women's material interest in pornography was presented as divided: if it hurts some women, other women love it, and stopping it hurts women more. Women against women subsequently became the pornographers' tactic of choice, as if women's oppression by pornography had been argued to be biological, as if biological females saying they were not hurt by it undercut that case. This choice of strategy was revealed in the orchestration of the ordinance referendum battle in Cambridge, Massachusetts, in November 1985, in which the ordinance narrowly lost, and even more graphically in evidence in the Boston, Massachusetts, hearing of March 1992. In Boston, speaking almost entirely through female mouthpieces, the corporate interests of the entertainment industry came out of the woodwork for the first time weighing in on the side of the pornography industry, arraying abstraction after evasion after obfuscation after self-interested, profit-oriented rationalization against survivors' simple, direct accounts of the role of pornography in their abuse. Much of the media persistently position women against women in their coverage, employing the pornographers' strategy in the way they report events and frame issues for public discussion. Corrective letters showing wide solidarity among women on the ordinance are routinely not published.

These hearings took place in public and on the record. The witnesses, unless they say otherwise, were fully identified to the governmental bodies before whom they testified. Some of the consequences to them show why it has taken so long and has been so hard to make this information public, and prefigure the onslaught that followed. Some of those who spoke in Minneapolis were hounded and punished for what they said. One woman's testimony was published by *Penthouse Forum* without her knowledge or permission, selling her assault for sexual use. A copy of *Penthouse's* pages with "We're going to get you, squaw" scrawled across it in red appeared in her mailbox. A dead rabbit appeared there a few days later; she was telephoned repeatedly by a man who appeared to be watching her in her home. Another witness was subsequently telephoned night after night at her unlisted telephone number: "The calls are not simply harassing phone calls. It is like someone is reading something out of the pornography books . . . we can't get away from it." These are techniques of terror.

By bringing forward festering human pain that had been denied, the hearings unleashed an explosion of reports by women and men desperate for help. A local organizing group formed after the Minneapolis hearing was deluged with them. Women told "about the time their boyfriend urinated on them while using pornography depicting 'golden showers.' " Rape victims reported that "their attacker took pictures during the rape and that she's afraid he is going to sell and distribute them." The group reported that "we have received a call from a man in Fort Collins, Colorado, terrified because a group of men were holding him captive and making pornography with him. He has called and sent us the pornography in hopes that it could be used as evidence, that the whip lashes would prove that he was forced." Some groups held more hearings. The National Organization for Women hosted testimony on pornography across the nation.

The Minneapolis hearings, circulated in photocopied transcript hand to hand, had a substantial impact on consciousness, politics, scholarship, theory, and policy. At the federal level, the first explosion of publicity surrounding the Minneapolis hearings revived a long-moribund proposal for a new national commission on pornography. Attorney General William French Smith created the Attorney General's Commission on Obscenity and Pornography and selected its members. The prior Commission on Obscenity and Pornography in 1970, appointed by President Nixon, had exonerated "obscenity" and "erotica" of a role in "crime," looking at no violent materials and looking for only violent effects. The President's Commission heard from not a single direct victim—offended moralists are not victims—and considered only evidence from "experts," meaning academics, on the question of harm. Understanding that asking the wrong questions of the wrong people might have produced the wrong answers, the Attorney General's Commission took extensive testimony from scores of survivors of all kinds of real abuse and investigated the effects of violent as well as nonviolent sexual materials. In other words, it investigated what those on the receiving end were in a position to know about the materials that are actually made and marketed by the pornography industry and consumed by its users. This commission was later named "the Meese Commission" by a hostile press in order to discredit it by association with an almost universally despised man who did announce the inquiry's formation but did not originate it and did virtually nothing with its results.

The *Final Report* of the Attorney General's Commission, which repeatedly footnoted the Minneapolis hearings, substantially adopted the civil rights approach in its approach, findings, and recommendations. The report included an entire chapter on harm to "performers"—of all survivors, the most ignored and, when noticed, blamed. It found that "the harms at which the ordinance is aimed are real and the need for a remedy for those harms is pressing." It concluded that "civil and other remedies ought to be available to those who have been in some way injured in the process of producing these materials." It endorsed a limited concept of civil remedies. It found that the civil rights approach "is the only legal tool suggested to the Commission which is specifically designed to provide direct relief to the victims of the injuries so exhaustively documented in our hearings throughout the country." The Commission also agreed that pornography, as made actionable in the ordinance, "constitutes a practice of discrimination on the basis of sex." In an embrace of the ordinance's specific causes of action as well as its approach, the Commission recommended that Congress "consider legislation affording protection to those individuals whose civil rights have been violated by the production or distribution of pornography . . . At a minimum, claims could be provided against trafficking, coercion, forced viewing, defamation, and assault, reaching the industry as necessary to remedy these abuses." Unable to find constitutional a legal definition of pornography that did not duplicate the existing obscenity definition, the Commission nonetheless found itself "in substantial agreement with the motivations behind the ordinance, and with goals it represents."

In the years soon following the Commission's Report, parts of the ordinance were introduced as bills in Congress. Senator Arlen Specter introduced a version of the ordinance's coercion provision as the Pornography Victim's Protection Act, making the coercion of an adult or the use of a child to make pornography civilly actionable. Senator Mitch McConnell introduced a rendition of the ordinance's assault provision as the Pornography Victims' Compensation Act, creating a civil action for assault or murder caused by pornography. Most stunningly, Congress in 1994 adopted the Violence Against Women act, providing a federal civil remedy for gender-based acts of violence such as rape and battering. In so doing, Congress made legally real its understanding that sexual violation is a practice of sex discrimination, the legal approach that the

antipornography civil rights ordinance pioneered in legislative form.

More broadly, the exposure of pornography's harms has moved the ground under social theory across a wide range of issues. The place of sex in speech, including literature and art, and its role in social action has been thrown open to reconsideration, historically and in the present. The implications of visual and verbal presentation and representation for the creation and distribution of social power—the relation between the way people are imaged and imagined to the ways they are treated—are being rethought. The buying and selling of human flesh in the form of pornography has given scholarship on slavery a new dimension. More has been learned about the place of sexuality in ideology and about the importance of sexual pleasure to the exercise of dominant power. The hearings are fertile ground for analyzing the role of visceral belief in inequality and inferiority in practical systems of discrimination, and of the role of denial of inequality in maintaining that inequality. The cultural legitimation of sexual force, including permission for and exoneration of rape and transformation of sexual abuse into sexual pleasure and identity, is being newly interrogated. New human rights theories are being built to respond to the human rights violations unearthed. As events that have been hidden come to light, the formerly unseen appears to determine more and more of the seen. The repercussions for theory, the requisite changes in thinking on all levels of society, have only begun to be felt.

For those who survived pornography, the hearings were like coming up for air. Now the water has closed over their heads once again. The ordinance is not law anywhere. Mayor Donald Fraser of Minneapolis vetoed it twice after passage by two different city councils. Minneapolis has dithered and done nothing to this day. The Indianapolis ordinance was declared unconstitutional by the Court of Appeals for the Seventh Circuit in a decision that inverted First Amendment law, saying that the harm of pornography only proved the importance of protecting it as speech, and reduced equality rights, by comparison, to a constitutional nullity. The U.S. Supreme Court summarily affirmed this result without hearing arguments, reading briefs, or issuing an opinion, using a now largely obsolete legal device for upholding a ruling without expressing a view on its reasoning. Although the Seventh Circuit decision is wrong in law, and the summary affirmance of it need not necessarily bind subsequent courts, the ordinance passed in Bellingham, Washington, by public referendum was invalidated by a federal court there, citing the Indianapolis decision as controlling. The Los Angeles ordinance was narrowly defeated, 3 to 2, in a vote delayed in order to be as inconspicuous as possible. The Massachusetts ordinance was maneuvered behind the scenes out of coming to a vote at all. Senators Specter and McConnell compromised their bills fundamentally. Neither bill—for all the purported political expediency of their sponsors in gutting them as tools against the pornography industry—passed or even made it out of committee.

The victims have been betrayed. To adapt George Eliot's words, "that roar which lies on the other side of silence" about sexual violation in the ordinary lives of women was heard in these hearings. Now society knows that is being done to the victims and has decided to turn away, close its mind, and, "well wadded with stupidity,"[15] go back to masturbating to the violation of their human rights. The debate over pornography that was reconfigured by the survivors' testimony to make harm to women indispensable to the discussion has increasingly regressed to its old right/left morality/ freedom rut, making sexual violence against women once again irrelevant and invisible.[16] Politicians are too cowed by the media even to introduce the bill. Truth be told, for survivor and expert both, it has become more difficult

than it was before to speak out against pornography, as those in these hearings did. The consequences are now known to include professional shunning and blacklisting, attacks on employment and publishing, deprivation of research and grant funding, public demonization, litigation and threats of litigation, and physical assault.[17] The holy rage of the pornographers at being publicly exposed, legalized through ACLU lawyers at every bend in the road and accompanied by the relentless beat of media lies, has made aggression against pornography's critics normative and routine, fighting back unseemly, seemingly impossible. The silencing is intentional, and it is effective. In this atmosphere, few stand up and say what they know.

The concerted attacks on anyone who dares to give even a respectful hearing to the critique of pornography from this point of view has been reminiscent of the left's vicious treatment of so-called "premature antifascists" during the period of the Hitler-Stalin pact, or of those who questioned Stalin including after the Moscow Trials. In the establishment today, support or at least tolerance for pornography, if slightly shaken, remains an article of faith among liberals and libertarians alike. The liberal establishment is its chief bastion but the right is actively complicit, its moralistic decency crusades and useless obscenity laws protecting pornography while pretending to stop it, contributing its share of judicial and other misogynists to the ranks of pornography's defenders, forever defending private concentrations of power and mistaking money for speech.

Against this united front, many a wellplaced and secure professional, upon taking a rather obvious position against exploitation and abuse, or upon simply describing what is in the pornography or in the research on its effects, has been startled to be screamed at by formerly rational colleagues, savaged by hostile mail (sometimes widely electronically disseminated), defamed by attacks on professional competence, subjected to false rumors, ostracized instead of respected, libeled in and out of pornography, sued for speech by those who say they oppose suits for speech, and investigated by journalists and committees—not to mention blandishments of money from pornographers, eviction from homes, and threats against families. Most fold. With intellectuals intimidated, what chance do prostituted women and raped children have?

In the defense of pornography against the ordinance—the first effective threat to its existence—the outline of a distinctive power bloc has become discernible in the shadows of American politics. Cutting across left and right, uniting sectors of journalism, entertainment, and publishing with organized crime, sprawling into parts of the academy and the legal profession, this configuration has emerged to act as a concerted political force. Driven by sex and money, its power is largely hidden and institutionally without limits. Most of those who could credibly criticize it either become part of it or collaborate through silence. No political or legal organ is yet designed or equipped to counter it. Existing structural restraints on excess power—such as the governmental power is formally controlled, as if the government is the only entity that can cohere power or abuse it. Private in the sense of nongovernmental in origin, this bloc uses government (such as First Amendment adjudications) as just one tool, wielding less visibly against dissenters a clout similar to the government's clout in the McCarthy era.

Politicians who live and die by spin and image grovel before this machine. Law has been largely impotent in the face of it and lacks the will and resources to resist it. Indeed, law has largely been created by it, the reality perceptions entrenched through the machine's distinctively deployed weapons of sex, money, and reputation being largely indelible and impervious to contrary proof. Academic institutions are often found cowering before it and

have ceded to it much of their role of credentialing the intelligentsia. Its concerted power defines what is taken as reality and aims to destroy those who challenge or deviate. Almost no one stands up to it. Those who testified in these hearings did.

One incident exposed the workings of this *de facto* machine accidentally. In 1986, a leaked memo from the public relations firm of Gray & Company proposed a press campaign for the Media Coalition, the group of trade publishers and distributors, including some pornographers, that is substantially funded by *Penthouse* and was behind the litigation against the ordinance in Indianapolis and Bellingham. Gray & Company proposed to "discredit the Commission on Pornography" and stop "self-styled anti-pornography crusaders" from creating "a climate of public hostility toward selected publications."[18] They got the contract, which budgeted about a million dollars to pursue their recommended lines of attack. As reflected in the press this campaign produced, this planned onslaught focused on two items of disinformation contained in the proposal. The first is that there is no evidence that pornography does harm. In their euphemistic PR language, "there is no factual or scientific basis for the exaggerated and unfounded allegations that sexually-oriented content in contemporary media is in any way a cause of violent or criminal behavior."[19] The second is that the campaign to stop pornography "is being orchestrated by a group of religious extremists."[20] The mainstream media slavishly published *as news* the spewings of the groups fronting this strategy, establishing both lies as conventional wisdom.

The false statement that scientific evidence on the harmful effects of exposure to pornography is mixed or inconclusive is now repeated like a mantra, even in court. It has become the official story, the baseline, the pre-established position against which others are evaluated, the standard against which deviations must defend themselves, the common sense view that needs no source and has none, the canard that individuals widely believe as if they had done the research themselves. Few read the scholarly literature or believe they need to. No amount of evidence to the contrary—and evidence to the contrary is all there is—is credible against the simple reassertion of what was believed, without evidence, to begin with. Associating all work against pornography with widely reviled extremists of the religious and political right—without regard for the lack of factual basis for this guilt by association—is similarly impervious to contrary proof and produces a self-righteous witch-hunt mentality. Individuals strategically singled out as threatening to the financial health of Gray & Company's "selected publications" are also used in pornography,[21] this cabal's ultimate weapon. Such attack-pornography potently and pervasively targets sexualized hostility at pornography's critics and destroys their status as credible speakers who have anything of value to say. The effect of lowering the human status of the critics can be relied upon to be discounted as having occurred by the norms of public discourse, which pervasively pretend that what is done in pornography occurs off stage in some twilight zone—coming from nowhere, meaning nothing, going noplace.

If this cabal acts in planned and organized ways at times, usually its common misogyny and attachment to pornography are themselves the conspiracy. The legitimate media act in their own perceived self-interest when they defend pornography, making common cause with mass sexual exploitation by calling pornography "speech." They seem to think that any restraint on pornography is a restraint on journalism. Their mistaken view that mainstream media and pornography are indistinguishable—the ordinance's definition of pornography distinguishes them, as does every pornography outlet in the world—pervasively distorts factual and legal reporting. The resulting tilt is inescapable and uncorrectable; other

than one's own experience to the contrary, which this process makes marginal, readers have no access to other information. That mainstream journalists tend to see their own power at stake in the legal treatment of pornography is particularly worth noting because they are not pornographers.

Sometimes the ax being ground is close to home, such as for journalists to whom Linda "Lovelace" was pimped when in captivity. Those who used her sexually have a specific stake in not believing that she was coerced to perform for the pornography film *Deep Throat*. They remain at large, mostly unidentified and writing. How often pornographer-manipulated news stories are concretely bought and planted can only be imagined, but how difficult can privileged access be for the pornographers and their point of view, given that they are often dealing with their own customers? Under these conditions, with access to information owned and controlled for content, with sex and money as potent motivators, the availability of unmediated original materials such as these hearings—these documents against the deluge—is as precious as it is rare. . . .

Every day the pornography industry gets bigger and penetrates more deeply and broadly into social life, conditioning mass sexual responses to make fortunes for men and to end lives and life chances for women and children. Pornography's up-front surrogates swallow more public space daily, shaping standards of literature and art. The age of first pornography consumption is young, and the age of the average rapist is ever younger. The acceptable level of sexual force climbs ever higher, women's real status drops ever lower. No law is effective against the industry, the materials, or the acts. Because the aggressors have won, it is hard to believe that they are wrong. When women can assert human rights against them, through a law they can use themselves, women will have a right to a place in the world.

12. American Booksellers v. Hudnut, 771 F.2d 323, 328 (7th Cir. 1985). "Therefore we accept the premises of this legislation. Depictions of subordination tend to perpetuate subordination. The subordinate status of women in turn leads to affront and lower pay at work, insult and injury at home, battery and rape on the streets."

13. E. R. Shipp, "A Feminist Offensive Against Exploitation," *The New York Times,* June 10, 1984, sec. 4, p. 2.

14. Minus the claim about Charlee Hoyt and plus many additional false or misleading details, essentially the same "report" was recycled six months later in Lisa Duggan, "Censorship in the Name of Feminism," *Village Voice,* October 16, 1984, p. 13, as if it were news.

15. George Eliot, *Middlemarch* (Bantam Books, 1985 ed. [from 1874 ed.]), p. 177.

16. See Catherine A. MacKinnon, "Pornography Left and right," 30 *Harvard Civil Rights-Civil Liberties Law Review* 143 (1995); Andrea Dworkin, "Woman-Hating Right and Left," in *The Sexual Liberals and the Attack on Feminism,* ed. Dorchen Leidholdt and Janice G. Raymond (Pergamon, 1990), p. 28.

17. The Attorney General's Commission on Pornography was sued as a whole, and its members individually, on the basis of a letter sent by the Executive Director asking distributors of adult magazines whether they were selling pornography. Penthouse International, Ltd. v. Meese et al., 939 F.2d 1011 (1991). The fact that the case was thrown out on appeal as baseless did not prevent it from operating as an instrument of intimidation and silencing of the commissioners.

Al Goldstein, editor of *SCREW,* a pornography magazine, sued Women Against Pornography and Frances Patai, an individual member of WAP, for libel for Patai's statement on WCBS-TV that *SCREW* "champion(ed) abuse of children." Goldstein said he did not champion or defend abuse of children. Goldstein and Milky Way Productions, Inc., et al. V. Patai and Women Against Pornography, Summons and Complaint (Supreme Court of the State of New York, County of New York, October 10, 1984). The defendants produced extensive examples of eroticization of incest and other sexual use of children in *SCREW* magazine over time. Having seriously damaged those sued, the case was settled.

Marty Rimm, undergraduate author of a sound and methodologically creative study, "Marketing Pornography on the Information Superhighway," 83 *Georgetown Law Journal* 1849 (1995), described accurately the pornography that is available on computer networks and measured patterns of its actual use. He found the simple truth of pornography's content and use, for example, that the more violating the materials are to women, the more popular they are. Once some of his findings were given visibility and credibility in a *Time* magazine cover story, he was hounded, harassed, and probed by journalists and attacked in *Playboy;* excoriated as a censor and subjected to intense rumor campaign of vilification on the Internet; likely deprived of a scholarship offer for graduate school at MIT; canceled before a Congressional committee, where he was to testify; and threatened with the loss of his degree by his sponsoring institution, Carnegie Mellon University, which convened a formal inquiry into bogus charges that went on for years, although he was eventually cleared of all the serious charges. His initially sought book proposal, an analysis of the approximately 85% of his data that was not discussed in the article, suddenly could not find a publisher. No lawyer could be found to defend his academic freedom.

Shots were fired into the windows of the office of Organizing Against Pornography in Minneapolis when the ordinance was pending there.

Andrea Dworkin and I have each been attacked in most of the ways described in this and subsequent paragraphs, and in others as well. Andrea Dworkin discusses some of her experiences in *Letters from a War Zone* (E. P. Dutton, 1988).

Exploring the attacks on Martin Garbus, a well-known defender of rights of free speech, for the sin of suing the press for a plaintiff in a libel case, *The New Yorker* said this: "Robert Sack, who represents the *Wall Street Journal,* likens First Amendment law to a religion. 'Switching sides,' he concludes, 'is close to apostasy.' " Reflecting the pressure brought on him, Garbus was also quoted as saying: "I've told my colleagues within the First Amendment world that I would *never* take another plaintiff's case." *The New Yorker* author commented, "[u]ndoubtedly, membership in the club does have its privileges . . ." Susie Linfield, "Exile on Centre Street," *The New Yorker,* March 11, 1996, pp. 40, 42.

18. Letter from Steve Johnson to John M. Harrington, June 5, 1986, pp. 2, 1.
19. Ibid., p. 4.
20. Ibid.
21. *Hustler* Magazine has often attacked critics of pornography in their "Asshole of the Month" feature. Peggy Ault, Dorchen Leidholdt, and Andrea Dworkin sued them for libel. Ault v. *Hustler* Magazine, Inc., 860 F.2d 877 (9th Cir. 1988); Leidholdt v. L.F.P. Inc., 860 F.2d 890 (9th Cir. 1988); Dworkin v. *Hustler* Magazine Inc., 867 F2d 1188 (9th Cir. 1989). All three cases were held legally insufficient before reaching the facts, holding in essence that pornography is unreal, hence not factual in nature, hence protected opinion. Both Gloria Steinem and Susan Brownmiller were used in pornography by *Hustler.* See Brief of *Amici Curiae* in Support of Plaintiff-Appellant, Dworkin v. *Hustler* Magazine Inc., 867 F.2d 1188 (9th Cir. 1989) (App. No. 87-6393) (pornography of both women in appendix). Andrea Dworkin and I have been used in visual pornography.

Discussion Questions

1. Professor MacKinnon maintains that pornography is an instance of sex discrimination, and thus, a violation of the civil rights of women. How does she support this position? Do you agree or disagree with her case? Explain and defend your answer.

2. Professor MacKinnon draws an analogy between the *Dred Scott* decision and the court decision that struck down an anti-pornography ordinance she and Ms. Dworkin had helped draft. How does she support this analogy? Do you think she succeeds? Why or why not? Explain and defend your answer.

3. Professor MacKinnon critiques the opinion of the Court of Appeals that struck down the Indianapolis ordinance. What are her main points against the court's opinion? Do you think she succeeds in making her case? Why or why not? Explain and defend your answer.

4. The authors of chapter 38 claim that Professor MacKinnon is mistaken in thinking that all pornography is degrading to women. Is this what Professor MacKinnon argues? Who makes the better argument? Explain and defend your answer.

5. The authors of chapter 38 question whether pornography is responsible for any more harm to women than much of the non-prohibited activity which is sexist and has been around for a much longer time. Present and explain Professor MacKinnon's argument against this claim. Do you think her use of first person accounts adequately addresses the concerns of the authors of chapter 38. Does her use of social science data? Explain and defend your answer.

You can locate InfoTrac-College Education articles about this chapter by accessing the InfoTrac-College Edition website (http://www.infotrac-college.com/wadsworth/). Using the InfoTrac-College Edition subject guide, enter the search terms relevant to this chapter, and then read abstracts for relevant articles.

40   The Case for Censorship

ROBERT H. BORK

Robert H. Bork is Professor of Law at Ave Maria School of Law (Ann Arbor, Michigan) as well as J. M. Olin Scholar in Legal Studies at the American Enterprise Institute (Washington, D.C.). The one-time Alexander M. Bickel Professor of Public Law at Yale Law School, Mr. Bork has served as Solicitor General and Acting Attorney General of the United States. His books include *Slouching Towards Gomorrah: Modern Liberalism and American Decline* (1996) and *The Tempting of America: The Political Seduction of the Law* (1991).

In this essay Mr. Bork argues that some form of censorship in the United States is legally and morally justified. He first clarifies what he thinks should be censored. He does not think censorship should be applied to speech that is appropriately protected by the First Amendment; this would include the speech of his liberal adversaries in the media, publishing, and entertainment industries. He believes censorship should be limited to only "the most violent and sexually explicit material" including that which is available on the Internet, in motion pictures, and in "the more degenerate lyrics of rap music." Bork argues that for over 175 years of the United States's history censorship of obscenity had been practiced, either informally (through custom) or formally (through statutes and ordinances). Some of it, he believes, was silly and should have been jettisoned. However, some of it was justified, for it protected the public good from being corrupted by images and texts that debase a nation's citizens and hence its civic culture, for a nondebased civic culture is necessary for the flourishing of our democratic institutions. According to Bork, a steady diet of obscenity and gratuitous violence, which appeal to the desires and not to the intellect, nurtures that aspect of our natures which makes it less likely that we will exhibit those virtues necessary for the preservation of our civic culture (e.g., fidelity, self-respect). If, according to conventional wisdom, the song, the printed word, and the motion picture can be uplifting and powerful instruments by which people and cultures can be moved, then, according to Bork, they can be employed to degenerate and debase as well.

THE DESTRUCTION OF STANDARDS is inherent in radical individualism, but it could hardly have been accomplished so rapidly or so completely without the assistance of the American judiciary. Wielding a false modern liberal version of the First Amendment, the courts have destroyed laws that created pockets of resistance to vulgarity and obscenity.

Sooner or later censorship is going to have to be considered as popular culture continues

---

Reprinted by permssion of the author from Robert H. Bork, Slouching Towards Gomorrah: Modern Liberalism and American Decline *(New York: HarperCollins, 1996).*

plunging to ever more sickening lows. The alternative to censorship, legal and moral, will be a brutalized and chaotic culture, with all that that entails for our society, economy, politics, and physical safety. It is important to be clear about the topic. I am *not* suggesting that censorship should, or constitutionally could, be employed to counter the liberal political and cultural propagandizing of movies, television, network news, and music. They are protected, and properly so, by the First Amendment's guarantees of freedom of speech and of the press. I *am* suggesting that censorship be considered for the most violent and sexually explicit material now on offer, starting with the obscene prose and pictures available on the Internet, motion pictures that are mere rhapsodies to violence, and the more degenerate lyrics of rap music.

Censorship is a subject that few people want to discuss, not because it has been tried and found dangerous or oppressive but because the ethos of modern liberalism has made any interference with the individual's self-gratification seem shamefully reactionary. Dole, Bennett, Tucker, and Leo, while denouncing some of the worst aspects of popular culture, were all quick to protest that they were not for censorship. That may be a tactical necessity, at least at this stage of the debate, since it has become virtually a condition of intellectual and social respectability to make that disclaimer. And it is true that there are a variety of actions short of censorship that should be tried. One is to organize boycotts of the other products sold by corporations that market filth. But what happens if a corporation decides it prefers the bottom line to responsibility? What happens if the company does not market other products that can be boycotted? So long as there exists a lucrative market for obscenity, somebody will supply it. That brings us back to "And then what?"

Is censorship really as unthinkable as we all seem to assume? That it is unthinkable is a very recent conceit. From the earliest colonies on this continent over 300 hundred years ago, and for about 175 years of our existence as a nation, we endorsed and lived with censorship. We do not have to imagine what censorship might be like; we know from experience. Some of it was formal, written in statutes or city ordinances; some of it was informal, as in the movie producers' agreement to abide by the rulings of the Hayes office. Some of it was inevitably silly—the rule that the movies could not show even a husband and wife fully dressed on a bed unless each had one foot on the floor—and some of it was no doubt pernicious. The period of Hayes office censorship was also, perhaps not coincidentally, the golden age of the movies.

The questions to be considered are whether such material has harmful effects, whether it is constitutionally possible to censor it, and whether technology may put some of it beyond society's capacity to control it.

It is possible to argue for censorship, as Stanley Brubaker, a professor of political science, does,[1] on the ground that in a republican form of government where the people rule, it is crucial that the character of the citizenry not be debased. By now we should have gotten over the liberal notion that its citizens' characters are none of the business of government. The government ought not try to impose virtue, but it can deter incitements to vice. "Liberals have always taken the position," the late Christopher Lasch wrote, "that democracy can dispense with civic virtue. According to this way of thinking, it is liberal institutions, not the character of citizens, that make democracy work."[2] He cited India and Latin America as proof that formally democratic institutions are not enough for a workable social order, a proof that is disheartening as the conditions in parts of large American cities approach those of the Third World.

Lasch stressed "the degree to which liberal democracy has lived off the borrowed capital of moral and religious traditions antedating the rise of liberalism."[3] Certainly, the great religions of the West—Christianity and Judaism—taught moral truths about respect for others, honesty, sexual fidelity, truth-speaking, the value of work, respect for the property of others, and self-restraint. With the decline of religious influence, the moral lessons attenuate as well. Morality is an essential soil for free and democratic governments. A people addicted to instant gratification through the vicarious (and sometimes not so vicarious) enjoyment of mindless violence and brutal sex is unlikely to provide such a soil. A population whose mental faculties are coarsened and blunted, whose emotions are few and simple, is unlikely to be able to make the distinctions and engage in the discourse that democratic government requires.

I find Brubaker and Lasch persuasive. We tend to think of virtue as a personal matter, each of us to choose which virtues to practice or not practice—the privatization of morality, or, if you will, the "pursuit of happiness," as each of us defines happiness. But only a public morality, in which trust, truth-telling, and self-control are prominent features, can long sustain a decent social order and hence a stable and just democratic order. If the social order continues to unravel, we may respond with a more authoritarian government that is capable of providing at least personal safety.

There is, of course, more to the case for censorship than the need to preserve a viable democracy. We need also to avoid the social devastation wrought by pornography and endless incitements to murder and mayhem. Whatever the effects upon our capacity to govern ourselves, living in a culture that saturates us with pictures of sex and violence is aesthetically ugly, emotionally flattening, and physically dangerous.

There are, no doubt, complex causes for illegitimacy and violence in today's society, but it seems impossible to deny that one cause is the messages popular culture insistently presses on us. Asked about how to diminish illegitimacy, a woman who worked with unmarried teenage mothers replied tersely: "Shoot Madonna." That may be carrying censorship a bit far, but one sees her point. Madonna's forte is sexual incitement. We live in a sex-drenched culture. The forms of sexual entertainment rampant in our time are overwhelming to the young, who would, even without such stimulations, have difficulty enough resisting the song their hormones sing. There was a time, coinciding with the era of censorship, when most did resist.

Young males, who are more prone to violence than females or older males, witness so many gory depictions of killing that they are bound to become desensitized to it. We now have teenagers and even subteenagers who shoot if they feel they have been "dissed" (shown disrespect). Indeed, the newspapers bring us stories of murders done for simple pleasure, the killing of a stranger simply because the youth felt like killing someone, anyone. That is why, for the first time in American history, you are more likely to be murdered by a complete stranger than by someone you know. That is why our prisons contain convicted killers who show absolutely no remorse and frequently cannot even remember the names of the persons they killed.

One response of the entertainment industry to criticisms has been that Hollywood and the music business did not create violence or sexual chaos in America. Of course not. But they contribute to it. They are one of the "root causes" they want us to seek elsewhere and leave them alone. The denial that what the young see and hear has any effect on their behavior is the last line of the modern liberal defense of decadence, and it is willfully specious. Accusing Senator Dole of "pandering to the right" in his speech deploring obscene and violent entertainment, the *New York Times* argued: "There is much in the movies and in hard-core rap music that is disturbing and demeaning to many Americans. Rap music, which often reaches the top of the charts, is also the music in which women are degraded and men seem to murder each other for sport. But no one has ever dropped dead from viewing 'Natural Born Killers,' or listening to gangster rap records."[4] To which George Will replied: "No one ever dropped dead reading 'Der Sturmer,' the Nazi anti-Semitic newspaper, but the culture it served caused six million Jews to drop dead."[5]

Those who oppose any form of restraint, including self-restraint, on what is produced insist that there is no connection between what people watch and hear and their behavior. It is clear why people who sell gangsta rap make that claim, but it is less clear why anyone should believe them. Studies show that the evidence of the causal connection between popular culture's violence and violent behavior is overwhelming.[6] A recent study, *Sex and the Mass Media*, asked: "Does the talk about and images of love, sex and relationships promote irresponsible sexual behavior? Do they encourage unplanned and unwanted pregnancy? Are the media responsible for teenagers having sex earlier, more frequently and outside of marriage?" The researchers concluded: "The answer to all these questions is a qualified 'yes'."[7] The answer was qualified because not enough research has as yet been done on the effects of sexual images. The authors relied in part on the analogous question of media depictions of violence and their effect on aggressive behavior, which would appear to be a parallel situation. Some of the studies found positive but relatively small effects, between 5 and 15 percent. "One of the most compelling of the naturalistic studies . . . found that the homicide rates in three countries (U.S., Canada, and South Africa) increased dramatically 10–15 years after the introduction of television." That study "estimated that exposure to television violence is a causal factor in about half of the 21,000 homicides per year in the United States and perhaps half of all rapes and assaults."[8]

The studies confirm what seems obvious. Common sense and experience are sufficient to reach the same conclusions. Music, for example, is used everywhere to create attitudes—armies use martial music, couples listen to romantic music, churches use organs, choirs, and hymns. How can anyone suppose that music (plus the images of television, movies, and advertisements) about sex and violence has no effect?

Indeed, Hollywood's writers, producers, and executives think popular entertainment affects behavior. It is not merely that they sell billions of dollars of advertising on television on the premise that they can influence behavior; they also think that the content of their programs can reform society in a liberal direction. They understand that no single program will change attitudes much, but they rely upon the cumulative impact of years of television indoctrination.[9] Why should we listen to the same people saying that their programs and music have no effect on behavior? That argument is over. The depravity sold by Hollywood and the record companies is feeding the depravity we see around us.

The television industry, under considerable political pressure, has agreed to a ratings system for its programs. Since assigning ratings to every program—including every episode in a series—will be much more difficult than assigning ratings to motion pictures, it is doubtful that the television rating system will add much except confusion and rancor. The movie ratings have not prevented underage children from freely seeing movies they were not meant to see. No doubt the same will be true of television ratings. The vaunted V chip will prove no solution. Aside from the fact that many parents simply will not bother with it, the V chip will likely lead to even more degrading programming by providing producers with the excuse that the chip adequately safeguards children, though it does not. And the chip certainly does nothing to prevent adults from enjoying the increasingly salacious and even perverted material that is on the way.

The debate about censorship, insofar as there can be said to be a debate, usually centers on the issue of keeping children away from pornography. There is, of course, a good deal of merit to that, but it makes the issue sound like one of child rearing, which most people would like the government to butt out of. Opponents say parents can protect their children by using control features offered by many services. Both sides are missing a major point. Aside from the fact that many parents will not use control features, censorship is also crucial to protect children—and the rest of us—from men encouraged to act by a steady diet of computerized pedophilia, murder, rape, and sado-masochism. No one supposes that every addict of such material will act out his fantasies, but it is willfully blind to think that none will. The pleasures the viewers of such material get from watching a thousand rape scenes or child kidnappings is not worth one actual rape or kidnapping.

There are those who say that the only solution is to rebuild a stable public culture. How one does that when the institutions we have long relied on to maintain and transmit such a culture—the two-parent family, schools, churches, and popular entertainment itself—are all themselves in decline it is not easy to say. Nevertheless, there is something to the point. Determined individuals and groups may be able to revitalize some of those institutions. For much that afflicts us, that is the only acceptable course. Law cannot be the answer in all or even most areas. And there are signs not just of resistance but of positive action against the forces of decadence. For the very worst manifestations of the culture, however, more directly coercive responses may be required. Whether as a society we any longer have the will to make such responses is very much in question.

Arguments that society may properly set limits to what may be shown, said, and sung run directly counter to the mood of our cultural elites in general, and in particular the attitude (it is hardly more than that) of our judges, many of whom, most unfortunately, are members in good standing of that elite. As constitutional law now stands, censorship would be extremely difficult, if not impossible. In *Miller* v. *California*,[10] the Supreme Court laid down a three-part test that must be met if sexually explicit material is to be banned. It must be shown that: (1) the average person, applying contemporary community standards, would find that the work, taken as a whole, appeals to the prurient interest; (2) the work depicts or describes, in a patently offensive way, sexual conduct specifically defined by the applicable state law; and (3) the work, taken as a whole, lacks serious literary, artistic, political, or scientific value.

The first two prongs of the test become increasingly difficult to satisfy as contemporary community standards decline and as fewer and fewer descriptions of sexual conduct are regarded as patently offensive. But it is the third part that poses the most difficulty. There is apparently nothing that a flummery of professors will not testify has "serious value." When Cincinnati prosecuted the museum that displayed Mapplethorpe's photographs, the jury deferred to defense witnesses who said the pictures were art and hence could not be obscene. Cincinnati was widely ridiculed and portrayed as benighted for even attempting to punish obscenity. One typical cartoon showed a furtive figure stepping out of an alley in the city to offer "feelthy pictures" to a surprised passerby. The picture was a reproduction of a Michelangelo. It is typical of our collapse of standards that Mapplethorpe's grotesqueries can be compared even in a cartoon to Michelangelo's art.

It is difficult to see merit in the serious value test. Serious literary, artistic, political, or scientific value can certainly be achieved without including descriptions of "patently offensive" sexual conduct. This third criterion serves merely as an escape hatch for pornographers whose "experts" can overbear juries. No doubt professors of literature can be found to testify to the serious literary value of the prose found in alt.sex.stories. Some of them are said to be very well written.

Without censorship, it has proved impossible to maintain any standards of decency. "[O]nly a deeply confused society," George Will wrote, "is more concerned about protecting lungs than minds, trout than black women. We legislate against smoking in restaurants; singing 'Me So Horny' is a constitutional right. Secondary smoke is carcinogenic; celebration of torn vaginas is 'mere words' "[11] The massive confusion Will describes is in large measure a confusion that first enveloped the courts, which they then imposed on us.

It will be said that to propose banning anything that can be called "expression" is an attempt to "take away our constitutional rights." A radio talk show host said that the proposal to censor obscenities on the Internet was a denial of the First Amendment rights of teenagers. Such reactions reveal a profound ignorance of the history of the First Amendment. Until quite recently, nobody even raised the question of that amendment in prosecutions of pornographers; it was not thought relevant even by the pornographers. As late as 1942, in the *Chaplinsky* decision, a unanimous Supreme Court could agree:

> There are certain well-defined and narrowly limited classes of speech, the prevention and punishment of which have never been thought to raise any Constitutional problem. These include the lewd and obscene, the profane, the libelous, and the insulting or "fighting" words—those which by their very utterance inflict injury or tend to incite an immediate breach of the peace. It has been well observed that such utterances are no essential part of any exposition of ideas, and are of such slight social value as a step to truth that any benefit that may be derived from them is clearly outweighed by the social interest in order and morality.[12]

Under today's constitutional doctrine, it would be difficult to impossible to prohibit or punish the lewd and obscene, or the profane. First Amendment jurisprudence has shifted from the protection of the exposition of ideas towards the protection of self-expression—however lewd, obscene, or profane. Time Warner, citing the authority of a 1992 statute, proposed to scramble sexually explicit programs on a New York cable channel (the channel, I believe, on which I watched the writhing, oily young woman mentioned earlier). Those who wanted the shows with strippers, excerpts from pornographic movies, and advertisements for phone sex and "escort" services would have to send in cards to the cable operator. A federal district judge in New York, disagreeing with the federal court of appeals in Washington, D.C., granted a preliminary injunction against Time Warner, saying that the statute probably violated the First Amendment. The plaintiffs who produce these shows said the scrambling would hurt their ability to reach their audience and stigmatize viewers who tune in to the shows. Both are results that would have been considered laudable rather than forbidden under the First Amendment not many years ago.

Yet it is clear that if there is something special about speech, something that warrants a constitutional guarantee, it is the capacity of speech to communicate ideas. There is no other distinction between speech and other human activities that go unprotected by the Constitution. That is the point the *Chaplinsky* Court grasped. Non-speech activities can give as much pleasure as speech, develop as many human faculties, and contribute to personal and social well-being. The only difference between speech and other behavior is speech's capacity to communicate ideas in the effort to reach varieties of truth. Celebration in song of the ripping of vaginas or forced oral sex or stories depicting the kidnapping, mutilation, raping, and murder of children do not, to anyone with a degree of common sense, qualify as ideas. And when something worthy of being called an idea is involved, there is no reason to protect its expression in lewd, obscene, or profane language. Such language adds nothing to the idea but, instead, detracts from it.

Today's Court majority would have difficulty understanding *Chaplinsky*'s statement that an utterance could inflict an injury to morality. Morality itself has become relativized in our constitutional jurisprudence, so that the Court no longer has the vocabulary to say that something is immoral and, for that reason, may be banned by the legislature. As Walter Berns wrote:

> The Court decontrolled the arts, so to speak, and the impact of that has been profound. It not only permitted the publication of sex but it *caused* the publication of sex—or, to coin a word, the "publification" of sex. . . . The immediate and obvious consequence of [the end of censorship] is that sex is now being made into the measure of existence, and such uniquely human qualities as modesty, fidelity, abstinence, chastity, delicacy, and shame, qualities that formerly provided the constraints on sexual activity and the setting within which the erotic passion was enjoyed, discussed, and evaluated, are today ridiculed as merely arbitrary interferences "with the health of the sexual parts."[13]

Berns wrote that in 1976, when he could have had no idea just how far the publification of sex would be carried. We may not know that even now. Our experience after the end of censorship suggests that there are few or no limits to depravity.

It may be too much to ask that the Supreme Court, as presently constituted, revisit and revise its First Amendment jurisprudence. Most people think of the Court as a legal institution because its pronouncements have the force of law. But the perception is flawed. The Court is also a cultural institution, one whose pronouncements are significantly guided not by the historical meaning of the Constitution but by the values of the class that is dominant in our culture. In our day, that means the cultural elite: academics, clergy, journalists, entertainers, foundation staffs, "public interest" groups, and the like. The First Amendment is central to the concerns of such folk because they are chatterers by profession, and their attitudes are relativistic and per-

missive. The mention of censorship, even of the most worthless and harmful materials, causes apoplexy in the members of that class.

The truth is that the judiciary's view of pornographic sex and pornographic violence will not change until the culture to which the Court responds changes. There is no sign that that will occur any time soon. The public debate in the area of the "arts" is not encouraging. Mapplethorpe's homoerotic photos and Serrano's "Piss Christ" were displayed with grants from the National Endowment for the Arts. So intimidating has the culture of modern liberalism become that cultural conservatives were reduced to complaining that works like these should not be subsidized with "taxpayers' dollars," as if taxpayers should never be required to subsidize things they don't like. If that were the case, government would have to close down altogether. Both spending and taxation would be at zero. To complain about the source of the dollars involved is to cheapen a moral position. The photographs would be just as offensive if their display were financed by a scatter-brained billionaire. We seem too timid to state that Mapplethorpe's and Serrano's pictures should not be shown in public, whoever pays for them. We are going to have to overcome that timidity if our culture is not to decline still further.

Libertarians join forces with modern liberals in opposing censorship, though libertarians are far from being modern liberals in other respects. For one thing, libertarians do not like the coercion that necessarily accompanies radical egalitarianism. But because both libertarians and modern liberals are oblivious to social reality, both demand radical personal autonomy in expression. That is one reason libertarians are not to be confused, as they often are, with conservatives. They are quasi- or semiconservatives. Nor are they to be confused with classical liberals, who considered restraints on individual autonomy to be essential.

The nature of the liberal and libertarian errors is easily seen in discussions of pornography. The leader of the explosion of porno-graphic videos, described admiringly by a competitor as the Ted Turner of the business, offers the usual defenses of decadence: "Adults have a right to see [pornography] if they want to. If it offends you, don't buy it."[14] Those statements neatly sum up both the errors and the (unintended) perniciousness of the alliance between libertarians and modern liberals with respect to popular culture.

Modern liberals employ the rhetoric of "rights" incessantly, not only to delegitimate the idea of restraints on individuals by communities but to prevent discussion of the topic. Once something is announced, usually flatly and stridently, to be a right—whether pornography or abortion or what have you—discussion becomes difficult to impossible. Rights inhere in the person, are claimed to be absolute, and cannot be diminished or taken away by reason; in fact, reason that suggests the non-existence of an asserted right is viewed as a moral evil by the claimant. If there is to be anything that can be called a community, rather than an agglomeration of hedonists, the case for previously unrecognized individual freedoms (as well as some that have been previously recognized) must be thought through and argued, and "rights" cannot win every time. Why there is a right for adults to enjoy pornography remains unexplained and unexplainable.

The second bit of advice—"If it offends you, don't buy it"—is both lulling and destructive. Whether you buy it or not, you will be greatly affected by those who do. The aesthetic and moral environment in which you and your family live will be coarsened and degraded. Economists call the effects an activity has on others "externalities"; why so many of them do not understand the externalities here is a mystery. They understand quite well that a person who decides not to run a smelter will nevertheless be seriously affected if someone else runs one nearby.

Free market economists are particularly vulnerable to the libertarian virus. They know that free economic exchanges usually benefit both parties to them. But they mistake that general rule for a universal rule. Benefits do not invariably result from free market exchanges. When it comes to pornography or addictive drugs, libertarians all too often confuse the idea that markets should be free with the idea that everything should be available on the market. The first of those ideas rests on the efficiency of the free market in satisfying wants. The second ignores the question of which wants it is moral to satisfy. That is a question of an entirely different nature. I have heard economists say that, as economists, they do not deal with questions of morality. Quite right. But nobody is just an economist. Economists are also fathers or mothers, husbands or wives, voters, citizens, members of communities. In these latter roles, they cannot avoid questions of morality.

The externalities of depictions of violence and pornography are clear. To complaints about those products being on the market, libertarians respond with something like "Just hit the remote control and change channels on your TV set." But, like the person who chooses not to run a smelter while others do, you, your family, and your neighbors will be affected by the people who do not change the channel, who do rent the pornographic videos, who do read alt.sex.stories. As film critic Michael Medved put it: "To say that if you don't like the popular culture, then turn it off, is like saying if you don't like the smog, stop breathing. . . . There are Amish kids in Pennsylvania who know about Madonna."[15] And their parents can do nothing about it.

Can there be any doubt that as pornography and depictions of violence become increasingly popular and increasingly accessible, attitudes about marriage, fidelity, divorce, obligations to children, the use of force, and permissible public behavior and language will change? Or that with the changes in attitudes will come changes in conduct, both public and private? We have seen those changes already and they are continuing. Advocates of liberal arts education assure us that those studies improve character. Can it be that only uplifting reading affects character and the most degrading reading has no effects whatever? "Don't buy it" and "Change the channel," however intended, are effectively advice to accept a degenerating culture and its consequences.

The obstacles to censorship of pornographic and violence-filled materials are, of course, enormous. Radical individualism in such matters is now pervasive even among sedate, upper middle-class people. At a dinner I sat next to a retired Army general who was now a senior corporate executive. The subject of Robert Mapplethorpe's photographs came up. This most conventional of dinner companions said casually that people ought to be allowed to see whatever they wanted to see. It would seem to follow that others ought to be allowed to do whatever some want to see.

The entertainment industry will battle ferociously against restraints, one segment of it because its economic interests would be directly threatened, the rest because, to avoid thinking, they have become absolutists about First Amendment freedoms. Then there are the First Amendment voluptuaries. The ACLU is to the First Amendment what the National Rifle Association is to the Second Amendment and the right to bear arms. The head of the ACLU announced in a panel discussion that the Supreme Court's failure to throw protection around nude dancing in night clubs was a terrible blow to our freedom of speech. Some years back, when I suggested to a law school audience that the courts had gone too far in preventing communities from prohibiting pornography, the then president of the organization compared me to Salazar of Portugal and the Greek colonels. Afterward he said he had called me a fascist. It is fascinating that when one calls for greater democratic control and less governance by a judicial oligarchy, one is immediately called a fascist. The ACLU seems to think democracy is tyranny and government by judges is freedom. That is a proposition that in the last half

of this century our judiciary has all too readily accepted. Any serious attempt to root out the worst in our popular culture may be doomed unless the judiciary comes to understand that the First Amendment was adopted for good reasons, and those reasons did not include the furtherance of radical personal autonomy.

It is not clear how effective censorship of the Internet or of digital films on home computers can be. Perhaps it is true, as has been said, that technology is on the side of anarchy. Violence and pornography can be supplied from all over the world, and it can be wireless, further complicating the problem of barring it. We may soon be at the mercy of a combination of technology and perversion. It's enough to make one a Luddite. But there are methods of presentation that can be censored. Lyrics, motion pictures, television, and printed material are candidates.

What we see in popular culture, from "Big Man with a Gun" to alt.sex.stories, is the product, though not, it is to be feared, the final product, of liberalism's constant thrust. Doing anything to curb the spreading rot would violate liberalism's central tenet, John Stuart Mill's "one very simple principle." Mill himself would be horrified at what we have become; he never intended this; but he bequeathed us the principle that modern liberals embrace and that makes it possible. We have learned that the founders of liberalism were wrong. Unconstrained human nature will seek degeneracy often enough to create a disorderly, hedonistic, and dangerous society. Modern liberalism and popular culture are creating that society.

NOTES

1. Stanley Brubaker, "In praise of censorship," *The Public Interest,* Winter 1994, p. 48.
2. Christopher Lasch, *The Revolt of the Elites and the Betrayal of Democracy* (New York: W.W. Norton, 1995), p. 85.
3. Ibid., p. 86.
4. "Mr. Dole's Entertainment Guide" *New York Times,* June 2, 1995, p. A28.

5. George Will, "This Week With David Brinkley," *ABC News,* June 4, 1995.

6. Michael Medved, *Hollywood vs. America: Popular Culture and the War on Traditional Values* (New York: HarperCollins, 1992), pp. 239–252; Vincent Ryan Ruggiero, *WARNING: Nonsense Is Destroying America* (Nashville: Thomas Nelson Publishers, 1994), pp. 91–125.

7. Jane D. Brown and Jeanne R. Steele, "Sexuality and American Social Policy," p. 1. A report prepared for the Henry J. Kaiser Family Foundation and the American Enterprise Institute, presented September 29, 1995.

8. Ibid., pp. 23–24.

9. S. Robert Lichter, Linda S. Lichter, and Stanley Rothman, *Prime Time: How TV Portrays American Culture* (Washington, DC: Regnery Publishing, 1994), pp. 425–31.

10. *Miller v. California,* 413 U.S. 15 (1973).

11. George Will, "America's Slide Into the Sewer," *Newsweek,* July 30, 1990, p. 64.

12. *Chaplinsky* v. *New Hampshire,* 315 U.S. 568, 571–2 (1942). (footnotes omitted)

13. Walter Berns, *The First Amendment and the Future of American Democracy* (New York: Basic Books, 1976), p. 221.

14. John R. Wilke, "A Publicly Held Firm Turns X-Rated Videos Into a Hot Business," *Wall Street Journal,* July 11, 1994, p. 8.

15. Michael Medved, "The Cultures of Hollywood," Bradley Lecture Series, American Enterprise Institute, January 12, 1993.

Discussion Questions

1. What type of speech does Professor Bork believe is protected by the First Amendment? Why does he believe that certain forms of "expression" are not really "speech"? If you disagree with Bork, explain and defend your position. If you agree with him, explain and defend where the line should be drawn between speech and nonspeech as well as what the government should do in borderline cases?

2. Why does Professor Bork believe that the U.S. Supreme Court's three-part test in *Miller v. California* (1973) is inadequate? Do you agree or disagree with him? Explain and defend your answer.

3. Why does Professor Bork not buy the retort of the anticensor, "if it offends, don't buy it"? Do you think that he adequately responds to this retort? Explain and defend your answer.

4. Professor Bork does not believe that the doctrine of the economic free market should be applied to non-economic questions such as access to obscene materials. What is his argument for this position? Do you agree or disagree with him? Explain and defend your answer.

5. What sort of materials does Professor Bork say it is appropriate for the government to censor?

6. Professor Bork writes that "morality is an essential soil for free and democratic governments." How does he defend this claim? Do you think that he is correct? Explain and defend your answer. Assuming he is correct about the importance of morality for government, do you think that it justifies some form censorship? Explain and defend your answer.

You can locate InfoTrac-College Education articles about this chapter by accessing the InfoTrac-College Edition website (http://www.infotrac-college.com/wadsworth/). Using the InfoTrac-College Edition subject guide, enter the search terms relevant to this chapter, and then read abstracts for relevant articles.

41   Pornography, Sex, and Censorship

FRED R. BERGER

Fred R. Berger, who died in 1988, was a Professor of Philosophy at the University of California, Davis. A social philosopher and civil libertarian, he published extensively in the areas of political philosophy, freedom of expression, and public policy. He has published in numerous academic journals. He is the author of *Freedom, Rights, and Pornographyy* (1991, edited by Bruce Russell) and *Happiness, Justice, and Freedom: The Moral and Political Philosophy of John Stuart Mill* (1984).

In this essay Professor Berger argues against the censorship of pornography. He begins by recognizing the difference between censorship and regulation, noting that he is arguing only against the former. He then moves on to define pornography: "[P]ornography [is] art or literature which explicitly depicts sexual activity or arousal in a manner having little or no artistic or literary value." He goes on to outline three forms of argument employed by conservatives who favor censorship. Professor Berger is concerned only with the third form: "[P]ornography promotes or leads to certain kinds of socially harmful attitudes and/or behavior." In reply to this form of argument, he first rebuts versions of the argument presented by George Steiner and Irving Kristol. Professor Berger then presents several other reasons to reject the conservative argument, including the rather novel argument that censorship rather than pornography may result in socially harmful attitudes and/or behavior. He concludes his essay by arguing that the censor has the burden of providing convincing reasons to interfere with someone's consumption of pornography.

AN OBSERVER OF AMERICAN attitudes toward pornography faces a bewildering duality: on the one hand, we buy and read and view more of it than just about anyone else, while, on the other hand, we seek to suppress it as hard as anybody else. I presume that these facts do not merely reflect a judgment of social utilities, namely, that the best balance of goods is achieved by having it available, but under conditions of prohibition![1] I believe, in fact, that this state of things reflects aspects of our attitudes toward sex, and much of the current controversy has tended to obscure this fact, and to ignore the important issues concerning sex and freedom to which the pornography issue points.

There is an important reason why the pornography controversy in the American context has tended to be narrowly focused. Our First Amendment prohibits government from abridging freedom of speech and press. Whatever interpretation is to be given that amendment, it is, in fact, stated in absolutist terms, and carries no mention of definition of obscenity or pornography. This difficulty is exacerbated by the fact that in the common-law

Reprinted by permission from Social Theory and Practice *4.2 (1977).*

background of our legal system, there is very little litigation which established clear legal definitions and doctrines. Obscenity convictions in the form we know them seem very much an invention of the 1800s, and of the late 1800s at that.[2] Moreover, in our experience with obscenity litigation, we have discovered that an enormous array of serious, even important, literature and art has fallen to the censor's axe. Thus, liberals and conservatives alike have feared that the removal of pornography from the protections of the First Amendment can endanger materials the Constitution surely ought to protect. This has given the constitutional issue great urgency.

The upshot has been that much of the debate has centered on the question of definition, and, moreover, that question has been pursued with legal needs in mind.

In this paper, I want to put aside the First Amendment to ask if there are any justifiable grounds for rejecting the arguments offered for the censorship of pornography independent of First Amendment considerations. Moreover, I shall be concerned with the *censorship* of pornography, not its *regulation*. The regulation of speech often has the same effect as censorship, and that is an important danger; nevertheless, censorship and regulation differ radically in intention, and that is an important difference.[3] I should also indicate that I shall suppose that those who favor censorship (I shall refer to them as "the censors") are not *generally* in favor of censorship, and would not prohibit what they regard as "true" art or literature.

Moreover, to lend further clarity to my discussion I shall propose a definition which is useful for the purposes of this paper, and which picks out most of what is usually regarded as pornographic, and that is all I claim for it. I define pornography as art or literature which explicitly depicts sexual activity or arousal in a manner having little or no artistic or literary value.[4] (I am assuming that scientific and medical texts are a kind of literature, with appropriate criteria of acceptability.)

The definition does, I believe, make pornography a relatively objective classification, insofar as there are clear cases on both sides of the divide, and there are relatively standard literary and artistic criteria by which to judge disputed cases.[5] In this respect, I am somewhat sympathetic to the conservatives who chide those liberals who claim they are not able to recognize standard cases of pornography as such.[6]

1. OBJECTIONS TO PORNOGRAPHY: CONFLICTING VIEWS ON SEX

Generally speaking, there are three forms of argument employed by the conservatives in favor of censorship. First, they simply hold that pornography itself is immoral or evil, irrespective of ill-consequences which may flow from it.[7] Second, they sometimes assert that, irrespective of its morality, a practice which most people in a community find abhorrent and disgusting may be rightfully repressed. Finally, they sometimes contend that pornography promotes or leads to certain kinds of socially harmful attitudes and/or behavior.

In this paper, I wish to concentrate on this last form of argument. The proponents of the first kind of claim cannot, for the most part, meet Ronald Dworkin's challenge to specify some recognizable sense of morality according to which their claims are true.[8] Though I am aware of one form of this argument which I think *can* meet that challenge, it is dealt with obliquely in my responses to the other claims. The second form of argument has been widely debated in the literature, and I have little to add to that debate.[9] The arguments do not turn on the nature of pornography as such, and, moreover, it is fairly clear that in contemporary America there is not an overwhelming abhorrence of pornography as such.[10] The last form of argument has been given new life, however, by claims based on analyses of pornographic materials as such. These new conservative arguments differ in important ways from the traditional views of the censors, and their arguments have been extremely influential. Each of the articles I shall discuss has been widely referred to; each has been reprinted a number of times, and all but one are cited in support of recent decisions in the courts.[11]

The traditional form of the claim can be labeled the "incitement to rape" theory. It holds that pornography arouses sexual desire, which seeks an outlet, often in antisocial forms such as rape. It is this version of the claim we are most familiar with, and the evidence which is available tends to refute it.[12] I shall have more to say about it later.

The conservative views I want to take up hold that the harms from pornography are somewhat long-range. These commentators maintain that the modes of sex depicted in pornography, and the manner of depiction, will result in altering our basic attitudes toward sex and to one another, so that in the end a climate of antisocial behavior will result. I have isolated four instances of such arguments in the literature of pornography.

The first claim I shall take up is put forth in an essay by George Steiner, entitled "Night Words," which has provoked considerable comment.[13] Though Steiner expressed disapproval of censorship because it is "stupid" and cannot work, his views have been taken as an argument supporting censorship. Steiner holds that pornography constitutes an invasion of privacy:

> Sexual relations are, or should be, one of the citadels of privacy, the night place where we must be allowed to gather the splintered, harried elements of our consciousness to some kind of inviolate order and repose. It is in sexual experience that a human being alone, and two human beings in that attempt at total communication which is also communion, can discover the unique bent of their identity. There we may find ourselves through imperfect striving and repeated failure, the

words, the gestures, the mental images which set the blood to racing. In that dark and wonder ever renewed both the fumblings and the light must be our own.

> The new pornographers subvert this last, vital privacy; they do our imagining for us. They take away the words that were of the night and shout them over the rooftops, making them hollow. The images of our lovemaking, the stammerings we resort to in intimacy come pre-packaged. . . . Natural selection tells of limbs and functions which atrophy through lack of use; the power to feel, to experience and realize the precarious uniqueness of each other's being, can also wither in a society.[14]

The second claim against pornography is made by Irving Kristol, in an article arguing for censorship. Kristol claims that pornography depersonalizes sex, reducing it to animal activity and thus debases it; that it essentially involves only the readers' or viewers' sexual arousal, and thus promotes an infantile sexuality which is dangerous to society:

> The basic psychological fact about pornography and obscenity is that it appeals to and provokes a kind of sexual regression. The sexual pleasure one gets from pornography and obscenity is autoerotic and infantile; put bluntly, it is a masturbatory exercise of the imagination, when it is not masturbation pure and simple. . . . Infantile sexuality is not only a permanent temptation for the adolescent or even the adult—it can quite easily become a permanent, self-reinforcing neurosis. It is because of an awareness of this possibility of regression toward the infantile condition, a regression which is always open to us, that all the codes of sexual conduct ever devised by the human race take such a dim view of autoerotic activities and try to discourage autoerotic fantasies. Masturbation is indeed a perfectly natural autoerotic activity. . . . And it is precisely because it is so perfectly natural that it can be so dangerous to the mature or maturing person, if it is not controlled or sublimated in some way.[15]

The danger is borne out, he thinks, in *Portnoy's Complaint*. Portnoy's sexuality is fixed in an infantile mode (he is a prolific and inventive masturbator), and he is incapable of an adult sexual relationship with a woman. The final consequences are quite dire, as Kristol concludes: "What is at stake is civilization and humanity, nothing less. The idea that 'everything is permitted,' as Nietzsche put it, rests on the premise of nihilism and has nihilistic implications."[16]

Professor Walter Berns, writing in the magazine *The Public Interest*, maintains that pornography breaks down the feelings of shame we associate with sex. This shame, he holds, is not merely a dictate of our society, it is natural in that it protects love, and promotes the self-restraint which is requisite for a democratic polity:

> Whereas sexual attraction brings man and woman together seeking a unity that culminates in the living being they together create, the voyeur maintains a distance; and because he maintains a distance he looks at, he does not communicate; and because he looks at he objectifies, he makes an object of that which it is natural to join; objectifying, he is incapable of uniting and is therefore incapable of love. The need to conceal voyeurism—the concealing shame—is corollary of the protective shame, the same that impels lovers to search for privacy and for an experience protected from the profane and the eyes of the stranger. . . . Shame, both concealing and protective, protects lovers and therefore love.[17]

The upshot, as we might have suspected, is catastrophic. Under the banner of "the forgotten argument," Bern writes:

> To live together requires rules and a governing of the passions, and those who are without shame will be unruly and unreliable; having lost the ability to restrain themselves by observing the rules they collectively give themselves, they will have to be ruled by others. Tyranny is the natural and inevitable mode of government for the shameless and the self-indulgent who have carried liberty beyond any restraint, natural and conventional.[18]

Finally, Professor Ernest van den Haag, in a series of articles, has argued for censorship on the grounds that pornography encourages "the pure libidinal principle," which leads to loss of empathy for others, and encourages violence and antisocial acts:

> By de-individualizing and dehumanizing sexual acts, which thus become impersonal, pornography reduces or removes the empathy and the mutual identification which restrain us from treating each other merely as objects or means. This empathy is an individual barrier to nonconsensual acts, such as rape, torture, and assaultive crimes in general. . . .
>
> By reducing life to varieties of sex, pornography invites us to regress to a premoral world, to return to, and to spin out, preadolescent fantasies—fantasies which reject reality and the burdens of individuation, of restraint, of tension, of conflict, of regarding others as more than objects of commitment, of thought, of consideration, and of love. These are the burdens which become heavy and hard to avoid in adolescence. By rejecting them, at least in fantasy, a return to the pure libidinal pleasure principle is achieved. And once launched by pornography, fantasy may regress to ever more infantile fears and wishes: people, together dehumanized, may be tortured, mutilated, and literally devoured.[19]

My response to these claims has two parts. First, I shall try to show that they reflect certain attitudes toward sex that are rejected by many, and that pornography will be judged differently by people with different attitudes toward sex. Second, I shall try to show why the gruesome results these writers foresee as the consequences of the state's failure to suppress dirty books and art are *not* likely consequences. Pornographic materials, *by their nature*, I shall contend, are an unlikely source or means of altering and influencing our basic attitudes toward one another.

Let us begin by noting certain features of pornography on which the conservative claims seem to hinge. First of all, by virtue of its lack of finesse, pornography is stark; it tends to remove those nuances of warmth and feeling which a more delicate approach is more apt to preserve. Second, there is some tendency of much pornography to assault our sensibilities and sense of the private, to estrange us somewhat. This is not difficult to understand, and it is not simply a result of our culture's attitudes toward sex. Sex, quite naturally, is associated with the notion of privacy because in sex we are in a vulnerable state, both emotionally and physically—we are very much in the control of our feelings and sensations, less aware of environmental factors, very much involved in and attending to our state of feeling and present activity.[20] Such vulnerability is the mark of private states—states on which we do not want others to intrude. This is reflected also in our attitudes toward grief and dying. Moreover, because we *want* to be totally taken with the activity itself, we do not usually want others present. So, we can concede that there is some truth to the conservative analyses of the nature of pornography.

These conservative arguments, however, involve and presuppose views on sex that many people reject. I think it is important to make these more explicit. Steiner, as we have seen, regards sex as a source of "inviolate order and repose," in which a sense of our identity is achieved by virtue of the private words, gestures, mental images which are shared with loved ones. (I envisage a hushed atmosphere.) For Van den Haag, sex, or mature sex, properly involves the burdens of "conflict, commitment, thought, consideration and love." And Kristol has distinguished mere "animal coupling" from making love, labeling the former "debased." Professor Berns's views about the nature of sex are, perhaps, clarified in a footnote:

> It is easy to prove that shamefulness is not the only principle governing the question of what may properly be presented on the stage; shamefulness would not, for example, govern the case of a scene showing the copulating of a married couple who love each other very much. That is not intrinsically shameful—on the contrary—yet it ought not to be shown. The principle here is, I think, an aesthetic one; such a scene is dramatically weak because the response of the audience would be characterized by prurience and not by a sympathy with what the scene is intended to portray, a beautiful love.[21]

The trouble with these views is that they see sex as normal or proper only within the context of deep commitment, shared responsibility, loving concern, and as involving restraint and repression of pure pleasure. Indeed, Professor Berns's footnote not only carries the suggestion that anything but married love is shameful, but also could be uncharitably interpreted as holding that "a beautiful love" is something which holds between disembodied souls, and in no way involves sexual communion, or the sharing of physical joy and pleasure. It seems to him that if we got some sense of the pleasure the couple take in one another physically, some hint of the physical forms of their communication and sense of mutuality, that this would somehow detract from our sympathy with their "beautiful love."

Now, many in our society reject these analyses of sex, either totally or partially. I want to sketch two possible views so that we might have a sense of the wider context of attitudes within which the pornography problem should be discussed. As many liberals share the conservative attitudes toward sex and many political conservatives do not, I shall label the views I discuss as "radical" or "radical-liberal," with no further political significance attached to them.

The radical maintains that the entire facade of sexual attitudes in contemporary society represents sham, hypocrisy, and unnecessary forms of social control. Sexual relations are governed by the notions of duty, shame, guilt. As such, there can be no honest sexuality, since mediating all sexual relations are feelings and associations which have nothing to do with our feelings *for* one another, and, often, little to do really with our sexual natures. The conservative picture of shared communication, in an aura of intimate connection, expressive of tender love, concern, commitment which are involved in mature (preferably married) sex, is an idealized, romanticized, unreal (perhaps even infantile) depiction of what really happens in sex. The fact is that most sex is routinized, dull, unfulfilling, a source of neurosis, precisely because its practice is governed by the restraints the conservatives insist on. Those constraints dictate with *whom* one has sex, *when* one has sex, how *often* one has sex, *where* one has sex, and so on. Moreover, the web of shame and guilt which is spun around sex tends to destroy its enjoyment, and thus to stunt our sexual natures—our capacity for joy and pleasure through sex. The result is a society which is highly neurotic in its attitudes toward and practice of sex—all of which interferes with honest communication and self-realization.

The radical solution to this perceived situation is to treat sex *as* a physical act, unencumbered with romanticized notions of love. Human sex just *is* a form of animal coupling, and to make more of it is to invite dishonesty and neurosis.

It seems to me that it is *this* sort of attitude which the conservative most fears. Though the conservative claims that such an attitude will result in devaluing humans, it is not clear why. He seems to infer that because the radical is willing to treat others as sources of pleasure, without the necessity of emotional commitment, he therefore perceives them as mere *instruments* of pleasure. This, of course, does not follow, either logically or as a matter of probability. Nor have I ever met a conservative who thought that correspondingly, if people are permitted to make profits from others in business dealings, they will come to view them as mere sources of profits. The point is that it

is absurd to suppose that one who no longer thinks of *sex* in terms of shame and guilt must lose the sense of shame and guilt at harming others, either through sex, or in other ways.

I do not wish to dwell on the radical position, however, because there is a more widespread view which I have labeled the "radical-liberal" view which I wish to consider. This conception accepts a large part of the radical critique, in particular the notion that guilt and shame, duty and commitment, are not necessary to fully human sex. The radical-liberal agrees that much of our ordinary sexual relations are marred by the inhibitions these impose. He or she need not, however, reject sex as an element in loving relationships, and he or she may well insist that love does engender special commitments and concern with which sex is properly entangled. But, the radical-liberal does not reject physical sex for its own sake as something debased or wicked, or shorn of human qualities. Indeed, he or she may insist that greater concern with the physical aspects of sexuality is needed to break down those emotional connections with sex which stand as barriers to its enjoyment, and as barriers to free open communication with others, and to one's development of a sense of one's sexual identity—a development in terms of one's own needs, desires, and life-style.

The intensity of such needs on the part of many people is, I believe, well-depicted in Erica Jong's contemporary novel, *Fear of Flying*. In the book, her heroine expresses her reaction to the attitude that a woman's identity is to be found in her relationship with a man. Female solitude is perceived as un-American and selfish. Thus, women live waiting to be half of something else, rather than being simply themselves. These American attitudes are perceived as inhibitions to the woman's self-discovery. . . .

The point is that to many people, the conservative's picture of sex, and the sorts of social relations in which he embeds it, has served to starve them of the unique development of their personalities, or an aspect of it. The anti-dote they see is a freer, more open attitude toward sex, removed from what they regard as a mystique of duty and guilt and shame.

People with the attitudes of the radical-liberal, or who see themselves as impeded in their full self-realization by the traditional views on sex, may well find pornography something of no consequence, or may even find it beneficial—a means of removing from their own psyches the associations which inhibit their sexual natures. The plain fact is that pornography is used for this effect by various therapists, who have thereby aided people to more fulfilled lives for themselves, and happier, healthier relations with loved ones.[22]

Will such a concern with physical pleasure result in nonattachment, in antihuman feelings, in the loss of loving relationships? It is at least as plausible that just the opposite is the probable result, that by virtue of lessened anxiety and guilt over sex, an important source of human communion is enhanced. In a Kinsey-type sex survey sponsored by *Playboy,* there was demonstrated a greatly heightened freedom in sex in America, and a greater emphasis on physical enjoyment, but this has not resulted in a significant lessening of the importance accorded to emotional ties.[23] Greater concern with pleasure has been used to *enhance* those relationships. Thus, it is no accident that among the millions who have lined up to see *Deep Throat, Behind the Green Door,* and *The Devil in Miss Jones,* have been a great many loving, married couples. Indeed, that there has come to be a body of "popular pornography"—porno for the millions—holds out some small hope that our culture will eventually develop a truly erotic artistic tradition, as explicitness becomes more natural, and tastes demand more of the productions.

We have seen that the conservative position presupposes attitudes toward sex which many reject, and that the alternative attitudes are consistent both with the acceptance of pornography and the values of care and concern for others. Let us turn now to the specific points the conservatives make concerning alleged harms.

2. THE RESPONSE TO CONSERVATIVE OBJECTIONS

I want to consider first the argument concerning privacy. It was Steiner's claim that pornography takes the "words of the night," and "by shouting them over the rooftops," robs us of the ability to use them or find them in private—sex becomes a matter in the public domain. Moreover, by dehumanizing the individual, people are treated as in concentration camps. As Steiner expressed it subsequent to the original publication of his essay: "Both pornography and totalitarianism seem to me to set up power relations which must necessarily violate privacy."[24]

If there is any plausibility to the first part of these claims, it must derive entirely from the metaphor of shouting the sacred night words over the rooftops. Were anyone to do such a thing with night words, day words, winter words, and so on, we would have a legitimate gripe concerning our privacy. But in what *way* is the voluntary perusal or viewing of pornography an invasion of privacy? His point *seems* to be that the constant consumption by the public of explicit sexual materials will come to make sex something "pre-packaged" for us, so that we will not discover how to do it ourselves, in our own ways. This is extraordinarily implausible, and if it were true, would constitute a reason for banning all literature dealing with human feelings and emotions, and ways of relating to one another. The evidence is that greater sexual explicitness is utilized as a means for people to have greater awareness of their sexuality and its possibilities, and to assimilate the experiences of others into their own lifestyles. The capacity to do this is *part* of what is involved in our being the unique individuals we are. At any rate, people who *want* the stimulation of erotic materials, who feel freer in expressing themselves through the influence of sexy art, who do not *want* an environment in which sex cannot be appreciated through explicit literature and art, will hardly be impressed with the manner in which the censor protects *their* privacy.

I want now to turn to Kristol's view that pornography is autoerotic, hence, infantile, and thus promotes a sexual regression which is a danger to civilization itself. The danger which this supposed form of infantilism poses is that it would destroy the capacity for an integral feature of mature relations (and ultimately civilized relations) if "not controlled or sublimated in some way."

Now the ultimate ground for censorship which the argument poses really has only secondary connections with the charges of autoeroticism and infantilism. Lots of things are "self-pleasuring" without being thought infantile or dangerous on that account. Consider the pleasures of the gourmet, or wine aficionado, or devotees of Turkish baths.

Kristol believes that masturbation, and pornography which is its mental form, has an appeal to us as adults, and this is dangerous. Because it *is so* attractive, it is liable to draw us away from real love, and this is why it must be headed off at the pass. The charge of infantilism, then, is only Kristol's way of making us feel bad about masturbating. By virtue of his claiming to know the rationale underlying "all the codes of sexual conduct ever devised by the human race," we are made to feel beyond the pale of civilized adult society. The argument turns, really, on the supposed dangers of an *overly* autoeroticized society, which he thinks the legalization of pornography will help produce.

In criticizing pornography on these grounds, Kristol has surely overshot his mark; for, there is nothing more masturbatory than masturbation itself. If Kristol is right, then his concern with pornography is too tepid a treatment of the danger. What the argument would show is that we must stamp out masturbation itself!

Moreover, Kristol is mistaken if he thinks that censorship of pornography will make one whit of difference to the incidence of masturbation. This is because the masturbatory imagination is perfectly limitless; it does not *need* explicit sexual stimuli. Deprived of that, it can make do with virtually anything—the impassioned kisses of film lovers, a well-filled female's sweater, or male's crotch,[25] even, we are told, a neatly displayed ankle or bare shoulder. The enormity of the problem Kristol faces is shown in the revelation of the *Playboy* survey that: "a large majority of men and women in every age group say that while they masturbate, they fantasize about having intercourse with persons they love."[26] The implications for the censor are staggering!

There are two further reasons why reasonable people will not take Kristol's view seriously. First, he underestimates the human capacity to assimilate varieties of sexual experience. People can enjoy pornography and intercourse without giving up one or the other.[27] Second, his entire argument grossly undervalues the appeal and attraction to us of the very thing he wants to preserve—mature sexual love which is fulfilling, rewarding, and integrated into the course of a loving relationship. Pornography may be in some sense autoerotic; it can be pleasant to be sexually stimulated. But it is rarely its own source of ultimate satisfaction; it usually stimulates to acquire further satisfactions. Indeed, this is presupposed by some of the conservative arguments. But there is no reason to assume that such satisfaction will be sought exclusively through masturbation, when a healthy sex relation is available with a loved one. I have *never* heard of anyone, male or female, complain that their love life had been ruined by their partner's turn to masturbation as a result of an excess of pornography. On the other hand, I have heard couples rave about sex had after viewing pornographic films.

Still, there does seem to be a lingering problem which the conservatives will regard as not adequately dealt with in anything said thus far. They think that literature and art *can* influence people's attitudes and beliefs, and also their behavior, and they cannot understand why the liberal, who believes this to be true in other cases, is unwilling to admit this with respect to pornography. Now, I believe the liberal *can* admit the possibility of a causal role for pornography with respect to people's attitudes and behavior. Such an admission does not, however, establish a case for censorship.

It would be quite extraordinary if literary and visual materials which are capable of arousing normal men and women did not also have some tendency to people already predisposed to harmful conduct, and especially people with an unstable psychological makeup. It is believable, even apart from any evidence, that such people might act from the fantasies such stimuli generate.

When the conservative is reasonable, however, he recognizes that the stimulation and consequent influence of pornography is a function not merely of the nature of the stimulus, but also of the person's background, upbringing, cultural environment, and his own genetic and personality structure and predispositions.[28] Put *this* way, the conservative has a somewhat plausible claim that pornography can sometimes be implicated as having some causal role in the etiology of social harms.

Put in its most reasonable form, however, the claim makes quite *un*reasonable the censorship of pornography. There are two primary reasons for this: (1) Pornography is not distinguishable from other materials in producing *direct* harms of this kind; it may, in fact, exert a counter-influence to other materials which are more likely to have these effects. (2) The *in*direct harms—those produced through the influence of altered attitudes and beliefs, are highly unlikely, and not of a kind a society which values freedom will allow to become the basis of suppression without strong evidence of

probably causal connections. It will seek to counter such remote influences with noncoercive means.

Let us turn to the first point—that other materials which no one would dream of suppressing are as likely to produce harms. Earl Finbar Murphy, writing in the *Wayne Law Review,* has given some graphic illustrations. He begins by pointing out that "everything, every idea, is capable of being obscene if the personality perceiving it so apprehends it." He continues:

> It is for this reason that books, pictures, charades, ritual, the spoken word, *can* and *do* lead directly to conduct harmful to the self indulging in it and to others. Heinrich Pommerenke, who was a rapist, abuser, and mass slayer of women in Germany, was prompted to his series of ghastly deeds by Cecil B. DeMille's *The Ten Commandments.* During the scene of the Jewish women dancing about the Golden Calf, all the doubts of his life came clear: women were the source of the world's trouble and it was his mission both to punish them for this and to execute them. Leaving the theater, he slew his first victim in a park nearby. John George Haigh, the British vampire who sucked his victims' blood through soda straws and dissolved their drained bodies in acid baths, first had his murder-inciting dreams and vampire-longings from watching the "voluptuous" procedure of—an Anglican High Church Service!

The prohibition and effective suppression of what the average consensus would regard as pornographic would not have reached these two. Haigh, who drank his own urine as well as others' blood, was educated to regard "all forms of pleasure as sinful, and the reading of newspapers undesirable." Pommerenke found any reference to sex in a film, however oblique, made him feel so intense inside that, "I had to do something to a woman." Albert Fish, who has been called the most perverse case known to psychiatry, decided he had a mission to castrate small boys and offer them as human sacrifices to God as a result of reading the Old Testament. Each of these had the common quality of being beyond the reach of the conventionally pornographic. They had altered the range of the erotically stimulating, and each illustrates how impossible it is to predict what will precipitate or form psycho-neurotic conduct. . . . The scope of pornography, so far from being in any way uniform, is as wide as the peculiarities of the human psyche.[29]

These are extreme cases, but they do represent a pattern on the part of people disposed to deviant behavior, as is borne out by studies of the personalities and backgrounds of sex offenders. In their book, *Pornography and Sexual Deviance,* Michael J. Goldstein and Harold S. Kant report:

A problem that arises in studying reactions to pornography among sex offenders is that they appear to generate their own pornography from nonsexual stimuli. . . . The sex offenders deduced a significantly greater number of sexual activities from the drawings (children playing near a tree, figure petting a dog, and three people standing unrelated to each other) than did the nonsex offenders. They also were more prone to incorporate recently viewed sexual pictures into a series of gradually more explicit drawings. These results imply that the sex offender is highly receptive to sexual stimuli, and reads sexual meanings into images that would be devoid of erotic connotations for the normal person. Certainly, this finding was borne out by our study of institutionalized pedophiles (child molesters), who found the familiar suntan lotion ad showing a young child, with buttocks exposed to reveal his sunburn as a dog pulls at his bathing suit, to be one of the most erotic stimuli they had encountered.[30]

Indeed, their studies seem to yield the conclusion that pornography itself does not tend to produce antisocial behavior, and that, at least in the case of rapists, other materials are likely to do so:

We must consider that sex offenders are highly receptive to suggestions of sexual behavior congruent with their previously formed desires and will interpret the material at hand to fit their needs. It is true, however, that while few, if any, sex offenders suggest that erotica played a role in the commission of sex crimes, stimuli expressing brutality, with or without concomitant sexual behavior, were often mentioned as disturbing, by rapists in particular. This raises the question of whether the stimulus most likely to release antisocial sexual behavior is one representing sexuality, or one representing aggression.[31]

In summarizing the evidence they gathered, and which is supported by other studies, they conclude that pornography does not seem to be a significant factor in the behavior of sex offenders. Moreover, there is some evidence that "for rapists, exposure to erotica portraying 'normal' heterosexual relations can serve to ward off antisocial sexual impulses."[32]

The point is that if we take the conservative's "harm" claim in its most plausible form, we must conclude that while pornography *can* play a causal role of this type, the evidence is that many other ordinary visual and literary depictions are more likely to do so. If we take seriously the claim that having this kind of causal role is sufficient for a case of censorship, then we must do a much greater housecleaning of our media offerings than we had imagined. The problem is that while we know where to begin—with unalloyed portrayals of violence, we can hardly know where to end.

A further serious difficulty for the conservative "harm" argument arises when we ask just what *kinds* of backgrounds and attitudes *do* predispose to the unwanted behavior. The studies of Kant and Goldstein are of help here, especially with respect to rapists:

The rapists, who found it very difficult to talk about sex, said there was little nudity in their homes while they were growing up and that sex was never discussed. Only 18 percent of the rapists said their parents had caught them with erotic materials; in those instances the parents had become angry and had punished them. (In the control group, 37 percent reported that their parents know they read erotic materials, but only 7 percent reported being punished. Most said their parents had been indifferent, and some said their parents had explained the materials to them—an occurrence not reported by any other group.)[33]

For the *rapists,* the data suggest very repressive family backgrounds regarding sexuality.[34]

Moreover: "It appears that all our noncontrol groups, no matter what their ages, education, or occupations, share one common characteristic: they had little exposure to erotica when they were adolescents."[35]

These results at the very least carry the suggestion that the very attitudes toward sex which motivate the censor are part of the background and psychological information of the personality of sex offenders—backgrounds which include the repression of sexual feelings, repression of exposure to explicit sexual stimuli, an overly developed sense of shame and guilt related to sex. As we have seen, some of the censors advocate *just* this sort of model for all of society, wherein suppression of pornography is just *one* way of safeguarding society. It may well be that they are in the paradoxical position of isolating a possible evil of great extent, and then recommending and fostering a response which will help produce that very evil.[36]

There is, however, a more profound reason why the admission of a possible causal role for pornography in affecting attitudes and behavior need not support the conservative view, and why the traditional liberal may well have been right in not taking pornography seriously.

To begin with, I believe we have granted the conservatives too much in admitting that pornography depersonalizes sex. While there is a measure of truth in this claim, it is not literally true. By concentrating on physical aspects of sex, pornography does, somewhat, abstract from the web of feelings, emotions, and needs which are usually attendant on sexual experience in ordinary life. Nonetheless, people are not depicted as mere machines or animals. Indeed, where there is explicit pornographic

purpose—the arousal of the reader or viewer— the end could not be accomplished were it not real fleshy people depicted. In addition, pornography almost always does have *some* human context within which sex takes place— a meeting in a bar, the bridegroom carrying his bride over the threshold, the window washer observing the inhabitant of an apartment. A study of pornography will reveal certain set patterns of such contexts: there is, indeed, a sort of orthodoxy among pornographers. And there is an obvious reason: pornography springs from and caters to sexual fantasies. This also explains why so little context is needed; the observer quickly identifies with the scene, and is able to elaborate it in his or her own mind to whatever extent he or she wishes or feels the need. That pornography is intimately tied to fantasy—*peopled* fantasy—also accounts for one of its worst features—its tendency to treat women in conventional male chauvinist ways. Pornography, as a matter of sociological fact, has been produced by and for men with such sexual attitudes.

There are further grounds for holding that pornography does not, by its nature, dehumanize sex in the feared ways. It usually depicts people as enjoying physical activity, that is, as mutually experiencing *pleasure*. Typical pornography displays sex as something people take fun in and enjoy. There is usually little doubt the persons involved are *liking* it. All of the censors we have discussed treat *Fanny Hill* as pornographic, but it is obvious to anyone who has read the book that it absolutely resists the claim that the characters are not portrayed as real people with the usual hopes and fears, who desire not to be harmed, and desire a measure of respect as persons. The book concentrates on sex and sexual enjoyment, and *that* is why it is taken as pornographic.[37] Even sadistic pornography, it should be noted, depicts people as having enjoyment; and, it is usually sado*masochistic* pleasures which are portrayed, with the resultant equalizing of the distribution of pleasure (if not of pain). In this respect, most pornography does not portray humans as *mere* instruments of whatever ends we have. And, in this respect, pornography does not express or evoke the genuinely immoral attitudes which a great deal of our movie, television, and literary materials cater to and reinforce.[38]

Indeed, much of what is found in the media *is* immoral in that it is expressive of, caters to, and fosters attitudes which *are* morally objectionable. People are treated as expendable units by international spies for whom *anything* is permitted in the name of national security; the typical laundry soap commercial treats women as idiotic house slaves; situation comedy typically portrays fathers as moronic bunglers who, nonetheless, rightfully rule their homes as dictators (albeit, benevolent ones); the various detective programs cater to the aggressive, dominating, *macho* image of male sexuality which is endemic within large portions of American society. Pornography cannot get off the hook merely by pointing out that it depicts *people*. On the other hand, most of it does not reflect or cater to attitudes as objectionable as one now finds dominating the output of television alone. And, where it does, it is not a result of the fact it is pornographic, but, rather, that it reflects conventional views widely expressed in other forms.[39]

There remains a final point to be made about the influence of pornography on attitudes. Pornography, when it does attract us, affect us, appeal to us, has a limited, narrowly focused appeal—to our sexual appetite. Such appeal tends toward short-lived enjoyments, rather than any far-reaching effects on the personality.[40] This is why pornography has essentially entertainment and recreational use and attraction; it is taken seriously by almost no one but the censors. It shows us people having sex, and that is it; we must do the rest. Serious literature and art, however, appeal to the whole person—to the entire range of his sensibilities, desires, needs, attitude patterns and beliefs and is thus far more likely to affect our ultimate behavior patterns. Even the limited reaction of sexual arousal is often better achieved through artistic technique. The conserva-tives deny this, but it is difficult to see on what grounds. Both in the essays of Van den Haag and of Walter Berns, there is the claim that aesthetic value would detract from the purely sexual appeal of a work.[41] I can only suppose that they think all people are possessed with, and exercise, the aesthetic sensibilities of literary and art critics, and thus readily separate out and analyze devices of technique in the experiencing of a work. This assuredly is not the case. Moreover, it is hardly plausible that artistic technique should enhance and further every *other* objective of an artist, and *not* be an accessory to the end of evoking sexual arousal. Real artistic value is unobtrusive in this respect.

Of course, television pap may well influence attitudes without having significant artistic value, merely by its sheer preponderance on the airwaves. But it is not *this* sort of role we need envisage for pornography liberated from censorship. Moreover, it is not clear its influence would be worse than that of other materials which now hog the channels.

It seems to me, however, that we have yet to make the most important response to the conservative's claims. For, up to now, we have treated the issue as if it were merely a matter of weighing up possible harms from pornography against possible benefits, and the likelihood of the occurrence of the harms. Unfortunately, this is the form the debate usually takes, when it is not strictly concerned with the First Amendment. But, something important is lost if we think the issue resolves into these questions. The more important issue turns on the fact that a great many people *like* and *enjoy* pornography, and *want* it as part of their lives, either for its enjoyment, or for more serious psychological purposes. This fact means that censorship is an interference with the freedom and self-determination of a great many people, and it is on this ground that the conservative harm argument must ultimately be rejected. For a society which accepts freedom and self-determination as centrally significant values cannot allow interferences with freedom on such grounds as these.

To give a satisfactory argument for these claims would require another paper. Moreover, I believe (with certain reservations) this has been adequately done in Mill's *On Liberty.* As the conservatives do not regard *that* as enunciating a clear, defensible body of doctrine,[42] I cannot hope to present an entirely convincing argument here. I want at the very least, however, to outline a minimal set of claims which I think bear on the issue, and which can provide ground for further debate.

The idea of a self-determining individual involves a person developing his or her own mode of life according to the person's own needs, desires, personality, and perceptions of reality. This conception has at least three features: (1) the person's desires are (so far as possible) expressions of his or her own nature—not imposed from without; (2) the manner of the development of his or her character and the pattern of the person's life, are, in large measure, a resultant of his or her own judgment, choice, and personal experience; and (3) the person's unique capacities and potentialities have been developed, or at least tried out.[43] Now, *if* one regards this as a valuable manner of living, and freedom as of value, *both* because it is intrinsic to treating others *as* self-determining agents, *and* because it is requisite for the realization of self-determination, then I think one will accept the following propositions concerning freedom:

1. The burden of producing convincing reasons and evidence is always on the person who would interfere with people's freedom and life-styles.
2. The person who would interfere with freedom must show that the activity interfered with is likely to harm others or interfere with their rights as individuals.[44]
3. Those who would deny freedom must show that the harm or interference threatened is one from which others have a superior right to protection.

Though these propositions are subject to considerable interpretation, it seems to me that one who accepts them will, at the least, recognize that the burden of proof is not symmetric either in structure or degree. The person who would deny freedom shoulders the burden, and, moreover, he or she does not succeed merely by showing *some* harms are likely to result. Accepting freedom and self-determination as central values entails accepting some risks, in order to *be* free. We do *not* presuppose that freedom will always produce good. And, insofar as the alleged harms are indirect and remote, we are committed to employing noncoercive means to combat them. Of course, we need not interpret this in a suicidal way—allowing interference only when the harm is inevitably upon us. But, at the least, we should require a strong showing of likely harms which are far from remote, and this is a burden which the censors of pornography *cannot* meet. Indeed, on this score, the conservative arguments are *many* times weaker than ones which can be made concerning many other kinds of communications, and such activities as hunting for sport, automobile racing, boxing, and so on.[45] If anyone wants a display of the extent to which our society allows recreation to instigate socially harmful attitudes and feelings, all he or she need do is sit in the stands during a hotly contested high school football or basketball game. And, of course these feelings quite often spill over into antisocial behavior.

Though I have defended pornography from criticisms based on its content or nature, I have certainly not shown that it is always unobjectionable. Insofar as it arises in a social context entirely infused with male sexism, much of it reflects the worst aspects of our society's approved conceptions of sexual relations. Too often, the scenes depicted involve male violence and aggression toward women, male dominance over women, and females as sexual servants. Moreover, there are aspects of the commercial institutions which purvey it in the market which are quite objectionable. My argument is has been that this is not necessary to pornography as such; where it is true, this reflects social and sexual attitudes already fostered by other social forces. Moreover, I have maintained that by virtue of a feature which does seem to characterize pornography—its break with certain inhibiting conceptions of sexuality, pornography may well play a role in people determining for themselves the lifestyle which most suits them. A society which values self-determination will interfere with it only under circumstances which the censors of pornography cannot show to hold.

Of course, I have said almost nothing about the nature of the specific freedoms we incorporate in our notion of freedom of speech. It may well be that that set of rights imposes even stricter obligations on those who would suppress forms of its exercise.

Notes

1. This proposition is argued for by one advocate of censorship. See Irving Kristol, "Pornography, Obscenity, and the Case for Censorship," *New York Times Magazine* (March 28, 1971): 23.
2. There are a number of brief summaries available on the development of the common-law approach to obscenity. See *The Report of the Commission on Obscenity and Pornography* (New York: Bantam, 1970), 348–54; Michael J. Goldstein and Harold S. Kant, *Pornography and Sexual Deviance* (Berkeley: University of California Press, 1973), 154–56; and an untitled essay by Charles Rembar in *Censorship: For and Against,* ed. Harold H. Hart (New York: Hart Publishing Co., 1971), 198–227.

Apparently, the leading case prior to the 18th century involved Sir Charles Sedley, who, with some friends, had become drunk in a tavern, appeared naked on a balcony overlooking Covent Garden, and shouted profanities at the crowd which gathered below; then he urinated upon, and threw bottles of urine on, the bystanders.

3. Regulation of speech is one of the most pressing problems for free speech in our contemporary, mass society, in which the control of the media is in relatively few hands, primarily concerned with the use of that media to produce profits. Moreover, the spectre of nonlegal controls, which Mill feared, is very much with us. It is surprising that so little attention has been given to the issue of the principles properly governing regulation. An indication of various forms of control utilized by government for the suppression of pornography is found by studying the development of censorship in the United States. See James C. N. Paul and Murray L. Schwartz, *Federal Censorship: Obscenity in the Mail* (New York: The Free Press, 1961).
4. I regard it as a serious drawback of the definition that it rules out by *fiat,* the claim that pornography *can* be, in and of itself, significant literature. This claim is convincingly argued for by Susan Sontag in her essay "The Pornographic Imagination," reprinted in *Perspectives on Pornography,* ed. Douglas A. Hughes (New York: St. Martin's Press, 1970), 131–69; also in her book *Styles of Radical Will* (New York: Farrar, Straus & Giroux, 1966). The argument for a broader, more inclusive definition is made convincingly by Morse Peckham in *Art and Pornography* (New York: Basic Books, 1969), chapter 1. Anyone with a serious interest in the subject of pornography will find this a most important work.
5. It is also clear that the definition would be a disaster in the legal context, since there is so great an area of *disagreement.* Moreover, there is a tremendous danger of a secondary form of censorship, in which literary critics come to watch closely how they criticize a work lest the critique be used by the censors.

That this in fact has happened is testified to in an eye-opening note by the English critic Horace Judson, in *Encounter* 30 (March 1968): 57–60. To his dismay, a critical review he wrote of Selby's *Last Exit to Brooklyn* was read into the record and used in banning that book in England.

6. See, for example, Ernest van den Haag, writing in *Censorship: For and Against,* 158. Also, in "Is Pornography a Cause of Crime?" *Encounter* 29 (December 1967): 54.

7. I believe that the minority report of the Presidential Commission on Obscenity and Pornography reduces to such a view, when it is not concerned specifically with possible harms. See, for example the rationale given on 498–500 of the report, for their legislative recommendations. Sense can be made of these passages *only* on the assumption the commissioners believe pornography is itself immoral. I might also note that if one looks up "pornography" in the *Readers' Guide,* he is advised "See immoral literature and pictures."

8. Ronald Dworkin, "Lord Devlin and the Enforcement of Morals," *Yale Law Journal* 75 (1966): 986–1005; reprinted in *Morality and the Law,* ed. Richard Wasserstrom (Belmont, Calif.: Wadsworth, 1971), 55–72.

9. For starters, one might review the essays in Wasserstrom, *Morality and the Law.*

10. In surveys done for the Presidential Commission, it was found that a (slim) majority of adults would not object to the availability of pornography if it could be shown it was not harmful. While hardly a declaration of adoration for pornography, this is not a demonstration of utter, overwhelming intolerance for it, either.

11. See, for example, Paris Adult Theatre I v. Slaton, 431 U.S. 49 (1973).

12. Report of the Commission on Obscenity, 26–32, in which the effects are summarized. Also, Goldstein and Kant, *Pornography and Sexual Deviance,* 139–53.

13. George Steiner, "Night Words: High Pornography and Human Privacy," in *Perspectives on Pornography,* 96–108.

14. Ibid., 106–07.

15. Kristol, "Pornography, Obscenity and the Case for Censorship," 113.

16. Ibid.

17. Walter Berns, "Pornography vs. Democracy: The Case for Censorship," *The Public Interest* 22 (Winter 1971): 12.

18. Ibid., 13. Berns cites Washington, Jefferson, and Lincoln as holding that democracy requires citizens of good character and self-restraint, and he seems to think that somehow this is a "forgotten argument" against pornography.

19. Van den Haag, in *Censorship: For and Against,* 146–48.

20. The extent to which feelings of vulnerability can be involved in sex is testified to by the kinds of fears which can inhibit orgasmic response. In her book reporting on techniques she has used with non- or preorgasmic women, Dr. Lonnie Garfield Barbach reports that among the factors which inhibit these women from having orgasms is the fear of appearing ugly, of their partners being repulsed by them, of losing control, fainting, or screaming. See Lonnie Garfield Barbach, *For Yourself: The Fulfillment of Female Sexuality* (Garden City, N.J.: Doubleday, 1975), 11–12.

21. Berns, "Pornography vs. Democracy," 12.

22. In *For Yourself,* Dr. Lonnie Garfield Barbach recommends the use of pornography for preorgasmic women seeking increased sexual responsiveness and fulfillment. See *For Yourself,* 75, 77, 85, 86. Dr. Wardell B. Pomeroy, one of Kinsey's collaborators, wrote *Playboy,* in reaction to a 1973 Supreme Court ruling on pornography:

> As a psychotherapist and marriage counselor, I sometimes recommend various erotic films, books and pictures to my patients. Many of them report that erotica helps them to free them of their inhibitions and, thus, helps them function better with their spouses. Now they will have more difficulty in seeing and reading such seriously valuable material, and I am afraid I must enlarge my own library for their perusal. *Playboy* 20 (October 1973): 57.

23. This point is made at length in the report. One example: "Despite the extensive changes that the liberation has made in the feelings that most Americans have about their own bodies, about the legitimacy of maximizing sexual pleasure and about the acceptability and normality of a wide variety of techniques of foreplay and coitus, sexual liberation has not replaced the liberal-romantic concept of sex with the recreational one. The latter attitude toward sex now coexists with the former in our society, and in many a person's feeling, but the former remains the dominant ideal." *Playboy* 20 (October 1973): 204.

24. Steiner, "Night Words," in *Perspectives*, 97.

25. That women look at, and are excited by, the bulges in men's trousers is given ample testimony in Nancy Friday's book on women's sexual fantasies. See *My Secret Garden* (New York: Pocket Books, 1974), the section entitled "Women Do Look," 214–22.

26. *Playboy*, 202.

27. See, for example, *Report of the Commission on Obscenity*, 28–29; also, Goldstein and Kant, *Pornography and Sexual Deviance*, 30.

28. Van den Haag seems to recognize this point. See "Is Pornography a Cause of Crime?" in *Encounter*, 53.

29. Earl Finbar Murphy, "The Value of Pornography," *Wayne Law Review* (1964): 668–69.

30. Goldstein and Kant, *Pornography and Sexual Deviance*, 31.

31. Ibid., 108–09.

32. Ibid., 152.

33. Ibid., 143.

34. Ibid., 145.

35. Ibid., 147.

36. To compound the paradox, if being a remote cause of harms is a prima facie ground for censoring literature, then we have some evidence that the conservative arguments ought to be censored. This is *not* a view I advocate.

37. I do not appeal to its conventional format—girl meets boy, girl loses boy, girl reunites with boy in marriage.

38. Professor Van den Haag holds that pornography "nearly always leads to sadistic pornography." It is not clear what this means; moreover, his argument is that this results *because* pornography dehumanizes sex. Since we have grounds for doubting this, we have grounds for doubting the alleged result. Also, since I am denying that pornography significantly dehumanizes sex, I am implicitly rejecting a further conservative argument I have not taken up, namely, that pornography is itself expressive of immoral attitudes irrespective of any further harmful effects. Since some liberals seem to be willing to silence Nazis or racists on such grounds, some conservatives think this argument will appeal to such liberals. I believe that both Kristol and Van den Haag maintain this view. See also Richard Kuh, *Foolish Figleaves?* (New York: Macmillan, 1967), 280ff. A position of this sort is maintained by Susan Brownmiller in her book *Against Our Will: Men, Women and Rape* (New York: Simon and Schuster, 1975), 201. Brownmiller regards pornography as an invention designed to humiliate women. I have not responded to her arguments as she gives none. Moreover, she employs a curious "double standard." She gives great weight to law enforcement officials' opinions about pornography, but would hardly be willing to take these same persons' views on rape at face value.

39. In this paragraph I have attempted to bring to bear on the argument some points made by Professor Ann Garry, in her commentary on the paper at the meeting of the Society for Philosophy and Public Affairs in San Diego, March 18, 1975.

40. *Report of the Commission on Obscenity*, 28; and Goldstein and Kant, *Pornography and Sexual Deviance*, 151.

41. Berns, in *The Public Interest*, 12 footnote, and Van den Haag, in *Perspectives*, 129.

42. See, for example, Gertrude Himmelfarb's recent critical account of Mill, *On Liberty and Liberalism: The Case of John Stuart Mill* (New York: Alfred A. Knopf, 1974). It appears to me that she has not really understood Mill. Ronald Dworkin has picked out some of the most glaring of her errors in his review in *The New York Review of Books* 21 (October 31, 1974): 21.

43. I believe this is Mill's conception. See also Sharon Hill's essay, Self-Determination and

Autonomy," in *Today's Moral Problems,* ed. Richard Wasserstrom (New York Macmillan, 1975), 171–86.

44. I want to note three points here. First, this view of freedom permits inferences for *moral* reasons; it does *not* insist on the moral neutrality of the law. It does, however, focus on the *kinds* of moral reasons allowed to count as grounds for the denial of freedom. Second, it does not rule out special legal recognition of modes of living which are central to the culture, for example, monogamous marriage. This will have indirect effects on freedom which a liberal theory would have to recognize and deal with, but it need not rule out such recognition out of hand. In addition, the notion of "harm" could be taken to include conduct or practices which are both intrusive on public consciousness, and offensive. This could provide a basis for *regulating* the sale and distribution of pornography, even if *prohibition* is not justified. Important discussion of the principles underlying the treatment of offensiveness in the law is to be found in an article by Joel Feinberg, "Harmless Immoralities and Offensive Nuisances," in *Issues in Law and Morality,* ed. Norman Care and Thomas Trelogan (Cleveland: Case Western Reserve University, 1973). Michael Bayles's commentary on that paper, also found in the same volume, is very useful. Third, valuing self-determination may entail a limited paternalism in circumstances where noninterference cannot possibly further autonomy. That it is at least possible for noninterference to promote self-determination seems to have been conceived by Mill as a presupposition for

applications of the principle of liberty. This helps explain some of his "applications" at the end of the essay. Just how to incorporate limited paternalism in a liberal theory is a thorny issue. The pornography issue, however, does not appear to significantly involve that issue. A useful treatment of paternalism is in Gerald Dworkin, "Paternalism," in *Morality and the Law,* 107–26.

45. So far as I can judge, the most telling "evidence" the conservatives have thus far come up with is: (a) *some* reasonable criticisms of the studies which have been done, and the interpretations which have been given them; and (b) a few, isolated, contrary studies (which are, coincidentally, open to similar or stronger objections). See especially the criticisms of Victor B. Cline in the minority report of the Presidential Commission on Obscenity and Pornography, 463–89. While I do not think the conservatives need produce ironclad scientific data demonstrating their claims, we surely cannot allow the suppression of freedom when the reasons offered are poor, and the weight of available evidence is heavily *against* those claims. The minority report (it may be Dr. Cline writing in this instance—it is unclear) asserts that the "burden of proof" is on the one who would change current law. This is an indefensible imprimatur of existing law as such; and it is absolutely inconsistent with the recognition of freedom and self-determination as important moral values. The mere *existence* of law cannot be allowed as a ground for its continued existence, if freedom is to have anything but secondary importance.

Discussion Questions

1. How does Professor Berger define pornography? Do you agree or disagree with his definition. Explain and defend your answer.
2. What is the form of conservative argument to which Professor Berger is responding? Professor Berger cites two approaches to this argument, one by George Steiner and the other by Irving Kristol. What are their arguments and how does Professor Berger respond to them? Do you agree or disagree with his responses? Explain and defend your answer.

3. In addition to his responses to Steiner and Kristol, Professor Berger presents several other reasons to reject the conservative argument. What are those reasons? Present and explain them in detail. Do you consider them plausible? Explain and defend your answer.

4. Professor Berger makes the rather provocative argument that censorship rather than pornography may result in socially harmful attitudes and/or behavior. How does he defend this position? Do you agree or disagree his defense? Explain and defend your answer.

5. Professor Berger concludes his essay by arguing that the censor has the burden of providing convincing reasons to interfere with someone's consumption of pornography. How does he argue for this position? Do you find his case compelling? Why or why not? Explain and defend your answer.

You can locate InfoTrac-College Education articles about this chapter by accessing the InfoTrac-College Edition website (http://www.infotrac-college.com/wadsworth/). Using the InfoTrac-College Edition subject guide, enter the search terms relevant to this chapter, and then read abstracts for relevant articles.

SECTION D

Homosexuality

Introduction to Section D

One of the most controversial issues in the United States today is the rights of homosexuals, or what is called, *gay rights*. Although no reasonable person denies that homosexuals should have equal rights under the law, the gay rights movement raises the controversial question of whether the state has an obligation to treat homosexual behavior as fundamental to the nature of homosexuals, as salient a feature as race. If the state does not have such an obligation, does it have a right to favor certain forms of behavior and certain lifestyles, such as heterosexual monogamy, because the state perceives such practices as furthering the "public good" or the "good of the community?" As of the publication of this book, the individual fifty states of the United States officially sanction only heterosexual monogamy by recognizing traditional marriage in property law, tax law, family law, and so on, and not recognizing other practices, such as polygamy and homosexual marriage. However, some jurisdictions allow for "domestic partnerships," in which same-sex couples, who cannot be legally married, and opposite-sex couples, who do not want to be married, may have many of the same benefits allotted to partners in a heterosexual marriage, from health insurance to inheritance. In 1999, the Vermont Supreme Court ordered the Vermont state legislature to either allow same-sex unions or to create something similar to marriage that would accommodate the rights of homosexuals. The legislature did just that in 2000, and created what it calls "civil unions." It was signed into law by the governer and soon afterward took effect.

Proponents of gay rights are claiming that the state's partiality toward heterosexual monogamy is inconsistent with our intuitions about justice, fairness, and personal autonomy. In fact, some of the changes in law called for by the gay rights movement assume that the latter intuitions along with mere individual consent are sufficient to invalidate as unethical and unconstitutional the state's preference for heterosexual monogamy.

Yet, there actually may be two issues in the question of gay rights. The first issue is whether the state should be forbidden from interfering with the private consensual sex of adults if no one outside the circle of consenters "gets hurt," even though such behavior violates the sensibilities of most people. The second issue is much more complex and is really at the heart of the above demands of the gay rights movement: Should the state be forbidden from giving legal and social preference to heterosexual monogamy while denying such to alternative lifestyles, including homosexuality, polygamy, or adult incest? The second is not the same as the first. In fact, one can say yes to the privacy rights implied in the first issue and no to what is suggested in the second, namely, that the state's institutions affirm moral equivalency of sexual practices. The differences between the first and second issues are not often appreciated or articulated in the popular debate over homosexual rights.

Many factions of the gay rights movement demand that homosexuals be given *minority status,* a status given by the federal government as well as state governments to groups whose members have suffered discrimination (e.g., African Americans, women, Hispanics) and because of this discrimination, it is argued, these groups have not advanced socially as far as they would have if they had not been discriminated against. Affirmative action policies, for example, apply only to members of groups that have minority status. Gay activists contend that homosexuals have suffered discrimination and therefore deserve minority status. Minority status for a group is established, according to the U.S. Supreme Court,[1] if the group fulfills at least three criteria:

> Criterion 1: A history of discrimination evidenced by lack of ability to obtain economic mean income, adequate education, or cultural opportunity . . .
> Criterion 2: Specially protected classes should exhibit obvious, immutable, or distinguishing characteristics, like race, color, gender, or national origin, that define them as a discrete group. . . .
> Criterion 3: "Protected classes" should clearly demonstrate political powerlessness. . . .[2]

Those who oppose applying minority status to homosexuals maintain that gay activists have failed to make a compelling case. For example, concerning the first criterion, it has been argued that on average homosexuals are disproportionately more wealthy, better educated, and more culturally adept and influential than heterosexuals or any racial or ethnic group that already has minority status. And, of course, criteria 2 and 3 have been challenged as well.[3]

The state of Colorado's controversial Amendment 2 concerned the issue of minority status. The amendment, as it appeared as a ballot question in 1992, reads: "Shall there be an amendment to Article II of the Colorado Constitution to prohibit the state of Colorado and any of its political subdivisions from adopting or enforcing any law or policy which provides that homosexual, lesbian, or bisexual orientation or conduct, or relationships constitutes or entitles a person to claim any minority or protected status, quota preference or discrimination?" Passing in a referendum with 54 percent of the popular vote, Amendment 2 was immediately challenged in the courts by gay groups. In 1996, in the case of *Romer v. Evans,* the U.S. Supreme Court declared Amendment 2 unconstitutional. An abridged version of that decision, including both majority and dissenting opinions, is included in this text as Chapter 43.

Interestingly, the Supreme Court, in *Boy Scouts of America v. Dale* (2000), in a 5-4 decision, overturned the New Jersey Supreme Court[4] and upheld the right of the Boy Scouts of America to exclude homosexual scoutmasters. Writing on behalf of the Court, Chief Justice Rehnquist admits that homosexuality is more accepted than it was years ago. However, he also maintains that this fact is no reason to deny the Boy Scouts' First Amendment right to freedom of association.[5]

There are three parts to this section, each dealing with a different aspect of gay rights. The first part (Chapters 42 and 43) deals with homosexuality and the law and consists of two pieces, excerpts from the Supreme Court's decision *Bowers v. Hardwick* (1986) as well as *Romer v. Evans*. In *Bowers* the Court ruled that the state of Georgia's statute that made engaging in homosexual sodomy (anal sex) illegal does not violate the right to privacy and is in fact constitutional. The majority opinion as well as a concurring and a dissenting opinion are included.

The second part of this section concerns the moral arguments for banning discrimination against homosexuals. In Chapter 44, Professor Richard Mohr defends the morality of homosexuality as well as the legal rights of homosexuals. He does this by covering four different moral and legal concerns. Professor Michael Pakaluk, in Chapter 45, takes a different perspective and argues that antidiscrimination laws to protect gays as well as permitting same-sex marriage will result in harm to society.

The issue of same-sex marriage is the focus of part three. In 1996, the Defense of Marriage Act (D.O.M.A.), passed by the U.S. Congress and signed into law by then-President Bill Clinton, was an attempt to legally resist same-sex marriage by doing two things: (1) it allows states to not honor same-sex marriages if such marriages are allowed in other states, and (2) it defines for the federal code that marriage "means only a legal union between one man and one woman as husband and wife."[6]

For the opponents of same-sex marriage, D.O.M.A. could not have arrived sooner. For it became federal law soon after the Supreme Court's *Romer* decision. In addition, D.O.M.A. became law in the midst of Hawaii's battle over same-sex marriage. In 1993, the Hawaii Supreme Court, in an opinion for which there is no precedent in the history of same-sex challenges to state marriage laws, ruled that Hawaii's marriage law, which defined marriage as a union between one man and one woman, was a form of sex discrimination and could only be a valid law if the state could show that it had a compelling interest to discriminate. In other words, the burden of proof shifted from the challengers of the marriage law to the state.[7] In 1996 a Hawaii trial court ruled that forbidding same-sex marriage violated Hawaii's constitution.[8] This decision was appealed to the Hawaii Supreme Court. However, on November 3, 1998, the citizens of Hawaii, in a statewide referendum, amended their state constitution to read: "The legislature shall have the power to reserve marriage to opposite-sex couples." This made the state's marriage law constitutional, for it is now in the constitution that the legislature may define marriage to include only opposite-sex couples. The vote was 69 to 31 percent in favor of the amendment. Also on November 3, 1998, the citizens of Alaska, in a 68 to 32 percent vote, agreed to include in their constitution an amendment that reads: "To be valid or recognized in this State, a marriage may exist only between one man and one woman." In 2000, California citizens overwhelmingly voted to define marriage in the same way as Alaska did two years earlier. Other states have passed similar laws, either by referendum or through the legislature. Yet, as pointed out above, Vermont, as a result of a ruling by its state Supreme Court, created for homosexuals an institution it calls "civil unions."

In Chapter 46, Professor Robert P. George argues that, contrary to the conventional wisdom, a state that permits same-sex marriage is not affirming a neutral position on the question of marriage, but is affirming a particular point of view. George presents a case for marriage being exclusively heterosexual and then presents what he believes are the philosophical beliefs that undergird the pro-same-sex marriage position. He then argues that a case for same-sex cannot be made by appealing to the "fundamental aspects of equality." Angela Bolte, in Chapter 47, examines both philosophical and legal arguments against same-sex marriage, concluding that legalizing same-sex marriage would strengthen, rather than weaken, the institution of marriage.

Key words: gays, lesbians, bisexuals, homosexuality, gender issues, heterosexuality, family law, marriage, same-sex marriage, gay marriage, marriage law, domestic partnerships, human sexuality, *Baehr v. Lewin, Baehr v. Miike, Boy Scouts of America v. Dale, civil unions*.

NOTES

1. The Court established these three criteria through a number of decisions with which civil rights experts are acquainted. See, for example, the application of these criteria in *Jantz v. Muci* 759 Fed. Supp. 1543 (1991).
2. Tony Marco, "Oppressed Minority, or Counterfeits?," *Citizen* 6 (April 20, 1992): 2, 3. Marco is a conservative writer who opposes the gay rights movement.
3. See Ibid., 1–4.
4. *Dale v. Boy Scouts of America,* 160 N.J. 562, 734 A.2d 1196 (1999).
5. See Chief Justice Rehnquist's majority opinion in *Boy Scouts of America v. Dale,* 120 S.Ct. 2446 (2000).
6. As quoted in Hadley Arkes, "Odd Couples: The Defense of Marriage Act Will Firm Up the Authority of the States to Reject Gay Marriage," *National Review* 48 (12 August 1996): 48.
7. *Baehr v. Lewin,* 852 P.2d 44 (1993).
8. *Baehr v. Miike,* Civ. No. 91-1394 (1996).

For Further Reading

Hadley Arkes, "Questions of Principle, Not Predictions: A Reply to Macedo," *The Georgetown Law Journal* 84 (1995).

David Orgon Coolidge, *Same-Sex Marriage?,* rev. ed. (Wynnewood, PA: Crossroads Monograph Series in Faith and Public Policy, 1997).

John G. Culhane, "Uprooting the Arguments Against Same-Sex Marriage," *Cardoza Law Review* 20 (March 1999).

William Eskridge, *The Case for Same-Sex Marriage* (New York: The Free Press, 1996).

Robert P. George and Gerard V. Bradley, "Marriage and the Liberal Imagination," *The Georgetown Law Journal* 84 (1995).

Harry V. Jaffa, *Homosexuality and the Natural Law* (Claremont, CA: The Claremont Institute for the Study of Statesmanship and Political Philosophy, 1990).

Marshall Kirk and Hunter Madsen, *After the Ball: How America Will Conquer Its Fear and Hatred of Gays in the 90s* (New York: Doubleday, 1989).

Stephen Macedo, "Homosexuality and the Conservative Mind," *The Georgetown Law Journal* 84 (1995).

Richard Mohr, "The Case for Gay Marriage," *Notre Dame Journal of Law, Ethics & Public Policy* 9 (1995).

———, *Gays/Justice: A Study of Ethics, Society, and Law* (New York: Columbia University Press, 1988).

Michael Ruse, *Homosexuality: A Philosophical Inquiry* (Oxford: Basil Blackwell, 1988).

Randy Shilts, *And the Band Played On: Politics, People, and the AIDS Epidemic* (New York: St. Martin's, 1987).

Christopher Wolfe, ed., *Homosexuality and American Public Life* (Dallas, TX: Spence Publishing, 1999).

D1

The Law and Homosexuality

Bowers v. Hardwick (1986)* 42

U.S. SUPREME COURT

In the state of Georgia in August 1992, Michael Hardwick was charged with violating that state's criminal statute forbidding homosexual sodomy. Mr. Hardwick was discovered committing an act of sodomy with another male in the bedroom of his home. The question before the U.S. Supreme Court in this case was whether the Georgia statute violated the right to privacy, which in a number of cases the Court has ruled is found in the U.S. Constitution (e.g., *Griswold v. Connecticut* [1965], *Roe v. Wade* [1973]). Justice Byron White delivered the opinion of the court, concluding, among other things, that the state of Georgia has the right, though not the obligation, to criminalize homosexual sodomy if it so chooses, since the right to privacy is not absolute. Although the right to privacy applies to such cases as the right to decide whether one wants to bear a child and a right to possess and read obscene material in the privacy of one's home, homosexual sodomy is more akin to the possession and use of illegal drugs for which private consent does not invalidate laws prohibiting such activity. In his concurring opinion, former Chief Justice Warren Burger stresses the moral condemnation of homosexual sodomy throughout the history of Western Civilization, firmly rooted in the Judeo-Christian tradition, Roman law, the English Reformation, and common law. In his dissenting opinion, Justice Harry Blackmun chastises his brethren in the majority for not truly appreciating the constitutional right to privacy and how it applies to intimate personal decisions about one's own sexuality. He understands the right to privacy in previous decisions as grounded in the right to be let alone, which would make it unconstitutional to legally forbid consenting adults from engaging in sodomy in the privacy of their own homes.

Most citations and all footnotes omitted.

JUSTICE WHITE DELIVERED THE opinion of the Court.

In August 1982, respondent Hardwick . . . was charged with violating the Georgia statute criminalizing sodomy by committing that act with another adult male in the bedroom of respondent's home. After a preliminary hearing, the District Attorney decided not to present the matter to the grand jury unless further evidence developed.

Respondent then brought suit in the Federal District Court, challenging the constitutionality of the statute insofar as it criminalized consensual sodomy. He asserted that he was a practicing homosexual, that the Georgia sodomy statute, as administered by the defendants, placed him in imminent danger of arrest, and that the statute for several reasons violates the Federal Constitution. . . .

This case does not require a judgment on whether laws against sodomy between consenting adults in general, or between homosexuals in particular, are wise or desirable. It raises no question about the right or propriety of state legislative decisions to repeal their laws that criminalize homosexual sodomy, or of the state-court decisions invalidating those laws on state constitutional grounds. The issue presented is whether the Federal Constitution confers a fundamental right upon homosexuals to engage in sodomy and hence invalidates the laws of the many States that still make such conduct illegal and have done so for a very long time. The case also calls for some judgment about the limits of the Court's role in carrying out its constitutional mandate.

We first register our disagreement with the Court of Appeals and with respondent that the Court's prior cases have construed the Constitution to confer a right of privacy that extends to homosexual sodomy and for all intents and purposes have decided this case. . . . [Three] cases were interpreted as construing the Due Process Clause of the Fourteenth Amendment to confer a fundamental individual right to decide whether or not to beget or bear a child. . . .

Accepting the decisions in these cases . . . we think it evident that none of the rights announced in those cases bears any resemblance to the claimed constitutional right of homosexuals to engage in acts of sodomy that is asserted in this case. No connection between family, marriage, or procreation on the one hand and homosexual activity on the other has been demonstrated, either by the Court of Appeals or by respondent. Moreover, any claim that these cases nevertheless stand for the proposition that any kind of private sexual conduct between consenting adults is constitutionally insulated from state proscription is unsupportable. . . .

Precedent aside, however, respondent would have us announce, as the Court of Appeals did, the fundamental right to engage in homosexual sodomy. This we are quite unwilling to do. It is true that despite the language of the Due Process Clauses of the Fifth and Fourteenth Amendments, which appears to focus only on the processes by which life, liberty, or property is taken, the cases are legion in which those Clauses have been interpreted to have substantive content, subsuming rights that to a great extent are immune from federal or state regulation or proscription. Among such cases are those recognizing rights that have little or no textual support in the constitutional language. . . .

Striving to assure itself and the public that announcing rights not readily identifiable in the Constitution's text involves much more than the imposition of the Justices' own choice of values on the States and the Federal Government, the Court has sought to identify the nature of the rights qualifying for heightened judicial protection. In *Palko v. Connecticut,* . . . it was said that this category includes those fundamental liberties that are "implicit in the concept of ordered liberty," such that "neither liberty nor justice would exist if [they] were sacrificed." A different description of fundamental liberties appeared in *Moore v. East Cleveland,* . . .

where they are characterized as those liberties that are "deeply rooted in this Nation's history and tradition." . . .

It is obvious to us that neither of these formulations would extend a fundamental right to homosexuals to engage in acts of consensual sodomy. Proscriptions against that conduct have ancient roots. . . . Sodomy was a criminal offense at common law and was forbidden by the laws of the original thirteen States when they ratified the Bill of Rights. In 1868, when the Fourteenth Amendment was ratified, all but 5 of the 37 States in the Union had criminal sodomy laws. In fact, until 1961, all 50 States outlawed sodomy, and today, 24 states and the District of Columbia continue to provide criminal penalties for sodomy performed in private and between consenting adults. . . . Against this background, to claim that a right to engage in such conduct is "deeply rooted in this Nation's history and tradition" or "implicit in the concept of ordered liberty" is, at best, facetious.

Nor are we included to take a more expansive view of our authority to discover new fundamental rights imbedded in the Due Process Clause. The Court is most vulnerable and comes nearest to illegitimacy when it deals with judge-made constitutional law having little or no cognizable roots in the language or design of the Constitution. That this is so was painfully demonstrated by the face-off between the Executive and the Court in the 1930's, which resulted in the repudiation of much of the substantive gloss that the Court had placed on the Due Process Clauses of the Fifth and Fourteenth Amendments. There should be, therefore, great resistance to expand the substantive reach of those Clauses, particularly if it requires redefining the category of rights deemed to be fundamental. Otherwise, the Judiciary necessarily takes to itself further authority to govern the country without express constitutional authority. The claimed right pressed on us today falls far short of overcoming this resistance.

Respondent, however, asserts that the result should be different where the homosexual conduct occurs in the privacy of the home. He relies on *Stanley v. Georgia,* . . . where the court held that the First Amendment prevents conviction for possessing and reading obscene material in the privacy of one's home: "If the First Amendment means anything, it means that a State has no business telling a man, sitting alone in his house, what books he may read or what films he may watch." . . .

Stanley did protect conduct that would not have been protected outside the home, and it partially prevented the enforcement of the state obscenity laws; but the decision was firmly grounded in the First Amendment. The right pressed upon us here has no similar support in the text of the Constitution, and it does not qualify for recognition under the prevailing principles of construing the Fourteenth Amendment. Its limits are also difficult to discern. Plainly enough, otherwise illegal conduct is not always immunized whenever it occurs in the home. Victimless crimes, such as the possession and use of illegal drugs, do not escape the law where they are committed at home. *Stanley* itself recognized that its holding offered no protection for the possession in the home of drugs, firearms, or stolen goods. . . . And if respondent's submission is limited to the voluntary sexual conduct between consenting adults, it would be difficult, except by fiat, to limit the claimed right to homosexual conduct while leaving exposed to prosecution adultery, incest, and other sexual crimes even though they are committed in the home. We are unwilling to start down that road.

Even if the conduct at issue here is not a fundamental right, respondent asserts that there must be a rational basis for the law and that there is none in this case other than the presumed belief of a majority of the electorate in Georgia that homosexual sodomy is immoral and unacceptable. This is said to be an inadequate rationale to support the law. The law, however, is constantly based on notions of morality, and if all laws representing essentially moral choices are to be invalidated under the Due Process Clause, the courts will be very busy indeed. Even respondent makes no such claim, but insists that majority sentiments about the morality of homosexuality should be declared inadequate. We do not agree, and are unpersuaded that the sodomy laws of some 25 States should be invalidated on this basis.

Accordingly, the judgment of the Court of Appeals is

Reversed.

CHIEF JUSTICE BURGER, concurring.

I join the Court's opinion, but I write separately to underscore my view that in constitutional terms there is no such thing as a fundamental right to commit homosexual sodomy.

As the Court notes, . . . the proscriptions against sodomy have very "ancient roots." Decisions of individuals relating to homosexual conduct have been subject to state intervention throughout the history of Western civilization. Condemnation of those practices is firmly rooted in Judeo-Christian moral and ethical standards. Homosexual sodomy was a capital crime under Roman law. . . . During the English Reformation when powers of the ecclesiastical courts were transferred to the King's Courts, the first English statute criminalizing sodomy was passed. . . . Blackstone described "the infamous *crime against nature*" as an offense of "deeper malignity" than rape, a heinous act "the very mention of which is a disgrace to human nature," and "ac rime not fit to be named." . . . The common law of England, including its prohibition of sodomy, became the received law of Georgia and the other Colonies. In 1816 the Georgia Legislature passed the statute at issue here, and that statute has been continuously in force in one form or another since that time. To hold that the act of homosexual sodomy is somehow protected as a fundamental right would be to cast aside millennia of moral teaching.

This is essentially not a question of personal "preferences" but rather of the legislative authority of the State. I find nothing in the Constitution depriving a State of the power to enact the statute challenged here. . . .

JUSTICE BLACKMUN, with whom JUSTICE BRENNAN, JUSTICE MARSHALL, and JUSTICE STEVENS join, dissenting.

This case is no more about a "fundamental right to engage in homosexual sodomy," as the Court purports to declare, . . . than *Stanley v. Georgia* . . . was about a fundamental right to watch obscene movies, or *Katz v. United States,* . . . was about a fundamental right to place interstate bets from a telephone booth. Rather, this case is about "the most comprehensive of rights and the right most valued by civilized men," namely, "the right to be let alone." . . .

The statute at issue, . . . denies individuals the right to decide for themselves whether to engage in particular forms of private, consensual sexual activity. The Court concludes that [the statute] is valid essentially because "the laws of . . . many States . . . still make such conduct illegal and have done so for a very long time." . . . But the fact that the moral judgments expressed by statutes like . . . [the Georgia statute] may be " 'natural and familiar . . . ought not to conclude our judgment upon the question whether statutes embodying them conflict with the Constitution of the United States.' " . . . Like Justice Holmes, I believe that "[i]t is revolting to have no better reason for a rule of law than that so it was laid down in the time of Henry IV. It is still more revolting if the grounds upon which it was laid down have vanished long since, and the rule simply persists from blind imitation of the past." . . . I believe we must analyze Hardwick's claim in the light of the values that underlie the constitutional right to privacy. If that right means anything, it means that, before Georgia can prosecute its citizens for making choices about the most intimate aspects of their lives, it must do more than assert that the choice they have made is an " 'abominable crime not fit to be named among Christians.' ". . .

In its haste to reverse the Court of Appeals and hold that the Constitution does not confe[r] a fundamental right upon homosexuals to engage in sodomy," . . . the Court relegates the actual statute being challenged to a footnote and ignores the procedural posture of the case before it. A fair reading of the statute and of the complaint clearly reveals that the majority has distorted the question this case presents.

. . . [T]he Court's almost obsessive focus on homosexual activity is particularly hard to justify in light of the broad language Georgia has used. Unlike the Court, the Georgia Legislature has not proceeded on the assumption that homosexuals are so different from other citizens that their lives may be controlled in a way that would not be tolerated if it limited the choices of those other citizens. . . . Rather, Georgia has provided that "[a] person commits the offense of sodomy when he performs or submits to any sexual act involving the sex organs of one person and the mouth or anus of another." . . . The sex or status of the persons who engage in the act is irrelevant as a matter of state law. In fact, to the extent I can discern a legislative purpose for Georgia's 1968 enactment . . . that purpose seems to have been to broaden the coverage of the law to reach heterosexual as well as homosexual activity. I therefore see no basis for the Court's decision to treat this case . . . solely on the grounds that it prohibits homosexual activity. Michael Hardwick's standing may rest in significant part on Georgia's apparent willingness to enforce against homosexuals a law it seems not to have any desire to enforce against heterosexuals. . . . But his claim that . . . [the Georgia statute] involves an unconstitutional intrusion into his privacy and his right of intimate association does not depend in any way on his sexual orientation. . . .

"Our cases long have recognized that the Constitution embodies a promise that a certain private sphere of individual liberty will be kept largely beyond the reach of government." . . . In construing the right to privacy, the Court has proceeded along two somewhat distinct, albeit complementary, lines. First, it has recognized a privacy interest with reference to certain *decisions* that are properly for the individual to make. . . . Second, it has recognized a privacy interest with reference to certain *places* without regard for the particular activities in which the individuals who occupy them are engaged. . . . The case before us implicates both the decisional and the spatial aspects of the right to privacy.

The Court concludes today that none of our prior cases dealing with various decisions that individuals are entitled to make free of governmental interference "bears any resemblance to the claimed constitutional right of homosexuals to engage in acts of sodomy that is asserted in this case." . . . While it is true that these cases may be characterized by their connection to protection of the family, . . . the Court's conclusion that they extend no further than this boundary ignores the warning in *Moore v. East Cleveland,* . . . against "clos[ing] our eyes to the basic reasons why certain rights associated with the family have been accorded shelter under the Fourteenth Amendment's Due Process Clause." We protect those rights not because they contribute, in some direct and material way, to the general public welfare, but because they form so central a part of an individual's life. "[T]he concept of privacy embodies the 'moral fact that a person belongs to himself and not others nor to society as a whole.' " . . . And so we protect the decision whether to marry precisely because marriage "is an association that promotes a way of life, not causes; a harmony in living, not political faiths; a bilateral loyalty, not commercial or social projects." . . . We protect the decision whether to have a child because parenthood alters so dramatically an individual's self-definition, not because of demographic considerations or the Bible's command to be fruitful and multiply. . . . And we protect the family because it contributes so powerfully to the happiness of individuals, not because of a preference for stereotypical households. . . . The Court recognized in *Roberts* . . . that the "ability independently to define one's identity is central to any concept of liberty" cannot truly be exercised in a vacuum; we all depend on the "emotional enrichment from close ties with others."

Only the most willful blindness could obscure the fact that sexual intimacy is "a sensitive, key relationship of human existence, central to family life, community welfare, and the development of human personality," . . . The fact that individuals define themselves in a significant way through their intimate sexual relationships with others suggests, in a Nation as diverse as ours, that there may be many "right" ways of conducting those relationships, and that much of the richness of a relationship will come from the freedom an individual has to *choose* the form and nature of these intensely personal bonds. . . .

In a variety of circumstances we have recognized that a necessary corollary of giving individuals freedom to choose how to conduct their lives is acceptance of the fact that different individuals will make different choices. For example, in holding that the clearly important state interest in public education should give way to a competing claim by the Amish to the effect that extended formal schooling threatened their way of life, the Court declared: "There can be no assumption that today's majority is 'right' and the Amish and others like them are 'wrong.' A way of life that is odd or even erratic but interferes with no rights or interests of others is not to be condemned because it is different." . . . The Court claims that its decision today merely refuses to recognize a fundamental right to engage in homosexual sodomy; what the Court really has

refused to recognize is the fundamental interest all individuals have in controlling the nature of their intimate associations with others.

The behavior for which Hardwick faces prosecution occurred in his own home, a place to which the Fourth Amendment attaches special significance. The Court's treatment of this aspect of the case is symptomatic of its overall refusal to consider the broad principles that have informed our treatment of privacy in specific cases. Just as the right to privacy is more than a mere aggregation of a number of entitlements to engage in specific behavior, so too, protecting the physical integrity of the home is more than merely a means of protecting specific activities that often take place there. Even when our understanding of the contours of the right to privacy depends on "reference to a 'place,'" . . . "the essence of a Fourth Amendment violation is 'not the breaking of [a person's] doors, and the rummaging of his drawers,' but rather is 'the invasion of his indefeasible right of personal security, personal liberty and private property.'" . . .

The Court's interpretation of the pivotal case of *Stanley v. Georgia*, . . . is entirely unconvincing. *Stanley* held that Georgia's undoubted power to punish the public distribution of constitutionally unprotected, obscene material did not permit the State to punish the private possession of such material. According to the majority here, *Stanley* relied entirely on the First Amendment, and thus, it is claimed, sheds no light on cases not involving printed materials. . . . But that is not what *Stanley* said. Rather, the *Stanley* Court anchored its holding in the Fourth Amendment's special protection for the individual in his home:

" 'The makers of our Constitution undertook to secure conditions favorable to the pursuit of happiness. They recognized the significance of man's spiritual nature, of his feelings and of his intellect. They knew that only a part of the pain, pleasure and satisfactions of life are to be found in material things. They sought to protect Americans in their beliefs, their thoughts, their emotions and their sensations.'

"These are the rights that appellant is asserting in the case before us. He is asserting the right to read or observe what he pleases— the right to satisfy his intellectual and emotional needs in the privacy of his own home." . . . quoting *Olmstead v. United States* . . .

The central place that *Stanley* gives Justice Brandeis' dissent in *Olmstead,* a case raising *no* First Amendment claim, shows that *Stanley* rested as much on the Court's understanding of the Fourth Amendment as it did on the matter how uncomfortable a certain group may make the majority of this Court, we have held that "[m]ere public intolerance or animosity cannot constitutionally justify the deprivation of a person's physical liberty." . . .

. . . Reasonable people may differ about whether particular sexual acts are moral or immoral, but "we have ample evidence for believing that people will not abandon morality, will not think any better of murder, cruelty and dishonesty, merely because some private sexual practice which they abominate is not punished by the law." . . . Petitioner and the Court fail to see the difference between laws that protect public sensibilities and those that enforce private morality. Statutes banning public sexual activity are entirely consistent with protecting the individual's liberty interest in decisions concerning sexual relations: the same recognition that those decisions are intensely private which justifies protecting them from governmental interference can justify protecting individuals from unwilling exposure to the sexual activities of others. But the mere fact that intimate behavior may be punished when it takes place in public cannot dictate how States can regulate intimate behavior that occurs in intimate places. . . .

This case involves no real interference with the rights of others, for the mere knowledge that other individuals do not adhere to one's value system cannot be a legally cognizable interest, . . . let alone an interest that can justify invading the houses, hearts, and minds of citizens who choose to live their lives differently.

. . . I can only hope that . . . the Court soon will reconsider its analysis and conclude that depriving individuals of the right to choose for themselves how to conduct their intimate relationships poses a far greater threat to the values most deeply rooted in our Nation's history than tolerance of nonconformity could ever do. Because I think the Court today betrays those values, I dissent.

Discussion Questions

1. Present and explain Justice White's opinion that homosexual sodomy is not protected by the right to privacy. Do you agree or disagree with the case he supports? Explain and defend your answer.
2. Present and explain former Chief Justice Burger's concurring opinion. Do you agree with the former Chief Justice that millennia of moral condemnation of homosexual sodomy counts against its permissibility? Explain and defend your answer.
3. Present and explain Justice Blackmun's dissenting opinion. Do you agree with Justice Blackmun's claim that the right to privacy entails the right to do anything in the privacy of one's home as long as it does not interfere with another's freedom? Explain and defend your answer.

You can locate InfoTrac-College Education articles about this chapter by accessing the InfoTrac-College Edition website (http://www.infotrac-college.com/wadsworth/). Using the InfoTrac-College Edition subject guide, enter the search terms relevant to this chapter, and then read abstracts for relevant articles.

43   Romer v. Evans (1996)

U.S. SUPREME COURT*

In this decision the U.S. Supreme Court ruled that the state of Colorado could not prohibit the state or any of its jurisdictions from granting protected status to homosexuals. Groups that have protected status are those such as African Americans and women. Society has tried to remedy the discrimination they have suffered by the use of such public policies as antidiscrimination laws, affirmative-action policies, and special scholarships to government schools. The Court in its decision overturned Colorado's Amendment 2, which had been passed by referendum in 1992 with 54 percent of the popular vote. The Colorado ballot contained the following question: "Shall there be an amendment to Article II of the Colorado Constitution to prohibit the state of Colorado and any of its political subdivisions from adopting or enforcing any law or policy that provides that homosexual, lesbian, or bisexual orientation or conduct, or relationships, constitutes or entitles a person to claim any minority or protected status, quota preference or discrimination?" The Court's majority opinion, written by Justice Anthony Kennedy (in which he is joined by Justices Sandra Day O'Connor, David Souter, Stephen Breyer, and Ruth Bader Ginsburg), maintains that Amendment 2 is unconstitutional because it violates the Equal Protection Clause of the Fourteenth Amendment. Kennedy draws this conclusion because the Colorado amendment singled out homosexuals as an identifiable group and denied them the opportunity to receive special protections. Thus gays were denied equal protection under the law since other groups, such as minorities, women, and the handicapped, were still permitted to enact statutes to receive special protections. This is why Justice Kennedy cites Justice John Marshall Harlan's famous dissent from the separate-but-equal case, *Plessy v. Ferguson* (1896): the Constitution "neither knows nor tolerates classes among citizens." Kennedy comments: "Unheeded then, those words now are understood to state a commitment to the law's neutrality where the rights of persons are at stake." And because the Colorado amendment, according to Kennedy, had no rational basis, it raises "the inevitable inference that the disadvantage is born of animosity toward the class of persons affected."

In his dissenting opinion (in which he is joined by Justice Clarence Thomas and Chief Justice William Rehnquist), Justice Antonin Scalia takes on Justice Kennedy's argument. Justice Scalia argues that Colorado's law has a rational basis, is not inconsistent with the Fourteenth Amendment's Equal Protection Clause (he cites prior case law in defense of this including *Bowers v. Hardwick* [Chapter 42] and cases that upheld antipolygamy statutes), and that the Court ought not to take a position in the "culture wars," but ought to leave the resolution of such disputes to democratic institutions (e.g., legislatures, Congress).

Most citations and all footnotes omitted.

JUSTICE KENNEDY delivered the opinion of the Court.

One century ago, the first Justice Harlan admonished this Court that the Constitution "neither knows nor tolerates classes among citizens." Plessy v. Ferguson, (1896) (dissenting opinion). Unheeded then, those words now are understood to state a commitment to the law's neutrality where the rights of persons are at stake. The Equal Protection Clause enforces this principle and today requires us to hold invalid a provision of Colorado's Constitution.

I

The enactment challenged in this case is an amendment to the Constitution of the State of Colorado, adopted in a 1992 statewide referendum. The parties and the state courts refer to it as "Amendment 2," its designation when submitted to the voters. The impetus for the amendment and the contentious campaign that preceded its adoption came in large part from ordinances that had been passed in various Colorado municipalities. For example, the cities of Aspen and Boulder and the city and County of Denver each had enacted ordinances which banned discrimination in many transactions and activities, including housing, employment, education, public accommodations, and health and welfare services. What gave rise to the statewide controversy was the protection the ordinances afforded to persons discriminated against by reason of their sexual orientation. Amendment 2 repeals these ordinances to the extent they prohibit discrimination on the basis of "homosexual, lesbian or bisexual orientation, conduct, practices or relationships."

Yet Amendment 2, in explicit terms, does more than repeal or rescind these provisions. It prohibits all legislative, executive or judicial action at any level of state or local government designed to protect the named class, a class we shall refer to as homosexual persons or gays and lesbians. The amendment reads:

"No Protected Status Based on Homosexual, Lesbian or Bisexual Orientation. Neither the State of Colorado, through any of its branches or departments, nor any of its agencies, political subdivisions, municipalities or school districts, shall enact, adopt or enforce any statute, regulation, ordinance or policy whereby homosexual, lesbian or bisexual orientation, conduct, practices or relationships shall constitute or otherwise be the basis of or entitle any person or class of persons to have or claim any minority status, quota preferences, protected status or claim of discrimination. This Section of the Constitution shall be in all respects self-executing."

Soon after Amendment 2 was adopted, this litigation to declare its invalidity and enjoin its enforcement was commenced in the District Court for the City and County of Denver. Among the plaintiffs (respondents here) were homosexual persons, some of them government employees. They alleged that enforcement of Amendment 2 would subject them to immediate and substantial risk of discrimination on the basis of their sexual orientation. Other plaintiffs (also respondents here) included the three municipalities whose ordinances we have cited and certain other governmental entities which had acted earlier to protect homosexuals from discrimination but would be prevented by Amendment 2 from continuing to do so. Although Governor Romer had been on record opposing the adoption of Amendment 2, he was named in his official capacity as a defendant, together with the Colorado Attorney General and the State of Colorado.

The trial court granted a preliminary injunction to stay enforcement of Amendment 2, and an appeal was taken to the Supreme Court of Colorado. Sustaining the interim injunction and remanding the case for further proceedings, the State Supreme Court held that Amendment 2 was subject to strict scrutiny under the Fourteenth Amendment because it infringed the fundamental right of gays and lesbians to participate in the political process. To reach this conclusion, the state court relied on our voting rights cases e.g., Reynolds v. Sims, (1964); Carrington v. Rash, (1965); Harper v. Virginia Bd. of Elections, (1966); Williams v. Rhodes, (1968), and on our precedents involving discriminatory restructuring of governmental decisionmaking, see, e.g., Hunter v. Erickson, (1969); Reitman v. Mulkey, (1967); Washington v. Seattle School Dist. No. 1, (1982); Gordon v. Lance, (1971). On remand, the State advanced various arguments in an effort to show that Amendment 2 was narrowly tailored to serve compelling interests, but the trial court found none sufficient. It enjoined enforcement of Amendment 2, and the Supreme Court of Colorado, in a second opinion, affirmed the ruling. We granted certiorari, and now affirm the judgment, but on a rationale different from that adopted by the State Supreme Court.

II

The State's principal argument in defense of Amendment 2 is that it puts gays and lesbians in the same position as all other persons. So, the State says, the measure does no more than deny homosexuals special rights. This reading of the amendment's language is implausible. We rely not upon our own interpretation of the amendment but upon the authoritative construction of Colorado's Supreme Court. The state court, deeming it unnecessary to determine the full extent of the amendment's reach, found it invalid even on a modest reading of its implications. The critical discussion of the amendment, is as follows:

"The immediate objective of Amendment 2 is, at a minimum, to repeal existing statutes, regulations, ordinances, and policies of state and local entities that barred discrimination based on sexual orientation. . . .

The 'ultimate effect' of Amendment 2 is to prohibit any governmental entity from adopting similar, or more protective statutes, regulations, ordinances, or policies in the future unless the state constitution is first amended to permit such measures."

Sweeping and comprehensive is the change in legal status effected by this law. So much is evident from the ordinances the Colorado Supreme Court declared would be void by operation of Amendment 2. Homosexuals, by state decree, are put in a solitary class with respect to transactions and relations in both the private and governmental spheres. The amendment withdraws from homosexuals, but no others, specific legal protection from the injuries caused by discrimination, and it forbids reinstatement of these laws and policies.

The change Amendment 2 works in the legal status of gays and lesbians in the private sphere is far reaching, both on its own terms and when considered in light of the structure and operation of modern anti-discrimination laws. That structure is well illustrated by contemporary statutes and ordinances prohibiting discrimination by providers of public accommodations. "At common law, innkeepers, smiths, and others who 'made profession of a public employment,' were prohibited from refusing, without good reason, to serve a customer." Hurley v. Irish-American Gay, Lesbian and Bisexual Group of Boston, Inc., (1995). The duty was a general one and did not specify protection for particular groups. The common-law rules, however, proved insufficient in many instances, and it was settled early that the Fourteenth Amendment did not give Congress a general power to prohibit discrimination in public accommodations. . . . In consequence, most States have chosen to counter discrimination by enacting detailed schemes.

Colorado's state and municipal laws typify this emerging tradition of statutory protection and follow a consistent pattern. The laws first enumerate the persons or entities subject to a duty not to discriminate. The list goes well beyond the entities covered by the common law. The Boulder ordinance, for example, has a comprehensive definition of entities deemed places of "public accommodation." They include "any place of business engaged in any sales to the general public and any place that offers services, facilities, privileges, or advantages to the general public or that receives financial support through solicitation of the general public or through governmental subsidy of any kind." Boulder Rev. Code § 12-1-1(j) (1987). The Denver ordinance is of similar breadth, applying, for example, to hotels, restaurants, hospitals, dental clinics, theaters, banks, common carriers, travel and insurance agencies, and "shops and stores dealing with goods or services of any kind," Denver Rev. Municipal Code, Art. IV, § 28-92 (1991).

These statutes and ordinances also depart from the common law by enumerating the groups or persons within their ambit of protection. Enumeration is the essential device used to make the duty not to discriminate concrete and to provide guidance for those who must comply. In following this approach, Colorado's state and local governments have not limited antidiscrimination laws to groups that have so far been given the protection of heightened equal protection scrutiny under our cases. Rather, they set forth an extensive catalog of traits which cannot be the basis for discrimination, including age, military status, marital status, pregnancy, parenthood, custody of a minor child, political affiliation, physical or mental disability of an individual or of his or her associates—and, in recent times, sexual orientation.

Amendment 2 bars homosexuals from securing protection against the injuries that these public-accommodations laws address. That in itself is a severe consequence, but there is more. Amendment 2, in addition, nullifies specific legal protections for this targeted class in all transactions in housing, sale of real estate, insurance, health and welfare services, private education, and employment.

Not confined to the private sphere, Amendment 2 also operates to repeal and forbid all laws or policies providing specific protection for gays or lesbians from discrimination by every level of Colorado government. The State Supreme Court cited two examples of protections in the governmental sphere that are now rescinded and may not be reintroduced. The first is Colorado Executive Order D0035 (1990), which forbids employment discrimination against " 'all state employees, classified and exempt' on the basis of sexual orientation." Also repealed, and now forbidden, are "various provisions prohibiting discrimination based on sexual orientation at state colleges." The repeal of these measures and the prohibition against their future reenactment demonstrate that Amendment 2 has the same force and effect in Colorado's governmental sector as it does elsewhere and that it applies to policies as well as ordinary legislation.

Amendment 2's reach may not be limited to specific laws passed for the benefit of gays and lesbians. It is a fair, if not necessary, inference from the broad language of the amendment that it deprives gays and lesbians even of the protection of general laws and policies that prohibit arbitrary discrimination in governmental and private settings. At some point in the systematic administration of these laws, an official must determine whether homosexuality is an arbitrary and, thus, forbidden basis for decision. Yet a decision to that effect would itself amount to a policy prohibiting discrimination on the basis of homosexuality, and so would appear to be no more valid under Amendment 2 than the specific prohibitions against discrimination the state court held invalid.

If this consequence follows from Amendment 2, as its broad language suggests, it would compound the constitutional difficulties the law creates. The state court did not decide whether the amendment has this effect, however, and neither need we. In the course of rejecting the argument that Amendment 2 is intended to conserve resources to fight discrimination against suspect classes, the Colorado Supreme Court made the limited observation that the amendment is not intended to affect many anti-discrimination laws protecting nonsuspect classes. In our view that does not resolve the issue. In any event, even if, as we doubt, homosexuals could find some safe harbor in laws of general application, we cannot accept the view that Amendment 2's prohibition on specific legal protections does no more than deprive homosexuals of special rights. To the contrary, the amendment imposes a special disability upon those persons alone. Homosexuals are forbidden the safeguards that others enjoy or may seek without constraint. They can obtain specific protection against discrimination only by enlisting the citizenry of Colorado to amend the State Constitution or perhaps, on the State's view, by trying to pass helpful laws of general applicability. This is so no matter how local or discrete the harm, no matter how public and widespread the injury. We find nothing special in the protections Amendment 2 withholds. These are protections taken for granted by most people either because they already have them or do not need them; these are protections against exclusion from an almost limitless number of transactions and endeavors that constitute ordinary civic life in a free society.

III

The Fourteenth Amendment's promise that no person shall be denied the equal protection of the laws must coexist with the practical necessity that most legislation classifies for one purpose or another, with resulting disadvantage to various groups or persons. We have attempted to reconcile the principle with the reality by stating that, if a law neither burdens a fundamental right nor targets a suspect class, we will uphold the legislative classification so long as it bears a rational relation to some legitimate end.

Amendment 2 fails, indeed defies, even this conventional inquiry. First, the amendment has the peculiar property of imposing a broad and undifferentiated disability on a single named group, an exceptional and, as we shall explain, invalid form of legislation. Second, its sheer breadth is so discontinuous with the reasons offered for it that the amendment seems inexplicable by anything but animus toward the class it affects; it lacks a rational relationship to legitimate state interests.

Taking the first point, even in the ordinary equal protection case calling for the most deferential of standards, we insist on knowing the relation between the classification adopted and the object to be attained. The search for the link between classification and objective gives substance to the Equal Protection Clause; it provides guidance and discipline for the legislature, which is entitled to know what sorts of laws it can pass; and it marks the limits of our own authority. In the ordinary case, a law will be sustained if it can be said to advance a legitimate government interest, even if the law seems unwise or works to the disadvantage of a particular group, or if the rationale for it seems tenuous. The laws challenged in the cases just cited were narrow enough in scope and grounded in a sufficient factual context for us to ascertain some relation between the classification and the purpose it served. By requiring that the classification bear a rational relationship to an independent and legitimate legislative end, we ensure that classifications are not drawn for the purpose of disadvantaging the group burdened by the law.

Amendment 2 confounds this normal process of judicial review. It is at once too narrow and too broad. It identifies persons by a single trait and then denies them protection across the board. The resulting disqualification of a class of persons from the right to seek specific protection from the law is unprecedented in our jurisprudence. The absence of precedent for Amendment 2 is itself instructive; "[d]iscriminations of an unusual character especially suggest careful consideration to determine whether they are obnoxious to the constitutional provision." Louisville Gas & Elec. Co. v. Coleman, (1928).

It is not within our constitutional tradition to enact laws of this sort. Central both to the idea of the rule of law and to our own Constitution's guarantee of equal protection is the principle that government and each of its parts remain open on impartial terms to all who seek its assistance. " 'Equal protection of the laws is not achieved through indiscriminate imposition of inequalities.' " Sweatt v. Painter, (1950) (quoting Shelley v. Kraemer (1948)). Respect for this principle explains why laws singling out a certain class of citizens for disfavored legal status or general hardships are rare. A law declaring that in general it shall be more difficult for one group of citizens than for all others to seek aid from the government is itself a denial of equal protection of the laws in the most literal sense. "The guaranty of 'equal protection of the laws is a pledge of the protection of equal laws.' " Skinner v. Oklahoma (1942) (quoting Yick Wo v. Hopkins, (1886)).

Davis v. Beason, (1890), not cited by the parties but relied upon by the dissent, is not evidence that Amendment 2 is within our constitutional tradition, and any reliance upon it as authority for sustaining the amendment is misplaced. In Davis, the Court approved an Idaho territorial statute denying Mormons, polygamists, and advocates of polygamy the right to vote and to hold office because, as the Court construed the statute, it "simply excludes from the privilege of voting, or of holding any office of honor, trust or profit, those who have been convicted of certain offences, and those who advocate a practical resistance to the laws of the Territory and justify and approve the commission of crimes forbidden by it." To the extent Davis held that persons advocating a certain practice may be denied the right to vote, it is no longer good law. Brandenburg v. Ohio (1969) (per curiam). To the extent it held that the groups designated in the statute may be deprived of the right to vote because of their status, its ruling could not stand without surviving strict scrutiny, a most doubtful outcome. Dunn v. Blumstein, (1972); cf. United States v. Brown, (1965); United States v. Robel, (1967). To the extent Davis held that a convicted felon may be denied the right to vote, its holding is not implicated by our decision and is unexceptionable.

A second and related point is that laws of the kind now before us raise the inevitable inference that the disadvantage imposed is born of animosity toward the class of persons affected. "[I]f the constitutional conception of 'equal protection of the laws' means anything, it must at the very least mean that a bare . . . desire to harm a politically unpopular group cannot constitute a legitimate governmental interest." Department of Agriculture v. Moreno, (1973). Even laws enacted for broad and ambitious purposes often can be explained by reference to legitimate public policies which justify the incidental disadvantages they impose on certain persons. Amendment 2, however, in making a general announcement that gays and lesbians shall not have any particular protections from the law, inflicts on them immediate, continuing, and real injuries that outrun and belie any legitimate justifications that may be claimed for it. We conclude that, in addition to the far-reaching deficiencies of Amendment 2 that we have noted, the principles it offends, in another sense, are conventional and venerable; a law must bear a rational relationship to a legitimate governmental purpose, Kadrmas v.

Dickinson Public Schools, (1988), and Amendment 2 does not.

The primary rationale the State offers for Amendment 2 is respect for other citizens' freedom of association, and in particular the liberties of landlords or employers who have personal or religious objections to homosexuality. Colorado also cites its interest in conserving resources to fight discrimination against other groups. The breadth of the amendment is so far removed from these particular justifications that we find it impossible to credit them. We cannot say that Amendment 2 is directed to any identifiable legitimate purpose or discrete objective. It is a status-based enactment divorced from any factual context from which we could discern a relationship to legitimate state interests; it is a classification of persons undertaken for its own sake, something the Equal Protection Clause does not permit. . . .

We must conclude that Amendment 2 classifies homosexuals not to further a proper legislative end but to make them unequal to everyone else. This Colorado cannot do. A State cannot so deem a class of persons a stranger to its laws. Amendment 2 violates the Equal Protection Clause, and the judgment of the Supreme Court of Colorado is affirmed.

It is so ordered.

JUSTICE SCALIA, with whom THE CHIEF JUSTICE and JUSTICE THOMAS join, dissenting.

The Court has mistaken a Kulturkampf for a fit of spite. The constitutional amendment before us here is not the manifestation of a " 'bare . . . desire to harm' " homosexuals, but is rather a modest attempt by seemingly tolerant Coloradans to preserve traditional sexual mores against the efforts of a politically powerful minority to revise those mores through use of the laws. That objective, and the means chosen to achieve it, are not only unimpeachable under any constitutional doctrine hitherto pronounced (hence the opinion's heavy reliance upon principles of righteousness rather than judicial holdings); they

have been specifically approved by the Congress of the United States and by this Court.

In holding that homosexuality cannot be singled out for disfavorable treatment, the Court contradicts a decision, unchallenged here, pronounced only 10 years ago, see Bowers v. Hardwick, (1986), and places the prestige of this institution behind the proposition that opposition to homosexuality is as reprehensible as racial or religious bias. Whether it is or not is precisely the cultural debate that gave rise to the Colorado constitutional amendment (and to the preferential laws against which the amendment was directed). Since the Constitution of the United States says nothing about this subject, it is left to be resolved by normal democratic means, including the democratic adoption of provisions in state constitutions. This Court has no business imposing upon all Americans the resolution favored by the elite class from which the Members of this institution are selected, pronouncing that "animosity" toward homosexuality is evil. I vigorously dissent.

Let me first discuss Part II of the Court's opinion, its longest section, which is devoted to rejecting the State's arguments that Amendment 2 "puts gays and lesbians in the same position as all other persons," and "does no more than deny homosexuals special rights." The Court concludes that this reading of Amendment 2's language is "implausible" under the "authoritative construction" given Amendment 2 by the Supreme Court of Colorado.

In reaching this conclusion, the Court considers it unnecessary to decide the validity of the State's argument that Amendment 2 does not deprive homosexuals of the "protection [afforded by] general laws and policies that prohibit arbitrary discrimination in governmental and private settings." I agree that we need not resolve that dispute, because the Supreme Court of Colorado has resolved it for us. In the case below, the Colorado court stated: "[I]t is significant to note that Colorado law currently proscribes discrimination against persons who are not suspect classes, including discrimination based on age; marital or family status; veterans' status; and for any legal, off-duty conduct such as smoking tobacco. Of course Amendment 2 is not intended to have any effect on this legislation, but seeks only to prevent the adoption of antidiscrimination laws intended to protect gays, lesbians, and bisexuals."

The Court utterly fails to distinguish this portion of the Colorado court's opinion. Colorado Rev. Stat. § 24-34-402.5 (Supp. 1995), which this passage authoritatively declares not to be affected by Amendment 2, was respondents' primary example of a generally applicable law whose protections would be unavailable to homosexuals under Amendment 2. The clear import of the Colorado court's conclusion that it is not affected is that "general laws and policies that prohibit arbitrary discrimination" would continue to prohibit discrimination on the basis of homosexual conduct as well. This analysis, which is fully in accord with (indeed, follows inescapably from) the text of the constitutional provision, lays to rest such horribles, raised in the course of oral argument, as the prospect that assaults upon homosexuals could not be prosecuted. The amendment prohibits special treatment of homosexuals, and nothing more. It would not affect, for example, a requirement of state law that pensions be paid to all retiring state employees with a certain length of service; homosexual employees, as well as others, would be entitled to that benefit. But it would prevent the State or any municipality from making death-benefit payments to the "life partner" of a homosexual when it does not make such payments to the long-time roommate of a nonhomosexual employee. Or again, it does not affect the requirement of the State's general insurance laws that customers be afforded coverage without discrimination unrelated to anticipated risk. Thus, homosexuals could not be denied coverage, or charged a greater premium, with respect to auto collision insurance; but neither the State nor any municipality could require that distinctive health insurance risks associated with homosexuality (if there are any) be ignored.

Despite all of its hand wringing about the potential effect of Amendment 2 on general antidiscrimination laws, the Court's opinion ultimately does not dispute all this, but assumes it to be true. The only denial of equal treatment it contends homosexuals have suffered is this: They may not obtain preferential treatment without amending the State Constitution. That is to say, the principle underlying the Court's opinion is that one who is accorded equal treatment under the laws, but cannot as readily as others obtain preferential treatment under the laws, has been denied equal protection of the laws. If merely stating this alleged "equal protection" violation does not suffice to refute it, our constitutional jurisprudence has achieved terminal silliness.

The central thesis of the Court's reasoning is that any group is denied equal protection when, to obtain advantage (or, presumably, to avoid disadvantage), it must have recourse to a more general and hence more difficult level of political decisionmaking than others. The world has never heard of such a principle, which is why the Court's opinion is so long on emotive utterance and so short on relevant legal citation. And it seems to me most unlikely that any multilevel democracy can function under such a principle. For whenever a disadvantage is imposed, or conferral of a benefit is prohibited, at one of the higher levels of democratic decisionmaking (i.e., by the state legislature rather than local government, or by the people at large in the state constitution rather than the legislature), the affected group has (under this theory) been denied equal protection. To take the simplest of examples, consider a state law prohibiting the award of municipal contracts to relatives of mayors or city councilmen. Once such a law is passed, the group composed of such relatives must, in order to get the benefit of city contracts, persuade the state legislature—unlike all other citizens, who need only persuade the municipality. It is ridiculous to consider this a denial of equal protection, which is why the Court's theory is unheard of.

The Court might reply that the example I have given is not a denial of equal protection only because the same "rational basis" (avoidance of corruption) which renders constitutional the substantive discrimination against relatives (i.e., the fact that they alone cannot obtain city contracts) also automatically suffices to sustain what might be called the electoral-procedural discrimination against them (i.e., the fact that they must go to the state level to get this changed). This is of course a perfectly reasonable response, and would explain why "electoral-procedural discrimination" has not hitherto been heard of: A law that is valid in its substance is automatically valid in its level of enactment. But the Court cannot afford to make this argument, for as I shall discuss next, there is no doubt of a rational basis for the substance of the prohibition at issue here. The Court's entire novel theory rests upon the proposition that there is something special—something that cannot be justified by normal "rational basis" analysis—in making a disadvantaged group (or a nonpreferred group) resort to a higher decisionmaking level. That proposition finds no support in law or logic.

II

I turn next to whether there was a legitimate rational basis for the substance of the constitutional amendment—for the prohibition of special protection for homosexuals. It is unsurprising that the Court avoids discussion of this question, since the answer is so obviously yes. The case most relevant to the issue before us today is not even mentioned in the Court's opinion: In Bowers v. Hardwick, (1986), we held that the Constitution does not prohibit what virtually all States had done from the founding of the Republic until very recent years—making homosexual conduct a crime. That holding is unassailable, except by those who think that the Constitution changes to suit current fashions. But in any event it is a given in the present case: Respondents' briefs did not urge overruling Bowers, and at oral argument respondents' counsel expressly disavowed any intent to seek such overruling. If it is constitutionally permissible for a State to make homosexual conduct criminal, surely it is constitutionally permissible for a State to enact other laws merely disfavoring homosexual conduct. (As the Court of Appeals for the District of Columbia Circuit has aptly put it: "If the Court [in Bowers] was unwilling to object to state laws that criminalize the behavior that defines the class, it is hardly open . . . to conclude that state sponsored discrimination against the class is invidious. After all, there can hardly be more palpable discrimination against a class than making the conduct that defines the class criminal." Padula v. Webster, (1987).) And a fortiori it is constitutionally permissible for a State to adopt a provision not even disfavoring homosexual conduct, but merely prohibiting all levels of state government from bestowing special protections upon homosexual conduct. Respondents (who, unlike the Court, cannot afford the luxury of ignoring inconvenient precedent) counter Bowers with the argument that a greater-includes-the-lesser rationale cannot justify Amendment 2's application to individuals who do not engage in homosexual acts, but are merely of homosexual "orientation." Some Courts of Appeals have concluded that, with respect to laws of this sort at least, that is a distinction without a difference. . . .

But assuming that, in Amendment 2, a person of homosexual "orientation" is someone who does not engage in homosexual conduct but merely has a tendency or desire to do so, Bowers still suffices to establish a rational basis for the provision. If it is rational to criminalize the conduct, surely it is rational to deny special favor and protection to those with a self-avowed tendency or desire to engage in the conduct. Indeed, where criminal sanctions are not involved, homosexual "orientation" is an acceptable stand-in for homosexual conduct. A State "does not violate the Equal Protection Clause merely because the classifications made by its laws are imperfect," Dandridge v. Williams, (1970). Just as a policy barring the hiring of methadone users as transit employees does not violate equal protection simply because some methadone users pose no threat to passenger safety, see New York City Transit Authority v. Beazer, 59 (1979), and just as a mandatory retirement age of 50 for police officers does not violate equal protection even though it prematurely ends the careers of many policemen over 50 who still have the capacity to do the job, see Massachusetts Bd. of Retirement v. Murgia, (1976) (per curiam), Amendment 2 is not constitutionally invalid simply because it could have been drawn more precisely so as to withdraw special antidiscrimination protections only from those of homosexual "orientation" who actually engage in homosexual conduct. As Justice KENNEDY wrote, when he was on the Court of Appeals, in a case involving discharge of homosexuals from the Navy: "Nearly any statute which classifies people may be irrational as applied in particular cases. Discharge of the particular plaintiffs before us would be rational, under minimal scrutiny, not because their particular cases present the dangers which justify Navy policy, but instead because the general policy of discharging all homosexuals is rational." Beller v. Middendorf (C.A.9 1980) (citation omitted).

Moreover, even if the provision regarding homosexual "orientation" were invalid, respondents' challenge to Amendment 2—which is a facial challenge—must fail. "A facial challenge to a legislative Act is, of course, the most difficult challenge to mount successfully, since the challenger must establish that no set of circumstances exists under which the Act

would be valid." United States v. Salerno, (1987). It would not be enough for respondents to establish (if they could) that Amendment 2 is unconstitutional as applied to those of homosexual "orientation"; since, under Bowers, Amendment 2 is unquestionably constitutional as applied to those who engage in homosexual conduct, the facial challenge cannot succeed. Some individuals of homosexual "orientation" who do not engage in homosexual acts might successfully bring an as-applied challenge to Amendment 2, but so far as the record indicates, none of the respondents is such a person. . . .

The foregoing suffices to establish what the Court's failure to cite any case remotely in point would lead one to suspect: No principle set forth in the Constitution, nor even any imagined by this Court in the past 200 years, prohibits what Colorado has done here. But the case for Colorado is much stronger than that. What it has done is not only unprohibited, but eminently reasonable, with close, congressionally approved precedent in earlier constitutional practice.

First, as to its eminent reasonableness. The Court's opinion contains grim, disapproving hints that Coloradans have been guilty of "animus" or "animosity" toward homosexuality, as though that has been established as un-American. Of course it is our moral heritage that one should not hate any human being or class of human beings. But I had thought that one could consider certain conduct reprehensible— murder, for example, or polygamy, or cruelty to animals—and could exhibit even "animus" toward such conduct. Surely that is the only sort of "animus" at issue here: moral disapproval of homosexual conduct, the same sort of moral disapproval that produced the centuries-old criminal laws that we held constitutional in Bowers. The Colorado amendment does not, to speak entirely precisely, prohibit giving favored status to people who are homosexuals; they can be favored for many reasons—for example, because they are senior citizens or members of racial minorities. But it prohibits giving them favored status because of their homosexual conduct—that is, it prohibits favored status for homosexuality.

But though Coloradans are, as I say, entitled to be hostile toward homosexual conduct, the fact is that the degree of hostility reflected by Amendment 2 is the smallest conceivable. The Court's portrayal of Coloradans as a society fallen victim to pointless, hate-filled "gay-bashing" is so false as to be comical. Colorado not only is one of the 25 States that have repealed their antisodomy laws, but was among the first to do so. But the society that eliminates criminal punishment for homosexual acts does not necessarily abandon the view that homosexuality is morally wrong and socially harmful; often, abolition simply reflects the view that enforcement of such criminal laws involves unseemly intrusion into the intimate lives of citizens. . . .

There is a problem, however, which arises when criminal sanction of homosexuality is eliminated but moral and social disapprobation of homosexuality is meant to be retained. The Court cannot be unaware of that problem; it is evident in many cities of the country, and occasionally bubbles to the surface of the news, in heated political disputes over such matters as the introduction into local schools of books teaching that homosexuality is an optional and fully acceptable "alternative life style." The problem (a problem, that is, for those who wish to retain social disapprobation of homosexuality) is that, because those who engage in homosexual conduct tend to reside in disproportionate numbers in certain communities, have high disposable income, and, of course, care about homosexual-rights issues much more ardently than the public at large, they possess political power much greater than their numbers, both locally and statewide. Quite understandably, they devote this political power to achieving not merely a grudging social toleration, but full social acceptance, of

homosexuality. See, e.g., Jacobs, The Rhetorical Construction of Rights: The Case of the Gay Rights Movement, 1969–1991, 72 Neb. L.Rev. 723, 724 (1993) ("[T]he task of gay rights proponents is to move the center of public discourse along a continuum from the rhetoric of disapproval, to rhetoric of tolerance, and finally to affirmation").

By the time Coloradans were asked to vote on Amendment 2, their exposure to homosexuals' quest for social endorsement was not limited to newspaper accounts of happenings in places such as New York, Los Angeles, San Francisco, and Key West. Three Colorado cities—Aspen, Boulder, and Denver—had enacted ordinances that listed "sexual orientation" as an impermissible ground for discrimination, equating the moral disapproval of homosexual conduct with racial and religious bigotry. The phenomenon had even appeared statewide: The Governor of Colorado had signed an executive order pronouncing that "in the State of Colorado we recognize the diversity in our pluralistic society and strive to bring an end to discrimination in any form," and directing state agency-heads to "ensure non-discrimination" in hiring and promotion based on, among other things, "sexual orientation." I do not mean to be critical of these legislative successes; homosexuals are as entitled to use the legal system for reinforcement of their moral sentiments as is the rest of society. But they are subject to being countered by lawful, democratic countermeasures as well.

That is where Amendment 2 came in. It sought to counter both the geographic concentration and the disproportionate political power of homosexuals by (1) resolving the controversy at the statewide level, and (2) making the election a single-issue contest for both sides. It put directly, to all the citizens of the State, the question: Should homosexuality be given special protection? They answered no. The Court today asserts that this most democratic of procedures is unconstitutional. Lacking any cases to establish that facially absurd proposition, it simply asserts that it must be unconstitutional, because it has never happened before. "[Amendment 2] identifies persons by a single trait and then denies them protection across the board. The resulting disqualification of a class of persons from the right to seek specific protection from the law is unprecedented in our jurisprudence. The absence of precedent for Amendment 2 is itself instructive. . . .

It is not within our constitutional tradition to enact laws of this sort. Central both to the idea of the rule of law and to our own Constitution's guarantee of equal protection is the principle that government and each of its parts remain open on impartial terms to all who seek its assistance."

As I have noted above, this is proved false every time a state law prohibiting or disfavoring certain conduct is passed, because such a law prevents the adversely affected group—whether drug addicts, or smokers, or gun owners, or motorcyclists—from changing the policy thus established in "each of [the] parts" of the State. What the Court says is even demonstrably false at the constitutional level. The Eighteenth Amendment to the Federal Constitution, for example, deprived those who drank alcohol not only of the power to alter the policy of prohibition locally or through state legislation, but even of the power to alter it through state constitutional amendment or federal legislation. The Establishment Clause of the First Amendment prevents theocrats from having their way by converting their fellow citizens at the local, state, or federal statutory level; as does the Republican Form of Government Clause prevent monarchists.

But there is a much closer analogy, one that involves precisely the effort by the majority of citizens to preserve its view of sexual morality statewide, against the efforts of a geographically concentrated and politically powerful minority to undermine it. The Constitutions of the States of Arizona, Idaho, New Mexico,

Oklahoma, and Utah to this day contain provisions stating that polygamy is "forever prohibited." Polygamists, and those who have a polygamous "orientation," have been "singled out" by these provisions for much more severe treatment than merely denial of favored status; and that treatment can only be changed by achieving amendment of the state constitutions. The Court's disposition today suggests that these provisions are unconstitutional, and that polygamy must be permitted in these States on a state-legislated, or perhaps even local-option, basis—unless, of course, polygamists for some reason have fewer constitutional rights than homosexuals.

The United States Congress, by the way, required the inclusion of these antipolygamy provisions in the Constitutions of Arizona, New Mexico, Oklahoma, and Utah, as a condition of their admission to statehood. (For Arizona, New Mexico, and Utah, moreover, the Enabling Acts required that the antipolygamy provisions be "irrevocable without the consent of the United States and the people of said State"—so that not only were "each of [the] parts" of these States not "open on impartial terms" to polygamists, but even the States as a whole were not; polygamists would have to persuade the whole country to their way of thinking.) Idaho adopted the constitutional provision on its own, but the 51st Congress, which admitted Idaho into the Union, found its Constitution to be "republican in form and . . . in conformity with the Constitution of the United States." Thus, this "singling out" of the sexual practices of a single group for statewide, democratic vote—so utterly alien to our constitutional system, the Court would have us believe—has not only happened, but has received the explicit approval of the United States Congress.

I cannot say that this Court has explicitly approved any of these state constitutional provisions; but it has approved a territorial statutory provision that went even further, depriving polygamists of the ability even to achieve a constitutional amendment, by depriving them of the power to vote. In Davis v. Beason, (1890), Justice Field wrote for a unanimous Court:

> "In our judgment, § 501 of the Revised Statutes of Idaho Territory, which provides that 'no person . . . who is a bigamist or polygamist or who teaches, advises, counsels, or encourages any person or persons to become bigamists or polygamists, or to commit any other crime defined by law, or to enter into what is known as plural or celestial marriage, or who is a member of any order, organization or association which teaches, advises, counsels, or encourages its members or devotees or any other persons to commit the crime of bigamy or polygamy, or any other crime defined by law . . . is permitted to vote at any election, or to hold any position or office of honor, trust, or profit within this Territory,' is not open to any constitutional or legal objection."

To the extent, if any, that this opinion permits the imposition of adverse consequences upon mere abstract advocacy of polygamy, it has, of course, been overruled by later cases. See Brandenburg v. Ohio, (1969) (per curiam). But the proposition that polygamy can be criminalized, and those engaging in that crime deprived of the vote, remains good law. See Richardson v. Ramirez, (1974). Beason rejected the argument that "such discrimination is a denial of the equal protection of the laws." Among the Justices joining in that rejection were the two whose views in other cases the Court today treats as equal protection lodestars—Justice Harlan, who was to proclaim in Plessy v. Ferguson, (1896) (dissenting opinion), that the Constitution "neither knows nor tolerates classes among citizens," and Justice Bradley, who had earlier declared that "class legislation . . . [is] obnox-

ious to the prohibitions of the Fourteenth Amendment." . . .

*651 This Court cited Beason with approval as recently as 1993, in an opinion authored by the same Justice who writes for the Court today. That opinion said: "[A]dverse impact will not always lead to a finding of impermissible targeting. For example, a social harm may have been a legitimate concern of government for reasons quite apart from discrimination. . . . See, e.g., . . . Davis v. Beason, (1890)." Church of Lukumi Babalu Aye, Inc. v. Hialeah, (1993). It remains to be explained how § 501 of the Idaho Revised Statutes was not an "impermissible targeting" of polygamists, but (the much more mild) Amendment 2 is an "impermissible targeting" of homosexuals. Has the Court concluded that the perceived social harm of polygamy is a "legitimate concern of government," and the perceived social harm of homosexuality is not?

IV

I strongly suspect that the answer to the last question is yes, which leads me to the last point I wish to make: The Court today, announcing that Amendment 2 "defies . . . conventional [constitutional] inquiry," and "confounds [the] normal process of judicial review," employs a constitutional theory heretofore unknown to frustrate Colorado's reasonable effort to preserve traditional American moral values. The Court's stern disapproval of "animosity" towards homosexuality might be compared with what an earlier Court (including the revered Justices Harlan and Bradley) said in Murphy v. Ramsey, (1885), rejecting a constitutional challenge to a United States statute that denied the franchise in federal territories to those who engaged in polygamous cohabitation:

> "[C]ertainly no legislation can be supposed more wholesome and necessary in the founding of a free, self-governing commonwealth, fit

to take rank as one of the co-ordinate States of the Union, than that which seeks to establish it on the basis of the idea of the family, as consisting in and springing from the union for life of one man and one woman in the holy estate of matrimony; the sure foundation of all that is stable and noble in our civilization; the best guaranty of that reverent morality which is the source of all beneficent progress in social and political improvement."

I would not myself indulge in such official praise for heterosexual monogamy, because I think it no business of the courts (as opposed to the political branches) to take sides in this culture war.

But the Court today has done so, not only by inventing a novel and extravagant constitutional doctrine to take the victory away from traditional forces, but even by verbally disparaging as bigotry adherence to traditional attitudes. To suggest, for example, that this constitutional amendment springs from nothing more than " 'a bare . . . desire to harm a politically unpopular group,' " is nothing short of insulting. (It is also nothing short of preposterous to call "politically unpopular" a group which enjoys enormous influence in American media and politics, and which, as the trial court here noted, though composing no more than 4% of the population had the support of 46% of the voters on Amendment 2. . . .)

When the Court takes sides in the culture wars, it tends to be with the knights rather than the villeins—and more specifically with the Templars, reflecting the views and values of the lawyer class from which the Court's Members are drawn. How that class feels about homosexuality will be evident to anyone who wishes to interview job applicants at virtually any of the Nation's law schools. The interviewer may refuse to offer a job because the applicant is a Republican; because he is an adulterer; because he went to the wrong prep school or belongs to the wrong country club; because he eats snails; because he is a womanizer; because she wears real-animal fur; or even because he hates the Chicago Cubs. But if the interviewer should wish not to be an associate or partner of an applicant because he disapproves of the applicant's homosexuality, then he will have violated the pledge which the Association of American Law Schools requires all its member schools to exact from job interviewers: "assurance of the employer's willingness" to hire homosexuals. This law-school view of what "prejudices" must be stamped out may be contrasted with the more plebeian attitudes that apparently still prevail in the United States Congress, which has been unresponsive to repeated attempts to extend to homosexuals the protections of federal civil rights laws, and which took the pains to exclude them specifically from the Americans with Disabilities Act of 1990.

Today's opinion has no foundation in American constitutional law, and barely pretends to. The people of Colorado have adopted an entirely reasonable provision which does not even disfavor homosexuals in any substantive sense, but merely denies them preferential treatment. Amendment 2 is designed to prevent piecemeal deterioration of the sexual morality favored by a majority of Coloradans, and is not only an appropriate means to that legitimate end, but a means that Americans have employed before. Striking it down is an act, not of judicial judgment, but of political will. I dissent.

Discussion Questions

1. Present and explain Justice Kennedy's argument that Amendment 2 violates the Equal Protection Clause of the Fourteenth Amendment. Do you agree or disagree with his argument? Explain and defend your answer.

2. Justice Kennedy claims that there is no "rational basis" for Amendment 2. How does he defend this claim. Do you think he is correct or incorrect? Explain and defend your answer.

3. Present and explain Justice Scalia's dissenting opinion. Do you agree or disagree with his argument? Explain and defend your answer.

4. Suppose that a religious homeowner, Mr. Saint, in the fictional city of Anytown, Colorado, places an advertisement in his local newspaper announcing that he is looking for a married couple to rent a room in his home. Mr. Saint is a friendly man, who is well-liked and well-known in his community for his generous and caring spirit. But he is also known as a devout religious man who believes that sexual relations are sacred and should only be practiced by a man and a woman within the confines of marriage. Suppose that based on Anytown's antidiscrimination ordinance (which includes a provision that forbids discrimination based on sexual orientation), Anytown's District Attorney decides to prosecute Mr. Saint on the grounds that his advertisement discriminates, because "married couple" excludes cohabitating singles, both heterosexual and homosexual. Given the Supreme Court's majority opinion in *Romer,* do you think that Mr. Saint's attorney could argue that Anytown's antidiscrimination ordinance discriminates *against* Mr. Saint and his First Amendment right to free exercise of religion? If so, support your position by proposing an argument. If not, explain and defend your answer.with the case he supports? Explain and defend your answer.

You can locate InfoTrac-College Education articles about this chapter by accessing the InfoTrac-College Edition website (http://www.infotrac-college.com/wadsworth/). Using the InfoTrac-College Edition subject guide, enter the search terms relevant to this chapter, and then read abstracts for relevant articles.

D2

Homosexuality and the Morality of Discrimination

Gay Basics: Some Questions, Facts, and Values   44

RICHARD D. MOHR

Richard D. Mohr is Professor of Philosophy at the University of Illinois–Urbana, specializing in ancient Greek thought. He has published widely in scholarly publications on the issue of homosexual rights. He is the author of the book *Gay/Justice: A Study of Ethics, Society, and Law* (1988).

In this essay, Professor Mohr defends the morality of homosexuality as well as the legal rights of homosexuals. He does this by dealing with four different areas of concern: (1) the "immorality" of homosexuality, (2) the "unnaturalness" of homosexuality, (3) the question of whether homosexuals freely choose the way they are, and (4) how society at large would be changed if homosexuals were socially accepted. Concerning the first area, Professor Mohr concludes that those who oppose homosexuality, although persuasively showing that homosexuality has been condemned by certain religious people and societies throughout history, have not shown that it is immoral in a prescriptive or a normative sense. In answer to the question of whether homosexuality is "unnatural," Mohr argues that the natural/unnatural distinction is ambiguous and in some cases presupposes a certain religious worldview, which would mean that such an opposition to homosexual behavior would be religiously based and a violation of the First Amendment if

Reprinted by permission from The Right Thing to Do: Basic Readings in Moral Philosophy, *ed. James Rachels (New York: Random House, 1989).*

made law. Concerning the fourth area, Professor Mohr maintains that although it is inconclusive as to whether homosexuality has a genetic component, he does not believe that homosexuality is a matter of "choice." He argues that once one begins to act in accordance with one's orientation (either homosexual or heterosexual), then one is on the road to personal well-being, hardly an immoral goal. In response to the question of how society would be changed if homosexuality were socially accepted, Mohr maintain that society would be richer, more open, and more just, extending its notion of family to include homosexual unions rather than threatening (as some detractors claim) the existence of the traditional family.

I. BUT AREN'T THEY IMMORAL?

MANY PEOPLE THINK SOCIETY'S treatment of gays is justified because they think gays are extremely immoral. To evaluate this claim, different senses of "moral" must be distinguished. Sometimes by "morality" is meant the overall beliefs affecting behavior in a society—its mores, norms, and customs. On this understanding, gays certainly are not moral: lots of people hate them and social customs are designed to register widespread disapproval of gays. The problem here is that this sense of morality is merely a *descriptive* one. On this understanding *every* society has a morality—even Nazi society, which had racism and mob rule as central features of its "morality," understood in this sense. What is needed in order to use the notion of morality to praise or condemn behavior is a sense of morality that is *prescriptive* or *normative*—a sense of morality whereby, for instance, the descriptive morality of the Nazis is found wanting.

As the Nazi example makes clear, that something is descriptively moral is nowhere near enough to make it normatively moral. A lot of people in a society saying something is good, even over eons, does not make it so. Our rejection of the long history of socially approved and state-enforced slavery is another good example of this principle at work. Slavery would be wrong even if nearly everyone liked it. So consistency and fairness require that we

abandon the belief that gays are immoral simply because most people dislike or disapprove of gays or gay acts, or even because gay sex acts are illegal.

Furthermore, recent historical and anthropological research has shown that opinion about gays has been by no means universally negative. Historically, it has varied widely even within the larger part of the Christian era and even within the church itself.[1] There are even societies—current ones—where homosexuality is not only tolerated but a universal compulsory part of social maturation.[2] Within the last thirty years, American society has undergone a grand turnabout from deeply ingrained, near total condemnation to near total acceptance on two emotionally charged "moral" or "family" issues: contraception and divorce. Society holds its current descriptive morality of gays not because it has to, but because it chooses to.

If popular opinion and custom are not enough to ground moral condemnation of homosexuality, perhaps religion can. Such argument proceeds along two lines. One claims that the condemnation is a direct revelation of God, usually through the Bible; the other claims to be able to detect condemnation in God's plan as manifested in nature.

One of the more remarkable discoveries of recent gay research is that the Bible may not be as univocal in its condemnation of homosexuality as has been usually believed.[3] Christ never mentions homosexuality. Recent interpreters of the Old Testament have pointed out that the story of Lot at Sodom is probably intended to condemn inhospitality rather than homosexuality. Further, some of the Old Testament condemnations of homosexuality seem simply to be ways of tarring those of the Israelites' opponents who happened to accept homosexual practices when the Israelites themselves did not. If so, the condemnation is merely a quirk of history and rhetoric rather than a moral precept.

What does seem clear is that those who regularly cite the Bible to condemn an activity like homosexuality do so by reading it selectively. Do ministers who cite what they take to be condemnations of homosexuality in Leviticus maintain in their lives all the hygienic and dietary laws of Leviticus? If they cite the story of Lot at Sodom to condemn homosexuality, do they also cite the story of Lot in the cave to praise incestuous rape? It seems then not that the Bible is being used to ground condemnation of homosexuality as much as society's dislike of homosexuality is being used to interpret the Bible.[4]

Even if a consistent portrait of condemnation could be gleaned from the Bible, what social significance should it be given? One of the guiding principles of society, enshrined in the Constitution as a check against the government, is that decisions affecting social policy are not made on religious grounds. If the real ground of the alleged immorality invoked by governments to discriminate against gays is religious (as it has explicitly been even in some recent court cases involving teachers and guardians), then one of the major commitments of our nation is violated.

II. BUT AREN'T THEY UNNATURAL?

The most noteworthy feature of the accusation of something being unnatural (where a moral rather than an advertising point is being made) is that the plaint is so infrequently made. One used to hear the charge leveled against abortion, but that has pretty much faded as anti-abortionists have come to lay all their chips on the hope that people will come to view abortion as murder. Incest used to be considered unnatural but discourse now usually assimilates it to the moral machinery of rape and violated trust. The charge comes up now in ordinary discourse only against homosexuality. This suggests that the charge is highly idiosyncratic and has little, if any, explanatory force. It fails to put homosexuality in a class with anything else so that one can learn by comparison with clear cases of the class just exactly what it is that is allegedly wrong with it.

Though the accusation of unnaturalness looks whimsical, in actual ordinary discourse when applied to homosexuality, it is usually delivered with venom aforethought. It carries a high emotional charge, usually expressing disgust and evincing queasiness. Probably it is nothing but an emotional charge. For people get equally disgusted and queasy at all sorts of things that are perfectly natural—to be expected in nature apart from artifice—and that could hardly be fit subjects for moral condemnation. Two typical examples in current American culture are some people's responses to mothers' suckling in public and to women who do not shave body hair. When people have strong emotional reactions, as they do in these cases, without being able to give good reasons for them, we think of them not as operating morally, but rather as being obsessed and manic. So the feelings of disgust that some people have to gays will hardly ground a charge of immorality. People fling the term "unnatural" against gays in the same breath and with the same force as when they call gays "sick" and "gross." When they do this, they give every appearance of being neurotically fearful and incapable of reasoned discourse.

When "nature" is taken in *technical* rather than ordinary usages, it looks like the notion also will not ground a charge of homosexual immorality. When unnatural means "by artifice" or "made by humans," it need only be pointed out that virtually everything that is good about life is unnatural in this sense, that the chief feature that distinguishes people from other animals is their very ability to make over the world to meet their needs and desires, and that their well-being depends upon these departures from nature. On this understanding of human nature and the natural, homosexuality is perfectly unobjectionable.

Another technical sense of natural is that something is natural and so, good, if it fulfills some function in nature. Homosexuality on this view is unnatural because it allegedly violates the function of genitals, which is to produce babies. One problem with this view is that lots of bodily parts have lots of functions and just because some one activity can be fulfilled by only one organ (say, the mouth for eating) this activity does not condemn other functions of the organ to immorality (say, the mouth for talking, licking stamps, blowing bubbles, or having sex). So the possible use of the genitals to produce children does not, without more, condemn the use of the genitals for other purposes, say, achieving ecstasy and intimacy.

The functional view of nature will only provide a morally condemnatory sense to the unnatural if a thing which might have many uses has but one proper function to the exclusion of other possible functions. But whether this is so cannot be established simply by looking at the thing. For what is seen is all its possible functions. The notion of function seemed like it might ground moral authority, but instead it turns out that moral authority is needed to define proper function. Some people try to fill in this moral authority by appeal to the "design" or "order" of an organ, saying, for instance, that the genitals are designed for the purpose of procreation. But these people cheat intellectually if they do not make explicit *who* the designer and orderer is. If it is God, we are back to square one—holding others accountable for religious beliefs.

Further, ordinary moral attitudes about childbearing will not provide the needed supplement which in conjunction with the natural function view of bodily parts would produce a positive obligation to use the genitals for procreation. Society's attitude toward a childless couple is that of pity not censure—even if the couple could have children. The pity may be an unsympathetic one, that is, not registering a course one would choose *for oneself*, but this does not make it a course one would *require* of others. The couple who discovers they cannot have children are viewed not as having thereby had a debt canceled, but rather as having to forgo some of the richness of life, just as a quadriplegic is viewed not as absolved from some moral obligation to hop, skip, and jump, but as missing some of the richness of life. Consistency requires then that, at most, gays who do not or cannot have children are to be pitied rather than condemned. What *is* immoral is the willful preventing of people from achieving the richness of life. Immorality in this regard lies with those social customs, regulations, and statutes that prevent lesbians and gay men from establishing blood or adoptive families, not with gays themselves.

Sometimes people attempt to establish authority for a moral obligation to use bodily parts in a certain fashion simply by claiming that moral laws are natural laws and vice versa. On this account, inanimate objects and plants are good in that they follow natural laws by necessity, animals by instinct, and persons by a rational will. People are special in that they must first discover the laws that govern them. Now, even if one believes the view—dubious in the post-Newtonian, post-Darwinian world—that natural laws in the usual sense ($E = mc^2$, for instance) have some moral content, it is not at all clear how one is to discover the laws in nature that apply to people.

On the one hand, if one looks to people themselves for a model—and looks hard enough—one finds amazing variety, including homosexuality as a social ideal (upper-class fifth-century Athens) and even as socially mandatory (Melanesia today). When one looks to people, one is simply unable to strip away the layers of social custom, history, and taboo in order to see what's really there to any degree more specific than that people are the creatures that make over their world and are capable of abstract thought. That this is so should raise doubts that neutral principles are to be found in human nature that will condemn homosexuality.

On the other hand, if one looks to nature apart from people for models, the possibilities are staggering. There are fish that change gender over their lifetimes: should we "follow nature" and be operative transsexuals? Orangutans, genetically our next of kin, live completely solitary lives without social organization of any kind: ought we to "follow nature" and be hermits? There are many species where only two members per generation reproduce: should we be bees? The search in nature for people's purpose, far from finding sure models for action, is likely to leave one morally rudderless.

III. BUT AREN'T GAYS WILLFULLY THE WAY THEY ARE?

It is generally conceded that if sexual orientation is something over which an individual—for whatever reason—has virtually no control, then discrimination against gays is especially deplorable, as it is against racial and ethnic classes, because it holds people accountable without regard for anything they themselves have done. And to hold a person accountable for that over which the person has no control is a central form of prejudice.

Attempts to answer the question whether or not sexual orientation is something that is reasonably thought to be within one's own control usually appeal simply to various claims of the biological or "mental" sciences. But the ensuing debate over genes, hormones, twins, early childhood development, and the like, is

as unnecessary as it is currently inconclusive.[5] All that is needed to answer the question is to look at the actual experience of gays in current society and it becomes fairly clear that sexual orientation is not likely a matter of choice. For coming to have a homosexual identity simply does not have the same sort of structure that decision making has.

On the one hand, the "choice" of the gender of a sexual partner does not seem to express a trivial desire that might be as easily well fulfilled by a simple substitution of the desired object. Picking the gender of a sex partner is decidedly dissimilar, that is, to such activities as picking the flavor of ice cream. If an ice-cream parlor is out of one flavor, one simply picks another. And if people were persecuted, threatened with jail terms, shattered careers, loss of family and housing, and the like, for eating, say, rocky road ice cream, no one would ever eat it; everyone would pick another easily available flavor. That gay people abide in being gay even in the face of persecution shows that being gay is not a matter of easy choice.

On the other hand, even if establishing a sexual orientation is not like making a relatively trivial choice, perhaps it is nevertheless relevantly like making the central and serious life choices by which individuals try to establish themselves as being of some type. Again, if one examines gay experience, this seems not to be the case. For one never sees anyone setting out to become a homosexual, in the way one does see people setting out to become doctors, lawyers, and bricklayers. One does not find "gays-to-be" picking some end—"At some point in the future, I want to become a homosexual"—and then setting about planning and acquiring the ways and means to that end, in the way one does see people deciding that they want to become lawyers, and then sees them plan what courses to take and what sort of temperaments, habits, and skills to develop in order to become lawyers. Typically gays-to-be simply find themselves having homosexual encounters and yet initially resisting quite strongly the identification of being homosexual. Such a person even very likely resists having such encounters, but ends up having them anyway. Only with time, luck, and great personal effort, but sometimes never, does the person gradually come to accept her or his orientation, to view it as a given material condition of life, coming as materials do with certain capacities and limitations. The person begins to act in accordance with his or her orientation and its capacities, seeing its actualization as a requisite for an integrated personality and as a central component of personal well-being. As a result, the experience of coming out to oneself has for gays the basic structure of a discovery, not the structure of a choice. And far from signaling immorality, coming out to others affirms one of the few remaining opportunities in ever more bureaucratic, mechanistic, and socialistic societies to manifest courage.

IV. HOW WOULD SOCIETY AT LARGE BE CHANGED IF GAYS WERE SOCIALLY ACCEPTED?

Suggestions to change social policy with regard to gays are invariably met with claims that to do so would invite the destruction of civilization itself: after all, isn't that what did Rome in? Actually Rome's decay paralleled not the flourishing of homosexuality but its repression under the later Christianized emperors.[6] Predictions of American civilization's imminent demise have been as premature as they have been frequent. Civilization has shown itself rather resilient here, in large part because of the country's traditional commitments to a respect for privacy, to individual liberties, and especially to people minding their own business. These all give society an open texture and the flexibility to try out things to see what works. And because of this one now need not speculate about what changes reforms in gay social policy might bring to society at large. For many reforms have already been tried.

Half the states have decriminalized homosexual acts. Can you guess which of the following states still have sodomy laws: Wisconsin, Minnesota; New Mexico, Arizona; Vermont, New Hampshire; Nebraska, Kansas. One from each pair does and one does not have sodomy laws. And yet one would be hard pressed to point out any substantial difference between the members of each pair. (If you're interested, it is the second of each pair with them.) Empirical studies have shown that there is no increase in other crimes in states that have decriminalized.[7] Further, sodomy laws are virtually never enforced. They remain on the books not to "protect society" but to insult gays, and for that reason need to be removed.

Neither has the passage of legislation barring discrimination against gays ushered in the end of civilization. Some 50 counties and municipalities, including some of the country's largest cities (like Los Angeles and Boston), have passed such statutes and among the states and colonies Wisconsin and the District of Columbia have model protective codes. Again, no more brimstone has fallen in these places than elsewhere. Staunchly anti-gay cities, like Miami and Houston, have not been spared the AIDS crisis.

Berkeley, California, has even passed domestic partner legislation giving gay couples the same rights to city benefits as married couples, and yet Berkeley has not become more weird than it already was.

Seemingly hysterical predictions that the American family would collapse if such reforms would pass proved false, just as the same dire predictions that the availability of divorce would lessen the ideal and desirability of marriage proved completely unfounded. Indeed if current discriminations, which drive gays into hiding and into anonymous relations, were lifted, far from seeing gays raze American families, one would see gays forming them.

Virtually all gays express a desire to have a permanent lover. Many would like to raise or foster children—perhaps those alarming numbers of gay kids who have been beaten up and thrown out of their "families" for being gay. But currently society makes gay coupling very difficult. A life of hiding is a pressure-cooker existence not easily shared with another. Members of non-gay couples are here asked to imagine what it would take to erase every trace of their own sexual orientation for even just one week.

Even against oppressive odds, gays have shown an amazing tendency to nest. And those gay couples who have survived the odds show that the structure of more usual couplings is not a matter of destiny but of personal responsibility. The so-called basic unit of society turns out not to be a unique immutable atom, but can adopt different parts, be adapted to different needs, and even be improved. Gays might even have a thing or two to teach others about division of labor, the relation of sensuality and intimacy, and stages of development in such relationships.

If discrimination ceased, gay men and lesbians would enter the mainstream of human community openly and with self-respect. The energies that the typical gay person wastes in the anxiety of leading a day-to-day existence of systematic disguise would be released for use in personal flourishing. From this release would be generated the many spinoff benefits that accrue to a society when its individual members thrive.

Society would be richer for acknowledging another aspect of human richness and diversity. Families with gay members would develop relations based on truth and trust rather than lies and fear. And the heterosexual majority would be better off for knowing that they are no longer trampling their gay friends and neighbors.

Finally and perhaps paradoxically, in extending to gays the rights and benefits it has reserved for its dominant culture, America would confirm its deeply held vision of itself as a morally progressive nation, a nation itself advancing and serving as a beacon for others—especially with regard to human rights. The words with which our national pledge ends—"with liberty and justice for all"—are not a description of the present but a call for the future. Ours is a nation given to a prophetic political rhetoric which acknowledges that morality is not arbitrary and that justice is not merely the expression of the current collective will. It is this vision that led the black civil rights movement to its successes. Those congressmen who opposed that movement and its centerpiece, the 1964 Civil Rights Act, on obscurantist grounds, but who lived long enough and were noble enough, came in time to express their heartfelt regret and shame at what they had done. It is to be hoped and someday to be expected that those who now grasp at anything to oppose the extension of that which is best about America to gays will one day feel the same.

NOTES

1. John Boswell, *Christianity, Social Tolerance and Homosexuality: Gay People in Western Europe from the Beginning of the Christian Era to the Fourteenth Century* (Chicago: University of Chicago Press, 1980).
2. See Gilbert Herdt, *Guardians of the Flute: Idioms of Masculinity* (New York: McGraw-Hill, 1981), pp. 232–239, 284–288; and see generally Gilbert Herdt, ed., *Ritualized Homosexuality in Melanesia* (Berkeley: University of California Press, 1984). For another eye-opener, see Walter L. Williams, *The Spirit and the Flesh: Sexual Diversity in American Indian Culture* (Boston: Beacon, 1986).
3. See especially Boswell, *Christianity,* ch. 4.
4. For Old Testament condemnations of homosexual acts, see Leviticus 18:22, 21:3. For hygienic and dietary codes, see, for example, Leviticus 15:19–27 (on the uncleanliness of women) and Leviticus 11:1–47 (on not eating rabbits, pigs, bats, finless water creatures,

legless creeping creatures, etc.). For Lot at Sodom, see Genesis 19:1–25. For Lot in the cave, see Genesis 19:30–38.

5. The preponderance of the scientific evidence supports the view that homosexuality is either genetically determined or a permanent result of early childhood development. See the Kinsey Institute's study by Alan Bell, Martin Weinberg, and Sue Hammersmith, *Sexual Preference: Its Development in Men and Women* (Bloomington: Indiana University Press, 1981); Frederick Whitam and Robin Mathy, *Male Homosexuality in Four Societies* (New York: Praeger, 1986), ch. 7.

6. See Boswell, *Christianity*, ch. 3.

7. See Gilbert Gels, "Reported Consequences of Decriminalization of Consensual Adult Homosexuality in Seven American States," *Journal of Homosexuality* 1, no. 4 (1976): 419–426; Ken Sinclair and Michael Ross, "Consequences of Decriminalization of Homosexuality: A Study of Two Australian States," *Journal of Homosexuality* 12, no. 1 (1985): 119–127.

Discussion Questions

1. Professor Mohr critiques the argument that homosexuality is immoral. Present and explain that argument, and then present and explain Professor Mohr's critique. Do you agree or disagree with his position? Explain and defend your answer.

2. Professor Mohr critiques the argument that homosexuality is unnatural. Present and explain that argument, and then present and explain Professor Mohr's critique. Do you agree or disagree with his position? Explain and defend your answer.

3. Professor Mohr maintains that picking the gender of one's sex partner is not something one "chooses" like one chooses a flavor of ice cream. Explain what he means by this analogy and how it ties into his view that homosexuality is not a choice. Also, why does Professor Mohr believe that if homosexuality is fully accepted by society, society will be better off? Do you agree or disagree with his assessment? Explain and defend your answer.

You can locate InfoTrac-College Education articles about this chapter by accessing the InfoTrac-College Edition website (http://www.infotrac-college.com/wadsworth/). Using the InfoTrac-College Edition subject guide, enter the search terms relevant to this chapter, and then read abstracts for relevant articles.

Homosexuality and the Common Good   45

MICHAEL PAKALUK

Michael Pakaluk is Associate Professor of Philosophy at Clark University in suburban Boston. He is the author of *Other Selves: Philosophers on Friendship* (1991) and translator of Aristotle's *Nicomachean Ethics: Books VIII and IX* (1999).

In this essay Professor Pakaluk argues that laws intending to prohibit discrimination against gays, including laws that permit same-sex marriage, "would undermine the family and society at large." He deals with four different types of legal changes: (1) the extension of civil rights antidiscrimination laws to include homosexuals; (2) the recognition of same-sex unions as equivalent to opposite-sex marriage; (3) the permitting of gay couples to become foster parents or adopt children; and (4) the eliminating of laws that prohibit sodomy. Pakaluk deals first with the last legal change. Although he believes that there may be prudential reasons for the legal change, he believes that the current political and social climate in the United States counts against it. Concerning changes 1 through 3, Professor Pakaluk argues that they are not merely changes in degree, that is, an expansion of our current rights and benefits to include gays, but rather, changes in kind. He makes his case for this conclusion by providing several reasons, among which are the following: (1) such changes will undermine the notion of the common good; (2) they will result in the state marginalizing and coercing those who have serious moral objections to homosexuality; (3) they are contingent on the belief that marriage and family are created by, and are not prior to, the state; (4) they depend on the belief that homosexuality has nothing to do with morality and character, a view, if implemented by the government, that would imply that the state promotes the shared belief that certain philosophical and religious positions (e.g., traditional Christianity, orthodox Judaism, and Islam) are mistaken; and (5) given the philosophical assumptions behind these proposed legal changes, it will likely lead to the belief that the state ought to raise people's children, for it is the state that creates the definition of "marriage" and "family" and it is unfair that only heterosexual couples have the natural means by which to procreate.

IT IS SOMETIMES CLAIMED that, if laws were uniformly changed to prohibit discrimination based upon sexual orientation or preference, or if same-sex partners were allowed by law to enter into contracts regarded as the equivalent of marriage and having similar privileges and rights, these changes would undermine the family and society at large. My purpose in this paper is to spell out some of the reasons why that claim is true, and what exactly the

Reprinted by permission from Homosexuality and American Public Life, *ed. Christopher Wolfe (Dallas, TX: Spence Publishing, 1999).*

claim means, that is, what the "undermining" of the family and society would amount to in this case.

We should acknowledge that the claim strikes many people, and not only "gay activists," as absurd. Fr. John F. Tuohey, described as being an assistant professor of moral theology at the Catholic University of America, provided a good example of this response in an article in *America* magazine.[1] Fr. Tuohey is criticizing a letter sent by the Vatican to American bishops, with the not very succinct title, "Some Considerations concerning the Catholic Response to Legislative Proposals on the Non-Discrimination of Homosexual Persons." That letter, echoing a 1986 Vatican document,[2] stated that "the view that homosexual activity is equivalent to, or as acceptable as, the sexual expression of conjugal love has a direct impact on society's understanding of the nature and rights of the family and puts them in jeopardy." Fr. Tuohey complains that "Nowhere does the statement attempt to show that recognizing the civil rights of gay and lesbian persons would harm the 'genuine' family or the common good." Indeed, "The absence of any evidence . . . that gay and lesbian persons pose a threat to society is easy to explain. No credible evidence exists. On the contrary, there is evidence to suggest exactly the opposite." He then describes the many contributions that homosexuals have made to their communities, implying that what they may do in private has no bearing on how they act as citizens and that, if so, they can hardly constitute any "threat" to anyone else.

Or, again, on a gay-activist web page, I encountered the following argument: "Giving gay couples the right to marry would not take away any of the rights heterosexual couples currently enjoy; it would only extend those rights and responsibilities to everyone in our society"—as if the proposed changes would only increase freedom, not limit it, and only add to the benefits people enjoy, not in any

way diminish them. But, if so, the changes would leave everything else intact: heterosexual couples and families could continue thriving and flourishing as much, or as little, as they were before. This is the way some people look at the matter, then, and any claims to the contrary strike them as exaggerated, even hysterical, and absurd.

Before proceeding, we should make clear the various sorts of legislative change that are at stake:

1. the extension of anti-discrimination laws, making it illegal to discriminate, especially in matters of housing or hiring, on the basis of sexual orientation or activity;
2. the legal recognition of same-sex couples as equivalent to marriage;
3. permitting same-sex couples to adopt or to serve as foster parents;
4. the repeal of anti-sodomy laws.

I want to say something about the last of these points in order to put the subject aside, since, although important, it is not my primary concern. In fact, the claim is *not* often made that repealing anti-sodomy laws would undermine the family or society. Although two dozen states presently retain anti-sodomy laws, it is not uncommon even for social conservatives to regard these laws as unwise and dispensable on the grounds that they are in general unenforceable.

But I think that view is a mistake. It is better to retain such laws where they exist, unless it were clear that they would be repealed as part of a what was a larger, *de facto* societal compromise, for anti-sodomy laws have a valuable function, even if they are unenforceable. First, they constitute a kind of link with the past, a link to society as it was *before* the sexual revolution, when our insight into matters sexual was clearer. We should retain such laws, then, as a kind of deference to the wisdom of the past. We accept them "on authority," so to speak, even if we do not directly grasp their point and force. And then, also, unenforceable laws may have the function of expressing a view and instructing: Anti-sodomy laws are an expression, in law, of the view that homosexual activity is inherently wrong—and that is the key truth that we have to preserve in the debates over each of the points I mentioned. Unenforceable or unenforced laws can also play an indirect role in deciding matters that *are* "enforceable." For example, in child custody decisions, it may become relevant that one parent rather than the other regularly engages in activity that is contrary to some unenforced law—the child then goes to the one who does *not* fornicate, or commit adultery, or engage in sodomy.

It is important not to acquiesce in *bad* reasons for repealing anti-sodomy laws, for instance, because they are argued to be excluded by an alleged constitutional right to privacy, or because they are claimed to be exceptions to Mill's harm principle. In fact, it is only if we hold that the state *could,* licitly and in principle, retain anti-sodomy laws, that we can then regard the repeal of such laws as an element in a stable compromise. John Finnis has referred, approvingly, to what he calls the "modern European consensus" on homosexuality, that is, the legal arrangement whereby, roughly, *private* homosexual acts are not proscribed, but public acts, and the public promotion of homosexuality, are proscribed. That arrangement, like indeed most stable social arrangements in which there are competing interests or desires, involves reciprocity: Society relinquishes legislation over homosexual acts in private, but those who engage in such acts relinquish any claim of right to them, which their public performance or advocacy would imply. Yet such an arrangement is not possible, once it is conceded, as it should not be, that society has no competence to legislate against homosexual acts in the first place.

PLUS ÇA CHANGE?

How can we make out the claim that the *other* sorts of legal changes *would* tend to undermine society or the family? A first step is to argue that the proposed changes would not be slight changes in degree—say, the extension of benefits or rights to a larger class—but rather changes in *kind,* of a very radical nature. This makes it more plausible, at least, that the changes might undermine society or the family: Presumably, a change that was not radical could not be the sort of thing that would pose such a threat. This, I take it, is the force of the argument that Hadley Arkes and others have advanced,[3] that if same-sex "marriages" were recognized, then there would be no reason, in principle, why a marriage should be between only two persons. There is a certain ambiguity in the current legal category of marriage. The old view remains vestigially that a marriage is the founding of a family; but alongside this is another competing view, that a marriage can be simply a long-term erotic friendship. The older view retains a kind of natural pride of place and in some sense overmasters the other. But once same-sex marriages are recognized, we resolve the ambiguity decisively in one direction, severing "marriage" from procreation—in which case there is no reason why only two should marry, any more than why only two should be friends. So the change, clearly, is a radical one—of the sort, we might suspect, which would be mischievous in unpredictable ways, even if its immediate effects do not appear so damaging. The change does not extend marriage but alters its nature.

That is the force, too, of the argument that, if anti-discrimination laws are extended to include sexual orientation, then we shall soon afterwards be met with affirmative action for professed homosexuals. Of course this will follow: If it is wrong, *now,* to take homosexuality into account in any decisions about hiring or housing, then it was wrong throughout past decades and centuries as well. But that is to say that homosexuals may claim a long history of unjust oppression, just as African-Americans and other minorities. And the recognized remedy for that sort of thing is affirmative action. It is clear, then, that we have, not a mere incremental change, which *allows* some additional citizens to do what they wish to do, but a radical change, namely, the mobilization of the entire apparatus of social justice, which originated in the civil rights movement, to *promote* and *advance* a certain way of life.

That is the first step, to argue that the proposed changes are radical, not slight. The second step is similar. We saw that proponents of gay rights legislation argue that the changes they favor would leave everything else in place, as before, while simply increasing the freedoms and benefits enjoyed by homosexuals. Therefore, one advances the argument to the contrary that the proposed changes would imply the use of the coercive power of the state, brought to bear against citizens who are not homosexual, precisely insofar as they act in support of marriage and the family as these are traditionally conceived. So, for instance, a Christian who lets a room in a small apartment building will no longer be allowed to refuse to provide, as he sees it, an "occasion for sin" (to use the traditional terminology) by renting to a same-sex couple: he finds his Christian sentiments blocked and checked by the force of law—by a law, one should recall, which was supposed merely to let others do what *they* wanted.[4] Or, again, parents who teach their children one thing about sexuality and the family will find that state funds are used, and regulations are established, directly in opposition to them in government schools, since, *of course,* if discrimination on the basis of sexual orientation is strictly analogous to that based on race, it will need to be similarly warned against in the schools, and this from the earliest ages.

The second step, then, is to argue that things are not at all left in place by the proposed changes; it is not simply a matter of

allowing an additional view. And then it begins to appear even more plausible that the proposed changes could undermine society and the family—if, that is, they are radical and imply the use of coercive state power against dispositions and actions that we regard as *good,* that is, those of honest citizens acting in accordance with their religious convictions, or simply aiming to teach their children well.

THE COMMON GOOD

But this leads to the third step of the argument, which is the most fundamental and, in a sense, the most obvious, but also the most subtle. At this point we need to go back and point out that Fr. Tuohey was not correct when he made his complaint. The Vatican letter he criticized *did* give an argument, albeit a very compressed one, for how the proposed legislative changes would harm society and the family. It gave the argument, in fact, in the very passage I quoted earlier: "the *view* that homosexual activity is equivalent to, or as acceptable as, the sexual expression of conjugal love has a direct impact on society's *understanding* of the nature and rights of the family and puts them in jeopardy" (my emphasis). What is at stake, most fundamentally, is a *view*—how it is that society looks upon something—and the view that we have is a part of the common good, and it involves immediate and manifold consequences.

Let me explain what I mean by saying something about the notion of a "common good" and what it is for society to have a *view* or belief about something. (This is in fact to explore the ancient idea of *concordia:* agreement on practical matters which is constitutive of social unity and civic friendship.)

I shall assume that people form associations, any association whatsoever, to procure or achieve something which they could not get at all, or could not get easily, if they acted each on his own. In that case, what they get through their association, and the instruments they use together in getting this, are, we can say, "common goods." For instance, in a large town or city, it would be either impossible or very difficult for each person to get water on his own—the water source is too small, or too far away, and hauling buckets takes too much time. So the town builds a system of reservoirs and pipes to supply water. The reserved water would then be a common good, and so too the reservoirs and supply system, the common instruments for procuring that good.

It should be noted that rarely is a common good simply a "thing" or material object. Even a water supply system, of any but the crudest sort, needs engineers to oversee it and skilled workers to maintain it. Their knowledge and habits of work—their virtues—have to be counted as part of that common good. But then, also, very often a *belief* is a common good. To give a simple example: Some commandos synchronize their watches and agree to rendezvous at a certain time. They must all believe that doing so is essential to their accomplishing their task; if an enemy could somehow befuddle some of them about that, he would foil their mission. Or, less trivially, it is a common good for both husband and wife to regard their marriage as indissoluble and for them to tailor their actions accordingly. If one member of the couple changes his mind about that, they both fail to achieve what they associated together for in the first place. Or, to take a political example, and one closer to our purposes, Lincoln held that the shared belief, among citizens in a republic, in the principles expressed in the Declaration of Independence, was essential to the practice of democracy. Their common belief in those "axioms of democracy," as Lincoln called them, is, we might say, an important common good. The shared belief in them is essential if citizens are to work together and assist one another, in a coordinated fashion, in maintaining and building up a free society.

A belief is held in common, we should note, not simply when each member of a group happens to hold it, but rather when each is furthermore *aware* that the others hold it, and is aware that the others are aware that *he* holds it. Typically, the way in which this sort of agreement is achieved in political society is through a law, a public resolution having the force of law, or some practice itself regulated by law. For instance, it is only after a declaration of war is passed by the legislature that everyone in a society becomes aware that a particular nation is regarded as a hostile power in the minds of all other fellow citizens as well. The declaration of war at once expresses and brings about this consensus. There are in fact many things which we thus believe in common, and which we must so believe, if our type of government is to work and endure. For example, we all believe that a life of productive work is better than one of listless unemployment, that literacy is a great good, and so on. It is an important mark of beliefs that are held in common, that they are transmitted effortlessly, with hardly any need of explicit teaching (which, by the way, is precisely why it is easy to neglect them). In a modern liberal state, in fact, it is typically left to religion to refresh and reinvigorate the shared beliefs most necessary to the state's existence, and rightly so; the government for its part has aimed, generally, not to place itself at odds with the promotion or encouragement of these beliefs.

We can say that a law implies a certain belief if the law could not be regarded as desirable or appropriate, except on that belief; also, that a law implies the *falsity* of a belief if it could be regarded as desirable or appropriate, *only* given the falsity of that belief. It was Lincoln's point against Douglas, for instance, that Douglas's idea of self-government implied a rejection of the principles of the Declaration of Independence: to accept a law which left it up to individual states, as something indifferent, whether they would be free or slave, was to abandon a shared belief in the basic equality of human beings, in virtue of their humanity. Douglas's conception of self-government could be regarded as desirable only given the falsity of the principles of the Declaration; thus it implied the rejection of those principles.

Finally, we can distinguish between beliefs which it is in some sense *natural* to hold in common, because they are regarded, correctly, as fulfillments or completions of other things believed, and those which it is not natural to hold in common, and which can be sustained, then, only artificially and through devices of coercion. For instance, the doctrine of communism, that all property should be held in common, proved itself to be unnatural, something which could not really be believed, and which therefore had to be upheld, if it was to be maintained at all, through extreme or illegitimate coercion. In this sense, the belief that the unborn child has a right to life is natural: It is the easy extension, to the unborn, of a belief we are prepared to hold as regards any human being. But the belief that a woman's so-called right to choose is more fundamental is like Douglas' view of self-government: It is unnatural and can only be maintained by the corruption of the institutions of medicine, the law, and the media.

Now, to apply these considerations to the case at hand. Consider first laws that would prohibit discrimination on the basis of sexual orientation. Such laws are, of course, modeled on civil rights legislation of the 1960s. Now it is necessary, if one is to *rule out* discrimination of some kinds as being inappropriate, to have in mind reasons on the basis of which discrimination, or the drawing of distinctions, or the assignment of rank, *would* be appropriate. You cannot rule out some types of features, as a basis of judgment, except to clear the way for others. The correct view in this matter was articulated by Martin Luther King, when he said famously that his ideal was a society in which people judged each other, not by the color of their skin, but by the content of their

character. And of course matters that have a bearing on morality are precisely those that, potentially, should enter into decisions about how we are to associate with others and on what conditions. If we grant this, then to say that a certain characteristic is *not* one that should be used for drawing distinctions is to say that it is *not* related to questions of morality or character. Anyone, then, who believed that homosexual acts were morally wrong, and who accepted this sound understanding of the point of anti-discrimination laws, could *not* regard it as appropriate or desirable to proscribe by law all discrimination on that basis; thus, laws which proscribe such behavior imply the view—and indeed propose it as a shared belief—that homosexual acts are not morally wrong. (Actually, one is left with an alternative: *either* homosexual acts are not morally wrong, *or* the apparatus of social justice originating in the civil rights movement works to no coherent purpose.)

What follows from this? If homosexual acts are not morally wrong, then, obviously, it is not the case that sexual activity *ought* to be confined to marriage. But that it ought to be is the correct view of the matter, and one that is most consistent with other deeply held common beliefs. Thus, for a society to accept such non-discrimination laws is for it to reject the true view of sexuality and marriage. We might say, then, that under the guise of a slight change in the law, motivated, apparently, by a concern for fairness, such laws embody or express the basic belief of the sexual revolution. They, so to speak, enshrine the sexual revolution in law.

THE CULTURE WAR

Of course it might be objected at this point that, if there is any threat to the family or society in this regard, it comes, rather, from the sexual revolution itself, and the evident change in society's mores then, not from some consequent change in law which assumes, as a *fait accompli,* the changes already introduced by the sexual revolution. But this objection underestimates the importance of law and fails to take into account the dividedness of society, that is, that there is indeed a culture war over sexual morality, which has continued to this point, and which will not be brought to a conclusion until the sexual revolution attains full legitimacy. Law is to society as principle and conscience are to an individual. A man may be a repeat adulterer, but so long as he recognizes that his marriage vow is binding upon him, he can reform. There are actually few, if any, legal changes since the 1960s which so directly imply the falsity of the view that sexual activity should be confined to marriage, as do gay rights laws. To accept such laws is to reject the principle, the claim of "conscience," by which, perhaps, the mores of the sexual revolution *could* be reversed.

Furthermore, although it is difficult to live in a society such as ours presently is, in which the true view of marriage and sexuality is hardly ever affirmed, it is much more difficult to live in one in which it is explicitly denied, and this with the power of the state. Currently, parents who wish to teach chastity and marital fidelity to their children are like the townspeople who needed water in our example, but where the water supply system has been disabled by a social upheaval, so that those who want water have to find a bucket and a water source and haul it in on their own. But once the negation of what such parents believe gets embodied into law—and law, too, which has the appearance of being righteous and progressive—it is as if the town then poisons its water supply, so that one has to be concerned, not only with getting fresh water, but also with not drinking the fouled water.

Consider next laws that would recognize same-sex couples as marriages. I consider it a telling fact that one never hears anyone saying, simply, that the proposed change is outright *impossible,* that two persons of the same sex *cannot* be married, whatever the state may say about it. Really, the only healthy reaction to the idea of same-sex "marriage" would be a kind of chuckle at the absurdity of it, and an internal resolve to ignore, as though nothing at all, both this fiction and anything any government might say in support of it. It is as though the government were to declare monkeys to be men, or men not to be men. Well, we have not done so well in resisting this last idea—the government *has* declared some men not to be men, and we go along with it—so I suppose it is not surprising that there are no signs of the appropriate response to the idea of men marrying men.

What these reflections suggest is the following. No one who thought that marriage had an objective character, prior to the state, could regard it as appropriate or desirable that there be a law by which the state defined and indeed altered, as by fiat, the character of marriage. Thus, laws recognizing gay marriage imply the falsity of the view that marriage is an objective reality prior to the state. Note too that parental authority must stand or fall with marriage. If the bond of husband and wife is not by nature, then neither is the government of those who share in that bond over any children that might result. Thus, laws recognizing gay marriage imply, similarly, that parents have no objective and natural authority over their children, prior to that of the state.

We are familiar with the idea, and, as I have said, we have acquiesced in it, that belief in the inherent dignity of all human beings is a subjective preference, a whim or fancy, which some fringe members of society—the right-to-life extremists—may perhaps regard as decisive in their *own* lives, because they hold to particular religious beliefs which involve this belief as a consequence. To accept gay "marriage," similarly, is to endorse the position that the belief in the family as having its own nature prior to the state is a mere whim or preference, springing from a religious viewpoint, perhaps, which the state is not bound to honor—in fact, which it cannot honor, without violating the separation of church and state.

If, indeed, gay "marriage" were to be recognised in law—a state of affairs which would itself be regrettable, since the required beliefs underlying it would be "unnatural" beliefs, in the sense I have explained, and which therefore could only be sustained by illegitimate force and coercion—then I do not doubt that it would not be long before it became regarded as unjust, that *some* couples, the heterosexual ones, can have children, but others cannot—just as, presently, women who accept the "pro-choice" ideology regard it as unjust that *they* can bear children, but men cannot. As much as possible, then, in a society in which the proposed changes have been fully implemented, children will be raised directly by the state. That biological parents have some special claim over their children will be seen as some kind of mysterious superstition, perhaps even a disguised animus against others, which can in any case be easily trumped by the state's concern for what it would regard as the well-being and proper education of citizens.

These are some of the developments that may be in store for us—at least we cannot say that we would be tending to avoid them—if we endorse gay rights and gay marriage. Of course, it might be objected that this is all fantastical and preposterous. But I am certain that gay marriage and partial birth abortion would have seemed much more fantastical and preposter-

ous in 1965. And in any case the burden has been discharged, the challenge overthrown. Why is it not absurd to hold that gay rights laws undermine society and the family? Because they imply beliefs which are incompatible with the common pursuit of goods which one wishes to obtain in marriage and family life. They remove a common good, a correct shared belief about the nature and good of marriage, which enables us to assist one another in realizing marriage and attaining its good, and they substitute—again, in the guise of something praiseworthy and just—a view which can only be sustained with coercion, and which will lead to suffering and unhappiness to the extent to which it is acted upon.

NOTES

1. "The C.D.F. and Homosexuals: Rewriting the Moral Tradition," in *America*, 167, n.6, September 12, 1992.
2. Congregation for the Doctrine of the Faith, "Letter to the Bishops of the Catholic Church on the Pastoral Care of Homosexual Persons," Rome, October 1, 1986, no.9.
3. See for instance Hadley Arkes, "The Implications of Gay Marriage," presented at a July 2, 1996 Capitol Hill briefing regarding the Defense of Marriage Act (DOMA).
4. See Richard Duncan, "Who Wants to Stop the Church: Homosexual Rights Legislation, Public Policy, and Religious Freedom," *Notre Dame Law Review* 69:3.

Discussion Questions

1. What does Professor Pakaluk mean by the common good and why does he believe that gay rights laws will undermine it?
2. Why does Professor Pakaluk believe that antisodomy laws serve an important purpose? Do you agree or disagree? Explain and defend your answer. Pakaluk recommends what John Finnis calls the "modern Euopean consensus." What does Finnis mean by this and do you think it is a good idea for North America to embrace it? Explain and defend your answer. Why does Pakaluk believe that Finnis's suggestion will not work in contemporary North America if we believe that antisodomy legislation is inherently unjust?

3. Why does Professor Pakaluk believe that the philosophical assumptions behind gay rights laws may open the door to numerous evils including state guardianship of children? Do you agree or disagree with his assesment? Explain and defend your answer.

4. How does Professor Pakaluk employ the words of Martin Luther King, Jr. to his advantage?

5. Do you agree or disagree with Professor Pakaluk that gay rights laws, if modeled after civil rights legislation, will result in the marginalization and coercian of citizens who believe that homosexuality is immoral? Explain and defend your answer.

6. Do you agree or disagree with Professor Pakaluk that gay rights laws are contingent on the belief that marriage and family are created by, and are not prior to, the state? Explain and defend your answer.

You can locate InfoTrac-College Education articles about this chapter by accessing the InfoTrac-College Edition website (http://www.infotrac-college.com/wadsworth/). Using the InfoTrac-College Edition subject guide, enter the search terms relevant to this chapter, and then read abstracts for relevant articles.

D3

The Debate Over Same-Sex Marriage

46   'Same-Sex Marriage' and 'Moral Neutrality'

ROBERT P. GEORGE

Robert P. George is the McCormick Professor of Jursiprudence at Princeton University, and a former member of the U.S. Civil Rights Commission. He has published widely in the areas of philosophy of law, moral philosophy, and political theory. His books include *Making Men Moral* (1993), *In Defense of Natural Law* (1999), and *Great Cases in Constitutional Law* (2000).

In this essay Professor George, an opponent of same-sex marriage, deals with the question of whether the state can, or ought to, be neutral on the question of the nature of marriage (see Part I Section D of this text for a general discussion of state neutrality when it comes to religious, moral and/or metaphysical beliefs). He begins with a brief discussion of both moral neutrality and the legal question of gay marriage. He then goes on to critique two arguments offered by proponents of same-sex marriage: (1) the argument from the unreasonableness of saying that a marriage is a union between one woman and one man; and (2) the argument that even if it may be morally correct that marriage is exclusively heterosexual and monogomous, such a moral judgment is not an appropriate basis on which to ground marriage law.

Professor George responds to the first argument by providing a sophisticated defense of male-female marriage, arguing for the proposition that "marriage is a

Reprinted by permission from Homosexuality and American Public Life, *ed. Christopher Wolfe (Dallas, TX: Spence Publishing, 1999), 141–53.*

two-in-flesh communion of persons that is consummated and actualized by acts which are reproductive *in type,* whether or not they are reproductive *in effect* (or are motivated, even in part, by a desire to reproduce)." In other words, marriage is inexorably linked to our natures as men and women, that there is a unity achieved in marriage that cannot be replicated in acts that simulate, but cannot duplicate, the consummation of marriage. George links this view to the moral status of children as subjects of justice rather than property or objects of desire. He then goes on to contrast the two-in-flesh communion view of marriage with what he calls liberal dualism, the view that one's body is merely an instrument of one's pleasure or desire to procreate rather than an aspect of one's integrated self. In response to the second argument— that the state should remain neutral on the question of marriage—Professor George makes two points. First, because the law is a teacher, if the law were to remain "neutral" on marriage, it would teach people something that undermines their ability to understand what he believes is the true meaning of marriage. In fact, he argues that most people, untouched by ideologies hostile to the traditional family, have no problem "seeing" the true meaning of marriage. Thus, if the state were to take a "neutral" posture it may harm people who need the reinforcement of the broader culture so that they are not distracted and lose their ability to "see" the true meaning of marriage.

Second, George argues that the state need not be neutral on the question of marriage in order to fulfill its requirement to uphold the "fundamental aspects of equality." For if marriage is by nature a two-in-flesh communion, to limit participation to male-female partners is not unjust. But if this view is false, that in fact same-sex unions are morally indistinguishable from male-female unions, then *that is the reason* same-sex marriages ought to be recognized.

FREQUENTLY I HEAR STUDENTS (and others) say, "I believe that marriage is a union of one man and one woman. But I think that it is wrong for the state to base its law of marriage on a controversial moral judgment, even if I happen to believe that judgment to be true. Therefore, I support proposals to revise our law to authorize same-sex 'marriages.'" The thought here is that the state ought to be neutral regarding competing understandings of the nature and value of marriage.

Of course, the claim that the law ought to be morally neutral about marriage or anything else is itself a moral claim. As such, *it* is not morally neutral, nor can it rest on an appeal to moral neutrality. People who believe that the law of marriage (or other areas of the law) ought to be morally neutral do not assert, nor does their position presuppose, that the law ought to be neutral regarding the view that the law ought to be neutral and competing moral views. It is obvious that neutrality between neutrality and unneutrality is logically impossible. Sophisticated proponents of moral neutrality therefore acknowledge that theirs is a controversial moral position whose truth, soundness, correctness, or, at least, reasonableness, they are prepared to defend against competing moral positions. They assert, in other words, that the best understanding of political morality, at least for societies such as ours, is one that includes a requirement that the law be morally neutral with respect to marriage. Alternative understandings of political morality, insofar as they fail to recognize the principle of moral neutrality, are, they say, mistaken and ought, as such, to be rejected.

Now, to recognize that any justification offered for the requirement of moral neutrality cannot itself be morally neutral is by no means to establish the falsity of the alleged requirement of moral neutrality. My purpose in calling attention to it is not to propose a retorsive argument purporting to identify self-referential inconsistency in arguments for moral neutrality. Although I shall argue that the moral neutrality of marriage law is neither desirable nor, strictly speaking, possible, I do not propose to show that there is a logical or performative inconsistency in saying that "the law (of marriage) ought to be neutral regarding competing moral ideas." It is not like saying "No statement is true." Nor is it like singing "I am not singing." At the same time, the putative requirement of moral neutrality is neither self-evident nor self-justifying. If it is to be vindicated as a principle of political morality, it needs to be shown to be true by a valid argument.

It is certainly the case that implicit in our matrimonial law is a (now controversial) moral judgment, namely, the judgment that marriage is inherently heterosexual—a union of one man and one woman. (In a moment, I will discuss the deeper grounds of that judgment.) Of course, this is not the only possible moral judgment. In some cultures, polygyny or (far less frequently) polyandry is legally sanctioned. Some historians claim that "marriages" (or their equivalent) between two men or two women have been recognized by certain cultures in the past.[1] However that may be, influential voices in our own culture today demand the revision of matrimonial law to authorize such "marriages." Indeed, the Supreme Court of the State of Hawaii has for some time been on the verge of requiring officials of that State to issue marriage licenses to otherwise qualified same-sex couples under the Equal Rights Amendment to the Hawaii Constitution. Unless the people of Hawaii are able to amend their state constitution to prevent the imposition of "same-sex marriage," it will then fall to the federal courts, and, ultimately, to the Supreme Court of the United States, to decide whether the "full faith and credit" clause of the Constitution of the United States requires every state in the Union to recognize such "marriages" contracted in Hawaii.

Anticipating the Hawaii Supreme Court's action, Congress passed the Defense of Marriage Act, which guarantees the right of states to refuse to recognize same-sex "marriages." The Act went to the President to sign or veto in the course of the 1996 presidential campaign. After denouncing the Act as both mean-spirited and unnecessary, Clinton quietly signed it into law, literally in the middle of the night. Of course, a second opportunity for a veto effectively rests with any five justices of the Supreme Court of the United States. Although it is impossible to say with confidence how the Supreme Court will ultimately rule on the inevitable constitutional challenge to the Defense of Marriage Act, the stated ground of the Court's decision in the 1996 case of *Romer v. Evans* (the so-called Colorado Amendment 2 Case) will surely inspire hope among those whom Clinton disappointed by failing to veto the Act. In *Romer*, the Court invalidated an amendment to the Constitution of the State of Colorado by which the people of that State sought to prevent its municipalities from enacting ordinances granting protected status or preferences based on homosexual or bisexual orientation. Six justices joined in an opinion written by Associate Justice Anthony Kennedy holding that Amendment 2 could only have been motivated by constitutionally impermissible "animus" against a politically vulnerable minority group.

There are two ways to argue for the proposition that it is unjust for government to refuse to authorize same-sex (and, for that matter, polygamous) "marriages." The first is to deny the reasonableness, soundness, or truth of the moral judgment implicit in the proposition that marriage is a union of one man and one woman. The second is to argue that this moral judgment cannot justly serve as the basis for the public law of matrimony, notwithstanding its reasonableness, soundness, or even its truth.

I maintain that the moral neutrality to which this way of arguing appeals is, and cannot but be, illusory. To that end, it will be necessary for me to explain the philosophical grounds of the moral judgment that marriage is a union of one man and one woman and to discuss the arguments advanced by certain critics of traditional matrimonial law in their efforts to undermine this judgment.

TWO IN ONE FLESH

Here is the core of the traditional understanding: Marriage is a two-in-one-flesh communion of persons that is consummated and actualized by acts which are reproductive *in type,* whether or not they are reproductive *in effect* (or are motivated, even in part, by a desire to reproduce). Reproductive-type acts have unique meaning, value, and significance because they belong to the class of acts by which children come into being. More precisely, these acts have their unique meaning, value, and significance because they belong to the *only* class of acts by which children can come into being, not as "products" which their parents choose to "make," but, rather, as perfective participants in the organic community (that is, the family) that is established by their parents' marriage. The bodily union of spouses in marital acts is the biological matrix of their marriage as a multi-level relationship that unites them at the bodily, emotional, dispositional, and spiritual levels of their being.

Marriage, precisely as such a relationship, is naturally ordered to the good of procreation (and to the nurturing and education of children), as well as to the good of spousal unity, and these goods are tightly bound together. The distinctive unity of spouses is possible *because* men and women, in reproductive-type acts, become a single reproductive principle. Although reproduction is a single act, in humans the reproductive act is performed not by individual members of the species, but by a mated pair as an organic unit. The point has been explained by Germain Grisez: "Though a male and a female are complete individuals with respect to other functions—for example, nutrition, sensation, and locomotion—with respect to reproduction they are only potential parts of a mated pair, which is the complete organism capable of reproducing sexually. Even if the mated pair is sterile, intercourse, provided it is the reproductive behavior characteristic of the species, makes the copulating male and female one organism."[2]

Although not all reproductive-type acts are marital,[3] there can be no marital act that is not reproductive in type. Masturbatory, sodomitical, or other sexual acts which are not reproductive in type cannot unite persons organically, that is, as a single reproductive principle.[4] Therefore, such acts cannot be intelligibly engaged in for the sake of marital unity as such: They cannot be marital acts. Rather, persons who perform such acts must be doing so for the sake of ends or goals which are *extrinsic* to themselves as bodily persons: Sexual satisfaction, or (perhaps) mutual sexual satisfaction, is sought as a means of releasing tension, or obtaining or sharing pleasure, either as an end in itself, or as a means to some other end, such as expressing affection. In any case, where one-flesh union cannot (or cannot rightly) be sought as an end in itself, sexual activity necessarily involves the instrumentalization of the bodies of those participating in such activity to extrinsic ends.

In marital acts, by contrast, the bodies of persons who unite biologically are not reduced to the status of mere instruments. Rather, the end, goal, and intelligible point of sexual union is the good of marriage itself. On this understanding, such union is not merely an instrumental good, that is, a reason for action whose intelligibility as a reason depends on other ends to which it is a means, but is, rather, an intrinsic good, that is, a reason for action whose intelligibility as a reason depends on no such other end. The central and justifying point of sex is not pleasure, or even the sharing of pleasure, *per se,* however much sexual pleasure is rightly sought as an aspect of the perfection of marital union. The point of sex, rather, is *marriage itself,* considered as a bodily union of persons consummated and actualized by acts which are reproductive in type. Because in marital acts sex is not instrumentalized,[5] such acts are free of the self-alienating and dis-integrating qualities of masturbatory and sodomitical sex. Unlike these and other nonmarital sex acts, marital acts establish no practical dualism which volitionally and, thus, existentially (though, of course, not metaphysically) separates the body from the conscious and desiring aspect of the self, understood as the "true" self that uses the body as its instrument.[6] As John Finnis has observed, marital acts are truly unitive, and in no way self-alienating, because the bodily or biological aspect of human beings is "part of, and not merely an instrument of, their *personal* reality."[7]

But, one may ask, what about procreation? On the traditional view, isn't the sexual union of spouses instrumentalized to the goal of having children? It is true that St. Augustine was an influential proponent of such a view. The strict Augustinian position was rejected, however, by the mainstream of philosophy and theology from the late Middle Ages forward, and the understanding of sex and marriage that came to be embodied in both the canon law of the Church and the civil law of matrimony does not treat marriage as a merely instrumental good. Matrimonial law has traditionally understood marriage to be consummated by, and only by, the reproductive-type acts of spouses. The sterility of spouses—so long as they are capable of consummating their marriage by a reproductive-type act (and, thus, of achieving bodily, organic unity)—has never been treated as an impediment to marriage,

even where sterility is certain, and even certain to be permanent (as in the case of the marriage of a woman who has been through menopause or has undergone a hysterectomy).[8]

According to the traditional understanding of marriage, then, it is the nature of marital acts as reproductive in type that makes it possible for such acts to be unitive in the distinctively marital way. And this type of unity has intrinsic, and not merely instrumental value. Thus, the unitive good of marriage provides a noninstrumental (and sufficient) reason for spouses to perform sexual acts of a type which consummates and actualizes their marriage. In performing marital acts, the spouses do not reduce themselves as bodily persons (or their marriage) to the status of means or instruments.

At the same time, where marriage is understood as a one-flesh union of persons, children who may be conceived in marital acts are understood, not as ends which are extrinsic to marriage (either in the Augustinian sense, or the modern liberal one), but rather as gifts which supervene on acts whose central justifying point is precisely the marital unity of the spouses.[9] It is thus that children are properly understood and treated—even in their conception—not as means to their parents' ends, but as ends-in-themselves; not as *objects* of the desire[10] or will of their parents, but as *subjects* of justice (and inviolable human rights); not as *property,* but as *persons.* It goes without saying that not all cultures have fully grasped these truths about the moral status of children. What is less frequently noticed is that our culture's grasp of these truths is connected to a basic understanding of sex and marriage that is not only fast eroding, but is now under severe assault from people who have no conscious desire to reduce children to the status of mere means, or objects, or property.

LIBERAL DUALISM

It is sometimes thought that defenders of traditional marriage law deny the possibility of something whose possibility critics of the law affirm. "Love," these critics say, "makes a family." And it is committed love that justifies homosexual sex as much as it justifies heterosexual sex. If marriage is the proper, or best, context for sexual love, the argument goes, then marriage should be made available as well to loving, committed same-sex partners on terms of strict equality. To think otherwise is to suppose that same-sex partners cannot really love each other, or love each other in a committed way, or that the orgasmic "sexual expression" of their love is somehow inferior to the orgasmic "sexual expression" of couples who "arrange the plumbing differently."

In fact, however, at the bottom of the debate is a possibility that defenders of traditional marriage law affirm and its critics deny, namely, the possibility of marriage as a one-flesh communion of persons. The denial of this possibility is central to any argument designed to show that the moral judgment at the heart of the traditional understanding of marriage as inherently heterosexual is unreasonable, unsound, or untrue. If reproductive-type acts in fact unite spouses interpersonally, as traditional sexual morality and marriage law suppose, then such acts differ fundamentally in meaning, value, and significance from the only types of sexual acts which can be performed by same-sex partners.

Liberal sexual morality that denies that marriage is inherently heterosexual necessarily supposes that the value of sex must be instrumental *either* to procreation *or* to pleasure. Proponents of the liberal view suppose that homosexual sex acts are indistinguishable from heterosexual acts whenever the motivation for such acts is something other than procreation. The sexual acts of homosexual partners, that is to say, are indistinguishable in motivation, meaning, value, and significance from the marital acts of spouses who know that at least one spouse is temporarily or permanently infertile. Therefore, the argument goes, traditional matrimonial law is guilty of unfairness in treating sterile heterosexuals as capable of marrying while treating homosexual partners as ineligible to marry.

Stephen Macedo has accused the traditional view and its defenders of precisely this apparent "double standard." He asks, "What is the point of sex in an infertile marriage? Not procreation: the partners (let us assume) know that they are infertile. If they have sex, it is for pleasure and to express their love, or friendship, or some other shared good. It will be for precisely the same reason that committed, loving gay couples have sex."[11]

But Macedo's criticism fails to tell against the traditional view because it presupposes as true precisely what the traditional view denies, namely, that the value (and, thus, the point) of sex in marriage can only be instrumental. On the contrary, it is a central tenet of the traditional view that the value (and point) of sex is the *intrinsic* good of marriage itself which is actualized in sexual acts which unite spouses biologically and, thus, interpersonally. The traditional view rejects the instrumentalization of sex (and, thus, of the bodies of sexual partners) to any extrinsic end. This does not mean that procreation and pleasure are not rightly sought in marital acts; it means merely that they are rightly sought when they are integrated with the basic good and justifying point of marital sex, namely, the one-flesh union of marriage itself.

It is necessary, therefore, for critics of traditional matrimonial law to argue that the apparent one-flesh unity that distinguishes marital acts from sodomitical acts is illusory, and, thus, that the apparent bodily communion of spouses in reproductive-type acts is not really possible. And so Macedo claims that "the 'one-flesh communion' of sterile couples would appear . . . to be more a matter of appearance than reality." Because of their sterility such couples cannot really unite biologically: "[T]heir bodies, like those of homosexuals, can form no 'single reproductive principle,' no real unity."[12] Indeed, Macedo goes so far as to argue that even fertile couples who conceive children in acts of sexual intercourse do not truly unite biologically, because, he asserts, "penises and vaginas do not unite biologically, sperm and eggs do."[13]

John Finnis has aptly replied that "in this reductivist, word-legislating mood, one might declare that sperm and egg unite only physically and only their pronuclei are biologically united. But it would be more realistic to acknowledge that the whole process of copulation, involving as it does the brains of the man and woman, their nerves, blood, vaginal and other secretions, and coordinated activity is biological through and through."[14]

Moreover, as Finnis points out, the organic unity which is instantiated in an act of the reproductive kind is not, as Macedo "reductively imagine[s], the unity of penis and vagina. It is the unity of the persons in the intentional, consensual *act* of seminal emission/reception in the woman's reproductive tract."[15]

The unity to which Finnis refers—unity of body, sense, emotion, reason, and will—is, in my view, central to our understanding of humanness itself. Yet it is a unity of which Macedo and others who deny the possibility of true marital communion can give no account. For their denial presupposes a dualism of "person" (as conscious and desiring self), on the one hand, and "body" (as instrument of the conscious and desiring self), on the other, which is flatly incompatible with this unity. Dualism is implicit in the idea, central to Macedo's denial of the possibility of one-flesh marital union, that sodomitical acts differ from what I have described as acts of the reproductive type only as a matter of the arrangement of the "plumbing." According to this idea, the genital organs of an infertile woman (and, of course, all women are infertile most of the time) or of an infertile man are not really reproductive organs"—any more than, say, mouths, rectums, tongues, or fingers are reproductive organs. Therefore, the intercourse of a man and a women where at least one partner is temporarily or permanently sterile cannot really be an act of the reproductive type.

But the plain fact is that the genitals of men and woman are reproductive organs all of the time—even during periods of sterility. And acts which fulfill the behavioral conditions of reproduction are acts of the reproductive type even where the nonbehavioral conditions of reproduction do not happen to obtain. Insofar as the object of sexual intercourse is marital union, the partners achieve the desired unity (become "two-in-one-flesh") precisely insofar as they mate, that is, fulfill the behavioral conditions of reproduction, or, if you will, perform the type of act—the only type of act—upon which the gift of a child may supervene.[16]

The dualistic presuppositions of the liberal position are fully on display in the frequent references of Macedo and its other proponents to sexual organs as "equipment." Neither sperm nor eggs, neither penises nor vaginas, are properly conceived in such impersonal terms. Nor are they "used" by persons considered as somehow standing over and apart from these and other aspects of their biological reality. The biological reality of persons is, rather, part of their personal reality. Hence, where a person treats his body as a subpersonal object, the practical dualism he thereby effects brings with it a certain self-alienation, a damaging of the intrinsic good of personal self-integration. In any event, the biological union of persons—which is effected in reproductive type acts but not in sodomitical ones—really is an interpersonal ("one-flesh") communion.

THE LAW AS TEACHER

Now, Macedo considers the possibility that defenders of the traditional understanding are right about all this: that marriage truly is a "one-flesh union" consummated and actualized by marital acts; that sodomitical and other intrinsically nonmarital sexual acts really are self-alienating and, as such, immoral; that the true conception of marriage is one according to which it is an intrinsically heterosexual (and, one might here add, monogamous) relationship. But even if the traditional understanding of marriage is the morally correct one—even if it is true—he argues, the state cannot justly recognize it as such. For, if disagreements about the nature of marriage "lie in . . . difficult philosophical quarrels, about which reasonable people have long disagreed, then our differences lie in precisely the territory that John Rawls rightly marks off as inappropriate to the fashioning of our basic rights and liberties."[17] And from this it follows that government must remain neutral as between conceptions of marriage as intrinsically heterosexual (and monogamous) and conceptions according to which "marriages" may be contracted not only between a man and a woman, but also between two men, two women (and, presumably, a man or a woman and multiple male or female "spouses"). Otherwise, according to Macedo, the state would "inappropriately" be "deny[ing] people fundamental aspects of equality based on reasons and arguments whose force can only be appreciated by those who accept difficult to assess [metaphysical and moral] claims."[18]

It seems to me, however, that something very much like the contrary is true. The true meaning, value, and significance of marriage are fairly easily grasped, even if people sometimes have difficulty living up to its moral demands, when a culture—including, critically, a legal culture—promotes and supports a sound understanding of marriage, both formally and informally. Ideologies and practices which are hostile to a sound understanding and practice of marriage in a culture tend to undermine the institution of marriage, making it difficult for people to grasp the true meaning, value, and significance of marriage. It is, therefore, extremely important that government eschew attempts to be "neutral" with regard to competing conceptions of marriage and try hard to embody in its law and policy the soundest, most nearly correct conception.

Moreover, any effort to achieve neutrality will inevitably prove to be self-defeating. For the law is a teacher: It will teach *either* that marriage is a reality that people can choose to participate in, but whose contours people cannot make and remake at will *or* the law will teach that marriage is a mere convention which is malleable in such a way that individuals, couples, or, indeed, groups, can choose to make of it whatever suits them. The result, given the biases of human sexual psychology, will be the development of practices and ideologies which truly do tend to undermine the sound understanding and practice of marriage, together with the pathologies that tend to reinforce the very practices and ideologies that cause them.

Joseph Raz, though himself a liberal who does not share my views on homosexuality or sexual morality generally, is rightly critical of forms of liberalism, including Rawlsianism, which suppose that law and government can and should be neutral with respect to competing conceptions of morality. In this regard, he has noted that "monogamy, assuming that it is the only valuable form of marriage, cannot be practised by an individual. It requires a culture which recognizes and supports it through the force of public opinion and its own formal institutions."[19]

Now, Raz does not suppose that in a culture whose law and public morality do not support monogamy a man who happens to believe in it will somehow be unable to restrict himself to having one wife or will be required to take additional wives. His point, rather, is that even if monogamy is a key element of a sound understanding of marriage, large numbers of people will fail to understand it or why it is the case—and will therefore fail to grasp the value of monogamy and the intelligible point of practicing it—unless they are assisted by a culture which supports, formally and informally, monogamous marriage. And what is true of monogamy is equally true of the other marks or aspects of a morally sound understanding of marriage. In other words, marriage is the type of good which can be participated in, or fully participated in, only by people who properly understand it and choose it with a proper understanding in mind; yet people's ability properly to understand it, and thus to choose it, depends upon institutions and cultural understandings that transcend individual choice.

But what about Macedo's claim that when matrimonial law deviates from neutrality by embodying the moral judgment that marriage is inherently heterosexual, it denies same-sex partners who wish to marry "fundamental aspects of equality?" Does a due regard for equality require moral neutrality? I think that the appeal to neutrality actually does no work here. If the moral judgment that marriage is between a man and a woman is false, then the reason for recognizing same-sex marriages is that such unions are as a matter of moral fact indistinguishable from marriages of the traditional type. If, however, the moral judgment that marriage is between a man and a woman is true, then Macedo's claim that the recognition of this truth by government "denies fundamental aspects of equality" simply cannot be sustained. If, in other words, the marital acts of spouses consummate and actualize marriage as a one-flesh communion, and serve thereby as the biological matrix of the relationship of marriage at all its levels, then the embodiment in law and policy of an understanding of marriage as inherently heterosexual denies no one fundamental aspects of equality. True, many persons who are homosexually oriented lack a psychological prerequisite to enter into marital relationships. But this is no fault of the law. Indeed, the law would embody a lie (and a damaging one insofar as it truly would contribute to the undermining of the sound understanding and practice of marriage in a culture) if it were to pretend that a marital relationship could be formed on the basis of, and integrated around, sodomitical or other intrinsically nonmarital (and, as such, self-alienating) sex acts.

It is certainly unjust arbitrarily to deny legal marriage to persons who are capable of performing marital acts and entering into the marital relationship. So, for example, laws forbidding interracial marriages truly were violations of equality. Contrary to the claims of Andrew Koppelman, Andrew Sullivan, and others, however, laws which embody the judgment that marriage is intrinsically heterosexual are in no way analogous to laws against miscegenation. Laws forbidding whites to marry blacks were unjust, not because they embodied a *particular* moral view and thus violated the alleged requirement of moral neutrality; rather, they were unjust because they embodied an *unsound* (indeed a grotesquely false) moral view—one that was racist and, as such, immoral.

NOTES

1. The late John Boswell, for example, claimed that brother/sister-making rituals found in certain early medieval Christian manuscripts were meant to give ecclesiastical recognition and approval to homosexual relationships. See *Same-Sex Unions in Premodern Europe* (New York: Villard Books, 1994). However, as Robin Darling Young has observed, "the reviews [of Boswell's work] after the early burst of hopeful publicity, have been notably skeptical—even from sources one would expect to be favorable." "Gay Marriage: Reimagining Church History," *First Things*, No. 47 (November, 1994): 48. Darling herself concludes that Boswell's "painfully strained effort to recruit Christian history in support of the homosexual cause that he favors is not only a failure, but an embarrassing one." Id.

2. Germain Grisez, "The Christian Family as Fulfillment of Sacramental Marriage," paper delivered to the Society of Christian Ethics Annual Conference, September 9, 1995.

3. Adulterous acts, for example, may be reproductive in type (and even in effect) but are intrinsically nonmarital.

4. Securely grasping this point, and noticing its significance, Hadley Arkes has remarked that " 'sexuality' refers to that part of our nature that

has as its end the purpose of begetting. In comparison, the other forms of 'sexuality' may be taken as minor burlesques or even mockeries of the true thing." Now, Professor Arkes is not here suggesting that sexual acts, in what he calls "the strict sense of 'sexuality,'" must be *motivated* by a desire to reproduce; rather, his point is that such acts, even where motivated by a desire for bodily union, must be reproductive in type if such union is to be achieved. This, I believe, makes sense of what Stephen Macedo and other liberal critics of Arkes's writings on marriage and sexual morality find to be the puzzling statement that "[e]very act of genital stimulation simply cannot count as a sexual act." See Hadley Arkes, "Questions of Principle, Not Predictions: A Reply to Stephen Macedo," *Georgetown Law Journal,* 84 (1995): 323.

5. This is by no means to suggest that married couples cannot instrumentalize and thus degrade their sexual relationship. See Robert P. George and Gerard V. Bradley, "Marriage and the Liberal Imagination," *Georgetown Law Journal,* 84 (1995): 301–320, esp. 303, n. 9.

6. On person-body dualism, its implications for ethics, and its philosophical untenability, see John Finnis, Joseph M. Boyle, Jr., and Germain Grisez, *Nuclear Deterrence, Morality and Realism* (Oxford: Oxford University Press, 1987), 304–09; and Patrick Lee, "Human Beings Are Animals," in Robert P. George, ed., *Natural Law and Moral Inquiry: Ethics, Metaphysics, and Politics in the Work of Germain Grisez* (Washington, D.C.: Georgetown University Press, forthcoming).

7. John Finnis, "Law, Morality, and Sexual Orientation," in John Corvino, ed., *Same Sex: Debating the Ethics, Science, and Culture of Homosexuality* (Lanham, Md.: Rowman and Littlefield, 1997), sec. III.

8. See George and Bradley, 307–09.

9. Ibid., 304.

10. I am not here suggesting that traditional ethics denies that it is legitimate for people to "desire" or "want" children. I am merely explicating the sense in which children may be desired or wanted by prospective parents under a description which, consistently with the norms of traditional ethics, does not reduce them to the status of "products" to be brought into existence at their parents' will and for their ends, but rather treats them as "persons" who are to be welcomed by them as perfective participants in the organic community established by their marriage. See George and Bradley, 306, n. 21. Also see Leon Kass, "The Wisdom of Repugnance: Why We Should Ban the Cloning of Humans," *The New Republic* (June 2, 1997): 17–26, esp. 23–24.

11. Stephen Macedo, "Homosexuality and the Conservative Mind," *Georgetown Law Journal,* 84 (1995): 278.

12. Ibid., 278.

13. Ibid., 280.

14. Finnis, "Law, Morality, and 'Sexual Orientation,'" sec. V.

15. Ibid.

16. John Finnis has carefully explained the point: "Sexual acts which are marital are 'of the reproductive kind' because in willing such an act one wills sexual behaviour which is (a) the very same as causes generation (intended or unintended) in every case of human *sexual* reproduction, and (b) the very same as one would will if one were intending precisely sexual reproduction as a goal of a particular marital sexual act. This kind of act is a 'natural kind,' in the morally relevant sense of 'natural,' not . . . if and only if one is intending or attempting to produce an *outcome,* viz. reproduction or procreation. Rather it is a distinct rational kind—and therefore in the morally relevant sense a natural kind—because (i) in engaging in it one is intending a *marital* act, (ii) its being of the reproductive kind is a necessary though not sufficient condition of its being marital, and (iii) marriage is a rational and natural kind of institution. One's reason for action—one's rational motive—is precisely the complex good of marriage. Finnis," "Law, Morality, and 'Sexual Orientation,'" sec. V.

17. Stephen Macedo, "Reply to Critics," *Georgetown Law Journal,* 84 (1995): 335.

18. Ibid., 335.

19. Joseph Raz, *The Morality of Freedom* (Oxford: Clarendon Press, 1986), 162.

Discussion Questions

1. What does Professor George mean by moral neutrality?
2. Explain and present Professor George's view of the nature of marriage. What does he mean by two-in-flesh communion? Do you agree or disagree? Explain and defend your answer.
3. What does Professor George mean by liberal dualism? What part, according to George, does liberal dualism play in the debate over gay marriage?
4. Present and explain the two arguments in support of same-sex marriage to which Professor George is responding?
5. Present and explain Professor George's response to the argument that even if it may be morally correct that marriage is exclusively heterosexual and monogomous, such a moral judgment is not an appropriate basis on which to ground marriage law. Do you agree with George's reply? Explain and defend your answer.

You can locate InfoTrac-College Education articles about this chapter by accessing the InfoTrac-College Edition website (http://www.infotrac-college.com/wadsworth/). Using the InfoTrac-College Edition subject guide, enter the search terms relevant to this chapter, and then read abstracts for relevant articles.

47   Do Wedding Dresses Come in Lavender?: The Prospects and Implications of Same-Sex Marriage

ANGELA BOLTE

Angela Bolte is currently a Ph.D. candidate in philosophy at Washington University in Saint Louis. She has published in the areas of social philosophy, philosophy of emotions, and philosophy of law. Her recent book is entitled *Legal Philosophy: Multiple Perspectives* (2000).

The following is a summary of the essay provided by the author:

To answer concerns regarding same-sex marriage, I will examin several issues. First, the concept of marriage must be defined. Opponents often argue that same-sex marriage violates the definition of marriage and, thus, same-sex marriage should not be legalized. Second, given the difficulty in defining the concept of marriage, I will undertake an examination of the features of marriage so as illustrate the compatibility of same-sex marriage with those features. Third, I will examine traditional legal arguments against same-sex marriage for their validity. Fourth, I will evaluate Claudia Card's arguments against same-sex marriage and offer a response to these arguments. Finally, I will explore domestic partnerships as a potential alternative to same-sex marriage. Once these steps are completed, it will be seen that same-sex marriage would be beneficial, rather than harmful, to the institution of marriage.

Reprinted by permission from Social Theory and Practice *24.1 (spring 1998). This essay has been edited for inclusion in this text.*

1.

ONE OF THE MOST important issues surrounding the same-sex marriage debate is whether or not same-sex marriages can even exist. All too often, same-sex marriages are discounted as impossible because marriage is viewed as existing only between a man and a woman. Gays and lesbians cannot meet the definition of marriage and, thus, "same-sex marriage" is an oxymoron.

One method of providing evidence for the possibility of same-sex marriages involves recognizing what is meant by the definition of marriage. Richard Mohr illustrates the difficulty of this task by pointing out the following:

Most commonly, dictionaries define marriage in terms of spouses, spouses in terms of husband and wife, and husband and wife in terms of marriage. In consequence, the various definitions do no work in explaining what marriage is and so simply end up assuming or stipulating that marriage must be between people of different sexes.[1]

It does seem that Mohr, for the most part, is correct. In most dictionaries marriage is defined in these terms, although at times any reference to "spouses" is dropped, but the point remains.[2] Dictionary definitions usually focus on the concepts of husband and wife and spend little time explaining anything about the actual nature of marriage.

The legal definition of marriage fares no better. Although the marriage laws in most states refer generically to spouses, *Blacks Law Dictionary* relies on the 1974 case *Singer v. Hara* to express the legal definition of marriage as "the legal union of one man and woman as man and wife."[3] Since the legal definition of marriage specifically excludes same-sex marriage, the courts have successfully argued that same-sex marriages cannot be allowed because these unions would destroy the very notion of marriage.

Some courts have tried to place an additional stipulation on the definition of marriage; namely, that marriage is a vehicle for the creation and raising of children. This traditional argument against same-sex marriage is also inadequate. With the elimination of the fertility clause in the marriage laws, the courts have removed the raising of children from the core of marriage law and the ability of spouses to create children together is no longer considered a requirement of marriage.[4] Thus, there is no legitimate legal basis from which to deny the right of marriage to gays and lesbians because they cannot create children together. Moreover, if this were legitimate, withholding marriage licenses from elderly or infertile couples would also be legitimate. In each of these cases, the couple cannot create children together and, to be consistent, denying the right of marriage to all of them would be necessary on these grounds. Due to the revised marriage laws, such a position would have little, if any, legal support.

It is also unclear how the stipulation that marriage is for the creation and raising of children truly excludes gays and lesbians. Gays and lesbians are increasingly becoming parents through new avenues such as adoption or artificial insemination. Many gays and lesbians also have children from previous marriages. This occurrence is presently so widespread that some mainstream and gay media have labeled this phenomenon a "gay baby boom."

It is estimated that there are three to four million gay and lesbian parents raising between six and fourteen million children.[5] This number is especially significant if it is argued that one of marriage's goals is the protection and care of the children that exist within it. There is an expectation that children are to be protected and cared for by the spouses while a marriage exists and this is reflected in the legal process that occurs when a marriage ends. The divorce laws are devised to help protect children by ensuring that child support is paid if necessary for the welfare of a particular child. Moreover, when a spouse dies, custody of the children is designed to pass to the living spouse, thus ensuring that the children are not removed from a familiar environment.

While traditional arguments claim that same-sex marriages should be banned because the children within those families will be subject to harm both through ridicule and confusion over sexual roles, it is rather the case that children are directly harmed through the banning of same-sex marriages. Currently, when a same-sex relationship ends, no institutions are in place to ensure the protection of the children, as there are when traditional marriages dissolve. A partner who leaves a same-sex relationship is under no obligation to provide financial support for children that he or she may have cared for and supported for years. In a case where the biological parent dies, the children could be left without either parent, if the living partner had not adopted them in a second-parent adoption. Moreover, in most states the courts do not allow second-parent adoptions by gays and lesbians. Given the vast numbers of children with same-sex parents, by not allowing same-sex marriage, many children are adversely affected.

As for the traditional arguments against same-sex marriage, Fredrick Elliston states that "in the case of . . . homosexual marriage, the source of the harm to children is social prejudice" against gays and lesbians.[6] Elliston argues that if same-sex marriages ware legalized, this social prejudice would be diminished. As for the second argument, that the children will suffer from confusion over sex roles, this is not necessarily a problem. According to feminist thinking, traditional sex roles are not desirable, and Elliston similarly argues that same-sex marriage "may help to combat this evil [of traditional sex roles]."[7]

Given the failure of legal definitions of marriage, perhaps sociology or anthropology would be a better source for a definition of marriage. Definitions from these areas are more informative, but do not provide a complete picture of marriage. For example, marriage is described in the following manner:

[M]arriage has been defined as a culturally approved relationship of one man and one woman (monogamy); or of one man and two or more women (polygyny/polygamy), in which sexual intercourse is usually endorsed between the opposite sex partners, and there is generally an expectation that children will be born of the union and enjoy the full birth status rights of their society. These conditions of sexual intercourse between spouses and reproduction of legitimate and socially recognized offspring are not, however, always fulfilled.[8]

The most important aspect of the above definition is the suggestion that a culture can define what is considered a marriage. In fact, a society could define and redefine marriage as often as it chooses.

Given that marriage is a perpetually evolving notion, same-sex marriages would not necessarily have a "negative" impact on the institution of marriage. The fear of such a negative impact is seen in a traditional argument that claims that the recognition of same-sex marriage would lead to the recognition of multiple forms of marriage, such as polygamy or group marriage, and traditional Western marriages would eventually be eradicated. If same-sex marriages lead to the eradication of traditional Western marriages, there is no reason to believe that this would somehow be negative. A move away from traditional Western marriages could be positive and stabilizing for the community because all citizens would be accepted, no matter what form their marriage takes.

Another traditional argument worries: "What if everybody did that [i.e., entered a same-sex marriage]?"[9] Although there eventually could be heterosexuals who choose to marry someone of the same sex, this would not necessarily be "negative." In fact, such marriages could be used to help provide basic needs and protections for those who are unable to support themselves. Unfortunately, in our society numerous citizens do not have equal access to basic rights and protections such as adequate housing or health insurance, because access to these rights and protections is limited by financial resources. If an individual lacks the financial means necessary to attain these rights and protections, he or she is usually forced to do without or to accept a substandard replacement.

Moreover, same-sex marriages would grant to gays and lesbians the rights attached to marriage that are presently denied to them. Unlike married opposite-sex couples, gays and lesbians with children are unable to have custody automatically passed to their partner at their death. Similarly, without a will, gays and lesbians cannot ensure that their estates will pass to their partner. Without being married, gays and lesbians cannot even file joint tax returns. Finally, the right of gays and lesbians to live in the community of their choice is limited, if the community specifies by law that only married couples may purchase a house within it. The denial of such rights to these citizens, while presently legal, is heterosexist and unjust.

Same-sex marriage could be used to provide access to these basic rights and protections. For example, a same-sex couple could pool their resources and attain adequate health insurance, better housing, or simply provide themselves financial security. Presently, many gays and lesbians enter traditional marriages with a heterosexual or a friend who is gay or lesbian to obtain these basic rights and protections. Heterosexuals could join a same-sex marriage for the same reason and this would not "make" them homosexual; just as gays or lesbians who are presently in traditional marriages for similar reasons are not "made" heterosexual.[10]

Although some heterosexuals could choose to enter same-sex marriages, the percentage of heterosexuals and homosexuals would not change greatly as some opponents of same-sex marriage fear. Most estimates of the actual number of gays and lesbians in the United States range between one and ten percent. This number would most likely stay the same,

although even if this number were to change, there is no reason to believe that this would be "negative."[11] If a person had not previously been attracted to someone of the same sex, the ability of gays and lesbians to marry would not alter the fundamental sexual behavior of this person. For example, with the advent of the gay and lesbian rights movement, gays and lesbians have become increasingly visible, but the percentage of gays and lesbians has not radically changed. What has happened is that gays and lesbians who had felt compelled to live a "straight" life have become more visible. If the legalization of same-sex marriage were to occur, the same phenomenon would be likely, with some gays and lesbians leaving, or not choosing, heterosexual marriages because of the more acceptable alternative.

Some might worry that by legalizing same-sex marriage, the number of children raised in such households would increase and those children would be more likely to be gay or lesbian. Given studies on the sexual orientation of the children of gays and lesbians, these children are no more likely to be gay or lesbian than other children. Moreover, it is unclear why an increase in the number of gays and lesbians would be a "negative." If those who construe the increase of gays and lesbians as negative are actually concerned about the extinction of the human race, it is unclear why this would necessarily happen. The increasing number of gays and lesbians with children illustrates that a reproductive drive exists within gays and lesbians and there is no reason to think that humans would disappear if everyone was gay or lesbian.

2.

Although society can redefine what is meant by the concept of marriage, it is possible that same-sex marriage can be accepted while retaining the key features of marriage as it is presently known within Western society.

Although describing marriage is difficult, the following list of features can be obtained.[12]

[Marriage] is usually a temporally extended relationship between or among two or more individuals; this usually involves (1) a sexual relationship; (2) the expectation of procreation; (3) certain expectations or even agreements to provide economic, physical, or psychological support for one another; and (4) a ceremonial event recognizing the condition of marriage.

Palmer points out, however, that "none of these is a necessary condition, and if they are logically sufficient conditions when taken jointly, it is probably because of the inclusion of feature number four."[13]

Richard Mohr characterizes marriage similarly. He believes that marriage is "intimacy given substance in the medium of everyday life, the day-to-day. Marriage is the fused intersection of love's sanctity and necessity's demand."[14] This characterization appears adequate to explain an institution infused with vagueness. Taken together, Palmer's and Mohr's conditions for marriage cover what the partners in a contemporary Western marriage generally expect. Moreover, their conditions for marriage dovetail with the definition from sociology and anthropology, but the following reduction is possible: an adequate level of commitment between partners; the joint raising of children, if the partners want them; and love. Although this reduction can be made, it is uncertain what each of these conditions entails for same-sex marriages.

The issue of commitment in marriage is interesting, yet controversial, and upon its discussion, questions concerning both the required amount of commitment and how best to define commitment immediately arise. These questions can be reduced to the following: either a committed marriage must be monogamous or it may be non-monogamous.[15] In the traditional Western view of marriage, monogamy in the form of sexual exclusivity is an essential ingredient in all marriages. Since gays and lesbians are often thought, under this traditional Western view, to be incapable of being sexually exclusive, it is claimed that they should not be allowed to marry, because they cannot meet a "necessary condition" of marriage.[16]

Although it is unclear that gays and lesbians are any less sexually exclusive or monogamous than heterosexuals, no marriage must be totally monogamous. If the partners in a marriage choose to have an "open" marriage, this does not mean that their marriage is somehow voided. The marriage is not voided, because monogamy is not a requirement of marriage; in fact, many types of marriage are non-monogamous by definition, such as polygamy or group marriage. Moreover, with the advent of no-fault divorce laws, the lack of monogamy within a marriage is no longer even legal ground for divorce. This shift in the law may be due to a recognition of the fact that the majority of society no longer considers monogamy a necessary condition of marriage. Therefore, if neither of the partners is coerced into giving assent to an open marriage, this decision should be respected.

Simultaneously, a decrease in monogamy need not amount to a decrease in commitment. While it is the case that a partner who is "cheating" on his or her partner most likely is guilty of a lack of commitment, if the relationship is open, a decrease in commitment is not necessary. While judging the degree of commitment in an open marriage is almost impossible, one indicator of commitment could simply be the continuation of the marriage.

In fact, Richard Mohr believes that if same-sex marriages were legalized, the marriages of gay men would help to improve mainstream views about monogamy. Mohr believes that monogamy is not essential for love and commitment in marriage, as evidenced by many long-term gay male relationships that incorporate non-monogamy.[17] Instead, Mohr believes that traditional couples should look at the relationships of gay men to rethink the traditional

Western model of the family. Mohr's basic position on monogamy and commitment seems correct. A lack of monogamy should not undermine commitment if the partners have agreed not to be monogamous.

Turning to the question of children, as argued above, no legitimate reason exists for preventing gays and lesbians from marrying simply because they are seen as "incapable" of having children. Moreover, nothing prevents gays and lesbians from having children; as previously mentioned, many gays and lesbians do have children. Finally, there is the condition of love. Although love is closely tied to the issue of commitment, love and monogamy are separate issues. Viewed on its own, love is probably the one issue where some agreement can be reached, because gays and lesbians can easily meet this feature of marriage.

With these partial characterizations of marriage, it can be seen that gays and lesbians can meet its features. This means that the courts should not dismiss cases regarding same-sex marriage because these marriages are viewed as impossible by virtue of being between same-sex couples. Instead, a rigorous examination of the legal arguments against same-sex marriage must be undertaken to see if legitimate legal and moral reasons exist for not allowing same-sex marriage.

3.

During the 1970s, several court cases were aimed directly at allowing same-sex marriage, but none succeeded.[18] Because of these failures, and the United States Supreme Court's majority opinion in *Bowers v. Hardwick,* no other major cases regarding same-sex marriage were filed until the early 1990s.[19] In 1993, *Baehr v. Lewin* was brought before the Hawaiian Supreme Court and the court sent the issue back to the lower courts, ruling that the state must demonstrate a compelling state interest to ban same-sex marriage. In December of 1996, a Hawaiian state court ruled that compelling state interest was not illustrated. . . .

With the possibility of the legalization of same-sex marriage, many traditional legal arguments against same-sex marriages have resurfaced. For example, in discussions of sodomy laws, two traditional arguments are often raised against homosexuality. The first argument claims that homosexual sex is not "natural" because it does not consist of penile-vaginal intercourse. Connected to this argument is a second argument that claims that homosexuality is intrinsically tied to perversion because it involves a misuse of body parts.[20] These arguments can be linked to the idea of "legal moralism" as advocated by Lord Patrick Devlin. Legal moralism states that the law ought to be based on the morality of the majority of society. Moreover, if a society wishes to continue, it must defend its moral code or potentially be destroyed.

Legal moralism and its connected arguments underlie discussions of how states can avoid, through "choice-of-law theory," recognizing same-sex marriages performed in sister states. Under choice-of-law, "any time application of the foreign state's law would violate a substantial public policy of the forum, the foreign law need not be applied," although there are constitutional restrictions to this.[21] Given the wording of choice-of-law theory, the substantial public policy could simply be the morality of a given state as expressed in law. In fact, the sodomy laws, which legal theorists believe will be used in an attempt to illustrate a substantial public policy against same-sex marriage, can be construed as a legal expression of what is presumed to be the morality of the state's citizens.[22]

While sodomy laws perhaps could be viewed as a clear expression of public morality and opinion toward homosexuality, it is unclear why this method is available when applications of the actual sodomy laws are examined. Sodomy laws are not enforced with regard to either homosexuals or heterosexuals in consensual relationships and, consequently, might not be accurate expressions of public opinion and morality. Given that the sodomy laws are ignored (even in *Bowers*, where an individual was caught in the act of violating the law and yet never charged), the argument can be made that these laws are no longer a part of public policy. Perhaps these laws ware once an expression of public morality, but, because these laws are not enforced, this connection no longer exists. Nevertheless, the alternative view must be examined, because the mere existence of these sodomy laws will no doubt be used to argue against the legalization of same-sex marriage.

While the sodomy laws might be viewed as an expression of public morality, the fact that these laws are applied differently to heterosexuals and homosexuals distorts their moral message. In fact, legal theorists argue that those states with sodomy laws that apply both to heterosexuals and homosexuals have a weaker ability to display a substantial public policy against same-sex marriage. This weaker ability is due to the fact that heterosexual couples in these states are subject to the sodomy laws and, presumably, some heterosexual couples also violate these laws; nevertheless, these couples are allowed to marry.

It may appear that *Bowers* allows such differential treatment with regard to sodomy laws, but this is not necessarily the case. In *Bowers,* the Supreme Court specifically held that there was no privacy right within the Constitution to homosexual sodomy, because the privacy rights of individuals are limited to the "liberties that are deeply rooted in this Nation's history and tradition," a clear statement of legal moralism.[23] At the same time, there is no explicit statement within *Bowers* that sodomy laws that pertain to heterosexuals are in violation of the right to privacy and thus violate the United States Constitution. This means that the sodomy laws ought to be equally applied to heterosexuals and homosexuals in all areas. For these states to disallow same-sex marriage because of broadly written

sodomy laws "would be indicative of differential treatment based on sexual orientation and arguably would be actionable under the Fourteenth Amendment if characterized as sex discrimination."[24] This strategy would be similar to the method presently being used in *Baehr* and would be available if *Baehr* is upheld.

Some might argue that homosexual sex is inherently in violation of the sodomy laws while heterosexual sex is not, and consequently it is not legitimate to apply broadly written sodomy laws to heterosexuals. This would mean that these states should have a good method for displaying a substantial public policy against same-sex marriage, but this argument is not necessarily correct. Depending on the wording of the statute, homosexual sex need not always violate sodomy statutes. For example, some sodomy laws are worded so that only anal sex is in violation of the law. Other sodomy laws are written so as either to make all intercourse illegal that is not penile-vaginal or to make oral sex illegal. Although some sodomy laws bar all of the above, not all sodomy laws are broadly worded. Given the variation of the laws, homosexual sex would not always be in violation of the sodomy statutes. Second, the question remains as to why heterosexuals should not be punished for violating sodomy laws. It seems that if states with broad sodomy laws are concerned with the violation of these laws, they should attempt to prevent all sodomy and not just apply the laws to gays and lesbians.

Another factor that would limit the demonstration of a substantial public policy against same-sex marriage by some states, but not all, is the presence of laws that protect gays and lesbians. Most relevant are the eight states that have laws forbidding discrimination against gays and lesbians, but there are several other important laws.[25] The courts in eleven states have rejected presumption against gays and lesbians in custody cases.[26] Eight states and the District of Columbia allow custody to gays and lesbians in second-parent adoptions.[27]

Finally, cities in ten states and the District of Columbia have domestic partnerships for gays and lesbians.[28] In each of these individual cases, the state would have a hard time proving a legitimate substantial public policy against gays and lesbians.

The presence of positive laws regarding homosexuality is particularly relevant when discussing legal moralism. Devlin's position relies on moral uniformity within society, but these laws illustrate that such uniformity does not exist. The law does not have a sound, uniform foundation that it can use to draw conclusions concerning homosexuality; thus, the law cannot be used for judging attitudes toward homosexuality. In addition, the law does not have a firm foundation concerning its position on sodomy for either homosexuals or heterosexuals. Most states have no laws concerning sodomy and only five have exclusively same-sex sodomy laws. If the law is to be based on the majority of society, the law ought to reflect the fact that most states do not hold any form of sodomy to be illegal. To base the law on the minority opinion that sodomy is immoral violates the basic tenets of legal moralism and, for that reason alone, ought to be rejected by advocates of legal moralism.

Moreover, as H.L.A. Hart pointed out regarding Devlin's argument, there is no way to judge if a society's morals have shifted or if the moral code has been destroyed.[29] The positive laws listed above, when conjoined with the elimination of the majority of state sodomy statutes, could illustrate that society's values regarding homosexuality have shifted and homosexuality is no longer viewed by the majority as abhorrent. This would mean that if same-sex marriage were legalized, the law would be in step with society's moral code.

Nevertheless, this does not mean that legal moralism is correct. Even if the law is in accord with society's moral code, this does not mean that the moral code is just. The moral code of a society must be subject to scrutiny, and cannot simply be relied upon to generate the law

without such scrutiny. It is not enough for tradition to support or deny any right; instead, a more neutral conception of justice must be used. If tradition were enough to support the law, numerous practices, such as slavery, would still be considered just. This fact alone illustrates the failure of legal moralism.

While some states may affirm same-sex marriages, this will not necessarily occur in all states. It could be that all states will be able both to eliminate laws that protect gays and lesbians and to put the necessary legislation in place to display a substantial public policy against same-sex marriage. Another scenario could be that the courts would allow any state to bar same-sex marriage due to the heterosexist tradition that exists regarding marriage within the United States. Only real challenges to the marriage laws of numerous states can demonstrate what will actually occur.

4.

Many within the gay and lesbian community also have articulated concerns regarding the acceptance of same-sex marriage. Claudia Card voices many of those concerns in her recent article "Against Marriage and Motherhood." Card believes that while it is wrong for the state to ban same-sex marriages, gays and lesbians should not be eager to enter marriage, because same-sex marriages will create multiple problems for the gay and lesbian community. Card rejects same-sex marriage because of the possible intrusiveness of the state into same-sex relationships, and she raises four specific problems that she believes should concern advocates of same-sex marriage.[30] First, gays and lesbians might be pressured into marriage to receive benefits such as health insurance. Second, once gays and lesbians enter these relationships, they could find the negative consequences of divorce too high because they could lose some of their economic resources. Third, marriage, due to its monogamous nature, will be too limiting and will distort the actual nature of many gay and lesbian relationships. Finally, Card claims that the legal access granted to spouses by marriage could open the door to all types of same-sex partner abuse. According to Card, instead of embracing flawed traditions, gays and lesbians should create their own traditions.

The problems that Card points out are significant but not overwhelming. As to her first two concerns, these problems are not specifically gay or lesbian in nature.[31] Many of those working for same-sex marriage realize that basic benefits such as health care should be available to everyone. The expansion of such benefits to everyone, not just to those who are married, is a major goal of these activists. Although the lack of such benefits for everyone within society should be a concern, it need not be tied only to the movement for same-sex marriage.

The basic problem underlying Card's second objection is one that is not new to the gay and lesbian community. Presently, palimony lawsuits often take place when a same-sex partnership dissolves. Card briefly mentions this fact and states that palimony is problematic specifically because it both prevents a partner from easily leaving a same-sex relationship and applies "the idea of 'common law' marriage to same-sex couples."[32] Card suggests that instead of palimony or marriage, couples who want a "contractual relationship" should engage in developing a specific legal contract that defines their relationship.

Although Card may find the restrictions placed on relationships both by divorce and palimony too limiting, these legal structures serve to protect both partners in ways that individualized "relationship contracts" might not. First, for such a move to be equitable to both partners, each partner would require a lawyer to ensure that the contract was fair. While this might be a simple requirement for some, many would find the lawyers' fees to be a burden and would reject a move toward a contract for that reason. Presumably, under Card's position, if the partners do not have a relationship contract, there would be no system in place to ensure a fair division of assets following a separation.[33] Second, some might attempt to negotiate their own contracts, and such a move could easily lead to one partner unwittingly accepting an unfair contract. Third, even with a contract negotiated by a lawyer, there is no guarantee that one partner will not be taken advantage of by the other. Fraud and deception often arise in other contractual situations, and there is no reason to believe that relationship contracts would be immune to such problems. Finally, circumstances surrounding a relationship can easily change, and there is no guarantee that the legal contract that encompasses the relationship is flexible enough to span the changes or, if it is not, that it will be altered in response to the changes in the relationship. While a few relationships would not greatly change over time, it cannot be assumed that this would be true for all relationships. Relationship contracts require additional expense, have the potential for unfairness and fraud, and can be made irrelevant by changing circumstances. Most important, by making relationship contracts the sole option for same-sex couples, those who are unable or unwilling to have such a contract will lose their current protections. Thus, while divorce and palimony may have some negative consequences, eliminating these institutions would cause even greater harm.

Card's third problem regarding the limiting nature of marriage is a common concern of some within the gay and lesbian rights movement.[34] Many of those in the gay and lesbian rights movement who stand opposed to same-sex marriage worry that marriage would become even more entrenched as the only acceptable type of relationship. They are concerned that those who are at the fringes of the gay and lesbian rights movement would be excluded because they choose not to live the more "acceptable" life of marriage.

I believe that this fear of accelerated exclusion due to the legalization of same-sex marriage is overstated. The fringe elements of the gay and lesbian rights movement are excluded currently by both the traditional and the gay and lesbian mainstreams with the ban on same-sex marriage. Since these elements are currently ostracized, legalizing same-sex marriage could not do a great deal more to harm those who are excluded.

It could be that those gays and lesbians who choose not to be married will be discriminated against, at times. Single and especially young heterosexuals are often thought not to be as stable as their married peers, and are, at times, at a disadvantage because they are not married.[35] The same would likely hold true for gays and lesbians. Nevertheless, it does seem that, overall, the legalization of same-sex marriage would have a liberalizing influence rather than cause a move toward increased conservatism.[36]

The legalization of same-sex marriage would bring what had once been determined to be "other," that is, what had been determined to be separate and inferior, into the mainstream. In other words, legalizing same-sex marriage would allow one form of difference to be included in what is deemed acceptable. By broadening the definition of what is considered acceptable, other forms of difference could become more accepted. For example, the gay and lesbian rights movement illustrates this occurrence. As gays and lesbians have become more visible and accepted, many issues surrounding their community have moved from unthinkable to potentially realizable. In fact, same-sex marriage has moved from unthinkable thirty years ago to potentially being legalized. In this manner, the legalization of same-sex marriage would lead to more rather than less acceptance of difference, and should therefore be supported by the gay and lesbian community.

Finally, Card's fourth concern claims that same-sex marriage could allow an abusive partner to abuse his or her same-sex spouse easily.

While same-sex marriages could potentially increase the control of an abusive partner, it is not clear that this would outweigh the potential benefit that marriage could bring to the issue of same-sex partner battering. Presently, gays and lesbians have difficulty finding help when they are in a battering relationship, for many reasons. Perhaps the main reason is the combination of homophobia and heterosexism. The gay and lesbian community does not wish to recognize the problem of same-sex partner battering, and for this reason "it is absolutely vital to work to eliminate homophobia and heterosexism in the shelter environment."[37] Although much of the theoretical groundwork on battering was done by lesbians, in conjunction with their work in developing many original shelters, these shelters are not always welcoming to those in the gay and lesbian community who need help.[38] Along with the fear and hatred of gays and lesbians that exists within the shelters, there is often disbelief that a woman could batter another woman or that a man could not defend himself against another man.

If same-sex marriages became widespread, there could be a profound effect on opinions regarding gays and lesbians, which would be beneficial for those gays and lesbians who are in battering relationships. Same-sex marriages could help to eliminate heterosexism and homophobia by elevating homosexuality to the level of acceptability. Through the legalization of same-sex marriage, gay and lesbian relationships would be acknowledged as legitimate. Moreover, gays and lesbians could become more visible due to the protections accorded to married couples. This visibility would further increase acceptance of gays and lesbians throughout society. Attributing increased acceptance of gays and lesbians to their growing visibility does seem possible. The gay and lesbian rights movement itself provides similar evidence, because as gays and lesbians have left the "closet," there has been a corresponding increase in their acceptance by society. In addition, when at least some people are aware that someone they know is gay or lesbian, they can be more accepting of gays and lesbians in general.

Same-sex marriage could also revolutionize the institution of marriage with regard to gender roles that support heterosexism and homophobia. Nan Hunter theorizes that same-sex marriage will cause a "subversion of gender."[39] Hunter believes that statements made by opponents of same-sex marriage—such as "Who would be the husband?"—illustrate the fear that exists regarding the revolutionary power of same-sex marriages.[40] While such statements are meant to ridicule the very idea of same-sex marriages, they also illustrate the speaker's fear that he or she will no longer be able to depend on the power granted by a social category such as "husband." Hunter believes that the subversion of gender would revolutionize marriage as it is known today and would begin the process of moving marriage away from its oppressive roots.

If gender roles were eroded; heterosexism and homophobia would be reduced, which would directly benefit those who are in abusive same-sex relationships by making shelter workers more willing to recognize and help them. Thus, it is likely that legalizing same-sex marriage would have a positive impact on abused gays and lesbians, regardless of their marital status.

5.

Although Card is concerned with any type of state regulation of same-sex relationships, she views domestic partnerships as less problematic, in some ways, than same-sex marriage.[41] In this respect Card agrees with many of those in the gay and lesbian community who have turned away from marriage and have embraced domestic partnerships.[42] While Card is not truly supportive of domestic partnerships, she is mistaken to consider them as a possible alternative to marriage.

Domestic partnerships may appear to be an attractive alternative to same-sex marriage, but the benefits of these partnerships are usually limited in scope. Municipalities offering the option of a domestic partnership usually offer the same benefits to both partners and spouses of employees. Non-employees, on the other hand, generally only have access to family memberships at city-owned attractions or the right to hospital or jail visitations. Private sector businesses offering domestic partnership policies usually restrict benefits to health insurance, although sometimes they are restricted further.

Although domestic partnerships are presently limited in their scope, advocates are working to expand their coverage. Their goal is to have the benefits attached to domestic partnerships equivalent to the benefits attached to traditional Western marriages. If domestic partnerships are implemented and expanded to become marriages by a different name, no fundamental difference between marriages and domestic partnerships would exist, because, presumably, domestic partnerships would be just as difficult to leave as marriages. If there were no difference between the two practices, there would be no real method by which to distinguish them. It appears that these advocates are engaged in self-deception, in that they want the rights and benefits of marriage, but not the label.

Supporters of domestic partnerships often claim that the problems surrounding domestic partnerships should be overlooked because these partnerships could be used to generate some significant benefits. One argument claims that domestic partnerships would be beneficial because they could be used to help educate the public in an effort to "pave the way" for same-sex marriages. A second argument is based on the idea that there is a much more realistic chance that domestic partnerships will become widespread than there is that same-sex marriage will be implemented soon. By having same-sex domestic partnerships in place, gays and lesbians can enjoy some actual benefits within their lifetimes, a guarantee that cannot be made regarding same-sex marriage.

While supporters of domestic partnerships try to illustrate their potential benefits, these relationships remain extremely problematic and could potentially contribute to the unjust treatment of gays and lesbians. If domestic partnerships are expanded, these partnerships could be viewed as "separate, but equal" to marriages between opposite-sex couples. As the civil rights movement illustrates, such situations are very rarely equal. Gays and lesbians must not be taken in by possible benefits, but must examine all the possibilities. There is a very real chance that domestic partnerships could be used to sidestep justice issues regarding the treatment of gays and lesbians. If domestic partnerships were granted, any request for the legalization of same-sex marriage could be seen as unnecessary and selfish. Moreover, while there might be an attempt to increase the legal rights of domestic partnerships, such as adding adoption or tax rights, access to these rights would have to occur at a state or national level through the legislative process. The prospects for state or nationwide same-sex domestic partnerships at the legislative level are no greater than the legalization of same-sex marriage. Thus, any promise of faster access to these rights is unlikely to be realized. These problems illustrate that domestic partnerships are not a legitimate alternative to same-sex marriage and it is only through marriage that gays and lesbians will achieve the rights they deserve as citizens.

6.

While it has been shown that major changes will occur in marriage when same-sex marriage is legalized, I do not feel that this would lead to the destruction of the institution itself. While some practices that marriage supports will be affected, marriage itself will continue. The polit-

ical right will argue that any change in marriage will serve to undermine the institution, but this argument is flawed. Change cannot simply be equated with undermining. If this were the case, then marriage has already been undermined. Marriage is significantly different from its original incarnation. Even in the past twenty years there have been many changes in marriage. From the elimination of fertility laws to the advent of no-fault divorce, marriage has changed, but it has not faded from existence. There is no legitimate reason to believe that by allowing gays and lesbians to marry, the institution of marriage will disappear. In fact, it could be that allowing everyone to marry the mate of his or her choice will strengthen marriage by furthering the natural evolution of this diverse and widespread institution.[43]

NOTES

1. Richard D. Mohr, "The Case for Same-Sex Marriage," *Notre Dame Journal of Law, Ethics & Public Policy* 95 (1995): 215–39; p. 219.
2. For an example of this usage, see *The American Heritage Dictionary,* 2nd ed., s.v. "marriage."
3. *Black's Law Dictionary,* 5th ed., s.v. "marriage." In Singer v. Hara [522 P.2d 1187 (Wash. 1974)], the court denied the following: The silence of the marriage statutes on this issue allowed same-sex marriage, denying that same-sex marriage violated Washington's Equal Rights Amendment, and a denial of the plaintiff's right to marry would violate the Eighth, Ninth, and Fourteenth Amendments to the Constitution.
4. In 1985, Hawaii became the last state to repeal this clause.
5. Deborah M. Henson, "Will Same-Sex Marriages Be Recognized in Sister States?: Full Faith and Credit and Due Process Limitations on States' Choice of Law Regarding the Status and Incidents of Homosexual Marriages Following Hawaii's *Baehr v. Lewin,*" *University of Louisville Journal of Family Law* 32 (1994): 551–600; p. 576.

6. Fredrick Elliston, "Gay Marriage," in Robert Baker and Fredrick Elliston (eds.), *Philosophy and Sex,* 2nd ed. (New York: Prometheus Books, 1984), pp. 146–66; p. 154.

7. Ibid.

8. *Social Science Encyclopedia,* 1st ed., s.v, "marriage."

9. Elliston, p. 160.

10. Although it may appear by this statement that I am advocating the position that homosexuality is genetic in origin, I do not hold this position. The "nature vs. nurture" debate is a controversy that I wish to put aside. Nevertheless, I do believe that anyone can choose to self-define as gay or lesbian. Such self-definition is done occasionally by feminists as a means of moving away from the male community. This is similar to cases in which someone who is attracted to the same sex, for whatever reason, chooses to ignore this attraction.

11. Ten percent was the number arrived at by the Kinsey studies and is the percentage generally used by the gay and lesbian rights movement, but other studies have arrived at lower numbers. This variation in percentages can be traced to two basic problems. First, arriving at a representative sample is often difficult due to "passing" by gays and lesbians. Second, there are also conflicting opinions on how to define what it means to be gay or lesbian.

12. David Palmer, "The Consolation of the Wedded," in Baker and Elliston, *Philosophy and Sex,* pp. 119–29; p. 119.

13. Ibid.

14. Mohr, p. 227.

15. Here, I am using monogamy in its more popular usage. Strictly speaking, a monogamous marriage is one in which there are only two marriage partners. Popularly speaking, a monogamous marriage is one in which the two partners are sexually exclusive to each other.

16. This view is based on old stereotypes held by the heterosexual community that homosexuals are "sexual animals" who are incapable of controlling their sexual desires. This view contrasts directly with the stereotype within the gay and lesbian community that lesbian relationships tend eventually to suffer from "bed death," that is, lesbian relationships become less sexual with time. For a discussion of men, lesbians, and sex, see Sarah Lucia Hoagland, *Lesbian Ethics: Toward New Values* (Palo Alto: Institute of Lesbian Studies, 1988), pp. 164–78.

17. Mohr, pp. 233–36. Mohr is citing evidence from David P. McWhirter and Andrew M. Mattison, *The Male Couple: How Relationships Develop* (Englewood Cliffs: Prentice Hall, 1984).

18. The first of these cases was *Baker v. Nelson* [191 N.W.2d 185 (Minn. 1971). Appeal dismissed 409 U.S. 810 (1972)]. The court denied the following: that the silence surrounding same-sex marriage was equal to permission, the Due Process Clause allowed same-sex marriage, and that by not allowing same-sex marriage the Equal Protection Clause was violated.

   Two years later in Jones v. Hallahan [501 S.W.2d 588 (Ky. 1973)], it was argued that the state's refusal of a marriage license to a same-sex couple denied the plaintiffs the following constitutional rights: the right to marry, the right of association, the free exercise of religion, and that a denial of a marriage license was cruel and unusual punishment. The court denied these claims and made the further claim that the state did not prevent the plaintiffs from marrying, instead, their sex did. The last major case in this era that attempted to allow same-sex marriage was *Singer v. Hara* (see n. 3).

19. 478 U.S. 186 (1986). Here, the United States Supreme Court upheld the constitutionality of the Georgia sodomy laws. The Court refused to include consensual homosexual sodomy in the zone of privacy identified as residing in the "penumbras" of the First, Third, Fourth, Fifth, and Ninth Amendments in the Court's ruling in *Griswold v. Connecticut* [381 U.S. 479 (1965)].

20. Michael Levin, "Why Homosexuality Is Immoral," in William H. Shaw (ed.), *Social and Personal Ethics* (Belmont, CA, Wadsworth, 1993), pp. 350–57

21. Henson, p. 553. There are limits to choice-of-law. The two main limits are the Full Faith and Credit and Due Process Clauses of the

United States Constitution. The Full Faith and Credit Clause requires for purposes of regulating interstate commerce, in most cases, that sister states recognize each other's laws. The Due Process Clause is relevant because, when a marriage is revoked, a host of other rights and benefits are revoked also and this potentially could violate a citizen's due process under the law. Although these restrictions exist, a state would not have to recognize a marriage that violated the state's substantial public policy. Choice of law in marriage is usually applied in the areas of incestuous and underage marriages.

22. Presently, only five states have exclusively homosexual sodomy laws, namely, Arkansas, Kansas, Missouri, Montana, and Oklahoma. Thirty states do not have sodomy laws and fifteen states have sodomy laws that pertain both to heterosexual and homosexual sodomy (Henson, p. 590).

23. Ibid., pp. 594–95.

24. Ibid., p. 590.

25. Ibid., p. 578. As of 1994, these states are Wisconsin, Massachusetts, Hawaii, Connecticut, New Jersey, Vermont, California, and Minnesota.

26. Jeffery J. Swart, "The Wedding Luau—Who is Invited?: Hawaii, Same-Sex Marriage, and Emerging Realities," *Emory Law Journal* 43 (1994): 1577–616; p. 1594. As of 1994, the states are Alaska, California, Indiana, Michigan, New Jersey, New York, South Carolina, Vermont, Washington, Massachusetts, and West Virginia. In New Mexico presumption was rejected in a custody case concerning a gay uncle. In Virginia, courts have both rejected and not rejected presumption against gay parents.

27. Ibid., p. 1597. As of 1994, the states are Alaska, Massachusetts, New York, California, Washington, Oregon, Vermont, and Minnesota.

28. Ibid., p. 1598. As of 1994, the states are Michigan, Georgia, Massachusetts, Connecticut, New York, California, Washington, Minnesota, Wisconsin, and Maryland.

29. H.L.A. Hart, "Immorality and Treason," in R.M. Dworkin (ed.), *The Philosophy of Law* (Oxford: Oxford University Press, 1977), pp. 83–88.

30. Claudia Card, "Against Marriage and Motherhood," *Hypatia* 11 (1996): 1–23; p. 8.

31. At the same time, it should be noted that Card's project is against marriage in general and not exclusively against same-sex marriage.

32. Card, p. 13.

33. In her proposal, Card would have legal contracts replace marriage and palimony for same-sex couples. Thus, the assumption that there would be no safety net of marriage and palimony laws for those rejecting relationship contracts is not far-fetched.

34. Paula L. Ettelbrick, "Since When is Marriage a Path to Liberation?," in Suzanne Sherman (ed.), *Lesbian and Gay Marriage: Private Commitments, Public Ceremonies* (Philadelphia: Temple University Press, 1992), pp. 20–26.

35. For example, promotions are often granted in the corporate and academic world only if the employee is married. Marriage is taken to mean that the employee has "settled down" and is now more serious and stable.

36. It should be noted that Card holds a contrasting position. Card believes that marriage could have a conservative effect by potentially making gays and lesbians less liberal and thus more "acceptable" to mainstream society.

37. Linda Geraci, "Making Shelters Safe for Lesbians," in Kerry Lobel (ed.), *Naming the Violence: Speaking Out About Lesbian Battering* (Seattle: Seal Press, 1986), pp. 77–79; p. 77.

38. Donna J. Cecere, "The Second Closet: Battered Lesbians," in Lobel (ed.), *Naming the Violence*, pp. 21–31.

39. Nan D. Hunter, "Marriage, Law and Gender: A Feminist Inquiry," in David S. Caudill and Steven Jay Gold (eds.), *Radical Philosophy of Law: Contemporary Challenges to Mainstream Legal Theory and Practice* (Englewood Cliffs, N.J.: Humanities Press, 1995), pp. 221–33; p. 225.

40. Ibid., p. 225.

41. Card, p. 12. It should be noted that Card is less critical of domestic partnerships, not because of any benefits that can be attached to these partnerships, but because the State is less involved in their regulation and because they are more readily dissolved than marriages.

42. For a discussion of domestic partnerships, see Barbara Findlen, "Is Marriage the Answer?," *Ms.,* May/June 1995, pp. 86–91.

43. I thank Irene Appelbaum, Claudia Card, Marilyn Friedman, Larry May, and Mark Rollins for extensive comments and suggestions on earlier versions of this paper. Earlier versions of this paper were read at the Thirteenth Annual International Social Philosophy Conference and at the 1996 Annual Meeting of the Society for Social and Political Philosophy. I thank those audiences for their criticisms and suggestions.

Discussion Questions

1. What are the reasons why Ms. Bolte believes that marriage is difficult to define? She maintains that marriage is a "perpetually evolving notion." Why is this important to her case for same-sex marriage?

2. Why does Ms. Bolte argue that from the features of marriage, same-sex marriage is a legitimate form of marriage? Do you agree or disagree? Explain and defend your answer.

3. What are the legal arguments against same-sex marriage that Ms. Bolte critiques? What are her responses to these arguments? Do you think she succeeds? Explain and defend your answer.

4. Present and explain Claudia Card's arguments against same-sex marriage. What are Ms. Bolte's responses to them? Do you think she is correct in her assessment of Professor Card's case? Explain and defend your answer.

5. What does Ms. Bolte think about domestic partnerships? Do you think that she is correct in her judgment? Why or why not?

6. Do you agree with Ms. Bolte's conclusion that same-sex marriage would be beneficial to the institution of marriage? Explain and defend your answer.

7. How do you think Michael Pakaluk (Chapter 44) would respond to Ms. Bolte's conclusion? Present and explain what sort of arguments you would imagine he would employ.

You can locate InfoTrac-College Education articles about this chapter by accessing the InfoTrac-College Edition website (http://www.infotrac-college.com/wadsworth/). Using the InfoTrac-College Edition subject guide, enter the search terms relevant to this chapter, and then read abstracts for relevant articles.